Time Series
Volume I

The International Library of Critical Writings in Econometrics

Series Editors: Mark Blaug
Professor Emeritus, University of London
Consultant Professor, University of Buckingham
Visiting Professor, University of Exeter
Adrian C. Darnell
Senior Lecturer in Economics, University of Durham

1. The Econometrics of Panel Data (Volumes I and II)
   G.S. Maddala

2. Macroeconometric Modelling (Volumes I and II)
   Kenneth F. Wallis

3. Simultaneous Equation Estimation
   Carl F. Christ

4. The History of Econometrics (Volumes I and II)
   Adrian C. Darnell

5. Time Series (Volumes I and II)
   Andrew Harvey

6. The Methodology of Econometrics (Volumes I and II)
   Dale J. Poirier

Future titles will include:

Bayesian Inference
George C. Tiao and Nicholas Polson

General to Specific Modelling
Neil R. Ericsson

Selection Bias
James J. Heckman

Specification Problems

Nonlinear Models

Time Series
Volume I

Edited by

Andrew Harvey

Professor of Econometrics, Department of Statistics
London School of Economics and Political Science

THE INTERNATIONAL LIBRARY OF CRITICAL WRITINGS IN ECONOMETRICS

An Elgar Reference Collection

Published by
Edward Elgar Publishing Limited
Gower House
Croft Road
Aldershot
Hants GU11 3HR
England

Edward Elgar Publishing Company
Old Post Road
Brookfield
Vermont 05036
USA

British Library Cataloguing in Publication Data
Time Series. – (International Library of
Critical Writings in Economics; Vol. 5)
I. Harvey, A.C. II. Series
330.0151955

Library of Congress Cataloguing in Publication Data
Time series / edited by Andrew Harvey.
p. cm. — (International library of critical writings in
econometrics : 5)
"An Elgar reference collection."
1. Time-series analysis. 2. Econometrics. I. Harvey, Andrew,
1947– . II. Series.
HB139.T53 1995
330'01'51955—dc20 94–27602
CIP

ISBN 1 85278 662 0 (2 volume set)

Printed in Great Britain at the University Press, Cambridge

Contents

Acknowledgements

The editor and publishers wish to thank the following who have kindly given permission for the use of copyright material.

American Statistical Association for articles: John F. Muth (1960), 'Optimal Properties of Exponentially Weighted Forecasts', *Journal of the American Statistical Association*, **55** (290), June, 299–306; G.E.P. Box and David A. Pierce (1970), 'Distribution of Residual Autocorrelations in Autoregressive-Integrated Moving Average Time Series Models', *Journal of the American Statistical Association*, **65** (332), December, 1509–26; Kenneth F. Wallis (1974), 'Seasonal Adjustment and Relations Between Variables', *Journal of the American Statistical Association*, **69** (345), March 18–31; G.E.P. Box and G.C. Tiao (1975), 'Intervention Analysis with Applications to Economic and Environmental Problems', *Journal of the American Statistical Association*, **70** (349), March, 70–79; David A. Dickey and Wayne A. Fuller (1979), 'Distribution of the Estimators for Autoregressive Time Series with a Unit Root', *Journal of the American Statistical Association*, **74** (366), June, 427–31; G.C. Tiao and G.E.P. Box (1981), 'Modeling Multiple Time Series with Applications', *Journal of the American Statistical Association*, **76** (376), December, 802–16; S.C. Hillmer and G.C. Tiao (1982), 'An ARIMA-Model-Based Approach to Seasonal Adjustment', *Journal of the American Statistical Association*, **77** (377), March, 63–70; W.R. Bell and S.C. Hillmer (1983), 'Modeling Time Series with Calendar Variation', *Journal of the American Statistical Association*, **78** (383), September, 526–34; Charles R. Nelson and Heejoon Kang (1984), 'Pitfalls in the Use of Time as an Explanatory Variable in Regression', *Journal of Business & Economic Statistics*, **2** (1), January, 73–82; Genshiro Kitigawa and Will Gersch (1984), 'A Smoothness Priors–State Space Modeling of Time Series with Trend and Seasonality', *Journal of the American Statistical Association*, **79** (386), June, 378–89; A.C. Harvey (1985), 'Trends and Cycles in Macroeconomic Time Series', *Journal of Business & Economic Statistics*, **3** (3), July, 216–27; Agustin Maravall (1985), 'On Structural Time Series Models and the Characterization of Components', *Journal of Business & Economic Statistics*, **3** (4), October, 350–55; Sastry G. Pantula (1991), 'Asymptotic Distributions of Unit Root Tests when the Process is Nearly Stationary', *Journal of Business & Economic Statistics*, **9** (1), January, 63–71.

Basil Blackwell Ltd for articles: G.E.P. Box and G.M. Jenkins (1962), 'Some Statistical Aspects of Adaptive Optimization and Control', *Journal of the Royal Statistical Society*, Series B, **24** (2), 297–331; G.E.P. Box and G.C. Tiao (1976), 'Comparison of Forecast and Actuality', *Applied Statistics*, Series C, **25** (3), 195–200; P.J. Harrison and C.F. Stevens (1976), 'Bayesian Forecasting', *Journal of the Royal Statistical Society*, Series B, **38** (3), 205–47; James E.H. Davidson, David F. Hendry, Frank Srba and Stephen Yeo (1978), 'Econometric Modelling of the Aggregate Time-Series Relationship between Consumers'

Expenditure and Income in the United Kingdom', *Economic Journal*, **88** (352), December, 661–92; John Geweke and Susan Porter–Hudak (1983), 'The Estimation and Application of Long Memory Time Series Models', *Journal of Time Series Analysis*, **4** (4), 221–38; A.C. Harvey and J. Durbin (1986), 'The Effects of Seat Belt Legislation on British Road Casualties: A Case Study in Structural Time Series Modelling', *Journal of the Royal Statistical Society*, Series A, **149** (3), 187–210.

Biometrika Trustees for articles: Paul Newbold (1974), 'The Exact Likelihood Function for a Mixed Autoregressive–Moving Average Process', *Biometrika*, **61** (3), December, 423–6; G.M. Ljung and G.E.P. Box (1978), 'On a Measure of Lack of Fit in Time Series Models', *Biometrika*, **65** (2), August, 297–303; D.S. Poskitt and A.R. Tremayne (1980), 'Testing the Specification of a Fitted Autoregressive-Moving Average Model', *Biometrika*, **67** (2), August, 359–63.

Econometric Society for articles: Robert F. Engle and C.W.J. Granger (1987), 'Co-Integrating and Error Correction: Representation, Estimation, and Testing', *Econometrica*, **55** (2), March, 251–76; P.C.B. Phillips (1987), 'Time Series Regression with a Unit Root', *Econometrica*, **55** (2), March, 277–301; James H. Stock (1987), 'Asymptotic Properties of Least Squares Estimators of Cointegrating Vectors', *Econometrica*, **55** (5), September, 1035–56; Christopher A. Sims, James H. Stock and Mark W. Watson (1990), 'Inference in Linear Time Series Models with Some Unit Roots', *Econometrica*, **58** (1), January, 113–44.

Elsevier Science Publishers B.V. for articles: Charles R. Nelson and Charles I. Plosser (1982), 'Trends and Random Walks in Macroeconomic Time Series: Some Evidence and Implications', *Journal of Monetary Economics*, **10** (2), September, 139–62; Søren Johansen (1988), 'Statistical Analysis of Cointegration Vectors', *Journal of Economic Dynamics & Control*, **12**, 231–54.

Elsevier Sequoia S.A. for article: A. Zellner and F. Palm (1974), 'Time Series Analysis and Simultaneous Equation Econometric Models', *Journal of Econometrics*, **2**, 17–54.

Institute of Management Science for article: Peter R. Winters (1960), 'Forecasting Sales by Exponentially Weighted Moving Averages', *Management Science*, **6** (3), April, 324–42.

Every effort has been made to trace all the copyright holders but if any have been inadvertently overlooked the publishers will be pleased to make the necessary arrangement at the first opportunity.

In addition the publishers wish to thank the Library of the London School of Economics and Political Science, the Marshall Library of Economics, Cambridge University and the Photographic Unit of the University of London Library for their assistance in obtaining these articles.

Introduction

Overview

The last twenty years has witnessed a considerable increase in the use of time series techniques in econometrics. Indeed many of the theoretical developments in the subject have been motivated by problems associated with economic and financial data. The articles in this volume have been chosen to illustrate what I feel to have been the main themes in time series work as it relates to econometrics.

In the following discussion, references denoted by an asterisk (*) appear in the volume. A dagger (†) indicates that the article appears in the companion volume by Wallis.

Ad hoc Forecasting Procedures

The EWMA is an *ad hoc* procedure for forecasting the level of a series by discounting past observations. Because this discounting is done exponentially, the current forecast can be updated very easily each time a new observation becomes available. The EWMA is therefore a simple recursion, in which only the current forecast needs to be stored. As a result it can be implemented with very primitive computing facilities and applied to a large number of series.

The EWMA can be extended so as to include trend and seasonal effects in the forecast function. This was done by Holt (1957), in an unpublished paper, and by Winters (1960)*. Hence the term 'Holt–Winters forecasting'. A somewhat different approach to generalizing the EWMA was taken by Brown (1963), who adopted a regression framework and used the method of discounted least squares.

Exponential smoothing techniques are intuitively appealing and have been used with considerable success, particularly in management science applications, such as forecasting inventories. However, the fact that they are applied in an *ad hoc* manner, without reference to an underlying statistical model, is a severe limitation. In the early 1960s, statistical models underlying exponential smoothing procedures were proposed. Apart from providing the basis for statistical inference and the construction of prediction intervals, these models could be generalized to give *classes* of models which could handle a much wider range of forecasting problems. The two main classes are ARIMA models and structural time series models.

ARIMA Modelling

The paper by Box and Jenkins (1962)* is concerned with developing the relationship between linear predictors and control theory. In doing so, it sets out the relationship between exponential smoothing procedures and certain linear time series models. Exponential smoothing procedures are concerned with forecasting nonstationary series, and Box and Jenkins (BJ) show how differencing enables the classical theory of stationary stochastic processes to be applied to the problem of forecasting nonstationary series. The resulting models belong to the autoregressive-integrated-moving average, or ARIMA, class. Box and Jenkins published a number of other papers in the 1960s and at the end of the decade provided a unified approach to ARIMA modelling in their book; see Box and Jenkins (1970).

The estimation of ARIMA models is relatively easy if certain simplifications are made to the initial conditions. Approximate maximum likelihood (ML) estimators can then be obtained by minimizing what is known as a conditional sum of squares function. Exact ML is more difficult, but a particularly insightful exposition is given by Newbold (1974)*.

An important part of the BJ approach to model building is diagnostic checking. This is now a standard feature of econometric and time series modelling, and its development owes a great deal to BJ. When a time series model is estimated, the residuals should indicate that it is picking up all the serial correlation in the series. As was pointed out by Durbin (1970), the properties of the residuals depend on the fitted model, and the portmanteau test of Box and Pierce (1970)* allows for this point. A modified test statistic proposed by Ljung and Box (1978)* has better small sample properties. An alternative approach to testing for residual serial correlation uses the Lagrange multiplier (LM) principle. Evidence on the effectiveness of the LM approach can be found in Poskitt and Tremayne (1980)*.

ARIMA models are based on taking differences. A generalization of the ARIMA class is obtained by considering the idea of fractional differencing. In other words, the degree of differencing need not be an integer. Geweke and Porter-Hudak (1983)* provide a discussion of the properties of such models and suggest an estimation procedure.

Structural Time Series Models

Muth (1960)* showed that the EWMA could be rationalized by a statistical model in which the observations are the sum of a random walk, representing the underlying level, and white noise, representing an irregular component. The rate of discounting then depends on the ratio of the variance of the disturbance driving the random walk to that of the white noise. The fact that the components in the model have an interpretation is appealing and this random walk plus noise, or local level, model is the simplest example of a structural time series model.

Theil and Wage (1964) and Nerlove and Wage (1964) extended Muth's work by writing down a model with a slope term. This local linear trend model gave forecasts equivalent to those obtained by the non-seasonal Holt–Winters procedure. However, the currently available technology was such that further development along these lines was not pursued until the 1970s. The key to handling structural time series models is the state space form; see Volume II Part II. The main work in this area was in engineering, and it was some time before statisticians appreciated the importance of papers such as Schweppe (1965)* which showed how the likelihood function could be obtained from the Kalman filter.

Although there was a lull in the development of structural time series models within the classical framework which Box and Jenkins had successfully adopted for ARIMA models, Harrison and Stevens (1971, 1976*) made progress along similar lines using a Bayesian approach. Their response to the problems posed by a classical treatment of what they called 'dynamic linear models' was to assume knowledge of certain key parameters and to start off the Kalman filter with proper prior distribution. They then considered a further class of models in which the data generation process switches between a finite number of regimes.

The development of structural time series models from the classical viewpoint regained its momentum in the late 1970s. Early contributions include the papers by Pagan (1975), Engle (1978), and Kitagawa and Gersch (1984)*. The net result has been a class of models and an associated modelling strategy which provide an alternative to ARIMA modelling; see the book by Harvey (1989). A structural time series model is defined as one which is formulated in terms of components which have a direct interpretation. Thus a typical model for a macroeconomic time series might include trend, seasonal, cyclical and irregular components, while a model for daily electricity demand might feature a day of the week effect. Such models can be regarded as regression models in which the explanatory variables are functions of time and the parameters are time-varying. This regression interpretation opens the way to a model selection methodology much more in keeping with that employed in modern econometrics. The contrast with ARIMA methodology is illustrated in Harvey (1985)*; see also Harvey and Durbin (1986)* in Part VI.

Unit Roots, Detrending and Non-stationarity

Autoregressive (AR) models can be estimated by ordinary least squares and the asymptotic distributional theory for stationary processes is relatively straightforward; see Mann and Wald (1944). This is no longer true when the underlying process is an AR in differences, but it is estimated in levels without imposing any restrictions on the parameters. The simplest example arises when the underlying process is a random walk, and a first order autoregression is estimated. The distribution of the OLS estimator of the AR parameter is not asymptotically normal; see Dickey and Fuller (1979)*. Furthermore, the simulation evidence presented in Fuller (1976) shows that in finite samples it tends to be much less than one, and that this tendency is exacerbated with the addition of a constant and a time trend. A test that the parameter is one must therefore be based on specially constructed tables. A number of authors have attacked the more general problem of testing for the appropriate degree of differencing. Some idea of the statistical theory needed to analyse these 'unit root' tests can be found in Phillips (1987)*. A study of their effectiveness can be found in Pantula (1991)*. Note that a structural time series modelling framework suggests different methods of testing for non-stationarity; see, for example, Nebaya and Tanaka (1988).

While it is clear that most economic time series are non-stationary, there has been some disagreement as to whether they can be best represented by a trend-stationary model, consisting of a stationary process around a deterministic time trend, or by a model, such as an ARIMA model, which is stationary in differences. Nelson and Plosser (1982)* present evidence based on unit root tests which comes down strongly in favour of the difference-stationary formulation; see also the paper by Harvey (1985)* referred to in the previous section. Note that the trend-stationary paradigm supports the common practice of detrending series by regressing on time prior to any analysis. As demonstrated in Nelson and Kang (1984)*, assuming trend-stationarity when it is inappropriate can lead to very misleading inferences being made.

Seasonality, Seasonal Adjustment and Calendar Effects

It is often necessary to decompose a series into trend, seasonal and irregular components. Structural time series models are explicitly formulated in terms of such components and so once a model has been fitted, a decomposition can be made almost immediately. It is less straightforward to decompose an ARIMA model into components, but Hillmer and Tiao (1982)* show how this may be done in certain special cases.

One of the main reasons for decomposing a time series is to remove the seasonal component. If a model, whether ARIMA or structural, is fitted to the data, this process is known as model-based seasonal adjustment. As such it may be contrasted with more mechanical approaches such as the widely used US Bureau of the Census X-11 procedure. Cleveland and Tiao (1976) derived an unobserved components model which would lead to components very close to those obtained by X-11. Maravall (1985)* compares and contrasts seasonal adjustment based on X-11, structural and ARIMA models.

Wallis (1974)* and Sims (1974) show how seasonally adjusting two series using different methods can distort the relationship between them.

The use of monthly observations raises certain issues which do not normally apply to quarterly data. These are termed calendar effects. There are two main sources of calendar effects: trading day variation and moving festivals. The former arises because business activity varies with the day of the week. Thus, for example, variables like total production or sales of some commodity will depend on which days of the week occur five times in a particular month in a given year. This information is known, and so may be incorporated in a time series model. Bell and Hillmer (1982)* describe how this may be done. They also discuss the treatment of one of the most important moving festivals, namely Easter. The timing of Easter can have a significant effect on the values of observations in March and April.

Dynamic Regression and Intervention Analysis

Explanatory variables may be included in a time series model. There may be lags in the response of the dependent variable to changes in the explanatory variables, and there are a number of ways of capturing distributed lags parsimoniously. ARIMA models may be extended to include explanatory variables by letting the lag structure depend on the ratio of two polynomials in the lag operator. This is known as a rational distributed lag, and when combined with an ARIMA disturbance it gives a transfer function model. Explanatory variables may be included in structural time series models. Rational distributed lags can also be used although they are less natural in this context and other lag structures, such as polynomial (Almon) distributed lags, or even unrestricted distributed lags may be entertained.

An important special case of an explanatory variable is a dummy, or intervention, variable which is used to represent a qualitative effect such as a particular event or a change in policy. Box and Tiao (1975)* call this kind of modelling 'intervention analysis'. The paper by Harvey and Durbin (1986)* develops intervention analysis within a structural framework, but also considers various diagnostic checking techniques which are applicable to intervention analysis carried out in other ways.

As a rule structural and transfer function models share the common feature of having nonstationary stochastic components. Thus, the explanatory variables do not explain all the long run movements in the dependent variable. A stochastic trend, explicit in a structural model and implicit in a transfer function, is therefore used. In classical econometrics, on the other hand, the explanatory variables explain all the long-run movements in the dependent variable. Thus the disturbance term is stationary, if not random white noise. In the autoregressive distributed lag framework, lagged values of the dependent variable are employed. A rearrangement of the lag structure in a model of this kind leads to the long-run, or equilibrium, relationship appearing explicitly in what is called an '*error correction term*'; see Davidson *et al* (1978)*. When the variables in the model are themselves nonstationary, the existence of an equilibrium relationship means that they are *co-integrated*. A full discussion of this concept can be found in the paper by Engle and Granger (1987)* which appears in the section on multivariate models. The article by Stock (1987)* explores the statistical implications of co-integration for single equation estimation. He establishes that a static regression gives a *superconsistent* estimator of the coefficient in the long-run relationship between two co-integrated variables.

Multivariate Models

In a multivariate time series model a set of variables are modelled jointly. There are no exogenous variables. Box and Tiao (1981)* discuss some of the ways in which ARIMA models may be generalized to multivariate series. Multivariate structural time series models may also be set up, and examples include Clark (1989). The relationship between dynamic simultaneous equation systems and time series models is explored in Zellner and Palm (1974)* and Wallis (1977)†.

It was pointed out in the previous section that a stable economic relationship between a set of economic variables implies that they are cointegrated. This has important implications for multivariate modelling. Engle and Granger (1987)* derive an important result, known as the Granger Representation Theorem which sets out the constraints which cointegration implies on the stationary multivariate time series model. A multivariate error correction model is then obtained. Granger and Engle also discuss a two-stage estimation procedure for single equations involving cointegrated variables. The first step is to carry out a simple static regression in levels; see the paper by Stock (1987)* in the previous section. A unit root test is then carried out on the residuals, and a rejection of the unit root is taken as evidence for cointegration. A second regression then estimates the short-run dynamics.

Autoregressive models are much easier to handle in a multivariate context than mixed ARIMA models, since they may be estimated unrestrictedly by OLS. In an influential paper, Sims (1980)† argued that the uncertainty surrounding economic theory makes vector auto-regressions an attractive alternative to traditional macroeconomic models. Since then they have become very popular. However, when some, or all, of the series are nonstationary, inference is complicated by the possibility of co-integration. Differencing in the presence of cointegration leads to strict noninvertibility, and so an AR representation is not possible. On the other hand, unconstrained estimation in levels leads to the kind of statistical problems associated with unit roots. Nevertheless, the theory surrounding inference in such cases has been worked out by Sims, Stock and Watson (1988)*. The constraints which cointegration implies for a levels autoregression can be imposed using the method described in Johansen (1988)*. He also sets out a procedure for testing for the order of cointegration, that is the number of stationary linear combinations of the series in the model.

Causality, Exogeneity and Expectations

A multivariate framework provides the basis for exploring issues which are important for understanding and modelling economic systems. For example, the notion of causality is central to a behavioural model. Granger (1969)* attempted to formulate ways in which the leads and lags between time series could provide evidence on the direction of a causal relationship. An application of these ideas can be found in Sims (1972)*. On the basis of causality tests, Sims concluded that changes in the money supply caused changes in GNP, but not *vice versa*. There have been a number of papers which have developed further tests for causality. However, whatever technique is applied, considerable care must be exercised regarding the conclusions which are drawn. An excellent discussion of the philosophical ideas underlying causality and the implications for causality testing can be found in Zellner (1978)*. While the notion of causality suggested by Granger is undoubtedly a useful concept, many econometricians prefer to use the term 'Granger causality' to indicate that a cause and effect relationship should not necessarily be inferred.

Granger causality also features in the article by Engle, Hendry and Richard (1983)*. The main focus of their paper is on exogeneity. They explore what this actually means in the context of economic modelling and its implications for estimation.

Economic theory imposes certain constraints on economic models. The most interesting from the time series point of view are those implied by rational expectations. Wallis (1980)* provides a good introduction to the nature of these constraints and the tools needed to handle them.

State Space Models and the Kalman Filter

The state space formulation is fundamental to time series modelling, in that it enormously expands the range of models which can be handled. For example it enables the parameters in structural time series models to be estimated, and provides the means for making forecasts and estimating the unobserved components such as trend and seasonal.

The Kalman filter is the basic recursion which allows the state vector to be updated as new observations become available. The classic article is Kalman (1960)*, but a more accessible introduction is provided by Meinhold and Singpurwalla (1983)*. Duncan and Horn (1972)* derive the filter without the assumption of normality. When normality is assumed, the Kalman filter enables the likelihood to be obtained in terms of one-step ahead prediction errors as pointed out by Schweppe (1965)*. The paper by de Jong (1991)* represents the current state of the art for the handling of statistical models by state space methods.

An early example of the use of Kalman filtering techniques in econometrics can be found in Rosenberg (1972)*. He estimates a multivariate model with time-varying parameters.

Recursive least squares in linear regression can be regarded as a special case of the Kalman filter. Brown, Durbin and Evans (1975)* used recursive least squares as a means of detecting structural change and it now features in many econometric packages.

A state space formulation allows data irregularities to be handled very easily. For example, Jones (1980)* estimates an ARIMA model with missing observations by putting it in state space form.

Non-Linear and Non-Gaussian Models

A non-linear time series model is basically one in which an observation cannot be expressed as a linear combination of current and past values of a series independent random variables. This opens up an enormous range of possibilities. Here we concentrate on a few models which are useful, or likely to be useful, in practice.

The class of models based on the idea of autoregressive conditional heteroscedasticity, or ARCH, has proved to be very popular as a means of capturing the changes in variance in financial time series, although the original paper, by Engle (1982)*, was actually concerned with inflation. Bollerslev (1986)* generalized the ARCH class of models to produce the GARCH class. The dynamic properties of these models with respect to variance are analogous to those of ARIMA models.

The model by Hamilton (1989)* is an example of how switches in regime can be handled by a non-linear model. He derives a filter which forms the basis of the statistical treatment.

A means of testing for non-linear effects is given by McLeod and Li (1983)*. They obtain the distribution of the portmanteau test statistic when it is constructed from the autocorrelations of squared residuals. Other tests are given by Tsay (1986)*.

Most time series models are based on an assumption of normality. Models for non-Gaussian observations are usually non-linear. Kitagawa (1987)* shows how filtering, smoothing and ML estimation can be carried out in a state space framework when the disturbances are non-normal. The method is computer intensive. West, Harrison and Migon (1985) approach the problem from a Bayesian perspective. Smith and Miller (1986)* extend an approach of J.Q. Smith (1980) and derive an analytic filter for observations following an exponential distribution.

References

Box, G.E.P. and Jenkins, G.M. (1970), *Time Series Analysis: Forecasting and Control*, San Francisco: Holden-Day

Brown, R.G. (1963), *Smoothing, Forecasting and Prediction*, Englewood Cliffs: Prentice Hall

Clark, P. (1989), 'Trend Reversion in Real Output and Unemployment', *Journal of Econometrics*, **40**, 15–32

Durbin, J. (1970), 'Testing for Serial Correlation in Least Squares Regression when Some of the Regressors are Lagged Dependent Variables', *Econometrica*, **38**, 410–21

Engle, R.F. (1978), 'Estimating Structural Models of Seasonality', in A. Zellner (ed.), *Seasonal Analysis of Economic Time Series*, Washington DC: Bureau of the Census, 281–308

Fuller, W.A. (1976), *Introduction to Statistical Time Series*, New York: John Wiley and Sons

Harrison, P.J. and Stevens, C.F. (1971), 'A Bayesian Approach to Short-term Forecasting', *Operational Research Quarterly*, **22**, 341–62

Harvey, A.C. (1989), *Forecasting, Structural Time Series Models and the Kalman Filter*, Cambridge: Cambridge University Press

Holt, C.C. (1957), 'Forecasting Seasonals and Trends by Exponentially Weighted Moving Averages', ONR Research Memorandum No. 52, Carnegie Institute of Technology, Pittsburgh, Pennsylvania

Mann, H.B. and Wald, A. (1943), 'On the Statistical Treatment of the Linear Stochastic Difference Equations', *Econometrica*, **11**, 173–220

Nabeya, S. and Tanaka, K. (1988), 'Asymptotic Theory of a Test for the Constancy of Regression Coefficients against the Random Walk Alternative', *Annals of Statistics*, **16**, 218–35

Nerlove, M. and Wage, S. (1964), 'On the Optimality of Adaptive Forecasting', *Management Science*, **10** (2), 207–29

Pagan, A.R. (1975), 'A Note on the Extraction of Components from Time Series', *Econometrica*, **43**, 163–8

Sims, C.A. (1974), 'Seasonality in Regression', *Journal of the American Statistical Association*, **69**, 618–27

Sims, C.A. (1980), 'Macroeconomics and Reality', *Econometrica*, **48**, 1–48

Smith, J.Q. (1979), 'A Generalization of the Bayesian Steady Forecasting Model', *Journal of the Royal Statistical Society*, **B 41**, 375–87

Theil, H. and Wage, S. (1964), 'Some Observations on Adaptive Forecasting', *Management Science*, **10**, 198–206

Wallis, K.F. (1977), 'Multiple Time Series Analysis and the Final Form of Econometric Models', *Econometrica*, **45**, 1481–97

West, M., Harrison, P.J. and Migon, H.S. (1985), 'Dynamic Generalised Linear Models and Bayesian Forecasting (with discussion)', *Journal of the American Statistical Association*, **80**, 73–97

Part I
Ad Hoc Forecasting Procedures

[1]

FORECASTING SALES BY EXPONENTIALLY WEIGHTED MOVING AVERAGES*†

PETER R. WINTERS

Graduate School of Industrial Administration, Carnegie Institute of Technology

The growing use of computers for mechanized inventory control and production planning has brought with it the need for explicit forecasts of sales and usage for individual products and materials. These forecasts must be made on a routine basis for thousands of products, so that they must be made quickly, and, both in terms of computing time and information storage, cheaply; they should be responsive to changing conditions. The paper presents a method of forecasting sales which has these desirable characteristics, and which in terms of ability to forecast compares favorably with other, more traditional methods. Several models of the exponential forecasting system are presented, along with several examples of application.

1. Introduction

Many forecasts of the future are made by people in the course of running a business, although in a large number of cases the forecasts are not called that, and the methods of making the forecasts are not clearly known even to the people making them. Forecasts are made for a variety of purposes, for example, for cash budgeting, establishing sales quotas, setting expense budgets, planning capital expenditures, and for production and inventory planning and control. The methods used to make the forecasts differ widely, as one would expect them to, because their uses differ widely. The kind of forecast requirement that this paper is particularly concerned with is the last mentioned above: forecasting sales of individual products for inventory control and production scheduling.

The need for forecasts of individual product (or item) sales most frequently arises because of an inventory control system, or a production scheduling system, consisting of decision rules which specify when to produce or order more of a particular item (triggers or order points) and how much to produce or order (lot sizes or order quantities). These decision rules are based in part on a prediction of sales or usage of each item in the near future. The rules are applied on a routine basis to many products, often tens of thousands, or even hundreds of thousands of them. Forecasts must be made frequently, monthly or weekly, on a routine basis.

* Received June 1959.

† This paper will appear in substantially the same form as a chapter in the forthcoming book: *Planning Production, Inventories and Employment*, by Charles C. Holt, John F. Muth, Franco Modigliani and Herbert A. Simon; Prentice-Hall, publishers. Earlier models of the exponential forecasting system appeared in ONR Research Memorandum No. 52, "Forecasting Seasonals and Trends by Exponentially Weighted Moving Averages", by Charles C. Holt, Carnegie Institute of Technology, April, 1957. William Gere assisted with the numerical calculations. This paper was written as part of the project "Planning and Control of Industrial Operations", sponsored by the Office of Naval Research, Contract No. ONR 27 T.O. 1, at Carnegie.

There are certain desirable characteristics of these forecasts that are implied by their use: they must be made quickly, cheaply, and easily; the forecasting technique must be clearly spelled out, so that it can be followed routinely, either manually or using an electronic computer. The number of pieces of information required to make a single forecast must be kept at a minimum, or else the total amount of information required for all products will be expensive to store and expensive to maintain. Finally, partly implicit in the above, is the need to be able to introduce the latest sales information easily and cheaply.

Quite a few forecasting techniques, or systems, are available or could be developed for predicting item sales. The ones discussed in this paper do not "predict" with a behavioral model of sales, but use an analysis of the sales time-series taken out of context. That is, the only input to the forecasting system is the past history of sales of the item, and not, for example, such information as what is happening in the market, the industry, the economy, sales of competing and complimentary products, price changes, advertising campaigns, and so on. A behavioral prediction model would have to be developed for each application, and would probably lack most of the desirable characteristics of a forecasting system that are listed above. Various forms of the exponential model have been used for a wide variety of forecasting applications with little modification.[1]

In its simplest form, the exponential system makes a forecast of expected sales in the next period by a weighted average of sales in the current period, and the forecast of sales for the current period made during the previous period. In the same way, the forecast for the current period was a weighted average of sales during the previous period and the forecast of sales for that period made in the period before. This same process continues back to the beginning of the sales data for the item. Thus a prediction made in any period is based on current sales data, and all the previous sales data for the item, but in such a way that only one number (the most recent estimate for the current period) must be retained to be combined with the latest incoming sales information.

This scheme obviously has the characteristics desired in a prediction method: current sales information is easily introduced, the forecast calculation is fast, and only a limited amount of information must be kept and maintained. For some products with stable sales rates and little seasonal influence, this simple exponential model proves quite satisfactory. Many products, however, have a marked trend in their sales, particularly when they are first introduced, or when competing products are introduced. And for many products there is a substantial seasonal pattern. It is usually worthwhile extending the exponential system to take into account long-run trends and seasonal effects. These two factors are handled in exactly the same way as the simple exponential system. More information is required with this more complete model, but the accuracy of prediction is also substantially increased for most kinds of products.

[1] For earlier types of exponential models see, for example, J. F. Magee, *Production Planning and Inventory Control*, McGraw-Hill, 1958. A more complete version of this model is given in *Statistical Forecasting*, by R. G. Brown, printed by Arthur D. Little, Inc., 1958.

Three forecasting models are used in a similar way in the paper to predict sales for three different time series. One of these is the (complete) exponential model; the other two are a naive model and a simple forecasting model of the more usual type. A comparison of "ability to predict" will be presented later in the paper to give a basis for evaluating the exponential model. The results of these comparisons show that the exponential system makes more accurate forecasts, requires less information storage, and requires slightly more time to compute, than the better of the two conventional models.

2. Development of the Exponential System

A number of variations of the exponential weighting method can be used. In this section we will present a sample of the possible variants, hopefully those which help demonstrate the method best and which are most generally useful. We will indicate other variants which might have more limited application.

2.1 *The Simplest Exponential Model*

The simplest application of an exponentially weighted moving average would be to the problem of making a forecast of the expected value of a stochastic variable whose mean (or expected value) does not change between successive drawings. This would correspond to predicting the expected sales for a product which had no definite seasonal pattern and no long-run trend. The following procedure is proposed: take a weighted average of *all* past observations and use this as a forecast of the present mean of the distribution, as

$$\bar{S}_t = AS_t + (1 - A)\bar{S}_{t-1} \tag{1}$$

where

S_t = actual sales during the t'th period
$\bar{S}_t$ = forecast of expected sales in the t'th period
$0 \leqq A \leqq 1$

Then

$$\bar{S}_{t-1} = AS_{t-1} + (1 - A)\bar{S}_{t-2},$$

so that

$$\bar{S}_t = AS_t + A(1 - A)S_{t-1} + (1 - A)^2\bar{S}_{t-2}. \tag{2}$$

Continuing this process, $\bar{S}_t$ can be expressed explicitly in terms of all the past observations of sales, that is, all the sales data available:

$$\bar{S}_t = A \sum_{n=0}^{M} (1 - A)^n S_{t-n} + (1 - A)^{M+1}\bar{S}_b \tag{3}$$

where $\bar{S}_b$ is the beginning value of $\bar{S}$. M is the number of observations in the series up to and including the current period, t. Even for relatively small A, if M is large enough, that is, if enough history is used, $(1 - A)^{M+1}$ becomes very small, and the last term can be ignored.

Since the process which generates the sales data is a stationary process, that is, there is no seasonal pattern and no trend, then $\bar{S}_t$ is an unbiased estimate of $E(S)$, the expected sales in any period:

$$(4) \qquad E(\bar{S}_t) = E(S)A \sum_{n=0}^{M} (1 - A)^n + (1 - A)^{M+1}\bar{S}_b$$

As noted above for large M, and most A, $(1 - A)^{M+1}\bar{S}_b$ approaches zero. Under these same conditions $A \sum_{n=0}^{M} (1 - A)^n$ approaches one. Thus

$$E(\bar{S}_t) \cong E(S)$$

with the degree of approximation depending on the values of M and A.

The statistical properties of $\bar{S}_t$ as an estimate of $E(S_t)$ will not be rigorously spelled out when the stochastic process is not stationary. But a weighted moving average with exponential weights is evidently a sensible mode of behavior for this simple forecasting problem. If the distribution mean is subject to a variety of short- and long-run systematic changes then the exponential model has some intuitive advantages. If the distribution mean changes slowly, then A should be small so as to keep the effect of older observations. If the distribution mean changes quickly, then A should be large so as to attenuate quickly the effect of older observations, but not too large, or else $\bar{S}_t$ will be subject to too much random variation. The problem of finding a satisfactory value of the weighting parameter, A, will not be solved in detail for this simple model. In a later section, however, we will discuss in substantial detail the effect on prediction accuracy of the set of weighting parameters for the more complete exponential model, which includes seasonal and trend effects.

An exploration of those time series for which the exponential system is optimal will not be considered.[2] A more relevant question here is whether this approach to forecasting holds promise for a variety of applications, compared with other methods. Before going to the complete forecasting model which includes both seasonal and trend, we will study a simpler version which includes only a seasonal effect.

2.2 *Forecasting With Ratio Seasonals*

It is possible to develop a forecasting model with either a multiplicative or an additive seasonal effect. If the amplitude of the seasonal pattern is independent of the level of sales, then an additive model is appropriate. More often, however, the amplitude of the seasonal pattern is proportional to the level of sales. This would indicate using the multiplicative, or ratio, seasonal effect. Figure 1 shows the sales for an individual product over a period of time. The actual sales in period t is given by S_t. The estimate of the smoothed and seasonally adjusted sales rate in period t is given by $\bar{S}_t$. The periodicity of the seasonal effect is L;

[2] For discussion of this subject see J. F. Muth, "Optimal Properties of Exponentially Weighted Forecasts," *Journal of the American Statistical Association*, forthcoming.

ITEM SALES: SEASONAL PATTERN

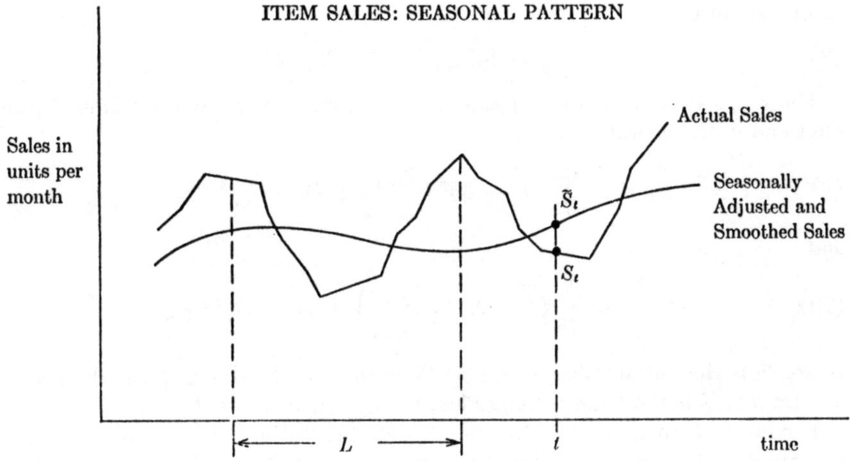

FIG. 1

if a period is a month, L would ordinarily be 12 months. The model is

$$(5) \qquad \bar{S}_t = A \frac{S_t}{F_{t-L}} + (1 - A)\bar{S}_{t-1}, \qquad 0 \leqq A \leqq 1$$

for the estimate of the expected deseasonalized sales rate in period t, and

$$(6) \qquad F_t = B \frac{S_t}{\bar{S}_t} + (1 - B)F_{t-L}, \qquad 0 \leqq B \leqq 1$$

for the current estimate of the seasonal factor for period t. In equation 5, $\bar{S}_t$ is a weighted sum of the current estimate obtained by deseasonalizing the current sales, S_t, and last period's estimate, $\bar{S}_{t-1}$, of the smoothed and seasonally adjusted sales rate for the series. (Note that in deseasonalizing current sales by S_t/F_{t-L}, the most recent estimate of the seasonal effect for periods in this position in the cycle has been used; the seasonal factor computed for May last year would be used to seasonally adjust this year's May data.) The value of $\bar{S}_t$ from Equation 5 is then used in forming a new estimate of the seasonal factor in Equation 6. This new estimate, F_t, is again a weighted sum of the current estimate, $S_t/\bar{S}_t$, and the previous estimate, F_{t-L}. A *forecast* of the expected sales in the following period would then be made using the following:

$$(7) \qquad S_{t,1} = \bar{S}_t F_{t-L+1}$$

where $S_{t,1}$ is the forecast made at the end of the current, or t'th period, for the following period. More generally, a forecast of expected sales T periods into the

[3] The forecasts can be readily extended beyond L periods in the future by *reusing* the L seasonal factors, $F_{t+1-L}, \cdots, F_t$.

future would be

$$S_{t,T} = \bar{S}_t F_{t-L+T}, \qquad T \leq L^3 \tag{8}$$

The weighted averages in Equations 5 and 6 may be written in terms of past data and initial conditions:

$$\bar{S}_t = A \sum_{n=0}^{M} (1-A)^n \frac{S_{t-n}}{F_{t-L-n}} + (1-A)^{M+1}\bar{S}_b \tag{9}$$

and

$$F_t = B \sum_{n=0}^{J} (1-B)^n \left(\frac{S_{t-nL}}{\bar{S}_{t-nL}}\right) + (1-B)^{J+1} F_{bt} \tag{10}$$

where $\bar{S}_b$ is the initial value of $\bar{S}$, and F_{bt} is the initial value of F for the period in question. J is the largest integer less than or equal to M/L.

The forecast, then, is a function of all past observations of the variable, of the weights A and B, and of the initial conditions $\bar{S}_b$ and the set of F_{bt}, L in number. The effect of the initial conditions on the forecast depends on the size of the weights and the length of the series preceding the current period, t. The effect of $\bar{S}_b$ will be usually attenuated sooner than the effect of the initial F's, because $\bar{S}_t$ is revised every period, but the F's are revised only once per cycle.

If this forecasting model with a seasonal but no trend effect is applied to a sales series for which the mean is subject to long and short-run systematic changes, or trends, then the seasonal factors, the F's, will quickly cease to be simple seasonal factors, and will soon contain some of the trend effect. For example, in application to a series of monthly observations, with a long-run upward trend, the set of twelve F's will begin to sum to more than 12.0, and compensate for the lack of a trend factor in the model. If, on the other hand, the model is applied to a series which includes short-run trends, of shorter duration than L, then the trend effect that is incorporated in the seasonal factor, F, is made up of short-run trend effects from the years previous to the use of the factor. Consequently, erratic behavior may be introduced into the seasonal adjustment and smoothing of S_t, and into the forecast itself. If the series for which the method is intended does have trend effects, and many sales series seem to, then we must introduce a specific trend factor.

2.3 *Forecasting with Ratio Seasonals and Linear Trend*

As with the preceding section it is possible to develop a forecasting model with either a ratio trend, or an additive, or linear trend. Because of the combination of short and long-run systematic changes in expected sales, it is more generally useful to work with the latter case. The form of the model for this "complete" forecasting scheme is similar to that given in Equations 5 and 6. First,

$$\bar{S}_t = A \frac{S_t}{F_{t-L}} + (1-A)(\bar{S}_{t-1} + R_{t-1}). \tag{11}$$

The only change in the definition of $\bar{S}_t$ is the addition of R_{t-1}, the most recent estimate of the additive trend factor, that is, the units per period that the expected sales rate, $\bar{S}_t$, is increasing (or decreasing). The expression for the revised estimate of the seasonal factor remains the same as it was in the previous section:

$$F_t = B\frac{S_t}{\bar{S}_t} + (1 - B)F_{t-L} \tag{12}$$

The expression for revising the estimate of the trend has the same form as Equations 11 and 12:

$$R_t = C(\bar{S}_t - \bar{S}_{t-1}) + (1 - C)R_{t-1} \tag{13}$$

weighting the estimate based on current data with the previous estimate. The forecast of sales T periods in the future would be obtained from the formula:

$$S_{t,T} = [\bar{S}_t + TR_t]F_{t-L+T} \qquad T = 1, 2, \cdots, L. \tag{14}$$

(Once again forecasts for future periods more distant than L can be made by reusing the appropriate F's.) Figure 2 illustrates the definition of variables.

In practice, the forecasting system would be used as follows to predict the sales of an individual product:

(1) At the end of the t'th (or current) period the actual sales of the product during the period, S_t, is recorded.

(2) Equation 11 is applied to evaluate $\bar{S}_t$, using $\bar{S}_{t-1}$ and A_{t-1} from the last period and the appropriate F_{t-L} computed during the previous cycle.

(3) Equation 12 is used to evaluate F_t, which can now replace F_{t-L}.

(4) Equation 13 is used to determine R_t, which can now replace R_{t-1}.

(5) Forecasts of future sales are made, using Equation 14.

(6) The value $\bar{S}_{t-1}$ is replaced by $\bar{S}_t$, and the data is ready for use at the end of the coming period.

ITEM SALES: SEASONAL AND TREND PATTERN

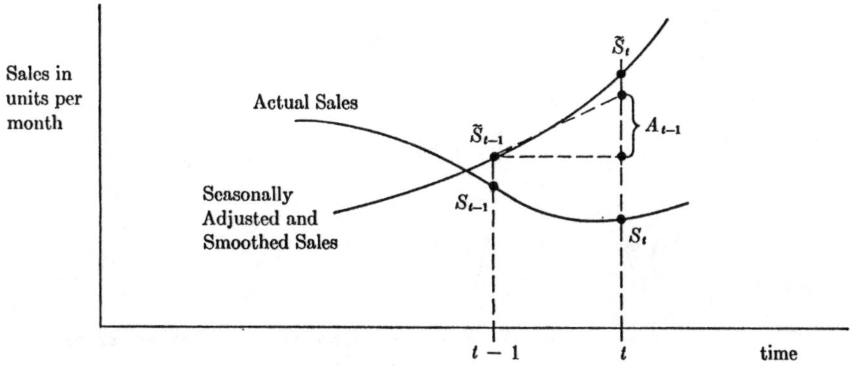

FIG. 2

Once again, the forecast is a function of past and current sales, of the weights A, B, C, and of the initial values of $\tilde{S}$, the F's, and R. And the quality, or accuracy, of forecasts depends upon these things, all of which except the sales history are at the command of the forecaster. In the next section we will discuss ways to select the weights and the initial conditions, and then we will demonstrate the use of the forecasting method.

3. Empirical Tests of Forecasting

3.1 *Selection of Weights and Initial Values*

First we will take up the problem of selecting initial values of $\tilde{S}$, the F's, and R, and the determination of the weights A, B, and C. Three series of sales are used to illustrate the application of the exponential system; these three are:

(1) Monthly sales of a cooking utensil, manufactured by Wearever, Inc. a subsidiary of the Aluminum Company of America; these are sales from the manufacturer's central warehouse to dealers; 7 years of data. See Figure 3.

(2) Bi-monthly sales of paint, one can-size of one color, manufactured by the paint division of Pittsburgh Plate Glass; sales are from one of the manufacturer's district warehouses to dealers; 5 years of data. See Figure 4.

(3) Monthly data of cellars excavated in one geographical area for the erection of prefabricated houses manufactured and sold by Admiral Homes, Inc. of West Newton, Pa.; 7 years of data. See Figure 5.

In each series the periods are numbered $t = 1, 2, \cdots, D$. For the cooking utensil, $D = 84$; for paint, $D = 30$; for cellars, $D = 84$. Each series has been divided into two parts, the first part of which was used to develop initial values of S, the F's, and R. The length of this first part of the series was H periods

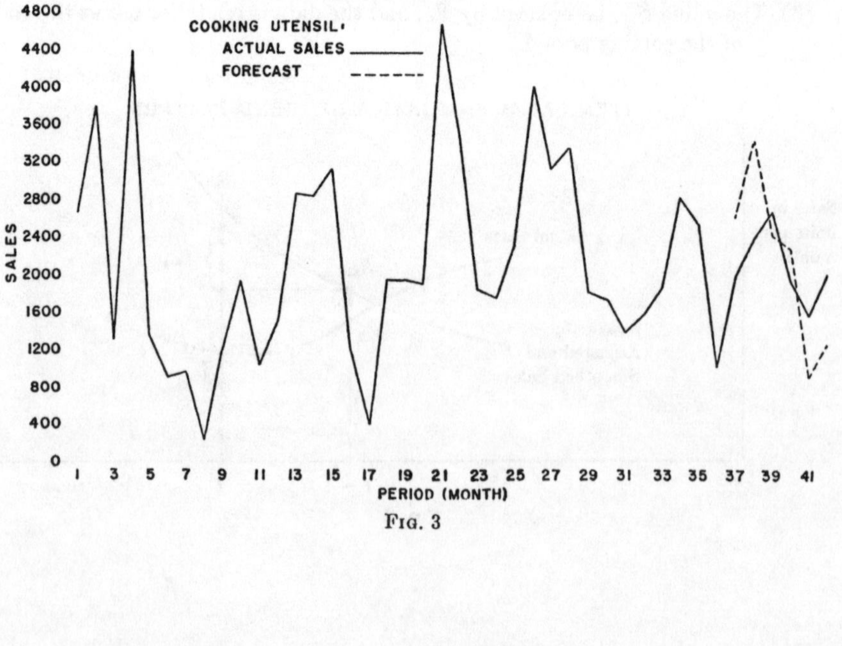

FIG. 3

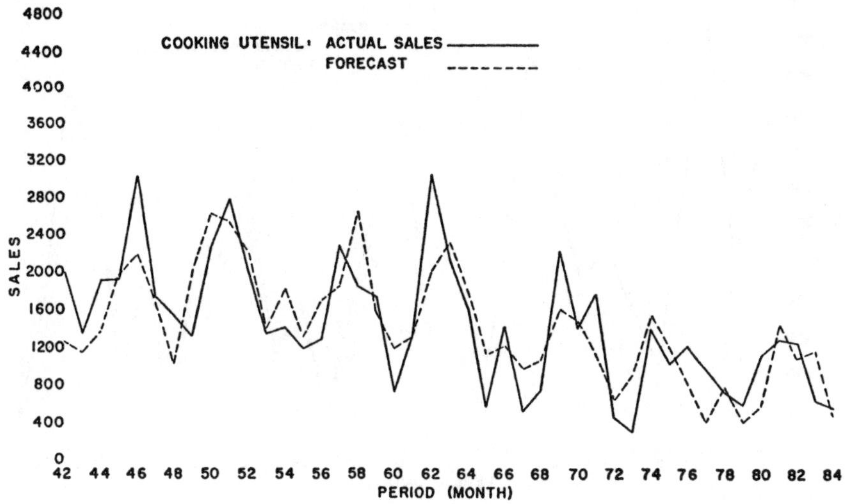

FIG. 3 (*Continued*)

($H = 36$, or 3 years, for the cooking utensil and cellars, and $H = 12$, or 2 years, for paint.) The second part of each series was then used to try out the forecasting method, by pretending that the future was unknown, making a forecast, moving along one period of actual sales data, comparing the forecast with actual sales, absorbing the actual sales data into the model, making another forecast, and so on. This is exactly as one would behave in practice, except for the advantage of collapsing several years of experience into a very short time, and the advantage of being able to experiment with a variety of values of the parameters, A, B, C.

The question immediately raised is how to compare one set of forecasts with another, that is, the effect of one set of parameters with the effect of another, or one forecasting method with another. Since the forecasts are predictions of expected values of sales it seems appropriate to choose as a criterion the standard deviation of forecast errors. If the forecast is unbiased, and this assumption is made here, then an estimate of the standard deviation of forecast errors is given by the sum of squared forecast errors. The forecast error is defined as

$$e_{t,T} = S_{t+T} - S_{t,T} \tag{15}$$

with S_{t+T} actual sales for the $(t + T)$ period, and $S_{t,T}$ the forecast for that period made in period t. If one is interested in forecasting only one period in the future, at any time, then the standard deviation of forecast errors is given by:

$$\sigma_e = \left\{ \frac{\sum_t e_{t,1}}{N - 1} \right\}^{1/2} \tag{16}$$

where t is summed over the set of N observations used for estimation. In practice forecasts are often made for several periods into the future, with the accuracy

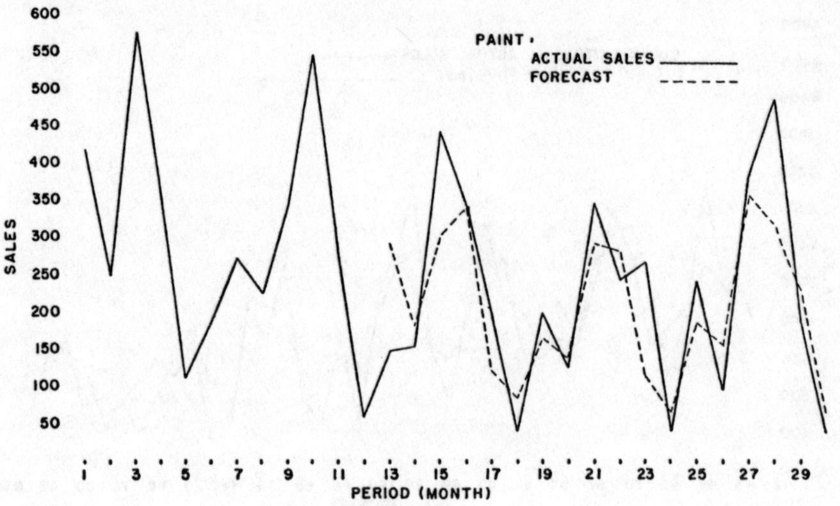

FIG. 4

of prediction most important for the coming period, and of declining importance for the later periods. In that case, a criterion function, U, which weights forecast errors such as the following can be used:

$$U = \sum_t (a_1 e_{t,1}^2 + a_2 e_{t,2}^2 + a_3 e_{t,3}^2) \tag{17}$$

with $a_1 > a_2 > a_3$, and possibly with $(a_1 + a_2 + a_3) = 1$. Investigation has shown that the set of weights (A, B, C) which given minimum σ_e is about the same as the set which gives minimum U for $a_1 = .6$, $a_2 = .3$, $a_3 = .1$. Because of this, we have used the simple criterion of Equation 16 for the empirical tests in the paper.

One can use any of a number of alternative methods to search for the set of (A, B, C) which minimizes σ_e. For example, we tried the method of steepest descent[4] and found it more or less satisfactory as a technique for finding the best weights for a single product. This method, however, gives only local information about the nature of σ_e, and it consumes enough time that it would not be feasible to use this method for each product, individually. We suspected that in fact σ_e is fairly "flat" near the minimum for any particular product, and that a single set of weights could be used for large classes of individual products. In order to find and present this kind of information, a grid of values of A, B, C was used for one series, the cooking utensil, and then additional points near the

[4] The method of steepest descent is sometimes called the gradient method. See, for example, *Modern Mathematics for the Engineer*, edited by E. F. Beckenbach, McGraw-Hill, 1956. Also, G. N. Lance, "Solution of Algebraic and Transcendental Equations on an Automatic Digital Computer," *Journal of the Association for Computing Machinery*, January, 1959.

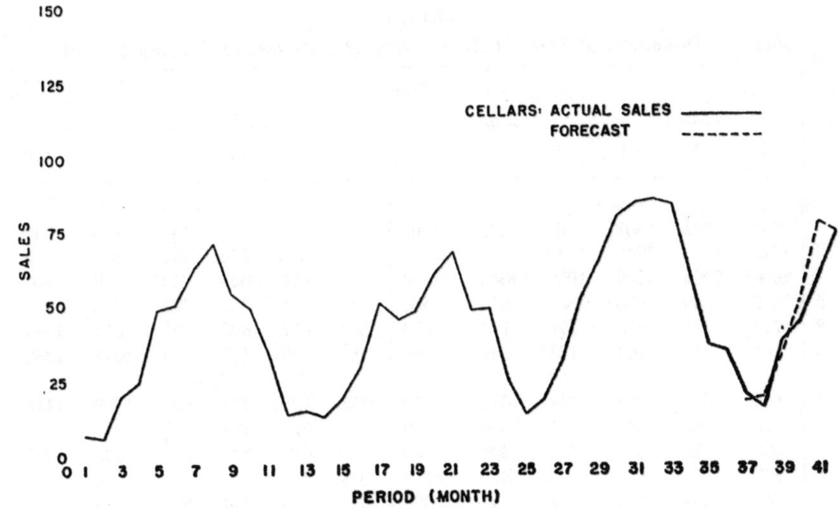

FIG. 5

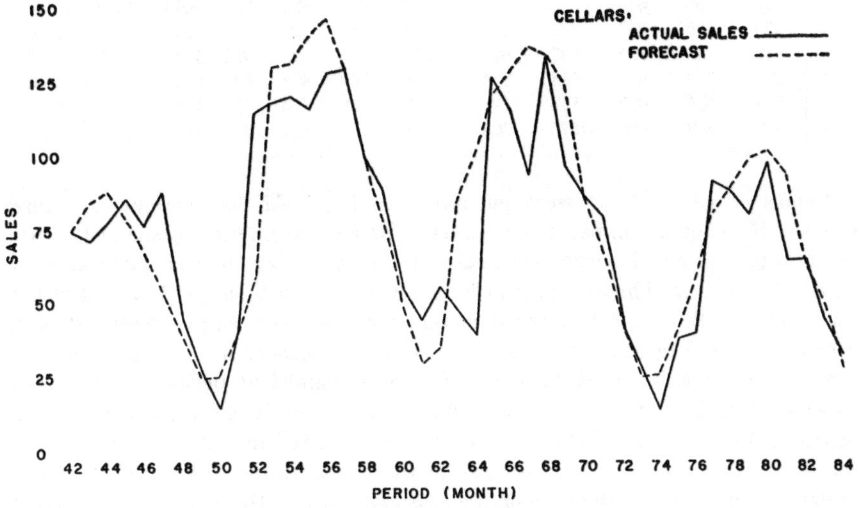

FIG. 5 (*Continued*)

minimum were used for each of the three series. The grid was made up of all possible combinations of 0, .2, .4, .6, .8, 1.0. The values of σ_e for these sets is given in Table 1. Table 2 shows the areas around the minimums of each series; the smallest division of the weights was a single decimal digit, i.e., (.1, .3, .2), but not (.13, .28, .24). It did in fact turn out that σ_e is flat near the minimum, but a detailed discussion of the results will be left until the method of calculation has been more fully described.

TABLE 1

Standard Deviations of Forecast Errors: Grid Results for the Cooking Utensil

B	C											
	0	.2	.4	.6	.8	1.0	0	.2	.4	.6	.8	1.0
	A = 0						A = .6					
0	1607	1607	1607	1607	1607	1607	630	663	717	781	855	940
.2	1249	1249	1249	1249	1249	1249	592	626	676	734	801	879
.4	1006	1006	1006	1006	1006	1006	567	603	655	713	780	864
.6	856	856	856	856	856	856	557	598	659	725	803	908
.8	778	778	778	778	778	778	566	617	698	791	915	1084
1.0	764	764	764	764	764	764	597	670	796	970	1294	1832
	A = .2						A = .8					
0	640	574	600	614	641	672	676	736	815	907	1009	1115
.2	570	518	539	557	599	649	650	710	784	871	967	1067
.4	531	488	510	541	622	752	630	689	761	845	938	1034
.6	523	*487**	522	605	849	4719	614	674	746	830	924	1019
.8	544	520	598	877	3592	20850	604	666	740	828	930	1029
1.0	603	617	840	2776	9282	11135	600	666	746	844	963	1077
	A = .4						A = 1.0					
0	607	609	641	678	719	768	738	825	930	1049	1178	1320
.2	559	565	597	637	679	726	738	825	930	1049	1178	1320
.4	532	543	582	637	698	767	738	825	930	1049	1178	1320
.6	532	550	607	698	816	958	738	825	930	1049	1178	1320
.8	558	595	691	863	1122	1483	738	825	930	1049	1178	1320
1.0	619	699	896	1578	4088	4424	738	825	930	1049	1178	1320

Values of $\sigma_e(A, B, C)$ were calculated on the IBM 650 computer. A flow chart of the program appears in Figure 6. The general procedure was as follows: the first part of a series was used in a common-sense way to get initial values of $\tilde{S}$, the F's, and R. The exponential model was then used on the *first part* of the series, $(t = 1, 2, \cdots, H)$, in the same manner as it was used in the second part, except that no forecasts were made, and thus no measure was made of forecast error. The values of $\tilde{S}$, the F's, and R that remained at period H were then considered initial values for the second half of a series. The added complication of using the first part of the series twice was incurred in order to wash out as far as possible the effects of the arbitrarily chosen initial values. This is particularly important in the case of the seasonal factors, the F's, because each is re-estimated only once a year; and it becomes increasingly important for each of the effects (smoothing, seasonal, and trend) as the weights become smaller. The best values of A, B, C are in fact relatively small so that this is a real problem. The method of obtaining values to start the first part of the series was the following.

(1) The average(sales per period)for each year, V_i, was computed. The i subscript refers to the year.

(2) R_{last}, the "previous" estimate of R (corresponds to R_{t-1} when in the t'th period) is $R_{last} = [V_{(H/L)} - V_1]/[H - L]$. In other words, R_{last} is

TABLE 2

Standard Deviations of Forecast Errors: Three Products and Composite Results

B	C																							
	Cooking Utensils						Paint						Cellars						Composite Rating—Three Products					
	0	.1	.2	.3	.4	.5	0	.1	.2	.3	.4	.5	0	.1	.2	.3	.4	.5	0	.1	.2	.3	.4	.5
A = .5																								
0	614	617	634				97.2	98.4	100.8				19.0*	19.8*	20.7				—	—	—			
.1	591	595	611				95.8	96.8	99.2				19.4*	20.4*	21.2				42	—	—			
.2	572	577	593				94.5	95.5	97.9				19.9*	20.9	21.9				39	—	—			
.3	557	563	579				93.4	94.3	96.7				20.4*	21.6	22.6				37	45	—			
A = .4																								
0	607	598	609				95.4	95.7	97.0				19.0*	19.8*	20.5*				42	45	—			
.1	580	574	584				93.7	93.8	95.1				19.4*	20.3*	21.1				38	41	—			
.2	559	554	565				92.2	02.2	93.4				19.9*	20.9	21.8				33	38	45			
.3	543	539	550				90.8	90.7	91.9				20.4*	21.6	22.6				31	36	45			
.4	532	530	543				89.7	89.5	90.7				20.9	22.2	23.4				30	36	—			
.5	529	527	542				88.8	88.6	89.8				21.5	23.0	24.4				32	40	—			
A = .3																								
0	611	584	589				93.9	93.2	93.3				19.5*	20.4*	20.9				44	42	45			
.1	580	557	562				91.9	91.1	91.0				19.7*	20.8*	21.4				37	37	39			
.2	555	535	540				90.2	89.2	89.2				20.1*	21.2	21.9				31	31	36			
.3	536	519	524	537	552		88.7	87.7	87.7	88.2	89.6		20.4*	21.7	22.5	23.5	24.9		26*	30	35	43	—	
.4	525	509	516	530	548		87.6	86.6	86.6	87.2	88.6		20.8	22.2	23.1	24.3	26.2		25*	28*	34	44	—	
.5	520	506	515	532	556		86.9	85.9	86.0	86.8	88.4		21.3	22.7	23.7	25.1	27.5		26*	29	36	—	—	
.6	523	510	522	546	577		86.5	85.7	86.0	87.0	89.0		21.8	23.2	24.3	25.9	28.9		29	33	40	—	—	
.7	533	522	540				86.7	86.1	86.8				22.3	23.8	24.9				34	39	—			
A = .2																								
0	640	583					93.3	92.1					20.8	21.8					—	—				
.1	602	552					91.2	89.8					20.6	21.8					45	39				
.2	570	526					89.4	88.0					20.6	21.8					36	31				
.3	547	506	500	510	520	528	88.0	86.5	85.7	84.8*	84.1*	84.1*	20.7	22.0	22.8	23.1	23.3	23.9	30	26*	28*	31	33	38
.4	531	493	488*	499	510	521	87.0	85.5	84.8*	84.0*	83.5*	83.6*	20.9	22.2	23.0	23.3	23.5	24.1	26*	24*	26*	29	31	37
.5	523	487*	484*	496	510	527	86.5	85.0*	84.4*	83.9*	83.6*	83.9*	21.2	22.6	23.4	23.6	23.6	24.3	26*	24*	26*	30	33	40
.6	523	488*	487*	503	522	550	86.5	85.1*	84.7*	84.5*	84.5*	85.1*	21.7	23.1	23.9	24.0	23.9	24.8	29	26*	30	34	37	—
.7	530	497	499	520	550	597	87.1	86.0	85.9	85.9	86.4	87.3	22.3	23.8	24.5	24.5	24.5	25.9	34	33	37	41	—	—
A = .1																								
.3	620	537	518	501	502	533	89.7	87.9	88.0	88.0	87.2	85.9	22.3	23.8	24.5	25.5	25.9	25.4	—	45	44	—	—	—
.4	594	521	502	486*	494	532	88.8	87.0	87.0	86.9	86.2	85.1*	22.3	23.9	24.7	25.7	26.0	25.6	—	40	40	43	45	—
.5	578	512	492	479*	494	538	88.5	86.6	86.5	86.4	85.8	84.8*	22.5	24.2	25.2	26.1	26.3	26.0	—	39	40	43	—	—
.6	569	509	488*	479*	502	551	88.6	86.8	86.6	86.5	86.0	85.3	22.9	24.8	25.8	26.7	26.8	26.6	—	42	42	45	—	—
.7	569	514	491	486*	517	573	89.3	87.6	87.4	87.3	87.1	86.6	23.5	25.5	26.7	27.4	27.6	27.7	—	—	—	—	—	—

The * marks indicate values of σ within 2% of minimum value for Cooking Utensils, within 2% for Paint, and within 8% for Cellars; they also indicate the best Composite Ratings.

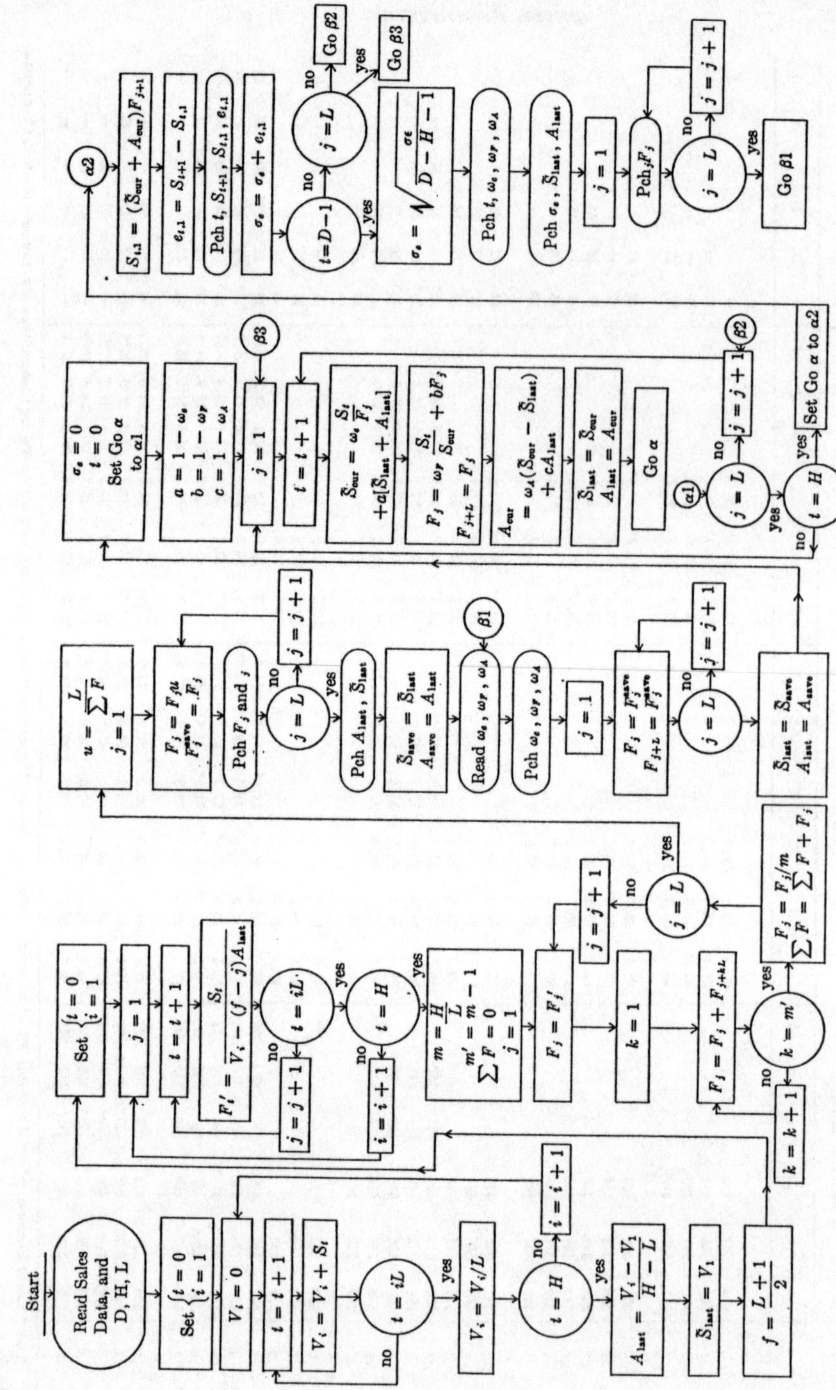
Start
Read Sales Data, and D, H, L
Set t = 0, i = 1
V_i = 0
t = t + 1
V_i = V_i + S_t
t = iL
yes
no
V_i = V_i/L
t = H
i = i + 1
A_last = (V_i − V_1)/(H − L)
S̄_last = V_1
f = (L + 1)/2
j = 1
j = j + 1
k = 1
k = k + 1
k = m′
j = L
Pch F_j and j
Pch A_last, S̄_last
Read ω_e, ω_F, ω_A
Pch ω_e, ω_F, ω_A
Go α
Set Go α to α1
Set Go α to α2
Go β1
Go β2
Go β3
α1
α2
β1
β2
β3
t = D−1
Pch σ_e, S̄_last, A_last

FIG. 6

the average trend between the first and last years, considering only these years.

(3) $\tilde{S}_{\text{last}}$, the "previous" estimate of $\tilde{S}$ (corresponds to $\tilde{S}_{t-1}$ when in the t'th period) is $\tilde{S}_{\text{last}} = V_1$, the average sales for the first year.

(4) Seasonal factors were computed for each period, $t = 1, \cdots, H$, as the ratio of actual sales for the period to average seasonally adjusted sales for that year, further adjusted by the trend, R_{last}:

$$F_t = \frac{S_t}{V_i - \left(\frac{L+1}{2} - j\right) R_{\text{last}}}$$

where V_i is the average sales in the appropriate year, and j is the position of the period within the year, e.g., for January, $j = 1$; for February, $j = 2$; etc.

(5) Seasonal factors for corresponding periods in each of the initial years were averaged to obtain one seasonal factor for each period in a year. For example, the F's were averaged for all Januarys to get one January seasonal factor.

(6) Finally, the seasonals were normalized so that they added to L; for 12 periods a year, $\sum_{j=1}^{12} F_j = 12$.

$$F_j = \text{Ave } F_j \left(\frac{L}{\sum_{j=1}^{L} \text{Ave } F_j} \right)$$

This last step was made to ensure that over a cycle the seasonal factors would make only seasonal adjustments, and not increase or decrease the average level of sales.

This process gave values of $\tilde{S}$, the F's, and R to use in period $t = 1$. At this point a set of values of (A, B, C) was read into the machine. The exponential system was applied starting as $t = 1$ and run through $t = H$ without making forecasts, and then through the rest of the data, $H + 1$ to L, making forecasts, and computing forecast errors. See Figure 6 for details.

3.2 *Results of Testing the Exponential System*

The results of the grid of (A, B, C) for the cooking utensil series are given in Table 1. The lowest σ_e is 487, at $(A = .2, B = .6, C = .2)$. The function σ_e is convex in the region of the minimum. Further search was conducted in the neighborhood of (.2, .6, .2), by taking a finer grid. These results are presented in Table 2. Slightly better values of σ_e were found, with the new minimum of 479 at two points: (.1, .5, .3) and (.1, .6, .3). Values of σ_e within 2% of the minimum are starred, and the minima are starred and underlined. The function σ_e is fairly "flat" in the neighborhood of the minima, as we suspected. Undoubtedly we could find lower values of σ_e, but the probable gain doesn't appear worth the effort.

A search was made, using the same finer grid size, for the minimum σ_e's of the other two series, using the assumption that they, too, were convex in a substantial region surrounding the minima. The results of this search is shown in Table 2, along with the cooking utensil values. Again, the best values are underlined, and values within 2% of the minimum for paint, and within 8%, for cellars, are starred. The minimum for paint is 83.5, at (.2, .4, .4); the minimum σ_e for cellars is 19.0, at (.4, 0, 0).[5] Values of zero for B and C mean that the original estimates of the seasonal and trend factors are never changed. The functions σ_e are, as in the case of the cooking utensil, quite "flat" in the neighborhoods of the minima, and are convex in these regions.

It is possible to get some idea of the accuracy of prediction from the standard deviation of forecast errors. The coefficient of variation of the distribution of sales rates, given the forecasting method, can be approximated by the ratio of σ_e to the average sales rate for that part of the series in which forecasts are made, i.e.,

$$\text{(18)} \qquad \text{Coefficient of variation} \cong \sigma_e \Big/ \left[\sum_{t=H+1}^{D} S_t/(D - H) \right] = \sigma_e/\bar{S}$$

For each of the three series, this value is

Cooking utensils	.31
Paint	.38
Cellars	.26

This means that, as an order of magnitude, about 65% of the forecasts will be within ±31%, 38%, and 26%, respectively, of the sales rates that actually occur.

To give some idea of the effect of different sets of values of (A, B, C) on all three series, a composite rating has been devised as follows. Given the minimum σ_e, all the other values can be expressed as a percentage above the minimum. This has been done for most of the sets of weights evaluated in Table 2, and percentages added across the three series. For example, for (.2, .4, .2) the percentage above the minimum is 2% for cooking utensils, 2% for paint, and 22% for cellars. The composite rating is the sum of these three, 26%, and appears in position (.2, .4, .2) in Table 2. The best composite rating is 24%, for (.2, .4, .1) and for (.2, .5, .1). Other good composite ratings are starred.

3.3 *General Comments on the Exponential Weights*

It is possible to make some general statements about the optimal weights that we would expect to find associated with various kinds of sales series. The best weights for cellars of (.4, 0, 0) seem strange at first. We might expect zero weights, which mean no weight to current estimates, in a situation where the random effect in current data is substantial. This would imply that accuracy of prediction would be low, but that is not the case with cellars. In fact, the coefficient of variation for cellars is the lowest of the three, indicating the best prediction.

[5] A comment on zero values will be made later in the section.

In order to shed light on this apparent paradox, some examples have been chosen which are a little extreme in order to make the point clear. One of the justifications for the exponential system is that if any of the basic parameters of a series changes or drifts over time, the forecasting system will soon pick up the new value; another justification is the ability to filter out substantial random effects in the observations. It is possible to imagine, however, a series in which some of the parameters are subject to little or no drift; and also series where there is little random effect. If there is no change in a parameter over the series then even if the random effect is small, the weight associated with that parameter would be very small, or even zero, because there is no value in changing, very much or at all, the original, and still accurate estimate of the parameter. If the drift in a parameter is large over the series, even to the point of abrupt changes in its value from time to time, there are two possibilities: a) little random effect would lead to large weights, weighting current estimates heavily; b) a large random effect would yield substantially smaller weights, depending on the relative importance of the changes in the parameter *versus* the random element. These intuitive conclusions are summarized in the following table:

Size of Weights Expected

Drift or change in parameters	Random Effect		
	None	Little	Large
None	indeterminate	very small	small
Little	large	very small to small	small
Large	large	medium	small to medium

Evidently, the cellars series is one in which there is not much change in the seasonal or trend parameters over the series, and at the same time, the random element in the series is not large. Also, note that A is somewhat larger for this series than for the other two; some of the change in $\tilde{S}$, not accounted for by a trend factor, is made up by the faster re-estimation of $\tilde{S}$ itself.

4. Comparison with Other Forecasting Models

As we mentioned in the first section of the paper, two other forecasting models were applied to the three series, cooking utensils, paint, cellars excavated, to make a comparison with the exponential system. We call these two more conventional models Comparison Model No. 1, and Comparison Model No. 2. Comparison Model No. 1 is quite simple. A prediction for any period is made by averaging sales in the two preceeding periods:

$$S_{t,1} = \tfrac{1}{2}(S_t + S_{t-1}) \tag{19}$$

Detailed results of this forecasting model will not be given, but a summary of the results appears in Table 3, along with the best forecast results of the exponential system. The standard deviations of forecast errors for Comparison Model No. 1

TABLE 3

Comparison of Forecasting Models

Exponential Forecast: Best Values			Standard Deviation of Forecast Errors		
A	B	C	Kitchen Utensils	Paint	Cellars Excavated
.1	.5	.3	479	—	—
.2	.4	.4	—	83.5	—
.4	0	0	—	—	19.0
Comparison Model No. 1............			733	177.9	28.6
Comparison Model No. 2............			512	97.5	22.6
Exponential Forecast Best Overall Weights					
A	B	C			
.2	.3	.1	507	86.5	22.0
.2	.4	.1	494	85.5	22.2
.3	.4	.1	509	86.6	22.2
Next Best Weights					
A	B	C			
.2	.3	.2	500	85.7	22.8
.2	.4	.2	488	84.8	23.0
.2	.5	.1	487	85.0	22.6
.2	.6	.1	488	85.1	23.1
.3	.3	.1	518	87.7	21.7
.3	.5	0	520	86.9	21.3
.3	.5	.1	506	85.9	22.7

are substantially higher for every series, and outstandingly so for the Paint series.

Comparison Model No. 2 is a more serious contender. It is in some ways similar to the variant of the exponential model with ratio seasonals and no trend factor. A forecast is made for a period by multiplying by a seasonal factor the average sales over the preceeding L periods:

$$S_{t,1} = \frac{1}{L}\left[\sum_{j=0}^{L-1} S_{t-j}\right] F_{t+1-L} \tag{20}$$

The seasonal factor, F, for the period in question was developed during the previous cycle, and is thus the latest estimate of a seasonal factor for the period being forecast.

The three series are handled in the same way for this model as for the exponential system: the first part of the data, through period H, is used to calculate seasonal factors. These seasonal factors are then used to forecast sales in the second part of the data ($H + 1$ to L), and are adjusted each year by weighting the current estimate by $\frac{1}{3}$, the previous estimate by $\frac{2}{3}$, and adding, exactly as with the exponential system. Initial F's are calculated by simply reversing Equation 20:

$$F_t = LS_t \Big/ \left[\sum_{j=1}^{L} S_{t-j} \right] \tag{21}$$

Because of this definition of the seasonal factor however, three years of data yields only two seasonal factors for corresponding periods, and two years of data given only one seasonal factor. Two or more estimates of an F are averaged. These seasonal factors are not normalized, of course, because they are intended to include some trend effect. If there is a consistent long-run trend, not normalizing leads to better forecasts.

Results of Comparison Model No. 2 are given in Table 3. The standard deviations of forecast errors for this model are higher for each of the three series than for the exponential model using the best set of weights for each series individually. There are three sets of weights which, when used for all of the series, yield standard deviations for each series lower than those from Comparison Model No. 2. These are shown as Best Overall Weights in Table 3. Finally, there are a number of sets of weights which yield better results for two out of the three series; these are shown as Next Best Weights in Table 3. In all of these latter cases, the exponential result that is worse for the one series is not much worse.

We conclude, then, that the exponential forecasting model has several advantages over more conventional forecasting models: (1) it gives better forecasts, (2) it requires less information and storage space, (3) it responds more rapidly to sudden shifts in the time series so that is routinely protects the forecaster.

Part II
ARIMA Modelling

[2]

Some Statistical Aspects of Adaptive Optimization and Control

By G. E. P. Box and G. M. Jenkins

University of Wisconsin, Madison *Imperial College, London*

[Read at a Research Methods Meeting of the Society, April 4th, 1962, Professor D. R. Cox in the Chair]

Summary

It is often necessary to adjust some variable X, such as the concentration of consecutive batches of a product, to keep X close to a specified target value. A second more complicated problem occurs when the independent variables X in a response function $\eta(X)$ are to be adjusted so that the derivatives $\partial\eta/\partial X$ are kept close to a target value zero, thus maximizing or minimizing the response. These are shown to be problems of prediction, essentially, and the paper is devoted mainly to the estimation from past data of the "best" adjustments to be applied in the first problem.

1. Introduction

1.1. *Experimentation as an Adaptive Process*

Our interest in adaptive systems arises principally because we believe that experimentation itself is an adaptive system. This iterative or adaptive nature of experimentation, as characterized by the closed loop, *conjecture–design–experiment–analysis* has been discussed previously by Box (1957).

In some circumstances, the probabilities associated with particular occurrences which are part of this iterative process may be of little direct interest, as may be the rightness or wrongness of particular "decisions" which are made along the way. For instance, on one admittedly idealized model of an evolutionary operation programme applied during the finite life of a chemical process, Box has shown in an unpublished report that if a virtually limitless number of modifications are available for trial, then to obtain maximum profit, each modification should be tested once and once only no matter what the standard deviation of the test procedure is.

Results of this kind are important but for the most part are not generally applicable to the experimental process itself. To see why this is so, we must distinguish between empirical and technical feedback.

1.2. *Empirical and Technical Feedback*

Empirical feedback occurs when we can give a simple rule which describes unequivocally what action should be taken and what new experiments should be done in every conceivable situation. In the above example the rule is: If after testing a modification once, it appears to give an improvement, then include it in the process and start to test another modification. If it fails to do this, leave it out and test another modification.

Technical feedback occurs when the information coming from the experiment interacts with technical knowledge contained in the experimenter's mind to lead to some form of action. The reasoning here is of a more complex kind not predictable by a simple rule. Inspection and analysis of data will often suggest to the trained scientist explanations which are far from direct. These will provide leads which he follows up in further work. To allow technical feedback to occur efficiently, the scientist must have a reasonably sure foundation on which to build his conjectures. To provide this, the effects about which he has to reason will need to be known with fairly good and stated precision and this may require considerable replication, hidden or direct. This is one reason why the $n = 1$ rule is not recommended for most applications of evolutionary operation, or for any other procedure which benefits heavily from technical as well as from empirical feedback.

However, when the feedback is essentially empirical, the use of conservative rules appropriate for technical feedback can lead to considerable inefficiency. Two problems which we feel should be considered from the empirical feedback point of view are those of adaptive optimization and adaptive quality control. It is hoped that the discussion of these problems here may provide a starting point for a study of the much wider adaptive aspects of the experimental method itself.

1.3. *Adaptive Quality Control*

Quality control undoubtedly has many different motivations and aims. Quality control charts are used to spotlight abnormal variations, to indicate when something went wrong and, perhaps most important of all, to give a pictorial and readily understandable representation of the behaviour of the process in a form which is continually brought to the notice of those responsible for running it. These are all examples of the technical feedback aspects of quality control, the importance of which cannot be easily overrated but which will not be considered here.

Quality control charts are, however, also used as part of an adaptive loop. With Shewhart charts, for example, some rule will be instituted that when a charted point goes outside a certain limit, or a succession of points fall between some less extreme limits, then a specified action is taken to adjust the mean value. In this circumstance we are clearly dealing with empirical rather than with technical feedback and the problem should be so treated.

A paper which pointed out the advantages of a new type of quality control chart using cumulative sums was recently read before this Society by Barnard (1959). In it the important feedback aspect of the quality control problem was clearly brought out and we owe much to this work.

1.4. *Adaptive Optimization*

Our interest in adaptive optimization was stimulated in the first place by experiences with evolutionary operation. By evolutionary operation we mean a simple technique used by plant operators by means of which over the life of the plant many modifications are tried and, where they prove to be useful, are included in the process. In practice, evolutionary operation, like quality control, is used for a number of rather different purposes. Its main purpose seems to be to act as a permanent incentive to ideas and as a device to screen these ideas as they are born, either spontaneously or out of previous work. As with quality control, many important advances are made here by the use of technical rather than empirical feedback.

However, evolutionary operation has occasionally also been used as a kind of manual process of adaptive optimization. It sometimes happens that there exist some unmeasurable and largely unpredictable variables, ξ, such as catalyst activity, whose levels change with time. When this happens, evolutionary operation is sometimes used to indicate continuously how the levels of some other controllable variables X should be moved so as to ensure, as nearly as possible, that the current maximum value in some *objective function*, or *response*, η is achieved at any given time t.

Other examples of variables which affect efficiency and, like catalyst activity, are not easily measured when the chemical process is running, and for which adaptive compensation in other variables may be desirable, are: degree of fouling of heat exchangers, permeability of packed columns, abrasion of particles in fluidized beds and, in some cases, quality of feed stock. When such uncontrollable and unmeasurable variables ξ occur as a permanent and inevitable feature of chemical processes, it may become worth while to install special equipment to provide automatic adaptive compensation of the controllable and measurable variables X (Box, 1960). It also becomes worth while to consider the theory of such systems so that the adaptive optimization may be made as efficient as possible.

1.5. *Scope of the Present Investigation*

In section 2 we consider a simplified discrete-time model for the adaptive optimization problem. We find that we are led to problems of adaptive control which lead in turn to problems of prediction and smoothing of a time-series. Our results are then applicable to the problem of adaptive statistical quality control, which is given special attention in sections 2 and 3. These sections incorporate ideas well known to control engineers. In section 4, the methods are illustrated by means of examples and in section 5 the results are expressed in terms of power spectra.

The problem of maximizing or minimizing a response will be considered in a later paper.

2. A DISCRETE-TIME MODEL

2.1. *Discrete Adaptive Optimization Model*

We shall first consider a simplified model in which data are available only at discrete and equal intervals of time each of which we call a *phase*. We suppose further that the situation remains constant during a phase but may change from phase to phase. The model is thus directly appropriate to a batch-type chemical process and provides a discrete approximation to the operation of a continuous process from which discrete data are taken at equal intervals of time.

Suppose the uncontrollable and immeasurable variables have levels ξ_p during the pth phase and these levels change from one phase to the next. Then the conditional response function $\eta(X|\xi_p)$ will change correspondingly as in Fig. 1. Suppose that in the pth phase it may be approximated by the quadratic equation

$$\eta_p = \eta(X|\xi_p) = \eta(\theta_p) - \tfrac{1}{2}\beta_{11}(X-\theta_p)^2, \qquad (2.1.1)$$

where $\theta_p = \{X_{\max}|\xi_p\}$ is the conditional maximal setting during the pth phase and β_{11} is known from prior calibration and does not change appreciably with ξ_p. We suppose finally that because of fluctuation in ξ_p, the conditional maximal value θ_p follows some stochastic process usually of a non-stationary kind. Let X_p be the *set-point* at which the controllable variable X is held in the pth phase (Fig. 1). Then the standardized slope of the response function at $X = X_p$,

$$\frac{1}{\beta_{11}}\left(\frac{d\eta_p}{dX}\right)_{X=X_p} = \theta_p - X_p = \epsilon_p,$$

measures the extent to which X_p deviates from θ_p. If experiments are performed at $X_p+\delta$ and at $X_p-\delta$ and the average response observed at these levels is $\bar{y}(X_p+\delta)$ and $\bar{y}(X_p-\delta)$, then an estimate e_p of $\epsilon_p=\theta_p-X_p$ is given by

$$e_p=\tfrac{1}{2}\{\bar{y}(X_p+\delta)-\bar{y}(X_p-\delta)\}/(\delta\beta_{11})=\epsilon_p+u_p, \tag{2.1.2}$$

where u_p is called the measurement error, although it will be produced partly by uncontrolled fluctuations in the process. Now

$$e_p=\epsilon_p+u_p=\theta_p-X_p+u_p=z_p-X_p, \tag{2.1.3}$$

where $z_p=\theta_p+u_p$ is an estimate of the position of the optimal setting θ_p during the pth phase.

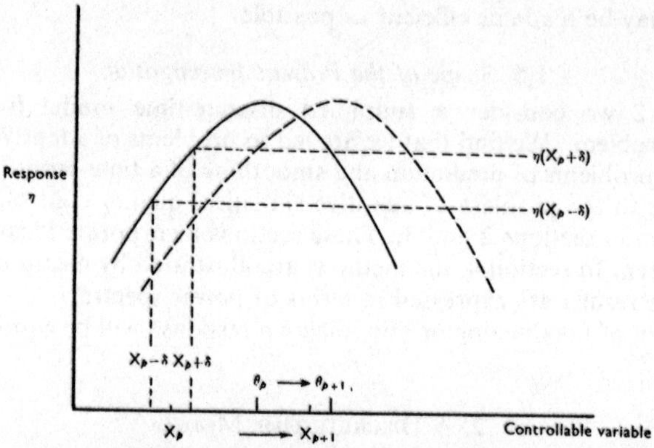

FIG. 1. Simple adaptive optimization.

If a series of adjustments has actually been made on some basis or other, we have a record of a sequence of set points $X_p, X_{p-1}, X_{p-2}, \ldots$ and of a sequence of deviations $e_p, e_{p-1}, e_{p-2}, \ldots$. From these it will be possible to reconstruct the sequence $z_p, z_{p-1}, z_{p-2}, \ldots$, of estimated positions of the maxima in phases $p, p-1, p-2, \ldots$. From such data we wish to make an adjustment x_{p+1} to the set point X_p so that the adjusted set point $X_{p+1}=X_p+x_{p+1}$ which will be maintained during the *coming* $(p+1)$th phase will be in some sense "best" in relation to the coming and unknown value of θ_{p+1}.

Now we suppose that the objective function η is such that the loss sustained during the $(p+1)$th phase is realistically measured by

$$\eta(\theta_{p+1})-\eta(X_{p+1}\,|\,\xi_{p+1})=\tfrac{1}{2}\beta_{11}(X_{p+1}-\theta_{p+1})^2, \tag{2.1.4}$$

the amount by which η falls short of the value theoretically attainable. The adjustment x_{p+1} will then minimize the expected loss if it is chosen so that $E(\theta_{p+1}-X_{p+1})^2$ is minimized. Thus our objective is attained if we set X_{p+1} equal to

$$\hat{\theta}_{p+1}=f(z_p, z_{p-1}, z_{p-2}, \ldots),$$

where $f(z_p, z_{p-1}, \ldots)$ is the minimum mean square estimate or *predictor* of θ_{p+1}, based on the observations $z_p, z_{p-1}, \ldots$.

For simplicity we take $\hat{\theta}_{p+1}$ to be a linear function of the z's,

$$\hat{\theta}_{p+1} = \sum_{j=0}^{\infty} \mu_j z_{p-j}, \tag{2.1.5}$$

and refer to the μ_j's as the *predictor* weights. If the model for the stochastic process $\{\theta_p\}$ is specified precisely, then it may well be that the best predictor is a non-linear function of the previous z's, as in the model used by Barnard (1959). In general, however, there is no empirical evidence for making such precise assumptions for the model so that the simplicity of the linear predictor is well worth maintaining.

At the beginning of the $(p+1)$th phase we should therefore apply to the previous setting X_p an adjustment $x_{p+1} = \hat{\theta}_{p+1} - \hat{\theta}_p$. Now in practice we do not observe the z's directly but only the e's. This means that we must calculate the adjustment from the estimated slopes $e_p, e_{p-1}, \ldots$, in the form

$$x_{p+1} = X_{p+1} - X_p = \hat{\theta}_{p+1} - \hat{\theta}_p = \sum_{j=0}^{\infty} w_j e_{p-j}, \tag{2.1.6}$$

where we call the w_j the *controller weights*. In section 2.3 we show that (2.1.5) and (2.1.6) imply that a definite relationship exists between the predictor weights μ_j and the controller weights w_j. The optimal adjustment is then obtained by choosing the w's, or equivalently the μ's, to minimize $E(\epsilon_{p+1}^2) = E(\theta_{p+1} - \hat{\theta}_{p+1})^2$.

Now $\hat{\theta}_{p+1} = f(z_p, z_{p-1}, \ldots)$ and $z_{p+1} = \theta_{p+1} + u_{p+1}$, so that if the "measurement error" u_{p+1} is distributed about zero with variance σ_u^2 *independently* of $u_p, u_{p-1}, \ldots$, and of $\theta_p, \theta_{p-1}, \ldots$, then

$$E(e_{p+1}^2) = E(z_{p+1} - \hat{\theta}_{p+1})^2 = E(\epsilon_{p+1}^2) + \sigma_u^2. \tag{2.1.7}$$

The loss $E(\epsilon_{p+1}^2)$ is then minimal when $E(z_{p+1} - \hat{\theta}_{p+1})^2 = E(e_{p+1})^2$ is minimized and $\hat{z}_{p+1}$, the best predictor of z_{p+1}, supplies in this case the best predictor $\hat{\theta}_{p+1}$ of θ_{p+1}. In general, σ_u^2 will depend on the number n of experiments performed in estimating the slope and also on δ, the magnitude of the perturbations. For any fixed values of n and δ, however, the best way of tracking θ_{p+1} is always to make an adjustment

$$x_{p+1} = \hat{\theta}_{p+1} - \hat{\theta}_p = \sum_{j=0}^{\infty} w_j e_{p-j}.$$

In those cases where the measurement errors u are independent of the θ's and of each other then $\hat{\theta}_{p+1} = \hat{z}_{p+1}$.

2.2. *Dynamics of Adjustment*

On our assumptions if, using data acquired during the pth and previous phases of operation, we wish to change the set point X_p of a controlled variable, such as temperature, to a level X_{p+1} so as to minimize the loss during the $(p+1)$th phase, we must set X_{p+1} equal to $\hat{\theta}_{p+1}$, the optimal value to be expected in the $(p+1)$th phase from the predictions of past data. In practice it would often not be possible to change a controlled variable X such as temperature directly. This would have to be done indirectly by adjusting some other variable X^* such as steam pressure. In general, we refer to the variable X^* which we can directly adjust as the manipulated variable. Now frequently, a change in the manipulated variable X^* (steam pressure) would not be immediately felt in the controlled variable X (temperature). The effect would build up over a considerable period of time.

It is convenient to suppose that the manipulated variable has been calibrated in units of its ultimate effect on the controlled variable. Then if we turn the steam valve forwards by "5 units", an increase of 5 units in temperature will ultimately result. Suppose that from data available in the pth phase an adjustment x^*_{p+1} can be made in the manipulated variable at a time such that proportions $v_0, v_1, v_2, \ldots$, of this change are experienced in the controlled variable in phases $p+1, p+2, p+3, \ldots$, where $v_0+v_1+\ldots=1$. Then we call $v_0, v_1, v_2, \ldots$ the *dynamic weights*.

It is shown in section 5.4 that we can induce the controlled variable X to undergo the optimal adjustment

$$x_{p+1} = \sum_{j=0}^{\infty} w_j e_{p-j}$$

if we adjust the manipulated variable in accordance with

$$x^*_{p+1} = \sum_{j=0}^{\infty} w^*_j e_{p-j}, \tag{2.2.1}$$

where the w^*_j's are such that the w_j's are the convolution of the controller and dynamic weights,

$$w_j = v_0 w^*_j + v_1 w^*_{j-1} + v_2 w^*_{j-2} + \ldots. \tag{2.2.2}$$

It follows that if we know the optimal w_j's and the dynamic weights v_i, then provided $v_0 \neq 0$ we can compute the w^*_j's which tell us how to change the manipulated variable X^*.

2.3. *Discrete Adaptive Quality Control*

In this section we retain the previous symbols but change the context in which they are used. Suppose we are now concerned with some "quality characteristic", such as the concentration of consecutive batches, and that if no steps were taken to control its behaviour, its observed value at the pth phase would be

$$z_p = \theta_p + u_p. \tag{2.3.1}$$

As before, we assume that θ_p follows some stochastic process, in general non-stationary, and u_p is a measurement error. Suppose that our object is to hold θ as closely as possible to some *target value* which, without loss of generality, we can take to be zero. To achieve this, suppose a method is available whereby the mean value of the stochastic process z can be adjusted up or down at will. Suppose that at the pth stage a *total correction* of $-X_p$ is being applied to the mean. Then the quantity actually observed is the apparent deviation from target

$$z_p - X_p = \theta_p - X_p + u_p = \epsilon_p + u_p = e_p.$$

We wish now to calculate a further adjustment x_{p+1} computed from data in the pth and previous phases so that when the total correction $-X_{p+1} = -(X_p + x_{p+1})$ is applied during the pth phase the actual deviation from target $\epsilon_{p+1} = \theta_{p+1} - X_{p+1}$ will be small.

We now assume a quadratic loss function, that is we suppose that the loss involved through θ being off-target by an amount ϵ_p is proportional to ϵ_p^2. On this assumption we must choose x_{p+1} as before so that $E(\epsilon_{p+1})^2 = E(\theta_{p+1} - X_{p+1})^2$ is minimized.

Once more then, this requires that

$$x_{p+1} = \hat{\theta}_{p+1} - \hat{\theta}_p = \sum_{j=0}^{\infty} w_j e_{p-j},$$

where the w_j's are chosen so that $\hat{\theta}_{p+1}$ is the minimum mean square error estimate of θ_{p+1}. As before, if the measurement errors are uncorrelated with each other and with the θ's, then $\hat{z}_{p+1} = \hat{\theta}_{p+1}$ and we can then take

$$x_{p+1} = \hat{z}_{p+1} - \hat{z}_p = \sum_{j=0}^{\infty} w_j e_{p-j},$$

where now we choose the w's so that $\hat{z}_{p+1} = \hat{\theta}_{p+1}$ is the minimum mean square error estimate of z_{p+1}.

Finally, suppose the mean value could only be controlled indirectly via a manipulated variable. Then, as before, with

$$x_{p+1} = \sum_{j=0}^{\infty} w_j e_{p-j}$$

denoting the adjustment induced into the controlled variable by a correction

$$x_{p+1}^* = \sum_{j=0}^{\infty} w_j^* e_{p-j}$$

directly applied to the manipulated variable, we should obtain optimal control by choosing the w^*'s so that the weights

$$w_j = \sum_{i=0}^{\infty} v_i w_{j-1}^*$$

were those required for optimal prediction of θ_{p+1}.

2.4. *Relation Between Optimization, Control and Prediction Problems*

We have seen that with the assumptions and simplifications introduced, the adaptive optimization and adaptive control problems are identical. Furthermore, in both cases optimal action on data accumulated during the pth and previous phases is taken when X_p is adjusted either directly or indirectly to a value

$$X_{p+1} = X_p + x_{p+1} = \hat{\theta}_{p+1},$$

where $\hat{\theta}_{p+1}$ is the mean square error predictor of θ_{p+1}.

In Table 1, the roles which the various elements play in the three problems are summarized and in Fig. 2 the simultaneous behaviour of the three series z_p, X_p, ϵ_p is displayed for a typical situation. By reference to Table 1 we can interpret Fig. 2 for each problem.

In the prediction problem the z's are directly observed and the predictor $\hat{\theta}_{p+1}$ can be conveniently calculated from

$$\hat{\theta}_{p+1} = \sum_{j=0}^{\infty} \mu_j z_{p-j}, \tag{2.4.1}$$

where the μ's are constants suitably chosen to minimize $E(\epsilon_{p+1}^2) = E(\theta_{p+1} - \hat{\theta}_{p+1})^2$.

In the optimization and control problems where optimal action is taken by setting X_{p+1} equal to $\hat{\theta}_{p+1}$ we do not observe the z's directly but only the e's. Now since $z_p = \hat{\theta}_p + e_p$ we could, as each new observation came to hand, reconstruct the z's and so use (2.4.1) to calculate the value $\hat{\theta}_{p+1}$. In practice, it is simpler to calculate

TABLE 1

Roles played by symbols in optimization, control and prediction problems

	e_p	$\epsilon_p = e_p - u_p$	z_p	$\theta_p = z_p - u_p$	X_p	x_{p+1}
Adaptive Optimization	Observed slope $\frac{\bar{y}(X_p+\delta)-\bar{y}(X_p-\delta)}{2\delta\beta_{11}}$ measures $\theta_p - X_p + u_p$, distance of X_p from max.; subject to error u_p	True slope, uncontaminated by measurement error u_p, measures $\theta_p - X_p$ distance of X_p from max.	Inferred position of max. can be calculated from $X_p + e_p$	Hypothetical true position of max. uncontaminated by error u_p	Set point of controlled variable	Calculated adjustment to be applied to set point X_p throughout pth phase
Adaptive control	Observed deviation of quality characteristic from its target	True deviation from target uncontaminated by measurement error u_p	Inferred value of quality characteristic if no control had been applied; can be calculated from $X_p + e_p$.	True value of quality characteristic if no control had been applied	Total correction applied negatively to mean	Calculated correction to be applied negatively to mean throughout the $(p+1)$th phase
Prediction	Observed deviation of z_p from prediction $\hat{\theta}_p = X_p$	True deviation from prediction uncontaminated by measurement error u_p	Directly observed characteristic	True value of characteristic uncontaminated by measurement error	Predicted value $\hat{\theta}_p$	Difference in predicted values $\hat{\theta}_{p+1} - \hat{\theta}_p$

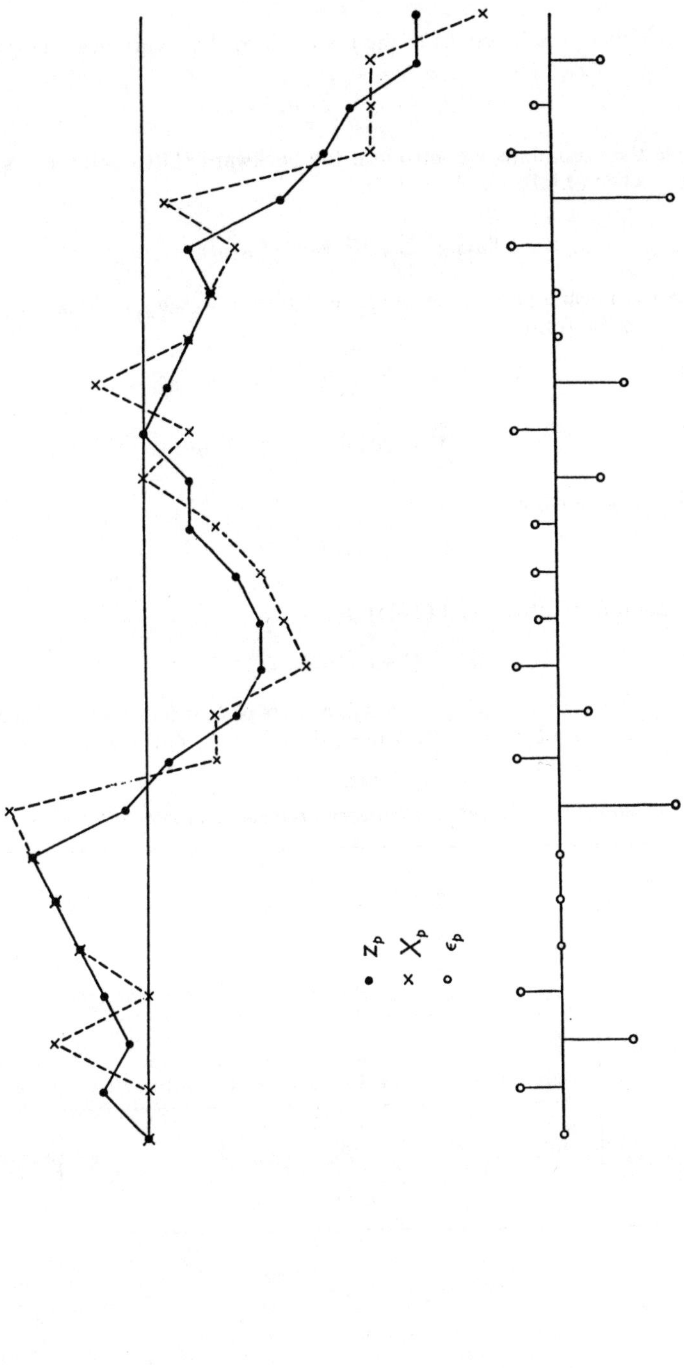

FIG. 2. Typical control and associated prediction problem.

the optimal adjustments $x_{p+1} = X_{p+1} - X_p = \hat{\theta}_{p+1} - \hat{\theta}_p$ from the directly observed e's according to

$$\hat{\theta}_{p+1} - \hat{\theta}_p = \sum_{j=0}^{\infty} w_j e_{p-j}, \tag{2.4.2}$$

where the weights w_j are functions of the μ's given by the recurrence relations

$$w_j = \mu_j - \mu_{j-1} + \sum_{k=0}^{j-1} \mu_k w_{j-1-k}. \tag{2.4.3}$$

To derive these relations we introduce the backward shift operator B such that $B^j z_p = z_{p-j}$. Then (2.4.1) may be written

$$\hat{\theta}_{p+1} = \sum_{j=0}^{\infty} \mu_j B^j z_p = \mathscr{L}_{\mu}(z_p), \tag{2.4.4}$$

where $\mathscr{L}_{\mu}$ is the linear operator on the z_p which produces $\hat{\theta}_{p+1}$. Similarly we may rewrite (2.4.2) in the form

$$(1-B)\,\hat{\theta}_{p+1} = \sum_{j=0}^{\infty} w_j B^j (z_p - \hat{\theta}_p),$$

so that

$$\left(1 - B + B \sum_{j=0}^{\infty} w_j B^j\right) \hat{\theta}_{p+1} = \sum_{j=0}^{\infty} w_j B^j z_p. \tag{2.4.5}$$

Denoting the linear operator

$$\sum_{j=0}^{\infty} w_j B^j$$

by $\mathscr{L}_w$, we obtain from (2.4.4) and (2.4.5) that

$$\mathscr{L}_w = (1 - B + B\mathscr{L}_w)\, \mathscr{L}_{\mu}. \tag{2.4.6}$$

Since the linear operators are infinite series in powers of B, it follows that this equality implies equality of every term in these series. If we identify coefficients of B^j on both

TABLE 2

Some examples of relationships between predictor and controller weights

Nature of weights	j	0	1	2	...	j
Exponentially weighted mean (proportional control)	μ_j	λ	$\lambda(1-\lambda)$	$\lambda(1-\lambda)^2$		$\lambda(1-\lambda)^j$
	w_j	λ	0	0		0
First order autoregressive	μ_j	a_1	0	0		0
	w_j	a_1	$-a_1(1-a_1)$	$-a_1^2(1-a_1)$		$-a_1^j(1-a_1)$
First order moving average (first difference control)	μ_j	β_1	$-\beta_1^2$	β_1^3		$(-1)^{j+1}\beta_1$
	w_j	β_1	$-\beta_1$	0		0

sides of (2.4.5) we are led to the recurrence relationship (2.4.3) between the controller weights w_j and the predictor weights μ_j. Some examples of this relationship are given in Table 2.

Example 1 corresponds to applying a weight λ to the current deviation and ignoring all the others and may be seen to correspond to the use of predictor weights which are exponentially weighted moving averages. These have been used with considerable success for the prediction of sales and production figures by Holt *et al.* (1960), Brown (1959), Muth (1960) and Cox (1961). The second and third examples take their names from the fact that they are best in a sense to be described in section 3 when the z_p process is of the type specified.

3. CHOICE OF WEIGHTS

3.1. *Choice of Predictor*

In this section we shall consider various specifications of the series z_p and how to choose the corresponding predictor weights with desirable properties. The associated controller weights obtained from the recurrence relation (2.4.3) will, of course, have the same desirable properties. The controller weights may be obtained directly but we adopt the present development via prediction partly because the prediction problem is of considerable interest in its own right.

As before, we suppose that the $(p-j)$th observation may be represented by

$$z_{p-j} = \theta_{p-j} + u_{p-j}, \tag{3.1.1}$$

where u_{p-j} is a measurement error and our object is to predict θ_{p+1} from previous values of z.

If our theory is to have practical value it would be unrealistic to assume that θ_{p-j} followed a stationary process. Instead we suppose that θ_{p-j} has a mean $E(\theta_{p-j}) = m_{p-j}$ which may vary. Our model can then be written

$$z_{p-j} = m_{p-j} + (\theta_{p-j} - m_{p-j}) + u_{p-j}. \tag{3.1.2}$$

The series $(\theta_{p-j} - m_{p-j})$ is assumed to be stationary and the $h \times h$ covariance matrix $\sigma_\theta^2 \mathbf{R}_h$ for h successive observations from this series is a Toeplitz matrix with elements $\{\rho_{|i-j|}\}\sigma_\theta^2$, where ρ_s is the autocorrelation of the θ's of lag s. The corresponding $h \times h$ covariance matrix for the u's, which we also assume stationary with mean zero, is denoted by $\sigma_u^2 \mathbf{S}_h$. The covariance matrix for the z's is thus $\sigma_\theta^2 \mathbf{T}_h$, where

$$\mathbf{T}_h = \mathbf{R}_h + \frac{\sigma_u^2}{\sigma_\theta^2}\mathbf{S}_h.$$

If the mean value $E(\theta_{p-j}) = m_{p-j}$ were known for every j then we should employ for our predictor of θ_{p+1} the quantity

$$m_{p+1} + \sum_{j=0}^{\infty} \mu_j\{z_{p-j} - m_{p-j}\}$$

and our prediction error would be

$$\epsilon_{p+1} = (\theta_{p+1} - m_{p+1}) - \sum_{j=0}^{\infty} \mu_j(z_{p-j} - m_{p-j}). \tag{3.1.3}$$

Now in most practical circumstances the predictor will place negligible weight on values of the series remote from the present time. Suppose all values of μ_j can be supposed zero for all $j \geqslant h$; then the predictor becomes

$$m_{p+1}+\sum_{j=0}^{h-1}\mu_j\{z_{p-j}-m_{p-j}\}.$$

The mean square error $E(\epsilon_{p+1})^2 = \text{var}(\epsilon_{p+1})$ may then be written in matrix form as

$$\text{var}(\epsilon_{p+1}) = \sigma_\theta^2\{1-2\boldsymbol{\mu}'\boldsymbol{\rho}+\boldsymbol{\mu}'\mathbf{T}\boldsymbol{\mu}\}, \tag{3.1.4}$$

where

$$\boldsymbol{\mu}_h' = (\mu_0, \mu_1, \ldots, \mu_{h-1})$$

and

$$\boldsymbol{\rho}_h' = (\rho_1, \rho_2, \ldots, \rho_h).$$

Differentiating with respect to the vector $\boldsymbol{\mu}$, we find that the mean square error is minimized when

$$\boldsymbol{\mu} = \mathbf{T}^{-1}\boldsymbol{\rho}. \tag{3.1.5}$$

The optimal predictor of θ_{p+1} is thus

$$\hat{\theta}_{p+1} = \mathbf{z}_p'\,\mathbf{T}^{-1}\boldsymbol{\rho}, \tag{3.1.6}$$

where

$$\mathbf{z}_p' = (z_p, z_{p-1}, \ldots, z_{p-h+1})$$

and this has variance $\boldsymbol{\rho}'\mathbf{T}^{-1}\boldsymbol{\rho}\sigma_\theta^2$. If in particular there were no measurement error and the z process, and hence the θ process, followed a kth order autoregressive scheme,

$$z_{p+1} = a_1 z_p + a_2 z_{p-1} + \ldots + a_{k+1} z_{p-k} \quad (k \leqslant h)$$

then we obtain the well-known result that $\boldsymbol{\mu} = \mathbf{a}$ where $\mathbf{a}' = (a_0, a_1, \ldots, a_{k+1})$.

3.2. *Constrained Predictors*

In most practical situations the mean m_{p-j} would not be known. If we employed the quantity $\mu_0 z_p + \mu_1 z_{p-1} + \ldots$ as a predictor of θ_{p+1} then the error of prediction would be

$$\epsilon_{p+1} = (\theta_{p+1}-m_{p+1}) - \sum_{j=0}^{h-1}\mu_j(z_{p-j}-m_{p-j}) + \left(m_{p+1}-\sum_{j=0}^{h-1}\mu_j m_{p-j}\right) \tag{3.2.1}$$

and the mean square error,

$$E(\epsilon_{p+1}^2) = \left(m_{p+1}-\sum_{j=0}^{h-1}\mu_j m_{p-j}\right)^2 + \text{var}(\epsilon_{p+1}), \tag{3.2.2}$$

would in general be inflated by an amount which depended on the behaviour of the mean m_{p-j}. One way in which this difficulty might be overcome would be to constrain the predictor weights μ_j so that the bias term

$$m_{p+1}-\sum_{j=0}^{h-1}\mu_j m_{p-j}$$

was eliminated or at least rendered small.

For example, if at the pth observation it was assumed that the mean, although unknown, was constant over the last h observations and would remain constant for one further observation, so that $m_{p+1} = m_p = m_{p-1} = \ldots = m_{p-h+1} = m$, then the bias term would vanish if the μ's were chosen subject to the restriction

$$\sum_{j=0}^{h-1}\mu_j = 1. \tag{3.2.3}$$

As observed by Cox (1961), by introducing this constraint we endow the predictor with the property of adjusting to the mean of the series. This is a property which is, of course, not possessed in general by the unrestricted Wiener predictors. For example, for predicting an autoregressive series the optimal weights $\boldsymbol{\mu} = \mathbf{a}$ will not in general sum to unity. This is because the existence of a known fixed mean is implicit in the assumption of an autoregressive series. For reasons which will be clear later, we would call the predictor constrained by (3.2.3) a *mean-projecting* predictor. More generally, if we can represent the behaviour of the $h+1$ values

$$m_{p+1}, m_p, m_{p-1}, \ldots, m_{p-h+1}$$

exactly by a polynomial of degree $0 \leqslant d \leqslant h-1$ then the bias term would vanish if

$$\sum_{j=0}^{h-1} j^k \mu_j = (-1)^k \quad (k = 0, 1, 2, \ldots, d). \tag{3.2.4}$$

Constrained predictors so obtained may be referred to as linear trend projecting, quadratic trend projecting, and so on.

Suppose then that the $h+1$ values $m_{p+1}, \ldots, m_{p-h+1}$ are exactly represented by a polynomial of degree $d < h-1$. Then since the bias term is now zero, the mean square error will be minimized by minimizing $\operatorname{var}(\epsilon_{p+1})$ subject to the constraints (3.2.4).

These constraints may be written

$$\mathbf{A}'\boldsymbol{\mu} = \mathbf{c}, \tag{3.2.5}$$

where $\mathbf{A}$ is an $h \times (d+1)$ matrix $\{a_{jk}\} = \{j^k\}$ with $j = 0, 1, \ldots, h-1$; $k = 0, 1, \ldots, d$, and $\mathbf{c}$ is a $(d+1) \times 1$ vector $\{(-1)^k\}$, $k = 0, 1, \ldots, d$. Introducing a vector of Lagrange multipliers $\boldsymbol{\lambda}' = (\lambda_0, \lambda_1, \ldots, \lambda_d)$, we have that the minimum mean square error is given by the unconditional minimum of

$$\{1 + 2\boldsymbol{\mu}'\boldsymbol{\rho} + \boldsymbol{\mu}'\mathbf{T}\boldsymbol{\mu}\} - 2(\boldsymbol{\mu}'\mathbf{A} - \mathbf{c})\boldsymbol{\lambda}. \tag{3.2.6}$$

On equating derivatives to zero, we obtain the simultaneous equations

$$\boldsymbol{\mu} = \mathbf{T}^{-1}\boldsymbol{\rho} + \mathbf{T}^{-1}\mathbf{A}\boldsymbol{\lambda}, \quad \mathbf{A}'\boldsymbol{\mu} = \mathbf{c}. \tag{3.2.7}$$

On multiplying the first equation by $\mathbf{A}'$ and substituting the result in the second, we obtain

$$\boldsymbol{\lambda} = (\mathbf{A}'\mathbf{T}\mathbf{A})^{-1}\{\mathbf{c} - \mathbf{A}'\mathbf{T}^{-1}\boldsymbol{\rho}\}; \tag{3.2.8}$$

hence finally

$$\boldsymbol{\mu}_c = \mathbf{T}^{-1}\boldsymbol{\rho} + \mathbf{T}^{-1}\mathbf{A}(\mathbf{A}'\mathbf{T}^{-1}\mathbf{A})^{-1}(\mathbf{c} - \mathbf{A}'\mathbf{T}^{-1}\boldsymbol{\rho}) \tag{3.2.9}$$

is the vector of optimal constrained predictor weights.

The corresponding predictor $\boldsymbol{\mu}_c'\mathbf{z}$ has variance

$$\{\boldsymbol{\rho}'\mathbf{T}^{-1}\boldsymbol{\rho} + (\mathbf{c} - \mathbf{A}'\mathbf{T}^{-1}\boldsymbol{\rho})'(\mathbf{A}'\mathbf{T}\mathbf{A})^{-1}(\mathbf{c} - \mathbf{A}'\mathbf{T}^{-1}\boldsymbol{\rho})\}\,\sigma_0^2, \tag{3.2.10}$$

where the second term in the curly brackets represents the inflation of the variance which occurs due to the constraints.

Given that the mean m_{p-j} follows a polynomial of the type assumed, this predictor $\boldsymbol{\mu}_c$ provides in fact the minimum variance linear unbiased predictor of θ_{p+1} as has been shown in an unpublished report by E. Parzen. We refer also to some earlier work on constrained predictors by Zadeh and Ragazzini (1950).

The predictor $\boldsymbol{\mu}_c$ has an alternative interpretation. Using it, the predicted value of θ_{p+1} may be written

$$\boldsymbol{\mu}_c'\mathbf{z} = \mathbf{c}'(\mathbf{A}'\mathbf{T}^{-1}\mathbf{A})^{-1}\mathbf{A}'\mathbf{T}^{-1}\mathbf{z}+\boldsymbol{\rho}\mathbf{T}^{-1}\{\mathbf{z}-\mathbf{A}(\mathbf{A}'\mathbf{T}^{-1}\mathbf{A})^{-1}\mathbf{A}'\mathbf{T}^{-1}\mathbf{z}\}. \quad (3.2.11)$$

Now we have seen that if the mean was known we should use as the predictor for θ_{p+1} the quantity

$$m_{p+1}+\boldsymbol{\mu}'(\mathbf{z}-\mathbf{m}) \quad \text{with } \boldsymbol{\mu}' = \boldsymbol{\rho}'\mathbf{T}^{-1}, \quad (3.2.12)$$

where $\mathbf{m}' = (m_p, m_{p-1}, \ldots, m_{p-h+1})$.

If in (3.2.12) we replace $m_{p+1} = \mathbf{c}'\boldsymbol{\beta}$ and $\mathbf{m} = \mathbf{A}'\boldsymbol{\beta}$ by the corresponding quantities where β is replaced by its best linear unbiased estimate

$$\hat{\boldsymbol{\beta}} = (\mathbf{A}'\mathbf{T}^{-1}\mathbf{A})^{-1}\mathbf{A}'\mathbf{T}^{-1}\mathbf{z},$$

then this is precisely the constrained predictor $\hat{\theta}_{p+1}$ given by (3.2.11).

Suppose, for example, we assume that over the last h observations z can be represented by a mean m subject to a linear trend, plus a stochastic variable $\theta-m$ for which the variance–covariance matrix $\mathbf{R}\sigma_\theta^2$ is known, plus a measurement error for which the variance–covariance matrix $\mathbf{S}\sigma_u^2$ is known.

Then the prediction of θ_{p+1} using the constrained predictor $\boldsymbol{\mu}_c'\mathbf{z}$ would be equivalent to the following:

(i) estimate m_{p+1} by projecting the line which best fits the last h z's through one further observation;

(ii) add to this an estimate of $\theta_{p+1}-m_{p+1}$, the deviation from the projected line at the next observation.

The latter estimate would be a weighted sum of the residuals from the line using the *unconstrained* predictor $\boldsymbol{\mu} = \mathbf{T}^{-1}\boldsymbol{\rho}$.

3.3. *A More Practical Predictor*

The above approach would be extremely difficult to apply in practice. To use it we would have to choose d and h, the degree of the polynomial and the length of series to which it was to be fitted. We should also need to know the covariance matrices $\mathbf{R}\sigma_\theta^2$ and $\mathbf{S}\sigma_u^2$. We are therefore led to seek an alternative approach which can be applied more readily whilst retaining so far as possible the advantages of the previous system.

We shall suppose in what follows either that the measurement errors u are uncorrelated one with another and with the θ's, so that $\hat{z}_{p+1} = \hat{\theta}_{p+1}$ or that the u's are negligible, in which case $z_{p+1} = \theta_{p+1}$ and again $\hat{z}_{p+1} = \hat{\theta}_{p+1}$.

Table 3 shows the optimal μ and w weights obtained for various series of interest. In each case the series is assumed to be represented over the last h observations by a polynomial of degree d, and the variation about the polynomial is assumed to follow the process indicated. In some instances the errors are supposed independent and in others that they follow a first order autoregressive series with coefficient a.

The first three series in the table are all examples of what may be called fully saturated predictors. We fit a polynomial of degree d to the last $h = d+1$ observations. The weight μ_j is then given by minus the coefficient of t^{j+1} in $(1-t)^{d+1}$. The form of the weights w_j is of special interest. In general, the change in the predictor $\hat{z}$ at the $(p+1)$th stage may be written as in (2.4.2) in the form

$$\Delta\hat{z}_{p+1} = \sum_{j=0}^{\infty} w_j e_{p-j}$$

TABLE 3

Some constrained predictors and their associated controller weights

Description	j	0	1	2	3	4	5	6	7	8	9
1 $d=0$ $h=1$ *Errors independent*	μ_j	1	.	.	.	.	.	.	.	.	.
	w_j	1	.	.	.	.	.	.	.	.	.
2 $d=1$ $h=2$ *Errors independent*	μ_j	2	−1	.	.	.	.	.	.	.	.
	w_j	2	1	1	1	1	1	1	1	1	1
3 $d=2$ $h=3$ *Errors independent*	μ_j	3	−3	1	.	.	.	.	.	.	.
	w_j	3	3	4	5	6	7	8	9	10	11
4 $d=0$ $h=\infty$ *Errors independent*	μ_j	γ_0	$\gamma_0(1-\gamma_0)$	$\gamma_0(1-\gamma_0)^2$	$\gamma_0(1-\gamma_0)^3$	.	.	.	.	.	.
	w_j	γ_0	0	0	0	0	0	0	0	0	0
5 $d=1$ $h=4$ *Errors independent*	μ_j	1·00	·50	·00	−·50	·00	·00	·00	·00	·00	·00
	w_j	1·00	·50	·50	·25	·38	·38	·44	·38	·38	·38
6 $d=1$ $h=4$ *First order A. R.* ($a_1=0·3$)	μ_j	1·14	·27	·04	−·45	·00	·00	·00	·00	·00	·00
	w_j	1·14	·43	·57	·32	·47	·45	·40	·45	—	—
7 $d=1$ $h=4$ *First order A. R.* ($a_1=0·5$)	μ_j	1·22	·15	·04	−·41	·00	·00	·00	·00	·00	·00
	w_j	1·22	·42	·58	·37	·47	·48	·43	·47	—	—
8 $d=1$ $h=4$ *First order A. R.* ($a_1=0·9$)	μ_j	1·33	·01	·00	−·34	·00	·00	·00	·00	·00	·00
	w_j	1·33	·45	·60	·46	·51	·53	·51	·52	—	—
9 $d=1$ $h=6$ *Errors independent*	μ_j	0·67	·47	·27	·07	−·13	−·33	·00	·00	·00	·00
	w_j	0·67	·24	·27	·27	·22	·08	·32	·21	·19	·20

and for the first three series in Table 3 this becomes

series 1, $\Delta\hat{z}_{p+1} = e_p$;

series 2, $\Delta\hat{z}_{p+1} = e_p + S^1 e_p$;

series 3, $\Delta\hat{z}_{p+1} = e_p + S^1 e_p + S^2 e_p$,

where
$$S^1 e_p = \sum_{j=0}^{\infty} e_{p-j}, \quad S^2 e_p = \sum_{j=0}^{\infty} \sum_{k=0}^{\infty} e_{p-j-k},$$

and in general $S^j e_p$ denotes the jth multiple sum over the past history of the e's. For a dth degree polynomial fitted to the last $h = d+1$ observations we would have

$$\Delta\hat{z}_{p+1} = e_p + S^1 e_p + S^2 e_p + \ldots + S^d e_p.$$

We now recall that a mean projecting predictor which has proved to be of great practical value is the exponentially weighted mean, shown here as series 4. Technically, $h = \infty$ for this predictor, but in practice the exponential weights become negligible after a moderate number of observations so that local changes in mean are satisfactorily followed. For this series

$$\Delta\hat{z}_{p+1} = \gamma_0 e_p.$$

This important mean projecting series does not fit naturally into our previous formulation but it is now seen to occur as a simple generalization of series 1.

In series 5, 6, 7, 8 and 9 we have tabulated sets of weights for various linear trend projectors. Bearing in mind that the properties of these series are not very sensitive to moderate changes in the weights, we see that all of them could be approximated by an obvious modification of series 2, namely

$$\Delta\hat{z}_{p+1} = \gamma_0 e_p + \gamma_1 S^1 e_p.$$

Finally, therefore, as a natural generalization, we consider the model where $\Delta\hat{z}_{p+1}$, the change to be applied at the $(p+1)$th stage to the previous predictor $\hat{z}_p$, is given by

$$\Delta\hat{z}_{p+1} = (\gamma_{-l} S^{-l} + \ldots + \gamma_{-2} S^{-2} + \gamma_{-1} S^{-1} + \gamma_0 + \gamma_1 S^1 + \gamma_2 S^2 + \ldots + \gamma_m S^m) e_p, \qquad (3.3.1)$$

where $S^{-j} e_p = \Delta^j e_p$.

3.4. *The Nature of the Stochastic Process for which the Predictor is Optimal*

We now ask the question: what stochastic process would z need to follow for such a predictor to be optimal? Consider a process generated by

$$z_{p+1} = \sum_{j=0}^{\infty} \eta_j z_{p-j} + \alpha_{p+1} \qquad (3.4.1)$$

which is, in general, non-stationary and where $\alpha_{p+1}, \alpha_p, \alpha_{p-1}, \ldots$ are uncorrelated identically distributed random variables, with mean zero. Suppose we predict the series using

$$\hat{z}_{p+1} = \sum_{j=0}^{\infty} \mu_j z_{p-j}. \qquad (3.4.2)$$

Then since

$$E(e_{p+1})^2 = E(z_{p+1} - \hat{z}_{p+1})^2 = E\left\{\sum_{j=0}^{\infty} (\eta_j - \mu_j) z_{p-j}\right\}^2 + E(\alpha_{p+1})^2, \qquad (3.4.3)$$

prediction is optimal if $\mu_j = \eta_j$ ($j = 0, 1, 2, \ldots$). It follows that the equivalent predictor

$$\Delta\hat{z}_{p+1} = \sum_{j=0}^{\infty} w_j \, e_{p-j}$$

is optimal for the equivalent stochastic process

$$\Delta z_{p+1} = \Delta\alpha_{p+1} + \sum_{j=0}^{\infty} w_j \, \alpha_{p-j}$$

and that when this optimal predictor is used the e's become α's and are uncorrelated.

In the present instance then our predictor is optimal for a series generated by

$$\Delta z_{p+1} = \Delta\alpha_{p+1} + \sum_{j=-l}^{m} \gamma_j \, S^j \, \alpha_p. \tag{3.4.4}$$

Differencing m times we have

$$\Delta^{m+1} z_{p+1} = \Delta^{m+1} \alpha_{p+1} + \sum_{j=0}^{l+m} \gamma_j \, \Delta^{l+m-j} \, \alpha_p.$$

On rearranging this expression, we find that our predictor would be optimal for any stochastic variable z whose $(m+1)$st difference may be represented by a moving average process of order $l+m+1$,

$$\Delta^{m+1} z_{p+1} = \alpha_{p+1} + \sum_{j=0}^{l+m} \delta_j \, \alpha_{p-j}, \tag{3.4.5}$$

so that all serial covariances after that of lag $l+m+1$ are zero. Thus we have a result which is of considerable practical value. If, after differencing our series z, which in general will be non-stationary, m times, we could render it stationary and if the population serial covariances of lag greater than some value $l+m+1$ were then zero, a predictor of the type (3.3.1) would be optimal.

The widely applied predictor obtained by taking an exponentially weighted mean

$$\hat{z}_{p+1} = \gamma_0 \sum_{j=0}^{\infty} (1-\gamma_0)^j \, z_{p-j}$$

corresponds simply to taking the single central term in our general series namely $\Delta\hat{z}_{p+1} = \gamma_0 \, e_p$. It is optimal for the stochastic process

$$\Delta z_{p+1} = \Delta\alpha_{p+1} + \gamma_0 \, \alpha_p = \alpha_{p+1} - (1-\gamma_0) \, \alpha_p,$$

$$\text{i.e.} \quad z_{p+1} = m + \alpha_{p+1} + \gamma_0 \, S^1 \, \alpha_p,$$

for which the first difference is a first order moving average. The addition of further terms can be thought of, therefore, as an appropriate generalization of this exponential predictor. In particular, for series which are highly non-stationary and exhibit marked trends, the additional term in $S^1 e_p$ will be of particular value since this will allow the predictor to adjust to changes in linear trend as well as to changes in mean.

Bearing in mind the great success of the exponential predictor, it might be expected that the simple generalization

$$\Delta\hat{z}_{p+1} = \gamma_{-1} \Delta e_p + \gamma_0 \, e_p + \gamma_1 \, S e_p \tag{3.4.6}$$

might be adequate for many practical purposes. Experience of two kinds indicates that this is so. Our own somewhat limited experience in applying this theory to industrial series has shown that for those series so far tried, this generalization has been adequate. In fact, so far as *prediction* is concerned, the term in Δe_p has not so far been needed. A further vast fund of experience in this area is possessed by control engineers. We have seen already that if there were no dynamics then the adjustment x_{p+1} of the control set point should be made equal to $\Delta\hat{z}_{p+1}$ the predicted change. A form of automatic control commonly used in industrial plants in continuous time makes a correction proportional to a linear combination of (i) the first derivative of the current deviation, (ii) the deviation itself, (iii) the integral of the deviations over all past history. If, therefore, we were using our predictor (3.4.6) for control purposes, we would employ a discrete time analogue of what control engineers have been using on automatic equipment for many years. The success of their efforts suggests that stochastic processes for which (3.4.6) is optimal adequately describe many industrial series.

The types of continuous control mentioned above are called *derivative*, *proportional* and *integral* respectively. For the discrete process we shall refer to the corresponding terms in (3.4.6) as *first difference*, *proportional* and *cumulative* terms and when we use the prediction equation for control purposes we shall talk of first difference control, proportional control and cumulative control. We shall adopt the three-term model in what follows bearing in mind that it is readily elaborated if need be.

3.5. *Fitting the Three-Term Model*

The stochastic process for which (3.4.6) is optimal is

$$z_{p+1} = m+\alpha_{p+1}+\gamma_{-1}\alpha_p+\gamma_0 S^1\alpha_p+\gamma_1 S^2\alpha_p. \tag{3.5.1}$$

For this process the second difference is the moving average of order 3,

$$\Delta^2 z_{p+1} = \alpha_{p+1}+(\gamma_1+\gamma_0+\gamma_{-1}-2)\alpha_p+(1-2\gamma_{-1}-\gamma_0)\alpha_{p-1}+\gamma_{-1}\alpha_{p-2}. \tag{3.5.2}$$

We notice

(i) that in those common cases where no difference term is needed, γ_{-1} would be zero and only the first and second serial correlations would be non-zero;

(ii) if $\gamma_1=\gamma_0=1$ and $\gamma_{-1}=0$ the terms in α_p, α_{p-1} and α_{p-2} are all zero, $\Delta^2 z_{p+1}=\alpha_{p+1}$, and predictor number 2 in Table 3 is optimal. For this choice of the γ's the second differences are uncorrelated. The nature of the serial correlation among the second differences indicates in what way and how far we must move away from this "pivotal" predictor.

To gain appreciation of the adequacy of a model of the kind assumed, a fairly long length of series would first be differenced $m+1$ times until it appeared stationary. In those cases studied, second differencing has always proved adequate. In two of the series discussed in section 4 first differencing would, in fact, have been adequate but nothing is lost by taking a higher order difference than is strictly necessary. In our calculations we have taken a "typical" run of two or three hundred observations and begun by calculating the first twelve serial covariances of the second differences. If, as a result of inspection, we find that these are small after the third we have proceeded with the estimation of the parameters $\gamma_{-1}, \gamma_0, \gamma_1$ in the three-term model. Inadequate differencing is indicated when positive serial correlation persists for higher lag s. If serial covariances of fourth or higher order were appreciable, but higher covariances were small, we would introduce further parameters corresponding to high derivative control as described above.

A spectral method of estimation of the parameters is described in section 5.5. An alternative method which we have used extensively is to evaluate the sum of squares $S(\gamma_1, \gamma_0, \gamma_{-1}) = e_1^2 + \ldots + e_n^2$ for a grid of values of $\gamma_1, \gamma_0, \gamma_{-1}$ and hence pick out the best values of $\gamma_1, \gamma_0, \gamma_{-1}$ by inspection. In practice we have found that the minimum is fairly flat. Typically, a rather large near-optimal region is found in the space of $\gamma_1, \gamma_0, \gamma_{-1}$ from which we can choose a convenient solution.

Suppose we have a set of data $z_1, z_2, \ldots, z_n$. To make the calculation of the sum of squares $e_1^2 + \ldots + e_n^2$ corresponding to a particular choice of γ_{-1}, γ_0 and γ_1 we note that if z_p, e_p, Δe_p and $S^1 e_p$ are known we may calculate

$$\hat{z}_{p+1} = z_p + \gamma_{-1} \Delta e_p + \gamma_0 e_p + \gamma_1 S^1 e_p$$

and then knowing z_{p+1}, the quantities e_{p+1}, Δe_{p+1} and $S^1 e_{p+1}$ can be easily obtained. To start the process we set $\hat{z}_1 = z_1$ so that $e_1 = \Delta e_1 = S^1 e_1 = 0$. This simple repetitive calculation is ideally suited for the electronic computer which we feel it safe to assume is now universally available.

Under the assumption that the e's are normally distributed, the sum of squares surface $S(\gamma_1, \gamma_0, \gamma_{-1})$ is, in fact, equivalent to the log-likelihood function conditional on $e_1 = \Delta e_1 = S^1 e_1 = 0$. The actual log-likelihood function could be obtained by integrating over the joint distribution of e_1, Δe_1 and $S^1 e_1$ as described by Barnard *et al.* (1962). We have not used this refinement since it would only be important for short series and further, if the choice of the best control parameters were very dependent on e_1, Δe_1 and $S^1 e_1$, we would be disinclined to use them for controlling the future behaviour of the series anyway.

In choosing our grid of values, it is necessary to restrict the $(\gamma_1, \gamma_0, \gamma_{-1})$ point to a certain region or else the control procedure will become *unstable*. It will be shown in section 5.4 that this occurs because the optimum predictors corresponding to the moving average process (3.2.5) lead to infinite prediction variances if the control parameters lie outside a certain region. For the general form of control typified by (3.2.2), the stability condition is that the roots of the characteristic equation

$$1 + \sum_{j=0}^{l+m} \delta_j x^{j+1} = 0$$

should not lie on or inside the unit circle with the possible exception of $m+1$ roots which could all be equal to unity.

The computer programme for the Control Data Corporation's 1604 machine at Madison, Wisconsin, produces the first twelve serial covariances of the second differences and obtains a sum of squares grid for $\gamma_{-1} = -0{\cdot}5\,(0{\cdot}25)\,0{\cdot}5$, $\gamma_0 = 0{\cdot}0\,(0{\cdot}1)\,2{\cdot}0$ and $\gamma_1 = 0{\cdot}0\,(0{\cdot}1)\,2{\cdot}0$ for a series of 300 terms in about 60 seconds. Some examples of these calculations will be discussed in the next section.

3.6. *Representation of Dynamics by Exponential Stages*

Suppose the control dynamics can be represented by an exponential transfer function so that $v_i = (1-\phi)\phi^i$ $(i = 0, 1, 2, \ldots)$.

From (2.2.2) it may be shown that to induce action in the controlled variable according to

$$x_{p+1} = \gamma_{-1} \Delta e_p + \gamma_0 e_p + \gamma_1 S^1 e_p \tag{3.6.1}$$

an adjustment

$$x^*_{p+1} = \gamma^*_{-2} \Delta^2 e_p + \gamma^*_{-1} \Delta e_p + \gamma^*_0 e_p + \gamma^*_1 S^1 e_p \tag{3.6.2}$$

must be applied to the manipulated variable, where $\gamma^*_{-2} = k\gamma_{-1}$, $\gamma^*_{-1} = \gamma_{-1}+k\gamma_0$, $\gamma^*_0 = \gamma_0+k\gamma_1$, $\gamma^*_1 = \gamma_1$ and $k = \phi/(1-\phi)$. In other words the matrix **T**, which transforms the γ's into γ^*'s when exponential dynamics apply, is given by the matrix relation

$$\boldsymbol{\gamma}^* = \mathbf{T}\boldsymbol{\gamma} \tag{3.6.3}$$

with

$$\mathbf{T} = \begin{bmatrix} k & \cdot & \cdot \\ 1 & k & \cdot \\ \cdot & 1 & k \\ \cdot & \cdot & 1 \end{bmatrix}. \tag{3.6.4}$$

The corresponding matrix **T** appropriate for the more general control model (3.3.1) is of the same form. We see that to compensate for exponential dynamics we must add difference control to the manipulated variable of one order higher than we require to be applied to the controlled variable. Furthermore, if we know

(i) the γ's required for optimal prediction,
(ii) the constant k of the exponential transfer,

then the γ^*'s, which determine the appropriate combination of the various kinds of control to be applied to the manipulated variable, are very easily obtained.

It frequently happens in practice that only the two terms involving γ_0 and γ_1 which produce proportional and cumulative action are needed for near-optimal prediction (and hence, in the absence of dynamics, for near-optimal control). Yet as soon as we must compensate for simple exponential dynamics our third term γ_{-1} will be equal to $k\gamma_0$ and so difference action is needed.

In some cases the dynamics are such that more than one exponential stage is involved. If the action x_{p+1} which it was desired to induce at the controlled variable was represented by an expression involving c terms and the dynamic behaviour was as if s exponential stages were involved with constants $k_1, k_2, \ldots, k_s$, then control involving differences of s orders higher would be required at the manipulated variable. If $\mathbf{T}_i$ is the $(c+i)\times(c+i-1)$ transfer matrix for the ith stage of the same form as (3.6.2) but containing the constant k_i, then the $(c+s)\times c$ matrix **T** representing the overall transfer matrix is given by $\mathbf{T} = \mathbf{T}_1\mathbf{T}_2\ldots\mathbf{T}_s$. For example, if an exponentially weighted mean with constant γ_0 adequately predicts the next observation, so that simple proportional control according to $x_{p+1} = \gamma_0 e_p$ is required to be applied to the controlled variable, and if the dynamics can be represented by two exponential stages with constants k_1 and k_2, then $\mathbf{T}' = [k_1 k_2, k_1+k_2, 1]$ and we control the manipulated variable in acccordance with

$$x^*_{p+1} = k_1 k_2 \gamma_0 \Delta^2 e_p + (k_1+k_2)\gamma_0 \Delta e_p + \gamma_0 e_p.$$

4. EXAMPLES

4.1. *A Study of Three Series*

In Fig. 3 are shown two or three hundred observations from each of three series associated with typical chemical operations. The series show values respectively of concentration, temperature and viscosity when no control was applied. Each series consists of discrete observations although the plotted points are joined in this figure by lines. Series II was obtained by temporarily disconnecting an automatic temperature controller, series I and III were obtained by reconstructing the uncontrolled series. In each of these latter cases some manual control had been employed. From (i) the values for the controlled series, (ii) the control action taken, and, where appropriate, (iii) the approximate system dynamics, the course which the series would have taken had no control been exerted could be calculated to a sufficient degree of approximation. The concentration of active ingredient in successive

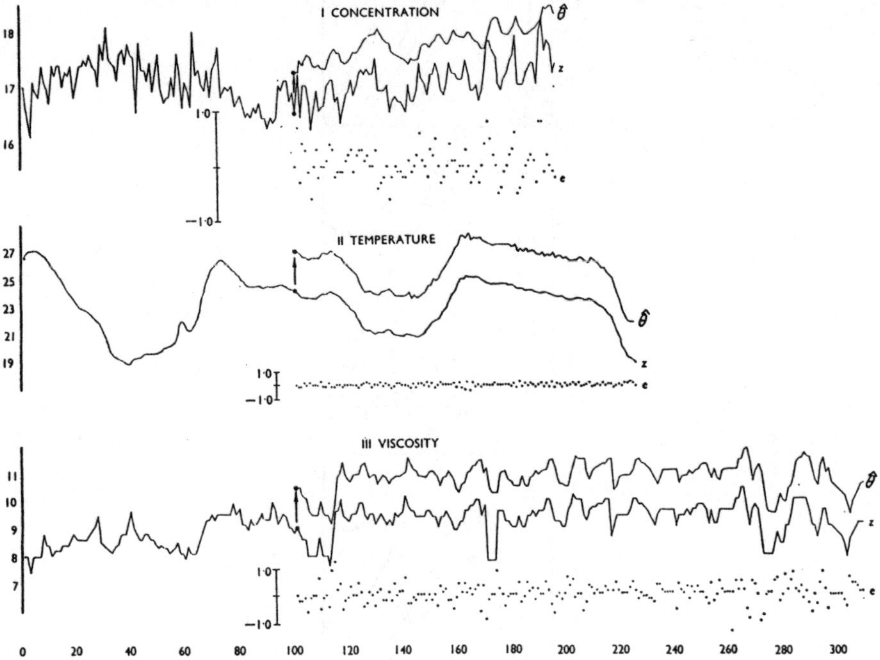

FIG. 3. Three uncontrolled industrial series, predicted series θ_p, and error e_p shown for latter sections.

batches shown in series I was controlled by the addition of the appropriate amount of pure chemical on a batch-to-batch basis. In this example, therefore, no dynamics had to be considered in reconstructing the series. The dynamics appropriate to series III are discussed later. It was found in each case that the serial covariances after the third are small, so that we feel justified in proceeding with our analysis based on the use of difference, proportional and cumulative control.

In Fig. 4 contour plots of the sums of squares surfaces are shown for different values of γ_0 and γ_1 when $\gamma_{-1} = 0$.

These diagrams show that:

(i) The choice of the coefficients is not very critical. A sum of squares very little greater than the smallest value can be obtained over a fairly wide area of the $(\gamma_{-1}, \gamma_0, \gamma_1)$ space.

(ii) For none of the series is there any strong indication that a difference term is necessary. Formal interpolation among the calculated sums of squares gives a minimum in each case in which γ_{-1} is slightly different from zero. However, the increase produced by setting $\gamma_{-1} = 0$ is entirely negligible.

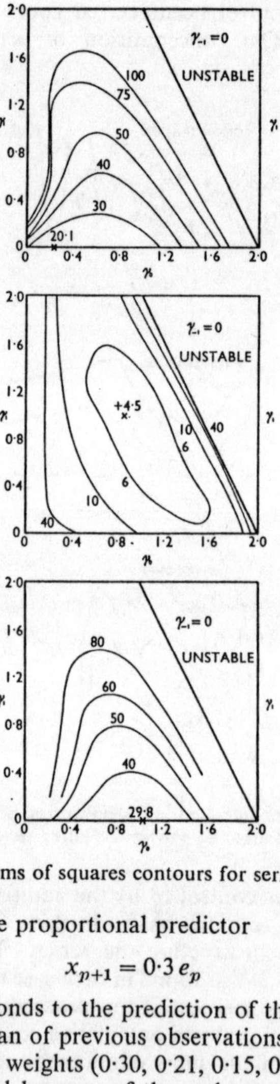

FIG. 4. Sums of squares contours for series I–III.

(iii) For series I the simple proportional predictor

$$x_{p+1} = 0{\cdot}3\, e_p$$

is near optimal. This corresponds to the prediction of the next value in the series by an exponentially weighted mean of previous observations. The small value $\gamma_0 = 0{\cdot}30$ ensures that the exponential μ weights (0·30, 0·21, 0·15, 0·10, 0·07, etc.) die out rather slowly. This is to be expected because of the rather noisy nature of the series. In general, the choice of the constant in a proportional (i.e. exponentially weighted) predictor is a compromise between the desirability of emphasis on "up-to-date values", obtained by choosing γ_0 close to unity and the desirability of "smoothing out the noise" obtained by taking a smaller value of γ_0.

(iv) For series II the necessity for cumulative control in addition to proportional control is clearly seen, the near-optimal predictor being

$$x_{p+1} = 1{\cdot}1\, e_p + 0{\cdot}8 \sum_{j=0}^{\infty} e_{p-j}.$$

Almost equally good prediction would be obtained by setting both γ_0 and γ_1 equal to unity. The corresponding μ weights would then be $\mu_0 = 2$, $\mu_1 = -1$ with all other values zero. The predictor $X_{p+1} = 2z_p - z_{p-1}$ is that obtained by projecting a straight line drawn through the last two observations and would be optimal when the second differences were independent random deviates. This type of prediction would be expected to be good for the present series (Fig. 3) in which linear trend extrapolation is clearly desirable and where the superimposed noise is small. We notice as expected that for this series the serial covariances of the second differences are *all* small in magnitude.

(v) For series III a near optimal predictor is $x_{p+1} = e_p$. This means that $X_{p+1} = z_p$ so that the previous observation is used to predict the next. Since an important characteristic of series III is the predominance of step changes, this is clearly sensible.

4.2. *Predicting the Series*

To illustrate the extent to which series of the various kinds can be predicted, we have applied predictors with optimal weights obtained from the first hundred values

TABLE 4

Serial correlations ρ_s and optimal control weights for series I–III

	Series I			*Series II*			*Series III*		
	1st 100 *obs.*	*2nd* 97 *obs.*	*Total* 197 *obs.*	*1st* 100 *obs.*	*2nd* 126 *obs.*	*Total* 226 *obs.*	*1st* 100 *obs.*	*2nd* 210 *obs.*	*Total* 310 *obs.*
Var (Δz^2)	·57	·22	·39	·032	·012	·020	17·7	22·2	20·7
ρ_1	−·69	−·53	−·67	·09	−·39	−·09	−·64	−·46	−·50
ρ_2	·22	·07	·22	−·18	·11	−·07	·25	−·07	·00
ρ_3	−·03	−·13	−·09	−·15	−·07	−·13	−·26	·08	·00
ρ_4	−·01	·22	·05	−·05	−·08	−·05	·30	−·13	−·01
ρ_5	·01	−·17	−·03	−·03	·10	·02	−·29	·06	−·02
ρ_6	−·06	−·02	−·06	·02	−·05	−·01	·25	−·01	·04
ρ_7	·12	·21	·15	·01	·17	·06	−·26	·06	−·02
ρ_8	−·05	−·24	−·12	−·07	−·05	−·06	·18	−·06	·01
ρ_9	·00	·14	·05	−·09	−·17	−·13	−·02	·03	·01
ρ_{10}	·03	·00	·03	·10	·14	·12	−·05	−·04	−·04
γ_0†	·30	·50	·30	1·20	1·00	1·10	·80	1·00	1·00
γ_1†	·00	·00	·00	·80	·60	·80	·00	·00	·00
Variance‡ before control		·139			2·313			29·0	
Variance‡ after control		·089			·013			11·0	

† Optimal values of γ_0 and γ_1, when $\gamma_{-1} = 0$.

‡ Variances refer to second part of series.

of each series to forecast values in the remainder. The predicted values are plotted above the second part of each series in Fig. 3. To avoid confusion between the original values and the predicted values, the latter have been moved upwards by the amount indicated and plotted above the original series. The errors of prediction are indicated by the series of dots plotted below each series. Table 4 shows for the first and the second part of each series, (i) the serial correlations of second differences, (ii) the optimal weights, (iii) the reduction in variance achieved by control of the second part of each series using weights calculated from the first part. Although no formal tests have been made there seems reason to doubt strict homogeneity particularly in the first series. The optimal weights for the first and second parts of each series agree remarkably well, however.

4.3. *An Example of an Adaptive Quality Control Scheme*

We now describe the institution of a practical adaptive quality control scheme based on the above discussion. For this we consider in more detail the system from which series III was obtained.

The values recorded in series III are hourly readings of viscosity. In a continuous reactor a gas was injected into a liquid to form a mixture of products which should have a viscosity between 86 and 98. The composition of the inlet gas was not constant and the reaction was controlled by feeding in more or less gas so as to achieve the required viscosity. Experiments with a gas of reasonably constant composition had shown that within the range considered a change in gas rate of 50 lb. per min. eventually produced a change in viscosity of about 10 units. After 82 min., 63 per cent. of this effect was produced and after 165 min. 86 per cent. If we assume a simple exponential response then this implies that approximately half the effect is achieved in one hour. Thus we may employ equation (3.5.3) with $\phi = \frac{1}{2}$, $\gamma_{-1} = 0$, $\gamma_0 = 1$, $\gamma_1 = 0$ to find the adjustment to be applied to the gas rate. We obtain simply

$$x^*_{p+1} = \Delta e_p + e_p = 2e_p - e_{p-1},$$

where x^*_{p+1} is the adjustment to be applied negatively to the gas rate measured in units of its *ultimate* effect on the viscosity. The logic of this control system is easily seen in this particularly simple example. Since only one half of the ultimate effect of any change realized will be produced at the next observation we must double the weight associated with e_p. However, the effect of having done this in the previous phase must also be undone; hence we must associate a weight of -1 with e_{p-1}.

The charts used to institute the scheme are shown in Fig. 5. The proportional (P) chart is simply a plot of hourly readings of viscosity. The origin is at the target value 92 midway between the limits 86 and 98 between which it is desired to control the response. A scale showing the "deviation from target value" is also shown. On the difference (D) chart is shown the difference between the last two readings plotted about an origin of zero. On the action (A) chart the sum of the deviations in charts P and D is plotted. This is referred to a scale showing directly the change in gas rate required. Each hour the operator obtains a new reading, he enters this on chart P, enters the difference from the previous reading on chart D, adds the two deviations and plots this on chart A. He then makes the appropriate adjustment to the gas rate which is shown on this last chart.

The above example happens to yield a particularly simple type of control. However, very little extra complication arises in other examples. When cumulative control is

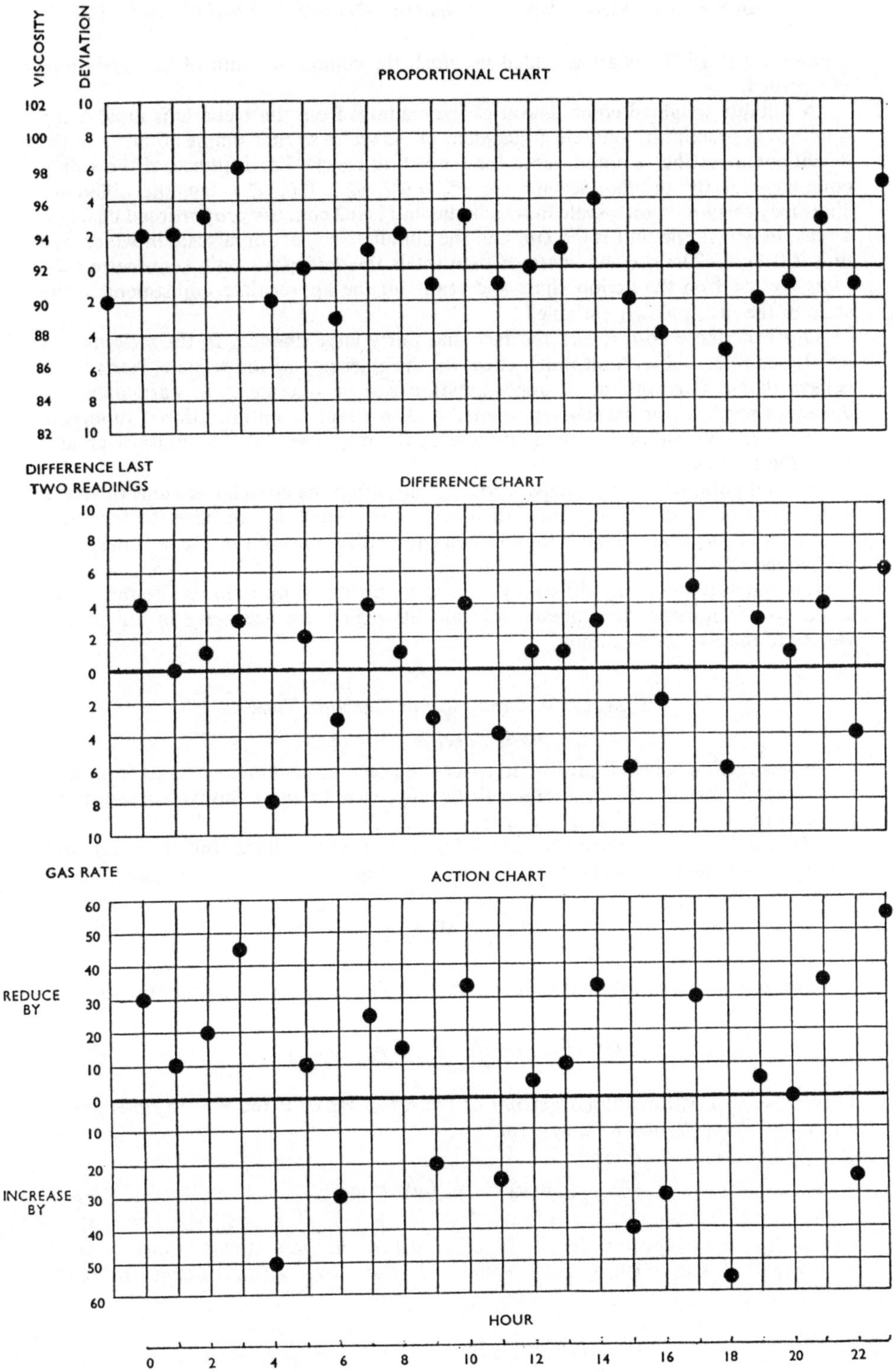

FIG. 5. Adaptive quality control chart for series III.

necessary a third (C) chart is added in which the cumulative sum of the deviations is recorded.

A suitably weighted combination of the readings from these charts is most easily obtained in practice by suitable adjustment of the scales so that simple addition of the deviations gives the required value for the action chart. For instance, if the values computed for the optimal scheme are $\gamma^*_{-1} = 0{\cdot}2$, $\gamma^*_0 = 0{\cdot}6$, $\gamma^*_1 = 0{\cdot}4$, the difference chart may be plotted on a scale in which one unit is 0·2 cm., the proportional chart on a scale in which one unit is 0·6 cm. and the cumulative chart on a scale in which one unit is 0·4 cm. The process operator then totals the deviations on a centimetre rule, plots the total on the action chart and reads off the appropriate adjustment in the scale of the manipulated variable.

Our experience so far, and the fact that fairly large changes in the weights can usually be tolerated without much effect on the efficiency of the scheme, leads us to believe that a fair amount of approximation can be tolerated. In particular, the dynamics need not be exactly represented and in adaptive optimization a moderate error in the estimate of β_{11}, the curvature of the response curve, would not greatly upset the scheme.

A small point which is perhaps worth noting is that the cumulative sums of errors which must be plotted when cumulative control is needed do not have the tendency to wander off the chart which is found when cumulative sums of the *original* deviations are plotted.

It is believed that many situations exist where a set of simple charts like the above could greatly improve the manual adjustments which are necessary in an infinite variety of industrial operations.

5. Spectral Approach in Discrete Time

5.1. *Basic Spectral Formulae*

In this section we shall present some of the previous results in spectral form and thus prepare the way for a more realistic approach to the adaptive optimization problem to be considered in a later paper.

We have shown that the error ϵ_p could be expressed as a linear function over past history of the random variables θ_p and u_p. We represent such a linear function by

$$T_l = \sum_{j=0}^{\infty} \phi_j^{(l)}\, \theta_{p-j}, \tag{5.1.1}$$

and a simple calculation shows that the covariance between two such linear functions is

$$\operatorname{cov}(T_l, T_m) = \sum_{p=0}^{\infty} \sum_{q=0}^{\infty} \phi_p^{(l)}\, \phi_q^{(m)}\, \zeta_{|p-q|}, \tag{5.1.2}$$

where $\zeta_s = \sigma_\theta^2\, \rho_s$ is the autocovariance of the θ's of lag s. If the θ's are observed at unit time intervals, then we may write

$$\zeta_s = \sigma_\theta^2 \int_{-\pi}^{+\pi} g_\theta^*(\omega)\, e^{i\omega s}\, d\omega, \tag{5.1.3}$$

where $g_\theta^*(\omega)$ is the spectral density function, defined in the frequency range $[-\pi, \pi]$ for operational convenience, and is equal to $\frac{1}{2} g_\theta(\omega)$, where $g_\theta(\omega)$ is defined in $[0, \pi]$.

If we now substitute for (5.1.3) in (5.1.2) we obtain

$$\operatorname{cov}(T_l, T_m) = \sigma_\theta^2 \int_{-\pi}^{+\pi} g_\theta^*(\omega)\, H_l(\omega)\, \bar{H}_m(\omega)\, d\omega, \tag{5.1.4}$$

where $H_l(\omega) = \sum_{j=0}^{\infty} \phi_j^{(l)}\, e^{-ij\omega}$

is the discrete Fourier transform of the weights $\phi_j^{(l)}$ and the bar denotes a complex conjugate. In the special case where $l = m$, (5.1.4) reduces to

$$\operatorname{var}(T_l) = \sigma_\theta^2 \int_{-\pi}^{+\pi} g_\theta^*(\omega) |H_l(\omega)|^2\, d\omega. \tag{5.1.5}$$

More generally, we may write the variance–covariance matrix of several such linear combinations in the form

$$\sigma_\theta^2 \mathbf{R} = \sigma_\theta^2 \int_{-\pi}^{+\pi} \mathbf{H}(\boldsymbol{\omega})\, \overline{\mathbf{H}}(\boldsymbol{\omega})'\, g_\theta^*(\omega)\, d\omega, \tag{5.1.6}$$

where $\mathbf{H}(\boldsymbol{\omega})' = \{H_1(\omega), H_2(\omega), \ldots, H_k(\omega)\}$ and the matrix $\mathbf{H}(\boldsymbol{\omega})\,\overline{\mathbf{H}}(\boldsymbol{\omega})'$ is Hermitian.

Equation (5.1.5) says that the variance of any linear combination may be expressed as a *spectral average* with weight function or kernel $|H_l(\omega)|^2$. The generating function $H_l(\omega)$ for the weights $\phi_j^{(l)}$ is important and is called the *frequency response function* of the linear operation performed by (5.1.1), or else the *transfer function* when expressed as a function of $p = i\omega$. In engineering language, (5.1.1) is called a *linear filter* and is characterized by the important property that if the input θ_p is periodic of the form $Ae^{ip\omega}$, then the output is given by $AH(\omega)\, e^{i\omega p}$, i.e. a periodic disturbance with the same frequency. Since $H(\omega) = G(\omega)e^{i\phi(\omega)}$, it follows that the output is multiplied by a factor $G(\omega)$, the *gain*, and phase-shifted by an amount $\phi(\omega)$. We may now interpret (5.1.5) heuristically as follows; the random variable θ_p may be decomposed into contributions $\theta_p(\omega)$ at each frequency with variance $\sigma_\theta^2 g_\theta^*(\omega)$ which when passed through the linear filter (5.1.1) will be multiplied by the factor $|H(\omega)|$, so that its variance is $\sigma_\theta^2 |H(\omega)|^2 g_\theta(\omega)$. The total variance is then obtained by adding up the contributions at each frequency.

The importance of these ideas to statistical estimation becomes apparent when it is realized that any linear estimate may be regarded as a filtering operation performed on the observations. We illustrate this by considering the estimation of a mean

$$\bar{\theta} = \frac{1}{2n+1} \sum_{p=-n}^{n} \theta_p \tag{5.1.7}$$

and a harmonic regression coefficient in the form

$$b = \frac{2}{2n+1} \sum_{p=-n}^{+n} \theta_p \cos(\omega_0 p). \tag{5.1.8}$$

For convenience we have arranged that the number of observations in the sample $N = 2n+1$ is odd and that the time origin occurs at the $(n+1)$st observation. Regarding (5.1.7) and (5.1.8) as filtering operations, it is readily seen that their frequency response functions $H_1(\omega)$ and $H_2(\omega)$ are respectively given by

$$H_1(\omega) = \sin(\tfrac{1}{2}N\omega)/\sin(\tfrac{1}{2}\omega) \tag{5.1.9}$$

and

$$H_2(\omega) = \frac{\sin\{\frac{1}{2}N(\omega-\omega_0)\}}{\sin\{\frac{1}{2}(\omega-\omega_0)\}} + \frac{\sin\{\frac{1}{2}N(\omega+\omega_0)\}}{\sin\{\frac{1}{2}(\omega+\omega_0)\}}. \tag{5.1.10}$$

By choice of time origin we have arranged that the phase-shift is zero and hence the frequency response function is a gain only. Also, these functions differ only in that (5.1.9) is centred about zero frequency and (5.1.10) about the frequency ω_0. The function (5.1.10) is exactly the same as the spectral window associated with the truncated periodogram estimate of the spectral density and has been plotted along with other forms of $H(\omega)$ in a paper recently published by one of us (Jenkins, 1961). It has the property that it is highly peaked about the frequency ω_0 and in fact behaves like a Dirac δ function as $n, N \to \infty$. It is not surprising, therefore, that it may be shown rigorously that

$$\lim_{N\to\infty} N \operatorname{var}(\bar{\theta}) = \pi\sigma_\theta^2 g_\theta(0) \tag{5.1.11}$$

and

$$\lim_{N\to\infty} N \operatorname{var}(b) = 2\pi\sigma_\theta^2 g_\theta(\omega_0), \tag{5.1.12}$$

so that the variances for large samples may be approximated respectively by $\pi\sigma_\theta^2 g_\theta(0)/N$ and $2\pi\sigma_\theta^2 g_\theta(\omega_0)/N$. However, this approximation may be seen to be a good one even for low values of N by observing that the width of the spectral window (5.1.10) will be narrow in general. Thus if the spectral density remains fairly constant over the width of the windows associated with the two estimates T_l and T_m, then

$$\operatorname{cov}(T_l, T_m) \sim \sigma_\theta^2 g_\theta(\omega_0) \int_{-\pi}^{+\pi} H_l(\omega)\, \bar{H}_m(\omega)\, d\omega = 2\pi\sigma_\theta^2 g_\theta(\omega_0) \sum_{j=0}^{\infty} \phi_j^{(l)} \phi_j^{(m)}. \tag{5.1.13}$$

In the case of a variance, if $g_\theta(\omega_0)$ remains fairly constant over the bandwidth of the window, then

$$\operatorname{var}(T_l) \sim 2\pi\sigma_\theta^2 g_\theta(\omega_0) \sum_{j=0}^{\infty} (\phi_j^{(l)})^2 \tag{5.1.14}$$

from which (5.1.11) and (5.1.12) are readily obtained. From (5.1.13) it may be seen that T_l and T_m are approximately uncorrelated provided the weights $\phi_j^{(l)}$ and $\phi_j^{(m)}$ are orthogonal, which is true for the estimators $\bar{\theta}$ and b.

5.2. *Prediction in Discrete Time*

Suppose that we can observe the mean process θ_p exactly without any measurement error u_p, so that $z_p = \theta_p$. Then the problem of pure prediction one step ahead as defined by (2.4.1) is to minimize the prediction error ϵ_p given by

$$\epsilon_{p+1} = \theta_{p+1} - \sum_{j=0}^{\infty} \mu_j\, \theta_{p-j}. \tag{5.2.1}$$

With

$$\mu(\omega) = \sum_{j=0}^{\infty} \mu_j e^{i\omega j},$$

the frequency response function associated with the predictor weights, it is readily seen that the $H(\omega)$ associated with the prediction error (5.2.1) is $1 - e^{-i\omega}\mu(\omega)$ and hence that

$$\operatorname{var}(\epsilon_{p+1}) = \sigma_\theta^2 \int_{-\pi}^{+\pi} |1 - e^{-i\omega}\mu(\omega)|^2 g_\theta^*(\omega)\, d\omega. \tag{5.2.2}$$

If it is now assumed that the spectral density may be written in the form

$$g_\theta(\omega) = \frac{\sigma_\epsilon^2}{2\pi\sigma_\theta^2} |\psi(\omega)|^{-2} \quad (-\pi \leqslant \omega \leqslant \pi), \tag{5.2.3}$$

then, using fairly standard techniques in the calculus of variations, it may be shown that the loss (5.2.2) is minimized with respect to variations in $\mu(\omega)$ when

$$1-e^{-i\omega}\mu(\omega)=\psi(\omega). \tag{5.2.4}$$

Two special cases are of interest:

(i) If the θ_p series represents an autoregressive process, then $\psi(\omega)$ is a polynomial of the form

$$\psi(\omega)=1-\sum_{j=1}^{k}a_j e^{-i\omega j}.$$

It follows that $\mu(\omega)=a_1+a_2e^{-i\omega}+\ldots+a_k e^{-i(k-1)\omega}$ so that the predictor weights μ_j are equal to a_j, as was shown in section 3.

(ii) If the θ_p series constitutes a moving average process

$$\theta_p=\epsilon_p+\beta_1\epsilon_{p-1}+\ldots+\beta_m\epsilon_{p-m}, \tag{5.2.5}$$

then
$$\psi^{-1}(\omega)=1+\beta_1e^{-i\omega}+\ldots+\beta_m e^{-im\omega} \tag{5.2.6}$$

and the solution for the optimum weights as given by (5.2.4) becomes extremely complicated. An example when $m=1$ has been given previously in Table 2.

5.3. *Control of the Mean when the Added Noise is Absent*

In this situation, $\epsilon_p=e_p$ and the *loop equation* (2.4.2) may be written

$$\Delta\epsilon_{p+1}=\Delta\theta_{p+1}-\sum_{j=0}^{\infty}w_j\epsilon_{p-j} \tag{5.3.1}$$

which may be expressed symbolically as

$$\epsilon_{p+1}=\left(1-\frac{B\mathscr{L}_w}{1-B+B\mathscr{L}_w}\right)\theta_{p+1}=(1-\mathscr{L}_\mu)\,\theta_{p+1}, \tag{5.3.2}$$

where $\mathscr{L}_w=\Sigma w_j B^j$ and B is the backward shift or delay operator. If the operator $\mathscr{L}_\mu$ is expanded in an infinite series in powers of B, then the terms of this series represent the weights given to previous θ's in obtaining a linear prediction of θ_{p+1}. The transform of these weights will be the frequency response function of the filter associated with (5.3.2) and this is obtained simply by replacing B by $e^{-i\omega}$, i.e.

$$H(\omega)=1-\frac{e^{-i\omega}W(\omega)}{1-e^{-i\omega}+e^{-i\omega}W(\omega)}, \tag{5.3.3}$$

where $W(\omega)=\Sigma w_j e^{-i\omega j}$ is the frequency response function of the controller weights. Since $H(\omega)=1-\mu(\omega)e^{-i\omega}$, it follows that the relation between the predictor and controller weights may be expressed in transforms by

$$\mu(\omega)=\frac{W(\omega)}{1-e^{-i\omega}+e^{-i\omega}W(\omega)} \tag{5.3.4}$$

yielding the inverse relation

$$W(\omega)=\frac{\mu(\omega)(1-e^{-i\omega})}{1-e^{-i\omega}\mu(\omega)}. \tag{5.3.5}$$

It follows from (5.2.4) that the optimum controller weights for the spectrum (5.2.3) are given by

$$W(\omega)=(e^{i\omega}-1)\{\psi^{-1}(\omega)-1\}. \tag{5.3.6}$$

In the case of an autoregressive scheme, $\psi^{-1}(\omega)$ is rather complicated, but for the moving average process with $\psi^{-1}(\omega)$ given by (5.2.6), the best controller weights are

$$W(\omega) = (e^{i\omega}-1)\sum_{j=1}^{m}\beta_j e^{-i\omega j}, \tag{5.3.7}$$

leading to various forms of difference control depending on the value of m. When $m = 1$, the weights correspond to first difference control. It is interesting to note the duality which exists between the autoregressive and moving average processes in so far as the optimum choice of predictor and controller weights is concerned.

If we use (5.3.4) and (5.3.5), it is possible to draw some general conclusions about the conditions which have to be satisfied in order for the predictor and controller weights to satisfy some of the constraints discussed in section 3, for example that they sum to unity. Since the sum of any set of weights is given by the value of the frequency response function at zero frequency, it follows from (5.3.5) that if the predictor weights do not sum to unity, the controller weights will always sum to zero. The disadvantages of the predictors which are not mean correcting are thus seen to carry over to the controller weights. If the latter sum to zero then in a situation where, for example, the last few deviations ϵ_p were all equal to some quantity δ, the controller would recommend no control action whereas a correction $-\delta$ is required for effective control.

When the predictor weights do add to unity, it is necessary to apply L'Hôpital's rule to evaluate the frequency response functions at zero frequency since both numerator and denominator vanish in (5.3.4) and (5.3.5). A simple calculation gives

$$\sum_{j=0}^{\infty}\mu_j = \sum_{j=0}^{\infty} j w_j \Big/ \left\{1+\sum_{j=0}^{\infty} j w_j\right\}, \tag{5.3.8}$$

$$\sum_{j=0}^{\infty} w_j = \sum_{j=0}^{\infty}\mu_j \Big/ \left\{\sum_{j=0}^{\infty}\mu_j+\sum_{j=0}^{\infty} j\mu_j\right\}. \tag{5.3.9}$$

It may be seen, therefore, that for a mean and trend correcting predictor, the controller weights must have an infinite sum and so we are led to some form of integral control.

5.4. *Control with Dynamics and Added Noise*

In discrete time there is a delay of one time unit before correction is made, so that even when all the correction becomes effective at the next instant, there are dynamic considerations present. For the moment we consider the dynamic aspects as referring to the extent to which the current correction becomes fully effective or not at the next instant, i.e. we ignore the initial delay of one time unit.

The loop equation may then be written, as before, in the form

$$\Delta\theta_{p+1} = \Delta\epsilon_{p+1}+x_{p+1}, \tag{5.4.1}$$

but now x_{p+1} is made up of two operations acting independently. The controller produces, from the past deviations ϵ_p, a correction whose negative value is $x^*_{p+1} = \mathscr{L}^*_w\,\epsilon_p$, where $\mathscr{L}^*_w$ is the linear operator associated with the controller. This is acted upon in turn by the dynamic characteristics of the process, characterized by a linear operator $\mathscr{L}_v$, finally producing $x_{p+1} = \mathscr{L}_v\mathscr{L}^*_w\,\epsilon_p$. From (5.4.1), it is seen that the linear operator connecting ϵ_{p+1} and the previous θ's is given by

$$\epsilon_{p+1} = \left(1 - \frac{B\mathscr{L}_v \mathscr{L}_w^*}{1-B+B\mathscr{L}_v \mathscr{L}_w^*}\right)\theta_{p+1}, \tag{5.4.2}$$

so that the loss may be written as

$$\operatorname{var}(\epsilon_{p+1}) = \int_{-\pi}^{+\pi} \left| 1 - \frac{e^{-i\omega} V(\omega) W^*(\omega)}{1-e^{-i\omega}+e^{-i\omega} V(\omega) W^*(\omega)} \right|^2 g_\theta^*(\omega)\, d\omega. \tag{5.4.3}$$

Hence the effect of the dynamics is to replace the controller frequency response function $W(\omega)$ in (5.3.4) by the product of the controller transfer function and the process or valve transfer function in (5.4.3).

By writing down explicitly what is meant by the operation $x_{p+1} = \mathscr{L}_v \mathscr{L}_w^* \epsilon_p$, it is possible to determine the weights which are actually applied to the errors ϵ_p. We may write this operation in the form

$$x_{p+1} = \sum_{r=0}^{\infty} v_r x_{p-r}^*$$

which in turn may be written as

$$x_{p+1} = \sum_{r=0}^{\infty} v_r \sum_{s=0}^{\infty} w_s^* \epsilon_{p-r-s} = \sum_{l=0}^{\infty} w_l \epsilon_{p-l},$$

where

$$w_l = \sum_{r=0}^{l} v_r w_{l-r}^*. \tag{5.4.4}$$

It follows that the effective weights which are applied to the errors ϵ_p are the convolution of the controller weights w_j^* and the weights v_j characterizing the dynamic response of the process.

In order to consider the effect of the added noise, it is necessary to derive the modified loop equation in this case. We must now distinguish between ϵ_{p+1} and e_{p+1} because if the u_p process is not white noise, then it is no longer true that $E(\epsilon_{p+1}^2)$ is minimized when $E(e_{p+1}^2)$ is minimized. Ignoring dynamics, the loop equation becomes

$$\epsilon_{p+1} = \epsilon_p + (\theta_{p+1} - \theta_p) - x_{p+1} + u_{p+1}. \tag{5.4.5}$$

This differs from the previous loop equation in that the added error u_{p+1} now inflates the loss. The linear operators connecting ϵ_{p+1} and the past history of the series and the u series may be obtained by rearranging (5.4.5) in the form

$$(1-B+B\mathscr{L}_w)\,\epsilon_{p+1} = (1-B)\,\theta_{p+1} + u_{p+1},$$

so that the loss may be written as

$$\operatorname{var}(\epsilon_{p+1}) = \sigma_\theta^2 \int_{-\pi}^{+\pi} \left| 1 - \frac{e^{-i\omega} W(\omega)}{1-e^{-i\omega}+e^{-i\omega} W(\omega)} \right|^2 g_\theta^*(\omega)\, d\omega$$

$$+ \sigma_u^2 \int_{-\pi}^{+\pi} \left| \frac{W(\omega)}{1-e^{-i\omega}+e^{-i\omega} W(\omega)} \right|^2 g_u^*(\omega)\, d\omega. \tag{5.4.6}$$

This formula shows that a compromise must now be set up between direct control of the θ_p series and smoothing out the effect of the u_p series, since a choice of $W(\omega)$ which makes the first integral small would tend to make the second integral large and vice versa.

5.5. *Estimation of the Control Parameters from Past Records*

In previous sections, we have shown that if the z series is stationary, then the optimum control parameters may be determined from a knowledge of the spectrum of the process. However, since most practical series display non-stationarity of various types, we were led to consider controller weights corresponding to constrained predictors designed to deal with short-term non-stationarity. In section 3 this led to the consideration of a mixture of cumulative proportional and first difference control. A series for which this form of control was optimal, whilst non-stationary itself, is such that its second differences are stationary and follow a third order moving average process. We now proceed to exhibit these results in spectral form.

In Table 5 we give the frequency response functions corresponding to these three forms of control in discrete time.

TABLE 5

Frequency response functions for various types of control

Control	*Controller weights*	*Frequency response function*
Cumulative	$w_j = \gamma_1$ (all j)	$\gamma_1/(1-e^{-i\omega})$
Proportional	$w_0 = \gamma_0$ $w_j = 0\ (j \geqslant 1)$	γ_0
First difference	$w_0 = \gamma_{-1}$ $w_1 = -\gamma_{-1}$ $w_j = 0\ (j \geqslant 2)$	$\gamma_{-1}(1-e^{-i\omega})$

It follows that a mixture of these three forms of control has a frequency response function

$$W(\omega) = \gamma_{-1}(1-e^{-i\omega})+\gamma_0+\gamma_1/(1-e^{-i\omega}). \tag{5.5.1}$$

Substituting for this in (5.4.6) and assuming that the added noise is white, we may express the loss in the form

$$\operatorname{var}(e_{p+1}) = \sigma_z^2 \int_{-\pi}^{+\pi} \frac{|1-e^{-i\omega}|^4\, g_z^*(\omega)}{|H(\omega)|^2}\, d\omega, \tag{5.5.2}$$

where $$H(\omega) = 1+e^{-i\omega}(\gamma_{-1}+\gamma_0+\gamma_1-2)+e^{-2i\omega}(1-2\gamma_{-1}-\gamma_0)+\gamma_{-1}e^{-3i\omega}. \tag{5.5.3}$$

From (5.5.2) it follows that $\operatorname{var}(e_{p+1})$ is finite only if the roots of $H(\omega)/(1-e^{-i\omega})^2$ lie outside the unit circle and this is the condition for stability mentioned earlier. We denote the second difference of the z_p series by d_p, and note that a second difference is equivalent to a filtering operation with frequency response function $(1-e^{-i\omega})^2$, which is a high pass filter removing low frequency trend. We may thus relate the spectrum of the second differences to that of the original series by a special case of a well-known formula relating the output and input spectral densities of a linear filter, viz.

$$\sigma_d^2 g_d(\omega) = \sigma_z^2 g_z(\omega)|1-e^{-i\omega}|^4. \tag{5.5.4}$$

It follows that the loss may be written as

$$\operatorname{var}(e_{p+1}) = \sigma_d^2 \int_{-\pi}^{+\pi} \frac{g_d^*(\omega)}{|H(\omega)|^2}\, d\omega. \tag{5.5.5}$$

This is similar to (5.2.2) and the converse of the result (5.2.4) shows that for fixed $H(\omega)$, this is minimized for variations in $g_d(\omega)$ of the form (5.2.3) when $\psi(\omega) = H(\omega)$, i.e. the second differences follow the third order moving average process whose generating function is given by (5.5.3).

At this stage we could proceed and find theoretically the values of $\gamma_{-1}, \gamma_0, \gamma_1$ which minimize (5.5.5) for a given $g_d(\omega)$. The variational argument no longer applies in this case and it would then be necessary to evaluate the integral (5.5.5) and find the values of $\gamma_{-1}, \gamma_0, \gamma_1$ which lead to minimum loss analytically or numerically.

From a practical point of view this is an academic exercise and needs to be replaced by a more empirical approach based on the following three stages:

(a) Given the reconstructed z series, to produce estimates of the parameters $\gamma_{-1}, \gamma_0, \gamma_1$.

(b) To keep a check on whether this form of control is adequate, i.e. whether the estimated deviations e_p after fitting the third order moving average are uncorrelated, or equivalently whether the spectrum of the e_p is effectively uniform or "white".

(c) To provide for updating or revision of the parameters as more information becomes available.

For (a) we may proceed as described in section 3.4 by evaluating the residual sum of squares $S(\gamma_{-1}, \gamma_0, \gamma_1)$ after fitting the third order moving average process for a grid of values of $\gamma_{-1}, \gamma_0, \gamma_1$ and then locate the best values of these parameters numerically. An alternative method is to write down the likelihood function of the second differences d_p. If the deviations e_p are independent, then the joint distribution P of these quantities in a sample of size N is given by

$$\log P = c - N \log \sigma_e - \frac{1}{2\sigma_e^2} \sum_{p=1}^{N} e_p^2.$$

Denoting by $c_s^{(e)}$ the serial covariance of lag s of the e's, then it is readily shown that, if N is even and equals $2n$,

$$c_s^{(e)} = \frac{\pi}{N} \sum_{j=-n}^{n-1} I_N(\omega_j)\, e^{i\omega_j s}, \tag{5.5.6}$$

where
$$I_N(\omega_j) = \frac{1}{\pi N} \left| \sum_{p=1}^{N} d_p\, e^{-i\omega_j p} \right|^2 \quad (\omega_j = 2\pi j/N)$$

is the sample periodogram of the second differences. Since the sum of squares of the e_p in (5.5.5) is simply $Nc_0^{(e)}$, it follows that the latter quantity may be expressed as a weighted sum of the periodogram ordinates. Using the following approximate relation between the periodograms of the e_p and d_p series,

$$I_N^{(d)}(\omega_j) = I_N^{(e)}(\omega_j) |H(\omega_j)|^2, \tag{5.5.7}$$

where $H(\omega)$ has been defined by (5.5.3), we obtain the following approximate form for the log likelihood of the d_p's:

$$\log L = c - N \log \sigma_e - \frac{\pi}{2\sigma_e^2} \sum_{j=0}^{n} \frac{\gamma_j I_N(\omega_j)}{|H(\omega_j)|^2}, \tag{5.5.8}$$

where
$$\gamma_j = \begin{matrix} 2 & (\omega_j \neq 0, \pi), \\ 1 & (\omega_j = 0, \pi). \end{matrix}$$

When N is odd, the expression is the same except that the ordinate $\omega_j = \pi$ does not appear. A similar form for the likelihood function has been derived previously by

Whittle (1950). Since

$$I_N(\omega_j) = \frac{1}{\pi}\left\{c_0 + 2\sum_{s=1}^{N-1} c_s \cos(\omega_j s)\right\}, \tag{5.5.9}$$

it is necessary, in order to evaluate the likelihood function, to calculate all the serial correlations in the sample. The expression (5.5.9) may be replaced to a high degree of accuracy by an estimate of the power spectral density, viz.

$$p_N(\omega_j) = \frac{1}{\pi}\left\{c_0 + 2\sum_{s=1}^{m} \lambda_s c_s \cos(\omega_j s)\right\}, \tag{5.5.10}$$

where the λ_s's are one of the sets of weights used in spectral analysis.

If we now substitute in (5.5.8) we have the following form for the log-likelihood function, accurate to a fairly high degree of approximation:

$$\log_e L \sim c - N \log \sigma_e - \frac{\pi N}{4k(m)\sigma_e^2} \sum_{j=0}^{k(m)} \frac{\gamma_j p_N(\omega_j)}{|H(\omega_j)|^2}, \tag{5.5.11}$$

where $\omega_j = \pi j / k(m)$ and $k(m)$ is the number of effectively independent spectral estimates which depends on λ_s and m and has been tabulated for the various weight functions used in spectral analysis by Jenkins (1961).

The advantage of (5.5.11) is that if the power spectrum $p_N(\omega)$ is known, the likelihood function may be calculated very easily for a grid of values of $\gamma_{-1}, \gamma_0, \gamma_1$ without recourse to any further calculations from the sample whilst the sum of squares method given in section 3.4 involves the fitting of the model to the data for each set of values of $\gamma_{-1}, \gamma_0, \gamma_1$. However, the latter method is easily programmed for an electronic computer and also gives information about the individual estimates e_p which would not be obtained directly in the likelihood-function approach.

The maximum likelihood estimator of σ_e^2 is readily seen from (5.5.11) to be

$$\hat{\sigma}_e^2 = \frac{\pi}{2k(m)} \sum_{j=0}^{k(m)} \frac{\gamma_j p_N(\omega_j)}{|H(\omega_j)|^2}, \tag{5.5.12}$$

and hence can be obtained easily when the optimum values of $\gamma_{-1}, \gamma_0, \gamma_1$ are available. An approximate test for the whiteness of the residual spectrum $g_e(\omega)$ may then be obtained by observing that

$$p_N(\omega) \sim \hat{\sigma}_e^2 g_N^{(e)}(\omega) |H(\omega)|^2 \tag{5.5.13}$$

and hence $g_N^{(e)}(\omega)$ may be estimated directly, since all the other quantities will have been evaluated in the calculation of the likelihood function.

Given the spectra of the second differences, it is also possible to draw some conclusions about the form of control which will be required. We illustrate this remark by referring to the spectra of series I–III which are plotted in Fig. 6. If no control is possible, i.e. $g_d(\omega)$ is a constant, then the second differences will have a spectrum of the form

$$\frac{2}{3\pi}(1 - \cos \omega)^2$$

which increases rapidly at higher frequencies and has been plotted as a base in Fig. 6. The need for proportional control is indicated by a boosting up of the lower and intermediate frequencies as in series I but more strongly in series III; however, the zero frequency spectral density will, in this case, be zero, subject to sampling fluctuations. The desirability of some form of integral control is indicated by the presence of non-zero spectral density at $\omega = 0$ and in higher density at the lower frequencies generally. For series II, this effect is quite marked since the spectrum is effectively

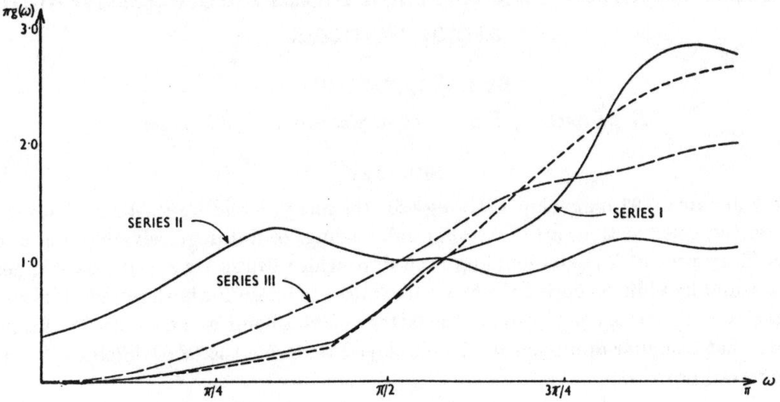

FIG. 6. Spectra of second differences for series I–III.

white and it is even possible for the spectrum to have a maximum at zero frequency if $\gamma_1 > 1$. This is due to the fact that the zero in the frequency response function of the second difference filter is compensated for by an effectively infinite spectral density at zero frequency in the original series due to the presence of trends.

ACKNOWLEDGEMENT

This research was supported by the National Science Foundation.

REFERENCES

BARNARD, G. A. (1959), "Control charts and stochastic processes", *J. R. statist. Soc.* B, **21**, 239–272.

—— JENKINS, G. M. and WINSTEN, C. B. (1962), "Likelihood inference and time-series", *J. R. statist. Soc.* A, **125**, 321–372.

BOX, G. E. P. (1957), "Integration of techniques in process development", *Trans. of the 11th Annual Convention of the Amer. Soc. Qual. Control*, 687.

—— (1960), "Some general considerations in process optimisation", *Trans. Am. Soc. mech. Engrs*, Ser. D (*Basic Eng.*), **82**, 113–119.

—— and CHANMUGAM, J. R. (1962), "Adaptive optimisation of continuous processes", *Industrial and Engineering Chemistry* (*Fundamentals*), **1**, 2–16.

BROWN, R. G. (1959), *Statistical Forecasting for Inventory Control*. New York: McGraw-Hill.

COX, D. R. (1961), "Prediction by exponentially weighted moving averages and related methods", *J. R. statist. Soc.* B, **23**, 414–422.

HOLT, C. C., MODIGLIANI, F., MUTH, T. F. and SIMON, H. A. (1960), *Planning Production, Inventories and Work Force*. London: Prentice-Hall.

JENKINS, G. M. (1961), "General considerations in the analysis of spectra", *Technometrics*, **3**, 133–166.

MUTH, J. F. (1960), "Optimal properties of exponentially weighted forecasts", *J. Amer. statist. Soc.*, **55**, 299–306.

WHITTLE, P. (1950), "The simultaneous estimation of a time-series harmonic components and covariance structure", *Trabajos de Estadistica*, **3**, 43–57.

ZADEH, L. A. and RAGAZZINI, J. R. (1950), "An extension of Wiener's theory of prediction", *J. appl. Phys.*, **21**, 645–655.

[3]

Biometrika (1974), 61, 3, *p.* 423
Printed in Great Britain

The exact likelihood function for a mixed autoregressive-moving average process

BY PAUL NEWBOLD
Department of Economics, University of Nottingham

SUMMARY

Box & Jenkins (1970) develop a strategy for the analysis and forecasting of time series, based on the construction, after suitable differencing, of autoregressive-moving average models. They present a model building procedure which works very well for most general purposes, and in addition derive the exact likelihood function for both pure autoregressive and pure moving average processes, in the latter case this being a new result. In this note it is shown that a similar approach can be employed to derive the exact likelihood function for the mixed process.

Some key words: Autoregressive-moving average models; Time series estimation.

1. INTRODUCTION

Let us suppose, following the notation of Box & Jenkins (1970), that the time series W_t is generated by the stationary mixed autoregressive-moving average process

$$W_t - \phi_1 W_{t-1} - \ldots - \phi_p W_{t-p} = a_t - \theta_1 a_{t-1} - \ldots - \theta_q a_{t-q}, \tag{1·1}$$

where $\{a_t\}$ constitutes a sequence of independent normal random variables each having mean zero and variance σ_a^2. Given an observed series $W_1, \ldots, W_n$, one requires to estimate the coefficients of (1·1) and to project this equation forward for the computation of forecasts of future values $W_{n+1}, W_{n+2}, \ldots$. Some difficulty is caused by the fact that (1·1) involves the unknown 'starting values' $W_0, W_{-1}, \ldots, W_{1-p}$ with $a_0, a_{-1}, \ldots, a_{1-q}$. Box & Jenkins approach this problem through the iterative cycle of 'back-forecasting' and forecasting. Such a treatment is adequate for general purposes, provided the iterative cycle is taken sufficiently far. However, three circumstances, which could arise either individually or collectively, can give difficulties:

(i) the roots of the polynomial equation $1-\phi_1 B - \ldots - \phi_p B^p = 0$ may lie near the unit circle;

(ii) the roots of the polynomial equation $1-\theta_1 B - \ldots - \theta_q B^q = 0$ may lie near, or indeed on, the unit circle;

(iii) the series of available data may be relatively short.

In situations of this kind it is worth-while to examine the possibility of a more direct treatment via the exact likelihood function, which, as we shall see, can be derived in a manner similar to that employed by Box & Jenkins in obtaining the corresponding function for a pure moving average process. For the autoregressive-moving average process of order (1, 1), Tiao & Ali (1971) give exact expressions for the elements of the inverse of the covariance matrix of the sample and its determinant. Shaman (1973) considers the more general mixed process and derives an expression for the elements of the inverse of the sample covariance matrix. His approach seems to require extremely heavy calculations, and no expression is given for the determinant of the matrix.

2. Derivation of the exact likelihood function

Consider first the nonsingular transformation from the set of $n+p+q$ variables a_t for $1-q \leqslant t \leqslant n$, W_t for $1-p \leqslant t \leqslant 0$ to the set of $n+p+q$ variables a_t for $1-q \leqslant t \leqslant 0$, W_t for $1-p \leqslant t \leqslant n$, following from (1·1), defined by

$$a_t = a_t \ (1-q \leqslant t \leqslant 0), \quad W_t = W_t \ (1-p \leqslant t \leqslant 0),$$
$$a_t = W_t - \phi_1 W_{t-1} - \ldots - \phi_p W_{t-p} + \theta_1 a_{t-1} + \ldots + \theta_q a_{t-q} \ (1 \leqslant t \leqslant n). \tag{2·1}$$

Now define the vector $e' = (e_{1-p-q}, \ldots, e_{-1}, e_0, e_1, \ldots, e_n)$, where

$$e_{1-p-j} = a_{1-j} \quad (j = 1, \ldots, q), \quad e_{1-j} = W_{1-j} \quad (j = 1, \ldots, p), \quad e_t = a_t \quad (t = 1, \ldots, n).$$

Let $W_n' = (W_1, \ldots, W_n)$ and $e_*' = (e_{1-p-q}, \ldots, e_{-1}, e_0)$. Then the set of equations (2·1) can be written as

$$e = LW_n + Xe_*, \tag{2·2}$$

where the $(n+p+q) \times n$ matrix L and the $(n+p+q) \times (p+q)$ matrix X involve only the coefficients $\phi_1, \ldots, \phi_p$ and $\theta_1, \ldots, \theta_q$. In fact, if we write $e_n' = (e_1, \ldots, e_n)$, equation (2·2) is of the form

$$\begin{pmatrix} e_* \\ \cdots \\ e_n \end{pmatrix} = \begin{pmatrix} 0 \\ \cdots \\ L_n \end{pmatrix} W_n + \begin{pmatrix} I \\ \cdots \\ X_n \end{pmatrix} e_*, \tag{2·3}$$

where L_n and X_n are respectively $n \times n$ and $n \times (p+q)$ matrices involving only $\phi_1, \ldots, \phi_p$ and $\theta_1, \ldots, \theta_q$.

Suppose now that

$$E(e_* e_*') = \sigma_a^2 \Omega, \tag{2·4}$$

where, for any particular model (1·1), the matrix Ω is readily calculated. Let T be a nonsingular square matrix such that

$$T\Omega T' = I. \tag{2·5}$$

We can then write $\Omega = T^{-1}(T')^{-1}$, and a matrix T^{-1} can be found by triangular resolution of Ω so that (2·5) is satisfied.

Multiplication of (2·3) by the matrix

$$\begin{bmatrix} T & 0 \\ 0 & I \end{bmatrix}$$

yields

$$\begin{pmatrix} u_* \\ \cdots \\ u_n \end{pmatrix} = \begin{pmatrix} 0 \\ \cdots \\ L_n \end{pmatrix} W_n + \begin{pmatrix} I \\ \cdots \\ X_n T^{-1} \end{pmatrix} u_*, \tag{2·6}$$

where $u_* = Te_*$ and $u_n = e_n$. By reverting to the formulation (2·2), we can write (2·6) as

$$u = LW_n + Zu_*, \tag{2·7}$$

where the $(n+p+q) \times (p+q)$ matrix Z involves only $\phi_1, \ldots, \phi_p$ and $\theta_1, \ldots, \theta_q$.

Now, u_* is independent of u_n since the elements of the former depend linearly only on the

a_t for $t \leqslant 0$. Further, $E(u_* u_*') = \sigma_a^2 T\Omega T' = \sigma_a^2 I$, by (2·5). Hence the joint density function of u is given by

$$p(u|\sigma_a) = (2\pi\sigma_a^2)^{-\frac{1}{2}(n+p+q)} \exp(-\tfrac{1}{2}u'u/\sigma_a^2).$$

Since the Jacobian of the transformation (2·7) is unity, it follows that

$$p(W_n, u_*|\phi, \theta, \sigma_a) = (2\pi\sigma_a^2)^{-\frac{1}{2}(n+p+q)} \exp\{-\tfrac{1}{2}S(\phi, \theta, u_*)/\sigma_a^2\}, \tag{2·8}$$

where $S(\phi, \theta, u_*) = (LW_n + Zu_*)'(LW_n + Zu_*)$, $\phi' = (\phi_1, \ldots, \phi_p)$ and $\theta' = (\theta_1, \ldots, \theta_q)$. Now, set

$$\hat{u}_* = -(Z'Z)^{-1} Z'LW_n. \tag{2·9}$$

Then $S(\phi, \theta, u_*) = S(\phi, \theta) + (u_* - \hat{u}_*)'Z'Z(u_* - \hat{u}_*)$, where

$$S(\phi, \theta) = (LW_n + Z\hat{u}_*)'(LW_n + Z\hat{u}_*). \tag{2·10}$$

Now, by writing (2·8) as

$$p(W_n, u_*|\phi, \theta, \sigma_a) = p(W_n|\phi, \theta, \sigma_a)\, p(u_*|W_n, \phi, \theta, \sigma_a),$$

it follows that

$$p(W_n|\phi, \theta, \sigma_a) = (2\pi\sigma_a^2)^{-\frac{1}{2}n} |Z'Z|^{-\frac{1}{2}} \exp\{-\tfrac{1}{2}S(\phi, \theta)/\sigma_a^2\}, \tag{2·11}$$

where $S(\phi, \theta)$ is given by (2·10) and (2·9). This is the required likelihood function. Further, it follows from the derivation that (2·11) can be written as

$$p(W_n|\phi, \theta, \sigma_a) = (2\pi\sigma_a^2)^{-\frac{1}{2}n} |Z'Z|^{-\frac{1}{2}} \exp\left(-\sum_{t=1-p-q}^{n} \tfrac{1}{2}u_t^{\dagger 2}/\sigma_a^2\right), \tag{2·12}$$

where $u_t^\dagger = E(u_t|W_n, \phi, \theta)$ and $u_* = \hat{u}_*$.

3. Autoregressive-moving average process of order (1, 1)

To illustrate the results of the previous section we consider the simplest case, i.e. where the series W_t is generated by the process

$$W_t - \phi W_{t-1} = a_t - \theta a_{t-1}.$$

In this case it is straightforward to verify that the matrices L and X of (2·2) are given by

$$L = \begin{bmatrix} 0 & 0 & 0 & \ldots & 0 & 0 \\ 0 & 0 & 0 & \ldots & 0 & 0 \\ 1 & 0 & 0 & \ldots & 0 & 0 \\ (\theta-\phi) & 1 & 0 & \ldots & 0 & 0 \\ \theta(\theta-\phi) & (\theta-\phi) & 1 & \ldots & 0 & 0 \\ \vdots & \vdots & \vdots & & \vdots & \vdots \\ \theta^{n-2}(\theta-\phi) & \theta^{n-3}(\theta-\phi) & \theta^{n-4}(\theta-\phi) & \ldots & (\theta-\phi) & 1 \end{bmatrix}, \tag{3·1}$$

$$X' = \begin{bmatrix} 1 & 0 & \theta & \theta^2 & \ldots & \theta^n \\ 0 & 1 & -\phi & -\theta\phi & \ldots & -\theta^{n-1}\phi \end{bmatrix}.$$

Now $e_*' = (a_0, W_0)$, and hence the matrix Ω of (2·4) is given by

$$\Omega = \begin{bmatrix} 1 & 1 \\ 1 & (1-\phi^2)^{-1}(1+\theta^2-2\phi\theta) \end{bmatrix}.$$

Then by triangular resolution of Ω we find that, if

$$T^{-1} = \begin{bmatrix} 1 & 0 \\ 1 & (\theta-\phi)(1-\phi^2)^{-\frac{1}{2}} \end{bmatrix},$$

T satisfies (2·5), and hence from (2·6) the matrix Z of (2·7) is given by

$$Z' = \begin{bmatrix} 1 & 0 & \theta-\phi & \theta(\theta-\phi) & \dots & \theta^{n-1}(\theta-\phi) \\ 0 & 1 & -\phi(\theta-\phi)\gamma & -\theta\phi(\theta-\phi)\gamma & \dots & -\theta^{n-1}\phi(\theta-\phi)\gamma \end{bmatrix}, \quad (3·2)$$

where $\gamma = (1-\phi^2)^{-\frac{1}{2}}$.

Thus, using (3·1) and (3·2) we can calculate $\hat{u}_*$ of (2·9) and hence by substitution in (2·11), or equivalently in (2·12), the exact likelihood function may readily be evaluated for any given values of ϕ and θ.

4. Summary and conclusions

In this note it has been shown that the exact likelihood function of a mixed autoregressive-moving average process can be derived in closed form and it has been illustrated how this function can, after some algebraic manipulation, be evaluated in any specific case. This result complements the derivation by Box & Jenkins (1970, Chapter 7) of the corresponding functions for pure autoregressive and pure moving average models. In fact, when considering the mixed process, Box & Jenkins extend their result for moving average models, essentially treating the general autoregressive-moving average process as an infinite order moving average. This leads to the likelihood function containing the sum of squares term

$$\sum_{t=-\infty}^{n} a_t^{\dagger 2},$$

where $a_t^\dagger = E(a_t|W_n, \phi, \theta)$. They propose that, in practice for sufficiently large Q, this sum of squares can be approximated by the sum from $1-Q$ to ∞. Further, they suggest employing back-forecasting to estimate the conditional expectations $a_t^\dagger$. Such a procedure works very well for most practically occurring situations. However, if a root of either the autoregressive or moving average polynomial operators lies close to the unit circle, it may be necessary to choose very large Q, in the former case, and/or to iterate a good many times in estimating the $a_t^\dagger$'s. In such a case the quality of their suggested approximation is in some doubt, particularly if the available time series is relatively short.

It is worth-while in such situations to consider the formulation (2·12) where the sum of squares in the exponent term extends over a finite range, and the conditional expectations involved can be evaluated directly using (2·9). Such a procedure would yield a check in specific situations of the validity of the approximations required in the application of the computationally more efficient procedure proposed by Box & Jenkins.

References

Box, G. E. P. & Jenkins, G. M. (1970). *Time Series Analysis, Forecasting and Control*. San Francisco: Holden Day.

Shaman, P. (1973). On the inverse of the covariance matrix for an autoregressive-moving average process. *Biometrika* **60**, 193–6.

Tiao, G. C. & Ali, M. M. (1971). Analysis of correlated random effects: linear model with two random components. *Biometrika* **58**, 37–51.

[*Received January* 1974. *Revised May* 1974]

[4]

© Journal of the American Statistical Association
December 1970, Volume 65, Number 332
Theory and Methods Section

Distribution of Residual Autocorrelations in Autoregressive-Integrated Moving Average Time Series Models

G. E. P. BOX and DAVID A. PIERCE*

Many statistical models, and in particular autoregressive—moving average time series models, can be regarded as means of transforming the data to white noise, that is, to an uncorrelated sequence of errors. If the parameters are known exactly, this random sequence can be computed directly from the observations; when this calculation is made with estimates substituted for the true parameter values, the resulting sequence is referred to as the "residuals," which can be regarded as estimates of the errors.

If the appropriate model has been chosen, there will be zero autocorrelation in the errors. In checking adequacy of fit it is therefore logical to study the sample autocorrelation function of the residuals. For large samples the residuals from a correctly fitted model resemble very closely the true errors of the process; however, care is needed in interpreting the serial correlations of the residuals. It is shown here that the residual autocorrelations are to a close approximation representable as a *singular* linear transformation of the autocorrelations of the errors so that they possess a singular normal distribution. Failing to allow for this results in a tendency to overlook evidence of lack of fit. Tests of fit and diagnostic checks are devised which take these facts into account.

1. INTRODUCTION

An approach to the modeling of stationary and non-stationary time series such as commonly occur in economic situations and control problems is discussed by Box and Jenkins [4, 5], building on the earlier work of several authors beginning with Yule [19] and Wold [17], and involves iterative use of the three-stage process of identification, estimation, and diagnostic checking. Given a discrete time series $z_t, z_{t-1}, z_{t-2}, \cdots$ and using B for the backward shift operator such that $Bz_t = z_{t-1}$, the general autoregressive—integrated moving average (ARIMA) model of order (p, d, q) discussed in [4, 5] may be written

$$\phi(B)\nabla^d z_t = \theta(B)a_t \tag{1.1}$$

where $\phi(B) = 1 - \phi_1 B - \cdots - \phi_p B^p$ and $\theta(B) = 1 - \theta_1 B - \cdots \theta_q B^q$, $\{a_t\}$ is a sequence of independent normal deviates with common variance σ_a^2, to be referred to as "white noise," and where the roots of $\phi(B) = 0$ and $\theta(B) = 0$ lie outside the unit circle. In other words, if $w_t = \nabla^d z_t = (1-B)^d z_t$ is the dth difference of the series z_t, then w_t is the stationary, invertible, mixed autoregressive (AR)—moving average (MA) process given by

$$w_t = \sum_{i=1}^{p} \phi_i w_{t-i} - \sum_{j=1}^{q} \theta_j a_{t-j} + a_t,$$

and permitting $d > 0$ allows the original series to be (homogeneously) nonsta-

* G. E. P. Box is professor of statistics, University of Wisconsin. David A. Pierce is on leave from the Department of Statistics, University of Missouri, Columbia, as statistician, Research Department, Federal Reserve Bank of Cleveland. This work was supported jointly by the Air Force Office of Scientific Research under Grant AFOSR-69-1803 and by the U. S. Army Research Office under Grant DA-ARO-D-31-124-G917.

tionary. In some instances the model (1.1) will be appropriate after a suitable transformation is made on z; in others z may represent the noise structure after allowing for some systematic model.

This general class of models is too rich to allow immediate fitting to a particular sample series $\{z_t\} = z_1, z_2, \cdots, z_n$, and the following strategy is therefore employed:

1. A process of identification is used to find a smaller subclass of models worth considering to represent the stochastic process.
2. A model in this subclass is fitted by efficient statistical methods.
3. An examination of the adequacy of the fit is made.

The object of the third or diagnostic checking stage is not merely to determine whether there is evidence of lack of fit but also to suggest ways in which the model may be modified when this is necessary. Two basic methods for doing this are suggested:

Overfitting. The model may be deliberately overparameterized in a way it is feared may be needed and in a manner such that the entertained model is obtained by setting certain parameters in the more general model at fixed values, usually zero. One can then check the adequacy of the original model by fitting the more general model and considering whether or not the additional parameters could reasonably take on the specified values appropriate to the simpler model.

Diagnostic checks applied to the residuals. The method of overfitting is most useful where the nature of the alternative feared model is known. Unfortunately, this information may not always be available, and less powerful but more general techniques are needed to indicate the way in which a particular model might be wrong. It is natural to consider the stochastic properties of the residuals $\hat{\mathbf{a}} = (\hat{a}_1, \hat{a}_2, \cdots, \hat{a}_n)'$ calculated from the sample series using the model (1.1) with estimates $\hat{\phi}_1, \hat{\phi}_2, \cdots, \hat{\phi}_p; \hat{\theta}_1, \hat{\theta}_2, \cdots \hat{\theta}_q$ substituted for the parameters. In particular their autocorrelation function

$$\hat{r}_k = \sum \hat{a}_t\hat{a}_{t-k} / \sum \hat{a}_t^2 \tag{1.2}$$

may be studied.

Now if the model were appropriate and the a's for the particular sample series were calculated using the *true* parameter values, then these a's would be uncorrelated random deviates, and their first m sample autocorrelations $\mathbf{r} = (r_1, r_2, \cdots, r_m)'$, where m is small relative to n and

$$r_k = \frac{\sum a_t a_{t-k}}{\sum a_t^2}, \tag{1.3}$$

would for moderate or large n possess a multivariate normal distribution [1]. Also it can readily be shown that the $\{r_k\}$ are uncorrelated with variances

$$V(r_k) = \frac{n-k}{n(n+2)} \approx 1/n, \tag{1.4}$$

from which it follows in particular that the statistic $n(n+2)\sum_{k=1}^{m}(n-k)^{-1}r_k^2$ would for large n be distributed as χ^2 with m degrees of freedom; or as a further approximation,

$$n\sum_{k=1}^{m} r_k^2 \sim \chi_m^2. \tag{1.5}$$

It is tempting to suppose that these same properties might to a sufficient approximation be enjoyed by the $\hat{r}$'s from the *fitted* model; and diagnostic checks based on this supposition were suggested by Box and Jenkins [4] and Box, Jenkins, and Bacon [6]. If this assumption were warranted, approximate standard errors of $1/\sqrt{n}$ [or more accurate standard errors of $\sqrt{n-k}/n(n+2)$] could be attached to the $\hat{r}$'s and a quality-control-chart type of approach used, with particular attention being paid to the $\hat{r}$'s of low order for the indication of possible model inadequacies. Also it might be supposed that Equation (1.5) with $\hat{r}$'s replacing r's would still be approximately valid, so that large values of this statistic would place the model under suspicion.

It was pointed out by Durbin [10], however, that this approximation is invalid when applied to the residual autocorrelations from a fitted autoregressive model. For example, he showed that $\hat{r}_1$ calculated from the residuals of a first order autoregressive process could have a much smaller variance than r_1 for white noise.

The present paper therefore considers in some detail the properties of the $\hat{r}$'s and in particular their covariance matrix, both for AR processes (Sections 2 and 3) and for MA and ARIMA processes (Section 5). This is done with the intention of obtaining a suitable modification to the above diagnostic checking procedures (Sections 4 and 5.3)

The problem of testing fit in time series models has been considered previously by several authors. Quenouille [14][1] developed a large-sample procedure for AR processes based on their sample partial autocorrelations, which possesses the same degree of accuracy as the present one.[2] Quenouille's test was subsequently extended [3, 15, 18] to cover MA and mixed models. Whittle [16] proposed tests based on the likelihood ratio and resembling the overfitting method above. The present procedure (a) is a unified method equally applicable to AR, MA, and general ARIMA models, (b) is motivated by the intuitive idea that the residuals from a correct fit should resemble the true errors of the process, and (c) can be used to suggest particular modifications in the model when lack of fit is found [5].

2. DISTRIBUTION OF RESIDUAL AUTOCORRELATIONS FOR THE AUTOREGRESSIVE PROCESS

In this section we obtain the joint large-sample distribution of the residual autocorrelations $\hat{\mathbf{r}} = (\hat{r}_1, \cdots, \hat{r}_m)'$ where $\hat{r}_k$ is given by (1.2), for an autoregressive process. This is done by first setting forth some general properties of AR processes, using these to obtain a set of linear constraints (2.9) satisfied by the $\{\hat{r}_k\}$, and then approximating $\hat{r}_k$ by a first order Taylor expansion (2.22) about the white noise autocorrelation r_k. Finally, these results are combined in matrix form to establish a linear relationship (2.27) between $\hat{\mathbf{r}}$ and $\mathbf{r}$ analogous to that between the residuals and true errors in a standard regression model, from which the distribution (2.29) of $\hat{\mathbf{r}}$ readily follows. Subsections 2.5–2.7 then discuss examples and applications of this distribution.

[1] See also [11].

[2] The authors are grateful to a referee for this observation.

2.1 The Autoregressive Process

The general AR process of order p,

$$\phi(B)y_t = a_t, \tag{2.1}$$

where B, $\phi(B)$, and $\{a_t\}$ are as in (1.1), can also be expressed as a moving average of infinite order by writing $\psi(B)=\phi^{-1}(B)=(1+\psi_1B+\psi_2B^2+\cdots)$ to obtain

$$y_t = \psi(B)a_t = \sum_{j=0}^{\infty}\psi_j a_{t-j}, \tag{2.2}$$

where $\psi_0=1$. By equating coefficients in the relation $\psi(B)\cdot\phi(B)=1$, it is seen that the ψ's and ϕ's satisfy the relation

$$\psi_\nu = \begin{cases}\phi_1\psi_{\nu-1}+\cdots+\phi_{\nu-1}\psi_1+\phi_\nu, & \nu\le p\\ \phi_1\psi_{\nu-1}+\cdots+\phi_p\psi_{\nu-p}, & \nu\ge p.\end{cases} \tag{2.3}$$

Therefore by setting $\psi_\nu=0$ for $\nu<0$, we have

$$\psi_0 = 1;\quad \phi(B)\psi_\nu = 0, \qquad \nu\neq 0. \tag{2.4}$$

Suppose then we have a series $\{y_t\}$ generated by the model (2.1) or (2.2), where in general $y_t=\nabla^d z_t$ can be the dth difference ($d=0, 1, 2, \cdots$) of the actual observations. Then for given values $\dot{\boldsymbol{\phi}}=(\dot\phi_1, \cdots, \dot\phi_p)'$ of the parameters we can define

$$\dot a_t = a_t(\dot{\boldsymbol{\phi}}) = y_t - \dot\phi_1 y_{t-1} - \cdots - \dot\phi_p y_{t-p} = \dot\phi(B)y_t \tag{2.5}$$

and the corresponding autocorrelation

$$\dot r_k = r_k(\dot{\boldsymbol{\phi}}) = \frac{\sum \dot a_t\dot a_{t-k}}{\sum \dot a_t^2}. \tag{2.6}$$

Thus, in particular,

1. $a_t(\boldsymbol{\phi})=a_t$ as in (2.1), (2.2);
2. $a_t(\hat{\boldsymbol{\phi}})=\hat a_t$ are the residuals when (2.1) is fitted and least squares estimated $\hat{\boldsymbol{\phi}}$ obtained; and
3. $r_k(\hat{\boldsymbol{\phi}})$ and $r_k(\boldsymbol{\phi})$ are respectively the residual and white noise autocorrelations (1.2) and (1.3).

2.2 Linear Constraints on the $\hat r$'s

It is known that the residuals $\{\hat a_t\}$ above satisfy the orthogonality conditions

$$\sum_{t=p+1}^{n}\hat a_t y_{t-j} = 0, \qquad 1\le j\le p. \tag{2.7}$$

Therefore if we let

$$\hat\psi(B) = \hat\phi^{-1}(B) = (1-\hat\phi_1B-\cdots-\hat\phi_pB^p)^{-1}, \tag{2.8}$$

then $y_t=\hat\psi(B)\hat a_t$, and from (2.7) we have

$$\begin{aligned}0 &= \textstyle\sum_t\sum_k \hat\psi_k\hat a_t\hat a_{t-k-j}\\ &= \textstyle\sum_k \hat\psi_k\hat r_{k+j}\\ &= \textstyle\sum \psi_k\hat r_{k+j} + O_p(1/n)\end{aligned} \tag{2.9}$$

where the symbol introduced in (2.9) denotes "order in probability" as defined in [13].

In leading up to (2.9) we have presumably summed an infinite number of autocorrelations from a finite series. However since $\{y_t\}$ is stationary we have $\psi_k \to 0$ as k becomes large; and unless ϕ is extremely close to the boundary of the stationarity region, this dying off of ψ_k is fast so that the summation can generally be stopped at a value of k much less than n. More precisely, we are assuming that n is larger than a fixed number N and for such n there exists a sequence of numbers m_n such that

(a) all ψ_j where $j \geq m_n - p$ are of order $1/\sqrt{n}$ or smaller, and
(b) the ratio m_n/n is itself of order $1/\sqrt{n}$.

Then in (2.9) and in all following discussion the error in stopping the summations at $k=m$ (we write m for m_n in the sequel) can to the present degree of approximation be ignored; and (b) also ensures that "end effects" (such as there being only $n-k$ terms summed in the numerator of $\hat{r}_k$ compared with n terms in the denominator) can also be neglected.

2.3 Linear Expansion of $\hat{r}_k$ about r_k

The root mean square error of $\hat{\phi}_j$, $1 \leq j \leq p$, defined by $\sqrt{E(\phi_j - \hat{\phi}_j)^2}$, is of order $1/\sqrt{n}$, and we can therefore approximate $\hat{r}_k$ by a first order Taylor expansion about $\hat{\phi} = \phi$ (evaluating the derivatives, however, at $\hat{\phi}$ rather than ϕ in order to obtain the simplification (2.12) below). Thus

$$\hat{r}_k = r_k + \sum_{j=1}^{p} (\phi_j - \hat{\phi}_j)\hat{\delta}_{jk} + O_p(1/n), \tag{2.10}$$

where

$$\hat{\delta}_{jk} = -\left.\frac{\partial \dot{r}_k}{\partial \dot{\phi}_j}\right|_{\dot{\phi}=\hat{\phi}}. \tag{2.11}$$

Now

$$\frac{\partial}{\partial \dot{\phi}_j}\left[\sum \dot{a}_t^2\right] = 0 \quad \text{at } \dot{\phi} = \hat{\phi}, \tag{2.12}$$

so that

$$\hat{\delta}_{jk} = -\left[\sum \hat{a}_t^2\right]^{-1} \left.\frac{\partial \dot{c}_k}{\partial \dot{\phi}_j}\right|_{\dot{\phi}=\hat{\phi}} \tag{2.13}$$

where

$$\begin{aligned} \dot{c}_k &= \sum \dot{a}_t \dot{a}_{t-k} = \sum [\dot{\phi}(B)y_t][\dot{\phi}(B)y_{t-k}] \\ &= \sum_t \sum_{i=0}^{p} \sum_{j=0}^{p} \dot{\phi}_i \dot{\phi}_j y_{t-i} y_{t-k-j}, \end{aligned} \tag{2.14}$$

where in (2.14) and below, $\phi_0 = \dot{\phi}_0 = -1$. From (2.13) and (2.14) it follows that

$$\begin{aligned} \hat{\delta}_{jk} &= -\frac{\sum y_t^2}{\sum \hat{a}_t^2} \sum_{i=0}^{p} \hat{\phi}_i [r^{(y)}_{k-i+j} + r^{(y)}_{k+i-j}] \\ &= -\frac{\sum_{i=0}^{p} \hat{\phi}_i [r^{(y)}_{k-i+j} + r^{(y)}_{k+i-j}]}{\sum_{i=0}^{p} \sum_{j=0}^{p} \hat{\phi}_i \hat{\phi}_j r^{(y)}_{i-j}}, \end{aligned} \tag{2.15}$$

where

$$r_\nu^{(y)} = \frac{\sum y_t y_{t-\nu}}{\sum y_t^2}.$$

Let us approximate $\hat{\delta}_{jk}$ by replacing $\hat{\phi}$'s and $r^{(y)}$'s in (2.15) by ϕ's and ρ's (the theoretical parameters and autocorrelations of the autoregressive process $\{y_t\}$) and denote the result by δ_{jk}. That is,

$$\delta_{jk} = \frac{\sum_{i=0}^{p} \phi_i[\rho_{k-i+j} + \rho_{k+i-j}]}{-\sum_{i=0}^{p}\sum_{j=0}^{p} \phi_i\phi_j\rho_{i-j}}. \tag{2.16}$$

Now from Bartlett's formula [2, Equation (7)] we have

$$r_k^{(y)} = \rho_k + O_p(1/\sqrt{n}), \tag{2.17}$$

and as in the discussion preceding (2.10), $\hat{\phi}_j = \phi_j + O_p(1/\sqrt{n})$;
thus

$$\hat{\delta}_{jk} = \delta_{jk} + O_p(1/\sqrt{n}), \tag{2.18}$$

so that equation (2.10) holds when $\hat{\delta}_{jk}$ is replaced by δ_{jk}.

By making use of the recursive relation which is satisfied by the autocorrelations of an autoregressive process, namely

$$\rho_\nu - \phi_1\rho_{\nu-1} - \cdots - \phi_p\rho_{\nu-p} = \phi(B)\rho_\nu = 0, \qquad \nu \geq 1, \tag{2.19}$$

expression (2.16) can be simplified to yield

$$\delta_{jk} = \frac{\sum_{i=0}^{p} \phi_i\rho_{k-j+i}}{\sum_{i=0}^{p} \phi_i\rho_i}. \tag{2.20}$$

Thus δ_{jk} depends only on $(k-j)$, and we therefore write $\delta_{k-j} = \delta_{jk}$. Then it is straightforward to show that

(a) $\delta_0 = 1$

(b) $\delta_\nu = 0, \quad \nu < 0,$ and thus

(c) $\phi(B)\delta_\nu = \dfrac{\sum_{i=0}^{p} \phi_i[\phi(B)\rho_{\nu+i}]}{\sum_{i=0}^{p} \phi_i\rho_i} = 0, \qquad \nu \geq 1.$

Comparing (a), (b), and (c) with the corresponding results (2.4) for ψ_ν, we therefore have $\delta_\nu = \psi_\nu$, that is

$$\delta_{jk} = \psi_{k-j}, \tag{2.21}$$

whence, for $k = 1, 2, \cdots, m$,

$$\hat{r}_k = r_k + \sum_{j=1}^{p} (\phi_j - \hat{\phi}_j)\psi_{k-j} + O_p(1/n). \tag{2.22}$$

2.4 Representation of $\hat{r}$ as a Linear Transformation of r

We can now establish a relationship between the residual autocorrelations $\hat{\mathbf{r}}$ and the white noise autocorrelations $\mathbf{r}$. Let

$$X = \begin{bmatrix} 1 & 0 & \cdots & 0 \\ \psi_1 & 1 & & \vdots \\ \psi_2 & \psi_1 & & 0 \\ \vdots & \vdots & & 1 \\ \vdots & \vdots & & \vdots \\ \psi_{m-1} & \psi_{m-2} & \cdots & \psi_{m-p} \end{bmatrix} \tag{2.23}$$

$$= [\mathbf{x}_1 \mid \mathbf{x}_2 \mid \cdots \mid \mathbf{x}_p].$$

Then to $O_p(1/n)$ we can write (2.22) in matrix form as

$$\hat{\boldsymbol{r}} = \boldsymbol{r} + X(\boldsymbol{\phi} - \hat{\boldsymbol{\phi}}), \tag{2.24}$$

where from (2.9)

$$\hat{\boldsymbol{r}}'X = \mathbf{0}. \tag{2.25}$$

If we now multiply (2.24) on both sides by

$$Q = X(X'X)^{-1}X', \tag{2.26}$$

then using (2.25) we obtain

$$\hat{\boldsymbol{r}} = (I - Q)\boldsymbol{r}. \tag{2.27}$$

It is known [1] that $\boldsymbol{r}$ is very nearly normal for n moderately large. The vector of residual autocorrelations is thus approximately a linear transformation of a multi-normal variable and is therefore itself normally distributed. Specifically,

$$\boldsymbol{r} \sim N(\mathbf{0}, (1/n)I), \tag{2.28}$$

and hence

$$\hat{\boldsymbol{r}} \sim N(\mathbf{0}, (1/n)[I - Q]). \tag{2.29}$$

Note that the matrix $I-Q$ is idempotent of rank $m-p$, so that the distribution of $\hat{\boldsymbol{r}}$ has a p-dimensional singularity.

2.5 Further Consideration of the Covariance Structure of the $\hat{r}$'s

It is illuminating to examine in greater detail the covariance matrix of $\hat{\boldsymbol{r}}$, or equivalently the matrix Q. The latter matrix is idempotent of rank p, and its non-null latent vectors are the columns of X. Also,

$$X'X = \begin{bmatrix} \sum \psi_j^2 & \sum \psi_j\psi_{j-1} & \cdots & \sum \psi_j\psi_{j-p+1} \\ \sum \psi_j\psi_{j-1} & \sum \psi_j^2 & \cdots & \sum \psi_j\psi_{j-p+2} \\ \vdots & \vdots & & \vdots \\ \sum \psi_j\psi_{j-p+1} & \sum \psi_j\psi_{j-p+2} & \cdots & \sum \psi_j^2 \end{bmatrix}$$

$$= \frac{\sigma_y^2}{\sigma_a^2} \begin{bmatrix} 1 & \rho_1 & \cdots & \rho_{p-1} \\ \rho_1 & 1 & \cdots & \rho_{p-2} \\ \vdots & \vdots & & \vdots \\ \rho_{p-1} & \rho_{p-2} & \cdots & 1 \end{bmatrix} \tag{2.30}$$

which when multiplied by σ_a^2 is the autocovariance matrix of the process itself. Let c^{ij} be the (ij)th element of $(X'X)^{-1}$ (given explicitly in [9]), and similarly q_{ij} for Q. If $\xi_j' = (\psi_{j-1}, \cdots, \psi_{j-p})$ denotes the jth row of X, then

$$\begin{aligned} q_{ij} &= \xi_i'(X'X)^{-1}\xi_j \\ &= \sum_{k=1}^{p} \sum_{l=1}^{p} \psi_{i-k} c^{kl} \psi_{j-l} \\ &= (-n)\operatorname{cov}[\hat{r}_i, \hat{r}_j] \quad \text{if } i \neq j. \end{aligned} \tag{2.31}$$

Since the elements of each column of X satisfy the recursive relation (2.4), we have $\phi(B)\xi_j = 0$, and hence

$$\phi(B)q_{ij} = 0, \tag{2.32}$$

where in (2.32) B can operate either on i or on j. This establishes an interesting recursive structure in the residual autocorrelation covariance matrix $(1/n) \cdot (I - Q)$ and provides an important clue as to how rapidly the covariances die out and the variances approach 1. Also, because of this property the entire covariance matrix is determined by specifying the elements

$$\begin{matrix} q_{11} & q_{12} & \cdots & q_{1p} \\ & q_{22} & \cdots & q_{2p} \\ & & \ddots & \vdots \\ & & & q_{pp} \end{matrix} \tag{2.33}$$

of Q, which are readily obtained by inverting the $X'X$ matrix (2.30).

2.6 Covariance Matrix of $\hat{r}$ for first and second order processes

Consider, for example, the first order autoregressive process $y_t = \phi y_{t-1} + a_t$, which in accordance with (2.2) we can write as

$$y_t = (1 - \phi B)^{-1} a_t = \sum_{j=0}^{\infty} \phi^j a_{t-j}. \tag{2.34}$$

For this process, $\psi_j = \phi^j$ and $(X'X)^{-1} = 1 - \phi^2$. From (2.31) the (ij)th element of Q is therefore $\phi^{i+j-2}(1-\phi^2)$, so that approximately the covariance matrix of the sample residual autocorrelations is

$$\Sigma_{\hat{r}} = (1/n)(I - Q) = 1/n \begin{bmatrix} \phi^2 & -\phi + \phi^3 & -\phi^2 + \phi^4 & \cdots \\ -\phi + \phi^3 & 1 - \phi^2 + \phi^4 & -\phi^3 + \phi^5 & \cdots \\ -\phi^2 + \phi^4 & -\phi^3 + \phi^5 & 1 - \phi^4 + \phi^6 & \cdots \\ \vdots & \vdots & \vdots & \end{bmatrix} \tag{2.35}$$

For the second order process

$$y_t = (1 - \phi_1 B - \phi_2 B^2)^{-1} a_t = \psi(B) a_t, \tag{2.36}$$

we have

$$X = \begin{bmatrix} 1 & 0 \\ \psi_1 & 1 \\ \psi_2 & \psi_1 \\ \vdots & \vdots \end{bmatrix}, \qquad X'X = \frac{\sigma_y^2}{\sigma_a^2} \begin{bmatrix} 1 & \rho_1 \\ \rho_1 & 1 \end{bmatrix},$$

$$(X'X)^{-1} = \frac{\sigma_a^2}{\sigma_y^2(1-\rho_1^2)}\begin{bmatrix} 1 & -\rho_1 \\ -\rho_1 & 1 \end{bmatrix}, \qquad \sigma_y^2 = \frac{(1-\phi_2)\sigma_a^2}{(1+\phi_2)[(1-\phi_2)^2-\phi_1^2]}.$$

Thus

$$q_{11} = 1 - \phi_2^2, \qquad q_{12} = -\phi_1\phi_2(1+\phi_2), \qquad q_{22} = 1 - \phi_2^2 - \phi_1^2(1+\phi_2)^2,$$

from which Q and $\sum \hat{r} = 1/n(I-Q)$ may be determined using (2.32). In particular,

$$\left.\begin{aligned} V(\hat{r}_1) &= 1/n\cdot\phi_2^2, \\ V(\hat{r}_2) &= 1/n[\phi_2^2 + \phi_1^2(1+\phi_2)^2], \quad \text{and} \\ V(\hat{r}_k) &= 1/n[1 - \phi_1 q_{k,k-1} - \phi_2 q_{k,k-2}], \; k \geq 3. \end{aligned}\right\} \tag{2.37}$$

From these examples we can see a general pattern emerging. As in (2.33) the first p variances and corresponding covariances will be heavily dependent on the parameters $\phi_1, \cdots, \phi_p$ and in general can depart sharply from the corresponding values for white noise autocorrelations, whereas for $k \geq p+1$ a "1" is introduced into the expression for variances (as in (2.35) and (2.37)), and the recursion (2.32) ensures that as k increases the $\{\hat{r}_k\}$ behave increasingly like the corresponding $\{r_k\}$ with respect to both their variances and covariances.

2.7 The distribution of $n\sum_1^m \hat{r}_k^2$

We have remarked earlier that if the fitted model is appropriate and the parameters ϕ are exactly known, then the calculated a_t's would be uncorrelated normal deviates, their serial correlations r would be approximately $N(0, (1/n)I)$, and thus $n\sum_1^m r_k^2$ would possess a χ^2 distribution with m degrees of freedom. We now see that if m is taken sufficiently large so that the elements after the mth in the latent vectors of Q are essentially zero, then we should expect that to the order of approximation we are here employing, the statistic

$$n\sum_1^m \hat{r}_k^2, \tag{2.38}$$

obtained when estimates $\hat{\phi}$ are substituted for the true parameters ϕ in the model, will still be distributed as χ^2, only now with $m-p$ rather than m degrees of freedom. This result is of considerable practical interest because it suggests that an overall test of the type discussed in [4] can in fact be justified when suitable modifications coming from a more careful analysis are applied. Later we consider in more detail the use of this test, along with procedures on individual $\hat{r}$'s, in diagnostic checking.

3. MONTE CARLO EXPERIMENT

We have made certain approximations in deriving the distribution of the residual autocorrelations, and it is therefore of interest to investigate this distribution empirically through repeated sampling and to compare the results with (2.29). This was done for the first order AR process for $\phi = 0, \pm.1, \pm.3, \pm.5, \pm.7, \pm.9$. For given ϕ, $s = 50$ sets of $n = 200$ random normal deviates were generated on the computer using a method described in [7], with separate aggregates of deviates obtained for each parameter value. For the jth set a series $\{y_t^{(j)}\}$ was generated using formula (2.34), $\hat{\phi}^{(j)}$ was estimated, $\{\hat{a}_t^{(j)}\}$ determined, and the quantities

$$\hat{r}_k^{(j)} = \frac{\sum \hat{a}_t^{(j)} \hat{a}_{t-k}^{(j)}}{\sum [\hat{a}_t^{(j)}]^2} \tag{3.1}$$

computed for $1 \leq k \leq m = 20$, $1 \leq j \leq s = 50$. This yielded sample variances and covariances

$$C_{kl} = \frac{1}{50} \sum_{j=1}^{50} \hat{r}_k^{(j)} \hat{r}_l^{(j)} \tag{3.2}$$

and sample correlations

$$R_{kl} = C_{kl}/\sqrt{C_{kk}C_{ll}} \,. \tag{3.3}$$

The results of this Monte Carlo sampling are set out in detail in [8] and in general confirm the adequacy of the approximations used. As an example of these calculations, Table 1 compares the empirical variances (3.2) of $\hat{r}_k$ and correlations (3.3) of $(\hat{r}_1, \hat{r}_k)$ with their theoretical counterparts obtained from (2.35). Allowing for the sampling error of the Monte Carlo estimates themselves, there is good agreement between the two sets of quantities, a phenomenon which occurred also for the other values of ϕ considered.

Since the large-sample variance ϕ^2/n of $\hat{r}_1$ departs the most from the common variance of $1/n$ for white noise autocorrelations, an examination of the empirical behavior of this quantity is of particular interest. Thus Figure 1 shows the sample variance of $\hat{r}_1$ for $\phi = 0, \pm.1, \pm.3, \pm.5, \pm.7, \pm.9$ in relation to the parabola $V(\hat{r}_1) = \phi^2/n$, with reasonable agreement between the two. (The coefficient of variation of the sample variance of $\hat{r}_k$ for $\phi \neq 0$ is approximately $\sqrt{2/s} = 1/5$, independent of k and n; at $\phi = 0$, $V(\hat{r}_1) = O(1/n^2)$.

Table 1. *THEORETICAL (AS IN (2.35)) AND EMPIRICAL (FROM MONTE-CARLO SAMPLING) VARIANCES AND CORRELATIONS OF SAMPLE RESIDUAL AUTOCORRELATIONS FROM FIRST-ORDER AR PROCESS WITH $\phi = .5$*

k	*Variance of $\hat{r}_k$ (multiplied by n)*		*Correlation between $\hat{r}_1$ and $\hat{r}_k$*	
	Theoretical	*Empirical*	*Theoretical*	*Empirical*
1	.250	.244	1.000	1.000
2	.813	.676	−.832	−.812
3	.953	.741	−.384	−.301
4	.988	.864	−.189	−.186
5	.997	1.240	−.094	−.366
6	.999	.967	−.047	−.221
7	1.000	.870	−.023	.083
8	1.000	1.203	−.012	−.148
9	1.000	.982	−.006	−.009
10	1.000	.881	−.003	−.080

Figure 1. THEORETICAL (LINE) AND EMPIRICAL (DOTS) VARIANCES OF $\hat{r}_1$

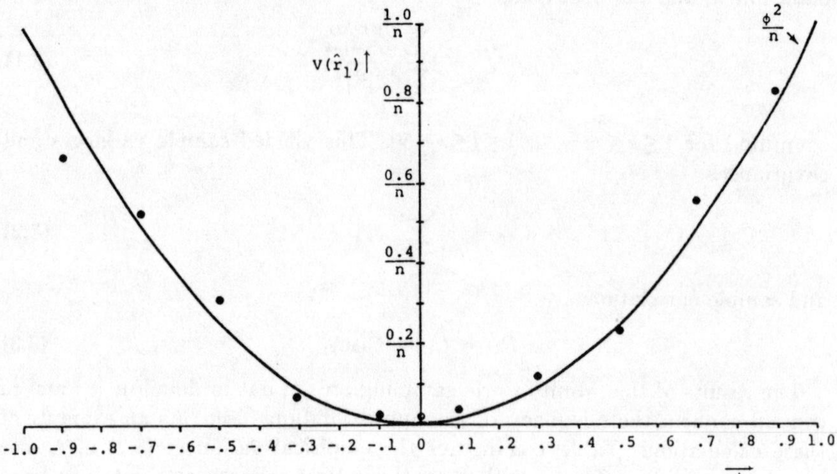

There are several additional comparisons which can be made based on certain functions of the $\hat{r}$'s. Thus we have seen that

$$\hat{l} = \sum \hat{\phi}^{k-1}\hat{r}_k = 0, \tag{3.4}$$

and in the course of our derivations we have had to make the approximation

$$l = \sum \phi^{k-1}\hat{r}_k = 0. \tag{3.5}$$

Some indication of the validity of this approximation is gained by examining the actual values of l from the sampling experiment, which were found to be distributed about zero with a variance of about one-hundredth that which would have been expected from the same linear form in white noise autocorrelations.

Of considerable importance because of its role in diagnostic checking is an examination of the quantity

$$n \sum_{k=1}^{m} \hat{r}_k^2 = 200 \sum_{k=1}^{20} \hat{r}_k^2, \tag{3.6}$$

which as in (2.38) should possess a χ^2—distribution with $\nu = m-1 = 19$ degrees of freedom. Such a distribution has a mean and variance of 19 and 38, respectively, with which the Monte Carlo values can be compared. When this was done, the overall or pooled empirical mean was found to be 18.1 and significantly different from 19. This difference is plausible, however, when it is realized that the statistic $n\sum_1^m \hat{r}_k^2$ possesses a χ^2_{m-p} distribution only insofar as the white noise autocorrelations $\mathbf{r} = (r_1, \cdots, r_m)'$ have a common variance of $1/n$; and from (1.4) it is seen that this approximation overestimates the true variance of a given r_k by a factor of $(n+2)/(n-k)$. In particular, for $n = 200$, $m = 20$, and a typical value of $k = 10$, the actual variance $V(r_k)$ is $190/202 \approx 94$ percent of the $1/n$ approximation. Since the residual autocorrelations $\hat{\mathbf{r}}$ are by (2.27) a linear transformation of $\mathbf{r}$, it is reasonable to expect that a comparable depression of the variances of $\{\hat{r}_k\}$ would occur, and this would account for the discrepancy between the theoretical and empirical means of the statistic $200 \sum_1^{20} \hat{r}_k^2$ encountered above. (This phenomenon would also explain the tendency for the empirical variances themselves, such as those in Table 1, to take on values averaging about 5 percent lower than those based on the matrix $(1/n)(I-Q)$ of (2.29).)

4. USE OF RESIDUAL AUTOCORRELATIONS IN DIAGNOSTIC CHECKING

We have obtained the large sample distribution of the residual autocorrelations $\hat{r}$ from fitting the correct model to a time series, and we have discussed the ways in which this distribution departs significantly from that of the white noise autocorrelations r. It is desirable now to consider the practical implications of these results in examining the adequacy of fit of a model.

First of all it appears that even though the $\hat{r}$'s have a variance/covariance matrix which can differ very considerably from that of the r's, the statistic $n\sum_{k=1}^{m} \hat{r}_k^2$ will (since the matrix $I-Q$ is idempotent) still possess a χ^2-distribution, only now with $m-p$ rather than m degrees of freedom. Thus the overall χ^2-test discussed in Section 1 may be justified to the same degree of approximation as before when the number of degrees of freedom is appropriately modified.

However, regarding the "quality-control-chart" procedure, that is the comparison of the $\{\hat{r}_k\}$ with their standard errors, some modification is clearly needed.

Figure 2 shows the straight-line standard error bands of width $1/\sqrt{n}$ associated with any set of white noise autocorrelations $\{r_k\}$. These stand in marked contrast to the corresponding bands for the residual autocorrelations $\{\hat{r}_k\}$, derived from their covariance matrix $(1/n)(I-Q)$ and shown in Figure 3 for selected first and second order AR processes. Since it is primarily the $\hat{r}$'s of small lags that are most useful in revealing model inadequacies, we see that the consequence of treating $\hat{r}$'s as r's in the diagnostic checking procedure can be a serious underestimation of significance, that is, a failure to detect lack of fit in the model when it exists. Of course, if the model would have been judged inadequate anyway, our conviction in this regard is now strengthened.

Suppose, for example, that we identify a series of length 200 as first order

Figure 2. STANDARD ERROR LIMITS FOR WHITE NOISE AUTOCORRELATIONS r_k

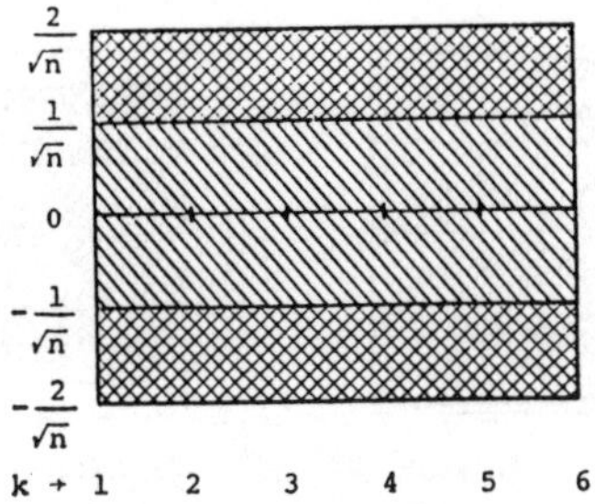

autoregressive and after fitting $\hat{\phi}=.5$. Suppose also that $\hat{r}_1=.10$. Now the standard error of r_1 for white noise is $1/\sqrt{n}=.07$, so that $\hat{r}_1$ is well within the limits in Figure 2. Therefore if we erroneously regarded these as limits on $\hat{r}_1$ we would probably not conclude that this model was inadequate. However, if the true process actually were first order autoregressive (say with $\phi=.5$), the standard error of $\hat{r}_1$ would be $|\phi|/\sqrt{n}=.035$; since the observed $\hat{r}_1=.10$ is almost three times this value, we should be very suspicious of the adequacy of this fit.

The situation is further complicated by the existence of rather high correlations between the $\hat{r}$'s, especially between those of small lags. For the first order process, the most serious correlation is

$$\rho[\hat{r}_1, \hat{r}_2] = -\frac{\phi}{|\phi|}\frac{1-\phi^2}{\sqrt{1-\phi^2+\phi^4}}$$

which, for example, approaches -1 as $\phi \rightarrow 0^+$ and is still as large as $-.6$ for $\phi=.7$. Correlation among the $\hat{r}$'s is even more prevalent in second and higher-order processes, where (as for variances) those involving lags up to $k=p$ can be particularly serious. From then on their magnitude is controlled by the recursive relationship (2.32); in particular, the closer ϕ is to the boundary of the stationarity region, the slower will be the dying out of $\text{cov}(\hat{r}_k, \hat{r}_l)$ or $\rho(\hat{r}_k, \hat{r}_l)$ although often in these situations the less serious will the initial correlations $\rho(\hat{r}_1, \hat{r}_2)$, $\rho(\hat{r}_2, \hat{r}_3)$, $\rho(\hat{r}_1, \hat{r}_3)$, etc., tend to be.

We have thus seen that the departure of the distribution of the residual autocorrelations $\hat{r}$ from that of white noise autocorrelations r is serious enough to

Figure 3. ***STANDARD ERROR LIMITS FOR RESIDUAL AUTOCORRELATIONS*** $\hat{r}_k$

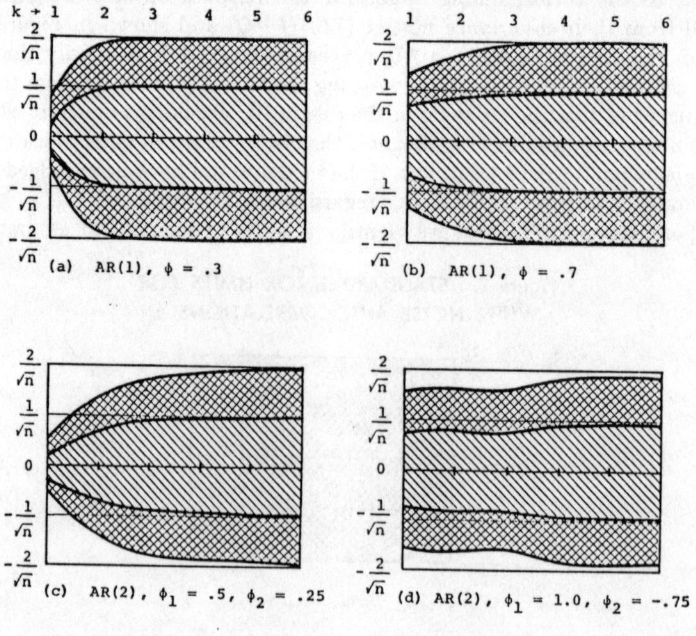

warrant some modifications in their use in diagnostic checking. The residual autocorrelation function, however, remains a powerful device for this purpose.

5. DISTRIBUTION OF RESIDUAL AUTOCORRELATIONS FOR THE MOVING AVERAGE AND GENERAL ARIMA PROCESSES

In obtaining the distribution of $\hat{r}=(\hat{r}_1, \cdots, \hat{r}_m)'$ for the pure autoregressive process in Section 2, considerable use was made of the recursive relation $\phi(B)\rho_k=0$, which is not satisfied by moving average models $y_t=\theta(B)a_t$, or more generally by mixed models of the form (1.1) with $w_t=\nabla^d z_t$ denoting the stationary dth difference.

It is fortunate, therefore, that these models have in common with the pure AR models (2.1) an important property (derived in Section 5.1) because of which the distribution of their residual autocorrelations can be found as an immediate consequence of the autoregressive solution (2.29). This property is that if two time series, (a) the mixed autoregressive—moving average series (1.1), and (b) an autoregressive series

$$\pi(B)x_t = (1 - \pi_1 B - \cdots - \pi_{p+q}B^{p+q})x_t = a_t \tag{5.1}$$

are both generated from the *same set* of deviates $\{a_t\}$, and moreover if

$$\pi(B) = \phi(B)\theta(B), \tag{5.2}$$

then when these models are each fitted by least squares, their residuals, and hence also their residual autocorrelations, will be very nearly the same. Therefore if a mixed model of order (p, d, q) is correctly identified and fitted, its residual autocorrelations for n sufficiently large will be distributed as though the model had been of order $(p+q, d, 0)$ with the relations between the two sets of parameters given by (5.2). In particular the ψ's comprising the X-matrix (2.23) for the model (1.1) are the coefficients in $\psi(B)=[\phi(B)\theta(B)]^{-1}$.

5.1 Equality of Residuals in AR and ARIMA Models

Let w_t and x_t be as in (1.1) and (5.1); (5.2) then implies

$$w_t = \theta^2(B)x_t. \tag{5.3}$$

As in (2.5), define

$$\dot{a}_t^{\text{AR}} = a_t^{\text{AR}}(\dot{\pi}) = \dot{\pi}(B)x_t = -\sum_{j=0}^{p+q}\dot{\pi}_j x_{t-j} \tag{5.4}$$

where $\dot{\pi}_0=-1$, and now also

$$\dot{a}_t^* = a_t^*(\dot{\phi}, \dot{\theta}) = \dot{\phi}(B)\dot{\theta}^{-1}(B)w_t = [\sum_{i=0}^{p}\dot{\phi}_i B^i][\sum_{j=0}^{q}\dot{\theta}_j B^j]^{-1}w_t, \tag{5.5}$$

where $\dot{\phi}_0=\dot{\theta}_0=-1$. We will expand these quantities about the true parameter values and go through a least squares estimation in each case which is analogous to writing the linear regression model $\mathbf{y}=X\boldsymbol{\beta}+\boldsymbol{\varepsilon}$ as

$$\dot{\mathbf{e}} = \mathbf{y} - \dot{\mathbf{y}} = X(\boldsymbol{\beta} - \dot{\boldsymbol{\beta}}) + \boldsymbol{\varepsilon} = X\boldsymbol{\delta} + \boldsymbol{\varepsilon}, \tag{5.6}$$

for fixed $\dot{\boldsymbol{\beta}}$, and then performing the regression directly on $\dot{\mathbf{e}}$ rather than on $\mathbf{y}$. The equality of the residuals in the two cases depends heavily on the fact that the derivatives in each expansion involve the same autoregressive variable x_t.

Thus

$$\frac{\partial \dot{a}_t^{AR}}{\partial \dot{\pi}_j} = -x_{t-j}, \qquad 1 \le j \le p+q, \text{ irrespective of } \dot{\pi};$$

$$\frac{\partial \dot{a}_t^*}{\partial \dot{\phi}_j} = -\dot{\theta}^{-1}(B)\dot{w}_{t-j}, \qquad 1 \le j \le p$$

$$= -\theta(B)x_{t-j} \quad \text{at } (\dot{\phi}, \dot{\theta}) = (\phi, \theta); \text{ and}$$

$$\frac{\partial \dot{a}_t^*}{\partial \dot{\theta}_j} = \dot{\phi}(B)\dot{\theta}^{-2}(B)w_{t-j}, \qquad 1 \le j \le q$$

$$= \phi(B)x_{t-j} \quad \text{at } (\dot{\phi}, \dot{\theta}) = (\phi, \theta).$$

Then

$$\dot{a}_t^{AR} = a_t^{AR} + \sum_{j=1}^{p+q} (\pi_j - \dot{\pi}_j)x_{t-j}, \tag{5.7}$$

and approximately

$$\dot{a}_t^* = a_t^* + \sum_{i=1}^{p} (\phi_i - \dot{\phi}_i)\theta(B)x_{t-i} - \sum_{j=1}^{q} (\theta_j - \dot{\theta}_j)\phi(B)x_{t-j} \tag{5.8}$$

$$= a_t^* + \sum_{i=1}^{p} (\phi_i - \dot{\phi}_i)x_{t-i} - \sum_{j=1}^{q} (\theta_j - \dot{\theta}_j)x_{t-j}$$
$$+ \sum_{i=1}^{p} \sum_{j=1}^{q} [\phi_i(\theta_j - \dot{\theta}_j) - \theta_j(\phi_i - \dot{\phi}_i)]x_{t-i-j}$$
$$= a_t^* + \sum_{i=1}^{p} (\phi_i - \dot{\phi}_i)x_{t-i} - \sum_{j=1}^{q} (\theta_j - \dot{\theta}_j)x_{t-j}$$
$$+ \sum_{i=1}^{p} \sum_{j=1}^{q} [\dot{\phi}_i(\theta_j - \dot{\theta}_j) - \dot{\theta}_j(\phi_i - \dot{\phi}_i)]x_{t-i-j} \tag{5.9}$$
$$= a_t^* + \sum_{j=1}^{p+q} (\beta_j - \dot{\beta}_j)x_{t-j}.$$

Thus letting $\boldsymbol{\beta} = (\beta_1, \cdots, \beta_{p+q})'$ and $\boldsymbol{\lambda} = \left[\begin{smallmatrix}\boldsymbol{\phi} \\ \boldsymbol{\theta}\end{smallmatrix}\right]$, we see that

$$\boldsymbol{\beta} = A\boldsymbol{\lambda}, \tag{5.10}$$

where A is a $(p+q)-$square matrix whose elements involve $\dot{\boldsymbol{\lambda}}$ but not the true parameter values $\boldsymbol{\lambda}$. For example, if $p=q=1$, we would have

$$\begin{bmatrix}\beta_1 \\ \beta_2\end{bmatrix} = \begin{bmatrix} 1 & -1 \\ -\dot{\theta} & \dot{\phi}\end{bmatrix}\begin{bmatrix}\phi \\ \theta\end{bmatrix} \tag{5.11}$$

Now equations (5.7) and (5.9) can be written as

$$\dot{\boldsymbol{a}}^{AR} = \boldsymbol{a} + X(\boldsymbol{\pi} - \dot{\boldsymbol{\pi}}) \tag{5.12}$$

$$\dot{\boldsymbol{a}}^* = \boldsymbol{a} + X(\boldsymbol{\beta} - \dot{\boldsymbol{\beta}}) \tag{5.13}$$

where the error in (5.13) is $O(|\boldsymbol{\beta} - \dot{\boldsymbol{\beta}}|^2)$, and where we have made use of the fact that, at $\dot{\boldsymbol{\pi}} = \boldsymbol{\pi}$, $\dot{\boldsymbol{\theta}} = \boldsymbol{\theta}$, and $\dot{\boldsymbol{\phi}} = \boldsymbol{\phi}$,

$$a_t^{AR} = a_t^* = a_t. \tag{5.14}$$

Thus in (5.12) the sum of squares

$$\boldsymbol{a}'\boldsymbol{a} = \sum a_t^2 = \sum [a_t^{AR}(\boldsymbol{\pi})]^2$$

is minimized as a function of $\boldsymbol{\pi}$ when

$$\boldsymbol{\pi} - \dot{\boldsymbol{\pi}} = \hat{\boldsymbol{\pi}} - \dot{\boldsymbol{\pi}} = (X'X)^{-1}X'\dot{\boldsymbol{a}}^{AR}, \tag{5.15}$$

while in (5.13) if we write

$$\mathbf{a}^* = \mathbf{a} + X[A(\boldsymbol{\lambda} - \dot{\boldsymbol{\lambda}})] = \mathbf{a} + Z(\boldsymbol{\lambda} - \dot{\boldsymbol{\lambda}}),$$

then the sum of squares

$$\mathbf{a}'\mathbf{a} = \sum a_t^2 = \sum [a_t^*(\boldsymbol{\lambda})]^2$$

is minimized as a function of $\boldsymbol{\lambda}$ when

$$\boldsymbol{\lambda} - \dot{\boldsymbol{\lambda}} = \hat{\boldsymbol{\lambda}} - \dot{\boldsymbol{\lambda}} = (Z'Z)^{-1}Z'\dot{\mathbf{a}}^* = A^{-1}(\hat{\boldsymbol{\beta}} - \dot{\boldsymbol{\beta}});$$

that is,

$$\hat{\boldsymbol{\beta}} - \dot{\boldsymbol{\beta}} = (X'X)^{-1}X'\dot{\mathbf{a}}^*. \tag{5.16}$$

Then by setting $\dot{\mathbf{a}} = \mathbf{a}$ in (5.15) and (5.16), we have from (5.14) the important equality

$$\hat{\boldsymbol{\pi}} - \boldsymbol{\pi} = (X'X)^{-1}X'\mathbf{a} = \hat{\boldsymbol{\beta}} - \boldsymbol{\beta}; \tag{5.17}$$

and finally by setting "." = "^" in (5.12) and (5.13), it follows from (5.17) that to $O_p(1/n)$

$$\hat{\mathbf{a}}^{\mathrm{AR}} = \mathbf{a} + X(\boldsymbol{\pi} - \hat{\boldsymbol{\pi}}) = \mathbf{a} + X(\boldsymbol{\beta} - \hat{\boldsymbol{\beta}}) = \hat{\mathbf{a}}^*, \tag{5.18}$$

and thus (to the same order) $\hat{\mathbf{r}}^{\mathrm{AR}} = \hat{\mathbf{r}}^*$, as we set out to show.

5.2 Monte Carlo Experiment

The equality (5.18) between the residuals from the autoregressive and mixed models depends on the accuracy of the expansion (5.8), that is, on the extent of linearity in the moving average model, between the true and estimated values $\boldsymbol{\theta}$ and $\hat{\boldsymbol{\theta}}$. It is therefore worthwhile to confirm this model-duality by generating and fitting pairs of series of the form (1.1) and (5.1) and comparing their residuals, or more to our purpose, their residual autocorrelations. This was done for $p+q=1$ and $p+q=2$ for series of length 200. Some indication of the close-

Table 2. RESIDUAL CORRELATIONS FROM FIRST ORDER AR AND MA TIME SERIES GENERATED FROM SAME WHITE NOISE ($n=200$)

k	$\phi=\theta=.1$		$\phi=\theta=.5$		$\phi=\theta=.9$	
	$\hat{r}_k^{AR}$	$\hat{r}_k^{MA}$	$\hat{r}_k^{AR}$	$\hat{r}_k^{MA}$	$\hat{r}_k^{AR}$	$\hat{r}_k^{MA}$
1	−.029	−.010	.003	−.005	−.048	−.057
2	.164	.169	.044	.045	.157	.151
3	.096	.099	−.098	−.096	.008	.009
4	−.050	−.049	.014	.021	−.126	−.127
5	−.003	−.006	.057	.058	.034	.035
6	−.143	−.144	.010	.012	−.091	−.090
7	−.023	−.026	−.004	.001	−.001	−.000
8	−.040	−.041	−.054	−.046	−.038	−.035
9	.010	.009	.052	.052	−.004	.000
10	−.049	−.049	−.065	−.067	.113	.116
$\hat{\phi}$ or $\hat{\theta}\rightarrow$	.159	.057	.543	.451	.922	.870

ness of the agreement is obtained from the few results for first order AR and MA processes shown in Table 2, where it is seen that the residual autocorrelation $\hat{r}_k^{AR}$ and $\hat{r}_k^{MA}$ are equal or nearly equal to the second decimal place.

A sampling experiment of the type described in Section 3 was also performed for the first order MA process. The results were very similar, which is to be expected in view of (5.18).

5.3 Conclusions

We have shown above that to a close approximation the residuals from any moving average or mixed autoregressive-moving average process will be the same as those from a suitably chosen autoregressive process. We have further confirmed the adequacy of this approximation by empirical calculation. It follows from this that we need not consider separately these two classes of processes; more precisely,

1. We can immediately use the AR result to write down the variance/covariance matrix of $\hat{r}$ for any autoregressive-integrated moving average process (1.1) by considering the corresponding variance/covariance matrix of $\hat{r}$ from the pure AR process

$$\pi(B)x_t = \theta(B)\phi(B)x_t = a_t. \tag{5.19}$$

2. All considerations regarding the use of residual autocorrelations in tests of fit and diagnostic checking discussed in Section 4 for the autoregressive model therefore apply equally to moving average and mixed models.
3. In particular it follows from the above that a "portmanteau" test for the adequacy of any ARIMA process is obtained by referring $n\sum_{k=1}^{m} \hat{r}_k^2$ to a χ^2 distribution with ν degrees of freedom, where $\nu = m - p - q$.

REFERENCES

[1] Anderson, R. L., "Distribution of the Serial Correlation Coefficient," *The Annals of Mathematical Statistics*, 13 (March 1942), 1–13.

[2] Bartlett, M. S., "On the Theoretical Specification and Sampling Properties of Autocorrelated Time Series," *Journal of the Royal Statistical Society*, Series B, 8 (April 1946), 27–41.

[3] ——— and Diananda, P. H., "Extensions of Quenouille's Tests for Autoregressive Schemes," *Journal of the Royal Statistical Society*, Series B, 12 (April 1950), 108–15.

[4] Box, G. E. P. and Jenkins, G. M., *Statistical Models for Prediction and Control*, Technical Reports #72, 77, 79, 94, 95, 99, 103, 104, 116, 121, and 122, Department of Statistics, University of Wisconsin, Madison, Wisconsin, 1967.

[5] ———, *Time Series Analysis Forecasting and Control*, San Francisco: Holden-Day, Inc., 1970.

[6] ——— and Bacon, D. W., "Models for Forecasting Seasonal and Non-Seasonal Time Series," in B. Harris, ed., *Spectral Analysis of Time Series*, New York: John Wiley & Sons, Inc., 1967.

[7] Box, G. E. P. and Muller, M. E., "Note on the Generation of Random Normal Deviates," *The Annals of Mathematical Statistics*, 29 (June 1958), 610–11.

[8] Box, G. E. P. and Pierce, D. A., "Distribution of Residual Autocorrelations in Integrated Autoregressive-Moving Average Time Series Models," Technical Report #154, Department of Statistics, University of Wisconsin, Madison, April, 1968.

[9] Durbin, J., "Efficient Estimation of Parameters in Moving Average Models," *Biometrika*, 46 (December 1959), 306–16.

[10] ———, "Testing for Serial Correlation in Least-Squares Regression When Some of the Regressors are Lagged Dependent Variables," *Econometrica*, 38 (May 1970), 410–21.

[11] Grenander, U. and Rosenblatt, M., *Statistical Analysis of Stationary Time Series*, New York: John Wiley & Sons, Inc., 1957.

[12] Mann, H. B. and Wald, A., "On the Statistical Treatment of Linear Stochastic Difference Equations," *Econometrica*, 11 (July 1943), 173–220.

[13] ——— "On Stochastic Limit and Order Relationships," *The Annals of Mathematical Statistics*, 14 (September 1943), 217–26.

[14] Quenouille, M. H., "A Large-Sample Test for the Goodness of Fit of Autoregressive Schemes," *Journal of the Royal Statistical Society*, Series A, 110 (June 1947), 123–9.

[15] Walker, A. M., "Note on a Generalization of the Large-Sample Goodness of Fit Test for Linear Autoregressive Schemes," *Journal of the Royal Statistical Society*, Series B, 12 (April 1950), 102-7.

[16] Whittle, P., "Tests of Fit in Time Series," *Biometrika*, 39 (December 1952), 309–18.

[17] Wold, H., *A Study in the Analysis of Stationary Time Series*, Stockholm: Almquist and Wiksell, 1938.

[18] ———, "A Large-Sample Test for Moving Averages," *Journal of the Royal Statistical Society*, Series B, 11 (April 1949), 297–305.

[19] Yule, G. U., "On a Method of Investigating Periodicities in Disturbed Series, with Special Reference to Wolfer's Sunspot Numbers," *Philosophical Transactions*, (A) 226 (July 1927), 267–98.

[5]

Biometrika (1978), **65**, 2, *pp.* 297–303
With 1 *text-figure*
Printed in Great Britain

On a measure of lack of fit in time series models

BY G. M. LJUNG
College of Business Administration, University of Denver, Colorado
AND G. E. P. BOX
Department of Statistics, University of Wisconsin, Madison

SUMMARY

The overall test for lack of fit in autoregressive-moving average models proposed by Box & Pierce (1970) is considered. It is shown that a substantially improved approximation results from a simple modification of this test. Some consideration is given to the power of such tests and their robustness when the innovations are nonnormal. Similar modifications in the overall tests used for transfer function-noise models are proposed.

Some key words: Autoregressive-moving average model; Residual autocorrelation; Test for lack of fit; Transfer function-noise model.

1. INTRODUCTION

Consider a discrete time series $\{w_t\}$ generated by a stationary autoregressive-moving average model

$$\phi(B)\,w_t = \theta(B)\,a_t,$$

where $\phi(B) = 1-\phi_1 B - \ldots - \phi_p B^p$, $\theta(B) = 1-\theta_1 B - \ldots - \theta_q B^q$, $B^k w_t = w_{t-k}$, and $\{a_t\}$ is a sequence of independent and identically distributed $N(0,\sigma^2)$ random deviates. The w_t's can in general represent the d-th difference or some other suitable transformation of a non-stationary series $\{z_t\}$.

After a model of this form has been fitted to a series $w_1, \ldots, w_n$, it is useful to study the adequacy of the fit by examining the residuals $\hat{a}_1, \ldots, \hat{a}_n$ and, in particular, their auto-correlations

$$\hat{r}_k = \sum_{t=k+1}^{n} \hat{a}_t \hat{a}_{t-k} \Big/ \sum_{t=1}^{n} \hat{a}_t^2 \quad (k = 1, 2, \ldots).$$

An informal graphical analysis of these quantities combined with overfitting (Box & Jenkins, 1970, §8.1) usually proves most effective in detecting possible deficiencies in the model. In addition, however, it is often worthwhile to look at an overall criterion of adequacy of fit. Box & Pierce (1970) noted that if the model were appropriate and the parameters were known, the quantity

$$\tilde{Q}(r) = n(n+2) \sum_{k=1}^{m} (n-k)^{-1} r_k^2, \tag{1·1}$$

where

$$r_k = \sum_{t=k+1}^{n} a_t a_{t-k} \Big/ \sum_{t=1}^{n} a_t^2,$$

would for large n be distributed as χ_m^2 since the limiting distribution of $r = (r_1, \ldots, r_m)'$ is multivariate normal with mean vector zero (Anderson, 1942; Anderson & Walker, 1964),

$\mathrm{var}(r_k) = (n-k)/\{n(n+2)\}$ and $\mathrm{cov}(r_k, r_l) = 0$ $(k \neq l)$. Using the further approximation $\mathrm{var}(r_k) = 1/n$, Box & Pierce (1970) suggested that the distribution of

$$Q(r) = n \sum_{k=1}^{m} r_k^2 \tag{1·2}$$

could be approximated by that of χ_m^2. Furthermore, they showed that when the $p+q$ parameters of an appropriate model are estimated and the $\hat{r}_k$'s replace the r_k's, then

$$Q(\hat{r}) = n \sum_{k=1}^{m} \hat{r}_k^2$$

would for large n be distributed as χ_{m-p-q}^2 yielding an approximate test for lack of fit.

In applications of this test, suspiciously low values of $Q(\hat{r})$ have sometimes been observed, and studies by the present authors, reported in a University of Wisconsin technical report, and by Davies, Triggs & Newbold (1977) have verified that the distribution of $Q(\hat{r})$ can deviate from χ_{m-p-q}^2. This observation was also made by Prothero & Wallis (1976) in the discussion of their paper. The observed discrepancies could be accounted for by several factors, for instance departures from normality of the autocorrelations. It appears, however, that the main difficulty is caused by the approximation of (1·1) by (1·2). A modified test based on the criterion

$$\tilde{Q}(\hat{r}) = n(n+2) \sum_{k=1}^{m} (n-k)^{-1} \hat{r}_k^2$$

was recommended by the present authors but its usefulness was questioned by Davies *et al.* (1977) on the ground that the variance of $\tilde{Q}(\hat{r})$ exceeds that of the χ_{m-p-q}^2 distribution. Our studies show however that the modified test provides a substantially improved approximation that should be adequate for most practical purposes.

2. Means and variances of $Q(r)$ and $\tilde{Q}(r)$

To examine the overall test, it is useful to consider initially the quantities $Q(r)$ and $\tilde{Q}(r)$ which involve the white noise autocorrelations r. Since the limiting distribution of r is $N(0, n^{-1} I_m)$, $Q(r)$ and $\tilde{Q}(r)$ are asymptotically distributed as χ_m^2 and have expectation m and variance $2m$. For finite values of n, $\tilde{Q}(r)$ has expectation m, whereas

$$E\{Q(r)\} = n \sum_{k=1}^{m} E(r_k^2) = \frac{mn}{n+2}\left(1 - \frac{m+1}{2n}\right). \tag{2·1}$$

Clearly, unless n is large relative to m, $E\{Q(r)\}$ can be much smaller than m.

The variances are

$$\mathrm{var}\{Q(r)\} = n^2 \sum_{k=1}^{m} \mathrm{var}(r_k^2) + 2n^2 \sum_{k=1}^{m-1} \sum_{l=k+1}^{m} \mathrm{cov}(r_k^2, r_l^2),$$

$$\mathrm{var}\{\tilde{Q}(r)\} = n^2(n+2)^2 \sum_{k=1}^{m} (n-k)^{-2} \mathrm{var}(r_k^2) + 2n^2(n+2)^2 \sum_{k=1}^{m-1} \sum_{l=k+1}^{m} (n-k)^{-1}(n-l)^{-1} \mathrm{cov}(r_k^2, r_l^2), \tag{2·2}$$

where, for fixed n, $\mathrm{cov}(r_k^2, r_l^2)$ is nonzero. The univariate and bivariate moments of the r_k's needed to evaluate (2·2) can be obtained using the identity

$$E(r_k^i r_l^j) = \frac{E\{(\Sigma a_t a_{t-k})^i (\Sigma a_t a_{t-l})^j\}}{E\{(\Sigma a_t^2)^{i+j}\}}, \tag{2·3}$$

which follows from independence of the r_k's and Σa_t^2 (Anderson, 1971, p. 304). Taking var $(a_t) = 1$ without loss of generality, we have that Σa_t^2 is distributed as χ_n^2 and $E(\Sigma a_t^2)^{i+j} = n(n+2)\ldots(n+2i+2j-2)$. The term in the numerator of (2·3) can be evaluated by multiplying term by term and taking the expected value. It can thus be verified that for $k < \frac{1}{2}n$

$$\operatorname{var}(r_k^2) = \frac{6(3n-5k)+3(n-k)^2}{n(n+2)(n+4)(n+6)} - \frac{(n-k)^2}{n^2(n+2)^2},$$

$$\operatorname{cov}(r_k^2, r_l^2) = \frac{(n-k)(n-l)+4(n-l)+8(n-k-l)}{n(n+2)(n+4)(n+6)} - \frac{(n-k)(n-l)}{n^2(n+2)^2}. \tag{2·4}$$

The exact variances of $Q(r)$ and $\tilde{Q}(r)$ are readily evaluated using (2·2) and (2·4). By ignoring terms of order higher than $1/n$ it may be shown that approximately, for n large relative to m,

$$\operatorname{var}\{Q(r)\} = 2m\left(1+\frac{m-10}{n}\right), \quad \operatorname{var}\{\tilde{Q}(r)\} = 2m\left(1+\frac{2m-5}{n}\right).$$

The variance of $\tilde{Q}(r)$ exceeds $2m$ but the absence of a location bias makes its distribution much closer to χ_m^2 than that of $Q(r)$. This is illustrated in Fig. 1 which compares Monte Carlo distributions of $Q(r)$ and $\tilde{Q}(r)$ based on 1000 replications to the χ_m^2 distribution for $m = 30$ and $n = 100$. The observed distribution of $Q(r)$ has mean 24·97 and variance 60·47; $\tilde{Q}(r)$ has mean 30·17 and variance 88·25. These values agree quite closely with the theoretical values 24·85, 63·15, 30·00 and 91·48, respectively. Also shown by dashed lines in Fig. 1 is a distribution of the form $a\chi_b^2$ for which both the mean and variance are adjusted to correspond with those of $\tilde{Q}(r)$. There is perhaps somewhat better agreement in the upper tail but the main improvement results from adjusting the mean.

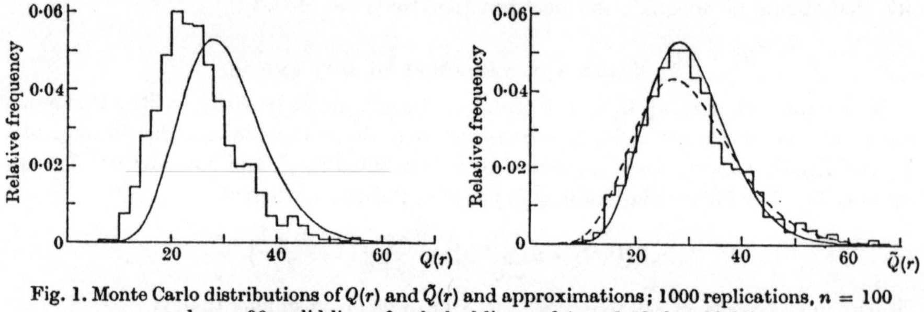

Fig. 1. Monte Carlo distributions of $Q(r)$ and $\tilde{Q}(r)$ and approximations; 1000 replications, $n = 100$ and $m = 30$; solid line, χ_{30}^2; dashed line, $a\chi_b^2$ ($a = 1·52$, $b = 19·68$).

3. The test statistics $Q(\hat{r})$ and $\tilde{Q}(\hat{r})$

Box & Pierce (1970) showed that the residual autocorrelations $\hat{r} = (\hat{r}_1, \ldots, \hat{r}_m)'$ from a correctly identified and fitted model can to a close approximation be represented as

$$\hat{r} \simeq (I-D)r,$$

where $I-D$ is an idempotent matrix of rank $m-p-q$. With this relationship the expectation of $Q(\hat{r})$ is

$$E\{Q(\hat{r})\} \simeq E\{nr'(I-D)r\} = \operatorname{tr}\{n(I-D)C\},$$

where C is the exact covariance matrix of r. The matrix D has its largest elements in the upper left corner with the remaining elements d_{ij} decreasing to zero as i and/or j increases. The matrix DC is therefore nearly equal to $n^{-1}D$. Using this approximation and noting that

$E\{Q(r)\} = \text{tr}(nC)$, we have

$$E\{Q(\hat{r})\} \simeq E\{Q(r)\} - p - q. \tag{3·1}$$

On combining (2·1) and (3·1), the expected value of $Q(\hat{r})$ is approximately

$$E\{Q(\hat{r})\} \simeq \frac{mn}{n+2}\left(1 - \frac{m+1}{2n}\right) - p - q, \tag{3·2}$$

which indicates that the distribution of $Q(\hat{r})$ can deviate markedly from χ^2_{m-p-q} unless n is large relative to m. However, using the same approximations it can be shown that

$$E\{\tilde{Q}(\hat{r})\} \simeq E\{\tilde{Q}(r)\} - p - q = m - p - q.$$

It may be expected therefore that the distribution of $\tilde{Q}(\hat{r})$ might be approximated by the χ^2_{m-p-q} distribution.

The adequacy of this approximation was questioned by Davies *et al.* (1977) on the ground that the variance of $\tilde{Q}(\hat{r})$ exceeds $2(m-p-q)$. However, results from a simulation study reported in the next section suggest that the reduction in the location bias results as before in a markedly improved approximation that should be adequate for most practical purposes It also appears that the expression for the variance given by Davies *et al.*, which is not exact, overestimates the variance of $\tilde{Q}(\hat{r})$. For example, for fitting a first-order autoregressive model to white noise, Davies *et al.* obtain for $m = 20$ and $n = 50$, 100 and 200, $\text{var}\{\tilde{Q}(\hat{r})\} = 58·80$, 50·08 and 44·20, respectively, while our study gives $\text{var}\{\tilde{Q}(\hat{r})\} = 46·84$, 43·20 and 41·97, respectively.

4. Some numerical results

4·1. *Comparison of the overall tests*

A Monte Carlo study was conducted by generating 4000 sets of observations $\{w_1, \ldots, w_n\}$ from the first-order autoregressive model $w_t - \phi w_{t-1} = a_t$, estimating ϕ by the approximate maximum likelihood estimator

$$(n-2)(n-1)^{-1} \sum_{t=2}^{n} w_t w_{t-1} \Big/ \sum_{t=2}^{n-1} w_t^2$$

(Box & Jenkins, 1970, p. 279), and calculating autocorrelations of the residuals $\hat{a}_1 = (1-\hat{\phi}^2)w_1$, $\hat{a}_t = w_t - \hat{\phi} w_{t-1}$ $(t = 2, \ldots, n)$. The statistics $Q(\hat{r})$ and $\tilde{Q}(\hat{r})$ were then calculated.

Table 1 shows the proportion of $Q(\hat{r})$ and $\tilde{Q}(\hat{r})$ values exceeding the upper 5, 10 and 25 percentage points of the χ^2_{m-1} distribution for a few combinations of n and m and for $\phi = 0·5$. The table also gives the means and variances of the observed distributions. It seems clear that although the variance of $\tilde{Q}(\hat{r})$ exceeds $2(m-1)$ a test based on this statistic would for smaller sample sizes provide a considerable improvement over the previously used $Q(\hat{r})$ test.

Table 1. *Empirical means, variances and significance levels of the statistics* $Q(\hat{r})$ *and* $\tilde{Q}(\hat{r})$; *data generated from the model* $w_t - \frac{1}{2}w_{t-1} = a_t$

		$Q(\hat{r})$					$\tilde{Q}(\hat{r})$				
					% level					% level	
n	m	Mean	Var.	5	10	25	Mean	Var.	5	10	25
50	10	7·48	13·79	2·3	4·7	13·4	8·82	19·11	5·3	9·5	23·0
	20	13·96	27·50	1·3	2·3	6·4	18·58	47·76	6·1	10·4	23·2
100	10	8·14	16·04	3·4	7·0	18·2	8·83	18·88	5·0	9·9	23·1
	20	16·26	35·45	2·5	5·0	13·1	18·63	46·46	5·8	10·2	22·8
	30	23·53	55·74	1·7	3·6	9·1	28·58	81·71	7·2	11·6	23·4
200	10	8·57	16·76	4·2	8·3	21·5	8·92	18·16	5·0	9·8	23·9
	20	17·46	36·36	3·5	6·9	17·6	18·66	41·51	5·4	10·0	22·7
	30	26·11	56·01	2·9	5·6	14·2	28·66	67·37	5·9	10·5	23·8

4·2. *An alternative test based on $Q(\hat{r})$*

The above results suggest that a closer approximation to the distribution of $Q(\hat{r})$ should be obtainable by appropriate adjustment of the mean of the approximating distribution. Furthermore, Table 1 shows values of var $\{Q(\hat{r})\}$ which are nearly twice the mean, suggesting the approximation $Q(\hat{r}) \sim \chi^2_{E\{Q(\hat{r})\}}$ with $E\{Q(\hat{r})\}$ given by (3·2). Empirical significance levels obtained using this approximation and the criterion $\tilde{Q}(\hat{r})$ are compared in Table 2. The agreement is quite close. It may however be more convenient generally to use $\tilde{Q}(\hat{r})$, since the test based on $Q(\hat{r})$ will have noninteger degrees of freedom.

Table 2. *Empirical significance levels based on the approximations $Q(\hat{r}) \sim \chi^2_{E\{Q(\hat{r})\}}$ and $\tilde{Q}(\hat{r}) \sim \chi^2_{m-1}$; data generated from the model $w_t - \phi w_{t-1} = a_t$*

		$Q(\hat{r}) \sim \chi^2_{E\{Q(\hat{r})\}}$						$\tilde{Q}(\hat{r}) \sim \chi^2_{m-1}$					
		$m = 10$			$m = 20$			$m = 10$			$m = 20$		
		% level						% level					
n	ϕ	5	10	25	5	10	25	5	10	25	5	10	25
50	0·1	4·1	8·3	21·2	4·6	8·1	20·9	4·7	9·3	21·4	5·9	10·1	22·5
	0·4	4·3	8·5	22·1	4·6	8·6	21·6	5·1	9·3	22·8	6·0	10·3	23·0
	0·7	4·7	9·5	23·3	5·1	9·6	22·6	5·4	10·1	23·6	6·7	11·3	24·0
100	0·1	4·3	8·8	23·4	5·1	9·3	22·2	4·7	9·3	23·5	5·9	10·0	22·7
	0·4	4·4	8·5	23·5	5·3	9·1	22·7	4·8	9·3	23·5	6·0	10·0	23·0
	0·7	4·7	9·0	24·1	5·6	9·6	22·7	4·9	9·4	24·0	6·2	10·3	23·2
200	0·1	5·0	9·6	24·1	5·2	9·8	22·7	5·2	9·9	24·2	5·5	10·2	23·2
	0·4	4·8	9·5	23·8	5·1	9·6	22·5	5·1	9·8	24·0	5·4	10·1	22·8
	0·7	4·8	9·9	24·1	4·9	10·0	22·5	5·0	10·1	24·2	5·3	10·5	22·8

4·3. *A power calculation*

The two criteria $Q(\hat{r})$ and $\tilde{Q}(\hat{r})$ differ in the weighting which is applied to the autocorrelations $\hat{r}_k$ with $\tilde{Q}(\hat{r})$ giving more emphasis to later autocorrelations than $Q(\hat{r})$. This would perhaps be an advantage if serial correlation occurs at high lags k. However, for large n this difference should be rather small. If the type of discrepancies to be expected is known, tests specifically aimed at detecting these discrepancies should be used. Such specific tests will of course be much more powerful. This point is illustrated in Table 3 which empirically compares the power of the overall tests and the method of "overfitting" (Box & Jenkins, 1970). The results are based on data generated from a second-order autoregressive model, with a first-order model being fitted to obtain $Q(\hat{r})$ and $\tilde{Q}(\hat{r})$. As might be expected, the overall tests

Table 3. *Empirical power of the overall tests and the method of overfitting for $n = 100$. Assumed model: $w_t - \phi w_{t-1} = a_t$; true model: $(1-0{\cdot}7B)(1-G_2 B)w_t = a_t$. Nominal significance level: 5%*

Test	m	$G_2 = 0$	$G_2 = 0{\cdot}1$	$G_2 = 0{\cdot}3$	$G_2 = 0{\cdot}5$	$G_2 = 0{\cdot}7$	$G_2 = 0{\cdot}9$
Overfitting		5·3	12·0	59·7	93·8	99·7	99·1
$Q(\hat{r}) \sim \chi^2_{E\{Q(\hat{r})\}}$	10	4·7	6·7	28·6	72·0	96·6	99·9
	20	5·6	7·3	24·4	62·8	93·7	99·7
	30	6·0	7·7	22·9	58·1	91·7	99·5
$\tilde{Q}(\hat{r}) \sim \chi^2_{m-1}$	10	4·9	7·0	28·9	71·6	96·2	99·9
	20	6·2	8·0	24·7	61·7	93·2	99·6
	30	7·0	9·0	23·7	57·0	90·5	99·3

are much less powerful than overfitting which tests the hypothesis that the second-order autoregressive coefficient is zero. A smaller value of m improves the power of the overall tests for this particular alternative.

4·4. *Effect of nonnormality of the a_t's*

In developing the overall test, it is assumed that the innovations a_t in the model are normally distributed. Circumstances occur where this assumption is not true. For example, it is known that stock price innovations often have highly leptokurtic distributions. Results by Anderson & Walker (1964) show that the asymptotic normality of the r_k's does not require normality of the a_t's, only that var (a_t) is finite. The overall test might therefore be expected to be insensitive to departures from normality of the a_t's. This is supported by Table 4, which shows the behaviour of $\tilde{Q}(\hat{r})$ when the a_t's have a double exponential and a uniform distribution. The results agree closely with those obtained under the normality assumption in Table 1.

Table 4. *Empirical means, variances and significance levels of $\tilde{Q}(\hat{r})$ when the innovations a_t have* (i) *a double exponential and* (ii) *a uniform distribution; data generated from the model*

$$w_t - \tfrac{1}{2}w_{t-1} = a_t$$

		(i) $a_t \sim$ double exponential					(ii) $a_t \sim$ uniform				
				% level					% level		
n	m	Mean	Var.	5	10	25	Mean	Var.	5	10	25
50	10	8·50	18·59	4·7	8·6	20·7	9·01	19·35	5·6	10·0	24·4
	20	17·77	47·00	5·4	8·8	19·6	18·95	52·39	7·3	12·1	24·3
100	10	8·80	18·70	5·0	9·1	22·4	9·11	19·41	5·5	10·8	25·3
	20	18·37	43·62	4·8	9·2	22·0	19·00	47·52	6·4	11·5	25·7
	30	27·94	76·60	6·3	10·1	21·9	28·98	81·72	7·5	12·4	25·3

5. Extension to transfer function noise models

To check the adequacy of the transfer function in the model

$$w_t = \frac{\omega(B)}{\delta(B)}\alpha_t + \frac{\theta(B)}{\phi(B)}a_t,$$

where

$$\omega(B)/\delta(B) = (\omega_0 - \omega_1 B - \ldots - \omega_u B^u)/(1 - \delta_1 B - \ldots - \delta_v B^v)$$

and where the input series $\{\alpha_t\}$ is assumed to be white noise and independent of $\{a_t\}$, it is useful to examine the cross-correlations between $\{\alpha_t\}$ and the residuals $\{\hat{a}_t\}$

$$\hat{r}_k^* = \sum_{t=k+1}^{n} \alpha_{t-k}\hat{a}_t \Big/ \left(\sum_{t=1}^{n} \alpha_t^2 \sum_{t=1}^{n} \hat{a}_t^2\right)^{1/2} \quad (k = 0, 1, \ldots).$$

D. A. Pierce in a University of Wisconsin technical report, Box & Jenkins (1970, § 11.3) and Pierce (1972) propose an overall test for lack of fit based on approximating the distribution of

$$S(\hat{r}^*) = n \sum_{k=0}^{m} (\hat{r}_k^*)^2$$

by the χ^2_{m-v-u} distribution. However, on arguing as above, it appears that a criterion of the form

$$\tilde{S}(\hat{r}^*) = n^2 \sum_{k=0}^{m} (n-k)^{-1}(\hat{r}_k^*)^2$$

would be more appropriate. The criterion $S(\hat{r}_k^*)$ is obtained by approximating the variance of the k-th sample cross-correlation between $\{\alpha_t\}$ and $\{a_t\}$ by $1/n$, while the actual variance is $(n-k)/n^2$.

The modification considered in the previous sections applies to the overall test for lack of fit in the noise model $\theta(B)/\phi(B)$ discussed by Box & Jenkins (1970, § 11.3).

This work was sponsored by the United States Army Research Office and the Air Force Office of Scientific Research.

References

Anderson, R. L. (1942). Distribution of the serial correlation coefficients. *Ann. Math. Statist.* **13**, 1–13.

Anderson, T. W. (1971). *The Statistical Analysis of Time Series*. New York: Wiley.

Anderson, T. W. & Walker, A. M. (1964). On the asymptotic distribution of the autocorrelations of a sample from a linear stochastic process. *Ann. Math. Statist.* **35**, 1296–303.

Box, G. E. P. & Jenkins, G. M. (1970). *Time Series Analysis Forecasting and Control*. San Francisco: Holden-Day.

Box, G. E. P. & Pierce, D. A. (1970). Distribution of residual autocorrelations in autoregressive-integrated moving average time series models. *J. Am. Statist. Assoc.* **65**, 1509–26.

Davies, N., Triggs, C. M. & Newbold, P. (1977). Significance levels of the Box–Pierce portmanteau statistic in finite samples. *Biometrika* **64**, 517–22.

Pierce, D. A. (1972). Residual correlations and diagnostic checking in dynamic-disturbance time series models. *J. Am. Statist. Assoc.* **67**, 636–40.

Prothero, D. L. & Wallis, K. F. (1976). Modelling macroeconomic time series (with discussion). *J. R. Statist. Soc.* A **139**, 468–500.

[*Received September* 1977. *Revised January* 1978]

[6]

Biometrika (1980), **67**, 2, *pp*. 359–63
Printed in Great Britain

Testing the specification of a fitted autoregressive-moving average model

BY D. S. POSKITT AND A. R. TREMAYNE
Department of Economics and Related Studies, University of York

SUMMARY

This paper provides an extension of the application of score, or Lagrangian multiplier, tests to diagnostic checking of ARMA, autoregressive-moving average, models. The score test procedure for testing the null hypothesis of an ARMA (p,q) process against certain ARMA $(p+r,q+s)$ alternatives is considered and shown to be of the form of a pure significance test.

Some key words: Autoregressive-moving average model; Significance test; Singular information matrix.

1. INTRODUCTION

Godfrey (1979) has provided a useful addition to the existing range of diagnostic checks for fitting an autoregressive-moving average, ARMA, model. We adopt the notation

$$\phi_{p+r}(B)\,x(t) = \theta_{q+s}(B)\,\varepsilon(t) \tag{1·1}$$

for the ARMA $(p+r, q+s)$ model, where

$$\phi_{p+r}(z) = 1-\phi_1 z-\phi_2 z^2-\ldots-\phi_{p+r}z^{p+r}, \quad \theta_{q+s}(z) = 1-\theta_1 z-\theta_2 z^2-\ldots-\theta_{q+s}z^{q+s}$$

have no common roots and B is the backward shift operator. It is further assumed that the standard stationarity and invertibility conditions hold and that $\varepsilon(t)$ is a Gaussian white noise process with mean zero and constant variance σ^2.

Godfrey's approach is to set up a hypothesis testing framework in which an assumed ARMA (p,q) model provides the null hypothesis $H(p,q)$ and the alternative is obtained by generalizing the form of the model, either to $H(p+r,q)$ or $H(p,q+s)$. It is then clear that the model of the null hypothesis simply imposes the restrictions $\phi_{p+i} = 0$ $(i = 1,\ldots,r)$ or $\theta_{q+i} = 0$ $(i = 1,\ldots,s)$ as appropriate. The adequacy of the assumed model is checked by employing the score or Lagrangian multiplier principle due to Rao (1948) and Silvey (1959) to test these restrictions using a sample of T observations. An advantage of using the score test is that, while it possesses the same desirable large sample properties as the likelihood ratio test, it requires estimation of only the most parsimonious model entertained and, furthermore, the test statistic is easily computed as T times a coefficient of determination from an auxiliary regression (Godfrey, 1979, pp. 68–9).

In many situations the researcher may wish to contemplate ARMA $(p+r,q+s)$ as the alternative model. Such an alternative is well known to lead to a singularity problem which means that standard large sample test procedures cannot be used. In the present paper we explore the usefulness of a procedure due to Silvey (1959) designed to modify the score test to cope with such problems. When testing $H(p,q)$ against a more general $H(p+r,q+s)$ alternative, it is necessary to impose restrictions on the parameter space of the alternative model to obtain identifiability. Alternatives restricted in this way will be termed admissible. It is demonstrated that the test is asymptotically insensitive to the particular set of restrictions chosen and that the same score test results as when explicitly testing the null hypothesis against alternative ARMA $(p+f, q)$ or ARMA $(p, q+f)$, where $f = \max(r, s)$. Consequently, the score test of $H(p,q)$ against any of the permitted range of alternatives may be viewed as a pure significance test (Cox & Hinkley, 1974, Chapter 3). Furthermore, it is shown that the useful computational device of representing the test statistic as T times a squared multiple correlation coefficient can be preserved when using the modified score test, and that, with this formulation, the invariance mentioned above is exact in finite samples. The practical implication of these results is that the researcher need only compute one statistic in order to test $H(p,q)$ against a range of alternative specifications.

2. TESTING ARMA $(p+r, q+s)$ ALTERNATIVES

To facilitate the development of score tests for autoregressive-moving average models it is useful to set $\beta = (\beta_0, \ldots, \beta_n)' = (\sigma^2, \phi_1, \ldots, \phi_{p+r}, \theta_1, \ldots, \theta_{q+s})'$. The log likelihood for the model (1·1) is

$$l(\beta) = k - \tfrac{1}{2}T \log \sigma^2 - (2\sigma^2)^{-1} \sum_{t=1}^{T} \varepsilon^2(t). \tag{2·1}$$

Let $\lambda = \partial l(.)/\partial \beta_i$ $(i = 1, \ldots, n)$ and let V be the $n \times n$ matrix of Fisher's information measure per observation corresponding to the parameters β_i $(i = 1, \ldots, n)$ of the ARMA $(p+r, q+s)$ model; see, for example, Box & Jenkins (1976, p. 240). In what follows an asterisk is used to denote evaluation of these quantities using the maximum likelihood estimates of the parameters of the ARMA (p,q) model of the null hypothesis. Godfrey's test statistic when either r or s equals zero is based upon

$$S_1 = T^{-1} \lambda^{*\prime} V^{*-1} \lambda^{*}. \tag{2·2}$$

Suppose that the order of both the autoregressive and moving average components is increased, that is $H(p,q)$ is to be tested against $H(p+r, q+s)$. In these circumstances, V is singular (Hannan, 1970, pp. 413–4). Let the theoretical autocovariance generating function of $x(t)$ be denoted by $\gamma_{xx}(z)$ and the theoretical cross-covariance generating function between $x(t)$ and $\varepsilon(t)$ be $\gamma_{x\varepsilon}(z)$; the singularity can be clearly seen by noting that the polynomial generating equations

$$\gamma_{xx}(z)\, \phi_p(z^{-1}) = \gamma_{x\varepsilon}(z)\, \theta_q(z^{-1}), \quad \gamma_{x\varepsilon}(z)\, \phi_p(z) = \sigma^2\, \theta_q(z) \tag{2·3}$$

imply that $V w_0 = 0$, where $w_0 = (1, -\phi_1, -\phi_2, \ldots, -\phi_p, 0, 0, \ldots, 0, 1, -\theta_1, -\theta_2 \ldots -\theta_q, 0, \ldots, 0)'$. A consequence of the singularity present is that conventional large sample test procedures are not available. The results of Silvey (1959, §6), however, suggest that if the rank of V is $n-g$, then a test may be based upon the statistic

$$S_2 = T^{-1} \lambda^{*\prime} (V^{*} + G_1 G_1')^{-1} \lambda^{*}, \tag{2·4}$$

where G_1 is an appropriate $n \times g$ submatrix of G, the matrix of partial derivatives of the restrictions implicit in the null hypothesis. This statistic is asymptotically distributed χ^2_{r+s-g}, a chi-squared variate with $r+s-g$ degrees of freedom, when the null hypothesis is true, significantly large values of S_2 indicating that the restrictions imposed are not consistent with the sample data.

Aitchison & Silvey (1960, §6) show that the adaptation of the score test procedure, using the matrix G_1 to circumvent the singularity problem, is equivalent to the requirement that g parameter restrictions hold in order to obtain identifiability. Equations (2·3) can be employed to show that $g = \min(r, s)$ and, for example, if the restrictions are simple exclusions, the form of G is such that the matrix $G_1 G_1'$ is null apart from $\min(r,s)$ ones placed appropriately along the diagonal. The position of a one implies that the corresponding element of β is assumed to be zero under null and alternative hypotheses. The choice of G_1, however, is not arbitrary in that one must ensure that $V+G_1 G_1'$ is nonsingular in order to employ the statistic (2·4), but, subject to this proviso, the relationship between the asymptotic properties of this statistic and that of Godfrey is presented in the following theorem.

THEOREM 1. *The score tests for testing $H(p,q)$ against $H(p+f,q)$ or $H(p,q+f)$ using* (2·2) *and against any admissable $H(p+r,q+s)$, $f=\max(r,s)$, using* (2·4) *are asymptotically identical. An alternative of this last form is admissable provided there exists a matrix G_1 such that $V+G_1 G_1'$ is nonsingular when the null hypothesis is true.*

Proof. The proof follows in two parts, first by demonstrating that the test statistic of (2·4) is asymptotically invariant with respect to the choice of G_1 and, secondly, by showing that the modified score test is asymptotically identical to the explicit test.

When the alternative is admissible we have (Rao, 1973, p. 34, problem 5) that $(V+G_1 G_1')^{-1} = V^-$, a generalized inverse of V, and, furthermore, λ asymptotically belongs to $\mathscr{M}(V)$, the vector space generated by the columns of V. The invariance property is now a consequence of Rao (1973, § 1b. 5, (vi), (c)). T. S. Breusch, in his unpublished Australian National Univ. thesis, notes that, if Silvey's modified score test satisfies conditions of the above form, then it is asymptotically unaffected by the choice of generalized inverse; see also Rao & Mitra (1971, § 10·4).

Legitimate choices of G_1 are made provided that $G_1 G_1'$ is not annihilated by any of the eigenvectors corresponding to zero eigenvalues of V, since this matrix and $G_1 G_1'$ are positive-semidefinite. The g such eigenvectors of V are given by $w_j = B^j w_0$ for $j=0, \min(r,s)-1$, where w_0 is as above and B is the block diagonal matrix, $\mathrm{diag}(C_{p+r}, C_{q+s})$, with C_m the $m \times m$ circulant with initial row $(0,0,\ldots,0,1)$. It follows that $H(p+f,q)$ and $H(p,q+f)$, $f=\max(r,s)$, are admissible alternatives. These hypotheses imply a matrix $G_1 G_1'$ whose rows and columns can be reordered to give

$$G_1 G_1' = \left[\begin{array}{c:c} 0 & 0 \\ \hdashline 0 & 1_g \end{array}\right],$$

where the rows and columns are partitioned into parts of sizes $p+q+f$ and g. Similarly V may be rearranged to obtain

$$\left[\begin{array}{c:c} V_{11} & V_{12} \\ \hdashline V_{21} & V_{22} \end{array}\right].$$

The matrix V_{11} is the nonsingular information matrix of the parameters of an implicitly specified ARMA $(p+f,q)$ or ARMA $(p,q+f)$ alternative. Recall that, asymptotically, $\lambda \in \mathscr{M}(V)$ and that the rank of V is $p+q+f$ and so, asymptotically,

$$\lambda = \begin{bmatrix} \lambda_1 \\ \lambda_2 \end{bmatrix} = \begin{bmatrix} V_{11} y \\ V_{21} y \end{bmatrix}$$

for some $p+q+f$ element vector y. After standard application of partitioned inversion formulae to $(V+G_1 G_1')$, it follows from straightforward but tedious algebra that $\lambda' V^- \lambda = \lambda_1' V_{11}^{-1} \lambda_1$, asymptotically, and thus the theorem is proved.

It seems likely in time series applications that the parameter restrictions imposed on the model of the alternative hypothesis will be of the simple exclusion type, although this need not be the case (Aitchison & Silvey, 1960, §§7, 8). When the restrictions are of this form,

$$G' = \begin{bmatrix} 0 & 1_r & 0 & 0 \\ 0 & 0 & 0 & 1_s \end{bmatrix},$$

where the columns are partitioned into sets of size p, r, q and s and the rows into r and s. It can be shown that $G_1 G_1' w_j \neq 0$ for $j = 0, \ldots, \min(r,s)-1$ provided that at least one of the $(i-j)$th columns for $j = 0, \ldots, \min(i-1,p)$ or the $(r+i-k)$th columns, $k = 0, \ldots, \min(i-1,q)$ for all $i = 1, \ldots, \min(r,s)$, are included in G_1. This condition may be equivalently stated in terms of the coefficients of the model in that restricting at least one of ϕ_{p+i-j}, for $j = 0, \ldots, \min(i-1,p)$, θ_{q+i-k} for $k = 0, \ldots, \min(i-1,q)$ both for all $i = 1, \min(r,s)$ to be zero ensures that the alternative model is identifiable when the null hypothesis is true.

An attractive feature of the tests of linear time series models advocated by Godfrey is that, apart from an asymptotically negligible nonzero sample mean correction, they are easily computed as T times a squared multiple correlation coefficient. We now show that the modified score test may also be represented in this way and, moreover, that the two statistics then yield the same value.

THEOREM 2. *When formulated as T times a coefficient of determination, the statistics* (2·2) *and* (2·4) *are numerically identical.*

Proof. Let $\varepsilon = \{\varepsilon(1), \ldots, \varepsilon(T)\}'$ and $X' = [\partial\varepsilon(t)/\partial\beta_i]$ $(i = 1, \ldots, n;\ t = 1, \ldots, T)$, where β has been reordered so that the first $p+q+f$ elements correspond to the parameters of either ARMA $(p+f, q)$ or ARMA $(p, q+f)$ models. Further, let $X = [X_1 : X_2]$, where X_1 is $T \times (p+q+f)$. Then we may write the statistic (2·3) of Godfrey (1979, p. 68) and (2·2) of the present paper as

$$S_1 = T\varepsilon^{*\prime} X_1^* (X_1^{*\prime} X_1^*)^{-1} X_1^{*\prime} \varepsilon^* / (\varepsilon^{*\prime}\varepsilon^*), \tag{2·5}$$

which is, with the caveat mentioned above, T times the R^2 obtained by regressing ε^* on X_1^*. Further setting $\varepsilon_a' = [\varepsilon' : 0]$ and $X_a' = [X' : G_1]$ we have that

$$S_2 = T\varepsilon_a^{*\prime} X_a^* (X_a^{*\prime} X_a^*)^{-1} X_a^{*\prime} \varepsilon_a^* / (\varepsilon_a^{*\prime}\varepsilon_a^*) \tag{2·6}$$

or TR^2 from the regression of ε_a^* on X_a^*. Clearly $\varepsilon_a^{*\prime} X_a^* = \varepsilon^{*\prime} X^*$ and $(X_a^{*\prime} X_a^*)^{-1}$ is a generalized inverse of $X^{*\prime}X^*$. As $\varepsilon^{*\prime}X^* \in \mathscr{M}(X^{*\prime}X^*)$ the quadratic form of (2·6) is invariant with respect to the choice of g-inverse. Finally, the $n \times n$ matrix with $(X_1^{*\prime}X_1^*)^{-1}$ in the north-west corner and zeros elsewhere is a g-inverse of $X^{*\prime}X^*$ and hence (2·5) and (2·6) are numerically equal.

3. Concluding remarks

A corollary of the results established in this paper is that Godfrey's statistic for testing $H(p,q)$ against either $H(p+r,q)$ or $H(p,q+r)$ is numerically invariant and, in fact, tests against a wide range of misspecifications. We conclude that, once the value of $f = \max(r,s)$ has been chosen, only one statistic need be computed to test the fitted model against any valid ARMA $(p+r, q+s)$ alternative. This suggests that, although when applying score in contrast to portmanteau tests, a hypothesis against which to test must be specified, the former may be thought of as resembling a pure significance test.

The authors thank T. S. Breusch, L. G. Godfrey and the referee for helpful comments and suggestions.

References

AITCHISON, J. & SILVEY, S. D. (1960). Maximum-likelihood estimation procedures and associated tests of significance. *J. R. Statist. Soc.* B **22**, 154–71.
BOX, G. E. P. & JENKINS, G. M. (1976). *Time Series Analysis: Forecasting and Control*, 2nd edition. San Francisco: Holden-Day.
COX, D. R. & HINKLEY, D. V. (1974). *Theoretical Statistics*. London: Chapman and Hall.
GODFREY, L. G. (1979). Testing the adequacy of a time series model. *Biometrika* **66**, 67–72.
HANNAN, E. J. (1970). *Multiple Time Series*. New York: Wiley.
RAO, C. R. (1948). Large sample tests of statistical hypotheses concerning several parameters with applications to problems of estimation. *Proc. Camb. Phil. Soc.* **44**, 50–9.
RAO, C. R. (1973). *Linear Statistical Inference and its Applications*, 2nd edition. New York: Wiley.
RAO, C. R. & MITRA, S. K. (1971). *Generalized Inverse of Matrices and its Applications*. New York: Wiley.
SILVEY, S. D. (1959). The Lagrangian multiplier test. *Ann. Math. Statist.* **30**, 389–407.

[*Received May* 1979. *Revised January* 1980]

[7]

Appl. Statist. (1976),
25, *No.* 3, p. 195

Comparison of Forecast and Actuality

By G. E. P. Box and G. C. Tiao
University of Wisconsin, Madison, U.S.A.
[Received February 1975. Revised November 1975]

Summary

The paper shows how possible change in a system generating a time series may be studied by comparing forecasts made from a model built on data prior to the suspected change with data actually occurring. An environmental example illustrates the decomposition of the overall criterion into relevant components and shows how difficulties can occur in distinguishing alternative models for change. The relation to surveillance problems and to intervention analysis is briefly discussed.

Keywords: FORECAST; PARAMETER CHANGES; SURVEILLANCE; INTERVENTION ANALYSIS; OZONE LEVEL; POLLUTION CONTROL

1. Introduction

Suppose a system has been subjected to a change. A natural way to consider the possible effect of that change is to compare, with actuality, forecasts made from a stochastic model which was appropriate before the change. Such a model determines the probability structure of its forecast errors and a specified change in the model results in a calculable change in that structure. Hence, appropriate functions of the forecast errors may be calculated which point to specific changes in the model.

The object of this paper is to illustrate this, using some environmental data. One point that emerges is that changes in the model of different kinds may not be easily distinguishable.

2. A Time Series Model for the Ozone Data

Following notation and methodology used for example in Box and Jenkins (1970), denote a time series by the sequence $\ldots z_{t-1}, z_t, z_{t+1}, \ldots$. Also define a *white noise* series $\ldots a_{t-1}, a_t, a_{t+1}, \ldots$ as a sequence of independently and normally distributed random *shocks* with mean zero and variance σ^2. The values z_t of the time series are then supposed to be generated by the *linear filtering* operation

$$z_t = \psi(B)\, a_t, \tag{1}$$

where $\psi(B) = 1+\psi_1 B+\psi_2 B^2+\ldots$ and B is the back shift operator such that $Ba_t = a_{t-1}$. Alternatively, the model may be written in the form $\pi(B)\, z_t = a_t$, where

$$\pi(B) = \psi^{-1}(B) = 1-\pi_1 B-\pi_2 B^2-\ldots.$$

For 180 successive values from January 1956 to December 1970 of the monthly average atmospheric ozone concentration at Azusa, California, Tiao *et al.* (1975), obtained a model with

$$\psi(B) = \frac{(1-\theta_1 B)(1-\theta_2 B^{12})}{1-B^{12}}, \quad \theta_1 = -0{\cdot}15,\ \theta_2 = 0{\cdot}91 \quad \text{and} \quad \sigma^2 = 1{\cdot}00. \tag{2}$$

This model was used to produce minimum mean square error forecasts (all from the origin December 1970) for the next 24 months. They are compared in Fig. 1 with what actually happened.

The comparison is of interest because new automobile emissions standards were introduced at the end of 1970. The diagram gives the impression that after 1970 the levels were lower than expected, but caution is needed because (i) forecasts are subject to error, (ii) for forecasts

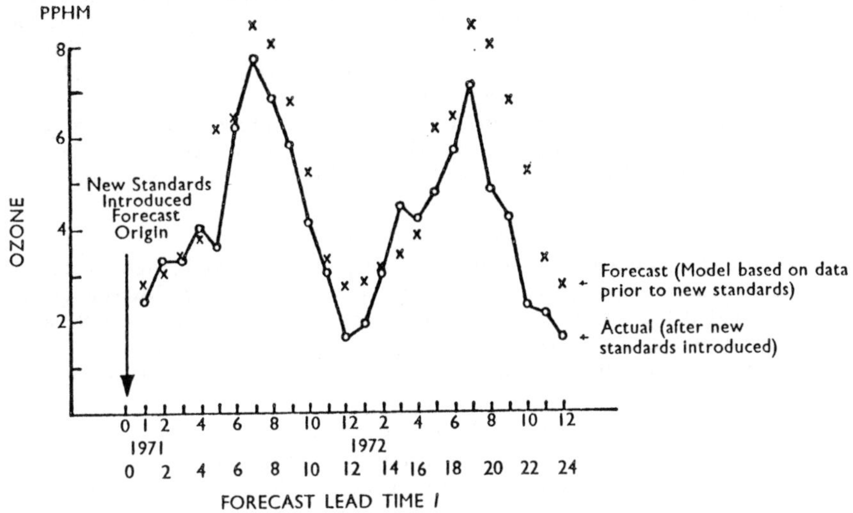

FIG. 1. Forecasts made in December 1970 of ozone concentration at Azusa, California, compared with actuality.

made from the same origin, successive forecast errors for the model in (2) are necessarily highly positively correlated giving a false impression of the consistency of discrepancies.

3. An Overall Check

The minimum mean square error forecast of z_l made at an origin conveniently taken to be zero is denoted by $\hat{z}(l)$, where $l = 1, 2, \ldots$, is called the lead time. It is readily shown that the lead l forecast error $e_l = z_l - \hat{z}(l)$ is given by

$$e_l = \sum_{j=1}^{l} \psi_{l-1} a_j, \tag{3}$$

where $\psi_0 = 1$. Now, for the forecasts of $z_1, \ldots, z_m$, writing $\mathbf{a}' = (a_1, \ldots, a_m)$ and $\mathbf{e}' = (e_1, \ldots, e_m)$ the transformation from random shocks to forecast errors is $\mathbf{e} = \boldsymbol{\psi}\mathbf{a}$, where $\boldsymbol{\psi}$ is an $m \times m$ lower triangular matrix with diagonal elements equal to unity, first subdiagonal elements equal to ψ_1, second subdiagonal element equal to ψ_2, and so on. Conversely, $\mathbf{a} = \boldsymbol{\pi}\mathbf{e}$ where $\boldsymbol{\pi} = \boldsymbol{\psi}^{-1}$, and it is readily confirmed that $\boldsymbol{\pi}$ is an $m \times m$ lower triangular matrix with diagonal elements equal to unity and the jth subdiagonal elements equal to $-\pi_j$, $j = 1, \ldots, m-1$.

Now the $m \times m$ covariance matrix for the vector $\mathbf{e}$ is $\mathbf{V} = E(\mathbf{ee}') = \boldsymbol{\psi}\boldsymbol{\psi}'\sigma^2$. It follows that if the original model is appropriate during the period $l = 1, \ldots, m$, then $Q = \mathbf{e}'\mathbf{V}^{-1}\mathbf{e}$ is distributed as χ^2 with m degrees of freedom, where $\mathbf{V}^{-1} = \boldsymbol{\pi}'\boldsymbol{\pi}/\sigma^2$. If, on the other hand, the model changes in some way we may expect that Q will be inflated.

Now rather than compute Q from the e_l, it is easier to employ the identity

$$Q = \mathbf{e}'\mathbf{V}^{-1}\mathbf{e} = \mathbf{e}'\boldsymbol{\pi}'\boldsymbol{\pi}\mathbf{e}/\sigma^2 = \mathbf{a}'\mathbf{a}/\sigma^2 = \sigma^{-2}\sum_{l=1}^{m} a_l^2. \tag{4}$$

Thus, Q is the standardized sum of squares of the one-step ahead forecast errors, $a_1, \ldots, a_m$, and as we suggested in our joint paper with Hamming, an overall test of the continuing appropriateness of the model during the period $l = 1, \ldots, m$ is achieved by referring Q to a χ^2 table with m degrees of freedom. Further, this is equivalent to the appropriate test applied to all the lead l forecast errors e_l, $l = 1, \ldots, m$.

Since in practice σ^2 is estimated from n data values to which, say, p parameters have been fitted, a closer approximation might refer $\hat{Q}/m$, where $\hat{Q} = \hat{\sigma}^{-2} \sum_{l=1}^{m} a_l^2$, to an F table with m and $n-p$ degrees of freedom. However, when n is large, this refinement would make little difference to the result which is in any case approximate since it does not allow† for errors of estimates of the parameters of the original series.

For the ozone data and with the model fitted to the 180 observations $z_{-180}, z_{-179}, \ldots, z_{-1}$, occurring before 1971, we find that $\hat{Q} = 36{\cdot}0$ which is close to the 5 per cent value of χ^2 with 24 degrees of freedom and suggests that the deviations from the forecast are real.

4. Components of χ^2

The quantity Q provides an overall criterion having, like all overall criteria, the advantage that it is unnecessary to be specific about the nature of the feared discrepancy, but the disadvantage that it lacks sensitivity when compared with a more specific criterion which *assumes* that we have guessed correctly what to be afraid of. We now illustrate how the Q statistic may be decomposed into components associated with various relevant alternatives.

4.1. *Relevant Alternatives*

The implication of the overall χ^2 test is that after 1970 the model has changed in some way or other. In speculating on *how* it has changed, we must on the one hand confront theoretical explanations (generated by knowledge of the system) with the data, and on the other allow examination of the data, and particularly of residuals, to suggest theoretical explanations. In particular, it becomes important to know the species of basic patterns which different kinds of discrepancies would inject into the residuals.

"Off the cuff" conjectures would certainly include (a) a change in level of z_t, (*b*) a change in one or both of the stochastic parameters θ_1 and θ_2. However, those having knowledge of the chemistry and meteorology involved pointed out that it was only during the "summer" months (June–October) that the new emission standard would be expected to make much difference; also, it was known that the number of cars fitted with the new control devices would be roughly twice as high in the second year as in the first. This suggested that we might expect (c) a shift in level of z_t in the summers only, with the shift in the second summer about twice that in the first. For reference purposes we refer to this last possibility as the "Met model".

Possibilities (a) and (c) above can be allowed for by substituting $z_t - \sum_{j=1}^{k} \beta_j x_{jt}$ for z_t in the model (1), where β_j are parameters and x_{jt} are appropriate indicator variables. In all cases, x_{jt} would be zero before $t = 0$. For example, to accommodate model (a) we can set $k = 1$, $x_{1l} = 1$, $l = 1, \ldots, 24$; and to accommodate model (c) we can set $k = 2$ with $\beta_1 = 0$ and $x_{2l} = 1$, for $l = 6, 7, 8, 9, 10$, $x_{2l} = 2$ for $l = 18, 19, 20, 21, 22$ and $x_{2l} = 0$ elsewhere. The same general device can, of course, be used to model other changes believed to affect z_t directly such as time trends and new exogenous variables. Allowing these possibilities our model can be written

$$a_t = \pi(B)\left(z_t - \sum_{j=1}^{k} \beta_j x_{jt}\right). \tag{5}$$

To determine the effect of changes in the parameters of the stochastic model, suppose that, prior to time zero, $\pi(B) = \pi_0(B)$ and the stochastic parameters included in the model had

† To gain some idea of how close the approximation is, a brief investigation of this source of error was made for an autoregressive process of order p. With estimates based on n initial observations, estimation errors inflate the mean value of χ^2 calculated from (4) by a factor approximating $1 + (p/n)$.

values $\theta_{10}, \ldots, \theta_{r0}$. Further, suppose that using these values the calculated shocks were $a_{0,1}, \ldots, a_{0,m}$.

Then, after expansion, approximately

$$a_{0,l} \doteq \sum_{j=1}^{k} \beta_j X_{jl} + \sum_{i=1}^{r} (\theta_i - \theta_{i0}) W_{il} + a_l, \tag{6}$$

where

$$X_{jl} = \pi_0(B)\, x_{jl}, \quad W_{il} = \left.\frac{-\partial a_l}{\partial \theta_i}\right|_0^{\prime}.$$

The values of $X_{1l}, X_{2l}, W_{1l}, W_{2l}$ corresponding to β_1, β_2, θ_1 and θ_2 for the ozone example are plotted in Fig. 2 together with the values of $a_{0,l}$. The speculations mentioned above imply that the residuals $a_{0,l}$ contain a deterministic component proportional either to X_{1l}, X_{2l}, W_{1l} or W_{2l} or to some linear combinations of them.

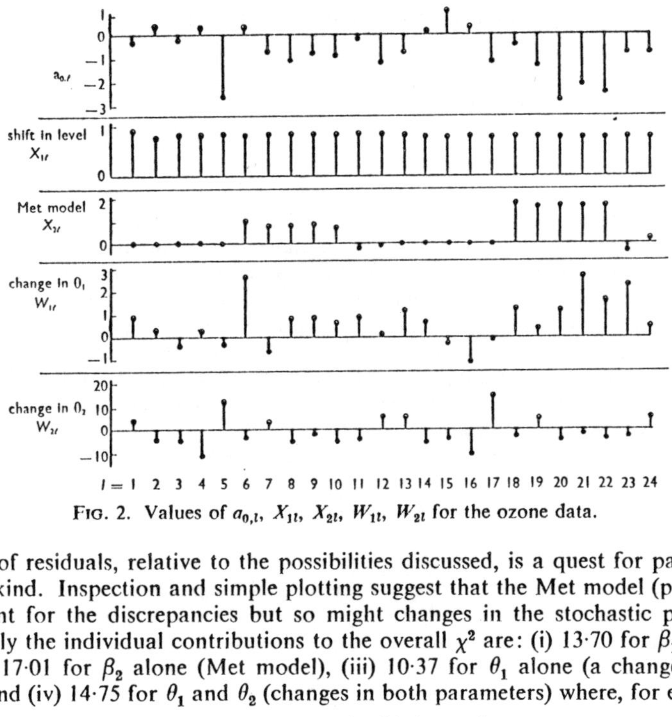

FIG. 2. Values of $a_{0,l}$, X_{1l}, X_{2l}, W_{1l}, W_{2l} for the ozone data.

Analysis of residuals, relative to the possibilities discussed, is a quest for patterns of the appropriate kind. Inspection and simple plotting suggest that the Met model (possibility (c)) might account for the discrepancies but so might changes in the stochastic parameter θ_1. More precisely the individual contributions to the overall χ^2 are: (i) 13·70 for β_1 alone (level change), (ii) 17·01 for β_2 alone (Met model), (iii) 10·37 for θ_1 alone (a change of the first parameter) and (iv) 14·75 for θ_1 and θ_2 (changes in both parameters) where, for example,

$$13{\cdot}70 = \left(\sum_{l=1}^{24} a_{0,l} X_{1l}\right)^2 \Big/ \left(\sum_{l=1}^{24} X_{1l}^2 \sigma^2\right).$$

If we fit equation (6) by least squares, we have

$$\hat{\beta}_1 = -0{\cdot}43, \quad \hat{\beta}_2 = -0{\cdot}71, \quad \theta_1 - \theta_{10} = -0{\cdot}11, \quad \theta_2 - \theta_{20} = -0{\cdot}07.$$
$$(0{\cdot}24) \qquad\quad (0{\cdot}24) \qquad\qquad\quad (0{\cdot}18) \qquad\qquad\quad (0{\cdot}02)$$

From the analysis of the overall χ^2 given in Table 1 it may be concluded that:

(i) much of the forecast discrepancy can be explained by the Met model associated with β_2 alone;

(ii) after the contribution of that model is taken account of, additional contributions from level shift β_1 and shift in θ_1 are not substantial;

(iii) there is, however, evidence of a slight but significant shift in θ_2.

In connection with this last component it must be remembered that the "Met model" given here is rather rough. Ideally it should take more accurate account of the increase in cars fitted with new engines, and also of the differential effectiveness of the new engines at different seasons. These inadequacies could produce pseudo-seasonal components and hence the apparent need for a slight change in θ_2 which was found.

TABLE 1

Analysis of χ^2 showing contributions of possible discrepancies

Source	*d.f.*	χ^2
Due to β_2 (Met model)	1	17·0
Extra for β_1 (Level shift)	1	2·5
Extra for shift in θ_1	1	0·7
Extra for shift in θ_2	1	5·0
Remainder	20	10·8
Total	24	36·0

A possibility which seems most worrisome to many users of time series analysis, and tends to come to mind first, is that the stochastic parameters determining the "memory" of the system may change by amounts sufficient to cause serious inaccuracies in forecasts. Now it should be noted that if the only possibility tested in the above example had been that θ_1 and θ_2 might have changed, the large contribution of 14·75 to χ^2 might have seemed totally convincing, and also θ_1 would have been identified as the major contributor. The above analysis cannot, of course, prove that a change in θ_1 has not occurred. It does show, however, that if level changes in z_t of a kind that makes practical sense are taken account of, the evidence that a change in θ_1 is needed, vanishes.

This is, of course, because the possibilities considered are closely related. Changes in level of z_t associated with such variables as X_{1t} and X_{2t} will obviously produce serial correlation in $a_{0,t}$. But consider also the residual component produced by a change in the parameter θ_1. This is

$$W_{1t} = -\frac{\partial a_t}{\partial \theta_1}\bigg|_0 = -(1-\theta_{10}B)^{-1}a_{0,t-1}.$$

Since θ_{10} is small in magnitude, the corresponding contribution to χ^2 is roughly

$$\left(\sum_{t=2}^{m} a_{0,t}a_{0,t-1}\right)^2 \bigg/ \left(\sum_{t=2}^{m} a_{0,t-1}^2\right)\sigma^2 = \sigma^{-2}\sum_{t=2}^{m} a_{0,t-1}^2 r_1^2,$$

where r_1 is the sample autocorrelation at lag 1 of the $a_{0,t}$. Thus, changes in level of z_t as well as changes in θ_1 are detected by the existence of serial correlation in the residuals. It follows that, although in this example the residuals $a_{0,t}$ are obviously serially correlated, this need not mean that θ_1 has changed.

Investigations as to whether, where and how often changes in stochastic parameters might occur *in real series* are not easy to carry out and little seems to have been done. One result that is clear, however, from the above discussion is that in any such investigation all plausible possibilities ought to be considered and we should not jump too hastily to the conclusion that shifts are necessarily due to changes in stochastic parameters.

5. Relation to Surveillance of Forecasting Systems

The ozone data used for illustration are here presented in the manner which we first received them—complete in December 1972. The problem we have discussed is, however, related to, but is different from, the problem of *sequential* surveillance of routine forecasting schemes. In that problem, data in the form of one-step ahead forecast errors from an operating scheme are available sequentially and a continuous monitoring is carried out to detect possible changes in the model. An early suggestion was that the a_t be plotted on a cumulative sum chart. This usually provides a good catch-all criterion and for the present data such a chart points strongly to the possibility of change although not, of course, to its specific nature. The essential idea involved in the CUSUM chart is the sequential plotting of the likelihood ratio statistic. If a change in *level* of the a_t themselves is being sought this leads at once to the criterion of the cumulative sum. However, as was pointed out, for example by Box and Jenkins (1966), for other alternatives such as a change in levels of one or more of the stochastic parameters, different cumulative plotting methods are appropriate. Some of these are discussed by Ledolter (1975) in a recent thesis.

6. Relation with Intervention Analysis

In our earlier work (1965, 1975) methods were described for estimating the effect of an "intervention" at a known point in a time series.

This situation differed from that discussed here in that the parameters of the time series model were estimated from substantial quantities of data available after, as well as before, the intervention.

However, these earlier methods can perfectly well be applied to examples like the present one and the results will be essentially similar if the period after the intervention is short. We believe the present procedure is worth separate consideration because of its simplicity and intuitive appeal. It is very natural to learn about a system by comparing a set of forecasts made at some point of possible change with actuality.

Acknowledgement

This research was supported in part by a grant from the American Petroleum Institute and in part by U.S. Army Research Office under Grant DA-ARO-D-31-124-72-G162.

References

Box, G. E. P. and Jenkins, G. M. (1966). Models for prediction and control. VI. Diagnostic checking. Tech. Report No. 99, Department of Statistics, University of Wisconsin, Madison.

—— (1970). *Time Series Analysis, Forecasting and Control.* San Francisco: Holden-Day.

Box, G. E. P. and Tiao, G. C. (1965). A change in level of a non-stationary time series. *Biometrika*, **52**, 181–192.

—— (1975). Intervention analysis with applications to economic and environmental problems. *J. Amer. Statist. Ass.*, **70**, 70–79.

Ledolter, J. (1975). Topics in time series analysis. Ph.D. Thesis, Department of Statistics, University of Wisconsin, Madison.

Tiao, G. C., Box, G. E. P. and Hamming, W. J. (1975). Analysis of Los Angeles photochemical smog data: a statistical overview. *J. Air Pollution Control Ass.*, **25**, 260–268.

[8]

THE ESTIMATION AND APPLICATION OF LONG MEMORY TIME SERIES MODELS

By John Geweke and Susan Porter-Hudak[1]

Department of Economics, Duke University

Abstract. The definitions of fractional Gaussian noise and integrated (or fractionally differenced) series are generalized, and it is shown that the two concepts are equivalent. A new estimator of the long memory parameter in these models is proposed, based on the simple linear regression of the log periodogram on a deterministic regressor. The estimator is the ordinary least squares estimator of the slope parameter in this regression, formed using only the lowest frequency ordinates of the log periodogram. Its asymptotic distribution is derived, from which it is evident that the conventional interpretation of these least squares statistics is justified in large samples. Using synthetic data the asymptotic theory proves to be reliable in samples of 50 observations or more. For three postwar monthly economic time series, the estimated integrated series model provides more reliable out-of-sample forecasts than do more conventional procedures.

Keywords. Fractional differencing, Long-memory, Integrated models

1. Introduction

In the most widely applied models for stationary time series the spectral density function is bounded at the frequency $\lambda = 0$ and the autocorrelation function decays exponentially. This is true in stable autoregressive moving average models, and it is characteristic of estimates obtained by nonparametric spectral methods, for example. Yet these properties do not appear widely characteristic of many time series (Hurst, 1951; Granger and Joyeux, 1980). The failure of these models to represent the spectral density at low frequencies adequately suggests that many-step-ahead forecasts obtained using these models could be inferior to those produced by models that permit unbounded spectral densities at $\lambda = 0$ and autocorrelation functions that do not decay exponentially. Limited empirical evidence to this effect has been reported by Granger and Joyeux, and is supported by somewhat more extensive investigations reported by Porter-Hudak (1982).

Attention has recently been given to two single-parameter models in which the spectral density function is proportional to λ^{-r}, $1 < r < 2$, for λ near 0, and the asymptotic decay of the autocorrelation function is proportional to τ^{r-1}. Because the spectral density function is unbounded at $\lambda = 0$—equivalently, the autocorrelation function is not summable—these are *long memory models* (defined by McLeod and Hipel, 1978).

The earlier model was introduced by Mandelbrot and Van Ness (1968) and Mandelbrot (1971) to formalize Hurst's empirical findings using cumulative river flow data. Let $Y_t = \int_{-\infty}^{t} (t-s)^{H-1/2}\, dB(s)$, where $B(s)$ is Brownian motion and $H \in (0,1)$. Then $X_t = Y_t - Y_{t-1}$ is a *simple fractional Gaussian noise*. (We have

0143-5782/83/04 0221-18 $02.50/0
JOURNAL OF TIME SERIES ANALYSIS Vol. 4, No. 4

added the word 'simple' to the definition given in the literature, to emphasize the difference between that model and the extension of it introduced here.) Jonas (1981) has shown that its spectral density is

$$f_1(\lambda; H) = \sigma^2(2\pi)^{-2H-2}\Gamma(2H+1)\sin(\pi H)4\sin^2(\lambda/2)\sum_{n=-\infty}^{\infty}|n+(\lambda/2\pi)|^{-2H-1}.$$

(We use the convention that the spectral density of a time series $\{X_t\}$ is $f(\lambda) = \sum_{s=-\infty}^{\infty} R_x(s)\exp(-i\lambda s)$, where $R_x(s)$ is the autocovariance function of $\{X_t\}$.) A little manipulation of this expression shows that

$$\lim_{\lambda\to 0}\lambda^{2H-1}f_1(\lambda; H) = (2\sigma^2/\pi)\Gamma(2H+1)\sin(\pi H).$$

The corresponding autocorrelation function is

$$\rho_1(\tau; H) = .5(|\tau-1|^{2H} - 2|\tau|^{2H} + |\tau+1|^{2H}).$$

A Taylor series expansion in $(\tau-1)/\tau$ and $(\tau+1)/\tau$ shows

$$\lim_{\tau\to\infty}\tau^{2-2H}\rho_1(\tau; H) = H(2H-1),$$

and from the Schwarz inequality $\rho_1(\tau; H) \gtreqless 0$ for $\tau \neq 0$ as $H \gtreqless .5$. In empirical work interest has centered on the cases $.5 < H < 1$.

The fractional Gaussian noise model is designed to account for the long term behaviour of the time series in question. Realistically, it seems unlikely that all the second moment properties of the series would be well described by any single-parameter function, but shorter term behaviour could be modelled by more conventional means. Toward this end, $\{X_t\}$ will be said to be a *general fractional Gaussian noise* if its spectral density is of the form $f_1(\lambda; H)f_u(\lambda)$ where $f_u(\lambda)$ is a positive continuous function bounded above and away from zero on the interval $[-\pi, \pi]$. The spectral density $f_u(\lambda)$ therefore is that of a short memory time series (McLeod and Hippel) with autoregressive representation (Rozanov, 1967, pp. 77–78). This class of models is broad: it includes, for example, time series arising from $\phi(B)X_t = \theta(B)X_t'$, where $\phi(B)$ and $\theta(B)$ are invertible polynomials of finite order in the lag operator B and X_t' is a simple fractional Gaussian noise.

The second long memory model was proposed independently by Granger and Joyeux (1980) and Hosking (1981). It can be motivated by the observation that some time series appear to have unbounded spectral densities at the frequency $\lambda = 0$, but the spectral densities of first differences of the same series appear to vanish at $\lambda = 0$. This suggests the model $(1-B)^d X_t = \varepsilon_t$, where $d \in (-.5, .5)$ and ε_t is serially uncorrelated. By this it is meant that the spectral density of $\{X_t\}$ is

$$f_2(\lambda; d) = (\sigma^2/2\pi)|1-e^{-i\lambda}|^{-2d} = (\sigma^2/2\pi)\{4\sin^2(\lambda/2)\}^{-d}.$$

A series with the spectral density $f_2(\lambda; d)$ will be called a *simple integrated series.* Clearly $\lim_{\lambda\to 0}\lambda^{2d}f_2(\lambda; d) = (\sigma^2/2\pi)$. The corresponding autocorrelation function (for $d \neq 0$) is

$$\rho_2(\tau; d) = \Gamma(1-d)\Gamma(\tau+d)/\{\Gamma(d)\Gamma(\tau+1-d)\},$$

and $\lim_{\tau\to\infty} \tau^{1-2d}\rho_2(\tau; d) = \Gamma(1-d)/\Gamma(d) = \pi/\sin(\pi d)$ (Granger and Joyeux, 1980, p. 17). A simple integrated series has the autoregressive representation

$$\sum_{j=0}^{\infty} a_2(j, d)X_{t-j} = \varepsilon_t, \qquad a_2(j; d) = \Gamma(j-d)/\{\Gamma(-d)\Gamma(j+1)\},$$

and moving average representation

$$X_t = \sum_{j=0}^{\infty} b_2(j; d)\varepsilon_{t-j}, \qquad b_2(j; d) = \Gamma(j+d)/\{\Gamma(j+1)\Gamma(d)\}$$

(Hosking, 1981, p. 167; Granger and Joyeux, 1980, equation (6) is in error). Since $\lim_{j\to\infty} j^{(1+d)}a_2(j; d) = 1/\Gamma(-d)$ and $\lim_{j\to\infty} b_2(j; d) = 1/\Gamma(d)$, $a_2(j; d)$ and $b_2(j; d)$ are each square summable; but $\sum_{j=0}^{\infty} |a_2(j; d)| > \infty$ if and only if $d > 0$, while $\sum_{j=0}^{\infty} |b_2(j; d)| < \infty$ if and only if $d < 0$.

It seems desirable to extend the integrated series model in the same way as the fractional Gaussian noise model. Hence $\{X_t\}$ will be called a *general integrated series* if its spectral density is of the form $f_2(\lambda; d)f_u(\lambda)$, where $f_u(\lambda)$ has the same characteristics as before. Whenever the process $\{\varepsilon_t\}$ is i.i.d. as well as being serially uncorrelated, we shall add the adjective *linear* to describe the process.

There are obvious similarities in simple fractional Gaussian noise and simple integrated series, to which Granger and Joyeux (1980), Hosking (1981), and Jonas (1981) have referred obliquely. In section 2 it is shown that the spectral density function of a general fractional Gaussian noise with parameter H is that of a general integrated series with parameter $H-\frac{1}{2}$, and vice versa. Which model one uses therefore depends on practical considerations, to which the rest of the paper is addressed. In section 3 a consistent, computationally efficient estimator $\hat{d}$ of the parameter d for general integrated series is introduced, and its asymptotic distribution is derived. (By virtue of the results of section 2, $\hat{H} = \hat{d}+\frac{1}{2}$ provides a consistent estimator of H, and $\hat{H}-H$ and $\hat{d}-d$ have the same asymptotic distribution.) Results with synthetic time series are reported in section 4, and with actual time series in section 5. On the basis of these results it can be concluded that the estimator $\hat{d}$ is at least as reliable in finite sample as any estimator of d and H suggested to date, and is more attractive computationally.

2. THE EQUIVALENCE OF GENERAL FRACTIONAL GAUSSIAN NOISE AND GENERAL INTEGRATED SERIES

We provide the following characterization of the relationship of the two models.

THEOREM 1. *$\{X_t\}$ is a general integrated series with parameter d ($-\frac{1}{2} < d < \frac{1}{2}$) if, and only if, it is also a general fractional Gaussian noise with parameter $H = d+\frac{1}{2}$.*

PROOF. Let $d=(L-2)/2$ and $H=(L-1)/2$, $1<L<3$.

$$f_1\{\lambda;(L-1)/2\}/f_2\{\lambda;(L-2)/2\}$$
$$=\pi^{-1}\Gamma(L)\sin\{\pi(L-1)/2\}|\sin(\lambda/2)|^L\sum_{n=-\infty}^{\infty}|n+(\lambda/2\pi)|^{-L}$$
$$=\pi(L)\sin\{\pi(L-1)/2\}|\sin(\lambda/2)/(\lambda/2)|^L\sum_{n=-\infty}^{\infty}|(\lambda/2\pi)/\{n+(\lambda/2\pi)\}|^L.$$

It suffices to show that this ratio is continuous in λ and bounded above and below by positive numbers on $[-\pi,\pi]$. The function $|\sin(\lambda/2)/(\lambda/2)|^L$ has these characteristics. Furthermore

$$1<\sum_{n=-\infty}^{\infty}|(\lambda/2\pi)/\{n+(\lambda/2\pi)\}|^L$$
$$=1+\sum_{n=1}^{\infty}|(\lambda/2\pi)/\{n+(\lambda/2\pi)\}|^L+\sum_{n=1}^{\infty}|(\lambda/2\pi)/\{n-(\lambda/2\pi)\}|^L$$
$$<1+2|(\lambda/2\pi)/\{1+(\lambda/2\pi)\}|^L\zeta(L),$$

where $\zeta(L)=\sum_{n=1}^{\infty}n^{-L}$ is Riemann's zeta function; $\zeta(L)<\infty$ for $L>1$. The function $\sum_{n=-\infty}^{\infty}|(\lambda/2\pi)/\{n+(\lambda/2\pi)\}|^L$ is therefore continuous and bounded above and below by positive numbers on $[-\pi,\pi]$ also.

The proof shows that $f_1(\lambda;(L-1)/2)/f_2(\lambda;(L-2)/2)$ is bounded uniformly in λ. It is not bounded uniformly in L, and its behaviour as $L\to 1$ and $L\to 3$ indicates potential complications in applied work. To examine the case $L\to 1$, write

$$f_1\{\lambda;(L-1)/2\}/f_2\{\lambda;(L-2)/2\}$$
$$=\sin(\lambda/2)\pi^{-1}\Gamma(L)\frac{\sin\{\pi(L-1)/2\}}{\sin(\pi L)}\sin(\pi L)\sum_{n=-\infty}^{\infty}|n+(\lambda/2\pi)|^{-L}.$$

Substitute $\sin(\pi L)=\pi/\{\Gamma(L)\Gamma(1-L)\}$ (Gradshteyn and Ryzhik, 1980, 8.334.3) and $\sum_{n=-\infty}^{\infty}|n+(\lambda/2\pi)|^{-L}=\zeta(L,\lambda/2\pi)+\zeta(L,-\lambda/2\pi)-(-|\lambda|/2\pi)^{-L}$ (where $\zeta(L,q)=\sum_{n=0}^{\infty}(n+q)^{-L}$ is Riemann's general zeta function) to obtain

$$\sin(\lambda/2)\pi^{-L+1}\Gamma(L)\frac{\sin\{\pi(L-1)/2\}}{\sin(\pi L)\Gamma(L)\Gamma(1-L)}$$
$$\times\{\zeta(L,\lambda/2\pi)+\zeta(L,-\lambda/2\pi)-(-|\lambda|/2\pi)^{-L}\}.$$

Since $\lim_{L\to 1}\zeta(L,q)/\Gamma(1-L)=-1$ (Gradshteyn and Ryzhik, 1980, 9.533.1) the limiting value of this expression as $L\to 1$ is $\sin(\lambda/2)$. Hence if a general integrated series were to be described as a general fractional Gaussian noise, then as $d\to-\frac{1}{2}$ a noninvertible moving average component would be required.

As $L\to 3$ the ratio approaches zero, but the approach is uniform in λ: $\lim_{L\to 3}f_1\{\lambda;(L-1)/2\}/[f_2(\lambda;(L-2)/2)\sin\{\pi(L-1)/2\}]$ is continuous and is bounded above and below by positive constants. This limiting case seems to pose no practical problems.

3. A SIMPLE ESTIMATION PROCEDURE FOR GENERAL INTEGRATED SERIES

Consider the problem of estimating the parameter d in the general integrated series model. Suppose $(1-B)^d X_t = u_t$, where u_t is a stationary linear process with spectral density function $f_u(\lambda)$ which is finite, bounded away from zero and continuous on the interval $[-\pi, \pi]$. The spectral density function of $\{X_t\}$ is $f(\lambda) = (\sigma^2/2\pi)\{4\sin^2(\lambda)\}^{-d} f_u(\lambda)$, and

$$\ln\{f(\lambda)\} = \ln\{\sigma^2 f_u(0)/2\pi\} - d\ln\{4\sin^2(\lambda/2)\} + \ln\{f_u(\lambda)/f_u(0)\}. \quad (1)$$

Suppose that a sample of $\{X_t\}$ of size T is available. Let $\lambda_{j,T} = 2\pi j/T$ $(j = 0, \ldots, T-1)$ denote the harmonic ordinates, and $I(\lambda_{j,T})$ denote the periodogram at these ordinates. Evaluate (1) at $\lambda_{j,T}$ and rearrange to obtain

$$\ln\{I(\lambda_{j,T})\} = \ln\{\sigma^2 f_u(0)/2\pi\} - d\ln\{4\sin^2(\lambda_{j,T}/2)\} + \ln\{f_u(\lambda_{j,T})/f_u(0)\} + \ln\{I(\lambda_{j,T})/f(\lambda_{j,T})\}. \quad (2)$$

The proposed estimate of d is motivated by the formal similarity of (2) and a simple linear regression equation: $\ln\{I(\lambda_{j,T}/2)\}$ is analogous to the dependent variable, $\ln\{4\sin^2(\lambda_{j,T})\}$ is the explanatory variable, $\ln\{I(\lambda_{j,T})/f(\lambda_{j,T})\}$ is the disturbance, the slope coefficient is $-d$, and the intercept term is $\ln\{\sigma^2 f_u(0)/2\pi\}$ plus the mean of $\ln\{I(\lambda_{j,T})/f(\lambda_{j,T})\}$. The term $\ln\{f_u(\lambda_{j,T})/f_u(0)\}$ becomes negligible as attention is confined to harmonic frequencies nearer to zero. The proposed estimator is the slope coefficient in the least squares regression of $\ln\{I(\lambda_{j,T})\}$ on a constant and $\ln\{4\sin^2(\lambda_{j,T}/2)\}$ in the sample $j = 1, \ldots, g(T)$; $g(T)$ will be described subsequently. It will be shown that when $d < 0$ the estimator is consistent, and the conventional interpretation of the standard error for the slope coefficient is appropriate asymptotically. We conjecture that the results remain true for $d \geq 0$, and experimental evidence to that effect will be provided subsequently.

To begin, consider (2) for $j = 1, \ldots, n$, for any arbitrarily chosen positive integer n. As T increases, the harmonic frequencies $\lambda_{j,T}$ all approach zero and the term $\ln\{f_u(\lambda_{j,T})/f_u(0)\}$ may be ignored. When $d < 0$ the coefficients in the moving average representation of $\{X_t\}$ are absolutely summable. Hence the random variables $Z_{j,T} = \sum_{t=1}^{T} X_t \exp(-i\lambda_{j,T})/\{f(\lambda_{j,T})\}^{1/2}$ are asymptotically i.i.d. normal (Hannan, 1973, theorem 3). The terms $\ln\{I(\lambda_{j,T})/f(\lambda_{j,T})\}$ are therefore also asymptotically i.i.d., and their distribution can be derived by change of variable techniques (Porter-Hudak, 1982, Appendix C). The distribution is of the Gumbel type; the asymptotic mean of $\ln\{I(\lambda_{j,T})/f(\lambda_{j,T})\}$ is $-C$ (C is Euler's constant, .57721 ...) and its variance is $\pi^2/6$. Consider invoking a conventional central limit theorem to obtain the asymptotic distribution of the least squares slope coefficient in (2). This requires that certain conditions on the regressors be met (to be discussed shortly) and that the disturbance term be i.i.d. with finite mean and variance. This condition will generally never be met for fixed *n or T*, but for fixed n it may be approximated to any specified degree of accuracy by choosing T sufficiently large. Once the accuracy criterion is met the number of ordinates can be increased to $n+1$, and T can then be further increased until the criterion of accuracy is again met. In this way a function $g(T)$ is defined, such that if $n = g(T)$ then the least squares slope estimator $\hat{d}$ of d is asymptotically normal. Clearly $g(T)$ must satisfy $\lim_{T\to\infty} g(T) = \infty$, $\lim_{T\to\infty} g(T)/T = 0$, but beyond this all that is known is that $g(T)$ exists.

Let $U(j, T) = \ln\{4\sin^2(\lambda_{j,T}/2)\}$, $\bar{U}(T, n) = n^{-1}\sum_{j=1}^{n} U(j, T)$. The asymptotic normality of $\hat{d}$ follows from the Lindberg-Levy central limit theorem (Kendall and Stuart, 1972, pp. 206–208).

$$\lim_{T\to\infty} \sum_{j=1}^{g(T)} \{U(j, T) - \bar{U}(T, g(T))\}^2 = \infty, \tag{3}$$

$$\lim_{T\to\infty} \{U(1, T)\}^2 \bigg/ \left[\sum_{j=1}^{g(T)} \{U(j, T) - \bar{U}(T, g(T))\}^2\right] = 0. \tag{4}$$

(In (4), use has been made of the fact that $\sup_{j=1,\dots,g(T)} \{U(j, T)\}^2 = \{U(1, T)\}^2$.) In showing (3) and (4) it is simpler to work with $W(j, T) = \ln(\lambda_{j,T})$ and $\bar{W}(T, n) = n^{-1}\sum_{j=1}^{n} W(j, T)$ in lieu of $U(j, T)$ and $\bar{U}(T, n)$, respectively. The substitution is justified by the fact that for any $g(T)$ that satisfies $\lim_{T\to\infty} g(T)/T = 0$, $\lim_{T\to\infty} U(j, T)/W(j, T) = 2$ $(j = 1, \dots, g(T))$ and

$$\lim_{T\to\infty} \left\{\sum_{j=1}^{g(T)} U(j, T) \bigg/ \sum_{j=1}^{g(T)} W(j, T)\right\}^2 = \lim_{T\to\infty} \sum_{j=1}^{g(T)} \{U(j, T)\}^2 \bigg/ \sum_{j=1}^{g(T)} \{Z(j, T)\}^2 = 4.$$

To simplify notation let $n = g(T)$. To establish (3) observe that

$$\sum_{j=1}^{n} \{W(j, T) - \bar{W}(j, T)\}^2 = \sum_{j=1}^{n} (\ln j)^2 - n^{-1}\left(\sum_{j=1}^{n} \ln j\right)^2. \tag{5}$$

Make the substitutions

$$\sum_{j=1}^{n} (\ln j)^2 = (n + \tfrac{1}{2})(\ln n)^2 - 2n\ln n + 2n + C_n$$

where $-(\ln 2)^2/2 - 2 < C_n < -2$ (Buck, 1978, p. 252), and

$$\sum_{j=1}^{n} \ln j = (n + \tfrac{1}{2})\ln n - n + D_n,$$

where $1 - \ln 2/2 < D_n < 1$ (Buck, 1978, p. 252). Expression (5) then reduces to

$$n - (\tfrac{1}{2} + \tfrac{1}{4}n^{-1})(\ln n)^2 + (1 - 2D_n - n^{-1}D_n)\ln n + C_n + 2D_n - n^{-1}D_n^2, \tag{6}$$

which for large n is dominated by $n \to \infty$. On the other hand, $\{W(1, T)\}^2 = (\ln 2\pi - \ln T)^2$. So long as

$$\lim_{T\to\infty} (\ln T)^2/g(T) = 0, \tag{7}$$

(4) will be satisfied. This appears to be a weak requirement: e.g., it is satisfied by $g(T) = cT^\alpha$, $0 < \alpha < 1$.

In inference about d from $\hat{d}$, use can be made of the known variance of the analogue of the disturbance term in (2): in large samples, the distribution of $\hat{d}$ is approximated by

$$N\left(d, \pi^2 \bigg/ \left[6\sum_{j=1}^{g(T)} \{U(j, T) - \bar{U}(T, g(T))\}^2\right]\right).$$

A natural, somewhat simpler procedure is to assume that $\hat{d}$ is normal with standard deviation given by the usual ordinary least squares arithmetic. This assumption is justified so long as s^2 consistently estimates $\text{var}\{I(\lambda_{j,T})/f(\lambda_{j,T})\}$ in (2), which will be guaranteed if the least squares intercept b_0 converges in probability to the population intercept $\ln\{\sigma^2 f_u(0)/2\pi\} - C$. Since $b_0 = n^{-1}\sum_{j=1}^{n} \ln\{I(\lambda_{j,T})\} - \hat{d}\bar{U}(T, n)$, this will occur if $\text{plim}\,(\hat{d} - d)\bar{U}(T, n) = 0$. As argued above, $\bar{U}(T, n)$ behaves like $n^{-1}\sum_{j=1}^{n} \ln(2\pi j/T) = \ln 2\pi - \ln T + \ln n + \ln n/2n - 1 + D_n/n$ when n is large, so $\lim \bar{U}(T, n)/\ln(n/T) = 1$. From (6), the asymptotic standard error of $\hat{d}$ is proportional to $n^{-1/2}$. Hence b_0 is consistent for the population intercept, and $\text{plim}\, s^2 = \pi^2/6$, if $\lim_{T\to\infty}\{g(T)\}^{-1/2} \ln\{g(T)/T\} = 0$. This condition is implied by (7).

These results are collected in the following theorem.

THEOREM 2. *Suppose* $\{X_t\}$ *is a general integrated linear process, with* $d < 0$. *Let* $I(\lambda_{j,T})$ *denote the periodogram of* $\{X_t\}$ *at the harmonic frequencies* $\lambda_{j,T} = \pi j/T$ *in a sample of size T. Let* $b_{1,T}$ *denote the ordinary least squares estimator of* β_1 *in the regression equation* $\ln\{I(\lambda_{j,T})\} = \beta_0 + \beta_1 \ln\{4\sin^2(\lambda_{j,T}/2)\} + u_{j,T}$, $j = 1, \ldots, n$. *Then there exists a function* $g(T)$ *(which will have the properties* $\lim_{T\to\infty} g(T) = \infty$, $\lim_{T\to\infty} g(T)/T = 0$) *such that if* $n = g(T)$ *then* $\text{plim}\, b_1 = -d$. *If* $\lim_{T\to\infty}(\ln T)^2/g(T) = 0$, *then* $(b_1 + d)/\{\widehat{\text{var}}(b_1)\}^{1/2} \to^{\mathcal{D}} N(0, 1)$, *where* $\widehat{\text{var}}(b_1)$ *is the usual least squares estimator of* $\text{var}(b_1)$.

Once the parameter 'd' is estimated, the relationship $f_u(\lambda) = f(\lambda)/f_2(\lambda; d)$ may be used to estimate $f_u(\lambda)$. This can be done as follows. First, the exact finite Fourier transform of the sequence $\{X_t, t = 1, \ldots, T\}$ is computed at the harmonic ordinates. The exact, rather than the fast, Fourier transform is used because the fast Fourier transform presumes circular stationarity; this presumption seems a poor approximation for long memory models, and in experiments along the lines of those reported in the next two sections the exact Fourier transform was a much more satisfactory (though more costly) procedure. Second, the Fourier transform of the series is multiplied by $(1 - \exp(-i\lambda))^{\hat{d}}$. Third, the exact inverse Fourier transform of this product is computed. In the final step conventional procedures—e.g., ARMA models, long autoregressions, or nonparametric spectral methods—are used to model $f_u(\lambda)$. Since $\hat{d}$ is consistent for d, the estimator (or the implicit estimator) of $f_u(\lambda)$ in the last step is consistent. The conventional distribution theory for the estimator will not be applicable, because $\hat{d}$ rather than d is used in the second step; indeed, because $\text{var}(\hat{d}) = O(g(T)^{-1})$ and $\lim_{T\to\infty} g(T)/T = 0$, conventional standard errors in the final step could be badly misleading.

Multi-step-ahead forecasting is straightforward. With $\hat{d}$ in hand, the autoregression coefficient estimates ($a_2(j; \hat{d})$, see Section 1) for the 'long memory' portion of the series can be computed. The estimated autoregressive representation for the 'short memory' portion of the series (corresponding to $f_u(\lambda)$) can also be computed. The convolution of the lag operators in these two representations provides the lag operator for the estimated autoregressive representation of $\{X_t\}$. Multi-step-ahead forecasts are then computed in the usual way.

It is clear that through suitable integer differencing the concept of integrated series can be extended, and these methods applied to cases $d \geq \frac{1}{2}$. The choice of 'suitable' integer involves subjective judgment and may become critical if d lies exactly between two integers and theorem 2 is to be invoked. An alternative in such cases is to fractionally difference the original series as in steps one through three of the estimation procedure for $f_u(\lambda)$, using a prespecified value of d in lieu of $\hat{d}$, to ensure that for the transformed series $d \in (-\frac{1}{2}, \frac{1}{2})$.

4. SIMULATION RESULTS

The results on estimation are asymptotic and restricted to the case $d < 0$. They leave open the questions of how large a sample is required for their reliability, how rapidly the number of ordinates used to estimate d, $g(T)$, should increase with sample size T, and whether they are valid for $d > 0$. Given the seemingly insurmountable difficulties in obtaining analytical answers to all of these questions, the most productive line of attack is to conduct some experiments with synthetic series. We report here the findings from a very limited simulation study; a more thorough investigation along these lines is warranted before these methods are used widely in empirical work.

The generation of synthetic data to mimic the realizations of long memory models has proved to be a challenge in its own right, precisely because widely separated points in the generated sample must be highly correlated. In early work, short memory approximations to long memory models were employed, with unsatisfactory results (see the discussion and citations in McLeod and Hipel, 1978, p. 497). A direct procedure (McLeod and Hipel, 1978) is to compute the pertinent $T \times T$ covariance matrix C for given values of the parameter H or d and sample size T, and then compute the Cholesky decomposition $C = MM'$. Given a standardized normal sequence of synthetic random variables $\underset{\sim}{e} = (e_1, \ldots, e_T)'$ the synthetic long memory series is then $M\underset{\sim}{e}$. The computation of M requires storage proportional to T^2 and time proportional to T^3, and is impractical for values of T exceeding 200 or so. In a variant on this method Granger and Joyeux (1980) used the Cholesky decomposition to obtain the first 100 values of the simulated sample, and then used the truncated autoregression $\sum_{j=0}^{100} a_2(j; d)x_{t-j} = e_t$ to obtain successive values of the series.

In our simulations we employed the recursion algorithm usually attributed to Levinson (1947) and Durbin (1960), as extended by Whittle (1963); Jonas (1981) has recognized the potential of this method in the simulation of long memory time series. The Levinson–Durbin–Whittle algorithm implicitly provides the Cholesky decomposition of a Toeplitz matrix. (The distinguishing feature of a Toeplitz matrix A is $a_{ij} = a_{i-j}$; the variance matrix of T successive realizations of a wide sense stationary process is a Toeplitz matrix.) Given the values of the autocovariance function $R(0), R(1), \ldots, R(T)$ for a wide sense stationary process $\{X_t\}$ the algorithm provides the coefficients in the linear projection of X_t on

$X_{t-1}, \ldots, X_{t-p}$ and the associated residual variance, for $p=1, \ldots, T$. Storage requirements and computation time are proportional to T^2; the advantage in computation time relative to the Cholesky decomposition stems from the exploitation of the fact that the variance matrix is a Toeplitz form. (For $T=400$, computation time with 64-bit double precision arithmetic is less than one minute using a VAX-11/780.)

Evidence on the characteristics of series generated in this way is provided in table I. For the example reported there, $T=265$. In each of 4000 replications the first 26 values of the sample autocovariance function were computed. The average of these values over the replications is the estimated autocovariance function of the simulated data reported in table I; standard errors for these estimates are reported parenthetically. Since at least one million pairs of generated data are involved in each average, the standard errors are quite small. In no case do the estimated means differ from the population values by more than two standard errors. These results compare quite favourably with those of Granger

TABLE I
AUTOCOVARIANCES FUNCTIONS ESTIMATED FROM SYNTHETIC DATA[a]

	$d=.25$		$d=.45$	
Lag	True Population	Synthetic Population Estimate[b]	True Population	Synthetic Population Estimate[c]
0	1.000	.998	1.000	1.017
1	.333	.332	.818	.835
2	.238	.238	.765	.782
3	.195	.194	.735	.752
4	.169	.168	.715	.731
5	.151	.150	.699	.715
6	.138	.137	.686	.702
7	.128	.126	.676	.692
8	.119	.117	.667	.683
9	.113	.112	.659	.674
10	.107	.106	.652	.667
11	.102	.101	.646	.661
12	.098	.097	.640	.655
13	.094	.092	.635	.650
14	.090	.089	.631	.645
15	.087	.087	.626	.641
16	.084	.084	.622	.637
17	.082	.082	.619	.634
18	.080	.079	.615	.630
19	.078	.078	.612	.627
20	.076	.075	.609	.624
21	.074	.073	.606	.620
22	.072	.071	.603	.618
23	.070	.068	.600	.616
24	.069	.069	.598	.613
25	.068	.068	.595	.611

[a] See text for data generation method.
[b] Standard errors for these estimates range from .0014 to .0019.
[c] Standard errors for these estimates range from .0096 to .0097.

and Joyeux (1980, pp. 25–26), and underscore the importance of using exact methods rather than short memory approximations in the synthesis of long memory time series.

The results of the experiments conducted are provided in table II. The experiments were designed to investigate the effects of alternative T, of alternative true models, and of using the known variance $\pi^2/6$ of the disturbance of the regression equation (2) as an alternative to the least squares estimator s^2, all for $d > 0$. The rule $g(T) = T^\alpha$ ($\alpha = .5, .6, .7$) was held fixed. The fractions reported in table II can be regarded as point estimates of the difference between one and the true size of the confidence intervals in finite sample; with 300 replications, the standard error of these point estimates is about .0125.

TABLE II

FRACTION OF REPLICATIONS IN WHICH TRUE d WAS OUTSIDE 95% CONFIDENCE INTERVAL FOR d BASED ON THEOREM 2

300 REPLICATIONS, $g(T) = T^\alpha$

$(1 - \phi B)(1 - B)^d X_t = \varepsilon_t$

Model	$d = .2, \phi = 0$			$d = .35, \phi = 0$			$d = .44, \phi = 0$			$d = .25, \phi = .5$		
α	.5	.6	.7	.5	.6	.7	.5	.6	.7	.5	.6	.7
$T = 50, \hat{\sigma}^2 = s^2$	.123	.073	.047	.107	.070	.070	.133	.100	.080	.136	.216	.390
$T = 50, \hat{\sigma}^2 = \pi^2/6$	.063	.057	.030	.033	.027	.040	.067	.057	.067	.070	.113	.356
$T = 100, \hat{\sigma}^2 = s^2$	.090	.067	.063	.087	.073	.053	.077	.083	.063	.103	.183	.446
$T = 100, \hat{\sigma}^2 = \pi^2/6$	.057	.060	.053	.053	.037	.040	.047	.057	.037	.083	.130	.473
$T = 200, \hat{\sigma}^2 = s^2$	.087	.117	.090	.063	.043	.053	.073	.100	.057	.090	.156	.566
$T = 200, \hat{\sigma}^2 = \pi^2/6$	.067	.080	.100	.023	.037	053	.050	.057	.043	.050	.117	.526
$T = 300, \hat{\sigma}^2 = s^2$	.057	.057	.047	.070	.060	.053	.060	.090	.053	.073	.103	.500
$T = 300, \hat{\sigma}^2 = \pi^2/6$	.067	.060	.047	.037	.033	.050	.050	.053	.060	.053	.070	.513

The results for simple integrated series, in the first three panels of table II, are better than those for the general integrated series in the fourth panel. Most markedly, confidence intervals evidently are more reliable when the true variance $\pi^2/6$ is used than when the conventional regression s^2 is employed to construct standard errors. Second, the reliability of confidence intervals is insensitive to the size of d. Finally—by comparison with these patterns—the effect of sample size on the reliability of the confidence intervals is negligible; in any event a sample size of 100 or more certainly seems adequate. Overall, the experimental results strongly suggest that the asymptotic results in Theorem 2 are adequate in samples of models size when the true variance $\pi^2/6$ is used. They also support the conjecture that those results are valid for $d > 0$ as well as for $d < 0$.

For the general integrated series considered these generalizations remain true: true variance leads to a more reliable confidence interval than s^2, and the effect of increasing sample size is small by comparison. When $g(t) = T^{.5}$ the results are much like those for the simple integrated series, but as more ordinates are incorporated in the log periodogram regression the reliability of the confidence intervals deteriorates. This is not surprising, since as ordinates are added the contribution of the term $\ln\{f_u(\lambda_j, T)/f_u(0)\}$ in (2) becomes non-negligible. The results in the last panel suggest that in empirical work $g(T)$ should be kept small if d appears sensitive to choice of $g(T)$.

5. FORECASTING WITH LONG MEMORY MODELS

The development of long memory models has been motivated, in part, by the hope that through providing a better description of the low frequency portion of the spectral density than is possible with conventional models, they will also provide better several-step-ahead forecasts. It should be revealing to compare the mean square error of several-step-ahead forecasts generated by these models with those of other models, using actual time series, estimated parameter values, and out-of-sample forecasts. We undertook such a comparison, using three postwar monthly price indices.

Four different models were used to produce forecasts. The first is a simple integrated series, in which the parameter d was estimated as described in section 3. The second is a general integrated series of the form

$$\phi(B)(1-B)^d X_t = \theta(B)\varepsilon_t$$

where $\phi(B)$ and $\theta(B)$ are polynomials of finite order. The parameter d was estimated as in the first model, and the series $(1-B)^d X_t$ was formed using the frequency domain methods described in section 3. Beginning with this series standard ARMA modelling procedures were used to identify and estimate $\phi(B)$ and $\theta(B)$. We have discussed reasons why these two particular models might produce good several-step-ahead forecasts if one of the long memory models is an appropriate description of the behaviour of the series. The third model is conventional ARIMA, in which only integer differencing of the series is presumed. Since parsimoniously parameterized ARIMA models are incapable of describing the low frequency behaviour of series with long memory properties, several-step-ahead forecasts for this model should be poor if a long memory is in fact appropriate. The final model is an autoregression of order fifty, estimated by ordinary least squares. A fiftieth order autoregression can describe a long memory model better than a parsimoniously parameterized ARIMA model. The larger the value of $d \in (-\frac{1}{2}, \frac{1}{2})$ the more closely it approximates a simple integrated series, and it may approximate a general integrated series better than a mixed fractional difference and ARMA model. In practice, the profligate parameterization of this model would presumably increase mean square error due to imperfectly estimated parameters to a greater extent than is the case with the other three models.

The estimation procedure in the first two models requires that the number of ordinates, $g(T)$, used in the periodogram regressions be specified. In the absence of any previous experience with this estimator, in each case we chose the number of ordinates for which the corresponding value of d minimized the mean square error of 20-step-ahead, in-sample forecasts. In most cases the plot of mean square error against the number of ordinates was a smooth parabola with a well defined minimum, and in all cases the number of ordinates selected was between $T^{.55}$ and $T^{.6}$. Forecasts were computed by calculating the autoregressive representation implied by the estimated model, truncating at the fiftieth term, and then recursively computing n-step-ahead forecasts.

TABLE III

ESTIMATED AUTOCORRELATION FUNCTION FOR PRICE SERIES

	Levels			Differences		
Lags	Food CPI	WPI	CPI	Food CPI	WPI	CPI
1	.985	.983	.985	.333	.294	.548
2	.970	.966	.969	.244	.317	.538
3	.956	.950	.954	.148	.321	.562
4	.942	.933	.938	.103	.156	.499
5	.928	.917	.922	.142	.276	.470
6	.915	.901	.906	.218	.292	.496
7	.903	.884	.891	.168	.186	.446
8	.891	.867	.875	.080	.209	.465
9	.879	.851	.860	.173	.210	.476
10	.867	.834	.844	.204	.085	.473
11	.855	.817	.829	.183	.268	.374
12	.842	.800	.815	.250	.245	.390
13	.829	.784	.800	.157	.046	.370
14	.817	.767	.786	.091	.232	.300
15	.804	.750	.771	.038	.103	.319
16	.792	.733	.757	.093	.072	.319
17	.780	.716	.743	.067	.179	.242
18	.768	.699	.729	.109	.128	.289
19	.757	.682	.715	.047	.063	.186
20	.747	.665	.702	.055	.164	.240
21	.736	.647	.689	.054	.014	.209
22	.725	.630	.677	.071	.007	.183
23	.714	.614	.665	.132	.093	.166
24	.702	.597	.653	.123	.062	.154
25	.690	.580	.641	.029	.080	.139
26	.679	.564	.629	.028	.114	.154
27	.667	.547	.618	.002	.029	.153
28	.655	.529	.608	.022	.128	.125
29	.644	.511	.597	.068	.142	.158
30	.632	.493	.587	.101	.155	.169
31	.619	.475	.577	.050	.140	.116
32	.607	.458	.567	.074	.167	.206
33	.594	.440	.557	.049	.079	.167
34	.582	.424	.548	.049	.084	.124
35	.569	.410	.539	.128	.153	.100
36	.557	.395	.529	.152	.091	.178
37	.543	.382	.520	.091	.161	.153
38	.531	.368	.512	.073	.123	.153
39	.519	.355	.503	.060	.077	.172
40	.507	.342	.495	.108	.123	.189

The consumer price index for food ('Food CPI', January 1947 to July 1978), the Wholesale Price Index ('WPI', January 1947 to February 1977) and the Consumer Price Index ('CPI', January 1947 to February 1976) were selected for study. This choice was motivated in part by Mandelbrot's argument (1973) that prices which are fractional Gaussian noise will remain so even with attempted arbitrage, and in part by Granger's demonstration (1980) that aggregates of first order Markov processes are (under certain assumptions about the distribution of parameters across the processes) simple integrated series. Granger and Joyeux have studied the mean square error of forecast for Food CPI from January 1947 to July 1978, using a simple integrated series model and a grid search estimator for d.

Sample autocorrelation functions for both levels and first differences of these series are provided in table III. For the differences, these functions exhibit the slow decay typical of long memory models but not of stable autoregressive moving average models with a few parameters. The first fifty sample autocorrelation

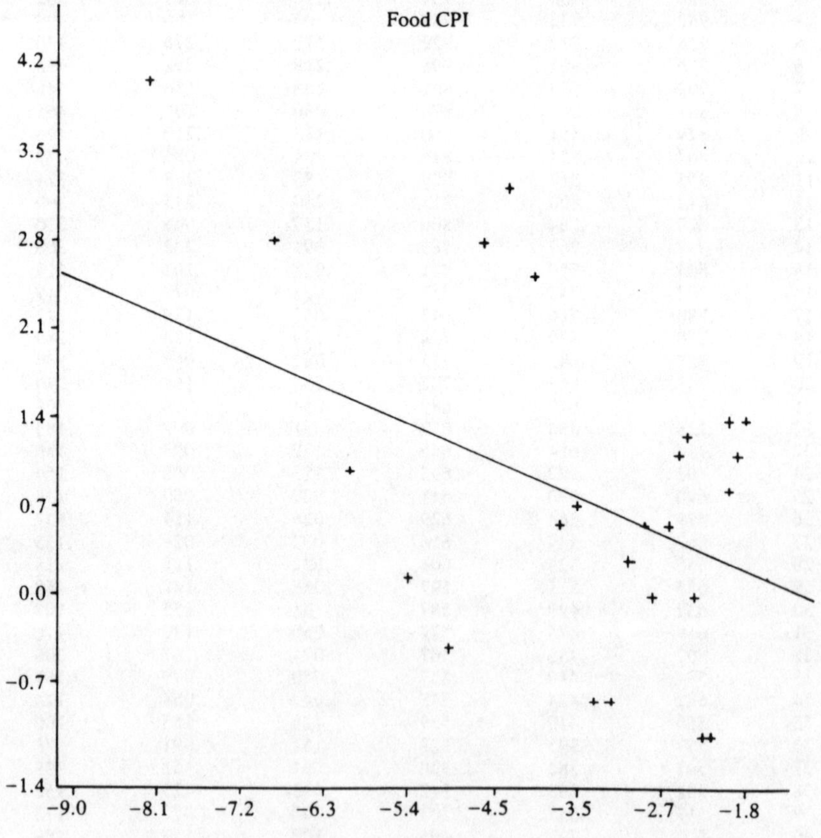

FIGURE 1. Linear plot of log periodogram vs. deterministic regressor.

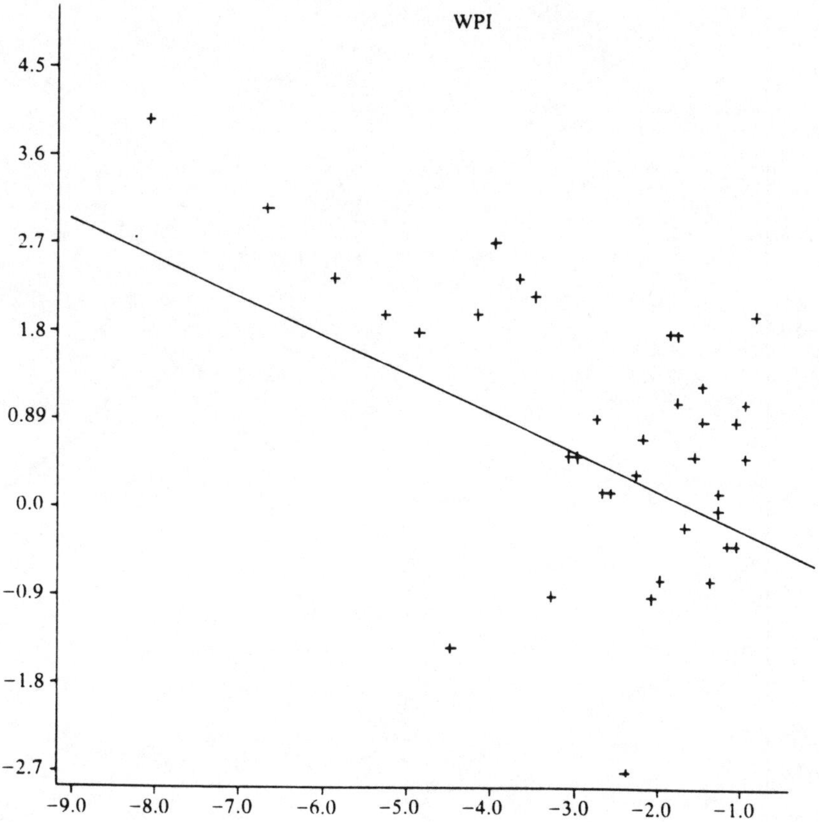

FIGURE 2. Linear plot of log periodogram vs. deterministic regressor.

coefficients are all positive in each case; for the Food CPI and the WPI over half of these are significantly different from zero by the usual rule of thumb, and for the CPI they are all significant. From table III it is clear that the CPI is more sluggish than the other two series. In the first two models, it was found necessary to begin with the series $(1-B)^{1.25}\mathrm{CPI}_t$ (formed as described in section 3) whereas for the other two only a conventional first difference was required.

Further evidence on the long memory characteristics of these series is provided in figs. 1 through 3, in which $\ln\{I(\lambda_{j,T})\}$ (the 'dependent variable' in equation (2)) is plotted against $\ln\{4\sin^2(\lambda_{j,T})\}$ (the 'regressor' in equation (2)). For each figure the periodogram ordinates were computed from the entire sample; the number of ordinates was selected as just described. If the series in question were in fact a general fractional Gaussian noise or a general integrated series, then the relationship should be approximately linear, and the standard deviation of the plotted points about the line should be about $\pi/\sqrt{6} \doteq 1.28$. These features

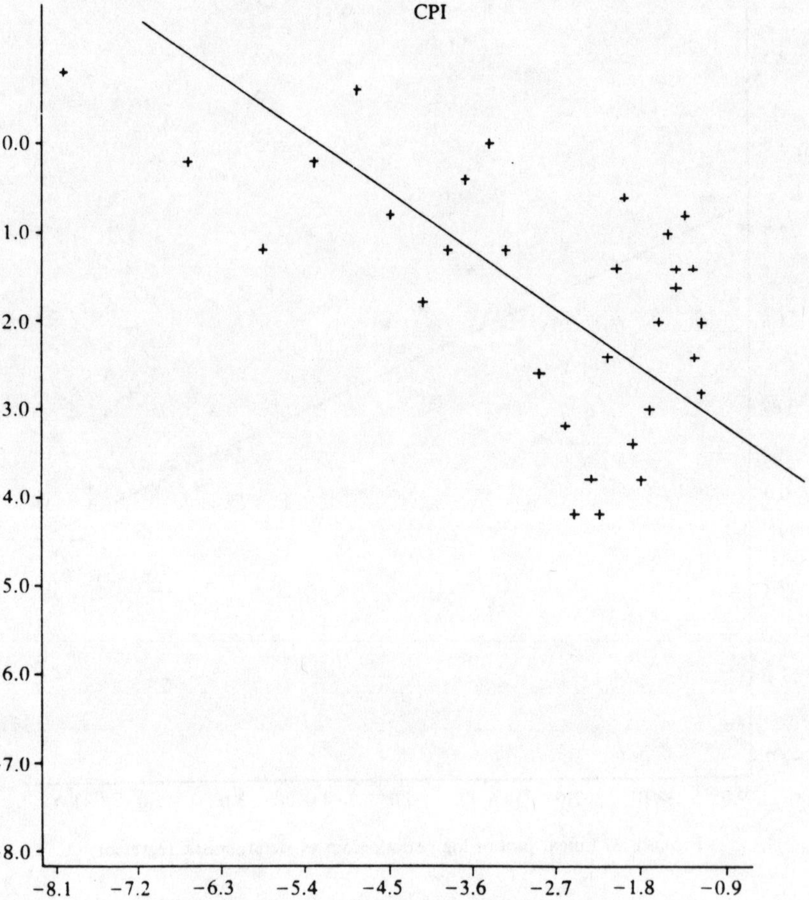

FIGURE 3. Linear plot of log periodogram vs. deterministic regressor.

seem characteristic of the plots for WPI and CPI (figs. 2 and 3), but more arguable for Food CPI (fig. 1).

For all three series 10- and 20-step-ahead forecasts were made beginning with March 1951 and at 10-month intervals thereafter. Forecasts were made using a 50 order autoregressive equation using the representation given in section 1. The parameter estimates based on the entire sample were used to produce the in-sample forecasts. For the out-of-sample forecasts parameter estimates are functions of the data preceding and including the month in which the forecast is made; the model is reestimated each time new forecasts are constructed. The mean square error of forecast is computed for the levels of the series. Results are reported in tables IV, V, and VI.

TABLE IV

COMPARISON OF MEAN SQUARE ERROR OF FORECAST CONSUMER FOOD PRICE INDEX, 1947–1978(6)

	Mean Square Error of Forecast			
	In Sample		Out of Sample	
Estimation Method	10-Step	20-Step	10-Step	20-Step
d[a]	8.359	17.837	26.310	36.223
d/ARMA[b]	7.804	16.996	34.174	46.305
ARMA[c]	8.969	18.647	41.727	56.732
AR50	8.046	16.754	24.017	33.477
$\hat{d}=.35$ (Granger and Joyeux)	8.361	17.923	28.360	37.443

[a] $\hat{d}=.423$, standard error $=.146$; $T=378$, $g(T)=26 \doteq T^{.55}$.
[b] $(1-B)^d X_t=(1-.188\,B-.03\,B^2-.1\,B^3-.15\,B^4)\varepsilon_t$, where X_t is the first differenced series.
[c] $(1-.33\,B)X_t=.26+\varepsilon_t$, where X_t is the first differenced series.

TABLE V

COMPARISON OF MEAN SQUARE ERROR OF FORECAST WHOLESALE PRICE INDEX, 1947–1977

	Mean Square Error of Forecast			
	In Sample		Out of Sample	
Estimation Method	10-Step	20-Step	10-Step	20-Step
d[a]	7.830	16.675	10.200	22.540
d/ARMA[b]	8.258	17.259	8.773	19.763
ARMA[c]	8.739	17.736	8.832	25.195
AR50	9.010	18.030	38.212	49.242

[a] $\hat{d}=.417$, standard error $=.112$; $T=363$, $g(T)=39 \doteq T^{.6}$.
[b] $(1-B)^d X_t=(1-.25\,B-.15\,B^2)(1+.14\,B^{12})\varepsilon_t$, where X_t is the first differenced series.
[c] $(1-.18\,B-.19\,B^2-.19\,B^3-.16\,B^5)X_t=.12+\varepsilon_t$, where X_t is the first differenced series.

For a given method of forecasting, it is always the case that the mean square error of the out-of-sample forecast exceeds that of the in-sample forecast, and of course 20-step-ahead forecasts are less accurate than 10-step-ahead forecasts. The comparatively sluggish CPI has a substantially lower mean square error of forecast (by whatever method) than the other two; the larger value of $\hat{d}$ for this series reflects the slower decay in the sample autocorrelation function reported in table III.

When comparisons across different forecasting procedures are made, the results are mixed but suggestive. The autoregression of order 50 ('AR50') provides the best out-of-sample forecasts for Food CPI and CPI, but performs miserably for WPI. Conventional ARMA models ('ARMA') generally perform badly: only for

TABLE VI

COMPARISON OF MEAN SQUARE ERROR OF FORECAST CONSUMER PRICE INDEX, 1947–1976

Estimation Method	Mean Square Error of Forecast			
	In Sample		Out of Sample	
	10-Step	20-Step	10-Step	20-Step
d[a]	.838	2.140	1.895	3.325
d/ARMA[b]	.732	1.852	2.775	4.792
ARMA[c]	1.311	2.782	3.751	7.474
AR50	1.402	2.717	1.417	3.079

[a] $\hat{d} = .701$, standard error $= .155$; $T = 351$, $g(T) = 34 \doteq T^{.6}$.
[b] $(1-B)^d X_t = (1-.5\,B)\varepsilon_t$, where X_t is the first differenced series.
[c] $(1-.22\,B-.19\,B^2-.26\,B^3-.1\,B^4-.06\,B^5)X_t = \varepsilon_t$, where X_t is the first differenced series.

WPI did they approach the performance of the long memory models. Mixed fractional differencing and ARMA representation ('d/ARMA') provides the best forecast for WPI, but for other series was superior only to the ARMA model. The forecasts provided by the simple integrated series model ('d') were never the best, but they were never markedly inferior to the others, either. The mean square error of 20-step-ahead forecasts for the simple integrated series model is on average 10% higher than that of the best set of forecasts (from whichever model). By contrast, for mixed integrated series and ARMA it is 31%, for ARMA 73%, and for an autoregression of order fifty 50%. The results suggest that use of a simple integrated series model may be a reasonable, conservative procedure for producing several-step-ahead univariate forecasts. Further experimentation along these lines with other series is clearly required to confirm this judgment.

This work was undertaken while the first author was Associate Professor and the second was a graduate student in the Department of Economics, University of Wisconsin-Madison. Portions of this article are taken from Susan Porter-Hudak's Ph.D thesis. Financial support from National Science Foundation grant SES-8207639 is acknowledged.

REFERENCES

BUCK, R. C. (1978) *Advanced Calculus*, McGraw-Hill: New York.
DURBIN, J. (1960) The Fitting of Time Series Models. *Rev. Int. Inst. Statist.* 28, 233–244.
GRADSHTEYN, I. S. and I. M. RYZHIK (1980) *Tables of Integrals, Series and Products*. Academic Press: New York.
GRANGER, C. W. G. and R. JOYEUX (1980) An Introduction to Long Memory Time Series Models and Fractional Differencing. *J. Time Series Anal.* 1 (1), 15–29.
GRANGER, C. W. G. (1980) Long Memory Relationships and the Aggregation of Dynamic Models. *J. Econometrics* 14, 227–238.
HANNAN, E. J. (1973) Central Limit Theorems for Time Series Regression. *Zeit. Wahrscheinlichkeitsth.* 26, 157–170.
HOSKING, J. R. M. (1981) Fractional Differencing. *Biometrika* 68 (1), 165–176.

HURST, H. E. (1951) Long Term Storage Capacity of Reservoirs. *Trans. Amer. Soc. Civil Engrs.* 116, 770–799.

JONAS, A. (June 1981) Long Memory Self Similar Time Series Models. Unpublished Harvard University manuscript.

KENDALL, M. and A. STUART (1977) *The Advanced Theory of Statistics*, Vol. 1, 4th ed. Charles Griffin: London.

LEVINSON, N. (1947) The Wiener RMS Criterion in Filter Design and Prediction. *J. Math. Phys.* 25, 261–278.

MANDELBROT, B. B. and J. W. VAN NESS (1968) Fractional Brownian Motion, Fractional Noises and Applications. *SIAM Rev.* 10, 422–437.

MANDELBROT, B. B. (1971) A Fast Fractional Gaussian Noise Generator. *Water Resources Research* 7, 543–553.

MANDELBROT, B. B. (1973) Statistical Methodology for Nonperiodic Cycles: From the Covariance to R/S Analysis. *Rev. Econ. Soc. Meas.* pp. 259–290.

MCLEOD, A. I. and K. W. HIPEL (1978) Preservation of the Rescaled Adjusted Range, I. A Reassessment of the Hurst Phenomenon. *Water Resources Research* 14 (3), 491–518.

PORTER-HUDAK, S. (1982) Long-Term Memory Modelling—A Simplified Spectral Approach. Unpublished University of Wisconsin Ph.D. thesis.

ROZANOV, Y. A. (1967) *Stationary Random Processes.* Holden-Day: San Francisco.

WHITTLE, P. (1963) On the Fitting of Multivariate Autoregressions, and the Approximate Canonical Factorization of a Spectral Density Matrix. *Biometrika* 50, 129–134.

Part III
Structural Time Series Models

[9]

OPTIMAL PROPERTIES OF EXPONENTIALLY WEIGHTED FORECASTS*

JOHN F. MUTH
Carnegie Institute of Technology

The exponentially weighted average can be interpreted as the expected value of a time series made up of two kinds of random components: one lasting a single time period (transitory) and the other lasting through all subsequent periods (permanent). Such a time series may, therefore, be regarded as a random walk with "noise" superimposed. It is also shown that, for this series, the best forecast for the time period immediately ahead is the best forecast for *any* future time period, because both give estimates of the permanent component. The estimate of the permanent component is imperfect, and so the estimate of a regression coefficient is inconsistent in a relation involving the permanent (e.g. consumption as a function of permanent income). Its bias is small, however.

1. INTRODUCTION

FORECASTS derived by weighting past observations exponentially (that is, geometrically) have been used with some success in operations research and economics. Magee [8], Winters [12],[1] and Brown [1] have used this approach in short-term forecasting of sales, primarily in inventory control. Distributed lags, while not always arising from explicit forecasts, have appeared in studies of capacity adjustment by Koyck [6], demand for cash balances during hyperinflations by Cagan [2], the consumption function by Friedman [3], and agricultural supply functions by Nerlove [11]. Its main *a priori* justification as a forecasting relation has been that it leads to correction of persistent errors, without responding very much to random disturbances.

Because exponentially weighted forecasts have been successful in a variety of applications, it is worth-while finding the statistical properties of time series for which the forecasting method would work well. The answer would allow the range of applicability of the forecasting method to be judged better and would ultimately lead to modifications when the conditions on the time series are not met. The methods we will use are related to those which have been moderately successful in control engineering.[2]

We shall consider only one estimation problem—the possible inconsistency in the regression coefficient of the forecasts because errors of measurement may be present. The reader is referred to Klein [5] and Koyck [6] for a discussion of other estimation problems.

2. "ADAPTIVE EXPECTATIONS" AND OPTIMAL PREDICTION

The exponentially weighted moving average forecast arises from the following model of expectations adapting to changing conditions. Let y_t represent

* This paper was written as part of the project, "The Planning and Control of Industrial Operations" under grant from the Office of Naval Research.

[1] See also Holt *et al.* [4], Ch. 14.

[2] Statistical problems in engineering control are ably discussed in Laning and Battin [7].

that part of a time-series which cannot be explained by trend, seasonal, or any other systematic factors; and let y_t^e represent the forecast, or expectation, of y_t on the basis of information available through the $(t-1)$st period. It is assumed that the forecast is changed from one period to the next by an amount proportional to the latest observed error. That is:

$$y_t^e = y_{t-1}^e + \beta(y_{t-1} - y_{t-1}^e), \qquad 0 \leq \beta \leq 1. \tag{2.1}$$

The solution of the above difference equation gives the formula for the exponentially weighted forecast:

$$y_t^e = \beta \sum_{i=1}^{\infty} (1 - \beta)^{i-1} y_{t-i}. \tag{2.2}$$

Since the weights attached to prior vaules of y_t add up to unity, the forecasting scheme does not in this respect introduce any systematic bias.

Now, suppose that the realizations of the random process can be written as some linear function of independent random shocks:

$$y_t = \epsilon_t + \sum_{i=1}^{\infty} w_i \epsilon_{t-i} \tag{2.3}$$

the shocks being independently distributed with mean zero and variance σ^2.

As long as the parameters w_i, which characterize the random process, are known, it is a relatively simple matter to find the expected value of y_t for any time period on the basis of previous outcomes. Suppose we wish to find the expectation of y_t given $\epsilon_{t-1}, \epsilon_{t-2}, \epsilon_{t-3}, \cdots$ (that is, the only information lacking to give the value of y_t exactly is the latest "shock," ϵ_t). Then we simply replace ϵ_t by its expected value, which is zero. Therefore we have:

$$\begin{aligned} y_t^e &= E(y_t \mid \epsilon_{t-1}, \epsilon_{t-2}, \epsilon_{t-3}, \cdots) \\ &= \sum_{i=1}^{\infty} w_i \epsilon_{t-i}. \end{aligned} \tag{2.4}$$

In order to relate the regression functions above to the expression for the exponentially weighted forecast, we need to be able to write (2.4) in terms of the observed variables $y_{t-1}, y_{t-2}, \cdots$. That is, we need to find the coefficients of the following function:

$$y_t^e = \sum_{j=1}^{\infty} v_j y_{t-j}. \tag{2.5}$$

Substituting from (2.3), and re-arranging terms, we obtain:

$$\begin{aligned} y_t^e &= \sum_{j=1}^{\infty} v_j \left(\epsilon_{t-j} + \sum_{i=1}^{\infty} w_i \epsilon_{t-i-j} \right) \\ &= v_1 \epsilon_{t-1} + \sum_{i=2}^{\infty} \left(v_i + \sum_{j=1}^{i-1} v_j w_{i-j} \right) \epsilon_{t-i} \end{aligned} \tag{2.6}$$

By comparing coefficients of Equations (2.4) and (2.6), we have the necessary relation between the parameters, w_i, associated with the latent shocks and those, v_j, associated with the observable past history of the process:

$$w_1 = v_1$$
$$w_i = v_i + \sum_{j=1}^{i-1} v_j w_{i-j}, \qquad i = 2, 3, 4, \cdots. \tag{2.7}$$

In order to characterize the time-series for which the exponentially-weighted forecast is optimal, we substitute the weights

$$v_j = \beta(1 - \beta)^{j-1}, \qquad j = 1, 2, 3, \cdots \tag{2.8}$$

from Equation (2.2) into Equations (2.7). The result of the substitutions is the system:

$$w_1 = \beta$$
$$w_i = \beta(1 - \beta)^{i-1} + \beta \sum_{j=1}^{i-1} (1 - \beta)^{j-1} w_{i-j}, \qquad i = 2, 3, 4, \cdots. \tag{2.9}$$

It follows that

$$w_i = \beta \qquad \text{for all } i \geq 1. \tag{2.10}$$

Writing y_t in terms of the independent shocks, as in Equation (2.3), we obtain:

$$y_t = \epsilon_t + \beta \sum_{i=1}^{\infty} \epsilon_{t-i}. \tag{2.11}$$

The shock associated with each time period has a weight of unity; its weight in successive time periods, however, is constant and somewhere between zero and one. Part of the shock in any period therefore, has a permanent effect, while the rest affects the system only in the current period.[3]

We have assumed that the forecasts given by Equation (2.2) were for the period immediately ahead. The best forecasts for all future periods, however, are the same. In order to prove this assertion, it is necessary to generalize the previous results. Let $y_{t,T}$ represent the value of y_{t+T}, forecasted on the basis of information available through period t (T is called the "forecast span"). By an argument similar to that leading to Equation (2.4), we have the relation:

$$\begin{aligned} y^e_{t,T} &= E(y_{t+T} \mid \epsilon_t, \epsilon_{t-1}, \epsilon_{t-2}, \cdots) \\ &= \sum_{i=0}^{\infty} w_{i+T} \epsilon_{t-i}. \end{aligned} \tag{2.12}$$

However, we wish to express the forecast in terms of the observables y_t, y_{t-1}, y_{t-2}, $\cdots$, rather than the latent variables ϵ_t, ϵ_{t-1}, ϵ_{t-2}, $\cdots$. The desired equation has the form:

[3] Some ways in which the economic system might generate time series of this form is examined in [10].

$$y_{t,T}^{e} = \sum_{j=0}^{\infty} v_{T,j} y_{t-j}. \tag{2.13}$$

From a knowledge of the weights w, we need to find the coefficients v.

The appropriate relations, which are found in the same way as Equations (2.7), are the following:

$$w_{i+T} = v_{T,i} + \sum_{j=0}^{i-1} v_{T,j} w_{i-j}, \qquad \begin{array}{l} i = 0, 1, 2, \cdots \\ T = 1, 2, 3, \cdots. \end{array} \tag{2.14}$$

To find the coefficients of Equations (2.13), substitute from (2.10) into (2.14) to obtain the following system:

$$\beta = v_{T,i} + \beta \sum_{j=0}^{i-1} v_{T,j}, \qquad i = 0, 1, 2, 3 \cdots. \tag{2.15}$$

Subtracting the conditions for $i=k-1$ from those for $i=k$ ($k=1, 2, 3, \cdots$), we obtain the difference equation:

$$v_{T,k} = (1-\beta) v_{T,k-1}, \qquad k = 1, 2, 3, \cdots. \tag{2.16}$$

Since, from Equation (2.15), $v_{T,0}=\beta$, we obtain the unique solution:

$$v_{T,k} = \beta(1-\beta)^k, \qquad k = 0, 1, 2, \cdots \tag{2.17}$$

The forecast weights are therefore independent of T, and the assertion is proved. This result is due to the fact that all prior shocks have the same weight, and that the forecasts only give an estimate of the permanent component of the shocks.

3. EXPECTATIONS WITH INDEPENDENT COMPONENTS

The same type of forecasting rule is appropriate if the permanent and transitory components in each period are statistically independent rather than perfectly correlated as in the preceding case. Let $\bar{y}_t$ represent the permanent component of y_t and η_t the transitory component, so that:

$$y_t = \bar{y}_t + \eta_t. \tag{3.1}$$

The transitory components are assumed to be independently distributed with mean zero and variance σ_η^2. The permanent components are defined by the relationships:

$$\bar{y}_t = \bar{y}_{t-1} + \epsilon_t = \sum_{i=1}^{t} \epsilon_i, \tag{3.2}$$

where the ϵ's are serially independent with mean zero and variance σ_ϵ^2. The η's and ϵ's are also assumed to be independent (this assumption is not, however, an essential one).

The forecasting problem, then, is to find the coefficients $v_1, v_2, \cdots$ in the equation:

$$\overset{\bullet}{y}_t = \sum_{j=1}^{\infty} v_j y_{t-j} \tag{3.3}$$

which minimize the error variance,

$$V = E(y_t - \overset{\bullet}{y}_t)^2. \tag{3.4}$$

The methods used in Section 2 are not appropriate for the independent components because it is impossible to measure both the ϵ_t and the η_t from the one set of observed variables. We can, however, proceed as follows. Substitute from Equations (3.1)–(3.3) and write the forecast error in terms of the weights attached to past observations:

$$V = \sigma_\epsilon^2 + \sigma_\eta^2 + \sigma_\epsilon^2 \sum_{j=1}^{\infty} \left(1 - \sum_{i=1}^{j} v_i\right)^2 + \sigma_\eta^2 \sum_{j=1}^{\infty} v_j^2. \tag{3.5}$$

Setting the derivatives of V with respect to v_k equal to zero, we have the following conditions on the optimal weights:

$$\frac{\partial V}{\partial v_k} = -2\sigma_\epsilon^2 \sum_{j=k}^{\infty} \left(1 - \sum_{i=1}^{j} v_i\right) + 2\sigma_\eta^2 v_k = 0, \qquad k = 1, 2, \cdots. \tag{3.6}$$

Taking second differences of the conditions above to eliminate the long summations, the optimal weights are the solution of the following difference equations:

$$\left(1 + \frac{\sigma_\epsilon^2}{\sigma_\eta^2}\right) v_1 = v_2 = \frac{\sigma_\epsilon^2}{\sigma_\eta^2} \tag{3.7a}$$

$$-v_{k-1} + \left(2 + \frac{\sigma_\epsilon^2}{\sigma_\eta^2}\right) v_k - v_{k+1} = 0, \qquad k = 2, 3, \cdots. \tag{3.7b}$$

The characteristic equation of the system above is

$$-\frac{(1 - \lambda)^2}{\lambda} + \frac{\sigma_\epsilon^2}{\sigma_\eta^2} = 0. \tag{3.8}$$

Because of the symmetry of Equation (3.7b), the characteristic roots occur in a reciprocal pair. Only the root less than unity, say λ_1, is relevant, because the infinite sums in Equations (3.5) and (3.6) would otherwise diverge. The relevant root may be written explicitly in terms of the variance ratio as follows:

$$\lambda_1 = 1 + \frac{1}{2}\frac{\sigma_\epsilon^2}{\sigma_\eta^2} - \frac{\sigma_\epsilon}{\sigma_\eta}\sqrt{1 + \frac{1}{4}\frac{\sigma_\epsilon^2}{\sigma_\eta^2}}\,. \tag{3.9}$$

The solution will then be of the form: $v_k = c\lambda_1^k$, where λ_1 is the relevant characteristic root and c is a constant to be determined from Equation (3.7a).

Substituting from Equation (3.8) into (3.7b), we find that $c=(1-\lambda_1)/\lambda_1$. The weights appearing in the forecasting formula would therefore be the following:

$$v_k = (1-\lambda_1)\lambda_1^{k-1}, \qquad k = 1, 2, 3, \cdots. \tag{3.10}$$

Note that the weights have the same form as those in Equation (2.2) if $\beta=1-\lambda_1$. The forecast for the next period is the forecast for all future periods as well because it is an estimate of the permanent component, $\bar{y}_t$.

If the changes in the permanent component are small relative to the "noise," then λ_1 will be very nearly unity. The forecast then gives nearly equal weights to all past observations in order that the transitory components tend to cancel each other out. The forecasts then do not depend very much on recent information because it says very little about the future. On the other hand, if changes in the permanent component are large relative to the noise, λ_1 would be small so as to weight the recent information heavily.

It is, incidentally, not necessary to assume that ϵ_t and η_t are uncorrelated. If $E\epsilon_t\eta_t=\sigma_{\epsilon\eta}$ and $E\epsilon_t\eta_s=0$ $(t\neq s)$, it is only necessary to replace the ratio $\sigma_\xi^2/\sigma_\eta^2$ in Equations (3.7)–(3.9) by $\sigma_\xi^2/(\sigma_\eta^2+\sigma_{\epsilon\eta})$.

4. PERMANENT AND TRANSITORY COMPONENTS OF INCOME

In the preceding sections we have characterized the time series for which the exponentially weighted moving average equals the conditional expected value. The important feature is that the time series consists of two random parts: one lasting a single time period, and the other lasting through all subsequent periods. The structure therefore resembles the hypothesis concerning permanent and transistory components of income, advanced by Friedman in his study of the consumption function [3]. The structure is not exactly the same, however, because Friedman intentionally left the definitions of "permanent" and "transitory" somewhat vague. We have had to be more specific in the definitions, according to Equations (3.1) and (3.2), although nothing in the analysis states how long a "period" must be. Nevertheless, it appears that the exponentially weighted moving average is an appropriate measure of pemanent income if Friedman's other hypotheses are true.

A problem which may be raised at this point concerns errors of estimating the marginal propensity to consume because of inaccurate measurements of the permanent component. Suppose that consumption depends on the true value of the permanent component of income, on the assumption that households can identify the two sources much better than is possible from aggregate time series. The propensity to consume estimated from the exponentially weighted moving average of income would then be biased downward because of the errors of measurement. We will show, however, that the bias should be small. The consumption model is:

$$c_t = \alpha\bar{y}_t + \delta_t, \tag{4.1}$$

where c_t is the consumption in the tth period, α the propensity to consume, and δ_t the error term of the equation assumed to be independent of the permanent component and its estimate.

The least-squares estimate of α (denoted by $\hat{\alpha}$) which results from using the value of the moving average, y^{e}_{t+1}, instead of the true permanent component, $\bar{y}_t$, is:

$$\hat{\alpha} = (\sum c_t y^{e}_{t+1})/(\sum y^{e\,2}_{t+1}). \tag{4.2}$$

Its probability limit is:

$$P \lim \hat{\alpha} = \alpha \operatorname{Cov}(\bar{y}_t, y^{e}_{t+1})/\operatorname{Var} y^{e}_{t+1}, \tag{4.3}$$

as long as δ_t is not correlated with y^{e}_t.

Assume that the process applies to the income of each household, with t denoting the age of the head of the household starting from the beginning of his working life.[4]

$$y_t = \eta_t + \sum_{i=1}^{t} \epsilon_i. \tag{4.4}$$

From Equations (3.3) and (3.10), y^{e}_{t+1} may similarly be expressed in terms of the independently-distributed shocks:

$$\begin{aligned} y^{e}_{t+1} &= (1-\lambda_1)\sum_{k=1}^{t} \lambda_1^{k-1} y_{t+1-k} \\ &= \sum_{k=1}^{t} [(1-\lambda_1)\lambda_1^{k-1}\eta_{t+1-k} + (1-\lambda_1^{k})\epsilon_{t+1-k}]. \end{aligned} \tag{4.5}$$

The variance of y^{e}_{t+1} is therefore:

$$\begin{aligned} \operatorname{Var} y^{e}_{t+1} &= (1-\lambda_1)^2 \frac{1-\lambda_1^{2t}}{1-\lambda_1^2}\sigma_\eta^2 + \left(t - 2\lambda_1\frac{1-\lambda_1^{t}}{1-\lambda_1} + \lambda_1^2\frac{1-\lambda_1^{2t}}{1-\lambda_1^2}\right)\sigma_\epsilon^2 \\ &= \left[t - \frac{\lambda_1}{1-\lambda_1}(1-\lambda_1^{t})^2\right]\sigma_\epsilon^2, \end{aligned} \tag{4.6}$$

the latter equation arising from the dependence of λ_1 on the ratio $\sigma_\epsilon^2/\sigma_\eta^2$ according to (3.8). The covariance between $\bar{y}_t$ and y^{e}_{t+1} may be similarly expressed as:

$$\operatorname{Cov}(\bar{y}_t, y^{e}_{t+1}) = \left[t - \frac{\lambda_1}{1-\lambda_1}(1-\lambda_1^{t})\right]\sigma_\epsilon^2. \tag{4.7}$$

The asymptotic bias, according to Equations (4.3), is determined by the ratio of (4.7) to (4.6). Since this ratio is very nearly unity for moderately large values of t, it appears that this kind of measurement error of the permanent component would introduce very little asymptotic bias in the estimate of the propensity to consume.

---

[4] This uses one of the ideas of Modigliani and Brumberg in their approach to the theory of the consumption [9].

REFERENCES

[1] Brown, R. G., *Statistical Forecasting for Inventory Control*, New York: McGraw-Hill Book Company, 1959.

[2] Cagan, P., "The Monetary Dynamics of Hyper-Inflation," in M. Friedman (Ed.), *Studies in the Quantity Theory of Money*, Chicago: University of Chicago Press, 1957.

[3] Friedman, M., *A Theory of the Consumption Function*, Princeton: Princeton University Press, 1957.

[4] Holt, C. C., Modigliani, F., Muth, J. F., and Simon, H. A., *Planning Production, Inventories, and Work Force*, Englewood Cliffs, New Jersey: Prentice-Hall, forthcoming.

[5] Klein, L. R., "The Estimation of Distributed Lags," *Econometrica* 26 (1958), 553–61.

[6] Koyck, L. M., *Distributed Lags and Investment Analysis*, Amsterdam: The North-Holland Publishing Company, 1954.

[7] Laning, J. H., Jr., and Battin, R. H., *Random Processes in Automatic Control*, New York: McGraw-Hill Book Company, 1956.

[8] Magee, J. F., *Production Planning and Inventory Control*, New York: McGraw-Hill Book Company, 1958.

[9] Modigliani, F., and Brumberg, R., "Utility Analysis and the Consumption Function: An Interpretation of Cross-Section Data," in K. K. Kurihara (Ed.), *Post-Keynesian Economics*, New Brunswick: Rutgers University Press, 1954.

[10] Muth, J. F., "Rational Expectations and the Theory of Price Movements," forthcoming.

[11] Nerlove, M., *The Dynamics of Supply: Estimation of Farmers' Response to Price*, Baltimore: The Johns Hopkins Press, 1958.

[12] Winters, P. R., "Forecasting Sales by Exponentially-Weighted Moving Averages," *Management Science*, forthcoming.

[10]

Bayesian Forecasting

By P. J. HARRISON and C. F. STEVENS

Warwick University *Independent Consultant*†

[Read before the ROYAL STATISTICAL SOCIETY at a meeting organized by the RESEARCH SECTION on Wednesday, May 5th, 1976, Professor S. D. SILVEY in the Chair]

SUMMARY

This paper describes a Bayesian approach to forecasting. The principles of Bayesian forecasting are discussed and the formal inclusion of "the forecaster" in the forecasting system is emphasized as a major feature. The basic model, the dynamic linear model, is defined together with the Kalman filter recurrence relations and a number of model formulations are given. Multi-process models introduce uncertainty as to the underlying model itself, and this approach is described in a more general fashion than in our 1971 paper. Applications to four series are described in a sister paper. Although the results are far from exhaustive, the authors are convinced of the great benefits which the Bayesian approach offers to forecasters.

Keywords: BAYESIAN FORECASTING; DYNAMIC LINEAR MODEL; KALMAN FILTER; MULTI-PROCESS MODELS; PREDICTION

1. INTRODUCTION

1.1. *Background*

ALTHOUGH the methods proposed in this paper are presented theoretically it is essential to say that they have developed from and during our many years of industrial experience as "operational" forecasters. This also explains our tendency to adopt language and examples appropriate to commercial applications even though the methods are generally applicable. Compared with current forecasting fashions our views may well appear radical but in order to extend facilities and to advance to the unfamiliar a fresh way of looking at the familiar is often required. We present an approach which we feel sure offers an extremely fruitful field for further practical application and theoretical research in areas that have previously been regarded as perhaps too difficult or whose practical importance has not been fully appreciated. This makes it necessary to remark on forecasting practice.

For well-understood reasons, theoreticians and teachers often limit themselves to studies amenable to theoretical analysis and to retrospective data analysis using simple fit and comparative criteria such as root mean squares. Such work is dominated by the past yet it is clear that operational forecasting is concerned with the present and the future; with the current situation and how it relates to what might happen rather than what did happen; and above all with creating a meaningful view of the future in the minds of the people who take decisions. The critical distinction is that between a statistical forecasting *method* and a forecasting *system*. The former transforms input data into output information in a purely mechanical way. The latter, however, includes people; the person responsible for the forecasts (who is rarely the systems designer) and all the people concerned with using the forecasts and supplying information relevant to the resulting actions.

To isolate oneself with a historical observation series in order to stimulate theory and in order to familiarize oneself with forecasting methods is natural enough, but it is a dangerous step to extrapolate to the conclusion that because a method produces the "best fit" on such a data series it is the best method to employ in a forecasting system. (Apart from the fact that time series data are so correlated that there is a tendancy to overfit a particular past realization

† Mr. C. F. Stevens, 5 Chestnut Close, Maidenhead, Berks.

at the expense of the unrealized future; apart from the fact that such time series analyses often ignore external information; and apart from the fact that the fitting criterion is usually far from reflecting the decision loss function, the analysis completely neglects the people who, in a forecasting system, will communicate with each other and with the forecasting model.) People have sources of information quite beyond the mere data history; for example, they will know perfectly well that a competitor's plant has been burned to the ground, that a competing product is being introduced, or that new legislation will come into force in 2 months' time. The effect of such events can often be well foreseen in a qualitative sense; at the simplest level, an increase or decrease of demand, temporary or sustained, is to be expected. The effects are, however, more difficult to express quantitatively and require probability distributions to describe the uncertainty. In these circumstances, no statistical forecasting method can be expected to predict such occurrences using only historical data. Rather it is necessary that people can communicate their information to the method and that the method clearly communicates the uncertain information in such a way that it is readily interpreted and accepted by decision makers. The essential qualities of a system are that it can respond quickly to major disturbances which threaten or occur but that it does not produce violently fluctuating forecasts in the "quiet periods" where there is little real movement in the underlying process. It is important to realize that to business people major disturbances are not pathological but are their meat and drink. That this is so is evident from the obvious fact that two of the most important marketing functions are (a) to bring about desirable changes and (b) to respond effectively to disturbances from causes beyond their control, such as may arise from economic, political or competitors' decisions or from such things as periods of untypical weather.

It is partly for these reasons that we do not consider such criteria as the RMS error over a data series as a valid measure of system performance. Published time series are nearly always carefully selected so that they do not contain major changes and so that they contain sufficient data to give good estimates of the model quantities. Rarely do these series feature cases of little or no data, or major discontinuities, and rarely do they even acknowledge subjective information, let alone try to incorporate it in the forecasting system. Consequently, it is not surprising that series selected to demonstrate the best features of particular methods which are only capable of responding satisfactorily to "well-behaved" data do not show the benefits of methods, such as this, designed not only to handle the well-behaved series but also the whole range of series that occur in practice. Furthermore, such "well-behaved" series are rarely followed up in the future; could this be because one of the major disturbances which "never happen" actually did occur?

1.2 *Foundations*

1.2.1. *General*

In this paper we present a Bayesian approach to forecasting which not only includes many conventional methods, such as linear regression, exponential smoothing and linear time series models as special cases, but possesses a remarkable range of additional facilities, not the least being its ability to respond effectively in the start-up situation where no prior data history (as distinct from information) is available.

The essential foundations of the method are:

(i) a *parametric* (or state space) model, as distinct from a functional model;
(ii) *probabilistic* information on the parameters at any given time;
(iii) a *sequential* model definition which describes how the parameters change in time, both systematically and as a result of random shocks;
(iv) *uncertainty* as to the underlying model itself, as between a number of discrete alternatives.

These are considered in more detail below.

1.2.2. *Parametric (State-space) Representation*

The benefits of the simplicity, structuring and insights afforded by the parametric representation of a process are far-reaching. For example, consider the following functional form for a process y_t $(t = 1,2,\ldots)$

$$2y_t - 3y_{t-1} + y_{t-2} = 0. \tag{1.2.1}$$

As is easily seen, a process which satisfies this equation is

$$\left.\begin{aligned} y_t &= \mu_t, \\ \mu_t &= \tfrac{1}{2}\mu_{t-1} + \beta_t, \\ \beta_t &= \beta_{t-1} \end{aligned}\right\} \tag{1.2.2}$$

where the parameters μ_t, β_t bear simple interpretations; μ_t is the "level" of the process at time t, and β_t the incremental growth in level, or slope, in the interval $(t-1, t)$.

The interpreted equations (1.2.2) logically imply (1.2.1) but (1.2.1) does not logically imply the interpreted form (1.2.2). The parametric structure has been used to introduce interpretation on the grounds that interpretation reduces ambiguity and the reduction of ambiguity increases meaning. This meaning has, however, been gained at some risk of misinterpretation and therefore benefit is to be derived through the use of a parametric structure only if there is a strong reason to view the process in a particular structural way. Such reasons naturally arise from the background context, from analogy and from the wish to increase understanding by proposing and using a given parametric structure.

In a forecasting system, structure has a great deal to offer. The statistical modeller who builds forecasting models often wishes to describe the situation he is modelling and not only needs to use mathematics as a language but, in larger model building, is almost forced into model decomposition where he builds sub-models and later joins these together (see Section 2.4). Another vital consequence of the parametric structural representation is that it permits communication between the forecaster and the forecasting method in both directions. The forecaster can both understand and evaluate inferences about the parameters (e.g. μ_t and β_t). And he can impart his own views on the parameters reflecting information external to the data history—a facility which is not only necessary initially when no data history is available but is also important in anticipating and dealing with major process changes.

1.2.3. *Probabilistic Parameter Description*

Consider now the deterministic system (1.2.2) modified by the addition of a random term into the observation equation and random disturbances $\delta\mu_t, \delta\beta_t$ into the system equations

$$y_t = \mu_t + \varepsilon_t, \tag{1.2.3}$$

$$\left.\begin{aligned} \mu_t &= \tfrac{1}{2}\mu_{t-1} + \beta_t + \delta\mu_t, \\ \beta_t &= \beta_{t-1} + \delta\beta_t, \end{aligned}\right\} \tag{1.2.4}$$

where $\text{var}(\varepsilon_t)$, $E(\delta\mu_t)$, $\text{var}(\delta\mu_t)$, $E(\delta\beta_t)$ and $\text{var}(\delta\beta_t)$ are known at time t, but not necessarily constant in time. (See Sections 5 and 3.4 for a discussion of the implications of non-zero values of $\delta\mu_t, \delta\beta_t$.) With such a system, the forecasting problem has two separate stages:

(i) to estimate the current parameter values μ_t, β_t from the available data $y_1, y_2, \ldots, y_t$; and then

(ii) to extrapolate this information forward in time to make inferences as to future values of the observation variable y_{t+k} $(k = 1,2,\ldots)$.

The Bayesian approach is natural since in commercial situations not only do people like to convey and receive their information on parameters in terms of cumulative probabilities, but they are concerned with making decisions in the face of uncertainty, which involves the combination of beliefs about the future with the consequential costs of decisions taken relative to possible future outcomes. It must also be stressed that a person's uncertainty about the future arises not simply because of future random terms but also because of uncertainty about the current parameter values and of the model's ability to link the present to the future.

Throughout this paper we çonsider the parametric vector to be a multivariate unknown random variable whose joint distribution we aim to infer from the data available at any given time. In the general case the observation y_t may also be a vector, and in this case the joint probability distributions offer an easy means of forecasting subject to constraints and of using data say on one product to inform about related products.

1.2.4. *Sequential Model Description*

This is the specification of the evolution of the system between discrete sample times $(t-1, t)$, the system (1.2.3) and (1.2.4) being an example, where evolution may be systematic (e.g. if $\delta\mu_t = \delta\beta_t = 0$ at any given time) or disturbed ($\delta\mu_t$, $\delta\beta_t \neq 0$). The implications of this are simply that in the approach used throughout this paper, the procedure for inferring the current parameter vector at time t needs only (i) the posterior parameter distribution at time $t-1$, (ii) the distributions of the *current* noise term ε_t and the *current* disturbances ($\delta\mu_t$, $\delta\beta_t$ in the present case); and, of course, the new data value y_t. *There is no requirement whatever for the transition model* $(t-1, t)$ *to be the same for all times* t. This is crucial since it gives enormous flexibility.

Different models would be appropriate, for example, if observations $t+1, \ldots, t+k-1$ were missing or if they were unequally spaced; for specifying changing variances; or if large disturbances were to be expected because of new legislation, say, or the introduction of a competing product.

1.2.5 *Multi-process Models*

Statistical methods of great power have been evolved to handle uncertainty as to parameter values for any given model, but the question of uncertainty as to the model itself does not seem to have received the same depth of treatment. Even in time-invariant analysis the data of a given experiment may be consistent with a number of possible models, the usual outcome being the selection of *a* model. Of course a good deal of thought is given to the selection, but it still seems strange that little attention has been paid to the case where there is genuine, irresolvable doubt as to which of a number of possible models actually obtains.

In time-ordered data the problem becomes more severe; not only may there be doubt as to the underlying model, but there is often reason to suppose that different models may obtain at different times, as has been hinted at in Section 1.2.4 above. This was the rationale underlying our first paper (Harrison and Stevens, 1971) and further practical experiences have confirmed our belief in the value of catering for occasional major disturbances. In this paper we distinguish between two broad types of model uncertainty, which are discussed in Sections 4 and 5.

(i) *Multi-process Models, Class I*: A unique process model obtains at all times, it not being known which one (of a set of discrete alternatives).

(ii) *Multi-process Models, Class II*: The generating model at any given time is a random choice from a number of discrete alternatives. For example, using this means it is possible to model sudden changes in level or slope, or the occurrence of occasional freak observation values.

Of the two classes, nearly all our practical experience to date has been with the Class II model, supplemented by a Class I model for the estimation of the noise variance.

1.3 *Schemata*

The general outline of this paper is as follows. In Section 2 we present the basic theory of the dynamic linear model (DLM); the model itself; its associated inferential method (the

Kalman filter, Kalman (1963)); its implications for prediction; and the principles of extension and superposition which increase immensely its potential range of application.

In Section 3 we give examples showing how a number of basic processes of interest to forecasters may be written in DLM form, and thus are amenable, either individually or in combination with other forms, to analysis by the Kalman filter.

Sections 4 and 5 are devoted to multi-process models, i.e. situations where there is uncertainty as to the generating process itself.

For reasons of space we regret that we are unable to conclude this paper with examples. For those interested, however, we have devoted the whole of a further paper to applications of the method to four genuine data series, none of which has been previously published.

By merely concentrating on a particular theme, a paper such as this necessarily gives an unbalanced impression, and there is always the danger that it will be inferred that the authors dismiss much previous work and consider their approach a panacea. We would like to correct any such impression at this stage by remarking that the Bayesian approach to time series is not a panacea but is a natural marriage of the theoretical work done in time series, linear models, Bayesian statistics and practical forecasting experience. Although we emphasize on-line identification and estimation this does not mean that we reject traditional data analysis methods such as correlation, cross-correlation, multivariate analysis, spectral analysis and general decomposition analysis. These methods are very valuable when sufficient data are available.

1.4. *Related Work*

It is necessary to mention some related work. Nearly all such work is related to the basic Kalman filter result of Section 2.2. Apart from the control theory literature, Whittle (1969) and Åström and Eykhoff (1971) have both mentioned the result to the Society and it is increasingly referred to in discussions of statistical papers, e.g. Brown *et al.* (1975), where the topic of changing regression parameters is discussed. In the discussion of that paper the very active Manchester school of Priestley, Subba Rao and Tong all give relevant references. We are not aware of any references to either the theory or the application of Bayesian methods to situations of abrupt changes in time series before our 1971 paper. However, Tong, who has developed a likelihood method, and Smith, who has developed a Bayesian method of detecting changes, have both spoken about their work at Warwick seminars. Both of them refer to their work in Brown *et al.* (1975) and quote references. The early work of Holt (1957), Brown (1963), our colleagues in I.C.I. (e.g. Coutie *et al.*, 1964) and many other practitioners who know so much and write so little must be mentioned as providing the foundations of our experience. So too must the major work of Box and Jenkins (1962, 1970) who, by their efforts have raised the consciousness of forecasters and brought theory and practice much closer together.

1.5. *Implementation*

In Section 3 we show how the Bayesian forecasting technique may be applied to a wide variety of situations. Unfortunately, we cannot at present claim to have had direct personal experience in all these cases. The bulk of our experience has been with the steady/linear growth models of Sections 3.4 and 3.5, with or without added seasonality, in the field of commercial demand forecasting. A number of operational systems for handling varying numbers of individual items (sometimes in the 10^3–10^4 range) have been or are being installed. One such scheme, we are pleased to report, has been in operation for 5 years, during which time its scope has been extended.

We are further aware of a number of applications by other workers, mainly in the socio-economic field, but few have been reported, with the notable exception of Beer (1974).

In all cases where we have been personally involved, the features of the method which users find attractive are (i) its "no data" capability, (ii) its ability to signal a variety of disturbances and to respond appropriately, either automatically or under user control, and (iii) its realistic estimates of forecast error, based on parameter uncertainty as well as observation noise.

We mention these things as evidence that there is a real need, at working levels, for the facilities offered by the Bayesian method; and that practical systems are capable of survival in the rough and tumble of reality. And if others are encouraged to develop and extend the methods further, both theoretically and practically, we shall be well pleased.

2. THE DYNAMIC LINEAR MODEL

2.1 *Definition*

The DLM is a system of equations specifying:

(i) how observations of a process are stochastically dependent on the current process parameters,

(ii) how the process parameters evolve in time, both as a result of the inherent process dynamics and from random shocks or disturbances.

The model is stated in terms of discrete, equally spaced intervals of time, although it is not difficult to extend it to unequal intervals of observations or to model missing values. Throughout the paper the following notion is standard:

t = time index ($t = 1, 2, \ldots$);

$\mathbf{y}_t = (m \times 1)$ vector of process observations made at time t;

$\boldsymbol{\theta}_t = (n \times 1)$ vector of process parameters at time t;

$\mathbf{F}_t = (m \times n)$ matrix of independent variables, *known at time* t;

$\mathbf{G} = (n \times n)$ known system matrix;

$\mathbf{v}_t, \mathbf{w}_t$ = random normal vectors, $(m \times 1)$ and $(n \times 1)$ respectively, with zero means and variances *known at time* t given by

$$\mathbf{V}_t = E[\mathbf{v}_t \mathbf{v}_t^T],$$

$$\mathbf{W}_t = E[\mathbf{w}_t \mathbf{w}_t^T].$$

Our DLM is:

The Dynamic Linear Model

$$\text{Observation equation:} \quad \mathbf{y}_t = \mathbf{F}_t \boldsymbol{\theta}_t + \mathbf{v}_t, \quad \{\mathbf{v}_t \sim N(\mathbf{0}, \mathbf{V}_t)\} \tag{2.1.1}$$

$$\text{System equation:} \quad \boldsymbol{\theta}_t = \mathbf{G}\, \boldsymbol{\theta}_{t-1} + \mathbf{w}_t, \quad \{\mathbf{w}_t \sim N(\mathbf{0}, \mathbf{W}_t)\} \tag{2.1.2}$$

The conventional linear normal model of classical statistics is the simple static case of the DLM in which $\boldsymbol{\theta}_t = \boldsymbol{\theta}$ and $\mathbf{V}_t$ are independent of time. This is equivalent to the redundant system equation $\boldsymbol{\theta}_t = \boldsymbol{\theta}_{t-1}$. In Section 3 we show how a number of process models of interest to forecasters can be expressed in DLM form. However, we would point out that there are two main interpretations for process parameters. A process parameter may express a relationship between the dependent variable $\mathbf{y}_t$ and an independent variable $\mathbf{F}_t$ in which case it extends the classical parametric interpretation of the static linear model, or, in say the case of a constant $\mathbf{F}_t$, the model is a state-space representation of a time series in which the parameters may be interpreted as process level, process growth and so on. The DLM may represent linear combinations of models, and hierarchic models, such as those of Lindley and Smith (1972), can also be formulated as DLM's.

The observation equation (2.1.1) specifies the stochastic dependence of the observation variable on the current (unknown) process parameters, it being assumed that this completely specifies the distribution of $\mathbf{y}_t$. In the system equation (2.1.2), the matrix $\mathbf{G}$, assumed to be a fixed characteristic of the process, defines the deterministic motion of the parameters from one moment to the next, superimposed on which is a random component specified by $\mathbf{w}_t$ which we term the "disturbance vector" at time t.

We would emphasize that, where quantities have been specified as being known at time t, we mean exactly that; there is no need to assume them constant. For example, the noise variance $\mathbf{V}_t$ is often a function of the process level (e.g. Poisson processes). The DLM can be generalized by allowing $\mathbf{G}$ to vary with time, and by considering a joint distribution and non-zero expectations for $\mathbf{v}_t$ and $\mathbf{w}_t$. We shall restrict ourselves to the above model since we believe that it will suffice for most applications.

2.2. *Estimation; The Kalman Filter*

We now state a very powerful result, originally given by Kalman (1963). It is assumed that initially at time $t = 0$, information concerning the parameter vector $\boldsymbol{\theta}_0$ was described in the form of a Normal probability distribution with mean $\mathbf{m}_0$ and variance $\mathbf{C}_0$. Then, if the process $\mathbf{y}_t$ is described through the DLM of Section 2.1, the Kalman result provides elegant recurrence relationships for updating or revising information concerning the parameter vectors. We write the result in the form most suitable for forecasting applications. Throughout the paper we will assume that the first observation is $\mathbf{y}_1$, and denote the entire sequence of values from $t = 1$ up to a specified time t by a superscript:

$$\mathbf{y}^t = (\mathbf{y}_1 \dots \mathbf{y}_t) = (\mathbf{y}^{t-1}, \mathbf{y}_t). \qquad (2.2.1)$$

The Kalman Filter

Let the DLM of Section 2.1 be the model description for an observation series $\mathbf{y}$. Then if the distribution of $\boldsymbol{\theta}_0$ prior to the first observation is $N(\mathbf{m}_0, \mathbf{C}_0)$, the posterior distribution of $\boldsymbol{\theta}_t$ at time t is also normally distributed, i.e.

$$(\boldsymbol{\theta}_t \,|\, \mathbf{y}^t, \mathbf{F}^t) \sim N(\mathbf{m}_t, \mathbf{C}_t), \qquad (2.2.2)$$

where the values of $\mathbf{m}_t$ and $\mathbf{C}_t$ are recursively obtained as follows. Let

$$\left.\begin{aligned} \hat{\mathbf{y}} &= \mathbf{F}_t \mathbf{G} \mathbf{m}_{t-1}, \\ \mathbf{e} &= \mathbf{y}_t - \hat{\mathbf{y}}, \\ \mathbf{R} &= \mathbf{G}\mathbf{C}_{t-1}\mathbf{G}^{\mathrm{T}} + \mathbf{W}_t, \\ \hat{\mathbf{Y}} &= \mathbf{F}_t \mathbf{R} \mathbf{F}_t^{\mathrm{T}} + \mathbf{V}_t, \\ \mathbf{A} &= \mathbf{R}\mathbf{F}_t^{\mathrm{T}} (\hat{\mathbf{Y}})^{-1}. \end{aligned}\right\} \qquad (2.2.3)$$

Then

$$\mathbf{m}_t = \mathbf{G}\mathbf{m}_{t-1} + \mathbf{A}\mathbf{e}, \qquad (2.2.4)$$

$$\mathbf{C}_t = \mathbf{R} - \mathbf{A}\hat{\mathbf{Y}}\mathbf{A}^{\mathrm{T}}. \qquad (2.2.5)$$

The recursive nature of the algorithm is important; in forecasting practice it means that the current posterior distribution may be calculated from the most recent observation value $(\mathbf{y}_t, \mathbf{F}_t)$, the posterior distribution $(\boldsymbol{\theta}_{t-1} \,|\, \mathbf{y}^{t-1}, \mathbf{F}^{t-1})$ and the current observation noise and disturbance variances $\mathbf{V}_t, \mathbf{W}_t$. The great advantage of this is that, for the first time, we have a rational, coherent framework for forecasting in situations where there is little or no prior history and for developing systems which require structured models to facilitate communication between man and "routine forecasting method".

The intermediate quantities in (2.2.3) are of some interest. For example, reference to Section 2.3 will show that $\hat{\mathbf{y}}, \hat{\mathbf{Y}}$ are the expectation and variance of $\mathbf{y}_t$ (conditional on $\mathbf{F}_t$), given data up to and including $\mathbf{y}^{t-1}, \mathbf{F}^{t-1}$ (i.e. the one-step ahead forecast) so that the quantity $\mathbf{e}$ is the (conditional) one-step ahead forecast error. The quantity $\mathbf{A}$ is closely analogous to the "smoothing constant" of many conventional systems, the main differences being that **A** is not in general a constant and that it is in fact a $(n \times m)$ matrix.

2.3. *Prediction*

Having obtained the results required to calculate the posterior distribution of the parameter vector $\boldsymbol{\theta}_t$ at any time $t = 1, 2, \ldots$, we now show how this information may be used to infer the distributions of future observations $\mathbf{y}_{t+k}$ $(k = 1, 2, \ldots)$. It is perhaps unnecessary to observe that these predictions are purely extrapolative in nature; our method, like other statistical forecasting methods, lays no claim to clairvoyance. We would also emphasize that our predictions are distributional in nature, and derived from the current parameter, uncertainty, future observation noises $\mathbf{V}_{t+k}$ and the disturbance variance $\mathbf{W}_{t+k} = \text{var}(\mathbf{w}_{t+k})$ $(k = 1, 2, \ldots)$. While it is natural to think of the expectations of the future variate values as "forecasts" there is no need to single out the expectation for this purpose; from the distributional information the user may derive whatever "forecasts" are appropriate to his situation. Thus, if the consequences of an error in one direction are more serious than an error of the same magnitude in the opposite direction, then the forecast can be biased to take this into account. This topic is developed further in Section 4.

From the equations of the DLM, (2.1.1) and (2.1.2), we may, at time t, write a future observation variable value as

$$\mathbf{y}_{t+k} = \mathbf{F}_{t+k}\,\boldsymbol{\theta}_{t+k} + \mathbf{v}_{t+k}, \tag{2.3.1}$$

$$\boldsymbol{\theta}_{t+k} = \mathbf{G}\boldsymbol{\theta}_{t+k-1} + \mathbf{w}_{t+k}. \tag{2.3.2}$$

Hence, from (2.3.1), assuming the variance of the random vectors $\mathbf{v}_{t+k}, \mathbf{w}_{t+k}$ is known, prediction of future values of $\mathbf{y}_{t+k}$ require inferences about the parameter vector $\boldsymbol{\theta}_{t+k}$ and the independent variable matrix $\mathbf{F}_{t+k}$. Let

$$\hat{\mathbf{m}}_{k,t} = E(\boldsymbol{\theta}_{t+k} \,|\, \mathbf{y}^t, \mathbf{F}^t),$$

$$\hat{\mathbf{C}}_{k,t} = \text{var}(\boldsymbol{\theta}_{t+k} \,|\, \mathbf{y}^t, \mathbf{F}^t),$$

where

$$\hat{\mathbf{m}}_{0,t} = \mathbf{m}_t = E(\boldsymbol{\theta}_t \,|\, \mathbf{y}^t, \mathbf{F}^t) \quad \text{and} \quad \hat{\mathbf{C}}_{0,t} = \mathbf{C}_t = \text{var}(\boldsymbol{\theta}_t \,|\, \mathbf{y}^t, \mathbf{F}^t),$$

are known from the Kalman filter algorithm.

Then, from (2.3.2)

$$\hat{\mathbf{m}}_{k,t} = \mathbf{G}\hat{\mathbf{m}}_{k-1,t}, \tag{2.3.3}$$

$$\hat{\mathbf{C}}_{k,t} = \mathbf{G}\hat{\mathbf{C}}_{k-1,t}\mathbf{G}^{\mathrm{T}} + \mathbf{W}_{t+k}, \tag{2.3.4}$$

so the mean and variance of the future parameter vector $\boldsymbol{\theta}_{t+k}$ can be calculated recursively from $k = 1, 2, \ldots$ using the known starting values $\hat{\mathbf{m}}_{0,t}, \hat{\mathbf{C}}_{0,t}$.

Let the prediction mean and variance of the k-step ahead process observation be written

$$\hat{\mathbf{y}}_{k,t} = E(\mathbf{y}_{t+k} \,|\, \mathbf{y}^t, \mathbf{F}^t),$$

$$\hat{\mathbf{Y}}_{k,t} = \text{var}(\mathbf{y}_{t+k} \,|\, \mathbf{y}^t, \mathbf{F}^t).$$

To calculate these values we need to distinguish between two cases, depending on whether $\mathbf{F}_{t+k}$ is or is not known at time t; in the latter case, equation (2.3.1) is non-linear in the unknowns $\boldsymbol{\theta}, \mathbf{F}$.

Prediction Case I: Known $\mathbf{F}_{t+k}$ $(k = 1, 2, \ldots)$

From (2.3.1) we can write immediately

$$\hat{y}_{k,t} = \mathbf{F}_{t+k}\,\hat{\mathbf{m}}_{k,t}, \tag{2.3.5}$$

$$\hat{\mathbf{Y}}_{k,t} = \mathbf{F}_{t+k}\,\hat{\mathbf{C}}_{k,t}\,\mathbf{F}_{t+k}^{\mathrm{T}} + \mathbf{V}_{t+k}, \tag{2.3.6}$$

where $\hat{\mathbf{m}}, \hat{\mathbf{C}}$ are obtained recursively from equations (2.3.3) and (2.3.4) above for $k = 1, 2, \ldots$, etc.

In the situation when $\mathbf{F}_{t+k}$ is not known at time t we must incorporate the further variability arising from the uncertainty of $\mathbf{F}_{t+k}$ itself. We suppose, therefore, that $\mathbf{F}_{t+k}$ can be expressed as an expected value $\hat{\mathbf{F}}$ and a stochastic term $\delta\mathbf{F}$, where, for simplicity, we drop the time suffix $t+k$, i.e.

$$\mathbf{F}_{t+k} = \hat{\mathbf{F}} + \delta\mathbf{F} = \begin{pmatrix} \hat{\mathbf{F}}_1 + \delta\mathbf{F}_1 \\ \vdots \\ \hat{\mathbf{F}}_m + \delta\mathbf{F}_m \end{pmatrix}, \tag{2.3.7}$$

where $\hat{\mathbf{F}}_i$, $\delta\mathbf{F}_i$ $(i = 1, \ldots, m)$ are $1 \times n$ vectors such that

$$\hat{\mathbf{F}} = E[\mathbf{F}_{t+k} \mid \mathbf{F}^t]$$

and with known covariances

$$\mathbf{\Phi}_{ij} = \operatorname{cov}(\delta\mathbf{F}_i, \delta\mathbf{F}_j^{\mathrm{T}}). \tag{2.3.8}$$

Effectively $\hat{\mathbf{F}}, \mathbf{\Phi}_{ij}$ constitute the prior distribution (at time t) of the future independent variable $\mathbf{F}_{t+k}$, and we say nothing as to how this is obtained. (It could derive, for example, from a forecasting process applied to the independent variables themselves.)

It is then not difficult, but rather cumbersome, to obtain the required results below, which we state without proof.

Prediction Case II: Unknown $\mathbf{F}_{t+k}$ $(k = 1, 2, \ldots)$

Let equations (2.3.7) and (2.3.8) define $\mathbf{F}_{k,t}$ and $\mathbf{\Phi}_{ij}$ $(i,j = 1, \ldots, m)$. Then

$$\hat{y}_{k,t} = \hat{\mathbf{F}}_{k,t}\,\hat{\mathbf{m}}_{k,t}, \tag{2.3.9}$$

$$\hat{\mathbf{Y}}_{k,t} = \hat{\mathbf{F}}_{k,t}\,\hat{\mathbf{C}}_{k,t}\,\hat{\mathbf{F}}_{k,t}^{\mathrm{T}} + \mathbf{V}_{t+k} + \mathbf{Z}, \tag{2.3.10}$$

where

$$\mathbf{Z} = \{Z_{ij}\} \text{ is } (m \times m)$$

and the element

$$Z_{ij} = \operatorname{trace}\,\{\mathbf{\Phi}_{ij}(\hat{\mathbf{m}}_{k,t}\hat{\mathbf{m}}_{k,t}^{\mathrm{T}} + \hat{\mathbf{C}}_{k,t})\}.$$

The result (2.3.10) has been given by Feldstein (1971) in the context of econometrics, the term $\mathbf{Z}$ representing the additional prediction uncertainty arising from the uncertainty associated with $\mathbf{F}_{t+k}$.

2.4. *Superposition*

The principle of superposition makes the seemingly trivial statement that a linear combination of linear models is itself a linear model. The obvious is singled out as a principle because of its far-reaching implications for the construction of large-scale and apparently complex models. The essential point is that a large linear model may be considered as the linear combination of a number of simpler linear models.

We show the principle in terms of just two models since the extension to three or more is easily appreciated. Suppose that the forecaster believes two distinct processes are at work in the generation of his data (e.g. a seasonal effect superimposed on a long-term process of growth or decline). The DLM's for each one individually may be written in general as

$$\mathbf{y}_{i,t} = \mathbf{F}_{i,t}\,\boldsymbol{\theta}_{i,t} \qquad (i = 1, 2), \tag{2.4.1}$$

$$\boldsymbol{\theta}_{i,t} = \mathbf{G}_i\,\boldsymbol{\theta}_{i,t-1} + \mathbf{w}_{i,t} \quad (i = 1, 2), \tag{2.4.2}$$

where no observation noise is specified in the observation equations, since $\mathbf{y}_{i,t}$ and $\mathbf{y}_{2,t}$ are idealized, noise-free quantities observable only in combination by $\mathbf{y}_t$, where

$$\mathbf{y}_t = \mathbf{y}_{1,t} + \mathbf{y}_{2,t} + \mathbf{v}_t \quad (\mathbf{v}_t \sim N(\mathbf{0}, \mathbf{V}_t)). \tag{2.4.3}$$

The joint system (2.4.1), (2.4.2) and (2.4.3) can then be written

$$\mathbf{y}_t = (\mathbf{F}_{1,t}, \mathbf{F}_{2,t}) \begin{pmatrix} \boldsymbol{\theta}_{1,t} \\ \boldsymbol{\theta}_{2,t} \end{pmatrix} + \mathbf{v}_t, \tag{2.4.4}$$

$$\begin{pmatrix} \boldsymbol{\theta}_{1,t} \\ \boldsymbol{\theta}_{2,t} \end{pmatrix} = \begin{pmatrix} \mathbf{G}_{11} & \mathbf{0} \\ \mathbf{0} & \mathbf{G}_{22} \end{pmatrix} \begin{pmatrix} \boldsymbol{\theta}_{1,t-1} \\ \boldsymbol{\theta}_{2,t-1} \end{pmatrix} + \begin{pmatrix} \mathbf{w}_{1,t} \\ \mathbf{w}_{2,t} \end{pmatrix}. \tag{2.4.5}$$

which is clearly a DLM in the new parameter vector $\boldsymbol{\theta}_t = (\boldsymbol{\theta}_{1,t}, \boldsymbol{\theta}_{2,t})^{\mathrm{T}}$. Coupling between the two systems may be introduced, if desired, by postulating non-zero system matrices $\mathbf{G}_{12}, \mathbf{G}_{21}$ and/or correlation between the disturbance vectors $\mathbf{w}_{1,t}, \mathbf{w}_{2,t}$.

2.5. *Extension*

The DLM assumes (equation 2.1.2) that $\boldsymbol{\theta}_t$ depends only on the immediately preceding parameter value $\boldsymbol{\theta}_{t-1}$. However, a higher order degree of dependence can easily be introduced as follows.

Let

$$\mathbf{y}_t = \mathbf{F}_t\,\boldsymbol{\theta}_t + \mathbf{v}_t,$$

$$\boldsymbol{\theta}_t = \sum_{i=1}^{p} \mathbf{G}_i\,\boldsymbol{\theta}_{t-i} + \mathbf{w}_t,$$

where $\mathbf{G}_i$ $(i = 1, \ldots, p)$ are known matrices. By writing this as

$$\mathbf{y}_t = (\mathbf{F}_t, \mathbf{0}, \ldots, \mathbf{0})\,\boldsymbol{\phi}_t + \mathbf{v}_t,$$

$$\boldsymbol{\phi}_t = (\boldsymbol{\theta}_t^{\mathrm{T}}, \ldots, \boldsymbol{\theta}_{t-p+1}^{\mathrm{T}})^{\mathrm{T}},$$

and

$$\boldsymbol{\phi}_t = \left(\begin{array}{c|c} \mathbf{G}_1 \ldots \mathbf{G}_{p-1} & \mathbf{G}_p \\ \hline \mathbf{I} & \mathbf{0} \end{array}\right) \boldsymbol{\phi}_{t-1} + \begin{pmatrix} \mathbf{w}_t \\ \mathbf{0} \end{pmatrix}, \tag{2.5.1}$$

the extended system is seen to be a DLM in $\boldsymbol{\phi}_t$.

3. RECIPES

3.1. *Introduction*

The DLM or state space representation is unfamiliar to many modellers and it is for this reason that we describe a number of models which, either in themselves or in linear combination, are useful to forecasters.

We will use the following conventions

(i) In each case the model will be first phrased in terms of its "natural" parameters and structure, and then translated into DLM form.

(ii) In all cases the observation equation is written as

$$\mathbf{y}_t = (\text{expression}) + \boldsymbol{\varepsilon}_t,$$

where $\mathbf{y}_t$ is the vector or univariate observation and $\boldsymbol{\varepsilon}_t$ is a random term with variance var$(\boldsymbol{\varepsilon}_t)$ known at time t.

(iii) It is convenient to use a δ-symbol to denote a random disturbance in the parameter variable specified, e.g.

$$\mu_t = \mu_{t-1} + \beta_t + \delta\mu_t \quad \text{or} \quad \boldsymbol{\beta}_t = \boldsymbol{\beta}_{t-1} + \delta\boldsymbol{\beta}_t,$$

and it will similarly be assumed that the variance–covariance matrix of the disturbances is known at time t. In many cases it is natural to assume independent disturbances, but if the modeller feels that the disturbances in any given process are correlated he is quite at liberty to specify this.

3.2. *Regression Models*

3.2.1. *The Static Model*

The familiar regression model is given by an observation equation

$$y_t = \mathbf{x}_t \boldsymbol{\beta} + \varepsilon_t,$$

where y_t is a univariate observation, $\mathbf{x}_t$ a $(1 \times n)$ independent variable vector and $\boldsymbol{\beta}$ an $(n \times 1)$ vector of unknown coefficients.

The static model is equivalent to a redundant system equation

$$\boldsymbol{\beta}_t = \boldsymbol{\beta}_{t-1} = \ldots \boldsymbol{\beta}_0 \quad \text{for all } t.$$

The filter algorithm affords a computationally neat and economical method of revising regression coefficient estimates as fresh data become available, without effectively re-doing the whole calculation all over again and without any matrix inversion. This has previously been pointed out by Plackett (1950) and others but its practical importance seems to have been almost completely missed. Further, since there is no requirement for the noise variance var(ε_t) to be constant, there is no need to seek for variance stabilizing transformations. Or, of equal importance, if the data have been transformed in order to obtain a convenient form of linear model then the implications of this transformation on the noise variance can be taken into account directly and simply.

3.2.2. *The Dynamic Model*

It is commonplace in econometrics to estimate the coefficients of linear models by fitting past data. This raises some difficulties since, even if such relationships actually obtain, there is no good reason to suppose that the coefficients, in "living" systems, should not be subject to changes in the course of time. This leads to a dilemma: if short series are used for parameter estimation, sampling errors will be large; whereas, if long data series are used, the resultant estimates will be, at best, several years out of date, or, at worst, totally misleading. The static model cannot cope with this situation but the following dynamic model offers a means of expressing this "moving" relationship.

$$y_t = \mathbf{x}_t \boldsymbol{\beta}_t + \varepsilon_t,$$

$$\boldsymbol{\beta}_t = \boldsymbol{\beta}_{t-1} + \delta\boldsymbol{\beta}_t.$$

This model is a DLM with $m = 1$, $\boldsymbol{\theta}_t = \boldsymbol{\beta}_t$, $\mathbf{F}_t = \mathbf{x}_t$ and $\mathbf{G} = \mathbf{I}$, the identity matrix. In accordance with our convention stated in Section 3.1, we do not specify $\mathbf{W}_t = \text{var}(\delta\boldsymbol{\beta}_t)$ since in the light of his knowledge of the structure of the process the modeller can choose this at his own discretion. Furthermore, there are so many options available to a skilful modeller that it is impossible to cover them all. For example, $\mathbf{W}_t$ may be chosen as a constant reflecting a constant decay with time of the value of previous information, or it may be chosen as a function of information in the independent variable space so that if there is a major change of socio-economic conditions to a region which has not previously been encountered then $\mathbf{W}_t$ becomes large reflecting the increased uncertainty and the urge to learn rapidly about this unusual state.

The possibilities are indeed vast. But the modeller does not need to decide *a priori* exactly what he is going to do, just as at the beginning of a game of chess he does not need to know exactly what he will do in all possible situations that might arise. He can deal with the situation which does arise when it arises.

Of course this state of affairs will worry people who like a fixed model for all times. But life is not often static. They can have a fixed procedure if they like within the DLM but the successful modeller will welcome flexibility, increased robustness and the opportunity to use his creativity and skill.

3.3. *The Steady Model*

This model is a simple polynomial model of zero degree and is widely used in practice although often with undue restriction in the sense that a limiting form of the recurrence relationship is employed as an exponentially weighted moving average (EWMA) assuming that the noise and disturbance variances are constant.

It is appropriate to the situation where the most important characteristic of the process in question is its current "true" level of demand, persistent growth or decline being either absent or unimportant (e.g. for short lead times with noisy data). Such a process can be written as

$$y_t = \mu_t + \varepsilon_t,$$
$$\mu_t = \mu_{t-1} + \delta\mu_t,$$

where μ_t is the true (unknown) level of demand at time t and $\delta\mu_t$ is a random demand disturbance at time t. This process, which is not as trivial as it may seem, is the simplest DLM we know, the equivalences being:

$$m = n = 1, \quad \boldsymbol{\theta}_t = (\mu_t), \quad \mathbf{F}_t = \mathbf{G} = (1), \quad \mathbf{V}_t = \operatorname{var}(\varepsilon_t), \quad \mathbf{W}_t = \operatorname{var}(\delta\mu_t).$$

In applying the Kalman filter, information on μ_{t-1} at time $t-1$, is described by

$$(\mu_{t-1} \mid y^{t-1}) \sim N(m_{t-1}, C_{t-1})$$

and the filter recurrence relation for the mean m_t is

$$m_t = m_{t-1} + A_t(y_t - m_{t-1}),$$

where

$$C_t = A_t \operatorname{var}(\varepsilon_t),$$
$$A_t = (C_{t-1} + \operatorname{var}(\delta\mu_t))/(C_{t-1} + \operatorname{var}(\delta\mu_t) + \operatorname{var}(\varepsilon_t)).$$

The facilities that this offers over the traditional EWMA will be evident. Given the model, it is clear that forecasts can be produced starting from no data, by using subjective values of m_0 and C_0 and that under restrictive conditions on the noise and disturbance variances A_t will progressively tend towards a limit (Harrison, 1967). We may also use this opportunity to show one way in which a decision maker can combine with the model. Suppose that, at time t, the model describes the level of product sales as $(\mu_t \mid y^t) \sim N(100, 400)$ with say the accompanying prior $(\mu_{t+1} \mid y^t) \sim N(100, 450)$. However, suppose that the decision maker is aware that next month a major new market opens for his product. He may think that this will roughly double the sales level but he will be very uncertain about the actual value of the new level. In this case he may over-ride the mechanical prior probability for μ_{t+1} with a subjective description $(\mu_{t+1} \mid t) \sim N(200, 1600)$. This clearly expresses his knowledge, the extra uncertainty associated with the unusual occurrence, and it also allows the filter to carry on combining new data with this probability description. The result is that a great deal of weight will be given to the next observation and that, as more data become available, under certain conditions on var ε and var $(\delta\mu_t)$, the weight (i.e. A_t) will tend to the limit of the corresponding EWMA. The effect of the subjective estimates will eventually die away but their practical importance at the time they are needed will be well appreciated by practitioners.

3.4. *The Linear Growth Model*

This model is highly relevant to applications. It extends the steady model by the addition of a slope term $\boldsymbol{\beta}_t$. As the data series develops with time then, provided there are no interventions from marketing and provided that the noise disturbance variances satisfy particular conditions (e.g. constant over time), the predictor will tend to a *limiting* form which is equivalent to Holt's (1957) linear growth predictor and to the ARIMA (0, 2, 2) predictor of Box and Jenkins (1970). The process equations are

$$y_t = \mu_t + \varepsilon_t,$$
$$\mu_t = \mu_{t-1} + \beta_t + \delta\mu_t,$$
$$\beta_t = \beta_{t-1} + \delta\beta_t.$$

The interpretation of μ_t is usually that of the level of the process at time t and β_t is the incremental growth of time t. The representation as a DLM is

$$y_t = (1,\ 0)\begin{pmatrix}\mu_t\\ \beta_t\end{pmatrix} + \varepsilon_t,$$

$$\begin{pmatrix}\mu_t\\ \beta_t\end{pmatrix} = \begin{pmatrix}1 & 1\\ 0 & 1\end{pmatrix}\begin{pmatrix}\mu_{t-1}\\ \beta_{t-1}\end{pmatrix} + \begin{pmatrix}\delta\mu_t + \delta\beta_t\\ \delta\beta_t\end{pmatrix}.$$

It is evident that even if the random disturbances $\delta\mu_t$, $\delta\beta_t$ are independent, covariance is introduced into the **W** matrix by the presence of the slope disturbance $\delta\beta_t$ in both elements of the disturbance vector.

3.5. *General Polynomial Models*

The steady and linear growth model may be generalized to include higher order terms and may be expressed as the DLM

$$y_t = (1, 0, \ldots, 0)\,\boldsymbol{\theta}_t + \varepsilon_t,$$
$$\boldsymbol{\theta}_t = \mathbf{T}\boldsymbol{\theta}_{t-1} + \mathbf{T}\delta\boldsymbol{\theta}_t,$$

where $\boldsymbol{\theta}_t = (\mu_t, \Delta_t^{(1)}, \ldots \Delta_t^{(p)})$, and $\mathbf{T} = [t_{ij}]$ is the upper triangular matrix; $t_{ij} = 1\ (i \leqslant j)$ and zero otherwise. Here μ_t is the level of the process at time t, and the Δ_t its first p differences. (The above system equation is merely a rephrasing of the equations defining the differences.) The DLM has $m = 1$, $n = p+1$, $\mathbf{F}_t = (1, 0, \ldots, 0)$, $\mathbf{G} = \mathbf{T}$ and $\mathbf{W}_t = \mathbf{T}\,\mathrm{var}\,(\delta\boldsymbol{\theta}_t)\,\mathbf{T}^{\mathrm{T}}$.

The limiting form of predictor is discussed in Harrison (1967) and equivalences are given in Godolphin and Harrison (1975).

3.6. *Seasonal Processes*

3.6.1. *General*

Processes exhibiting seasonality are commonplace in industrial, commercial and social data, often due wholly or partially, directly or indirectly, to the motion of the earth round the sun. Seasonality may also arise from secular effects such as feast days and public holiday periods. We adopt the following notation for seasonal data: T the data period (i.e. number of data points *per annum*); $m(t)$ is the "month" associated with any given time $t (m = 1, \ldots, T)$, where we generally use "month" for the data interval.

3.6.2. *Additive Seasonal Vector Model*

In this representation the effect of seasonality is represented by a vector of unknown additive seasonal terms, one for each period of the annual cycle T. The model is:

$$y_t = \rho_{m(t),t} + \varepsilon_t,$$
$$\rho_{i,t} = \rho_{i,t-1} + \delta\rho_{i,t} \quad (i = 1, \ldots, T)$$

where, since the sum of the seasonal terms must sum to zero over a complete cycle,

$$\sum_{i=1}^{T} \rho_{i,t} = \sum_{i=1}^{T} \delta\rho_{i,t} = 0 \quad (t = 1, 2, \ldots).$$

This can be expressed as a DLM by writing it as

$$y_t = (0, \ldots, 0, 1, \ldots, 0)\, \boldsymbol{\rho}_t + \varepsilon_t,$$

$$\boldsymbol{\rho}_t = \boldsymbol{\rho}_{t-1} + \delta\boldsymbol{\rho}_t.$$

It may be of interest to note that, in contrast to the polynomial models of Sections 3.3–3.5, the **F**-matrix $\mathbf{F}_t = (0, \ldots, 0, 1, 0, \ldots, 0)$, which has one in the position $m(t)$ and zeros elsewhere, is not now a constant but varies with time. (Of course, it varies quite systematically, and its value is known for any time t.)

3.6.3. *Periodic Function Model*

The above model implies a need for T unknown parameters for the representation of seasonality alone, and in certain cases this may make unwarrantable demands for computer time and/or storage, as, for example, with weekly data ($T = 52$) or for detail items of low individual turnover. In such cases the following type of model is not only necessary but also useful in its own right on account of its ability to maintain desired forms of seasonal patterns. (In fact we would recommend it for consideration as an alternative to the seasonal vector model above even when the choice is not dictated by necessity.) In this model seasonality is represented by a number of periodic functions

$$f_i(t) = f_i(t + kT) \quad (t = 1, 2, \ldots, k = \pm 1, \pm 2, \ldots, n)$$

the observation equation being

$$y_t = \sum_{i=1}^{n} \alpha_{i,t} f_i(t) + \varepsilon_t.$$

the α's being unknown coefficients subject to disturbances

$$\boldsymbol{\alpha}_t = \boldsymbol{\alpha}_{t-1} + \delta\boldsymbol{\alpha}_t.$$

Here $m = 1$, $\boldsymbol{\theta}^t = (\alpha_{1,t}, \ldots, \alpha_{n,t})^{\mathrm{T}}$, $\mathbf{F}_t = (f_1(t), \ldots, f_n(t))$ and $\mathbf{G} = \mathbf{I}$. This is a valid DLM because the independent vector $\mathbf{F}_t$, while not constant, is known for all times t.

An obvious candidate for the f-functions is the group of harmonic terms cos/sin $(2\pi it/T)$ $(i = 1, 2, \ldots, T/2)$ but there is no necessity for this; tabular representation is another possibility. In using this model in practice it is sometimes necessary to make special provision for certain exceptional periods, especially the moving Easter weekend.

It is not of course necessary or even usual to employ *all* the possible harmonic terms (e.g. Harrison, 1965). One case of which we have had experience required only the fundamental and first harmonic (i.e. only four coefficients) for adequate representation of seasonality for each of a large number of detail items weekly.

3.7. *Autoregressive Models*

The autoregressive model AR(p) is generally defined as

$$y_t = \sum_{i=1}^{p} \phi_i y_{t-i} + \varepsilon_t, \tag{3.7.1}$$

the ϕ-coefficients and $V_t = \operatorname{var}(\varepsilon_t)$ being unknowns to be estimated from the data (if any). Estimates, once made, are customarily used for prediction purposes as if they are known precisely, and they are not usually subject to frequent revision. The DLM representation

$$y_t = (y_{t-1}, \ldots, y_{t-p})\, \boldsymbol{\phi}_t + \varepsilon_t, \tag{3.7.2}$$

$$\boldsymbol{\phi}_t = \boldsymbol{\phi}_{t-1} + \delta\boldsymbol{\phi}_t \tag{3.7.3}$$

surmounts both difficulties with ease; estimates are continually revised, and the Kalman filter yields, not only the precision of the estimates, but their covariances as well, both of which are highly relevant to prediction. (Since *future* observation values are not known, the Case II prediction method of Section 2.3 is indicated for this model.) As a final "plus", the system equation (3.7.2) permits changes in the ϕ-coefficients to be modelled, if required.

With the current great effort being devoted to a time series approach named *adaptive filtering* we would point out that apart from its conceptual weaknesses and its lack of practical robustness, its adherents seemed to have missed the point that it need be no more than an AR(p) model with constant coefficients (i.e. var $\boldsymbol{\delta\phi}_t = \mathbf{0}$). Thus there is no need to bother with arbitrary "training constants" since the Kalman filter automatically provides the appropriate recurrence estimates and additionally gives forecasters the many other facilities of the Bayesian approach.

3.8. *Moving Average Models*

The estimation problems in the moving average MA(q) model

$$y_t = \varepsilon_t + \sum_{i=1}^{q} \psi_i \varepsilon_{t-i}, \tag{3.8.1}$$

where the ψ coefficients are unknown, are well known, and are discussed at some length by Durbin (1959) and Kendall and Stuart (1968). The difficulty arises from the non-linearity of the model in the unknowns, and Box and Jenkins (1970) propose a search method to estimate the ψ coefficients. For the same reason (i.e. non-linearity) (3.8.1) is not a DLM as it stands. There are, however, a number of possible ways which can be suggested to overcome this difficulty, at least in part.

(i) AR *Approximation.* Since a MA system of finite degree q can be represented as an AR model of infinite degree, and vice versa, one possibility is simply to use the AR model (3.7), finding the appropriate degree by trial and error. The lack of parsimony this implies is offset to some extent by the joint covariance information supplied by the Kalman filter.

(ii) *Learning about the relevant* ε*'s.* This formulation assumes that the values of ψ_i $(i = 1, \ldots, q)$ are known so that

$$y_t = (1, \psi_1, \ldots, \psi_q)\,\boldsymbol{\theta}_t,$$

$$\boldsymbol{\theta}_t = \begin{pmatrix} \mathbf{0}^{\mathrm{T}} & 0 \\ \mathbf{I} & \mathbf{0} \end{pmatrix} \boldsymbol{\theta}_{t-1} + \begin{pmatrix} \varepsilon_t \\ \mathbf{0} \end{pmatrix}.$$

Here one uses information to *revise* estimates of relevant earlier random shocks {that is, $\boldsymbol{\theta}_t^{\mathrm{T}} = (\varepsilon_t, \ldots, \varepsilon_{t-q})$}.

(iii) *Learning about the* ψ*'s.* This formulation assumes that the observation equation is

$$y_t = e_t + \sum_{i=1}^{q} \psi_{it} e_{t-i},$$

where e_t is the observed one-step ahead forecasting error ($e_t = y_t - \hat{y}_{1,t-1}$) at time t. The system equation is then

$$\boldsymbol{\psi}_t = \boldsymbol{\psi}_{t-1} + \boldsymbol{\delta\psi}_t,$$

which allows the estimates of ψ_i $(i = 1, \ldots, q)$ to be updated and to adapt to movements in $\boldsymbol{\psi}_t$. The classical time series forecasting method uses the above observation equation but assumes the ψ_i to be known. This approach is only possible with sufficient data history to estimate the errors $e_1, e_2, \ldots, e_{t-1}$.

3.9. *Joint Demand Models*

A quite common situation in the commercial field occurs when the individual items in a given product line are subject to external effects which apply, *pro rata*, to all of them. For example, if something in the environment were to cause an increase in the demand for a certain style of shoe, then it might be reasonable to suppose that this would be reflected in the demand for individual sizes and fittings within the range. This type of situation can be modelled as follows. Let:

y_{it} = observed demand for product i at time t;

μ_{it} = "true" demand;

ε_{it} = random observation noise peculiar to ith item;

η_t = random term applicable to range as a whole;

$\delta\mu_{it}$ = random disturbance in demand peculiar to the ith term;

ξ_t = random disturbance in demand for range as a whole;

k_i = proportion applicable to ith term $\simeq E(\mu_{it})/\sum_{i=1}^{p} E(\mu_{it})$.

Then a model is

$$y_{it} = \mu_{it} + \varepsilon_{it} + k_i \eta_t,$$
$$\mu_{it} = \mu_{it-1} + \delta\mu_{it} + k_i \xi_t \quad (i = 1, \ldots, p).$$

This may be expressed as a DLM

$$\mathbf{y}_t = \boldsymbol{\mu}_t + \boldsymbol{\nu}_t, \quad \boldsymbol{\mu}_t = \boldsymbol{\mu}_{t-1} + \boldsymbol{\omega}_t,$$

where $\nu_{it} = \varepsilon_{it} + k_i \eta_t$, and $\omega_{it} = \delta\mu_{it} + k_i \xi_t$ $(i = 1, \ldots, p)$. The effect of the common disturbance and random noises is to introduce correlations into the covariance matrices $V_t, \mathbf{W}_t$, since, for example,

$$\mathbf{V} = (V_{ij}) = \begin{cases} E(\nu_{it}\nu_{jt}) & (i,j = 1, \ldots, p), \\ \operatorname{var}(\varepsilon_{it}) + k_i^2 \operatorname{var}(\eta_t) & (i = j), \\ k_i k_j \operatorname{var}(\eta_t) & (i \neq j) \end{cases}$$

with similar results for disturbance variance $E(\omega_{it}\omega_{jt})$ $(i,j = 1, \ldots, p)$. The practical implications of this correlation are interesting; it means that the forecasts for any single item in the range use data from all the other items. This throws light on the well-known "top-down" or "bottom-up" dilemma; if, as in the present instance, information from the range as a whole is of value in forecasting single items, then, if the user is in fact forecasting each item independently then the independent forecasts should be constrained to be consistent with the total forecast. Such constraints are easy to apply since all that is involved is a conditional probability distribution based on the joint distribution. A further interesting consequence of this model has been noted by Stevens (1974), and Green and Harrison (1972) have investigated some aspects of aggregate forecasting.

3.10. *Smoothing*

The Kalman filter has been presented as a means of infering the current unknown parameter value $\boldsymbol{\theta}_t$ as a new data value $(\mathbf{y}_t, \mathbf{F}_t)$ becomes available. A moment's reflection should, however, convince one that a new observation throws new light on previous parameter values as well as the current one, and therefore these estimates can be revised also, if desired. This can be done by defining a new model in terms of the entire parameter sequence to date as follows, which again is a DLM (of steadily increasing dimension):

$$\mathbf{y}_t = \mathbf{F}_t \boldsymbol{\phi}^t + \boldsymbol{\varepsilon}_t,$$

$$\boldsymbol{\phi}^t = \left(\frac{\mathbf{G} \quad \mathbf{0} \quad \dots \quad \mathbf{0}}{\mathbf{I}}\right) \boldsymbol{\phi}^{t-1} + \begin{pmatrix} \boldsymbol{\delta\phi}_t \\ \mathbf{0} \end{pmatrix},$$

where

$$\boldsymbol{\phi}^t = (\boldsymbol{\theta}_t, \boldsymbol{\theta}_{t-1}, \dots, \boldsymbol{\theta}_0)^{\mathrm{T}}.$$

In practice the vector $\boldsymbol{\phi}^t$ would probably be truncated; the random disturbances implicit in the structure of the DLM ensure that current observations carry little further information as to the state of the process in the remote past.

4. MULTI-PROCESS MODELS: CLASS I

4.1. *Introduction*

A DLM is characterized by **F**, **G**, **V** and **W**, where, for simplicity, we drop the time suffix. The matrix **F** defines how the process is "observed"; **G** is an inherent characteristic of the system governing its motion; **V** is the observation noise variance var$(\mathbf{v}_t)$; and **W** is the disturbance noise variance var$(\mathbf{w}_t)$.

In many cases the **F**, **G** matrices will suggest themselves in the light of the situation, analogy, knowledge and experience. For example, with commercial monthly demand data, a simple linear growth seasonal model is always a strong candidate for short-term forecasting. The noise variances **V**, **W** are more difficult to estimate, although, in the case of sales products, variance "laws" across a company's products can often be derived; these laws will generally relate the noise variances to turnover and unit sales size and can be applied to new products at the product launch. Zellner (1971) has given a good treatment of the static case $\mathbf{W} = \mathbf{0}$ but the general DLM clearly gives rise to problems of much larger magnitude. However, there are many possibilities for reducing the problems with the main information coming from structural form and meaning. For example, in a straightforward regression model **W** indicates the rate of decay with time of information on the regression coefficients; in the polynomial models of Sections 3.3–3.5 the interpretation of the structure in a way analogous to derivatives immediately gives a sense of magnitude; and general canonical forms of the system equations, such as a Jordan form, give the model-builder as much guidance on the noise as they do on the behaviour of the system. Again it may be desirable to parameterize the **W** matrix and Godolphin and Harrison (1975) have shown what this means in relation to exponentially weighted polynomial regression. In this paper we present an identification approach based on discrete methods which may be applied to "on-line" identification after exhausting the *a priori* information. We define $M = \{\mathbf{F}, \mathbf{G}, \mathbf{V}, \mathbf{W}\}$ as the specification of a given model M and suppose that the uncertainty about the model and its parameters can be adequately described by a set of discrete alternative models $M^{(j)}$ $(j = 1, \dots, N)$ with associated probabilities, where N is such as to keep the problem manageable. We then make our inferences in terms of the discrete alternatives by wholly computational methods. We do not pretend that the methods are as elegant as we would wish, but the simplicity has the advantage of affording a means of doing something without having to make grossly unrealistic assumptions simply for the sake of tractability.

In this section we consider the class of model in which the forecaster assumes that there is a single (unknown) model which adequately represents the process at all times $(t = 1, 2, \dots)$. We then make the distinction between two types of problem:

(i) from the set of possible models $M^{(j)}$ $(j = 1, \dots, N)$ it is required to choose a single model to represent the process;

(ii) it is required that forecasts and decisions be based on information relating to the whole set of models.

An example of the first type of problem would be that in which a fashion product is to be marketed; initially there is no sales data but only subjective information; the product is expected to display a fashion or seasonal periodicity but there is uncertainty about which of two standard seasonal forms it will follow; a final purchasing decision must be made at time $t = 6$ and it is then desired to base this on the most probable model. Here the two models might specify different values of **F** and **G**. An example of the second type of situation is where one is forecasting a product using the steady model of Section (3.3) but is uncertain about the value of $\mathbf{V} = \text{var}(\varepsilon_t)$. Here the approach might be to specify a small number of discrete values $\mathbf{V}^{(1)}, \mathbf{V}^{(2)}, \ldots, \mathbf{V}^{(N)}$ which are thought to cover the likely value of **V**, to assign these prior probabilities, to update these probabilities with time and to estimate future observations using information on all the models. If **V** is to be constant, its value will not usually coincide with any of the $\mathbf{V}^{(i)}$ and this is one reason for employing all models. Another advantage of this approach is that if by any chance **V** is not constant but varies then the method is adaptive to these changes within the stated range and by an extension of the method, which is particularly useful in quality control, the variance adaptation can be specified.

These two types of problem are singled out merely for illustration; there are, of course, situations where the two types are mixed and where one wishes to eliminate some models but to forecast using a subset of the original set. We would remark that Newbold and Granger (1974) have looked at a particular set of problems concerning the combination of forecasts.

4.2. *Basic Probability Results*

In Section 2, the results concerning the information at time t relating to the parameter vector $\boldsymbol{\theta}_t$ and future observations $\mathbf{y}_t$ were established *conditional* on a single specified DLM. In considering a range of models we define:

$$p_{j,0} = \text{the probability at } t = 0 \text{ that } M^{(j)} \text{ is the model we are seeking,}$$

$$p_{j,t} = P\{M = M^{(j)} \mid \mathbf{y}^t, \mathbf{F}^t, p_{j,0}\} \text{ to be the (4.2.1) corresponding posterior probability at time } t,$$

$$\mathbf{p}_0 = (p_{1,0}, p_{2,0}, \ldots, p_{N,0}).$$

We then use the notation established in Section 2 but often with addition of a bracketed superscript (j) to show that we are conditioning the interpretation to model $M^{(j)}$ (e.g. $\mathbf{G}^{(j)}$ refers to the system matrix **G** specified for model $M^{(j)}$).

Bayes' theorem may be applied with the usual "chain-rule" to give the joint and conditional distributions of $\boldsymbol{\theta}_t$ and M as

$$P(\boldsymbol{\theta}_t, M \mid \mathbf{y}^t, \mathbf{F}, \mathbf{p}_0) = P(\boldsymbol{\theta}_t \mid M, \mathbf{y}^t, \mathbf{F}^t) P(y_t \mid M, \mathbf{y}^{t-1}, \mathbf{F}^t) P(M \mid \mathbf{y}^{t-1}, \mathbf{F}^t, \mathbf{p}_0) \tag{4.2.2}$$

and the marginal distribution

$$P(M \mid \mathbf{y}^t, \mathbf{F}^t, \mathbf{p}_0) \propto L(\mathbf{y}_t \mid M, \mathbf{y}^{t-1}, \mathbf{F}^t) P(M, \mathbf{y}^{t-1}, \mathbf{F}^t, \mathbf{p}_0), \tag{4.2.3}$$

where L denotes the likelihood or probability density.

The conditional distribution of $(\boldsymbol{\theta}_t \mid M, \mathbf{y}^t, \mathbf{F}^t, \mathbf{p}_0)$ is $N(\mathbf{m}_t, \mathbf{C}_t)$ obtained recursively from (2.2.2) to (2.2.5), using the DLM on which one is conditioning. Remembering from Sections 2.2 and 2.3 that, using the particular model, M, the conditional distribution of $(\mathbf{y}_t \mid M, \mathbf{y}^t, \mathbf{F}_t)$ is $N(\hat{\mathbf{y}}, \hat{\mathbf{Y}})$ and noting that

$$p_{j,t-1} = P(M = M^{(j)} \mid \mathbf{y}^{t-1}, \mathbf{F}^{t-1}, \mathbf{p}_0) = P(M = M^{(j)} \mid \mathbf{y}^{t-1}, \mathbf{F}^t, \mathbf{p}_0), \tag{4.2.4}$$

it is seen that the above likelihood of $\mathbf{y}_t$ and the joint and conditional distributions of $\boldsymbol{\theta}_t$ and M are readily obtained.

Similarly, as in Sections 2.3 and 2.4,

$$(\mathbf{y}_{t+L}\,|\,\mathbf{y}^t, \mathbf{F}^t, M^{(j)}) \sim N(\hat{\mathbf{y}}^{(j)}_{L,t}, \hat{\mathbf{Y}}^{(j)}_{L,t}) \tag{4.2.5}$$

so that the information about future observation values is readily obtained.

4.3. *Decisions*

Since we express our concern about practice we need to remark that in many situations the problem is not actually one of forecasting but is one of decision; of what to do *now*. A full treatment of this problem is extremely complex and difficult involving, for example, consideration of the likely implications of the current decision on decisions which will arise at future times and the further information arising from future data. It is for this reason that most forecasting studies compare methods in terms of forecast accuracy, usually the mean square error.

The spirit of Bayesian statistics is to describe uncertainty in terms of probability distributions and to combine these with utility functions in order to reach decisions. We shall sketch this approach which comes a little nearer to giving a more adequate basis for the comparison of methods. Our reason is that in nearly all commercial cases the utility function is asymmetric, since gross overforecasting leads to one kind of loss, say stock and waste costs and labour redundancies whereas gross underforecasting leads to another kind of loss, say lost profit and overtime labour. Furthermore, reasonably sized errors often incur insignificant penalties whereas large errors which occur, particularly in situations of sudden sustained change, can bring extremely serious losses of an importance well beyond that reflected by least squares—sometimes because the utility function has marked discontinuities. Let

L = known forecast lead time ($L = 1, 2, \ldots$),

x_t = L-ahead forecast at time t (i.e. to time $t+L$),

$u(x, y)$ = utility associated with a forecast x and an actual outcome y,

$U_t(x, j)$ = expected utility of forecast x if model $M^{(j)}$ obtains,

$x^*_{t,j}$ = the Bayesian forecast at time t, given model $M^{(j)}$: then $x^*_{t,j}$ is found by maximizing over x_t the expected utility

$$U_t(x_{t,j}) = E\{u(x_t, y_{t+L})\}^{(j)} \tag{4.3.1}$$

which is found using the distribution of y_{t+L} conditional on model $M^{(j)}$, given in (4.2.5). We now briefly discuss the two distinct types of problem stated in Section 4.1.

4.3.1. *Choice of a Single Model*

The problem here is that of choosing a particular model to maximize the *cumulative* expectation

$$E\left[\sum_{i=1}^{\infty} u(x^*_{t+i,j}, y_{t+i})\right] \tag{4.3.2}$$

over future unknown observations having unknown values $y_{t+i}\ldots$. If the data series to hand can be regarded as representative of future data, one means of proceeding is simply to perform the minimization process over this series. Thus the selection of a model is based on the function $\tilde{U}(j) = \sum_{i=1}^{t-L} U_i(x^*_{ij}, j)$. We choose $M^{(k)}$, where

$$\tilde{U}(k) = \max_{1 \leqslant j \leqslant N} \tilde{U}(j). \tag{4.3.3}$$

Of course if $u(x_t, y_{t+L}) = -(x_t - y_{t+L})^2$ then we have the well-used lead time least-squares error criterion.

4.3.2. *Using the Set of Models*

The approach is to define the utility of a forecast x_t as

$$U(x_t) = \sum_{j=1}^{N} U_t(x_t, j)\, p_{j,t} \tag{4.3.4}$$

and select the forecast x_t^* such that $U(x_t)$ is maximized.

4.4. *Comments*

This section has been confined to the case in which a single unique model adequately represents the process at all times $t = 1, 2, \ldots$. We have previously stated that a single DLM representation of a socio-economic process is a rather hopeful assumption although it can be useful in combination with a good "management information system". We would make now the following comments:

(i) The procedures are analogous to the model identification and parameter estimation in conventional practice. However, the identification is "on-line", using a DLM rather than a static model. We place a greater emphasis on description in model formulation but do not snub traditional data analysis which, when data are available, can be very useful in preliminary model selection and the derivation of prior information.

(ii) The formal introduction of a utility function and the consequent use of Bayesian decisions naturally extends the relevance of a forecasting system. We feel that, while theory needs "nice" criteria for assessing methods analytically, practitioners must not succumb to the siren call of MSE in cases when it is totally inappropriate.

(iii) If the results in case (i) of Section 4.4 seem obvious we would reply that it introduces not only a general utility function, but also includes the lead time. It is often not appreciated that in a practical situation a model that is good for a short lead time is not necessarily good for a longer one and vice-versa. In theory, there is usually the assumption of a unique generating model so that theory is correct to insist that in the limit, there is one model for forecasting the hypothetical data. But this assumption is nonsense in socio-economics; the model is just the way we decide to view an observation series and its context.

5. MULTI-PROCESS MODELS: CLASS II

5.1. *Introduction*

One of the advantages of using a DLM is that at any time, $t-1$, the only information required to forecast an observation at the next period, t, is a DLM which describes the evolution of the process in the time interval $(t-1, t)$ together with the probability description of the relevant parameters $(\boldsymbol{\theta}_{t-1} \mid \mathbf{y}^{t-1})$. It is thus clear that, if desired, the DLM used to describe the evolution of the process at one time can be different from that used by the modeller at other times; this is a very important feature of the Bayesian approach. However, we have already seen in Section 4 that there may be uncertainty as to which model obtains at any given time. We thus introduced multi-process models.

The case we wish to deal with now is one in which no single DLM adequately describes what might happen to the process in the next time interval. And let it be very clear that a forecaster should concern himself with what might happen in the future not what did (or did not) happen in any past time period. This case is by no means unusual but nearly always represents the real situation in socio-economic applications and also in many production process applications. For example, maverick or outlier observations frequently occur in sales data without prior warning. The process level may suddenly and unexpectedly change; in commercial situations for any of a number of market, promotion or consumer production reasons, and in process control for reasons of mechanical failure, wear or variation in raw materials. Again the noise and disturbance variation may change. As far as these latter changes are linked to process parameters this may be adequately expressed as part of a single DLM, but apart from these cases some changes in **V** and/or **W** are hard to anticipate and are not associated with *a priori* defined measurable quantities. For example, in quality control the whole or partial aim may be to detect those sudden and gradual changes in quality variation which give rise to an unacceptable proportion of low quality product.

The variety of descriptions available to the Bayesian modeller is enormous. In a related paper (Harrison and Stevens, 1975) we give some applications of a particular and widely applicable mixed model. In this paper we confine our more detailed discussion to models which at any time t comprises a set of DLM's each of which has a definite form but differs from each of the others either in its definition of the noise variance **V** or in the disturbance variance **W**.

5.2. *An Illustration*

In order to illustrate the implications of the random terms $\mathbf{v}_t, \mathbf{w}_t$, consider the DLM of linear growth (Section 3.4):

$$y_t = \mu_t + \varepsilon_t,$$
$$\mu_t = \mu_{t-1} + \beta_t + \delta\mu_t,$$
$$\beta_t = \beta_{t-1} + \delta\beta_t.$$

Assume, for clarity rather than reality, that the random terms $\varepsilon_t, \delta\mu_t, \delta\beta_t$ are all identically zero for all times except $t = 5$. Consider three distinct happenings at $t = 5$:

$$\text{(i) } \varepsilon_5 = 10, \quad \text{(ii) } \delta\mu_5 = 10, \quad \text{(iii) } \delta\beta_5 = 10$$

and always

$$\begin{pmatrix} \mu_0 \\ \beta_0 \end{pmatrix} \Bigg\| \; \mathbf{y}^0 \Bigg) \sim \left(\begin{matrix} 10 \\ 2{\cdot}5 \end{matrix}; \; 0 \right)$$

so that μ_0 and β_0 are precisely known. Then the data values generated by the model are shown in Fig. 1.

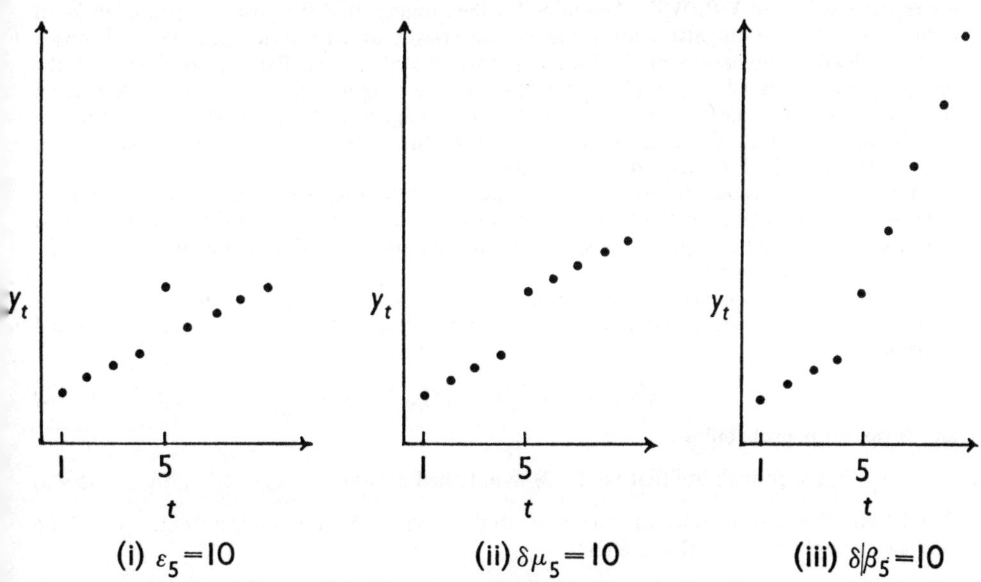

FIG. 1. The effect of a process disturbance at time $t = 5$.

As $t = 5$ it is clear that in (i) we have the situation of a maverick observation since after this "wild" observation the process continues in an unaffected way; in (ii) the non-zero $\delta\mu_5$ produces a permanent upward shift in level with a subsequent undisturbed growth; and in (iii) the non-zero $\delta\beta_5$ produces a permanent change in slope.

This simple idealistic example will enable an appreciation of the role of $\mathbf{V}_t = \text{var}(\mathbf{v}_t)$ and $\mathbf{W}_t = \text{var}(\mathbf{w}_t)$ in the general DLM. If at time t, $\mathbf{W}_t = \mathbf{0}$ then the expected future system behaviour is that it proceeds on its way in an undisturbed fashion; if $\mathbf{W}_t$ is exceptionally large then this indicates a significant sudden change in the underlying system which will have a sustained effect on the expected value of future observations; and if $\mathbf{V}_t$ is large then at time t this indicates a wild observation value at that time but one which has no sustained effect in that it does not affect the expectations of future observations. Since $\mathbf{w}_t$ is an $(n \times 1)$ vector, it follows that by specifying different values of $\mathbf{w}_t$, n distinct types of disturbance can be modelled as well as their combinations.

5.3. *The Multi-state Model*

Consider a model $M^{(j)}$ which defines a state j and which, at any time t, may characterize the process evolution by $M_t^{(j)} = \{\mathbf{F}_t, \mathbf{G}, \mathbf{V}_t^{(j)}, \mathbf{W}_t^{(j)}\}$ $(j = 1, \ldots, N)$, where $\mathbf{V}_t^{(j)}, \mathbf{W}_t^{(j)}$ are known at time t. The multi-state model comprises the set of models $M^{(j)}$ $(j = 1, \ldots, N)$ and describes the state which obtains at time t by a Markov process. The general description is by a square matrix $[\pi_{ij,t}]$ where $\pi_{ij,t}$ denotes the probability that if model $M^{(i)}$ obtained at time $t-1$ then model $M^{(j)}$ obtains at time t. We shall confine ourselves to the models we have actually used, so that we deal with the simple case where the probability that model $M^{(j)}$ obtains at any time t is π_j and is independent of the time and process history. Thus we shall only deal with N state probabilities $\boldsymbol{\pi} = (\pi_1, \pi_2, \ldots, \pi_N)$.

5.4. *A Practical Procedure*

It will be clear that if the distribution of $\boldsymbol{\theta}_{t-1}$ is normal, then, for any given model $M^{(j)}$ the resultant posterior distribution of $\boldsymbol{\theta}_t$ is to be found directly from the Kalman filter, using the appropriate values of $\mathbf{V}_t^{(j)}$, $\mathbf{W}_t^{(j)}$. Assuming for the moment that the posterior probabilities of each state $j = 1, \ldots, N$ are also known, the resultant posterior distribution at time t will consist of a weighted combination of N distinct normal distributions. Passing to time $t+1$ the updating is still possible, by applying the Kalman filter algorithm for each possible current state to each component of the time t posterior, thus generating a distribution comprising N^2 distinct normal components. Clearly this procedure cannot long continue; some means must be found to inhibit this explosive proliferation.

A number of possible approximation techniques can be suggested; our solution is not the only one, nor perhaps even the best. It has, however, been found to work successfully in a large number of practical applications, and might therefore be a suitable starting point for the investigation of alternatives.

Our practical procedure depends upon approximations in order, at any time $t-1$, to summarize the parameter and model information relevant to future times as N normal distributions

$$(\boldsymbol{\theta}_{t-1} \mid M_{t-1}^{(j)}, \mathbf{y}^{t-1}) \sim N(\mathbf{m}_{t-1}^{(j)}, \mathbf{C}_{t-1}^{(j)}) \tag{5.4.1}$$

and N posterior probabilities

$$P_{t-1}^{(j)} = \text{probability that model } M^{(j)} \text{ obtained at time } t-1 \; (j = 1, \ldots, N). \tag{5.4.2}$$

Based upon this information and the next observation $\mathbf{y}_t$, N^2 normal distributions may be derived by applying the Kalman filter:

$$(\boldsymbol{\theta}_t \mid \mathbf{y}^t, M_{t-1}^{(i)}, M_t^{(j)}) \sim N(\mathbf{m}_t^{(i,j)}, \mathbf{C}_t^{(i,j)}) \quad \text{for } (i = 1, \ldots, N, j = 1, \ldots, N), \tag{5.4.3}$$

and the N^2 probabilities

$$P_t^{(i,j)} = P\{M_{t-1}^{(i)}, M_t^{(j)} \mid \mathbf{y}^t\} \tag{5.4.4}$$

may be calculated by Bayes' theorem since

$$P_t^{(i,j)} \propto L(\mathbf{y}_t \mid M_{t-1}^{(i)}, M_t^{(j)}, \mathbf{y}^{t-1})\, \pi_j\, P_{t-1}^{(i)}. \tag{5.4.5}$$

The likelihood is easily calculated using the results of Section 2.2, with the obvious notation, so that

$$(\mathbf{y}_t \mid M_{t-1}^{(i)}, M_t^{(j)}, \mathbf{y}^{t-1}) \sim N(\hat{\mathbf{y}}^{(i,j)}, \hat{\mathbf{Y}}^{(i,j)}). \tag{5.4.6}$$

To complete the procedure, it remains to reduce the N^2 posteriors to N. The "collapsing" process we employ for applications is as follows:

$$P_t^{(j)} = \sum_{i=1}^{N} P_t^{(i,j)}, \tag{5.4.7}$$

$$\mathbf{m}_t^{(j)} = \sum_{i=1}^{N} P_t^{(i,j)}\, \mathbf{m}_t^{(i,j)} / P_t^{(j)}, \tag{5.4.8}$$

$$\mathbf{C}_t^{(j)} = \sum_{i=1}^{N} P_t^{(i,j)} \{\mathbf{C}_t^{(i,j)} + (\mathbf{m}_t^{(i,j)} - \mathbf{m}_t^{(j)})(\mathbf{m}_t^{(i,j)} - \mathbf{m}_t^{(j)})^{\mathrm{T}}\} / P_t^{(j)}. \tag{5.4.9}$$

ACKNOWLEDGEMENTS

The authors wish to thank Imperial Chemical Industries and the S.R.C. for generously supporting the work in its early stages. Much of the development was undertaken while one of us was at University College London. The excellence of their computing facilities is gratefully acknowledged and so is the advice and encouragement from Professor D. V. Lindley and his staff.

REFERENCES

ÅSTROM, K. J. and EYKHOFF, P. (1971). Systems identification—a survey. *Automatica*, **7**, 123–162.
BEER, S. (1975). *Platform for Change*. New York: Wiley.
BOX, G. E. P. and JENKINS, G. M. (1962). Some statistical aspects of adaptive optimization and control. *J. R. Statist. Soc.* B, **24**, 297–343.
—— (1970). *Time Series Analysis, Forecasting and Control*. San Francisco: Holden-Day.
BROWN, R. G. (1963). *Smoothing, Forecasting and Prediction*. Englewood Cliffs: Prentice-Hall.
BROWN, R. L., DURBIN, J. and EVANS, J. M. (1975). Techniques for testing the constancy of regression relationships. *J. R. Statist. Soc.* B, **37**, 149–192.
COUTIE, G. A., *et al.* (1964). *Short-term Forecasting*. I.C.I. monograph No. 2. Edinburgh: Oliver and Boyd.
DURBIN, J. (1959). Efficient estimation of parameters in moving average models. *Biometrika*, **46**, 306–316.
EDWARDS, A. W. F. (1972). *Likelihood*. Cambridge: University Press.
FELDSTEIN, M. S. (1971). The error of forecasting econometric models when the forecast-period exogenous variables are stochastic. *Econometrika*, **39**, 55–60.
GODOLPHIN, E. J. and HARRISON, P. J. (1975). Equivalence theorems for polynomial-projecting predictors. *J. R. Statist. Soc.* B, **37**, 205–215.
GREEN, M. and HARRISON, P. J. (1972). On aggregate forecasting. Warwick: Statistics Research Report No. 2.
—— (1973). Fashion forecasting for a mail-order company using a Bayesian approach. *Oper. Res. Quart.*, **24**, 193–205.
HARRISON P. J. (1965). Short-term sales forecasting. *J. R. Statist. Soc. C, Appl. Statist.*, **14**, 102–139.
—— (1967). Exponential smoothing and short-term sales forecasting. *Manag. Sci.*, **13**, 821–842.
HARRISON, P. J. and STEVENS, C. F. (1971). A Bayesian approach to short-term forecasting. *Oper. Res. Quart.*, **22**, 341–362.
—— (1975). Bayes forecasting in action: case studies. Warwick: Statistics Research Report No. 14.
HOLT, C. C. (1957). Forecasting seasonals and trends by exponentially weighted moving averages. Carnegie Institute of Technology: ONR Memorandum 52.

KALMAN, R. E. (1963). New methods in Wiener filtering theory. In *Proceedings of the First Symposium on Engineering Application of Random Function Theory and Probability* (J. L. BOGDANOFF and F. KOZIN, eds). New York: Wiley.
KENDALL, M. G. and STUART, A. (1968). *The Advanced Theory of Statistics*, Vol. 3. London: Griffin.
LINDLEY, D. V. and SMITH, A. F. M. (1972). Bayes' estimates for the linear model. *J. R. Statist. Soc.* B, **34**, 1–41.
NEWBOLD, P. and GRANGER, C. W. J. (1974). Experience with forecasting univariate time series and the combination of forecasts. *J. R. Statist. Soc.* A, **137**, 131–165.
PLACKETT, R. L. (1950). Some theorems in least squares. *Biometrika*, **37**, 149–157.
STEVENS, C. F. (1974). On the variability of demand for families of items. *Oper. Res. Quart.*, **25**, 411–420.
TELKSNYS, L. (1973). Determination of changes in properties of random processes by the Bayes method. In *Identification and System Parameter Estimation* (P. EYKHOFF, ed.). Amsterdam: North Holland.
WHITTLE, P. (1969). A view of stochastic control theory. *J. R. Statist. Soc.* A, **132**, 320–334.
ZELLNER, A. (1971). *An Introduction to Bayesian Inference in Econometrics*. New York: Wiley.

DISCUSSION ON THE PAPER BY PROFESSOR HARRISON AND MR STEVENS

Professor M. B. PRIESTLEY (University of Manchester Institute of Science and Technology): The subject of forecasting seems to hold a peculiar fascination for both probabilists and statisticians. Ever since Wiener and Kolmogorov first gave a complete solution to the least squares prediction problem probabilists have had great fun solving and re-solving it, and generalizing it to spaces of greater and greater abstraction. Statisticians, on the other hand, have concentrated on producing a variety of "packages" which use techniques of varying degrees of cunning to compute the least squares predictors given that the observed series belongs to a certain class of finite parameter models. However, apart from a few isolated attempts to develop a general form of prediction theory for non-stationary processes, all this intensive effort has hardly advanced the fundamental ideas beyond the point at which Wiener and Kolmogorov left them in the 1940's. In fact, virtually all previous studies are based on the following assumptions:

a. the observed series is stationary, or can be reduced to stationarity by a suitable transformation,
b. the predictors are linear functions of past observations,
c. the criterion of optimality is the mean square prediction error.

Given these three assumptions there is really little left to do—apart from the (in principle) "trivial" problem of actually computing the optimal predictor. (Of course, in practice this operation involves the far from trivial ancillary problem of model fitting—but at a fundamental level the problem of model fitting is quite distinct from the problem of prediction.)

It is therefore a particular pleasure to welcome the present paper. Here we have an approach which really does attempt to offer us something quite different from the Wiener–Kolmogorov theory. Out goes the assumption of stationarity, and the mean square error criterion has apparently gone too—although whether it is really there lurking in the background is a moot point which I shall take up later. Admittedly, the models are still linear (in a general sense), but otherwise the basic approach is essentially new. The main mathematical tool which the authors use is that of the *Kalman filter* and although, as they say, this basic result has been around for quite some time, it is, I think, the first time that this algorithm has been advocated as a data orientated forecasting technique. Originally the Kalman filter was developed within the context of control theory problems and it is interesting to compare the formulation of the authors DLM (equations (2.1.1) and (2.1.2)) with the conventional state space models used by control engineers. At first sight the formulation of the DLM looks rather odd and does not appear to be consistent with the standard state space formulation. The difficulty arises from the interpretation of $\boldsymbol{\theta}_t$, and, as the authors point out, this "time-dependent parameter" can be interpreted in various ways. If (2.1.1) and (2.1.2) are interpreted in the conventional control theory context then $\boldsymbol{\theta}_t$ would be regarded as the (unobservable) state of the system at time t, and $\mathbf{F}_t$ would then describe how the components of the state vector are transformed into the observation vector $\mathbf{y}_t$. However, it is clear from the subsequent discussion that this is not the way in which the authors interpret these equations (except in the case of a constant $\mathbf{F}_t$), the emphasis being primarily on the interpretation of $\boldsymbol{\theta}_t$ as a vector of time-dependent stochastic parameters. In the case of a constant parameter system the standard state-space description is based on a Markovian representation of the state vector, $\mathbf{x}_t$, (say) coupled with an observation equation, i.e. takes the form,

$$\mathbf{y}_t = \mathbf{H}\mathbf{x}_t + \boldsymbol{\varepsilon}_t, \tag{1}$$

$$\mathbf{x}_t = \boldsymbol{\theta}\mathbf{x}_{t-1} + \mathbf{v}_t. \tag{2}$$

If now $\boldsymbol{\theta}$ is allowed to be time dependent then one would have the further equation, e.g.

$$\boldsymbol{\theta}_t = \mathbf{G}\boldsymbol{\theta}_{t-1}+\mathbf{w}_t. \quad (3)$$

The authors' description is equivalent to using only equations (1) and (3), with $\boldsymbol{\theta}_t$ replacing $\mathbf{x}_t$ and $\mathbf{H}$ becoming the time-dependent matrix, $\mathbf{F}_t$. However, the dynamics of the complete system involve both the evolution of $\boldsymbol{\theta}_t$ *and* the evolution of $\mathbf{y}_t$, given $\boldsymbol{\theta}_t$. The evolution of $\boldsymbol{\theta}_t$ is given explicitly by (2.1.2) (corresponding to (3) above) but the evolution of $\mathbf{y}_t$ is now concealed inside the observation matrix $\mathbf{F}_t$ instead of being given explicitly by (1) and (2). In the usual Kalman theory, $\mathbf{F}_t$ is certainly allowed to be time dependent, but is normally assumed to be functionally independent of the $\mathbf{y}_t$ process. If $\mathbf{F}_t$ is allowed to *involve past values of* $\mathbf{y}_t$ (as is required in, for example, the autoregressive case) then the validity of the recursive relations (2.2.3) might need further investigation. The authors allow $\mathbf{F}_t$ to be defined generally as "any set of variables known at time t", but when these variables are, in fact, past values of $\mathbf{y}_t$ then why not use the Markovian representation as given in (2)? This point emerges, more clearly, in their treatment of the autoregressive model in (3.7), and the representation of y_t given by (3.7.2) can be easily adapted to the conventional state-space form by setting $\mathbf{y}_t = (y_t, y_{t-1}, \ldots, y_{t-p+1})'$ and then writing $\mathbf{y}_t = \boldsymbol{\phi}_t \mathbf{y}_{t-1}$, etc.

Incidentally, there is a simple interpretation of the Kalman filter algorithm (equation (2.2.3)) which it might be useful to mention—although I am sure that the authors themselves are familiar with it. Given observations only up to time $t-1$, the obvious "predictor", $\mathbf{m}_t$, of $\boldsymbol{\theta}_t$ is, from (2.1.2), $\mathbf{m}_t = \mathbf{G}\mathbf{m}_{t-1}$, and the corresponding "predictor" of $\mathbf{y}_t$ is, from (2.1.1), $\hat{\mathbf{y}}_t = \mathbf{F}_t\mathbf{G}\mathbf{m}_{t-1}$. When the next observation, $\mathbf{y}_t$, becomes available we can compare this with the predicted value and compute the error, $\mathbf{e}_t = \mathbf{y}_t - \hat{\mathbf{y}}_t$. The "up-dated" predictor of $\boldsymbol{\theta}_t$ is then simply a linear combination of the previous predictor ($\mathbf{G}\mathbf{m}_{t-1}$) and the error, $\mathbf{e}_t$. Even in its general form this result is very similar to the exponentially weighted moving average scheme, and it reduces exactly to the EWMA form under a sufficiently simple model for y_t—as explained in Section 3.3. This, presumably, is the reason for the authors' comment that the matrix $\mathbf{A}$ may be regarded as a "smoothing constant".

The authors claim that their approach enjoys the merit of flexibility and it is certainly true that their method allows the user to modify forecasts in an extremely general way in the light of any additional information—either quantitative or qualitative—which may come to light. However, as in all things one has to pay for luxuries of this kind and the cost is, of course, a loss of precision or reliability in the forecasts. To follow this point to an extreme situation one can argue that the most flexible method imaginable would simply be to look at the data, think about them, and then write down the forecast. What could be more flexible than this? The user here has complete freedom to take account of whatever sources of information or hunches may come his way, but, of course, such a method is totally lacking in precision. One is tempted to say that (borrowing a phrase from another branch of time series analysis) there is an obvious *uncertainty principle* which would be something like "the more flexibility the less reliability", and the real question now is what is the best compromise between these two desirable objectives. It may be noted also that any recursive forecasting scheme (such as those advocated by Box and Jenkins) can be made "flexible" in the way the authors propose simply by allowing the user to change the forecast at the previous stage if he feels it to be appropriate. This feature does not, therefore, seem to be dependent on the fact that the authors have chosen a Bayesian approach.

The authors did not say very much about the problem of model identification, but clearly even with a Bayesian approach and a built-in mechanism for using several alternative models, there is still the question as to which model or class of models one uses in any particular case. This particular problem has been studied extensively in connection with "standard" forecasting techniques, but I would be interested to hear how the authors would identify their class of models. A closely related problem is that of choosing the prior distributions and of determining what effect changes of priors have on the early forecasts.

The use of models involving stochastic parameters is, I suppose, inevitable with a Bayesian approach, but I am anything but clear as to the logical distinction between the stochastic parameters and time-dependent *deterministic* parameters. Models involving time-dependent deterministic parameters have been studied quite extensively in recent years and prediction methods have been developed for these. This approach does not require any specific model for the evolution of the parameters over time as long as this is, in a sense, sufficiently smooth. In some ways it could be argued that the use of time-dependent deterministic parameters provides more flexibility than a stochastic parameter tied down to a first-order Markov model.

Finally, may I return to the point which I raised earlier in the discussion, namely, are the authors using some hidden form of mean square error criterion? The point is that, e.g. in the scalar case, $\hat{y}_{k,t}$ as given by (2.3.5) is that value which minimizes $E[y_{t+k}-\hat{y}_{k,t}]^2$, where the expectation is taken with respect to the posterior distribution. In the classical Wiener–Kolmogorov theory the optimal (not necessarily linear) predictor is given by minimizing $E[y_{t+k}-\hat{y}_{k,t}]^2$, leading to $\hat{y}_{k,t} = E[y_{t+k} \mid \mathbf{y}^t]$, i.e. the conditional expectation of y_{t+k} given all the observations available. There is obviously a very close relationship between these two quantities and, bearing in mind that the authors' models are all linear, one wonders whether—at least in the particular case where the parameters are known and independent of time—the two approaches might be much closer than they at first appear.

In conclusion may I say that I have enjoyed reading the authors' paper very much indeed. They have presented us with some thought-provoking ideas expressed in a stimulating, lucid and highly readable form. Very sensibly, they do not claim that their approach provides the answer to all forecasting problems, but in situations for which it was designed it clearly produces good results—as shown in their companion paper on case studies. There is no point in arguing about whether a forecasting technique based on one class of models is "better" than a technique based on a different class of models; each will produce optimal forecasts (according to the criterion chosen) provided the data conform to the selected models. The real question, therefore, is whether the models considered can give more accurate descriptions of certain types of data than other models. The answer to this will emerge only in the light of practical experience. I have great pleasure in proposing the vote of thanks.

Dr B. J. N. BLIGHT (Birkbeck College, University of London): The authors are to be congratulated on presenting an interesting and challenging paper which brings theory and practice together. The Kalman filter and its many offshoots have, of course, been studied for some time; there have, for example, been a number of papers in the *Journal of the American Statistical Association* on dynamic regression models and the text by Aoki is based on Kalman filter models. I know of no other work, however, that classifies the Kalman filter and its variants in such a clear and comprehensive manner. I have two comments to make; one on the general line of adaptive inference adopted by the authors with regard to the inclusion of the forecaster in the forecasting system, and the other a more detailed point on the autoregressive process as a special case of the dynamic linear model.

One of the most interesting aspects of this paper is the authors' continual advocation of the inclusion of subjective knowledge as it becomes available. It seems to me that the DLM approach has a distinct advantage over ARIMA models in this respect since the Markov property of the model allows an easier interpretation of the model parameters with the result that subjective knowledge is more easily assimilated into the scheme. This enters in two ways; partly through the model itself in the user's selection of $\mathbf{V}_t$ and $\mathbf{W}_t$ (and, possibly, $\mathbf{F}_t$) at each time stage, and partly in situations such as that described at the end of Section 3.3. In this case the subjective knowledge is *directly* about the process parameter and comes from outside the process itself. The authors consider an extreme example where the subjective knowledge completely overrules the knowledge of μ_{t+1} based on the past, whereas in many cases we would wish to marry these two sources of knowledge in some reasonable fashion. The Bayesian does this by selecting his prior on the basis of his subjective knowledge and then combines it with the data information *via* Bayes' theorem. The likelihood approach, on the other hand, regards the likelihood function and subjective knowledge as two separate entities and bases judgment on these as such. The dynamic situation, however, appears to require something in between these two approaches. Likelihood is inappropriate because the parameter in question is truly stochastic so that the posterior distribution is certainly the correct function to study. A strict Bayesian approach, however, would be impractical for if we denote the subjective knowledge that becomes available at time t by S_t, then a strict Bayesian approach would involve forming a prior for the μ_t based on *all* the subjective knowledge available at time t and then it would be combined with $\mathbf{y}^t$ by Bayes' theorem. This approach is very unattractive as it loses all the nice updating features of the Kalman filter. The authors' suggestion, which seems very practical, is to treat S_t and $f(\mu_t \mid \mathbf{y}^t)$ as two separate entities and form a new posterior, $f^*(\mu_t \mid \mathbf{y}^t)$ from them. A few queries arise in this approach, however, as there are reasonable alternatives to this. We could, for example, combine S_t with $f(\mu_t \mid \mathbf{y}^{t-1})$ to form $f^*(\mu_t \mid \mathbf{y}^{t-1})$ and then update this using y_t and Bayes' theorem. Also, if we wish to predict μ_{t+k} should we derive $f(\mu_{t+k} \mid \mathbf{y}^t)$ from $f^*(\mu_t \mid \mathbf{y}^t)$ or should we combine S_t with $f(\mu_{t+k} \mid \mathbf{y}^t)$ to form the predictive distribution? The answer to this would seem to be that the subjective knowledge should be incorporated at the point where it makes most sense to the user; that is where he feels most confident about combining it with the posterior.

My second point is concerned with k-step prediction for the autoregressive models of Section 3.7. Let us, for simplicity, consider the case when $p = 1$ so that we then have the doubly stochastic Markov model,

$$y_t = y_{t-1}\phi_t + \varepsilon_t,$$
$$\phi_t = \phi_{t-1} + \delta\phi_t.$$

If we write $F_t = y_{t-1}$ then we see, as the authors correctly assert, that this is a special case of the DLM. It is rather a complicated case, however, since the F and y series are now the same so that not only is F stochastic but it depends on the past of the y series. For one-step prediction this causes no problems since $\mathbf{y}^{t-1} = \mathbf{F}^t$ are known and the Kalman filter applies. For $k(>1)$ step prediction the problem is more difficult and Case II of Section 2.3 does not apply in the simplest form represented by equations (2.3.9) and (2.3.10). To see this, for k-step prediction we have

$$\hat{y}_{k,t} = E(y_{t+k} \mid \mathbf{y}^t) = E(F_{t+k}\phi_{t+k} \mid \mathbf{y}^t),$$

and since $F_{t+k} = y_{t+k-1}$ is correlated with ϕ_{t+k} then we do not get the factorization of (2.3.9). Recurrence relations which generate $\hat{y}_{k,t}$ can be obtained in this case and it can be shown that $\hat{y}_{k,t}$ is a function of the first k moments of $f(\theta_t \mid \mathbf{y}^t)$. In conclusion I would like, once again, to express my appreciation to the authors for their stimulating paper.

The vote of thanks was passed by acclamation.

Professor D. R. Cox (Imperial College, London): It is a pleasure to join in congratulating the authors on an important and interesting piece of work. Some miscellaneous comments are as follows:

(i) The use of what in other statistical contexts would be called latent structure models is undoubtedly very fruitful in constructing plausible models; I wonder whether the authors would like to comment on the dangers of over-elaboration.
(ii) A different kind of system to which these ideas can be applied is the forecasting of point processes (Snyder, 1975; Vere-Jones, 1975) and in as yet an unpublished work by Dr M. H. A. Davis. The calculations tend to be difficult. My own work (Cox, 1975) has been concentrated on determining in an empirical Bayes context whether a finite Poisson process has terminated.
(iii) There are interesting applications of ideas close to the present paper in meteorology, notably in the forecasting of the path of typhoons (Takeuchi, 1976).
(iv) The criticisms of mean square error as an overriding criterion apply also to simpler statistical problems; for instance, inverse estimation and binary dose-response curves. Even so it is, of course, sometimes useful; a point related to the work of Holt (1957) is that in using a trend-corrected exponentially weighted moving average much better results tend to be obtained if the trend correction is shrunk towards zero.

Dr C. Chatfield (University of Bath): This is an important paper which will be of interest to anyone concerned with forecasting.

Two features of the paper may inhibit its widespread use. Firstly, it uses the Kalman filtering technique with which many statisticians are unfortunately unfamiliar. This technique is a powerful recursive method of estimating the present state of a system and has applications in control and regression as well as time-series analysis. It is well worth reading the introductory paper by Young (1974).

The second feature of the paper which may be inhibiting is the word "Bayesian" in the title, so may I emphasize that you do not need to be a Bayesian to adopt the method. If, as the authors suggest, the general purpose default priors work pretty well for most time series, then one does not need to supply prior information. So, despite the use of Bayes' theorem inherent in Kalman filtering, I wonder if *Adaptive Forecasting* would be a better description of the method. What the paper does not perhaps make clear is that subjective information can be incorporated as one goes along as well as in the priors. When a freak observation occurs in, for example, a series of sales figures, one can usually find out why by asking the sales manager. He will be able to say if it is caused by a strike, a stockout or some other factor, and will probably be able to tell you if it is a transient or not. This information can be used to alter the probabilities of the different models. The examples quoted by the authors, which treat freak observations automatically, are perhaps rather misleading in that I do not think freak values *should* be treated automatically, except when large numbers of items are involved.

I am unhappy about the distinction between what the authors call "functional models" and "parametric (state-space) models". I can see nothing "functional" about (1.2.1), and I see a clear distinction between parametric models, such as multiple regression models, and state-space models. In the latter, $\boldsymbol{\theta}_t$ are to be interpreted as state-space variables, not process parameters, while $\mathbf{F}_t$ is an observation matrix of 0's and 1's and not a matrix of independent variables.

One problem the paper leaves unanswered is the identification problem. The authors show that their DLM contains nearly every other forecasting procedure but we are not told how to select the appropriate model for a particular case. Perhaps their model is *too* general. In their companion paper on applications, a simple multiplicative model appears "out of a hat" and is applied to all four series with little explanation.

An annoying feature of the paper is the authors' notation, which, in my view, is very hard to follow. I counted at least 73 different symbols, some of them chosen very confusingly. For example $M^{(j)}$ denotes a model, M_t a level, $\mathbf{m}_t$ a mean, $m(t)$ a month and m the number of variables.

Despite these misgivings, this is clearly an important paper which will repay careful study.

Dr H. Tong (University of Manchester Institute of Science and Technology): I would like to congratulate Professor Harrison and Mr Stevens on a very interesting paper.

As some of the points that I wanted to raise have already been raised by the previous speakers, I shall restrict myself to the following point.

Also due to Kalman are the concepts of controllability and observability, which play an immensely important role in systems theory in general, and filtering (and hence forecasting) and identification in particular. (See, for example, Silverman, 1966.) In fact, I have been informed that Professor Kalman would like to be remembered for these ideas than for anything else.

Interpreting equations (2.1.1) and (2.1.2) as the *observation equation* and the *state equation* respectively in the Kalman sense, we can give necessary and sufficient conditions for the DLM to be completely observable and completely controllable. To simplify discussions, let us assume that the matrix coefficients G and F are t-independent and that $\mathbf{V}_t$ is absent. (For the more general case we can refer to, for example, Bucy and Joseph, 1968, Chapter 3.) Then the DLM is completely controllable if and only if the matrix $[\mathbf{I}_n, \mathbf{G}, \mathbf{G}^2, \ldots, \mathbf{G}^{n-1}]$ is of rank n; the DLM is completely observable if and only if the matrix $[\mathbf{F}^{\mathrm{T}}, \mathbf{G}^{\mathrm{T}}\mathbf{F}^{\mathrm{T}}, \ldots, (\mathbf{G}^{n-1})^{\mathrm{T}}\mathbf{F}^{\mathrm{T}}]$ is of rank n. Checking some of the cases in Section 3 of the paper, I found that the dynamic model of Section 3.2.2 is not completely observable although completely controllable, when $\mathbf{F}_t = \mathbf{x}_0$ say, for all t. It is well known in the context of minimal realization theory that a system is completely controllable and completely observable if and only if the state-space description, constructed from a given transfer function (matrix) relating the "inputs" ($\mathbf{w}_t$) and outputs ($\mathbf{y}_t$), is of *minimal* dimension. This result, essentially due to Kalman, is obviously important also in the context of identification in view of the identifiability consideration. In a somewhat related study, Akaike (1974) has discussed the concept of block identifiability of autoregressive moving average processes, utilizing Hannan's result (1969).

I would be interested to know if Professor Harrison and Mr Stevens could offer their comments on the non-observability of the case mentioned above, bearing in mind the importance of observability. More generally, what is the precise role (if any) played by the concept of controllability and observability in their DLM?

Mr G. J. A. Stern (ICL): In my view, Section 1.1 of this paper ought to be set up as a permanent block of type and incorporated in all subsequent papers and books on forecasting, or maybe inscribed on brass over the portals of the Society. As the authors rightly say, a forecasting system should consist both of a technique, and of the expertise and knowledge of the user of the forecast. As they rightly say, a forecast needs to create "a meaningful view of the future in the minds of the people who take decisions". One can agree also with the doubtfulness of the least squares criterion often used in fitting to past data, and on the generally rather academic approach taken by many forecasters. In short, I think that the aims of the authors are absolutely right, and I am sure too that their achievements in forecasting are well up to their aims. I only have some slight doubts as to whether this paper lives up to both their aims and their undoubted achievements. These are doubts only, which I am quite prepared to believe are unjustified, and I also take their point that their work is by no means complete.

It seems to me that one needs roughly three types of forecast:

(1) Very short-term forecasts of a mechanical rule of thumb kind. The typical application is forecasting one period ahead for each of several thousand items for stock control. All one is trying to do there is to improve slightly on some yet cruder rule applied by the manual system, and there can be little possibility of giving individual attention to most of the items. A simple automatic process, no more complex than Holt–Winters, at most, is all that can be used here.

(2) Medium-term forecasts, often needed for control purposes. Typically a sales manager wants to assess from sales so far whether he will meet his target. Again, Professor Harrison mentioned the mail order house case of forecasting sales of dresses for the rest of the season from sales so far, a case I happen to have worked on. Here again, all that was needed by the decision-makers, as I understood it, was to be warned that they were very over-stocked or very under-stocked, or about right—no precise numbers were needed. In cases like this the decision-maker wants to be personally involved because he may need to take fairly drastic action as a result of the forecast, and he may only accept a forecast if he understands how it was made, and if he can modify it with the sort of knowledge which he has, as Professor Harrison described so vividly. Will such a manager accept anything more than some simple model like saying that in a season the first week's sales are 10 per cent of the whole, and the second week's sales 5 per cent, etc?

(3) One also has very complex long-term forecasts usually based on regression or econometric modelling. It is relevant to recall the paper by Coen *et al.* (1969) where it was claimed that stock exchange levels could be predicted more than a year in advance by levels of economic indicators like car production—a very useful discovery if authentic. Box and Newbold (1971) pointed out that the relationship was only apparent and arose from the assumption that the error structure was as for regression, whereas it appeared in fact to be a random walk, in which case there was no longer any relationship. One could comment that such forecasting is evidently very hazardous if even Sir Maurice Kendall can be tripped up; but to make a comment more directly relevant here, I would like to ask the present authors if their formulation allows of error structures such as those often needed for econometric work. If, as I understand, it does not, then this may sharply limit the usefulness of the part of the formulation allowing independent variables.

If the above analysis of forecasting has any relationship to reality, one could say that the first two types of forecast are not, in any real sense, sub-sets of the authors' formulation. Of course I accept that in a formal sense they could specify the forecasting methods to fit in with their formulation, but this is rather like saying that Newton's dynamics is a sub-set of Einstein's general theory of relativity. When astronauts wanted to get to the moon, they used Newton's theory, not Einstein's, which, however interesting theoretically, is not usable in practice for most problems. With regard to the third type of forecasting, there seems to me a doubt as to whether the authors' formulation could tackle it adequately in many cases.

Even if the authors are too modest to say so, it could be argued that as they are among our most eminent and experienced forecasters with many successes to their credit, the method they advocate and use must be a good one. I would like to ask if their undoubted success does not largely spring from their general knowledge of the subject matter of the forecast, their experience, systematic approach, etc., rather than from any specific technique, other than the simplest. I would like to see an experiment, in which the authors use their method in its full extension, someone else not so eminent does the same, and then both parties forecast using very crude methods like trend plus seasonal and the like, modifying the forecast according to their knowledge and experience. May it not turn out that success in forecasting depends largely on the knowledge and ability of the forecasters and little on the system used? Nevertheless, even if all these strictures are upheld in their entirety, the authors can still claim a unified theory covering several techniques, and this is both appealing to the human mind, and can be the source of advances in the art.

Dr A. O'Hagan (University of Warwick): The problem of unknown variances appears to be crucial to the successful implementation of the ideas of this paper. The authors' approach seems to be to use a discrete approximation to the current posterior distribution of **V** and **W**, whereas this distribution should surely be continuous. Surely this is precisely a case of making "grossly unrealistic assumptions simply for the sake of tractability"? The updating procedure (4.2.3) is too cumbersome to allow many discrete values of **V** and **W** to be used and the approximation is correspondingly poor. In particular, in obtaining the marginal posterior distribution of $\boldsymbol{\theta}_t$ the authors perform what amounts to a very crude numerical integration over the true continuous distribution of **V** and **W**.

However, I would like to make a constructive suggestion. Although the marginal density of **V** and **W** given $\mathbf{y}^t$ is hideously complicated, their conditional posterior distributions $P(\mathbf{V}, \mathbf{W} \mid \boldsymbol{\phi}^t, \mathbf{y}^t)$ given the whole vector $\boldsymbol{\phi}^t$ (Section 3.10) of current and past $\boldsymbol{\theta}_t$ are independent inverse Wishart if their conditional prior distributions are of this form. Furthermore, the distribution of $\boldsymbol{\phi}^t$ given **V**, **W**, $\mathbf{y}^t$ is Normal with mean and covariance matrix easily derived from Section 3.10. This combination of Normal and Wishart means that equations for the joint mode of $\boldsymbol{\phi}^t$, **V** and **W** are easily written down, and other modes may be derived using the methods of O'Hagan (1976). In complicated models, when the dimensionality of **V** and **W** becomes too large for any reasonable numerical integration, the modal approach remains feasible. Indeed, by computing various kinds of mode and searching for multimodality we can in fact build up a useful description of the posterior distribution.

Dr T. Leonard (University of Warwick): I would like to add my congratulations to the authors for describing the first approach to forecasting to allow the practitioner to utilize fully his conceptual ideas, common sense and intuition, instead of referring to somewhat irrelevant standard criteria and grinding out a fairly meaningless data-fitting procedure. Whilst the authors mainly concentrate their energies on normal linear situations in discrete time, where the variance is known, a principal strength of their approach is that its underlying concepts readily generalize to less restrictive situations. For example, if $y(t)$ is a continuous time Gaussian process with mean value function $\theta(t)$ and covariance kernel $K(s, t)$, it is possible to assign a second stage to the model by taking $\theta(t)$ to be a Gaussian process, say with mean value function $\mu(t)$ and covariance kernel $C(s, t)$. It is then well known (e.g. Kimeldorf and Wahba, 1970) that the posterior mean of $\theta(t)$, given n observations, $y(t_1), \ldots, y(t_n)$, is denoted by

$$\theta^*(t) = \mu(t) + \boldsymbol{\xi}^T \boldsymbol{\Sigma}^{-1} \boldsymbol{\lambda}(t),$$

where the jth elements of $\boldsymbol{\xi}$ and $\boldsymbol{\lambda}(t)$ are

$$\xi_j = y(t_j) - \mu(t_j)$$

and

$$\lambda_j(t) = C(t_j, t),$$

respectively, and

$$\boldsymbol{\Sigma} = \{K(t_j, t_k) + C(t_j, t_k)\}.$$

This defines a very simple general method for both filtering and prediction in the continuous time situation, and it is possible to generalize it to the time-dependent Poisson process. When the variances in the authors' models are unknown it is possible to assign continuous priors to the variances generalizing the discrete mixtures in Section 1.2.5. Particular care should be taken in choosing the priors, and I have strong reservations about finite discrete mixtures, owing to the thickness of the tails of the marginal likelihood of the variances. For continuous priors, unconditional predictors for the process parameters will sometimes be easily computable via numerical integrations.

Finally, if the data are not normal, transformations often lead us back to the standard linear results. For example, if $y(t)$ has a Poisson distribution with mean $\theta(t)$, it is possible to employ the authors' second stage set-up for $\gamma(t) = \log \theta(t)$ and then to proceed as if $\log y(t)$ is normally distributed with mean $\gamma(t)$ and variance $\{y(t)\}^{-1}$. A more accurate routine is available when there are zeros in the data. When the variances in the normal linear model are unequal, logarithmic transformations are also available (Leonard, 1975). Similar transformations may be used to introduce the ideas of the mixed model Kalman filter into histogram smoothing and the non-parametric estimation of a continuous probability density function.

Dr R. J. BHANSALI (University of Liverpool): I would also like to congratulate the authors on a thought-provoking paper. However, I would like to make a brief comment concerning the problem of model selection referred to in Section 1.2.5.

For the time-invariant models this problem can be solved using the information-theoretic criterion suggested by Akaike (1971). Shibata (1976) has shown that for the class of autoregressive models the use of Akaike's criterion fits the correct order model with a high probability. To use this criterion for the more general problem of model selection, it is necessary to estimate the parameters of several competing models by the method of maximum likelihood. The particular model which gives the minimum of Akaike's criterion is then chosen. Now, the choice available for modelling the behaviour of a stationary time series is rather wide. Apart from the autoregressive, the moving average and the autoregressive-moving average models, the use of the exponential model suggested by Bloomfield (1973) may be considered. Alternatively one could follow Parzen (1974) and consider the use of a non-parametric autoregressive model. Because of this rather wide choice of models, the traditional likelihood method of estimating the parameters of these models may be computationally too expensive to apply in practice. A computationally efficient alternative would be to use the spectral factorization procedure. It can be shown that (Bhansali, 1975) by using a spectral factorization procedure all these different models can be fitted efficiently. Hence, using this frequency domain approach the implementation of Akaike's information-theoretic criterion for model selection may be carried out quickly and efficiently.

Professor A. M. WALKER (University of Sheffield): My question relates to Sections 4.3 and in particular 4.3.1, p. 223, which refer to the use of utility in connection with the choice of a single model. I have not had time to think out in any detail what I would do about this, but I cannot see how comparison of utilities, or cumulative utilities as given by expressions such as equation (4.3.2), on the assumption that a particular model is true, can lead to a reasonable way of selecting models. Something seems rather strange about the logic, and I would be grateful if the authors could describe their argument in more detail at this point.

Professor D. V. LINDLEY (University College London): Tonight's paper makes important contributions to the theory and practice of statistics and will hopefully mark a significant turning point in the Society's affairs. (May I incidentally regret the decision of the Committee—of which I am a member—to cut the paper down to conventional length by the removal of the examples. Conventions should give way to distinction.) The authors provide powerful tools for forecasting, but it is in a wider context that I would like to discuss their results. It might be argued that most statistical tasks are forecasting, for what is an agricultural experiment in partially balanced randomized blocks but an aid to forecasting the yield that a farmer might get from a new variety or insecticide?

They show very clearly that, contrary to an oft-repeated view, the Bayesian method is not model-specific. It has always been apparent that the "ideal" coherent person has a probability specification over everything, but tonight we see how a "real" person can come close to this view and yet remain operational. The authors' device is to discretize the situation and use a probability distribution over a finite number of models. This could be used in robustness studies, for example, where the model would refer to the error distribution; long-tailed, short-tailed or normal, to mention but three possibilities. Mention of normality reminds me to ask the authors whether they feel that their assumptions of normality are restrictive. The assumptions not merely affect the distributions but play an important role in the sufficiency and linearity of the Kalman filter. (For example, try the process model on discrete data.)

A second contribution is to show how all forms of uncertainty can be incorporated into the situation and not just the restricted ones that are conventionally used. This may be expressed by saying that the likelihood of the data is only part of the Bayesian story. Modern statistical methods tend seriously and consistently to *underestimate* the variability in the system by ignoring elements other than the sampling variation, thereby giving a spurious sense of precision to the results.

In the riches of the paper the ingenious technical device of the final paragraph should not go unnoticed. Mixtures are notoriously difficult to handle because of the complexity of the recurrence relations. An example is in signal-detection theory, where the observed datum is known to come from one of a number of sources. Various devices, such as the decision-directed approach, have been suggested to overcome the complexity and yet not lose efficiency. The authors' suggestion looks as if it may be an improvement.

I am not alone in thinking that British management is not as good as it might be and that its incompetence is partly to blame for Britain's position today. Is it significant that ICI can let two such able people leave; or is it the case that the only place to do really imaginative practical work is in academea?

The following contributions were received in writing after the meeting.

Dr O. D. ANDERSON (Civil Service College): Harrison–Stevens (HS), coming from the back, may or may not have the potential to outstrip the current forecasting front runner, Box–Jenkins (BJ). However, any improvement needs to be established both at the Giant's level, that of Professors Harrison and Jenkins, and at Jack's—yours and mine. The Giants can fight it out on the pages of this *Journal* or through the pull of their consultancies; but, in the end, it is Jack who has to be won over, by an approach which works for *him*, if a Giant is not to be toppled.

BJ has on the whole satisfied Jack, but only after many years of effort, development and persuasion by the two Giants involved and some of their satellites. A most notable factor has been the emphasis that Professor Jenkins has given to the running of courses for Jack, on the methodology and application of BJ.

The outcome is that much investment has gone into making BJ widely operational, and this considerable capital should not be lightly rendered obsolete, even should HS be later shown to offer a definite advantage. The costs to Jacks of switching bandwagons might well outweigh the gains. They will have to halt their present horses and then break in their new team. Certainly there will be effectively a step back, before two paces forward can again be taken.

I hope very much that HS and BJ do not set up in competition. For though this would interest giantologists, it will not help Jack much. Far better if HS recognizes that BJ has a long head-start, so that BJ is perhaps helped to develop in the direction of HS. The object being assimilation rather than a battle.

In fact it seems that a number of implicit criticisms of BJ, contained in this paper, are unfounded if one looks at current practice, especially allowing for the fact that the latest BJ model is not fully described by the 1970 manual. Thus extra information, such as having satisfactorily had your competitor's factory rased, can be straightforwardly incorporated into the forecast in the form of a favourable "intervention".

Finally, though the greater apparent flexibility of HS is an attractive sales feature, it does give Jack even more rope to get tangled up in. Given his present state of knowledge and expertise, it would seem more sensible to look for modifications in the BJ specification, such as allowing time-varying parameters; rather than throwing Jack into the air and telling him "you learnt to swim once—now learn to fly!"

However, here is surely the stuff that Guy medals are made of. It is indeed with extreme regret that I was unable to attend this meeting. It can only have been that such a brilliant contribution was greeted with the appreciation it undoubtedly deserved. I can find little exception to the mathematical formulation and am able to accept, on trust, that Professor Harrison and Mr Stevens find their extremely versatile DLM delivers the goods in "messy" situations—at least, when *they* are holding the reins.

Professor JAMES M. DICKEY (University College of Wales): The present work by Harrison and Stevens promises to be a landmark. General and tractable theory is developed with a close eye to real forecasting contexts. In my opinion these methods will be found useful in practice. I expend some effort in the following trying to explain what I mean by "useful". Further details will be published in a future report on joint work with Joseph B. Kadane. Such explanation is necessary because this theory—any theory—does not refer *literally* to a practical context, and we have little or no meta-theory for the relation between theory and practice. (See, though, Berk, 1966.)

It has long been recognized in some circles that in practice the "true model" is infinitely complicated, in the sense that the larger the sample size the greater the number of parameters which appear to be needed for realistic modelling. Any null model is an oversimplified fiction and is sure to be "rejected" for a large enough sample size. (This may be a kind of analogue for stochastic models of the recognition that stochastic models are more realistic in practice than simple deterministic ones.)

In effect, there is no true model. But the authors, in harmony with much of statistical theory and practice, continually refer to one in an operational sense: "which of a number of possible models actually obtains"; "different models may obtain at different times"; "$M^{(j)}$ is the model we are seeking"; "model $M^{(j)}$ obtains"; and "the multi-state model . . . describes the state which obtains at time t by a Markov process". Of course, the authors realize that a language of pretence is being used, for they write, "the model is just the way we decide to view an observation series and its context".

The Bayesian and frequentist approaches make distinct uses of language, but both involve pretence. The frequentist statistician argues within an explicit sampling model; invokes theorems on consistency and efficiency; hopes that his sampling model is approximately true in some sense, whereby his procedures will still be consistent and almost efficient; and he is completely lost for meaning without the existence of a true model.

The Bayesian statistician is able to model subjective uncertainty as well as sampling fiction; and if the existence of the sampling model is questioned too closely he can admit that it merely consists of a public conditional distribution in a joint subjective distribution. It is often overlooked, as in the following quotation from Cox and Hinkley (1974, p. 48), that if his sampling model is actual, the Bayesian statistician has all of the consistency and most of the efficiency of the frequentist (Ferguson, 1967).

> The Bayesian coherency principle is a requirement for a certain kind of self-sufficiency. It contains no direct guarantee that the answers we obtain are related to the objective truth about the system under study. On the other hand, the repeated sampling principles are concerned with the relation between the data and a model of the real world. They deal with the question of how close to the "true" answer we are likely to get by repeated use of a particular technique.

Of course, for the frequentist to *say* he knows something about the behaviour of his procedure in the real world is entirely different than *actually* knowing as recognized by Good (1970, p. 124).

> The subjectivist states his judgments, whereas the objectivist sweeps them under the carpet by calling assumptions *knowledge*, and he basks in the glorious objectivity of science.

Both the Bayesian statistician and the frequentist are cut off from any *necessary* relation to the real world. Neither can rely on his sampling model for *actual* reference to the world. In addition, the Bayesian's "prior" distribution, also, is an oversimplification that usually does not exist prior to the choice of a sampling model, made after informal analysis of the realized data. The view underlying Pratt *et al.* (1964) is that the assessment of a prior distribution is itself a decision act (personal communication from Pratt and Schlaifer).

Of course, the frequentist statistician's "procedure" is also a fiction, which does not apply to the whole sample space, and hence cannot be evaluated by a risk integral, following as it usually does an informal data analysis with diagnostic checking. For discussion of this point, see Dickey (1976a, b).

To return to the methods of Harrison and Stevens, while tail area tests may be useless because any model tested is already known to be false, what should one make of the posterior odds between two models which are both known to be false? In Section 4.3.2 they wisely take the view that the probabilities of the models should be merely one ingredient in an attempted comprehensive combination of models useful to evaluate any forecasting function. In Section 4.3.1 they unfortunately compare the forecasters given as optimal within models, on the basis of the expected utilities within the respective models, asking in effect, "How good would I believe my best predictor under this model to be if I believed this model?" That would be to bury the ostrich's head in his own house's sandy foundations.

A useful compromise when a simple forecasting function is desired might be to compare those forecasters which are optimal under the component models on the basis of their expected performance under the composite model. This leads in the standard regression situation with a pair of nested models and squared-error loss to the decision criterion: "Choose that forecasting function whose model has the higher posterior probability." In this case, of course, the *overall* optimal forecaster under the composite model is the posterior mean, the average of the posterior means under the individual models, weighted by the posterior probabilities of the models.

The authors are right to warn against squared-error loss in favour of more reasonable utilities. The distinction is not strongly enough made, however, between the two kinds of models: (i) the forecast function; and (ii) the model of the inference or evaluation of the forecast. The work to be reported with Kadane treats choice of model as choice of forecast function; and the criteria derived differ importantly from the criteria for deciding which model is "true". The traditional significance test for $H: \mu = \mu_0$ for the mean μ of a simple normal sample $(y_1, ..., y_n)$ has a threshold on $|y - \mu_0|/n^{\frac{1}{2}}$ independent of the sample size n. Constant Bayesian posterior odds in favour of H implies a threshold on the same deviate proportional to $(\log n)^{\frac{1}{2}}$. Whereas, the corresponding threshold is proportional to $n^{\frac{1}{2}}$ for the criterion of maximum expected predictive utility.

I have not succeeded here in indicating that the forecasting methods of Harrison and Stevens will give information about the real world; but I think that they will. One important way in which they may do so is merely by enabling the forecasting statistician to get on with the business of analysing his data and contemplating its relation to the probable future.

Mr E. J. GODOLPHIN (Royal Holloway College): My remarks on this interesting paper are confined to a point of detail on the DLM model. It appears that, to apply the authors' procedure, it is generally required to specify not just the variances of individual elements of $\mathbf{v}_t$ and $\mathbf{w}_t$ but also the cross- and autocovariances of these elements. This may seem desirable, for example, when using the steady-state model of Section 3.3. For simplicity, but without affecting the general point, consider the limiting case with time-independent second moments. Using an argument which generalizes a result of Muth (1960), this model can be expressed in the well-known form which leads to the EWMA predictor, namely

$$\nabla y_t = a_t - \theta a_{t-1}.$$

Now the real parameter θ can be expressed in several ways dependent upon the prior specification of variances and covariances in the model:

(1) $\operatorname{cov}(\varepsilon_t, \delta\mu_t) \neq 0$, $\operatorname{cov}(\delta\mu_t, \delta\mu_{t-1}) = 0$. Then

$$\theta = \{1 + \tfrac{1}{2}\phi + \tfrac{1}{2}(\phi^2 + 4\phi)^{\frac{1}{2}}\}^{-1} = 1 + \tfrac{1}{2}\phi - \tfrac{1}{2}(\phi^2 + 4\phi)^{\frac{1}{2}}$$

with

$$\phi = \operatorname{var}(\delta\mu_t)/\{\operatorname{var}(\varepsilon_t) + \operatorname{cov}(\varepsilon_t, \delta\mu_t)\}.$$

Thus if $\operatorname{cov}(\varepsilon_t, \delta\mu_t) > -\operatorname{var}(\varepsilon_t)$ then $\phi > 0$ so that $0 < \theta < 1$; in addition the random walk model $\theta = 0$ corresponds to $\operatorname{cov}(\varepsilon_t, \delta\mu_t) = -\operatorname{var}(\varepsilon_t)$ whilst $-1 < \theta < 0$ occurs when $-\tfrac{1}{4}\operatorname{var}(\delta\mu_t) - \operatorname{var}(\varepsilon_t) < \operatorname{cov}(\varepsilon_t, \delta\mu_t) < -\operatorname{var}(\varepsilon_t)$.

(2) $\operatorname{cov}(\varepsilon_t, \delta\mu_t) = 0$, $\operatorname{cov}(\delta\mu_t, \delta\mu_{t-1}) \neq 0$. Then

$$\theta = 2(1 - \rho v)/[(v+2) + \{(1 - 4\rho^2)v^2 + 4(1 + 2\rho)v\}^{\frac{1}{2}}]$$

with

$$v = \operatorname{var}(\delta\mu_t)/\operatorname{var}(\varepsilon_t) \quad \text{and} \quad \rho = \operatorname{cov}(\delta\mu_t, \delta\mu_{t-1})/\operatorname{var}(\delta\mu_t)$$

so that $|\rho| < \tfrac{1}{2}$. Therefore $0 \leqslant \theta < 1$ and $-1 < \theta \leqslant 0$ when $\operatorname{cov}(\delta\mu_t, \delta\mu_{t-1}) \leqslant \operatorname{var}(\varepsilon_t)$ and

$$\operatorname{cov}(\delta\mu_t, \delta\mu_{t-1}) \geqslant \operatorname{var}(\varepsilon_t)$$

respectively.

The authors are doubtless aware of results of this kind, although in the paper they specify $\operatorname{cov}(\varepsilon_t, \delta\mu_t) = \operatorname{cov}(\delta\mu_t, \delta\mu_{t-1}) = 0$ and so restrict themselves to positive values of θ (note also that in the non-limiting time-dependent case the smoothing constant $A_t = 1 - \theta$ is bounded by $0 < A_t < 1$). Perhaps it may be argued in this case that positive parameter values are more likely to occur in many applications, though this would avoid such cases as that derived by Box and Jenkins (1970, p. 239) for their IBM data.

But in some more general DLM models, if the prior assumption is made that the elements of $\mathbf{v}_t$ and $\mathbf{w}_t$ are neither cross- nor autocorrelated then this can result in fairly severe restrictions on the choice of possible models. Consider, for example, the DLM

$$y_t = \mu_t + \varepsilon_t,$$
$$\mu_t = g\mu_{t-1} + \beta_t + \delta\mu_t,$$
$$\beta_t = \beta_{t-1} + \delta\beta_t,$$

where $0 < g \leqslant 1$, which contains the examples of Section 1.2.3 ($g = \tfrac{1}{2}$) and Section 3.4 ($g = 1$).

Making the same assumptions as previously, and also that ε_t, $\delta\mu_t$, $\delta\beta_t$ are independent sets of uncorrelated random disturbances, then $\nabla y_t - g\nabla y_{t-1}$ has the same correlation structure as an ARIMA (1, 1, 2) or (0, 2, 2) process

$$\nabla y_t - g\nabla y_{t-1} = a_t - \theta_1 a_{t-1} - \theta_2 a_{t-2}.$$

It follows from a result of Godolphin (1976) that θ_1 is necessarily positive and that $-g < \theta_2 < 0$, in contrast to the invertibility region $|\theta_1| < 1 - \theta_2$ and $|\theta_2| < 1$, and to widen the bounds it seems essential to specify correlated disturbances. Of course these comments do not detract at all from the flexibility of the authors' models resulting from the use of information beyond the available time-series realization; but do the authors have any suggestions with regard to prior specification of covariances in typical forecasting applications?

Dr W. D. RAY (Birkbeck College, London): This paper comes to the forecasting field at an opportune time. The simple reason is that the classical models used for forecasting have, up to the present, been static ones, static in their parameters but not necessarily in the way they operate; some of them could adapt to changing circumstances but in a fairly constrained fashion. The methodology presented here gives much more flexibility but at a price which has yet to be evaluated.

The authors are to be commended for on the one hand exposing the statistical community to the Kalman-type dynamic linear model (DLM), and on the other to the possibilities of choice of models in a formal sequential way. They must not imagine, however, that the first of these ideas has not been appreciated and indeed used prior (if the reader will forgive the word) to this paper. Dr Young (1971, 1975) in his discussions of recent papers in this *Journal* gave some elegant reminders of what has been done in this field. It is also known that dynamic regression using the Plackett–Kalman algorithms was used by one chemical company (not ICI) in the mid-sixties, both rolling on with new observations added, and old observations discarded. Further, whilst the authors do a service in listing the classical models in their DLM forms some of these again were known to some statisticians, many control people and not a few econometricians.

It has always amused and intrigued me that whilst it took a decade or more for control engineers to "discover" the method of maximum likelihood to assist in their system parameter estimation problem, equally it has taken statisticians about as long to "borrow" the Kalman filter. Technically there is not a lot to say about the DLM and its analysis. Kalman invented it with the physical state-space in mind, Åström modified it to the parameter state-space form and the present authors have laid it all out for us to see and use. Some theoretical loose ends may need tidying up, for example Professor Priestley's remarks on conditional means and least squares estimators seem pertinent and at least one of the classical models does not fall so simply into the DLM package. Basically however the theory, given its assumptions, stands firm.

It is the second theme of the paper, the multi-process modelling, which may be contentious. This idea with choice of model, accompanying priors and loss functions for decision, whilst admirably desirable for flexibility of thought and action, could produce so much of it as to make the method somewhat impractical with the limited data available. This would be a pity. What I am saying is that knowledge comes in different quality packages. Historical data are pure. It may well be hilarious, full of wildies and mavericks. No matter, it has happened, there is no uncertainty. Knowledge however which comes from external sources is much more precarious. True, some of it may be pure; however, a lot will be conjectural and some may be unintentionally misleading. It is the problem of the observer who thinks he has the first category but in reality has the third which has to be faced. As our new President emphasized in her recent address to the Society, "there is the innate variability of *Homo sapiens*" and "we all behave irrationally".

I agree with the authors that, in the event, it is the Multi-process Models Class II which matter most in practice. Those of Class I and a unique model hardly exist. This being so Section 5 is at once the most relevant and yet the most sketchy; not without reason, since it is of considerable difficulty.

No method will find favour until tested in competition as I am sure the Kalman filter part of this one will. From an isolated brief comparative study of using Box–Jenkins, Holt–Winters and the Kalman method on my pet "nasty" time series the race ended in a tie; it very much depended upon where you were in the series which method turned out best. A second trial of the method, on a series whose structure and parameters were known, showed that a fairly large sample was necessary before estimates of the parameters converged on the true values. Furthermore, as the forecasting continued the estimates diverged from the true values, later taking up biased positions. Thus if this method is used for estimation some care will be required.

Notwithstanding the latter experiences, I found the paper most interesting.

Dr P. Newbold (University of Nottingham): I would like to congratulate the authors of this most stimulating paper. They remind us that, in the industrial forecasting context, one often meets situations where there is worthwhile prior information, very little data, unstable underlying structure through time and a need for a more relevant criterion of evaluation than root mean squared error. The natural tendency in situations where these factors are present is to resort to *ad hoc* methods, and the outstanding achievement of this paper is the demonstration that a formal structure can be imposed on the problem. It is hardly surprising that in doing so a "radical" view is required and readers are urged to look at forecasting in a "fresh way". I regret that my subsequent comments reflect a sluggishness on my part in making the necessary mental adjustments, but perhaps contemplation of the unfamiliar in terms of lessons derived from the familiar is of some value.

I wish to take up two aspects of the proposed methodology—its ability to deal with very short time series and the problem of forecast evaluation.

Although the theoretical results derived in the paper are applicable to a wide range of model structures, it appears from the companion paper that in practice one is required to choose, somewhat arbitrarily, a specific underlying model. Various possible states of this underlying model are then contemplated and probabilities assessed for each one at any point in time. Of course, given sufficient data, procedures exist whereby the evidence of the data is allowed to suggest a model. The need to produce a system which forecasts from short series disqualifies this approach here, but it must be added that the possibility of using an inappropriate model is greatly increased. This suggests that research on the consequences of using mis-specified time series models would be of great value. Work along these lines, mainly by Neville Davies of Trent Polytechnic, is currently in progress at Nottingham. For evidence that certain kinds of mis-specification of time series can have serious consequences in regression analysis see Box and Newbold (1971) and Granger and Newbold (1974); also Newbold and Davies' as yet unpublished paper on error mis-specification.†

I fully sympathize with the authors' resaons for disliking root mean squared error as a criterion for the evaluation of forecasts. The difficulty, of course, is to know what to put in its place, and here the authors are not completely convincing. For example, in the companion paper, actual values and 1-step forecasts are graphed together. However, as noted by Granger and Newbold (1973), if the underlying process is integrated the results can often appear over-flattering. For such series a more realistic (though less flattering) view is obtained by graphing actual changes and predicted changes. The point is well illustrated by examination of Case III for which it appears at first glance as if the forecasts follow the pattern of the actuals very impressively. However, closer inspection suggests that the 1-step forecast errors are strongly positively autocorrelated (a positive error is generally followed by another positive error). Hence, of course, these errors are predictable and it would appear that the forecasts could be improved upon. The implication in such circumstances is that the assumed underlying model is incorrect, which brings us back to the previous point.

The authors replied in writing, as follows.

We wish to thank the numerous contributors to the discussion for their evident interest in the subject, for their valuable suggestions and for the clarity of their comments. We hope they will understand that for reasons of space we are not able to answer all their comments individually.

Professor Priestley focuses attention on some of the fundamental differences between Bayesian forecasting and most other current forecasting methods. As he says, stationarity has gone; there is no requirement that either the original series or some postulated derivation of the observation series, such as a finite difference, is stationary. The Bayesian approach does not tie the evolution of the future wholly to that of past observations, nor to a single model. Professor Priestley also points out that, as a restricting criterion of optimality, the mean square prediction error has also gone. We believe that he retained slight doubts about this because in the paper we occasionally regress into the traditional habit of referring to the posterior mean as the "forecast". It is of course fundamental that at any time our information is the whole of the posterior distribution and its extension in time, which, when combined with an appropriate utility function, leads to decision.

† Available in MS from the University of Nottingham.

The question of model identification has been raised by a number of speakers. This is a far-reaching topic which illustrates some of the major differences between Bayesian and other methods. First of all we would agree that if the observation or a derivative series is stationary and if there are sufficient data then existing identification methods are appropriate. The difference arises since other methods tend to regard these conditions as virtually axiomatic whereas we regard them as unusual. To begin with every series of observations has a first observation and a (usually very important) period when data are scarce. Further, in commercial situations, we regard the assumption of stationarity to be too severe since, in identification, this assumes that because something has never (or always) happened in the past it will never (always) happen in the future. It is in this sense that we say that we are more concerned with the future than the past. In the general modelling situation this leads to an identification procedure which, in addition to data, considers such practicalities as context, analogies and robustness of the model.

To illustrate, in the context of short-term forecasting for stock control, most people are aware that, where there is no marked growth or decay, a "Steady Model" (Section 3.3) will usually give better performance than a "Linear Growth Model" (Section 3.4). However, should conditions change and a significant growth set in then the Steady Model will not only be poorer, but, with respect to cost consequences, substantially poorer than the Growth Model. The question then centres around the likelihood of such a slope change together with its consequences. In many applications a small sacrifice of performance in the steady conditions is worth paying for the insurance against the possibility of the outcome of such a significant change.

The method proposed is the use of either or both of the Multi-Process Models of Section 5, it being suggested that the user can span the likely model-space by means of a relatively small number of distinct models. The principles involved can be illustrated by the diagram below, where four models are displayed symbolically. Since the Bayesian approach can calculate the posterior model probabilities $P_{j,t}$ $(j = 1, 2, 3, 4)$ the resultant "mix" can be thought of as corresponding with the convex hull of the set $M^{(1)}, M^{(2)}, M^{(3)}, M^{(4)}$, i.e. a potentially much larger set of models than the original set. Furthermore, should the model of the process change, this will involve a shift (permanent or temporary) in the operating point, and it is this which gives the Bayesian method its remarkable ability of adaption which we have observed in many applications. We feel that further research in this area would be most rewarding.

In the case of little or no past data, formal procedures for model identification are simply not applicable; the data they require do not exist. To have no data is not, however, the same thing as to have no *information*, whether derived from experience, analogy or whatever, and again we have found that it is usually possible to postulate a number of distinct models sufficiently wide to span the required model space and allow the method to "home-into" a suitable operating point quite quickly. Indeed, the performance of the method in the case of no data is one of its most impressive features. However, we are not religious Bayesians; we are fully prepared to scrap or revise our original formulations if subsequent results show them to be invalid or inadequate.

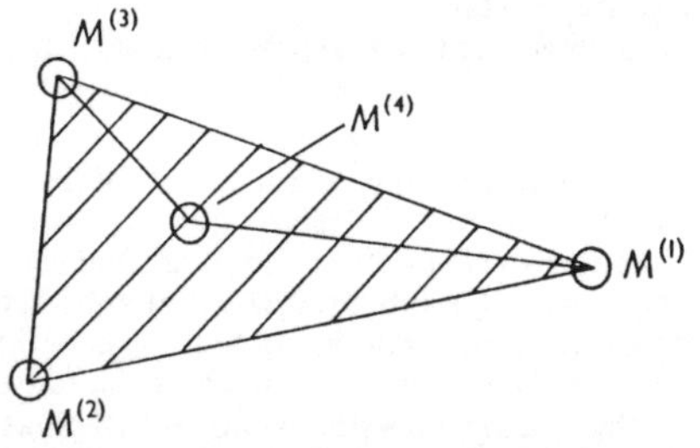

The question of model criteria is mentioned by a number of speakers. Professor Cox asks about the dangers of over-elaboration and Professor Dickey, who has made a number of relevant contributions in the area of Bayesian models, also raises the topic. It is another major area; one in which there are many differences of opinion. There is the whole question of the important but often neglected descriptive criteria, particularly in macro-modelling where meaning, simplicity and economy are often as important as quantitative criteria. However, here we restrict ourselves to comments on quantitative criteria since this cannot be avoided in the comparison of different methods or techniques. In the paper we queried the usefulness of the commonly used mean square error for this purpose, and a number of people expressed agreement with this view. Our reasons were twofold, namely:

(i) symmetric quadratic loss is often inappropriate to the decision problem involved (e.g. in stock control);

(ii) by giving heavy weight to occasional large errors, this method can lead to false or misleading conclusions as to the methods under comparison.

We believe that the speakers who agreed with us did so on the basis of the first point; we are not sure whether the second is understood as well. To illustrate it, consider the following hypothetical sequence of data, with forecasts generated by alternative models M^1, M^2.

Obs.	100	100	200	100	100	...
$M^1 FC$	90	110	90	110	90	...
$M^2 FC$	110	90	110	90	110	...

The sums of the squared forecast errors are 12,500 for M^1 and 8,500 for M^2, leading to the conclusion that M^2 is considerably better than M^1. This is in fact due merely to the accident of the timing and magnitude of the freak value; this apart, the two methods perform equally well. More generally the major contributors to the error mean square are the occasional large disturbances. The contribution to the mean square error of the large disturbances masks the subsequent responses of alternative systems; which, given that they cannot predict the disturbances as such (though together with people, they often can), constitutes the true measure of system performance.

Professor Priestley points out some of the differences between control engineers and ourselves in the formulations of a single model. He has selected an important topic which may well be responsible for much of the current confusion about dynamic linear modelling. Engineers tend to talk in terms of a state-space vector $\mathbf{x}_t$, a control vector $\mathbf{u}_t$ and an observation vector $\mathbf{z}_t$. Their objective usually centres around future values of the state-space vector whereas in most statistical work our parameter vector $\boldsymbol{\theta}_t$ is only *incidental* since interest is generally concerned with future values of the observation vector $\mathbf{y}_t$ and the corresponding decision utilities. There is no neat correspondence. Dependent upon the context and using the notation of (2.1.1) and (2.1.2), elements of $\mathbf{F}_t$ may be found in $\boldsymbol{\theta}_t$ or hidden as the *expectations* of functions of the random observation vector $\mathbf{y}_t$ and non-zero expectations of the noise disturbances may also be used to introduce control variables $\mathbf{u}_t$. We used the particular DLM formulation simply because it developed naturally from a statistician's way of viewing statistical linear models, Markov processes, distributional information, sufficiency and decisions.

It may be useful to classify the DLM in three distinct sets although acknowledging mixtures and elaborations:

(i) Constant DLM ($\mathbf{F}_t$, $\mathbf{V}_t$, $\mathbf{W}_t$, $\mathbf{G}$ are constant);

(ii) independent variable DLM (each element of $\mathbf{F}_t$ represents a particular independent variable at all times).

(iii) The specific control formulation.

In (i) there is an equivalence between DLMs and classical models of linear time series including all the ARIMA processes and extending beyond to "explosive" non-stationary processes. That this equivalence is true may simply be shown by using well-known canonical eigenvalue representations of the system equation, together with a map of $\mathbf{F}$ into (1, 0, 0, ..., 0) and then appropriately reducing the equations to at most an nth order difference equation in both observations and disturbances. In this case the engineer's formulation and the DLM would tend to be the same. However, the use is somewhat different; to the engineer this is a system with no controls whereas to the Bayesian forecaster it is a system open to information since, as Blight discusses, the observer may intervene with subjective information about the parameter vector. This is a crucial practical point in that the Bayesian formulation retains all we are used to in classical time series but provides many new facilities.

Taking the independent variable case, the parameter vector may be interpreted either as stochastic parameter, as stochastic factor effects or as a combination of the two. The first case has been sufficiently covered in Section 3.2. Stochastic factor effects are worthy of further research since, from our industrial experience, we known that in the analysis of production data the use of a static linear model instead of a dynamic linear model may lead to false and costly conclusions about the significance of factor effects.

In looking at the specific control formulation (iii), engineers usually write their model in a form similar to the following:

$$\text{observation equation:} \quad \mathbf{z}_t = \mathbf{H}\mathbf{x}_t + \mathbf{v}_t,$$

$$\text{system equation:} \quad \mathbf{x}_t = \mathbf{A}\mathbf{x}_{t-1} + \mathbf{B}\mathbf{u}_t + \mathbf{w}_t,$$

where for simplicity we will take A, B and H as constant, $\mathbf{u}_t$ as the control vector, $\mathbf{x}_t$ as the state vector, $\mathbf{z}_t$ as the observation vector. Control literature deals with this formulation and we acknowledge its economy especially where transfer responses are needed to relate the control to future states.

Dr Tong mentions Kalman's important concepts of observability and controllability and asks about their meaning with respect to the DLM. Consider the above deterministic formulation with $\mathbf{v}_t = \mathbf{0}$ and $\mathbf{w}_t = \mathbf{0}$ for all t and a univariate series of observations. Briefly, observability can be described as: "a state $\mathbf{x}_t$ is observable if knowledge of $\mathbf{u}^{t-1}$, $\mathbf{z}^{t-1}$ completely determines $\mathbf{x}_t$". Controllability may be thought as: "a given state $\mathbf{x}_t$ is controllable if for all possible $\mathbf{x}_0$, there exists a finite control vector $\mathbf{u}^t$ which results in the system achieving the state $\mathbf{x}_t$ at time t." Kalman defined his concepts in the deterministic case but these have been extended to the stochastic case and have proved key concepts in investigating stability and the correspondence between state space models and input–output models. Looking first at an interpretation of observability in our constant models (i), and substituting the word relatedness for observability, the meaning of Tong's conditions becomes clear since an element of $\boldsymbol{\theta}_t$ is not "observable" with respect to $\mathbf{y}^t$ if it is unrelated to $\mathbf{y}^t$. But if this element is unrelated to $\mathbf{y}^t$ then, in case (i) models, it is unrelated to future observation values, so that the element is redundant and the model over-specified with respect to future observations. Consequently for the constant DLM, forecasters may think of unobservability in terms of an over-specification of the parameter vector whereas engineers, whose main interest is the state vector, might think of observability in terms of an under-specification or instability of the observation vector.

Dr Tong is right in saying that the dynamic model of Section 3.2.2 is not completely observable although completely controllable if $\mathbf{F}_t = \mathbf{x}_0$ for all t. In such a case and considering the forecasting of just a univariate observation series, the model may be reduced from dimension n to dimension 1 and represented as a steady model of Section 3.3. Considering cases in which we are able to select $\mathbf{F}_t$ over a design space, the link between observability and design information may be seen. This is of great importance to statisticians who, in the particular case of the static linear model, are well aware of the meaning of linear independence of the independent variable design matrices formed by the $\mathbf{F}_t$'s. The case which Dr Tong quotes is typically found in production where so-called optimal operating conditions $\mathbf{x}_0$ are initially found from full-scale plant experiments and from then on the plant manager operates persistently with these conditions since he is reluctant to experiment further in case he drops below the output target. Suppose initially that information relating output to plant operating conditions is expressed through the prior $(\boldsymbol{\theta}_0 \mid \mathbf{y}^0) \sim N(\mathbf{m}_0; \mathbf{C}_0)$. Then by taking the special case ($n > 1$, $\mathbf{G} = \mathbf{I}$, $\mathbf{F}_t = \mathbf{x}_0 = (1, 0, 0, \ldots, 0)$ for all t) it is clear that when the rank of $\mathbf{W}$ is n, one continually loses information on all elements of $\boldsymbol{\theta}_t$ other than on the first until one eventually becomes entirely ignorant of the effects and interactions of all the plant variables. The only information one then has concerns the yield relating to the adopted operating conditions $\mathbf{x}_0$ and nothing at all about variation away from these conditions. Professor Box was well aware of this from his ICI experiences which largely motivated his development of Evolutionary Operation (EVOP). The DLM formulation might help to further an understanding of Box's important contribution to practical statistics which advocates continual or periodic experiments designed to maintain information where response surfaces evolve in time.

We do not see an alternative useful practical interpretation of Kalman's concept of controllability. Taking just the stock control situation in which say the steady or growth models of Section 3 are used, it is evident that we cannot control the parameter vector $\boldsymbol{\theta}_t$ and that our objectives are phrased in terms of future observations of $\mathbf{y}$ and not $\boldsymbol{\theta}$. It is, of course, true that the problems of optimal control are identical with those of the control engineers in the sense that one must select a production and stock decision now knowing that this influences future decisions, but there is rarely any way of controlling the *externals* reflected by $\boldsymbol{\theta}_t$. Thus in dealing with open systems of this type we conclude that the systems are generally not controllable. Further, even in the case of macro socio-economic systems we would venture the opinion that whereas these may be partially controllable they are rarely completely controllable.

Professor Priestley raises a point about the autoregressive process. As Dr Blight indicates, our inferential procedure on the autoregressive parameter ϕ_t is correct since ϕ_t only depends upon known observations. Furthermore, there is no difficulty with the one-step-ahead probability distribution. But we are grateful to Dr Blight for revealing an error in our thinking. The point at issue is how the recursive equation is used for lead times extending beyond the next time period when our knowledge about the value of the parameter is uncertain and where the two general prediction forms of Section 2.3 are not directly applicable. We look forward to Dr Blight's forthcoming paper on the subject.

Dr Blight also discusses the incorporation of subjective information and we would like to indicate an alternative method to that illustrated in Section 3.3. Consider a generalization of the DLM as

$$\mathbf{y}_t = \mathbf{F}_t \boldsymbol{\theta}_t + \mathbf{v}_t, \qquad \mathbf{v}_t \sim N(\bar{\mathbf{v}}_t; \mathbf{V}_t),$$
$$\boldsymbol{\theta}_t = \mathbf{G}\boldsymbol{\theta}_{t-1} + \mathbf{w}_t, \quad \mathbf{w}_t \sim N(\bar{\mathbf{w}}_t; \mathbf{W}_t),$$

in which the disturbances do not necessarily have zero means. Defining

$$\hat{\mathbf{y}}_t = \mathbf{F}_t(\mathbf{G}\mathbf{m}_{t-1} + \bar{\mathbf{w}}_t) + \bar{\mathbf{v}}_t,$$
$$\mathbf{e}_t = \mathbf{y}_t - \hat{\mathbf{y}}_t$$

the reccurrence relationships follow through as usual. Thus subjective information can be introduced through specification of the disturbance distribution at time t. For example with the linear growth model of Section 3.4, if it is thought that at time t the level of the process will jump by 100 and the associated uncertainty is characterized by a variance of 400, then an appropriate specification of the relevant element of $\mathbf{w}_t$ might be

$$\delta\mu_t \sim N(100; 400).$$

This still preserves the former covariance structure of $\mathbf{C}_{t-1}$ and offers an easy means of handling observer information.

Dr Stern says that "one needs roughly three types of forecast". His first type relates to stock control situations and we agree that here the need is for a robust system which, when required, caters for level, growth and seasonality but we believe that such a system should extend to situations with no or little data, should be designed to intereact with subjective information and should be capable of coping with major disturbances on the management by exception principle. With respect to Dr Stern's second point we would refer him to Green and Harrison (1973). The third point concerns economic models and we believe that the superposition of our regression DLM's and "time series" type models will provide the independent variable linear models and error structures he requires.

One of Professor Cox's points concerns a shrinking trend. This has sometimes been adopted in practice because of the wish to use Holt's growth model for updating in cases where it is not appropriate to use the Holt forecasting function over the forecast lead time. One model which overcomes this unsatisfactory procedure is

$$y_t = \mu_t + \varepsilon_t,$$
$$\mu_t = \mu_{t-1} + \beta_t + \delta\mu_t,$$
$$\beta_t = g\beta_{t-1} + \delta\beta_t,$$

where $0<g<1$, generally with g closer to 1 than zero, so that

$$E(\beta_{t+k} \mid \mathbf{y}^t) = g^k E(\beta_t \mid \mathbf{y}^t) \to 0 \text{ as } k \to \infty.$$

Dr Chatfield suggests that you do not have to be a Bayesian to adopt the proposed methodology. This may be true but there is generally no avoiding integration over the parameter space and it is somewhat philosophical, although important, as to how this is explained away. Whilst we are not extreme Bayesians we do feel that in nearly all applications the natural specification of the prior information will be as a distribution function and that adoption of the Bayesian formulation is by far the easiest and most satisfactory. Dr Chatfield also questions the automatic handling of freaks.

To answer this properly, the context of the forecasting system has to be discussed. In situations where there are many products to be forecast and where marketing people's time is scarce there is clearly a case for an automatic method so that marketing need only intervene by exception; that is when they know the automatic method will not be able to handle the situation quickly enough. A number of Bayesian systems have been in operation for some years now and one of the notable comments from a user is: "the system response is almost human". Such systems have, of course, been designed to consider the general desired response to "discontinuities" and act in accordance with these desires. One point that is so often missed by theoreticians is the uncertainty and confusion amongst decision-makers caused by discontinuities. In retrospect it is easy to identify a freak or a jump and to explain it, whereas at the moment it happens all sorts of explanations are ventured leading to widely different conjectures about the future. Without experiencing the heightened emotions and distortions of these times it is easy to adopt a false picture of the context and propose utopian solutions. Thus an automatic safety-net which increases confidence in periods of major "change" may be valued simply for operational reasons. We feel this relevant to Dr Newbold's comments on the predictability of errors which are retrospectively seen as positively correlated. These comments seem to stem from a preoccupation with stationarity. Yes it is quite true if, in the broad sense, the series is stationary but this series is clearly non-stationary. Furthermore, it is quite true if one performs a retrospective analysis, since one knows exactly the values one is trying to forecast.

Mr Godolphin asks about the prior specification of covariances in typical forecasting applications. We would not expect marketing people to specify much more than means and, indirectly, variances. Usually the covariances are then generated by the system equation as it progresses in time. With respect to his point about severe restrictions we would refer him to Section 2.5 which deals with one way of formulating the models he discusses. Naturally the case of cross-covariances between $\mathbf{v}_t$ and $\mathbf{w}_t$ are straightforwardly dealt with using the usual approach of joint and conditional distributions to give slightly amended recurrence relationships.

Professor Lindley, Professor Cox and Dr Leonard mention the cases of non-normality and non-lognormality. There are a variety of methods for handling such cases. The multi-process models allow the specification of error distributions which are satisfactorily described by mixtures of a small number of Normal distributions and this can be particularly useful for characterizing "fatter than Normal" tails. Professor Lindley asks us about the role of sufficiency and linearity in the Kalman filter. The concept of sufficiency will probably be a key concept in the extension to the general non-Normal case but continued adherence to additivity and linearity may prove an obstruction and will almost certainly have to go. One possible approach towards extending the methods may be the following. The system equations may be thought of as constraints. For example, equation (2.1.2) can be used to give us information on $\boldsymbol{\theta}_t$ given that we have a posterior distribution for $(\boldsymbol{\theta}_{t-1} \mid \mathbf{y}^{t-1})$ and knowledge of the mean and covariance of $\mathbf{W}_t$. In other words the information $\mathbf{y}^{t-1}$ constrains our views about $\boldsymbol{\theta}_t$. This immediately suggests the possibility of describing $\boldsymbol{\theta}_t$ using the "least prejudiced" or maximum entropy distribution which satisfies the information constraints over the parametric sample space. Furthermore, if the distribution $(\mathbf{y}_t \mid \boldsymbol{\theta}_t)$ is conjugate to $(\boldsymbol{\theta}_t \mid \mathbf{y}^{t-1})$ then simple updating recurrence relationships might be expected. In the case of constraints on the mean and variance over a parametric space R^n, and with $\mathbf{v}_t$ normally distributed, this approach is equivalent to that of the quoted DLM and a Kalman filter. However, it is clear that this approach may lead to interesting models extending beyond the normal distribution, many of which may be non-linear in the observations. The link between maximum entropy distributions and sufficiency is well known and thus if this approach offers fruitful results it will be sufficiency that is the key concept, whereas in the general theory additivity and linearity may well be only of interest in particular cases. Yet another possible approach involves transformations to normality with assumed additivity, as mentioned by Dr Leonard. He also mentions the continuous case of the Kalman filter and both he and Dr O'Hagan raise the possibility of dealing with continuous priors of variances. We agree that this is possible but for reasons of cost and operation we would be reluctant to use numerical integration and lose the simple recurrence relationships. Not wishing to give offence, either to Professor Lindley or the company in question, we are somewhat embarrassed by his remark concerning ourselves and ICI. We wish to say, however, that the work described in our paper could never have been started, let alone completed, without the active support and encouragement of the company, as we acknowledge in the paper. Our departures were motivated by a desire to pursue our own personal interests, of which this paper is but one aspect, and we regard ourselves as fortunate in still retaining strong links with ICI.

We are grateful to Dr Bhansali for his comments and references. We have taken the opportunity of altering equation (4.3.2) in the light of the comments of Professors Walker and Dickey. We agree that we were in error; tripped up by our own notation Dr Chatfield. We take seriously Dr Anderson's points about Box-Jenkins and we agree that Jack is the man who finally decides things. Bayesian forecasting is in its infancy and nobody would expect a newborn babe to compete with a fifteen year old. But here we are involved in the dynamics of change and, as Piaget says, this involves accommodation, assimilation and denial before a new phase is reached. Only time will tell whether the fundamentals of the Bayesian approach will constitute such a new accepted phase which themselves will eventually be superseded by further developments. This is relevant to Dr Ray's comments on the length of time it takes for changes to occur. It is one of our tenets that there are three stages in the outsider's view of research: (i) impossible; (ii) obvious (when it is accomplished) and (iii) we knew it all the time (when it is accepted). But this is how it should be, for new developments are often important not for their creativeness but for their destruction of the clutter which previously hindered a clear view.

References in the Discussion

Akaike, H. (1971). Information theory and an extension of the maximum likelihood principle. In *2nd Int. Symp. of Information Theory* (B. N. Petrov and F. C. Saki, eds), pp. 267–281. Budapest: Akademia Kiado.

—— (1974). Markovian representation of stochastic processes and its application to the analysis of autoregressive moving average processes. *Ann. Inst. Statist. Maths.*, **26**, 363–387.

Berk, R. H. (1966). Limiting behavior of posterior distributions when the model is incorrect. *Ann. Math. Statist.*, **37**, 51–58.

Bhansali, R. J. (1975). Fitting time series models in the frequency domain. *Bull. Int. Statist. Inst.* **40**. (in press).

Bloomfield, P. (1973). An exponential model for the spectrum of a scalar time series. *Biometrika*, **60**, 217–226.

Box, G. E. P. and Newbold, P. (1971). Some comments on a paper by Coen, Gomme and Kendall. *J. R. Statist. Soc.* A, **134**, 229–240.

Bucy, R. S. and Joseph, P. D. (1968). *Filtering for Stochastic Processes with Applications to Guidance*. New York: Interscience.

Coen, P. J., Gomme, E. D. and Kendall, M. G. (1969). Lagged relationships in economic forecasting. *J. R. Statist. Soc.* A, **132**, 133–163.

Cox, D. R. (1975). A note on empirical Bayes inference in a finite Poisson process. *Biometrika*, **62**, 709–711.

Cox, D. R. and Hinkley, D. V. (1974). *Theoretical Statistics*. London: Chapman & Hall. New York: Wiley.

Dickey, J. M. (1976a). Comment on a paper by Mervyn Stone. *J. Amer. Statist. Ass.*, **71**, 117–119.

—— (1976b). Approximate posterior distributions. *J. Amer. Statist. Ass.*, **71** (in press).

Ferguson, T. S. (1967). *Mathematical Statistics*. New York: Academic Press.

Godolphin, E. J. (1976). On the Cramér–Wold factorization. *Biometrika*, **63**, 367–380.

Good, I. J. (1970). The probabilistic explication of information, evidence, surprise, causality, explanation and utility. In *Foundations of Statistical Inference* (V. P. Godambe and D. A. Sprott, eds). Toronto: Holt, Rinehart and Winston. (Proceedings of the 1970 Waterloo Symposium.)

Granger, C. W. J. and Newbold, P. (1974). Spurious regressions in econometrics. *J. Econometrics*, **2**, 111–120.

Hannan, E. J. (1969). The identification of vector mixed autoregressive moving average systems. *Biometrika*, **56**, 223–225.

Kimeldorf, G. S. and Wahba, G. (1970). A correspondence between Bayesian estimation on stochastic processes and smoothing by splines. *Ann. Math. Statist.*, **41**, 495–502.

Leonard, T. (1975). A Bayesian approach to the linear model with unequal variances. *Technometrics*, **17**, 95–102.

Muth, J. F. (1960). Optimal properties of exponentially weighted forecasts. *J. Amer. Statist. Ass.*, **55**, 299–306.

O'Hagan, A. (1976). On posterior joint and marginal modes. *Biometrika*, **63**, 329–333.

Parzen, G. (1974). Some recent advances in time modelling. *IEEE Trans. on Automatic Control*, **AC 19**, 723–730.

Pratt, J. W., Raiffa, H. and Schlaizer, R. (1964). The foundations of decision under uncertainty: and elementary exposition. *J. Amer. Statist. Ass.*, **59**, 353–375.

Shibata, R. (1976). Selection of an autoregressive model by Akaike's information criterion. *Biometrika*, **68**, 117–126.

Silverman, L. M. (1966). Representation and realisation of time variable linear systems. Technical Report 94, Office of Naval Research, Columbia University.

SNYDER, D. L. (1975). *Random Point Processes.* New York: Wiley.
TAKEUCHI, K. (1976). Application of the Kalman filter to cyclone forecasting. *I.I.A.S.A. Res. Mem.*, 76, 9.
VERE-JONES, D. (1975). On updating algorithms and inference for stochastic point processes. In *Perspectives in Probability and Statistics* (J. Gani, ed.), pp. 239–259. London: Academic Press.
YOUNG, P. C. (1971). Comments on a paper by J. Bray. *J. R. Statist. Soc.* A, 134, 220–223.
—— (1974). Recursive approaches to time series analysis. *Bull. Inst. Maths & Applicns*, 10, 209–224.
—— (1975). Comments on a paper by R. L. Brown, J. Durbin and J. M. Evans. *J. R. Statist. Soc.* B, 37, 168–174.

[11]

A Smoothness Priors–State Space Modeling of Time Series With Trend and Seasonality

GENSHIRO KITAGAWA and WILL GERSCH*

A smoothness priors modeling of time series with trends and seasonalities is shown. An observed time series is decomposed into local polynomial trend, seasonal, globally stationary autoregressive and observation error components. Each component is characterized by an unknown variance–white noise perturbed difference equation constraint. The constraints or Bayesian smoothness priors are expressed in state space model form. Trading day factors are also incorporated in the model. A Kalman predictor yields the likelihood for the unknown variances (hyperparameters). Likelihoods are computed for different constraint order models in different subsets of constraint equation model classes. Akaike's minimum AIC procedure is used to select the best model fitted to the data within and between the alternative model classes. Smoothing is achieved by using a fixed-interval smoother algorithm. Examples are shown.

KEY WORDS: Bayesian modeling; Box-Jenkins; Smoothing; Seasonal adjustment; Kalman filter; Likelihood; Trading day adjustment.

1. INTRODUCTION

This article is addressed to the problem of modeling and smoothing time series with trend and seasonal mean value functions and stationary covariances. A modeling approach is taken. We were motivated by the Shiller-Akaike smoothness priors solution to the smoothing problem originally posed by Whittaker (1923). (Some of our earlier work is in Kitagawa 1981 and Brotherton and Gersch 1981.)

Let the observations of a discrete time series be

$$y(n) = f(n) + \epsilon(n); n = 1, \ldots, N \qquad (1.1)$$

with $\epsilon(n)$ iid from $\mathcal{N}(0, \sigma^2)$, σ^2 unknown, and $f(\cdot)$ an unknown smooth function. The smoothing problem is to estimate $f(n)$, $n = 1, \ldots, N$ in a statistically satisfactory manner. Whittaker suggested that the solution for $f(n)$, $n = 1, \ldots, N$ balance a tradeoff between infidelity to the data and infidelity to a kth-order difference equation constraint on $f(n)$. The choice of a tradeoff parameter was left to the investigator. For a fixed value of the tradeoff parameter, the solution to Whittaker's problem can be expressed in terms of constrained least squares computations, which are parametric in that tradeoff parameter.

A spline smooth–generalized cross validation to determine the smoothness tradeoff parameter approach to the smoothing problem was developed and extensively exploited in applications by Wahba (1977) and Wahba and Wold (1975) and their colleagues. That solution is of computational complexity $O(N^3)$. Wahba (1977) pointed out that the two critical facets of a solution to the smoothing problem are the determination of the smoothness tradeoff parameter and the realization of a computational procedure. In Akaike (1980a), Shiller's (1973) Bayesian smoothness prior idea is fully developed to yield a likelihood computation for determining the smoothness tradeoff parameter. Akaike (1980a) gives an explicit solution to the problem posed by Whittaker. His constrained least squares computational solution is also $O(N^3)$. Akaike (1980b) and Akaike and Ishiguro (1980, 1983) smooth time series with trends and seasonalities in the BAYSEA seasonal adjustment program. Initially motivated by Akaike (1980a), we achieved an $O(N)$ computational solution to the smoothing problem, extended some of the ideas of BAYSEA to include a provision for the presence of a stationary stochastic component in the trend and seasonal model, and achieved reliable prediction performance of time series with trends and seasonalities (Gersch and Kitagawa (1983). Our approach is also a Bayesian–smoothness prior approach that yields the smoothness tradeoff parameters as a likelihood computation.

Stochastically perturbed difference equation constraints on the trend, seasonal, stationary time series, and trading day components of the observed time series are expressed in a state space model. The computation of the likelihood of the hyperparameters that balance the smoothness tradeoffs of the trend, seasonal, stationary stochastic, and observation error components of the data is facilitated by an $O(N)$ computational complexity—recursive computational Kalman predictor. Akaike's (1973, 1974) minimum AIC procedure is used to determine the best of alternative trend and stochastic component

* Genshiro Kitagawa is a Researcher at the Institute of Statistical Mathematics, 4-6-7 Minami Azabu, Minato Ku, Tokyo, Japan, and Will Gersch is Professor, Department of Information and Computer Sciences, University of Hawaii, Honolulu, HI 96822. The work reported here was begun in 1981–1982, when the authors were American Statistical Association Fellows at the U.S. Bureau of the Census. Enthusiastic encouragement from, and conversations with, Dr. David Findley are gratefully acknowledged. The authors are also grateful for valuable comments by referees.

June 1984, Volume 79, Number 386
Theory and Methods Section

difference equation orders and to determine the best model of alternative model classes. Finally, the AIC best modeled data is smoothed by a fixed-interval smoother algorithm.

Fitting the trend plus seasonal plus stochastic component model to the observed data $y(1), \ldots, y(N)$ implicitly estimates $3N$ parameters (one each for the trend, seasonal, and stochastic components at times $n = 1, \ldots, N$). With Bayesian smoothness priors constraints imposed on those components, they are estimated as the solution of stochastically perturbed difference equations. The hyperparameters, or more precisely the perturbation to observation variance ratios, are the essential parameters of the model. It is the likelihood of the hyperparameters that is computed by the Kalman filter.

The subject treated in this article is very closely related to the subject of seasonal adjustment of time series that is treated, for example, in Shiskin, Young, and Musgrave (1967); Cleveland and Tiao (1976); Pierce (1978); Hillmer, Bell, and Tiao (1983); and Hillmer and Tiao (1982). The smoothing problem approach is closely related to work by Wahba (1977) and Wahba and Wold (1975), and to the maximum penalized likelihood method of Good and Gaskins (1980) and references therein. Young and Jakeman (1979) and Wecker and Ansley (1983) are also of interest.

In Section 2 the Shiller-Akaike smoothness prior solution to the smoothing problem is reviewed. In Section 3 state space smoothness priors models for time series that include trend, seasonality, stationary stochastic, trading day effects, and observation error components are shown. Also included are the minimum AIC method for selecting the best of alternative candidate state space models and the Kalman predictor and smoother formulas. Examples are shown in Section 4; some of the phenomenology of our smoothing problem approach to the modeling of time series with trends and seasonalities is illustrated there as well. In Section 5 we discuss the examples and compare our smoothness priors–minimum AIC procedure with the Box-Jenkins-Tiao (BJT) procedure for the modeling of time series with trends and seasonalities.

2. A BAYESIAN SOLUTION TO THE SMOOTHING PROBLEM

A smoothing problem and an approach to its solution, attributed to Whittaker (1923), is as follows: Let

$$y(n) = f(n) + \epsilon(n) \quad n = 1, \ldots, N \tag{2.1}$$

denote a sequence of observations, where $f(n)$ is an unknown smooth function, and $\epsilon(n)$, $n = 1, \ldots, N$ are iid normal random variables with zero mean and unknown variance σ^2. The problem is to estimate $f(n)$, $n = 1, \ldots, N$ from the observations, $y(1), \ldots, y(N)$, in a statistically sensible way. Here the number of parameters to be estimated is equal to the number of observations. Ordinary least squares or maximum likelihood estimates yield computationally unstable or meaningless results.

Whittaker suggested that the solution $f(n)$, $n = 1, \ldots, N$ balance a tradeoff between infidelity to the data and infidelity to a kth-order difference equation constraint. For fixed values of λ and k, the solution satisfies

$$\min_f \left[\sum_{n=1}^{N} (y(n) - f(n))^2 + \lambda^2 \sum_{n=1}^{N} (\nabla^k f(n))^2 \right]. \tag{2.2}$$

The first term in the brackets in (2.2) is the infidelity-to-the-data measure, the second is the infidelity-to-the-constraint measure, and λ is the smoothness tradeoff parameter. Whittaker left the choice of λ to the investigator.

Akaike's (1980a) smoothness priors solution explicitly solves the problem posed by Whittaker (1923). A version of that solution follows: Multiply (2.2) by $-\frac{1}{2}\sigma^2$; consider σ^2, λ^2, and k known and exponentiate (2.2). Then the solution that maximizes (2.2) achieves the maximization of

$$l(f) = \exp\left\{\frac{-1}{2\sigma^2} \sum_{n=1}^{N} (y(n) - f(n))^2\right\} \cdot \exp\left\{\frac{-\lambda^2}{2\sigma^2} \sum_{n=1}^{N} (\nabla^k f(n))^2\right\}. \tag{2.3}$$

Under the assumption of normality, (2.3) yields a Bayesian posterior distribution interpretation

$$\pi(f \mid y, \lambda, \sigma^2, k) \propto p(y \mid \sigma^2, f)\pi(f \mid \lambda, \sigma^2, k), \tag{2.4}$$

with $\pi(f \mid \lambda, \sigma^2, k)$ the smoothness prior distribution of f and $p(y \mid \sigma^2, f)$ the data distribution, conditional on σ^2 and on f, and $\pi(f \mid y, \lambda, \sigma, k)$ the posterior of f. Akaike (1980a) obtained the marginal likelihood for λ and k by integrating (2.4) with respect to f. He showed the application of this method to several interesting data analysis problems. In Bayesian terminology, λ is a hyperparameter (Lindley and Smith 1972). This "type II maximum likelihood method" of estimation was suggested by Good (1965). (See Good and Gaskins 1980 and references therein.)

3. A KALMAN FILTER–MINIMUM AIC CRITERION SOLUTION TO THE SMOOTHING PROBLEM

Motivated by Akaike (1980a), we developed an equivalent state space smoothness priors approach, which is shown in this section. The time series is decomposed into local polynomial trend, global stochastic trend, seasonal, trading day effect, and observation error components. Difference equation constraints for those components are expressed in state space model form. The state space Kalman filter recursive computation yields the likelihood of the tradeoff parameters. Akaike's (1973,1979) minimum AIC procedure is used to select the best of the alternative state space models. The state space models, Akaike's minimum AIC procedure, and the recursive computational Kalman filtering and smoothing are discussed. (Akaike's least squares computations are of computational complexity $O(N^3)$; ours are of $O(N)$.)

3.1 The Models

The generic state space or signal model for the observations $y(n)$, $n = 1, \ldots, N$ is

$$x(n) = Fx(n-1) + Gw(n),$$
$$y(n) = H(n)x(n) + \epsilon(n), \qquad (3.1)$$

where F, G, and $H(n)$ are $M \times M$, $M \times L$, and $1 \times M$ matrices, respectively, and $w(n)$ and $\epsilon(n)$ are assumed to be zero mean independent and identically distributed normal random variables. $x(n)$ is the state vector at time n, and $y(n)$ is the observation at time n. For any particular model of the time series, the matrices F, G, and $H(n)$ are known, and the observations are generated recursively from an initial state that is assumed to be normally distributed with mean $\bar{x}(0)$ and covariance matrix $V(0)$.

In particular, the general state space model for the time series $y(1), \ldots, y(N)$ that includes the effects of local polynomial trends, stationary AR processes, seasonal components, trading day effects, and observation errors is written in the following schematic form:

$$x(n) = Fx(n-1) + Gw(n)$$

$$x(n) = \begin{bmatrix} F_1 & 0 & 0 & 0 \\ 0 & F_2 & 0 & 0 \\ 0 & 0 & F_3 & 0 \\ 0 & 0 & 0 & F_4 \end{bmatrix} x(n-1) + \begin{bmatrix} G_1 & 0 & 0 & 0 \\ 0 & G_2 & 0 & 0 \\ 0 & 0 & G_3 & 0 \\ 0 & 0 & 0 & G_4 \end{bmatrix} w(n)$$

$$y(n) = [H_1 \;\; H_2 \;\; H_3 \;\; H_4(n)]x(n) + \epsilon(n). \qquad (3.2)$$

In (3.2) the overall state space model $(F, G, H(n))$ is constructed by the component models (F_j, G_j, H_j), $(j = 1, \ldots, 4)$. In order $(j = 1, \ldots, 4)$ these models represent the polynomial trend, stationary AR, seasonal, and trading day effects component models, respectively. The number of state components in the particular model (F_j, G_j, H_j) is designated by M_j, $(j = 1, \ldots, 4)$. (The F_j matrices are square.) By the orthogonality of the representation in (3.2), $(2^4 - 1)$ alternative model classes of trend and seasonality may be constructed from combinations of F_j, G_j, H_j, $(j = 1, \ldots, 4)$. The component models F_j, G_j, H_j, $(j = 1, \ldots, 4)$ satisfy particular difference equation constraints on the components. Some of the particular trend, seasonal, AR, and trading day difference equation constraints that we have employed, and that have representations as the F_j, G_j, H_j, $(j = 1, \ldots, 4)$ matrices in (3.2), are shown immediately following.

1. *Local Polynomial Trend Model:* (F_1, G_1, H_1). The polynomial trend component satisfies a kth-order stochastically perturbed difference equation

$$\nabla^k t(n) = w_1(n);\; w_1(n) \sim \mathcal{N}(0, \tau_1^2), \qquad (3.3a)$$

where $\{w_1(n)\}$ is an iid sequence and ∇ denotes the difference operator defined by $\nabla t(n) = t(n) - t(n-1)$. For $k = 1, 2, 3$, those constraints and the values of M_1, the corresponding F_1, G_1, H_1 matrices, and the state vector components are

$k = 1 = M_1$: $t(n) = t(n-1) + w_1(n)$

$$F_1 = [1],\; G_1 = [1],\; H_1 = [1];\; x(n) = t(n). \qquad (3.3b)$$

$k = 2 = M_1$: $t(n) = 2t(n-1) - t(n-2) + w_1(n)$

$$F_1 = \begin{bmatrix} 2 & -1 \\ 1 & 0 \end{bmatrix},\; G_1 = \begin{bmatrix} 1 \\ 0 \end{bmatrix},\; H_1 = \begin{bmatrix} 1 \\ 0 \end{bmatrix}';$$

$$x(n) = \begin{bmatrix} t(n) \\ t(n-1) \end{bmatrix}. \qquad (3.3c)$$

$k = 3 = M_1$: $t(n) = 3t(n-1) - 3t(n-2) + t(n-3) + w_1(n)$

$$F_1 = \begin{bmatrix} 3 & -3 & 1 \\ 1 & 0 & 0 \\ 0 & 1 & 0 \end{bmatrix},\; G_1 = \begin{bmatrix} 1 \\ 0 \\ 0 \end{bmatrix},\; H_1 = \begin{bmatrix} 1 \\ 0 \\ 0 \end{bmatrix}';$$

$$x(n) = \begin{bmatrix} t(n) \\ t(n-1) \\ t(n-2) \end{bmatrix}. \qquad (3.3d)$$

The subsequent stochastic, seasonal, and trading day constraints correspond to the state space matrices F_j, G_j, $H_j(n)$, $j = 2, 3, 4$, respectively. For brevity, only the difference equation constraints on those components are shown. The state vector $x(n)$ contains lagged versions of those components. An example of a state space signal model that incorporates each of the constraints is given in (3.9).

2. *Stochastic Trend Model:* (F_2, G_2, H_2). The stationary stochastic component $v(n)$ is assumed to satisfy an autoregressive (AR) model of order p. That is,

$$v(n) = \alpha_1 v(n-1) + \cdots + \alpha_p v(n-p) + w_2(n);$$
$$w_2(n) \sim \mathcal{N}(0, \tau_2^2). \qquad (3.4)$$

In (3.4) $\{w_1(n)\}$ is an iid sequence. The AR model is constrained to be stationary.

3. *Local Polynomial Seasonal Component Models:* (F_3, G_3, H_3). Often we use the seasonal component model

$$\sum_{i=0}^{L-1} s(n-i) = w_3(n);\; w_3(n) \sim \mathcal{N}(0, \tau_3^2), \qquad (3.5a)$$

where L is the number of periods in a season ($L = 4$, $L = 12$ for quarterly and monthly data, respectively), and $\{w_3(n)\}$ is an iid sequence. Then

$$s(n) = -\sum_{i=1}^{L-1} s(n-i) + w_3(n) \qquad (3.5b)$$

or

$$s(n) = -\sum_{i=1}^{L-1} B^i s(n) + w_3(n), \qquad (3.5c)$$

where B^i is the backwards shift operator defined by $B^i s(n) = s(n - i)$. Other seasonal component models that we occasionally employ are

$$\left(1 - \sum_{i=1}^{L-1} B^i\right)^2 s(n) = w_3(n) \tag{3.5d}$$

and

$$s(n) = s(n - L) + w_3(n). \tag{3.5e}$$

The seasonal models in (3.5a) and (3.5e) have been used for comparatively regular and changing seasonal effects, respectively. The seasonal model in (3.5d) is satisfactory for increasing or decreasing seasonal components.

4. *Trading Day Effect Model:* $(F_4, G_4, H_4(n))$. The trading day effect model is an adjustment used because there are a different number of ith days of the week ($i = 1, \ldots, 7$) per month for each successive month (Cleveland and Devlin 1980, Cleveland and Grupe 1983, and Hillmer and Tiao 1982). The adjustment corresponds to the removal of a fixed calendar day effect component from the observed time series. We achieve the trading day adjustment via a state space–Kalman filter regression on fixed regressors. (The use of the Kalman filter for regression on fixed regressors was first suggested by Harvey and Phillips 1979.) The trading day is expressed by

$$\sum_{i=1}^{7} \beta_i(n) d_i^*(n) = \sum_{i=1}^{6} \beta_i(n)(d_i^*(n) - d_7^*(n))$$
$$= \sum_{i=1}^{6} \beta_i(n) d_i(n), \tag{3.6}$$

where $d_i^*(n)$ denotes the number of ith days of the week in the nth month $d_i = d_i^* - d_7^*$, and $\beta_i(n)$ denotes the trading day factor of ith days of the week at time n. Furthermore, we apply the constraint $\sum_{i=1}^{7} \beta_i(n) = 0$ so that $\beta_7(n) = -\sum_{i=1}^{6} \beta_i(n)$. The nonperturbed difference equation constraint on the trading days is

$$\beta_i(n) = \beta_i(n - 1);\ i = 1, \ldots, 6. \tag{3.7}$$

(The trading day effect constraints in (3.6) and (3.7) are shown as functions of n. In fact, the $\beta_i(n)$ converge to steady state values β_i, and the corresponding regression is a fixed-effects regression.)

For a general model including local polynomial and stochastic trends, local polynomial seasonal and trading day components, the state or noise vector $w(n)$, and observation noise $\epsilon(n)$ are assumed to be normal iid with zero mean and diagonal covariance matrix

$$\begin{bmatrix} w(n) \\ \epsilon(n) \end{bmatrix} \sim \mathcal{N}\left[\begin{bmatrix}0\\0\\0\\0\end{bmatrix}, \begin{bmatrix} \tau_1^2 & 0 & 0 & 0 \\ 0 & \tau_2^2 & 0 & 0 \\ 0 & 0 & \tau_3^2 & 0 \\ 0 & 0 & 0 & \sigma^2 \end{bmatrix}\right] \tag{3.8}$$

The variances $\tau_1^2, \tau_2^2, \tau_3^2$, and σ^2 are unknown. The other potentially unknown parameters in the state space model are $\alpha_1, \ldots, \alpha_p$, the AR coefficients of the AR model for the stochastic trend component. Comparatively small values of the τ_1^2, τ_2^2, and τ_3^2 terms imply comparatively strict adherence to the corresponding difference equation constraint.

Model class types fitted to data can be designated by a notation that reveals the constraint orders for the components. For example, $M = (2, 2, 11, 0)$ and $M = (2, 0, 11, 6)$ designate, respectively, the model with trend constraint order 2, AR model order 2 and (monthly) seasonal order 11 without trading day effect, and the model with trend constraint order 2, no AR component monthly seasonal order 11, and the trading day effect component. The vector M plus the values of the hyperparameters for a particular model completely specifies the candidate model to be fitted.

For a specific example, the state and state space structure of a model with $M = (2, 2, 11, 6)$ and observation equation are respectively as in (3.9a) and (3.9b) below.

$$x(n) = \begin{bmatrix} t(n) \\ t(n-1) \\ \hline v(n) \\ v(n-1) \\ \hline s(n) \\ \vdots \\ s(n-10) \\ \hline \beta_1(n) \\ \vdots \\ \beta_6(n) \end{bmatrix} = \left[\begin{array}{c|c|c|c} \begin{matrix} 2 & -1 \\ 1 & 0 \end{matrix} & 0 & 0 & 0 \\ \hline \begin{matrix} 0 & 0 \\ 0 & 0 \end{matrix} & \begin{matrix} \alpha_1 & \alpha_2 \\ 1 & 0 \end{matrix} & 0 & 0 \\ \hline 0 & 0 & \begin{matrix} -1 & \cdots & -1 \\ 1 & & 0 \\ & \ddots & \vdots \\ & 1 & 0 \end{matrix} & 0 \\ \hline 0 & 0 & 0 & \begin{matrix} 1 & & \\ & \ddots & \\ & & 1 \end{matrix} \end{array}\right] x(n-1) + \begin{bmatrix} 1 & 0 & 0 \\ 0 & 0 & 0 \\ \hline 0 & 1 & 0 \\ 0 & 0 & 0 \\ \hline 0 & 0 & 1 \\ \vdots & \vdots & \vdots \\ 0 & 0 & 0 \\ \hline 0 & 0 & 0 \\ \vdots & \vdots & \vdots \\ 0 & 0 & 0 \end{bmatrix} w(n) \tag{3.9a}$$

$$y(n) = [1\ 0\ 1\ 0\ 1\ \ldots\ 0\ d_1(n) \ldots d_6(n)]\, x(n) + \epsilon(n). \tag{3.9b}$$

The state process noise vector $w(n)$ and the observation noise $\epsilon(n)$ make up an iid vector with distribution properties given by (3.8). The observation equation (3.9a) explains the observed data $y(n)$ in terms of the contribution of the local polynomial trend, stationary AR process, seasonal, trading day effect, and error components.

If only the trend, $t(n)$, the trend plus AR, $t(n)$, or the seasonal component, $s(n)$, are to be considered, the observation equations revert from the general time form variable $H(n)x(n)$ (as in 3.9b), respectively, to the stationary $Hx(n)$ forms:

$$Hx(n) = [1\ 0\ \ \ \ldots]x(n)$$
$$Hx(n) = [1\ 0\ 1\ 0\ \ \ldots]x(n)$$
$$Hx(n) = [0\ 0\ 0\ 0\ 1\ \ldots]x(n). \qquad (3.10)$$

In the context of the original Whittaker problem, for the situation in which only the trend and seasonal components are considered, the smoothness priors problem corresponds to the maximization of

$$l(f) = \exp\left\{\frac{-1}{2\sigma^2}\sum_{n=1}^{N}[y(n) - s(n)]^2\right\}$$
$$\times \exp\left\{\frac{-\tau_1^2}{2\sigma^2}\sum_{n=1}^{N}[\nabla^k t(n)]^2\right\}$$
$$\times \exp\left\{\frac{-\tau_3^2}{2\sigma^2}\sum_{n=1}^{N}\left[\sum_{i=0}^{L-1} s(n-i)\right]^2\right\}. \qquad (3.11)$$

That context emphasizes the role of the hyperparameters τ_1^2 and τ_3^2 as a measure of the uncertainty of belief in the prior. Relatively small τ_1^2 (τ_3^2) imply relatively wiggly trend (seasonal) components. Relatively large τ_1^2 (τ_3^2) imply relatively smooth trend (seasonal) components. Also, the ratio of $\tau_j^2/\sigma^2, j = 1$ or 3, can be interpreted as signal-to-noise ratios. This interpretation suggests that in the vicinity of the maximized likelihood, the likelihood is a rather flat function of the hyperparameters. Indeed, this has been our experience, which suggests an alternative to the usual computationally expensive nonlinear optimization procedures that yield estimates of the hyperparameters via a maximization of the likelihood. We compute the likelihoods, using the efficient Kalman filter algorithm, over a coarse grid of the hyperparameters. Estimation of the hyperparameters is then reduced to a search over the discrete likelihood parameter space. (The value of σ^2 in (3.11) is essentially estimated free of computational charge in the Kalman filter procedures. See the references cited in the section following.)

3.2 The Minimum AIC Procedure

Akaike's (1973,1974) minimum AIC procedure is a statistical estimation procedure for determining the best of alternative parametric models fitted to the data. The AIC of a particular fitted model is

$$\text{AIC} = -2\log(\text{maximized likelihood})$$
$$+\ 2(\text{the number of fitted parameters}). \qquad (3.12)$$

In fitting state space models of the kind described in Section 3.1, the total number of parameters fitted is $(M_1 + 2M_2 + M_3 + M_4) + [\delta(M_1) + \delta(M_2) + \delta(M_3)]$, where $(M_1 + M_2 + M_3 + M_4)$ is the dimensionality of the state space, $\delta(M) = 1$ if $M_j \neq 0$, and $\delta(M_j) = 0$ if $M_j = 0$. That is, $M_j = 1$ indicates that the F_j component is included in the signal model. Then the likelihood of the vector of unknown parameters and the initial state given the data is

$$L(\theta, \tilde{x}(0)) = \prod_{n=2}^{N} f(y(n) \mid y(n-1), \ldots, y(1),$$
$$\theta, \tilde{x}(0))f(y(1) \mid \theta, \tilde{x}(0)), \qquad (3.13)$$

where θ is the parameter vector defined by $\theta = (\tau_1^2, \tau_2^2, \tau_3^2, \sigma^2, \alpha_1, \ldots, \alpha_p)$.

Under the Gaussian assumption, we can exploit the innovations representation achieved with the Kalman predictor as follows:

$$L(\theta, \tilde{x}(0))$$
$$= \prod_{n=1}^{N}(2\pi v(n|n-1))^{-1/2}\exp\left\{\frac{-v(n)^2}{2v(n \mid n-1)}\right\}. \qquad (3.14)$$

In (3.14), $v(n) = y(n) - Hx(n \mid n-1)$ and $v(n \mid n-1)$ are, respectively, the innovations and the conditional variance of $v(n)$ at time n. Also, $x(n \mid n-1)$ is the conditional mean of the state vector $x(n)$. The conditioning is on the data $y(n-1), \ldots, y(1)$. The variance of the innovations $v(n \mid n-1)$ is obtained from

$$v(n \mid n-1) = H(n)V(n \mid n-1)H(n)' + \sigma^2, \qquad (3.15)$$

where $V(n \mid n-1)$ is the conditional variance of the state vector $x(n)$ given the observations up to time $n-1$.

The likelihood for the hyperparameters is computed for the discrete point set of the values $2^{(j-1)}$ ($j = 1, \ldots, 5$) for each of τ_1^2, τ_3^2 ($\tau_4^2 = 0$). When the stationary AR component is included in the model, τ_2^2 is also searched over $\tau_2^2 = 2^{(j-1)}$, ($j = 1, \ldots, 5$) and the $\alpha_1, \ldots, \alpha_p$ are computed by a quasi-Newton-Raphson type of procedure for each of the points in the $\tau_1^2, \tau_2^2, \tau_3^2$ space. The parameters $\alpha_1, \ldots, \alpha_p, \tau_1^2, \tau_2^2, \tau_3^2$ for which the AIC is smallest specify the AIC best model of the data.

Some comments on computational complexity are appropriate here. The basic computation for the minimum AIC procedure, (3.12), is the computation of the maximized likelihood for particular classes of parametric models. With correlated data, the likelihood computation usually requires the inversion of an $N \times N$ covariance matrix that needs $O(N^3)$ computations. Equation (3.13), the formula for the likelihood as computed by the Kalman predictor, reveals that the joint density for the observations $y(1), \ldots, y(N)$ has been factored into the product of densities for the innovations $v(n)$, $n = 1, \ldots, N$. The orthogonalization achieved by the recursive Kalman predictor accounts for the $O(N)$ complexity.

Additional material on the recursive predictor/smoother computations is summarized in the next section.

3.3 Recursive Kalman Filtering and Smoothing

There is a very extensive Kalman methodology literature. Only the barest details and formulas required for our computations are indicated here. Kalman (1960) is the original paper on this subject. Meditch (1969) and Anderson and Moore (1979) give very satisfactory treatments. An early paper in the statistical literature on the Kalman predictor is Duncan and Horn (1972). Chan, Goodwin, and Sin (1982) proved the convergence of the Ricatti equations (equivalently, the convergence of the Kalman gain $K(\cdot)$ in (3.18)) for systems that, like our trend and seasonal models, have zeros on the unit circle. This result provides the theoretical basis for the Kalman filter computations of the likelihoods for our models.

The state space model is

$$x(n) = Fx(n-1) + Gw(n),$$
$$y(n) = H(n)x(n) + \epsilon(n). \quad (3.16)$$

The Kalman methodology yields recursive computations for the predicted, filtered, and smoothed estimates of the state vector $x(n)$ and the signal $H(n)x(n)$ for $n = 1, \ldots, N$. The predicted, filtered, and smoothed state vector and signal are denoted by

$$\begin{array}{ll} \text{predicted} & x(n \mid n-1) \\ & y(n \mid n-1) \\ \text{filtered} & x(n \mid n) \\ & y(n \mid n) \\ \text{smoothed} & x(n \mid N) \\ & y(n \mid N). \end{array} \quad (3.17)$$

In the notation above, $x(n \mid n-1)$ and $y(n \mid n-1)$ denote the estimates of the state vector and the observation at time n given the past observations $y(n-1), \ldots, y(1)$; $x(n \mid n)$ and $y(n \mid n)$ are estimates of the state and observations at time n given the current and past data $y(n), y(n-1), \ldots, y(1)$; and $x(n \mid N)$ and $y(n \mid N)$ are estimates of the state and observation at time n given all the data $y(1), \ldots, y(N)$.

Given the initial vector $x(0 \mid 0)$ and the initial covariance $V(0 \mid 0)$, the quantities required for the computation of the likelihood (3.14) are obtained recursively:

$$x(n \mid n-1) = Fx(n-1 \mid n-1)$$
$$x(n \mid n) = x(n \mid n-1) + K(n)[y(n) - H(n)x(n \mid n-1)], \quad (3.18)$$

where $K(n)$ is the Kalman gain vector

$$K(n) = V(n \mid n-1)H'(n)v(n \mid n-1)^{-1}. \quad (3.19)$$

In (3.19) and subsequently, B' denotes the transpose of B. The updated equations for the variance of the state vector are

$$V(n \mid n-1) = FV(n-1 \mid n-1)F' + GQG',$$
$$V(n \mid n) = (I - K(n)H(n))V(n \mid n-1). \quad (3.20)$$

The likelihood for each of the particular values of τ_1^2, τ_2^2, τ_3^2 is computed, and the parameter set for which the AIC is smallest specifies the AIC criterion best model of the data. For that model, the filtered data are smoothed over the interval $n = N-1, \ldots, 1$ by the fixed interval smoothing formulas

$$x(n \mid N) = x(n \mid n) + A(n)(x(n+1 \mid N) - x(n+1 \mid n)), \quad (3.21a)$$
$$V(n \mid N) = V(n \mid n) + A(n)(V(n+1 \mid N) - V(n+1 \mid n))A(n)', \quad (3.21b)$$

where

$$A(n) = V(n \mid n)F'V(n+1 \mid n)^{-1}. \quad (3.21c)$$

Some comments on the initializing procedure are appropriate here. The Kalman filter algorithm requires the initial values $x(0 \mid 0)$ and $V(0 \mid 0)$. For a stationary system, we can use the theoretical mean value and covariance matrix of the state vector. They are easily computed from the assumed model. For a nonstationary system the theoretical mean and covariance cannot be defined. We use $x(0 \mid 0)$ and $V(0 \mid 0)$, a diagonal matrix with large diagonal values, and then do a first run of the Kalman filter over a time-reversed version of the data to estimate $x(0 \mid 0)$ and $V(0 \mid 0)$. This is equivalent to estimating the initial values from the entire data set.

4. EXAMPLES

In this section some of the phenomenology of the modeling of time series with the additive local polynomial, AR, seasonal, and observation noise components is shown.

Example 1. BLSAGEMEN, $N = 162$. These are Bureau of Labor Statistics data for male agricultural workers 20 years and older. Computational results are shown in Figure 1 for the models indicated in Table 1.

Figures 1A1, 1B1, and 1C1 show the original data and the fitted trends of the corresponding models. The seasonal components of the A and B models are in Figures 1A2 and 1B2, respectively. Figure 1C2 shows the local polynomial plus global autoregressive trend. Prediction results are shown in Figures 1A3, 1B3, 1C3, 1A4, 1B4, and 1C4. The model is fitted to the data $y(1), \ldots, y(N)$, $N = 138$. Prediction is done to estimate the data $y(N+1), \ldots, y(N+K)$, $N = 138$, $K = 24$. Two kinds of predictions are considered. In one-step-ahead prediction, the quantity $y(n+1 \mid n)$, $(n = N, N+1, \ldots, N+K-1)$, is computed. In increasing-horizon prediction, the quantity $y(N+i \mid N)$, $(i = 1, \ldots, K)$, is computed. In

Table 1. Trend and Seasonal Models Fitted to the BLSAGEMEN Data

Model	M	T	$\hat{\sigma}^2$	AIC
A	(2, 0, 11, 0)	(32, 0, 1)	2,014	1,997
B	(2, 0, 11, 0)	(1, 0, 32)	656	1,830
C	(2, 2, 11, 0)	(16, 1, 16)	587	1,789

384 Journal of the American Statistical Association, June 1984

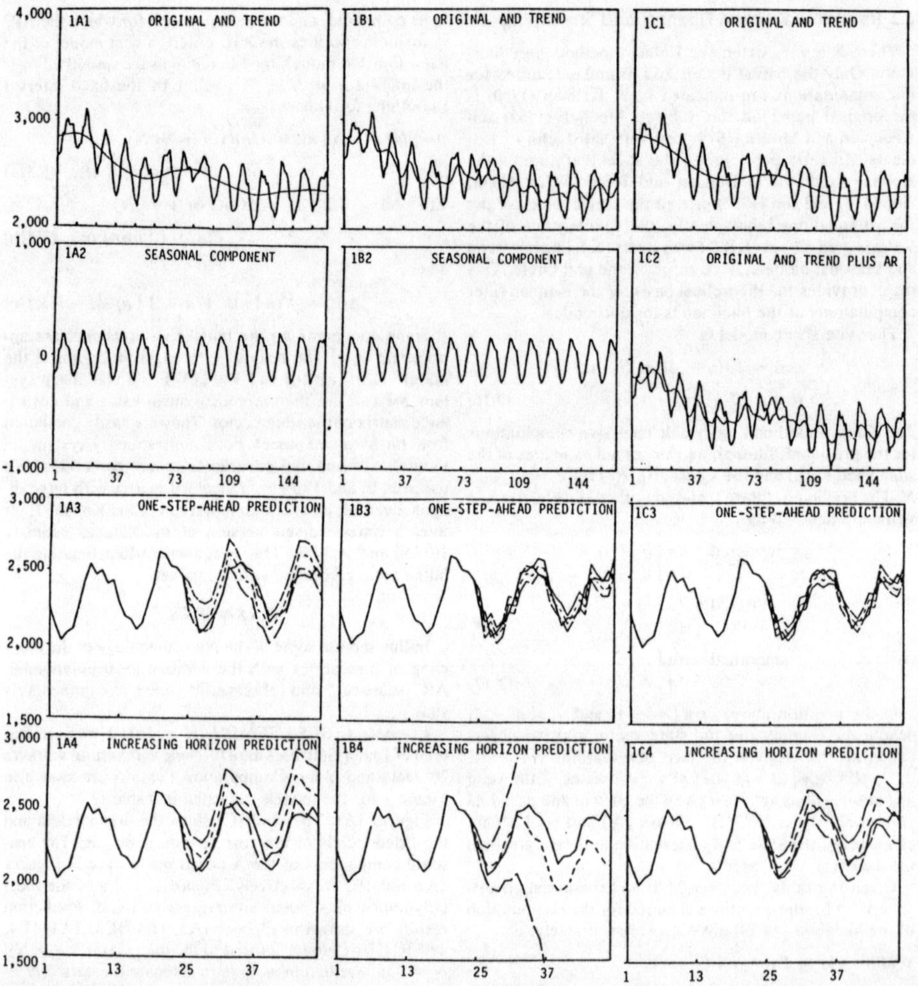

Figure 1. BLSAGEMEN data 1967–October 1980, N = 162. Trend and seasonal components, predictions, true values, and plus and minus one-sigma confidence intervals. (A) Model M = (2, 0, 11, 0), T = (32, 0, 1), $\hat{\sigma}^2$ = 2014, AIC = 1997. A1: Original data and trend; A2: Seasonal component; A3: One-step-ahead predictions; A4: Increasing horizon predictions. (B) Model M = (2, 0, 11, 0), T = (1, 0, 32), $\hat{\sigma}^2$ = 656, AIC = 1830. B1: Original data and trend; B2: Seasonal component; B3: One-step-ahead predictions; B4: Increasing horizon predictions. (C) Model M = (2, 2, 11, 0), T = (16, 1, 16), $\hat{\sigma}^2$ = 587, AIC = 1789. C1: Original data and trend; C2: Original data and trend plus AR component; C3: One-step-ahead predictions; C4: Increasing horizon predictions.

these and all subsequent illustrations showing predictions, the true value, the predicted value (dashed lines), and the computed plus and minus one sigma observation standard deviation (dotted lines) are shown. Figures 1A3, 1B3, and 1C3 are the one-step-ahead predictions for the A, B, and C models, respectively. Figures 1A4, 1B4, and 1C4 are the increasing-horizon predictions for the A, B, and C models, respectively.

Figures 1A1 and 1B1 reveal that the local polynomial trend is smoother for larger values of τ_1^2. Figures 1A2 and 1B2 reveal that the seasonal component is smoother for larger values of τ_2^2. The AIC values of the A, B, and

C models are respectively AIC(A) = 1997, AIC(B) = 1830, and AIC(C) = 1789. The width of the one-step-ahead one-sigma intervals are ranked in order with the AIC, model C having the narrowest one-sigma interval. The AIC ordering of the one-step-ahead prediction performance models does not have any necessary implications on the ordering of increasing horizon prediction performance. In this example, however, the AIC best model, C, does achieve the best increasing horizon prediction performance and does exhibit the narrowest one-sigma prediction interval. The subject of one-step-ahead and k-step-ahead prediction models and their implications for increasing horizon prediction are shown in Gersch and Kitagawa (1983).

Example 2. BLSUEM 16–19. These are Bureau of Labor Statistics data for unemployed males ages 16–19.

Table 2. Models Fitted to the BLSUEM *16–19 Data*

Model	*M*	*N*	*T*	$\hat{\sigma}^2$	AIC
A	(2, 0, 11, 0)	180	(1, 0, 4)	628.7	2,014.2
B	(2, 2, 11, 0)	180	(64, 1, 16)	763.9	1,952.5
C	(2, 0, 11, 0)	48	(16, 0, 16)	—	—

Computational results are shown in Figure 2 for the models indicated in Table 2.

These data were also analyzed by a different method in Hillmer and Tiao (1981). The trend and seasonal components of model A, shown in Figures 2A1 and 2A2, are very similar in appearance to those shown in the Hillmer-Tiao analysis. This is not the AIC best M = (2, 0, 11, 0) model. The overall AIC best of model types M = (2, 0,

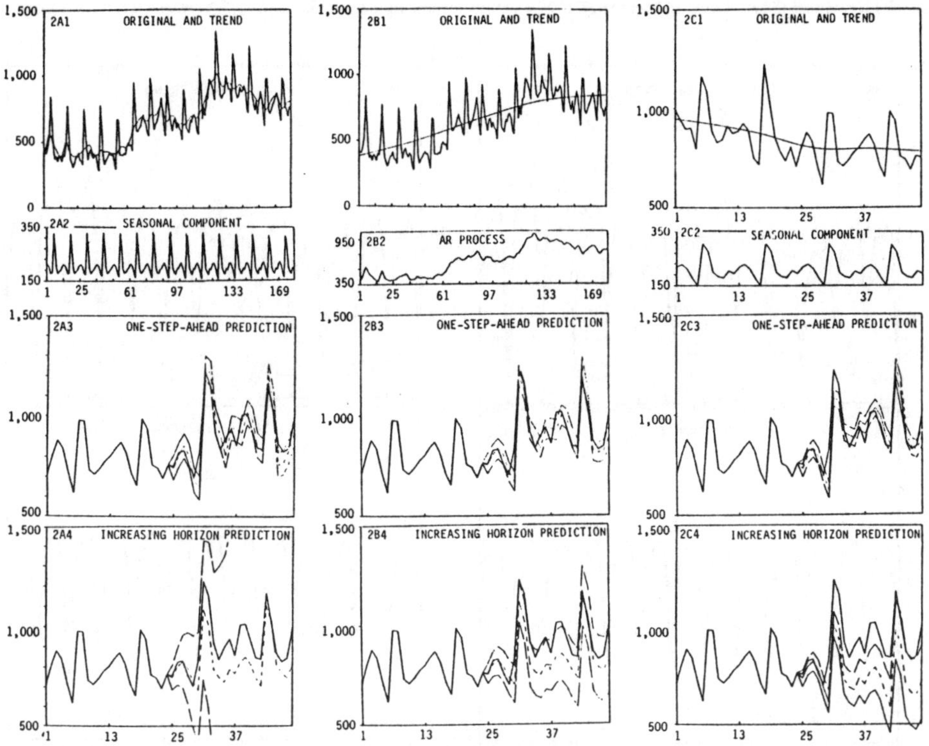

Figure 2. BLSUEM 16–19 Trend and seasonal components, predictions, true values, and plus and minus one-sigma confidence intervals. (A) Model M = (1, 0, 11, 0), T = (1, 0, 4), $\hat{\sigma}^2$ *= 628.7,* AIC *= 2014.2, N = 180, K = 24. A1: Original data and trend; A2: Seasonal component; A3: One-step-ahead predictions; A4: Increasing horizon predictions. (B) Model M = (2, 2, 11, 0), T = (64, 1, 16),* $\hat{\sigma}^2$ *= 763.9,* AIC *= 1952.5, N = 180, K = 24. B1: Original data and trend; B2:* AR *component; B3: One-step-ahead prediction; B4: Increasing horizon prediction. (C) Model M = (2, 0, 11, 0), T = (16, 0, 16), N = 48, K = 24. C1: Original data and trend; C2: Seasonal component; C3: One-step-ahead prediction; C4: Increasing horizon prediction.*

11, 0) and M = (2, 2, 11, 0) considered in Table 2 is Model B, the M = (2, 2, 11, 0) model. (Model C was fitted to a different data span than models A and B, so that its AIC's cannot be compared.) The original data, trend, and autoregressive components estimated by model B, are shown in Figures 2B1, and 2B2, respectively. The seasonal component for Model B is very similar to the seasonal component for Model A, Figure 2A2. The trend plus AR component for Model B is very similar to the trend component of Model A, Figure 2A1. The one-step-ahead and increasing horizon prediction performance of Models A and B are shown in Figures 2A3 and 2A4, and 2B3 and 2B4, respectively. The one-step-ahead one-sigma interval width of Model B is slightly narrower than that of Model A. The increasing horizon prediction one-sigma interval of Model B is much narrower than that of Model A. The models were computed on N = 156 data points and predicted for K = 24 data points. Some of the computational results for Model C are shown in Figures 2C1–2C4. This model was computed on N = 24 data points and predicted for K = 24 data points.

Table 3. Trend and Seasonal Models Fitted to the CONHSN *Data*

Model	*M*	*T*	$\hat{\sigma}^2$	AIC
A	(2, 0, 11, 0)	(16, 0, 16)	.301	76.85
B	(2, 0, 22, 0)	(16, 0, 8,192)	.287	68.25

Example 3. CONHSN, N = 156, Alternative Seasonal Models. These are Census Bureau construction series data for housing starts. Computational results are shown in Figure 3. They correspond to the models for the CONHSN data shown in Table 3.

Figures 3A1 and 3B1 show the trends of the A and B models to be very similar. The seasonal component shown in Figures 3A2 and 3B2 correspond to the constraint models (3.5a) and (3.5d), respectively, with cor-

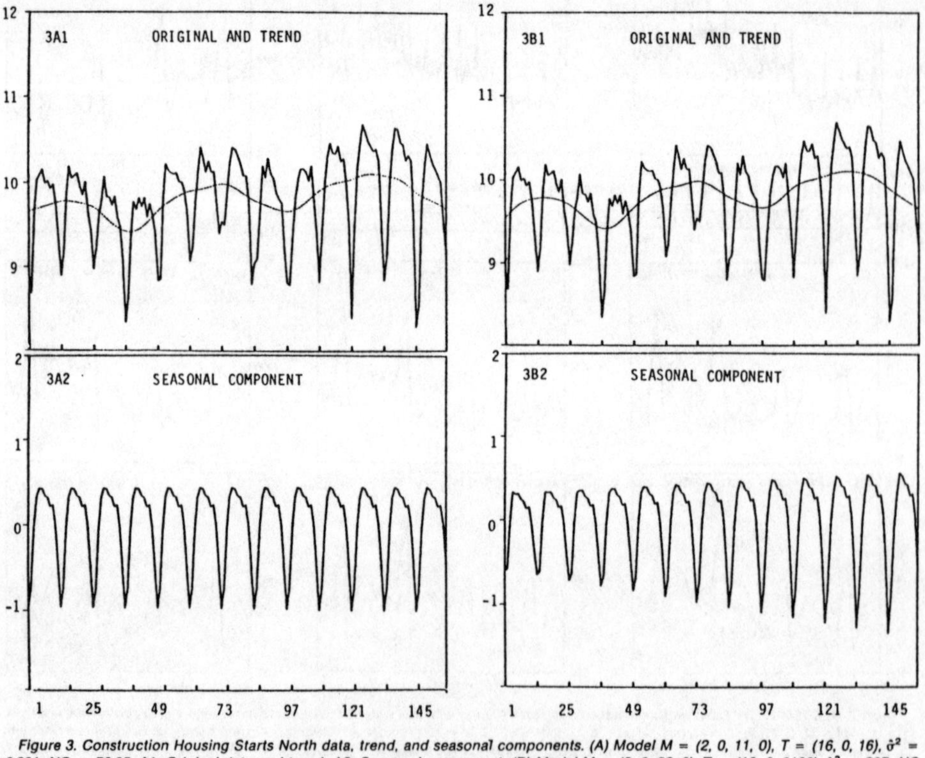

Figure 3. Construction Housing Starts North data, trend, and seasonal components. (A) Model M = (2, 0, 11, 0), T = (16, 0, 16), $\hat{\sigma}^2$ = 0.301, AIC = 76.85. A1: Original data and trend; A2: Seasonal component. (B) Model M = (2, 0, 22, 0), T = (16, 0, 8192), $\hat{\sigma}^2$ = 287, AIC = 68.25. B1: Original data and trend; B2: Seasonal component.

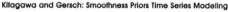

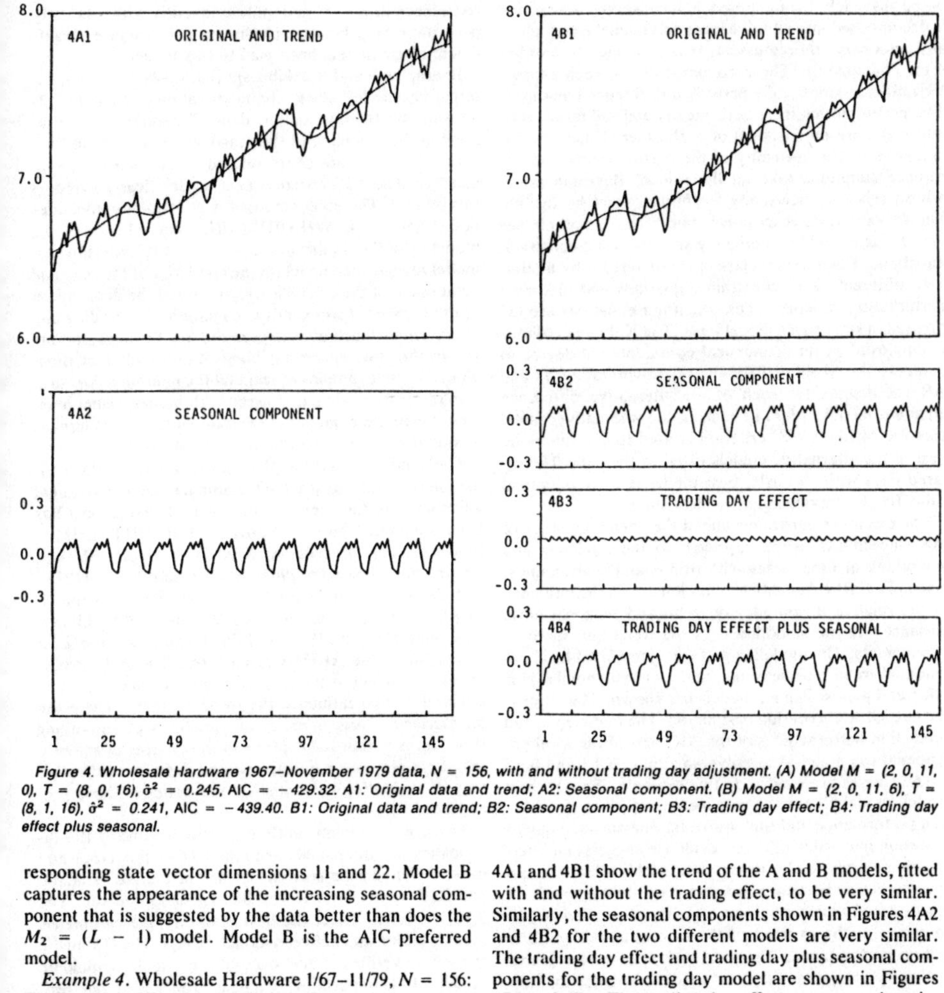

Figure 4. Wholesale Hardware 1967–November 1979 data, N = 156, with and without trading day adjustment. (A) Model M = (2, 0, 11, 0), T = (8, 0, 16), $\hat{\sigma}^2$ = 0.245, AIC = −429.32. A1: Original data and trend; A2: Seasonal component. (B) Model M = (2, 0, 11, 6), T = (8, 1, 16), $\hat{\sigma}^2$ = 0.241, AIC = −439.40. B1: Original data and trend; B2: Seasonal component; B3: Trading day effect; B4: Trading day effect plus seasonal.

responding state vector dimensions 11 and 22. Model B captures the appearance of the increasing seasonal component that is suggested by the data better than does the $M_2 = (L - 1)$ model. Model B is the AIC preferred model.

Example 4. Wholesale Hardware 1/67–11/79, $N = 156$: Trading Day Effect Model. This is Census Bureau data. Computational results are shown in Figure 4. Those results correspond to the models shown in Table 4. Figures 4A1 and 4B1 show the trend of the A and B models, fitted with and without the trading effect, to be very similar. Similarly, the seasonal components shown in Figures 4A2 and 4B2 for the two different models are very similar. The trading day effect and trading day plus seasonal components for the trading day model are shown in Figures 4B3 and 4B4. The trading day effect appears to be minuscule. The superposition of the trading day effect on the seasonal component reveals the irregularizing effect of the number of trading days on the seasonality. The trading day effect model is the AIC criterion best model.

Table 4. Trading Day Effect Model, Wholesale Hardware Data

Model	*M*	*T*	$\hat{\sigma}^2$	AIC
A	(2, 0, 11, 0)	T = (8, 0, 16)	.245	−429.32
B	(2, 0, 11, 6)	T = (8, 0, 16)	.241	−439.40

5. SUMMARY AND DISCUSSION

A smoothness priors–Kalman filter–Akaike AIC criterion approach to the modeling of time series with trends and seasonalities was shown. Like the Box-Jenkins procedure, the smoothness priors procedure is a model-based approach. In our approach, an observed time series is decomposed into additive local polynomial trend, globally stationary autoregressive, seasonal, and observation error components. These components are each characterized by stochastically perturbed difference equations. The perturbations have zero means and unknown variances and are independent of each other. Under the assumption of the normality of the perturbations, the difference equations take on the role of Bayesian priors whose relative uncertainty is characterized by the unknown variances. Alternative time series model classes are characterized by alternative subsets of the constraint equations. Each model class is characterized by models with different order constraint equations and unknown perturbation variances. The constraint equations are expressed in state space model form. The Kalman predictor is employed as an economical computational device to compute the likelihood for the unknown variances and AR coefficients for each of the alternative difference equation model orders in each of the alternative model classes. Akaike's AIC criterion is used to determine the best of the alternative models fitted to the data. The filtered data with this AIC best model is then smoothed using fixed-interval smoother algorithms.

The examples illustrate some of the phenomenology of this smoothness priors approach to the modeling and smoothing of time series with trends and seasonalities. Example 1, BLSAGEMEN data, illustrates the influence of the relative magnitudes of trend and seasonal noise variances on the smoothness of the trend and seasonal components. The modeling performance of two local polynomial trend plus seasonal, and local polynomial plus AR trend plus seasonal, models are shown. The latter is the overall AIC criterion best model. The one-step-ahead prediction performances of the AIC best of the local polynomial trend and local polynomial plus AR trend both model classes are similar. In this example, the AIC best model, model C, has the best increasing horizon prediction performance and the narrowest one-sigma standard deviation interval width. The evidence suggests an interpretation. A relatively smooth trend yields relatively narrow increasing horizon one-sigma prediction intervals. A wiggly trend yields good one-step-ahead prediction performance at the expense of the increasing horizon prediction performance. The local polynomial plus global stationary plus seasonal signal model combines the best predictor properties of the smooth and wiggly trend models.

The BLSUEM 16–19 data were analyzed by Hillmer and Tiao (1982), using a different model analysis. As shown in the example, the trends obtained by the "Wisconsin School" approach are known to be more wiggly than those obtained by the Census X-11 procedure. From the vantage point of our own analysis, the Wisconsin trends appear to be equivalent to some combination of what we refer to as local polynomial and global stochastic components, almost invariably with accompanying relatively wide increasing horizon prediction performance confidence intervals, and quite frequently with relatively poor increasing horizon prediction performance. Insufficient attention has been paid to this tendency.

Examples 3 and 4 exhibit special attributes of our alternative model class characterizations. Example 3, housing starts construction data, illustrates two variations in the modeling of the seasonal component of time series. The data are characterized by an increasing seasonality. The AIC criterion best model clearly captures this pattern. The other seasonality constraint model does not. Example 4, WHARDWARE data, illustrates the modeling of the trading day effect. The AIC criterion best model reveals the impact on the regularity of the seasonal component of the calendar irregularity of the distribution of the number of weekends each month. The trading day effects model achieves regression on fixed regressors within the state space modeling–Kalman filter methodology. These examples reveal that the minimum AIC procedure yields models that agree with human visual judgment when the evidence is clear and also selects models in situations that cannot be handled by the human eye.

The models and examples shown relate to the estimation of trend and seasonal components in the seasonal adjustment of time series. Treatment of that subject has been dominated by the Census X-11 and BJT ARIMA-type modeling procedures. See, for example, Shiskin, Young, and Musgrave (1967), Shiskin and Plewes (1978), and Cleveland and Tiao (1976) for treatments of the X-11 procedure, and see Box and Jenkins (1970), Hillmer, Bell, and Tiao (1983), and Hillmer and Tiao (1982) for treatment of the ARIMA procedures. The X-11 procedures are subject to certain practical public data reporting constraints that influence the trend estimate. There are an extremely large number of variations of smoothing procedures within X-11. Many of the choices of smoothing filters are done subjectively, and there is no effective way of evaluating the statistical properties of those procedures.

There is a critically different attitude toward the diagnostics of modeling between the BJT methodology and ours, which can be seen in our use of the AIC statistic and BJT's use of the Pierce-Box-Ljung Q statistic. The AIC is used to select the best of alternative parametric models within and between model classes. The Q statistic is used to verify the adequacy of a particular candidate model. A distinguishing practical property of our procedure in comparison with the BJT procedure is that ours is essentially a semiautomatic extensive model alternative procedure. The BJT procedure seems to require extensive expert human intervention to achieve satisfactory modeling. Some evidence in support of this appraisal can be seen in the history of the modeling of the Wisconsin telephone data in Thompson and Tiao (1971) and Hillmer (1982). The Thompson-Tiao model is sophisticated, and considerable expertise was required to arrive at that model. Expert experience in the modeling of time series justified Hillmer's use of the trading day effect model. The Q statistic does not.

In addition, the successful AIC criterion modeling of the BLSUEM 16–19, $N = 24$ data point series seems to support the interpretation of our procedure as a semiautomatic procedure even on short-duration series. The small sample–large variability properties of the Q statistic do not lend themselves to reliable diagnostic appraisals of such short duration series. Finally, we suggest that the appropriate testing ground for any time series modeling procedure is in the evaluation of the predictive properties of models fitted by that procedure. A maximization of the expected entropy of the predictive distribution interpretation of the minimum AIC procedure was exhibited in Gersch and Kitagawa (1983) for AIC minimum one-step-ahead and twelve-step-ahead modeling and prediction of time series with trends and seasonalities. Some of that prediction performance analysis appears to transcend the BJT ARIMA model approach.

[*Received July 1982. Revised November 1983.*]

REFERENCES

AKAIKE, H. (1973), "Information Theory and an Extension of the Maximum Likelihood Principle," in *Second International Symposium on Information Theory*, eds. B.N. Petrov and F. Csaki, Budapest: Akademiai Kiado, 267–281.

——— (1974), "A New Look at the Statistical Model Identification," *IEEE Transactions on Automatic Control*, AC-19, 716–723.

——— (1980a), "Likelihood and the Bayes Procedure in Bayesian Statistics," in *Bayesian Statistics*, eds. J.N. Bernado, M.H. DeGroot, D.V. Lindley, and A.F.M. Smith, Valencia, Spain: University Press, 141–166.

——— (1980b), "Seasonal Adjustment by a Bayesian Modeling," *Journal of Time Series Analysis*, 1, 1–13.

AKAIKE, H., and ISHIGURO, M. (1980), "BAYSEA, A Bayesian Seasonal Adjustment Program," *Computer Science Monographs*, No. 13, Tokyo: The Institute of Statistical Mathematics.

——— (1983), "Comparative Study of the X-11 and BAYSEA Procedures of Seasonal Adjustment," in *Applied Time Series Analysis of Economic Data*, ed. A. Zellner, Washington, D.C.: U.S. Department of Commerce, Bureau of the Census.

ANDERSON, B.D.O., and MOORE, J.B. (1979), *Optimal Filtering*, Englewood Cliffs, N.J.: Prentice Hall.

BOX, G.E.P., and JENKINS, G.M. (1970), *Time Series Analysis, Forecasting and Control*, San Francisco: Holden-Day.

BROTHERTON, T., and GERSCH, W. (1981), "A Data Analytic Approach to the Smoothing Problem and Some of Its Variations," in *Proceedings of the 20th IEEE Conference on Decision and Control*, 1061–1099.

CHAN, S.W., GOODWIN, G.C., and SIN, K.S. (1982), "Convergence Properties of the Solutions of the Ricatti Difference Equation," *Proceedings of the 21st IEEE Conference on Decision and Control*, 300–305.

CLEVELAND, W.S., and DEVLIN, S.J. (1980), "Calendar Effects in Monthly Time Series; Detection by Spectrum Analysis and Graphical Methods," *Journal of the American Statistical Association*, 75, 487–496.

CLEVELAND, W.P., and GRUPE, M.R. (1983), "Modeling Time Series When Calendar Effects Are Present," in *Applied Time Series Analysis of Economic Data*, ed. A. Zellner, Washington, D.C.: Department of Commerce, Bureau of the Census.

CLEVELAND, W.P., and TIAO, G.C. (1976), "Decomposition of Seasonal Time Series: A Model for the Census X-11 Program," *Journal of the American Statistical Association*, 71, 581–587.

DUNCAN, D., and HORN, S. (1972), "Linear Dynamic Recursive Estimation From the Viewpoint of Regression Analysis," *Journal of the American Statistical Association*, 67, 815–821.

GERSCH, W., and KITAGAWA, G. (1983), "The Prediction of Time Series With Trends and Seasonalities," *Journal of Business & Economic Statistics*, 1, 253–264.

GOOD, I.J. (1965), *The Estimation of Probabilities*, Cambridge, Mass.: MIT Press.

GOOD, I.J., and GASKINS, R.A. (1980), "Density Estimation and Bump Hunting by the Penalized Likelihood Method Exemplified by Scattering and Meteorite Data," *Journal of the American Statistical Association*, 75, 42–73.

HARVEY, A.C., and PHILLIPS, G.P.A. (1979), "Maximum Likelihood Estimation of Regression Models With Autoregressive-Moving Average Disturbances," *Biometrika*, 66, 49–58.

HILLMER, S.C. (1982), "Forecasting Time Series With Trading Day Variation," *Journal of Forecasting*, 1, 385–395.

HILLMER, S.C., BELL, W.R., and TIAO, G.C. (1983), "Modeling Considerations in the Seasonal Adjustment of Economic Time Series," in *Applied Time Series Analysis of Economic Data*, ed. A. Zellner, Washington, D.C.: U.S. Department of Commerce, Bureau of the Census.

HILLMER, S.C., and TIAO, G.C. (1982), "An ARIMA-Based Approach to Seasonal Adjustment," *Journal of the American Statistical Association*, 77, 63–70.

KALMAN, R.E. (1960), "A New Approach to Linear Filtering and Prediction Problems," *Trans. ASME, Journal of Basic Engineering*, Ser. D, 80, 35–45.

KITAGAWA, G. (1981), "A Nonstationary Time Series Model and Its Fitting by a Recursive Technique," *Journal of Time Series Analysis*, 2, 103–116.

LINDLEY, D.V., and SMITH, A.F.M. (1972), "Bayes Estimate for the Linear Model," *Journal of the Royal Statistical Society*, Ser. B, 34, 1–41.

MEDITCH, J.S. (1969), *Stochastic Optimal Linear Estimation and Control*, New York: McGraw Hill.

PIERCE, D.A. (1978), "Seasonal Adjustment When Both Deterministic and Stochastic Seasonality Are Present," in *Seasonal Analysis of Economic Time Series*, ed. A. Zellner, Washington, D.C.: U.S. Department of Commerce, Bureau of the Census.

SHILLER, R. (1973), "A Distributed Lag Estimator Derived From Smoothness Priors," *Econometrica*, 41, 775–778.

SHISKIN, J., and PLEWES, T.J. (1978), "Seasonal Adjustment of the U.S. Employment Rate," *The Statistician*, 27, 181–202.

SHISKIN, J., YOUNG, A.H., and MUSGRAVE, J.C. (1967), "The X-11 Variant of Census Method II Seasonal Adjustment Program," Technical Paper 15, Washington, D.C.: U.S. Bureau of the Census.

THOMPSON, H.E., and TIAO, G.C. (1971), "Analysis of Telephone Data: A Case of Forecasting Seasonal Time Series," *The Bell System Journal of Economics and Management Science*, 2, 515.

WAHBA, G. (1977), "A Survey of Some Smoothing Problems and the Method of Generalized Cross-Validation for Solving Them," in *Applications of Statistics*, ed. P.R. Krishnaiah, Amsterdam: North Holland, 507–524.

WAHBA, G., and WOLD, S. (1975), "A Complete Automatic French Curve: Fitting Spline Functions by Cross Validations," *Communications in Statistics*, 4, 1–17.

WECKER, W.E., and ANSLEY, C.F. (1983), "The Signal Extraction Approach to Nonlinear Regression and Spline Smoothing," *Journal of the American Statistical Association*, 78, 81–89.

WHITTAKER, E.T. (1923), "On a New Method of Graduation," *Proceedings of the Edinborough Mathematical Society*, 41, 63–75.

YOUNG, P.C., and JAKEMAN, A.J. (1979), "The Estimation of Input Variables in Stochastic Dynamic Systems," Report No. AS/R28, Canberra, Australia: Australian National University, Centre for Resource and Environmental Studies.

[12]

Journal of Business & Economic Statistics, July 1985, Vol. 3, No. 3

Trends and Cycles in Macroeconomic Time Series

A. C. Harvey
London School of Economics, Houghton St., London WC2A 2AE, England

Two structural time series models for annual observations are constructed in terms of trend, cycle, and irregular components. The models are then estimated via the Kalman filter using data on five U.S. macroeconomic time series. The results provide some interesting insights into the dynamic structure of the series, particularly with respect to cyclical behavior. At the same time, they illustrate the development of a model selection strategy for structural time series models.

KEY WORDS: Autoregressive integrated moving average model; Kalman filter; Model selection; State-space model; Structural time series model; Unobserved components.

1. INTRODUCTION

The decomposition of economic time series into trend and cyclical components plays an important role in much of macroeconomics. For example, it is common practice to regard the trend as a deterministic function of time and the cyclical component as a stationary process that exhibits transitory movements around the trend. This view leads economists to analyze detrended data and construct models relating different variables from such data. If the trend components in economic time series are not deterministic, however, Nelson and Kang (1981, 1984) showed that such an approach can lead to very misleading inferences being drawn.

Nelson and Plosser (1982) provided some empirical evidence on the properties of U.S. macroeconomic time series. They set up two models: the trend stationary (TS) model in which

$$y_t = \alpha + \beta t + w_t, \tag{1.1}$$

where y_t is the natural logarithm of the observations and w_t is a stationary and invertible autoregressive moving average (ARMA) process, and the difference stationary (DS) model

$$\Delta y_t = \beta + v_t, \tag{1.2}$$

where v_t is a stationary and invertible ARMA process (see also Beveridge and Nelson 1981). The evidence from the testing procedure of Dickey and Fuller (1979) indicates that for no series is it possible to confidently reject the null hypothesis of the DS model against the alternative of a TS model. As Nelson and Plosser were careful to point out, however, acceptance of the null hypothesis is not disproof of the alternative. They therefore examined the correlograms to see what these suggest about the nature of the series. For most of the series, the correlograms of first differences (of the logarithms) have sample autocorrelations that are positive and significant at lag one but not significant at higher lags. Nelson and Plosser argued that this constitutes strong evidence in favor of the DS model. They then argued further that if the autocorrelation function of the first differences of a process exhibits a positive first-order autocorrelation and zero higher-order autocorrelations, this seems to preclude the possibility of constructing a sensible unobserved components model in which y_t is the sum of a *stochastic* trend and a stationary process.

The aim of this article is to examine these questions further by adopting a somewhat different methodological stance. Nelson and Plosser followed the approach pioneered by Box and Jenkins (1976) in which the observations themselves are used to identify a suitably parsimonious model from the class of autoregressive integrated moving average (ARIMA) processes. Thus they effectively identified an ARIMA(0, 1, 1) process as being appropriate for virtually all of their series, and they then drew conclusions about the nature of these series on the basis of the properties of this process. The view taken here is that the ARIMA class is a very broad one and that attempts to identify suitable models on the basis of the data alone can lead to unsatisfactory results. In some cases, as argued in Harvey and Todd (1983), the models may yield poor forecasts. More generally, there is no guarantee that an ARIMA model identified from the data will have the kind of properties that a particular economic time series is postulated to exhibit. As a rule, there will be several ARIMA models that are consistent with a given set of data, in the sense that they exhibit a good fit, or to put it another way, have an autocorrelation function (at the appropriate degree of differencing) that has similar properties to the observed correlogram. It is often difficult to see exactly what properties these different ARIMA specifications will have, particularly with regard to potential decompositions into trend, cycle, and seasonal components. An alternative approach is therefore to work with a class of unobserved components models that have these properties explicitly built into their structure.

The plan of this article is as follows: After a preliminary discussion of the data in Section 2, the evidence in the correlogram is reexamined in Section 3 in the light of various formulations of trend plus cycle models, of which (1.1) is a special case. An alternative class of models in which the cycle is incorporated into the trend is also proposed. Both classes of models, which in the terminology of Harvey and Todd (1983) and Engle (1978) are "structural" models, are shown to be consistent with correlograms found for the series in question. In Section 4, the statistical properties of these structural models are discussed. The series are analyzed in Sections 5 and 6, and estimates of the unknown structural parameters are computed by a maximum likelihood procedure based on the Kalman filter. Conclusions and extensions are presented in Section 7.

2. THE DATA

The data used by Nelson and Plosser (1982) consist of 14 U.S. macroeconomic time series. The series are annual, with starting dates from 1860 to 1909. The final year is 1970 in all cases. In this study attention is concentrated on just five of these series, primarily because many of the series—for example real GNP, nominal GNP, and real per capita GNP—display fairly similar characteristics. The series considered are real GNP, industrial production, the unemployment rate, consumer prices, and common stock prices. Details of sources can be found in Nelson and Plosser (1982, p. 146).

The figures for real GNP are of particular interest in a study of cycles. Figure 1 shows the natural logarithm of real GNP and the first differences of the logarithms. It is apparent from these graphs that there is a fairly dramatic change in the series after about 1947. As one might expect, the movements in postwar GNP are much smoother. (The years 1946 and 1947 represent a settling down period after the war). This shows up clearly in the correlograms of the logs of first differences for the period up to and including 1947 and the post-1947 period (see Figure 2). The correlogram for the earlier period is very similar to the correlogram that Nelson and Plosser (1982, table 3) gave for the whole period. The correlogram for the later period is not. In

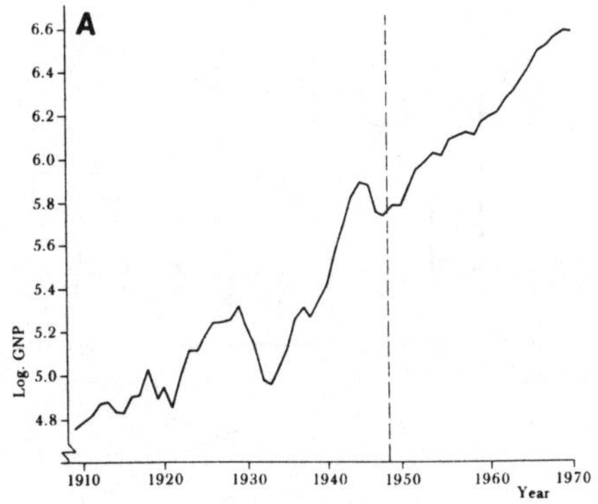

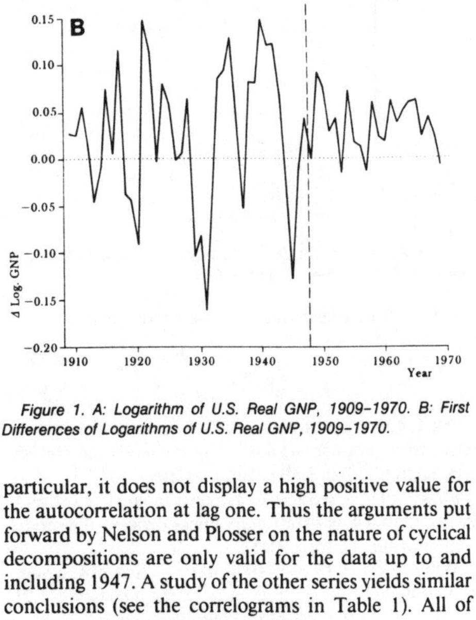

Figure 1. A: Logarithm of U.S. Real GNP, 1909–1970. B: First Differences of Logarithms of U.S. Real GNP, 1909–1970.

particular, it does not display a high positive value for the autocorrelation at lag one. Thus the arguments put forward by Nelson and Plosser on the nature of cyclical decompositions are only valid for the data up to and including 1947. A study of the other series yields similar conclusions (see the correlograms in Table 1). All of them were therefore split at 1947.

3. TREND AND CYCLE MODELS

The traditional formulation of an annual economic time series is

$$y_t = \mu_t + \psi_t + \epsilon_t, \qquad t = 1, \ldots, T, \tag{3.1}$$

where y_t is the logarithm of the observed value, μ_t is a trend, ψ_t is a cycle, and ϵ_t is an irregular component. In what follows, ψ_t will always be a stationary linear process, ϵ_t will denote a white noise disturbance term with variance σ^2, and all of the components will be assumed to be uncorrelated with each other.

218 Journal of Business & Economic Statistics, July 1985

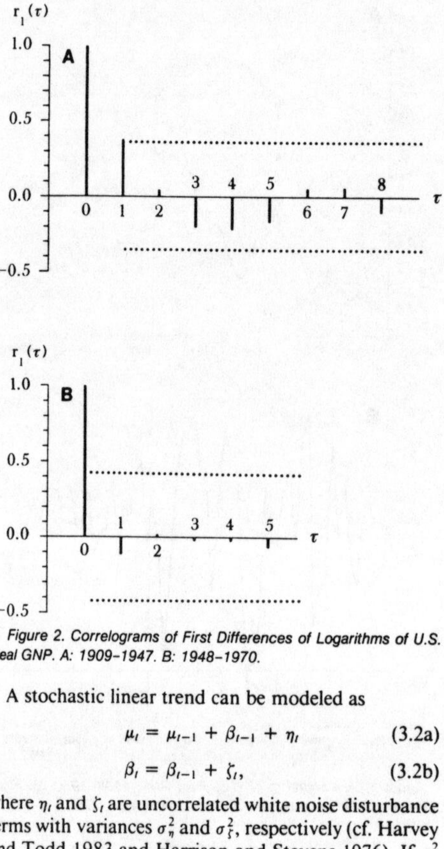

Figure 2. Correlograms of First Differences of Logarithms of U.S. Real GNP. A: 1909–1947. B: 1948–1970.

A stochastic linear trend can be modeled as

$$\mu_t = \mu_{t-1} + \beta_{t-1} + \eta_t \qquad (3.2a)$$

$$\beta_t = \beta_{t-1} + \zeta_t, \qquad (3.2b)$$

where η_t and ζ_t are uncorrelated white noise disturbance terms with variances σ_η^2 and σ_ζ^2, respectively (cf. Harvey and Todd 1983 and Harrison and Stevens 1976). If $\sigma_\eta^2 = \sigma_\zeta^2 = 0$, then μ_t reduces to a deterministic linear trend. Provided that ψ_t is a stationary linear process, the model is then of the TS form (1.1).

When $\sigma_\zeta^2 = 0$, (3.1) is stationary in first differences; and provided that $\sigma_\eta^2 > 0$, it is of the DS form (1.2), with $\beta_t = \beta$. In the rest of this section it will be assumed that $\sigma_\zeta^2 = 0$. This assumption will be relaxed in Section 4, but since it appears that σ_ζ^2 is quite small in practice, any conclusions reached under the assumption that it is zero are unlikely to be misleading.

3.1 The Correlogram of First Differences

Let $\rho_d(\tau)$ denote the autocorrelation at lag τ from the dth difference of a stochastic process and $r_d(\tau)$ denote the corresponding sample autocorrelation. Nelson and Plosser (1982) found that $r_1(1)$ is strongly positive and that most of the higher-order autocorrelations are statistically insignificant at the 5% level. This is illustrated by the correlogram in Figure 2A, where the dotted lines indicate ±2 standard errors on the assumption that $\rho_1(1) = r_1(1)$ and $\rho_1(\tau) = 0$ for $\tau \geq 2$. If the data were, in fact, generated by a process in which $\rho_1(\tau) = 0$ for $\tau \geq 2$, this would imply that $\psi_t = 0$ in (3.1). Furthermore, a positive $\rho_1(1)$ means that (3.1) must be ruled out completely unless there is a strong negative correlation between ϵ_t and η_t (see Nelson and Plosser 1982, pp. 152–158). If ϵ_t and η_t are uncorrelated, then $\rho_1(1)$ must be less than or equal to zero.

The above conclusions rest on the assumption that $\rho(\tau) = 0$ for $\tau \geq 2$, that is, that the process generating the series is ARIMA(0, 1, 1) with a constant. Although a standard application of the Box–Jenkins methodology suggests this model as a prime candidate on the grounds of parsimony, it might well be considered unacceptable, since it is unable to generate cyclical behavior of the kind that is plausible from an inspection of Figure 1A. Once the assumption that $\rho_1(\tau) = 0$ for $\tau \geq 2$ is relaxed, the fact that $\rho_1(1)$ is positive is still consistent with a wide range of stationary stochastic processes for ψ_t. In fact for any stationary stochastic process, it follows directly that

$$\begin{aligned}\gamma_1(1) &= E[(y_t - y_{t-1})(y_{t-1} - y_{t-2})] \\ &= 2\gamma_0(1) - \gamma_0(0) - \gamma_0(2),\end{aligned}$$

and so $\gamma_1(1)$, and hence $\rho_1(1)$, will be positive if

$$2\rho_0(1) > 1 + \rho_0(2). \qquad (3.3)$$

Suppose for the sake of simplicity that $\sigma_\eta^2 = \sigma^2 = 0$; that is, the model is of the TS form (1.1), with $w_t = \psi_t$. If ψ_t follows an AR(2) (autoregressive) process—that is, if $\psi_t = \phi_1\psi_{t-1} + \phi_2\psi_{t-2} + \omega_t$, where ω_t is white noise—

Table 1. Correlograms of First Differences of Logarithms

Series	Period	Number of observations	Sample autocorrelations, $r_1(\tau)$: 1	2	3	4	5	6	7	8	Q statistic[a]	Variance × 10^4
Real GNP	1909–1947	39	.37	.04	−.20	−.21	−.17	.04	.05	−.09	10.73	62.2
	1948–1970	23	−.11	−.00	−.02	−.01	−.06				.43	8.87
Industrial production	1860–1947	88	−.06	−.11	−.03	−.12	−.27	.07	.14	−.01	9.74	122
	1948–1970	23	−.30	−.06	.07	−.03	−.04				2.57	34.4
Unemployment rate	1890–1947	58	.11	−.30	.02	−.06	−.18	.06	.16	−.17	8.58	3120
	1948–1970	23	−.13	−.24	−.16	.17	.08				3.70	670
Consumer prices	1860–1947	88	.57	.16	.01	−.03	.02	−.01	.00	.02	31.71	39.9
	1948–1970	23	.32	−.13	−.05	−.09	.00				3.33	4.19
Common stock prices	1871–1947	77	.21	−.16	−.10	−.27	−.32	.00	.13	.01	20.90	295
	1948–1970	23	.03	−.21	−.04	.41	.11				6.54	126

[a] Q denotes the Box–Ljung form of the portmanteau test statistic [see (4.1)], with P = 5 df; 5% significance value = 11.07; 10% = 9.24.

it follows from (3.3) that $\rho_1(1)$ will be positive if $\phi_1(2 - \phi_1) > 1 - \phi_2^2$. It is not difficult to find parameters within the stationarity region that satisfy this constraint. In fact for real GNP in the pre-1948 period, regressing y_t on y_{t-1} and y_{t-2} together with time t gives estimates of these parameters of $\hat{\phi}_1 = 1.27$ and $\hat{\phi}_2 = -.48$. The autocorrelation function of the differenced observations can be calculated by noting that the following equation can be derived from (3.3):

$$\rho_1(\tau) = \frac{2\rho_0(\tau) - \rho_0(\tau - 1) - \rho_0(\tau + 1)}{2(1 - \rho_0(1))}, \quad \tau = 0, 1, 2, \ldots . \quad (3.4)$$

The autocorrelation function of Δy_t satisfies the same difference equation as that of ψ_t, but with starting values at $\tau = 1$ and 2. For the parameter estimates just given, it exhibits a damped cycle with a period of 15.3 years. This is shown in Figure 3, and it can be seen that the pattern is not dissimilar to that of the observed correlogram in Figure 2A. Relaxing the assumption that σ_η^2 and σ^2 are zero can only lead to an autocorrelation function of Δy_t that is even closer to the observed correlogram.

The conclusion therefore is that although the sample autocorrelations at lags higher than one are not statistically significant (at the 5% level), they are not negligible, and the overall pattern is not inconsistent with trend plus cycle models of the form (3.1). Even a deterministic trend, that is, the TS model, cannot be ruled out. Similar results can be found for many of the other series besides GNP.

3.2 The Cyclical Trend Model

Given the findings in Section 3.1, the next question is whether there is an alternative class of models, also reflecting the cyclical behavior of the series, that can be set against the trend plus cycle models of (3.1). One

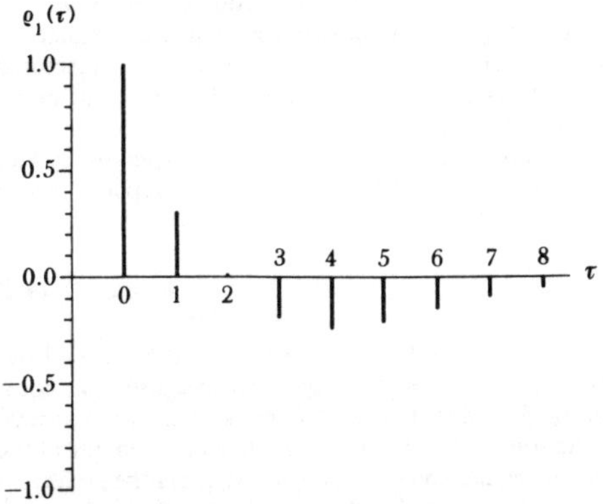

Figure 3. Autocorrelation Function for First Differences From a Deterministic Linear Trend With AR(2) Disturbances.

possibility is to incorporate the cycle within the trend. Thus (3.1) is replaced by

$$y_t = \mu_t + \epsilon_t, \quad (3.6)$$

and

$$\mu_t = \mu_{t-1} + \beta_{t-1} + \psi_{t-1} + \eta_t, \quad (3.7)$$

and ψ_t is a stationary linear stochastic process. Equation (3.2b) remains the same, but when $\sigma_\zeta^2 = 0$, the model corresponds to the DS form of (1.2).

3.3 Modeling the Cyclical Component

So far the two general models, (3.1) and (3.6), have left the form of ψ_t unspecified, apart from a requirement that it should be a stationary linear process capable of displaying pseudocyclical behavior. The AR(2) process was used as an illustration simply because it is the best-known process of this kind and relatively easy to handle. An alternative specification, which has certain attractions within the context of the more general formulations of (3.1) and (3.6), involves modeling the cyclical process explicitly. It takes the form

$$\begin{bmatrix} \psi_t \\ \psi_t^* \end{bmatrix} = \rho \begin{bmatrix} \cos\lambda & \sin\lambda \\ -\sin\lambda & \cos\lambda \end{bmatrix} \begin{bmatrix} \psi_{t-1} \\ \psi_{t-1}^* \end{bmatrix} + \begin{bmatrix} \omega_t \\ \omega_t^* \end{bmatrix}, \quad (3.8)$$

where ψ_t is the cyclical component, ω_t and ω_t^* are uncorrelated white noise disturbance terms with variances σ_ω^2 and σ_ω^{*2}, respectively, and ψ_t^* appears by construction (cf. Harrison and Akram 1983). The parameters $0 \leq \lambda \leq \pi$ and $0 \leq \rho \leq 1$ have a direct interpretation as the frequency of the cycle and the damping factor on the amplitude, respectively. The disturbances make the cycle stochastic rather than deterministic, and if ρ is strictly less than one, the process is stationary. The model can be written as

$$\psi_t = \frac{(1 - \rho\cos\lambda \cdot L)\omega_t + (\rho\sin\lambda \cdot L)\omega_t^*}{1 - 2\rho\cos\lambda \cdot L + \rho^2 \cdot L^2}, \quad (3.9)$$

where L is the lag operator. This reveals it to be an ARMA(2, 1) process; but if $\sigma_\omega^2 = 0$, it becomes AR(2). It is a rather special case of an AR(2), however, in that when $0 < \lambda < \pi$, the parameters are constrained to lie within the region corresponding to complex roots. (The modulus of these roots is ρ.) Since the aim is to model a stochastic cycle, this is a desirable constraint to impose. Note that the AR(1) model is obtained when λ is equal to 0 or π.

The preceding cyclical model was estimated both with and without the constraint that $\sigma_\omega^2 = \sigma_\omega^{*2}$. It appeared that very little, if anything, was lost in terms of goodness of fit by imposing this constraint. From the point of view of numerical optimization, having one parameter rather than two was found to be a considerable advantage. Hence in the results reported in the Section 4, this constraint was always imposed, and estimates are given for a single parameter, σ_ω^2. A theoretical rationale for the constraint, in terms of an underlying continuous time model, can be found in Harvey (1983).

3.4 ARIMA Models and the Reduced Form

Consider the trend plus cycle model (3.1), with trend (3.2) and cycle (3.8). When $\sigma_\zeta^2 = 0$, taking first differences yields the reduced or canonical form

$$\Delta y_t = \beta + \eta_t + \Delta\psi_t + \Delta\epsilon_t. \tag{3.10}$$

Since $\psi_t \sim$ ARMA(2, 1), it follows that the right side of (3.10) is ARMA(2, 3). It is an ARMA model, however, in which the AR and MA parameters are subject to strong restrictions. These restrictions fulfill two important roles. In the first place, they ensure that the model displays the desired characteristics. In the second place, provided that $\rho > 0$, they ensure that there are no common factors in the AR and MA polynomials; that is, the model is locally identifiable. (If the constraint $\sigma_\omega^2 = \sigma_\omega^{*2}$ is not imposed in the cycle, the model can also cease to be identifiable in the special case when $\lambda = 0$ or π. This provides yet another reason for imposing it.)

The cyclical trend model can also be expressed as an ARIMA(2, 1, 3) model when $\sigma_\zeta^2 = 0$, and the condition that $\rho > 0$ is again necessary for identifiability.

If $\sigma_\zeta^2 > 0$, both (3.1) and (3.6) can be expressed as ARIMA(2, 2, 4) models without a constant term.

4. ESTIMATION, TESTING, AND MODEL EVALUATION

Unobserved components models can be estimated in a number of ways (see Nerlove et al. 1979 and Harvey and Peters 1984). In this article, direct estimation of the structural parameters is carried out in the time domain by casting the model in state-space form. The same state-space form can be used to make predictions of future observations and to construct optimal estimates of the various unobserved components in the model by smoothing.

4.1 Maximum Likelihood Estimation

Both the trend plus cycle and the cyclical trend models can be written in state-space form very easily by defining the state vector to be $\alpha_t = (\mu_t, \beta_t, \psi_t, \psi_t^*)'$. The Kalman filter is then initiated by setting the mean squared errors of the initial estimators of μ_t and β_t equal to large but finite numbers. Since ψ_t is stationary, the initial mean squared error matrix of $(\psi_t, \psi_t^*)'$ is equal to the unconditional covariance matrix of $(\psi_t, \psi_t^*)'$. The summations in the prediction error decomposition form of the likelihood function then run from $t = 3$ to T. Maximization of this likelihood function with respect to the unknown parameters $\sigma^2, \sigma_\eta^2, \sigma_\zeta^2, \sigma_\omega^2, \lambda$, and ρ can be carried out numerically as in Harvey and Todd (1983).

4.2 Tests and Model Evaluation

Asymptotic standard errors of the maximum likelihood (ML) estimates can be computed by evaluating the Hessian numerically. This enables confidence intervals to be constructed for ρ and λ. Tests can also be carried out, although it should be remembered that if $\rho = 0$, the model ceases to be identifiable. Tests that any of the variance components $\sigma_\eta^2, \sigma_\zeta^2$, and σ_ω^2 are zero are also subject to problems, though for a different reason—namely that the usual asymptotic normality of the ML estimators does not hold under the null hypothesis. (This difficulty does not arise with σ_η^2 if $\sigma_\zeta^2 >$ 0.) Within the ARIMA framework, hypotheses of this kind involve the degree of differencing and are not normally tested (cf. Plosser and Schwert 1977 and Sargan and Bhargava 1983). It is possible to construct exact tests, as in Franzini and Harvey (1983), but it is difficult to apply such an approach here because of the possible presence of a cyclical component.

Comparison of various models, including those such as (3.1) and (3.6), that are nonnested can be made on the basis of the maximized likelihood function. The prediction error variance $\bar{\sigma}_p^2$, defined as the steady-state variance of the one-step ahead prediction error, can also be used to give an indication of goodness of fit.

Diagnostic checking tests could, in theory, be constructed using the Lagrange multiplier (LM) principle. Since both (3.1) and (3.6) are relatively rich models anyway, however, there is no obvious alternative hypothesis. In any case, LM tests for unobserved components models are best formulated in the frequency domain (see Harvey and Hotta 1982), and a detailed discussion of this is beyond the scope of this article. An alternative approach to diagnostic checking is to use the more conventional Box–Ljung Q statistic

$$Q = T^*(T^* + 2) \sum_{\tau=1}^{P} (T^* - \tau)^{-1} r^2(\tau), \tag{4.1}$$

where T^* is the number of residuals (usually $T - 2$) and $r(\tau)$ is the τth autocorrelation in the residuals. If the model contains n parameters, it may be conjectured that Q has a χ^2 distribution with $P - n + 1$ df under the null hypothesis.

A simple diagnostic test for heteroscedasticity can also be constructed from the residuals. Suppose that m is $T^*/3$ or the nearest integer to it. The test statistic is

$$H = \left[\sum_{t=T-m+1}^{T} (\nu_t^2/f_t)\right] \Big/ \sum_{t=k+1}^{m+k} (\nu_t^2/f_t), \tag{4.2}$$

where $k = T - T^*$. A naive test could be carried out by comparing H with the appropriate significance point of an $F_{m,m}$ distribution. Of course, this is not strictly valid unless all of the parameters, apart from one of the variances, are known. Nevertheless, it may be preferable to the large sample alternative of treating mH as χ_m^2 under the null hypothesis.

Subject to satisfactory diagnostics, a fitted model will

be evaluated not only on its goodness of fit but also on the basis of the numerical values of estimated parameters. Thus as in model building in econometrics, the question of statistical significance (at an arbitrary significance level of 5%) is not necessarily as important as the consideration of whether the estimated parameters give a model with a sensible interpretation.

4.3 Preliminary Analysis

If there is some doubt as to whether a cyclical model is appropriate, it may be wise to conduct a preliminary analysis of the data. One reason for doing this is to avoid unnecessary computing, particularly as (3.1) and (3.6) are not identifiable when $\rho = 0$.

As was demonstrated in Section 3, a good deal of information can be obtained by looking at the correlogram of Δy_t. A cyclical pattern in the sample autocorrelations suggests the possibility of either (3.1) or (3.6). In the case of (3.6) it can be shown that when $\sigma_\zeta^2 = \sigma^2 = 0$, the LM test for $\rho = 0$ is based simply on $r_1(1)$ (see the Appendix). The LM principle can be extended to carry out tests of $\rho = 0$ in more complicated models. Thus if no clear pattern emerges from the correlogram of Δy_t—perhaps because σ_ζ^2 is positive—a stochastic trend, (3.2), can be fitted to the data and an LM test of $\rho = 0$ carried out. As already indicated, such tests are best developed in the frequency domain, and a detailed consideration of them is beyond the scope of this particular article. Instead, the Box–Ljung test was used to give an indication of model inadequacy in such cases.

Returning to the correlogram of Δy_t, it should be borne in mind that when this indicates white noise, the appropriate model is random walk plus drift; that is,

$$y_t = y_{t-1} + \beta + \eta_t, \qquad t = 2, \ldots, T. \qquad (4.3)$$

Thus in terms of (3.1) and (3.6), all of the parameters apart from σ_η^2 are zero. This model is known to give a reasonable fit to many economic time series, and in Harvey (1984) it is used as a yardstick in the R_D^2 measure of goodness of fit:

$$R_D^2 = 1 - T^*\tilde{\sigma}_p^2 \Big/ \sum_{t=2}^{T} (\Delta y_t - \Delta\bar{y})^2. \qquad (4.4)$$

4.4 Prediction

Given estimates of the unknown parameters σ_η^2, σ_ζ^2, σ_ω^2, σ^2, λ, and ρ, the Kalman filter produces the minimum mean squared estimators (MMSE's) of the elements in the state vector at time T. The estimator of β_T is the current estimate of the long-run growth rate, that is, the slope of the final forecast function for the log of the variable in question. For both (3.1) and (3.6), the forecast function exhibits damped cyclical behavior before settling down to a linear trend. The difference is that in (3.6) the intercept term in the final forecast function depends on the cyclical component, whereas in (3.1) it does not.

5. EMPIRICAL RESULTS FOR SERIES BEFORE 1948

The ML estimates for the following models are presented in Table 2: (a) the stochastic trend model, that is, (3.1) and (3.2), but without the cyclical component, ψ_t; (b) the trend plus cycle model, (3.1), (3.2), and (3.8); and (c) the cyclical trend model, (3.6), (3.7), and (3.8). The series contained observations up to and including 1947. A detailed analysis of the results obtained for each series is given in Sections 5.1–5.5.

The following points should be noted:

1. The period of a cycle corresponding to a frequency of λ radians is $2\pi/\lambda$ years. This is also, by definition, the period of the damped cycle in the autocorrelation and forecast functions. The peak in the power spectrum is usually at a slightly different fre-

Table 2. Maximum Likelihood Estimates of Parameters for (a) Stochastic Trend, (b) Trend Plus Cycle, and (c) Cyclical Trend for Pre-1948 Period

		Estimates (× 10⁴)											
Series	Model	σ_η^2	σ_ζ^2	σ_ω^2	σ^2	ρ	λ	$2\pi/\lambda$	Log L	$\tilde{\sigma}_p^2$ (× 10³)	Q[a]	H[b]	R_D^2
GNP	(a)	62.2	.0	—	.0	—	—	—	73.66	6.22	19.15* (10)	1.62	.00
(P = 10, m = 12)	(b)	23.7	6.1	3.3	.0	.97	.90	7.0	76.49	5.88	5.10 (6)	.82	.05
	(c)	.0	.0	24.3	4.9	.73	.72	8.7	77.83	4.98	5.90 (7)	.87	.20
Industrial	(a)	122	.0	—	.0	—	—	—	144.5	122	14.48 (9)	5.88*	.00
production	(b)	39.2	.0	52.9	.0	.79	.45	14.0	146.3	116	14.20* (6)	6.67*	.05
(P = 10, m = 28)	(c)	106.0	.0	.3	.0	1.00	.99	6.3	147.5	115	12.6* (6)	5.00*	.06
Unemployment	(a)	3120	.0	—	.0	—	—	—	2.59	312	15.55 (10)	.90	.00
rate	(b)	1810	.0	500	.0	.77	.91	6.9	3.81	297	13.78 (7)	1.00	.05
(P = 10, m = 18)	(c)	.0	.0	2140	.0	.56	1.38	4.5	5.58	283	7.81 (8)	1.11	.09
Consumer	(a)	.0	32.4	—	.0	—	—	—	203.4	3.24	11.70 (9)	.88	.19
prices	(b)	.0	5.6	6.8	.0	.87	.77	8.2	209.1	2.84	7.01 (6)	.83	.29
(P = 9, m = 28)	(c)	.0	2.1	15.6	.0	.69	.79	8.0	212.3	2.62	2.76 (6)	.98	.34
Common stock	(a)	295.0	.0	—	.0	—	—	—	92.4	295	21.80* (8)	4.76*	.00
prices	(b)	.0	.0	176	.0	.83	.47	13.3	99.3	234	8.85 (6)	5.88*	.21
(P = 8, m = 25)	(c)	229	.0	1.8	.0	1.00	.69	9.1	97.8	259	13.30* (5)	3.65*	.12

[a] Box–Ljung Q statistic: degrees of freedom (i.e., $P - n + 1$) are in parentheses; values of P are given under the series name; asterisks in this column indicate a significant value at the 5% level.

[b] Heteroscedasticity statistic: values of m are given under the series name; asterisks in this column indicate significant values at the 10% level for a two-sided test based on the F distribution of (m, m) df.

quency. This is, of course, similar to the situation that arises with a pure AR(2) process (see Box and Jenkins 1976, p. 63).

2. In assessing the degrees of freedom for the Q statistic, it is suggested that a degree of freedom not be deducted when a parameter is estimated as zero. If a degree of freedom is deducted, the Box–Ljung tests may give contradictory results. An example is provided by the fitting of model (a) to GNP. Since the estimates of σ_ζ^2 and σ^2 are both zero, the correlogram of residuals is identical to the correlogram of first differences, as given in Table 1. Thus the degrees of freedom of the Q statistic are best taken as P rather than $P - 2$. Of course, numerical values close to but not equal to zero present something of a dilemma in this respect, but there is obviously no clear-cut solution to the problem.

5.1 Real GNP

As already noted, the correlogram of first differences shows evidence of a cyclical movement, and an examination of the series itself indicates that a cycle with a period of, say, six to nine years might not be unreasonable. Models (b) and (c) give a cyclical component with a period within this range, and both are satisfactory with respect to the diagnostics. The estimate of ρ, however, is close to unity for the trend plus cycle model, and this indicates that the model may be inappropriate. The superiority of the cylical trend is confirmed by its better goodness of fit.

The standard errors of the estimators of ρ and λ in the cyclical trend model were estimated numerically as .15 and .16, respectively. If the distribution of the ML estimator of λ is taken to be approximately normal, then a 95% confidence interval for λ translates into a confidence interval of 6.0–15.7 years for the period. It may well be, however, that the distribution of the estimator of the period is closer to normality, in which case the confidence interval would be different. This question clearly requires further investigation, as indeed does that of the distribution of the estimators of the variance parameters.

The cyclical trend model has the estimate of σ_ζ^2 equal to zero. Taken together with σ^2 equal to zero, this suggests that the model can also be interpreted as ARIMA(2, 1, 2). Furthermore, the fact that the estimated value of σ_ω^2 is much greater than that of σ_η^2 indicates that an ARIMA(2, 1, 1) or even an ARIMA(2, 1, 0) model may not be a bad approximation. Fitting the second of these models by ordinary least squares gave a prediction error variance of 5.28×10^{-3}, which is not much more than that of the full model. The estimated parameters were $\hat{\phi}_1 = .417$ and $\hat{\phi}_2 = -.115$, and these yield a damped cyclical autocorrelation function with a period of 7.0 years. The model therefore displays some of the desirable characteristics for this series. The interesting question is whether the standard ARIMA-model selection methodology would lead to its being selected. As already noted, Nelson and Plosser (1982) felt that the correlogram indicated an ARIMA(0, 1, 1) model. (Fitting this model gives $\tilde{\sigma}_p^2 = 5.40 \times 10^{-3}$.) It is conceivable, however, that it could have been taken to indicate an ARIMA(2, 1, 0) model. But since the t statistic associated with ϕ_2 is only $-.65$, many researchers would have then dropped this term and estimated an ARIMA(1, 1, 0) model. On reexamining the correlogram, they might then have been led back to the choice of ARIMA(0, 1, 1), since the correlogram is certainly not consistent with the autocorrelation function of a first-order AR process.

5.2 Industrial Production

The correlogram of first differences given in Table 1 shows no obviously discernible pattern. This suggests that a random walk with drift, (4.3), may be the best one can do. The estimates for the more general models reported in Table 2 seem to confirm that this is the case. The stochastic trend model collapses directly to the random walk plus drift model, and the cyclical trend model has only a 6% better fit, coupled with an estimate of ρ equal to unity and a very small estimate of the cyclical variance σ_ω^2. This apparently indicates something close to a deterministic cycle. The estimates of the cyclical parameters in model (b) are more acceptable, although the period is 14 years and there is no improvement on model (c) in terms of goodness of fit. Furthermore, the value of the Q statistic is much the same as when no cycle is fitted.

The major problem with all of the models fitted lies in the unacceptably high values for the H statistic. This indicates increased volatility of the observations in the later years, a fact that is not immediately apparent from a casual inspection of the graph. In order to investigate this matter further, the series was split at 1909 (since the first observation on GNP is at 1909). The correlograms of first differences showed the following results: for 1860–1908, $Q(5) = 5.72$, $H(15) = 1.79$, $\tilde{\sigma}_p^2 = 57 \times 10^{-4}$; and for 1909–1947, $Q(5) = 5.14$, $H(12) = 1.45$, $\tilde{\sigma}_p^2 = 206 \times 10^{-4}$, where the figures in parentheses after Q and H denote P and m, respectively. There is still a slight indication of heteroscedasticity, but it is not significant, nor is the Box–Ljung statistic. The random walk plus drift model therefore seems appropriate for both parts of the series. It is interesting that when the cyclical trend model, (c), was fitted to the period 1909–1947, it collapsed to the random walk plus drift model. Thus the cycle found in GNP during that period apparently cannot be found in industrial production.

5.3 Unemployment Rate

Both cyclical models give sensible results, but the Q statistic for model (c) is lower, and the goodness of fit is better. The period of the cycle in model (c) is only

4.5 years, but it must be remembered that the series contains nineteen more observations than the GNP series.

Fitting an AR(2) process to first differences gives an almost identical fit to model (c), with the period of the implied cycle being 4.4 years.

5.4 Consumer Price Index

The interesting point about the consumer price series is that all three models have σ_ζ^2 positive. This is presumably because the series is much more volatile than real series, such as GNP and industrial production. A positive σ_ζ^2 indicates that second differencing is needed to render the series stationary, although this would not be apparent from the correlogram of first differences, which dies away in classical fashion. Presumably, part of the explanation lies in the exceptionally high value of .57 for $r_1(1)$. In any case, the results show that the correlogram can display some ambiguity in this respect. Having said that, it must be conceded that the obvious Box–Jenkins choice, namely ARIMA(0, 1, 1) plus constant, actually gives a better fit than either of the cyclical models. Specifically: $\tilde{\theta} = .69$ (.08), $\tilde{\beta} = .011$ (.009), $\tilde{\sigma}_p^2 = 2.47 \times 10^{-3}$, $R_D^2 = .38$, $Q = 4.38$, and $H = 1.08$, where β is the constant term, the figures in parentheses indicate asymptotic standard errors, the Q statistic is based on 8 df, and $m = 29$ in the H statistic.

Of the two cyclical models, the cyclical trend is to be preferred on the grounds of better goodness of fit and less residual serial correlation. The fact that the ARIMA(0, 1, 1) model gives a slightly better fit than the cyclical trend model and would clearly be selected on grounds of parsimony is perhaps, however, a little disconcerting. Nevertheless, model (c) does have a cyclical component that is remarkably consistent with the cycle found for GNP.

5.5 Stock Prices

This series is very erratic, and the results from fitting time series models, both structural and ARIMA, are not very convincing. The correlogram in Table 1 displays no clearly discernible pattern, yet the random walk plus drift model appears to be ruled out by the high Q statistic. Fitting the cyclical trend model, (c), is unsatisfactory because of the estimate of ρ equal to unity and the high value of Q. Curiously enough, the trend plus cycle model, (b), fares best, and the zero estimates for σ_η^2 and σ_ζ^2 actually seem to indicate that the trend is deterministic! An examination of a graph of the series shows that this is a plausible result, although it is also clear that such a deterministic trend could not possibly carry over into the post-1947 period.

Finally, observe that the H statistic indicates strong heteroscedasticity for all models. This seems to be due to the violent fluctuations in stock prices of the 1920s and 1930s, and it provides further evidence that fitting univariate time series models to the full period is not satisfactory.

5.6 General Comments

The following general comments can be made on the basis of the analysis of the five series discussed in Sections 5.1–5.5.

1. In all but one instance, the variance of the irregular component was found to be zero.
2. The variance parameter, σ_ζ^2, was found to be zero for all series except consumer prices (cf. the results of Harvey and Todd 1983).
3. The stochastic trend model, (a), reduced to a random walk plus drift model for all series, apart from consumer prices.
4. With the exception of the stock price series, the cyclical trend model is to be preferred to the trend plus cycle model. This means that the trend and cycle components cannot be separated. Instead, the growth rate of the trend decomposes into a long-run component, a transitory cyclical component, and a random component. In the case of GNP, the fact that σ_η^2 and σ_ζ^2 are both zero means that the growth rate in the trend is equal to a constant term plus the cyclical component.
5. The fact that the cyclical trend model is preferred in most cases is, in itself, evidence against the TS model of (1.1). Furthermore, when the trend plus cycle model is fitted, the possibility of a deterministic trend is effectively ruled out by a clear positive estimate of σ_η^2 or σ_ζ^2. The only exception is stock prices, but as already noted, the model is not really very convincing.
6. The assumption that after appropriate differencing, a series is stationary throughout its length is not one that can be taken for granted. For industrial production and stock prices, the lack of homogeneity is indicated by the diagnostics. Once this has been noticed, this finding also becomes apparent from a close inspection of the graphs of levels and first differences.
7. The structural models are more convincing for the real series—namely GNP, industrial production, and unemployment—than they are for consumer and stock prices.

6. EMPIRICAL RESULTS FOR THE POSTWAR PERIOD

The correlograms presented in Table 1 show the properties of the series in the postwar period (or more precisely, 1948–1970) to be very different from the properties of the same series before 1948. Unfortunately, the relatively small number of observations makes time series modeling difficult. Of course, the data set could be extended by including observations beyond 1970 or obtaining observations on a quarterly basis, or both. Doing this, however would have widened the scope of this article considerably and introduced a number of new issues.

Table 3. Maximum Likelihood Estimates of Parameters for (a) Stochastic Trend, (b) Trend Plus Cycle, and (c) Cyclical Trend for 1948–1970

		Estimates ($\times 10^4$)				Estimates							
Series	Model	σ_η^2	σ_ζ^2	σ_ω^2	σ^2	ρ	λ	$2\pi/\lambda$	Log L	$\tilde{\sigma}_p^2$ ($\times 10^{-4}$)	Q^a	H^b	R_D^2
GNP	(a)	7.52	.0	—	.65	—	—	—	61.74	8.77	9.26	.58	.01
	(c)	6.89	.0	1.68	.0	.37	3.14	2.0	61.80	8.77	9.00	.58	.01
Industrial production	(a)	12.6	.0	—	10.4	—	—	—	48.55	29.8	10.33	.88	.13
Unemployment rate	(a)	311	.0	—	188	—	—	—	16.58	632	4.95	.33	.06
	(b)	217	.0	99	49	.72	1.34	4.7	17.45	576	7.88	.45	.14
	(c)	24	.0	207	126	.68	1.43	4.4	17.38	578	7.66	.45	.14
Consumer prices	(a)	2.5	.73	—	.0	—	—	—	70.68	4.19	6.66	.06*	.00
	(c)	.0	.28	2.1	.0	.60	1.05	6.0	72.28	3.64	10.33	.13*	.13
Common stock prices	(a)	25.1	4.4	.0	44	—	—	—	34.36	126	12.55	1.06	.00
	(c)	.6	.68	8.09	202	.94	1.48	4.3	37.16	103	1.53	.81	.18

[a] For all series $P = 8$.
[b] For all series $m = 7$; asterisks indicate significant values at the 10% level.

Table 3 presents the ML estimates of the same models as Table 2 except that the series contain data from 1948 to 1970.

6.1 Real GNP

The correlogram of first differences in Table 1 indicates a random walk plus drift model, with the Q statistic taking the very low value of .43. Fitting the stochastic trend model (a) does, however, give a positive value for σ^2, as well as for σ_η^2. Although it is nice to note that the positive value is consistent with the negative (but insignificant) value of $r_1(1)$, the overall improvement in goodness of fit is very small.

6.2 Industrial Production

The sample autocorrelations of first differences are all small except for the one at lag one, which is $-.30$. This suggests a stochastic trend model with $\sigma^2 > 0$. The results show that such a model gives a reasonable fit with $R_D^2 = .13$. As with real GNP, no improvement in goodness of fit could be obtained by including a cyclical component in the model.

6.3 Unemployment Rate

The unemployment series shows evidence of a cycle, albeit a fairly weak one. The period of between four and five years is not unreasonable, and there is no strong indication of residual serial correlation or heteroscedasticity.

6.4 Consumer Prices

As with the pre-1948 price series, the estimate of σ_ζ^2 is positive for both (a) and (c). The period of the cycle for (c), however, is perhaps too big to make the model attractive, and in terms of goodness of fit, (a) shows no gain over the random walk plus drift model. Model (b), as usual, was even less attractive than (c). As with the pre-1948 observations, an ARIMA(0, 1, 1) model gives a better fit than the structural cyclical models. The extremely strong heteroscedasticity (with high variances at the beginning) casts doubt, however, on the validity of any of these models.

6.5 Common Stock Prices

For this series the message in the correlogram of first differences is not at all clear. The Q statistic is not significant at the 5% level of significance, but $r_1(2) = -.21$ and $r_1(4) = .41$. The stochastic trend model, (a), and the trend plus cycle model, (b), give the same result. There is no improvement, however, over the random walk plus drift model in terms of goodness of fit. The cyclical trend model, on the other hand, has $R_D^2 = .18$, and the estimated period of 4.3 years suggests that the model may provide a reasonable description of the series. Nevertheless one can hardly be enthusiastic about it on grounds of parsimony.

6.6 General Remarks

For most of the series it is possible to estimate models that are somewhat more complex than the random walk plus drift model and have a positive R_D^2. On a statistical criterion, however, such as the Akaike information criterion (AIC), the random walk plus drift model is to be preferred in all cases. On the other hand, it must be remembered that the sample size is small. Furthermore, the fact that for several series, the additional parameters estimated have a sensible interpretation is not without interest.

Regarding a deterministic trend, it is again very clear that the TS model of (1.1) cannot possibly hold.

Finally, as with the pre-1948 data, the structural models seem relatively less convincing when applied to consumer and stock prices.

7. CONCLUSIONS AND EXTENSIONS

The results of this research have implications on two fronts. In the first place, they provide useful information on the nature of economic time series. Second, they demonstrate the development of a new methodology for analyzing and modeling time series.

7.1 Statistical Methodology

In the prevailing Box–Jenkins approach, the idea is to select a parsimonious model from the class of ARIMA processes. This is done on the basis of the data themselves, with statistical tools such as the correlogram playing a prominent role in model selection. The structural approach, on the other hand, is based on a class of models containing unobserved components that have a direct interpretation. These include trend, seasonal, and cycle components. All are known to exist, to a greater or lesser extent, in economic time series, and so strong consideration is given to actually including such components in the model at the outset. The result is a change in emphasis in model selection. The reduced form of a structural model is still an ARIMA model, but it is subject to restrictions imposed by a priori considerations. Thus the "flexibility" of the Box–Jenkins approach to select models that may have unacceptable properties is lost. This does not mean that the information in the data, as reflected, say, in the correlogram, should be ignored; and there is certainly no case for fitting a structural model that is inconsistent with the correlogram. The argument is, perhaps, the other way round, however, in the sense that the correlogram may be very difficult to interpret in the absence of some prior notion of the sort of model that may be reasonable. The correlogram in Figure 2A provides an excellent example.

The construction of a structural time series model has two purposes. The first is to make forecasts. The second is to provide a way of presenting the "stylized facts" associated with the movements of a particular economic time series (cf. Ashenfelter and Card 1982). The structural time series model is not intended to represent the underlying data generation process. Rather, it aims to present the "facts" about the series in terms of a decomposition into trend, cycle, seasonal, and irregular components. These quantities are of interest to economists in themselves. Furthermore, they highlight the features of a series that must be accounted for by a properly formulated behavioral econometric model (cf. the "encompassing principle" advocated for econometric model building by Hendry and Richard 1983 and Mizon 1984). Of course, the two roles of a structural model are not entirely independent. A model that reflects the main features of a series is also likely to be good for forecasting.

7.2 Macroeconomic Time Series

In their 1982 article, Nelson and Plosser concluded that the deterministic trend with a stationary disturbance term (or cycle) superimposed on it was not a tenable model for economic time series. This article questions the methodology used to arrive at that conclusion. In particular, objections have been raised against the way in which Nelson and Plosser used the principle of parsimony to effectively identify an ARIMA(0, 1, 1) model for the time series in question and against the fact that they assumed a constant structure throughout the whole time period. Nevertheless, the results obtained here using the structural methodology strongly support the conclusion reached by Nelson and Plosser.

For the data up to 1947, the most interesting conclusion is that a stochastic cycle is best modeled within the trend. In other words, the cycle is an intrinsic part of the trend rather than a separate component that can just be added on afterwards. For the period 1948–1970, a faint cycle can be detected in some series, but it is difficult to justify on statistical grounds the inclusion of a cyclical component anywhere in the model. A stochastic trend model is sufficient, and in many cases (e.g., real GNP) this model effectively reduced to a random walk plus drift model. The absence of a significant cycle explains why, for many postwar series, a trend plus seasonal plus irregular components model can be adopted for monthly and quarterly observations (e.g., see Harvey and Todd 1983). Within a Box–Jenkins framework, the widespread adoption of the airline model [i.e., ARIMA(0, 1, 1) × $(0, 1, 1)_s$] is a reflection of the same phenomenon. Of course, after 1970 many economic time series became more volatile again and it could be argued that the reintroduction of a cyclical component is desirable.

7.3 Extensions

The model building in this article has been based on annual data. The extension of the state-space model to handle quarterly or monthly observations, however, is relatively straightforward. Another interesting extension is to include more than one cyclical component in the model. If it is felt that there may be a 20-year cycle as well as a 5-year cycle, then both components may be modeled by (3.8) and incorporated into the overall structure as appropriate.

Structural models other than those described here may be appropriate in other circumstances, particularly when one moves away from economic time series. There is nothing necessarily restrictive about the structural class; the only requirement is that the model be set up in terms of components that have some kind of interpretation.

In the examples reported here, the Box–Ljung test was used as a diagnostic for serial correlation. As already noted, the LM principle may yield more satisfactory tests, and this is currently being investigated. A rather rough-and-ready heteroscedasticity test was also used. Heteroscedasticity is rarely tested for in time series modeling, and the original motivation for including it here was to check on the suitability of the logarithmic transformation. Further analysis prompted by significant values of the test statistic, however, revealed that the assumption of homoscedasticity cannot always be taken for granted in economic time series. This then raises the question of how heteroscedasticity is best modeled. One possibility is to develop the autoregressive conditional heteroscedasticity (ARCH) framework of Engle (1982) and Weiss (1984).

As Figures 1B and 2 reveal, the stationarity of an economic time series (after appropriate differencing) may not be a tenable assumption. Indeed, the remarkable thing about differenced economic time series is not that they are sometimes nonstationary, but rather that they are occasionally stationary! One of the attractions of the state-space approach in this context is that it provides a framework for incorporating changing structures into the model. The question of exactly how this should be done and how various types of change might be detected clearly warrants further research.

ACKNOWLEDGMENTS

The author would like to thank Charles Nelson for supplying the data used in this study and Simon Peters for carrying out the computations. The author would also like to thank both of them for their comments on the original draft of the article. The work was supported by the Economic and Social Research Council as part of the Dynamic Econometric Models, Expectations, Innovations, and Choice econometrics project at the London School of Economics.

APPENDIX: LAGRANGE MULTIPLIER TEST FOR A CYCLE

Consider model (3.6) with $\sigma^2 = \sigma_\xi^2 = 0$ and with $\sigma_\omega^2 = \sigma_\omega^{2*}$ in the cycle (3.9). We wish to test H_0: $\rho = 0$ against H_1: $\rho > 0$. Since the model is not identifiable under H_0, it is also necessary to set $\sigma_\eta^2 = 0$ (cf. the use of a similar device in Poskitt and Tremayne 1980).

Although tests of this kind are generally best developed in the frequency domain (as in Harvey and Hotta 1982), the present test can also be derived in the time domain by noting that the canonical form of the model is

$$(1 - 2\rho\cdot\cos\lambda\cdot L + \rho^2L^2)\Delta y_t^* = \xi_t + \theta(\rho)\xi_{t-1}, \quad \text{(A.1)}$$

where ξ_t is a white noise disturbance term and Δy_t^* is Δy_t in deviation from the mean form. The moving average parameter, $\theta(\rho)$, is a nonlinear function of ρ, and so $\partial\theta(\rho)/\partial\rho = 0$ when $\rho = 0$. Furthermore, it will be clear from (3.9) that when $\rho = 0$, $\xi_t = \omega_t$ and $\theta(\rho) = 0$.

Suppose that λ is regarded as being known. Although (A.1) is an ARMA(2, 1) process, it depends on a single unknown parameter, and a Lagrange multiplier test can be constructed by regressing ξ_t on $\partial\xi_t/\partial\rho$, with both evaluated at $\rho = 0$. This suggests a test statistic of TR^2, where R^2 is the coefficient of (multiple) correlation from a regression of $\hat{\xi}_t = \Delta y_t$ on $(-2\cos\lambda)\Delta y_{t-1}^*$. The result is exactly the same, however, if Δy_t^* is simply regressed on Δy_{t-1}^*. This regression does not depend on λ. Hence it is valid for all λ, and so it is immaterial whether λ is known or not.

This argument suggests a test based on $Tr_1^2(1)$, with the distribution under the null hypothesis being χ_1^2. Alternatively, the von Neumann ratio may be used, although it must be remembered that the test is two-sided, since $\rho_1(1)$ may be negative or positive for (3.9). Note that in a somewhat wider context, the same argument can be used to show that the Durbin–Watson test is appropriate when the disturbance term in a static linear regression is assumed to follow (3.9).

[*Received August 1984. Revised December 1984.*]

REFERENCES

Ashenfelter, O., and Card, D. (1982), "Time Series Representations of Economic Variables and Alternative Models of the Labour Market," *Review of Economic Studies*, 49, 761–782.

Beveridge, S., and Nelson, C. R. (1981), "A New Approach to Decomposition of Economic Time Series Into Permanent and Transitory Components With Particular Attention to Measurement of the 'Business Cycle,'" *Journal of Monetary Economics*, 7, 151–174.

Box, G. E. P., and Jenkins, G. M. (1976), *Time Series Analysis: Forecasting and Control* (rev. ed.), San Francisco: Holden-Day.

Dickey, D. A., and Fuller, W. A. (1979), "Distribution of the Estimators for Autoregressive Time Series With a Unit Root," *Journal of the American Statistical Association*, 74, 427–431.

Engle, R. F. (1978), "Estimating Structural Models of Seasonality," in *Seasonal Analysis of Economic Time Series*, ed. A. Zellner, Washington, DC: U.S. Dept. of Commerce, Bureau of the Census, pp. 281–308.

——— (1982), "Autoregressive Conditional Heteroscedasticity With Estimates of the Variance of UK Inflation," *Econometrica*, 50, 987–1007.

Franzini, L., and Harvey, A. (1983), "Testing for Deterministic Trend and Seasonal Components in Time Series Models," *Biometrika*, 70, 673–682.

Harrison, P. J., and Akram, M. (1983), "Generalised Exponentially Weighted Regression and Parsimonious Dynamic Linear Modelling," in *Time Series Analysis: Theory and Practice* (Vol. 3), ed. O. D. Anderson, Amsterdam: North-Holland, pp. 19–50.

Harrison, P. J., and Stevens, C. F. (1976), "Bayesian Forecasting," *Journal of the Royal Statistical Society*, Ser. B, 38, 205–247.

Harvey, A. C. (1983), "The Formulation of Structural Time Series Models in Discrete and Continuous Time," *Questiio*, 7, 563–575.

——— (1984), "A Unified View of Statistical Forecasting Procedures," *Journal of Forecasting*, 3, 245–275.

Harvey, A. C., and Hotta, L. (1982), "Specification Tests for Dynamic Models With Unobserved Components," unpublished manuscript, London School of Economics, Dept. of Statistics.

Harvey, A. C., and Peters, S. (1984), "Estimation Procedures for Structural Time Series Models," Econometrics Programme Discussion Paper A44, London School of Economics, Dept. of Economics.

Harvey, A. C., and Todd, P. H. J. (1983), "Forecasting Economic Time Series With Structural and Box-Jenkins Models" (with discussion), *Journal of Business & Economic Statistics*, 1, 299–315.

Hendry, D. F., and Richard, J.-F. (1983), "The Econometric Analysis of Economic Time Series," *International Statistical Review*, 51, 111–164.

Mizon, G. E. (1984), "The Encompassing Approach in Econometrics," in *Econometrics and Quantitative Economics*, eds. D. F. Hendry and K. F. Wallis, Oxford: Blackwell, pp. 135–172.

Nelson, C. R., and Kang, H. (1981), "Spurious Periodicity in Inappropriately Detrended Time Series," *Econometrica*, 49, 741–751.

——— (1984), "Pitfalls in the Use of Time as an Explanatory Variable in Regression," *Journal of Business & Economic Statistics*, 2, 73–82.

Nelson, C. R., and Plosser, C. I. (1982), "Trends and Random Walks in Macroeconomic Time Series," *Journal of Monetary Economics*, 10, 139–162.

Nerlove, M., Grether, D. M., and Carvalho, J. L. (1979), *Analysis of Economic Time Series*, New York: Academic Press.

Plosser, C. I., and Schwert, C. W. (1977), "Estimation of a Noninvertible Moving Average Process: The Case of Overdifferencing," *Journal of Econometrics*, 6, 199–224.

Poskitt, D. S., and Tremayne, A. R. (1980), "Testing the Specification of a Fitted Autoregressive-Moving Average Model," *Biometrika*, 67, 359–363.

Sargan, J. D., and Bhargava, A. (1983), "Maximum Likelihood Estimation of Regression Models With First-Order Moving Average Errors When the Root Lies on the Unit Circle," *Econometrica*, 51, 799–820.

Weiss, A. A. (1984), "ARMA Models With ARCH Errors," *Journal of Time Series Analysis*, 5, 129–143.

Part IV
Unit Roots, Detrending and Non-stationarity

[13]

Distribution of the Estimators for Autoregressive Time Series With a Unit Root

DAVID A. DICKEY and WAYNE A. FULLER*

Let n observations $Y_1, Y_2, \ldots, Y_n$ be generated by the model $Y_t = \rho Y_{t-1} + e_t$, where Y_0 is a fixed constant and $\{e_t\}_{t=1}^n$ is a sequence of independent normal random variables with mean 0 and variance σ^2. Properties of the regression estimator of ρ are obtained under the assumption that $\rho = \pm 1$. Representations for the limit distributions of the estimator of ρ and of the regression t test are derived. The estimator of ρ and the regression t test furnish methods of testing the hypothesis that $\rho = 1$.

KEY WORDS: Time series; Autoregressive; Nonstationary; Random walk; Differencing.

1. INTRODUCTION

Consider the autoregressive model

$$Y_t = \rho Y_{t-1} + e_t\ , \quad t = 1, 2, \ldots, \tag{1.1}$$

where $Y_0 = 0$, ρ is a real number, and $\{e_t\}$ is a sequence of independent normal random variables with mean zero and variance σ^2 [i.e., e_t NID$(0, \sigma^2)$].

The time series Y_t converges (as $t \to \infty$) to a stationary time series if $|\rho| < 1$. If $|\rho| = 1$, the time series is not stationary and the variance of Y_t is $t\sigma^2$. The time series with $\rho = 1$ is sometimes called a random walk. If $|\rho| > 1$, the time series is not stationary and the variance of the time series grows exponentially as t increases.

Given n observations $Y_1, Y_2, \ldots, Y_n$, the maximum likelihood estimator of ρ is the least squares estimator

$$\hat{\rho} = (\sum_{t=1}^{n} Y_{t-1}^2)^{-1} \sum_{t=1}^{n} Y_t Y_{t-1}\ . \tag{1.2}$$

Rubin (1950) showed that $\hat{\rho}$ is a consistent estimator for all values of ρ. White (1958) obtained the limiting joint-moment generating function for the properly normalized numerator and denominator of $\hat{\rho} - \rho$. For $|\rho| \neq 1$ he was able to invert the joint-moment generating function to obtain the limiting distribution of $\hat{\rho} - \rho$. For $|\rho| < 1$ the limiting distribution of $n^{\frac{1}{2}}(\hat{\rho} - \rho)$ is normal. For $|\rho| > 1$ the limiting distribution of $|\rho|^n(\rho^2 - 1)^{-1}(\hat{\rho} - \rho)$ is Cauchy. For $\rho = 1$, White was able to represent the limiting distribution of $n(\hat{\rho} - 1)$ as that of the ratio of two integrals defined on the Wiener process.

Rao (1961) extended White's results to higher-order autoregressive time series whose characteristic equations have a single root exceeding one and remaining roots less than one in absolute value. Anderson (1959) obtained the limiting distributions of estimators for higher-order processes with more than one root exceeding one in absolute value.

The hypothesis that $\rho = 1$ is of some interest in applications because it corresponds to the hypothesis that it is appropriate to transform the time series by differencing. Currently, practitioners may decide to difference a time series on the basis of visual inspection of the autocorrelation function. For example, see Box and Jenkins (1970, p. 174). The autocorrelation function of the deviations from the fitted model is then investigated as a test of the appropriateness of the model. Box and Jenkins (1970, p. 291) suggested the Box and Pierce (1970) test statistic

$$Q_K = n \sum_{k=1}^{K} r_k^2\ , \tag{1.3}$$

where

$$r_k = (\sum_{t=1}^{n} \hat{e}_t^2)^{-1} \sum_{t=k+1}^{n} \hat{e}_t \hat{e}_{t-k}$$

and the $\hat{e}_t$'s are the residuals from the fitted model. Under the null hypothesis, the statistic Q_K is approximately distributed as a chi-squared random variable with $K - p$ degrees of freedom, where p is the number of parameters estimated. If $\{Y_t\}$ satisfies (1.1) then $p = 0$ under the null hypothesis and $\hat{e}_t = Y_t - Y_{t-1}$.

The likelihood ratio test of the hypothesis H_0: $\rho = 1$ is a function of

$$\hat{\tau} = (\hat{\rho} - 1)S_e^{-1}(\sum_{t=2}^{n} Y_{t-1}^2)^{\frac{1}{2}}\ ,$$

where

$$S_e^2 = (n-2)^{-1} \sum_{t=2}^{n} (Y_t - \hat{\rho} Y_{t-1})^2\ .$$

In this article we derive representations for the limiting distributions of $\hat{\rho}$ and of $\hat{\tau}$, given that $|\rho| = 1$. The representations permit construction of tables of the percentage points for the statistics. The statistics $\hat{\rho}$ and $\hat{\tau}$

* Wayne A. Fuller is Professor of Statistics at Iowa State University, Ames, IA 50011. David A. Dickey is Assistant Professor of Statistics at North Carolina State University, Raleigh, NC 27650. This research was partially supported by Joint Statistical Agreement No. 76-66 with the Bureau of the Census.

© Journal of the American Statistical Association
June 1979, Volume 74, Number 366
Theory and Methods Section

are also generalized to models containing intercept and time terms.

In Section 4 the Monte Carlo method is used to compare the power of the statistics $\hat{\tau}$ and $\hat{\rho}$ with that of Q_K. Examples are given in Section 5.

2. MODELS AND ESTIMATORS

The class of models we investigate consists of (a) the model (1.1), (b) the model

$$Y_t = \mu + \rho Y_{t-1} + e_t \ , \quad t = 1, 2, \ldots \qquad (2.1)$$
$$Y_0 = 0$$

and (c) the model

$$Y_t = \mu + \beta t + \rho Y_{t-1} + e_t \ , \quad t = 1, 2, \ldots \qquad (2.2)$$
$$Y_0 = 0 \ .$$

Assume n observations $Y_1, Y_2, \ldots, Y_n$ are available for analysis and define the $(n-1)$ dimensional vectors,

$$\mathbf{1}' = (1, 1, 1, \ldots, 1) \ ,$$
$$\mathbf{t}' = (1 - (n/2), 2 - (n/2), 3 - (n/2), \ldots, n - 1 - (n/2)) \ ,$$
$$\mathbf{Y}_t' = (Y_2, Y_3, Y_4, \ldots, Y_n) \ ,$$
$$\mathbf{Y}_{t-1}' = (Y_1, Y_2, Y_3, \ldots, Y_{n-1}) \ .$$

Let $\mathbf{U}_1 = \mathbf{Y}_{t-1}$, $\mathbf{U}_2 = (\mathbf{1}, \mathbf{Y}_{t-1})$, and $\mathbf{U}_3 = (\mathbf{1}, \mathbf{t}, \mathbf{Y}_{t-1})$. We define $\hat{\rho}_\mu$ as the last entry in the vector

$$(\mathbf{U}_2'\mathbf{U}_2)^{-1}\mathbf{U}_2'\mathbf{Y}_t \ , \qquad (2.3)$$

and define $\hat{\rho}_\tau$ as the last entry in the vector

$$(\mathbf{U}_3'\mathbf{U}_3)^{-1}\mathbf{U}_3'\mathbf{Y}_t \ . \qquad (2.4)$$

The statistics analogous to the regression t statistics for the test of the hypothesis that $\rho = 1$ are

$$\hat{\tau} = (\hat{\rho} - 1)(S_{e1}^2 c_1)^{-\frac{1}{2}} \ , \qquad (2.5)$$

$$\hat{\tau}_\mu = (\hat{\rho}_\mu - 1)(S_{e2}^2 c_2)^{-\frac{1}{2}} \ , \qquad (2.6)$$

$$\hat{\tau}_\tau = (\hat{\rho}_\tau - 1)(S_{e3}^2 c_3)^{-\frac{1}{2}} \ , \qquad (2.7)$$

where S_{ek}^2 is the appropriate regression residual mean square

$$S_{ek}^2 = (n - k - 1)^{-1}[\mathbf{Y}_t'(\mathbf{I} - \mathbf{U}_k(\mathbf{U}_k'\mathbf{U}_k)^{-1}\mathbf{U}_k')\mathbf{Y}_t] \qquad (2.8)$$

and c_k is the lower-right element of $(\mathbf{U}_k'\mathbf{U}_k)^{-1}$.

3. LIMIT DISTRIBUTIONS

As the first step in obtaining the limit distributions we investigate the quadratic forms appearing in the statistics. Because the estimators are ratios of quadratic forms we lose no generality by assuming $\sigma^2 = 1$ in the sequel.

3.1 Canonical Representation of the Statistics

Given that $\rho = 1$, the quadratic form $\sum_{t=2}^n Y_{t-1}^2$ can be expressed as $\mathbf{e}_n'\mathbf{A}_n\mathbf{e}_n$, where $\mathbf{e}_n' = (e_1, e_2, \ldots, e_{n-1})$, the elements α_{ij} of $\mathbf{A}_n^{-1}$ satisfy $\alpha_{11} = 1$, $\alpha_{jj} = 2$ for $j > 1$, $\alpha_{j,j-1} = \alpha_{j,j+1} = -1$ for all j, and $\alpha_{ij} = 0$ otherwise. By a result of Rutherford (1946), the roots of $\mathbf{A}_n$ are

$$\lambda_{in} = (\tfrac{1}{4}) \sec^2((n - i)\pi/(2n - 1)) \ , \quad i = 1, 2, \ldots, n - 1 \ .$$

Let $\mathbf{M}$ be the $n - 1$ by $n - 1$ orthonormal matrix whose ith row is the eigenvector of $\mathbf{A}_n$ corresponding to λ_{in}. The itth element of $\mathbf{M}$ is

$$m_{it} = 2(2n - 1)^{-\frac{1}{2}} \cdot \cos[(4n - 2)^{-1}(2t - 1)(2i - 1)\pi] \ , \qquad (3.1)$$

and we can express the normalized denominator sum of squares appearing in $\hat{\rho}$ as

$$\Gamma_n = n^{-2} \sum_{t=2}^{n} Y_{t-1}^2 = n^{-2} \sum_{i=1}^{n-1} \lambda_{in} Z_{in}^2 \ , \qquad (3.2)$$

where $\mathbf{Z} = (Z_{1n}, Z_{2n}, \ldots, Z_{n-1,n})' = \mathbf{M}\mathbf{e}_n$.

Let

$$\mathbf{H}_n = n^{-\frac{1}{2}} \cdot \begin{bmatrix} n^2 & n^2 & n^2 & & n^2 \\ n(n-1) & n(n-2) & n(n-3) & \ldots & n \\ 0 & n-2 & 2(n-3) & \ldots & n-2 \end{bmatrix}$$

and

$$(T_n, W_n, V_n)' = n^{-\frac{1}{2}}(Y_{n-1}, n^{-1} \sum_{t=2}^{n} Y_{t-1}, n^{-2} \sum_{j=1}^{n-1} (n - j)(j - 1)e_j)' = \mathbf{H}_n\mathbf{e}_n = \mathbf{H}_n\mathbf{M}^{-1}\mathbf{Z} \ . \qquad (3.3)$$

Then

$$n(\hat{\rho} - 1) = (2\Gamma_n)^{-1}(T_n^2 - 1) + O_p(n^{-\frac{1}{2}}) \ , \qquad (3.4)$$

$$n(\hat{\rho}_\mu - 1) = (2\Gamma_n - 2W_n^2)^{-1}(T_n^2 - 1 - 2T_nW_n) + O_p(n^{-\frac{1}{2}}) \ , \qquad (3.5)$$

$$n(\hat{\rho}_\tau - 1) = [2(\Gamma_n - W_n^2 - 3V_n^2)]^{-1} \cdot [(T_n - 2W_n)(T_n - 6V_n) - 1] + O_p(n^{-\frac{1}{2}}) \ . \qquad (3.6)$$

3.2 Representations for the Limit Distributions

Having expressed $n(\hat{\rho} - 1)$, $n(\hat{\rho}_\mu - 1)$, and $n(\hat{\rho}_\tau - 1)$ in terms of $(\Gamma_n, T_n, W_n, V_n)$ we obtain the limiting distribution of the vector random variable. The following lemma will be used in our derivation of the limit distribution.

Lemma 1: Let $\{Z_i\}_{i=1}^\infty$ be a sequence of independent random variables with zero means and common variance σ^2. Let $\{w_i; i = 1, 2, \ldots\}$ be a sequence of real numbers and let $\{w_{in}; i = 1, 2, \ldots, n-1; n = 1, 2, \ldots\}$ be a triangular array of real numbers. If

$$\sum_{i=1}^{\infty} w_i^2 < \infty \ ,$$

$$\lim_{n\to\infty} \sum_{i=1}^{n-1} w_{in}^2 = \sum_{i=1}^{\infty} w_i^2 \ ,$$

and

$$\lim_{n\to\infty} w_{in} = w_i ,$$

then $\sum_{i=1}^{\infty} w_i Z_i$ is well defined as a limit in mean square and

$$p \lim \{\sum_{i=1}^{n} w_{in} Z_i\} = \sum_{i=1}^{\infty} w_i Z_i .$$

Proof: Let $\epsilon > 0$ be given. Then we can choose an M such that

$$\sigma^2 \sum_{i=M+1}^{\infty} w_i^2 < \epsilon/9$$

and

$$\sigma^2 |\sum_{i=1}^{n} w_{in}^2 - \sum_{i=1}^{\infty} w_i^2| < \epsilon/9 ,$$

for all $n > M$. Furthermore, given M, we can choose $N_0 > M$ such that $n > N_0$ implies

$$\sigma^2 \sum_{i=1}^{M} (w_{in} - w_i)^2 < \epsilon/9$$

and

$$\sigma^2 \sum_{i=M+1}^{n} w_{in}^2 < 3\epsilon/9 .$$

Hence, for all $n > N_0$,

$$\text{var}\{\sum_{i=1}^{n} w_{in} Z_i - \sum_{i=1}^{\infty} w_i Z_i\} < \epsilon ,$$

and the result follows by Chebyshev's inequality.

Theorem 1: Let $\{Z_i\}_{i=1}^{\infty}$ be a sequence of NID(0, 1) random variables. Let $\eta_n' = (\Gamma_n, T_n, W_n, V_n)$, where the elements of the vector are defined in (3.2) and (3.3). Let

$$\eta' = (\Gamma, T, W, V) ,$$

where

$$(\Gamma, T) = (\sum_{i=1}^{\infty} \gamma_i^2 Z_i^2, \sum_{i=1}^{\infty} 2^{\frac{1}{2}} \gamma_i Z_i) ,$$

$$(W, V) = (\sum_{i=1}^{\infty} 2^{\frac{1}{2}} \gamma_i^2 Z_i, \sum_{i=1}^{\infty} 2^{\frac{1}{2}} [2\gamma_i^3 - \gamma_i^2] Z_i) ,$$

$$\gamma_i = (-1)^{i+1} \sqrt{\gamma_i^2} ,$$

and

$$\gamma_i^2 = \lim_{n\to\infty} n^{-2} \lambda_{in} = 4[(2i-1)\pi]^{-2} .$$

Then η_n converges in distribution to η, that is,

$$\eta_n \xrightarrow{\mathcal{L}} \eta .$$

Proof: Note that η is a well-defined random variable because $\sum_{i=1}^{\infty} \gamma_i^k < \infty$ for $k = 2, 3, \ldots, 6$. Let ξ_{in} be the ith column of $\mathbf{H}_n \mathbf{M}^{-1}$, where

$$\xi_{in} = (a_{in}, b_{in}, g_{in})'$$
$$= [\text{cov}(T_n, Z_{in}), \text{cov}(W_n, Z_{in}), \text{cov}(V_n, Z_{in})]' .$$

For fixed i,

$$\lim_{n\to\infty} \xi_{in} = \xi_i = (a_i, b_i, g_i)'$$
$$= 2^{\frac{1}{2}}(\gamma_i, \gamma_i^2, 2\gamma_i^3 - \gamma_i^2)' . \quad (3.7)$$

By Jolley (1961, p. 56, #307,308) we have

$$\sum_{i=1}^{\infty} (a_i^2, b_i^2, g_i^2) = (1, 1/3, 1/30) .$$

Let

$$(\Gamma_n^*, T_n^*) = (\sum_{i=1}^{n-1} n^{-2} \lambda_{in} Z_i^2, \sum_{i=1}^{n-1} a_{in} Z_i) ,$$

$$(W_n^*, V_n^*) = (\sum_{i=1}^{n-1} b_{in} Z_i, \sum_{i=1}^{n-1} g_{in} Z_i) .$$

Now, for example, by (3.3)

$$\lim_{n\to\infty} \sum_{i=1}^{n-1} a_{in}^2 = \lim_{n\to\infty} \text{var}\{T_n^*\} = \lim_{n\to\infty} \text{var}\{T_n\} = 1 .$$

Therefore, by (3.7) and Lemma 1, T_n^* converges in probability to T. It follows by analogous arguments that $(\Gamma_n^*, T_n^*, W_n^*, V_n^*)$ converges in probability to (Γ, T, W, V). Because the distribution of $(\Gamma_n^*, T_n^*, W_n^*, V_n^*)$ is the same as that of η_n we obtain the conclusion.

Corollary 1: Let Y_t satisfy (1.1) with $\rho = 1$. Then

$$n(\hat{\rho} - 1) \xrightarrow{\mathcal{L}} \tfrac{1}{2}(\Gamma^{-1}(T^2 - 1) ,$$

$$n(\hat{\rho}_\mu - 1) \xrightarrow{\mathcal{L}} \tfrac{1}{2}(\Gamma - {}^2W)^{-1}[(T^2 - 1) - 2TW] ,$$

$$\hat{\tau} \xrightarrow{\mathcal{L}} \tfrac{1}{2}\Gamma^{-\frac{1}{2}}(T^2 - 1) ,$$

and

$$\hat{\tau}_\mu \xrightarrow{\mathcal{L}} \tfrac{1}{2}(\Gamma - W^2)^{-\frac{1}{2}}[(T^2 - 1) - 2TW] .$$

Let Y_t satisfy (2.1) with $\rho = 1$. Then

$$n(\hat{\rho}_\tau - 1) \xrightarrow{\mathcal{L}} \tfrac{1}{2}(\Gamma - W^2 - 3V^2)^{-1} \cdot[(T - 2W)(T - 6V) - 1]$$

and

$$\hat{\tau}_\tau \xrightarrow{\mathcal{L}} \tfrac{1}{2}(\Gamma - W^2 - 3V^2)^{-\frac{1}{2}}[(T - 2W)(T - 6V) - 1] .$$

Proof: The proof is an immediate consequence of Theorem 1 because the denominator quadratic forms in $\hat{\rho}$, $\hat{\rho}_\mu$, $\hat{\rho}_\tau$ are continuous functions of η that have probability 1 of being positive and the S_{ek}^2 of (2.8) converge in probability to σ^2.

The numerator and denominator of the limit representation of $n(\hat{\rho} - 1)$ are consistent with White's (1958) limit joint-moment generating function.

Note that the limiting distributions of $\hat{\rho}_\mu$ and $\hat{\tau}_\mu$ are obtained under the assumption that the constant term μ is zero. Likewise, the limiting distributions of $\hat{\rho}_\tau$ and $\hat{\tau}_\tau$ are derived under the assumption that the coefficient for time, β, is zero. The distributions of $\hat{\rho}_\tau$ and $\hat{\tau}_\tau$ are unaffected by the value of μ in (2.2). If $\mu \neq 0$ for (2.1) or $\beta \neq 0$ for (2.2), the limiting distributions of $\hat{\tau}_\mu$ and $\hat{\tau}_\tau$ are normal. Thus if (2.1) is the maintained model and the statistic $\hat{\tau}_\mu$ is used to test the hypothesis $\rho = 1$, the hypothesis will be accepted with probability greater than the nominal level where $\mu \neq 0$.

By the results of Fuller (1976, p. 370), the limiting distributions of $\hat{\rho}$, $\hat{\rho}_\mu$, and $\hat{\rho}_\tau$, given that $\rho = -1$, are identical and equal to the mirror image of the limiting distribution of $\hat{\rho}$ given that $\rho = 1$. Likewise, the limiting distributions of $\hat{\tau}$, $\hat{\tau}_\mu$, and $\hat{\tau}_\tau$ for $\rho = -1$ are identical and equal to the mirror image of the limiting distribution of $\hat{\tau}$ for $\rho = 1$.

In our derivations Y_0 is fixed. The distributions of $\hat{\rho}_\mu$ and $\hat{\tau}_\mu$ do not depend on the value of Y_0. The limiting distribution of $\hat{\rho}$ does not depend on Y_0, but the small-sample distribution of $\hat{\rho}$ will be influenced by Y_0.

In the derivations we assumed the e_t to be NID$(0, \sigma^2)$. The limiting distributions also hold for e_t that are independent and identically distributed nonnormal random variables with mean zero and variance σ^2. White (1958) and Hasza (1977) have discussed this generalization.

The statistic $\hat{\tau}$ is a monotone function of the likelihood ratio when Y_0 is fixed under the null model of $\rho = 1$ and under the alternative model of $\rho \neq 1$. Tests based on the τ statistics are not likelihood ratios and not necessarily the most powerful that can be constructed if, for example, the alternative model is that $(Y_0, Y_1, \ldots, Y_n)$ is a portion of a realization from a stationary autoregressive process.

A set of tables of the percentiles of the distributions is given in Fuller (1976, pp. 371,373) and a slightly more accurate set in Dickey (1976). Dickey also presents details of the table construction and gives estimates of the sampling error of the estimated percentiles.

4. POWER COMPARISONS

The powers of the statistics studied in this article were compared with that of the Box-Pierce Q statistic in a Monte Carlo study using the model

$$Y_t = \rho Y_{t-1} + e_t \ , \quad t = 1, 2, \ldots, n \ ,$$

where the $e_t \sim \text{NID}(0, \sigma^2)$ and $Y_0 = 0$. Four thousand samples of size $n = 50$, 100, 250 were generated for $\rho = .80$, .90, .95, .99, 1.00, 1.02, 1.05. The random-number generator SUPER DUPER from McGill University was used to create the pseudonormal variables.

Eight two-sided size .05 tests of the hypothesis $\rho = 1$ were applied to each sample. The tests were $\hat{\rho}$, $\hat{\tau}$, $\hat{\rho}_\mu$, $\hat{\tau}_\mu$, Q_1, Q_5, Q_{10}, Q_{20}, where Q_K is the Box-Pierce Q statistic defined in (1.3) with $\hat{e}_t = Y_t - Y_{t-1}$.

There are several conclusions to be drawn from the results presented in the table. First, the Q statistics are less powerful than the statistics introduced in this article. For example, when $n = 250$ and $\rho = .8$ the worst of the statistics introduced in this article rejected the null hypothesis 100 percent of the time, while the best of the Q statistics rejected the null hypothesis in only 45 percent of the samples.

Second, the performances of $\hat{\rho}$ and $\hat{\tau}$ were similar, and they were uniformly more powerful than the other test

Monte Carlo Power of Two-Sided Size .05 Tests of $\rho = 1$

		ρ						
n	*Test*	*.80*	*.90*	*.95*	*.99*	*1.00*	*1.02*	*1.05*
50	Q_1	.09	.05	.05	.04	.04	.07	.47
	Q_5	.07	.04	.03	.03	.04	.08	.53
	Q_{10}	.05	.04	.03	.03	.03	.09	.54
	Q_{20}	.03	.02	.02	.02	.02	.08	.52
	$\hat{\rho}$	.57	.18	.08	.05	.05	.14	.71
	$\hat{\tau}$	.57	.18	.08	.04	.05	.23	.70
	$\hat{\rho}_\mu$	.28	.10	.06	.05	.06	.11	.67
	$\hat{\tau}_\mu$	.18	.06	.04	.04	.05	.13	.68
100	Q_1	.15	.07	.05	.04	.05	.26	.94
	Q_5	.13	.08	.05	.04	.04	.34	.95
	Q_{10}	.11	.06	.05	.03	.04	.37	.95
	Q_{20}	.08	.05	.04	.03	.03	.38	.95
	$\hat{\rho}$	.99	.55	.17	.05	.05	.54	.98
	$\hat{\tau}$	.99	.55	.17	.04	.05	.59	.97
	$\hat{\rho}_\mu$	.86	.30	.10	.05	.05	.49	.98
	$\hat{\tau}_\mu$	.73	.18	.06	.04	.05	.51	.98
250	Q_1	.34	.12	.06	.05	.06	.94	1.00
	Q_5	.45	.13	.07	.04	.05	.95	1.00
	Q_{10}	.34	.12	.06	.04	.05	.95	1.00
	Q_{20}	.24	.10	.05	.04	.04	.95	1.00
	$\hat{\rho}$	1.00	1.00	.74	.08	.05	.98	1.00
	$\hat{\tau}$	1.00	1.00	.74	.08	.05	.97	1.00
	$\hat{\rho}_\mu$	1.00	.96	.43	.06	.05	.98	1.00
	$\hat{\tau}_\mu$	1.00	.89	.28	.04	.05	.98	1.00

statistics. It is not surprising that $\hat{\rho}$ and $\hat{\tau}$ are superior to $\hat{\rho}_\mu$ and $\hat{\tau}_\mu$ because $\hat{\rho}$ and $\hat{\tau}$ use the knowledge that the true value of the intercept in the regression is zero.

Third, for $\rho < 1$ the statistic $\hat{\rho}_\mu$ yielded a more powerful test than the statistic $\hat{\tau}_\mu$. For $\rho > 1$ the ranking was reversed and the $\hat{\tau}_\mu$ statistic was more powerful.

For sample sizes of 50 and 100, and $\rho < 1$, Q_1 was the most powerful of the Q statistics studied. For sample size 250, Q_5 was the most powerful Q statistic. The size of the Q tests for $K \geq 5$ was considerably less than .05 for $n = 50$.

There is evidence that $\hat{\tau}$ and $\hat{\tau}_\mu$ are biased tests, accepting the null hypothesis more than 95 percent of the time for ρ close to, but less than, one. Because the tests are consistent, the minimum point of the power function is moving toward one as the sample size increases.

5. EXAMPLES

Gould and Nelson (1974) investigated the stochastic structure of the velocity of money using the yearly observations from 1869 through 1960 given in Friedman and Schwartz (1963). Gould and Nelson concluded that the logarithm of velocity is consistent with the model $X_t = X_{t-1} + e_t$, where $e_t \sim N(0, \sigma^2)$ and X_t is the velocity of money.

Two models,

$$X_t - X_1 = \rho(X_{t-1} - X_1) + e_t \qquad (5.1)$$

and

$$X_t = \mu + \rho X_{t-1} + e_t \ , \qquad (5.2)$$

were fit to the data. For (5.1) the estimates were

$$\hat{X}_t - X_1 = \underset{(.0094)}{1.0044}(X_{t-1} - X_1) \ , \quad \hat{\sigma}^2 = .0052$$

and for (5.2),

$$\hat{X}_t = \underset{(.0176)}{.0141} + \underset{(.0199)}{.9702}X_{t-1} \ , \quad \hat{\sigma}^2 = .0050 \ .$$

Model (5.1) assumes that it is known that no intercept enters the model if X_1 is subtracted from all observations. Model (5.2) permits an intercept in the model. The numbers in parentheses are the "standard errors" output by the regression program. For (5.1) we compute

$$n(\hat{\rho} - 1) = 91(.0044) = .4004$$

and

$$\hat{\tau} = (.0094)^{-1}(.0044) = .4681 \ .$$

Using either Table 8.5.1 or 8.5.2 of Fuller (1976), the hypothesis that $\rho = 1$ is accepted at the .10 level.

For (5.2) we obtain the statistics

$$n(\hat{\rho}_\mu - 1) = 92(.9702 - 1) = -2.742$$

and

$$\hat{\tau}_\mu = (.0199)^{-1}(.9702 - 1.0) = -1.50 \ .$$

Again the hypothesis is accepted at the .10 level.

As a second example we study the logarithm of the quarterly Federal Reserve Board Production Index for the period 1950–1 through 1977–4. We assume that the time series is adequately represented by the model

$$Y_t = \beta_0 + \beta_1 t + \alpha_1 Y_{t-1} + \alpha_2 Y_{t-2} + e_t \ ,$$

where e_t are NID(0, σ^2) random variables.

On the basis of the results of Fuller (1976, p. 379) the coefficient of Y_{t-1} in the regression equation

$$Y_t - Y_{t-1} = \beta_0 + \beta_1 t + (\alpha_1 + \alpha_2 - 1)Y_{t-1} - \alpha_2(Y_{t-1} - Y_{t-2}) + e_t$$

can be used to test the hypothesis that $\rho = \alpha_1 + \alpha_2 = 1$. This hypothesis is equivalent to the hypothesis that one of the roots of the characteristic equation of the process is one. The least squares estimate of the equation is

$$\hat{Y}_t - Y_{t-1} = \underset{(.15)}{.52} + \underset{(.00034)}{.00120}t - \underset{(.033)}{.119}Y_{t-1} + \underset{(.081)}{.498}(Y_{t-1} - Y_{t-2}), \quad \sigma^2 = .033 \ .$$

There are 110 observations in the regression. The numbers in parentheses are the quantities output as "standard errors" by the regression program. On the basis of the results of Fuller, the statistic $(n - p)(\hat{\rho} - 1)(1 + \hat{\alpha}_2)^{-1}$, where $\hat{\rho}$ is the coefficient of Y_{t-1} and p is the number of parameters estimated, is approximately distributed as $n(\hat{\rho}_\tau - 1)$. Also the "t statistic" constructed by dividing the coefficient of Y_{t-1} by the regression standard error is approximately distributed as $\hat{\tau}_\tau$. For this example we have

$$(n - p)(\hat{\rho} - 1)(1 + \hat{\alpha}_2)^{-1} = 106(-.119)(.502)^{-1} = -25.1$$

and

$$\hat{\tau}_\tau = (.033)^{-1}(-.119) = -3.61 \ .$$

Both statistics lead to rejection of the null hypothesis of a unit root at the 5 percent level if the alternative hypothesis is that both roots are less than one in absolute value. The Monte Carlo study of Section 4 indicated that tests based on the estimated ρ were more powerful for tests against stationarity than the $\hat{\tau}$ statistics. In this example the test based on $\hat{\rho}$ rejects the hypothesis at a smaller size (.025) than that of the $\hat{\tau}$ statistic (.05).

[*Received November 1976. Revised November 1978.*]

REFERENCES

Anderson, Theodore W. (1959), "On Asymptotic Distributions of Estimates of Parameters of Stochastic Difference Equations," *Annals of Mathematical Statistics*, 30, 676–687.

Box, George E.P., and Jenkins, Gwilym M. (1970), *Time Series Analysis Forecasting and Control*, San Francisco: Holden-Day.

Box, George E.P., and Pierce, David A. (1970), "Distribution of Residual Autocorrelations in Autoregressive-Integrated Moving Average Time Series Models," *Journal of the American Statistical Association*, 65, 1509–1526.

David, Herbert A. (1970), *Order Statistics*, New York: John Wiley & Sons.

Dickey, David A. (1976), "Estimation and Hypothesis Testing in Nonstationary Time Series," Ph.D. dissertation, Iowa State University.

Friedman, Milton, and Schwartz, A.J. (1963), *A Monetary History of the United States 1867–1960*, Princeton, N.J.: Princeton University Press.

Fuller, Wayne A. (1976), *Introduction to Statistical Time Series*, New York: John Wiley & Sons.

Gould, John P., and Nelson, Charles R. (1974), "The Stochastic Structure of the Velocity of Money," *American Economic Review*, 64, 405–417.

Hasza, David P. (1977), "Estimation in Nonstationary Time Series," Ph.D. dissertation, Iowa State University.

Jolley, L.B.W. (1961), *Summation of Series* (2nd ed.), New York: Dover Press.

Rao, M.M. (1961), "Consistency and Limit Distributions of Estimators of Parameters in Explosive Stochastic Difference Equations," *Annals of Mathematical Statistics*, 32, 195–218.

Rao, M.M. (1978), "Asymptotic Distribution of an Estimator of the Boundary Parameter of an Unstable Process," *Annals of Statistics*, 6, 185–190.

Rubin, Herman (1950), "Consistency of Maximum-Likelihood Estimates in the Explosive Case," in *Statistical Inference in Dynamic Economic Models*, ed. T.C. Koopmans, New York: John Wiley & Sons.

Rutherford, D.E. (1946), "Some Continuant Determinants Arising in Physics and Chemistry," *Proceedings of the Royal Society of Edinburgh*, Sect. A, 62, 229–236.

White, John S. (1958), "The Limiting Distribution of the Serial Correlation Coefficient in the Explosive Case," *Annals of Mathematical Statistics*, 29, 1188–1197.

[14]

Econometrica, Vol. 55, No. 2 (March, 1987), 277-301

TIME SERIES REGRESSION WITH A UNIT ROOT

BY P. C. B. PHILLIPS[1]

This paper studies the random walk, in a general time series setting that allows for weakly dependent and heterogeneously distributed innovations. It is shown that simple least squares regression consistently estimates a unit root under very general conditions in spite of the presence of autocorrelated errors. The limiting distribution of the standardized estimator and the associated regression t statistic are found using functional central limit theory. New tests of the random walk hypothesis are developed which permit a wide class of dependent and heterogeneous innovation sequences. A new limiting distribution theory is constructed based on the concept of continuous data recording. This theory, together with an asymptotic expansion that is developed in the paper for the unit root case, explain many of the interesting experimental results recently reported in Evans and Savin (1981, 1984).

KEYWORDS: Unit root, time series, functional limit theory, Wiener process, weak dependence, continuous record, asymptotic expansion.

1. INTRODUCTION

AUTOREGRESSIVE TIME SERIES with a unit root have been the subject of much recent attention in the econometrics literature. In part, this is because the unit root hypothesis is of considerable interest in applications, not only with data from financial and commodity markets where it has a long history but also with aggregate time series. The study by Hall (1978) has been particularly influential with regard to the latter, advancing theortical support for the random walk hypothesis for consumption expenditure and providing further empirical evidence. Moreover, the research program on vector autoregressive (VAR) modeling of aggregate time series (see Doan et al. (1984) and the references therein) has actually responded to this work by incorporating the random walk hypothesis as a Bayesian prior in the VAR specification. This approach has helped to attenuate the dimensionality problem of VAR modeling and seems to lead to decided improvements in forecasting performance (Litterman (1984)).

At the theoretical level there has also been much recent research. This has concentrated on the distribution theory that is necessary to develop tests of the random walk hypothesis under the null and the analysis of the power of various tests under interesting alternatives. Investigations by Dickey (1976), Dickey and Fuller (1979, 1981), Fuller (1976), and Evans and Savin (1981, 1984) have been at the forefront of this research. Related work on regression residuals has been done by Sargan and Bhargava (1983) and by Bhargava (1986). Recently, attention has also been given to more general ARIMA models by Solo (1984) and by Said and Dickey (1985).

[1] I am grateful to Gary Chamberlain, two referees, Robert Engle, Gene Savin, and C. Z. Wei for comments on the first version of this paper. Helpful discussions with Donald Andrews and David Pollard are also acknowledged. My thanks, as always, go to Glena Ames for her skill and effort in typing the manuscript of this paper. The research reported here was supported by the NSF under Grant No. SES 8218792.

All of the research cited in the previous paragraph has been confined to the case where the sequence of innovations driving the model is independent with common variance. Frequently, it is assumed that the innovations are iid $(0, \sigma^2)$ or, further, that they are iid $N(0, \sigma^2)$. Independence and homoskedasticity are rather strong assumptions to make about the errors in most empirical econometric work; and there are good reasons from economic theory (as shown in Hall (1978)) for believing them to be false in the context of aggregate time series that may be characterized as a random walk. For both empirical and theoretical considerations, therefore, it is important to develop tests for unit roots that do not depend on these conditions.

One aim of the present paper is to develop such tests. In doing so, we provide an asymptotic theory for the least squares regression estimator and the associated regression t statistic which allows for quite general weakly dependent and heterogenously distributed innovations. The conditions we impose are very weak and are similar to those used recently by White and Domowitz (1984) in the general nonlinear regression context. However, the limiting distribution theory that we employ here is quite different from that of White and Domowitz (1984). It belongs to a general class of functional limit theory on metric spaces, rather than the central limit theory on Euclidean spaces that is more conventionally used in econometrics (as in the excellent recent treatment by White (1984)). Our approach unifies and extends the presently known limiting distribution theory for the random walk and more general ARIMA models with a single unit root. It would seem to allow for most of the data we can expect to encounter in time series regression with aggregate economic series. A particularly interesting feature of the new test statistics that we propose in this paper is that their limiting distributions are identical to those found in earlier work under the assumption of iid errors. Thus, we discover that much of the work done by the authors cited in the earlier paragraph (particularly Fuller (1976), Dickey and Fuller (1979), and Evans and Savin (1981)) under the assumption of iid errors remains relevant for a very much larger class of models.

Another aim of the paper is to present a new limiting distribution theory that is based on the concept of continuous data recording. This theory, together with the asymptotic expansion that is developed in Section 7 of the paper for the unit root case, help to explain many of the interesting experimental results reported in the recent papers by Evans and Savin (1981, 1984) in this journal.

2. FUNCTIONAL LIMIT THEORY FOR DEPENDENT HETEROGENEOUSLY DISTRIBUTED DATA

Let $\{y_t\}_{t=1}^{\infty}$ be a stochastic process generated in discrete time according to:

(1) $$y_t = \alpha y_{t-1} + u_t \qquad (t = 1, 2, \ldots);$$

(2) $$\alpha = 1.$$

Under (2) we have the representation $y_t = S_t + y_0$ in terms of the partial sum $S_t = \sum_1^t u_j$ of the innovation sequence $\{u_j\}$ in (1) and the initial condition y_0. We may define $S_0 = 0$. The three alternatives commonly proposed for y_0 are (c.f. White (1958)):

(3a) $y_0 = c$, a constant, with probability one;

(3b) y_0 has a certain specified distribution;

(3c) $y_0 = y_T$, where $T =$ the sample size.

Equation (3c) is a circularity condition, due to Hotelling, that is used mainly as a mathematical device to simplify distribution theory (c.f. Anderson (1942)). (3b) is a random initial condition that is frequently used to achieve stationarity in stable models ($|\alpha| < 1$). In this paper, we shall employ (3b). This permits the greatest flexibility in the specification of (1). It allows for nonstationary series (with $|\alpha| \geqslant 1$) and it includes (3a) as a special case (and, in particular, the commonly used condition $y_0 = 0$).

Our concern in this section will be with the limiting distribution of standardized sums such as:

(4a) $$X_T(r) = \frac{1}{\sqrt{T}\sigma} S_{[Tr]} = \frac{1}{\sqrt{T}\sigma} S_{j-1}, \quad (j-1)/T \leqslant r < j/T \quad (j = 1, \ldots, T),$$

(4b) $$X_T(1) = \frac{1}{\sqrt{T}\sigma} S_T,$$

where [ ] denotes the integer part of its argument and σ is a certain constant defined later (see Assumption 2.1 below). Observe that the sample paths $X_T(r) \in D = D[0, 1]$, the space of all real valued functions on [0, 1] that are right continuous at each point of [0, 1] and have finite left limits. That is, jump discontinuities (or discontinuities of the first kind) are allowable in D. It will be sufficient for our purpose if we endow D with the uniform metric defined by $\|f - g\| = \sup_r |f(r) - g(r)|$ for any $f, g \in D$.

$X_T(r)$ is a random element in the function space D. Under certain conditions, $X_T(r)$ can be shown to converge weakly to a limit process which is popularly known either as standard Brownian motion or the Wiener process. This result is often referred to as a *functional central limit theorem* (CLT) (i.e. a CLT on a function space) or as an *invariance principle*, following the early work of Donsker (1951) and Erdos and Kac (1946). The limit process which we denote by $W(r)$, has sample paths which lie in $C = C[0, 1]$, the space of all real valued continuous functions on [0, 1]. Moreover, $W(r)$ is a Gaussian process (for fixed r, $W(r)$ is $N(0, r)$) and has independent increments ($W(s)$ is independent of $W(r) - W(s)$ for all $0 < s < r \leqslant 1$). We shall denote the weak convergence of the process $X_T(r)$ to $W(r)$ by the notation $X_T(r) \Rightarrow W(r)$; and, when the meaning is clear from the context, we shall sometimes suppress the argument r and simply write $X_T \Rightarrow W$. Here and elsewhere in the paper the symbol "$\Rightarrow$" is used to signify the weak convergence of the associated probability measures as $T \uparrow \infty$. Note that many finite dimensional CLT's follow directly from this result (e.g., the case in which $r = 1$ yields the Lindeberg-Lévy theorem when the u_j are iid $(0, \sigma^2)$). The reader is referred to Billingsley (1968) for a detailed introduction to the subject and to Pollard (1984) for an excellent recent treatment.

The conditions under which $X_T \Rightarrow W$ are very general indeed and extend to a wide class of nonstationary, weakly dependent, and heterogeneously distributed innovation sequences $\{u_t\}_1^\infty$. Billingsley (1968, Ch. 4) proves a number of such results for strictly stationary series satisfying weak dependence conditions. His results have recently been extended by many authors in the probability literature (see Hall and Heyde (1980, Ch. 5) for a good discussion of this literature and some related results for martingales and near martingales). Amongst the most general results that have been established are those of McLeish (1975a, 1977) and Herrndorf (1983, 1984a, 1984b). We shall employ a result of Herrndorf (1984b) in our own development because it applies most easily to the weakly dependent and heterogeneously distributed innovations that we wish to allow for in the context of time series such as (1).

To begin we must be precise about the sequence $\{u_t\}_1^\infty$ of allowable innovations in (1). In what follows we shall assume that $\{u_t\}_1^\infty$ is a sequence of random variables that satisfy the following Assumption.

ASSUMPTION 2.1: (a) $E(u_t)=0$, *all* t; (b) $\sup_t E|u_t|^\beta<\infty$ *for some* $\beta>2$; (c) $\sigma^2=\lim_{T\to\infty} E(T^{-1}S_T^2)$ *exists and* $\sigma^2>0$; (d) $\{u_t\}_1^\infty$ *is strong mixing with mixing coefficients* α_m *that satisfy*:

$$(5) \qquad \sum_1^\infty \alpha_m^{1-2/\beta}<\infty.$$

These conditions allow for both temporal dependence and heteroskedasticity in the process $\{u_t\}_1^\infty$. For the definition of strong mixing and the mixing coefficients α_m that appear in (d) the reader is referred, for example, to White (1984). Condition (d) controls the extent of the temporal dependence in the process $\{u_t\}_1^\infty$, so that, although there may be substantial dependence amongst recent events, events which are separated by long intervals of time are almost independent. In particular, the summability requirement (5) on the mixing coefficients is satisfied when the mixing decay rate is $\alpha_m=O(m^{-\lambda})$ for some $\lambda>\beta/(\beta-2)$. The summability condition (5) also controls the mixing decay rate in relation to the probability of outliers as determined by the moment existence condition (b). Thus, as β approaches 2 and the probability of outliers rises (under the weakening moment condition (b)) the mixing decay rate increases and the effect of outliers is required under (5) to wear off more quickly. This tradeoff between moment and mixing conditions was first developed by McLeish (1975b) in the context of strong laws for dependent sequences. Condition (b) also controls the allowable heterogeneity in the process by ruling out unlimited growth in the βth absolute moments of u_t.

Condition (c) is a convergence condition on the average variance of the partial sum S_T. It is a common requirement in much central limit theory although it is not strictly a necessary condition (see, for example, Herrndorf (1983)). However, if $\{u_t\}$ is weakly stationary, then

$$\sigma^2 = E(u_1^2) + 2\sum_{k=2}^{\infty} E(u_1 u_k) \tag{6}$$

and the convergence of the series is implied by the mixing condition (5) (see Ibragimov and Linnik (1971), Theorem 18.5.3). Even in this case, however, we still require $\sigma^2 > 0$ to exclude degenerate results. Once again, this is a conventional requirement.

Assumption 2.1 allows for a wide variety of possible generating mechanisms for the sequence of innovations $\{u_t\}_1^{\infty}$. These include all Gaussian and many other stationary finite order ARMA models under very general conditions on the underlying errors (see Withers (1981)).

We shall make extensive use of the following two results in our theoretical development. The first is a functional central limit theorem that is due to Herrndorf, and the second is the continuous mapping theorem, which is given a very thorough treatment in Billingsley (1968, Section 5).

LEMMA 2.2: *If $\{u_t\}_1^{\infty}$ satisfies Assumption 2.1, then as $T\uparrow\infty$ $X_T \Rightarrow W$, a standard Wiener process on C.*

LEMMA 2.3: *If $X_T \Rightarrow W$ as $T\uparrow\infty$ and h is any continuous functional on D (continuous, that is, except for at most a set of points $D_h \subset D$ for which $P(W\in D_h)=0$), then $h(X_T)\Rightarrow h(W)$ as $T\uparrow\infty$.*

3. LARGE SAMPLE ($T\uparrow\infty$) ASYMPTOTICS

We denote the ordinary least squares (OLS) estimator of α in (1) by $\hat{\alpha} = \sum_1^T y_t y_{t-1} / \sum_1^T y_{t-1}^2$. Appropriately centered and standardized we have

$$T(\hat{\alpha}-1) = \left\{T^{-1}\sum_1^T y_{t-1}(y_t - y_{t-1})\right\} \Big/ \left\{T^{-2}\sum_1^T y_{t-1}^2\right\} \tag{7}$$

and we shall consider the limiting behavior of this statistic as $T\uparrow\infty$. We shall also consider the conventional regression t statistic:

$$t_\alpha = \left(\sum_1^T y_{t-1}^2\right)^{1/2} (\hat{\alpha}-1)/s \tag{8}$$

where

$$s^2 = T^{-1}\sum_1^T (y_t - \hat{\alpha} y_{t-1})^2. \tag{9}$$

Both (7) and (8) have been suggested as test statistics for detecting the presence of a unit root in (1). The distributions of these statistics under both the null hypothesis $\alpha = 1$ and certain alternatives $\alpha \neq 1$ have been studied recently by Dickey and Fuller (1979, 1981), Evans and Savin (1981, 1984) and Nankervis and Savin (1985). The work of these authors concentrates altogether on the special case in which the innovation sequence $\{u_t\}_1^\infty$ is iid $(0, \sigma^2)$. In related work, Solo (1984) has studied the asymptotic distribution of the Lagrange multiple (LM) statistic in a general ARIMA setting. His results are also established under the assumption that iid innovations drive the model.

Our approach relies on the theory of weak convergence on D. It leads to rather simple characterizations of the limiting distributions of (7) and (8) in terms of functionals of a Wiener process. The main advantage of the approach is that the results hold for a very wide class of error processes in the model (1).

THEOREM 3.1: *If* $\{u_t\}_1^\infty$ *satisfies Assumption* 2.1 *and if* $\sup_t E|u_t|^{\beta+\eta} < \infty$ *for some* $\eta > 0$ (*where* $\beta > 2$ *is the same as that in Assumption* 2.1), *then as* $T \uparrow \infty$:

(a) $$T^{-2}\sum_1^T y_{t-1}^2 \Rightarrow \sigma^2 \int_0^1 W(r)^2\, dr;$$

(b) $$T^{-1}\sum_1^T y_{t-1}(y_t - y_{t-1}) \Rightarrow (\sigma^2/2)(W(1)^2 - \sigma_u^2/\sigma^2);$$

(c) $$T(\hat{\alpha} - 1) \Rightarrow (1/2)(W(1)^2 - \sigma_u^2/\sigma^2) \Big/ \int_0^1 W(r)^2\, dr;$$

(d) $$\hat{\alpha} \underset{p}{\rightarrow} 1;$$

(e) $$t_\alpha \Rightarrow (\sigma/2\sigma_u)(W(1)^2 - \sigma_u^2/\sigma^2) \Big/ \left\{\int_0^1 W(r)^2\, dr\right\}^{1/2};$$

where

$$\sigma_u^2 = \lim_{T\to\infty} T^{-1}\sum_1^T E(u_t^2),$$

$$\sigma^2 = \lim_{T\to\infty} E(T^{-1}S_T^2),$$

and $W(r)$ *is a standard Wiener process on* C.

When the innovation sequence $\{u_t\}_1^\infty$ is iid$(0, \sigma^2)$ we have $\sigma_u^2 = \sigma^2$, leading to the following simplification of part (c) of Theorem 3.1:

(10) $$T(\hat{\alpha} - 1) \Rightarrow (1/2(W(1)^2 - 1)) \Big/ \int_0^1 W(r)^2\, dr.$$

Result (10) was first given by White (1958, p. 1196), although his expression is incorrect as stated since his standardization of $\hat{\alpha}$ is $g(T)(\hat{\alpha} - 1)$ with $g(T) = T/\sqrt{2}$. Unfortunately, this rather minor error recurs at several points in the paper by Rao (1978, pp. 187-188). Lai and Wei (1982) and Lai and Seigmund (1984) also give (10) as stated above.

Theorem 3. 1 extends (10) to the very general case of weakly dependent and heterogeneously distributed data. Interestingly, our result shows that the limiting distribution of $T(\hat{\alpha}-1)$ has the same general form for a very wide class of innovation processes $\{u_t\}_1^\infty$.

The differences between (c) of Theorem 3.1 and (10) may be illustrated with a simple example. Suppose that the generating process for $\{u_t\}$ is the moving average

$$u_t = \varepsilon_t + \theta\varepsilon_{t-1} \qquad (t=1,2,\ldots),$$

with ε_t iid$(0, \sigma_\varepsilon^2)$. Then

$$\sigma_u^2 = \operatorname*{plim}_{T\to\infty} T^{-1}\sum_1^T u_t^2 = (1+\theta^2)\sigma_\varepsilon^2,$$

$$\sigma^2 = \lim_{T\to\infty} T^{-1}E(S_T^2) = (1+\theta)^2\sigma_\varepsilon^2,$$

and we have

$$T^{-1}\sum_1^T y_{t-1}u_t \Rightarrow \frac{\sigma_\varepsilon^2}{2}[(1+\theta)^2W(1)^2-(1+\theta^2)],$$

which can also be verified by direct calculation. In this case

$$T(\hat{\alpha}-1)\Rightarrow(1/2)[W(1)^2-(1+\theta^2)/(1+\theta)^2]\Big/\int_0^1 W(r)^2\,dr,$$

generalizing (10) and, of course, reducing to it when $\theta=0$.

Part (d) of Theorem 3.2 shows that, unlike the stable AR(1) with $|\alpha|<1$, OLS retains the property of consistency when there is a unit root even in the presence of substantial serial correlation. This extremely simple result seems not to have been derived at this level of generality before, although closely related results for ARIMA models have been obtained recently by Tiao and Tsay (1983) and by Said and Dickey (1984). The robustness of the consistency of $\hat{\alpha}$ in this case is rather extraordinary, allowing for a wide variety of error processes that permit serious misspecifications in the usual random walk formulation of (1) with white noise errors. Intuitively, when the model (1) has a unit root, the strength of the signal (as measured by the sample variation of the regressor y_{t-1}) dominates the noise by a factor of $O(T)$, so that the effects of any regressor-error correlation are annihilated in the regression as $T\uparrow\infty$.

Part (e) of Theorem 3.1 gives the limiting distribution of t_α. This distribution, like that of the coefficient estimator, depends on the variance ratio σ_u^2/σ^2. We note that in the Lagrange multiplier approach (c.f. Evans and Savin (1981) and Solo (1984)) we would employ the variance estimator $s'^2 = T^{-1}\sum_1^T(y_t-y_{t-1})^2$ in the test statistic, using the null hypothesis (2). Writing the Lagrange multiplier statistic as $LM = t'^2$ where $t' = (\sum_1^T y_{t-1}^2)^{1/2}(\hat{\alpha}-1)/s'$, we deduce from part (e) of Theorem 3.1 that

$$LM \Rightarrow (\sigma/2\sigma_u)^2[W(1)^2-\sigma_u^2/\sigma^2]^2\Big/\int_0^1 W(r)^2\,dr. \qquad (11)$$

Solo (1984) derived the special case of (11) in which $\sigma^2=\sigma_u^2$.

Theorem 3.1 provides an interesting example of a functional of a partial sum that does not necessarily converge weakly to the same functional of Brownian motion. To show this, it is most convenient to replace $X_T(r)$ as defined by (4) by its close relative, the random element

$$Y_T(r)=\frac{1}{\sqrt{T}\sigma}S_{[Tr]}+\frac{Tr-[Tr]}{\sqrt{T}\sigma}u_{[Tr]+1}, \qquad (j-1)/T\leq r<j/T \quad (j=1,\dots,T),$$

$$Y_T(1)=\frac{1}{\sqrt{T}\sigma}S_T,$$

which lies in $C[0, 1]$. In fact, $Y_T(r)\Rightarrow W(r)$ under the same conditions as those prescribed earlier for $X_T(r)$ in Lemma 2.2. However, the sample path of $Y_T(r)$ is continuous and of bounded variation on [0, 1] so that we may define and evaluate by partial integration the following Riemann Stieltjes integral:

$$\int_0^1 Y_T(r)\,dY(r)=\tfrac{1}{2}[Y_T^2(r)]_0^1=\tfrac{1}{2}Y_T(1)^2. \tag{12}$$

The corresponding integral for the limit process $W(r)$ must be defined as a stochastic integral, for which the rule of partial integration used in (12) does not apply. Instead, we have the well known result (see, for example, Hida (1980, p. 158)):

$$\int_0^1 W\,dW=(1/2)(W(1)^2-1) \tag{13}$$

which may be obtained directly from the Ito formula. On the other hand, we deduce from (12) and Lemma 2.3 that

$$\int_0^1 Y_T\,dY_T\Rightarrow(1/2)\,W(1)^2. \tag{14}$$

The problem arises because all elements of $C[0, 1]$ except for a set of Wiener measure zero are of unbounded variation (Billingsley (1968, p. 63)). In particular, the sample paths of $W(t)$ are almost surely of unbounded variation and thus the integral $\int_0^1 W\,dW$ does not exist in the same sense as the integral $\int_0^1 Y_T\,dY_T$. It follows that the latter integral does not define a continuous mapping $C[0, 1]$ and we cannot appeal to the continuous mapping theorem to deduce that $\int Y_T\,dY_T\Rightarrow \int W\,dW$ when $Y_T\Rightarrow W$. In fact, as (13) and (14) demonstrate, the result is not correct.

We may, however, proceed as in the proof of Theorem 3.1 in the Appendix. Alternatively, since $dY_T(t)=\sqrt{T}u_j\,dt/\sigma$ we find by direct integration that:

$$\int_{(j-1)/T}^{j/T} Y_T\,dY_T=\frac{1}{T\sigma^2}S_{j-1}u_j+\frac{u_j^2}{2T\sigma^2}$$

and summing over $j=1,\dots,T$ we deduce that

$$T^{-1}\sum_1^T S_{j-1}u_j=\sigma^2\int_0^1 Y_T\,dY_T-\sum_1^T u_j^2/2T\Rightarrow(\sigma^2/2)\,W(1)^2-\sigma_u^2/2, \tag{15}$$

as given by part (b) of Theorem 3.1. Note also, in view of (13), that the sum (15) converges to $\sigma^2 \int_0^1 W\,dW$ if and only if $\sigma_u^2 = \sigma^2$.

4. ESTIMATION OF (σ_u^2, σ^2)

The limiting distributions given in Theorem 3.1 depend on unknown parameters σ_u^2 and σ^2. These distributions are therefore not directly useable for statistical testing. However, both these parameters may be consistently estimated and the estimates may be used to construct modified statistics whose limiting distributions are independent of (σ_u^2, σ^2). As we shall see, these new statistics (given below by (21) and (22)) provide very general tests for the presence of a unit root in (1).

As shown in the proof of Theorem 3.1, $T^{-1}\sum_1^T u_t^2 \to \sigma_u^2$ a.s. as $T\uparrow\infty$. This provides us with the simple estimator

$$(16) \qquad s_u^2 = T^{-1}\sum_1^T (y_t - y_{t-1})^2 = T^{-1}\sum_1^T u_t^2,$$

which is consistent for σ_u^2 under the null hypothesis (2). Since $\hat{\alpha} \xrightarrow[p]{} 1$ by Theorem 3.1 we may also use $T^{-1}\sum_1^T (y_t - \hat{\alpha} y_{t-1})^2$ as a consistent estimator of σ_u^2.

Consistent estimation of $\sigma^2 = \lim_{T\to\infty} E(T^{-1}S_T^2)$ is more difficult. The problem is essentially equivalent to the consistent estimation of an asymptotic covariance matrix in the presence of weakly dependent and heterogeneously distributed observations.[2] The latter problem has recently been examined by White and Domowitz (1984). A detailed treatment is also available in Chapter VI of White (1984).

We start by defining

$$\begin{aligned}\sigma_T^2 &= \operatorname{var}(T^{-1/2}S_T)\\ &= T^{-1}\sum_1^T E(u_t^2) + 2T^{-1}\sum_{\tau=1}^{T-1}\sum_{t=\tau+1}^{T} E(u_t u_{t-\tau})\end{aligned}$$

and by introducing the approximant

$$\sigma_{Tl}^2 = T^{-1}\sum_1^T E(u_t^2) + 2T^{-1}\sum_{\tau=1}^{l}\sum_{t=\tau+1}^{T} E(u_t u_{t-\tau}).$$

We shall call l the lag truncation number. For large T and large $l < T$, σ_{Tl}^2 may be expected to be very close to σ_T^2 if the total contribution in σ_T^2 of covariances such as $E(u_t u_{t-\tau})$ with long lags $\tau > l$ is small. This will be true if $\{u_t\}_1^\infty$ satisfies Assumption 2.1. Formally, we have the following lemma.

LEMMA 4.1: *If the sequence $\{u_t\}_1^\infty$ satisfies Assumption* 2.1 *and if $l\uparrow\infty$ as $T\uparrow\infty$, then $\sigma_T^2 - \sigma_{Tl}^2 \to 0$ as $T\uparrow\infty$.*

[2] This is most easily seen by noting that $S_T/\sqrt{T} \Rightarrow N(0, \sigma^2)$, according to the invariance principle Lemma 2.2.

This Lemma suggests that under suitable conditions on the rate at which $l\uparrow\infty$ as $T\uparrow\infty$ we may proceed to estimate σ^2 from finite samples of data by sequentially estimating σ_{Tl}^2. The problem is explored by White (1984, Ch. 6). We define

$$s_{Tl}^2 = T^{-1}\sum_1^T u_t^2 + 2T^{-1}\sum_{\tau=1}^{l}\sum_{t=\tau+1}^{T} u_t u_{t-\tau}. \tag{17}$$

The following result establishes that s_{Tl}^2 is a consistent estimator of σ^2.

THEOREM 4.2: *If* (a) $\{u_t\}_1^\infty$ *satisfies Assumption* 2.1(*a*), (*c*), *and* (*d*), *and part* (*b*) *of Assumption* 2.1 *is replaced by the stronger moment condition*: $\sup_t E|u_t|^{2\beta} < \infty$, for some $\beta > 2$; (b) $l\uparrow\infty$ *as* $T\uparrow\infty$ *such that* $l = o(T^{1/4})$; *then* $s_{Tl}^2 \underset{p}{\rightarrow} \sigma^2$ *as* $T\uparrow\infty$.

According to this result, if we allow the number of estimated autocovariances to increase as $T\uparrow\infty$ but control the rate of increase so that $l = o(T^{1/4})$ then s_{Tl}^2 yields a consistent estimator of σ^2. White and Domowitz (1984) provide some guidelines for the selection of l. Inevitably the choice of l will be an empirical matter. In our own case, a preliminary investigation of the sample autocorrelations of $u_t = y_t - y_{t-1}$ will help in selecting an appropriate choice of l. Since the sample auto-correlations of first differenced economic time series usually decay quickly it is likely that in moderate sample sizes quite a small value of l will be chosen.

Rather than using the first differences $u_t = y_t - y_{t-1}$ in the construction of s_{Tl}^2, we could have used the residuals $\hat{u}_t = y_t - \hat{\alpha} y_{t-1}$ from the least squares regression. Since $\hat{\alpha} \underset{p}{\rightarrow} 1$ as $T\uparrow\infty$ this estimator is also consistent for σ^2 under the null hypothesis (2). Moreover, this estimator is consistent for σ^2 under explosive alternatives to (2) (i.e. when $\alpha > 1$) and may, therefore, be preferred to s_{Tl}^2 when such cases seem likely.

We remark that s_{Tl}^2 is not constrained to be nonnegative as it is presently defined in (17). When there are large negative sample serial covariances, s_{Tl}^2 can take on negative values. In a related context, Newey and West (1985) have recently suggested a modification to variance estimators such as s_{Tl}^2 which ensures that they are nonnegative. In the present case, the modification yields:

$$\tilde{s}_{Tl}^2 = T^{-1}\sum_1^T u_t^2 + 2T^{-1}\sum_{\tau=1}^{l} w_{\tau l}\sum_{t=\tau+1}^{T} u_t u_{t-\tau} \tag{18}$$

where

$$w_{\tau l} = 1 - \tau/(l+1). \tag{19}$$

It is simple to motivate the weighted variance estimator (18). When $\{u_t\}_1^\infty$ is weakly stationary, $\sigma^2 = 2\pi f_u(0)$ where $f_u(\lambda)$ is the spectral density of u_t. In this case, $(1/2\pi)\tilde{s}_{Tl}^2$ is the value at the origin $\lambda = 0$ of the Bartlett estimate

$$\hat{f}_u(\lambda) = (1/2\pi)\sum_{\tau=-l-1}^{l+1} [1 - |\tau|/(l+1)]C(\tau)\, e^{-i\lambda\tau}, \tag{20}$$

$$C(\tau) = T^{-1}\sum_{t=|\tau|+1}^{T} u_t u_{t-|\tau|}$$

of $f_u(\lambda)$ (see, for example, Priestley (1981, pp. 439-440)). Since the Bartlett estimate (20) is nonnegative everywhere, we deduce that $\tilde{s}^2_{Tl} \geq 0$ also. Of course, weights other than (19) are possible and may be inspired by other choices of lag window in the density estimate (20).

5. NEW TESTS FOR A UNIT ROOT

The consistent estimates s^2_u and s^2_{Tl} may be used to develop new tests for unit roots that apply under very general conditions. We define the statistics:

$$\text{(21)} \qquad Z_\alpha = T(\hat{\alpha}-1) - (1/2)(s^2_{Tl} - s^2_u) \Big/ \left(T^{-2} \sum_1^T y^2_{t-1} \right)$$

and

$$\text{(22)} \qquad Z_t = \left(\sum_1^T y^2_{t-1} \right)^{1-2} (\hat{\alpha}-1)/s_{Tl} - (1/2)(s^2_{Tl} - s^2_u) \left[s_{Tl} \left(T^{-2} \sum_1^T y^2_{t-1} \right)^{1/2} \right]^{-1}.$$

Z_α is a transformation of the standardized estimator $T(\hat{\alpha}-1)$ and Z_t is a transformation of the regression t statistic (8).

The limiting distributions of Z_α and Z_t are given by:

THEOREM 5.1: *If the conditions of Theorem* 4.2 *are satisfied, then as* $T \uparrow \infty$,

$$\text{(a)} \qquad Z_\alpha \Rightarrow \frac{(W(1)^2 - 1)/2}{\int_0^1 W(t)^2 \, dt}$$

and

$$\text{(b)} \qquad Z_t \Rightarrow \frac{(W(1)^2 - 1)/2}{\{\int_0^1 W(t)^2 \, dt\}^{1/2}}$$

under the null hypothesis that $\alpha = 1$ *in* (1).

Theorem 5.1 demonstrates that the limiting distributions of the two statistics Z_α and Z_t are invariant within a very wide class of weakly dependent and possibly heterogeneously distributed innovations $\{u_t\}_1^\infty$. Moreover, the limiting distribution of Z_α is identical to that of $T(\hat{\alpha}-1)$ when $\sigma^2_u = \sigma^2$ (see (10) above). The latter distribution has recently been computed by Evans and Savin (1981) using numerical methods. These authors present tabulations and graphical plots of the limiting pdf and their article also contains a detailed tabulation of the limiting cdf, which is suitable for testing purposes. Since Evans and Savin work with the normalization $g(T)(\hat{\alpha}-1)$, in which $g(T) = T/\sqrt{2}$, the modified statistic

$$\text{(23)} \qquad Z'_\alpha = (1/\sqrt{2}) Z_\alpha$$

may be used to ensure compatibility with their published tables. Fuller (1976, p. 371) provides a tabulation of the limiting distribution (10) for the standardization $T(\hat{\alpha}-1)$, so that his table may be used directly in significance testing with our statistic Z_α.

The limiting distribution of Z_t given in Theorem 5.1 is identical to that of the regression t statistic when $\sigma^2 = \sigma_u^2$ (see Theorem 3.1). This is, in fact, the limiting distribution of the t statistic when the innovation sequence $\{u_t\}_1^\infty$ is iid $(0, \sigma^2)$. The latter distribution has been calculated using Monte Carlo methods by Dickey (1976) and tabulations of percentage points of the distribution are reported in Fuller (1976, Table 8.5.2, p. 373).

Theorem 5.1 shows that much of the work of these authors on the distribution of the OLS estimator $\hat{\alpha}$ and the regression t statistic under iid innovations remains relevant for a very much larger class of models. In fact, our results show that their tabulations appear to be relevant in almost any time series with a unit root. To test the unit root hypothesis (2) one simply computes (21), (23), or (22) and compares these to the relevant critical values given by Evans and Savin (1981) and Fuller (1976).

6. CONTINUOUS RECORD ASYMPTOTICS

In certain econometric applications a near-continuous record of data is available for empirical work. Prominent examples occur in various financial, commodity, and stock markets as well as in certain recent energy usage experiments. Undoubtedly, trends in this direction will accelerate in the next decade with ongoing computerizations of banking and credit facilities and electronic monitoring of sales activity. Moreover, financial and foreign exchange markets, in particular, now offer empirical researchers the opportunity of working with data recorded at many different frequencies (weekly, daily, hourly or even minute by minute in some cases). For these reasons, it is of intrinsic interest to study the behavior of econometric estimators and test statistics as the time interval (h) between sampled observations is allowed to vary and, possibly, to tend to zero. When $h \downarrow 0$, we obtain in the limit a continuous record of observations over a finite time span, comparable to a seismographic recording. We shall call asymptotics of this type continuous record asymptotics.[3]

As we shall show below, there is a very interesting relationship, at least in certain cases, between the behavior of the statistics we have been considering when the sample size $T \uparrow \infty$ and when the sampling interval $h \downarrow 0$. This relationship, together with the results of Section 7, help to explain many of the recent Monte Carlo results reported by Evans and Savin (1981, 1984). Moreover, continuous record ($h \downarrow 0$) asymptotics have an additional advantage in that they bring into prominence the role of initial observation conditions. Such conditions can be of considerable importance in the statistical behavior of certain econometric estimators and tests in finite samples of data. Yet their effects normally disappear entirely in conventional large sample ($T \uparrow \infty$, h fixed) asymptotic theory. We shall

[3] Note that earlier work on continuous time econometric modeling (see, for instance, Bergstrom (1984) and the articles published in Bergstrom (1976)) used small sampling interval ($h \downarrow 0$) methods in a different context: viz., to compare various estimation procedures by considering how their conventional ($T \uparrow \infty$) asymptotic properties differed as $h \downarrow 0$.

illustrate the effects of such initial conditions in the context of autoregressions such as (1) in the presence of a unit root.

We start by considering a triangular array of random variables $\{\{y_{nt}\}_{t=1}^{T_n}\}_{n=1}^{\infty}$ defined as follows. Given n, the sequence $\{y_{nt}\}_1^{T_n}$ is generated by the random walk

$$y_{nt} = y_{nt-1} + u_{nt} \qquad (t = 1, \ldots, T_n;\ y_{n0} = y(0)), \tag{24}$$

where the innovations $\{u_{nt}\}_{t=1}^{T_n}$ are iid $(0, \sigma^2 h_n)$ are independent of $y(0)$, and $T_n h_n = N$ is a fixed positive constant for all n. Moreover, as $n \uparrow \infty$ we shall require $T_n \uparrow \infty$ and $h_n \downarrow 0$ so that $T_n h_n = N$ remains constant and $T_n \in Z^+$. The sequence $\{\{u_{nt}\}_1^{T_n}\}_1^{\infty}$ will be called a triangular array of iid $(0, \sigma^2 h_n)$ variates and $\{\{y_{nt}\}_1^{T_n}\}_1^{\infty}$ will be called a triangular array of random walks.

Each row of the triangular array $\{\{y_{nt}\}_1^{T_n}\}_1^{\infty}$ may be interpreted as a sequence of random variables generated by a random walk in discrete time with a sampling interval $= h_n$. The array itself represents a sequence of random walks with sampling intervals that decrease ($h_n \downarrow$) as we get deeper ($n \uparrow$) into the array. The convergence of the sampling interval $h_n \downarrow 0$ as $n \uparrow \infty$ and the requirement that $h_n T_n = N$ be fixed are the only connections that link the random variables in different rows of the array. The interval $[0, N]$ may be regarded as a fixed time span over which we observe the random walk at discrete points in time determined by the sampling interval h_n. The triangular array $\{\{y_{nt}\}_1^{T_n}\}_1^{\infty}$ then provides a formal framework within which h_n may vary and by means of which we may investigate limiting behavior as $h_n \downarrow 0$.

Let $S_{ni} = \sum_{j=1}^{i} u_{nj}$ $(1 \leq i \leq T_n)$ with $S_{n0} = 0$ as usual. We form the random function

$$Y_n(r) = \sigma^{-1} S_{ni-1}, \qquad (i-1)/T_n \leq r < i/T_n \qquad (i = 1, \ldots, T_n),$$
$$Y_n(1) = \sigma^{-1} S_{nT_n},$$

and observe that $Y_n \in D$. As $n \uparrow \infty$ $Y_n(r)$ converges weakly to a constant multiple of a standard Wiener process. Specifically, we have the following lemma.

LEMMA 6.1: *If* (a) $\{\{u_{nt}\}_1^{T_n}\}_1^{\infty}$ *is a triangular array of iid* $(0, \sigma^2 h_n)$ *variates*; (b) $T_n \in Z^+$, $T_n \uparrow \infty$, *and* $h_n \downarrow 0$ *as* $n \uparrow \infty$ *in such a way that the product* $T_n h_n = N > 0$ *remains constant*; *then* $Y_n(r) \Rightarrow N^{1/2} W(r)$ *as* $n \uparrow \infty$ *where* $W(r)$ *is a standard Wiener process.*

Let

$$\hat{\alpha}_n = \sum_1^{T_n} y_{nt} y_{nt-1} \Big/ \sum_1^{T_n} y_{nt-1}^2$$

be the coefficient and

$$t_{\alpha_n} = \left(\sum_1^{T_n} y_{nt-1}^2 \right)^{1/2} (\hat{\alpha}_n - 1)/s_n$$

be the associated t ratio in a least squares regression on (24). Here,

$$s_n = \left\{ T_n^{-1} \sum_1^{T_n} (y_{nt} - \hat{\alpha}_n y_{nt-1})^2 \right\}^{1/2}$$

is the standard error of the regression. The limiting behavior of these statistics as $h_n \downarrow 0$ is given in our next result.

THEOREM 6.2: *If $\{\{y_{nt}\}_1^{T_n}\}_1^\infty$ is a triangular array of random walks for which the innovation sequence $\{\{u_{nt}\}_1^{T_n}\}_1^\infty$ satisfies the conditions of Lemma 6.1, then as $n \uparrow \infty$:*

(a) $$h_n \sum_1^{T_n} y_{nt-1}^2 \Rightarrow N^2\sigma^2\left\{\int_0^1 W(r)^2\,dr + 2(y(0)/\sigma N^{1/2})\int_0^1 W(r)\,dr + y(0)^2/\sigma^2 N\right\};$$

(b) $$\sum_1^{T_n} y_{nt-1}(y_{nt}-y_{nt-1}) \Rightarrow (N\sigma^2/2)\{W(1)^2 - 1 + 2(y(0)/\sigma N^{1/2})W(1)\};$$

(c) $$h_n^{-1}(\hat{\alpha}_n - 1) \Rightarrow (1/N)\left[\int_0^1 W(r)^2\,dr + 2(y(0)/\sigma N^{1/2}) \cdot \int_0^1 W(r)\,dr + y(0)^2/\sigma^2 N\right]^{-1} \cdot [(1/2)(W(1)^2 - 1) + (y(0)/\sigma N^{1/2})W(1)];$$

(d) $$t_{\alpha_n} \Rightarrow \left[\int_0^1 W(r)^2\,dr + 2(y(0)/\sigma N^{1/2})\int_0^1 W(r)\,dr + y(0)^2/\sigma^2 N\right]^{-1/2} \cdot [(1/2)(W(1)^2 - 1) + (y(0)/\sigma N^{1/2})W(1)];$$

where $W(r)$ is a standard Wiener process.

Theorem 6.2 shows that for small h_n the distribution of $\hat{\alpha}_n$ and that of t_{α_n} may be approximated by suitable functionals of Brownian motion. These functionals involve the initial condition $y(0)$, which may be either constant or random. If $y(0)$ is random then it is independent of the Wiener process $W(r)$ that appears in the functionals given in parts (c) and (d) (recall that $y(0)$ is independent of innovation sequence $\{\{u_{nt}\}_1^{T_n}\}_1^\infty$). For large N the distributions may be well approximated by:

(25) $$h_n^{-1}(\hat{\alpha}_n - 1) \sim N^{-1}\left[\int_0^1 W(r)^2\,dr\right]^{-1}[(1/2)(W(1)^2 - 1)];$$

(26) $$t_{\alpha_n} \sim \left[\int_0^1 W(r)^2\,dr\right]^{-1/2}[(1/2)(W(1)^2 - 1)].$$

(25) and (26) correspond, as we would expect, to the conventional large sample ($T \uparrow \infty$) asymptotics and are special cases of our earlier results in Theorem 3.1 with $\sigma^2 = \sigma_u^2$.

When the time span N is not large, (25) and (26) may not be good approximations. Theorem 6.2 suggests that the initial value $y(0)$ or, more specifically, the ratio $c=y(0)/\sigma$ plays an important role in the determining of the adequacy of these approximations. Thus, when c is large the effect on the limiting distributions given in parts (c) and (d) of Theorem 6.2 is substantial. In fact as $c\uparrow\infty$ it is easy to deduce from these expressions that:

(27) $$h_n^{-1}(\hat{\alpha}_n-1)\sim(1/cN^{1/2})W(1)\equiv N(0,1/c^2N);$$

(28) $$t_{\alpha_n}\sim W(1)\equiv N(0,1).$$

Theorem 6.2 helps to explain several of the phenomena discovered in the experimental investigation of Evans and Savin (1981). These authors found: (i) that the finite sample distribution of $\hat{\alpha}$ was very well approximated by its asymptotic distribution (using conventional large sample $(T\uparrow\infty)$ asymptotics with h fixed) even for quite small samples when the initial value $y(0)=0$; and (ii) that changes in $c=y(0)/\sigma$ precipitate substantial changes in the distribution of $\hat{\alpha}$; specifically, the distribution of $T(\hat{\alpha}-1)$ noticeably concentrates as c increases.

Observation (ii) is well explained by Theorem 6.2, which shows that c is an important parameter in the limiting distribution of $h_n^{-1}(\hat{\alpha}_n-1)$ as $h_n\downarrow 0$ over finite data spans $[0, N]$. This is to be contrasted with the usual $(T\uparrow\infty)$ asymptotic theory, which obscures the dependence of the distribution of $\hat{\alpha}$ on $y(0)/\sigma$. The second phenomenon noted by Evans-Savin, that the distribution of $T(\hat{\alpha}-1)$ concentrates as c increases, is directly corroborated by (27). Thus, using $N=T_nh_n$, we deduce from (27) that:

$$T_n(\hat{\alpha}_n-1)\sim(N^{1/2}/c)W(1)\equiv N(0,N/c^2)\xrightarrow[p]{}0, \quad \text{as} \quad c\uparrow\infty.$$

The fact that the asymptotic $(T\uparrow\infty)$ distribution of $\hat{\alpha}$ is a very good approximation in finite samples when $y(0)=0$ and the innovations are iid (Evans-Savin observation (i) above) is also well explained by our analytical results. In particular, Theorem 6.2 shows that the asymptotic distribution applies not only as $T\uparrow\infty$ in the conventional sense with h fixed (our Theorem 3.1(c) with $\sigma^2=\sigma_u^2$) but also as $h_n\downarrow 0$ with a fixed data span N (our Theorem 6.2(c) with $y(0)=0$). Thus, the limiting distribution theory operates in two different directions with identical results when $y(0)=0$ and the innovations are iid. Moreover, this limiting distribution is actually the finite sample distribution of the least squares continuous record estimator when the (continuous) stochastic process is Gaussian.

To show this we observe that the natural limit of (24) as $n\uparrow\infty$ may be regarded as the stochastic differential equation

(29) $$dy(t)=\theta y(t)\,dt+\zeta(dt) \qquad (0\leq t\leq N)$$

with $\theta=0$. In (29) $y(t)$ is now a random function of continuous time over $[0, N]$ and $\zeta(dt)$ is a σ-additive random measure which is defined on all subsets of the real line with finite Lebesgue measure such that:

(30) $$E(\zeta(dr))=0, \qquad E(\zeta(dr)^2)=\sigma^2\,dr$$

(see, for example, Rozanov (1967, p. 8)). The stochastic integral $\int_0^t \zeta(dr)$ has zero mean, variance $= \sigma^2 t$, and uncorrelated increments. We note that (24) may be regarded as a random walk in discrete time that is satisfied by equispaced observations over intervals of length h_n generated by (29) with $\theta = 0$. Then we may write, for example,

$$u_{nt} = \int_{th_n - h_n}^{th_n} \zeta(dr)$$

and $\{u_{nt}\}_1^{T_n}$ is an orthogonal sequence with common variance $\sigma^2 h_n$. If we go further in the specification of (29) and require that the increments of $\int_0^t \zeta(dr)$ be independent, then the continuous stochastic process $y(t)$ defined by (29) is Gaussian and $\sigma^{-1}\int_0^t \zeta(dr)$ $(0 \leq t \leq N)$ is a Wiener process on $C[0, N]$. This is proved by Billingsley (1968, Theorem 19.1, p. 154) and is also a consequence of our Lemma 6.1. In particular, from Lemma 6.1 we have $Y_n(r) \Rightarrow N^{1/2}W(r)$ $(0 \leq r \leq 1)$ as $n \uparrow \infty$. Now set $t = Nr$ $(0 \leq t \leq N)$, $y_n(t) = \sigma Y_n(t/N)$ and define $V(t) = N^{1/2}W(t/N)$. Clearly, $V(t)$ is a Wiener process on $C[0, N]$. Moreover, as $n \uparrow \infty$, $y_n(t) \Rightarrow \sigma V(t) \equiv y(t)$ $(0 \leq t \leq N)$, where "$\equiv$" signifies equality in distribution. Thus, the triangular array $\{\{y_{nt}\}_1^{T_n}\}_1^{\infty}$ $(T_n h_n = N, y_{n0} = 0)$ converges weakly as $n \uparrow \infty$ to the continuous Gaussian process $y(t)$ $(0 \leq t \leq N)$ generated by the stochastic differential equation (29) with $\theta = 0$, $y(0) = 0$.

If we now consider the problem of estimating the parameter θ in (29) from the continuous record $\{y(t); 0 \leq t \leq N\}$ least squares suggests the criterion

$$\text{(31)} \qquad \min_\theta \int_0^N (\dot{y} - \theta y)^2 \, dt.$$

Here we write $\dot{y} = dy(t)/dt$ in a purely formal way since this is all that is needed for our present purpose. (31) leads to the estimator:

$$\text{(32)} \qquad \hat{\theta} = \int_0^N y\dot{y} \, dt \Big/ \int_0^N y^2 \, dt = \int_0^N y \, dy \int_0^N y^2 \, dt.$$

Provided the integral $\int_0^N y \, dy$ in the numerator of (32) is interpreted as a stochastic integral it is not necessary to be more specific about the interpretation of $\dot{y}$ as a generalized stochastic process.

The estimator $\hat{\theta}$ was originally suggested by Bartlett (1946). Its properties were subsequently studied by Grenander (1950) and more recently by Brown and Hewitt (1975) and by Feigin (1979). As our next result shows the distribution of $\hat{\theta}$ can be simply expressed in terms of the initial value $y(0)$ and a standard Wiener process.

THEOREM 6.3: *If $y(t)$ $(0 \leq t \leq N)$ is generated by* (29) *where $\zeta(dr)$ is Gaussian and independent of $y(0)$, then $\hat{\theta}$ has the same distribution in finite samples (i.e. finite N) as the functional*

$$\text{(33)} \qquad (1/N)\left[\int_0^1 W(r)^2 \, dr + 2(y(0)/\sigma N^{1/2}) \int_0^1 W(r) \, dr + y(0)^2/\sigma^2 N\right]^{-1}$$

$$\cdot [(1/2)(W(1)^2-1)+(y(0)/\sigma N^{1/2})W(1)]$$

of the standard Wiener process $W(r)$.

This verifies the result we stated earlier: viz., the limiting distribution of $h_n^{-1}(\hat{\alpha}_n-1)$ as $n\uparrow\infty$ (Theorem 6.2(c)) is the same as the finite sample (fixed N) distribution of the continuous record estimator $\hat{\theta}$. Since the triangular array $\{\{y_{nt}\}_1^{T_n}\}_1^{\infty}$ converges weakly to the Gaussian process $y(t)$ as $n\uparrow\infty$ and since both estimators $\hat{\alpha}_n$ and $\hat{\theta}$ are obtained by least squares, this is a result that may well have been anticipated. Interestingly, while the limiting distribution of $h_n^{-1}(\hat{\alpha}_n-1)$ and the distribution of $\hat{\theta}$ are equivalent, the distribution of $\hat{\alpha}_n$ is degenerate in the limit as $n\uparrow\infty$. In fact, $\hat{\alpha}_n \underset{p}{\rightarrow} 1$ as $n\uparrow\infty$ and $h_n\downarrow 0$. $\hat{\theta}$, on the other hand, is a consistent estimator of $\theta=0$ only as $N\uparrow\infty$. The consistency of $\hat{\alpha}_n$ is explained by the fact that, although there is not an infinite span of data (N is fixed), there is, in the limit as $n\uparrow\infty$, an infinite amount of independent incremental data on the random walk (24) (and, hence, on the coefficient $\alpha=1$) because the triangular array $\{\{u_{nt}\}_1^{T_n}\}_1^{\infty}$ has iid innovations in every row. This is sufficient to ensure that $\hat{\alpha}_n \underset{p}{\rightarrow} 1$ as $n\uparrow\infty$.

7. AN ASYMPTOTIC EXPANSION OF THE DISTRIBUTION OF $T(\hat{\alpha}-1)$

A general refinement (to higher order) of the functional central limit theorem discussed in Section 2 does not yet appear to be available in the probability literature. However, it is relatively easy to develop asymptotic expansions in special cases such as the limit Theorem 3.1. In order to proceed one needs to endow the random sequence $\{u_t\}_1^{\infty}$ with somewhat stronger properties than those of Assumption 2.1. To facilitate our analysis here, we shall consider the special case in which the u_t are iid $N(0,\sigma^2)$. In this case it is easy to see that, for fixed $r\in[0,1]$, $X_T(r)$ is $N(0,[Tr]/T)$. In fact, when $r=0$ we have $X_T(0)=W(0)=0$ and when $0<r\leqslant 1$ we have:

$$\begin{aligned} X_T(r) &= W(r)([Tr]/Tr)^{1/2} \\ &= W(r)\{1-(Tr-[Tr])/Tr\}^{1/2} \qquad (34)\\ &\equiv W(r)\left\{1-\frac{1}{2}\frac{Tr-[Tr]}{Tr}\right\}+O_p(T^{-2}), \end{aligned}$$

where, as before, "$\equiv$" signifies equality in distribution. Equation (34) provides a simple asymptotic expansion for the finite dimensional (in fact, one dimensional) distribution of $X_T(r)$ with r fixed. Note that, since $W(r)/r \underset{\text{a.s.}}{\rightarrow} 0$ as $r\downarrow 0$ (see, for example, Hida (1980, p. 57)), the expansion (34) remains well defined in the neighborhood of $t=0$. Higher order finite dimensional distributions of $X_T(r)$ may be treated in a similar way. The error on the approximation $X_T(r)\sim W(r)$ is seen to be of $O_p(T^{-1})$ in (34). This suggests that certain functionals of $X_T(r)$ may be expected to differ from the same functionals of $W(r)$ by quantities of the same order. In particular

$$\int_0^1 X_T(r)^2\,dr \equiv \int_0^1 W(r)^2\,dr + O_p(T^{-1}) \tag{35}$$

and this expansion may be verified directly by developing an expansion for the characteristic function of $\int_0^1 X_T(r)^2\,dr$. Since the algebra is lengthy we shall not report it here.

Our main concern is to develop an expansion for the distribution of $T(\hat{\alpha}-1)$. We therefore consider next the numerator of this statistic, viz.

$$T^{-1}\sum_1^T y_{t-1}(y_t - y_{t-1}) = (\sigma^2/2)X_T(1)^2 - (2T)^{-1}\sum_1^T u_i^2 + y_0\bar{u}, \tag{36}$$

using formula (A3) from the Appendix. We shall confine our attention to the case where the initial value $y_0 = 0$. Since $X_T(1)^2 \equiv W(1)^2 + O_p(T^{-1})$, (36) becomes (in distribution):

$$\begin{aligned}&(\sigma^2/2)(W(1)^2-1) - (1/2T)\sum_1^T (u_i^2 - \sigma^2) + O_p(T^{-1})\\ &\quad\equiv (\sigma^2/2)(W(1)^2-1) - (\sigma^2/\sqrt{2T})\xi + O_p(T^{-1})\end{aligned}$$

where $\xi \equiv N(0, 1)$ and is independent of the Wiener process $W(r)$. The distribution of ξ follows directly from the Lindeberg-Levy theorem. Note that ξ is dependent on a quadratic function of the u_i, whereas $W(r)$ depends on partial sums which are linear in the u_i. Hence, ξ and $W(r)$ are uncorrelated and, being normal, are therefore independent. We deduce the following result.

THEOREM 7.1: *If y_t is generated from the random walk* (1) *with $\alpha = 1$ and initial value $y_0 = 0$ and if the u_i are iid $N(0, \sigma^2)$, then*

$$T(\hat{\alpha}-1) \equiv \frac{(1/2)(W(1)^2-1) - (1/\sqrt{2T})\xi}{\int_0^1 W(r)^2\,dr} + O_p(T^{-1}) \tag{37}$$

where $W(r)$ is a standard Wiener process and ξ is $N(0, 1)$ and independent of $W(r)$.

(37) provides the first term in the asymptotic expansion of the distribution of $T(\hat{\alpha}-1)$ about its limiting distribution. We observe that the term of $1/\sqrt{T}$ in this expansion contributes no adjustment to the mean of the limiting distribution. This is to be contrasted with the expansion of the distribution of $\sqrt{T}(\hat{\alpha}-\alpha)$ when $|\alpha| < 1$ that was obtained in earlier work by the author (1977). In the latter case the mean adjustment of the $O(1/\sqrt{T})$ term in the expansion was substantial for α less than but close to unity.

The expansion (37) suggests that the location of the limiting distribution should be an accurate approximation in moderate samples. This is confirmed in the results of the sampling experiment in Evans and Savin (1981). It will be of interest to discover the extent to which (37) improves upon the asymptotic distribution of $\hat{\alpha}$ at various finite sample sizes. The numerical computations that are necessary to explore this question will be performed at a later date.

8. CONCLUSION

The model (1) and (2) that we have considered above is much more general than it may appear. It applies, for example, to virtually any ARMA model with a unit root and even ARMAX systems with a unit root and with stable exogenous processes that admit a Wold decomposition. In the former case, we may write

$$a(L)(1-L)y_t = b(L)e_t \tag{38}$$

for given finite order lag polynomials $a(L)$ and $b(L)$ in the lag operator L. Then, upon inversion, (38) becomes

$$y_t = y_{t-1} + u_t, \qquad u_t = a(L)^{-1}b(L)e_t, \tag{39}$$

and u_t will satisfy the weak dependence and heteroskedasticity conditions of Assumption 2.1 under very general conditions on the innovations and lag polynomials of (38). In the latter case, we may write

$$a(L)(1-L)y_t = b(L)x_t + c(L)e_t \tag{40}$$

with

$$d(L)x_t = f(L)v_t$$

and then upon inversion we have

$$y_t = y_{t-1} + u_t, \qquad u_t = a(L)^{-1}c(L)e_t + a(L)^{-1}b(L)d(L)^{-1}f(L)v_t$$

which is once again of the form (1) with u_t satisfying the required assumptions under general conditions on e_t, v_t, and the lag polynomials.

Our results show that in quite complicated time series models such as (38) and (40) it is not necessary to estimate the model or even to identify the model in order to consistently estimate or test for a unit root in the time series. One needs only to construct the first order serial correlation coefficient and associated test statistics (21) or (22) and use the appropriate limiting distributions given in Theorems 3.1 and 5.1 for statistical testing. This approach applies under conditions that are of even wider applicability than the models (38) and (40). In a certain sense, this general idea is already implicit in the Box-Jenkins modeling approach. However, none of the traditional theory in this research (given, for example, by Box and Jenkins (1976) or Granger and Newbold (1977)) allows for estimation or testing procedures that have anything approaching the range of applicability of the approach developed here.

The research reported in this paper is currently being extended in various ways. First, the methods that we have developed make it very easy to perform similar analyses on models like (1) with a drift and a time trend. The new tests for the presence of a unit root given here may also be extended to such models. Second, multivariate generalizations of time series models such as (1) may also be studied by our methods. This generalization opens the way to a detailed asymptotic analysis of nonstationary vector autoregressions, spurious regressions of the type considered by Granger and Newbold (1974, 1977), and co-integrating regressions of the type advanced recently by Granger and Engle (1985). Third, the asymptotic local power properties of the tests developed herein and those of other authors such as Dickey and Fuller (1976, 1981) may be studied by procedures which are entirely analogous to those devised here but which allow for local departures from unit root formulations. Finally, the methods outlined in Section 7 for the refinement of the first order asymptotic theory may be extended to apply in quite general time series models with a unit root. All of these extensions are currently under investigation by the author.

Department of Economics, Yale University, New Haven, CT 06520, U.S.A.

Manuscript received April, 1985; final revision received March, 1986.

MATHEMATICAL APPENDIX

PROOF OF LEMMA 2.2: See Herrndorf (1984b, Corollary 1, p. 142).

PROOF OF LEMMA 2.3: See Billingsley (1968, Corollary 1, p. 31).

PROOF OF THEOREM 3.1: To prove (a) and (b) we write each statistic as a functional of $X_T(r)$ on $D[0,1]$. Thus, in the case of (a), we have

$$\text{(A1)}\quad T^{-2}\sum_1^T y_{t-1}^2 = T^{-2}\sum_{i=1}^T\left(\sum_{j=1}^{i-1} u_j + y_0\right)^2$$

$$= T^{-2}\sum_1^T (S_{i-1}^2 + 2y_0 S_{i-1} + y_0^2)$$

$$= \sigma^2\sum_1^T\int_{(i-1)/T}^{i/T}(1/T\sigma^2)S_{[Tr]}^2\,dr + 2y_0\sigma T^{-1/2}\sum_1^T\int_{(i-1)/T}^{i/T}(1/\sqrt{T}\sigma)S_{[Tr]}\,dr + y_0^2/T$$

$$= \sigma^2\int_0^1 X_T^2(r)\,dr + 2y_0\sigma T^{-1/2}\int_0^1 X_T(r)\,dr + y_0^2/T$$

$$\Rightarrow \sigma^2\int_0^1 W(r)^2\,dr, \quad \text{as} \quad T\uparrow\infty$$

by Lemmas 2.2–2.3. Note that (A1) holds whether y_0 is a constant (see (3a)) or is random (see (3b)).

In the above derivation

$$\text{(A2)}\quad \sigma^2 = \lim_{T\to\infty} E(T^{-1}S_T^2)$$

as in part (a) of Assumption 2.1.

To prove (b) we have:

$$\text{(A2)}\quad T^{-1}\sum_1^T y_{t-1}(y_t - y_{t-1}) = \sum_{i=1}^T (1/\sqrt{T})(S_{i-1}+y_0)(u_i/\sqrt{T})$$

$$= T^{-1}\sum_1^T S_{i-1}u_i + y_0\bar{u}$$

$$= (2T)^{-1}\sum_1^T (S_i^2 - S_{i-1}^2 - u_i^2) + y_0\bar{u}$$

$$= (\sigma^2/2)\sum_1^T [X_T(r)^2]_{(i-1)/T}^{i/T} - (2T)^{-1}\sum_1^T u_i^2 + y_0\bar{u}$$

$$\text{(A3)}\quad = (\sigma^2/2)X_T(1)^2 - (2T)^{-1}\sum_1^T u_i^2 + y_0\bar{u}.$$

Under the conditions of the theorem (in particular, the requirement that $\sup_t E|u_t|^{\beta+\eta}<\infty$ for some $\beta>2$ and $\eta>0$) we deduce that:

(A4) $$T^{-1}\sum_1^T u_t^2 \xrightarrow[\text{a.s.}]{} \sigma_u^2 = \lim_{T\to\infty} T^{-1}\sum_1^T E(u_t^2)$$

and

(A5) $$\bar{u} \xrightarrow[\text{a.s.}]{} 0$$

by the strong law of McLeish (1975b, Theorem 2.10 with condition (2.12). Now $X_T(1)\Rightarrow W(1)$ by Lemma 2.2. It follows from (A3)-(A5) and the continuous mapping theorem (Lemma 2.3) that as $T\uparrow\infty$,

(A6) $$T^{-1}\sum_1^T y_{t-1}u_t \Rightarrow (\sigma^2/2)W(1)^2-(\sigma_u^2/2)=(\sigma^2/2)\{W(1)^2-\sigma_u^2/\sigma^2\},$$

proving (b) of the theorem.

In view of (A1) and (A6), result (c) of the theorem is also a direct consequence of the continuous mapping theorem. Part (d) of the theorem follows immediately from result (c).

To prove part (e) we first write

$$s^2=T^{-1}\sum(y_t-\hat{\alpha}y_{t-1})^2=T^{-1}\sum_1^T u_t^2-2(\hat{\alpha}-1)T^{-1}\sum_1^T y_{t-1}u_t+(\hat{\alpha}-1)^2T^{-1}\sum_1^T y_{t-1}^2.$$

Then, in view of (A4) and parts (a), (b), and (d) of the theorem we deduce that $s^2\xrightarrow[p]{}\sigma_u^2$ as $T\uparrow\infty$. Thus, it is of no consequence in the limiting distribution whether we use s^2 or $s'^2=T^{-1}\sum(y_t-y_{t-1})^2$ (as in the LM approach) in the construction of the t_α statistic (8). Part (e) of the theorem now follows directly from the continuous mapping theorem using parts (a) and (c).

PROOF OF LEMMA 4.1: The proof follows the same line as the proof of Lemma 6.17, pp. 149-152 of White (1984). We need only note that, since $\{u_t\}_1^\infty$ is strong mixing and $\sup_t E|u_t|^\beta<\infty$, the following inequality:

$$|E(u_tu_{t-\tau})|\leq c\alpha_\tau^{1-2/\beta}$$

holds for some constant c (see, for example, Ibragimov and Linnik (1971, Theorem 17.2.2, p. 307)). Thus

$$\left|2T^{-1}\sum_{\tau=l+1}^{T-1}\sum_{t=\tau+1}^{T}E(u_tu_{t-\tau})\right|\leq 2cT^{-1}\sum_{\tau=l+1}^{T-1}(T-\tau)\alpha_\tau^{1-2/\beta}$$

and the right side of this inequality tends to zero as $T\uparrow\infty$ since $l\uparrow\infty$ and $\sum_1^\infty\alpha_m^{1-2/\beta}<\infty$. We deduce that $\sigma_T^2-\sigma_{Tl}^2\to 0$ as $T\uparrow\infty$.

PROOF OF THEOREM 4.2: The proof follows the same lines as the proof of Theorem 6.20, pp. 155-159 of White (1984), although we have no need to treat estimated residuals here. We first note that the assumptions of the theorem ensure that the conditions of Lemma 4.1 hold. Thus, $\sigma_T^2-\sigma_{Tl}^2\to 0$ as $T\uparrow\infty$. Next we have

$$s_{Tl}^2-\sigma_{Tl}^2=T^{-1}\sum_1^T\{u_t^2-E(u_t^2)\}+2T^{-1}\sum_{s=1}^{l}\sum_{t=s+1}^{T}\{u_tu_{t-s}-E(u_tu_{t-s})\}$$

and

$$T^{-1}\sum_1^T\{u_t^2-E(u_t^2)\}\xrightarrow[\text{a.s.}]{}0,\quad T\uparrow\infty,$$

as in the proof of Theorem 3.1. Writing $Z_{ts}=u_tu_{t-s}-E(u_tu_{t-s})$, it remains to show that $T^{-1}\sum_{s=1}^{l}\sum_{t=s+1}^{T}Z_{ts}\xrightarrow[p]{}0$ as $T\uparrow\infty$. But this part of the proof follows as in the proof given by White (1984, pp. 155-157). It is necessary, however, to correct the error that occurs on page 156 of White (1984) in the use of his Lemma 6.19. When one allows for the fact that s may increase with T, the conclusion of Lemma 6.19 should be amended to

$$E\left(\sum_{t=s+1}^{T}Z_{ts}\right)\leq s(T-s)B<sTB$$

for a suitable constant B. It follows that (see p. 156 of White (1984) for details):

$$P\left[\left|T^{-1}\sum_{s=1}^{l}\sum_{t=s+1}^{T} Z_{ts}\right| \geq \varepsilon\right] \leq \sum_{s=1}^{l} sTBl^2/\varepsilon^2T^2$$

$$= Bl^3(l+1)/2\varepsilon^2 T$$

which tends to zero if $l = o(T^{1/4})$. We deduce that $s_{Tl}^2 \underset{p}{\rightarrow} \sigma^2$ as required.

PROOF OF THEOREM 5.1: By Theorems of 3.1 and 4.2 we have as $T\uparrow\infty$:

$$T(\hat{\alpha}-1) \Rightarrow \frac{(1/2)(W(1)^2 - \sigma_u^2/\sigma^2)}{\int_0^1 W(r)^2\,dr},$$

$$T^{-2}\sum_1^T y_{t-1}^2 \Rightarrow \sigma^2 \int_0^1 W(r)^2\,dr,$$

$$s_{Tl}^2 \underset{p}{\rightarrow} \sigma^2 \quad \text{and} \quad s_u^2 \underset{p}{\rightarrow} \sigma_u^2.$$

Part (a) now follows directly by the continuous mapping theorem. In the same way we deduce that

$$Z_t \Rightarrow \frac{(W(1)^2 - \sigma_u^2/\sigma^2)/2}{\{\int_0^1 W(r)^2\,dr\}^{1/2}} - \frac{(\sigma^2 - \sigma_u^2)/2}{\sigma^2\{\int_0^1 W(r)^2\,dr\}^{1/2}}$$

and part (b) follows as required.

PROOF OF LEMMA 6.1: Define $\xi_{nt} = \sigma^{-1}h_n^{-1/2}u_{nt}$. Then

$$Y_n(r) = h_n^{1/2}\sum_1^{i-1}\xi_{nt}, \quad (i-1)T_n \leq r < i/T_n \qquad (i=1,\ldots,T_n)$$

$$= N^{1/2}T_n^{-1/2}\sum_1^{i-1}\xi_{nt}.$$

But $\{\{\xi_{nt}\}_1^{T_n}\}_1^{\infty}$ is a triangular array of iid (0, 1) variates so that

$$W_n(r) = T_n^{-1/2}\sum_1^{i-1}\xi_{nt}, \qquad (i-1)/T_n \leq r < i/T_n,$$

$$\Rightarrow W(r)$$

as $n\uparrow\infty$ (see, for example, McLeish (1977, Corollary 2.11)). It follows that as $n\uparrow\infty$ $Y_n(r) \Rightarrow N^{1/2}W(r)$ as required.

PROOF OF THEOREM 6.2: Using (24), Lemma 6.1, and the continuous mapping theorem, we obtain:

$$h_n\sum_1^{T_n} y_{nt-1}^2 = (N/T_n)\sum_1^{T_n}\left\{\sum_1^{t-1} u_{ni} + y(0)\right\}^2$$

$$= (N/T_n)\sum_1^{T_n}\{S_{nt-1}^2 + 2y(0)S_{nt-1}\} + Ny(0)^2$$

$$= N\sigma^2\int_0^1 Y_n(r)^2\,dr + 2N\sigma y(0)\int_0^1 Y_n(r)\,dr + Ny(0)^2$$

$$\Rightarrow N^2\sigma^2\int_0^1 W(r)\,dr + 2N^{3/2}\sigma y(0)\int_0^1 W(r)\,dr + Ny(0)^2$$

as $n\uparrow\infty$. This proves part (a).

To prove part (b) we write:

$$\sum_1^{T_n} y_{nt-1}(y_{nt}-y_{nt-1}) = \sum_1^{T_n}\left\{\sum_1^{t-1} u_{ni}+y(0)\right\} u_{nt}$$
$$= h_n\sigma^2 \sum_1^{T_n}\left(\sum_1^{t-1}\xi_{ni}\right)\xi_{nt}+\sigma y(0)h_n^{1/2}\sum_1^{T_n}\xi_{nt}$$
$$= N\sigma^2\sum_1^{T_n}\left(T_n^{-1/2}\sum_1^{t-1}\xi_{ni}\right)(T_n^{-1/2}\xi_{nt})+\sigma y(0)N^{1/2}T^{-1/2}\sum_1^{T_n}\xi_{nt}$$
$$= (N\sigma^2/2)\sum_1^{T_n}\{[W_n(r)^2]_{(t-1)/T}^{t/T}-T_n^{-1}\xi_{nt}^2\}+\sigma y(0)N^{1/2}W_n(1)$$
$$= (N\sigma^2/2)W_n(1)^2-(N\sigma^2/2)T_n^{-1}\sum_1^{T_n}\xi_{nt}^2$$
$$\Rightarrow (N\sigma^2/2)W(1)^2-(N\sigma^2/2)+\sigma y(0)N^{1/2}W(1)$$

by the strong law of large numbers, Lemma 6.2, and the continuous mapping theorem.

Part (c) follows directly from the expression

$$\hat{\alpha}_n-1=\sum_1^{T_n} y_{nt-1}(y_{nt}-y_{nt-1})\Big/\sum_1^{T_n} y_{nt-1}^2$$

and parts (a) and (b) above.

To prove part (d) we note first, after a simple calculation, that

$$(1/h_n)s_n^2\Rightarrow\sigma^2T_n^{-1}\sum_1^{T_n}\xi_{nt}^2+2(h_n/N)(1-\hat{\alpha}_n)\sum_1^{T_n}y_{nt-1}u_{nt}+(h_n/N)(\hat{\alpha}_n-1)^2\sum_1^{T_n}y_{nt-1}^2$$
$$\underset{p}{\rightarrow}\sigma^2$$

as $n\uparrow\infty$. Then

$$t_{\alpha_n}=\left(h_n\sum_1^{T_n}y_{nt-1}^2\right)^{1/2}(1/h_n)(\hat{\alpha}_n-1)/(h_n^{-1/2}s_n)$$
$$\Rightarrow[(1/2)(W(1)^2-1)+(y(0)/\sigma N^{1/2})W(1)]$$
$$\div\left[\int_0^1 W(r)^2\,dr+2(y(0)/\sigma N^{1/2})\int_0^1 W(r)\,dr+y(0)^2/\sigma^2N\right]^{1/2}$$

as required.

Proof of Theorem 6.3: From the solution of (29) we have (under the null hypothesis $\theta=0$) $y(t)=\int_0^t\zeta(dr)+y(0)$. Thus,

$$y(t)/\sigma=V(t)+y(0)/\sigma.$$

Since $\int_0^t\zeta(dr)$ is Gaussian by assumption $V(t)$ is here a Wiener process on $C[0,N]$. Transform $t\to Nu=t$ with $u\in[0,1]$. Note that $V(t)=V(Nu)\equiv N(0,Nu)$ so that we may write $V(Nu)\equiv N^{1/2}W(u)$ where $W(u)$ is a Wiener process on $C[0,1]$. Now

$$\int_0^N y^2\,dt=\sigma^2\int_0^N V(t)^2\,dt+2\sigma y(0)\int_0^N V(t)\,dt+y(0)^2N$$
$$\equiv\sigma^2N^2\int_0^1 W(u)\,du+2\sigma y(0)N^{3/2}\int_0^1 W(u)\,du+y(0)^2N$$

and

$$\int_0^N y\,dy=\sigma^2\int_0^N V\,dV+\sigma y(0)\int_0^N dV$$
$$=\sigma^2N\int_0^1 W\,dW+\sigma y(0)N^{1/2}W(1)$$

$$= (\sigma^2 N/2)\{W(1)^2 - 1\} + \sigma y(0) N^{1/2} W(1)$$

and the required result follows.

REFERENCES

ANDERSON, R. L. (1942): "Distribution of the Serial Correlation Coefficient," *Annals of Mathematical Statistics*, 13, 1-13.

BARTLETT, M. S. (1946): "On the Theoretical Specification and Sampling Properties of Autocorrelated Time Series," *Journal of the Royal Statistical Society*, 7, 27-41.

BERGSTROM, A. R. (1976): *Statistical Inference in Continuous Time Economic Models*. Amsterdam: North Holland.

——— (1984): "Continuous Time Stochastic Models and Issues of Aggregation Over Time," Ch. 20 in *Handbook of Econometrics*, Vol. 2, ed. by M. D. Intriligator and Z. Griliches. Amsterdam: North Holland, pp. 1145-1212.

BHARGAVA, A. (1986): "On the Theory of Testing for Unit Roots in Observed Time Series," mimeographed, University of Pennsylvania.

BILLINGSLEY, P. (1968): *Convergence of Probability Measures*. New York: John Wiley.

BOX, G. E. P., AND G. M. JENKINS (1976): *Time Series Analysis: Forecasting and Control*. San Francisco: Holden Day.

BROWN, B. M., AND J. I. HEWITT (1975): "Asymptotic Likelihood Theory for Diffusion Processes," *Journal of Applied Probability*, 12, 228-238.

DICKEY, D. A. (1976): "Estimation and Hypothesis Testing for Nonstationary Time Series," Ph.D. Thesis, Iowa State University, Ames, Iowa.

DICKEY, D. A., AND W. A. FULLER (1976): "Distribution of the Estimators for Autoregressive Time Series with a Unit Root," *Journal of the American Statistical Association*, 74, 427-431.

——— (1981): "Likelihood Ratio Statistics for Autoregressive Time Series with a Unit Root," *Econometrica*, 49, 1057-1072.

DOAN, T., R. B. LITTERMAN, AND C. SIMS (1984): "Forecasting and Conditional Projection Using Realistic Prior Distributions," *Econometric Reviews*, 3, 1-100.

DONSKER, M. D. (1951): "An Invariance Principle for Certain Probability Limit Theorems," *Memoirs of the American Mathematical Society*, 6, 1-12.

ERDÖS, P., AND M. KAC (1946): "On Certain Limit Theorems in the Theory of Probability," *Bulletin of the American Mathematical Society*, 52, 292-302.

EVANS, G. B. A., AND N. E. SAVIN (1981): "Testing for Unit Roots: 1," *Econometrica*, 49, 753-779.

——— (1984): "Testing for Unit Roots: 2," *Econometrica*, 52, 1241-1269.

FEIGIN, P. D. (1979): "Some Comments About a Curious Singularity," *Journal of Applied Probability*, 16, 440-444.

FULLER, WAYNE A. (1976): *Introduction to Statistical Time Series*. New York: John Wiley & Sons.

GRANGER, C. W. J., AND P. NEWBOLD (1974): "Spurious Regressions in Econometrics," *Journal of Econometrics*, 2, 111-120.

——— (1977): *Forecasting Economic Time Series*. New York: Academic Press.

GRANGER, C. W. J., AND R. F. ENGLE (1985): "Dynamic Model Specification with Equilibrium Constraints: Cointegration and Error Correction," UCSD Discussion Paper No. 85-18.

GRENANDER, U. (1950): "Stochastic Processes and Statistical Inference," *Arkiv För Matematik*, 1, 195-275.

HALL, P., AND C. C. HEYDE (1980): *Martingale Limit Theory and its Application*. New York: Academic Press.

HALL, R. E. (1978): "Stochastic Implication of the Life Cycle-Permanent Income Hypothesis: Theory and Evidence," *Journal of Political Economy*, 86, 971-987.

HERRNDORF, N. (1983): "The Invariance Principle for φ-Mixing Sequences," *Z. Wahrscheinlichkeitstheorie Verw. Gebiete*, 63, 97-108.

——— (1984a): "A Functional Central Limit Theorem for ρ-Mixing Sequences," *Journal of Multivariate Analysis*, 15, 141-146.

——— (1984b): "A Functional Central Limit Theorem for Weakly Dependent Sequences of Random Variables," *Anals of Probability*, 12, 141-153.

HIDA, T. (1980): *Brownian Motion*. New York: Springer-Verlag.

IBRAGIMOV, I. A., AND Y. V. LINNIK (1971): *Independent and Stationary Sequences of Random Variables*. Groningen: Wolters-Noordhoff.

LAI, T. L., AND C. Z. WEI (1982): "Least Squares Estimates in Stochastic Regression Models with Applications to Identification and Control of Dynamic Systems," *Annals of Statistics*, 10, 154-166.

LAI, T. L., AND D. SEIGMUND (1983): "Fixed Accuracy Estimation of an Autoregressive Parameter," *Annals of Statistics*, 11, 478-485.

LITTERMAN, R. B. (1984): "Forecasting with Bayesian Vector Autoregressions: Four Years of Experience," mimeographed, Federal Reserve Bank of Minneapolis.

MCLEISH, D. L. (1975a): "Invariance Principles for Dependent Variables," *Z. Wahrscheinlichkeitstheorie und Verw. Gebiete*, 32, 165-178.

——— (1975b): "A Maximal Inequality and Dependent Strong Laws," *Annals of Probability*, 3, 829-839.

——— (1977): "On the Invariance Principle for Nonstationary Mixingales," *Annals of Probability*, 5, 616-621.

NANKERVIS, J. C., AND N. E. SAVIN (1985): "Testing the Autoregressive Parameter with the t Statistic," *Journal of Econometrics*, 27, 143-162.

NEWEY, W. K., AND K. D. WEST (1985): "A Simple Positive Definite Heteroskedasticity and Autocorrelation Consistent Covariance Matrix," Princeton Discussion Paper No. 92.

PHILLIPS, P. C. B. (1977): "Approximations to Some Finite Sample Distributions Associated with a First-Order Stochastic Difference Equation," *Econometrica*, 45, 463-485.

POLLARD, D. (1984): *Convergence of Stochastic Processes.* New York: Springer-Verlag.

PRIESTLEY, M. B. (1981): *Spectral Analysis and Time Series*, Vol. 1. New York: Academic Press.

RAO, M. M. (1978): "Asymptotic Distribution of An Estimator of the Boundary Parameter of An Unstable Process," *Annals of Statistics*, 6, 185-190.

ROZANOV, Y. A. (1967): *Stationary Random Processes.* San Francisco: Holden Day.

SAID, S. E., AND D. A. DICKEY (1985): "Testing for Unit Roots in Autoregressive-Moving Average Models of Unknown Order," *Biometrika*, 71, 599-608.

SARGAN, J. D., AND A. BHARGAVA (1983): "Testing Residuals from Least Squares Regression for Being Generated by a Gaussian Random Walk," *Econometrica*, 51, 153-174.

SOLO, V. (1984): "The Order of Differencing in ARIMA Models," *Journal of the American Statistical Association*, 79, 916-921.

TIAO, G. C., AND R. S. TSAY (1983): "Consistency Properties of Least Squares Estimates of Autoregressive Parameters in ARMA Models," *Annals of Statistics*, 11, 856-871.

WHITE, H. (1984): *Asymptotic Theory for Econometricians.* New York: Academic Press.

WHITE, H., AND I. DOMOWITZ (1984): "Nonlinear Regression with Dependent Observations," *Econometrica*, 52, 143-162.

WHITE, J. S. (1958): "The Limiting Distribution of the Serial Correlation Coefficient in the Explosive Case," *Anals of Mathematical Statistics*, 29, 1188-1197.

WITHERS, C. S. (1981): "Conditions for Linear Processes to be Strong Mixing," *Z. Wahrscheinlichkeitstheorie und Verw. Gebiete*, 57, 477-480.

[15]

Journal of Business & Economic Statistics, January 1991, Vol. 9, No. 1

Asymptotic Distributions of Unit-Root Tests When the Process Is Nearly Stationary

Sastry G. Pantula
Department of Statistics, North Carolina State University, Raleigh, NC 27695-8203

Several test criteria are available for testing the hypothesis that the autoregressive polynomial of an autoregressive moving average process has a single unit root. Schwert (1989), using a Monte Carlo study, investigated the performance of some of the available test criteria. He concluded that the actual levels of the test criteria considered in his study are far from the specified levels when the moving average polynomial also has a root close to 1. This article studies the asymptotic null distribution of the test statistics for testing $\rho = 1$ in the model $Y_t = \rho Y_{t-1} + e_t - \theta e_{t-1}$ as θ approaches 1. It is shown that the test statistics differ from one another in their asymptotic properties depending on the rate at which θ converges to 1.

KEY WORDS: Autoregressive and moving average processes; Limiting distributions; Random walk; White noise.

Fuller (1976) and Dickey and Fuller (1979) proposed simple tests for testing the hypothesis that the characteristic equation of an autoregressive process has a single unit root. The test criteria proposed by Dickey and Fuller (1979), however, are not valid when the process is an autoregressive moving average process. The moving average parameters in the model introduce some bias into the Dickey–Fuller test statistics, which are constructed assuming that the model is a pure autoregressive process. Said and Dickey (1984, 1985) proposed two methods for testing for a single unit root in an autoregressive moving average process. Phillips (1987a) and Phillips and Perron (1988) suggested alternate criteria, which asymptotically correct the bias in the Dickey–Fuller test statistics. Hall (1989), on the other hand, suggested a criterion based on the instrumental variable (IV) approach that avoids the bias in the Dickey–Fuller criteria.

Schwert (1989) and Hall (1989) considered the model

$$Y_t = \rho Y_{t-1} + e_t - \theta e_{t-1}, \qquad \rho = 1, \qquad (1)$$

where e_t is a sequence of iid $N(0, 1)$ variables. Schwert (1989) cited several examples of economic data that are well approximated by Model (1) with θ close to 1. See also Schwert (1987). Schwert (1989) considered the test statistics for testing the null hypothesis $\rho = 1$ proposed by Dickey and Fuller (1979), Said and Dickey (1984, 1985), Phillips (1987a) and Phillips and Perron (1988). Using a Monte Carlo study, he compared the empirical level with the specified level of different test criteria. He concluded that the performance of the test criteria is poor when θ is close to 1. When $\theta = .8$, the empirical levels of different test criteria are observed to be much higher than the specified level. Hall (1989) observed that his criteria based on the IV approach also reject the null hypothesis more often than expected when θ is close to unity. (See Table 2 in Sec. 3 for the empirical levels of different test criteria when $\theta = .8$.) Similar results were also observed by Phillips and Perron (1988) and Perron (1988).

The main goal of this article is to study the asymptotic properties of some of the unit-root test criteria when θ approaches unity. Note that the model (1), when $\rho = 1$ and $\theta = 1$, reduces to $Y_t = \mu + e_t$, where e_t is a white-noise process. The null hypothesis H_0: $\rho = 1$ ($|\theta| < 1$) includes processes that are arbitrarily close to a white-noise process. If the process were a white-noise process, one should reject this null hypothesis. In finite samples, it may not be reasonable to expect that the preceding test criteria hold the proper level for all values of θ, especially when θ is arbitrarily close to 1. To study the behavior of the test statistics when θ is close to 1, I consider the model (1) when $\rho = 1$ and $\theta = \theta_n = 1 - n^{-\delta}$, where $\delta \geq 0$. If $\delta = 0$, we get $\theta = 0$ and the process is a random-walk process. As δ increases, θ gets closer to 1 and the process behaves like a white-noise process. This line of research was also suggested by Perron (1988).

In Section 1, I discuss the model and some of the unit-root test statistics. In Section 2, I present the asymptotic distributions of the test statistics for different values of δ. The results of a Monte Carlo study are given in Section 3. I conclude with some remarks in Section 4. An outline of the proofs of the main results is given in an appendix. Interested readers may obtain a complete set of detailed proofs from me.

1. THE MODEL AND THE TEST STATISTICS

Consider the simple model

$$Y_t(n) = \rho Y_{t-1}(n) + e_t - \theta_n e_{t-1}, \qquad t = 1, 2, \ldots, n, \qquad (2)$$

where $\rho = 1$, $\theta_n = 1 - n^{-\delta}$, $\delta \geq 0$, and e_t is a sequence of iid random variables with mean 0, variance σ^2, and

64 Journal of Business & Economic Statistics, January 1991

bounded fourth moments. Since the effect of e_0 and Y_0 is asymptotically negligible, I assume throughout the article that $\sigma^2 = 1$, $e_0 = 0$, and $Y_0 = 0$. Note that

$$Y_t(n) = Y_{t-1}(n) + e_t - e_{t-1} + n^{-\delta}e_{t-1}$$
$$= e_t + n^{-\delta}X_{t-1}, \tag{3}$$

where $X_t = \Sigma_{i=1}^t e_i$ is a random-walk process; so the process $Y_t(n)$ is a combination of a white-noise process and a random-walk process. For the sake of convenience, in the rest of the article I use Y_t for $Y_t(n)$. If $\delta = 0$, then Y_t is a nonstationary (random-walk) process given by $Y_t = Y_{t-1} + e_t$. As δ increases to infinity, Y_t behaves more and more like a white-noise process. (In fact, if $\delta > .5$, then $\max_{1\le t\le n} n^{-\delta}\|X_{t-1}\|$ converges to 0 almost surely.) In this sense, the process is *nearly stationary* (in fact, nearly white noise). Model (2) is motivated by the examples of economic data cited by Schwert (1989).

Ahtola and Tiao (1984), Phillips (1987b), and Chan and Wei (1987) considered an analogous specification of the autoregressive coefficient. They considered processes that are nearly nonstationary in which $\rho = \rho_n$ converges to 1 as n increases. The purpose of their studies was to investigate the asymptotic power of the unit-root tests under a sequence of local alternatives. I, on the other hand, am considering a sequence of models in the null hypothesis that approach the alternative (stationary models) and study the asymptotic level of the tests.

Now let us consider the behavior of the sample autocovariance function $\hat\gamma(h)$ of the Y_t process given in (2). Note that

$$\hat\gamma(h) = n^{-1}\sum_{t=h+1}^{n} Y_tY_{t-h}$$
$$= n^{-1}\sum_{t=h+1}^{n} e_te_{t-h} + n^{-2\delta+1}n^{-2}$$
$$\times \sum_{t=h+1}^{n} X_{t-1}^2 + 0_p(n^{-\delta}).$$

Therefore, if $0 < \delta < .5$, $n^{2\delta-1}\hat\gamma(h) \xrightarrow{\mathcal{L}} \Gamma$ ($h = 0, 1, 2, \ldots$), where $\Gamma = \int_0^1 W^2(t)\,dt$ and $W(t)$ is a standard Brownian motion. Therefore, for $0 < \delta < .5$, $\hat\rho(h) = [\hat\gamma(0)]^{-1}\hat\gamma(h) \xrightarrow{P} 1$. (We use $\xrightarrow{\mathcal{L}}$ to indicate the convergence in distribution and $\xrightarrow{P}$ to denote the convergence in probability. I will also use $\Rightarrow$ to signify weak convergence of the probability measures on the function space $D[0, 1]$, where $D[0, 1]$ is the space of real valued functions on the interval $[0, 1]$ that are right continuous and have finite limits.) On the other hand, if $\delta > .5$, then $\hat\gamma(h) \xrightarrow{P} 0$ for $h > 0$ and $\hat\gamma(0) \xrightarrow{P} 1$. In fact, if $\delta > .75$, then from corollary 6.3.5.1 of Fuller (1976), it follows that, for any fixed h, $n^{1/2}[\hat\rho(1), \ldots, \hat\rho(h)] \xrightarrow{\mathcal{L}} N(0, I_h)$, where I_h denotes an identity matrix of size h. Therefore, when $\delta > .75$, an α-level test criterion based on the Q statistic suggested by Ljung and Box (1978) is expected to reject the hypothesis that the process is *white noise* only $100\alpha\%$ of the time; that is, when $\delta > .75$, in practice one would tend to believe that the process is white noise. A limited simulation of the processes Y_t in (2) with $\delta > .75$ indicates that the time plot and the sample correlogram resemble that of a white-noise process.

I now present some of the test statistics that exist in the literature for testing the null hypothesis H_0: $\rho = 1$, $|\theta| < 1$, against the alternative hypothesis H_a: $|\rho| < 1$, $|\theta| < 1$, in Model (1) and present the asymptotic distributions under the null hypothesis.

1. *The $\hat\tau$ statistic suggested by Dickey and Fuller (1979):* The regression t statistic for testing that the coefficient of Y_{t-1} is 1 in the regression of Y_t on Y_{t-1},

$$\hat\tau = s_1^{-1}\left(\sum_{t=2}^{n} Y_{t-1}^2\right)^{1/2}(\hat\rho - 1), \tag{4}$$

where

$$s_1^2 = (n-2)^{-1}\sum_{t=2}^{n}(Y_t - \hat\rho Y_{t-1})^2$$

and

$$\hat\rho = \left(\sum_{t=2}^{n} Y_{t-1}^2\right)^{-1}\sum_{t=2}^{n} Y_{t-1}Y_t.$$

Dickey and Fuller (1979) considered the test statistic $\hat\tau$ only for the case in which $\delta = 0$. They showed that, under Model (2) when $\rho = 1$ and $\delta = 0$,

$$\hat\tau \xrightarrow{\mathcal{L}} \Gamma^{-1/2}\xi, \tag{5}$$

where $\Gamma = \int_0^1 W^2(t)\,dt$, $\xi = \frac{1}{2}W^2(1) - \frac{1}{2}$, and $W(t)$ is a standard Brownian motion. Fuller (1976) gave the percentiles of the limiting distribution given in (5). The test statistic $\hat\tau$ is not appropriate for testing the hypothesis of nonstationarity when the process is a mixed model (e.g., $\delta > 0$). I study the statistic $\hat\tau$ only to see what happens to it when the model is *incorrectly* specified to be a first-order autoregressive process.

2. *The t_k statistic suggested by Said and Dickey (1984):* The regression t statistic for testing that the coefficient of Y_{t-1} is 0 in the regression of $u_t = Y_t - Y_{t-1}$ on Y_{t-1} ($u_{t-1}, \ldots, u_{t-k+1}$), where $k = 0(n^{1/4})$; that is,

$$t_k = (s_k^2G^n)^{-1/2}\hat\eta_1, \tag{6}$$

where $\hat\eta_1$ is the first coordinate of $\hat\eta = G_k^{-1}g_k$,

$$G_k = \sum_{t=k+1}^{n} \mathbf{L}_{t-1}\mathbf{L}_{t-1}',$$

$$\mathbf{L}_{t-1}' = (Y_{t-1}, u_{t-1}, \ldots, u_{t-k+1}),$$

$$\mathbf{g}_k = \sum_{t=k+1}^{n} \mathbf{L}_{t-1}u_t,$$

$$s_k^2 = (n-2k)^{-1}\sum_{t=k+1}^{n}(u_t - \mathbf{L}_{t-1}\hat\eta)^2, \tag{7}$$

and G'' is the (1, 1)th element of G_k^{-1}. Note that $(s_k^2 G'')^{1/2}$ is the estimated standard error of $\hat{\eta}_1$ and t_k is the usual regression statistic for testing that the coefficient of Y_{t-1} is 0 in the regression of u_t on $\mathbf{L}'_{t-1}$. Said and Dickey (1984) showed that under Model (2), when $\rho = 1$ and $\delta = 0$, $t_k \xrightarrow{\mathcal{L}} \Gamma^{-1/2}\xi$.

3. *The Z_α statistics proposed by Phillips (1987a):* Let $\hat{\rho}$ denote the least squares estimator in the regression of Y_t on Y_{t-1}. Then, under Model (1), when $\rho = 1$, the estimator $\hat{\rho}$ is not consistent for ρ when $\theta \neq 0$. Phillips (1987a) and Phillips and Perron (1988) suggested modifications to $n(\hat{\rho} - 1)$ given by

$$Z_\alpha = n(\hat{\rho} - 1) - \left[n^{-2}\sum_{t=2}^{n} Y_{t-1}^2\right]^{-1}\left[n^{-1}\sum_{j=1}^{k}\sum_{t=j+1}^{n} \hat{u}_t\hat{u}_{t-j}\right] \quad (8)$$

and

$$Z_\alpha^{(1)} = Z_\alpha + \left[n^{-2}\sum_{t=2}^{n} Y_{t-1}^2\right]^{-1} \times \left[n^{-1}\sum_{j=1}^{k}(k+1)^{-1}j\sum_{t=j+1}^{n}\hat{u}_t\hat{u}_{t-j}\right], \quad (9)$$

where $\hat{u}_t = Y_t - \hat{\rho}Y_{t-1}$. They proved that Z_α and $Z_\alpha^{(1)}$ converge asymptotically to $\Gamma^{-1}\xi$ when $k = 0(n^{1/4})$. The percentiles of the distribution of $\Gamma^{-1}\xi$ are tabulated in table 8.5.1 of Fuller (1976).

4. *Z_{IV} statistic suggested by Hall (1989):* Let $\hat{\rho}_{IV} = (\Sigma_t Y_{t-1}Y_{t-2})^{-1}(\Sigma_t Y_{t-2}Y_t)$ denote the instrumental-variable estimator of ρ in the regression of Y_t on Y_{t-1}, where Y_{t-2} is used as an instrument. [Hall (1989) actually suggested a class of estimators in which Y_{t-l} ($l > 1$) is used as an instrument. Note that, under Model (1), Y_{t-l} is uncorrelated with $e_t - \theta e_{t-1}$ for $l > 1$. Pantula (1989) showed that among the IV estimators for ρ in Model (1) considered by Hall (1989) the IV estimator with Y_{t-2} as the instrument has the smallest asymptotic variance when $|\rho| < 1$.) Then, under Model (2) when $\rho = 1$ and $\delta = 0$, the statistic

$$Z_{IV} = n(\hat{\rho}_{IV} - 1) \xrightarrow{\mathcal{L}} \Gamma^{-1}\xi. \quad (10)$$

It is more common in practice to consider the alternative hypothesis to be either H_a: $Y_t = \mu + \rho Y_{t-1} + e_t - \theta e_{t-1}$ ($|\rho| < 1$, $|\theta| < 1$) or H_a: $Y_t = \beta_0 + \beta_1 t + \rho Y_{t-1} + e_t - \theta e_{t-1}$ ($|\rho| < 1$, $|\theta| < 1$). In the literature, there are several other test statistics [e.g., the $t_{k,\mu}$ and $t_{k,\tau}$ statistics of Said and Dickey (1984); the Z_t, $Z_{\alpha\mu}$, $Z_{t\mu}$, $Z_{\alpha\tau}$, and $Z_{t\tau}$ statistics of Phillips and Perron (1988), and the IV versions of Phillips and Perron (1988) test statistics proposed by Hall (1989)] to test the null hypothesis H_0: $\rho = 1$, $|\theta| < 1$ against the preceding alternative hypotheses. The purpose of this article is to give *some* indication of what happens to some of the test statistics when the process is nearly stationary. The ideas presented here can be routinely extended to other test statistics and hence such extensions will not be presented here.

2. MAIN RESULTS

For different values of δ in Model (2), I now present the asymptotic distribution of the test statistics described in Secton 1. Recall that under Model (2) $Y_t = e_t + n^{-\delta}X_{t-1}$, where $X_t = \Sigma_{i=1}^{t} e_i$. As noted earlier, if $\delta > .5$, then $n^{-\delta}\max_{1\le t\le n}|X_{t-1}|$ converges to 0 almost surely. This indicates that the behavior of Y_t (and hence of the statistics) may depend on whether $\delta > .5$ or not.

Note also that the test statistics t_k, Z_α, and $Z_\alpha^{(1)}$ depend on k, which is of order $n^{1/4}$. In fact, the t statistic t_k is based on approximating the integrated moving average processes in (1) by a kth-order autoregressive process. From (2), we have that

$$\begin{aligned} u_t &= Y_t - Y_{t-1} \\ &= -(1 - n^{-\delta})e_{t-1} + e_t \\ &= -\sum_{l=1}^{k-1}(1 - n^{-\delta})^l u_{t-l} + e_t - (1 - n^{-\delta})^k e_{t-k}. \quad (11) \end{aligned}$$

The remainder term $(1 - n^{-\delta})^k e_{t-k}$ in the autoregressive approximation may or may not converge to 0. Since $k = 0(n^{1/4})$, the coefficient $(1 - n^{-\delta})^k$ converges to 0 or 1 depending on whether $0 < \delta < .25$ or $\delta > .25$. Therefore, in presenting the limiting distributions of the test statistics, we consider three intervals: (a) $0 < \delta < .25$, (b) $.25 < \delta < .5$, and (c) $\delta > .5$. See Figure 1 and Table 1 for a summary of the orders in probability of various test statistics as a function of δ.

2.1 Results for the Case in Which $0 < \delta < .25$: Nonstationary Region

The asymptotic distributions of the test statistics are summarized in the following theorem.

Theorem 2.1. Consider Model (2) when $\rho = 1$ and $0 < \delta < .25$:

1. $n^{-\delta}\hat{\tau} \xrightarrow{\mathcal{L}} -[2\Gamma]^{-1/2}$
2. $t_k \xrightarrow{\mathcal{L}} \Gamma^{-1/2}\xi$
3. (a) $Z_\alpha \xrightarrow{\mathcal{L}} \Gamma^{-1}\xi$ for $0 < \delta < .1875$
   (b) $k^{-1}n^{1-4\delta}Z_\alpha \xrightarrow{\mathcal{L}} -[\Gamma]^{-2}$ for $.1875 < \delta < .25$
   (c) $Z_\alpha^{(1)} \xrightarrow{\mathcal{L}} \Gamma^{-1}\xi$ for $0 < \delta < .1875$
   (d) $k^{-1}n^{1-4\delta}Z_\alpha^{(1)} \xrightarrow{\mathcal{L}} -.5[\Gamma]^{-2}$ for $.1875 < \delta < .25$
4. $Z_{IV} \xrightarrow{\mathcal{L}} \Gamma^{-1}\xi$,

where the test statistics Γ and ξ are as defined in Section 1.

Notice that the test statistic $\hat{\tau}$ diverges to negative infinity. Moreover, Z_α and $Z_\alpha^{(1)}$ diverge to negative infinity when $\delta > .1875$. More important, note that the remaining statistics have the *same* asymptotic distributions as in the case in which $\delta = 0$; that is, even if the process is nearly stationary, the test statistics have the asymptotic distributions as in the case when the process is nonstationary, provided that the rate at which the moving average parameter $\theta_n = 1 - n^{-\delta}$ converges to 1 is not faster than $n^{1/4}$. In this sense, the test criteria

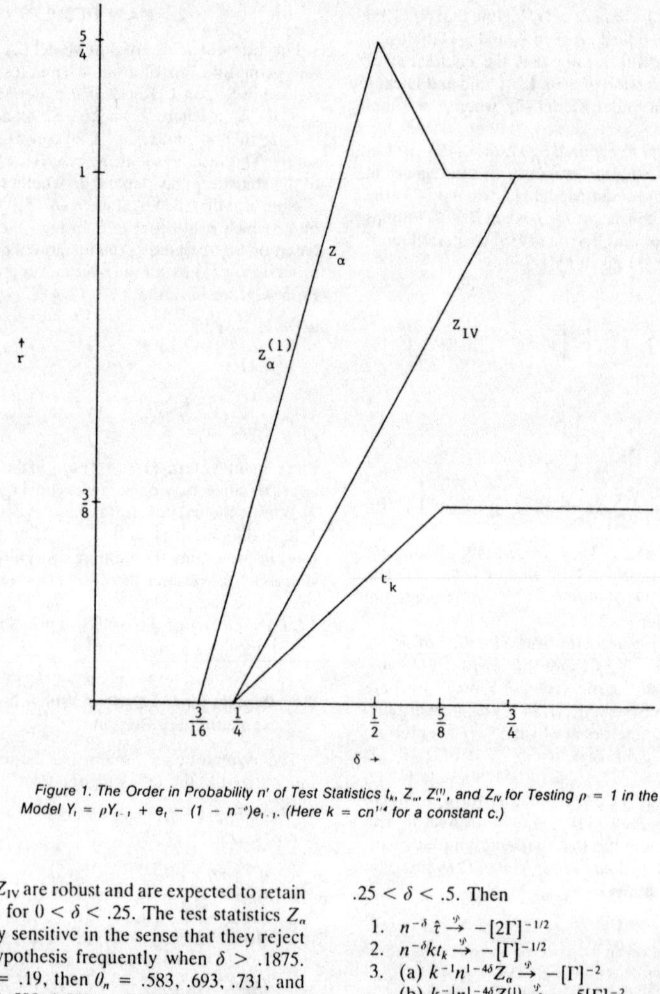

Figure 1. The Order in Probability n^r of Test Statistics t_k, Z_α, $Z_\alpha^{(1)}$, and Z_{IV} for Testing $\rho = 1$ in the Model $Y_t = \rho Y_{t-1} + e_t - (1 - n^{-\delta})e_{t-1}$. (Here $k = cn^{1/4}$ for a constant c.)

based on t_k and Z_{IV} are robust and are expected to retain the proper level for $0 < \delta < .25$. The test statistics Z_α and $Z_\alpha^{(1)}$ are very sensitive in the sense that they reject the unit-root hypothesis frequently when $\delta > .1875$. (Note that if $\delta = .19$, then $\theta_n = .583, .693, .731$, and .826 for $n = 100, 500, 1{,}000$, and 10,000, respectively.)

2.2 Results for the Case in Which $.25 < \delta < .5$: Gray Zone

The following theorem summarizes the limiting distributions of the test statistics given in Section 1 for processes satisfying (2) when $\rho = 1$ and $.25 < \delta < .5$. Note that if $\delta = .25$, then $\theta_n = .684, .789, .822$, and .900 for $n = 100, 500, 1{,}000$, and 10,000, respectively. Moreover, if $\delta = .5$, then $\theta_n = .9, .955, .968$, and .99 for $n = 100, 500, 1{,}000$, and 10,000, respectively.

Theorem 2.2. Consider Model (2) when $\rho = 1$ and $.25 < \delta < .5$. Then

1. $n^{-\delta}\,\hat{\tau} \xrightarrow{\mathcal{D}} -[2\Gamma]^{-1/2}$
2. $n^{-\delta} k t_k \xrightarrow{\mathcal{D}} -[\Gamma]^{-1/2}$
3. (a) $k^{-1} n^{1-4\delta} Z_\alpha \xrightarrow{\mathcal{D}} -[\Gamma]^{-2}$
   (b) $k^{-1} n^{1-4\delta} Z_\alpha^{(1)} \xrightarrow{\mathcal{D}} -.5[\Gamma]^{-2}$
4. $n^{-2\delta+.5} Z_{IV} \xrightarrow{\mathcal{D}} [\Gamma]^{-1}(N_1 - N_0)$,

where N_0 and N_1 are independent $N(0, 1)$ random variables independent of Γ and ξ.

Notice that the test statistics $\hat{\tau}$ and t_k diverge to negative infinity. Note that $|Z_{IV}|$ diverges to infinity at the rate $n^{2\delta-.5}$, whereas the test statistic t_k diverges to negative infinity at the rate $n^{\delta-.25}$. This indicates that the test statistic Z_{IV} is more unstable than the test statistic t_k. Moreover, the statistics Z_α and $Z_\alpha^{(1)}$ diverge to negative infinity at the rate $n^{4\delta-.75}$. This partly explains the Monte Carlo results of Schwert (1989). He observed that the Phillips and Perron (1988) test statistics reject

Table 1. Summary of the Asymptotic Distributions of Unit-Root Test Statistics in the Model $Y_t = \rho Y_{t-1} + e_t - (1 - n^{-\delta})e_{t-1}$

		Test statistic[a]				
δ		$\hat{\tau}$	t_k	Z_α	$Z_\alpha^{(1)}$	Z_{IV}
$(0, \frac{3}{16})$	Multiplier	$n^{-\delta}$	1	1	1	1
	Limit[b]	$-[2\Gamma]^{-1/2}$	$\Gamma^{-1/2}\xi$	$\Gamma^{-1}\xi$	$\Gamma^{-1}\xi$	$\Gamma^{-1}\xi$
$(\frac{3}{16}, \frac{1}{4})$	Multiplier	$n^{-\delta}$	1	$k^{-1}n^{1-4\delta}$	$k^{-1}n^{1-4\delta}$	1
	Limit	$-[2\Gamma]^{-1/2}$	$\Gamma^{-1/2}\xi$	$-\Gamma^{-2}$	$-.5\Gamma^{-2}$	$\Gamma^{-1}\xi$
$(\frac{1}{4}, \frac{1}{2})$	Multiplier	$n^{-\delta}$	$kn^{-\delta}$	$k^{-1}n^{1-4\delta}$	$k^{-1}n^{1-4\delta}$	$n^{-2\delta+0.5}$
	Limit	$-[2\Gamma]^{-1/2}$	$-\Gamma^{-1/2}$	$-\Gamma^{-2}$	$-0.5\Gamma^{-2}$	$\Gamma^{-1}(N_1 - N_0)$
$(\frac{1}{2}, \frac{5}{8})$	Multiplier	$n^{-1/2}$	$kn^{-\delta}$	$k^{-1}n^{-2+2\delta}$	$k^{-1}n^{-2+2\delta}$	$n^{-2\delta+0.5}$
	Limit	-1	$-\Gamma^{-1/2}$	$-\Gamma$	$-.5\Gamma$	$\Gamma^{-1}(N_1 - N_0)$
$(\frac{5}{8}, \frac{3}{4})$	Multiplier	$n^{-1/2}$	$k^{1/2}n^{-1/2}$	n^{-1}	n^{-1}	$n^{-2\delta+0.5}$
	Limit	-1	-1	-1	-1	$\Gamma^{-1}(N_1 - N_0)$
$(\frac{3}{4}, \infty)$	Multiplier	$n^{-1/2}$	$k^{1/2}n^{-1/2}$	n^{-1}	n^{-1}	n^{-1}
	Limit	-1	-1	-1	-1	$-1 + N_1^{-1}N_0$

[a] Here $k = 0(n^{1/4})$.
[b] N_0 and N_1 are independent $N(0, 1)$ variables independent of $\Gamma = \int_0^1 W^2(t)\,dt$ and $\xi = .5[W^2(1) - 1]$, where $W(t)$ is a standard Brownian motion.

the unit roots very often. Note that $\theta_n = .8$ [one of the values considered by Schwert (1989)] corresponds to δ ranging from .5 to .23 as n ranges from 25 to 1,000. See Figure 1 for a graphical comparison of the test criteria.

2.3 Results for the Case in Which $\delta > .5$: Stationary Region

The limiting distributions of the test statistics given in Section 1 for processes satisfying (2) when $\delta > .5$ are summarized in the following theorem.

Theorem 2.3. Consider Model (2) when $\rho = 1$ and $\delta > .5$. Then

1. $n^{-1/2}\hat{\tau} \xrightarrow{P} -1$
2. (a) $n^{-\delta}kt_k \xrightarrow{\mathcal{D}} -[\Gamma]^{-1/2}$ if $.5 < \delta < .625$
   (b) $n^{-1/2}k^{1/2}t_k \xrightarrow{P} -1$ if $\delta > .625$,
3. (a) $n^{-2+2\delta}k^{-1}Z_\alpha \xrightarrow{\mathcal{D}} -\Gamma$ for $.5 < \delta < .625$,
   (b) $n^{-1}Z_\alpha \xrightarrow{P} -1$ for $\delta > .625$,
   (c) $n^{-2+2\delta}k^{-1}Z_\alpha^{(1)} \xrightarrow{\mathcal{D}} -.5\Gamma$ for $.5 < \delta < .625$,
   (d) $n^{-1}Z_\alpha^{(1)} \xrightarrow{P} -1$ for $\delta > .625$
4. (a) $n^{-2\delta+.5}Z_{IV} \xrightarrow{\mathcal{D}} [\Gamma]^{-1}[N_1 - N_0]$ if $.5 < \delta < .75$
   (b) $n^{-1}Z_{IV} \xrightarrow{\mathcal{D}} -1 + N_1^{-1}N_0$ if $\delta > .75$,

where N_0 and N_1 are independent $N(0, 1)$ variables independent of Γ and ξ.

Note that $\hat{\tau}$ and t_k diverge to negative infinity and the Z_α tests diverge to negative infinity much faster than the other test statistics. It is interesting to note that the rate at which Z_α diverges decreases with δ as δ increases from .5 to .625. The test criterion based on t_k almost always rejects the hypothesis that the process is nonstationary when $\delta > .5$. Recall that when $\delta > .5$, the process $Y_t(n)$ behaves more like a stationary process than like a nonstationary process and hence it is not unreasonable if test statistics reject the nonstationarity in favor of stationarity. If you interpret the probability of rejecting nonstationarity of Model (*2*) as the *level* of the test for nonstationarity of Model (*1*), however, then the statistics Z_α and t_k will have levels close to 1.

The order in probability of Z_{IV} is smaller than that of Z_α. Moreover, the order in probability of Z_α is greater than that of t_k, indicating that t_k is more stable than Z_α and Z_{IV}. Note also that the estimator $\hat{\rho}_{IV} = 1 + n^{-1}Z_{IV}$ converges in distribution to a Cauchy random variable. See Figure 1 for a summary of the orders in probability of various test statistics.

3. A MONTE CARLO STUDY

In this section, I present the results from a small Monte Carlo study that support my theoretical results. I consider the model given in (2)

$$Y_t = \rho Y_{t-1} + e_t - (1 - n^{-\delta})e_{t-1}, \qquad (12)$$

where $e_t \sim \text{NID}(0, 1)$. Empirical levels of various test statistics, based on 1,000 Monte Carlo replications for $n = 50$ and 100 are presented in Tables 2–5. For $n =$

Table 2. Empirical Levels of .05-Level Unit-Root Test Criteria When $\theta = .8$ [$n = 50$; 100 (based on 1,000 replications); $n = 500$ (based on 100 replications)]

Test statistic	$n = 50$, $\delta = .411$	$n = 100$, $\delta = .349$	$n = 500$, $\delta = .259$
t_4	.440	.359	.44
t_8	.142	.111	.33
$Z_{\alpha,4}$	.889	.894	.76
$Z_{\alpha,8}$	.872	.940	.78
$Z_{\alpha,4}^{(1)}$	.946	.878	.82
$Z_{\alpha,8}^{(1)}$	.908	.913	.79
Z_{IV}	.292	.212	.15

NOTE: The model is $Y_t = \rho Y_{t-1} + e_t - \theta e_{t-1}$ ($\rho = 1$, $\theta = .8$). t_4, $Z_{\alpha,4}$, and $Z_{\alpha,4}^{(1)}$ correspond to $k = 3$, 4, and 5 for $n = 50$, 100, and 500, respectively. Similarly, t_8, $Z_{\alpha,8}$, and $Z_{\alpha,8}^{(1)}$ correspond to $k = 6$, 8, and 11 for $n = 50$, 100, and 500, respectively.

Table 3. Empirical Levels of .05-Level Unit-Root Test Criteria (based on 1,000 replications)

Test statistic	δ = .125, θ_n = .387	δ = .250, θ_n = .624	δ = .375, θ_n = .769	δ = .500, θ_n = .859	δ = .625, θ_n = .913	δ = .750, θ_n = .947
t_3	.079	.143	.350	.620	.824	.952
t_6	.051	.053	.116	.212	.390	.554
$Z_{\alpha,3}$	.221	.543	.822	.966	1.000	1.000
$Z_{\alpha,6}$	.213	.514	.819	.964	1.000	1.000
$Z^{(1)}_{\alpha,3}$	.293	.639	.896	.986	1.000	1.000
$Z^{(1)}_{\alpha,6}$	.235	.569	.856	.978	1.000	1.000
Z_{IV}	.078	.109	.229	.374	.513	.623

NOTE: The model is $Y_t = \rho Y_{t-1} + e_t - (1 - n^{-\delta})e_{t-1}(\rho = 1, n = 50)$.

500, the results are based on 100 Monte Carlo replications.

In Table 2, the empirical levels of unit-root test criteria are presented when the process is generated according to (12) and when $\rho = 1$ and $\theta_n = 1 - n^{-\delta} = .8$ for $n = 50$, 100, and 500. Table 3 contains the results for the processes that are generated according to (12) when $\rho = 1$; $\delta = .125, .25, .375, .5, .625$, and .75, and $n = 50$. Similarly, Tables 4 and 5 contain the results for $n = 100$ and $n = 500$. The test statistics t_4, $Z_{\alpha,4}$, and $Z^{(1)}_{\alpha,4}$ correspond to k given by k_4 = integer part of $[4(.01n)^{.25}]$. Similarly, t_8, $Z_{\alpha,8}$, and $Z^{(1)}_{\alpha,8}$ correspond to k given by k_8 = integer part of $[8(.01n)^{.25}]$. Note that k_4 = 3, 4, and 5 for n = 50, 100, and 500, respectively, and k_8 = 6, 8, and 11 for n = 50, 100, and 500, respectively. Note that, for a fixed n, the probability of rejecting the unit-root hypothesis increases as δ increases. Moreover, for a fixed δ, the empirical level of the unit-root hypothesis increases as n increases. The choice of k plays an important role in the performance of the criteria based on t_k, Z_α, and $Z^{(1)}_\alpha$. Even though the t_k statistic is more stable in terms of the order in probability than the Z_{IV} statistic, the empirical levels of Z_{IV} are observed to be more stable than that of the t_k statistic. This may be because of the choice of k used and the fact that t_k diverges to *negative* infinity, whereas only the absolute value of Z_{IV} diverges. The limiting distribution of Z_{IV}, when properly normalized, has a support on both negative and positive parts of the real line.

4. SUMMARY AND REMARKS

Schwert (1989) cited several examples of economic data that appear to be integrated first-order moving average processes in which the moving average parameter is close to 1. Using an extensive Monte Carlo study, he compared the performance of some of the existing test criteria for testing the hypothesis that the autoregressive parameter is equal to 1 when the moving average parameter is close to 1. He observed that the empirical levels of the test criteria are far from the specified levels, even for large sample sizes. Similar results were also observed by Phillips and Perron (1988), Perron (1988), and Hall (1989). This article provides the asymptotic distributions of some of the test statistics as the moving average parameter approaches 1.

We have considered nearly stationary (white-noise) processes given by $Y_t = Y_{t-1} + e_t - (1 - n^{-\delta})e_{t-1}$. A nearly stationary process is a combination of a white-noise process and a random-walk process. If δ is small, the random-walk part is dominant and Y_t behaves like a nonstationary process. If δ is large, the process behaves like a white-noise process. [Note that if $\theta_n = 1 - n^{-\delta}$, then $\delta = -[\ln n]^{-1}[\ln(1 - \theta_n)]$. For example, the parameter $\theta = .8$ corresponds to δ ranging from .5 to .23 as n changes from 25 to 1,000, and the parameter $\theta = .5$ corresponds to δ ranging from .22 to .1 as n ranges from 25 to 1,000. The values $\theta = .8$ and .5 were considered by Schwert (1989) and Hall (1989).]

I have shown that the test statistics t_k and Z_{IV} have the same asymptotic distributions for $0 < \delta < .25$ as when $\delta = 0$ (which corresponds to a pure random-walk process). The statistics Z_α and $Z^{(1)}_\alpha$, however, have the same asymptotic distributions as when $\delta = 0$, for only $0 < \delta < .1875$. The test statistics Z_α and $Z^{(1)}_\alpha$ diverge to negative infinity when $\delta > .1875$, and hence they are very sensitive to processes with moving average parameter θ_n close to 1. I have also shown that all of the test

Table 4. Empirical Levels of .05-Level Unit-Root Test Criteria (based on 1,000 replications)

Test statistic	δ = .125, θ_n = .438	δ = .250, θ_n = .684	δ = .375, θ_n = .722	δ = .500, θ_n = .900	δ = .625, θ_n = .944	δ = .750, θ_n = .968
t_4	.061	.170	.454	.738	.948	.998
t_8	.042	.061	.125	.350	.603	.828
$Z_{\alpha,4}$	.250	.641	.923	.999	1.000	1.000
$Z_{\alpha,8}$	.331	.745	.964	1.000	1.000	1.000
$Z^{(1)}_{\alpha,4}$	.237	.620	.920	.999	1.000	1.000
$Z^{(1)}_{\alpha,8}$	.275	.665	.937	1.000	1.000	1.000
Z_{IV}	.062	.130	.257	4.09	.560	.680

NOTE: The model is $Y_t = \rho Y_{t-1} + e_t - (1 - n^{-\delta})e_{t-1}(\rho = 1, n = 100)$.

Table 5. Empirical Levels of .05-Level Unit-Root Test Criteria (based on 100 replications)

Test statistic	$\delta = .125$, $\theta_n = .540$	$\delta = .250$, $\theta_n = .789$	$\delta = .375$, $\theta_n = .903$	$\delta = .500$, $\theta_n = .955$	$\delta = .625$, $\theta_n = .979$	$\delta = .750$, $\theta_n = .991$
t_5	.09	.32	.85	.98	1.00	1.00
t_{11}	.09	.21	.65	.96	1.00	1.00
$Z_{\alpha 5}$	.27	.76	.99	1.00	1.00	1.00
$Z_{\alpha 11}$	.29	.79	1.00	1.00	1.00	1.00
$Z^{(1)}_{\alpha 5}$	.37	.88	1.00	1.00	1.00	1.00
$Z^{(1)}_{\alpha 11}$	.31	.82	1.00	1.00	1.00	1.00
Z_{IV}	.08	.14	.29	.42	.57	.73

NOTE: The model is $Y_t = \rho Y_{t-1} - (1 - n^{-\delta})e_{t-1} + e_t (\rho = 1, n = 500)$.

statistics are unstable when $\delta > .25$; that is, the order in probability of the statistics increases with the sample size n. The t statistic t_k in particular diverges to negative infinity for $\delta > .25$. Recall that for $\delta > .5$, the process behaves like a white-noise process and the criterion based on t_k rejects the hypothesis of nonstationarity almost always. Similar behavior is expected by the Z_α and $Z^{(1)}_\alpha$ test statistics. On the other hand, the test statistics Z_α and Z_{IV} have definite computational advantages over the test statistic t_k. The matrix that needs to be inverted in the computation of t_k is converging to a singular matrix asymptotically. This may cause some computational problems.

The test statistic $\hat{\tau}$ is not appropriate for testing the hypothesis of nonstationarity when the process is a mixed model. I included $\hat{\tau}$ in the article only to indicate what happens to the test statistic $\hat{\tau}$ when the model is incorrectly specified to be a first-order autoregressive model.

The performance of the test statistics t_k and different versions of Z_α depends on the number of lags k used in the computation. I have taken $k = O(n^{1/4})$. The orders of k and $1 - \theta_n$ both affect the asymptotic distributions of t_k and Z_α. Consider for example $\delta = .3$ (>.25). For $\delta = .3$, one may be able to show that the t statistic t_k has the same asymptotic distribution as in the case of $\delta = 0$, provided that k is taken to be of order $n^{.31}$. As one expects, when θ is closer to 1, it takes a larger number of lags to approximate an integrated moving average process by a higher order autoregressive process. This is also evident in the Monte Carlo results of Schwert (1989). In practice it is, however, difficult to decide what the value of δ is and which multiplier of $n^{1/4}$ one should use to select k. Comparing the rates of convergence of different test statistics in Figure 1, it is clear that t_k is expected to perform better than the other test statistics, and hence I recommend the use of t_k statistic when $\theta_n > 0$. [Perron (1988) and Schwert (1989) also made similar recommendations.]

As pointed out earlier, the composite hypothesis that the process has a single unit root (nonstationary) includes processes that are close to white noise. This article studies the asymptotic behavior of the different test statistics as the models in the null hypothesis approach stationary models. My article concentrates on test statistics that do not include an intercept and/or a trend. For processes satisfying (2), with minor modifications, the results can be extended to test statistics in which an intercept (and a trend) is estimated. Moreover, the results for $\delta = .25$, .5, .625, and .75 are not difficult. The important point here is the rates of divergence of various statistics, and these rates are continuous in δ. The extensions to higher order autoregressive and moving average processes, however, are not immediate and will be considered elsewhere.

ACKNOWLEDGMENTS

I am grateful to David Dickey, Graciela Gonzalez-Farias, two referees, and an associate editor for their comments and suggestions. My thanks also go to the National Science Foundation for research support. Finally, my thanks go to Janice Gaddy for her skill and effort in typing the manuscript.

APPENDIX: AN OUTLINE OF PROOFS

In this appendix, I present the proofs for the asymptotic distributions of $\hat{\tau}$ and Z_{IV} given in Section 2. The asymptotic distributions for t_k, Z_α, and $Z^{(1)}_\alpha$ can be obtained similarly, and the proofs are available from me. I will first present simple expressions for the test statistics, considered in Section 1, that will be useful in deriving the asymptotic distributions.

1. Consider the $\hat{\tau}$ statistic proposed by Dickey and Fuller (1979),

$$\hat{\tau} = s_1^{-1}\left(\sum_{t=2}^{n} Y_{t-1}^2\right)^{1/2}(\hat{\rho} - 1),$$

where

$$\hat{\rho} = \left(\sum_{t=2}^{n} Y_{t-1}^2\right)^{-1}\left(\sum_{t=2}^{n} Y_{t-1}Y_t\right).$$

It is easy to see that

$$\hat{\tau} = \left(s_1^2 \sum_{t=2}^{n} Y_{t-1}^2\right)^{-1/2} \sum_{t=2}^{n} Y_{t-1}u_t, \qquad \text{(A.1)}$$

where

$$s_1^2 = (n - 2)^{-1} \sum_{t=2}^{n} u_t^2 - (\hat{\rho} - 1)^2(n - 2)^{-1} \sum_{t=2}^{n} Y_{t-1}^2, \qquad \text{(A.2)}$$

and $u_t = Y_t - Y_{t-1}$.

2. The test statistic Z_{IV} given in (10) can be written as

$$Z_{IV} = n\left(\left(\sum_{t=2}^{n} Y_{t-2}Y_{t-1}\right)^{-1} \sum_{t=2}^{n} Y_{t-2}u_t\right). \quad (A.3)$$

Proof of Theorem 2.1. Recall that $Y_t = e_t + n^{-\delta}X_{t-1}$, $X_t = \Sigma_{i=1}^{t} e_i$, and we assume that $0 < \delta < .25$. (a) Note that

$$\sum_{t=2}^{n} Y_{t-1}^2 = \sum_{t=1}^{n-1} e_t^2 + n^{-2\delta} \sum_{t=1}^{n-1} X_{t-1}^2 + 2n^{-\delta} \sum_{t=1}^{n-1} X_{t-1}e_t, \quad (A.4)$$

and with

$$u_t = Y_t - Y_{t-1} = e_t - (1 - n^{-\delta})e_{t-1},$$

$$\sum_{t=2}^{n} Y_{t-1}u_t = -(1 - n^{-\delta}) \sum_{t=2}^{n} e_{t-1}^2 + n^{-2\delta} \sum_{t=2}^{n} X_{t-1}e_t$$

$$+ (1 - n^{-\delta}) \sum_{t=2}^{n} e_{t-1}e_t + n^{-\delta}X_{n-1}e_n. \quad (A.5)$$

Therefore,

$$n^{-1} \sum_{t=2}^{n} Y_{t-1}u_t \xrightarrow{P} -1, \quad \text{and for } 0 < \delta < .25,$$

$$n^{-2+2\delta} \sum_{t=2}^{n} Y_{t-1}^2 \xrightarrow{\mathcal{L}} \Gamma.$$

Moreover, note that

$$n^{-1} \sum_{t=2}^{n} u_t^2 = n^{-1} \sum_{t=2}^{n} e_t^2 + (1 - n^{-\delta})^2 n^{-1} \sum_{t=2}^{n} e_{t-1}^2$$

$$- 2(1 - n^{-\delta})n^{-1} \sum_{t=2}^{n} e_{t-1}e_t \xrightarrow{P} 2. \quad (A.6)$$

Therefore, from (A.1),

$$n^{-\delta}\hat{\tau} = \left(s_1^2 n^{-2+2\delta} \sum_{t=2}^{n} Y_{t-1}^2\right)^{-1/2} n^{-1}$$

$$\times \sum_{t=2}^{n} Y_{t-1}u_t \xrightarrow{\mathcal{L}} -[2\Gamma]^{-1/2}.$$

(b) To find the distribution of Z_{IV} given in (A.3), consider

$$\sum_{t=3}^{n} Y_{t-2}Y_{t-1} = \sum_{t=2}^{n-1} e_{t-1}e_t + n^{-2\delta}$$

$$\times \sum_{t=2}^{n} X_{t-1}^2 + 0_p(n^{-\delta+1}), \quad (A.7)$$

and

$$\sum_{t=3}^{n} Y_{t-2}u_t = \sum_{t=3}^{n} e_{t-2}e_t - \sum_{t=2}^{n-1} e_{t-1}e_t$$

$$+ n^{-2\delta} \sum_{t=2}^{n} X_{t-1}e_t + 0_p(n^{-\delta+.5}). \quad (A.8)$$

Therefore, from (A.3), (A.7), and (A.8), we get for $0 < \delta < .25$,

$$Z_{IV} = \left[n^{-2+2\delta} \sum_{t=3}^{n} Y_{t-2}Y_{t-1}\right]^{-1}$$

$$\times \left[n^{-1+2\delta} \sum_{t=3}^{n} Y_{t-2}u_t\right] \xrightarrow{\mathcal{L}} \Gamma^{-1}\xi.$$

The following lemma is used to prove Theorems 2.2 and 2.3.

Lemma A.1. Let $\{e_t\}$ be a sequence of iid (0, 1) random variables with bounded fourth moments. Consider the random variables,

$$(S_n(r), N_n')' = n^{-1/2}\left(\sum_{t=1}^{[nr]} e_t, \sum_{t=1}^{n} \varepsilon_t^{*\prime} e_t\right)',$$

where $\varepsilon_t^* = (e_{t-2}, e_{t-1})'$, $[nr]$ denotes the integer part of nr, and $0 \le r \le 1$. Then $(S_n(r), N_n')' \Rightarrow (W(r), N_1, N_0)'$, where $W(\cdot)$ is a standard Brownian motion and N_0 and N_1 are independent $N(0, 1)$ variables independent of $W(\cdot)$.

Proof. The result follows from theorem 2.2 of Chan and Wei (1988) and theorem 3.3 of Helland (1982).

Proof of Theorem 2.2. Recall that the process Y_t satisfies $Y_t = e_t + n^{-\delta}X_{t-1}$ $(.25 < \delta < .5)$, where $X_t = \Sigma_{i=1}^{t} e_i$.

1. From (A.4), (A.5), and (A.6) we get, for $.25 < \delta < .5$,

$$n^{-2+2\delta} \sum_{t=2}^{n} Y_{t-1}^2 \xrightarrow{\mathcal{L}} \Gamma,$$

$$n^{-1} \sum_{t=2}^{n} Y_{t-1}u_t \xrightarrow{P} -1,$$

and

$$n^{-1} \sum_{t=1}^{n} u_t^2 \xrightarrow{P} 2.$$

Therefore, from (A.1) we have

$$n^{-\delta}\hat{\tau} \xrightarrow{\mathcal{L}} -[2\Gamma]^{-1/2}.$$

2. From (A.7) and (A.8), we have, for $.25 < \delta < .5$,

$$n^{-2+2\delta} \sum_{t=3}^{n} Y_{t-2}Y_{t-1} = n^{-2} \sum_{t=3}^{n} X_{t-1}^2 + o_p(1)$$

and

$$n^{-1/2} \sum_{t=3}^{n} Y_{t-2}u_t = n^{-1/2} \sum_{t=3}^{n} e_{t-2}e_t - n^{-1/2} \sum_{t=3}^{n} e_{t-1}e_t + o_p(1).$$

Therefore, from Lemma A.1 we get

$$n^{-2\delta+0.5}Z_{\text{IV}} \xrightarrow{\mathcal{L}} [\Gamma]^{-1}(N_1 - N_0).$$

Proof of Theorem 3.3. Here we assume that $Y_t = e_t + n^{-\delta}X_{t-1} (\delta > .5)$, where $X_t = \sum_{i=1}^{t} e_i$.

1. For $\delta > .5$, note that

$$n^{-1} \sum_{t=2}^{n} Y_{t-1}^2 \xrightarrow{P} 1,$$

$$n^{-1} \sum_{t=2}^{n} Y_{t-1}u_t \xrightarrow{P} -1,$$

$$n^{-1} \sum_{t=2}^{n} u_t^2 \xrightarrow{P} 2,$$

and

$$s_1^2 = n^{-1} \sum_{t=2}^{n} u_t^2 - \left[n^{-1} \sum_{t=2}^{n} Y_{t-1}^2\right]^{-1} \times \left[n^{-1} \sum_{t=2}^{n} Y_{t-1}u_t\right]^2 \xrightarrow{P} 1.$$

Therefore, from (A.1), we get

$$n^{-1/2}\hat{\tau} \xrightarrow{P} -1.$$

2. (a) For $.5 < \delta < .75$, from the arguments used in the proof of Theorem 2.2, we get

$$n^{-2\delta+.5}Z_{\text{IV}} \xrightarrow{\mathcal{L}} [\Gamma]^{-1}(N_1 - N_0).$$

(b) For $\delta > .75$,

$$n^{-1}Z_{\text{IV}} + 1 = \left[\sum_{t=3}^{n} Y_{t-2}Y_{t-1}\right]^{-1} \left[\sum_{t=3}^{n} Y_{t-2}Y_t\right]$$

$$= \left[n^{-1/2} \sum_{t=3}^{n} e_{t-2}e_t\right]^{-1} \left[n^{-1/2} \sum_{t=3}^{n} e_{t-1}e_t\right] + o_p(1) \xrightarrow{\mathcal{L}} N_1^{-1}N_0.$$

[*Received June 1989. Revised March 1990.*]

REFERENCES

Ahtola, J. A., and Tiao, G.C. (1984), "Parametric Inference for a Nearly Nonstationary First Order Autoregressive Model," *Biometrika*, 71, 263–272.

Chan, N. H., and Wei, C. Z. (1987), "Asymptotic Inference for Nearly Nonstationary AR(1) Processes," *The Annals of Statistics*, 15, 1050–1063.

——— (1988), "Limiting Distributions of Least Squares Estimates of Unstable Autoregressive Processes," *The Annals of Statistics*, 16, 367–401.

Dickey, D. A., and Fuller, W. A. (1979), "Distribution of the Estimators for Autoregressive Time Series With a Unit Root," *Journal of the American Statistical Association*, 74, 427–431.

Fuller, W. A. (1976), *Introduction to Statistical Time Series*, New York: John Wiley.

Hall, A. (1989), "Testing for a Unit Root in the Presence of Moving Average Errors," *Biometrika*, 76, 49–56.

Ljung, G. M., and Box, G. E. P. (1978), "On a Measure of Lack of Fit in Time Series Models," *Biometrika*, 65, 99–107.

Pantula, S. G. (1989), "Optimal Instrumental Variable Estimator of the AR Parameter of an ARMA (1, 1) Process, Problem 89.1.2," *Econometric Theory*, 5, 173.

Perron, P. (1988), "Trends and Random Walks in Macroeconomic Time Series," *Journal of Economic Dynamics and Control*, 12, 297–332.

Phillips, P. C. B. (1987a), "Time Series Regression With a Unit Root," *Econometrica*, 55, 277–301.

——— (1987b), "Towards a Unified Asymptotic Theory for Autoregression," *Biometrika*, 74, 535–547.

Phillips, P. C. B., and Perron, P. (1988), "Testing for a Unit Root in Time Series Regression," *Biometrika*, 75, 335–346.

Said, S. E., and Dickey, D. A. (1984), "Testing for Unit Roots in Autoregressive Moving Average Models of Unknown Order," *Biometrika*, 71, 599–607.

——— (1985), "Hypothesis Testing in ARIMA(p, 1, q) Models," *Journal of the American Statistical Association*, 80, 369–374.

Schwert, G. W. (1987), "Effects of Model Specification on Tests for Unit Roots in Macroeconomic Data," *Journal of Monetary Economics*, 20, 73–103.

——— (1989), "Tests for Unit Roots: A Monte Carlo Investigation," *Journal of Business and Economic Statistics*, 7, 147–160.

[16]

Journal of Monetary Economics 10 (1982) 139–162. North-Holland Publishing Company

TRENDS AND RANDOM WALKS IN MACROECONMIC TIME SERIES

Some Evidence and Implications

Charles R. NELSON

University of Washington, Seattle, WA 98195, USA

Charles I. PLOSSER*

University of Rochester, Rochester, NY 14627, USA

This paper investigates whether macroeconomic time series are better characterized as stationary fluctuations around a deterministic trend or as non-stationary processes that have no tendency to return to a deterministic path. Using long historical time series for the U.S. we are unable to reject the hypothesis that these series are non-stationary stochastic processes with no tendency to return to a trend line. Based on these findings and an unobserved components model for output that decomposes fluctuations into a secular or growth component and a cyclical component we infer that shocks to the former, which we associate with real disturbances, contribute substantially to the variation in observed output. We conclude that macroeconomic models that focus on monetary disturbances as a source of purely transitory fluctuations may never be successful in explaining a large fraction of output variation and that stochastic variation due to real factors is an essential element of any model of macroeconomic fluctuations.

1. Introduction

It is common practice in macroeconomics to decompose real variables such as output, and sometimes nominal variables, into a secular or growth component and a cyclical component. In the case of output, the secular component is viewed as being in the domain of growth theory with real factors such as capital accumulation, population growth, and technological change as the primary determinants. The cyclical component, on the other hand, is assumed to be transitory (stationary) in nature with monetary and, to a lesser extent, real factors being featured as primary causes. Since cyclical fluctuations are assumed to dissipate over time, any long-run or permanent

*We have received helpful comments from Robert Barro, Stephen Beveridge, David Dickey, Robert King, Levis Kochin, Robert Lucas, John Makin, Robert Mendelsohn, William Schwert, Robert Shiller, George Tiao, an anonymous referee, and others, but responsibility for all errors is entirely ours. Heejoon Kang, Gordon McDonald and Nejat Seyhun assisted in programming and computation. Nelson's participation in this research was supported by the National Science Foundation under grant SOC-7906948 and Plosser's by the Center for Research in Government Policy and Business at the University of Rochester.

0304–3902/82/0000–0000/$02.75

movement (non-stationarity) is necessarily attributed to the secular component.

The notion that the secular component does not fluctuate much over short periods of time, such as a year or a quarter, but rather moves slowly and smoothly relative to the cyclical component has led to the practice of 'detrending' time series by regression on time (or perhaps a polynomial in time). The residuals are then interpreted as the cyclical component to be explained by business cycle theory.[1] For example, Bodkin (1969), Lucas (1973), Barro (1978), Sargent (1978), Taylor (1979), Hall (1980), and Kydland and Prescott (1980) all implicitly or explicitly regard residuals from fitted linear or quadratic time trends as the relevant data for business cycle analysis.[2]

Secular movement, however, need not be modeled by a deterministic trend. For example, the class of integrated stochastic processes exemplified by the random walk, also exhibit secular movement but do not follow a deterministic path. If the secular movement in macroeconomic time series is of a stochastic rather than deterministic nature, then models based on time trend residuals are misspecified.[3]

The types of misspecification that arise from inappropriate detrending can be illustrated by considering the properties of residuals from a regression of a random walk on time. These properties are investigated in recent papers by Chan, Hayya and Ord (1977) and Nelson and Kang (1981). The autocorrelation function of the residuals is shown to be a statistical artifact in the sense that it is determined entirely by sample size and it implies strong positive autocorrelation at low lags with pseudo-periodic behavior at long lags.[4] Empirical investigations of output fluctuations that do not consider the possible source of this autocorrelation might be led to over-estimate both the persistence and variance of the business cycle. Conversely, the importance of real factors that influence the secular component would be under-estimated.

In this paper we investigate whether macroeconomic times series are consistent with the time trend decomposition usually employed. Section 2 discusses the statistical issues involved in testing for deterministic trends and section 3 presents the results of formal and informal tests using long historical time series for the U.S. We are unable to reject the hypothesis that

[1]Or equivalently, time is included as an explanatory variable.

[2]Burns and Mitchell (1946), in their pioneering empirical investigation of business cycles, were concerned with the method of trend removal and went to great lengths to justify their procedures (see pp. 37–41, and ch. 7).

[3]Hall's (1980) use of the time trend model for real GNP is particularly puzzling since in previous work [Hall (1978)] he argues that aggregate consumption behaves like a random walk. Without some rather implausible restrictions on the other components of GNP, aggregate GNP will then include random walk characteristics and linear detrending is likely to be inappropriate.

[4]It is interesting to note that McCulloch (1975) finds evidence of periodicity in logs of real income, investment, and consumption after fitting a linear trend, but does not find periodicity in their first differences.

these series are non-stationary stochastic processes with no tendency to return to a trend line. The implications of this finding are explored in sections 4 and 5. Assuming that any stochastic fluctuations in output of a permanent variety must be associated with secular movements, and thus real factors, the evidence presented in section 3 leads us to the inference that (i) real shocks associated with the secular component contribute substantially to the variation in observed output, and (ii) either these shocks are correlated with the innovations in the cyclical component or the secular component contains transitory fluctuations (or both). We conclude that macroeconomic models that focus on monetary disturbances as a source of purely transitory (stationary) fluctuations may never be successful in explaining a very large fraction of output fluctuations and that stochastic variation due to real factors is an essential element of any model of economic fluctuations. Some recent efforts in this direction include the equilibrium stochastic growth models studied by Black (1979), Long and Plosser (1980), King and Plosser (1981) and Kydland and Prescott (1981).

2. Statistical background

The basic statistical issue is the appropriate representation of non-stationarity in economic time series. We are primarily concerned with non-stationarity in the mean of the series. Such behavior implies that the series lacks a fixed long-term mean, or put positively, has a tendency to move farther away from any given initial state as time goes on.

We consider two fundamentally different classes of non-stationary processes as alternative hypotheses. The first class of processes consists of those that can be expressed as a deterministic function of time, called a trend, plus a *stationary* stochastic process with mean zero. We refer to these as trend-stationary (TS) processes. The tendency of economic time series to exhibit variation that increases in mean and dispersion in proportion to absolute level motivates the transformation to natural logs and the assumption that trends are linear in the transformed data. We also assume that the deviations from trend have a representation as a stationary and invertible ARMA process. Denoting the natural logs of the series by z_t and the deviations from trend by c_t, the linear TS class has the form

$$\begin{aligned} z_t &= \alpha + \beta t + c_t, \\ \phi(L)c_t &= \theta(L)u_t;\ u_t \sim \text{i.i.d.}(0, \sigma_u^2), \end{aligned} \tag{1}$$

where α and β are fixed parameters, L is the lag operator, and $\phi(L)$ and $\theta(L)$ are polynomials in L that satisfy the conditions for stationarity and invertibility.

The fundamental determinism of the process is captured in the properties of long-term forecasts and uncertainty around such forecasts. While autocorrelation in c_t can be exploited in short-term forecasting, it is clear that over long horizons the only information about a future z is its mean ($\alpha + \beta t$). Therefore neither current nor past events will alter long-term expectations. Further, the long-term forecast error must be c which has finite variance. Thus uncertainty is bounded, even in the indefinitely distant future.

The second class of non-stationary process considered in this paper is that class for which first or higher order differences is a stationary and invertible ARMA process (DS processes). The counterpart of the linear TS process is the first-order DS process in natural logs written as

$$(1-L)z_t = \beta + d_t,$$
$$\delta(L)d_t = \lambda(L)u_t;\; u_t \sim \text{i.i.d.}(0, \sigma_u^2), \tag{2}$$

where $(1-L)$ is the difference operator and $\delta(L)$ and $\lambda(L)$ are polynomials satisfying the stationarity and invertibility conditions. The simplest member of the class is the random walk for which the changes are serially uncorrelated, that is $d_t = u_t$.

To see the fundamental difference between the TS and DS classes it is useful to express z_t as the value at some reference point in the past, time zero, plus all subsequent changes,

$$z_t = z_0 + \beta t + \sum_{j=1}^{t} d_j. \tag{3}$$

Eqs. (3) and (1) indicate that the two types of processes can be written as a linear function of time plus the deviation from it. The intercept in (1), however, is a fixed parameter while in (3) it is a function of historical events, and the deviations from trend in (1) are stationary while in (3) they are accumulations of stationary changes. The accumulation in (3) is not stationary but rather its variance increases without bound as t gets large. It is not difficult to see that the long-term forecast of a DS process will always be influenced by historical events and the variance of the forecast error will increase without bound.

The DS class is purely stochastic in nature while the TS class is fundamentally deterministic. When one assumes the latter class is appropriate one is implicitly bounding uncertainty and greatly restricting the relevance of the past to the future. Empirical tests may be quite sensitive to this distinction. For example, Shiller (1979) finds that the variance of holding period returns on long-term bonds is larger than would be consistent with a particular efficient markets (rational expectations) version of term structure theory if short rates are assumed to be stationary around a fixed mean. They are not too large, however, if short-term rates are assumed stationary only after differencing. The crucial factor causing the discrepancy is that under the DS assumption any movement in short rates will have some impact on the long-term expectations embodied in long rates, but will have very little impact under the TS assumption.[5]

The fundamental difference between the two classes of processes can also be expressed in terms of the roots of the AR and MA polynomials. If we first-difference the linear TS model the result is

$$\phi(L)[(1-L)z_t]=\beta\phi(L=1)+(1-L)\theta(L)u_t, \tag{4}$$

where $\phi(L=1)$ is a constant obtained by evaluating the polynomial $\phi(L)$ at $L=1$. Eq. (4) indicates that a unit root will be present in the MA part of the ARMA process describing the first differences $[(1-L)z_t]$. The simplest example would be the case of a linear trend plus random noise ($c_t=u_t$). The presence of the unit root implies that the process is not invertible; that is, it does not have a convergent autoregressive representation. Recall that the first differences of a DS process are both stationary and invertible.

Correspondingly, when we write the DS in terms of levels we obtain from (2)

$$\delta(L)(1-L)z_t=\beta\delta(L=1)+\lambda(L)u_t, \tag{5}$$

which contains a unit root in the AR polynomial. It would appear then that if a series is generated by a member of the linear TS subclass we should fail to reject the hypothesis of a unit MA root in the ARMA model for its first difference, and if it is generated by a member of the first order DS subclass we should fail to reject the hypothesis of a unit AR root in the ARMA model for its levels.[6]

Unfortunately, the standard asymptotic theory developed for stationary and invertible ARMA models is not valid for testing the hypotheses that either polynomial contains a unit root. To get some idea of the problem, consider the simplest version of (5) where the null hypothesis is that z_t is a random walk with drift,

$$z_t=\rho z_{t-1}+\mu+u_t,$$

so $\rho=1$ is the hypothesis we wish to test. The standard expression for the

[5] In a subsequent paper Shiller (1981) finds the variance of linearly detrended stock returns is similarly excessive if dividends are also assumed to be stationary around a linear trend (both variables deflated and in logs), but he does not report the impact of the TS assumption on the results.

[6] Pierce (1975) discusses a technique for distinguishing between deterministic and stochastic non-stationarity by inspection of sample autocorrelation functions.

large sample variance of the least square estimator $\hat{\rho}$ is $[(1-\rho^2)/T]$ which would be zero under the null hypothesis. The true variance of course is not zero; the problem is that the conventional asymptotic theory is inappropriate in this case. Dickey (1976) and Fuller (1976) develop the limiting distribution of $\hat{\rho}$ and the conventionally calculated least squares t-statistic, which we denote τ for the null hypothesis $\rho=1$, and tabulate the distributions. They demonstrate that if $\mu=0$ then the distribution of $\hat{\rho}$ is biased towards zero and skewed to the left, that is towards stationarity.[7]

In addition, Dickey and Fuller provide a set of results that allow us to test the DS hypothesis against the TS hypothesis as long as we are willing to assume that only AR terms are required to obtain satisfactory representations. The strategy is to embed both hypotheses in a common model. The simplest alternatives are a TS process with first order AR deviations and a random walk (DS process) with drift which are both special cases of

$$z_t=\alpha+\beta t+u_t/(1-\phi L),$$

or equivalently, after multiplication by $(1-\phi L)$, of

$$z_t=\phi z_{t-1}+[\alpha(1-\phi)+\phi\beta]+\beta(1-\phi)t+u_t. \tag{6}$$

If the TS hypothesis is correct then $|\phi|<1$. If the DS hypothesis is correct then $\phi=1$ and (6) reduces to

$$z_t=z_{t-1}+\beta+u_t.$$

It would appear then that one would want to run the regression

$$z_t=\mu+\rho z_{t-1}+\gamma t+u_t \tag{7}$$

and test the null hypothesis $\rho=1$, $\gamma=0$ which is equivalent to $\phi=1$ in (6). Under this null hypothesis the usual t-ratios are not t-distributed but Dickey and Fuller provide tabulations of the distribution of the t-ratio for ρ, again denoted τ, for testing the null hypothesis $\rho=1$.[8] Dickey and Fuller (1979)

[7]The problem of testing for unit roots in MA polynomials is more discouraging. MA processes are only identified under the restriction that the roots lie on or outside the unit circle; therefore estimates will be bounded away from the unit root. Plosser and Schwert (1977) have demonstrated in the first-order MA case that application of t-tests or likelihood ratio tests, which would be appropriate for null hypotheses within the invertibility region, lead to rejection in the vast majority of instances when the null hypothesis of a unit root is true.

[8]They do not develop a statistic for the joint test or for γ alone. However, a test on ρ alone is sufficient given that we do not consider a process with $\rho=1$ and $\gamma\neq 0$ as part of the model space. A process with $\rho=1$ and $\gamma\neq 0$ would be one in which differences in logs (rates of change) followed a deterministic path, implying ever increasing ($\gamma>0$) or even decreasing ($\gamma<0$) rates of change. We rule out this kind of behavior in economic time series on a priori grounds. Similarly we rule out quadratic or higher degree time polynomial trends.

state that the distributions of $\hat{\rho}$ and $\tau(\hat{\rho})$ is not affected by whether μ is zero or not, but $\tau(\hat{\rho})$ would be normal if $\gamma \neq 0$ (the case we have excluded). To illustrate these properties we have conducted a Monte Carlo experiment which is summarized in table 1. The sample length is 100 observations with 500 replications. In Case I the generating process is a random walk with a zero drift; in Case II there is non-zero drift. As indicated by Dickey and Fuller, customary testing procedures reject the null in favor of stationarity far too often in both cases. The distribution of $\hat{\rho}$ is centered around 0.9 instead of 1.0 in both cases. In addition, it is clear that the t-ratio for testing the hypothesis that $\gamma=0$ [denoted $t(\hat{\gamma})$], is biased towards indicating a trend. Thus, standard testing procedures are strongly biased towards finding stationarity around a trend; they tend to reject the hypothesis $\rho=1$ when it is true in favor of $\rho<1$ and tend to reject the hypothesis $\gamma=0$ when it is true.

Results of Fuller (1976) allow us to use the distributions of $\hat{\rho}$ and $\tau(\hat{\rho})$ in higher order cases. In general we want to distinguish between a TS process with AR component of order k and a DS process with AR representation of order $(k-1)$. In levels we write the DS model as an AR of order k with one

Table 1

Sampling distributions for the estimators in regression model (7),[a]

$$z_t = \hat{\mu} + \hat{\rho} z_{t-1} + \hat{\gamma} t + \hat{u}_t,$$

Case I: $\mu=0, \quad \rho=1.0, \quad \gamma=0,$

Case II: $\mu=1.0, \quad \rho=1.0, \quad \gamma=0.$

	Mean	Standard deviation	Skewness	Excess Kurtosis	Studentized range	Percent rejections
Case I						
$\hat{\mu}$	−0.007	0.525	0.490	4.12	10.73	
$t(\hat{\mu})$	−0.049	1.84	0.079	−0.615	5.97	32.8
$\hat{\rho}$	0.895	0.064	−1.11	1.53	6.15	
$\tau(\hat{\rho})$	−2.26	0.863	−0.237	0.655	7.41	65.2
$\hat{\gamma}$	−0.001	0.013	0.212	2.27	7.91	
$t(\hat{\gamma})$	−0.093	1.84	0.124	−0.807	5.08	35.6
Case II						
$\hat{\mu}$	0.878	0.503	−0.390	0.732	6.70	
$t(\hat{\mu})$	4.00	2.18	−0.524	−0.569	4.94	79.0
$\hat{\rho}$	0.900	0.054	−0.757	0.493	5.67	
$\tau(\hat{\rho})$	−2.22	0.769	0.196	0.284	6.35	66.0
$\hat{\gamma}$	0.099	0.054	0.698	0.303	5.49	
$t(\hat{\gamma})$	2.22	0.777	−0.202	0.454	6.94	65.0

[a]The sampling distributions are based on 500 replications of a random walk of sample size 100, with (Case II) and without (Case I) drift. $t(\hat{\mu})$ and $t(\hat{\gamma})$ are the ratios of $\hat{\mu}$ and $\hat{\gamma}$ to their respective standard errors and $\tau(\hat{\rho})$ is the ratio of $(\hat{\rho}-1)$ to its standard error. The percent rejections are computed based on the frequency that $|t(\hat{\mu})|$, $|\tau(\hat{\rho})|$, and $|t(\hat{\gamma})|$ are greater than 1.96.

root on the unit circle. The alternatives are imbedded in the model

$$z_t=\phi_1 z_{t-1}+\cdots+\phi_k z_{t-k}+\mu+\gamma t+u_t, \tag{8}$$

where $\sum\phi_i=1$ and $\gamma=0$ if the DS hypothesis is true. The terms in lagged z's can be rearranged in the format

$$z_t=\left(\sum_{i=1}^{k}\phi_i\right)z_{t-1}+\left(-\sum_{i=2}^{k}\phi_i\right)(z_{t-1}-z_{t-2})$$

$$+\cdots+(-\phi_k)(z_{t-k+1}-z_{t-k})+\mu+\gamma t+\mu_t. \tag{9}$$

Fuller (1976, p. 374) shows that if the coefficient of z_{t-1} is unity in (9), as it would be under the DS hypothesis, then the least squares estimator of that coefficient has the same large sample distribution as $\hat{\rho}$ in model (7), and similarly for its τ-ratio.[9]

We note that in the Dickey–Fuller procedure the *null* hypothesis is the DS specification while the alternative is the TS specification. As usual, acceptance of the null hypothesis is not disproof of the alternative hypothesis. It is important therefore to have a check on the power of the test. To provide this check we include in our data set a series that on *a priori* grounds is likely to be a member of the TS class (albeit with zero slope) rather than the DS class, namely the unemployment rate.

3. Analysis of U.S. historical data

We turn now to the analysis of the U.S. historical time series listed in table 2 which include measures of output, spending, money, prices, and interest rates.[10] The data are annual, generally averages for the year, with starting dates from 1860 to 1909 and ending in 1970 in all cases. All series except the bond yield are transformed to natural logs.

Sample autocorrelations of the levels are tabulated in table 2 and typically start at around 0.96 at lag one and decay slowly with increasing lag. This is consistent with the behavior of sample autocorrelations from a random walk as indicated by the values calculated from a formula due to Wichern (1973). One exception to this characterization is the unemployment rate which exhibits more rapid decay as would be expected of a stationary

[9]Dickey and Fuller (1981) have recently extended their analysis to likelihood ratio statistics.

[10]Data cources are as follows. GNP series, industrial production, employment 1929–1970, unemployment rate, consumer prices, and stock prices: *Long Term Economic Growth*, (1973). Wages, money stock, and bond yield: *Historical Statistics of the U.S., Colonial Times to 1970*, (1975). Velocity: Friedman and Schwartz (1963) with revisions kindly provided by Anna Schwartz. Employment 1890–1928: Lebergott (1964). Data files available from the authors upon request.

Table 2

Sample autocorrelations of the natural logs of annual data.[a]

			Sample autocorrelations					
Series	Period	T	r_1	r_2	r_3	r_4	r_5	r_6
Random walk[b]		100	0.95	0.90	0.85	0.81	0.76	0.70
Time aggregated[b] random walk		100	0.96	0.91	0.86	0.82	0.77	0.73
Real GNP	1909–1970	62	0.95	0.90	0.84	0.79	0.74	0.69
Nominal GNP	1909–1970	62	0.95	0.89	0.83	0.77	0.72	0.67
Real per capita GNP	1909–1970	62	0.95	0.88	0.81	0.75	0.70	0.65
Industrial production	1860–1970	111	0.97	0.94	0.90	0.87	0.84	0.81
Employment	1890–1970	81	0.96	0.91	0.86	0.81	0.76	0.71
Unemployment rate	1890–1970	81	0.75	0.47	0.32	0.17	0.04	−0.01
GNP deflator	1889–1970	82	0.96	0.93	0.89	0.84	0.80	0.76
Consumer prices	1860–1970	111	0.96	0.92	0.87	0.84	0.81	0.77
Wages	1900–1970	71	0.96	0.91	0.86	0.82	0.77	0.73
Real wages	1900–1970	71	0.96	0.92	0.88	0.84	0.80	0.75
Money stock	1889–1970	82	0.96	0.92	0.89	0.85	0.81	0.77
Velocity	1869–1970	102	0.96	0.92	0.88	0.85	0.81	0.79
Bond yield	1900–1970	71	0.84	0.72	0.60	0.52	0.46	0.40
Common stock prices	1871–1970	100	0.96	0.90	0.85	0.79	0.75	0.71

[a]The natural logs of all the data are used except for the bond yield. T is the sample size and r_i is the ith order autocorrelation coefficient. The large sample standard error under the null hypothesis of no autocorrelation is $T^{-\frac{1}{2}}$ or roughly 0.11 for series of the length considered here.

[b]Computed by the authors from the approximation due to Wichern (1973).

series. Sample autocorrelations of first differences are presented in table 3 and in each instance are positive and significant at lag one, but in many cases are not significant at longer lags.

One explanation of positive autocorrelation at lag one only is that the annual series are constructed by averaging shorter interval observations which themselves are generated by a DS process. Working (1960) demonstrates this effect of time aggregation on a random walk and shows that positive autocorrelation at lag one approaches +0.25 as the number of underlying observations being aggregated becomes large. Tiao (1972) shows that the Working result generalizes to the temporal aggregation of any DS process as long as the span of serial dependence in the underlying process is shorter than the interval of aggregation, in this case one year.

The autocorrelation structures of real GNP, nominal GNP, real per capita GNP, employment, nominal and real wages, and common stock prices display positive autocorrelation at lag one only which is characteristic of first-order MA processes. This representation of the data is inconsistent with the TS model. The only TS process that gives rise to autocorrelation only at lag one is the case of serially random deviations around the trend. The value of the lag one autocorrelation, however, would be −0.50. To salvage a TS

Table 3

Sample autocorrelations of the first difference of the natural logs of annual data.[a]

Series	Period	T	Sample autocorrelations r_1	r_2	r_3	r_4	r_5	r_6	$s(r)$
Time aggregated random walk[b]			0.25	0.00	0.00	0.00	0.00	0.00	
Real GNP	1909–1970	62	0.34	0.04	−0.18	−0.23	−0.19	0.01	0.13
Nominal GNP	1909–1970	62	0.44	0.08	−0.12	−0.24	−0.07	0.15	0.13
Real per capita GNP	1909–1970	62	0.33	0.04	−0.17	−0.21	−0.18	0.02	0.13
Industrial production	1860–1970	111	0.03	−0.11	−0.00	−0.11	−0.28	0.05	0.09
Employment	1890–1970	81	0.32	−0.05	−0.08	−0.17	−0.20	0.01	0.11
Unemployment rate	1890–1970	81	0.09	−0.29	0.03	−0.03	−0.19	0.01	0.11
GNP deflator	1889–1970	82	0.43	0.20	0.07	−0.06	0.03	0.02	0.11
Consumer prices	1860–1970	111	0.58	0.16	0.02	−0.00	0.05	0.03	0.09
Wages	1900–1970	71	0.46	0.10	−0.03	−0.09	−0.09	0.08	0.12
Real wages	1900–1970	71	0.19	−0.03	−0.07	−0.11	−0.18	−0.15	0.12
Money stock	1889–1970	82	0.62	0.30	0.13	−0.01	−0.07	−0.04	0.11
Velocity	1869–1970	102	0.11	−0.04	−0.16	−0.15	−0.11	0.11	0.10
Bond yield	1900–1970	71	0.18	0.31	0.15	0.04	0.06	0.05	0.12
Common stock prices	1871–1970	100	0.22	−0.13	−0.08	−0.18	−0.23	0.02	0.10

[a]The first differences of the natural logs of all the data are used except for the bond yield. T is the sample size and r_i is the estimated ith order autocorrelation coefficient. The large sample standard error for r is given by $s(r)$ under the null hypothesis of no autocorrelation.

[b]Theoretical autocorrelations as the number of aggregated observations becomes large; result due to Working (1960).

representation for these series we would need to hypothesize the presence of an autoregressive component in the deviations from trend that has a root close enough to unity to obscure the effect of differencing on the autocorrelation structure. For example, suppose the deviations from trend were generated by the ARMA process

$$(1-\phi L)c_t=(1-\theta L)u_t \tag{10}$$

so that the first difference of z_t have the representation

$$(1-L)z_t=\beta+\frac{(1-L)(1-\theta L)}{(1-\phi L)}u_t. \tag{11}$$

The ratio $(1-L)/(1-\phi L)$ has the expansion $[1-(1-\phi)L-\phi(1-\phi)L^2-\ldots]$, which may be difficult to distinguish empirically from unity if ϕ is close to one, leaving the appearance of a first order MA process $(1-\theta L)$ for $\{(1-L)z_t\}$.

The GNP deflator, consumer prices, the money stock, and the bond yield, exhibit more persistent autocorrelation in first differences. None, however, shows evidence of being generated from a process containing MA terms with a unit root or AR terms arising from inversion of such an MA term as one would expect to find in a TS process that has been differenced. The presence of strong positive autocorrelation in deviations from trend (or from a fixed mean) may again be the explanation. The conclusion we are pointed toward is that if these series do belong to the TS class, then the deviations from trend must be sufficiently autocorrelated to make it difficult to distinguish them from the DS class on the basis of sample autocorrelations.

The evidence against the TS representation from levels and differences is reinforced by the sample autocorrelations of the deviations from fitted trend lines presented in table 4. The pattern is strikingly similar across series (except for the unemployment rate) starting at about 0.9 at lag one and declining roughly exponentially. The first two lines in table 4 give the expected sample autocorrelations for deviations of random walks of 61 and 101 observations from a fitted trend line [Nelson and Kang (1981)] and again suggest the consistency of the data with a simple form of the DS hypothesis.[11] Nelson and Kang also show that these results are rather insensitive to moderate autocorrelation in first differences, such as would be present in a time aggregated DS process.

[11]The approximate expected sample autocorrelations are based on the ratios of expected sample autocovariances. Simulation experiments by Nelson and Kang (1981) for 100 observations suggest that the exact expected sample autocorrelations are smaller. At lag one the mean sample autocorrelation was 0.88 instead of 0.91 and at lag 6 it was 0.43 instead of 0.51.

Table 4

Sample autocorrelations of the deviations from the time trend.[a]

		Sample autocorrelations						
Series	Period	T	r_1	r_2	r_3	r_4	r_5	r_6
Detrended random		61	0.85	0.71	0.58	0.47	0.36	0.27
walk[b]		101	0.91	0.82	0.74	0.66	0.58	0.51
Real GNP	1909–1970	62	0.87	0.66	0.46	0.26	0.19	0.07
Nominal GNP	1909–1970	62	0.93	0.79	0.65	0.52	0.43	0.05
Real per capita GNP	1909–1970	62	0.87	0.65	0.43	0.24	0.11	0.04
Industrial production	1860–1970	111	0.84	0.67	0.53	0.40	0.30	0.28
Employment	1890–1970	81	0.89	0.71	0.55	0.39	0.25	0.17
Unemployment rate	1890–1970	81	0.75	0.46	0.30	0.15	0.03	−0.01
GNP deflator	1889–1970	82	0.92	0.81	0.67	0.54	0.42	0.30
Consumer prices	1860–1970	111	0.97	0.91	0.84	0.78	0.71	0.63
Wages	1900–1970	71	0.93	0.81	0.67	0.54	0.42	0.31
Real wages	1900–1970	71	0.87	0.69	0.52	0.38	0.26	0.19
Money stock	1889–1970	82	0.95	0.83	0.69	0.53	0.37	0.21
Velocity	1869–1970	102	0.91	0.81	0.72	0.65	0.59	0.56
Bond yield	1900–1970	71	0.85	0.73	0.62	0.55	0.49	0.43
Common stock prices	1871–1970	100	0.90	0.76	0.64	0.53	0.46	0.43

[a]The data are residuals from linear least squares regression of the logs of the series (except the bond yield) on time. See footnote for table 3.

[b]Approximate expected sample autocorrelations based on Nelson and Kang (1981).

To carry out the formal tests of Dickey and Fuller we must estimate regressions of the form of eq. (9) which may be rewritten as

$$z_t = \mu + \gamma t + \rho_1 z_{t-1} + \sum_{j=2}^{k} \rho_j (z_{t+1} - z_{t-j}) + u_t. \tag{12}$$

To specify the maximum lag k we consider both the values that would be suggested by the autocorrelations of first differences and by the partial autocorrelations of the deviations from trend. In cases where MA models for first differences seem appropriate we fit AR approximations. In general the latter procedure indicates higher order autoregressions and our rule is to utilize the higher order models on the grounds that leaving out relevant terms might bias our results but inclusion of irrelevant ones would only reduce efficiency.[12]

The results of these regressions are reported in table 5. Recall that we are interested in testing whether ρ_1 differs from unity. The values of $\hat{\rho}$ range

[12]We do not report the sample partial autocorrelations of the deviations from trend. However, the pattern is very similar across almost all of the series; a sharp cut-off after lag two where there is negative and generally significant partial autocorrelation. These characteristics suggest second-order AR representations with complex roots and therefore pseudoperiodic behavior in the trend deviations, again a property of detrended random walks [Nelson and Kang (1981)].

Table 5

Tests for autoregressive unit roots[a]

$$z_t = \hat{\mu} + \hat{\gamma}t + \hat{\rho}_1 z_{t-1} + \hat{\rho}_2(z_{t-1} - z_{t-2}) + \cdots + \hat{\rho}_k(z_{t-k+1} - z_{t-k}) + \hat{\mu}_t.$$

Series	T	k	$\hat{\mu}$	$t(\hat{\mu})$	$\hat{\gamma}$	$t(\hat{\gamma})$	$\hat{\rho}_1$	$\tau(\hat{\rho}_1)$	$s(\hat{u})$	r_1
Real GNP	62	2	0.819	3.03	0.006	3.03	0.825	−2.99	0.058	−0.02
Nominal GNP	62	2	1.06	2.37	0.006	2.34	0.899	−2.32	0.087	0.03
Real per capita GNP	62	2	1.28	3.05	0.004	3.01	0.818	−3.04	0.059	−0.02
Industrial production	111	6	0.103	4.32	0.007	2.44	0.835	−2.53	0.097	0.03
Employment	81	3	1.42	2.68	0.002	2.54	0.861	−2.66	0.035	0.10
Unemployment rate	81	4	0.513	2.81	−0.000	−0.23	0.706	−3.55*	0.407	0.02
GNP deflator	82	2	0.260	2.55	0.002	2.65	0.915	−2.52	0.046	−0.03
Consumer prices	111	4	0.090	1.76	0.001	2.84	0.986	−1.97	0.042	−0.06
Wages	71	3	0.566	2.30	0.004	2.30	0.910	−2.09	0.060	0.00
Real wages	71	2	0.487	3.10	0.004	3.14	0.831	−3.04	0.034	−0.01
Money stock	82	2	0.133	3.52	0.005	3.03	0.916	−3.08	0.047	0.03
Velocity	102	1	0.052	0.99	−0.000	−0.65	0.941	−1.66	0.067	0.11
Interest rate	71	3	−0.186	−0.95	0.003	1.75	1.03	0.686	0.283	−0.02
Common stock prices	100	3	0.481	2.02	0.003	2.37	0.913	−2.05	0.158	0.20

[a] z_t represents the natural logs of annual data except for the bond yield. $t(\hat{\mu})$ and $t(\hat{\gamma})$ are the ratios of the OLS estimates of μ and γ to their respective standard errors. $\tau(\hat{\rho}_1)$ is the ratio of $\hat{\rho}_1 - 1$ to its standard error. $s(\hat{u})$ is the standard error of the regression and r_1 is the first-order autocorrelation coefficient of the residuals. The values of $\tau(\hat{\rho}_1)$ denoted by an (*) are smaller than the 0.05 one tail critical value of the distribution of $\tau(\hat{\rho}_1)$ and similarly for $\hat{\rho}_1$. It should also be noted that $t(\hat{\mu})$ and $t(\hat{\gamma})$ are not distributed as normal random variables.

from a low of 0.706 for the unemployment rate to a high of 1.03 for the bond yield. The majority of the estimates fall in the range 0.85 to 0.93 which is quite consistent with the mean of 0.900 and standard deviation of 0.054 reported in table 1 for realizations of a random walk. Also of interest is that all but two of the t-statistics for the hypothesis $\rho_1 = 1$ [i.e., $\tau(\hat{\rho})$] are significant by conventional standards. However, we know from the sampling experiments in table 1 that $\tau(\hat{\rho}_1)$ has a mean of about -2.22 under the null hypothesis that ρ_1 is unity. Using the distributions tabulated by Fuller (1976), only the unemployment rate exhibits a value of $\tau(\hat{\rho})$ below the 0.05 critical value of -3.45 for samples sizes of 100. In this case, $\hat{\rho}$ is also smaller than the 0.05 critical value given by Fuller. Moreover, there is no evidence from this regression that the slope is non-zero and we conclude that the series is well described as a stationary process.

To sum up, the evidence we have presented is consistent with the DS representation of non-stationaruty in economic time series.[13] We recognize that none of the tests presented, formal and informal, can have power against a TS alternative with an AR root arbitrarily close to unity. However, if we are observing stationary deviations from linear trends in these series then the tendency to return to the trend line must be so weak as to avoid detection even in samples as long as sixty years to over a century.

4. Stochastic representations of the secular component

Our tests in section 3 suggest that economic time series do not contain deterministic time trends but contain stochastic trends characteristic of the DS class of processes. To investigate the implications of this finding it is useful to focus on the behavior of output. Pursuing the decomposition discussed earlier we assume that actual output (presumably logged) can be viewed as the sum of a secular or growth component, $\bar{y}_t$, and a cyclical component, c_t. If the cyclical component is assumed to be transitory (stationary), then any underlying non-stationarity in output must be attributable to the secular component. Thus, if actual output can be viewed

[13]The contrasting implications of the TS and DS models for long-run uncertainty can be illustrated by real per capita GNP. Under the TS hypothesis, uncertainty about future values is founded by the marginal standard deviation of fluctuations around a linear trend which is estimated to be 0.133 (in natural logs) over the sample period. According to the DS model for this series, however, the standard deviation of forecast errors is given by $SD[e_t(k)] = 0.062[1+(k-1)1.711]^{\frac{1}{2}}$, where $e_t(k)$ denotes the forecast error for k years in the future. This standard deviation exceeds 0.133 for any more than four years in the future and obviously grows without bound but at a decreasing rate. Taking into account an estimated mean growth rate of 0.016, the lower point of a 95% confidence interval reaches its minimum when the forecast horizon is 24 years. At a horizon of 24 years the standard deviation is 0.39 compared with accumulated mean growth of 0.38. Thus the possibility that actual real per capital would not only show no increase 24 years hence but decline by about 33% from its current level is not excluded in 95% interval.

as belonging to the DS class, then so must the secular component. This decomposition of output can be expressed as

$$y_t = \bar{y}_t + c_t$$
$$= (1-L)^{-1}\theta(L)v_t + \psi(L)u_t, \tag{13}$$

where $\bar{y}_t = (1-L)^{-1}\theta(L)v_t$ or $(1-L)\bar{y}_t = \theta(L)v_t$, and $c_t = \psi(L)u_t$. The (possibly infinite order) polynomials $\theta(L)$ and $\psi(L)$ are assumed to satisfy the conditions for stationarity and invertibility and v_t and u_t are mean zero serially uncorrelated random variables. Eq. (13) assigns the non-stationarity of y to $\bar{y}$ through the factor $(1-L)^{-1}$. (Also note that we are ignoring any drift in $\bar{y}$ for convenience.) Separation of the secular component from observed data may be thought of as a problem in signal extraction when only information in the observed series itself is used, or it may be cast as a regression problem when determinants of the growth process are regarded as known and observable.

4.1. Regression strategies

Perhaps the ideal method of dealing with non-stationarity in output (i.e., growth or secular movements) is to include the variables in a regression that would account for such behavior. For example, Perloff and Wachter (1979), among many others, fit real GNP to labor, capital, and energy as inputs in a translog production function and represent technological change as a time trend. The first-order autocorrelation coefficient of the residuals, however, is reported to be 0.881, roughly the value expected from regression of a random walk on time given the number of observations in question. It would seem then that measured input and time trend variables may not adequately account for the growth component in real GNP.[14] Another regression strategy is to work in per capita values under the assumption that population is the primary source of non-stationarity. We can reject this strategy based on our results in section 3 that indicate per capita real GNP also belongs to the DS class. Thus, using observable variables to account for growth components seems unsatisfactory since neither factor inputs nor population seem to suffice and direct measures of technology are not readily available.[15]

[14]Plosser and Schwert (1979) discuss this issue and others that must be considered when intepreting regressions such as those estimated by Perloff and Wachter (1979).

[15]It is interesting that the DS nature of technological change is evident in the early empirical estimates of the implied stock of technology calculated by Solow (1957) for the period 1909–1949 as corrected by Hogan (1958). The log of Solow's $A(t)$ variable exhibits little autocorrelation in first differences ($Q(12) = 8.8$) and $\hat{\rho}$ and its τ-ratio for regression (12) are both close to their expected values under the Fuller/Dickey distribution, suggesting that the stock of technology is well characterized as a random walk.

4.2. Signal extraction and an unobservable components model of output

Signal extraction procedures imply, or are implied by, some model of the underlying component structure of the series. Therefore, it seems that prior to adoption of an unobserved components model, it should be investigated for consistency with the data, or, perhaps preferably, an attempt should be made to identify a class of models from the observed sample autocorrelations.

The classic example of signal extraction in economics is the permanent income model of Friedman (1957).[16] One version measures permanent income as an exponentially weighted average of past observed incomes. Muth (1960) shows that an optimal estimate of permanent income has that form if permanent income follows a random walk and transitory income is serially random and independent of changes in permanent income. The Friedman/Muth permanent income model may be written as a special case of (13) with $\theta(L)=\psi(L)=1$

$$y_t=\bar{y}_t+u_t, \qquad \bar{y}_t=\bar{y}_{t-1}+v_t, \tag{14}$$

where $\bar{y}_t$ is now the permanent component, generated by a random walk with innovations v_t, and u_t is the transitory component, a purely random series that is independent of v_t. The first differences are the stationary process

$$(1-L)y_t=v_t+u_t-u_{t-1}, \tag{15}$$

illustrating the general fact that differencing does not 'remove the trend' since the innovation in the permanent component, v_t, is part of the first difference. The first differences are autocorrelated at lag one only with coefficient

$$\rho_1=-\sigma_u^2/(\sigma_v^2+2\sigma_u^2), \tag{16}$$

which is confined to the range $-0.05\leqq\rho_1\leqq 0$ and depends on the relative variances of u and v. Apparently, this model cannot account for the positive autocorrelation at lag one only observed in the first difference of the historical series studied in section 3.

In general, if an unobserved components version of (13) is restricted *a priori* by assuming that (i) $\bar{y}_t$ is a random walk [i.e., $\theta(L)=1$] and (ii) v_t and u_t are independent, then the parameters of the unobserved components model will be identified. This is clearly the case for the permanent income model

[16]For a general discussion of signal extraction in economic time series see Pierce (1978) and Nerlove, Grether, and Carvalho (1979). Some recent examples of signal extraction techniques applied to unobserved components models are Beveridge and Nelson (1981) and Hodrick and Prescott (1980).

since σ_u^2 is computable from the autocovariance of the first differences at lag one [the numerator of (16)] and σ_v^2 from the variance of the first differences [the denominator of (16)] and the computed value of σ_u^2. If the cyclical or stationary component of (13) has the MA representation $\psi(L)u_t$ and is of order q, then the first difference will be

$$(1-L)y_t = v_t + (1-L)\psi(L)u_t \tag{17}$$

with non-zero autocovariances through lag $(q+1)$. The value of $(q+1)$ can in principle be inferred from a realization of y. There are then $(q+2)$ parameters to be solved for from the $(q+2)$ autocovariance relations implied by (17), using values for the autocovariances computed from the data.[17]

It is clear from our discussion, however, that a decomposition satisfying both the above restrictions is not always feasible. The simplest example is a process with positive autocorrelation in first differences at lag one only. Eq. (17) implies that the Friedman/Muth model is the only linear model that satisfies both restrictions and leads to non-zero autocorrelation at lag one only. However, it is unable to account for positive autocorrelation at lag one only. To do so we must relax either the assumption that $\bar{y}$ is a random walk (i.e., containing no transitory, only permanent movements) or the assumption that v and u are independent. In general, if either of these assumptions is relaxed the parameters of the unobserved components model are not identified.

Nevertheless, the assumption that the cyclical component is stationary combined with the observation that autocorrelations in the first differences of output are positive at lag one and zero elsewhere are sufficient to imply that the variation in actual output changes is dominated by changes in secular component $\bar{y}_t$ rather than the cyclical component c_t.

The above proposition can be demonstrated by considering first differences of (13)

$$(1-L)y_t = \theta(L)v_t + (1-L)\psi(L)u_t. \tag{18}$$

The presence of first-order autocorrelation only in $(1-L)y_t$ implies (barring fortuitous cancelations) that $\theta(L)$ is first-order and $\psi(L)$ is zero-order so that we can write

$$(1-L)y_t = v_t + \theta v_{t-1} + u_t - u_{t-1}, \tag{19}$$

[17]The argument is easily extended to the case where the stationary component includes AR terms since they may be inferred from the autocovariances of the first differences for lags greater than $(q+1)$ using Yule–Walker equations. We note, however, that we do not have a formal proof that the non-linear autocovariance equations will always have a solution or unique solution in terms of invertible values of the ψ's.

with $|\theta|<1$ being required by invertibility. While u_t and v_t may be contemporaneously correlated, lagged cross-correlations would imply higher than first-order autocorrelation in $(1-L)y_t$ and therefore are ruled out. The autocovariance of output changes at lag one is therefore

$$\gamma_1=\theta\sigma_v^2-(1-\theta)\sigma_{uv}-\sigma_u^2, \tag{20}$$

where σ_{uv} is the contemporaneous covariance between u and v. Note that γ_1 consists of the autocovariance of the change in the secular component, $\bar{y}$, at lag one, $\theta\sigma_v^2$, the sum of the cross-covariances at lag one, $-(1-\theta)\sigma_{uv}$, and the autocovariance of the change is the cyclical component, c, at lag one, $-\sigma_u^2$, which is necessarily negative. The factors that would account for the positive value of γ_1 we observe are therefore (1) a positive value of θ (positive autocorrelation in first differences of the secular component) combined with a sufficiently large value of σ_v^2, and/or (2) a sufficiently large negative value of the covariance σ_{uv} which also puts a lower bound on σ_v^2 due to the familiar inequality $\sigma_u\sigma_v \geqq |\sigma_{uv}|$. We now prove that if $\gamma_1>0$ then $\sigma_v^2>\sigma_u^2$.

Since the value of σ_{uv} is unknown, consider first the case $\sigma_{uv} \geqq 0$. For $\gamma_1>0$ and $\sigma_{uv} \geqq 0$, eq. (20) implies that $\theta>0$, i.e., the secular component must be positively autocorrelated. Given this, eq. (20) also implies

$$\sigma_v^2>\theta^{-1}\sigma_u^2+(\theta^{-1}-1)\sigma_{uv}>\sigma_u^2,$$

using the fact that $0<\theta<1$. The other possible case is $\sigma_{uv}<0$. Using the fact that $\sigma_u\sigma_v \geqq |\sigma_{uv}|$, we have

$$\theta\sigma_v^2+(1-\theta)\sigma_u\sigma_v-\sigma_u^2 \geqq \theta\sigma_v^2-(1-\theta)\sigma_{uv}-\sigma_u^2>0.$$

Factoring the first expression yields

$$(\theta\sigma_v+\sigma_u)(\sigma_v-\sigma_u)>0$$

and hence both factors must be positive or negative. If they are both positive then the second factor gives us $\sigma_v>\sigma_u$. Note that there is nothing in this case to prevent θ from being negative since if the first factor is positive we have only that $\theta>-(\sigma_u/\sigma_v)$. If both factors are negative then the first factor would imply $\theta<0$ but also that $\sigma_v>-\theta^{-1}\sigma_u>\sigma_u$ (again using the fact that $0<\theta<1$), however, the second factor would imply $\sigma_v<\sigma_u$ thus leading to a contradiction that rules out negative factors. We conclude therefore that the standard deviation of innovations in the secular or growth component is larger than the standard deviation of innovations in the cyclical component.

We can now use these results to obtain a plausible range of values of σ_v/σ_u under alternative assumptions. Consider first the case $\sigma_{uv}=0$, so that the growth and cyclical components are uncorrelated. From (19) and (20) it is easy to show that

$$\rho_1 = \frac{\theta\sigma_v^2 - \sigma_u^2}{(1+\theta^2)\sigma_v^2 + 2\sigma_u^2}, \quad \text{or}$$

$$\sigma_v/\sigma_u = [-(1+2\rho_1)/\rho_1(1+\theta^2-\rho_1^{-1}\theta)]^{\frac{1}{2}}. \tag{21}$$

Our empirical results give us a relevant range of values for ρ_1 and we know that $0<\theta<1$ when $\sigma_{uv}=0$. Computed values of the ratio of the standard deviations are given in the following table:

Values of σ_v/σ_u for various values of ρ_1 and θ when $\sigma_{uv}=0$.

	θ			
ρ_1	0.3	0.5	0.6	0.8
0.1	2.5	1.8	1.6	1.4
0.3	—	3.6	2.9	2.3
0.4	—	∞	5.7	3.5

The blanks in the table are due to the fact that ρ_1 cannot be larger than $\theta/(1+\theta^2)$ regardless of how large we make σ_v^2/σ_u^2. The values in the table suggest that the standard deviation of innovations in the non-stationary component may be several times larger than the standard deviation of innovations in the cyclical component.

Now consider the case where the secular or non-stationary component is a strict random walk, so that $\theta=0$. The value of ρ_1 is then given by

$$\rho_1 = \frac{-\rho_{uv} - (\sigma_v/\sigma_u)^{-1}}{(\sigma_v/\sigma_u) + 2(\sigma_v/\sigma_u)^{-1} + 2\rho_{uv}},$$

where ρ_{uv} is the contemporaneous correlation between u and v. To account for positive values of ρ_1, ρ_{uv} must be negative, in fact $\rho_{uv} < -(\sigma_v/\sigma_u)^{-1} < 0$. Thus, imposing the random walk assumption on $\bar{y}$ implies either strong negative correlation between u and v, or a large variance ratio, or both. This is borne out by the values of ρ_{uv} and (σ_v/σ_u) consistent with observed values of ρ_1 presented in the following table:

Values of σ_v/σ_u for various values of ρ_1 and ρ_{uv} when $\theta=0$.

	ρ_{uv}		
ρ_1	−0.2	−0.6	−0.9
0.0	5.0	1.7	1.1
0.1	—	4.5	1.2
0.3	—	—	1.8

The blanks indicate values of ρ_1 and ρ_{uv} that are inconsistent with any σ_v/σ_u. It is interesting to note that the magnitude of σ_v/σ_u implied by assuming $\sigma_{uv}=0$ or $\theta=0$ are similar.

The above results are dependent on the stochastic structure of output being a first-order MA process with positive autocorrelation at lag one. As mentioned in section 3, the positive autocorrelation could be attributed entirely to temporal aggregation. If this is the case then our inferences about σ_v/σ_u are distorted since it is well-known that time aggregation amplifies low frequency (i.e., long-run) movements relative to high frequency (i.e., short-run) movements. However, we are somewhat reluctant to accept this interpretation of the results since it implies that the short-run or cyclical variability we are reducing through aggregation is variation that is dissipated within the aggregation interval of a year [see Tiao (1972)]. Another way of making this point is to say that by looking at annual data, we can make no inference regarding the variance of components whose memory (or life) is less than a year. We do not believe, however, this is a significant disadvantage of the annual time interval since most economists probably identify business cycles (transitory components) with periods that are longer than a year.[18]

It is instructive to contrast our analysis to the signal extraction strategy proposed by Hodrick and Prescott (1980). Hodrick and Prescott decompose observed variables into growth and cyclical components under the maintained hypothesis that the growth component moves smoothly through time. The standard deviation of innovations in the growth component is assumed to be very small relative to the standard deviation of innovations in the cyclical component (specifically 1/40th). Optimal estimates are chosen through a criterion function that penalizes variance in the second differences of the growth component as well as variance in the cycle. A linear time trend emerges as a limiting case.

The Hodrick and Prescott strategy implicitly imposes a components model on the data without investigating what restrictions are implied (a difficult task in their model) and whether those restrictions are consistent with the data. Our strategy, on the other hand, is to use the data as an aid in identifying certain characteristics of an appropriate components model. Our results suggest that the ratio of the standard deviations of growth to cyclical innovations has a minimum in the neighborhood of one with likely values up to five or six rather than the value of 1/40th assumed by Hodrick and Prescott.

[18]Although we have not carried out an analysis using quarterly data, our experience with such data suggests that our conclusions are not likely to be sensitive to the interval of observation. In other words, the autocorrelation structure of the quarterly data are not much different from that observed in the annual data.

5. Some implications for business cycle theorizing

The analysis of unobserved components models leads us to the inference that if (a) output is the sum of a non-stationary component of the DS class and a stationary (transitory) component, and (b) we observe non-negative autocorrelation at lag one only in the first differences of output then (i) the variance of the innovations in the non-stationary component must be as large or larger than that of the purely stationary or transitory component, and (ii) either the non-stationary component contains significant transitory components (i.e., it is not a random walk) or, if the non-stationary component is assumed to be a random walk, the innovations in the random walk are correlated with the transitory component.

These inferences have potentially important implications for business cycle research. For example, most of the recent developments in business cycle theory stress the importance of monetary disturbances as a source of output fluctuations.[19] However, the disturbances are generally assumed to have only transitory impact (i.e., monetary disturbances have no permanent real effects).[20] Therefore, the inference that the innovations in the non-stationary component have a larger variance than the innovations in a transitory component implies that real (non-monetary) disturbances are likely to be a much more important source of output fluctuations than monetary disturbances.[21] This conclusion is further strengthened if monetary disturbances are viewed as only one of several sources of cyclical disturbances. In addition, while we have focused on real GNP, we believe the fact that other real variables such as real per capita GNP, employment, and real wages have similar characteristics provides some corroborating evidence. In fact, by investigating in detail several series jointly one might be able to get a more complete picture of the relative sizes of various shocks.[22] Several additional points are worth noting. First there is nothing in theory or in our empirical results that implies that the unobserved components model of (13) is economically meaningful. For example, we cannot reject the hypothesis that actual output contains only one non-stationary component (i.e., $\sigma_u^2=0$) and thus observed autocorrelation simply reflects autocorrelation in movements in a stochastic growth component. Indeed, a stochastic growth process that contains both permanent and

[19]For example, see the models of Lucas (1975) and Barro (1976).

[20]We are ignoring in this discussion the potential permanent effects of inflation in the models described by Tobin (1965), Stockman (1982), and others.

[21]As noted near the end of section 3, given the observed behavior of output, this result holds even if monetary disturbances and real (non-stationary) disturbances are correlated (perhaps through policy response).

[22]For example one might be able to use a known decomposition of output to in turn decompose the unemployment rate into 'natural' and 'cyclical' movements in the unemployment rate. Such an effort, however, would probably require more structure to the problem that we have used here.

transitory characteristics can arise in the models developed by Long and Plosser (1980) and Kydland and Prescott (1981). In these models, dynamic competitive equilibrium is capable of generating fluctuations in a 'natural rate of output' that, in many ways, mimics the behavior of observed output.

Second, we also cannot prove empirically that cyclical fluctuations are stationary. The stationarity of this component is also an assumption, but one we believe most economists would accept. Nevertheless, the hypothesis that the business cycle is a stochastic process of the DS class is not refutable from the empirical evidence. The general point is that some unobserved components representations are rejected by the data, but the data by itself cannot reveal the true structure.

6. Summary and conclusions

In this paper we try to distinguish between two alternative hypotheses concerning the nature of non-stationarity in macroeconomic time series, one is the widely held view that such series represent stationary fluctuations around a deterministic trend and the other is that non-stationarity arises from the accumulation over time of stationary and invertible first differences. Our test results are consistent with the latter hypothesis and would be consistent with the former only if the fluctuations around a deterministic trend are so highly autocorrelated as to be indistinguishable from non-stationary series themselves in realizations as long as one hundred years.

The distinction between the two classes of processes is fundamental and acceptance of the purely stochastic view of non-stationarity has broad implications for our understanding of the nature of economic phenomena. For example, if aggregate output is thought of as consisting of a non-stationary growth component plus a stationary cyclical component, then the growth component must itself be a non-stationary stochastic process rather than a deterministic trend as has been generally assumed in empirical work. Instead of attributing all variation in output changes to the cyclical component, the stochastic model allows for contributions from variations in both components. Therefore, empirical analyses of business cycles based on residuals from fitted trends lines are likely to confound the two sources of variation, greatly overstating the magnitude and duration of the cyclical component and understating the importance of the growth component. Moreover, to impose the trend specification is to assume away long-run uncertainty in these variables and to remove much of their variation *a priori*.

We also remind the reader that first differencing does not remove a stochastic growth component although it may render the series stationary. The first differences of the observed series will consist of the sum of the first differences of both the secular and cyclical components. While first differences do not exhibit the spurious periodicity of trend residuals neither do they discard variation in the secular component; the problem of inferring the behavior of each unobserved component from the sum remains.

Finally, the empirical observation that changes on real output (as well as employment and real wages) displays non-negative autocorrelation at lag one and zero elsewhere suggests that shocks to the secular or non-stationary component account for a substantial portion of the variation observed. Assigning a major portion of variance in output to innovations in this non-stationary component gives an important role to real factors in output fluctuations and places limits on the importance of monetary theories of the business cycle.

References

Barro, Robert J., 1976, Rational expectations and the role of monetary policy, Journal of Monetary Economics 2, 1–32.

Barro, Robert J., 1978, Unanticipated money, output, and the price level in the United States, Journal of Political Economy 86, 549–580.

Beveridge, Stephen and Charles R. Nelson, 1981, A new approach to decomposition of economic time series into permanent and transitory components with particular attention to measurement of the 'business cycle', Journal of Monetary Economics 7, 151–174.

Black, Fischer, 1979, General equilibrium and business cycles, Working paper (Sloan School of Management, Massachusetts Institute of Technology, Cambridge, MA).

Bodkin, Ronald G., 1969, Real wages and cyclical variations in employment, An examination of the evidence, Canadian Economic Journal 2, 353–374.

Burns, Arthur F. and Wesley C. Mitchell, 1946, Measuring business cycles (National Bureau of Economic Research, New York).

Chan, K. Hung, Jack C. Hayya and J. Keith Ord, 1977, A note on trend removal methods: The case of polynomial versus variate differencing, Econometrica 45, 737–744.

Dickey, David A., 1976, Estimation and hypothesis testing in nonstationary time series, Unpublished doctoral dissertation (Iowa State University, Ames, IA).

Dickey, David A. and Wayne A. Fuller, 1979, Distribution of the estimators for autoregressive time series with a unit root, Journal of the American Statistical Association 74, 427–431.

Dickey, David A. and Wayne A. Fuller, 1981, Likelihood ratio statistics for autoregressive time series with a unit root, Econometrica 49, 1057–1072.

Friedman, Milton, 1957, A theory of the consumption function (Princeton University Press, Princeton, NJ).

Friedman, Milton and Anna J. Schwartz, 1963, A monetary history of the United States, 1867–1960 (Princeton University Press, Princeton, NJ).

Fuller, Wayne A., 1976, Introduction to statistical time series (Wiley, New York).

Hall, Robert E., 1978, Stochastic implications of the life cycle permanent income hypothesis: Theory and evidence, Journal of Political Economy 86, 971–988.

Hall, Robert E., 1980, Labor supply and aggregate fluctuations, Carnegie-Rochester Conference Series on Public Policy 12, 7–35.

Historical Statistics of the U.S., Colonial Times to 1970, 1975, (U.S. Dept. of Commerce, Bureau of the Census, Washington, DC).

Hodrick, Robert J. and Edward C. Prescott, 1980, Post-war U.S. business cycles: An empirical investigation, Working paper (Carnegie-Mellon University, Pittsburgh, PA).

Hogan, Warren P., 1958, Technological progress and production functions, The Review of Economics and Statistics 40, 407.

King, Robert G. and Charles I. Plosser, 1981, The behavior of money, credit, and prices in a real business cycle, Working paper GPB 81-8 (University of Rochester, Rochester, NY).

Kydland, Finn and Edward C. Prescott, 1980, A competitive theory of fluctuations and the feasibility and desirability of stabilization policy, in: Stanley Fisher, ed., Rational expectations and economics policy (University of Chicago Press, Chicago, IL).

Kydland, Finn and Edward C. Prescott, 1981, Time to build and the persistence of unemployment, Working paper (Carnegie-Mellon University, Pittsburgh, PA).

Lebergott, Stanley, 1964, Manpower in economic growth (McGraw-Hill, New York).

Long, John B. and Charles I. Plosser, 1980, Real business cycles, Working paper (University of Rochester, Rochester, NY).

Long Term Economic Growth, 1973 (U.S. Dept. of Commerce, Washington, DC).

Lucas, Robert E., Jr., 1973, Some international evidence on output–inflation tradeoffs, American Economic Review 63, 326–334.

Lucas, Robert E., Jr., 1975, An equilibrium model of the business cycle, Journal of Political Economy 83, 1113–1144.

McCulloch, J. Huston, 1975, The Monte Carlo cycle in business activity, Economic Inquiry 13, 303–321.

Muth, John F., 1960, Optimal properties of exponentially weighted forecasts, Journal of the American Statistical Association 55, 299–306.

Nelson, Charles R. and Heejoon Kang, 1981, Spurious periodicity in inappropriately detrended time series, Econometrica 49, 741–751.

Nerlove, Marc, David M. Grether and Jose L. Carvalho, 1979, Analysis of economic times series: A synthesis (Academic Press, New York).

Perloff, Jeffrey M. and Michael L. Wachter, 1979, A production function — nonaccelerating inflation approach to potential output: Is measured potential output too high? Carnegie-Rochester Conference Series on Public Policy 10, 113–164.

Pierce, David A., 1975, On trend and autocorrelation, Communications in Statistics 4, 163–175.

Pierce, David A., 1978, Signal extraction error in nonstationary time series, Federal Reserve Board Special Studies Papers, 112.

Plosser, Charles I. and G. William Schwert, 1977, Estimation of a noninvertible moving average process: The case of overdifferencing, Journal of Econometrics 6, 199–224.

Plosser, Charles I. and G. William Schwert, 1979, Potential GNP: Its measurement and significance — A dissenting opinion, Carnegie-Rochester Conference on Public Policy 10, 179–186.

Sargent, Thomas J., 1978, Estimation of dynamic labor demand schedules under rational expectations, Journal of Political Economy 86, 1009–1044.

Shiller, Robert J., 1979, The volatility of long term interest rates and expectations models of the term structure, Journal of Political Economy 87, 1190–1219.

Shiller, Robert J., 1981, Do stock prices move too much to be justified by subsequent changes in dividends? American Economic Review 71, 421–436.

Solow, Robert M., 1957, Technical change and the aggregate production function, The Review of Economics and Statistics 39, 312–320.

Stockman, Alan C., 1981, Anticipated inflation and the capital stock in a cash-in-advance economy, Journal of Monetary Economics 8, 387–393.

Taylor, John B., 1979, Estimation and control of a macroeconomic model with rational expectations, Econometrica 47, 1267–1286.

Tiao, George C., 1972, Asymptotic behaviour of temporal aggregates of time series, Biometrika 59, 525–531.

Tobin, James, 1965, Money and economic growth, reprinted in ch. 9 of Essays in Economics, Volume 1: Macroeconomics, 1971 (North-Holland, Amsterdam).

Wichern, Dean W., 1973, The behavior of the sample autocorrelation function for an integrated moving average process, Biometrika 60, 235–239.

Working, Holbrook, 1960, A note on the correlation of first differences of averages in a random chain, Econometrica 28, 916–918.

[17]

©Journal of Business & Economic Statistics, Vol. 2, No. 1, January 1984

Pitfalls in the Use of Time as an Explanatory Variable in Regression

Charles R. Nelson
Department of Economics, University of Washington, Seattle, WA 98105

Heejoon Kang
Department of Business Economics and Public Policy, School of Business, Indiana University, Bloomington, IN 47405

Regression of a trendless random walk on time produces R-squared values around .44 regardless of sample length. The residuals from the regression exhibit only about 14% as much variation as the original series even though the underlying process has no functional dependence on time. The autocorrelation structure of these "detrended" random walks is pseudo-cyclical and purely artifactual. Conventional tests for trend are strongly biased toward finding a trend when none is present, and this effect is only partially mitigated by Cochrane-Orcutt correction for autocorrelation. The results are extended to show that pairs of detrended random walks exhibit spurious correlation.

KEY WORDS: Detrending; Regression; Random walk; Autocorrelation; Spurious correlation.

1. INTRODUCTION

A stationary time series is one that fluctuates around a mean value. More technically, it has a mean value, variance and autocovariances which are finite and constant through time. Many economic time series, however, are clearly nonstationary in the sense that they tend to depart even farther from any given value as time goes on. When movement in a series appears to be predominantly in one direction it is often said to exhibit "trend." In applied work, trend is often attributed to a functional dependence on time. Accordingly, nonstationary time series are frequently "detrended" by regressing the series on time or a function of time. The residuals are then treated as a stationary time series with well defined variance, autocovariances and covariances with other detrended variables. The model or representation implicit in these procedures is

$$Y_t = f(t) + u_t, \tag{1.1}$$

where $\{Y_t\}$ is an observed nonstationary time series and $\{u_t\}$ is the stationary series of deviations around the trend function $f(t)$. In the case of a linear trend, $f(t)$ has the form $\alpha + \beta t$.

An alternative hypothesis consistent with nonstationarity is the one popularized by Box and Jenkins (1970), namely that the observed series represents the accumulation (integration) of changes or first differences that are a stationary time series. A series of this type evolves according to the relation

$$Y_t = Y_{t-1} + \beta + \epsilon_t, \tag{1.2}$$

where $\{\epsilon_t\}$ is a stationary series with mean zero and constant variance σ_ϵ^2, and where β is the (fixed) mean of the first differences, often called the drift. The simplest member of this class is the random walk in which the steps, ϵ_t, are serially random. Accumulating changes in Y from any initial value, say Y_0, we have

$$Y_t = Y_0 + \beta t + \sum_{i=1}^{t} \epsilon_i, \tag{1.3}$$

which has the same form as a linear version of (1.1). It is fundamentally different from (1.1), however. The intercept is not a fixed parameter but rather depends on the initial value Y_0. The disturbance is not stationary; rather the variance and autocovariances depend on time. In the random case the variance is just to $t\sigma_\epsilon^2$. The width of a confidence interval for future values of Y in (1.1) is limited in width by the finite dispersion of u, while in (1.3) it increases without bound (in proportion to $\sqrt{t}$ for a random walk with normally distributed errors). We follow Nelson and Plosser (1982) in referring to the first class of models (1.1) as trend stationary processes (TSP) and the second class (1.2) as difference stationary processes (DSP).

A test for the hypothesis that a time series belongs to

the DSP class against the alternative that it belongs to the TSP class has been developed by Dickey and Fuller (1979). In the simplest case one estimates by least squares the coefficients in the model,

$$Y_t = \alpha + \rho Y_{t-1} + \beta t + \epsilon_t, \quad (1.4)$$

which belongs to the DSP class if $\rho = 1$ and $\beta = 0$, and to the TSP class if $|\rho| < 1$. Dickey and Fuller show that the least squares estimate of ρ is not distributed around unity under the DSP hypothesis but rather around a value less than one. The negative bias diminishes with the number of observations. Nelson and Plosser applied this testing procedure to a wide range of historical time series for the U.S. economy and found that the DSP hypothesis was accepted in all cases with the exception of the unemployment rate, which, not surprisingly, appears to be stationary, and population, which was not consistent with linear versions of either hypothesis. Furthermore, many variables such as real GNP and employment were found to be reasonably characterized as random walks with drift.

In this article we explore the pitfalls inherent in regression models in which time is included as an explanatory variable under the TSP hypothesis when in fact the time series we are interested in explaining belongs to the DSP class. We take as our benchmark the case in which the series is generated by a random walk. In Section 2 of the article we investigate the properties of standard regression statistics including R^2, t ratios, and sample autocorrelations of residuals when time is the only explanatory variable as it is in detrending regressions. In Section 3 we extend the investigation to regressions that include other explanatory variables. Particular attention is focused on the danger of spurious regression relationships among variables that are unrelated.

2. GOODNESS OF FIT AND RESIDUAL VARIANCE IN LINEAR TIME TREND REGRESSIONS

The simplest example of regression on time and the one most often encountered in practice is the linear detrending regression

$$Y_t = \alpha + \beta t + u_t, \quad (2.1)$$

in which the nonstationarity in Y is assumed to be explained by a linear dependence on time, with the remaining variation in Y being due to a stationary "cyclical" component $\{u_t\}$. If the series is one that grows exponentially it is often transformed to natural logarithms prior to detrending. Regression (2.1) is properly specified if the series belongs to the TSP class and account is taken of autocorrelation in the disturbances prior to drawing inferences about β. However, if Y belongs to the DSP class, then the disturbance in (2.1) is not stationary and the appropriate transformation to produce a stationary series would be differencing. Suppose one nevertheless fits the linear trend to a DSP series. What can we say about the properties of the usual regression statistics and the resulting detrended data?

We begin by noting that a DSP has the form of a linear regression with cumulative errors, as in (1.3). The initial value Y_0 may be regarded as an unknown parameter, say α, so we have

$$Y_t = \alpha + \beta t + \sum_{i=1}^{t} \epsilon_i; \quad t = 1, \ldots, N. \quad (2.2)$$

In this context, the realization $(Y_1, \ldots, Y_N)$ is thought of as resulting from a random drawing from the joint distribution of disturbances $(\epsilon_1, \ldots, \epsilon_N)$. This joint distribution implies a joint distribution for the cumulative errors in (2.2). These regression errors have mean zero and a $N \times N$ covariance matrix, say Ω. The properties of the ordinary least squares (OLS) coefficients $\hat{\alpha}$ and $\hat{\beta}$ and the resulting residuals are of considerable practical interest since it is these residuals that are often interpreted as detrended data in applied work.

Standard least squares regression theory provides us with some immediate and useful results, namely, (a) $\hat{\alpha}$ and $\hat{\beta}$ are unbiased, (b) sampling errors $(\hat{\alpha} - \alpha)$ and $(\hat{\beta} - \beta)$ in a given sample depend only on the ϵ's underlying that sample and not on α or β, and (c) the particular residuals, or detrended data, obtained from a given sample depend only on the ϵ's and not on α or β. These properties imply that we can investigate the distributions of $(\hat{\alpha} - \alpha)$, $(\hat{\beta} - \beta)$, the detrended data, and derived statistics such as standard errors and t-ratios by Monte Carlo methods without being concerned that our results depend on arbitrarily chosen values of α and β.

To make our investigation operational we need to choose a particular DSP process as an archetype, and our choice is the random walk for which the ϵ's are independent and identically distributed. The random walk is the simplest member of the DSP class and also provides a reasonable characterization of many economic time series. For this case the elements of Ω are just $\Omega_{j,k} = \min(j, k)\, \sigma_\epsilon^2$ so that Ω is completely determined by the number of observations and σ_ϵ^2.

The covariances between errors in this model are all positive, and standard analysis of regression with positively correlated disturbances suggests that conventional standard errors and t statistics will mislead by overstating significance of coefficient estimates. Correspondingly, R^2 will exaggerate the extent to which movement of the data is actually accounted for by time. This is analogous to the spurious regression phenomenon discussed by Granger and Newbold (1974) in the context of pairs of stochastic time series. To see how the spurious regression phenomenon works in our situation, consider the case where $\beta = 0$, so that the level of Y does not have any functional dependence on time. The population value of R^2 is zero since time does not in fact account for any of the variation in Y. If we nevertheless run the regression of Y on time we will obtain a sample value of R^2 which is given by

$$R^2 = 1 - (\text{SSE}/\text{SST}), \quad (2.3)$$

where SSE is the conventional error sum of squares and SST the total sum of squares. Using the *true* parameters we will have SSE = SST and $R^2 = 0$. As we shall see, the sample R^2 will be wrong on both counts; that is, both SSE and SST are distorted in the sample.

Taking the SST part of R^2 first, we note that by definition the sample variance of N observations is

$$\text{SST}/(N-1) \equiv (N-1)^{-1}(\sum Y^2) - [N(N-1)]^{-1}(\sum Y)^2. \quad (2.4)$$

For model (2.2) with $\beta = 0$ the expected value of the first term is readily shown to be

$$E[(N-1)^{-1}(\sum Y^2)] = [N(N+1)/2(N-1)]\sigma_\epsilon^2 \approx (N/2)\sigma_\epsilon^2, \quad (2.5)$$

which is the correct average variance of Y over the sample, since the variances of Y_1, Y_2, Y_N are $\sigma_\epsilon^2, 2\sigma_\epsilon^2, \ldots, N\sigma_\epsilon^2$, respectively. The distortion of SST comes with the second term, which arises from using the sample mean of Y in calculating SST, since

$$E(\sum Y)^2 = (1 + 2^2 + \ldots + N^2)\sigma_\epsilon^2 = [N(N+1)(2N+1)/6]\sigma_\epsilon^2, \quad (2.6)$$

which is of order N^3 instead of order N as would be the case in a random sampling situation. Thus, we have

$$E[(\sum Y)^2/(N-1)N] = (N+1)(2N+1)/6(N-1)]\sigma_\epsilon^2, \quad (2.7)$$

which combined with (2.5) gives us

$$E[\text{SST}/(N-1)] = [(N+1)/6]\sigma_\epsilon^2. \quad (2.8)$$

Comparing (2.8) with (2.5) we see that the effect of using the sample mean of Y instead of the true mean, zero, in calculating the sample variance of Y cuts the measured variation in the data by an average of two-thirds.

In studying the behavior of SSE we are able to make use of a formula given in Nelson and Kang (1981), based on work by Chan, Hayya, and Ord (1977), for the expected values of the autocovariances of residuals from regression of a random walk on time. This result does not depend on whether the mean of the changes, β, is zero or not. Recognizing that the variance of the residuals is their autocovariance at lag zero, equation (2.1) of Nelson and Kang (1981) yields the approximation

$$E[\text{SSE}/(N-1)] \approx [(N+1)/15]\sigma_\epsilon^2. \quad (2.9)$$

Comparing this result with (2.5), which gives the true variance of Y for a realization of length N, we see that the variance of detrended data is only 2/15 as large. Thus, even when no trend or drift is present, regression detrending will remove about 86% of the variation from the original data.

If it were true that $E(R^2) = 1 - E(\text{SSE})/E(\text{SST})$ instead of $1 - E(\text{SSE}/\text{SST})$, we could combine results (2.8) and (2.9) to obtain $E(R^2) = 3/5 = .6$ for regression of a random walk with zero drift on time. As we shall see from the results of sampling experiments, $E(R^2)$ is not that large, but rather around .44 because of the difference between $E(\text{SSE})/E(\text{SST})$ and $E(\text{SSE}/\text{SST})$. The fact that $E(\text{SSE})$ and $E(\text{SST})$ are both of order N *does* suggest that $E(R^2)$ does not depend importantly on sample size, a result that is confirmed by sampling experiments. To explore the sampling characteristics of sample R^2, t ratios, residual variance, and residual autocorrelation, we have performed a set of experiments in which the trend model was fitted by OLS to 1000 independent replications of a random walk with $\alpha = 0$, $\beta = 0$, and ϵ_t iid $N(0, 1)$. The basic results for $N = 100$ observations are presented in Table 1. Only the results for R^2 and the mean values of $\hat{\alpha}$ and $\hat{\beta}$ depend on α and β.

Note first that the mean sample R^2 is .443, although Y does not in fact depend on t. The R^2 obtained in each realization is a lower bound on the R^2 that would have been obtained in the multiple OLS regression, which included other independent variables. The minimum observed value of R^2 was .000+ and the maximum was .978. This occurs in spite of the fact that $\hat{\beta}$ is unbiased.

The mean sample variance of residuals, $[\text{SSE}/(N-1)]$, is 6.79, which agrees closely with the value given by approximation (2.9) for $N = 100$ and $\sigma_\epsilon^2 = 1$, namely 6.73. Since the true variance of Y averaged over the sample is 50, the detrending procedure has indeed

Table 1. Empirical Moments of Summary Statistics for OLS Regression of a Zero-Drift Random Walk on Time with 100 Observations, Based on 1,000 Replications: $Y_t = \hat{\alpha} + \hat{\beta}t + \hat{u}_t$.

Statistic	*Mean*	*Variance*	*Standard Deviation*
R^2	.443	.092	.304
SSE/(N−1)	6.7	18.32	4.28
$\hat{\beta}$	−.002	.013	.115
Est. Var. ($\hat{\beta}$)	.81 E−4	.26 E−8	.51 E−4
$t(\hat{\beta})$	−.16	220.2	14.84
$\hat{\alpha}$	.02	13.81	3.72
Est. Var. ($\hat{\alpha}$)	.28	.03	.17
$t(\hat{\alpha})$	−.005	50.41	7.10
D.W.	.198	.011	.104
r_1	.88	.28 E−2	.532 E−1
r_2	.77	.91 E−2	.956 E−1
r_3	.68	.17 E−1	.129
r_{22}	−.04	.01	.09
r_{23}	−.02	.01	.09

NOTE: $\hat{\alpha}$ and $\hat{\beta}$ are computed by OLS and their estimated variances and t-ratios under the (inappropriate) assumptions of the classical linear regression model. In this situation $\hat{\alpha}$ and $\hat{\beta}$ are unbiased (have expected value zero).

removed 86 percent of the variation in the data. This attenuation effect does not depend on σ_ϵ^2.

The spurious regression phenomenon is further reflected in the large dispersion of t ratios for $\hat{\beta}$ and $\hat{\alpha}$, their standard deviations being about 15 and 7 times, respectively, what they would be in a properly specified regression model. As a result, the true null hypotheses $\beta = 0$ and $\alpha = 0$ are rejected with frequencies of 87% and 80%, respectively, at a nominal 5% significance level.

Earlier papers by Chan, Hayya, and Ord (1977) and Nelson and Kang (1981) discuss the behavior of sample autocorrelations of residuals from regression of a random walk on time. An approximation is developed in which the expected sample autocorrelation for a given lag is a function only of the ratio of the lag to the length of the series, except for terms of order N^{-1} and smaller. For example, at lag one the expected autocorrelation is roughly $(1 - 10/N)$. Thus, the shape of the sample autocorrelation function is effectively an artifact of detrending, with the value of the autocorrelation for given lag depending on the particular sample length. Furthermore, the function is shown by Nelson and Kang to resemble a damped sine wave, as can be seen in Figure 1, where the function is plotted for $N = 101$. This resemblance implies pseudo-periodic behavior in the detrended series where none is present in the underlying data. At lags that are small relative to sample size, however, the function declines roughly exponentially. These results do not depend on either the true value of β or σ_ϵ^2.

In our experimental case with $N = 100$ the empirical means of the first three sample autocorrelations of residuals, denoted by r_1, r_2 and r_3 in Table 1, are .88, .77, and .68, respectively. The values predicted by the approximation formula, .91, .82, and .74, are somewhat too high. The empirical mean values do decline roughly exponentially. This decline suggests that an investigator versed in time series model identification would usually specify a stationary first order AR process for this

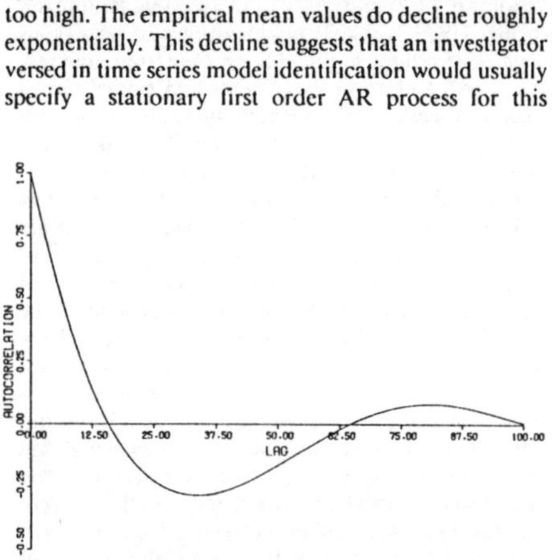

Figure 1. Theoretical Autocorrelations for Detrended Random Walk.

detrended series even though the original data are not stationary around a trend. This conjecture is supported by values of the partial autocorrelations at lags two and three, denoted by r_{22} and r_{33} in Table 1. The means are −.04 and −.02, respectively, which should be compared with a standard error of $[1/\sqrt{N}]$ or .100 in this case. We conclude that an investigator who takes the time trend model seriously is likely to specify an AR(1) process for the residuals with a coefficient typically around .88 in the case of 100 observations, or in general about $(1 - 10/N)$.

To check the sensitivity of our results to sample size we also ran the experiment for $N = 20$ observations, again with 1000 replications. Mean R^2 was nearly the same, .435, as expected. The mean sample variance of residuals was 1.40, so detrending again removed about 86% of the variation in the data. In accordance with the smaller number of observations, t ratios are reduced in absolute size, with standard deviations falling to about 6 and 3 for $\hat{\beta}$ and $\hat{\alpha}$ respectively, the true null hypotheses being rejected 73% and 54% of the time, respectively, at a 5 percent nominal significance level. The means of r_1, r_2, and r_3 were .50, .17, and −.04, compared with corresponding values from the approximation formula of .59, .28, and .05. Thus, with only 20 observations the oscillatory character of the autocorrelation function becomes more evident at low lags. This is further evident in the partial autocorrelations r_{22} and r_{33}, which have mean values −.18 and −.13, although the appropriate standard error is now .22. If a second order autoregression is specified for the residuals, the coefficients implied by sample autocorrelations indicate complex roots (oscillatory behavior) in 69% of the cases. By comparison, complex roots were indicated in less than 1% of the cases for $N = 100$.

An alert investigator would presumably recognize the presence of autocorrelation in the trend regression residuals and would rerun the regression after correction for autocorrelation if the objective was to test for the presence of trend rather than simply detrending. Under the hypothesis of AR(1) errors, the appropriately transformed regression would be

$$(Y_t - \rho Y_{t-1})$$
$$= \alpha(1 - \rho) + \beta[t - \rho(t - 1)] + (u_t - \rho u_{t-1}), \quad (2.10)$$

where ρ is the AR coefficient for the OLS residuals. Indeed, (2.10) would be a correctly specified regression if ρ were set at unity which corresponds to first differencing. However, an investigator who believed the errors were stationary would presumably use the value of r_1 from the OLS residuals. Estimation of (2.10) with r_1 in place of ρ amounts to a two-step Cochrane-Orcutt (1949) procedure. The transformation of course undercorrects for autocorrelation, since r_1 is typically around .88 for $N = 100$. As a result, the spurious regression phenomenon by no means disappears. In the same set of experiments with $N = 100$ the standard deviation of the t ratio for the trend coefficient $\hat{\beta}$ dropped to only 4.57 after transformation, with the true null hypothesis being rejected in 58% of the realizations at a nominal 5% level. Similarly, the standard deviation of $t(\hat{\alpha})$ fell to 2.67 and the rejection frequency fell to 45%. The mean R^2 in these regressions was .122. The residuals in the transformed regressions give no hint of trouble: the mean Durbin-Watson statistic was 1.88, corresponding to a mean autocorrelation at lag one of only .05.[1]

The Cochrane-Orcutt procedure is often iterated using successive estimates of (α, β) and ρ until convergence occurs. In the special case of time trend regression, convergence effectively occurs at the first iteration. The algebraic reasons for this are explored in the Appendix. This result is entirely due to the algebra of least squares and the special nature of the time trend variable, and it is not dependent on the data being generated by a TSP, DSP, or whatever.

To sum up, an investigator following standard methodology will tend to find evidence of a trend in random walk data when none is in fact present. This error occurs essentially because testing for trend in the regression framework takes as a maintained hypothesis the assumption that the time series is *stationary*, apart from a deterministic trend (if any). Since trend lines fit random walk data well in an ex post sense, the detrending procedure will tend to remove much variation in the data, which is in fact stochastic rather than deterministic. As Nelson and Kang (1981) have demonstrated, the autocorrelation properties of the detrended data will be dominated by the effects of detrending, thereby obscuring evidence of any actual autocorrelation in first differences. We conclude that the appropriate test for trend developed by Dickey and Fuller (1979) should be conducted prior to analysis of nonstationary series. At a minimum, the alternative that the series are stationary in differences should be considered.

It is doubtless true that many economic time series such as output, sales, and prices do in fact exhibit a positive rate of drift, which would mean $\beta > 0$ in our simple model. If this is the case, does it mitigate any of our objections to time trend regression? Not at all. As noted previously, the properties of estimation errors $(\hat{\alpha} - \alpha)$ and $(\hat{\beta} - \beta)$, the residuals, and statistics constructed from them do not depend on β; residual variance will understate the true stochastic variation in the data to the same degree, residual autocorrelations will display the same pseudoperiodicity, and conventional measures of significance will be overstated. R^2 will still reflect the spurious regression phenomenon. The behavior of R^2 in the case $\beta > 0$ is illuminated by considering the effect of β on SSE or SST. While SSE does not depend on β at all, E(SST) is augmented by a term that is a function of β^2 and N and is of order N^3. The ratio $E(\text{SSE})/E(\text{SST})$ is then of order N^{-1}, implying that R^2 will tend toward one as N increases in the case $\beta \neq 0$, instead of toward a constant. Denoting by $\tilde{R}^2$ the expression $[1 - E(\text{SSE})/E(\text{SST})]$, it is easy to show that

$$\tilde{R}^2 = [\tilde{R}_0^2 + (N/2)(\beta^2/\sigma_\epsilon^2)]/[1 + (N/2)(\beta^2/\sigma_\epsilon^2)], \tag{2.11}$$

where $\tilde{R}_0^2$ is the previously derived value of $\tilde{R}^2$ for $\beta = 0$. Note that $\tilde{R}^2$ exceeds $\tilde{R}_0^2$ if $\beta \neq 0$, the difference increasing with the ratio $(\beta^2/\sigma_\epsilon^2)$ and N. It is the case for postwar annual U.S. real GNP in logs that β and σ_ϵ are roughly equal. For $\beta^2 = \sigma_\epsilon^2$, we have

$$\tilde{R}^2 = [\tilde{R}_0^2 + (N/2)]/(1 + N/2), \tag{2.12}$$

which is always greater than $N/(N + 2)$. This suggests that for economic time series, R^2 will be driven close to unity very rapidly as N increases. The high values of R^2 reported in the literature for regressions that include time are therefore not surprising. Obviously, R^2 gives us little useful information about the explanatory power of the independent variables in such regressions.

To check on the validity of (2.11) as an approximation we reran our Monte Carlo experiments setting $\beta^2 = \sigma_\epsilon^2$ and N at 20 and 100. The mean sample R^2 in the case $N = 20$ was .953, compared with the .949 implied by (2.12), with $\tilde{R}_0^2$ replaced by the Monte Carlo mean for $\beta = 0$. At $N = 100$ the mean R^2 rose to .992, which compares with .989 predicted by (2.12).

An example from the literature may help to emphasize some of the points made in this section. Perloff and Wachter (1979, Table 3) report a series of regressions of aggregate output in the U.S. on time, time squared, time cubed, and an index of labor and capital inputs constructed under various assumptions about the form of the aggregate production function. The polynomial trend function is intended to capture the effects of technological change. The data cover the 92 quarters from 1955 through 1977. The reported R^2 values are about .995. Using (2.12), we would expect an R^2 of about .998 in a regression of output on time *alone* if output were a random walk and did not depend on the index of inputs, assuming $(\beta/\sigma_\epsilon) = 1$ and taking $\tilde{R}_0^2 = .44$. Thus, the reported R^2 in itself provides no real information about the relationship. The t ratios for time squared and time cubed are not significant, but for time they are in the range of 8 to 10, which is within one standard deviation of zero for the results reported in our Table 1 for the case of a random walk with zero drift. The t ratios for the input index are ten or larger, however. This suggests that the upward drift in output may be largely due to the upward drift in the index of

[1] The alert reader will recognize that the Durbin-Watson statistic is not strictly appropriate in testing for random disturbances in regression (2.10) since ρ is estimated from the data. In effect, the model includes a lagged dependent variable, Y_{t-1}. Following Durbin (1970), one could estimate ρ with α and β and compute the h statistic, which takes into account the estimated variance of the estimate of ρ. However, this variance will tend to be small for large values of ρ, such as those we have in this situation. See the discussion in Durbin (1970, p. 419).

inputs. However, Perloff and Wachter warn that "because of autocorrelation, these statistical tests should be viewed with caution" (p. 130, fn. 25). Indeed, the Durbin-Watson statistic for the preferred model is .231, corresponding to an r_1 of .884, very close to the mean values recorded in our Table 1 for a slightly larger number of observations. Therefore, we interpret the Perloff and Wachter results as consistent with the hypothesis that the contribution of technology (inputs other than labor and capital) to output is not stationary around a deterministic trend, but is rather a nonstationary stochastic process akin to a random walk. If this hypothesis is correct, then technological change occurs in an irregular stochastic fashion rather than in a smooth deterministic one.

3. SPURIOUS REGRESSION RELATIONSHIPS BETWEEN NONSTATIONARY VARIABLES RESULTING FROM INAPPROPRIATE USE OF TIME AS AN INDEPENDENT VARIABLE

In situations where the relationship between nonstationary variables is of primary interest, one often encounters regression equations of the form

$$Y_t = \alpha + \beta t + \gamma X_t + u_t, \qquad (3.1)$$

where $\{Y_t\}$ is a nonstationary variable such as output, $\{X_t\}$ is a nonstationary independent variable (or set of such variables) such as a production input, and $\{u_t\}$ is a sequence of disturbances. The role of time is to account for growth in Y not attributable to X, for example the impact of technological change on output. The parameters of (3.1) are estimated by ordinary or generalized least squares procedures that make the assumption that the errors $\{u_t\}$ are stationary. Equivalently, another way to state this assumption that the part of Y not explained by X, that is $(Y_t - \gamma X_t)$, is a TSP variable. If this quantity is instead a DSP variable, then first differencing of the relationship, that is,

$$\Delta Y_t = \beta + \gamma(\Delta X_t) + \epsilon_t, \qquad (3.2)$$

would put it in the form suitable for estimation by standard procedures. What we are interested in here is the consequence of estimating the relationship in levels (3.1) when the differenced relationship (3.2) is in fact the one with stationary disturbances.

We begin by noting, as in Section 2, that a relationship between levels of the variables including time is obtained by accumulating changes given by (3.2) from an arbitrary time period zero, which gives

$$Y_t = Y_0 + \beta t + \gamma X_t + \sum_{i=1}^{t} \epsilon_i. \qquad (3.3)$$

This equation has the same form as (3.1) except that the disturbance is cumulative rather than stationary, and the intercept is given by the arbitrary initial value Y_0 rather than being a fixed parameter. Standard results in regression theory tell us that OLS estimates of β and γ in (3.3) will be unbiased but inefficient since the disturbances in (3.3) will be correlated across time periods. In the case that the ϵ_t's are serially random, the disturbance in (3.3) is a random walk. The covariance matrix Ω for these N disturbances would then have elements $\Omega_{j,k} = \min(j, k)\sigma_\epsilon^2$; $j, k = 1, \ldots, N$, and an appropriate GLS estimator could be constructed for Y_0, β, and γ that would recognize this covariance structure. Alternatively, the equation could be estimated efficiently in first differences by OLS, which is much simpler.

Estimation of γ by OLS in levels will be subject to the spurious regression phenomenon discussed by Granger and Newbold (1974). The classical formula will understate the sampling variance of $\hat{\gamma}$ and therefore overstate its significance. A heuristic explanation of this is as follows. Lovell (1963) showed that the OLS coefficient $\hat{\gamma}$ obtained in a regression of Y on time and X is numerically identical to the OLS coefficient obtained in the regression of detrended Y on detrended X. The detrended values of any time series may be expressed as the product of an $N \times N$ matrix, say T, times the vector of observations for the series. Note that T depends only on N and is the same for all series of length N. Multiplying (3.3) in vector form through by T we have

$$TY = \gamma TX + Tu, \qquad (3.4)$$

where Y, X and u denote column vectors of the respective time series, and we use the fact that the detrended values of the intercept variable and time are identically zero. Using tildes to denote the detrended variables, we have

$$\tilde{Y}_t = \gamma \tilde{X}_t + \tilde{u}_t. \qquad (3.5)$$

If $\{X_t\}$ and $\{u_t\}$ are both random walks, then $\{Y_t\}$ is also a random walk and (3.5) is the regression of a detrended random walk on another detrended random walk with a disturbance that is also a detrended random walk. In short, estimating γ by least squares in (3.3) is equivalent to a regression where the independent variable and the error term have the same autocorrelation function. A standard textbook result, originally noted by Wold (1953), is that the effect of autocorrelation in regression errors is to inflate the variance of the OLS coefficient by a factor of the form $(1 + \sum \rho_i r_i)$, where ρ_i is the autocorrelation of the disturbance at lag i and r_i is the sample autocorrelation of the independent variable at lag i. Since ρ_i and r_i will tend to be the same in our situation, the variance of $\hat{\gamma}$ will be larger than the classical formula would indicate. Furthermore, since these autocorrelation coefficients become larger with sample size (recall that is is roughly $(1 - 10/N)$ at lag 1), the spurious regression effect will be *more* pronounced in larger samples.

To get an idea of the magnitude of the spurious

Table 2. Empirical Moments of Summary Statistics for OLS Regression of a Zero-Drift Random Walk on an Unrelated Zero-Drift Random Walk and Time with 100 Observations. Based on 1,000 Replications: $Y_t = \hat{\alpha} + \hat{\beta}t + \hat{\gamma}X_t + \hat{u}_t$.

Statistic	Mean	Variance	Standard Deviation
R^2	.501	.077	.278
SSE/(N−3)	5.830	14.131	3.759
$\hat{\gamma}$	−.011	.177	.421
Std. Error ($\hat{\gamma}$)	.102	.002	.045
$t(\hat{\gamma})$	−.054	20.164	4.490
$\hat{\beta}$	.005	.014	.117
Std. Error ($\hat{\beta}$)	.013	.000+	.007
$t(\hat{\beta})$	.324	133.556	11.557
D.W.	.260	.016	.128
r_1	.852	.004	.064
r_2	.721	.013	.112
r_3	.604	.021	.146

NOTE: See Note to Table 1.

regression phenomenon in this situation for sample sizes typically encountered in economics, we have conducted a Monte Carlo experiment corresponding to that reported in Table 1 but with the addition of an independent variable that is a random walk. Since the spurious regression phenomenon depends on the random walk nature of the variables and not on specific parameter values, we have set β and γ equal to zero so that the R^2 obtained provides a lower bound for the general case. $\{X_t\}$ and $\{u_t\}$ are zero-drift random walks with unit variance Normal disturbances. The primary results are given in Table 2. As in the detrending regressions, only the means of $\hat{\alpha}$, $\hat{\beta}$, and $\hat{\gamma}$ and values of R^2 depend on α, β, and γ.

Note that the empirical mean of the conventional standard error for $\hat{\gamma}$ is about one-fourth as large as the empirical standard deviation of $\hat{\gamma}$, which implies that the precision of the estimate of γ will be greatly overstated if serial correlation in the regression errors is ignored. Correspondingly, the empirical standard deviation of the conventional t ratio is too large by a factor of about 4. If a t table is used to assess significance, $\hat{\gamma}$ is significant at the 5% level or better 64% of the time and at the 1% level or better 55% of the time. The spurious relationship with time is reduced somewhat by the inclusion of X, as one would expect, but the rejection frequency for the true null hypothesis is nevertheless 83% at a nominal 5% level, compared with the 87% frequency we obtained when time was the only regressor.

The values of R^2 are of course higher than in the simple time trend regressions of Section 2, since inclusion of an additional variable cannot lower R^2 in a given sample. The empirical mean rises to .501 from .443. Thus, time and a random walk variable will typically explain about 50% of the variation in a random walk that is in fact unrelated to either. This further reinforces our conclusion reached in Section 2 that R^2 values are highly misleading, or at least uninformative, in regressions involving time as a variable. The increase in R^2 due to inclusion of X will, of course, typically appear "significant" by conventional criteria, since the F test used to assess its significance under classical regression assumptions will correspond to the t test for $\hat{\gamma}$.

Finally, we note that the empirical means of sample autocorrelations of the residuals reported in Table 2 are somewhat smaller than those reported in Table 1 in the absence of X; for example, at lag one we obtain .852 instead of .883. The mean Durbin-Watson statistic is correspondingly somewhat larger, .260 compared with .198. Nevertheless, an alert investigator would again usually reject the hypothesis of serially random errors. Believing the regression disturbances to be stationary, and noting the roughly exponential decline of the sample autocorrelations in a typical realization, our imaginary investigator would presumably follow the popular procedure of assuming a first-order AR process for the errors and use r_1 as an estimate of the AR coefficient. The transformed regression equation would be

$$(Y_t - r_1 Y_{t-1}) = \alpha(1 - r_1) + \beta(t - r_1(t - 1)) + \gamma(X_t - r_1 X_{t-1}) + (u_t - r_1 u_{t-1}). \quad (3.6)$$

Now (3.6) would be a properly specified classical regression if r_1 were set at unity (corresponding to first differences), since $(u_t - u_{t-1})$ is indeed random in our situation. Sample values of r_1 are, however, rarely close to unity, since the empirical standard deviation is only .064 around the mean of .852. The transformed regression would still suffer from the problem of nonrandom, indeed nonstationary, disturbances.

The corresponding results for the transformed regressions (3.6) using a first round estimate of r_1 are reported in Table 3. Note that the empirical standard deviation of the t ratio for $\hat{\gamma}$ is reduced by the transformation from 4.490 to 1.287, although the standard deviation

Table 3. Empirical Moments of Summary Statistics for Transformed Regressions (3.6) Based on the Same One Thousand Samples Used in Table 2.

Statistic	Mean	Variance	Standard Deviation
R^2	.162	.032	.178
SSE/(N−3)	.970	.024	.153
$\hat{\gamma}$	.003	.016	.126
Std. Error ($\hat{\gamma}$)	.100	.000+	.012
$t(\hat{\gamma})$	.044	1.656	1.287
$\hat{\beta}$	.005	.014	.118
Std. Error ($\hat{\beta}$)	.031	.000+	.014
$t(\hat{\beta})$	.142	22.010	4.692
D.W.	1.820	.038	.195
r_1	.079	.009	.097
r_2	.064	.010	.099
r_3	.052	.010	.098

NOTE: See Note to Table 1.

for a t-distributed variable with 96 degrees of freedom is 1.010. Thus, the frequency of rejection of the true null hypothesis on γ is still too large, in particular 11.3% at a nominal 5% level and 5.4% at a nominal 1% level. This overstatement of significance is reflected in the comparison of the empirical standard deviation of $\hat{\gamma}$, .126, with the mean standard error, .100. The spurious relationship of Y to time is also diminished by the transformation, although it is still very strong. The empirical standard deviation of the t ratio for $\hat{\beta}$ is 4.69. Rejection frequencies are 60% at a nominal 5% level and 51.5% at a nominal 1% level.

The autocorrelation coefficients of the residuals in the transformed regressions are of course considerably diminished relative to those obtained for the original regressions, averaging only .079 at lag one with a standard deviation of .097. An investigator using the standard error $1/\sqrt{N} = .100$ would rarely reject the hypothesis of serially random errors. The mean Durbin-Watson statistic of 1.820 is similarly well inside the acceptance region (see footnote 1). We conclude, then, that an investigator who believed the disturbances in the levels regression to be stationary would usually find the results of the transformed regression to be satisfactory in the sense of passing the usual tests of random errors, and would therefore run a substantial risk of finding a significant relationship between Y and X where none exists.

Unlike the case of the detrending regression, however, continued iteration of the Cochrane-Orcutt procedure does alter the estimates and improve their properties. The frequency of rejection of the true null hypothesis on γ drops to 6.7% at a nominal 5% level and to 2.5% at a nominal 1% level, reflecting the fact that estimated standard errors are closer to the actual standard deviation. The effect on inference about β is less dramatic. The frequencies of rejection fall only to 51.5% and 39.8% for the 5% and 1% tests, respectively.

4. SUMMARY AND CONCLUSIONS

It is common practice in applied regression to attribute nonstationarity or "trend" in a time series to a functional dependence on time, with the remaining variation in the series assumed to be stationary. In this article we have considered the consequences of such an assumption when the time series is not stationary around a function of time, but rather is stationary in first differences. The results reported by Nelson and Plosser (1982) are consistent with this hypothesis for a wide range of economic variables. The prototypical example of such nonstationary stochastic processes is the random walk process which forms the basis for our exploratory analysis.

The primary findings are as follows.

1. Regression of a random walk on time by least squares will produce R^2 values of around .44 regardless of sample size when the variable has, in fact, no dependence whatever on time (zero drift). For random walks with drift, the R^2 will be higher and will increase with sample size, reaching 1 in the limit regardless of the actual rate of drift of the series or its variability.

2. Residuals from regression of a random walk on time will have a variance that is, on average, only about 14% of the true stochastic variance of the series. This result holds regardless of sample length or the true rate of drift (mean rate of change) of the series. If these residuals are mistakenly interpreted as a detrended series, then their variance will greatly understate the actual variance of the series. Equivalently, stochastic variation is mistakenly attributed to dependence on time, which is present in only an ex post sense and not an ex ante one.

3. The mean values of sample autocorrelations of a "detrended" random walk are a function of sample length, being roughly $(1 - 10/N)$ at lag one, for example, and they are therefore purely artifactual. Since the function oscillates with a period of roughly $(2/3)N$, the detrended data will appear to exhibit a long cycle that is spurious. Nelson and Kang (1981) showed that this result is quite robust with respect to serial correlation in the first differences of the series.

4. A conventional t statistic for the least squares coefficient of time is a very poor test for the presence of trend in the sense of a dependence on time. Such tests lead to rejection of the null hypothesis of no dependence in 87% of the cases for a sample length of 100 at a nominal 5% level, when in fact there is no dependence on time. Attempts to correct for serial correlation in the residuals only partially correct this effect. An investigator applying a first order AR correction based on sample autocorrelations of the residuals would still reject the true hypothesis at a nominal 5% level with 73% probability. The correct procedure would be to take first differences, in which case the size of the test would be correct.

5. Regression of one random walk on another, with time included to account for trend, is strongly subject to the spurious regression phenomenon. That is, a conventional t test will tend to indicate a relationship between the variables when none is present. Since such regressions can be thought of as regression of one detrended random walk on another, the phenomenon can be viewed in the framework developed by Wold (1953) for stationary autocorrelated series. For the case of zero drift (unrelated random walks), the true null hypothesis of no relationship is rejected with a frequency of 64% at a nominal 5% level using 100 observations. The true null hypothesis of no dependence on time is correspondingly rejected with an 83% frequency. Attempts to correct for serial correlation on the assumption that the disturbances are stationary and first order autoregressive only partially alleviate the problem; the rejection frequencies drop to 11.3% and 60% respectively. Continued iteration reduces these to

6.7% and 51.5% respectively. First differencing would, of course, correct the size of the tests.

Our advice to practitioners, based on this investigation, is to regard stationarity around a function of time as a tentative rather than a maintained hypothesis. It is certainly not a harmless assumption, but rather one fraught with potential pitfalls. Regression models involving nonstationary time series should be estimated in differenced form and the results carefully compared with those for the regression in levels with time as an explanatory variable. Two recent papers by Plosser and Schwert (1977, 1978) suggest that the consequences of unnecessary differencing to achieve stationarity are much less costly in the present context than those of failing to difference when it is appropriate. In addition, the tests for stationarity in differences as opposed to stationarity around a trend line developed by Dickey and Fuller (1979) are strongly recommended as a guide to the appropriate transformation of time series data.

APPENDIX: RAPID CONVERGENCE OF SLOPE AND AUTOREGRESSIVE PARAMETERS IN LINEAR TIME TREND REGRESSION

The familiar regression model with AR(1) errors is

$$Y_t = \beta X_t + \epsilon_t \tag{A.1}$$

and

$$\epsilon_t = \rho\epsilon_{t-1} + \nu_t, \tag{A.2}$$

where Y and X are deviations from means. Following Cochrane and Orcutt (1949), one obtains a first round estimate of β by OLS, say $\hat{\beta}$, and then runs an autoregression on the residuals to get a first round estimate of ρ, say $\hat{\rho}$. The data are then transformed to $(Y_t - \rho Y_{t-1})$ and $(X_t - \rho X_{t-1})$, from which a second round estimate of β is obtained, and so forth. Convergence is effectively immediate in the special case of time trend regression for which $X_t = t; t = -n, \ldots, +n$.

Consider first the least squares estimate of β given a value of ρ, say β^*. It can be shown to be

$$\beta^* = \frac{\begin{array}{c}\sum Y_tX_t + \rho^2 \sum Y_{t-1}X_{t-1} \\ - \rho \sum Y_tX_{t-1} - \rho \sum X_tY_{t-1}\end{array}}{\sum X_t^2 + \rho^2 \sum X_{t-1}^2 - 2\rho \sum X_tX_{t-1}}, \tag{A.3}$$

where the summations run from $t = -n + 1$ to $+n$. Consider dividing each term by $\sum X_t^2$, in which case we have

$$\beta^* \doteq \frac{\begin{array}{c}\hat{\beta} + (\rho^2 \sum Y_{t-1}X_{t-1} \\ - \rho \sum Y_tX_{t-1} - \rho \sum X_tY_{t-1})/\sum X_t^2\end{array}}{1 + \rho^2 - 2\rho(\sum X_tX_{t-1})/\sum X_t^2}, \tag{A.4}$$

with the approximation caused by leaving the first observation out of $\hat{\beta}$. Obviously, we can say little in general about the difference between β^* and $\hat{\beta}$, the OLS estimate with $\rho = 0$. This difference depends on autocorrelation in X and cross-correlation between Y and X at lags (+1) and (−1). However, in the time trend case we have $X_t = t = X_{t-1} + 1$, which implies

$$\beta^* \doteq \frac{\hat{\beta} + \rho^2\hat{\beta} - 2\rho\hat{\beta}}{1 + \rho^2 - 2\rho} = \hat{\beta}. \tag{A.5}$$

The degree of approximation is the order of difference between $\sum t(t-1)/\sum t^2$ and unity, which is $1/N$. Thus, the nature of the independent variable in the time trend case implies that the slope estimate is insensitive to the value of ρ.

Similarly, consider estimating ρ on the basis of a given value for β, say $(\hat{\beta} + \Delta\beta)$. In the general case we have

$$\rho^* = \frac{\begin{array}{c}\sum \hat{e}_t\hat{e}_{t-1} - (\Delta\beta)\sum \hat{e}_tX_{t-1} \\ + (\Delta\beta)\sum X_t\hat{e}_{t-1}\end{array}}{\begin{array}{c}\sum \hat{e}_{t-1}^2 + (\Delta\beta)^2 \sum X_{t-1}^2 \\ - 2(\Delta\beta)\sum \hat{e}_{t-1}X_{t-1}\end{array}}, \tag{A.6}$$

where the summations run from $t = -n + 1$ to $+n$, and $\hat{e}$ denotes OLS residuals associated with $\hat{\beta}$. Now dividing each term by $\sum \hat{e}_{t-1}^2$ and noting that the third term in the denominator becomes negligible, we have

$$\rho^* \doteq \frac{\hat{\rho} + (\Delta\beta)(\sum X_t\hat{e}_{t-1} - \sum \hat{e}_tX_{t-1})/\sum \hat{e}_{t-1}^2}{1 + (\Delta\beta)^2 \sum X_{t-1}^2/\sum \hat{e}_{t-1}^2}, \tag{A.7}$$

which will differ from $\hat{\rho}$ depending on $(\Delta\beta)$, cross-correlation between X and $\hat{e}$ at lags (+1) and (−1), and the variance ratio of X and e. In the special case $X_t = t = X_{t-1} + 1$, we see that the approximation reduces to

$$\rho^* = \hat{\rho}/(1 + (\Delta\beta)^2 \sum X_{t-1}^2/\sum e_{t-1}^2), \tag{A.8}$$

since $\sum X_t\hat{e}_{t-1}$ becomes $(\sum X_{t-1}\hat{e}_{t-1} + \sum \hat{e}_{t-1})$, which differs from zero only by end terms (by the algebra of least squares), and the same for $\sum e_tX_{t-1}$. Since $(\Delta\beta)$ tends to be small in the time trend case, the adjustments to $\hat{\rho}$ will be small.

To sum up, iteration of trend line coefficients and autoregressive coefficients for detrended data will be rapid because of the special nature of the independent variable. In our experience, widely-used computer programs for Cochrane-Orcutt have never gone beyond one iteration. This result is entirely due to the algebra of least squares. The true nature of the underlying data is irrelevant, whether it be a TSP, a DSP, or something else. Furthermore, the result implies that rapid convergence will occur whenever the independent variables are closely approximated by linear trends. The result also generalizes to higher order autoregressive schemes for the residuals.

ACKNOWLEDGMENTS

The authors wish to thank Dennis F. Kraft for thoughtful comments and useful suggestions for improvement. This research was supported by the National Science Foundation under Grants SES-7906948 and SES-8112687.

Received September 1982. Revised August 1983.

REFERENCES

BOX, GEORGE E. P., and JENKINS, GWILYM M. (1970), *Time Series Analysis and Control, Forecasting*, San Francisco: Holden-Day.

CHAN, K. HUNG, HAYYA, JACK C., and ORD, J. KEITH (1977), "A Note on Trend Removal Methods: The Case of Polynomial Regression Versus Variate Differencing," *Econometrica*, 45, 737-744.

COCHRANE, D., and ORCUTT, G. H. (1949), "Application of Least Squares Regression to Relationships Containing Autocorrelated Error Terms," *Journal of the American Statistical Association*, 44, 32-61.

DICKEY, DAVID A., and FULLER, WAYNE A. (1979), "Distribution for the Estimators for Autoregressive Time Series With a Unit Root," *Journal of the American Statistical Association*, 74, 427-431.

DURBIN, J. (1970), "Testing for Serial Correlation in Least-Squares Regression When Some of the Regressors are Lagged Dependent Variables," *Econometrica*, 38, 410-421.

GRANGER, C. W. J., and NEWBOLD, P. (1974), "Spurious Regressions in Econometrics," *Journal of Econometrics*, 2, 111-120.

LOVELL, MICHAEL C. (1963), "Seasonal Adjustment of Economic Time Series and Multiple Regression Analysis," *Journal of the American Statistical Association*, 58, 993-1010.

NELSON, CHARLES R., and KANG, HEEJOON (1981), "Spurious Periodicity in Inappropriately Detrended Time Series," *Econometrica*, 49, 741-751.

NELSON, CHARLES R., and PLOSSER, CHARLES I. (1982), "Trends and Random Walks in Macroeconomic Time Series: Some Evidence and Implications," *Journal of Monetary Economics*, 10, 139-162.

PERLOFF, JEFFREY M., and WACHTER, MICHAEL L. (1979), "A Production Function-Nonaccelerating Inflation Approach to Potential Output: Is Measured Potential Output Too High?" *Carnegie-Rochester Conference Series on Public Policy*, 10, 113-164.

PLOSSER, CHARLES I., and SCHWERT, G. WILLIAM (1977), "Estimation of a Non-Invertible Moving Average Process: The Case of Overdifferencing," *Journal of Econometrics*, 6, 199-224.

———, (1978), "Money, Income, and Sunspots: Measuring Economic Relationships and the Effects of Differencing," *Journal of Monetary Economics*, 4, 637-660.

WOLD, HERMAN (1953), *Demand Analysis*, New York: John Wiley.

Part V
Seasonality, Seasonal Adjustment and Calendar Effects

[18]

An ARIMA-Model-Based Approach to Seasonal Adjustment

S. C. HILLMER and G. C. TIAO*

This article proposes a model-based procedure to decompose a time series uniquely into mutually independent additive seasonal, trend, and irregular noise components. The series is assumed to follow the Gaussian ARIMA model. Properties of the procedure are discussed and an actual example is given.

KEY WORDS: ARIMA model; Seasonal adjustment; Census X-11 program; Pseudospectral density function; Model-based decomposition; Canonical decomposition.

1. INTRODUCTION

Business and economic time series frequently exhibit seasonality—periodic fluctuations that recur with about the same intensity each year. It has been argued (c.f., Nerlove, Grether, and Carvalho 1979, p. 147) that seasonality should be removed from economic time series so that underlying "business cycles" can be more easily studied and current economic conditions can be appraised. Of the large number of seasonal adjustment procedures, the most widely used is the Census X-11 method described in Shiskin, Young, and Musgrave (1967). The X-11 program and other methods that have been empirically developed tend to produce what their developers feel are desirable seasonal adjustments, but their statistical properties are difficult to assess from a theoretical viewpoint. Recently, there has been considerable interest in developing model-based procedures for the decomposition and seasonal adjustment of time series (see, e.g., the work of Grether and Nerlove 1970; Cleveland and Tiao 1976; Pierce 1978, 1980; Box, Hillmer, and Tiao 1978; Tiao and Hillmer 1978; and Burman 1980). Following this line of work and motivated in part by the considerations in the X-11 program, this article proposes a model-based approach that decomposes a time series into seasonal, trend, and irregular components.

We suppose that an observable time series at time t, Z_t, can be represented as

$$Z_t = S_t + T_t + N_t, \qquad (1.1)$$

where S_t, T_t, and N_t are unobservable seasonal, trend, and noise components. It may be the case that a more accurate representation for Z_t would be as the product of S_t, T_t, and N_t. In that situation the model (1.1) would be appropriate for the logarithms of the original series. We assume that each of the components follows an ARIMA model,

$$\begin{aligned}\phi_S(B)S_t &= \eta_S(B)b_t\\ \phi_T(B)T_t &= \eta_T(B)c_t \qquad (1.2)\\ \phi_N(B)N_t &= \eta_N(B)d_t,\end{aligned}$$

where B is the backshift operator such that $BS_t = S_{t-1}$, each of the pairs of polynomials $\{\phi_S(B), \eta_S(B)\}$, $\{\phi_T(B), \eta_T(B)\}$, and $\{\phi_N(B), \eta_N(B)\}$ have their zeros lying on or outside the unit circle and have no common zeros, and b_t, c_t, and d_t are three mutually independent white noise processes, identically and independently distributed as $N(0, \sigma_b^2)$, $N(0, \sigma_c^2)$, and $N(0, \sigma_d^2)$, respectively. Then it is readily shown that the overall model for Z_t is the ARIMA model

$$\varphi(B)Z_t = \theta(B)a_t, \qquad (1.3)$$

where $\varphi(B)$ is the highest common factor of $\phi_S(B)$, $\phi_T(B)$, and $\phi_N(B)$, and $\theta(B)$ and σ_a^2 can be obtained from the relationship

$$\frac{\theta(B)\theta(F)\sigma_a^2}{\varphi(B)\varphi(F)} = \frac{\eta_S(B)\eta_S(F)\sigma_b^2}{\phi_S(B)\phi_S(F)} + \frac{\eta_T(B)\eta_T(F)\sigma_c^2}{\phi_T(B)\phi_T(F)} + \frac{\eta_N(B)\eta_N(F)\sigma_d^2}{\phi_N(B)\phi_N(F)}, \qquad (1.4)$$

where $F = B^{-1}$. We also assume that the parameters in (1.3) are known. In practice a model for the observable series Z_t can be built from the data, and the estimated parameter values used as if they were the true values.

The ARIMA form has been found flexible enough to describe the behavior of many actual nonstationary and seasonal time series (Box and Jenkins 1970). There are situations in which such models by themselves may not be adequate; for example, a series describing employment may be dramatically affected by a strike and the model (1.3) does not cover such contingencies. However,

* S.C. Hillmer is Assistant Professor, School of Business, University of Kansas, Lawrence, KS 66044. G.C. Tiao is Professor of Statistics and Business, Department of Statistics, University of Wisconsin, Madison, WI 53706. This research was partially supported by the U.S. Bureau of the Census, Washington, D.C. under JSA No. 80-10; Army Research Office, Durham under grant No. DAAG29-78-G-0166; the ALCOA Foundation; and University of Kansas research allocation 3139-X0-0038. The article was completed when G.C. Tiao was on leave at the University of Chicago.

© Journal of the American Statistical Association
March 1982, Volume 77, Number 377
Theory and Methods Section

in these situations ARIMA models can frequently be modified to approximate reality; for instance, intervention analysis techniques described in Box and Tiao (1975) might be used to account for the effects of strikes and other exogenous events.

Given the observable Z_t and the structure in (1.1), (1.2), and (1.3), the problem is to decompose Z_t into S_t, T_t, and N_t. Our approach is as follows: (a) We first impose restrictions on $\phi_S(B)$ and $\phi_T(B)$ for the component models (1.2) based in part on considerations in the Census X-11 program. (b) A model for Z_t is derived from observable data. (c) A principle is adopted that uniquely specifies the component models in a manner consistent with the imposed restrictions and the model derived for Z_t. (d) Given the component models, known signal extraction methods are applied to decompose Z_t into (estimates of) the components. Properties of the procedure are explored and an illustration using an actual time series is presented.

2. DECOMPOSITION WHEN THE COMPONENT MODELS ARE KNOWN

If in (1.1) the stochastic structures of S_t, T_t, and N_t in (1.2) are known, then estimates of S_t and T_t can be readily obtained (see, e.g., Whittle 1963 and Cleveland and Tiao 1976). Specifically, Cleveland and Tiao have shown that, when all the zeros of $\phi_S(B)$, $\phi_T(B)$, and $\phi_N(B)$ are on or outside of the unit circle, the minimum mean squared estimates of the seasonal and trend components S_t and T_t are, respectively,

$$\hat{S}_t = W_S(B)Z_t \quad \text{and} \quad \hat{T}_t = W_T(B)Z_t, \qquad (2.1)$$

where

$$W_S(B) = \frac{\sigma_b^2}{\sigma_a^2}\frac{\varphi(B)\varphi(F)\eta_S(B)\eta_S(F)}{\theta(B)\theta(F)\phi_S(B)\phi_S(F)}$$

and

$$W_T(B) = \frac{\sigma_c^2}{\sigma_a^2}\frac{\varphi(B)\varphi(F)\eta_T(B)\eta_T(F)}{\theta(B)\theta(F)\phi_T(B)\phi_T(F)}.$$

Because in practice the S_t, T_t, and N_t series are unobservable, it is usually unrealistic to assume that the component models in (1.2) are known. As a result, the weight functions $W_S(B)$ and $W_T(B)$ cannot be determined and the values $\hat{S}_t$ and $\hat{T}_t$ cannot be calculated. We can, however, get an accurate estimate of the model (1.3) from the observable Z_t series. Consequently, it is of interest to investigate to what extent a known model for Z_t will determine the models for the component series.

3. PROPERTIES OF SEASONAL AND TREND COMPONENTS

It is well known that the Census X-11 procedure may be approximated by a linear filter (for instance see Young 1968 and Wallis 1974). One important feature of the X-11 filter weights for the trend and the seasonal components is that the weights applied to observations more removed from the current time period decrease. This feature was incorporated into the X-11 program probably because of the belief that the trend and seasonal components of many series change over time; consequently the information about the current trend or seasonal is contained in the values of Z_t close to current time. Therefore, in developing a decomposition procedure we should allow for evolving trend and seasonal components.

Stochastic Trend

Economic data often exhibit underlying movements that drift over time. While *locally* such movements might be adequately modeled by a polynomial in time, a fixed polynomial time function is clearly inappropriate over the *entire* time span. Thus a stochastic trend model is needed, and we assume that the trend component, T_t, follows the nonstationary model

$$(1 - B)^d T_t = \eta_T(B)c_t, \qquad (3.1)$$

where $\eta_T(B)$ is a polynomial in B of degree at most d, and c_t are iid $N(0, \sigma_c^2)$. Box and Jenkins (1970, p. 149) have shown that the minimum mean squared error forecast function of (3.1) is a polynomial time function of degree $(d - 1)$ whose coefficients are updated as the origin of forecast is advanced; therefore (3.1) can be regarded as a polynomial model with stochastic coefficients.

It is also of interest to consider the trend component in the frequency domain. Intuitively, the spectral density function of a trend component should be large for the low frequencies and small for higher frequencies. Since the model (3.1) is nonstationary, the spectral density function is strictly speaking not defined. However, we can define a pseudospectral density function (psdf) for (3.1) by

$$f_T(w) = \sigma_c^2\eta_T(e^{iw})\eta_T(e^{-iw})/(1 - e^{iw})^d(1 - e^{-iw})^d,$$
$$0 \le w \le \pi. \qquad (3.2)$$

Now the psdf (3.2) is infinite at $w = 0$ and very large for small w. This is consistent with what could be viewed as a stochastic trend component.

Stochastic Seasonal

A deterministic seasonal component S_t of period s would have the property that it repeats itself every s periods and that the sum of any s consecutive components should be a constant, that is,

$$S_t = S_{t-s} \quad \text{and} \quad U(B)S_t = c, \qquad (3.3)$$

where $U(B) = 1 + B + \ldots + B^{s-1}$ and c is an arbitrary constant that can be taken as zero. Such a model, however, implies that the seasonal pattern is fixed over time. For business and economic time series, it seems reasonable to require that the seasonal component should be capable of evolving over time but that *locally* a regular seasonal pattern should be preserved. In other words, $U(B)S_t$ should be random but cluster about zero. Consider the nonstationary model

$$U(B)S_t = \eta_S(B)b_t, \qquad (3.4)$$

where $\eta_S(B)$ is a polynomial in B of degree at most $s - 1$ and b_t are iid $N(0, \sigma_b^2)$. That is, the consecutive moving sum of s components, $U(B)S_t$, follows a moving average model of order (at most) $s - 1$. It is readily shown that the forecasting function of (3.4) at a given time origin follows a fixed seasonal pattern of period s, but the pattern is updated as the origin is advanced. Also, $EU(B)S_t = E\eta_S(B)b_t = 0$. Thus, the model (3.4) preserves a local cyclical pattern but allows seasonality to evolve over time.

It is also informative to consider the psdf, $f_S(w)$, of the model in (3.4)

$$f_S(w) = \sigma_b^2 \frac{\eta_S(e^{iw})\eta_S(e^{-iw})}{U(e^{iw})U(e^{-iw})}. \tag{3.5}$$

It can be shown that $f_S(w)$ has the following properties: (a) $f_S(w)$ is infinite at the seasonal frequencies $w = 2k\pi/s$ for $k = 1, \ldots, [s/2]$, where $[x]$ denotes the greatest integer less than or equal to x; (b) $f_S(w)$ has relative minimum at $w = 0$ and near the frequencies $w = ((2k - 1)\pi)/s$ for $k = 2, \ldots, [s/2]$. Therefore, the psdf of (3.4) has infinite power at the seasonal frequencies and relatively small power away from the seasonal frequencies.

4. MODEL-BASED SEASONAL DECOMPOSITION

From considerations in the previous section, we require $\varphi(B)$ to contain the factor $U(B)$ before we impose a seasonal component S_t and to contain the factor $(1 - B)^d$ before we impose a trend component T_t for Z_t. We further require that in (1.2) the autoregressive polynomial of N_t, $\phi_N(B)$, has no common zeros with either $(1 - B)^d$ or $U(B)$, because otherwise it would imply the existence of additional seasonal and trend components that could then be absorbed into S_t and T_t. Thus, we shall suppose that in (1.3)

$$\varphi(B) = (1 - B)^d U(B)\phi_N(B), \tag{4.1}$$

where the three factors on the right side have no common zeros. In other words, knowing the model for Z_t and assuming that a decomposition is possible, the autoregressive polynomials of S_t, T_t, and N_t can be uniquely determined. Also, the relationship (1.4) becomes

$$\frac{\theta(B)\theta(F)}{\varphi(B)\varphi(F)}\sigma_a^2 = \frac{\eta_S(B)\eta_S(F)}{U(B)U(F)}\sigma_b^2 + \frac{\eta_T(B)\eta_T(F)}{(1 - B)^d(1 - F)^d}\sigma_c^2 + \frac{\eta_N(B)\eta_N(F)}{\phi_N(B)\phi_N(F)}\sigma_d^2. \tag{4.2}$$

The more difficult task is to determine the moving average polynomials and the innovation variances. Within the class of $\eta_S(B)$ and $\eta_T(B)$ whose degrees are at most $(s - 1)$ and d as required by (3.1) and (3.4), any choice of the three moving average polynomials $\eta_S(B)$, $\eta_T(B)$, and $\eta_N(B)$ and the three variances σ_b^2, σ_c^2, and σ_d^2 satisfying (4.2) will be called an *acceptable* decomposition because it is consistent with information provided by the model for the observed data Z_t.

We now give a necessary and sufficient condition for the existence of an acceptable decomposition. Assuming that $\varphi(B)$ takes the form (4.1), we may perform a unique partial fraction decomposition of the left side of (4.2) to yield

$$\frac{\theta(B)\theta(F)}{\varphi(B)\varphi(F)}\sigma_a^2 = \frac{Q_S(B)}{U(B)U(F)} + \frac{Q_T(B)}{(1 - B)^d(1 - F)^d} + \frac{Q_N(B)}{\phi_N(B)\phi_N(F)}, \tag{4.3}$$

where

$$Q_S(B) = q_{0S} + \sum_{i=1}^{s-2} q_{iS}(B^i + F^i),$$

$$Q_T(B) = q_{0T} + \sum_{i=1}^{d-1} q_{iT}(B^i + F^i),$$

and $Q_N(B)$ can be obtained by subtraction. The uniqueness in (4.3) results from the fact that the degrees of $Q_S(B)$ and $Q_T(B)$ are lower than the degrees of the corresponding denominator. Now for $0 \le w \le \pi$, let

$$\epsilon_1 = \min_w \frac{Q_S(e^{-iw})}{|U(e^{-iw})|^2},$$

$$\epsilon_2 = \min_w \frac{Q_T(e^{-iw})}{|1 - e^{-iw}|^{2d}}, \tag{4.4}$$

and

$$\epsilon_3 = \min_w \frac{Q_N(e^{-iw})}{|\phi_N(e^{-iw})|^2}.$$

We now show that an acceptable decomposition exists if and only if $\epsilon_1 + \epsilon_2 + \epsilon_3 \ge 0$.

Proof. By writing $B = e^{-iw}$, $0 \le w \le \pi$, each of the three terms on the right side of (4.2) is a psdf.

Since $\eta_S(B)$ is of degree at most $s - 1$ and $\eta_T(B)$ is of degree at most d, by comparing (4.2) with (4.3) we can write

$$\frac{|\eta_S(e^{-iw})|^2\sigma_b^2}{|U(e^{-iw})|^2} = \frac{Q_S(e^{-iw})}{|U(e^{-iw})|^2} + \gamma_1,$$

$$\frac{|\eta_T(e^{-iw})|^2\sigma_c^2}{|1 - e^{-iw}|^{2d}} = \frac{Q_T(e^{-iw})}{|1 - e^{-iw}|^{2d}} + \gamma_2, \tag{4.5}$$

and

$$\frac{|\eta_N(e^{-iw})|^2\sigma_d^2}{|\phi_N(e^{-iw})|^2} = \frac{Q_N(e^{-iw})}{|\phi_N(e^{-iw})|^2} + \gamma_3,$$

where γ_1, γ_2, and γ_3 are three constants such that $\gamma_1 + \gamma_2 + \gamma_3 = 0$. The constants γ_i provide a means to change from the initial partial fractions decomposition (4.3) to an acceptable decomposition if one exists. Thus, an acceptable decomposition implies and is implied by the fact that $\gamma_i + \epsilon_i \geq 0$ for $i = 1, 2, 3$ or equivalently that $\epsilon_1 + \epsilon_2 + \epsilon_3 \geq 0$.

From the previous discussion, when $\epsilon_1 + \epsilon_2 + \epsilon_3 \geq 0$, every set of γ_i's corresponds to a unique acceptable decomposition; thus a unique decomposition exists if and only if $\epsilon_1 + \epsilon_2 + \epsilon_3 = 0$. On the other hand, when $\epsilon_1 + \epsilon_2 + \epsilon_3 > 0$, there are an infinite number of ways of adding constants to the three terms on the right side of (4.3) to obtain acceptable decompositions.

5. A CANONICAL DECOMPOSITION

In the absence of prior knowledge about the precise stochastic structure of the trend and seasonal components, all of the information in the known model of Z_t, (1.3), about S_t and T_t is embodied in (4.2). However, when $\epsilon_1 + \epsilon_2 + \epsilon_3 > 0$, this information is not sufficient to uniquely determine the models for S_t and T_t. To perform seasonal adjustment of the data, an arbitrary choice must be made. Considering that the seasonal and trend components should be slowly evolving, it seems reasonable to extract as much white noise as possible from the seasonal and trend components subject to the restrictions in (4.2). Thus, we seek to maximize the innovation variance σ_d^2 of the noise component N_t. Therefore, we define the *canonical decomposition* as the decomposition that maximizes σ_d^2 subject to the restrictions in (4.2).

Properties of the Canonical Decomposition

In the following we denote the canonical seasonal component by $\tilde{S}_t$, the canonical trend component by $\tilde{T}_t$, and use the same convention when referring to the moving average polynomials and innovation variances of the canonical decompositions. We prove the following properties of the canonical decomposition in the appendix. (a) The canonical decomposition is unique. (b) It minimizes the innovation variances σ_b^2 and σ_c^2. (c) The polynomials $\tilde{\eta}_S(B)$ and $\tilde{\eta}_T(B)$ have at least one zero on the unit circle so that the models for $\tilde{S}_t$ and $\tilde{T}_t$ are noninvertible. (d) If $\hat{S}_t$ and $\hat{T}_t$ are any acceptable seasonal and trend components other than the canonical decomposition, then $\hat{S}_t = \tilde{S}_t + e_t$ and $\hat{T}_t = \tilde{T}_t + \alpha_t$, where e_t and α_t are white noise series. (e) The variance of $U(B)S_t$ is minimized for the canonical decomposition.

One may lend justification of the (arbitrary) choice of the canonical decomposition on the basis of these properties. In particular, property (b) is intuitively pleasing since the randomness in S_t arises from the sequence of b_t's and the randomness in T_t arises from the sequence of c_t's. Thus, minimizing σ_b^2 and σ_c^2 makes the seasonal and trend components as deterministic as possible while remaining consistent with the information in the observable Z_t series. Also, from property (d) any acceptable seasonal component can be viewed as the sum of the canonical seasonal and white noise. But $\tilde{S}_t$ is a highly predictable component that accounts for all of the seasonality in the original series and e_t is a completely unpredictable component. Thus, one might argue that the choice of an acceptable decomposition other than the canonical decomposition only produces a more confused seasonal component than necessary. Finally, property (e) is intuitively pleasing since $E[U(B)S_t] = 0$ and a small value for $\text{var}[U(B)S_t]$ will help ensure that the sum of s consecutive seasonal components remains close to zero.

6. APPLICATION TO SOME SPECIAL SEASONAL MODELS

We now illustrate the results in the preceding sections with the following three special cases of (1.3). These models have been frequently used in practice to fit seasonal data (see, e.g., Box and Jenkins 1970, and Tiao, Box, and Hamming 1975).

$$(1 - B^s)Z_t = (1 - \theta_2 B^s)a_t, \tag{6.1}$$

$$(1 - B)(1 - B^s)Z_t = (1 - \theta_1 B)(1 - \theta_2 B^s)a_t, \tag{6.2}$$

and

$$(1 - B^s)Z_t = (1 - \theta_1 B)(1 - \theta_2 B^s)a_t. \tag{6.3}$$

Without loss of generality, we assume that $\sigma_a^2 = 1$. For these models, the general approach is as follows. We first divide the denominator of the left side of (4.3) into the numerator to obtain $Q_N(B)$ and a remainder term $R(B)$; we then perform a partial fractions expansion of $R(B)/\varphi(B)\varphi(F)$ to obtain $Q_S(B)$ and $Q_T(B)$; and finally we find the minimum values ϵ_1, ϵ_2, and ϵ_3 in order to investigate whether an acceptable decomposition exists.

The model (6.1)

In this case, $d = 1$ and $\phi_N(B) = 1$. By partial fraction, (4.3) becomes

$$\frac{(1 - \theta_2 B^s)(1 - \theta_2 F^s)}{(1 - B^s)(1 - F^s)} = \frac{Q_S(B)}{U(B)U(F)} + \frac{Q_T(B)}{(1 - B)(1 - F)} + \theta_2, \tag{6.4}$$

where

$$Q_T(B) = \frac{1}{s^2}(1 - \theta_2)^2$$

and

$$Q_S(B) = (1 - \theta_2)^2 \left[1 - \frac{1}{s^2} U(B)U(F)\right] \Big/ (1 - B)(1 - F)$$

$$= \frac{1}{6s^2}(1 - \theta_2)^2 \times \left[\sum_{l=2}^{s-1} (l - 1)l(l + 1)(B^{s-l} + F^{s-l}) + (s - 1)s(s + 1)\right].$$

For the trend component, we see that $Q_T(e^{-iw}) \mid 1 - e^{-iw} \mid^{-2}$ is monotonically decreasing in w and

$$\epsilon_2 = \frac{1}{4s^2}(1 - \theta_2)^2.$$

For the seasonal component, it is easy to show that $Q_S(e^{-iw}) \mid U(e^{-iw}) \mid^{-2} \geq 0$ and has a local minimum at $w = 0$. Also, we conjecture that $w = 0$ is in fact the global minimum. This conjecture is verified analytically for $s \leq 3$ and numerically for s from 4 to 20. Assuming this is true for all s we find that

$$\min_w \left\{1 - \frac{1}{s^2} \mid U(e^{-iw}) \mid^2\right\} \Big/ \mid 1 - e^{-iw} \mid^2 = (s^2 - 1)/12 \qquad (6.5)$$

so that $\epsilon_1 = (1 - \theta_2)^2(s^2 - 1)/12s^2$. Since $\epsilon_3 = \theta_2$, for an acceptable decomposition to exist it is required that

$$\epsilon_1 + \epsilon_2 + \epsilon_3 = \theta_2 + \frac{(1 - \theta_2)^2}{4s^2} + \frac{(s^2 - 1)(1 - \theta_2)^2}{12s^2} \geq 0$$

or equivalently

$$\theta_2 \geq -\frac{(5s^2 - 2) + 2s\sqrt{6(s^2 - 1)}}{(s^2 + 2)}. \qquad (6.6)$$

Values of the lower bound of θ_2 for selected values of s are given in the following tabulation:

s	2	4	6
l.b.θ_2	−.1716	−.1170	−.1080
8	10	12	∞
−.1049	−.1035	−.1027	−.1010

Therefore, there are values of θ_2 for which the model (6.1) is not consistent with an additive decomposition as we have defined it; however, a value of $\theta_2 > -.1010$ will always lead to an acceptable decomposition.

When strict inequality is obtained in (6.6), there will be an infinite number of acceptable decompositions. The canonical decomposition corresponds to

$$\frac{\bar{\sigma}_b^2 \bar{\eta}_S(B)\bar{\eta}_S(F)}{U(B)U(F)} = \frac{Q_S(B)}{U(B)U(F)} - \frac{s^2 - 1}{12s^2}(1 - \theta_2)^2$$

and (6.7)

$$\frac{\bar{\sigma}_c^2 \bar{\eta}_T(B)\bar{\eta}_T(F)}{(1 - B)(1 - F)} = \frac{1}{4s^2}(1 - \theta_2)^2 \frac{(1 + B)(1 + F)}{(1 - B)(1 - F)}.$$

The Model (6.2)

For this model, $d = 2$ and $\phi_N(B) = 1$. After some algebraic reduction, we find

$$\frac{(1 - \theta_1 B)(1 - \theta_2 B^s)(1 - \theta_1 F)(1 - \theta_2 F^s)}{(1 - B)(1 - B^s)(1 - F)(1 - F^s)} = \frac{Q_S(B)}{U(B)U(F)} + \frac{Q_T(B)}{(1 - B)^2(1 - F)^2} + \theta_1\theta_2, \qquad (6.8)$$

where

$$Q_T(B) = \frac{(1 - \theta_1)^2(1 - \theta_2)^2}{s^2} \times \left\{1 + \left[\frac{\theta_2 s^2}{(1 - \theta_2)^2} + \frac{(s^2 - 4)}{12} + \frac{(1 + \theta_1)^2}{4(1 - \theta_1)^2}\right] \times (1 - B)(1 - F)\right\}$$

and

$$(1 - \theta_2)^{-2}(1 - B)^2(1 - F)^2 Q_S(B) = (1 - \theta_1)^2\left\{1 - \frac{1}{s^2}U(B)U(F)\right\} + \theta_1(1 - B)(1 - F) - \left\{\frac{s^2 - 4}{12s^2}(1 - \theta_1)^2 + \frac{(1 + \theta_1)^2}{4s^2}\right\}(1 - B^s)(1 - F^s).$$

We now show that an acceptable decomposition exists if $\theta_2 \geq 0$.

Proof. First, setting $B = -1$ (or $w = \pi$ in $B = e^{-iw}$) in $Q_T(B)(1 - B)^{-2}(1 - F)^{-2}$, we have

$$\frac{Q_T(-1)}{16} = \frac{(1 - \theta_2)^2}{48s^2} \times \{(1 - \theta_1)^2(s^2 - 1) + 3(1 + \theta_1)^2\} + \frac{\theta_2(1 - \theta_1)^2}{4} = C \qquad (6.9)$$

say. The right side of (6.8) can now be written as

$$\frac{Q_S^*(B)}{U(B)U(F)} + \frac{Q_T^*(B)}{(1 - B)^2(1 - F)^2} + \theta_2\frac{(1 + \theta_1)^2}{4}, \qquad (6.10)$$

where

$$Q_T^*(B) = Q_T(B) - C(1 - B)^2(1 - F)^2$$

and

$$Q_S^* = Q_S(B) + U(B)U(F)\left\{C - \frac{\theta_2(1 - \theta_1)^2}{4}\right\}.$$

Also, it can be verified that

$$(1 - \theta_2)^{-2}(1 - B)^2(1 - F)^2 Q_S^*(B) = \frac{(1 - \theta_1)^2}{4}(1 + B)(1 + F) \times \left\{1 - \frac{1}{s^2}U(B)U(F) - \frac{s^2 - 1}{12s^2}(1 - B^s)(1 - F^s)\right\} + \frac{(1 + \theta_1)^2}{4}(1 - B)(1 - F) \times \left\{1 - \frac{1}{4s^2}U(B)U(F)(1 + B)(1 + F)\right\}. \qquad (6.11)$$

When $\theta_2 \geq 0$, one can readily show that $Q_T(e^{-iw}) \mid 1 - e^{-iw} \mid^{-2}$ is monotonically decreasing in w so that the

68 Journal of the American Statistical Association, March 1982

second term in (6.10) is nonnegative for all w. Now, on the right side of the equation in (6.11), the second term with $B = e^{-iw}$ is clearly nonnegative for all w and, from (6.5), so is the first term. Thus, an acceptable decomposition exists and is given by (6.10).

The Model (6.3)

In this case, $d = 1$ and $\phi_N(B) = 1$. By partial fraction, we find

$$\frac{(1-\theta_1 B)(1-\theta_1 F)(1-\theta_2 B^s)(1-\theta_2 F^s)}{(1-B^s)(1-F^s)} = \frac{Q_S(B)}{U(B)U(F)} + \frac{Q_T(B)}{(1-B)(1-F)} + Q_N(B), \tag{6.12}$$

where

$$Q_T(B) = \frac{1}{s^2}(1-\theta_1)^2(1-\theta_2)^2,$$

$$(1-\theta_2)^{-2}(1-B)(1-F)Q_S(B) = \frac{(1+\theta_1)^2}{4}(1-B)(1-F) + (1-\theta_1)^2\left\{\frac{1}{4}(1+B)(1+F) - \frac{1}{s^2}U(B)U(F)\right\},$$

and

$$Q_N(B) = \theta_2(1-\theta_1 B)(1-\theta_1 F).$$

Noting that

$$\min_w Q_T(e^{-iw})\,|1-e^{-iw}|^{-2} = \frac{1}{4s^2}(1-\theta_1)^2(1-\theta_2)^2,$$

we can express the right side of (6.12) alternatively as

$$\frac{Q_S^*}{U(B)U(F)} + \frac{Q_T^*(B)}{(1-B)(1-F)} + Q_N^*(B), \tag{6.13}$$

where

$$Q_T^*(B) = Q_T(B) - \frac{1}{4s^2}(1-\theta_1)^2 \times (1-\theta_2)^2(1-B)(1-F),$$

$$Q_N^*(B) = Q_N(B) + \frac{1}{4s^2}(1+\theta_1)^2(1-\theta_2)^2,$$

and

$$(1-\theta_2)^{-2}(1-B)(1-F)Q_S^*(B) = (1-\theta_1 B)(1-\theta_1 F)\left\{1 - \frac{1}{s^2}U(B)U(F)\right\}.$$

Similar to the model (6.2), when $\theta_2 \geq 0$, all three terms in (6.13) are nonnegative for all w so that acceptable decompositions exist.

For the models (6.2) and (6.3), acceptable decompositions also exist for negative values of θ_2 near zero. The precise lower bounds are difficult to determine analytically. However, for these as well as for any model of the form (1.3) satisfying the condition (4.1), the existence of acceptable decompositions and the corresponding canonical form can always be determined by numerical methods. A computer program to determine the canonical component models and to compute the estimates $\hat{S}_t$, $\hat{T}_t$, and $\hat{N}_t$ is available on request.

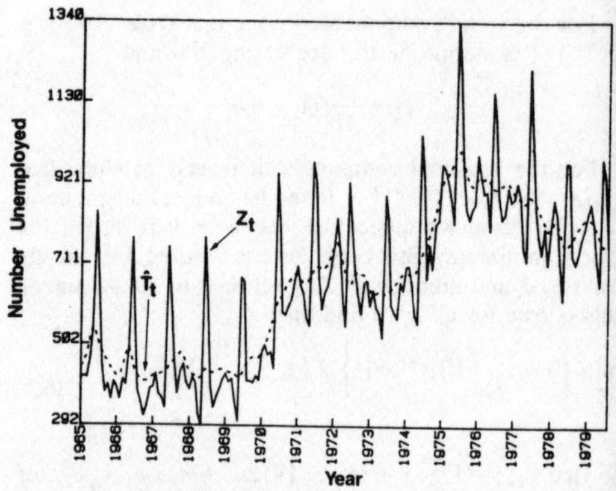

Figure 1. Monthly Unemployed Males Aged 16 to 19 (January 1971–August 1979) and the Estimated Trend Component Series

7. AN EXAMPLE

We now apply the model-based decomposition procedure to the monthly series of U.S. unemployed males aged 16 to 19 from January 1965 to August 1979, obtained from the Bureau of Labor Statistics. The series is a component used in constructing the monthly unemployment index.

The series is plotted in Figure 1. The variability of the series appears relatively constant over time; thus we decided to model the series in the original metric. It is found that the data can be adequately represented by the model (6.2) with

$$s = 12, \quad \hat{\theta}_1 = \underset{(.075)}{.313}, \quad \text{and} \quad \hat{\theta}_2 = \underset{(.035)}{.817}. \tag{7.1}$$

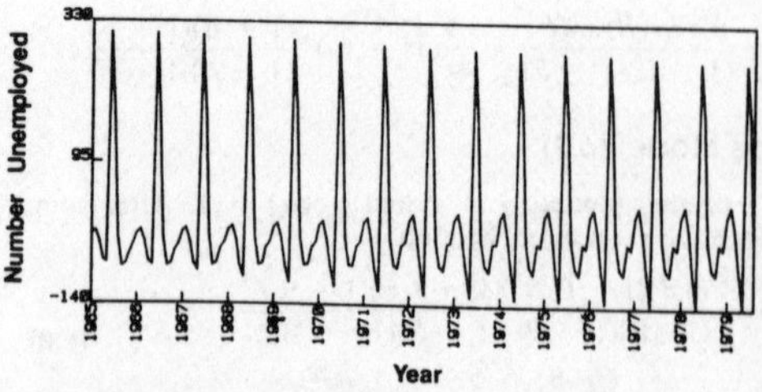

Figure 2. Estimated Seasonal Component Series for the Unemployed Males Data

Table 1. Weight Function for Estimating the Seasonal Component: Unemployed Males Data

Lag j	w_j											
0–11	.085	−.007	−.008	−.008	−.008	−.008	−.008	−.007	−.007	−.007	−.007	−.007
12–23	.076	−.007	−.007	−.007	−.006	−.006	−.006	−.006	−.006	−.006	−.006	−.006
24–35	.062	−.006	−.005	−.005	−.005	−.005	−.005	−.005	−.005	−.005	−.005	−.005
36–47	.051	−.005	−.004	−.004	−.004	−.004	−.004	−.004	−.004	−.004	−.004	−.004

with the standard errors of the parameter estimates given in parentheses below the estimates.

Assuming the estimates in (7.1) are the true values, we computed the corresponding canonical decomposition and, from (2.3), the associated weights for the estimates of the seasonal and trend components. These weights are given in Tables 1 and 2 from the center through lag 47. In both cases the remaining weights can be obtained by using the equation $w_j = .313\ w_{j-1} + .817\ w_{j-12} - .256\ w_{j-13}$. We observe that the weights associated with the seasonal component die out slowly and span a large number of years. This is in contrast to the weights associated with the standard Census X-11 program whose weights die out in about three years (see, e.g., Wallis 1974). We note that the rate at which the weight in the model-based approach decreases is primarily determined by the value of the parameter $\hat{\theta}_2 = .817$, which is determined from the original series.

The estimated trend component $\hat{T}_t$ is shown in Figure 1 and the estimated seasonal component $\hat{S}_t$ is plotted in Figure 2. We make the following observations. (a) The estimated trend component appears to capture the basic underlying movements of the series. (b) The seasonal component seems to have been adequately removed by the model-based decomposition. (c) The estimated seasonal component varies around a zero level and it is slowly changing over time. Therefore, for this particular series it appears that the model-based seasonal adjustment procedure has led to intuitively pleasing results.

8. DISCUSSION

In this article, we have proposed a model-based procedure to decompose a time series uniquely into mutually independent seasonal, trend, and irregular noise components. The method can be readily extended to models other than the ones discussed. For example, when $s = 12$, the autoregressive part of the seasonal component need not be $U(B)$, but can be any product of the factors $(1 + B)$, $(1 + B^2)$, $(1 + B + B^2)$, $(1 - B + B^2)$, $(1 + \sqrt{3}B + B^2)$, and $(1 - \sqrt{3}B + B^2)$. Also, the trend component may be augmented into a "trend-cycle" component by allowing the autoregressive part to take the form $(1 - B)^d \phi_T^*(B)$, where $\phi_T^*(B)$ has all its zeros lying on the unit circle (but distinct from $B = 1$ and those of the seasonal component). The possibilities are unlimited, depending on the form of the known model of Z_t and the nature of the problem.

Finally, we remark here that in illustrating the decomposition procedure with the models (6.1) to (6.3), in each case the values of θ_2 are restricted essentially to be nonnegative to yield acceptable decompositions. While we have rarely seen in practice a negative estimate of θ_2, it is conceivable that this could happen. One possible explanation for a negative θ_2 is that the white noise b_t and c_t for the seasonal and trend components are correlated. As an extreme example of the model (6.1) with $s = 2$, suppose the component models are

$$(1 + B)S_t = (1 - B)b_t,$$
$$(1 - B)T_t = (1 + B)c_t, \tag{8.1}$$

and

$$N_t \equiv 0.$$

The reader can readily verify that if $\sigma_b^2 = \sigma_c^2$ and b_t and c_t are perfectly positively correlated, then $\theta_2 = -1$. Thus, by allowing the component models to be dependent, we could increase the range of the models of Z_t for which acceptable decompositions exist. This seems to be an interesting topic for further study.

APPENDIX

In this appendix we sketch the proof of the properties of the canonical decomposition given in Section 5. Upon multiplying each expression in (4.5) by the denominator on the left side of the corresponding equation, we obtain

Table 2. Weight Function for Estimating the Trend Component: Unemployed Males Data

j	w_j											
0–11	.318	.212	.072	.028	.014	.010	.008	.008	.007	.005	.001	−.012
12–23	−.021	−.012	.001	.005	.006	.006	.006	.006	.006	.004	.001	−.009
24–35	−.018	−.010	.001	.004	.005	.005	.005	.005	.005	.004	.001	−.008
36–47	−.014	−.008	.001	.003	.004	.004	.004	.004	.004	.003	.001	−.006

$$|\eta_S(e^{-iw})|^2 \sigma_b^2 = Q_S(e^{-iw}) + \gamma_1 | U(e^{-iw})|^2 = f_S(w, \gamma_1),$$

$$|\eta_T(e^{-iw})|^2 \sigma_c^2 = Q_T(e^{-iw}) + \gamma_2 | 1 - e^{-iw}|^{2d} = f_T(w, \gamma_2), \quad \text{(A.1)}$$

$$|\eta_N(e^{-iw})|^2 \sigma_d^2 = Q_N(e^{-iw}) + \gamma_3 | \phi_N(e^{-iw})|^2 = f_N(w, \gamma_3).$$

Using a result of Hannan (1970, p. 137), we have that

$$\sigma_b^2(\gamma_1) = \exp\left\{\frac{1}{2\pi}\int_{-\pi}^{\pi} \ln f_S(w, \gamma_1)\, dw\right\},$$

$$\sigma_c^2(\gamma_2) = \exp\left\{\frac{1}{2\pi}\int_{-\pi}^{\pi} \ln f_T(w, \gamma_2)\, dw\right\}, \quad \text{(A.2)}$$

$$\sigma_d^2(\gamma_3) = \exp\left\{\frac{1}{2\pi}\int_{-\pi}^{\pi} \ln f_N(w, \gamma_3)\, dw\right\}.$$

Now in (A.1), $f_N(w, \gamma_3)$ does not depend on γ_3 if $\phi_N(e^{-iw}) = 0$ and is otherwise strictly increasing in γ_3; thus σ_d^2 is maximized when $\gamma_3 = \epsilon_1 + \epsilon_2$. From the restrictions that $\gamma_1 + \gamma_2 + \gamma_3 = 0$ and $\gamma_i + \epsilon_i \geq 0$, $i = 1, 2, 3$, we have that for the canonical decomposition $\gamma_1 = -\epsilon_1$ and $\gamma_2 = -\epsilon_2$. Therefore, the canonical decomposition is unique and furthermore, from (A.1) and (A.2), the innovation variances $\sigma_b^2(\gamma_1)$ and $\sigma_c^2(\gamma_2)$ are minimized for the canonical decomposition. In addition, if we take $\gamma_1 = -\epsilon_1$ and $\gamma_2 = -\epsilon_2$ in (A.1), both $f_S(w, -\epsilon_1)$ and $f_S(w, -\epsilon_2)$ are zero for some $0 \leq w \leq \pi$ implying that $\bar{\eta}_S(B)$ and $\bar{\eta}_T(B)$ are not invertible.

If we let

$$f_{\bar{S}}(w) = Q_S(e^{-iw}) | U(e^{-iw})|^{-2} - \epsilon_1$$

denote the psdf of $\bar{S}$, and let $f_{\tilde{S}}(w)$ denote the psdf of any other acceptable decomposition $\tilde{S}_t$, then it follows that

$$f_{\tilde{S}}(w) = f_{\bar{S}}(w) + \sigma_e^2 \quad \text{(A.3)}$$

with $\sigma_e^2 > 0$. Equation (A.3) implies $\tilde{S}_t = \bar{S}_t + e_t$, where e_t is white noise with variance σ_e^2.

Finally, from (4.5) the variance of $U(B)S_t$ is

$$\text{var}[U(B)S_t] = \frac{1}{2\pi}\int_{-\pi}^{\pi} [Q_S(e^{-iw}) + \gamma_1 | U(e^{-iw})|^2]\, dw. \quad \text{(A.4)}$$

It is evident that (A.4) is minimized when γ_1 is made as small as possible or $\gamma_1 = -\epsilon_1$, the value corresponding to the canonical decomposition.

[Received October 1980. Revised June 1981.]

REFERENCES

BOX, G.E.P., HILLMER, S.C., and TIAO, G.C. (1978), "Analysis and Modeling of Seasonal Time Series," in *Seasonal Analysis of Economic Time Series*, ed. Arnold Zellner, U.S. Department of Commerce, 309.

BOX, G.E.P., and JENKINS, G.M. (1970), *Time Series Analysis: Forecasting and Control*, San Francisco: Holden-Day.

BOX, G.E.P., and TIAO, G.C. (1975), "Intervention Analysis With Applications to Economic and Environmental Problems," *Journal of the American Statistical Association*, 70, 70.

BURMAN, J.P. (1980), "Seasonal Adjustment by Signal Extraction," *Journal of the Royal Statistical Society*, Ser. A, 143, 321.

CLEVELAND, W.P., and TIAO, G.C. (1976), "Decomposition of Seasonal Time Series: A Model for the Census X-11 Program," *Journal of the American Statistical Association*, 71, 581.

GRETHER, D.M., and NERLOVE, M. (1970), "Some Properties of 'Optimal' Seasonal Adjustment," *Econometrica*, 38, 682.

HANNAN, E.J. (1970), *Multiple Time Series*, New York: John Wiley.

NERLOVE, M., GRETHER, D.M., and CARVALHO, J.L. (1979), *Analysis of Economic Time Series*, New York, Academic Press.

PIERCE, D.A. (1978), "Seasonal Adjustment When Both Deterministic and Stochastic Seasonality Are Present," in *Seasonal Analysis of Economic Time Series*, ed. Arnold Zellner, U.S. Department of Commerce, 242.

——— (1980), "Data Revisions With Moving Average Seasonal Adjustment Procedures," *Journal of Econometrics*, 14, 95.

SHISKIN, J., YOUNG, A.H., and MUSGRAVE, J.C. (1967), "The X-11 Variant of Census Method II Seasonal Adjustment Program," Technical Paper 15, Bureau of the Census, U.S. Dept. of Commerce.

TIAO, G.C., and HILLMER, S.C. (1978), "Some Consideration of Decomposition of a Time Series," *Biometrika*, 65, 497.

TIAO, G.C., BOX, G.E.P., and HAMMING, W. (1975), "A Statistical Analysis of the Los Angeles Ambient Carbon Monoxide Data 1955–1972," *Journal of the Air Pollution Control Association*, 25, 1130.

WALLIS, K.F. (1974), "Seasonal Adjustment and the Relations Between Variables," *Journal of the American Statistical Association*, 69, 18.

WHITTLE, P. (1963), *Prediction and Regulation*, New York: D. Van Nostrand.

YOUNG, A.H. (1968), "Linear Approximations to the Census and BLS Seasonal Adjustment Methods," *Journal of the American Statistical Association*, 63, 445.

[19]

Journal of Business & Economic Statistics, October 1985, Vol. 3, No. 4

On Structural Time Series Models and the Characterization of Components

Agustin Maravall
Servicio de Estudios, Banco de España, Alcala 50, Madrid 28014, Spain

This article analyzes certain properties of a class of recently proposed structural time series models in which particular structures are imposed upon the unobserved components of an observed time series. It is shown how the overall model can be expected to fit series, such as those for which the X-11 or Airline models are appropriate. As for the components, identification of the model is achieved by assigning a certain amount of white noise variation to the trend and seasonal components. It is shown that the structural approach can be modified to avoid trend and seasonal components contaminated by noise.

KEY WORDS: Seasonal adjustment; X-11; ARIMA models; Airline model: Unobserved components; Canonical decomposition.

1. INTRODUCTION

Applied time series analysts, such as those working to satisfy the demands of economic policy makers, rely heavily on X-11 for unobserved components estimation (most often, for seasonal adjustment) and on autoregressive integrated moving average (ARIMA) models for short-term forecasting. Over the last few years, thanks to the recent work of Bell, Box, Burman, Cleveland, Hillmer, Tiao, and others, there has been a move toward the integration of both operations, that is, in the direction of using ARIMA models for signal extraction also. Two advantages of this approach are, first, that it permits one to overcome the limitations of the relatively fixed X-11 filters and, second, that the specification of a model offers a systematic framework for analysis.

Several problems still remain, however. First, on occasion, the ARIMA models identified through the usual Box–Jenkins criteria offer unsatisfactory spectral decompositions. Second, the analytical expressions for the components can be complicated, which limits the usefulness of the model. Moreover, it may be desirable to avoid—as much as possible—the identification stage, either because one wishes to avoid the pernicious effects of data mining, or because a large number of series has to be frequently analyzed.

A class of parametric time series models was proposed recently under the name of "structural time series models" (Harvey 1981, 1984; Harvey and Todd 1983). Following the work of Engle (1978) and Nerlove et al. (1979), a particular structure is imposed on the traditional trend, seasonal, and irregular components; this structure depends on a few parameters. Thus, on the one hand, the structural model has the limitation that the overall implied structure for the series is subject to certain constraints; hence it may be unsuitable for some series. On the other hand, these models possess some convenient features. First, by skipping the identification stage, they avoid the problem of data mining while presenting more versatility than the filters of X-11. Second, they provide components that should be expected to behave properly as trend, seasonal, and irregular components. These models also offer some computational virtues, such as easily providing the mean squared error of the estimated components.

From the point of view of applications, these features are important. They will only be meaningful, however, if it is indeed the case that the structural models can adequately represent a large number of series encountered in practice. The purpose of this article is to first look into this question and then to compare the structural model components with those obtained from the X-11 and the ARIMA-based signal extraction methods.

2. THE BASIC STRUCTURAL MODEL

We shall analyze the so-called "basic structural model" (BSM) and consider monthly time series. The series of interest (or a suitable transformation) is the sum of a trend, a seasonal, and an irregular component:

$$y_t = p_t + s_t + u_t. \tag{2.1}$$

The trend component can be expressed as

$$\nabla p_t = \beta_{t-1} + \eta_t, \tag{2.2}$$

where $\nabla = 1 - B$ and B is the lag operator. Thus the trend component is locally linear, and the slope β_t

follows the random walk

$$\nabla \beta_t = \zeta_t. \quad (2.3)$$

The seasonal component satisfies the equation

$$S(B) s_t = \omega_t, \quad (2.4)$$

where $S(B) = 1 + B + \cdots + B^{11}$. Thus the sum of 12 consecutive seasonal components oscillates randomly around 0. (In Harvey 1984 an alternative model for the seasonal component, which uses a series of sines and cosines, is also advocated.) The three variables η_t, ζ_t, and ω_t, plus the irregular u_t, are assumed to be independent white noises. The only unknown parameters of the model are the four variances

$$\sigma_u^2, \sigma_\eta^2, \sigma_\zeta^2, \sigma_\omega^2. \quad (2.5)$$

In terms of ARIMA representation, it is easily seen that the trend component can be expressed as the integrated moving average (IMA) (2.1) model

$$\nabla^2 p_t = (1 - \mu B)\, d_t, \quad (2.6)$$

where μ and σ_d^2 are related to σ_η^2 and σ_ζ^2 through the equations

$$\sigma_\zeta^2 = (1 - \mu)^2 \sigma_d^2 \quad \text{and} \quad \sigma_\eta^2 = \mu \sigma_d^2. \quad (2.7)$$

Considering (2.1), (2.2), (2.3), and (2.4), the overall series can be expressed as

$$z_t = S(B)\zeta_{t-1} + \nabla_{12}\eta_t + \nabla^2 \omega_t + \nabla\nabla_{12} u_t, \quad (2.8)$$

where $z_t = \nabla\nabla_{12} y_t$. Hence z_t follows a moving average (MA) (13) model, with the parameters and the variance of the innovation being functions of the parameters in (2.5).

From (2.8), the autocovariance function (ACVF) of z_t can be computed, and letting γ_k denote the k-lag autocovariance, it is given by

$$\begin{aligned}
\gamma_0 &= 12\sigma_\zeta^2 + 2\sigma_\eta^2 + 6\sigma_\omega^2 + 4\sigma_u^2 \\
\gamma_1 &= 11\sigma_\zeta^2 \qquad - 4\sigma_\omega^2 - 2\sigma_u^2 \\
\gamma_2 &= 10\sigma_\zeta^2 \qquad + \sigma_\omega^2 \\
\gamma_3 &= 9\sigma_\zeta^2 \\
\gamma_4 &= 8\sigma_\zeta^2 \\
\gamma_5 &= 7\sigma_\zeta^2 \\
\gamma_6 &= 6\sigma_\zeta^2 \\
\gamma_7 &= 5\sigma_\zeta^2 \\
\gamma_8 &= 4\sigma_\zeta^2 \\
\gamma_9 &= 3\sigma_\zeta^2 \\
\gamma_{10} &= 2\sigma_\zeta^2 \\
\gamma_{11} &= \sigma_\zeta^2 \qquad + \sigma_u^2 \\
\gamma_{12} &= -\sigma_\eta^2 \qquad - 2\sigma_u^2 \\
\gamma_{13} &= \qquad + \sigma_u^2. \quad (2.9)
\end{aligned}$$

with all other γ_k being 0.

These equations imply a set of restrictions on the ACVF of z_t. They overidentify the parameters, and in terms of the autocorrelations, the equations in (2.9) imply the following constraints:

$$\begin{aligned}
&\rho_k/\rho_{k+1} = (12 - k)/(11 - k),\ k = 3, \ldots, 9 \\
&\rho_k > 0,\ k = 2, \ldots, 11 \\
&\rho_{12} < 0 \\
&\rho_{11} > \rho_{13} \\
&|\rho_{12}| > \rho_{13}. \quad (2.10)
\end{aligned}$$

Obviously, many ARIMA models will not satisfy (2.10). The question is, Are these constraints likely to be reasonably in agreement with a large number of series encountered in practice?

3. COMPARISON WITH X-11

If y_t denotes a series for which X-11 is appropriate, the autocorrelation function (ACF) of $\nabla\nabla_{12} y_t$ is that given in the X-11 column of Table 1 (Cleveland 1972). It can be seen that all of the constraints in (2.10) are satisfied. In particular, when setting

$$\begin{aligned}
\sigma_\zeta^2 &= .025\gamma_0 \qquad \sigma_\eta^2 = .020\gamma_0 \\
\sigma_\omega^2 &= .010\gamma_0 \qquad \sigma_u^2 = .050\gamma_0, \quad (3.1)
\end{aligned}$$

the BSM has the ACF displayed in the last column of Table 1. Both ACF are practically identical. Thus the BSM could be applied to series for which X-11 is appropriate, and we know from experience that there are many such series.

Although the overall implied ACF may be the same, the components are not. From (2.7), $\mu = 1 - \sigma_\zeta/\sigma_d$ and $\sigma_d^2 - \sigma_d\sigma_\zeta - \sigma_\mu^2 = 0$, which for the variances in (3.1), yield $\mu = .34$, $\sigma_d^2 = .058\gamma_0$. Hence the trend component for the BSM becomes, from (2.6),

$$\nabla^2 p_t = (1 - .34B)\, d_t. \quad (3.2)$$

The BSM seasonal component is given by (2.4), and the irregular component is white noise. Let (2.1) rep-

Table 1. ACF: Comparison With X-11

k	*X-11**	*BSM*
1	−.061	−.065
2	.266	.260
3	.226	.225
4	.201	.200
5	.175	.175
6	.150	.150
7	.125	.125
8	.100	.100
9	.075	.075
10	.046	.050
11	.178	.175
12	−.326	−.320
13	.153	.150
14	−.004	0

* From Cleveland 1972.

resent the X-11 decomposition of the series into trend, seasonal, and irregular components. Using Cleveland's (1972) approximation again, the trend and seasonal components are given by

$$\nabla^2 p_t = (1 + .26B + .30B^2 - .32B^3)b_t \quad (3.3)$$

$$S(B)s_t = (1 + .26B^{12})c_t, \quad (3.4)$$

where b_t, c_t, and u_t (the irregular component) are independent white noises. Comparing the two trend and seasonal components, X-11 is seen to imply additional MA terms, which are likely to induce additional smoothing for both components.

Cleveland's (1972) characterization of X-11 also includes the ratios $(\sigma_u^2/\sigma_b^2) = 10.1$ and $(\sigma_c^2/\sigma_b^2) = .3$. Write $\nabla\nabla_{12}y_t = P_t + S_t + U_t$, where

$$P_t = S(B)(1 + .26B + .30B^2 - .32B^3)b_t$$

$$S_t = \nabla^2(1 + .26B^{12})c_t$$

$$U_t = \nabla\nabla_{12}u_t$$

are the parts of the stationary transformation associated with the trend, seasonal and irregular components. Hence

$$\text{var}(P_t) = 1.877\sigma_u^2$$

$$\text{var}(S_t) = .190\sigma_u^2$$

$$\text{var}(U_t) = 4\sigma_u^2$$

and

$$\text{var}(\nabla\nabla_{12}y_t) = 6.067\sigma_u^2. \quad (3.5)$$

A similar decomposition of $\nabla\nabla_{12}y_t$ for the BSM is given by (2.8), where P_t, S_t and U_t are, respectively, the first two, the third, and the fourth components of the right side. From (3.1) and the first equation in (2.9), the following results are obtained:

$$\text{var}(P_t) = 2.267\sigma_u^2$$

$$\text{var}(S_t) = .400\sigma_u^2$$

$$\text{var}(U_t) = 4\sigma_u^2$$

and

$$\text{var}(\nabla\nabla_{12}y_t) = 6.667\sigma_u^2. \quad (3.6)$$

From (3.5) and (3.6), $\sigma_u^2(\text{X-11}) = 1.1\sigma_u^2(\text{BSM})$. Hence the variance of the X-11 irregular component is approximately 10% larger than that of the BSM. All things considered, although the components are relatively close for X-11 and the BSM, the former seems to remove some of the series variation from the trend and seasonal components and transfer it to the irregular component.

4. COMPARISON WITH THE ARIMA-BASED METHOD; THE AIRLINE MODEL

Looking at the results obtained by Harvey and Todd (1983) for the Prothero–Wallis series, it can be seen that in all six cases, $\sigma_\zeta^2 = 0$. They attribute this result to the small sample bias of exact maximum likelihood estimation. Be that as it may, it is interesting to analyze the BSM for this case.

When $\sigma_\zeta^2 = 0$, the equations in (2.9) become

$$\begin{aligned}
\gamma_0 &= 2\sigma_\eta^2 + 6\sigma_\omega^2 + 4\sigma_u^2 \\
\gamma_1 &= \quad - 4\sigma_\omega^2 - 2\sigma_u^2 \\
\gamma_2 &= \quad \sigma_\omega^2 \\
\gamma_{11} &= \quad \sigma_u^2 \\
\gamma_{12} &= -\sigma_\eta^2 \quad - 2\sigma_u^2 \\
\gamma_{13} &= \quad \sigma_u^2
\end{aligned} \quad (4.1)$$

where $\gamma_k = 0$ for other values of k. Again, the numerical values will depend on the variances of η_t, ω_t, and u_t, but it will always be true that

$$\begin{aligned}
&\gamma_1 < 0 \\
&\gamma_{11} = \gamma_{13} > 0 \\
&\gamma_{12} < 0 \\
&|\gamma_{12}| > |\gamma_{11}|.
\end{aligned} \quad (4.2)$$

Consider now the "Airline model" (Box–Jenkins 1970): $\nabla\nabla_{12}y_t = (1 - \theta_1 B)(1 - \theta_{12}B^{12})a_t$.

The ACVF for $\nabla\nabla_{12}y_t$ is given by:

$$\begin{aligned}
\gamma_0 &= (1 + \theta_1^2)(1 + \theta_{12}^2)\sigma_a^2 \\
\gamma_1 &= -\theta_1(1 + \theta_{12}^2)\sigma_a^2 \\
\gamma_{11} &= \theta_1\theta_{12}\sigma_a^2 \\
\gamma_{12} &= -\theta_{12}(1 + \theta_1^2)\sigma_a^2 \\
\gamma_{13} &= \theta_1\theta_{12}\sigma_a^2
\end{aligned} \quad (4.3)$$

with all other γ_k equal to 0. If $\theta_1, \theta_{12} \geq 0$—an acceptable decomposition exists if $\theta_{12} \geq 0$ (Hillmer and Tiao 1982)—it can be seen that all constraints in (4.2) are satisfied.

A difference between (4.1) and (4.3) is that in the former, $\gamma_2 > 0$, while in the latter, $\gamma_2 = 0$. Since (4.1), however, implies that $\rho_2 = \sigma_\omega^2/(2\sigma_\eta^2 + 6\sigma_\omega^2 + 4\sigma_u^2)$, ρ_2 will typically be very small.

Table 2 compares the ACF's of the BSM and the Airline model for different values of the parameters: the two models display ACF's that are quite close. After all, both are three-parameter models. One of the param-

Table 2. ACF: Comparison With the Airline Model

Model	ρ_1	ρ_2	ρ_{11}	ρ_{12}	ρ_{13}
Airline					
$\theta_1 = .8$, $\theta_{12} = .8$	−.488	-	.238	−.488	.238
$\theta_1 = .8$, $\theta_{12} = .4$	−.488	-	.168	−.345	.168
$\theta_1 = .4$, $\theta_{12} = .8$	−.345	-	.168	−.488	.168
$\theta_1 = .4$, $\theta_{12} = .4$	−.345	-	.119	−.345	.119
BSM					
$\sigma_\eta^2 = 1$, $\sigma_\omega^2 = .25$, $\sigma_u^2 = 20$	−.490	.003	.239	−.490	.239
$\sigma_\eta^2 = 1$, $\sigma_\omega^2 = .75$, $\sigma_u^2 = 3$	−.486	.040	.162	−.378	.162
$\sigma_\eta^2 = 1$, $\sigma_\omega^2 = .01$, $\sigma_u^2 = 1.13$	−.350	.001	.172	−.495	.172
$\sigma_\eta^2 = 1$, $\sigma_\omega^2 = .25$, $\sigma_u^2 = .70$	−.380	.039	.111	−.380	.111

eters—θ_1 or σ^2_η (more precisely, σ^2_η/σ^2_u)—is associated with the stability of the trend component. Similarly, θ_{12} and $\sigma^2_\omega/\sigma^2_u$ are associated with the stability of the seasonal component. The third parameter determines, in both cases, the size of the one-step-ahead forecast error. Since the BSM implies (for $\sigma^2_\zeta = 0$) a unit root in the MA expression of $\nabla\nabla_{12}y_t$, the approximation should work better for larger values of θ_1 or θ_{12} in (4.3), which is exactly what Table 2 indicates. (Notice that for large values of σ^2_ω, the BSM can have values of ρ_1 larger than .5, the maximum that can be obtained in the Airline model.)

Thus the BSM can generate ACF's similar to those of the Airline model, and our experience is that this ACF characterizes many economic time series. (Ansley 1983 also shows how some modification of the BSM may approximate the Airline model.)

5. CHARACTERIZATION OF THE COMPONENTS

With observations on y_t alone, identification of the models generating p_t, s_t and u_t in (2.1) poses some problems. The ad hoc characterization of the components in the BSM guarantees that the models are uniquely identified. This is easily seen by considering (2.9): since the four unknown parameters (σ^2_ζ, σ^2_η, σ^2_ω, σ^2_u) can be expressed as functions of the observable covariances, the model is identified and the parameters can be estimated consistently. (For example, the first four equations can be solved recursively, and the four unknown variances can be expressed as linear functions of the observable covariances γ_0, γ_1, γ_2, and γ_3.)

The BSM offers therefore an example in which a priori considerations of the components' structure identify the model. This is fundamentally due to the limitations on the orders of the MA terms of the components, relative to those of the autoregressive (AR) terms (see Maravall 1978).

For the ARIMA-based procedure, however, the fact that for both components, p_t and s_t, the order of the AR polynomial is (at most) equal to that of the MA polynomial implies that the model is not identified. Identification is then achieved with an additional assumption: the variance of the irregular component is to be maximized; this yields the "canonical decomposition" of Hillmer–Tiao (1982). (The assumption of maximum irregular variance was first introduced by Pierce 1978 and Box et al. 1978.)

The specification of models for the signal with AR polynomials of larger order than that of MA, implied in the Harvey–Todd (1983) approach, is a well-established practice. (To quote a few examples, see Harrison and Stevens 1976, Fuller 1976, Engle 1978, Nerlove et al. 1979, and Gersch and Kitagawa 1983; it is also implicit in the literature on AR signals, such as Pagano 1974, and an elaborate application can be found in Porter et al. 1978.) In all of these cases, by removing MA terms from the models for p_t, or s_t, or both identification is achieved without having to maximize the variance of the irregular component.

In the final analysis, the selection of a specific decomposition depends basically on the a priori beliefs that the analyst has about the desirable properties of a trend, seasonal, and irregular components. There is a point, however, that is worth discussing. I illustrate it for the BSM specification.

5.1 The Trend Component

Consider the trend component given by (2.6), and write

$$p_t = \pi_t + \epsilon_t, \tag{5.1}$$

where ϵ_t is white noise, orthogonal to π_t. From (2.6) and (5.1),

$$(1 - \mu B)\, d_t = \nabla^2\pi_t + \nabla^2\epsilon_t, \tag{5.2}$$

which implies that $\nabla^2\pi_t$ has to be an MA(2), say, $\nabla^2\pi_t = (1 - \alpha_1 B - \alpha_2 B^2)b_t$.

Thus the system of covariance equations corresponding to (5.2) is given by

$$\begin{aligned} 1 + \mu^2 &= (1 + \alpha_1^2 + \alpha_2^2)\sigma^2_b + 6\sigma^2_\epsilon \\ -\mu &= (-\alpha_1 + \alpha_1\alpha_2)\sigma^2_b - 4\sigma^2_\epsilon \\ 0 &= -\alpha_2\sigma^2_b + \sigma^2_\epsilon \end{aligned} \tag{5.3}$$

where, without loss of generality, we have assumed that $\sigma^2_d = 1$.

Since there is an infinite number of values for the parameters (α_1, α_2, σ^2_b, and σ^2_ϵ) that satisfy the system (5.3), the models for π_t and ϵ_t are not identified. There is thus an infinite number of ways in which the BSM trend component can be split into trend and (orthogonal) noise components.

The pseudospectrum of p_t is given by

$$f_p(\lambda) = (1 + \mu^2 - 2\mu \cos \lambda)/4(1 - \cos \lambda)^2,$$

a monotonically decreasing function in $0 \leq \lambda \leq \pi$. Hence $\min_{0\leq\lambda\leq\pi} f_p(\lambda) = f_p(\pi) = (1 + \mu)^2/16$.

Setting $\sigma^2_\epsilon = (1 + \mu)^2/16$, the system (5.3) becomes identified. It can then be seen that the first equation minus twice the difference between the second and third yields $1 + \alpha_1 - \alpha_2 = 0$, or $\alpha(-1) = 0$, where $\alpha(B) = 1 - \alpha_1 B - \alpha_2 B^2$. Thus all white noise is removed from the trend component when π_t is of the type $\nabla^2\pi_t = (1 + B)(1 - \alpha_2 B)b_t$, and in terms of the parameters in equations (2.2) and (2.3), the variance of the irregular component is then increased by $\sigma^2_\epsilon = (\sigma^2_\zeta + 4\sigma^2_\eta)/16$.

5.2 The Seasonal Component

A similar reasoning applies to the BSM seasonal component, given by $(1 + B + \cdots + B^{r-1})s_t = \omega_t$, where r is the number of observations in a year. This is easily seen by considering the simplest case $r = 2$ (i.e., the seasonality is of period 2, appropriate for semiannual data), in which case $(1 + B)s_t = \omega_t$. Writing, as before,

$$s_t = \pi_t + \epsilon_t, \tag{5.4}$$

it is apparent that $\omega_t = (1 + B)\pi_t + (1 + B)\epsilon_t$, which implies that $(1 + B)\pi_t$ is an MA(1), say, $(1 + B)\pi_t = (1 - \alpha B)c_t$. Setting $\sigma_\omega^2 = 1$, the system of covariance equations becomes $1 = (1 + \alpha^2)\sigma_c^2 + 2\sigma_\epsilon^2$, $0 = -\alpha\sigma_c^2 + \sigma_\epsilon^2$, and again, the BSM seasonal component can be decomposed into "seasonal plus noise" in an infinite number of ways.

The pseudospectrum of s_t is equal to $f_s(\lambda) = 1/2(1 + \cos\lambda)$, a monotonically increasing function in $0 \le \lambda \le \pi$; hence $\min_{0\le\lambda\le\pi} f_s(\lambda) = f_s(0) = \frac{1}{4}$. Setting $\sigma_\epsilon^2 = \sigma_\omega^2/4$, it follows that all white noise is removed from the seasonal component when π_t is given by $(1 + B)\pi_t = (1 - B)c_t$, and $\sigma_c^2 = \sigma_\omega^2/4$.

For $r > 2$ the previous discussion is easily generalized. The BSM seasonal component has the pseudospectrum

$$f_s(\lambda) = \sigma_\omega^2\{r + 2[(r - 1)\cos\lambda + (r - 2) \times \cos 2\lambda + \cdots + \cos(r - 1)\lambda]\}^{-1},$$

which can be rewritten as

$$f_s(x = \cos\lambda) = \sigma_\omega^2[h_1 + h_2 x + \cdots + h_r x^{r-1}]^{-1}.$$

Since, for $0 \le \lambda \le \pi$, $\min f_s(\lambda) = f_s(0) = \sigma^2/r^2 > 0$, the identity

$$\frac{1}{h_1 + h_2 x + \cdots + h_r x^{r-1}} = \frac{m(x)}{h_1 + h_2 x + \cdots + h_r x^{r-1}} + k \tag{5.5}$$

will be satisfied for $k \ge 0$ and $m(x)$, in general, of order $(r - 1)$. Setting the two components of the right side of (5.5) equal to the spectra of π_t and ϵ_t in (5.4), it follows that the model for π_t will be of the type $S(B)\pi_t = \beta(B)b_t$, with $\beta(B)$ of order $(r - 1)$. The two seasonal components s_t and π_t will have parallel spectra, and k (i.e., the variance of ϵ_t) will be a maximum when $\beta(B)$ can be factorized as $\beta(B) = (1 - B)\beta^*(B)$, with $\beta^*(B)$ being of order $(r - 2)$, in which case $f_\pi(0) = 0$.

5.3 Conclusion

We have seen that the BSM, given by equations (2.1)–(2.4) with u_t white noise, has (for $r = 2$) the same reduced form as the model

$$y_t = p_t^* + s_t^* + u_t^*$$
$$\nabla^2 p_t^* = (1 + B)(1 - \alpha B)b_t$$
$$S(B)s_t^* = (1 - B)c_t \tag{5.6}$$

and u_t^* white noise. The two decompositions represent two alternative, observationally equivalent, structural models. Hence maximizing the irregular term variance is something that can be applied to structural models. The four unknown parameters in (5.6)—α, σ_b^2, σ_c^2, and $\sigma_{u^*}^2$—can be expressed as single-valued functions of the four unknown BSM parameters, given in (2.5). Specifically, $\sigma_{u^*}^2 = \sigma_u^2 + \frac{1}{16}\sigma_\zeta^2 + \frac{1}{4}\sigma_\eta^2 + \frac{1}{4}\sigma_\omega^2$, $\sigma_c^2 = \sigma_\omega^2/4$, α is the root of the equation $\alpha^2 - 2\delta\alpha + 1 = 0$ (with $\delta = 1 + 2\sigma_\zeta^2/(\sigma_\zeta^2 + 4\sigma_\eta^2)$) that is smaller than 1, and $\sigma_b^2 = (\sigma_\zeta^2 + 4\sigma_\eta^2)/16\alpha$.

It is therefore possible to move from one parameterization to the other, so that, for example, having estimated the BSM, the components p_t^* and s_t^* can be derived and used for smoothing.

By directly specifying identified models for the components (reducing a priori the order of the MA polynomial relative to the AR polynomial), the BSM components will be equal to the sum of another component with the same spectral profile plus orthogonal white noise. Thus identification in the BSM is achieved by removing white noise variation from the irregular component and superimposing it on the trend, or seasonal, or both components.

If the objective of the analysis is forecasting, it is obvious that interchanging noise among the components has no effect on the aggregated forecast. On the contrary, from the point of view of unobserved components estimation, the two decompositions will differ. In the final analysis, the choice of the component models relies on arbitrary assumptions. Since their characterization is based purely on stochastic behavior, however, if we define the irregular component to be white noise variation, why only a certain part of it? To allow the trend and seasonal components to include (separable) white noise is to introduce unnecessary ambiguity. Why should purely white noise variation be part of a trend or seasonal component? As we have seen, components clean of noise could be easily incorporated into a structural approach by allowing for larger MA's in the component models, with those MA's containing the factor $(1 + B)$ in the trend case, and (possibly) the factor $(1 - B)$ in the seasonal case [so as to impose $f_p(\pi) = f_s(0) = 0$, respectively.]

ACKNOWLEDGMENTS

Thanks are due to A. C. Harvey and two anonymous referees for their helpful comments.

[*Received January 1985. Revised March 1985.*]

REFERENCES

Ansley, C. F. (1983), Comment on "Forecasting Economic Time Series With Structural Box–Jenkins Models: A Case Study," by A. C. Harvey and P. H. J. Todd, *Journal of Business & Economic Statistics*, 1, 307–309.

Box, G. E. P., and Jenkins, G. M. (1970), *Times Series Analysis: Forecasting and Control*, San Francisco: Holden-Day.

Box, G. E. P., Hillmer, S. C., and Tiao, G. C. (1978), "Analysis and Modeling of Seasonal Time Series," in *Seasonal Analysis of Economic Time Series*, ed. A. Zellner, Washington, DC: U.S. Dept. of Commerce, Bureau of the Census, pp. 309–334.

Cleveland, W. P. (1972), "Analysis and Forecasting of Seasonal Time Series," unpublished Ph.D. dissertation, University of Wisconsin–Madison, Dept. of Statistics.

Engle, R. F. (1978), "Estimating Structural Models of Seasonality," in *Seasonal Analysis of Economic Time Series*, ed. A. Zellner, Washington, DC: U.S. Dept. of Commerce, Bureau of the Census, pp. 281–297.

Fuller, W. A. (1976), *Introduction to Statistical Time Series*, New York: John Wiley, pp. 170–174.

Gersch, W., and Kitagawa, G. (1983), "The Prediction of Time Series With Trends and Seasonalities," *Journal of Business & Economic Statistics*, 1, 253–264.

Harrison, P. J., and Stevens, C. F. (1976), "Bayesian Forecasting," *Journal of the Royal Statistical Society*, Ser. B, 38, 205–247.

Harvey, A. C. (1981), *Time Series Models*, Oxford: Philip Allan.

——— (1984), "A Unified View of Statistical Forecasting Procedures," *Journal of Forecasting*, 3, 245–275.

Harvey, A. C., and Todd, P. (1983), "Forecasting Economic Time Series With Structural and Box–Jenkins Models: A Case Study," *Journal of Business & Economic Statistics*, 1, 299–307.

Hillmer, S. C., and Tiao, G. C. (1982), "An ARIMA-Model-Based Approach to Seasonal Adjustment," *Journal of the American Statistical Association*, 77, 63–70.

Maravall, A. (1978), "Comment on Modeling Considerations in the Seasonal Adjustment of Economic Time Series," in *Seasonal Analysis of Economic Time Series*, ed. A. Zellner, Washington, DC: U.S. Dept. of Commerce, Bureau of the Census, pp. 470–471.

Nerlove, M., Grether, D. M., and Carvalho, J. L. (1979), *Analysis of Economic Time Series*, New York: Academic Press.

Pagano, M. (1974), "Estimation of Models of Autoregressive Signal Plus White Noise," *Annals of Statistics*, 2, 99–108.

Pierce, D. A. (1978), "Seasonal Adjustment When Both Deterministic and Stochastic Seasonality Are Present," in *Seasonal Analysis of Economic Time Series*, ed. A. Zellner, Washington, DC: U.S. Dept. of Commerce, Bureau of the Census, pp. 242–269.

Porter, R. D., Maravall, A., Parke, D. W., and Pierce, D. A. (1978), "Transitory Variation in the Monetary Aggregates," in *Improving the Monetary Aggregates*, Washington, DC: Federal Reserve Board of Governors, pp. 1–33.

[20]

Seasonal Adjustment and Relations Between Variables

KENNETH F. WALLIS*

This article studies the effect of official seasonal adjustment procedures on the relations between variables. By considering time-invariant linear filters, and in particular a linear approximation to the Census Method II adjustment program, the effect of adjusting one or both of the variables in a distributed lag relation is examined, and the distortions which can arise are described. Applying the actual (nonlinear) adjustment procedure to artificial data indicates that at least for the particular x-series used, the results of the linear filter analysis provide a good guide to the behavior of estimates obtained from data adjusted by the official method.

1. INTRODUCTION

Discussion of seasonal adjustment procedures has generally proceeded in terms of their effect on a single economic time series. Official statisticians (Brown, *et al.* [1], Burman [2, 3], Shiskin, *et al.* [22], U.S. Bureau of Labor Statistics [27]) have been concerned with designing seasonal adjustment procedures which satisfy various criteria, and they, together with others (Godfrey and Karreman [7], Nerlove [17, 18], Rosenblatt [20, 21]), have evaluated by various means the extent to which these and other criteria are met. Underlying much of this work is the "classical" additive or multiplicative components model, where the time series is taken to comprise trend-cycle, seasonal, and irregular components. Seasonality is seldom defined rigorously; one of the more explicit statements is that of Nerlove [17], who defines seasonality as "that characteristic of a time series that gives rise to spectral peaks at seasonal frequencies." In the time domain, following Thomas and Wallis [26], "by seasonal variation we understand those systematic though not necessarily regular intra-year movements in economic time series which are often caused by non-economic phenomena, such as climatic changes and the regular timing of religious festivals." Broadly speaking, the objective of seasonal adjustment is to remove the seasonal component without distorting the remainder, which perhaps provides an ex-post definition of the seasonal component as the difference between the original and adjusted series. The predominant uses are those of short-term forecasting and policy analysis, where the implicit view seems to be that the seasonal component is of little interest, being not only exogenous to the economic system but also uncontrollable, yet predictable. Thus, most macroeconomic aggregates are appraised in their adjusted forms. However, there are exceptions to this, such as total unemployment, which is taken to be politically sensitive irrespective of season, and at a less aggregated level, various stock-flow relationships, where the existence of a seasonal peak in demand is explicitly acknowledged (as with banks' reserve ratios and retailers' inventories).

In general, little attention has been paid to the effect that seasonal adjustment of separate time series has on the relations between them, although changes in dynamic specification when moving between adjusted and unadjusted data have been observed.[1] Perhaps this neglect results from the view that the seasonal component of a given series is noise, and even if correlated with the seasonal component of another series, it is still noise. Also, the nonlinear nature of the official adjustment procedures, largely based on ratio-to-moving-average methods, makes theoretical investigation difficult, although at the simplest level it is clear that they preserve neither sums nor ratios, so that an adjusted aggregate is not generally equal to the total of the adjusted components, and an adjusted unemployment rate is not generally equal to the ratio of the adjusted number unemployed to the adjusted labor force. Regression methods of seasonal adjustment are easier to investigate, and Lovell [14] has developed a rationale for their use; a number of their implications for the regression analysis of the relations between variables in adjusted or original form are described by Thomas and Wallis [26]. However, such techniques have found little use, "since no regression models have yet been demonstrated empirically to provide sufficiently accurate estimates of the trend-cycle and the seasonal, particularly in the current period" (Shiskin, *et al.* [22]).

* Kenneth F. Wallis is with the London School of Economics, Houghton Street, London WC2A 2AE, England. A preliminary version of this article was presented at the European meeting of the Econometric Society, Budapest, September 1972. The author wishes to thank David Elliot for computational assistance, the Central Statistical Office for making their program available, and an anonymous referee, J.P. Burman, E.J. Hannan, A. Lancaster, and C.A. Sims for helpful comments. Related, contemporaneous, but independent work by Sims is described in [24].

[1] For example, in the London Business School quarterly model of the U.K. economy, on switching from unadjusted to adjusted data, the consumption function for nondurables moved from an equation containing current and one- and two-quarter lagged values of income, estimated in four-quarter differences, to a more conventional form with current income and the one-quarter lagged dependent variable, the implied adjustment of consumption to income becoming much slower. At the same time the consumption function for durable goods became a static equation, the stock of durable goods dropping out, being highly collinear with income in the adjusted data. (Source: various discussion papers of the LBS Econometric Forecasting Unit.)

© Journal of the American Statistical Association
March 1974, Volume 69, Number 345
Applications Section

A. Weights for Linear Adjustment Filters

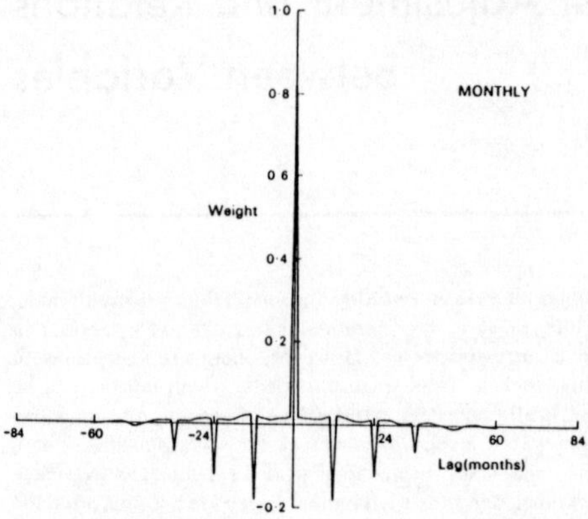

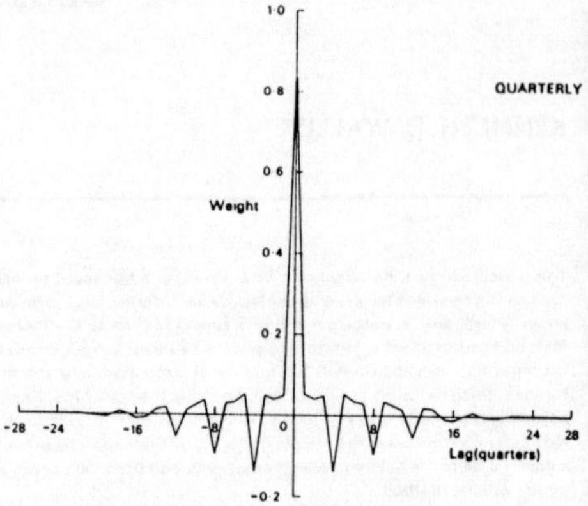

This article studies the effect of official seasonal adjustment procedures on the relations between series. For the present purposes, "official" means the U.S. Bureau of the Census Method II, Variant X-11 [22], as modified by the British Central Statistical Office. The view taken is that seasonality in one economic variable is not necessarily an isolated phenomenon, but may be related to the seasonality in other economic variables with which that variable interacts. Thus the seasonal components themselves may contain information about the relationships between series. Various possibilities are considered, and the effects of separate seasonal adjustments on the underlying relationship between two series and on the statistical estimation procedures employed to detect that relationship are investigated. The investigation proceeds by means of a linear filter approximation to the official procedure in Section 2, and by the analysis of artificial data in Section 3, where the actual official method is applied. Some concluding remarks are presented in Section 4.

2. LINEAR FILTERS AND RELATIONS BETWEEN VARIABLES

2.1 An Approximation to the Official Adjustment Procedure

A linear filter approximation to the official adjustment procedure is first presented, and then the characteristics of the actual procedure which are neglected in the approximation are described. Given an original series $\{x_t\}$, the adjusted series is obtained as

$$\overset{a}{x}_t = \sum_{-m}^{m} a_j x_{t-j} \quad (a_j = a_{-j}) \tag{2.1}$$

and the linear filter or adjustment coefficients $\{a_j\}$ summarize the following steps (a monthly series is assumed, and "moving average" is abbreviated m.a.):

a. Compute the differences between the original series and a centered 12-term m.a. (a 2 × 12 m.a., that is, a 2-term average of a 12-term average), as a first estimate of the seasonal and irregular components.
b. Apply a weighted 5-term m.a. to each month separately (a 3 × 3 m.a.), to obtain an estimate of the seasonal component.
c. Adjust these seasonal components to sum to zero (approximately) over any 12-month period by subtracting a centered 12-term m.a. from them.
d. Subtract the adjusted seasonal component from the original series, to give a preliminary seasonally adjusted series.
e. Apply a 9-, 13- or 23-term Henderson m.a. to the seasonally adjusted values, and subtract the resulting trend-cycle series from the original series to give a second estimate of the seasonal and irregular components.
f. Apply a weighted 7-term m.a. (a 3 × 5 m.a.) to each month separately, to obtain a second estimate of the seasonal component.
g. Repeat step (c).
h. Subtract these final estimates of the seasonal component from the original series, giving the seasonally adjusted series.

The net effect of these eight steps is represented as the $2m + 1$ term m.a. given in (2.1), where the "half-length" m is the sum of the half-lengths of the component m.a.'s, namely, 82, 84, or 89, depending on the choice made at (e). In actual practice this choice depends on the relative contributions of the trend-cycle and irregular components to the variability of the preliminary seasonally adjusted series obtained at (d)—the greater the irregular contribution, the longer the moving average used. With quarterly data this choice is not available, and step (e) comprises a 5-term Henderson m.a.; otherwise, replacing centered 12-month m.a.'s by centered 4-quarter m.a.'s where appropriate gives the linear filter approximation for the adjustment of quarterly data ($m = 28$). The coefficients for the monthly ($m = 84$) and quarterly adjustment filters are shown in Figure A.[2] In both illustrations a seasonally adjusted observation is obtained as a moving average of original observations

[2] These coefficients are analogous to the weights for seasonal factor, trend-cycle, and irregular estimates in the present method and the BLS method presented by Young [30].

up to seven years before and after, although the weights attached to the more distant observations are very small.

There are four important features of the official adjustment procedure which are not captured in this representation.

1. *Multiplicative models* are often employed in place of the additive model implicit above. Thus, seasonal components are estimated as average ratios to, rather than average differences from, the trend-cycle, and the result is a set of seasonal adjustment factors which average 100.0% over a year.
2. *Graduation of extreme values* is undertaken in order to improve the estimation of seasonal and trend-cycle components by preventing the moving averages from responding "too much" to a single outlier. Each value of a preliminary estimated irregular component is compared to the standard deviation, σ, computed over a moving 5-year period. Values between $1\frac{1}{2}\sigma$ and $2\frac{1}{2}\sigma$ distant from 0.0 (100.0 for multiplicative models) are weighted, decreasing linearly from full weight at $1\frac{1}{2}\sigma$ to zero weight at $2\frac{1}{2}\sigma$, and values outside $(-2\frac{1}{2}\sigma, +2\frac{1}{2}\sigma)$ are discarded as extreme. The original series is then modified by adding this graduated irregular component back to the other two components, and trend-cycle and seasonal components are reestimated. The new irregular component is studied for extreme values once again, and after this second modification of the original series, final estimates of the trend-cycle and seasonal are developed. Thus steps (a)—(h) or their multiplicative equivalents are followed three times, each time beginning with a slightly different input series; the choice of $1\frac{1}{2}$ and $2\frac{1}{2}$ as σ limits is in practice optional, and if these limits were set sufficiently wide, no irregular component values would be considered extreme, and identical calculations would result at each of the three iterations.
3. *Calendar-year totals* of the adjusted series are constrained to equal the calendar-year totals of the original series by making a further adjustment to the output from step (h). This could be done by simply adding one-twelfth of the discrepancy to each month's figure, but the actual corrections are smoothed by a piecewise cubic to avoid discontinuities at year-ends.
4. *End-corrections* are necessary, since seven years of data on either side of an observation to be adjusted are never available; hence, asymmetrical "equivalent" moving averages are constructed. This general heading covers the important problem of the adjustment of current observations, and the possible need to revise estimated or extrapolated seasonal factors as subsequent observations become available. That problem is not considered in this article, where the focus of interest is the econometric analysis of historical time series. Nevertheless, in Section 3 it is assumed that a limited series of original observations is available over, say, 15 years, and a corresponding adjusted series is required over the whole period.

These four features will be of no further concern in Section 2 of this paper, but are described here to emphasize those elements of the official procedure to be used in Section 3 that the linear filter approximation does not capture.[3]

[3] "Trading-day" corrections also feature in practical seasonal adjustment programs, variations in the number of working days per month having an impact on certain 'flow' variables, and changes in the day of the week on which accounts are closed being relevant for certain 'stock' variables. In the Census Bureau method, the necessary corrections can be either imposed *a priori* or estimated by regression; for the present purposes it is assumed that any required corrections have been made.

2.2 Filtering a Single Time Series

The properties of the linear filter (2.1) can be described in a number of ways, and it is convenient to introduce some further time series concepts and notation. The generating function or z-transform of a sequence $\{a_j\}$ is defined as

$$A(z) = \sum a_j z^j.$$

The backward shift or lag operator L is defined by $L^j x_t = x_{t-j}$, hence (2.1) may be written

$$x_t^a = A(L)x_t.$$

The effect of the filter on particular frequencies ω of the input series is given by the frequency response function

$$A(\omega) = \sum a_j e^{-i\omega j} = |A(\omega)|e^{i\theta(\omega)}.$$

$|A(\omega)|$ represents the gain of the filter and $\theta(\omega)$ the phase shift; the latter is zero for the symmetric moving averages considered here, as $A(\omega)$ is real:

$$A(\omega) = a_0 + 2\sum_{j=1}^{m} a_j \cos \omega j.$$

The autocovariances of a zero-mean stationary time series are given by

$$\gamma_k = E(x_t x_{t-k}), \quad \gamma_k = \gamma_{-k},$$

with generating function

$$\Gamma(z) = \sum \gamma_k z^k.$$

The autocorrelation coefficients γ_k/γ_0, $k = 0, 1, \cdots$ give the correlogram of the series. The autocovariance generating function of a filtered series is obtained from that of the input series and the coefficients of the filter as

$$\Gamma(z)^a = A(z)\Gamma(z)A(z^{-1}). \tag{2.2}$$

The spectral density function is given by

$$f(\omega) = \frac{1}{2\pi}\sum \gamma_k e^{-ik\omega} = \frac{1}{2\pi}\Gamma(e^{-i\omega}),$$

thus the spectra of the original and filtered series are related by

$$f^a(\omega) = |A(\omega)|^2 f(\omega).$$

The squared gain $|A(\omega)|^2$, or transfer function of the filter, represents the extent to which the contribution of the component of frequency ω to the total variance of the series is modified by the action of the filter, and the transfer function of the monthly filter is plotted in Figure B.[4] It is seen that the filter completely removes the seasonal frequencies $\pi k/6$, $k = 1, \cdots, 6$, all of them being treated equally. Of course if a particular seasonal pattern can be adequately represented by sine and cosine waves at fewer than six seasonal frequencies,[5] then the filter is in effect overadjusting by unnecessarily modifying certain frequencies.

[4] Similar functions are calculated for two other seasonal adjustment procedures by Hext [13].

[5] For an example, see Brown, *et al.* [1].

B. Transfer Function of Monthly Filter

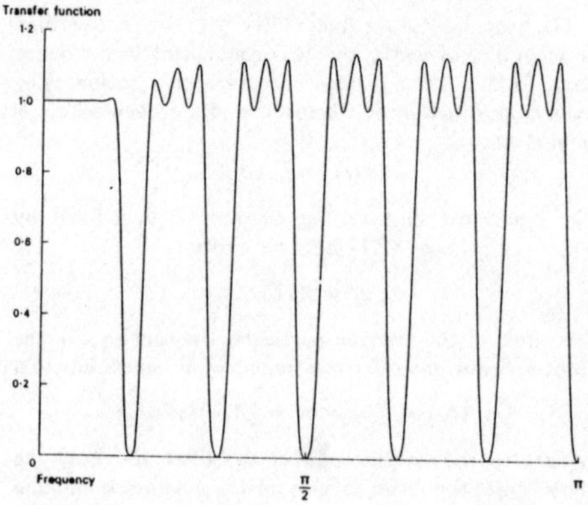

In the time domain the effect of the quarterly version of the filter is illustrated in Figure C, which compares the correlograms of original and filtered series, computed as in (2.2), for three simple examples. The first is a "white noise" or independent input series, with $\gamma_k = 0$ for $k \neq 0$; the resulting "adjusted" series has small positive autocorrelation coefficients at lags of 1–3, 5–7, $\cdots$ quarters, and somewhat larger negative correlations between observations 4, 8, $\cdots$ quarters apart. The second illustration uses as input series the familiar first-order autoregression or AR(1) process, with autocorrelation coefficients $\rho^{|k|}$, and the correlograms when $\rho = 0.7$ are shown in the central panel of Figure C. The moving average increases the autocorrelations overall, inducing little seasonal effect. As ρ decreases from this value, the picture moves towards that of the first illustration, thus when $\rho = 0.5$, the autocorrelations at multiples of 4 lags are negative, though small. The final example takes the simple AR(4) process

$$x_t = \rho x_{t-4} + \epsilon_t,$$

for which the autocorrelation coefficient is zero unless k is an integer multiple of 4, in which case it is $\rho^{k/4}$. It can be seen from the final panel of Figure C (where $\rho = 0.9$) that the autocorrelation at lags 4, 8, $\cdots$ is reduced, but substantial autocorrelation at all other lags is introduced by the moving average procedure. The first-order autocorrelation coefficient is almost equal to the fourth; indeed, for $\rho \leq 0.65$, the largest coefficient is the first, which might result in a filtered fourth-order scheme being identified as a first-order scheme.

The correlogram values at $k = 1$ are the (asymptotic) expected values of least squares coefficients when fitting a first-order autoregesssive model. Thus if the correct model, as used in the second illustration, is

$$x_t = \rho x_{t-1} + \epsilon_t,$$

then the filtered data give

$$x_t^a = \rho x_{t-1}^a + \epsilon_t^a,$$

and the least squares coefficient $\sum x_t^a x_{t-1}^a / \sum x_{t-1}^{a^2}$ provides an asymptotically biased estimate of ρ, for although x_{t-1} and ϵ_t are independent, the same is not true for the moving averages x_{t-1}^a and ϵ_t^a. The extent of the asymptotic bias is given by the difference between the two correlogram values at $k = 1$, and is reported for a range of values of ρ and both monthly and quarterly versions in Table 1. This indicates that the parameter ρ will always tend to be overestimated (asymptotically). However, the opposite is true when the simple fourth-order autoregression

C. Correlograms of Filtered Series

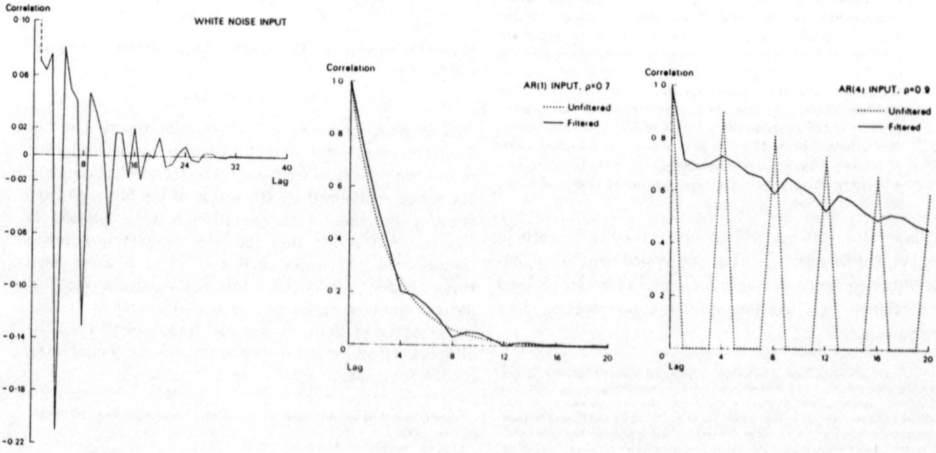

is considered, as suggested by the comparison at $k = 4$ in the final panel of Figure C; the parameter estimate calculated from filtered data is downward biased, and this applies for all values of ρ.

1. Asymptotic Bias in Estimates of First Order Autoregression from Filtered Data

Filter	ρ									
	−.9	−.7	−.5	−.3	−.1	.1	.3	.5	.7	.9
Monthly (m = 84)	.033	.011	.013	.018	.024	.029	.033	.037	.036	.019
Quarterly	.184	.110	.075	.062	.066	.076	.080	.070	.047	.017

The same effects as those described in the preceding paragraphs are obtained with the monthly filter, provided that 4 is replaced by 12 at appropriate points in the discussion.

2.3 Relations Between Variables

The relation between two variables is represented by the distributed lag model, familiar in econometrics, of the general form

$$y_t = \textstyle\sum_0^\infty \beta_j x_{t-j} + u_t. \qquad (2.3)$$

It is assumed that x_t and u_s are independent for all t and s, and the relationship between y and x is generally represented as a *one-sided* time invariant filter, as indicated. The sequence of distributed lag coefficients $\{\beta_j\}$ is required to converge to zero at some suitable rate for theoretical reasons, and further restrictions are often imposed for practical estimation purposes, such as requiring the coefficients to be functions of a small number of parameters. If the coefficients are all positive, an "average lag" is given by $\sum j\beta_j/\sum \beta_j$, and estimates of this quantity are often reported in empirical work.

Following previous notational conventions, the model can be written

$$y_t = \sum \beta_j L^j x_t + u_t = B(L)x_t + u_t$$

and the distributed lag frequency response function is

$$B(\omega) = \sum \beta_j e^{-ij\omega}.$$

Introducing the cross-covariance function

$$\gamma_{yx}(k) = E(y_t x_{t-k}) \quad \text{(independent of } t)$$

and the spectral density functions

$$f_{yx}(\omega) = \frac{1}{2\pi}\sum \gamma_{yx}(k)e^{-ik\omega}, \qquad f_{xx}(\omega) = \frac{1}{2\pi}\sum \gamma_{xx}(k)e^{-ik\omega},$$

then

$$f_{yx}(\omega) = B(\omega)f_{xx}(\omega).$$

Assuming now that the two series are adjusted or filtered, possibly using different filters

$$y_t^a = A_y(L)y_t, \quad x_t^a = A_x(L)x_t,$$

then the relation between the adjusted variables is

$$y_t^a = \frac{A_y(L)B(L)}{A_x(L)} x_t^a + A_y(L)u_t,$$

i.e.,

$$y_t^a = \sum \beta_j^* x_{t-j}^a + u_t^a,$$

where

$$B^*(L) = \frac{A_y(L)B(L)}{A_x(L)}. \qquad (2.4)$$

Although $B(L)$ is one-sided, $B^*(L)$ is in general doubly infinite. The spectral functions for filtered data are

$$f_{yx}^a(\omega) = A_y(\omega)\overline{A_x(\omega)}f_{yx}(\omega), \quad f_{xx}^a(\omega) = |A_x(\omega)|^2 f_{xx}(\omega),$$

and the frequency domain expression corresponding to (2.4) is

$$B^*(\omega) = \frac{A_y(\omega)B(\omega)}{A_x(\omega)}, \qquad (2.5)$$

which is not defined at seasonal frequencies. It is seen that the effect of the filtering operations is to change the lag function to $B^*(L)$ and the error term to u_t^a. Of course if the same linear filter adjustment procedure is applied to both series ($A_y = A_x$), then the relationship between them is not changed, and the only effect is on the error term—if u_t is nonautocorrelated, then u_t^a is a high-order moving average process, and least squares estimates with adjusted data will not be fully efficient.[6] This is virtually the situation which applies in this section, for the adjustment procedure under consideration amounts to the application of the same linear filter to both series.[7]

A further consequence of converting an independent u-series to an autocorrelated u^a-series is that the usual formula for calculating the covariance matrix of the estimated coefficients is invalid when applied to adjusted data. As indicated by Malinvaud [15, Sect. 13.5], whether the application of the standard least squares formula leads to an underestimate or overestimate of the actual variances depends on the product of the autocorrelation coefficients of the error term and the explanatory variable. The first panel of Figure C indicates that if u is an independent series, then u^a has small positive autocorrelation coefficients at lags of 1–3, 5–7, ···

[6] This corresponds to the case discussed by Thomas and Wallis [26, Sect. 3], where the loss in efficiency due to the unnecessary inclusion of seasonal variables in a regression equation is evaluated. In the framework introduced by Watson [29], the lower bound to the efficiency of least squares estimates with adjusted data is zero, being attained when x is composed only of seasonal harmonics, so that the filter not only produces an autocorrelated error term but also annihilates the explanatory variable!

[7] The only departure from this lies in the choice of a 9-, 13-, or 23-term weighted moving average at Step (e), with monthly data, and different choices for the x and y series would be made if the relative contributions of the irregular components of the two series differed substantially. The distributed lag functions found in empirical work are generally very smooth, hence the irregular component of x contributes relatively little to irregularities in y, the main source being the random error term u. Thus the longer options will tend to be selected the greater the relative variance of u, or the proportion of variance in y unexplained by x (assuming u to be white noise). Nevertheless the overall differences between the three options at this stage are very small, this being only one of many steps in the procedure. The main effect is on the rate of decline of the transfer function to the value of 0 at the seasonal frequencies from the value of 1 at frequencies $\pi/30$ on either side (see Figure B), but even here there is little variation, and consequently B^* is very close to B even when one filter has $m = 82$ and the other $m = 89$.

quarters, offset by rather larger negative coefficients at lags of 4, 8, $\cdots$ quarters. Since an adjusted x-series will typically exhibit positive autocorrelation, with low-order coefficients dominating, in determining the net effect on the variance matrix some canceling will occur. Thus the overall effect may be positive or negative but is likely to be small, so that in this situation the standard inference procedures are unlikely to go seriously awry when applied to adjusted data.

A simple case in which B^* differs from B, corresponding to one which is often found in empirical work, occurs when the explanatory variable is nonseasonal and hence is not adjusted. Examples are found with prices or interest rates as explanatory variables, displaying no seasonality, while the dependent variable is used in its adjusted form, seasonality arising from the error term. Thus $A_x(L) = 1$ and (2.4) becomes

$$B^*(L) = A_y(L)B(L).$$

The estimated relationship differs from the true relationship, and an illustration of the distortion is given in Figure D, where the original distributed lag function is the familiar geometrically declining function, $B(L) = 1/(1 - \lambda L)$, with $\lambda = 0.7$, and $A_y(L)$ is the quarterly adjustment filter. While $B^*(L)$ appears to be longer and flatter than $B(L)$ for positive lags, the most striking features are the pronounced seasonal dips in the new lag function, and the coefficients which appear at negative lags and which might suggest to the unwary that x_{t+j} influences y_t. A simpler example is obtained if the original model is static [$B(L) = 1$], whereupon adjusting y produces a "dynamic" model. As already seen, these distortions can be avoided by applying the same filter to both or neither of the series, and which course is adopted depends on the postulated nature of the error term. It is assumed in this case that u is seasonal, this being the source of the seasonality in y, and so direct estimation (say by ordinary least squares) using the original data will not be fully efficient. The efficient estimator is a generalized least squares-type estimator, which is usually implemented in the time domain by applying OLS to transformed data, the transformation being that required to convert $\{u_t\}$ to an independent series. Thus to the extent that the adjustment filter deseasonalizes u, adjusted data provide more efficient estimates.[8] Note that in order to accomplish these objectives, the same filter is applied to both series irrespective of their nature. Although the success of this procedure requires successful adjustment of the unobservable error term, in the present context of linear models and methods this is achieved whenever the y series is successfully adjusted.

[8] It is interesting that in this case there does not appear to be a regression counterpart, for if the true regression model is $y = X\beta + D\alpha + u$, where D is a matrix of seasonal variables, but these are erroneously excluded and y is simply regressed on the X-variables, then the resulting coefficient estimates are not only unbiased but also efficient when D and X are orthogonal, that is when X is nonseasonal.

D. Distributed Lag Function for Adjusted Y-Series

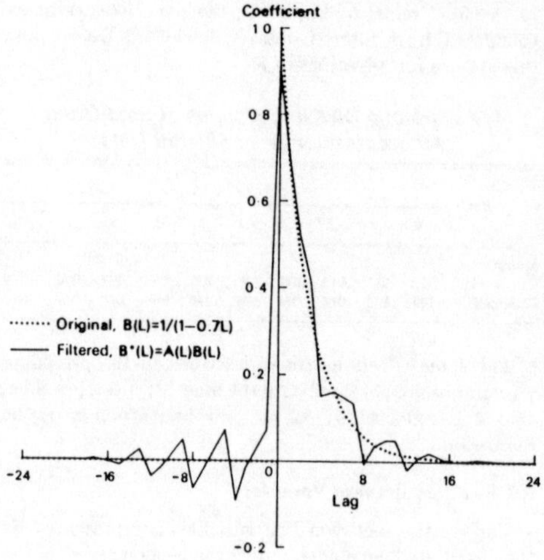

2.4 Seasonal and Nonseasonal Components of the x-Variable

To analyze further the possible effects of seasonal adjustment on the various relations between series, the notion that the different components of the two series may be related differently is introduced, following Nerlove [19]: "It is plausible, for example, that a manufacturer deciding on inventory levels will react somewhat differently to a change in sales he regards as being purely seasonal in character than he will to one he regards as more permanent or longer lasting or one he regards as exceptionally ephemeral." For present purposes the x-variable is divided into two unobservable components, the seasonal and other-than-seasonal components,

$$x_t = x_t^o + x_t^s,$$

and the distributed lag model is written

$$y_t = \sum \beta_{1j} x_{t-j}^o + \sum \beta_{2j} x_{t-j}^s + u_t. \qquad (2.6)$$

(It might be assumed that the second term gives the seasonal component of y, and the first term the rest, but little is gained by separating these, which would ignore the role of the error term.) Assuming that x^o and x^s are uncorrelated, the spectral density function of x can be similarly split up,

$$f_{xx}(\omega) = f_{xx}^o(\omega) + f_{xx}^s(\omega),$$

whereupon

$$f_{yx}(\omega) = B_1(\omega) f_{xx}^o(\omega) + B_2(\omega) f_{xx}^s(\omega).$$

As before, the filtered series obey the relation

$$y_t^a = \sum \beta_j^* x_{t-j}^a + u_t^a,$$

but now

$$B^*(\omega) = \frac{A_y(\omega)}{A_x(\omega)}\left(\frac{f^{o}_{xx}(\omega)}{f_{xx}(\omega)}B_1(\omega) + \frac{f^{s}_{xx}(\omega)}{f_{xx}(\omega)}B_2(\omega)\right). \quad (2.7)$$

This provides an extension of (2.5), which represents the special case $B_1 = B_2$. The situation discussed in the preceding paragraph arises when $f^s_{xx}(\omega) = 0$. One further special case is now discussed.

If $B_2 = 0$, then the seasonal component of x is truly noise, being unrelated to y. In terms of observable variables, (2.6) now becomes

$$y_t = \sum \beta_{1j}x_{t-j} + (u_t - \sum \beta_{1j}x^s_{t-j}), \quad (2.8)$$

which is of the standard errors-in-variables form. Whether y is seasonal (which depends on u), setting $B_2 = 0$ in (2.7) indicates that the relation between the observed variables provides underestimates of B_1. If no adjustment is made, then the observed variables give the relation

$$B(\omega) = \frac{f_{yx}(\omega)}{f_{xx}(\omega)} = B_1(\omega)\left(\frac{1}{1 + f^{s}_{xx}(\omega)/f^{o}_{xx}(\omega)}\right)$$

where f^s_{xx}/f^o_{xx} is the noise-to-signal ratio for x. Thus estimates of B_1 obtained by replacing f_{yx} and f_{xx} by their sample equivalents are inconsistent. An obvious possibility is the adjustment of x so that the actual regressor is "closer" to the true explanatory variable; however, this does not entirely work. From (2.7), the observed relation between y and x^a is then

$$B^*(\omega) = B_1(\omega)\frac{f^{o}_{xx}(\omega)}{A_x(\omega)f_{xx}(\omega)}, \quad (2.9)$$

and since $f^a_{xx}(\omega) = |A_x(\omega)|^2 f_{xx}(\omega)$, whether the ratio on the right side is close to 1 depends on (a) whether $A_x(\omega) \simeq A^2_x(\omega)$, which is approximately true since A is in general close to either 0 or 1, and (b) whether $f^a_{xx}(\omega) \simeq f^o_{xx}(\omega)$. This raises the general question of how "good" the seasonal adjustment is, and although not much can be said in the absence of specific time series models, it is clear that the relationship will not hold exactly, for $x^a = Ax^o + A\dot{x}^s \neq x^o$.

In (2.6), the distributed lag function relating the observable variables is a hybrid, whether or not the adjustment assumed in (2.7) is applied. While it might be convenient to assume that B^* is given by B_2 at seasonal frequencies and by B_1 elsewhere, i.e., that the ratios f^o_{xx}/f_{xx} and f^s_{xx}/f_{xx} are accordingly zero or one, this can only be an approximation. In practice, there is not a single seasonal frequency but a narrow band of frequencies around $k\pi/6$ at which seasonal effects are manifested. This also applies to the models of seasonal components introduced by Hannan [12] and Grether and Nerlove [9], which moreover have non-zero power at all frequencies; on the other hand the typical spectral shape (see [8]) which might represent x^o certainly has power at seasonal frequencies. Nevertheless an analysis at separate frequencies with unadjusted data might indicate whether B_1 and B_2 differ substantially, although a sample of the size common in applied econometrics might not offer sufficient resolution.

For adjusted data, the lag function is given by (2.7), with attendant difficulties and distortions already discussed. As before, some distortion can be avoided by using either the same adjustment filter ($A_x = A_y$) or none at all, and which course is adopted depends, for reasons of efficiency, on the nature of the error term. This can be assessed by tests such as that described by Wallis [28] or, more generally, by means of the cumulated periodogram of regression residuals (see Durbin [6]). The observation that were the unobservable x^o and x^s suddenly to become available then (2.6) could be estimated directly (either as it stands or taking x^o and x^s separately, for they are assumed independent) might suggest that the components x^o and x^s be replaced by their estimates x^a and $(x - x^a)$. However, not only are these estimates inexact, as indicated above, but the assumed independence of the components, used in deriving (2.7), is not reproduced in the estimates.[9] The adjusted series has spectral density function $|A(\omega)|^2 f_{xx}(\omega)$, that of the estimated seasonal component is $|1 - A(\omega)|^2 f_{xx}(\omega)$, and their cross-spectrum is $A(\omega)\{1 - A(\omega)\}f_{xx}(\omega)$,[10] which is, however, small except within $\pi/30$ on either side of the six seasonal frequencies (monthly data).

Implicit in (2.6) is the assumption that, while the components x^o and x^s are unobservable by the investigator, they are nevertheless known to the economic agent, and form the basis of his separate reactions. However, in some situations it might be more plausible to assume that the components are equally not observed by the economic agent, who consequently has to form his own estimates; such an assumption seems more in keeping with the previously cited quotation from Nerlove [19]. Thus actual decisions are based on estimates of the seasonal and nonseasonal components, calculated from the observed past of the series in a manner which can be represented as a *one-sided* filtering operation, current estimates being based on current and past data. Writing $C(L)$ for the agent's "adjustment" filter, so that

$$\hat{x}^o_t = C(L)x_t = \sum_0^\infty c_j x_{t-j}, \quad \hat{x}^s_t = \{1 - C(L)\}x_t,$$

then replacing the unobserved components in (2.6) by these estimates yields the following relation between observable variables:

$$y_t = [B_1(L)C(L) + B_2(L)\{1 - C(L)\}]x_t + u_t.$$

This can be regarded as a generalization of the simple adaptive expectations model, which arises when $B_1(L) = \beta$, $B_2(L) = 0$, and $C(L)$ is the exponentially

[9] This precludes the use of x^s as an instrumental variable in the errors-in-variables problem (2.8), for although it is clearly correlated with x, it is not independent of x^s.

[10] Note from Figure B that erroneously assuming independence and calculating the spectrum of the estimated seasonal component as $\{1 - A^2(\omega)\}f_{xx}(\omega)$ would result in some negative values.

weighted moving average operator. The overall effect is a one-sided lag function of the initial form (2.2), though rather complex. Separate estimation of B_1 and B_2 would require knowledge of C, or an assumption about the prediction method applied. For the "official" adjusted series x^a to be of use, it would be necessary to assume that the two filters produced similar results, or that the economic agent reacted to the current value of the official seasonally adjusted series, re-introducing considerations of end-corrections and one-sided m.a.'s previously discussed.

In Section 3 the linear filter approximation is replaced by the official adjustment procedure, and the various cases discussed in the preceding paragraphs are constructed from artificial time series.

3. A SIMULATION STUDY

In this section we describe simulation experiments carried out by generating data according to the various models discussed in Sections 2.3 and 2.4, adjusting the series where appropriate by the official procedure described in Section 2.1, and comparing the results of estimation using adjusted and unadjusted data.

A single x-process is used, namely that designed by Grether and Nerlove [9] and employed by Stephenson and Farr [25]:

$$x_t = \frac{(1 + 0.8L)}{(1 - 0.95L)(1 - 0.75L)} \zeta_t + \frac{(1 + 0.6L)}{(1 - 0.9L^{12})} \eta_t + \xi_t,$$

where $\{\zeta_t\}$, $\{\eta_t\}$, $\{\xi_t\}$ are mutually uncorrelated normally distributed random variables, with variances chosen so that the three terms have variances 8.5, 1.0, and 0.5, respectively. Where separate components are required, the second term is taken as the seasonal component x_t^s, and the first and third terms as x_t^o. While it is conceptually helpful to keep the three components separate, by giving the rational lag operators a common denominator $(1 - 0.95L)(1 - 0.75L)(1 - 0.9L^{12})$ it can be seen that the x-process has a standard autoregressive-moving average representation, of order (14, 14), although one subject to considerable restrictions on its parameters. The effective sample size is 180, corresponding to 15 years of monthly data, and each experiment consists of 50 replications, in each of which a new x-series is generated. On inspecting the x-series, it is immediately clear that the seasonal pattern changes much more rapidly than is observed in practice. This feature could be removed by making the coefficient of 0.9 in the x_t^s lag operator much closer to 1, but it presents no difficulty in the present circumstances since the adjustment procedure is designed to cope with changing seasonal patterns; nevertheless it would render useless any comparison with simple dummy variable methods, which assume a fixed seasonal pattern. The adjustment procedure is applied incorporating all the features omitted from the linear approximation as described earlier. Thus the filter is truly symmetric only in the eighth of our fifteen years, for only then are there seven years of data on either side of an observation, and the adjustment procedure is entirely one-sided for the first and last observations. Since the multiplicative form is used, a constant term is added to the model presented above, in order to ensure that the series is positive-valued. The estimated spectrum of the x-process, calculated by averaging the periodograms of the fifty series, and the implied transfer function of the seasonal adjustment procedure are presented in Figure E. The latter is calculated as the ratio of the "before" and "after" estimated spectral density functions, thus the spectrum presented on the left of Figure E is the denominator of this ratio. The actual transfer function differs from the linear filter approximation (Figure B) in not reaching zero at seasonal frequencies, although the correspondence is close.

The distributed lag functions used are the simple geometric $1/(1 - \lambda L)$, and an inverted V (see [5]), beginning with $\beta_1 = \frac{1}{12}$, increasing linearly to $\beta_6 = 6/12$,

E. Estimated Spectral Density and Adjustment Transfer Function for Grether-Nerlove Model

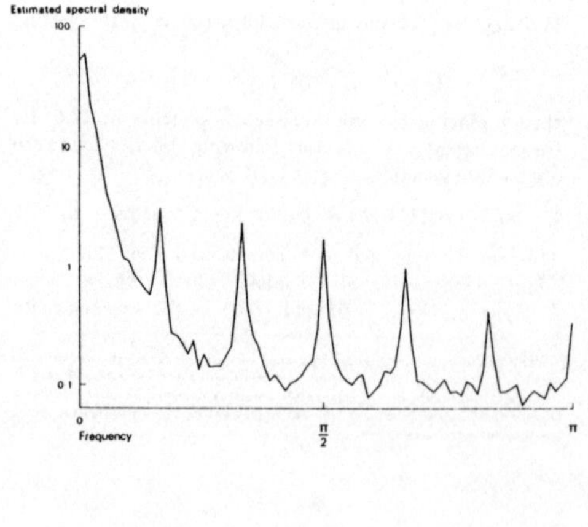

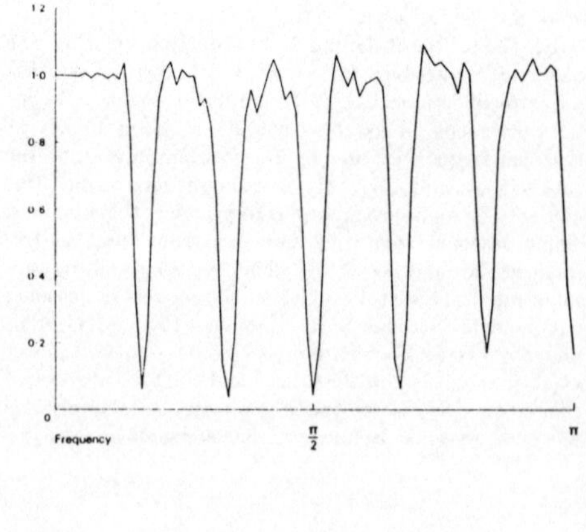

and decreasing to $\beta_{11} = \frac{1}{12}$. The independent random error term ϵ_t has unit variance throughout. For a parameter θ, the mean and standard deviation of the 50 estimates, $\bar{\hat{\theta}}$ and SD$(\hat{\theta})$ are reported, thus $\bar{\hat{\theta}} - \theta$ is an estimate of the bias $E(\hat{\theta}) - \theta$, with standard error SD$(\hat{\theta})/\sqrt{50}$. In some cases the inconsistency plim $(\hat{\theta}) - \theta$ has been evaluated to provide a yardstick for the finite sample results. The estimation methods employed are ordinary least squares (OLS) and the spectral distributed lag estimator (see [11]). In all cases an intercept term is estimated, although its value is not reported.

3.1 Experiment A

$$y_t = B(L)x_t + \epsilon_t$$

We begin with the general case of Section 2.3, and consider the adjustment of both x and y series.

(i) $B(L) = \beta/(1 - \lambda L)$, $\beta = 1.0$, $\lambda = 0.7$.

Equation estimated: $y_t = \lambda y_{t-1} + \beta x_t + u_t$.

This is the familiar geometric lag function for which OLS provides inconsistent estimates, the estimated equation having a first-order moving average error $u_t = \epsilon_t - \lambda\epsilon_{t-1}$. The probability limits of OLS estimates are 1.093 and .666, and the results with the original data (sample size 180) correspond very closely, as shown in Table 2. The effect of the seasonal adjustment is a small increase in these biases, although the observed biases are smaller than the asymptotic biases calculated assuming that the linear filter approximation is employed.

2. Experiment A(i), Geometric Lag Function

Statistic	Parameter			
	β	λ	β	λ
	Original data		Adjusted data	
Mean estimate	1.093	.663	1.108	.658
Bias	.093	−.037	.108	−.042
SD	.051	.019	.057	.020
Inconsistency	.093	−.034	.146[a]	−.049[a]

[a] Calculated for linear filter.

(ii) $B(L) = \sum_{j=1}^{11} \beta_j L^j$, $\{\beta_j\} = \frac{1}{12}\{1, 2, \cdots, 6, 5, \cdots, 1\}$.

The equation is estimated by OLS ignoring information about the shape of the distribution, and the results are presented in Table 3. The original data produce unbiased estimates, as expected. Although the estimated biases with adjusted data are slightly greater, the estimates remain unbiased overall. The variances increase, thus the linear filter result that adjustment in this case reduces efficiency without inducing bias is reproduced by the official adjustment procedure.[11] The final row of Table 3 presents the means of the coefficient standard errors calculated by applying the usual OLS formula in each replication. A comparison with the standard deviation of the estimated coefficients indicates a slight tendency for the standard errors to underestimate, but overall the correspondence is close, as suggested in Section 2.3.

3.2 Experiment B

$$y_t = B(L)x_t^o + x_t^s$$

This gives an example of a nonseasonal explanatory variable and a seasonal dependent variable, being the special case discussed in Section 2.3. The seasonal component of the Grether-Nerlove model serves as the "unobservable" error term, while x_t^o is the observed explanatory variable.

(i) $B(L) = \beta/(1 - \lambda L)$, $\beta = 1.0$, $\lambda = 0.7$.

Equations estimated: (a) $y_t = \lambda y_{t-1} + \beta x_t^o + u_{1t}$
(b) $y_t^a = \lambda y_{t-1}^a + \beta x_t^o + u_{2t}$
(c) $y_t^a = \lambda y_{t-1}^a + \beta (x_t^o)^a + u_{3t}$.

Again OLS estimates of Equation (a) are inconsistent, and from the results given in Table 4 we see that the probability limits once more provide a good guide to the finite sample results. Adjusting only the dependent variable, the sole seasonal variable, retains substantial biases, although the signs are reversed and the variance is somewhat reduced. Finally, adjusting both variables, despite the nonseasonal nature of the explanatory variable, substantially reduces the biases and further reduces the variances to about one quarter of the original variances.

(ii) $B(L) = \sum_{j=1}^{11} \beta_j L^j$, $\{\beta_j\} = \frac{1}{12}\{1, 2, \cdots, 6, 5, \cdots, 1\}$.

The results presented in Table 5 show that here the original data produce unbiased estimates, as in Experiment A(ii). If just the dependent variable is adjusted, conforming to a commonly-observed practice, significant biases result, the general tendency being a flattening of the inverted V shape. Adjusting both variables not only restores unbiasedness but also reduces the variances, in accordance with the linear filter results, noting that as the error term is seasonal, the efficient estimator is a generalized least squares-type estimator.

3.3 Experiment C

Errors-in-variables:

$$y_t = B_1(L)x_t^o + u_t.$$

Turning to the situations discussed in Section 2.4, the case $B_2 = 0$ is first considered. The observed explanatory variable exhibits seasonal variation, but the seasonal

[11] A substantially greater increase in the variances is observed when simple dummy variables are used in conjunction with the original data. However, the present x-series exhibits a changing seasonal pattern, as noted above, and so simple dummy variable adjustment is not appropriate. Studies with more extensive sets of seasonal variables (such as those employed by Stephenson and Farr [25]) have not been performed, for the main point of interest is the behavior of the official procedure, nor has an x-series with a constant pattern been constructed, for such a series is somewhat unrealistic.

3. Experiment A(ii), Inverted V Lag Function

Statistic	β_1	β_2	β_3	β_4	β_5	β_6	β_7	β_8	β_9	β_{10}	β_{11}	$\Sigma\beta_j$
Original data												
Mean estimate	.082	.173	.235	.348	.430	.480	.417	.324	.258	.166	.084	2.997
Bias	−.001	.006	−.015	.015	.013	−.020	.000	−.009	.008	−.001	.001	
SD	.063	.078	.076	.081	.079	.069	.049	.080	.069	.065	.061	
Adjusted data												
Mean estimate	.089	.166	.254	.325	.434	.473	.400	.350	.249	.155	.103	2.998
Bias	.006	−.001	.004	−.008	.017	−.027	−.017	.017	−.001	−.012	.020	
SD	.072	.095	.100	.113	.102	.085	.081	.110	.092	.094	.087	
Mean std error	.078	.090	.092	.093	.093	.093	.093	.093	.092	.090	.078	

component is unrelated to the dependent variable, which is nonseasonal given the nature of the error term, thus the relative seasonality of x and y is the reverse of that in Experiment B.

(i) $B_1(L)=\beta/(1-\lambda L)$ $\beta=1.0$, $\lambda=0.7$, $u_t=B_1(L)\epsilon_t$.

Estimated equation (original data):

$$y_t = \lambda y_{t-1} + \beta x_t + (\epsilon_t - \beta x_t^s)$$

(adjusted data):

$$y_t = \lambda y_{t-1} + \beta x_t^a + v_t.$$

To focus attention on the errors-in-variables problem, this experiment is run with a first-order autoregressive error term $u_t = \lambda u_{t-1} + \epsilon_t$, to give an estimated equation of the partial adjustment form with independent error, and the results are presented in Table 6. The estimates with the original x-series are badly biased as expected, with $\hat{\beta}$ coming off worst. The estimated average lag $\hat{\lambda}/(1-\hat{\lambda})$ has a mean of 4.3 months, compared with the true value of $2\frac{1}{3}$ months. The use of the adjusted x-series improves matters considerably, reducing the biases to less than one-third of their former values, although they are still by no means negligible. An improvement also occurs in the variance of the estimates. Using x^a as an instrumental variable in estimating the original equation

4. Experiment B(i), Geometric Lag Function, Nonseasonal x

Statistic	β (Original data)	λ (Original data)	β (Adjusted y-series)	λ (Adjusted y-series)	β (Adjusted y and x^a)	λ (Adjusted y and x^a)
Mean estimate	1.067	.675	.928	.720	.991	.702
Bias	.067	−.025	−.072	.020	−.009	.002
SD	.053	.018	.034	.011	.026	.009
Inconsistency	.065	−.022				

achieves results which show slightly greater biases than those obtained when x^a is used directly, although the correspondence is close. The essential elements in determining the biases, namely the covariances of y_{-1} and x^a with the equation's error term, are very similar in the two approaches, given the relatively small seasonal variance, thus this particular instrumental variable has little to commend it (see Footnote 9).

(ii) $B_1(L) = \sum_{j=1}^{11} \beta_j L^j$,

$$\{\beta_j\} = \tfrac{1}{12}\{1, 2, \cdots, 6, 5, \cdots, 1\} \quad u_t = \epsilon_t$$

As shown in Table 7, the original estimates are again badly biased, the inverted V being considerably flattened,

5. Experiment B(ii), Inverted V Lag Function, Nonseasonal x

Statistic	β_1	β_2	β_3	β_4	β_5	β_6	β_7	β_8	β_9	β_{10}	β_{11}	$\Sigma\beta_j$
Original data: y on x^o												
Mean estimate	.078	.173	.273	.333	.402	.483	.421	.325	.247	.177	.088	3.000
Bias	−.005	.006	.023	.000	−.015	−.017	.004	−.008	−.003	.010	.005	
SD	.076	.063	.088	.083	.109	.091	.087	.073	.078	.067	.078	
Adjusted y-series: y^a on x^o												
Mean estimate	.113	.190	.263	.321	.391	.462	.395	.317	.251	.184	.121	3.008
Bias	.030	.023	.013	−.012	−.026	−.038	−.022	−.016	.001	.017	.038	
SD	.040	.034	.028	.033	.039	.042	.031	.036	.037	.033	.043	
Adjusted data: y^a on $(x^o)^a$												
Mean estimate	.085	.175	.259	.329	.413	.487	.411	.330	.253	.164	.093	2.999
Bias	.002	.008	.009	−.004	−.004	−.013	−.006	−.003	.003	−.003	.010	
SD	.034	.034	.031	.036	.030	.042	.032	.043	.040	.031	.045	

6. Experiment C(i), Geometric Lag Function, Nonseasonal y

Statistic	Parameter					
	β	λ	β	λ	β	λ
	Original data		Adjusted data		x^a as instrumental variable	
Mean estimate	.624	.807	.885	.732	.879	.734
Bias	−.376	.107	−.115	.032	−.121	.034
SD	.100	.030	.072	.023	.070	.021

although the total multiplier is surprisingly well-estimated on average. The adjusted x-series (note that the y-series is nonseasonal) achieves a great improvement: taking coefficients singly, only $\hat{\beta}_6$ is significantly biased, although the variances have increased. Thus the ratio on the right side of (2.9) is apparently close to 1 when the official adjustment procedure is applied to this particular x-series.

3.4 Spectral Distributed Lag Estimation

The results to be reported here, based on runs with unadjusted data, are less conclusive. Spectra and cross-spectra are estimated by applying a modified Daniell window to the corresponding periodograms, calculated by a fast Fourier transform algorithm.

First, the "Hannan inefficient" estimator is applied, calculating coefficients as in Hannan [11, Sec. 7] for lags of 0–19 months. The results given in Table 8 are based on the original data of Experiment A(ii), with $B(L) = \sum_{j=1}^{11} \beta_j L^j$, but are not directly comparable to those given in Table 3, where an efficient method and a correct specification were employed.

In general, the method performs moderately well. The overall pattern of coefficients emerges somewhat smoothed, with relatively little noise introduced at lags where the true coefficient is zero. However a number of the individual coefficients appear to be biased, and the sum of the coefficients β_1 to β_{11} of 2.872 underestimates the true value of 3, even neglecting the negative estimates on either side of the inverted V.

The method is then applied to (2.6),

$$y_t = B_1(L)x_t^o + B_2(L)x_t^s + \epsilon_t,$$

where $B_1(L)$ is the geometric lag function ($\beta = 1.0$, $\lambda = 0.7$) and $B_2(L)$ is the inverted V. Estimation of B_1 is attempted by omitting seasonal frequencies from the calculation of distributed lag coefficients using unadjusted data.[12] The periodograms are calculated at frequencies $\pi k/90$, $k = 0, \cdots, 90$, and in smoothing these to obtain spectral estimates prior to calculating $\hat{\beta}$'s, the (seasonal) points $k = 15, 30, \cdots$ together with one point on either side are omitted. Of course this method does not provide efficient estimates of β and λ; the main objective is to see how well the general form of B_1 is estimated.

The results in Table 9 indicate that the general shape of B_1 is reproduced, although the initial values after the first are underestimated and the subsequent geometric decline is correspondingly too slow. The relatively large downward bias at lag 12 suggests that deleting the seasonal frequencies in an attempt to pick out B_1 alone may nevertheless produce seasonal dips in the estimated distribution analogous to those obtained in Figure D. The possibility remains, however, that the Grether-Nerlove x-process is not well suited to an investigation of this particular point, for the seasonal component has spectral peaks not only at seasonal frequencies but also at the origin, and some contamination of the estimate of B_1 may result. In the context of this model an alternative approach is to use adjusted data and regress y on x^a and $x - x^a$ by least squares without constraining the lag functions. The resulting estimate of B_2 is very erratic, the high variances of the estimates corresponding to the relatively small contribution of the seasonal component, but as indicated in Table 10 the estimate of B_1 corresponds a little more closely to the true geometric lag function and the variances are slightly smaller than those of the spectral estimator using unadjusted data, although a direct comparison is not possible since fewer coefficients could be estimated in the OLS approach.

On turning to the "Hannan efficient" estimator (see [11, Sec. 1]) further difficulties emerge. Calculation of spectra and cross-spectra for each individual explanatory variable, in this case each lagged x-value, is required. When these are obtained by the short-cut method of

[12] Frequency-band regression analysis is described by Groves and Hannan [10]. An example of spectral distributed lag estimation in which "seasonal adjustment" is accomplished by omitting bands of seasonal frequencies is presented by Sims [23].

7. Experiment C(ii), Inverted V Lag Function, Nonseasonal y

Statistic	Parameter											
	β_1	β_2	β_3	β_4	β_5	β_6	β_7	β_8	β_9	β_{10}	β_{11}	$\Sigma\beta_j$
	Original data											
Mean estimate	.207	.195	.250	.317	.338	.381	.343	.295	.266	.255	.193	3.010
Bias	.124	.028	.000	−.016	−.079	−.119	−.074	−.038	.016	.058	.110	
SD	.088	.076	.079	.072	.082	.100	.102	.082	.076	.091	.094	
	Adjusted x-series											
Mean estimate	.100	.166	.250	.354	.396	.452	.399	.317	.251	.201	.101	2.987
Bias	.017	−.001	.000	.021	−.021	−.048	−.018	−.016	.001	.034	.018	
SD	.104	.080	.110	.091	.096	.121	.135	.107	.099	.105	.111	

8. Hannan Inefficient Estimates of Inverted V Lag Function

Statistic	Lag																			
	0	1	2	3	4	5	6	7	8	9	10	11	12	13	14	15	16	17	18	19
Mean estimate	−.005	.118	.196	.255	.346	.428	.465	.385	.294	.215	.115	.055	−.007	−.006	−.023	−.009	−.015	−.014	−.026	.006
Bias	−.005	.035	.029	.005	.012	.011	−.035	−.031	−.039	−.035	−.052	−.028	−.007	−.006	−.023	−.009	−.015	−.014	−.026	.006
SD	.099	.104	.075	.096	.094	.092	.081	.106	.087	.086	.093	.086	.085	.082	.088	.087	.089	.089	.078	.084

9. Hannan Inefficient Estimates of "Seasonally Adjusted" Geometric Lag Function

Statistic	Lag																			
	0	1	2	3	4	5	6	7	8	9	10	11	12	13	14	15	16	17	18	19
Mean estimate	1.047	.598	.384	.287	.186	.141	.128	.096	.091	.078	.060	−.006	−.089	−.033	−.003	.019	−.008	.001	.008	.011
Bias	.047	−.102	−.106	−.056	−.054	−.027	.010	.014	.034	.038	.032	−.026	−.103	−.043	−.009	.015	−.012	−.001	.006	.010
SD	.258	.146	.121	.166	.151	.134	.148	.143	.155	.130	.116	.132	.138	.107	.108	.124	.099	.101	.106	.094

10. Regression Estimates of "Seasonally Adjusted" Geometric Lag Function

Statistic	Lag												
	0	1	2	3	4	5	6	7	8	9	10	11	12
Mean estimate	.942	.642	.485	.349	.246	.230	.146	.115	.074	.071	.036	.002	−.029
Bias	−.058	−.058	−.005	.006	.006	.062	.029	.032	.016	.031	.008	−.018	−.043
SD	.130	.108	.109	.097	.121	.099	.113	.104	.106	.116	.122	.111	.105

11. Hannan Efficient Estimates of Inverted V Lag Function

Statistic	Lag												
	0	1	2	3	4	5	6	7	8	9	10	11	12
Mean estimate	.010	.117	.173	.214	.324	.364	.431	.420	.343	.289	.206	.108	−.029
Bias	.010	.033	.006	−.036	−.009	−.053	−.069	.003	.009	.039	.039	.025	−.029
SD	.497	.233	.234	.188	.178	.218	.203	.213	.202	.209	.211	.175	.375

estimating $f_{yx}(\omega)$ and $f_{xx}(\omega)$, and then calculating the cross-spectrum between y_t and x_{t-k} as $e^{ik\omega}f_{yx}(\omega)$ and that between x_{t-j} and x_{t-k} as $e^{i(k-j)\omega}f_{xx}(\omega)$, a significant spurious contemporaneous coefficient ($\hat{\beta}_0$) appears in the estimated lag function. This disappears when separate spectral and cross-spectral estimates for $x_t, x_{t-1}, \ldots, x_{t-12}$ are calculated,[13] as indicated in the results presented in Table 11, which again are based on the original data of Experiment A(ii). Overall, the biases are little different from those given by the Hannan inefficient estimator, and the inverted V is again rather smoothed.[14] But the standard deviations are most striking. Not only are they substantially greater than those obtained in Experiment A(ii) (OLS estimates are best linear unbiased in finite samples in this model), they are also greater than those of the inefficient estimator,[15] notwithstanding differences in the number of coefficients estimated. This feature, together with the high computational burden of this estimator, has precluded further investigation of its behavior.

4. CONCLUSION

The foregoing discussion has considered the problems which arise in estimating a distributed lag relation using seasonally adjusted data. In Section 2 the argument was constructed in terms of linear filters, and various distortions which might result from filtering one or both of the series were described. While most of the results

[13] The author is indebted to Christopher A. Sims for the suggestion that the short-cut method biases $\hat{\beta}_0$ via its biased spectral estimates. Frequency-domain methods treat a series as wrapping around back on itself, and the short-cut method of calculating the cross spectrum between y_t and x_{t-k} implicitly aligns the sequence $y_1, \cdots, y_T$ with the sequency $x_{T-k+1}, \cdots, x_T, x_1, \cdots, x_{T-k}$, creating a bias if the values at the end of the series are substantially different from those at the beginning (as is often the case). This problem does not arise in the direct estimate of the cross-spectrum, for the offending observations are deleted, and the effective sample size becomes $T - k$.

In computing the coefficient estimates, a direct estimate of the OLS residual spectrum is used.

[14] This smoothing of lag functions in the Hannan estimates is present in the simulation results of Cargill and Meyer [4]. They also find that in cases with an autocorrelated error term, the efficient procedure gives little improvement over the inefficient procedure in terms of bias in samples of 100 observations.

[15] E.J. Hannan has pointed out that the number of frequency bands used in computing the estimates is rather larger than would normally be recommended for samples of this size, but recomputing with a much smaller number did not lead to any improvement. However, the present combination of a white noise error and a sharp-peaked regressor spectrum is the worst possible case for the Hannan efficient estimator.

are perfectly general, and not specifically concerned with filters designed for seasonal adjustment, the introduction of spurious "future" coefficients as illustrated in Figure D is a direct consequence of the two-sided nature of the filter under consideration. A one-sided adjustment filter would not produce this particular distortion, and would also enable one to answer the question, "For what autoregressive-moving average input series is the filtered series white noise?" The "optimal" seasonal adjustment of Grether and Nerlove [9], based on the theory of minimum mean-square error extraction and prediction, can indeed produce a one-sided adjustment filter, though the optimal prediction theory argument is not so compelling when parameters have to be estimated from a finite sample of data and, moreover, the correct autoregressive-moving average representation of the series is not known. So to retain practical relevance we concentrated on the official adjustment procedure. In Section 3 the actual official method was applied, in contrast to the linear filter approximation, but the conclusion in the cases studied is that the approximation is a good guide to the performance of the actual nonlinear method. In particular the nonlinearities were not sufficiently pronounced to negate the argument of Section 2 that applying the same linear filter to both series prevents distortion of the lag relationship. The problem of detecting different (non-zero) relations for the seasonal and nonseasonal components requires further investigation; while some success was achieved with the nonseasonal relationship, the particular seasonal component used presented difficulties.

The practical investigator typically has little prior knowledge of the nature of the seasonal relationships, and which of our experimental results is most representative or relevant must be determined in the specific context. The economist's usual *a priori* theorizing, if specifically focussed on short-run adjustment problems, would be helpful in some applications, such as the theory of the behavior of firms. More generally, which of our cases is likely to apply can be determined by examining the x and y series themselves, to see what seasonality they exhibit—this would allow one to discriminate between the cases considered in experiments A, B, and C, for example. Second-stage diagnostic devices such as examination of the residuals of the first estimates, or reestimation subject to high-order autoregressive error terms, then permit further discrimination. As we have seen, filtering or the use of adjusted data is appropriate in some circumstances, although it should be seen more as an adjustment to the model than an adjustment to the data. The indiscriminate use of filters, or the non-availability of unadjusted data, will inevitably lead to mistaken inferences about the strength and dynamic pattern of relationships. Naturally, other techniques such as the use of dummy variables should be included in the list of possible approaches, and it should be noted finally that such variables can be used to relax one particular assumption of the foregoing analysis, namely that the distributed lag relationship is time-invariant. Cases in which the seasonality in y is caused by coefficients changing from season to season remain to be investigated, although some empirical instances have already been noted.[16]

[*Received May 1973. Revised October 1973.*]

REFERENCES

[1] Brown, R.L., Cowley, A.H. and Durbin, J., *Seasonal Adjustment of Unemployment Series*, Studies in Official Statistics, Research Series No. 4, London: HMSO, 1971.

[2] Burman, J.P., "Moving Seasonal Adjustment of Economic Time Series," *Journal of the Royal Statistical Society, Ser. A*, 128, Part 4 (1965), 534–58.

[3] ———, "Moving Seasonal Adjustment of Economic Time Series: Additional Note," *Journal of the Royal Statistical Society, Ser. A*, 129, Part 2 (1966), 274.

[4] Cargill, Thomas F. and Meyer, Robert A., "A Simulation Study of Hannan's Procedures for Estimating a Distributed Lag Process," *Proceedings of the Business and Economic Statistics Section*, American Statistical Association, 1971, 316–23.

[5] de Leeuw, Frank, "The Demand for Capital Goods by Manufactures: A Study of Quarterly Time Series," *Econometrica*, 30 (July 1962), 407–23.

[6] Durbin, J., "Tests for Serial Correlation in Regression Analysis Based on the Periodogram of Least-Squares Residuals," *Biometrika*, 56 (March 1969), 1–15.

[7] Godfrey, Michael D. and Karreman, Herman F., "A Spectrum Analysis of Seasonal Adjustment," in Martin Shubik, ed., *Essays in Mathematical Economics in Honor of Oskar Morgenstern*, Princeton: University Press, 1967, 367–421.

[8] Granger, C.W.J., "The Typical Spectral Shape of an Economic Variable," *Econometrica*, 34 (January 1966), 150–61.

[9] Grether, D.M. and Nerlove, M., "Some Properties of 'Optimal' Seasonal Adjustment," *Econometrica*, 38 (September 1970) 682–703.

[10] Groves, Gordon W. and Hannan, E.J., "Time Series Regression of Sea Level on Weather," *Reviews of Geophysics*, 6 (May 1968), 129–74.

[11] Hannan, E.J., "Regression for Time Series," in Murray Rosenblatt, ed., *Time Series Analysis*, New York: John Wiley and Sons, Inc., 1963, 17–37.

[12] ———, "The Estimation of a Changing Seasonal Pattern," *Journal of the American Statistical Association*, 59 (December 1964), 1063–77.

[13] Hext, George R., "Transfer Functions for Two Seasonal Adjustment Filters," Technical Report No. 3 under NSF Grant GS-142, Institute for Mathematical Studies in the Social Sciences, Stanford University, 1964.

[14] Lovell, Michael C., "Seasonal Adjustment of Economic Time Series and Multiple Regression Analysis," *Journal of the American Statistical Association*, 58 (December 1963), 993–1010.

[15] Malinvaud, E., *Statistical Methods of Econometrics*, Chicago: Rand McNally and Co., 1966.

[16] Modigliani, Franco and Sauerlender, Owen H., "Economic Expectations and Plans of Firms in Relation to Short-Term Forecasting," in *Short-Term Economic Forecasting* (NBER Studies in Income and Wealth, Vol. 17), Princeton: University Press, 1955, 261–351.

[17] Nerlove, Marc, "Spectral Analysis of Seasonal Adjustment Procedures," *Econometrica*, 32 (July 1964), 241–86.

[16] For example, Tony Lancaster has shown that the problems of handling seasonality in the U.S. cement industry example of Wallis [28, Sect. 3.4] can be resolved by considering output-sales-inventory relations which differ between quarters. This approach was used by Modigliani and Sauerlender [16], but they did not complete the analysis of all four quarters.

[18] ———, "A Comparison of a Modified 'Hannan' and the BLS Seasonal Adjustment Filters," *Journal of the American Statistical Association*, 60 (June 1965), 442–91.

[19] ———, "Distributed Lags and Unobserved Components in Economic Time Series," in W. Fellner, *et al.*, *Ten Economic Studies in the Tradition of Irving Fisher*, New York: John Wiley and Sons, Inc., 1967, 127–69.

[20] Rosenblatt, Harry M., "Spectral Analysis and Parametric Methods for the Seasonal Adjustment of Economic Time Series," *Proceedings of the Business and Economic Statistics Section*, American Statistical Association, 1963, 94–133.

[21] ———, "Spectral Evaluation of BLS and Census Revised Seasonal Adjustment Procedures," *Journal of the American Statistical Association*, 63 (June 1968), 472–501.

[22] Shiskin, Julius, Young, Allan H. and Musgrave, John C., *The X-11 Variant of the Census Method II Seasonal Adjustment Program*, Bureau of the Census Technical Paper No. 15 (revised), Washington D.C.: U.S. Department of Commerce, 1967.

[23] Sims, Christopher A., "Are There Exogenous Variables in Short-Run Production Relations?" *Annals of Economic and Social Measurement*, 1 (January 1972), 17–36.

[24] ———, "Seasonality in Regression," Discussion Paper No. 23, Center for Economic Research, University of Minnesota, 1972.

[25] Stephenson, James A. and Farr, Helen T., "Seasonal Adjustment of Economic Data by Application of the General Linear Statistical Model," *Journal of the American Statistical Association*, 67 (March 1972), 37–45.

[26] Thomas, J.J. and Wallis, Kenneth F., "Seasonal Variation in Regression Analysis," *Journal of the Royal Statistical Society, Ser. A*, 134, Part 1 (1971), 57–72.

[27] U.S. Bureau of Labor Statistics, *The B.L.S. Seasonal Factor Method*, Washington, D.C.: U.S. Department of Labor, 1966.

[28] Wallis, Kenneth F., "Testing for Fourth Order Autocorrelation in Quarterly Regression Equations," *Econometrica*, 40 (July 1972), 617–36.

[29] Watson, G.S., "Serial Correlation in Regression Analysis I," *Biometrika*, 42 (December 1955), 327–41.

[30] Young, Allan H., "Linear Approximations to the Census and BLS Seasonal Adjustment Methods," *Journal of the American Statistical Association*, 63 (June 1968), 445–71.

[21]

Modeling Time Series With Calendar Variation

W. R. BELL and S. C. HILLMER*

The modeling of time series data that include calendar variation is considered. Autocorrelation, trends, and seasonality are modeled by ARIMA models. Trading day variation and Easter holiday variation are modeled by regression-type models. The overall model is a sum of ARIMA and regression models. Methods of identification, estimation, inference, and diagnostic checking are discussed. The ideas are illustrated through actual examples.

KEY WORDS: Calendar variation; Trading day variation; Easter holiday variation; ARIMA models; Monthly time series.

1. INTRODUCTION

Suppose we observe a time series Z_t that follows the model (perhaps after transformation)

$$Z_t = f(\mathbf{X}_t;\xi) + N_t. \tag{1.1}$$

Here f is a function of ξ, a vector of parameters, and of $\mathbf{X}_t$, a vector of fixed independent variables observed at time t, and N_t is a noise series. If N_t is white noise, then (1.1) is the familiar linear or nonlinear regression model. However, when one deals with time series, N_t will generally be autocorrelated and frequently nonstationary. Numerous authors have warned against the consequences of using standard regression theory when N_t is autocorrelated, the problem being well established as long ago as Anderson (1954).

In this article we are concerned with the converse problem—that of the effects of ignoring $f(\mathbf{X}_t; \xi)$ when analyzing a time series. In the particular case we consider, $f(\mathbf{X}_t; \xi)$ represents trading day and holiday effects. For this case we illustrate the important points that (a) pure ARIMA models should not be applied blindly to all time series, (b) to ignore known, relevant independent variables is to invite difficulties, and (c) substantial improvements in models can be obtained when relevant independent variables are incorporated in the model.

* W. R. Bell is Mathematical Statistician, U.S. Census Bureau, Washington, DC 20233. S. C. Hillmer is Assistant Professor, School of Business, University of Kansas, Summerfield Hall, Lawrence, KS 66045. This research was partially supported while the authors were participants in the ASA-Census Research Fellowship Program. This program was funded by the U.S. Census Bureau and the National Science Foundation, and their support was instrumental in completing this research. The authors also acknowledge the many stimulating discussions with Census Bureau employees that helped shape the ideas of the research, and they wish to thank the referees and an associate editor for a number of helpful suggestions. The second author was partially supported by the Department of Commerce (Census Bureau) through JSA 81-2.

2. MODEL-BUILDING PROCEDURES

In developing models of the form (1.1) for a specific set of data we follow the three-stage model-building procedure of identification, estimation, and diagnostic checking presented in Box and Jenkins (1976). In (1.1) we assume that N_t follows the ARIMA model

$$\phi(B)\delta(B)N_t = \theta(B)a_t, \tag{2.1}$$

where B is the backshift operator ($BN_t = N_{t-1}$), $\phi(B) = 1 - \phi_1 B - \cdots - \phi_p B^p$ and $\theta(B) = 1 - \theta_1 B - \cdots - \theta_q B^q$ have all their zeros outside the unit circle, $\phi(B)$ and $\theta(B)$ have no common zeroes, $\delta(B)$ is a differencing operator (all zeroes on the unit circle) such as $(1 - B)$ or $(1 - B)(1 - B^{12})$, and $\{a_t\}$ is a sequence of independent, identically distributed (iid) random variables with mean 0 and variance σ^2. Some of the ϕ's and θ's may be 0 or otherwise constrained, so that (2.1) could be a multiplicative seasonal model.

2.1 Model Identification

The regression portion of the model, $f(\mathbf{X}_t; \xi)$, can be identified by consideration of the nature of the independent variables, which in our case are describing the trading day or holiday variation. To identify the noise model (2.1) we first examine the sample autocorrelation function (SACF) of the time series Z_t. In our experience with series containing trading day or holiday variation, examination of the SACF of Z_t is useful for determining the degree of differencing, $\delta(B)$, in N_t. We believe this is so because the effect of the nonstationary N_t on the computed sample autocorrelations dominates the effect of the trading day or holiday variation. In contrast, after Z_t (and thus N_t) has been appropriately differenced, the effect of the differenced N_t on the computed sample autocorrelations no longer dominates the effect of the differenced $f(\mathbf{X}_t; \xi)$. The SACF and sample partial autocorrelation function (SPACF) of the differenced Z_t series are usually confused. At this stage we must at least approximately remove the effects of $f(\mathbf{X}_t; \xi)$ from Z_t. To do this we fit the model

$$\delta(B)Z_t = \delta(B)f(\mathbf{X}_t; \xi) + e_t \tag{2.2}$$

by least squares regression (linear or nonlinear) and examine the SACF and SPACF of the residuals from this regression in order to tentatively identify the noise model. A justification for this procedure is that the sample au-

September 1983, Volume 78, Number 383
Applications Section

tocorrelations and hence the sample partial autocorrelations of the residuals from the least squares fit of (2.2) differ from those of $\delta(B)N_t$ by an amount that converges in probability to zero (see Fuller 1976, p. 399). This procedure is illustrated by two examples later in this article.

2.2 Model Estimation

Combining (1.1) and (2.1), we can write our model as

$$\delta(B)Z_t = \delta(B)f(\mathbf{X}_t; \xi) + \frac{\theta(B)}{\phi(B)} a_t. \qquad (2.3)$$

We can then estimate ξ, ϕ, and θ, in (2.3) by maximum likelihood methods assuming normality of the a_t's We estimate σ^2 by $\hat{\sigma}^2 = (n - r)^{-1} \sum \hat{a}_t^2$ where n is the number of observations less the degree of $\delta(B)\phi(B)$, r is the number of parameters in (2.3), and

$$\hat{a}_t = \hat{\theta}(B)^{-1}\hat{\phi}(B)\delta(B)[Z_t - f(\mathbf{X}_t, \hat{\xi})].$$

Since the model for N_t is invertible this is asymptotically equivalent to nonlinear least squares.

Pierce (1971) discusses inference for the model (1.1) for the case in which $f(\mathbf{X}_t; \xi)$ is linear in ξ. He shows that under some conditions on the a_t's and the $\mathbf{X}_t$'s that the least squares estimates $\hat{\nu} = (\hat{\xi}, \hat{\phi}, \hat{\theta})$ are consistent and asymptotically normal, $\hat{\xi}$ is asymptotically independent of $(\hat{\phi}, \hat{\theta})$, and $\hat{\sigma}^2$ is a consistent estimator of σ^2. Also, the (i, j)th element of the inverse of the asymptotic covariance matrix of $\hat{\nu}$ can be approximated numerically by $-(\partial^2 L/\partial\nu_i\partial\nu_j) \mid \hat{\nu}$, where L is the log-likelihood. Hannan (1971) and Gallant and Goebel (1976) obtain results analogous to those of Pierce for the case in which $f(\mathbf{X}_t; \xi)$ is nonlinear in ξ, although they do not explicitly consider the asymptotic properties of $\hat{\phi}$ and $\hat{\theta}$. They require the additional assumptions of continuity of $f(\mathbf{X}_t; \xi)$ for the consistency of $\hat{\xi}$ (Hannan 1971) and twice differentiability for the asymptotic normality.

2.3 Diagnostic Checking

In general, the adequacy of both the assumed formulation of $f(\mathbf{X}_t;\xi)$ and the assumed noise model $\phi(B)\delta(B)N_t = \theta(B)a_t$ should be checked. To check the form of $f(\mathbf{X}_t; \xi)$ the residuals, $\hat{a}_t$, can be plotted against the X_{it} and any other possible independent variables. The $\hat{a}_t$ should be plotted against time to check for outliers, constancy of variance, and trends. The SACF of the residuals should be examined for any large autocorrelations. Ljung and Box (1978) show that under the hypothesis that the model is correct, for large n the statistic

$$Q = n(n + 2) \sum_{k=1}^{L} r_k(\hat{a})^2/(n - k)$$

has approximately a $\chi^2(L - s)$ distribution, where $r_k(\hat{a})$ is the lag k sample autocorrelation of $\hat{a}_t$, and s equals the number of parameters in the noise model. The noise model is judged inadequate if Q exceeds $\chi^2{}_\gamma(L - s)$ for some suitable γ.

3. TRADING DAY AND HOLIDAY VARIATION

The variation in a monthly time series that is due to the changing number of times each day of the week occurs in a month is called *trading day variation*. Trading day variation occurs when the activity of a business or industry varies with the days of the week so that the activity for a particular month partially depends on which days of the week occur five times. In addition, Young (1965) notes that accounting and reporting practices can create trading day effects in a time series. For example, stores that perform their bookkeeping activities on Fridays tend to report higher sales in months with five Fridays than in months with four Fridays. *Holiday variation* refers to fluctuations in economic activity due to changes from year to year in the composition of the calendar with respect to holidays. The primary example of this for U.S. economic series is the increased buying that takes place in some retail sales series just before Easter. This is a holiday effect since Easter falls on various dates in March and April. Holiday effects must be distinguished from seasonal effects, which are attributable to the same month every year. For instance, the increase in retail sales in December prior to Christmas each year is a seasonal effect and not a holiday effect.

Almost all of the previous research on trading day and holiday effects has dealt with their relation to seasonal adjustment. Young (1965) describes the procedures that are used in the Census X-11 seasonal adjustment program to adjust time series for trading day variation, and briefly discusses the adjustments made for holiday variation. Cleveland and Devlin (1980,1982) have reported on methods to identify times in which trading day effects are present in a time series and on methods to remove these effects. Pfefferman and Fisher (1980) discuss adjustments for both trading day and holiday variation. All of these authors use a two-stage approach in which a regression model is fitted to data that have been preprocessed to remove the trend and seasonality. We prefer to postulate a model of the form (1.1) and ARIMA noise structure and simultaneously estimate the regression and ARIMA parameters. Once a model of the form (1.1) has been developed, it can be used for a variety of purposes including forecasting and seasonal adjustment.

4. MODELING TRADING DAY VARIATION IN TIME SERIES

Trading day variation arises in part because the activity for a monthly time series varies with the days of the week. We assume that trading day effects can be approximated by a deterministic model. We deal only with flow series for which the data are the accumulation of the daily values (flows) over the calendar months. (Cleveland and Grupe (1982) discuss modeling of trading day effects for other types of series such as stock series, e.g., inventories.) If ξ_i, $i = 1, \ldots, 7$, represent the average rates of activity on Monday, Tuesday, Wednesday, Thursday, Friday, Saturday, and Sunday for the series being modeled (i.e., the daily effects), then the effect attributable to the number of times each day of the week occurs in month t is

$$TD_t = \sum_{i=1}^{7} \xi_i X_{it}, \tag{4.1}$$

where X_{it}, $i = 1, \ldots, 7$, are, respectively, the number of Mondays, Tuesdays, and so on in month t. A similar model was used by Young (1965), Cleveland and Devlin (1982), and Pfefferman and Fisher (1980). The model (4.1) accounts for variations in level due to differing month lengths, and allows for variations in level due to differing day of the week compositions for months of the same length. A model for the time series that incorporates trading day effects is

$$Z_t = TD_t + N_t, \tag{4.2}$$

where TD_t is as defined in (4.1) and N_t as in (2.1).

We obtain a useful reparameterization of (4.1) as follows. Let $\bar{\xi} = 1/7 \sum_{i=1}^{7} \xi_i$, $T_{it} = X_{it} - X_{7t}$, $i = 1, \ldots, 6$, and let $T_{7t} = \sum_{i=1}^{7} X_{it}$ denote the length of month t. Then we can write (4.1) as

$$\begin{aligned} TD_t &= \sum_{i=1}^{7} (\xi_i - \bar{\xi})(X_{it} - X_{7t}) \\ &\quad + \sum_{i=1}^{7} (\xi_i - \bar{\xi})X_{7t} + \bar{\xi}\sum_{i=1}^{7} X_{it} \\ &= \sum_{i=1}^{7} \beta_i T_{it}, \end{aligned} \tag{4.3}$$

where $\beta_i = \xi_i - \bar{\xi}$, $i = 1, \ldots, 6$, and $\beta_7 = \bar{\xi}$. Our model then becomes

$$Z_t = \sum_{i=1}^{7} \beta_i T_{it} + \frac{\theta(B)}{\phi(B)\delta(B)} a_t. \tag{4.4}$$

We get the same estimate for TD_t whether we use the parameterization (4.1) or (4.3); however, we have observed that estimates of the ξ_i's tend to be highly correlated while estimates of $\beta_1, \ldots, \beta_6$ are less so and are not highly correlated with the estimate of β_7. The parameters $\beta_i = \xi_i - \bar{\xi}$, $i = 1, \ldots, 6$, measure the differences between the Monday, Tuesday, . . . , Saturday effects and the average of the daily effects, $\beta_7 = \bar{\xi}$. The difference between the Sunday effect and the average of the daily effects is then

$$\begin{aligned} \xi_7 - \bar{\xi} &= \sum_{1}^{7} \xi_i - \bar{\xi} - \sum_{1}^{6} \xi_i \\ &= 6\bar{\xi} - \sum_{1}^{6} (\beta_i + \bar{\xi}) = -\sum_{1}^{6} \beta_i, \end{aligned}$$

and one may solve for the Sunday effect, ξ_7, using $\beta_7 - \sum_1^6 \beta_i$.

4.1 An Example

As an example, consider the series retail sales of lumber and building materials from January 1967 to September 1979, (the data for which may be obtained from the U.S. Census Bureau). Examination of a plot of the series reveals that the amplitude of the seasonality increases with the level. Therefore, we have determined that it is appropriate to model the natural logarithms, which we denote by Z_t. Examination of the SACF of the logged data and the SACF of the first differenced logged data indicated that first and twelfth differences are needed to achieve stationarity. The SACF of $(1 - B)(1 - B^{12})Z_t$ together with plus and minus two standard error limits are reported in Figure 1. Figure 1 does not exhibit a recognizable pattern. In order to identify the noise model we note that (2.2) for this example can be written

$$(1 - B)(1 - B^{12})Z_t = \sum_{1}^{7} \beta_i(1 - B)(1 - B^{12})T_{it} + e_t,$$

so we examine the SACF of the residuals from the regression of $(1 - B)(1 - B^{12})Z_t$ on $(1 - B)(1 - B^{12})T_{it}$ for $i = 1, \ldots, 7$. From this SACF, Figure 2, the presence of the large negative value at lag 12 suggests the noise

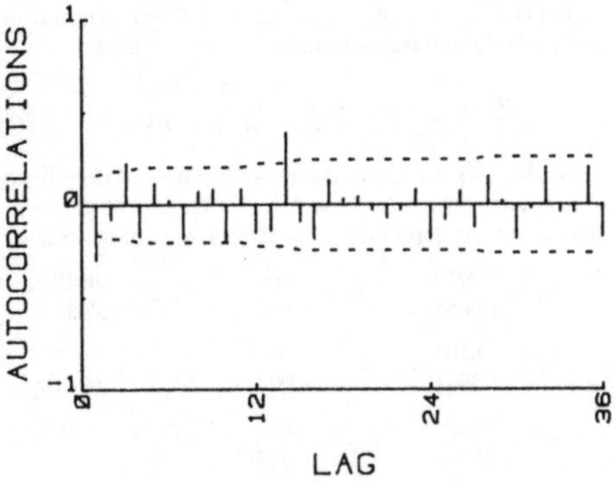

Figure 1. SACF of $(1 - B)(1 - B^{12})Z_t$.

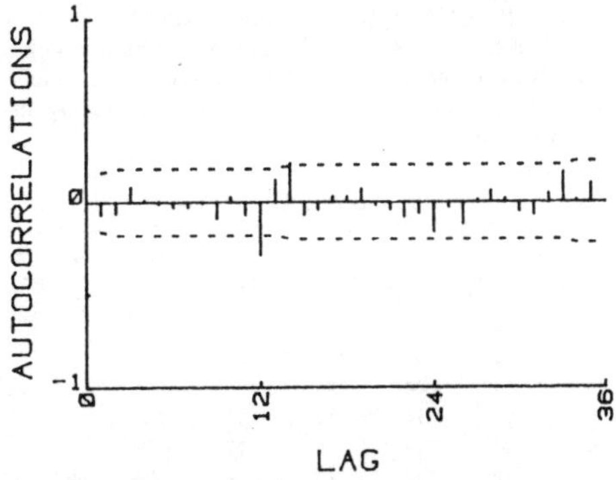

Figure 2. SACF of Regression Residuals.

model $(1 - B)(1 - B^{12})N_t = (1 - \theta_{12}B^{12})a_t$. Therefore, a tentatively entertained model for this series is

$$Z_t = \sum_{i=1}^{7} \beta_i T_{it} + \frac{(1 - \theta_{12}B^{12})}{(1 - B)(1 - B^{12})} a_t. \quad (4.5)$$

The BMDQ2T program (Liu 1979) was used to estimate the parameters in the model (4.5). The parameter estimates and corresponding standard errors are as follows:

$$\hat\beta_1 = \underset{(.0042)}{.0055} \quad \hat\beta_2 = \underset{(.0041)}{.0068} \quad \hat\beta_3 = \underset{(.0042)}{.0017}$$

$$\hat\beta_4 = \underset{(.0041)}{.0103} \quad \hat\beta_5 = \underset{(.0041)}{.0061} \quad \hat\beta_6 = \underset{(.0041)}{-.0098}$$

$$\hat\beta_7 = \underset{(.014)}{.037} \quad \hat\theta_{12} = \underset{(.028)}{.87} \quad \hat\sigma^2 = .00101.$$

The sample autocorrelations of the residuals from this model are all within plus or minus two standard errors of zero, and other diagnostic checks reveal no inadequacies with this model. The correlation matrix for the parameter estimates $\hat\beta_i$ $i = 1, \ldots, 7$ are reported in Table 1. The parameter estimates $\hat\beta_1, \ldots, \hat\beta_6$ are correlated so that individual inferences about these parameters must be made with caution. In contrast, $\hat\beta_7$ appears to be nearly uncorrelated with $\hat\beta_1, \ldots, \hat\beta_6$. This correlation pattern is typical of others that we have observed.

Inferences about the parameters in (4.5) can be made based on the asympotic theory referenced in Section 2. We first examine whether the daily effects (ξ_i) are different for the different days of the week by testing

$$H_0\colon\ \xi_1 = \cdots = \xi_7 \text{ vs.}$$

$$H_1\colon\ \text{not all } \xi_i \text{ are equal.}$$

This is equivalent to testing

$$H_0\colon\ \beta_1 = \cdots = \beta_6 = 0 \text{ vs.}$$

$$H_1\colon\ \text{not all } \beta_i = 0\ i = 1, \ldots, 6. \quad (4.6)$$

If $\mathbf{A}$ is the estimated covariance matrix of $\hat{\boldsymbol\beta} = (\hat\beta_1, \ldots, \hat\beta_6)'$, then under H_0 in (4.6) the asymptotic distribution of $\hat{\boldsymbol\beta}'\mathbf{A}^{-1}\hat{\boldsymbol\beta}$ is chi-squared with 6 degrees of freedom. Because $\hat{\boldsymbol\beta}'\mathbf{A}^{-1}\hat{\boldsymbol\beta} = 147.63$ is larger than 12.6, which is the .05 critical value of a chi-squared distribution with 6 degrees of freedom, we reject H_0 in (4.6) and conclude that the different days of the week have significantly different effects.

Table 1. Correlation Matrix of $\hat\beta$

	$\hat\beta_1$	$\hat\beta_2$	$\hat\beta_3$	$\hat\beta_4$	$\hat\beta_5$	$\hat\beta_6$	$\hat\beta_7$
$\hat\beta_1$	1.						
$\hat\beta_2$	−.54	1.					
$\hat\beta_3$	−.12	−.50	1.				
$\hat\beta_4$	.14	−.09	−.53	1.			
$\hat\beta_5$	.07	.14	−.12	−.51	1.		
$\hat\beta_6$	−.04	.05	.15	−.07	−.55	1.	
$\hat\beta_7$	.12	−.11	.13	−.14	.05	.09	1.

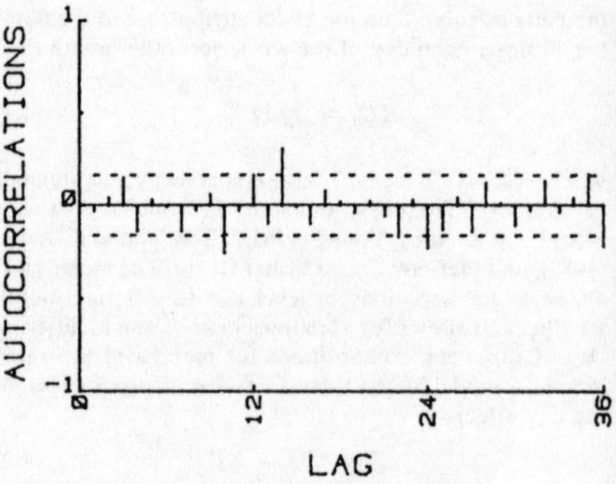

Figure 3. SACF of Residuals From (4.9).

It is also of interest to test

$$H_0\colon\ \beta_7 = 0 \text{ vs.}$$

$$H_1\colon\ \beta_7 \neq 0. \quad (4.7)$$

Since $\hat\beta_7$ divided by its standard error equals 2.6, we reject the null hypothesis in (4.7). When $\beta_7 \neq 0$, the term $\beta_7 T_{7t}$ in (4.5) accounts for an effect due to leap-year Februaries. To see this, notice from (4.5) that when we apply $1 - B^{12}$ to the data Z_t, we obtain

$$(1 - B^{12})Z_t = \sum_{i=1}^{7} \beta_i(1 - B^{12})T_{it} + \frac{(1 - \theta_{12}B^{12})}{1 - B} a_t.$$

Since T_{7t} equals the length of month t, $(1 - B^{12})T_{7t} = 0$ except in a leap-year February and the February of the following year.

4.2 Ignoring Trading Day Effects

From the preceding analysis it is clear that the model (4.5) is an adequate description of this time series. It is of interest to get an idea of the effect of ignoring the trading day variables in this particular example. With this idea in mind we estimated the model

$$(1 - B)(1 - B^{12})Z_t = (1 - \theta_{12}B^{12})a_t. \quad (4.8)$$

Examination of the residual autocorrelations from (4.8) revealed a number of significant values, including a significant autocorrelation at lag one. We therefore tried the model

$$(1 - B)(1 - B^{12})Z_t = (1 - \theta_1 B)(1 - \theta_{12}B^{12})a_t. \quad (4.9)$$

The parameter estimates for (4.9) are $\hat\theta_1 = .40$, $\hat\theta_{12} = .88$, and $\hat\sigma^2 = .0017$. The residual autocorrelations are plotted in Figure 3. By comparing the results of the fit for (4.5) with those of the fit for (4.9), we can judge the impact of the trading day effects upon this data set. While the residual autocorrelations from model (4.9) did not reveal any specific pattern, there are a number of moderately large sample autocorrelations. Futhermore, the value of the Ljung-Box Q based on 36 lags is 96.9, which greatly exceeds $\chi^2_{.01}(34) = 56.1$. We conclude that the residuals from (4.9) are not random. In contrast the model (4.5) passes the diagnostic checks and there is about a 40 percent reduction in the residual sum of squares from model (4.9) to (4.5). For this particular example the trading day effects are substantial and ignoring these effects is inappropriate.

5. MODELING HOLIDAY (EASTER) EFFECTS IN TIME SERIES

The Census Bureau adjusts certain retail sales series for holiday effects due to Easter, Labor Day, and Thanksgiving-Christmas (Young 1965). However, the Labor Day and Thanksgiving-Christmas adjustments are rather negligible, so we deal here only with modeling the effects of changing Easter dates. Techniques similar to those discussed here could be used to model other holiday effects, if necessary. For example, Liu (1980) discussed the problems involved with modeling a time series affected by the varying placement of the Chinese New Year.

The earliest and latest dates on which Easter can fall are March 22 and April 25. Thus, for series in which increased buying takes place before Easter we expect the March and April values in any particular year to depend on the date of Easter.

Specifying a functional form for the effect of Easter is not as simple as doing so for trading day effects. To be rather general, let $\tilde{\alpha}_i$ denote the effect on the series being modeled on the ith day before Easter; let $h(i, t)$ be 1 when the ith day before Easter falls in the month corresponding to time point t, and 0 otherwise. Then the Easter effect at t, E_t, is

$$E_t = \sum_{i=1}^{K} \tilde{\alpha}_i h(i, t), \qquad (5.1)$$

where K denotes some suitable upper bound on the length of the effect in days. Since many time series that contain Easter variation also contain trading day variation, we consider the model

$$Z_t = TD_t + E_t + N_t, \qquad (5.2)$$

where TD_t is given by (4.3), N_t by (2.1), and E_t by (5.1), although we will need to simplify E_t.

The relationship (5.1) was derived by consideration of the daily impact of Easter on the level of the series. Unfortunately, in most situations the only data available are monthly values of the series; as a consequence, in practice we cannot estimate effects as general as (5.1). To illustrate, consider the placement of Easter for the years 1967 to 1979. We chose these particular years because they correspond to the time frame of an actual set of data that is considered later; however, conclusions similar to those that we draw for these years are relevant for other time periods. Figure 4 shows the Easter dates for these years and constitutes the experimental design for determining the effect of Easter. From the diagram it is evident

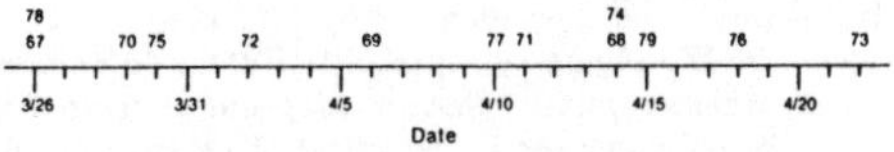

Figure 4. The Placement of Easter for 1967 to 1979.

that not all of the $\tilde{\alpha}_i$ in (5.1) can be estimated. For example, in these years whenever the fourth day before Easter fell in March so did the fifth day before Easter; otherwise, they both fell in April. Thus we cannot distinguish the effect of $\tilde{\alpha}_4 h(4, t)$ from that of $\tilde{\alpha}_5 h(5, t)$, using the data from 1967–1979. Since we cannot estimate all of the $\tilde{\alpha}_i$ in (5.1), we must look for special patterns in the $\tilde{\alpha}_i$.

We initially use the simple pattern $\tilde{\alpha}_1 = \cdots = \tilde{\alpha}_\tau = \tilde{\alpha}$, $\tilde{\alpha}_{\tau+1} = \cdots = \tilde{\alpha}_K = 0$ for some value τ. This implies

$$E_t = \alpha \cdot H(\tau, t), \qquad (5.3)$$

where $\alpha = \tilde{\alpha}\tau$ and $H(\tau, t) = 1/\tau \sum_{i=1}^{\tau} h(i, t)$. Given τ, $H(\tau, t)$ can be defined as the proportion of the time period τ days before Easter that falls in the month corresponding to time point t. With this definition $H(\tau, t)$ can be defined for any $\tau > 0$. For fixed t, $H(\tau, t)$ is in general a continuous but nondifferentiable function of τ. Figure 5 shows $H(\tau, t)$ for t corresponding to March 1969 and April 1969, Easter having been on April 6 that year.

Patterns other than that leading to (5.3) are possible. However, because Easter seldom occurred in early April from 1967 to 1979 (see Figure 4), it is unlikely that complex patterns can be detected from the data. This situation may change as additional data covering different Easter dates become available. We illustrate an approach to checking the adequacy of our assumed pattern in Section 5.3.

5.1 Noise Model Identification

It is of interest to consider the effect of E_t on the ACF of the original series and its differences. Figure 6 shows the SACF of $(1 - B)(1 - B^{12})H(14, t)$ (using January 1967 through September 1975 data), its most unusual features being the spikes at and near lags 36 and 48. Patterns in the SACF's for $H(\tau, t)$ for other τ and other time periods are similar. The degree to which these characteristics are transmitted to the original series depends on the magnitude of the Easter effect relative to TD_t and N_t. However, spikes at these lags can be taken as a possible indication of Easter effects in a series, especially when they show up in the SACF of a residual series from a model that has no terms to account for Easter effects.

To illustrate noise model identification, we consider the example of monthly retail sales of shoe stores (U.S.) from January 1967 through September 1979, which is available from the Census Bureau. (The observation for January 1970 ($t = 37$) was found to be an outlier and was modified from 243 to 270.3 (millions of dollars). The effect of the outlier was estimated by fitting the model with an indicator variable at $t = 37$.) We found it appropriate to analyze natural logarithms (denoted by Z_t) and to take $(1 - B)(1 - B^{12})Z_t$. Figure 7 gives the SACF of the differenced series, which exhibits behavior very similar to that in Figure 6, reflecting the Easter effect. To approximately remove E_t we choose a preliminary value of τ in (5.3), such as $\tau = 14$, and regress $(1 - B)(1 - B^{12})Z_t$ on $(1 - B)(1 - B^{12})H(14, t)$ and $(1 - B)(1 - B^{12})T_{it}$ $i = 1, \ldots, 7$. The SACF of the residuals from this regression, shown in Figure 8, does not show any influence of Easter or trading day effects. From this we identify a tentative noise model:

$$(1 - B)(1 - B^{12})N_t = (1 - \theta_1 B)(1 - \theta_{12}B^{12})a_t. \quad (5.4)$$

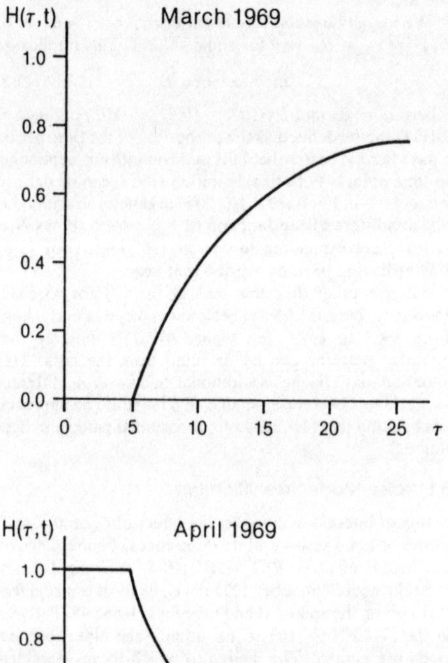

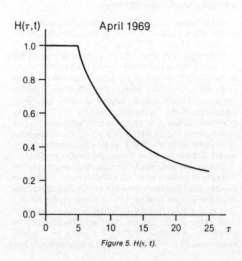

Figure 5. $H(\tau, t)$.

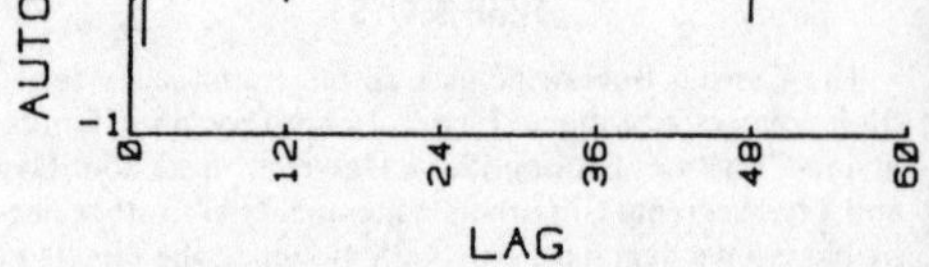

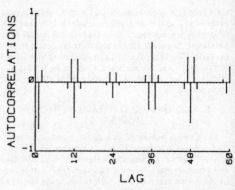

Figure 6. SACF of $(1 - B)(1 - B^{12})H(14, t)$.

5.2 Estimation of the Holiday Model

We demonstrate estimation of the model

$$Z_t = \sum_{i=1}^{7} \beta_i T_{it} + \alpha H(\tau, t) + \frac{\theta(B)}{\phi(B)\delta(B)} a_t \quad (5.5)$$

with the shoe stores example begun in Section (5.1). Notice that (5.5) is linear in $\beta_1, \ldots, \beta_7$, and α for fixed τ, so for fixed τ estimation may proceed in a manner analogous to that for the trading day model (4.4). We can obtain maximum likelihood estimators for the parameters of (5.5), including τ, by defining the asymptotic log-likelihood

$$L_{\max}(\tau) = \max_{\beta,\alpha,\phi,\theta,\sigma^2} L(\beta,\alpha,\tau,\phi,\theta,\sigma^2)$$

$$= -\frac{n}{2}\ln\hat{\sigma}^2(\tau) + \text{constant}$$

(where $\hat{\sigma}^2(\tau)$ is the estimate of σ^2 for fixed τ) and maximizing this over τ. Table 2 gives $\hat{\sigma}^2(\tau)$ for the shoe store

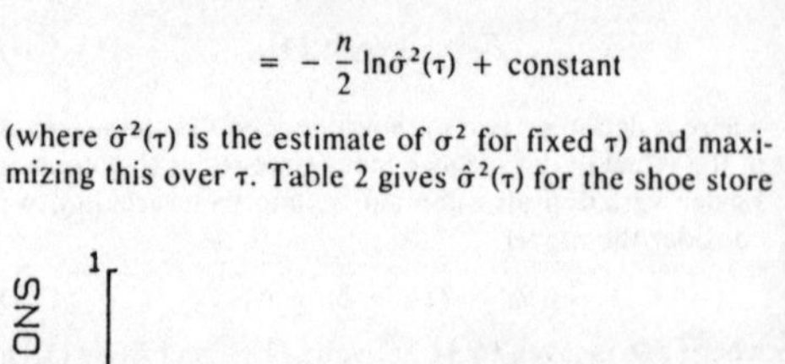

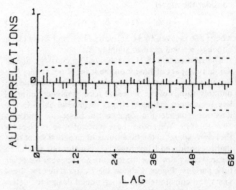

Figure 7. SACF of $(1 - B)(1 - B^{12})Z_t$.

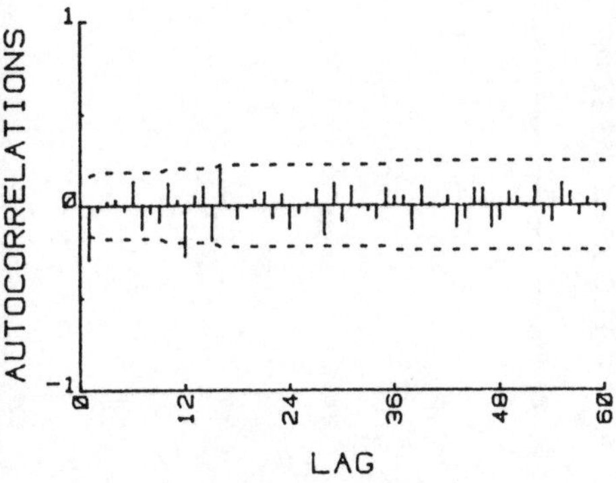

Figure 8. SACF of Regression Residuals.

series for $\tau = 1, \ldots, 25$. The MLE of τ is $\hat{\tau} = 10$ (approximately) and the estimates of the other parameters together with their standard errors are (from the fit with $H(10, t)$ in the model) as follows:

$$\hat{\beta}_1 = \frac{.0036}{(.0066)} \qquad \hat{\beta}_2 = \frac{-.0024}{(.0062)} \qquad \hat{\beta}_3 = \frac{-.0035}{(.0063)}$$

$$\hat{\beta}_4 = \frac{-.0087}{(.0062)} \qquad \hat{\beta}_5 = \frac{.0213}{(.0063)} \qquad \hat{\beta}_6 = \frac{.0131}{(.0065)}$$

$$\hat{\beta}_7 = \frac{.045}{(.021)} \qquad \hat{\theta}_1 = \frac{.32}{(.079)} \qquad \hat{\theta}_{12} = \frac{.86}{(.029)}$$

$$\hat{\alpha} = \frac{.166}{(.012)} \qquad \hat{\sigma}^2 = .00160.$$

It is of interest to note that for this series there is not much difference in the values of $\hat{\sigma}^2(\tau)$ for values of τ near 10.

Since $H(\tau, t)$ is continuous, $\hat{\tau}$ should be a consistent estimator of τ; however, since $H(\tau, t)$ is not differentiable for all t, the asymptotic normality need not hold. For fixed τ the results cited in Section 2.2 apply to the estimators of the other parameters, so that we can make inferences conditional on τ. If $\hat{\tau}$ were approximately independent of the estimators of the other parameters, then we could fix τ at 10 to make inferences. This can be checked by examining the parameter estimates and their standard errors for various τ. (in computing the standard errors, the parameter σ was estimated using the residual standard error for $\tau = 10$ because we considered this value to be a better estimator of σ than the residual standard error for other values of τ.) For this example the standard errors of $\hat{\beta}_1(\tau), \ldots, \hat{\beta}_7(\tau)$ are quite nearly constant for $\tau = 1, \ldots, 25$. Also, $\hat{\beta}_3(\tau), \ldots, \hat{\beta}_7(\tau)$ vary little for $\tau = 2, \ldots, 25$ and $\hat{\beta}_1(\tau)$ and $\hat{\beta}_2(\tau)$ vary little for $\tau = 7, \ldots, 25$. The estimates at the lower values of τ differ more from the others, although the differences are not large relative to the standard errors. The standard errors for $\hat{\theta}_1(\tau)$ and $\hat{\theta}_{12}(\tau)$ show little variation (no more than 10 percent) for $\tau = 2, \ldots, 25$ and $\tau = 2, \ldots, 16$ respectively, and are slightly lower outside these ranges. The estimates $\hat{\theta}_1(\tau)$ and $\hat{\theta}_{12}(\tau)$ vary little with τ, except possibly for $\tau = 1$. It seems for this series that $\hat{\beta}_1, \ldots, \hat{\beta}_7, \hat{\theta}_1, \hat{\theta}_{12}$, and their standard errors are relatively independent of $\hat{\tau}$, at least for a large part of the range of τ considered; thus we can make inferences on $\beta_1, \ldots, \beta_7, \theta_1$, and θ_{12} conditional on $\tau = 10$.

Table 2 shows that $\hat{\alpha}(\tau)$ and its estimated standard error depends more or τ. Still, we note that for this example there appears to be a fairly wide range of values of τ for which the estimates of α and their standard errors are fairly constant. These results are partially due to the experimental design given in Figure 4. Thus for data covering approximately the same years as this particular example, it may be reasonable to choose an approximate value for τ (for example, $\tau = 10$) and proceed with the inference conditional upon the value of τ chosen.

5.3 Checking the Easter Model

One way that the model (5.5) can be inadequate is if the Easter effect is more complex than that described by the simple pattern $\bar{\alpha}_1 = \cdots = \bar{\alpha}_\tau, \bar{\alpha}_{\tau+1} = \cdots = \bar{\alpha}_k = 0$. We cannot estimate all the $\bar{\alpha}_i$ in (5.1), but can estimate a somewhat general pattern by grouping some of the terms in (5.1) together. We used the grouping

$$\begin{aligned} E_t = {} & \alpha_1[h(1, t) + h(2, t)] \\ & + \alpha_2[h(3, t) + \cdots + h(6, t)] \\ & + \alpha_3[h(7, t) + \cdots + h(10, t)] \\ & + \alpha_4[h(11, t) + \cdots + h(14, t)] \\ & + \alpha_5[h(15, t) + \cdots + h(18, t)] \\ & + \alpha_6[h(19, t) + \cdots + h(22, t)]. \end{aligned} \tag{5.6}$$

Table 2. Estimation of τ

τ	1	2	3	4	5	6	7	8	9	10	11	12	13
$100\hat{\sigma}^2(\tau)$	.212	.182	.177	.176	.175	.167	.163	.162	.161	.160	.161	.164	.167
$\hat{\alpha}(\tau)$	.13	.15	.15	.15	.15	.16	.16	.16	.16	.17	.17	.17	.17
$\hat{\sigma}(\hat{\alpha}(\tau))$	.0129	.0127	.0125	.0124	.0123	.0123	.0123	.0122	.0122	.0123	.0126	.0128	.0130

τ	14	15	16	17	18	19	20	21	22	23	24	25
$100\hat{\sigma}^2(\tau)$	.171	.171	.173	.175	.176	.178	.180	.183	.183	.183	.183	.183
$\hat{\alpha}(\tau)$	.17	.18	.18	.19	.19	.20	.21	.21	.22	.23	.24	.25
$\hat{\sigma}(\hat{\alpha}(\tau))$	.0135	.0141	.0146	.0151	.0157	.0164	.0169	.0176	.0183	.0192	.0200	.0209

Any grouping of the $h(i, t)$ can be used as long as it produces explanatory variables that are linearly independent over the span of the data. For our example we have 26 March and April observations for estimating the Easter effect. So as not to spread the observations too thin, we decided to use six groups, and chose the grouping in (5.6) to yield groups of equal length, except for a first group of length two to allow for a possibly important effect immediately before Easter.

Our general model at this point is (5.2) with TD_t given by (4.3), E_t by (5.6), and N_t by (2.1). We investigate how complex an Easter effect is needed by sequentially testing

$$H_0: \quad \alpha_j = \alpha_{j+1} = \cdots = \alpha_6 = 0 \text{ vs.}$$

$$H_1: \quad \alpha_j \neq 0, \alpha_{j+1} = \cdots = \alpha_6 = 0$$

for $j = 1, \ldots, 6$. When H_0 is rejected we can investigate whether a simple pattern of the form $\hat{\alpha}_1 = \cdots = \hat{\alpha}_\tau = \hat{\alpha}$, $\hat{\alpha}_{\tau+1} = \cdots = \hat{\alpha}_k = 0$ is adequate by testing (for $j > 1$)

$$H_0': \quad \alpha_1 = \cdots = \alpha_j, \alpha_{j+1} = \cdots = \alpha_6 = 0$$

against H_1. Table 3 presents (asymptotic) likelihood ratio test statistics for the shoe stores example computed as

$$\frac{[\mathrm{RSS}(H_0) - \mathrm{RSS}(H_1)]/\nu_1}{\mathrm{RSS}(H_1)/\nu_2}$$

and similarly for H_0', where RSS denotes the residual sum of squares. The numerator degrees of freedom, ν_1, is 1 for testing H_0 and $j - 1$ for testing H_0'. The denominator degrees of freedom, ν_2, is 153 − 13 (for differencing) − 1 (outlier) − 7 (*TD* parameters) − 2 (θ_1 and θ_{12}) $-j = 130 - j$. The 5% and 1% critical values for the $F(\nu_1, \nu_2)$ distribution are also reported. The test statistics do not indicate that $\alpha_j \neq 0$ for $j > 3$. Also, there is no reason to reject the assumption that $\alpha_1 = \alpha_2 = \alpha_3$. We conclude that for this example the data give no evidence that the simplified Easter effect given by (5.3) is inadequate.

In addition to checking the Easter effect, we also should check the adequacy of the noise model (5.4). The sample autocorrelations of the residuals for the shoe stores series (using the model (5.5) with $\tau = \hat{\tau} = 10$) are all within plus or minus two standard errors of zero with the exception of $r_8(\hat{a})$, which is 2.7 standard errors below zero. The Ljung-Box Q statistic for 36 lags is 46.3. Since this is less than 48.6, the $\chi^2_{.05}(34)$ critical value, we conclude that the residuals appear to be white noise.

Table 3. Investigating $\alpha_1 = \cdots = \alpha_j, \alpha_{j+1} = \cdots = \alpha_6 = 0$

j	*F-statistic for* H_0	*F-statistic for* H_0'	$F_{.05}(j-1, 130)$	$F_{.01}(j-1, 130)$
1	90.3	—	—	—
2	12.1	.9	3.9	6.8
3	5.7	.6	3.0	4.8
4	.0	—	—	—
5	2.7	—	—	—
6	.3	—	—	—

$F_{.05}(1,130) = 3.9 \quad F_{.01}(1,130) = 6.8$

NOTE: The $F(\nu_1, 130-j)$ critical values are very close to the $F(\nu_1, 130)$ critical values.

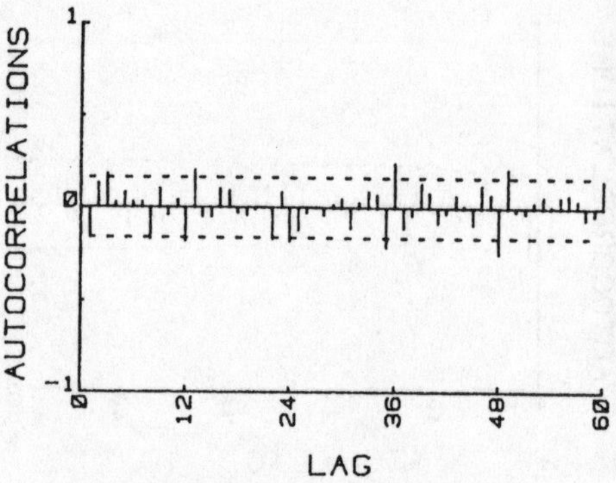

Figure 9. SACF of Residuals From (5.7).

5.4 Ignoring Trading Day and Easter Effects

As in the example of Section 4 it is of interest to investigate the influence of the trading day and Easter holiday terms in model (5.5) by fitting the model without these terms, which is

$$(1 - B)(1 - B^{12})Z_t = (1 - \theta_1 B)(1 - \theta_{12} B^{12})a_t. \quad (5.7)$$

The parameter estimates for model (5.7) are $\hat{\theta}_1 = .68$, $\hat{\theta}_{12} = .93$, and $\hat{\sigma}^2 = .00333$. The residual autocorrelations are plotted in Figure 9. From Figure 9 there appear to be a number of moderately large $r_k(\hat{a})$'s at low lags, but there is not a recognizable pattern that would suggest a modification if a pure ARIMA model is to be used. Also, the behavior of the $r_k(\hat{a})$'s near lags 36 and 48 resembles that in Figure 6, indicating the presence of the Easter effect. The Ljung-Box Q statistic based upon 36 lags is 79.5, which is larger than $\chi^2_{.01}(34) = 56.1$. Thus, we would reject the hypothesis that the residuals from model (5.7) were white noise. The model (5.7) has obvious inadequacies, and there is about a 50 percent reduction in the residual sum of squares when the trading day and Easter influences are appropriately modeled.

6. CONCLUSIONS

In the time series literature the model (1.1) has been considered from a theoretical viewpoint; however, in many applications there has been an apparent tendency either to consider pure regression models or to consider pure ARIMA time series models. We have argued that there are situations in which a combination of these two models is superior. As particular examples we considered in detail the cases of time series that include trading day variation and Easter holiday variation. These two particular examples are important because there are many time series that contain one or both of these effects. The actual time series we considered indicate that substantial improvements over pure ARIMA models can be achieved if trading day and Easter effects are appropriately modeled. We hope that from this research more model builders will become aware of trading day and Easter variations and, as a result, will be in a better position to handle them.

[*Received March 1981. Revised February 1983.*]

REFERENCES

ANDERSON, R.L. (1954), "The Problem of Autocorrelation in Regression Analysis," *Journal of the American Statistical Association*, 49, 113–129.

BOX, G.E.P., and JENKINS, G.M. (1976), *Time Series Analysis: Forecasting and Control*, San Francisco: Holden Day.

CLEVELAND, W.P., and GRUPE, M.R. (1982), "Modeling Times Series When Calendar Effects are Present," to appear in *Proceedings of the Conference on Applied Time Series Analysis of Economic Data*, ed. Arnold Zellner.

CLEVELAND, W.S., and DEVLIN, S.J. (1980), "Calendar Effects in Monthly Time Series: Detection by Spectrum Analysis and Graphical Methods," *Journal of the American Statistical Association*, 75, 487–496.

——— (1982), "Calendar Effects in Monthly Time Series: Modeling and Adjustment," *Journal of the American Statistical Association*, 77, 520–528.

FULLER, W. (1976), *Introduction to Statistical Time Series*, New York: John Wiley and Sons.

GALLANT, A.R., and GOEBEL, J.J. (1976), "Non-linear Regression with Autocorrelation Errors," *Journal of the American Statistical Association*, 71, 961–967.

HANNAN, E.J. (1971), "Non-linear Time Series Regression," *Journal of Applied Probability*, 8, 767–780.

LIU, L.M. (1979), "User's Manual for BMDQ2T Time Series Analysis," BMDP Technical Report.

——— (1980), "Analysis of Time Series with Calendar Effects," *Management Science*, 26, 106–112.

LJUNG, G.M., and BOX, G.E.P. (1978), "On a Measure of Lack of Fit in Time Series Models," *Biometrika*, 65, 297–303.

PFEFFERMAN, D., and FISHER, J. (1980), "Festival and Working Days Prior Adjustments in Economic Time Series," in *Time Series*, ed. O.D. Anderson, New York: North-Holland.

PIERCE, D.A. (1971), "Least Squares Estimation in the Regression Model With Autoregressive-moving Average Errors," *Biometrika*, 58, 299–312.

YOUNG, A.H. (1965), "Estimating Trading-Day Variation in Monthly Economic Time Series," Technical Paper 12, Bureau of the Census.

Part VI
Dynamic Regression and Intervention Analysis

[22]

Intervention Analysis with Applications to Economic and Environmental Problems

G. E. P. BOX and G. C. TIAO*

This article discusses the effect of interventions on a given response variable in the presence of dependent noise structure. Difference equation models are employed to represent the possible dynamic characteristics of both the interventions and the noise. Some properties of the maximum likelihood estimators of parameters measuring level changes are discussed. Two applications, one dealing with the photochemical smog data in Los Angeles and the other with changes in the consumer price index, are presented.

1. INTRODUCTION

Data of potential value in the formulation of public and private policy frequently occur in the form of time series. Questions of the following kind often arise: "Given a known intervention,[1] is there evidence that change in the series of the kind expected actually occurred, and, if so, what can be said of the nature and magnitude of the change?"

For example, in early 1960 two events occurred, here referred to jointly as the intervention, which might have been expected to reduce the oxidant (denoted by O_3) pollution level in downtown Los Angeles. These events were the diversion of traffic by the opening of the Golden State Freeway and the coming into effect of a new law (Rule 63) which reduced the allowable proportion of reactive hydrocarbons in the gasoline sold locally. The expected effect of this intervention would be to produce a more or less immediate reduction (i.e., a step change) in the oxidant level in early 1960. Figure A shows the monthly averages of oxidant concentration level from 1955–72 in downtown Los Angeles [6]. Using this highly variable and seasonal time series, is there evidence for a change in level and, if so, what is its magnitude?

Many other problems of this kind have come to our attention in recent years. These have included the possible effect of the opening of a nuclear power station on measurements made on river samples, the possible effect of the Nixon Administration's Phases I and II on an economic indicator, and the possible effect of promotions, advertising campaigns and price changes on the sale of a product.

Available procedures such as Student's t test for estimating and testing for a change in mean have played an important role in statistics for a very long time.

A. Monthly Average of Hourly Readings of O_3 (pphm) in Downtown Los Angeles (1955–1972)[a]

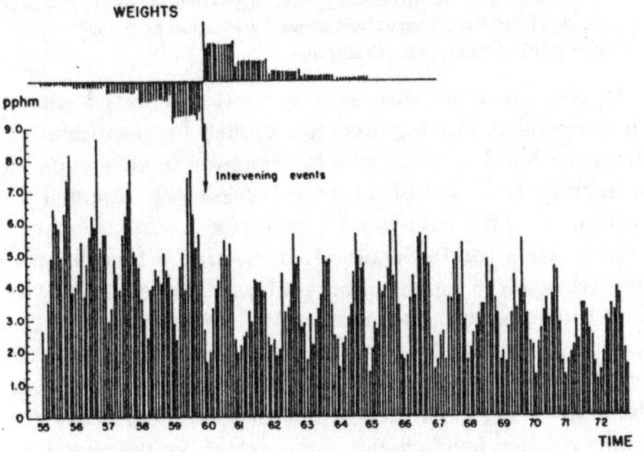

[a] With the weight function for estimating the effect of intervening events in 1960.

However, the ordinary t test would be valid only if the observations before and after the event of interest varied about means μ_1 and μ_2, not only normally and with constant variance but *independently*. In the examples quoted, however, the data are in the form of time series in which successive observations are usually serially dependent and often nonstationary, and there may be strong seasonal effects. Thus the ordinary parametric or nonparametric statistical procedures which rely on independence or special symmetry in the distribution function are not available nor are the blessings endowed by randomization.

An approach we initiated earlier [2] was to build a stochastic model which included the possibility of change of the form expected. Such model building is necessarily iterative and, as discussed, e.g., in [3], involves inferences from a tentatively entertained model alternating with criticism of the appropriate tentative analysis. The process proceeds [1] by successive use of Identification (tentative specification of the model form), Fitting, and Diagnostic Checking. Using these ideas in the present context, we come to the following general strategy:

1. Frame a model for change which describes what is expected to occur given knowledge of the known intervention;

* G.E.P. Box is R. A. Fisher professor and G. C. Tiao is professor and chairman, Department of Statistics, University of Wisconsin, Madison, Wis. 53706. This research was supported in part by a grant from the American Petroleum Institute and in part by U.S. Army Research Office under Grant DA-ARO-D-31-124-72-G162.

[1] A term introduced in [5], based on our earlier work [2].

© Journal of the American Statistical Association
March 1975, Volume 70, Number 349
Invited Paper, Theory and Methods Section

2. Work out the appropriate data analysis based on that model;
3. If diagnostic checks show no inadequacy in the model, make appropriate inferences; if serious deficiencies are uncovered, make appropriate model modification, repeat the analysis, etc.

Suppose the data ... $Y_{t-1}, Y_t, Y_{t+1}, \ldots$ are available as a series obtained at equal time intervals. Following, e.g., [1], we will employ models of the general form

$$y_t = f(\kappa, \xi, t) + N_t \tag{1.1}$$

where:

$y_t = F(Y_t)$ is some appropriate transformation of Y_t, say $\log Y_t$, $(Y_t)^{\frac{1}{2}}$ or Y_t itself;
$f(\kappa, \xi, t)$ can allow for deterministic effects of time, t, the effects of exogenous variables, ξ, and in particular, interventions;
N_t represents stochastic background variation or noise;
κ is a set of unknown parameters.

In Section 2 we discuss a general integrated mixed autoregressive moving average model for representing the noise N_t. A class of general dynamic models capable of representing the effect of interventions is given in Section 3. The associated parameter estimation procedures are given in Section 4. In Section 5 two illustrative examples of intervention analysis are presented. The first concerns the Los Angeles oxidant data, and the second considers possible effects on the consumer price index of recent government actions. Finally, in Section 6, the nature of the maximum likelihood estimators for some specific level-change parameters is discussed in some detail.

2. A STOCHASTIC MODEL FOR THE NOISE

We suppose that the noise $N_t = y_t - f(\mathbf{k}, \xi, t)$ may be modeled by a mixed autoregressive moving average process

$$\varphi(B)N_t = \theta(B)a_t \tag{2.1}$$

where:

1. B is the backshift operator such that $By_t = y_{t-1}$;
2. $\ldots a_{t-1}, a_t, a_{t+1}, \ldots$ is a sequence of independently distributed normal variables having mean zero and variance $(\sigma_a)^2$ which for brevity we refer to as "white" noise;
3. $\theta(B) = 1 - \theta_1 B - \theta_2 B^2 \cdots - \theta_q B^q$, $\varphi(B) = 1 - \varphi_1 B - \varphi_2 B^2 \cdots - \varphi_p B^p$ are "moving average" and "autoregressive" polynomials in B of degrees q and p, respectively;
4. the roots of $\theta(B)$ lie outside, and those of $\varphi(B)$ lie on or outside the unit circle.

For the representation of certain kinds of homogeneous nonstationary series, the operator $\varphi(B)$ is factored so that

$$\varphi(B) = (1 - B)^d \phi(B) \tag{2.2}$$

where the roots of $\phi(B)$ all lie outside the unit circle. This corresponds to the use of a stationary model in the dth difference. Also, for seasonal data with period s (e.g., monthly data with $s = 12$), it is often helpful to write $\varphi(B) = \varphi_1(B)\varphi_2(B^s)$ and $\theta(B) = \theta_1(B)\theta_2(B^s)$ with $\varphi_2(B^s) = (1 - B^s)^D \phi_2(B^s)$ to allow for seasonal nonstationarity.

Finally, we entertain a class of noise model of the form

$$\phi_1(B)\phi_2(B^s)(1 - B)^d(1 - B^s)^D N_t = \theta_1(B)\theta_2(B^s)a_t \tag{2.3}$$

where the polynomials $\phi_1(B)$, $\phi_2(B^s)$, $\theta_1(B)$, $\theta_2(B^s)$ are of degrees p_1, p_2, q_1, q_2, respectively.

3. A DYNAMIC MODEL FOR INTERVENTION

Frequently the effects of exogenous variables ξ can be represented by a dynamic model of the form

$$f(\delta, \omega, \xi, t) = \sum_{j=1}^{k} \mathcal{Y}_{tj} = \sum_{j=1}^{k} \{\omega_j(B)/\delta_j(B)\}\xi_{tj} \tag{3.1}$$

where:

1. The $\mathcal{Y}_{tj}$ represent the dynamic transfer from ξ_{tj};
2. The parameters κ previously lumped together are now denoted by δ and ω;
3. The polynomials in B

$$\delta_j(B) = 1 - \delta_{1j}B - \cdots - \delta_{r_j j}B^{r_j} \quad \text{and}$$
$$\omega_j(B) = \omega_{0j} - \omega_{1j}B - \cdots - \omega_{s_j j}B^{s_j}$$

are of degrees r_j and s_j, respectively;
4. We shall normally assume that $\omega_j(B)$ has roots outside, and $\delta_j(B)$, outside or on, the unit circle.

In general, the individual ξ_{tj} could be exogenous time series whose influence needs to be taken into account. For the present purpose, however, some or all of them will be indicator variables taking the values 0 and 1 to denote the nonoccurrence and occurrence of intervention.

For illustration, suppose for a single exogenous variable ($k = 1$) the model is

$$y_t = \mathcal{Y}_t + N_t = (\omega(B)/\delta(B))\xi_t + (\theta(B)/\varphi(B))a_t \; ; \tag{3.2}$$

then the transfer $\mathcal{Y}_t$ to the output from ξ_t is generated by the linear difference equation

$$\delta(B)\mathcal{Y}_t = \omega(B)\xi_t \; .$$

Figures B(a), B(b) and B(c) show the response $\mathcal{Y}_t$ transmitted to the output for various simple dynamic systems by an indicator variable representing a step. We can denote such an indicator by $\xi_t = S_t^{(T)}$ where

$$S_t^{(T)} = \begin{cases} 0, & t < T \\ 1, & t \geq T \end{cases} . \tag{3.3}$$

Similarly, we use $P_t^{(T)}$ for a pulse indicator where

$$P_t^{(T)} = \begin{cases} 0, & t \neq T \\ 1, & t = T \end{cases} . \tag{3.4}$$

Referring to the figure for the case we have discussed for the Los Angeles 1960 intervention, we would expect that the change could be modelled as in Figure B(a), so that immediately following the known step change in the input, an output step change of unknown magnitude would be produced according to

$$\mathcal{Y}_t = \omega B S_t^{(T)} \; .$$

Sometimes a step change would not be expected to produce an immediate response but rather a "first order" dynamic response like that in Figure B(b). The appropriate transfer function model is then

$$\mathcal{Y}_t = \{\omega B/(1 - \delta B)\}S_t^{(T)} \; ,$$

($\delta < 1$). It is readily shown that the time constant of this system is estimated by $\{-\log_e \delta\}^{-1}$ and the steady state gain is $\omega/(1-\delta)$. When δ approaches the value unity, we have the transfer function model

$$\mathcal{Y}_t = \{\omega B/(1-B)\} S_t^{(T)}$$

in which a step change in the input produces a "ramp" response in the output (Figure B(c)).

Note that since

$$(1-B)S_t^{(T)} = P_t^{(T)} \ , \qquad (3.5)$$

any of these transfer functions could equally well be discussed in terms of the unit pulse $P_t^{(T)}$, and sometimes matters are best thought of directly in terms of $P_t^{(T)}$. Thus, suppose we have monthly sales data and wish to represent the effect of a promotion or advertising campaign lasting less than a month. The simple first order model

$$\mathcal{Y}_t = \{\omega_1 B/(1-\delta B)\} P_t^{(T)}$$

might do this (Figure B(d)) with ω_1 indicating the initial increase in sales immediately following the intervention and δ representing the rate of decay of this increase.

This particular model implies that no lasting effect will occur as a result of the intervention. When this might not be so, the model $B(e)$

$$\mathcal{Y}_t = \{(\omega_1 B/(1-\delta B)) + (\omega_2 B/(1-B))\} P_t^{(T)}$$

could be used in which the possibility is entertained that a residual gain (or loss) in sales ω_2 persists.

B. Responses to a Step and a Pulse Input[a]

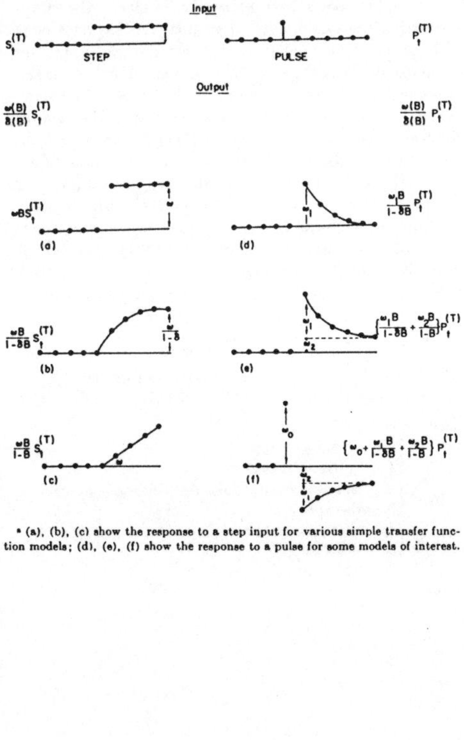

[a] (a), (b), (c) show the response to a step input for various simple transfer function models; (d), (e), (f) show the response to a pulse for some models of interest.

If it were believed that the full impact of intervention might not be felt until the second month, after which there would be a decay and possibly a residual effect as in the previous case, the model

$$\mathcal{Y}_t = \{\omega_0 B + (\omega_1 B^2/(1-\delta B)) + (\omega_2 B^2/(1-B))\} P_t^{(T)}$$

might be appropriate. This would insert a preliminary value ω_0 into the output (which in the preceding context would usually be less than ω_1). The same form of model, shifted forward and with some sign changes in the parameters, could be useful to represent the effect of price changes. In the application shown in Figure B(f), ω_0 would be positive and would represent an immediate rush of buying when a prospective price change was announced. The reduction in buying immediately after the change occurred would be represented by $\omega_1 + \omega_2$ and the final effect of the change would be represented by ω_2 which is shown as negative but, of course, could have a zero or positive value.

Obviously, these difference equation models may be readily extended to represent many situations of potential interest.

The following points are worthy of note:

(i) The function $\mathcal{Y}_t$ represents the *additional* effect of the intervention over the noise. In particular, when N_t is nonstationary, large changes could occur in the output even with no intervention. Fitting the model can make it possible to distinguish between what can and what cannot be explained by the noise.

(ii) Intervention extending over several time intervals can be represented by a series of pulses. A three month advertising campaign might be represented, for example, by three pulses whose magnitude might represent expenditure in the three months.

4. CALCULATIONS BASED ON THE LIKELIHOOD

Suppose we entertain a model of the form

$$y_t = \sum_{j=1}^{k} \mathcal{Y}_{tj} + N_t \qquad (4.1)$$

where $\sum_{j=1}^{k} \mathcal{Y}_{tj}$ is the transfer function given in (3.1) associated with known interventions, N_t assumes the form in (2.3), and a time series is available of length $n + d + sD$. Then the likelihood may be obtained in terms of an n dimensional vector $\mathbf{w}$ whose tth element is $w_t = (1-B)^d(1-B^s)^D(y_t - \sum_{j=1}^{k} \mathcal{Y}_{tj})$. The corresponding model for w_t,

$$w_t = \{\theta_1(B)\theta_2(B^s)/\phi_1(B)\phi_2(B^s)\} a_t \ , \qquad (4.2)$$

is stationary. Thus, following the argument given, e.g., in [1, p. 273], and with the vector $\boldsymbol{\beta}$ having for its g elements the stochastic and dynamic parameters in the model, the likelihood function may be written

$$L(\boldsymbol{\beta}, (\sigma_a)^2 | \mathbf{y}) = (2\pi(\sigma_a)^2)^{-(n/2)} |\mathbf{M}|^{\frac{1}{2}} \cdot \exp\{-S(\boldsymbol{\beta})/2(\sigma_a)^2\} \qquad (4.3)$$

where $\mathbf{M}^{-1}(\sigma_a)^2$ is the covariance matrix of the vector w and

$$S(\beta) = \mathbf{w}'\mathbf{M}\mathbf{w} = \sum_{t=-\infty}^{n} [a_t|\mathbf{y}, \beta]^2 \quad (4.4)$$

with $[a_t|\mathbf{y}, \beta]$ as the expected value of a_t conditional on β and $\mathbf{y}$.

If none of the roots in (4.2) is close to the unit circle, then for moderate and large n, the likelihood is dominated by the exponent. The values of the elements of β minimizing (4.4), which we shall call the *least squares* values, are to a close approximation also the maximum likelihood values. Alternatively, if we introduce a prior distribution such that in the neighborhood where the likelihood is nonnegligible $p(\beta, \sigma_a) \propto p(\beta)(\sigma_a)^{-1}$, we obtain the posterior distribution

$$p(\beta|\mathbf{y}) \propto p(\beta)|\mathbf{M}|^{\frac{1}{2}}\{S(\beta)\}^{-(n/2)} . \quad (4.5)$$

Again for moderate or large samples and for a noninformative distribution $p(\beta)$, the term involving $S(\beta)$ dominates and approximately

$$p(\beta|\mathbf{y}) \dot{\propto} \{S(\beta)\}^{-(n/2)} \quad (4.6)$$

so that the least square estimates correspond with the point of maximum posterior density.

Now if, over the region where the density is appreciable, $S(\beta)$ is approximately quadratic (and in any given case it is easy to check this numerically), then the posterior distribution is approximately a multivariate t. Then,

$$p(\beta|\mathbf{y}) \dot{\propto} \{1 + (\sum_{ij} S_{ij}(\beta_i - \hat{\beta}_i)(\beta_j - \hat{\beta}_j)/ (n-g)(s_a)^2)\}^{-(n/2)} \quad (4.7)$$

where

$$S_{ij} = \tfrac{1}{2}\partial^2\{S(\beta)\}/\partial\beta_i\partial\beta_j|_{\beta=\hat{\beta}}$$

and $(s_a)^2 = S(\hat{\beta})/(n-g)$. Thus, for moderate or large n, β is approximately distributed as multivariate normal with mean $\hat{\beta}$ and covariance matrix

$$V(\beta) = (s_a)^2\{S_{ij}\}^{-1} .$$

The square roots of the diagonal elements of $V(\beta)$ will be referred to as standard errors (S.E.).

In practice we may obtain $\hat{\beta}$, $V(\beta)$ and $(s_a)^2$ using a standard nonlinear least squares computer program for the numerical minimization of $S(\beta)$. To do this we need only to be able to compute the quantities $[a_t|\mathbf{y}, \beta]$ for any β and we may proceed as follows. Since the model for w_t is stationary, $[a_t|\mathbf{y}, \beta]$ will be negligible for values $t \leq -Q$ where Q is some suitably chosen positive number. We, therefore, replace $S(\beta)$ by the finite sum $\sum_{t=-Q}^{n} [a_t|\mathbf{y}, \beta]^2$. It is shown in [1] that the initial values $[a_0]$, $[a_{-1}]$, $\cdots$, $[a_{-Q}]$ may often be obtained conveniently by a process of "back forecasting" which also indicates an appropriate value for Q.

5. TWO ILLUSTRATIVE EXAMPLES

The theory developed here is illustrated in this section by two examples, one employing the Los Angeles oxidant data and the other, the rate of change in the United States consumer price index, to determine the effect of known interventions.

5.1 Example 1: The Los Angeles Oxidant Data

Monthly averages of the oxidant (O_3) level in Downtown Los Angeles from January 1955 to December 1972 are shown in Figure A.

Identification (Specification) of the Model. The periods 1955–60 and 1960–65 were regarded as containing no major intervention which would affect the O_3 level. The series themselves and the sample autocorrelation functions within these periods suggest nonstationary and highly seasonal behavior. The autocorrelation functions of such differences $(1 - B^{12})y_t$ taken twelve months apart show significant correlations only at lags 1 and 12. This suggests the following model for the noise N_t:

$$(1 - B^{12})N_t = (1 - \theta_1 B)(1 - \theta_2 B^{12})a_t . \quad (5.1)$$

Interventions I_1 and I_2 of potential major importance are:

I_1: In 1960 the opening of the Golden State Freeway and the coming into effect of a new law (Rule 63) reducing the allowable proportion of reactive hydrocarbons in locally sold gasoline.

I_2: From 1966 onwards regulations required engine design changes in new cars which would be expected to reduce the production of O_3.

As already argued, I_1 might be expected to produce a step change in the O_3 level at the beginning of 1960. The effect of I_2 might be most accurately represented if we knew, for example, the proportion of new cars having specified engine changes which were in the pool of all cars driven at any point in time. Unfortunately, such data are not available to us presently. We have, therefore, represented the possible effect of intervention as a constant intervention change from year to year reflecting the increased proportion of "new design vehicles" in the car population. As explained more fully in [6], the engine changes would be expected to slow down the photochemical reactions which produce O_3 and, because of the summer-winter atmospheric temperature inversion differential and the difference in the intensity of sunlight, the net effect would be different in winter when oxidant pollution is low from that in summer when it is high.

A model form was, therefore, tentatively entertained for all the available monthly O_3 data from January 1955 to December 1972, which may be conveniently written as:

$$y_t = \omega_{01}\xi_{t1} + \omega_{02}\frac{\xi_{t2}}{1 - B^{12}} + \omega_{03}\frac{\xi_{t3}}{1 - B^{12}} + \frac{(1 - \theta_1 B)(1 - \theta_2 B^{12})}{(1 - B^{12})} a_t \quad (5.2)$$

where

$$\xi_{t1} = \begin{cases} 0, & t < \text{January, 1960} \\ 1, & t \geq \text{January, 1960} \end{cases}$$

$$\xi_{t2} = \begin{cases} 1, & \text{"summer" months June–October beginning 1966} \\ 0, & \text{otherwise} \end{cases}$$

$$\xi_{t3} = \begin{cases} 1, & \text{"winter" months November–May beginning 1966} \\ 0, & \text{otherwise.} \end{cases}$$

This allows for a step change in the level of O_3 beginning in 1960 of size ω_{01} associated with I_1 and for progressive yearly increments in the O_3 level beginning 1966 of ω_{02} and ω_{03} units, respectively, for the summer and the winter months. This representation is admittedly somewhat crude, and we hope to improve on it as more data become available.

Estimation Results. The maximum likelihood estimates and the associated standard errors are as follows:

Parameter	*MLE*	*S.E.*
ω_{01}	−1.09	.13
ω_{02}	−0.25	.07
ω_{03}	−0.07	.06
θ_1	−0.24	.03
θ_2	0.55	.04

Since examination of residuals $\hat{a}_t$ fails to show any obvious inadequacies in the model, we interpret the results as follows. The marginal distributions *a posteriori* of ω_{01}, ω_{02} and ω_{03} are very nearly normal and centered at the maximum likelihood estimate values with the approximate standard deviations shown.

Thus, there is evidence that

(i) associated with I_1 is a step change of approximately $\hat{\omega}_0 = -1.09$ units in the level of O_3;

(ii) associated with I_2 there is a progressive reduction in O_3. Over the period studied, there is a yearly increment of approximately $\hat{\omega}_{02} = -.25$ in the summer months, but the increment (if any) in the winter is slight.

5.2 Example 2: The Rate of Change in the U.S. Consumer Price Index

A second example supplies further intuitive appreciation for the kind of calculations being performed.

Figure C shows the latter part of a record of the monthly rate of change in the consumer price index (CPI) given more completely in [4]. The complete (July 1953 to December 1972) data include 234 successive values, 218 of which occurred prior to the institution of

C. *Monthly Rate of Inflation of the U.S. Consumer Price Index: January 1964–December 1972*

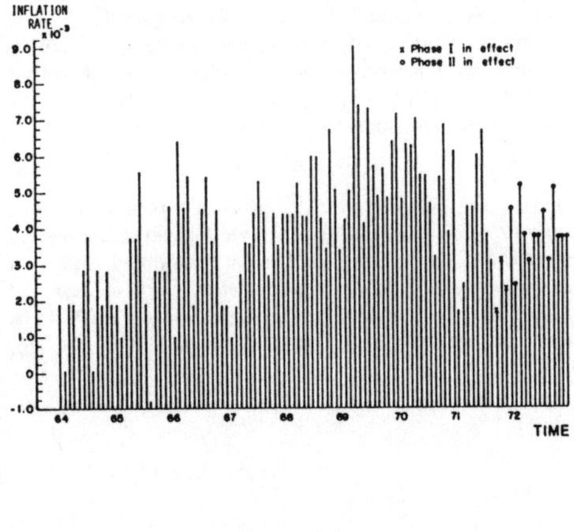

controls in August 1971. As indicated in the figure, in the three months beginning September 1971, Phase I control was applied; and after that to the end of the recorded period, Phase II was in effect.

Inspection of the autocorrelation functions of the first 218 observations and their differences prior to Phase I suggests a noise model of the form

$$(1 - B)N_t = (1 - \theta B)a_t \ . \tag{5.3}$$

The maximum likelihood values for the parameters are:

Parameter	*MLE*	*S.E.*
θ	0.84	.04
σ_a	0.0019	

Inspection of the residuals and their autocorrelations reveals no obvious inadequacies of this model, so we adopt it.

We now ask the question, "What are the possible effects of Phases I and II?" To answer, we suppose:

(i) that Phases I and II can be expected to produce changes in level of the rate of change of the CPI,

(ii) that the form of the noise model remains essentially the same.

On these assumptions, the approximate model (ignoring estimation errors in the noise structure) is

$$y_t = \omega_{01}\xi_{t1} + \omega_{02}\xi_{t2} + \{(1 - .84B)/(1 - B)\}a_t \tag{5.4}$$

where

$$\xi_{t1} = \begin{cases} 1, & t = \text{September, October and November 1971} \\ 0, & \text{otherwise} \end{cases}$$

$$\xi_{t2} = \begin{cases} 1, & t \geq \text{December 1971} \\ 0, & \text{otherwise} \end{cases}$$

which may be written

$$z_t = \omega_{01}x_{t1} + \omega_{02}x_{t2} + a_t \ . \tag{5.5}$$

The sequences $\{z_t\}$, $\{x_{t1}\}$, $\{x_{t2}\}$ may be readily calculated from the equations

$$(1 - .84B)z_t = (1 - B)y_t$$
$$(1 - .84B)x_{t1} = (1 - B)\xi_{t1}$$
$$(1 - .84B)x_{t2} = (1 - B)\xi_{t2}$$

using, e.g., the initial approximation $z_1 = x_{11} = x_{12} = 0$.

Also, since

$$(1 - B)/(1 - \theta B) = 1 - B(1 - \theta)(1 + \theta B + \theta^2B^2 + \cdots) \ ,$$

we have

$$z_t = y_t - \bar{y}_{t-1} \ , \quad x_{t1} = \xi_{t1} - \bar{\xi}_{t-1,1} \ , \quad x_{t2} = \xi_{t2} - \bar{\xi}_{t-1,2}$$

where $\bar{y}_{t-1}$, $\bar{\xi}_{t-1,1}$ and $\bar{\xi}_{t-1,2}$ are exponentially weighted moving averages of values prior to time t, e.g.,

$$\bar{y}_{t-1} = (1 - \theta)(y_{t-1} + \theta y_{t-2} + \theta^2 y_{t-3} + \cdots) \ .$$

We see that (5.5) is very much like the regression equations we are all familiar with in which the deviation of y_t from its average is related to the deviations of ξ_{t1} and ξ_{t2} from their averages. Notice, however, that the model copes with nonstationarity by using not the usual arithmetic averages, but local exponentially weighted averages which change as the series progresses.

Using (5.5), the constants ω_{01} and ω_{02} may now be estimated by ordinary linear least squares as

Parameter	*MLE*	*SE*
ω_{01}	−0.0022	0.0010
ω_{02}	−0.0007	0.0009

Alternatively, a nonlinear least squares program may be employed to estimate ω_{01}, ω_{02} and θ simultaneously from the complete set of 234 data values yielding the estimates (essentially as before):

Parameter	*MLE*	*SE*
θ	0.85	.05
ω_{01}	−0.0022	0.0010
ω_{02}	−0.0008	0.0009

The analysis suggests that a real drop in the rate of increase of the CPI is associated with Phase I, but the effect of Phase II is less certain.

6. NATURE OF THE MAXIMUM LIKELIHOOD ESTIMATORS FOR SOME LEVEL CHANGE PARAMETERS

The maximum likelihood estimators of parameters such as ω_{01}, ω_{02} and ω_{03} in (5.2) and (5.4) which measure level changes are functions of the data. It is instructive to consider the nature of these functions. Several results in the summation of series useful in the following discussion are given in the appendix.

6.1 One Parameter "Linear" Dynamic Model

Consider first the dynamic model in (3.2). Formally, it can be written

$$Q(B)y_t = (\varphi(B)/\theta(B))(\omega(B)/\delta(B))\xi_t + a_t \quad (6.1)$$

where $Q(B) = \varphi(B)/\theta(B)$, even though in practice the y_t are only available for $t = 1, \cdots, n$. Since the roots of $\theta(B)$ all lie outside the unit circle, $Q(B)$ can be expressed as a power series in B which converges for $|B| = 1$.

Here we discuss the situation where

$$(\varphi(B)/\theta(B))(\omega(B)/\delta(B)) = \beta R(B) \quad (6.2)$$

and investigate the nature of the maximum likelihood estimator of β, assuming that (i) the coefficients in $Q(B)$ and $R(B)$ are known and (ii) the power series $R(B)$ converges for $|B| = 1$.

Letting

$$z_t = Q(B)y_t \quad \text{and} \quad x_t = R(B)\xi_t ,$$

we can write (6.1) in the form of the usual linear model

$$z_t = \beta x_t + a_t \quad (6.3)$$

so that the maximum likelihood estimator of β is

$$\hat{\beta} = \sum_{t=1}^{n} z_t x_t / \sum_{t=1}^{n} (x_t)^2$$

with

$$\text{Var}(\hat{\beta}) = (\sigma_a)^2 (\sum_{t=1}^{n} (x_t)^2)^{-1} . \quad (6.4)$$

For large n, we apply the results (A.6) and (A.7) in the appendix to obtain

$$\sum_{t=1}^{\infty} z_t x_t = \sum_{t=1}^{\infty} Q(B)y_t R(B)\xi_t = \sum_{t=1}^{\infty} \xi_t R(F)Q(B)y_t = R(F)Q(B)C_{\xi y}(0)$$

where $F = B^{-1}$ and

$$\sum_{t=1}^{n} (x_t)^2 = \sum_{t=1}^{\infty} R(B)\xi_t R(B)\xi_t = R(F)R(B)C_{\xi\xi}(0) ,$$

where

$$C_{\alpha\beta}(k) = \sum_{t=1}^{\infty} \beta_t \alpha_{t-k} , \quad k = 0, \pm 1, \pm 2, \cdots ,$$

and for a given k

$$B^l C_{\alpha\beta}(k) = C_{\alpha\beta}(k - l) , \quad l = 0, \pm 1, \pm 2, \cdots .$$

Thus,

$$\hat{\beta} = R(F)Q(B)C_{\xi y}(0)/R(F)R(B)C_{\xi\xi}(0) \quad (6.5)$$

and

$$\text{Var}(\hat{\beta}) = (\sigma_a)^2/R(F)R(B)C_{\xi\xi}(0) .$$

Making use of (A.10) in the appendix, we can write $R(B)R(F)$ as

$$R(B)R(F) = r_0 + \sum_{l=1}^{\infty} r_l(B^l + F^l) . \quad (6.6)$$

Suppose that $\xi_t = P_t^{(T)}$ is a pulse at time T, and a large number of observations are available before and after T. In this case

$$C_{\xi\xi}(k) = \begin{cases} 1, & k = 0 \\ 0, & k \neq 0 \end{cases} \quad \text{and} \quad C_{\xi y}(k) = y_{T-k} , \quad (6.7)$$

so that

$$\hat{\beta} = (r_0)^{-1}R(F)Q(B)y_T \quad \text{and} \quad \text{Var}(\hat{\beta}) = (\sigma_a)^2(r_0)^{-1} \quad (6.8)$$

where it is understood that B is operating on T.

Now, nonstationarity in time series data can often be removed by differencing. In what follows we suppose that the polynomial $\varphi(B)$ in (6.1) is divisible by $(1 - B)$. We consider two special cases of interest.

Case (i). $\quad \omega(B)/\delta(B) = \beta B , \quad (6.9)$

that is, the pulse input $P_t^{(T)}$ gives rise to a response at time $(T + 1)$ measured by β which dissipates completely after the $(T + 1)$th period. It should be noted that with any number of periods of pure delay, the response will follow the same pattern but be appropriately shifted. In this case, $Q(B) = R(B)F$ so that, from (6.6) and (6.8),

$$\hat{\beta} = y_{T+1} - \tfrac{1}{2} \sum_{l=1}^{\infty} \lambda_l(y_{T+1+l} + y_{T+1-l}) , \quad (6.10)$$

where $\lambda_l = -2r_l/r_0$. Also, since $\varphi(B)$ is assumed divisible by $(1 - B)$, $r_0 + 2\sum_{l=1}^{\infty} r_l = 0$, and hence $\sum_{l=1}^{\infty} \lambda_l = 1$.

As an example, consider the integrated moving average model of order one for the noise term N_t for which

$$\varphi(B) = 1 - B \quad \text{and} \quad \theta(B) = 1 - \theta B \; . \qquad (6.11)$$

Since

$$R(B)R(F) = \frac{(1 - B)(1 - F)}{(1 - \theta B)(1 - \theta F)}$$

$$= (1 + \theta)^{-1} \cdot [2 - (1 - \theta) \sum_{l=1}^{\infty} \theta^{l-1}(B^l + F^l)] \; ,$$

we find that

$$\lambda_l = (1 - \theta)\theta^{l-1} \; . \qquad (6.12)$$

Thus, $\hat{\beta}$ represents a comparison between y_{T+1} and the mean of two exponentially weighted averages, one of the observations before time $(T + 1)$ and the other after, with the magnitude of the weights $(1 - \theta)\theta^{l-1}$ monotonically decreasing as l increases.

This formulation is applicable to situations where the response to the pulse input is expected to be short-lived, e.g., the effect on the demand for electricity during a sudden heat wave in the summer or the sale of beer in Wisconsin should the Packers win the Super Bowl. Essentially, we are comparing the observation y_{T+1} with the neighboring ones to determine if y_{T+1} is an "aberrant" or "outlying" observation. The results in (6.10) and (6.12) are appealing since, in forming the comparison, more weight is given to observations close to the intervening event and less and less weight to observations remote from the time of the event.

Case (ii). $\omega(B)/\delta(B) = \beta B/(1 - B)$. (6.13)

Here, the response to the pulse $P_t^{(T)}$ is a step change in the level of the observations measured by β. Thus

$$Q(B) = (1 - B)R(B)F \qquad (6.14)$$

and, from (6.6), (6.8) and (A.11), we have that

$$\hat{\beta} = (r_0)^{-1}R(B)R(F)(1 - B)y_{T+1}$$

$$= \sum_{l=0}^{\infty} \alpha_l y_{T+1+l} - \sum_{l=0}^{\infty} \alpha_l y_{T-l} \qquad (6.15)$$

where $\alpha_l = (r_0)^{-1}(r_l - r_{l+1})$ so that $\sum_{l=0}^{\infty} \alpha_l = 1$.

The quantity $\hat{\beta}$ is, therefore, a contrast between two weighted averages, one of observations before the intervening pulse $P_t^{(T)}$ and the other afterward, where the weights are symmetrical.

As a first example, consider again the integrated moving average model in (6.11). We find

$$\hat{\beta} = (1 - \theta) \sum_{l=0}^{\infty} \theta^l y_{T+1+l} - (1 - \theta) \sum_{l=0}^{\infty} \theta^l y_{T-l} \qquad (6.16)$$

as obtained in [2].

As a second example, we return to the model in (5.2) for the monthly averages of ozone in downtown Los Angeles. For illustration, we shall ignore the effect of interventions after 1966 and discuss the step change

$$(\beta B/(1 - B))P_t^{(T)} = \omega_{01}\xi_{t1} \; , \quad T = \text{December 1959}$$

in the level of the series due to the intervening events around that time. In this case, the noise model is such that

$$\varphi(B) = (1 - B^{12})$$

and

$$\theta(B) = (1 - \theta_1 B)(1 - \theta_2 B^{12}) \; .$$

Thus,

$$R(B)R(F) = \frac{(\sum_{j=0}^{11} B^j)(\sum_{j=0}^{11} F^j)}{(1 - \theta_1 B)(1 - \theta_2 B^{12})(1 - \theta_1 F)(1 - \theta_2 F^{12})}$$

$$= (\sum_{j=0}^{\infty} \pi_j B^j)(\sum_{j=0}^{\infty} \pi_j F^j) \qquad (6.17)$$

so that from (A.10),

$$r_l = \sum_{j=0}^{\infty} \pi_j \pi_{j+l} \; .$$

The π_j can be obtained from the relationship

$$(1 - \theta_1 B)(1 - \theta_2 B^{12}) \sum_{j=0}^{\infty} \pi_j B^j = \sum_{j=0}^{11} B^j \; .$$

By writing $\pi_j = 12n + m$, we find

$$\pi_{12n+m} = (1 - \theta_1)^{-1}(\phi - \theta_2)^{-1}[(\theta_1)^{m+1}\{(1 - \phi)\phi^n - (1 - \theta_2)(\theta_2)^n\} + (\phi - \theta_2)(\theta_2)^n] \; ,$$
$$m = 0, \cdots, 11; n = 0, \cdots, \infty \qquad (6.18)$$

where $\phi = (\theta_1)^{12}$.

From (6.18) and after some algebraic reduction, we obtain, on setting $l = 12k + s$,

$$r_{12k+s} = (1 - \theta_1)^{-2}(1 - (\theta_2)^2)^{-1} \cdot \left[12 - s(1 - \theta_2) + \frac{\theta_1(1 - \theta_2)^2}{1 - (\theta_1)^2} \cdot \left(\frac{\phi(\theta_1)^{-s}}{1 - \phi\theta_2} - \frac{(\theta_1)^s}{\phi - \theta_2}\right)\right](\theta_2)^k + (1 - \theta_1)^{-2}$$
$$\cdot (\phi - \theta_2)^{-1}(1 - \phi\theta_2)^{-1}(1 - (\theta_1)^2)^{-1} \cdot (1 - \phi)^2(\theta_1)^{s+1}\phi^k \; , \qquad (6.19)$$

$$s = 0, \cdots, 11; \quad k = 0, \cdots, \infty \; .$$

The resulting weight function for the Los Angeles data is shown in Figure A above the observations.

6.2 The General "Linear" Dynamic Model

The result in (6.5) can be readily extended to the case of more than one parameter. In the general dynamic model with k inputs in (4.1), letting

$$(\varphi(B)/\theta(B))(\omega_j(B)/\delta_j(B)) = \beta_j R_j(B) \qquad (6.20)$$

we can write

$$Q(B)y_t = \sum_{j=1}^{k} \beta_j R_j(B)\xi_{tj} + a_t, \quad t = 1, \cdots, n \qquad (6.21)$$

where, as before in (6.1), $Q(B) = \varphi(B)/\theta(B)$. Assuming that all the coefficients in $Q(B)$ and $R_j(B)$ are known and these $k+1$ power series converge for $|B| = 1$, the model is then linear in the k parameters $\boldsymbol{\beta} = (\beta_1, \cdots, \beta_k)'$. It readily follows that, for large n, the maximum likelihood estimator $\hat{\boldsymbol{\beta}}$ satisfies the normal equations

$$\mathbf{A}\hat{\boldsymbol{\beta}} = \mathbf{b} \qquad (6.22)$$

where $\mathbf{A}$ is a $k \times k$ matrix and $\mathbf{b}$ a $k \times 1$ vector such that

$$\mathbf{A} = [a_{ij}] , \quad a_{ij} = R_i(F)R_j(B)C_{\xi_i\xi_j}(0)$$
$$\mathbf{b} = (b_1, \cdots, b_k)'$$

with

$$b_j = R_j(F)Q(B)C_{\xi_j y}(0) ; \quad i, j = 1, \cdots, k .$$

In what follows, we investigate the special case having two parameters,

$$y_t = \{\beta_1\eta(B)B + \beta_2(1 - B)^{-1}B\}P_t^{(T)} + (\theta(B)/\varphi(B))a_t . \qquad (6.23)$$

In this model, $\beta_1\eta(B)BP_t^{(T)}$, where $\eta(B)$ is assumed to converge for $|B| = 1$, measures the transient effect, and β_2 represents the eventual change in the level of the observations induced by the pulse input $P_t^{(T)}$ (see Figure B(e) for the special case $\eta(B) = (1 - \delta B)^{-1}$). When $\beta_1 = 0$, the model reduces to that considered in (6.13). It is, therefore, of particular interest to know to what extent the nature and precision of the estimator of β_2 is affected by the presence of β_1. We again suppose that the noise term is nonstationary so that $\varphi(B)$ is divisible by $(1 - B)$.

To facilitate comparison with the model (6.13) we again define a quantity $R(B)$ such that

$$Q(B) = (1 - B)R(B)F ,$$

so that in (6.22)

$$R_1(B) = Q(B)\eta(B)B = R(B)\eta(B)(1 - B)$$

and

$$R_2(B) = R(B) .$$

It follows that, provided $|\mathbf{A}| \neq 0$,

$$\hat{\beta}_1 = |\mathbf{A}|^{-1}\{a_{22}b_1 - a_{12}b_2\} ,$$
$$\hat{\beta}_2 = |\mathbf{A}|^{-1}\{a_{11}b_2 - a_{12}b_1\} \qquad (6.24)$$

where

$$|\mathbf{A}| = a_{11}a_{22} - (a_{12})^2 ,$$
$$b_1 = R(B)R(F)(1 - F)\eta(F)(1 - B)y_{T+1} ,$$
$$b_2 = R(B)R(F)(1 - B)y_{T+1} ,$$

and a_{11}, a_{12} and a_{22} are, respectively, the coefficients of B^0 in the power series

$$R(B)R(F)\eta(B)\eta(F)(1 - B)(1 - F) ,$$
$$R(B)R(F)\eta(B)(1 - B) ,$$
$$R(B)R(F) .$$

Some Properties of $\hat{\beta}_1$ and $\hat{\beta}_2$.

(i) Both b_1 and b_2 are linear functions of the observations y_t. By setting $B = F = 1$, the sum of the coefficients associated with y_t is zero for both of these functions. Thus, $\hat{\beta}_1$ and $\hat{\beta}_2$ are linear contrasts in y_t.

(ii) The estimator $\hat{\beta}_2$ can be expressed in the form

$$\hat{\beta}_2 = \sum_{l=0}^{\infty} \alpha_{1l}y_{T+1+l} - \sum_{l=0}^{\infty} \alpha_{2l}y_{T-l}$$

where (6.25)

$$\sum_{l=0}^{\infty} \alpha_{1l} = \sum_{l=0}^{\infty} \alpha_{2l} = 1 ,$$

i.e., a contrast between two weighted averages, one of observations on or before the pulse input and the other afterward. To see this, since $\hat{\beta}_2$ is a linear contrast, it suffices to show that $\sum_{l=0}^{\infty} \alpha_{1l} = 1$.

From the expression for b_2 in (6.24), letting

$$G(B) = R(B)R(F) , \quad H(B) = 1 - B$$

and

$$b_2 = \sum_{l=-\infty}^{\infty} d_l y_{T+1-l}$$

it follows from (A.11) that $\sum_{l=-\infty}^{0} d_l = a_{22}$.

Further, making use of (A.12) and (A.13), we see that a_{12} in (6.24) is also the coefficient of B^0 in $R(B)R(F) \cdot (1 - F)\eta(F)$. If we now set

$$G_1(B) = R(B)R(F)(1 - F)\eta(F) , \quad H_1(B) = 1 - B$$

and

$$b_1 = \sum_{l=-\infty}^{\infty} d_l^* y_{T+1-l} ,$$

we then have $\sum_{l=-\infty}^{0} d_l^* = a_{12}$. The desired result follows since

$$\sum_{l=0}^{\infty} \alpha_{1l} = |\mathbf{A}|^{-1}\{a_{11} \sum_{l=-\infty}^{0} d_l - a_{12} \sum_{l=-\infty}^{0} d_l^*\} = 1 .$$

This property is similar to that of $\hat{\beta}$ in (6.15) for the model (6.13), except that the weight functions are no longer symmetrical. From least squares theory, we have

$$\hat{\beta}_2 = \hat{\beta} - (a_{12}/|\mathbf{A}|)(b_1 - a_{12}\hat{\beta}) , \qquad (6.26)$$

and the second term on the right side measures the effect of the presence of the term $\beta_1\eta(B)BP_t^{(T)}$ in the model.

(iii) One would expect that addition of the parameter β_1 to the model would reduce the precision with which β_2 could be estimated. A useful measure of the loss of information is the variance ratio Var $(\hat{\beta}_2)$/Var$(\hat{\beta})$ where it is understood that the denominator corresponds to the model in (6.13). Now

$$\text{Var }(\hat{\beta}_2)/\text{Var }(\hat{\beta}) = (1 - \rho^2)^{-1}$$

where (6.27)

$$\rho = a_{12}/(a_{11}a_{22})^{\frac{1}{2}} .$$

We illustrate these results in terms of a specific example. Consider the case of (6.23) in which

$$\eta(B) = (1 - \delta B)^{-1}, \quad \varphi(B) = 1 - B \text{ and } \theta(B) = 1 - \theta B.$$

We find

$$\hat{\beta}_2 = \hat{\beta} - \frac{(1-\theta)(1+\delta)}{(\theta-\delta)} \sum_{l=0}^{\infty} [(1-\delta)\delta^l - (1-\theta)\theta^l] y_{T+1+l} , \quad (6.28)$$

where $\hat{\beta}$ is given in (6.16). In this case only the weights associated with the observations after the intervening pulse $P_t^{(T)}$ are affected by the presence of $\beta_1(1-\delta B)^{-1}BP_t^{(T)}$ in the model. The weight function is shown in Figure D for $\theta = .5$ and $\delta = .25$.

D. Comparison of Weights Associated with y_{T+1+l} $\hat{\beta}_2$ and for $\hat{\beta}$ ($\theta = .05$, $\delta = .25$, $l = 0, 1, 2, \ldots$)

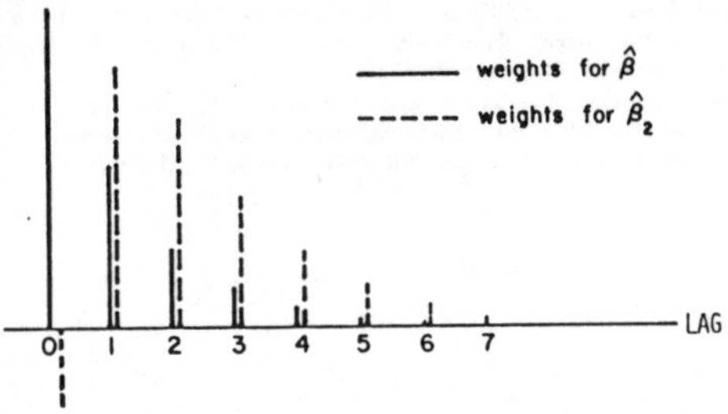

Also, for this model the variance ratio is

$$V = \text{Var}(\hat{\beta}_2)/\text{Var}(\hat{\beta}) = 1 + ((1-\theta)(1+\delta)/(1+\theta)(1-\delta)) . \quad (6.29)$$

The value of this ratio for various values of θ and δ is shown in the following tabulation:

θ	δ: −.5	−.25	0	.25	.5
−.5	2.00	2.80	4.00	6.00	10.00
−.25	1.56	2.00	2.67	3.78	6.00
0	1.33	1.60	2.00	2.67	4.00
.25	1.20	1.36	1.60	2.00	2.80
.5	1.11	1.20	1.33	1.56	2.00

Thus, the presence of β_1 in the model can cause large increases in the variance of $\hat{\beta}_2$, compared with $\hat{\beta}$, when θ is negative and δ is positive.

7. CONCLUDING REMARKS

In the past, much attention has been given to statistical analysis linking phenomena which are coincidental in time. In practice, it is perhaps more often the case that a response at a given point of time depends on events, both known and unknown, which have occurred not necessarily coincidentally but over the recent past. Statistical methods have, in a word, "lacked memory." The dynamic characteristics of both the transfer function and the noise parts of the model have tended to be ignored. The application of time series methods can amend this situation. This is illustrated in this article in the particular case where the object is to study the possible effect of interventions in the presence of dependent noise structure.

APPENDIX

We here state some useful results in the summation of series.

Lemma 1: Let $\{v_k\}_0^\infty$ be a sequence of numbers and let $\{x_t\}_{-\infty}^\infty$ and $\{y_t\}_{-\infty}^\infty$ be two sequences of numbers such that $x_t \equiv y_t \equiv 0$ for $t \leq 0$. If one of the following three double sums is absolutely convergent,

$$S_1 = \sum_{t=1}^{\infty}\sum_{k=0}^{\infty} x_t v_k y_{t-k} , \quad S_2 = \sum_{u=1}^{\infty}\sum_{k=0}^{\infty} y_u v_k x_{u+k} , \quad (A.1)$$

$$S_3 = \sum_{k=0}^{\infty}\sum_{u=1}^{\infty} v_k y_u x_{u+k},$$

the other two are absolutely convergent and

$$S_1 = S_2 = S_3 .$$

Proof of the lemma can be found in any standard text on infinite series.

It is convenient to express S_1, S_2 and S_3 in terms of the backshift operator B and its reciprocal, the forward shift operator $F = B^{-1}$. Letting

$$V(B) = \sum_{k=0}^{\infty} v_k B^k \quad \text{and} \quad V(F) = \sum_{k=0}^{\infty} v_k F^k \quad (A.2)$$

we can then write

$$S_1 = \sum_{t=1}^{\infty} x_t V(B) y_t \quad \text{and} \quad S_2 = \sum_{t=1}^{\infty} y_t V(F) x_t . \quad (A.3)$$

Further, suppose we define

$$C_{xy}(k) = \sum_{t=1}^{\infty} y_t x_{t-k} , \quad C_{yx}(k) = \sum_{t=1}^{\infty} x_t y_{t-k} , \quad k = 0, \pm 1, \pm 2, \cdots$$

so that

$$C_{xy}(k) = C_{yx}(-k) . \quad (A.4)$$

The quantity S_3 in (6.1) can be expressed as

$$S_3 = \sum_{k=0}^{\infty} v_k C_{xy}(-k) ,$$

and, by letting $C_{xy}(-k) = B^k C_{xy}(0)$, we have

$$S_3 = V(B) C_{xy}(0) . \quad (A.5)$$

It follows that when the conditions of Lemma 1 hold,

$$\sum_{t=1}^{\infty} x_t V(B) y_t = \sum_{t=1}^{\infty} y_t V(F) x_t = V(B) C_{xy}(0) . \quad (A.6)$$

This result can be readily extended to the following:

Lemma 2: Suppose $W(B) = V_1(B) + V_2(F)$ where $V_1(B)$ and $V_2(F)$ are two power series in B and F, respectively, such that the sum $\sum_{t=1}^{\infty} x_t W(B) y_t$ is absolutely convergent. Then

$$\sum_{t=1}^{\infty} x_t W(B) y_t = W(B) C_{xy}(0) . \quad (A.7)$$

Lemma 3: Let $G(B) = \sum_{j=-\infty}^{\infty} g_j B^j$ and $H(B) = \sum_{k=-\infty}^{\infty} h_k B^k$ be two power series in B and converge for $|B| = 1$, and let $D(B)$

$= G(B)H(B)$. Then

$$D(B) = \sum_{l=-\infty}^{\infty} d_l B^l \tag{A.8}$$

where $$d_l = \sum_{j=-\infty}^{\infty} g_j h_{l-j} \ .$$

In particular

(i) if $g_j = g_{-j}$ and $h_k = h_{-k}$, then

$$d_l = d_{-l} = \sum_{u=0}^{\infty} h_u g_{u+l} + \sum_{u=1-l}^{\infty} g_u h_{u+l} \ , l = 0, \cdots, \infty \ ; \tag{A.9}$$

(ii) if $g_j = 0, j \leq -1$ and $H(B) = G(F)$, then

$$d_l = d_{-l} = \sum_{j=0}^{\infty} g_j g_{j+l} \ , \quad l = 0, \cdots, \infty \ ; \tag{A.10}$$

(iii) if $H(B) = 1 - B$, then

$$d_l = g_l - g_{l-1} \qquad l = 0, \pm 1, \cdots, \pm \infty \ , \tag{A.11}$$

so that $\sum_{l=1}^{\infty} d_l = -g_0$ and $\sum_{l=-\infty}^{0} d_l = g_0$;

(iv) if $g_j = g_{-j}$ and $h_j = 0 \ \ j \leq -1$, then

$$d_0 = \sum_{j=0}^{\infty} h_j g_j \ ; \tag{A.12}$$

(v) if $g_j = g_{-j}$ and $h_j = 0 \ \ j \geq 1$, then

$$d_0 = \sum_{j=-\infty}^{0} h_j g_j \ . \tag{A.13}$$

[Received October 1973. Revised August 1974.]

REFERENCES

[1] Box, G.E.P. and Jenkins, G.M., *Time Series Analysis, Forecasting and Control*, San Francisco: Holden-Day, Inc., 1970.

[2] ——— and Tiao, G.C., "A Change in Level of a Non-stationary Time Series," *Biometrika*, 52 (June 1965), 181–92.

[3] ——— and Tiao, G.C., *Bayesian Inference in Statistical Analysis*, Reading, Mass.: Addison-Wesley Publishing Co., 1973.

[4] Feige, E. and Pearce, D.K., "Inflation and Income Policy: An Application of Time Series Models," Report #7318, Social Systems Research Institute, University of Wisconsin, Madison, 1973.

[5] Glass, G.V., "Estimating the Effects of Intervention into a Nonstationary Time Series," *American Educational Research Journal*, 9, No. 3 (1972), 463–77.

[6] Tiao, G.C., Box, G.E.P. and Hamming, W.J., "Analysis of Los Angeles Photochemical Smog Data: A Statistical Overview," *Journal of Air Pollution Control Association*, 25 (March 1975).

J. R. Statist. Soc. A. (1986)
149, *Part* 3, *pp.* 187–227

The Effects of Seat Belt Legislation on British Road Casualties: A Case Study in Structural Time Series Modelling

By A. C. HARVEY and J. DURBIN†
London School of Economics and Political Science, UK

[*Read before* the Royal Statistical Society *on Wednesday, March 15th, 1986, Professor M. J. R. Healy in the Chair*]

SUMMARY

Monthly data on road casualties in Great Britain are analysed in order to assess the effects on casualty rates of the seat belt law introduced on January 31st, 1983. Such analysis is known technically as intervention analysis. The form of intervention analysis used in this paper is based on structural time series modelling and differs in significant respects from standard intervention analysis based on *ARIMA* modelling. The relative merits of the two approaches are compared. Structural modelling intervention techniques are used to estimate the changes in casualty rates for various categories of road users following the introduction of the seat belt law.

Keywords: ROAD CASUALTIES; SEAT BELT LAW; STRUCTURAL MODELS; ARIMA MODELS; INTERVENTION ANALYSIS; KALMAN FILTER; DIAGNOSTICS; CUSUM; RECURSIVE RESIDUALS; RISK COMPENSATION

1. INTRODUCTION

The wearing of seat belts by front seat occupants of cars and light goods vehicles was made compulsory in the UK on January 31 1983. The law was introduced initially for an experimental period of three years with the intention that Parliament would consider extending the legislation before the expiry of this period. The Department of Transport undertook to monitor the effect of the law on road casualties and as part of this monitoring exercise they invited us early in 1985 to conduct an independent technical assessment of the statistical evidence.

A full description of the findings of the investigation and the methods used has been given in our report to the Department (Durbin and Harvey, 1985). The purposes of the present paper are:

(a) to provide an opportunity for public discussion of the results of our analysis of the effects of the seat belt law on road casualties: and
(b) to invite a technical debate on the methodology we used and in particular on the relative merits of structural modelling and *ARIMA* modelling for this type of investigation.

The main data we examined consisted of numbers killed and numbers seriously injured each month for various categories of road users for the period from January 1969 to December 1984. Our task was to investigate changes in casualty rates attributable to the introduction of the seat belt law. The standard way for time series analysts to tackle problems of this type in recent years has been to use Box-Tiao (1975) intervention analysis based on Box-Jenkins (1970) *ARIMA* modelling. However, we have become increasingly dissatisfied with various aspects of standard *ARIMA* modelling. In particular, we have become disenchanted with the notion that the appropriate way to deal with trend and seasonal components is to eliminate

† *Present address*: Dept of Statistical and Mathematical Sciences, London School of Economics and Political Science, Houghton St., London WC2A 2AE, UK.

 0035–9238/86/149187 $2.00

them by differencing. We are also sceptical about the emphasis on stationarity of the differenced series.

Our views on time series modelling are consistent with our general attitude to statistical modelling. We believe that the statistician should seek to identify the main observable features of the phenomena under study and should then attempt to incorporate in his model an explicit allowance for each of these main features. Visual inspection of graphs of time series usually reveal trends and seasonals as important observable features of the data, and it seems desirable to model these features explicitly. By analogy with usage in econometrics this procedure is called structural modelling. In a structural model of an economic system each component or equation is intended to represent a specific feature or relationship in the system under study. Sometimes it is convenient to transform the structural model into a particular alternative form for specific purposes, such as forecasting, and this is called the reduced form of the model. In the time series case it is possible to transform a linear structural model into an *ARIMA* model and this may then be referred to as the reduced form of the structural model.

The historical development of the structural models used in this work can be traced in papers by Muth (1960), Theil and Wage (1964), Harrison (1967), Harrison and Stevens (1976), Engle (1978), Kitagawa (1981), Harvey and Todd (1983), Durbin (1984) and Harvey (1984, 1985a) together with further references given in these papers. At the time we received the invitation from the Department of Transport to analyse the road casualty data, one of us (ACH) had been developing techniques and computer programs for time series structural modelling during the previous two or three years as part of an ESRC funded research programme in econometrics at the London School of Economics. It turned out that with relatively little modification these techniques and programs could be used for the road casualties analysis and we concluded that they were better suited to the purpose than standard *ARIMA* intervention analysis. We have therefore used them throughout, though we did in fact carry out some parallel *ARIMA* analyses for comparative purposes.

The paper is organised as follows. In Section 2 we present the models used in the paper and refer briefly to the Kalman filter techniques used for fitting them. Section 3 discusses the data used in the study. In Section 4 we explain how an appropriate model is selected for a particular series and discuss the diagnostic techniques used to assess the fit of models to the data. For this purpose we illustrate by considering monthly numbers of car drivers killed and seriously injured. Section 5 considers how the effect of an intervention is assessed in structural modelling. In this application the intervention is the introduction of the seat belt law. Section 6 summarises the results obtained. In Section 7 we discuss our conclusions.

2. STRUCTURAL TIME SERIES MODELS

2.1. *The Basic Structural Model*

The starting point for the construction of structural models is the traditional representation of a time series as a sum of trend, seasonal and irregular components

$$y_t = \mu_t + \gamma_t + \varepsilon_t, \quad t = 1, \ldots, T \tag{2.1}$$

where y_t denotes the tth observation, possibly after some transformation such as the logarithmic, and μ_t, γ_t and ε_t are the trend, seasonal and irregular components. A simple special case is that in which μ_t is the deterministic linear trend $\alpha + \beta t$ and γ_t is a strictly periodic function of period s where s is the number of months per year. However, this form is of very limited application since usually some provision is needed to permit the structure to evolve over time.

The basic idea of how this can be achieved came from Muth (1960) who considered the case where there is no seasonal and the trend has no slope but the level μ_t evolves over time in a random walk, giving the model

$$y_t = \mu_t + \varepsilon_t, \qquad \mu_t = \mu_{t-1} + \eta_t, \tag{2.2}$$

where ε_t and η_t are independent white noise terms. It is easy to show that (2.2) is equivalent to a model in which the first differences $y_t - y_{t-1} = \Delta y_t$ follow an $MA(1)$ model. Muth then showed that the one-step ahead forecasts produced by the simplest form of exponentially weighted moving average given by Holt (1957) and Winters (1960) are minimum mean-square error ($MMSE$) forecasts for observations generated by model (2.2) and hence for the equivalent $ARIMA$ (0, 1, 1) model.

Subsequently, Theil and Wage (1964) extended Muth's model to include a trend that is locally linear, but where both level and slope are determined by random walks. This gives the model

$$y_t = \mu_t + \varepsilon_t \tag{2.3a}$$

$$\mu_t = \mu_{t-1} + \beta_{t-1} + \eta_t, \quad \beta_t = \beta_{t-1} + \zeta_t. \tag{2.3b}$$

where ζ_t is a white noise disturbance term independent of ε_t and η_t.

They showed that the $MMSE$ forecasts for this model are given by the first two Holt-Winters recursions for the special case $\sigma_\eta^2 = 0$. Nerlove and Wage (1964) then showed that second differences of observations generated by (2.3) follow an $MA(2)$ model.

At this point in the early or mid 1960's it appears using hindsight that the theory of $MMSE$ forecasting might have developed either by extension of structural models (2.2) and (2.3) or alternatively by extension of the differencing method to deal with higher-order trends and seasonals. In this connection the following quotation from p. 207 of Nerlove and Wage (1964) is of considerable interest. "We believe, therefore, that the results of this paper illustrate a general approach to the prediction of non-stationary time series, and these are, after all, the type mainly encountered in ecnomic or management problems. Thus the paper may have a somewhat wider significance than its title or primary purpose might suggest". In the event Box and Jenkins followed the $ARIMA$ route.

The key to the handling of the computations needed for structural models of great generality is the Kalman filter and it is worth noting that Kalman's (1960) paper was already available when work on $ARIMA$ modelling began. Nevertheless, with the computational technology available at the time the calculations required would have been extremely burdensome. Furthermore, it was a long time after the publication of Schweppe's (1965) paper before statisticians realised that the likelihood function could be constructed for quite complex models by means of the Kalman filter.

Independent work on structural modelling was being done in the 1960's by P. J. Harrison and some of this work for non-seasonal series is described in Harrison (1967). There are various ways in which seasonal components can be incorporated into structural models and two general techniques are described by Harrison and Stevens (1976).

Our preferred technique for handling seasonality is to employ the trigonometric model

$$\gamma_t = \sum_{j=1}^{s/2} \gamma_{jt} \tag{2.4a}$$

where, with s even and $\lambda_j = 2\pi j/s$,

$$\begin{bmatrix} \gamma_{jt} \\ \gamma_{jt}^* \end{bmatrix} = \begin{bmatrix} \cos\lambda_j & \sin\lambda_j \\ -\sin\lambda_j & \cos\lambda_j \end{bmatrix} \begin{bmatrix} \gamma_{j,t-1} \\ \gamma_{j,t-1}^* \end{bmatrix} + \begin{bmatrix} \omega_{jt} \\ \omega_{jt}^* \end{bmatrix}, j = 1, \ldots, \tfrac{1}{2}s - 1, \tag{2.4b}$$

$$\gamma_{jt} = (\cos\lambda_j)\gamma_{j,t-1} + \omega_{jt}, j = \tfrac{1}{2}s, \tag{2.4c}$$

and where the ω_{jt}'s and ω_{jt}^*'s are both $NID(0, \sigma_\omega^2)$ and are independent of each other. In a more general formulation, the variances of ω_{jt} and ω_{jt}^* are permitted to vary with j. The rationale for (2.4) is that if the disturbances ω_{jt} and ω_{jt}^* are set equal to zero the seasonal pattern is constant and (2.4) then provides updating formulae from one time period to the next for each trigonometric component of the seasonal pattern. The introduction of the disturbances permits the seasonal pattern to vary over time.

Our basic structural model (BSM) is specified by the relations (2.1), (2.3b) and (2.4). Its reduced from is obtained by taking first difference Δ followed by seasonal differences Δ_s. The resulting series $\Delta\Delta_s y_t$ is found to follow an $MA(s+1)$ process where the $s+1$ moving average coefficients are complicated functions of the variances of the disturbances σ_ε^2, σ_η^2, σ_ζ^2 and σ_ω^2.

2.2. *Explanatory Variables and Intervention Effects*

The structural model may be extended by adding exogenous explanatory variables to the right hand side of (2.1) giving

$$y_t = \mu_t + \gamma_t + \sum_{j=1}^{k} \delta_j x_{jt} + \varepsilon_t, \tag{2.5}$$

where x_{jt} is the value of the jth explanatory variable at time t and δ_j is its coefficient. There is no necessity for the x_{jt} series to have any stationarity properties either before or after differencing. If $\sigma_\eta^2 = \sigma_\zeta^2 = \sigma_\omega^2 = 0$, the model collapses to a standard regression model with a linear time trend and seasonal dummies in addition to the explanatory variables x_{jt}.

We now consider how to use structural modelling to estimate the effect of an intervention, such as the introduction of the seat belt law, at a particular point of time $t = \tau$. Within the $ARIMA$ system the appropriate technique is called intervention analysis and was introduced by Box and Tiao (1975). The ideas from which this approach was developed can easily be incorporated into the structural framework. In the simplest case we assume that the effect of the intervention occurs instantaneously at time τ and leads to an immediate change in the level of the series which remains constant at an amount λ say. Other possibilities are that there is an instantaneous response at time τ which increases or decreases subsequently or that the response builds up gradually following the intervention.

These possibilities can be accommodated by extending the model (2.5) to the form

$$y_t = \mu_t + \gamma_t + \sum_{j=1}^{k} \delta_j x_{jt} + \lambda w_t + \varepsilon_t \tag{2.6}$$

where we refer to w_t as the intervention variable. In the simplest case where the response in instantaneous and constant, w_t is the dummy variable defined by

$$w_t = \begin{cases} 0, & t < \tau, \\ 1, & t \geqslant \tau. \end{cases} \tag{2.7}$$

The formulation (2.6) is the model used for most of the work in this paper. There are many ways in which the model could be modified or extended. For example, claendar effects and higher order local polynomials can be allowed for, and cycles can be incorporated into the model as in Harvey (1985a). Extensions can be made to handle weekly or even daily data.

2.3. *Statistical Treatment*

Structural time series models of great apparent complexity can be efficiently fitted by powerful but straightforward general techniques. The key to these techniques is that the models can be put into state space form and then handled routinely by the Kalman filter. In its general univariate form the state space model consists of the following two equations:

$$y_t = z_t'\alpha_t + \varepsilon_t, \quad t = 1, \ldots, T \tag{2.8a}$$

called the measurement or observation equation, and

$$\alpha_t = T_t\alpha_{t-1} + \eta_t, \quad t = 1, \ldots, T \tag{2.8b}$$

called the transition or state equation. Here, y_t is the observation of interest, z_t is a non-stochastic vector, α_t is an $m \times 1$ state vector, T_t is a non-stochastic $m \times m$ matrix and ε_t, η_t are independent $NID(0, \sigma^2 h_t)$ and $NID(0, \sigma^2 Q_t)$ disturbances where h_t, Q_t are a scalar and an $m \times m$ matrix respectively and σ^2 is a positive scalar.

The advantage of this formulation is that there is a routine mechanical procedure for updating estimates, generally referred to as the Kalman filter. Maximum likelihood estimation can be performed either in the time domain, using the Kalman filter, or in the frequency domain, see Harvey and Peters (1984) for details and Nerlove *et al.* (1979) pp. 132–139 for a general discussion of estimation in the frequency domain.

3. DATA

The principal data used for the analyses in this paper are monthly observations of (i) numbers killed and seriously injured and (ii) numbers killed for the following categories of road users: (a) car drivers, (b) car front seat passengers, (c) car rear seat passengers, (d) pedestrians and (e) cyclists. The period covered was January 1969 to December 1984. The data refer to the whole of Great Britain. We also had data for various periods on seat belt wearing rates, indices of traffic densities for various categories of vehicles and on the real cost of petrol.

To give the reader an impression of the magnitudes involved we give in Table 1 the annual totals for 1982 and 1984 as representing two complete years before and after the completion of the seat belt law.

TABLE 1
Numbers killed and seriously injured and numbers killed 1982 *and* 1984

	Killed and seriously injured 1982	1984	*Killed* 1982	1984
Car drivers	19,460	16,421	1,472	1,228
Car front seat passengers	9,458	7,047	658	539
Car rear seat passengers	4,706	5,062	297	372
Pedestrians	18,963	19,168	1,869	1,821
Cyclists	5,967	6,506	294	337

4. MODEL SELECTION

In the first two sections we argued that the attraction of structural time series models is that they are formulated in terms of components which have a direct interpretation. In this section we set out what we feel is an appropriate model selection methodology for structural models both with and without explanatory variables. Some of the diagnostic checking techniques are appropriate for *ARIMA* as well as structural models. However, as we shall show at various points in the discussion, there are important differences in emphasis in structural and *ARIMA* model selection.

The introduction of intervention effects raises further issues of model selection. These issues are considered separately in Section 5. The present section concentrates on selecting an appropriate model for various casualty series based on data from January 1969 to December 1982, i.e. before the intervention took place. Our basic approach was first to fit the model for the period up to December 1981 and then to use the 1982 data for post-sample predictive tests.

4.1. *Univariate Time Series Models*

Fig. 1 shows the numbers of car drivers killed and seriously injured (*KSI*) in each month in Great Britain over the period January 1969 to December 1984. There is a clear seasonal pattern and although it could be argued that the inclusion of a slope component in the trend — β_t in (2.3) — is unnecessary, our preference is to at least start off with the more general

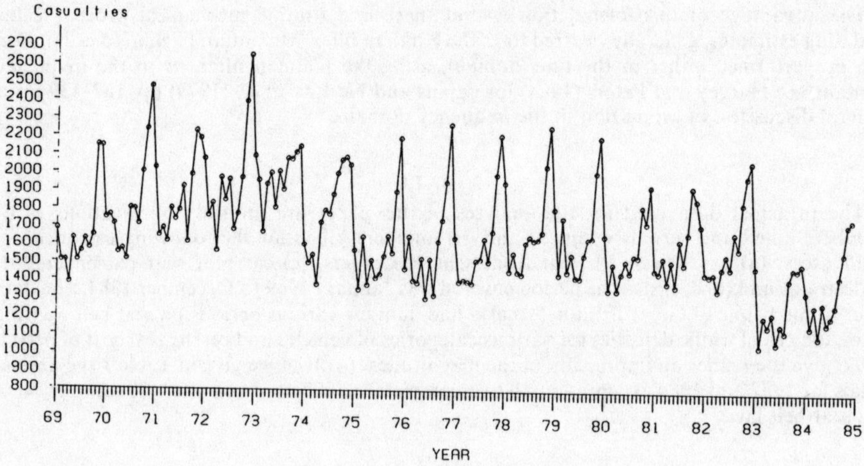

Fig. 1. Car drivers killed and seriously injured.

local linear trend model. Little is lost by proceeding in this way, but more could be lost if the slope were incorrectly constrained to be zero throughout the period.

The first model fitted was the basic structural model (*BSM*), (2.1), (2.3b) and (2.4). Estimating this model by exact *ML* for the (natural) logarithm of drivers *KSI* using data from January 1969 to December 1981 gave the following estimates:

$$\tilde{\sigma}_\varepsilon^2 = \underset{(0.582 \times 10^{-3})}{3.871 \times 10^{-3}}, \quad \tilde{\sigma}_\eta^2 = \underset{(0.252 \times 10^{-3})}{0.609 \times 10^{-3}}, \quad \tilde{\sigma}_\zeta^2 = 0, \quad \tilde{\sigma}_\omega^2 = 0$$

with

$$\tilde{\sigma} = 0.076 \qquad R^2 = 0.76 \qquad R_s^2 = 0.27$$
$$H(47) = 1.025 \qquad Q(15) = 16.80 \qquad \text{Normality} = 1.87,$$

where the figures in parentheses under the parameter estimates are asymptotic standard errors, calculated by the frequency domain method given in Harvey and Peters (1984).

The standardized residuals from fitting the model will be denoted by $\tilde{v}_t = v_t/f_t^{1/2}$, $t = s + 2, \ldots, T$, where v_t is the one step ahead prediction error and f_t is the estimate of its variance. Both v_t and f_t are obtained from the Kalman filter. The various statistics presented under the above parameter estimates are as follows:

(a) $\tilde{\sigma}^2$ is the estimated one step ahead prediction error variance,

(b) R^2 is, as usual, one minus the ratio of $(T - s - 1)\,\tilde{\sigma}^2$ to the sum of squares of y_t about its mean,

(c) R_s^2 is one minus $(T - s - 1)\tilde{\sigma}^2$ divided by the sum of squares of first differences around the seasonal means of first differences; see Harvey (1984, Appendix 1).

(d) H is a heteroscedasticity test statistic defined by

$$H(m) = \sum_{t=T-m+1}^{T} \tilde{v}_t^2 \Bigg/ \sum_{t=s+2}^{s+1+m} \tilde{v}_t^2. \tag{4.1}$$

The integer m is approximately $(T - s - 1)/3$. If the relative variances $\sigma_\eta^2/\sigma_\varepsilon^2$, $\sigma_\zeta^2/\sigma_\varepsilon^2$ and $\sigma_\omega^2/\sigma_\varepsilon^2$

were known, the distribution of H would be $F_{m,m}$ under the null hypothesis that the model is correctly specified.

(e) $Q(P)$ is the Box-Ljung statistic constructed from the first P autocorrelations of the standardised residuals. Under the null hypothesis $Q(P)$ should be treated as having a χ^2 distribution with P-3 degrees of freedom. However, when σ^2_ω and σ^2_ζ are both zero the appropriate number of degrees of freedom is P-1.

(f) 'Normality' is the test statistic for testing normality given by

$$\text{Normality} = \frac{(T-s-1)}{6} b_1 + \frac{(T-s-1)}{24}(b_2-3)^2 \tag{4.2}$$

where $\sqrt{b_1}$ is the third moment of the standardised residuals about the mean and b_2 is the fourth moment; see Jarque and Bera (1980) and Bowman and Shenton (1975). The distribution of the test statistic under the null is asymptotically χ^2_2.

None of the diagnostics indicates that the model is inappropriate and the plot of the residuals, $\tilde{v}_t$, $t = s+2, \ldots, T$, showed nothing unusual.

The model was used to predict casualties in 1982, using the estimates calculated from 1969 to 1981 data. The goodness of fit in this post-sample period was then tested using the post-sample predictive test statistic

$$\xi(l) = \sum_{t=T+1}^{T+l} \tilde{v}_t^2/l \tag{4.3}$$

which is similar to the Chow test for regression; see Harvey and Todd (1983) and Box and Tiao (1976). The statistic $\xi(l)$ approximately follows an F-distribution with $(l, T-s-1)$ degrees of freedom. For the data in question $\xi(12)$ was 0.450, which is clearly not significant. In fact it indicates rather better predictions than in the sample period.

The above analysis suggests that the basic structural model is indeed appropriate for the drivers *KSI* series. Furthermore, re-estimating the model using data up to December 1982 changes the parameter estimates very little.

The level of the trend and its slope, together with the seasonal pattern normally change over time and they could be estimated by a smoothing algorithm. The final estimates at the end of the sample are, however, produced by the Kalman filter and these are usually the figures of most interest. In fact in the present example the slope of the trend and the seasonal pattern remain constant over time. At the end of 1981 the components of the trend were estimated as follows:

Level ($\tilde{\mu}_T$) : 7.337 (0.036) Slope ($\tilde{\beta}_T$) : -0.0005. (0.0020)

The figures in parentheses are root mean square errors (rmse's). Bearing in mind that the observations are in logarithms, the estimated (level of the) trend at the end of 1981 was exp(7.337) = 1536. The growth rate was -0.05% which is clearly insignificant.

The seasonal effects are also produced. Exponentiating these figures gives a set of multiplicative seasonal factors. For car drivers *KSI* these are

J	*F*	*M*	*A*	*M*	*J*	*J*	*A*	*S*	*O*	*N*	*D*
1.020	0.908	0.934	0.866	0.946	0.916	0.967	0.969	0.993	1.073	1.204	1.281

As can be seen the main adverse seasonal effects occur in November and December.

4.2. *Correlograms and ARIMA Model Selection*

As we have just seen, the diagnostics confirm the choice of the basic structural model as a reasonable one for the car drivers *KSI* series. In the Box-Jenkins approach, on the other hand, no prior ideas about the nature of the series are involved and the idea is to use statistics such as the correlogram to select a model in the (seasonal) *ARIMA* class. Our contention is firstly that this class is itself somewhat arbitrary, and secondly that by following the model selection approach advocated in Box and Jenkins (1970) one can be led to the selection of models within that class which have unacceptable properties.

Fig. 2 shows the correlogram of $\Delta\Delta_{12}y_t$, where y_t is the logarithm of car drivers *KSI* for January 1969 to December 1982. The first point to note is that although this correlogram was not used in the selection of a structural model, it is quite consistent with the theoretical autocorrelation function implied by the basic structural model fitted in the previous sub-section. We would like to stress that the *BSM* is only one model within the structural class, and we would not advocate fitting it if its implied autocorrelation function was incompatible with the observed correlogram.

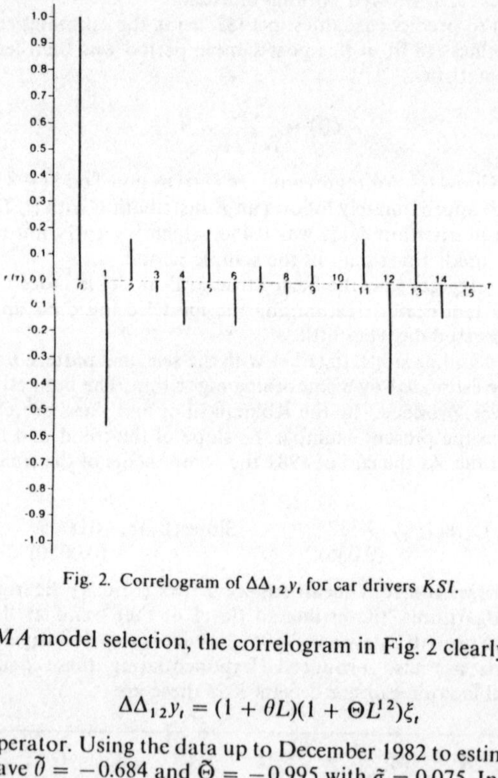

Fig. 2. Correlogram of $\Delta\Delta_{12}y_t$ for car drivers *KSI*.

As regards *ARIMA* model selection, the correlogram in Fig. 2 clearly leads to the choice of the airline model

$$\Delta\Delta_{12}y_t = (1 + \theta L)(1 + \Theta L^{12})\xi_t \tag{4.4}$$

where *L* is the lag operator. Using the data up to December 1982 to estimate such a model with the SAS package gave $\tilde{\theta} = -0.684$ and $\tilde{\Theta} = -0.995$ with $\tilde{\sigma} = 0.075$. In fact this is compatible with the *BSM* we fitted in sub-section 4.1 since the reduced form of a *BSM* with $\sigma_\zeta^2 = \sigma_\omega^2 = 0$ is an airline model with $\Theta = -1$. The parameter estimates reported for the *BSM* fitted in sub-section 4.1 (to the data up to December 1981) imply $\theta = -0.674$ in the airline model.

The prevalence of the airline model in applied work suggests that this model is appropriate for many economic time series. Indeed although the airline model is not normally equivalent to the *BSM*, as it is in the example cited here, its properties are usually fairly similar; see Maravall (1985). However, despite the appeal of the airline model it is not clear that an *ARIMA* model builder would necessarily select it in this case. The reason is that when Θ is minus one, the model is strictly noninvertible. The $\Delta\Delta_{12}$ transformation then leads to overdifferencing since only the Δ_{12} operator is needed to make the series stationary.

Fig. 3 shows the correlogram of $\Delta_{12}y_t$. (The broken lines should be ignored for the moment). Although the sample autocorrelations die away in a manner compatible with a stationary series, it is not clear what *ARIMA* model would be selected. There is a fairly wide range of possibilities involving various mixtures of *AR*, *MA* and seasonal *MA* polynomials. However, it is unlikely that any of these would be a suitable parsimonious model. If the data really are generated by an airline model with $\Theta = -1$, or equivalently by a *BSM* with $\sigma_\zeta^2 = \sigma_\omega^2 = 0$, then

$$\Delta_{12}y_t = (1 + \theta L)S(L)\xi_t \quad (4.5a)$$

$$= S(L)\eta_t + \Delta_{12}\varepsilon_t, \quad (4.5b)$$

where $S(L) = 1 + L + \ldots + L^{s-1}$. Setting $\theta = -0.684$ in (4.5a) leads to the implied autocorrelation function shown by the broken lines in Fig. 3.

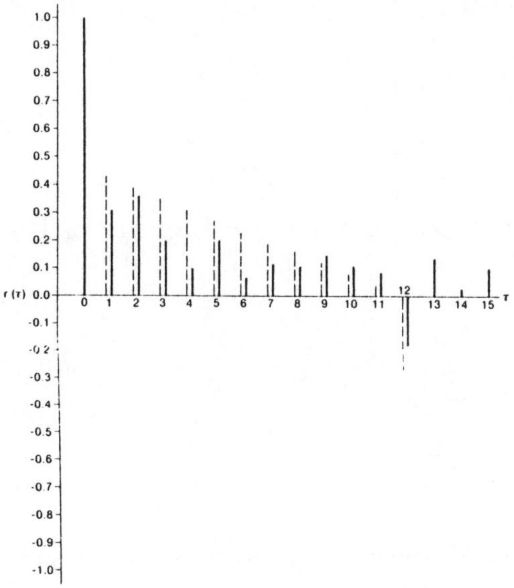

Fig. 3. Correlogram of $\Delta_{12}y_t$ for car drivers KSI.

The use of the seasonal difference operator by itself is not uncommon in *ARIMA* modelling. However an autocorrelation function such as that displayed in Fig. 3 suggests that seasonal differencing only would potentially lead to a wide range of inappropriate *ARIMA* models being chosen. As a specific case we cite the study by Bhattacharyya and Layton (1979). Their work is an investigation, using quarterly data, of the effects of the seat belt law in Queensland on deaths of car drivers. It represents a well carried out example of the use of *ARIMA* and intervention analysis techniques. The authors found that the Δ_4 operator was sufficient to reduce the observations to stationarity and on the basis of the correlogram of $\Delta_4 y_t$ they selected the following model for the pre-intervention period:

$$\Delta_4 y_t = \theta_0 + (1 + \theta_4 L^4)(1 + \theta_3 L^3 + \theta_5 L^5)\xi_t. \quad (4.6)$$

The properties of this model are not particularly appealing and the fact that Bhattacharyya and Layton report that it failed the Chow test (albeit marginally) could well be an indication of its overparameterization and inappropriateness.

A transformation which we have found to be useful for analysing economic time series is to take first differences and then to remove the seasonal means. The value of this transformation was implicitly recognised by Pierce (1978) and, as already noted in the previous sub-section, it is the sum of squares from this transformation which provides the baseline for the R_s^2 measure of goodness of fit. Applying this transformation to the car drivers *KSI* series gives the correlogram shown in Fig. 4. The dotted horizontal lines show ± 2 s.d.'s on the assumption that the first-order autocorrelation is the only non-zero one and its theoretical value is equal to the sample value of $r(1) = -0.475$. In contrast to the correlogram of $\Delta_s y_t$, the message in Fig. 4 is clear. It indicates an $MA(1)$ process and this is consistent with the fitted basic structural and airline models.

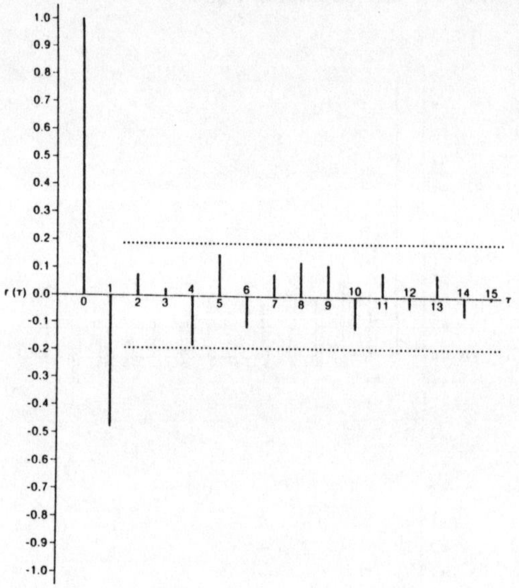

Fig. 4. Correlogram of Δy_t minus seasonal means for car drivers KSI.

4.3. *Explanatory Variables*

Suppose that it is felt that some of the movements in the series can be accounted for by observable exogenous explanatory variables. This leads to consideration of a model of the form (2.7). If $\sigma_\eta^2 = \sigma_\zeta^2 = \sigma_\omega^2 = 0$, then the model collapses to a standard regression with a linear time trend and seasonal dummies in addition to the x_j's. This was the model used by Scott and Willis (1985) in their analysis of the effects of the seat belt law. However, assuming such a structure at the outset can result in misleading inferences being drawn if the assumption that σ_η^2, σ_ζ^2 and σ_ω^2 are zero is not true; see Nelson and Kang (1984).

As in most areas of the social sciences, there is no firm theory indicating which explanatory variables should appear in a model. It is therefore important to adopt a methodology which guards against what is known as 'data mining'. This term refers to uncritical examination of data sets for evidence of relationships without adequate prior consideration of potential behavioural hypotheses and without proper allowance for the process of selection of relationships when carrying out statistical tests. The methodology we use here involves formulating a general model which includes all potentially useful explanatory variables, and then testing down to obtain a parsimonious representation. At all stages the model is checked using the diagnostics described in the previous section and the coefficients are examined to see that they are consistent with what any theory would suggest.

In modelling the series on car drivers *KSI* two explanatory variables are available for inclusion. These are:

(i) the car traffic index, which measures the number of kilometres travelled by cars in a month, and

(ii) the real price of petrol, i.e. the price of petrol per litre at the pump divided by the retail price index.

The use of the car traffic index as an explanatory variable calls for no explanation, but perhaps a little should be said about the inclusion of the real price of petrol. During the period under review there were substantial changes in this variable and one effect of petrol price increases was probably to induce some drivers to drive more slowly and with less braking and acceleration. This could be expected to reduce accident rates. The variable can also be regarded as a proxy for such factors as petrol rationing and the introduction of lower speed limits during the oil crisis period of 1973–74. Lagged values of the petrol price index were originally included but their coefficients were found to be small and statistically insignificant.

Estimating (2.5) for the period January 1969 to December 1981 by exact *ML* in the time domain with the logarithms of both the above variables included gave the following results:

$$\tilde{\sigma}_\varepsilon^2 = 4.198 \times 10^{-3}, \tilde{\sigma}_\eta^2 = 0.308 \times 10^{-3}, \tilde{\sigma}_\zeta^2 = 0, \tilde{\sigma}_\omega^2 = 0.$$

$$\text{Car traffic index coefficient} = \underset{(0.14)}{0.08}, \quad \text{Petrol price coefficient} = \underset{(0.11)}{-0.31}$$

with

$$\tilde{\sigma} = 0.074 \qquad R^2 = 0.78 \qquad R_s^2 = 0.31$$

$$H(47) = 1.43 \qquad Q(15) = 17.35 \qquad \text{Normality} = 1.19.$$

Because the variables are in logarithms the coefficients of the car traffic index and the petrol price may be interpreted as elasticities. Thus a 1% rise in the traffic index gives a 0.08% rise in casualties, while a 1% rise in the price of petrol gives a 0.31% fall in casualties. The coefficient of the traffic index is statistically insignificant, and when we refitted the model without it, we obtained virtually the same results for the other parameters; see Durbin and Harvey (1985, p.A7). The diagnostics were satisfactory and the post sample predictive test statistic is $\xi(12) = 0.562$ indicating that the model gives good predictions for 1982.

On a technical point it should be noted that the diagnostics H, Q and Normality for a model of the form (2.7) are constructed from the residuals obtained by applying the Kalman filter to the 'observations' $y_t - x_t'\tilde{\delta}$, $t = 1, \ldots, T$. This Kalman filter is the same as the Kalman filter appropriate for the *BSM* and so the number of residuals is $T - s - 1$. However, if the explanatory variable coefficient vector, δ, is included in an augmented state vector only $T - s - 1 - k$ residuals are obtained. These residuals are known as generalized recursive residuals; see Harvey and Peters (1984). When explanatory variables are present in the model, the Chow statistic, (4.3), is computed using generalized recursive residuals.

4.4. *Detecting Model Breakdown*

The use of CUSUMs of recursive residuals for detecting structural change over time in linear regression models was first suggested by Brown, Durbin and Evans (1975). Similar techniques can also be used to see whether a structural time series model with explanatory variables is breaking down. The residuals used are the generalized recursive residuals described at the end of the previous sub-section.

Let $\tilde{v}_t^\dagger$, $t = s + k + 2, \ldots, T$ denoted the standardized generalized recursive residuals. Then

$$CUSUM(t, \tau) = \sum_{j=\tau+1}^{t} \tilde{v}_j^\dagger, \; t = \tau + 1, \ldots, T. \tag{4.7}$$

If the relative variances $\sigma_\eta^2/\sigma_\varepsilon^2$, $\sigma_\zeta^2/\sigma_\varepsilon^2$ and $\sigma_\omega^2/\sigma_\varepsilon^2$ were known, the generalized recursive residuals would have the same properties as the recursive residuals in linear regression, i.e. they would be normally and independently distributed with mean zero and constant variance. Fig. 5 shows an example of a *CUSUM* for the model fitted to pedestrians killed, the variance parameters having been estimated using data from January 1969 to December 1982. The steady rise in the *CUSUM* from the beginning of 1982 onwards suggests that the model may have started to break down at this point, since it was systematically underpredicting. The fact that the significance lines are not crossed is not critical since the *CUSUM* is best regarded as a diagnostic rather than a formal test procedure.

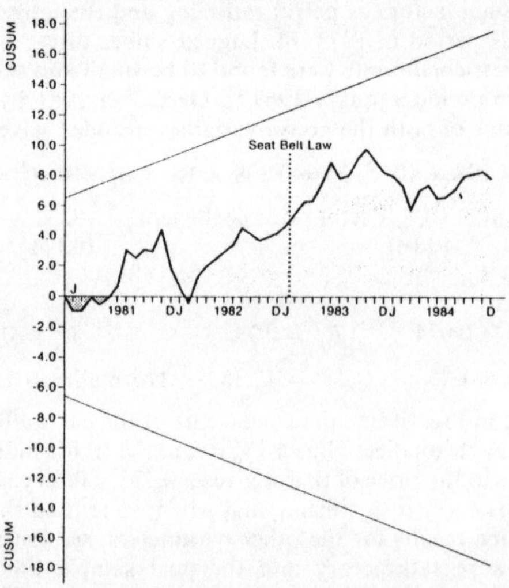

Fig. 5. Cusum of standardised recursive residuals for pedestrians killed from January 1981 onwards with 10 per cent significance lines.

A second example of the use of a *CUSUM* is given in Fig. 6. This shows the *CUSUM* for rear seat passengers killed starting at τ = January 1983. In this case the *CUSUM* line soon crosses the significance line, clearly indicating that the model began to break down in early 1983.

As already indicated, the *CUSUM* is best regarded as a diagnostic rather than a formal test, particularly when the investigator has no prior knowledge as to the point at which a model is liable to break down. However for investigation of change after a given value of τ, there are other more formal and possibly more powerful tests which may be applied. Two possibilities are (a) the recursive residual t-test which was suggested by Harvey in the discussion to Brown, Durbin and Evans (1975, p. 179) and (b) the Chow test based on (4.3).

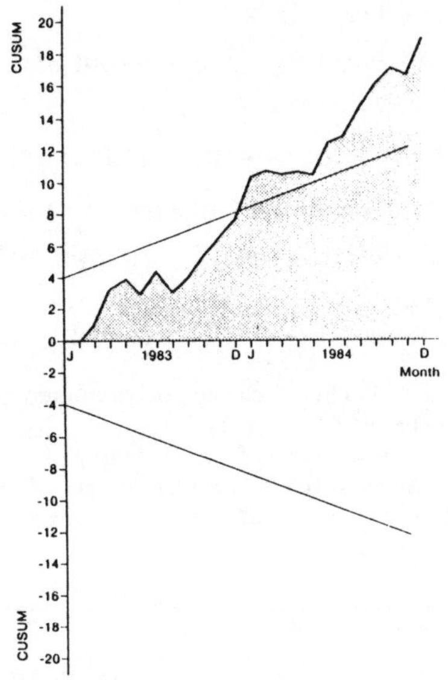

Fig. 6. Plot of cusum of standardised residuals for car rear seat passengers killed from February 1983 onwards with 10 per cent significance lines (intervention variable not included in the model).

5. ASSESSING THE EFFECTS OF INTERVENTIONS

The effect of an intervention on the series of interest can be assessed by including a variable, w_t, in the model as in (2.6). The actual form of w_t will depend on the effect which the intervention is assumed to have on the series. The final effect may involve a shift in the level or the slope of the trend, or a combination of both. Alternatively the effect may be transient. In addition there is the question of the dynamic pattern of the response.

The use of intervention variables introduces features into estimation which raise special problems for model selection. These arise because the intervention is normally a once and for all event. In subsection 5.1 we discuss estimation in some detail before suggesting a model selection strategy. The general conclusions apply irrespective of whether or not explanatory variables are present in the model.

5.1. *Estimation*

Suppose that the relative variances $\sigma_\eta^2/\sigma_\varepsilon^2$, $\sigma_\zeta^2/\sigma_\varepsilon^2$ and $\sigma_\omega^2/\sigma_\varepsilon^2$ are known or, alternatively, that the sample size prior to the intervention is large so that they can effectively be treated as known. Unless the trend and seasonal components in (2.6) are all deterministic, i.e. $\sigma_\eta^2 = \sigma_\zeta^2 = \sigma_\omega^2 = 0$, the following results hold for the estimator of λ:

(a) the influence of observations beyond the intervention tends to zero as the time beyond the intervention tends to infinity; and

(b) the estimator is not consistent, even though it is the *MVUE*.

In order to explore the implications of the above results further, consider the simple random walk plus noise model, (2.2), with a step intervention, (2.7), at time $t = \tau$, i.e.

$$y_t = \mu_t + \lambda w_t + \varepsilon_t, \mu_t = \mu_{t-1} + \eta_t, \quad t = 1, \ldots, T \tag{5.1}$$

with $\varepsilon_t \sim NID(0, \sigma_\varepsilon^2)$, $\eta_t \sim NID(0, \sigma_\eta^2)$ and $\sigma_\eta^2/\sigma_\varepsilon^2 = q \geqslant 0$. The reduced form of the random walk plus noise model is *ARIMA* (0, 1, 1), i.e.

$$\Delta y_t = \xi_t + \theta\xi_{t-1}, \quad \xi_t \sim NID(0, \sigma^2), \tag{5.2}$$

with

$$\theta = -2/\{2 + q + \sqrt{(q^2 + 4q)}\} \quad \text{and} \quad \sigma^2 = -\sigma_\varepsilon^2/\theta. \tag{5.3}$$

It is not difficult to see that for a given value of q the variance of the *GLS* estimator of λ is

$$\text{var}(\tilde{\lambda}) = \sigma^2\{1 - (-\theta)^2\}/\{1 - (-\theta)^{2(T-\tau+1)}\}. \tag{5.4}$$

In the limit as $T - \tau \to \infty$

$$\text{var}(\tilde{\lambda}) \underset{T-\tau\to\infty}{\to} \sigma^2\{1 - (-\theta)^2\} \tag{5.5}$$

since for $0 < q \leqslant \infty$, $-1 < \theta \leqslant 0$. Thus λ cannot be estimated consistently unless $q = 0$ in which case $\theta = -1$ and $\text{var}(\tilde{\lambda}) = \sigma^2/(T - \tau + 1)$.

It is interesting to compare the variance of the estimator of λ based on a finite number of observations after the intervention with its variance for an infinite number of observations after the intervention. Thus for $q = 0.1$ we have the following relative variances for different values of $l = T - \tau + 1$:

l	1	2	3	4	5	6	7	12
Rel. var	.47	.72	.85	.92	.96	.98	.99 ...	1

A more extensive table can be found in Harvey (1985b).

The above comparisons are basically applicable to the models for car drivers *KSI* reported in Section 4 for large sample sizes. For the basic structural model $q = 0.157$, but when explanatory variables were added q fell to $q = 0.080$. In both cases q is close enough to 0.1 to make the table above informative. As can be seen it is the first four or five observations after the intervention which contain most of the relevant information.

During our study the question of whether to use annual or monthly data was raised with us a number of times. There seemed to be a feeling that results from using annual totals might be more reliable because the annual observations tend to average out the irregularities in the monthly observations. In fact this is not an argument for using annual data and it is worth considering briefly the loss in efficiency which arises in large samples when estimating a step intervention effect from annual, rather than monthly, observations. Again we use model (5.1). As shown in Tiao (1972), the reduced form of the model is still *ARIMA* (0, 1, 1) although now the range of the moving average parameter is $[-1, 0.268]$. For $q = 0.1$ the loss of efficiency from using annual observations is approximately one third. On the other hand if $q = \infty$, i.e. $\sigma_\varepsilon^2 = 0$ and the monthly observations follow a random walk, the efficiency of the annual estimator is only 0.14.

The main conclusion from this sub-section is that discounting can be quite considerable. The solution is to try and find exogenous variables, possibly control variables, which reduce the variation in the nonstationary stochastic part of the model. Thus in terms of (5.1) we would ideally like to find an exogenous variable to add to the right hand side of (5.1a), the effect of which would be to send q to zero. The theory underlying the use of control variables as explanatory variables in equations like (2.6) is developed in Harvey (1985b).

5.2. *Model Selection*

The model selection problem surrounding the specification of an intervention effect has special features because the event only occurs once. This makes it virtually impossible to set up a general model for the intervention effect involving, say, slope, level and transient effects each with a lag structure, estimating such a model and then testing down to obtain a parsimonious specification. Instead it is necessary to proceed by specifying an intervention model on the basis of *a priori* considerations. Special diagnostics are then used to check the model. If *a priori* considerations suggest more than one possible specification, a choice between them can be made on their ability to satisfy the diagnostics and their goodness of fit. Clearly it is the pattern of residuals immediately after the intervention which is of prime importance. Several diagnostic tests are developed below. It is assumed that a fairly long series is available prior to the intervention and that this series has been used to select and estimate a suitable model. If this is not the case then some modification to the overall strategy is necessary, although the general principle remains the same.

The diagnostics we suggest are all based on generalized recursive residuals. Thus the explanatory variables are included in the state vector. In addition the intervention variable is also included in the state vector. However, it is only brought into the state vector at time τ. As a result, the prediction error at time τ is identically equal to zero; cf Brown, Durbin and Evans (1975, p. 152-3). This fact must be borne in mind when constructing test statistics. Our suggested diagnostics, apart from an examination of the plot of the residuals in the post intervention period, are as follows.

(a) *Post intervention predictive test*—The test statistic has a similar form to the Chow statistic, (4.3), i.e. the post-sample predictive test statistic. The sample size is taken to be τ-1 while the post-intervention period consists of the observations at time $t = \tau + 1, \tau + 2, \ldots, \tau + l$. The statistic is

$$\xi_\tau(l) = \sum_{t=\tau+1}^{\tau+l} \tilde{v}_t^{\dagger 2}/l \tag{5.6}$$

It is approximately distributed as $F(l, \tau\text{-}2\text{-}s\text{-}k)$,

(b) *Recursive t-test*—If *a priori* theory suggests that the residuals after the intervention may all be of a certain sign, a recursive t-test could be appropriate. The test statistic is defined as

$$\psi(l) = l^{-1/2} \sum_{t=\tau+1}^{\tau+l} \tilde{v}_t^{\dagger}. \tag{5.7}$$

This is distributed approximately as Student's t with τ-2-s-k-degrees of freedom.

(c) *CUSUM test*—The post-intervention *CUSUM* is

$$CUSUM(h) = \sum_{t=\tau+1}^{\tau+h} \tilde{v}_t^{\dagger}, h = 1, \ldots, l. \tag{5.8}$$

Boundary lines can be constructed as for the *CUSUM* defined in Section 4. As before a one-sided boundary may be appropriate.

5.3. *The Effect of the Seat Belt Law on Car Drivers*

We now turn to the application of these techniques to the series of car drivers *KSI* and car drivers killed. The most straightforward hypothesis to adopt is that the introduction of the seat belt law on January 31st, 1983, induced a once and for all downward shift in the level of each series. This implies a model of the form (2.6) with w_t defined by (2.7). However, since the seat belt wearing rate rose from 40% in December 1982 to 50% in January 1983 in anticipation of the introduction of the law, we modified (2.7) slightly by setting $w_t = 0.18$ in January 1983.

The model for car drivers *KSI* was developed earlier in Section 4.3. The relative variances were re-estimated using data up to the end of 1982. The estimates did not change very much and it was these estimates which were used when the intervention parameter, λ, was estimated using the data up to and including December 1984. The resulting estimate of λ was

$$\tilde{\lambda} = \underset{(0.053)}{-0.262}.$$

Since exp(-0.262) = 0.770, the estimated reduction in drivers *KSI* is 23.0%. The 50% confidence interval for this reduction is 20.2 to 25.8% while the 95% confidence interval is 14.7% to 30.6%. The relationship between the normal and lognormal distributions suggests the use of $\exp\{\tilde{\lambda} + \frac{1}{2}\,\mathrm{var}(\tilde{\lambda})\}$ instead of $\exp(\tilde{\lambda})$. However the value of this gives an estimated reduction of 22.9% so the difference is negligible.

The diagnostics are based on the residuals for February 1983 onwards, i.e. τ = Jan 1983. The post intervention predictive test statistics for l = 3, 6 and 23 were as follows:

$$\xi_\tau(3) = 1.28, \quad \xi_\tau(6) = 0.93, \quad \xi_\tau(23) = 0.67.$$

None of these indicates a statistically significant increase in the variance of the residuals following the intervention. Similarly the *CUSUM* up to Dec. 1984, which can be found plotted in Figure 7, does not cross either the 5% or 10% boundary lines. Finally Figure 8 shows the predictions for 1983 and 1984. These are obtained using observations of the explanatory variables for 1983 and 1984 but not using observations of the car drivers *KSI* series itself for 1983 and 1984. Including the intervention variable which was subsequently estimated from the 1983 and 1984 data gives very accurate results.

5.4. *Sensitivity Analysis*

One of the attractions of structural time series models is that they lend themselves to sensitivity analysis. As an example of such analysis, consider the series for the logarithm of pedestrians killed by cars using the logarithm of pedestrians *KSI* by heavy goods vehicles (HGVs) and public service vehicles (PSVs) as an explanatory variable. (The reason for the choice of this variable as a control variable is discussed in more detail in Durbin and Harvey (1985); the details are not important in the present context.) The result of fitting this model to data up to Dec 1982 was to produce deterministic trend and seasonal components, i.e. $\sigma_\eta^2 = \sigma_\zeta^2 = \sigma_\omega^2 = 0$. The diagnostics were acceptable and $\tilde{\sigma} = 0.149$ while $R_s^2 = 0.44$ and $R^2 = 0.76$.

In view of our discussion in Section 2 of this paper, a deterministic trend must be regarded as being somewhat unusual and needs to be handled with some care. Thus some caution is needed in assessing the estimate of the intervention effect of the seat belt law which is

$$\tilde{\lambda} = \underset{(0.066)}{0.133}$$

and is statistically significant at the 5% level in a two-sided test. We therefore decided to examine the sensitivity of this estimate to changes in the variance parameters. The key parameter in this respect is σ_η^2, since in most of the models we fitted this tended to be significantly different from zero. Setting $\sigma_\eta^2/\sigma_\varepsilon^2 = 0.1$ yields

$$\tilde{\lambda} = \underset{(0.098)}{0.095}$$

Making this modification therefore yields an estimate smaller than the original estimate and this new estimate is not statistically significant at any reasonable level. Nevertheless it does indicate a non-negligible increase in this series and so we conclude that our original result is fairly robust.

Another aspect of sensitivity analysis concerns the treatment of outliers. There is no general agreement amongst statisticians on how to deal with outliers. In the present context observations with relatively large residuals are often associated with extreme weather conditions, as in the exceptionally cold month of December 1981. One way of dealing with the problem is to estimate models both including and excluding such outlying observations in order to determine whether the results are unduly sensitive to their presence. Handling a missing observation by the Kalman filter is straightforward. We fitted a number of our models with the December 1981 value included and excluded but the differences were negligible.

5.5 *Dynamic Response*

The effect of an intervention may be dynamic, that is the response to the intervention changes over time. Determining the form of the response in the absence of any *a priori* information is difficult because the intervention only happens once. The most satisfactory way to proceed it to postulate a pattern for the response based on theoretical grounds. The methods described in sub-section 5.2 can then be used to test whether the chosen specification is acceptable.

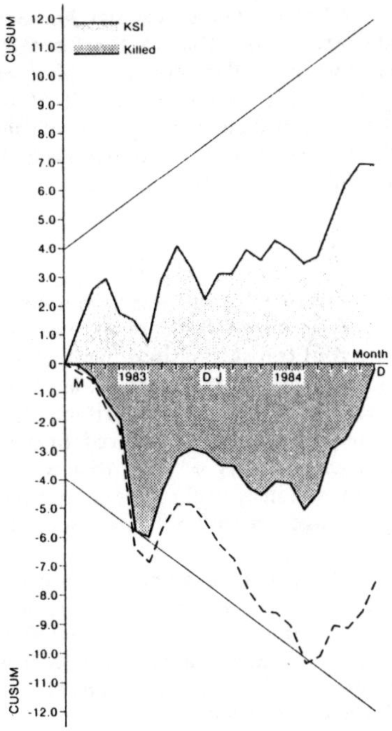

Fig. 7. Plot of *CUSUM* of standardised residuals for car drivers *KSI* and killed from March 1983 onwards with 10 per cent significance lines. Lower broken line shows CUSUM for drivers killed under the risk homeostasis hypothesis.

In the context of the seat belt law, the risk homeostasis hypothesis advocated by Wilde (1982) states that car drivers will eventually re-adjust their driving behaviour so as to keep the probability of their being killed constant. Stated in this general form the risk homeostasis hypothesis is virtually impossible to prove or disprove for a time series with a stochastic trend component. The reason is the discounting of observations as one moves further away from the time at which the intervention occured; see sub-section 5.1. However, if a specific hypothesis is put forward it can be tested. Thus suppose that the effect of the seat belt law declines linearly until it is eliminated after two years. This means that the intervention variable w_t is defined as

$$w_t = \begin{cases} 0, & t < \text{Jan. '83} \\ 0.18, & t = \text{Jan. '83} \\ 1-(t\text{-Feb. '83})/24, & t = \text{Feb. '83}, \ldots, (\text{Feb. '83}) + 24. \end{cases} \quad (5.19)$$

Fitting (2.6) to the series of car drivers killed with w_t defined by (5.9) gave

$$\tilde{\lambda} = -0.206$$
$$(0.075)$$

with the post-intervention test statistic $\xi_\tau(23)$, taking the value 1.240. This is not statistically significant at any conventional level of significance, and it is not much higher than the value of 1.207 obtained when the original intervention variable was fitted. Thus although one would prefer the original model on grounds of goodness of fit in the post-intervention period, the fit is not dramatically better than that of the postulated risk homeostasis model and the forecast errors from the latter model are comparable to the forecast errors obtained before the intervention. However, where this particular version of the dynamic risk homeostasis model does break down is in the *CUSUM*. Fig. 7 shows the *CUSUM* as a broken line. As can be seen it clearly crosses the lower 10% significance line. Again a one sided test is appropriate as one would expect the dynamic risk homeostasis model to overpredict if the seat belt law had led to a once and for all downward shift in the level of fatalities.

6. RESULTS

The methodology in the previous two sections was used to select models for the categories of road users we considered. This involved trials of different combinations of explanatory variables and use of the square root transformations in appropriate cases as an alternative to the logarithmic transformation, as well as an examination of residuals and inspection of the results of various diagnostic tests. In the event the logarithmic transformation was adopted for all the cases considered in this paper. The results achieved for the models we finally selected are summarised in Table 2. For each category of road user we give the estimated percentage change in numbers killed and seriously injured, and numbers killed, attributed to the introduction of the seat belt law, together with 50% confidence limits and values of diagnostic statistics.

We shall comment on the results in detail in the next section. Here, we merely draw attention to a few points of special interest. The most surprising feature of the results is the large increase of 26.7 per cent in the numbers of rear seat passengers killed. Because this increase is so much larger than expected we checked the analysis rather carefully from several points of view. For example, we put the series through the univariate *ARIMA* identification and estimation procedure and emerged with the fitted airline model

$$\Delta\Delta_{12} y_t = \underset{(0.081)}{0.212} w_t + (1-0.96L)(1-0.89L^{12})\xi_t,$$

This indicated an increase of 23.6 per cent which is close to that estimated by the corresponding structural model.

The largest departure from normality occurred for pedestrians *KSI* and this suggests the possibility of outliers. A plot of the residuals indicated two outliers with normalised values of 3.02 and -3.53 respectively. However, we concluded that these values were not inconsistent with the distribution of the full set of residuals and decided not to make any correction. A similar outcome was found for cyclists *KSI* and the same decision was taken.

Deficiencies in the fit of the model for pedestrians killed are indicated by the significantly high value of 27.2 for the Box-Ljung statistic. The fit of the model up to 1981 showed that, after

TABLE 2

Percentage changes in casualty rates and values of diagnostic statistics

	Percentage increase	*50% confidence limits*		R^2	R_s^2	*Heteroscedasticity H*	*Box-Ljung Q*	*Normality*	*Explanatory variables included*
Drivers *KSI*	−23.0	−25.8,	−20.2	0.78	0.31	1.54	16.7	1.15	*P*
Drivers killed	−18.0	−21.6,	−14.3	0.52	0.34	0.97	18.9	3.55	*TP*
FSPs *KSI*	−30.3	−33.1,	−27.5	0.75	0.19	0.71	9.3	1.76	*TP*
FSPs killed	−25.1	−28.0,	−21.9	0.49	0.50	1.25	11.1	2.26	*TP*
RSPs *KSI*	2.9	−0.4,	6.4	0.81	0.50	1.10	10.5	4.39	*TP*
RSPs killed	26.7	21.5,	32.2	0.45	0.45	0.80	7.3	3.37	*TP*
Pedestrians *KSI*	−0.5	−2.3,	2.3	0.89	0.24	0.79	11.9	13.1	*T**
Pedestrians killed	7.8	4.1,	11.2	0.85	0.53	1.19	27.2	2.66	*T**
Cyclists *KSI*	4.8	0.7,	8.7	0.84	0.40	0.63	10.3	8.52	*T*C*
Cyclists killed	13.4	6.0,	21.3	0.35	0.39	0.95	17.4	2.49	*T*C*
5% significance points						0.57/1.75	21.0	5.99	

FSP = Front seat passenger
RSP = Rear seat passenger
T = Car traffic index
*T** = Total motor traffic index
P = Petrol price index
C = Cycle traffic index

allowing for the increase in road traffic, pedestrian fatalities were decreasing at a steady rate of 6.9 per cent per annum. However, the numbers for 1981 and 1982 were almost the same at 1874 and 1869. These facts, together with the examination of plots of the residuals and the *CUSUM* of the standardised recursive residuals given in Fig. 5, suggested that the decline in pedestrian fatalities which had been taking place during the 1970's may have started to level out in 1982. The effect of this would be that the model would tend to underpredict in the post-law period, thus leading to an overestimate of the effect of the law. A further point is that the standard error of the estimate of the intervention coefficient in 0.051 while the estimate of $\tilde{\lambda}$ itself is 0.075. Thus for a one-sided test $\tilde{\lambda}$ is not significant at the 5% level although it is significant at the 10% level. These reservations should be borne in mind when interpreting the estimated increase of 7.8% in pedestrian fatalities.

The values of 0.35 for R^2 and 0.39 for R_s^2 indicate that the explanatory power of the model for cyclists killed is relatively poor. On the other hand the diagnostic tests gave satisfactory results. The estimated intervention coefficient $\tilde{\lambda}$, is 0.126 with an estimated standard error of 0.100. Thus $\tilde{\lambda}$ is almost significant at the 10% level. We attribute the relative lack of precision in the estimation of λ as due more to the intrinsic variability of the series than to any deficiencies of the model.

The coefficients of the explanatory variables used in the equations reported in Table 2 provide some interesting subsidiary results. The most striking of these is that the car traffic index appears to have little effect on car drivers *KSI*, but it does affect front seat passengers and it affects rear seat passengers even more. The estimated elasticities for front and rear seat passengers are 0.33 and 0.75 respectively, with estimated standard errors of 0.16 and 0.18. For the fatality series on drivers, front seat passengers and rear seat passengers the figures are 0.32, 0.68 and 1.09 respectively. Thus the car traffic index has more of an effect on the killed series, but the ordering between the three types of car occupants remains the same. The analysis of light goods vehicles casualty series showed a similar pattern. As regards the petrol price index we found an elasticity of around minus 0.3 for the *KSI* and killed series for drivers and front seat passengers, while the elasticities for rear seat passengers *KSI* and killed were small and statistically insignificant.

The estimated elasticities of pedestrians *KSI* and killed with respect to the total motor traffic

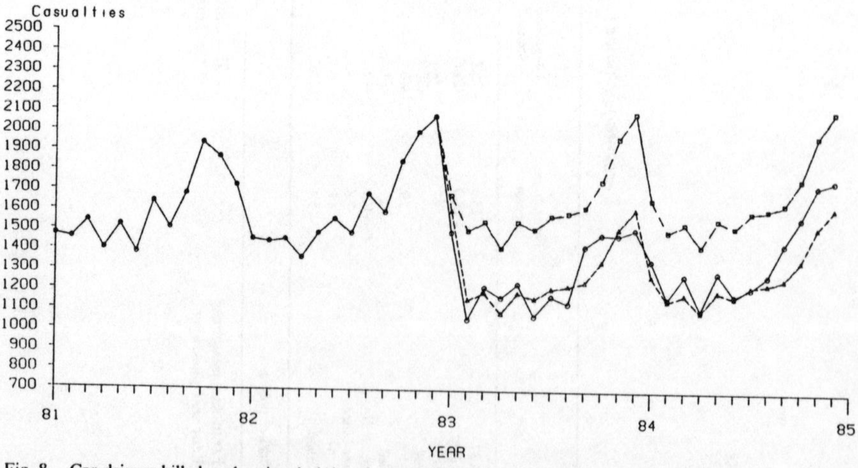

Fig. 8. Car drivers killed and seriously injured. ○, actual values of series (as in Fig. 1); △, predictions with intervention effect included; □, predictions with intervention effect removed.

index are 0.62 and 0.93 respectively. For cyclists *KSI* we found elasticities of 0.77 for the total motor traffic index and 0.14 for the cycle index. For cyclists killed the corresponding figures are 1.12 and 0.05. Thus the motor traffic index seems to be a much more important determinant of cyclist casualties than is the cycle index.

Substantially more information about our analyses and the results than space permits here is given in Appendix 1 of Durbin and Harvey (1985).

7. CONCLUSIONS

7.1. *Discussion of Results*

We first note the high rate of compliance with the seat belt law. By February 1983 the wearing rate had jumped to 90 per cent and the rate has remained at approximately 95 per cent from March 1983 onwards. There can therefore be no doubt about the success of the law as regards compliance.

In considering the casualty figures we distinguish between those directly affected by the law, namely car drivers and front seat passengers, and those not directly affected by the law, that is car rear seat passengers, pedestrians and cyclists.

Taking first numbers killed and seriously injured, we found a reduction of 23 per cent for car drivers and 30 per cent for front seat passengers. Thus for those directly affected by the law, there have been substantial reductions. For rear seat passengers *KSI* we found a rise of 3 per cent, for pedestrians a fall of one half per cent, and for cyclists an increase of 5 per cent, all three values being statistically insignificant. We conclude that there is no significant evidence of change in numbers *KSI* of those not directly affected.

For numbers killed, we found for those directly affected a reduction of 18 per cent for car drivers and 25 per cent for front seat passengers. While these reductions are not as large as for numbers *KSI* they remain substantial. Taking now those indirectly affected by the law, our model gave an increase of 27 per cent for rear seat passengers, 8 per cent for pedestrians and 13 per cent for cyclists. The value for rear seat passengers is highly significant and the other two values are on the borderline of significance. We conclude that there was an increase in fatalities of those not directly affected.

We are unable to provide a completely satisfactory explanation of the difference between the figures for *KSI* and killed for rear seat passengers, pedestrians and cyclists. As has been indicated, we found that the performance of our models for pedestrians and cyclists killed was not as good as with other data sets. The fact remains that we find the large proportionate increase in rear seat passengers killed hard to understand. We have ruled out under-reporting in 1983 and 1984 of serious injuries as an explanation, because this would have shown up in the Rutherford *et al.* (1985) analysis as an increase in numbers of rear seat passengers treated in hospitals; in fact, they found a slight decrease. We are reluctant to accept changes in driving behaviour as an explanation since these would be expected to lead to a corresponding increase in numbers seriously injured and there is no evidence of such an increase. For a similar reason the transfer of passengers from the front to the rear seats in response to the law is not a completely satisfactory explanation. We must therefore leave the sharp rise in the number of rear seat passengers killed relative to the number *KSI* as an unexplained mystery, at least until more evidence is available.

We now consider how to estimate the overall net effect of the seat belt law on numbers *KSI* and numbers killed. So far as front seat occupants are concerned, there is a clearly understood mechanism by which the wearing of a seat belt prevents or reduces the severity of injury and saves lives. Thus it seems reasonable to attribute changes in casualty rates for front seat occupants as due almost entirely to the effect of the law. However, for rear seat passengers, pedestrians and cyclists, the situation is more complicated. One has to try and assess whether changes in driving behaviour have taken place as a result of the law, and then attempt to disentangle the effect of any such changes from any other factors involved, such as possible changes in underlying trends, as in the case of pedestrians killed, and possible changes in passenger seating positions, as in the case of rear seat passengers killed. Direct evidence on either changes in driving behaviour or the other factors scarcely exists. Thus one feels less confident in attributing changes in casualty rates to the seat belt law than in the case of front seat occupants.

Overall, for the twenty three month period from February 1983 to December 1984, we estimate the reduction due to the law in numbers *KSI* for drivers and front seat passengers as 15,600. The estimated reduction in numbers killed is 879. We have included here figures for occupants of light goods vehicles, which are analysed in our Report though not in this paper. When casualties to rear seat passengers, pedestrians and cyclists are added, the estimated reduction in numbers *KSI* changes to 14,890 and the estimated reduction in numbers killed changes to 397. We conclude that, whether we concentrate on those directly affected or also include those indirectly affected, there have been substantial net reductions in numbers *KSI* and numbers killed due to the introduction of the seat belt law.

7.2. *Evidence on Changes in Driving Behaviour*

Some opponents of compulsory wearing of seat belts have argued that while casualties to front seat occupants will undoubtedly go down due to the introduction of the seat belt law, casualties to other road users, particularly rear seat passengers, pedestrians and cyclists, will increase to such an extent that the overall gains will be very substantially reduced or even cancelled out altogether. The reason given is that the protection conferred by wearing a seat belt will tend to make drivers feel safer and as a result some of them will change their driving behaviour in a way that will increase the risk of accidents. This theory is called the theory of risk compensation. The theory has been extensively discussed and there is a large literature on it. The leading exponent of the theory in this country is J.G.U. Adams and in Adams (1984, 1985) he discusses it using an interesting variety of evidence from a number of countries. An extensive review of work in the field is given by Ashton and others (1985). They concluded that "the available evidence indicates that risk compensation probably does not occur when drivers are compelled to wear seat belts".

Our own work was not directly concerned with testing the risk compensation hypothesis, and it will be apparent from the discussion in the previous sub-section that our evidence is somewhat contradictory. The figures for *KSI* casualties lead one to reject the risk compensation hypothesis. On the other hand, the killed figures do lend support to the hypothesis although, as we have noted, a careful look at the evidence indicates some reservations in arriving at such a conclusion.

7.3. *Statistical Methodology*

So far as methodology is concerned we have based our analysis on structural modelling instead of one the more conventional *ARIMA* system. Univariate *ARIMA* modelling is based on the idea that by differencing and other transformations a stationary series can be obtained. A parsimonious *ARMA* model is then selected by using statistical tools based mainly on the correlogram. Our experience is that truly stationary behaviour is often hard to achieve from real time series and one has to be content with approximations to stationarity that are not well defined. Moreover, the correlogram is rather treacherous as an instrument for model selection because of its high sampling variability for series of moderate length. Thus apart from straightforward cases such as those leading to the "airline model" the *ARIMA* model identification procedure is often quite hard to operate. Explanatory variables are incorporated into the *ARIMA* system by the transfer function technique. Even for a single explanatory variable this is not always feasible since the technique depends on the achievement of approximate stationarity by differencing and other transformations; see Harvey (1981, pp. 244–246). Moreover the basic identification tool is the cross-correlogram, which is even harder to interpret than the univariate correlogram and may be a very inefficient way of determining the form of a lag structure. The difficulties multiply as the number of explanatory variables increases.

The structural approach that we have adopted represents, we believe, a more direct and transparent technique for time series modelling. The basis idea is that one looks at the behaviour of an observed time series and where the series appears to contain trend and seasonal components one aims at modelling these directly. Allowance can be made for changes over time in the behaviour of these and other components as needed. Explanatory and intervention variables can be added in a direct manner. Because the models can be put in state-space form and thus can be handled computationally by the Kalman filter it is possible to accommodate a considerable amount of apparent complexity.

7.4. *Miscellaneous Points*

In our Report we mention at various points some difficulties that arose because of under-reporting of some accidents involving fatalities in the Metropolitan Police area. After submitting the Report we re-analysed data for Great Britain excluding this area but found that no differences of any consequence emerged. We have not therefore taken up space in this paper by discussing this re-analysis.

The data we used are available for research purposes from the Head of Computer Services, London School of Economics, Houghton Street, London WC2A 2AE. A nominal charge of £10 is made to cover handling charge and the cost of the floppy disc (available for IBM PC or BBC micro).

ACKNOWLEDGEMENTS

We are grateful to Mr E. J. Thompson, Director of Statistics at the Department of Transport, for inviting us to undertake this study, and to him and his colleagues, particularly Mr H. M. Dale and Mr P. J. Hathaway for their helpfulness at all stages. Our main debt is to our research assistant, Simon Peters, for carrying out the large amount of computing and data processing needed for this work. We also thank Richard Snell, Manuel Arellano and Javier Fernandez who played valuable supporting roles in this respect. Much of the methodology used was developed as part of the Economic and Social Research Council supported DEMEIC Econometrics programme.

REFERENCES

Adams, J. G. U. (1984) Smeed's law, seat belts and the emperor's new clothes. In *Human Behaviour and Traffic Safety* (C. Evans and R. C. Schwing, eds). Proceedings of International Symposium sponsored by General Motors. To appear.

——(1985) *Risk and Freedom: The Record of Road Safety Regulation.* Cardiff: Transport Publishing Projects.

Ashton, S. J., Thomas, P. D., Harms, P., Mackay, G. M. and Galer, M. D. (1985) The effects of mandatory seat belt use in Great Britain. Paper presented at the 10th International Conference on Experimental Safety Vehicles,Oxford, 1985.

Bhattacharyya, M. N. and Layton, A. P. (1974) Effectiveness of seat belt legislation on the Queensland road toll—an Australian case study in intervention analysis. *J. Amer. Statist. Ass.*, **74**, 596-603.

Bowman, K. O. and Shenton, L. R. (1975) Omnibus test contours for departures from normality based on $\sqrt{b_1}$ and b_2. *Biometrika*, **62**, 243-250.

Box, G. E. P. and Jenkins, G. M. (1970) *Time Series Analysis: Forecasting and Control.* San Francisco: Holden-Day.

Box, G. E. P. and Tiao, G. C. (1975) Intervention analysis with applications to economic and environmental problems. *J. Amer. Statist. Ass.*, **70**, 70-79.

——(1976) Comparison of forecast with actuality. *Appl. Statist.*, **25**, 195-200.

Brown, R. L., Durbin, J. and Evans, J. M (1975) Techniques for testing the constancy of regression relationships over time (with Discussion). *J. R. Statist. Soc.* B, **37**, 149-192.

Durbin, J. (1984) Time series analysis. *J. R. Statist. Soc.* A, **147**, 161-173.

Durbin, J. and Harvey, A. C. (1985) The effects of seat belt legislation on road casualties in Great Britain: Report on Assessment of Statistical Evidence. Annex to *Compulsory Seat Belt Wearing Report by the Department of Transport*. London: HMSO.

Engle, R. F. (1978) Estimating structural models of seasonality. In *Seasonal Analysis of Economic Time Series* (A. Zellner, ed.), pp. 281-308. Washington, D.C.: Bureau of the Census.

Harrison, P. J. (1967) Exponential smoothing and short-term sales forecasting. *Manag. Sci.*, **13**, 821-842.

Harrison, P. J. and Stevens, C. F. (1976) Bayesian forecasting (with Discussion). *J. R. Statist. Soc.* B, **38**, 205-247.

Harvey, A. C. (1981) *The Econometric Analysis of Time Series*. Oxford: Philip Allen. New York: Wiley.

——(1984) A unified view of statistical forecasting procedures. *J. Forecasting*, **3**, 245-275.

——(1985a) Trends and cycles in macroeconomic time series. *J. Bus. Econ. Statist.*, **3**, 216-227.

——(1985b) Multivariate time series models, control groups and intervention analysis. CSE Econometrics Programme Discussion Paper No. A.53, London School of Economics.

Harvey, A. C. and Todd, P. (1983) Forecasting economic time series with structural and Box-Jenkins models: a case study (with Discussion). *J. Bus. Econ. Statist.*, **1**, 299-315.

Harvey, A. C. and Peters, S. (1984) Estimation procedures for structural time series models. LSE Econometrics Programme Discussion Paper No. A.44, London School of Economics.

Holt, C. C. (1957) Forecasting seasonals and trends by exponentially weighted moving averages. Carnegie Institute of Technology, Pittsburgh, Pennsylvania. ONR Research Memorandum No. 52.

Jarque, C. M. and Bera, A. K. (1980) Efficient tests for normality, homoscedasticity and serial independence of regression residuals. *Econ. Lett.*, **6**, 255-259.

Kalman, R. E. (1960) A new approach to linear filtering and prediction problems. *Trans. ASME J. Basic Engning*, **82**, 35-45.

Kitagawa, G. (1981) A nonstationary time series model and its fitting by a recursive filter. *J. Time Ser. Anal.*, **2**, 103-116.

Ljung, J. and Caines, P. E. (1979) Asymptotic normality and prediction error estimators for approximate system models. *Stochastics*, **3**, 29-46.

Maravall, A. (1985) On structural time series models and the characterization of components. *J. Bus Econ. Statist.*, **3**, 350-355.

Muth, J. F. (1960) Optimal properties of exponentially weighted forecasts. *J. Amer. Statist. Ass.*, **55**, 299-305.

Nelson, C. and Kang, H. (1984) Pitfalls in the use of time as an explanatory variable. *J. Bus. Econ. Statist.*, **2**, 73-82.

Nerlove, M. and Wage, S. (1964) On the optimality of adaptive forecasting. *Manag. Sci.*, **10**, 2, 207-229.

Nerlove, M., Grether, D. M., and Carvalho, J. L. (1979) *Analysis of Economic Time Series*. New York: Academic Press.

Pierce, D. A. (1978) Seasonal adjustment when both deterministic and stochastic seasonality are present. In *Seasonal Analysis of Economic Time Series* (A. Zellner, ed.), pp. 242-269. Washington, D.C.: Bureau of the Census.

Road Accidents in Great Britain, 1983 (1984) London: HMSO.

Rutherford, W. H., Greenfield, A. A., Hayes, H. R. M. and Nelson, J. K. (1985) *The Medical Effects of Seat Belt Legislation in the United Kingdom*. Research Report No. 13, Office of the Chief Scientist, DHSS. London: HMSO.

Schweppe, F. (1965) Evaluation of likelihood functions for Gaussian signals. *IEEE Trans. Inform. Theory*, **11**, 61-70.

Scott, P. P. and Willis, P. A. (1985) Road casualties in Great Britain—the first year with seat belt legislation. TRRL Research Report 9, Department of Transport.

Theil, H. and Wage, S. (1964) Some observations on adaptive forecasting. *Manag. Sci.*, **10**, 198-206.

Tiao, G. C. (1972) Asymptotic behaviour of temporal aggregates of time series. *Biometrika*, **59**, 525-531.

Wilde, G. J. S. (1982) The theory of risk homeostasis: implications for safety and health. *Risk Analysis*, **2**, 209-225.

Winters, P. R. (1960) Forecasting sales by exponentially weighted moving averages. *Manag. Sci.*, **6**, 324-342.

[24]

THE ECONOMIC JOURNAL

DECEMBER 1978

The Economic Journal, **88** (*December* 1978), 661–692
Printed in Great Britain

ECONOMETRIC MODELLING OF THE AGGREGATE TIME-SERIES RELATIONSHIP BETWEEN CONSUMERS' EXPENDITURE AND INCOME IN THE UNITED KINGDOM*

I. INTRODUCTION

Although the relationship between Consumers' Expenditure and Disposable Income is one of the most thoroughly researched topics in quantitative economics, no consensus seems to have emerged in the United Kingdom about the short-run dynamic interactions between these two important variables. In support of this contention, we would cite the plethora of substantially different quarterly regression equations which have been reported by Byron (1970), Deaton (1972, 1977), Hendry (1974), Ball *et al.* (1975), Bispham (1975), Shepherd *et al.* (1975), Wall *et al.* (1975), Townend (1976) and Bean (1977). Moreover, this list of studies is representative, rather than exhaustive.

The diversity of the published estimates is really surprising since most of the investigators seem to have based their regression equations on similar economic theories and seem to have used approximately the same data series. Specifically, therefore, we wish to explain why their results manifest quite dissimilar short-run multipliers, lag reactions and long-run responses. This requires examining the extent to which the estimates are mutually incompatible as well as their inconsistency with the empirical evidence. More generally, we hope to be able to specify which aspects of the methodology used were primarily responsible for creating the differences in the published results.

Close inspection of the above list of studies reveals that despite their superficial similarities, they differ in many respects the importance of which is not obvious *a priori*. Initially, therefore, to highlight the issues involved we concentrated on three studies only (Hendry (1974), Ball *et al.* (1975) and Wall *et al.* (1975), denoted *H*, *B*, *W* respectively). Rather than use the elegant but very technical theory recently developed for testing "non-nested" models (see Pesaran and Deaton, 1978) we have chosen to "standardise" those aspects of the three studies which do not seem crucial to explaining the original differences between the results. This allows analogues of the contending models to be embedded in

* This research was financed in part by a grant from the Social Science Research Council to the Econometric Methodology Project at the London School of Economics. Preparation of the initial draft of the paper was supported by grants from the National Science and Ford Foundations while the second author visited at the Cowles Foundation, Yale University. The fourth author gratefully acknowledges the financial assistance of a Canada Council Doctoral Fellowship. We are grateful to Gordon Anderson, Charles Bean, Jeremy Bray, Angus Deaton, John Flemming, Grayham Mizon and John Muellbauer for helpful comments on previous drafts.

a common framework within which nested tests are feasible. By stressing the implications for each model of the results obtained by others it will be seen below that our approach assigns a major role to mis-specification analysis (see Hendry, 1977*a*, for a discussion of mis-specification theory in dynamic systems).

A proliferation of non-nested models is symptomatic of certain inappropriate aspects of present practice in econometrics. We would suggest that this problem can be mitigated to some extent by adopting the following principles. First, we consider it an essential (if minimal) requirement that any new model should be related to existing "explanations" in a constructive research strategy such that previous models are only supplanted if new proposals account (so far as possible) for previously understood results, and also explain some new phenomena. Second, to avoid directionless "research" and uninterpretable measurements, a theoretical framework is also essential. Unfortunately, much existing economic analysis relates to hypothetical constructs (for example, "permanent income") and/or is based on unclearly specified but stringent *ceteris paribus* assumptions, and leaves many important decisions in formulating an operational model to *ad hoc* considerations (e.g. functional form, dynamic specification, error structure, treatment of seasonality, etc.). Nevertheless, economic theory does furnish some helpful postulates about behaviour in steady-state environments and to guide an empirical analysis it seems sensible to incorporate such information as is available explicitly. Third, to be empirically acceptable, an econometric model obviously must account for the properties of the data (e.g. the autocorrelation function in a time-series study). It is not valid to "accomplish" this aim simply by not looking for counter-evidence (for example, by claiming the absence of autocorrelation in a dynamic equation on the basis of an insignificant value for a Durbin–Watson *d*-statistic).

The combination of not encompassing previous findings, introducing *ad hoc* auxiliary assumptions and not rigorously testing data compatibility leaves plenty of room for a diversity of outcomes from model building even in a common theoretical framework with a common data set. Indeed, one could characterise "econometric modelling" as an attempt to match the hypothetical data generation process postulated by economic theory with the main properties of the observed data. Any model which fails to account for the "gestalt" of results which are obtained from the data set cannot constitute the actual data generation process. Consequently, a further minimal requirement when modelling from a common data set is that the chosen model should explain both the *results* obtained by other researchers and *why* their research methods led to their published conclusions. The former usually can be achieved through the appropriate mis-specification analysis from a sufficiently general model which could be based on *a priori* theory (see, for example, Hendry and Anderson, 1977) or empirical considerations. Any theory gains some plausibility by an explanation of different empirical results, but a data-based construction always must be susceptible to a potential *post hoc ergo propter hoc* fallacy. However, given the research methods which any investigator claimed to use it is not trivial even from a data based general model to explain why they reached certain conclusions. That the general model is not obtained by every investigator seems to depend on the operation of (self-imposed) constraints limiting the range of specifications, estimators, diagnostic tests, etc., which are employed. Such arbitrary and unnecessary constraints can play a large role in determining the final equations selected and a further major objective of this paper is to illustrate the advantages of using a wide range of different techniques (including both "econometric" and "time-series" methods) when analysing aggregate economic data.

We believe that considerable insight can be achieved by trying to explain the interrelationships between the consumption function studies of Hendry (1974), Ball *et al.* (1975) and Wall *et al.* (1975). Our analysis proceeds by noting seven potential explanations for the main differences between these three studies, namely the choice of (i) data series, (ii) methods of seasonal adjustment, (iii) other data transformations, (iv) functional forms, (v) lag structures, (vi) diagnostic statistics and (vii) estimation methods. It proves possible to "standardise" the models on a common basis for (i)–(iv) such that the major differences between the studies persist. This allows us to nest the standardised contending theories as special cases of a general hypothesis and test to see which (if any) are acceptable on statistical grounds. Such an approach leads to the selection on *statistical criteria* of the equation which we consider to be the least reasonable of the three on the basis of *economic theory* considerations. To account for this outcome we investigate the role of measurement errors in the data, but draw a blank. Next, we develop an econometric relationship (which was originally obtained as an empirical description of the data series) and show that it satisfies our desired theory criteria, fits as well as the previously best fitting equation and includes the rejected models as special cases. Moreover, this relationship is such that if it were the true model, then it is reasonably easy to see in retrospect why the alternative research methods led to their various conclusions. Finally, we conduct a variety of tests on a modified version of our chosen model and show that it adequately accounts for the atypical consumption behaviour observed over the period 1971–5.

The data and the three econometric studies are described in Sections II and III respectively. Sections IV and V investigate the standardisation aspects and multicollinearity respectively and in Section VI we consider the selection of the equation which performs "best" on statistical criteria. Section VII discusses the effects of certain of the data transformations on measurement errors. In Section VIII we propose a possible explanation for all the previous results through a serious, but hard to detect, dynamic mis-specification, and conditional on this interpretation, re-evaluate the role of (v)–(vii) above. Inflation effects are considered in Section IX and Section X concludes the study.

It should be noted that throughout the paper we are only concerned with expenditure excluding durables. Also, we must stress that most of the modelling described below was carried out during 1974/5 using data series in 1963 prices and estimating up to the end of 1970 only. Re-estimation using an extended data set in 1970 prices was undertaken in early 1977 without re-specifying any of the earlier equations and still terminating the estimation period in 1970. The data to the end of 1975 was used for testing and the additional equations based on Deaton (1977) were included at this stage.

II. THE DATA

Let Y_t denote personal disposable income, Cd_t consumers' expenditure on durable goods, S_t personal saving and C_t consumers' expenditure on all other goods and services, all variables being in constant prices. The main series used in this study are taken from *Economic Trends* (1976 Annual Supplement) and are quarterly, seasonally unadjusted in £ million at 1970 prices. Although C_t and Cd_t are separately deflated, the series are such that $Y_t = C_t + Cd_t + S_t$. Fig. 1 shows the time series of Y_t and C_t for the period 1958 (i) to 1976 (ii) (the data for 1957 were used to create variables like $C_t - C_{t-4}$).

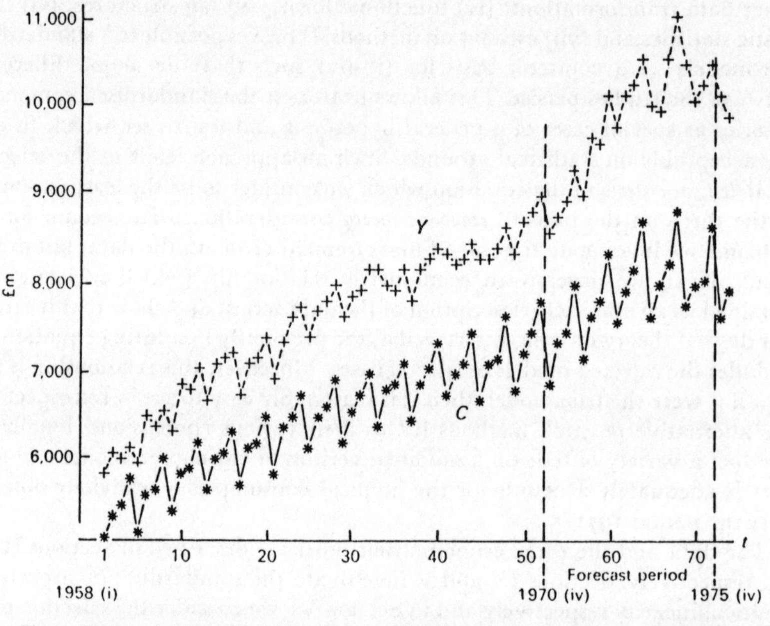

Fig. 1. Time paths of personal disposable income (Y) and consumers' expenditure (C).

The salient features of the data are the strong trends in both C_t and Y_t, the magnitude and stability of the seasonal pattern in C_t compared to that of Y_t (although the seasonal shape has tended to become increasingly "elongated" over time), the regularity of the "output" series C_t compared to the "input" series Y_t, and the marked change in the behaviour of the Y_t series after 1972. Detailed scrutiny reveals the presence of "business cycles" which are more clearly seen in the transformed series $\Delta_4 Y_t = Y_t - Y_{t-4}$ and $\Delta_4 C_t$ graphed in Fig. 2 (Δ_4 is referred to below as the four period or annual difference as compared with the fourth difference Δ_1^4). Fig. 2 also confirms the greater variance of the income series, and casual inspection suggests that using annual differences has removed most of the seasonality in both series. As shown in Fig. 3, the average propensity to consume (C_t/Y_t denoted APC) has fallen steadily over the sample

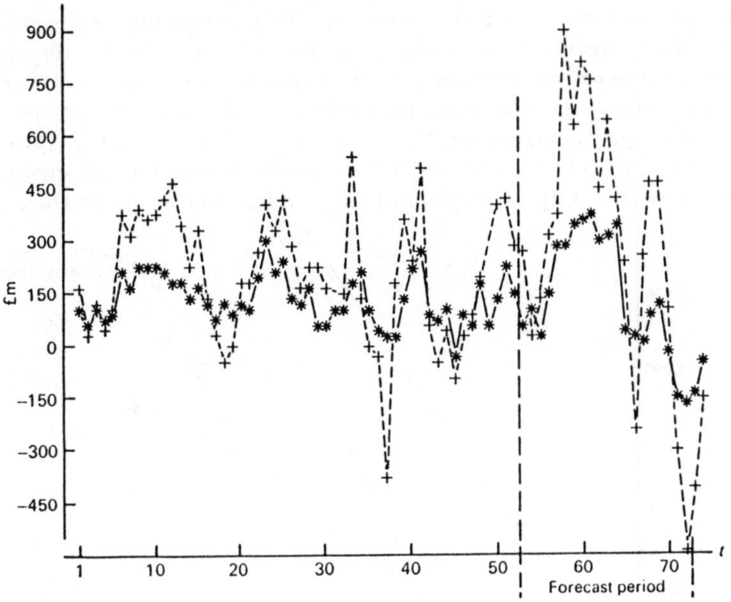

Fig. 2. Four period changes in data series. *——*, $\Delta_4 C$; +——+, $\Delta_4 Y$.

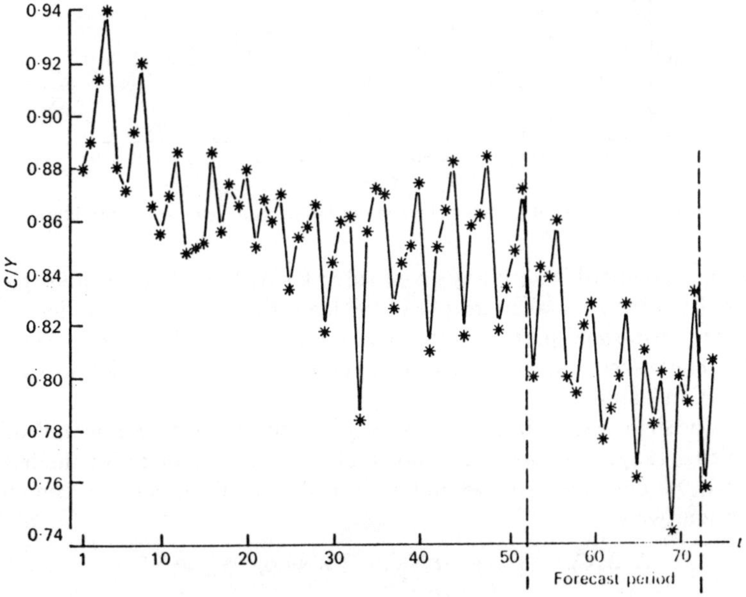

Fig. 3. The average propensity to consume.

period from around 0·9 to under 0·8, although as explained below, this evidence is still consonant with a long-run income elasticity of expenditure close to unity. If C_t is plotted against Y_t as in Fig. 4, marked differences in the average propensities to consume in the various quarters are clear. The upper and lower lines show the patterns of observations for the fourth and first quarters respectively. Finally, plotting $\Delta_4 C$ against $\Delta_4 Y$ yields a scatter diagram (see Fig. 5) in which the slope (*MPC*) of the "short-run" consumption function is much smaller than that of the relationship portrayed in Fig. 4, and a wide range of values of $\Delta_4 C$

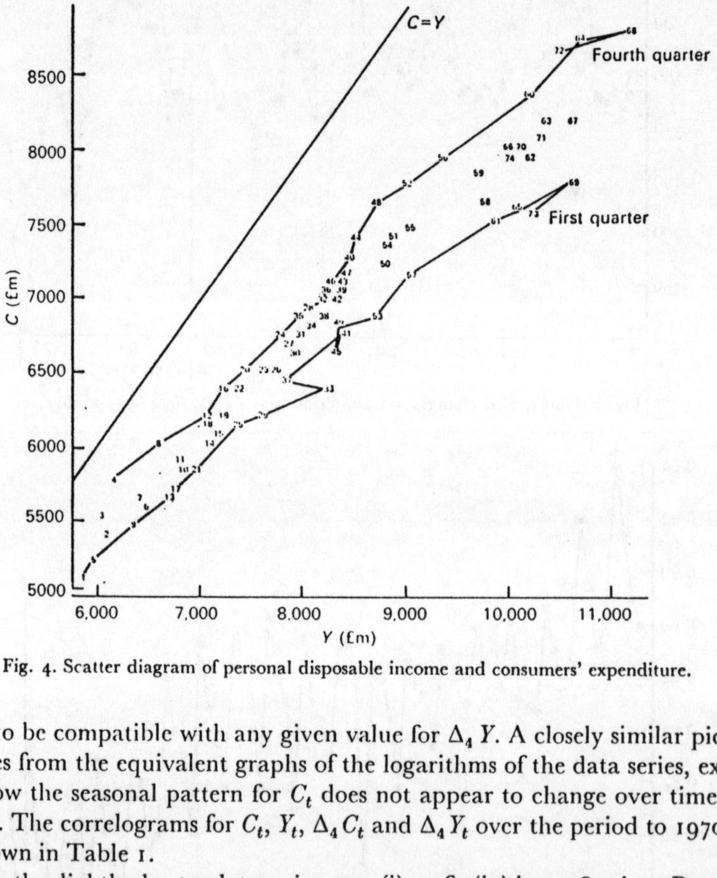

Fig. 4. Scatter diagram of personal disposable income and consumers' expenditure.

seems to be compatible with any given value for $\Delta_4 Y$. A closely similar picture emerges from the equivalent graphs of the logarithms of the data series, except that now the seasonal pattern for C_t does not appear to change over time (see Fig. 6). The correlograms for C_t, Y_t, $\Delta_4 C_t$ and $\Delta_4 Y_t$ over the period to 1970 (iv) are shown in Table 1.

From the slightly shorter data series 1957 (i)–1967 (iv) in 1958 prices, Prothero and Wallis (1977) obtained a number of univariate time-series models for C_t and Y_t, no one of which was uniformly superior. Their most parsimonious descriptions were:

$$\Delta_1 \Delta_4 C_t = (1 - \underset{(0\cdot14)}{0\cdot59} L^4)\, \epsilon_t, \quad \hat{\sigma} = 32\cdot0, \quad \chi^2_{15} = 6\cdot8, \tag{1}$$

$$\Delta_1 \Delta_4 Y_t = (1 - \underset{(0\cdot18)}{0\cdot58} L^4)\, \epsilon_t, \quad \hat{\sigma} = 103\cdot0, \quad \chi^2_{15} = 9\cdot6. \tag{2}$$

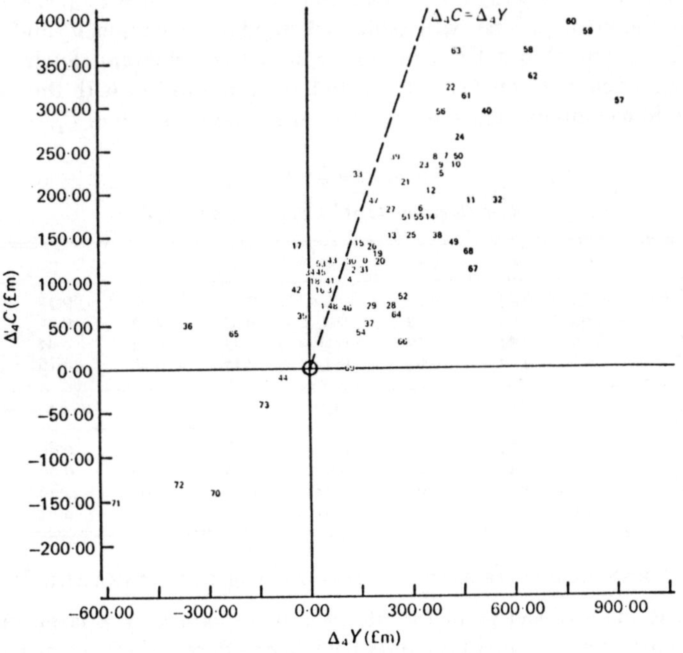

Fig. 5. Scatter diagram of four period changes.

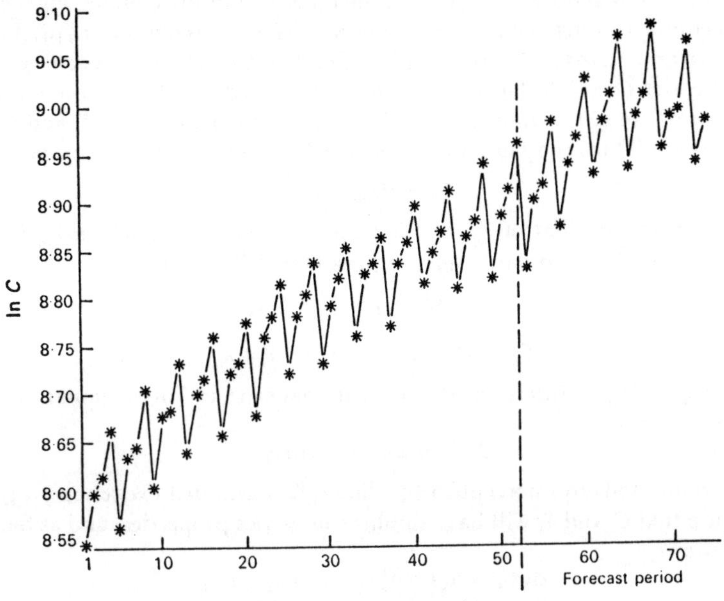

Fig. 6. Logarithms of consumers' expenditure.

In (1) and (2), L denotes the lag operator such that $L^jC_t = C_{t-j}$, ϵ_t represents a white-noise error process with estimated standard deviation $\hat{\sigma}$, and χ^2_{15} is the Box–Pierce (1970) test for a random residual correlogram. Such time-series descriptions show C_t and Y_t to obey similar equations but with the variance of the random component of Y_t nearly ten times as large as that of C_t.

Table 1

Correlograms for C_t, Y_t, $\Delta_4 C_t$ and $\Delta_4 Y_t$

Lag...	1	2	3	4	5	6	7	8
C	0·79	0·80	0·75	0·99	0·76	0·76	0·72	0·99
Y	0·95	0·95	0·93	0·97	0·93	0·93	0·91	0·96
$\Delta_4 C$	0·49	0·24	−0·02	−0·28	−0·23	−0·24	−0·02	−0·07
$\Delta_4 Y$	0·50	0·24	0·04	−0·33	−0·17	−0·16	−0·16	−0·02
Lag...	9	10	11	12	13	14	15	16
C	0·72	0·73	0·67	0·99	0·68	0·68	0·60	0·98
Y	0·92	0·92	0·89	0·96	0·91	0·90	0·86	0·95
$\Delta_4 C$	−0·05	0·09	0·02	0·04	0·02	0·06	0·20	0·35
$\Delta_4 Y$	−0·03	0·01	−0·02	−0·03	−0·04	−0·08	0·04	0·18

III. THREE ECONOMETRIC STUDIES AND THEIR RESEARCH METHODS

Since the main objective of this study is to explain why a large number of econometric descriptions of the data have been offered, there seems no need for a long section dealing with relevant economic theories. However, we do wish to stress that most theories of the consumption function were formulated to reconcile the low short-run *MPC* with the relative stability claimed for the *APC* over medium to long data periods (see *inter alia* Duesenberry, 1949; Brown, 1952; Friedman, 1957; Ando and Modigliani, 1963). Broadly speaking, all of these theories postulate lag mechanisms which mediate the response of C_t to changes in Y_t (e.g. previous highest C_t, C_{t-1}, "permanent income" and wealth respectively). Thus, the Permanent Income Hypothesis (*PIH*) assumes that:

$$C_t = \theta Y_{pt} + u_t, \tag{3}$$

where u_t is independent of Y_{pt} and has finite variance, and where Y_{pt} is "permanent income". Friedman (1957) approximated Y_{pt} using.

$$(1-\lambda L)\, Y_{pt} = (1-\lambda)\, Y_t \tag{4}$$

to obtain

$$C_t = \theta(1-\lambda)\,(1-\lambda L)^{-1}\, Y_t + u_t, \tag{5}$$

while Sargent (1977) interprets this as a rational expectations formulation when Y_t is generated by

$$\Delta_1 Y_t = a + (1-\lambda L)\,\epsilon_t, \tag{6}$$

which would add an intercept to (5). Since Y_t is assumed exogenous, (3) and (6) ensure that C_t and Y_t will have similar time-series properties, and as Sargent (1977) shows,

$$\begin{aligned}\Delta_1 C_t &= \theta(1-\lambda)\,\epsilon_t + \theta a + u_t - u_{t-1}\\ &= \theta a + (1-\lambda^* L)\,\epsilon_t^*, \end{aligned} \tag{7}$$

where ϵ_t^* is white noise and λ^* depends on θ, λ, σ_u^2 and σ_ϵ^2. Since $\sigma_{\epsilon^*}^2 > \sigma_u^2$, it is of course more efficient to analyse (5) than (7).

At the aggregate level, a steady-state form of the Life Cycle Hypothesis (*LCH*) is exposited by Modigliani (1975) as:

$$C_t = \alpha Y_t + (\delta - r) A_t, \tag{8}$$

where A_t is end period private wealth and r (the rate of return on assets), α and δ are constant. Out of steady-state, α and δ (like θ in (3)) vary with a number of factors including the rate of interest and the expected growth of productivity. If capital gains and interest are included in income, then from (8) and the identity

$$A_t = A_{t-1} + Y_{t-1} - C_{t-1} \tag{9}$$

we can obtain

$$\Delta_1 C_t = \alpha \Delta_1 Y_t + (\delta - r)(Y_{t-1} - C_{t-1})$$

or

$$C_t = \alpha Y_t + (\delta - r - \alpha) Y_{t-1} + (1 - \delta + r) C_{t-1}, \tag{10}$$

which again produces a distributed lag model of C_t on Y_t.[1]

It is noticeable that neither the *PIH* nor the *LCH* is much concerned with seasonal patterns of expenditure and models based on such theories are often estimated from annual or from seasonally adjusted quarterly data series.

Against this background we can consider the three econometric studies.

(*H*) Hendry (1974) estimated several equations of the form

$$C_t = a_0 + a_1 Y_t + a_2 C_{t-1} + \sum_{j=1}^{3} b_j Q_{jt} + \sum_{j=1}^{4} d_j Q_{jt} t + \epsilon_t \quad (t = 1, \ldots, T), \tag{11}$$

where Q_{jt} denotes a dummy variable for the jth quarter. He imposed various restrictions on the parameters, used a number of different estimators and considered various autocorrelation structures for ϵ_t. For example, assuming a constant seasonal pattern ($d_j = 0$, $j = 1, \ldots, 4$), no autocorrelation and using raw data, 1957(i)–1967(iv) in 1958 prices, least-squares estimation yielded (see *H*, table 1):

$$\underset{(76)}{\hat{C}_t = 377} + \underset{(0{\cdot}06)}{0{\cdot}10 Y_t} + \underset{(0{\cdot}09)}{0{\cdot}84 C_{t-1}} + \hat{S}_t, \tag{12}$$

$$R^2 = 0{\cdot}994, \quad \hat{\sigma} = 30{\cdot}4, \quad \text{dw} = 2{\cdot}6.$$

In (12) the numbers in parentheses are standard errors,

$$\hat{S}_t = \sum_{j=1}^{3} \hat{b}_j Q_{jt},$$

R^2 is the squared coefficient of multiple correlation, $\hat{\sigma}$ is the standard deviation of the residuals and dw is the Durbin–Watson statistic. Then testing (12) for (i) fourth-order autoregressive residuals, (ii) omitted four period lagged values of C_t, Y_t and C_{t-1} and (iii) an evolving seasonal pattern, *H* found that each of these three factors was present if allowed for *separately*. When included in com-

[1] The derivation of (10) is less convincing if a white noise error is included in (8), since the error on (10) would be a first-order moving average with a root of minus unity, reflecting the inappropriateness of differencing (8).

binations, however, they appeared to act as substitutes since only the last remained significant in the three sets of pairwise comparisons.

Consequently, H selected (11) (with ϵ_t assumed serially independent) as the best description of his data and obtained the following least squares estimates (instrumental variables estimates were similar):

$$\hat{C}_t = \underset{(369)}{1994} + \underset{(0{\cdot}04)}{0{\cdot}19}Y_t + \underset{(0{\cdot}14)}{0{\cdot}22}C_{t-1} + \hat{S}_t + \sum_{j=1}^{4} \hat{d}_j Q_{jt} t, \qquad (13)$$

$$R^2 = 0{\cdot}998, \quad \hat{\sigma} = 17{\cdot}6, \quad \text{dw} = 2{\cdot}2.$$

When selecting this outcome, all other potential mis-specifications were apparently deliberately ignored by H to highlight the problems of stochastic specification. Even granting this escape from sins of omission, there are several important drawbacks to econometric formulations like (11)–(13), and many of the following criticisms apply to other published regression equations. First, the assumed seasonal pattern is *ad hoc* and would yield meaningless results if extrapolated much beyond the sample period. Moreover, one of the more interesting aspects of the data (the regular seasonal pattern of C_t) is attributed to unexplained factors, where by contrast a model like

$$C_t = \sum_{i=1}^{4} \alpha_i Q_{it} Y_t$$

would at least correspond to the possible behavioural hypothesis of a different *MPC* in each quarter of the year. Secondly, since the derived mean lag and long-run (static equilibrium) marginal propensity to consume coefficients in (12) are given by $\hat{a}_2/(1-\hat{a}_2)$ and $\hat{a}_1/(1-\hat{a}_2)$ respectively, these can be altered considerably by minor changes in $\hat{a}_2$ when that coefficient is close to unity. In turn, $\hat{a}_2$ can vary markedly with different treatments of residual autocorrelation. Next, both the short-run and long-run *MPC*'s are very small in (13) (yielding a long-run elasticity of about 0·2) and are radically different from the corresponding estimates in (12) although only the treatment of seasonality has changed. In part this is due to the inclusion of a trend in (13), but this is hardly an explanation and simply prompts the question as to why the trend is significant when one believes that the economic variables are actually determining the behaviour of C_t (most of the very close fit of (13) is due to the trend and seasonals). Finally, it is difficult to evaluate the plausibility of the results *as presented* in (12) and (13). For example, R^2 is unhelpful since the data are trending (see Granger and Newbold, 1974). Also, dw has both low power against high-order residual autocorrelation in static equations and an incorrect conventional significance level in dynamic equations[1] (see Durbin, 1970). No forecast or parameter stability tests are presented and the appropriateness of least squares is not obvious (although Hendry, 1974, did in fact publish forecast tests, other diagnostic checks, and used less restrictive estimators).

Overall, with or without evolving seasonals, (11) does not seem to be a useful

[1] dw is quoted below as a conventional statistic (from which, for example, Durbin's h test could be calculated if desired).

specification for studying consumption–income responses, however well it may happen to describe the data for a short time period.

(*B*) Ball *et al.* (1975) present an equation rather like (12), but based on seasonally adjusted data (abbreviated to *SA* below and denoted by a superscript *a*) for the period 1959 (ii)–1970 (iv), estimated by least squares:

$$\widehat{(C-G)}_t^a = \underset{(65)}{185} + \underset{(0{\cdot}07)}{0{\cdot}23}(Y-G)_t^a + \underset{(0{\cdot}09)}{0{\cdot}69}(C-G)_{t-1}^a + (\hat{\phi}_1 D_t + \hat{\phi}_2 D_{t-1}), \quad (14)$$

$$\bar{R}^2 = 0{\cdot}99, \quad \hat{\sigma} = 29{\cdot}3, \quad \text{dw} = 2{\cdot}3,$$

D_t represents a dummy variable with zero values everywhere except for 1968 (ii) when it is unity (1968 (i) and (ii) are anomalous quarters owing to advance warning in the first quarter of 1968 of possible purchase tax increases in the second quarter; these duly materialised, and considerable switching of expenditure between these quarters resulted). G_t denotes direct transfer payments to individuals, and as specified in (14), G_t is immediately and completely spent. $\bar{R}^2$ is the adjusted value of R^2.

Many of the criticisms noted in *H* apply to (14) and in addition, the use of *SA* data must be considered. Seasonal adjustment methods can be interpreted as filters applied to time series to remove frequency components at or near seasonal frequencies, such filters often being many-period weighted moving averages (e.g. 24 periods for quarterly data in the commonly used Bureau of Census Method II version X-11 program). In published statistics, single series tend to be separately adjusted. However, as documented by Wallis (1974), *separate* adjustment of series can distort the relationship between pairs of series and in particular can alter the underlying dynamic reactions. Thus, Wallis records a case of *four* period lags being incorrectly identified as *one* period after *SA* and the possibility of such a dynamic mis-specification applying to (14) merits investigation since earlier variants of (14) in the London Business School model based on unadjusted data used C_{t-4} as a regressor.

Note that the estimates in (14) again seem to imply a long-run (static equilibrium) elasticity of less than unity ($MPC = 0{\cdot}74$, $APC = 0{\cdot}84$) which is consistent with Fig. 3 and reasonably similar to (12) despite the very different treatment of seasonality.

(*W*) Wall *et al.* (1975) analyse total consumers' expenditure $C_t^* = Cd_t^a + C_t^a$ using *SA* data for 1955 (i)–1971 (iv) with estimation based on the transfer function methodology proposed by Box and Jenkins (1970). Their published model is

$$\hat{\dot{C}}_t^* = 0{\cdot}21 + \underset{(0{\cdot}08)}{0{\cdot}31}\dot{Y}_t^a + \underset{(0{\cdot}08)}{0{\cdot}24}\dot{Y}_{t-1}^a \quad \text{where} \quad \dot{x}_t = 100(x_t - x_{t-1})/x_{t-1}, \quad (15)$$

$$R^2 = 0{\cdot}56, \quad \hat{\sigma} = 0{\cdot}74.$$

The relative first difference transformation was adopted to make the variables "stationary". Given their advocacy of Box–Jenkins methods, we assume that *W* estimated (15) with the residuals treated as "white noise" because they had found no evidence of residual autocorrelation.

However, (15) has *no static equilibrium* solution and is only consistent with a steady-state growth rate of about 2% pa. Indeed, the *ad hoc* mean correction of 0·21 is 35% of the mean of $\dot{C}^*$ and as a consequence, the conventionally calculated long-run elasticity is 0·55. Moreover, (15) implies that any adjustment to income changes is completed within six months and is independent of any disequilibrium between the *levels* of C_t and Y_t. Also, the use of $C_t^* = C_t^a + Cd_t^a$ may entail some aggregation bias in view of the extra variables usually included in models of durables purchases (see, for example, Williams, 1972, and Garganas, 1975). However, it is not surprising that (15) results from estimation based on data like that in Fig. 5.

IV. A STANDARDISED FRAMEWORK

The studies listed as *H*, *B* and *W* above satisfy the requirement that approximately the same data set (*C*, *Y*) is involved in all three cases. Nevertheless, the *results* differ in many respects and are conditioned by very different auxiliary hypotheses. Indeed, the first problem is to find enough common elements to allow direct comparisons to be made! Our approach is to re-estimate close equivalents of (13)–(15) in a standard framework which tries to isolate which factors do, and which do not, induce differences in the results. We begin by examining the roles of the data period, seasonal adjustment procedures, data transformations and functional forms since it might be anticipated that small alterations to these should not greatly change the findings of any particular study.

We chose the data series graphed in Fig. 1, with the 20 observations for 1971 (i)–1975 (iv) being used purely for forecast tests.[1] The choice of data period did not seem to be too important, and we preferred raw to *SA* data for the reasons noted in the discussion of *H* and *B*, namely "Wallis' effects" and our desire to "model" the seasonal behaviour of *C* rather than filter it out. Sims (1974) has pointed out that the use of raw data involves a potential risk of "omitted seasonals" bias if there is also seasonal noise in the error on the equation of relevance; however, the estimates recorded below do not suggest the presence of such a problem.

A major assumption which we made in order to develop analogues of the various equations is that the closest equivalent of a transformation of the form $\Delta_1 Z_t^a = Z_t^a - Z_{t-1}^a$ (in *SA* data) is $\Delta_4 Z_t = Z_t - Z_{t-4}$ (in raw data), since both transformed variables represent changes net of seasonal factors (we have also estimated most of the analogue equations using *SA* data and report below on the negligible changes this induces). The *converse* equivalence is not valid, however, since dynamics should be unaltered when a linear filter is *correctly* applied to a relationship (see Wallis, 1974; Hendry and Mizon, 1978). Also,

[1] We ignored the two observations for 1976 as being liable to considerably larger revisions than the earlier data.

we assumed that $\Delta_1 \ln x_t \simeq \Delta_1 x_t/x_{t-1}$ (where ln denotes $\log_e$) and so could approximate W's variable $\dot{C}_t^*$ in SA data by $\Delta_4 \ln (C_t + Cd_t)$ in raw data.

Finally, models in differences can be related to those in levels, by noting that there are two distinct interpretations of "differencing", a point most easily demonstrated by the following relationship:[1]

$$x_t = \beta_1 w_t + \beta_2 w_{t-4} + \beta_3 x_{t-4} + \sum_{j=1}^{4} (\theta_j + \mu_j t)\, Q_{jt} + v_t, \tag{16}$$

where w_t is an exogenous regressor generated by a stationary stochastic process and v_t is a stationary error.

(a) Differencing as a Filter or Operator

Applying the operation Δ_4 to equation (16) yields

$$\Delta_4 x_t = \beta_1 \Delta_4 w_t + \beta_2 \Delta_4 w_{t-4} + \beta_3 \Delta_4 x_{t-4} + \sum_{j=1}^{4} 4\mu_j Q_{jt} + \Delta_4 v_t \tag{17}$$

and hence the features which are altered comprise:

– the elimination of trends and the re-interpretation of the constant seasonal pattern in (17) as corresponding with the evolving pattern in (16);

– the autocorrelation properties of v_t (e.g. if $v_t = v_{t-4} + \nu_t$, where ν_t is white noise, then $\Delta_4 v_t$ is white noise, whereas if $v_t = \nu_t$, $\Delta_4 v_t$ is a four period simple moving-average with a coefficient of -1);

– the form of all the non-dummy variables in (16) (which reoccur as annual differences in (17)).

(b) Differencing as a Set of Coefficient Restrictions

Applying the restrictions $\beta_1 = -\beta_2$ and $\beta_3 = 1$ to (16) yields:

$$\Delta_4 x_t = \beta_1 \Delta_4 w_t + \sum_{j=1}^{4} (\theta_j + \mu_j t)\, Q_{jt} + v_t. \tag{18}$$

Now, the changes from (16) are the elimination of w_{t-4} and x_{t-4} as independent regressors and the occurrence of the transformed variables $\Delta_4 x_t$ and $\Delta_4 w_t$. The interpretation of the constant and the seasonal pattern is unaltered and when the restrictions are valid the autocorrelation properties of v_t are unaffected – if v_t in (16) is white noise then so is v_t in (18) (contrast the arguments presented in Granger and Newbold, 1974). One immediate and obvious application of interpretation (*b*) is the converse step of deriving (16) from (18) which allows valid comparisons of models involving differenced variables with those using level variables.

Combining all of the above approximations, we move from (15) via the equivalence of $\dot{C}_t^a$ with $\Delta_4 \ln C_t$ to:

$$\begin{aligned}\Delta_4 \ln C_t &= \delta_0 + \delta_1 \Delta_4 \ln Y_t + \delta_2 \Delta_4 \ln Y_{t-1} + e_t \\ &= \delta_0 + (\delta_1 + \delta_2)\, \Delta_4 \ln Y_t - \delta_2 \Delta_1 \Delta_4 \ln Y_t + e_t,\end{aligned} \tag{19}$$

[1] Equations involving variables denoted by x_t and w_t are used to illustrate simplified versions of principles which can be generalised validly to the relationship between C and Y.

which provides our version of (15). For comparison with equations in log-levels we use the unrestricted version of (19), namely

$$\ln C_t = \lambda_1 \ln Y_t + \lambda_2 \ln Y_{t-4} + \lambda_3 \ln Y_{t-1} + \lambda_4 \ln Y_{t-5} + \lambda_5 \ln C_{t-4} + \lambda_6 + e_t, \qquad (20)$$

where (19) corresponds to imposing $\lambda_1 = -\lambda_2$, $\lambda_3 = -\lambda_4$ and $\lambda_5 = 1$ in (20). Since no seasonal dummy variables are introduced in (20) this procedure requires that Δ_4 in (19) removes any seasonal factors; some support for such a proposition is provided in Fig. 2 but this issue will be reconsidered below. We assumed that it was reasonable to use C_t in place of C_t^* in developing (19) for reasons presented above. Throughout, we have estimated most specifications in both linear and log-linear forms, comparing these where necessary using the likelihood criterion proposed by Sargan (1964). Thus (19) can be compared through (20) and the linear-log mapping with whatever equivalents are chosen for (13) and (14) (we chose to use C_t rather than $(C_t - G_t)$ when approximating (14) to maintain closer comparison with both (15) and (11)).

The main justification for adopting the above approximations is simply that the important features of and differences between the results in (13)–(15) survive the standardisation sequence. Firstly, to illustrate the effects of changing the sample period to 1958(ii)–1970(iv) and using 1970 prices, re-estimation of (13) by least-squares yields:

$$\underset{(537)}{\hat{C}_t = 2556} + \underset{(0{\cdot}05)}{0{\cdot}20 Y_t} + \underset{(0{\cdot}12)}{0{\cdot}35 C_{t-1}} + \underset{(33)}{83 D_t^0} - \underset{(60)}{514 Q_{1t}} - \underset{(57)}{74 Q_{2t}}$$

$$- \underset{(38)}{187 Q_{3t}} + \underset{(3{\cdot}7)}{16{\cdot}3 t} - \underset{(1{\cdot}3)}{6{\cdot}7 Q_{1t} t} - \underset{(1{\cdot}2)}{2{\cdot}2 Q_{2t} t} - \underset{(1{\cdot}2)}{0{\cdot}3 Q_{3t} t}, \qquad (21)$$

$$R^2 = 0{\cdot}996, \quad \hat{\sigma} = 39{\cdot}4, \quad \text{dw} = 2{\cdot}2, \quad z_1(20) = 130, \quad z_2(15) = 25.$$

In (21), $D^0 = (D_{t-1} - D_t)$, which assumes that the 1968(i) announcement caused a switch in expenditure between quarters.[1] $z_1(k)$ is a test of parameter stability or one period ahead forecast accuracy using the actual future values of the regressors for the next k quarters. Letting f_t denote the forecast error, then

$$z_1(k) = \sum_{t=T+1}^{T+k} (f_t/\hat{\sigma})^2,$$

which would be distributed as χ_k^2 in large samples if the parameters in (21) remained constant.[2] $z_2(l)$ is the Pierce (1971) residual correlogram statistic, distributed as χ_l^2 in large samples when the residuals are serially independent.[3]

[1] The introduction of VAT in 1973 was treated as being similar to the 1968(i)/(ii) budget effect and hence we projected D_t^0 as $+1$, -1 in 1973(i)/(ii). This improved the forecast accuracy in these quarters and demonstrated the value of investigating "special effects".

[2] A significant value for z_1 indicates *both* an incorrect model *and* a change in the stochastic properties of the variables in the "true" data generation process of C_t, whereas an insignificant value for z_1 only shows that the latter has not occurred and is fully consistent with an incorrect model for C_t (see Hendry, 1977*a*). Note that a large value of z_1 occurs when the variance of the forecast errors is large relative to the variance of the sample residuals.

[3] The results of Hendry (1977*b*) and Davis *et al.* (1977) suggest that "small" values of z_2 should be treated with caution, and do not necessarily indicate the absence of residual autocorrelation.

The only noticeable differences between (13) and (21) are the change in $\hat{\sigma}$ due to the change in the base of the implicit deflator for C, and the increase in the coefficient of C_{t-1}. However, z_2 indicates the presence of significant autocorrelation (actually, of fourth order) and z_1 strongly rejects parameter stability (when comparing equations, it should be noted that z_1 is *not* a measure of ***absolute*** forecast accuracy).

Next, we estimated two analogues of (14) from the same sample, namely

$$\underset{}{\hat{C}_t} = \underset{(142)}{509} + \underset{(0\cdot08)}{0\cdot18}Y_t + \underset{(0\cdot11)}{0\cdot75}C_{t-1} + \underset{(49)}{68}D_t^0 - \underset{(63)}{812}Q_{1t} + \underset{(46)}{32}Q_{2t} - \underset{(26)}{169}Q_{3t}, \tag{22}$$

$$R^2 = 0\cdot990, \quad \hat{\sigma} = 62\cdot0, \quad \mathrm{dw} = 2\cdot1, \quad z_1(20) = 190, \quad z_2(15) = 86,$$

which is, not surprisingly, also similar to (12); and

$$\hat{C}_t = \underset{(112)}{734} + \underset{(0\cdot06)}{0\cdot28}Y_t - \underset{(0\cdot06)}{0\cdot09}\Delta_1 Y_t + \underset{(0\cdot08)}{0\cdot59}C_{t-4} + \underset{(44)}{71}D_t^0 - \underset{(58)}{251}Q_{1t} - \underset{(27)}{92}Q_{2t} - \underset{(27)}{81}Q_{3t} \tag{23}$$

$$R^2 = 0\cdot993, \quad \hat{\sigma} = 53\cdot2, \quad \mathrm{dw} = 1\cdot3, \quad z_1(20) = 129, \quad z_2(12) = 21,$$

which is reasonably similar to (14). ($\Delta_1 Y_t$ was included in (23) to allow for a one-lag income effect but dw still indicates considerable first-order residual autocorrelation.) Lastly, for (15):

$$\Delta_4 \hat{C}_t = \underset{(10\cdot1)}{78\cdot5} + \underset{(0\cdot04)}{0\cdot34}\Delta_4 Y_t - \underset{(0\cdot04)}{0\cdot14}\Delta_1 \Delta_4 Y_t + \underset{(22)}{61}\Delta_4 D_t^0, \tag{24}$$

$$R^2 = 0\cdot70, \quad \hat{\sigma} = 40\cdot5, \quad \mathrm{dw} = 1\cdot7, \quad z_1(20) = 94\cdot0, \quad z_2(16) = 20.$$

We have quoted (24) in linear (rather than log) form for immediate comparison with (21)–(23) but despite this change of functional form, (24) reproduces the main features of (15) (a long-run elasticity of about 0·5, a large and significant intercept and "white noise" errors). All of the re-estimated analogues are rejected by the forecast test, although this does not affect our ability to choose between them; an explanation for the overall poor forecasts is provided in Section IX. Equation (22) also exhibits very marked four period autocorrelation and re-estimation assuming an error of the form $u_t = \rho_4 u_{t-4} + \epsilon_t$, yielded $\hat{\rho}_4 = 0\cdot98(0\cdot03)$, $z_2(12) = 22$ and $\hat{\sigma} = 42\cdot9$. Consequently, all of the models estimated from the raw data require some allowance for four-period effects.

A similar story emerges if *SA* data are used and seasonal dummies are omitted from all of the models. Specifically for (22), (23) and (24) we obtained (for the rather different data period 1963 (i)–1973 (i), forecasting 1973 (ii)–1975 (ii)):

$$\hat{C}_t^a = \underset{(154)}{250} + \underset{(0\cdot04)}{0\cdot18}Y_t^a + \underset{(0\cdot06)}{0\cdot75}C_{t-1}^a + \underset{(29)}{101}D_t^0, \tag{22a}$$

$$R^2 = 0\cdot990, \quad \hat{\sigma} = 39\cdot3, \quad \mathrm{dw} = 2\cdot5, \quad z_1(8) = 35\cdot5, \quad z_2(9) = 8\cdot4;$$

$$\hat{C}_t^a = \underset{(145)}{567} + \underset{(0\cdot03)}{0\cdot41}Y_t^a - \underset{(0\cdot05)}{0\cdot20}\Delta_1 Y_t^a + \underset{(0\cdot05)}{0\cdot44}C_{t-4}^a + \underset{(30)}{81}D_t^0, \tag{23a}$$

$$R^2 = 0\cdot990, \quad \hat{\sigma} = 41\cdot2, \quad \mathrm{dw} = 1\cdot5, \quad z_1(8) = 138, \quad z_2(6) = 6\cdot3;$$

$$\Delta_4 \hat{C}^a_t = \underset{(11)}{66} + \underset{(0{\cdot}03)}{0{\cdot}37}\Delta_4 Y^a_t - \underset{(0{\cdot}04)}{0{\cdot}16}\Delta_1 \Delta_4 Y^a_t + \underset{(23)}{86}\Delta_4 D^0_t, \tag{24a}$$

$$R^2 = 0{\cdot}80, \quad \hat{\sigma} = 43{\cdot}9, \quad \text{dw} = 1{\cdot}8, \quad z_1(8) = 26{\cdot}2, \quad z_2(10) = 20;$$

$$\Delta_1 \hat{C}^a_t = \underset{(8{\cdot}6)}{21} + \underset{(0{\cdot}08)}{0{\cdot}31}\Delta_1 Y^a_t - \underset{(0{\cdot}05)}{0{\cdot}11}\Delta^2_1 Y^a_t + \underset{(19)}{69}\Delta_1 D^0_t, \tag{15a}$$

$$R^2 = 0{\cdot}52, \quad \hat{\sigma} = 44{\cdot}5, \quad \text{dw} = 2{\cdot}9, \quad z_1(8) = 7{\cdot}3, \quad z_2(10) = 24.$$

These results support our contention that the choices of the exact data period and of the seasonal adjustment procedures do not markedly affect the *estimates* obtained, although it should be noted that the goodness of fit ranking of the models on *SA* data is the *opposite* of that prevailing with raw data. Only (24*a*) has an error variance close to its raw data counterpart, and hence the *selection* of equations is greatly altered by *SA*.

Thus (i)–(iv) can be eliminated as the *main* factors accounting for the differences in (13)–(15) and we can proceed to consider (v)–(vii) which represent more important differences in methodology. At this stage, our standardised analogues of (13)–(15) can be nested as special cases of the model

$$C_t = \xi_0 + \xi_1 Y_t + \xi_2 Y_{t-4} + \xi_3 \Delta_1 Y_t + \xi_4 \Delta_1 Y_{t-4} + \xi_5 C_{t-4}$$
$$+ \sum_{j=1}^{3} \xi_{5+j} Q_{jt} + \xi_9 D^0_t + \xi_{10} D^0_{t-4} + \xi_{11} C_{t-1} + \xi_{12} t$$
$$+ \sum_{j=1}^{3} \xi_{12+j} Q_{jt}\, t + \epsilon_t, \tag{25}$$

and hence (21)–(24) can all be tested directly against the estimated version of (25).

V. ON MULTICOLLINEARITY

Can sensible estimates of (25) be obtained given the general misapprehension that "severe collinearity problems are bound to be present"? To resolve this, consider the well-known formula (see, for example, Theil, 1971, p. 174):

$$\xi^2_i / \widehat{\text{var}(\xi_i)} = (T-m)\, r^2_i / (1 - r^2_i) \quad (i = 1, \ldots, m), \tag{26}$$

where r_i is the partial correlation between the regressand and the *i*th regressor allowing for the influence of the other $(m-1)$ regressors in the equation. The left-hand side of (26) is the square of the conventionally calculated t statistic to test $H_0 : \xi_i = 0$.

A crucial point is that a partial correlation like r_i can *increase* as m increases to $m+n$ even if the n added variables are highly (but not perfectly) collinear *provided they are relevant to explaining the regressand.* Thus t values can increase even though the moment matrix requiring inversion in least squares becomes "more singular" in the sense of having a smaller determinant or a smaller ratio of the least to the greatest eigenvalue (compare, for example, the analysis assuming that the true model is known in Johnston, 1972, ch. 5.7). In effect, the issue is that "collinearity problems" are likely to occur in conjunction with omitted variables problems. If the n initially excluded regressors are important in determining the regressand, then adding them may well help resolve what appears to be a collinearity problem between the m originally included variables, since "small" t values can arise from downward biases in ξ_i as well as from "large" values of $\widehat{\text{var}}\,(\xi_i)$. Consequently, it is *not* universally valid to assume that a group of badly determined estimates indicates the presence of collinearity (to be solved by *reducing* the dimensionality of the parameter space) rather than omitted variables bias (solved by *increasing* the dimensionality of the parameter space). To illustrate these points consider the following estimates of a special case of (25) (which incidentally immediately demonstrates some mis-specification of (23)):

$$\underset{}{\hat{C}_t} = \underset{(627)}{2516} + \underset{(0{\cdot}06)}{0{\cdot}24} Y_t - \underset{(0{\cdot}06)}{0{\cdot}07}\Delta_1 Y_t + \underset{(0{\cdot}12)}{0{\cdot}38} C_{t-4} + \underset{(4)}{13}t + \underset{(40)}{65} D_t^0 + \hat{S}_t, \qquad (27)$$

$$R^2 = 0{\cdot}994, \quad \hat{\sigma} = 48{\cdot}8, \quad \text{dw} = 1{\cdot}6, \quad z_1(20) = 119, \quad z_2(12) = 37.$$

Conventionally, $\Delta_1 Y_t$ is "insignificant" (but see Bock *et al.*, 1974, for an analysis of some of the consequences of using a "preliminary test" estimator in which "insignificant" regressors are excluded prior to re-estimation), and the trend coefficient is significant. Now compare (27) with the equation in which every regressor also re-occurs with a four-period lag:[1]

$$\begin{aligned}\hat{C}_t = {} & \underset{(695)}{921} + \underset{(0{\cdot}05)}{0{\cdot}31} Y_t - \underset{(0{\cdot}05)}{0{\cdot}09}\Delta_1 Y_t + \underset{(0{\cdot}13)}{0{\cdot}65} C_{t-4} + \underset{(5)}{4}t - \underset{(0{\cdot}06)}{0{\cdot}25} Y_{t-4} \\ & + \underset{(0{\cdot}05)}{0{\cdot}16}\Delta_1 Y_{t-4} + \underset{(0{\cdot}11)}{0{\cdot}16} C_{t-8} + \underset{(33)}{67} D_t^0 - \underset{(34)}{46} D_{t-4}^0 + \hat{S}_t, \qquad (28)\end{aligned}$$

$$R^2 = 0{\cdot}997, \quad \hat{\sigma} = 38{\cdot}7, \quad \text{dw} = 2{\cdot}1, \quad z_1(20) = 110, \quad z_2(8) = 12.$$

Patently, despite including three more regressors, the t values for Y_t, $\Delta_1 Y_t$ and C_{t-4} are *all* considerably larger in (28) than in (27), whereas the trend coefficient has become negligible in (28), and reveals the possibility of explaining the behaviour of C_t by economic variables alone (the seasonal dummies are also insignificant in (28)).

VI. SELECTION OF THE "BEST" EQUATION

We now return to choosing between the various equations on statistical criteria. Even before estimating (25) it can be seen that (28) encompasses (23) and allows immediate rejection of the latter. Moreover, adding C_{t-1} to (28) cannot worsen the goodness of fit and so (22) can be rejected also. Testing (21) proves more of a problem since in Hendry (1974), (21) was chosen in preference to an equation similar to (28) (but excluding $\Delta_1 Y_t$, $\Delta_1 Y_{t-4}$ and C_{t-8}) whereas for the present data, (28) fits marginally better. Strictly, (28) is not nested within the (initially)

[1] Equation (28) can be derived from (27) by assuming that the residuals in (27) follow a simple fourth order autoregressive process, then carrying out the usual "Cochrane–Orcutt" transformation, but ignoring the parameter restrictions implied by the autoregressive transform.

general equation (25), although this is only due to the presence of the insignificant regressor C_{t-8} and so can be ignored. Direct estimation of (25) yields:

$$\hat{C}_t = \underset{(692)}{1618} + \underset{(0\cdot06)}{0\cdot28Y_t} + \underset{(0\cdot15)}{0\cdot14C_{t-1}} + \underset{(0\cdot15)}{0\cdot40C_{t-4}} - \underset{(0\cdot06)}{0\cdot15Y_{t-4}} - \underset{(0\cdot06)}{0\cdot09\Delta_1 Y_t}$$
$$+ \underset{(0\cdot06)}{0\cdot11\Delta_1 Y_{t-4}} + \underset{(34)}{91D_t^0} - \underset{(34)}{11D_{t-4}^0} + \underset{(4\cdot4)}{7\cdot6t} + \underset{(129)}{212Q_{1t}} + \underset{(77)}{180Q_{2t}}$$
$$+ \underset{(104)}{278Q_{3t}} + \underset{(1\cdot87)}{2\cdot95Q_{1t}t} + \underset{(1\cdot60)}{3\cdot88Q_{2t}t} + \underset{(1\cdot52)}{4\cdot63Q_{3t}t}, \quad (29)$$

$$R^2 = 0\cdot997, \quad \hat{\sigma} = 36\cdot2, \quad \text{dw} = 2\cdot0, \quad z_1(20) = 114.$$

The fit of (29) is little better than either of (21) or (28) even though many of the four lagged variables and evolving seasonals appear to be significant on t tests. Thus, given either set of variables, the additional explanatory power of the other set is small and so to a considerable extent we re-confirm their substitute roles. Relative to Hendry (1974), the four period lags are more important in the larger sample.

The most interesting outcome is that (24) cannot be rejected against (29) by testing the joint significance of all the restrictions using an F-test based on the residual sums of squares ($F(12, 31) = 1\cdot9$). Thus at the chosen significance level (using, for example, the S-method discussed by Savin, 1977) no other subset of the restrictions can be judged significant either; alternatively, individual t tests on restrictions would need to be significant at (at least) the 0·4 % level to preserve the overall size of the test at 5 % when considering 12 restrictions. On this basis, (24) seems to provide an adequate parsimonious description of the data (although other equations are also not significantly worse than (29) at the 5 % level), and it seems that the Δ_4 transform satisfactorily removes seasonality.

Moreover, if (24) were close to the correct data generation process then we would expect just the sort of result shown in (28) (the fits are similar, the lag polynomial in C_t has a root near unity, the seasonal dummies are insignificant and four period lags of income variables have roughly equal magnitudes, opposite signs to current dated equivalents). Tentatively accepting such a hypothesis, (22) and (23) would constitute poor approximations to (24) and hence are easy to reject whereas (21) is a reasonable approximation and is not easily discarded (see Figs. 1 and 4). Also, the relationship between (24) and (28) corresponds closely with the interpretation of differences as arising from coefficient restrictions but does not cohere with the "filtering" interpretation. The large change in the constant term is probably due to collinearity, since the exact unrestricted equivalent of (24) is:

$$\hat{C}_t = \underset{(76)}{150} + \underset{(0\cdot04)}{0\cdot32Y_t} - \underset{(0\cdot04)}{0\cdot33Y_{t-4}} - \underset{(0\cdot04)}{0\cdot12\Delta_1 Y_t} + \underset{(0\cdot04)}{0\cdot16\Delta_1 Y_{t-4}}$$
$$+ \underset{(0\cdot04)}{0\cdot995C_{t-4}} + \hat{\phi}_1 D_t^0 + \hat{\phi}_2 D_{t-4}^0, \quad (30)$$

$$R^2 = 0\cdot996, \quad \hat{\sigma} = 40\cdot7, \quad \text{dw} = 1\cdot8, \quad z_1(20) = 82\cdot9, \quad z_2(12) = 19.$$

The coefficients of (30) correspond very closely with those of the unrestricted equation which would be anticipated if (24) validly described the expenditure relationship, although the large standard error of the intercept in (30) compared to (24) is a distinct anomaly requiring explanation in due course. In summary, the evidence points strongly to accepting (24) as the best simple description of the data despite the loss of long-run information and the theoretical drawbacks discussed in Section III.

VII. MEASUREMENT ERRORS

Zellner and Palm (1974) note that difference transformations can substantially alter the ratio of the "systematic" variance to the measurement error variance of time series. Since large measurement error variances in regressors can cause large downward biases in estimated coefficients (see for example, Johnston, 1972, ch. 9.3) it is possible that the low-income elasticities in (24) could be caused by the effects of the Δ_4 transform enhancing relative measurement errors.

A formal mis-specification analysis of a simple model where observations are generated by a first-order autoregressive process with coefficient ψ_1 and first-order autoregressive measurement error with coefficient ψ_2, reveals that $\psi_1 > \psi_2$ is a necessary and sufficient condition for differencing to induce a relative increase in measurement error variance. The amount by which the measurement error bias in the coefficient of a differenced regression exceeds the corresponding bias in the regression in levels depends directly and proportionately on $(\psi_1 - \psi_2)$. Davidson (1975) found that data revisions were highly autoregressive, and although by itself this does not imply that the unknown errors also will be autoregressive, two other factors argue for the magnitude of $(\psi_1 - \psi_2)$ being small for Y_t. First, if there were large measurement errors in $\Delta_4 Y_t$ these would occur one period later in $\Delta_4 Y_{t-1}$ which would create a negative first order moving average error on (24) and we could find no evidence of this – nor did Wall *et al.* (1975) in their similar equation (15). Secondly, we re-estimated (24) by weighted least squares assuming a measurement error variance of 50 % of the variance of $\Delta_4 Y_t$ yet there was no noticeable increase in the coefficients. All of these points together, though individually rather weak, suggest that errors-in-variables biases do *not* explain the low long-run elasticities. Conversely, any simultaneity bias which might arise from least squares estimation would tend to cause upward biased coefficients and hence can be discarded as an explanation also. Thus we return to Figs. 2 and 5 which originally indicated the source of the problem: the variance of $\Delta_4 Y_t$ is much larger than that of $\Delta_4 C_t$ and so any model like (24) must end up having "small" coefficients.

VIII. A SIMPLE DYNAMIC MODEL

In one sense, the above results simply reproduce the familiar problem of reconciling short-run and long-run consumption behaviour. However, there is a more serious difficulty since the original set of models included several distributed lag variants of permanent income and/or life-cycle theories (see Section III above) yet in a direct comparison, the statistical evidence favoured the model which accounted for only short-run behaviour. Clearly, therefore, either some new implementation of the *PIH* or *LCH* is required or (assuming that we do not wish to canvass a new theory) an account must be provided of why the evidence takes the form which it does. Naturally, we prefer the latter course.

Fisher (1962) advocated using equations involving only differenced variables to facilitate the study of short-run behaviour without having to specify trend dominated long-run components. The main defects in this strategy are that one loses almost all *a priori* information from economic theory (as most theories rely on steady-state arguments) and all long-run information in the data (yet Granger's "typical spectral shape" suggests that economic data are highly informative about the long-run: see Granger, 1966). Moreover, as noted when discussing (15), it seems inappropriate to assume that short-run behaviour is independent of disequilibria in the levels of the variables.

A simple modification of equations in differences can resolve these three problems. Consider a situation in which an investigator accepts a non-stochastic steady-state theory that $X_t = KW_t$, where K is constant on any given growth path, but may vary with the growth rate. In logs, letting $x_t = \ln X_t$, etc., the theory becomes:

$$x_t = k + w_t. \tag{31}$$

The differenced variable equivalent is:

$$\Delta_1 x_t = \Delta_1 w_t. \tag{32}$$

However, to assume that (32) had a white-noise error would deny the existence of any "long-run" relationship like (31), and to assume that (31) had a stationary error process would cause a negatively autocorrelated error to occur on (32). Furthermore, the Δ_1 operator in (32) could just as validly have been Δ_4 – on all of these points the theory is unspecific.

On the basis of (31), the investigator wishes to postulate a stochastic disequilibrium relationship between x_t and w_t, which will simplify to (31) in steady state. In the absence of a well-articulated theory of the dynamic adjustment of x_t to w_t, it seems reasonable to assume a general rational lag model of the form:

$$\alpha(L)\, x_t = k^* + \beta(L)\, w_t + v_t, \tag{33}$$

where $\alpha(L)$ and $\beta(L)$ are polynomials in the lag operator L of high enough order that v_t is white noise. For simplicity of exposition we consider the situation where both polynomials are first order:

$$x_t = k^* + \beta_1 w_t + \beta_2 w_{t-1} + \alpha_1 x_{t-1} + v_t. \tag{34}$$

Clearly, (31) and (32) are the special cases of (34) when $\beta_2 = \alpha_1 = 0$, $\beta_1 = 1$, and $\beta_1 = -\beta_2 = 1$, $k^* = 0$, $\alpha_1 = 1$ respectively; these coefficient restrictions force behaviour to be in steady state at all points in time. However, to ensure that for *all* values of the estimated parameters, *the steady-state solution of* (34) *reproduces* (31) one need only impose the coefficient restriction $\beta_1 + \beta_2 + \alpha_1 = 1$ or

$$\beta_1 = -\beta_2 + \gamma \quad \text{and} \quad \alpha_1 = 1 - \gamma$$

yielding the equation:

$$\Delta_1 x_t = k^* + \beta_1 \Delta_1 w_t + \gamma(w_{t-1} - x_{t-1}) + v_t \tag{35}$$

(which is more general than (31) or (32) but less general than (34)). The specification of (35) is, therefore, guided by the long-run theory; there is no loss of long-run information in the data since (35) is a reformulated "levels equation"; and compared with the "short-run" model:

$$\Delta_1 x_t = k^* + \beta_1 \Delta_1 w_t \tag{36}$$

the vital "initial disequilibrium" effect is provided by $\gamma(w_{t-1} - x_{t-1})$. Consequently, (35) does indeed resolve the three problems noted above (it is straightforward to generalise the analysis to equations of the form of (33)). An important example of this class of model is the real-wage variable formulation used by Sargan (1964).

In (35) consider any steady-state growth path along which

$$\Delta_1 \ln X_t = \Delta_1 x_t = g = \Delta_1 w_t,$$

then the solution of (35) with $v_t = 0$ is:

$$g = k^* + \beta_1 g + \gamma(w_{t-1} - x_{t-1}) \tag{37}$$

or assuming $\gamma \neq 0$,

$$X_t = KW_t \quad \text{where} \quad K = \exp\{[k^* - g(1 - \beta_1)]/\gamma\} \tag{38}$$

(implicitly, in (31) $k = [k^* - g(1 - \beta_1)]/\gamma$). Thus for any constant growth rate, if $\gamma \neq 0$, (35) automatically generates a long-run elasticity of unity for all values of the parameters, whereas if $\gamma = 0$, the elasticity is β_1. (Interpreting X_t as C_t and W_t as Y_t, then the derived APC ($= MPC$ in steady-state growth) is a decreasing function of the growth rate g, consonant with inter-country evidence (see Modigliani, 1975). Note that the above analysis remains valid even if $k^* = 0$ (in which case $K < 1$ for $\gamma, g > 0$ and $1 > \beta_1 > 0$), so that the theory entails no restrictions on the presence or absence of an intercept in (35).[1]

If, from the steady-state solution (38), the growth rate of W_t changes from g to g_1 the ratio of X to W will gradually change from K to

$$K_1 = \exp\{[k^* - g_1(1 - \beta_1)]/\gamma\}$$

and hence even prolonged movements in one direction of the observed X/W ratio do not rule out a long-run unit elasticity hypothesis for a *given* growth rate. If g is a variable, then $(X/W)_t$ will not be constant either, although the data will be consistent with a model like (35). The important implication of this is that a variable, or even trending, observed APC does not by itself refute a unit-elasticity model (the unit elasticity restriction is easily tested in (35) by including w_{t-1} as a separate regressor and testing its coefficient for significance from zero). Estimation of (31) requires that the *data* satisfy a unit elasticity restriction (this will be false out of steady state) whereas estimation of (35) only requires that the *model* satisfy this restriction and that the data are consonant with the model.

[1] If $k^* = 0$, then $K = 1$ when $g = 0$. Consequently, care must be exercised when simulating to *equilibrium* a model containing equations of the form of (35) for a subcategory of expenditure.

The estimation of restricted dynamic models like (35) from finite samples does not seem to have been the subject of any investigations to date. Consequently, we undertook a pilot simulation study of least-squares estimation of δ_1 and δ_2 in

$$\Delta_1 x_t = \delta_1 \Delta_1 w_t + \delta_2(w_{t-1} - x_{t-1}) + v_t \quad (t = 1, \ldots, T) \qquad (35)^*$$

for

$$(\delta_1, \delta_2) = (0{\cdot}5, 0{\cdot}1), \quad v_t \sim NI(0, 1)$$

and

$$w_t = 0{\cdot}8 w_{t-1} + u_t \quad \text{with} \quad u_t \sim NI(0, 9), \quad \text{independent of } v_t.$$

The results are shown in Table 2 for 100 random replications. For $T \geqslant 34$, the biases are very small, S.E. provides an accurate estimate of S.D. and $H_0: \delta_i = 0$

Table 2

*Simulation Findings for (35)**

	$(\hat{\delta}_1 - \delta_1)$				$(\hat{\delta}_2 - \delta_2)$			
T	14	34	54	74	14	34	54	74
Bias	0·010	−0·013	−0·003	0·003	−0·026	−0·009	−0·004	−0·007
S.D.	0·106	0·062	0·041	0·044	0·108	0·060	0·043	0·038
S.E.	0·090	0·058	0·044	0·038	0·105	0·060	0·045	0·039
H_0 rejected	99	100	100	100	15	41	60	82

S.D. denotes the sampling standard deviation, S.E. the average estimated standard error and "H_0 rejected" shows the frequency with which the null hypothesis $H_0: \delta_i = 0$ was rejected when the nominal test size was 0·05. The values for δ_1, δ_2, and σ_v^2/σ_u^2 were based on empirical estimates of analogous consumption functions.

is rejected with considerable frequency. This contrasts favourably both with the bias which would arise from estimating μ in a simple dynamic model of the form:

$$x_t = \mu x_{t-1} + u_t$$

(where the bias is approximately equal to $-2\mu/T$ and so has the same sign but is about 5 times as large as the corresponding bias in $\hat{\delta}_2$ in Table 2) as well as with the biases and the variances which would be obtained from unrestricted estimation of:

$$x_t = \beta_1 w_t + \beta_2 w_{t-1} + \alpha_1 x_{t-1} + v_t. \qquad (34)^*$$

Thus there may be an "estimation" advantage from formulating dynamic equations as in (35), although for small δ_2, it may not be easy to establish $\hat{\delta}_2$ as significant at the 0·05 level unless T is relatively large.

When the appropriate lag length in (35) is four periods, the resulting model can be written as:

$$(X/W)_t = K^*(X/W)_{t-4}^{1-\gamma}(W_t/W_{t-4})^{\beta_1 - 1}. \qquad (39)$$

For small γ the historical seasonal pattern of the *APC* will persist with modifications from any "seasonality" in $\Delta_4 \ln W_t$. Note that (35) and (39) are stable dynamic processes for $2 > \gamma > 0$, and that K is relatively robust to changes in the values of β_1 and $\gamma > 0$ (contrast the properties of the solved long-run *MPC* from (12)). However, K is not a continuous function of γ at $\gamma = 0$ (switching from zero to infinity) which reflects dynamic instability in (39) at $\gamma = 0$.

The solved distributed lag representation of (35) is:

$$x_t = k^*/\gamma + \sum_{j=0}^{\infty} \mu_j w_{t-j} + u_t, \tag{40}$$

where

$$u_t = (1-\gamma)\, u_{t-1} + v_t \quad \text{and} \quad \mu_0 = \beta_1, \quad \mu_j = (1-\gamma)^{j-1}\gamma(1-\beta_1) \quad (j \geqslant 1).$$

The mean lag is $(1-\beta_1)/\gamma$ which could be very large for γ close to zero, but, depending on the magnitude of β_1, much of the adjustment could occur instantaneously (for example, the median lag could be less than one period). If v_t is white noise, then (40) will manifest considerable autocorrelation for small γ, no matter how long a distributed lag is used for w_t.

The final feature of (35) is of crucial importance; *if* the growth rate g is relatively constant, then X_t will be approximately equal to KW_t and hence from (31), $(x_{t-1} - w_{t-1}) \simeq k$. In such a state of the world, the intercept and $(w_{t-1} - x_{t-1})$ would be almost perfectly collinear in (35). A similar collinearity also must affect any attempt to estimate (34) unrestrictedly. Although either regressor could be dropped without much loss to the goodness of fit, setting $k^* = 0$ does not affect the long-run behaviour (see (38) above) but setting $\gamma = 0$ *does*. This phenomenon at last provides a potential explanation both for the discrepant behaviour of the standard error of the intercept between (24) and (30) *and* for the low elasticity of the former equation since *the initial disequilibrium effect has been excluded from* (24), *but is still indirectly present in* (30).

However, before considering empirical variants of (35) it seems worth commenting on the relationship between equations like (35) and the four main theories of consumers' behaviour discussed in Section III. First, it is clear that both (34) and (35) resemble Brown's (1952) model; also, the term $\gamma(w_{t-1} - x_{t-1})$ could be interpreted as a "ratchet" to the "short-run" relationship (36) (compare Duesenberry, 1949) although it is a "ratchet" which operates in either direction for any sustained change in the growth rate of w_t. The distributed lag form (40) could be interpreted as an empirical approximation to "permanent income" in a model which always satisfies a long-run steady-state unit elasticity postulate (see Friedman, 1957). Moreover, using $C_t = x_t$ and $Y_t = w_t$, (35) corresponds to a transformed "life-cycle" model. For example, the wealth model of Ball and Drake (1964) is the special case of (35) in which $\beta_1 = \gamma$ and Deaton (1972) presents a modified life-cycle model of the same form but with revaluations of wealth as an additional variable. More recently, Deaton (1977) presents a savings equation closely similar to (35) but with the rate of inflation as an additional regressor (this study is discussed in Section IX below). Similar reasoning applies to models using changes in liquid assets in consumption equations (see Townend, 1976).

Nevertheless, as stressed above, the transformations involved in deriving the *PIH* and *LCH* (or eliminating any stock variable) significantly affect the properties of the error process, and it is possible (at least in principle) to distinguish between the contending hypotheses on this basis, subject to requiring that the error on the "true" model is white noise. Even so, it is exceedingly hard in practice to decide in a time-series context *alone* which relationships are "autonomous" and which are merely "good approximations". In terms of modelling any relationship between C and Y, the only really definite conclusion is that it seems vital to include some factor to account for the effect represented by $(w_{t-1} - x_{t-1})$.

Returning to the problem of reconciling the estimates in (24) and (30), consider the alternative restriction of dropping the intercept and retaining $(C_{t-4} - Y_{t-4})$, which in log terms yields:

$$\Delta_4 \ln \hat{C}_t = \underset{(0 \cdot 04)}{0 \cdot 49} \Delta_4 \ln Y_t - \underset{(0 \cdot 05)}{0 \cdot 17} \Delta_1 \Delta_4 \ln Y_t - \underset{(0 \cdot 01)}{0 \cdot 06} \ln (C/Y)_{t-4} + \underset{(0 \cdot 004)}{0 \cdot 01} \Delta_4 D_t^0, \quad (41)$$

$$R^2 = 0 \cdot 71, \quad \hat{\sigma} = 0 \cdot 0067, \quad \text{dw} = 1 \cdot 6, \quad z_1(20) = 80 \cdot 7, \quad z_2(12) = 23.$$

A relationship like (41) can be derived from a simple "feedback" theory in which consumers plan to spend in each quarter of a year the same as they spent in that quarter of the previous year ($\ln C_t = \ln C_{t-4}$) modified by a proportion of their annual change in income ($+0 \cdot 49 \Delta_4 \ln Y_t$), and by whether that change is itself increasing or decreasing ($-0 \cdot 17 \Delta_1 \Delta_4 Y_t$) (compare Houthakker and Taylor, 1970); these together determine a "short-run" consumption decision which is altered by $-0 \cdot 06 \ln (C_{t-4}/Y_{t-4})$, the feedback from the previous C/Y ratio ensuring coherence with the long-run "target" outcome $C_t = KY_t$. The parameterisation of (41) is determined by the choice of a set of plausible decision variables which incorporate relatively independent items of information, allowing agents to assess their reactions separately to changes in each variable. This seems a "natural" parameterisation to adopt, and as the small standard errors in (41) show, the resulting parameters are precisely estimated. Moreover, if any omitted decision variables can be re-formulated as orthogonal to the already included regressors, then the potentially serious problem of "omitted variables bias" is transformed to a problem of estimation efficiency. In practical terms, previously estimated coefficients will not change radically as new explanatory variables are added (see equation (45) below). The use of transformed variables like $\Delta_4 \ln C_t$, etc., is *not* because we want to "seasonally adjust" and/or achieve "stationarity" (with the attendant loss of spectral power at low frequencies noted by Sims, 1974) but because $\Delta_4 \ln C_t$ represents a sensible decision variable when different commodities are being purchased in different quarters of the year.

The significant value of z_1 in (41) reveals that other factors need to be included to provide a full account of the behaviour of C_t and this aspect is considered in Section IX. Nevertheless, (41) seems consistent with the salient features of the data in Figs. 1–6 and straightforwardly explains the large difference between the short-run and long-run *MPC*. The impact elasticity is 0·32, rising to 0·49 after one quarter, the remaining 51 % of the adjustment taking a considerable time to occur, which matches the relatively small value of the variance of consumption relative to that of income noted earlier. With only three "economic" variables, the model seems a reasonably parsimonious explanation of trend, cycle and seasonal components. Also it provides a suitable basis for discussing why the studies by *H*, *B* and *W* reached their published results.

First, a model like (41) could never be detected by any methodology in which the first step was to difference data and then only investigate the properties of the differenced series (as Wall *et al.*, 1975, do). Subject to that restriction, (24) (or its log equivalent) provides an excellent approximation in terms of goodness of fit despite its apparent lack of coherence with steady-state theory and long-run evidence.

Next, the lag structure of (41) could not be detected by researchers who only investigated lags of one or two periods and never used diagnostic tests for higher order residual autocorrelation (see Ball *et al.*, 1975). *The use of SA data does not justify neglecting higher-order lags.* If a model like (39) constitutes the true data generation process then this should not be greatly altered by filtering out seasonal frequencies from the data. Indeed, re-estimating (41) on the *SA* data used earlier yields:

$$\underset{}{\Delta_4 \ln \hat{C}_t^a} = \underset{(0{\cdot}04)}{0{\cdot}44\Delta_4 \ln Y_t^a} - \underset{(0{\cdot}05)}{0{\cdot}19\Delta_1 \Delta_4 \ln Y_t^a} - \underset{(0{\cdot}01)}{0{\cdot}06 \ln (C^a/Y^a)_{t-4}} + \underset{(0{\cdot}003)}{0{\cdot}01\Delta_4 D_t^0}, \quad (41\,a)$$

$$R^2 = 0{\cdot}79, \quad \hat{\sigma} = 0{\cdot}0063, \quad \mathrm{dw} = 1{\cdot}7, \quad z_1(8) = 29{\cdot}0, \quad z_2(6) = 18.$$

The coefficients are very similar to (41), but the use of *SA* data has created considerable negative fourth-order residual autocorrelation (e.g. a coefficient at four lags of $-0{\cdot}7$ in a tenth-order residual autoregression) which would induce any investigator who did not *previously* believe in a model like (41) to select an equation with considerably less emphasis on four period effects.

Lastly, despite estimating equations with four period lags similar to unrestricted variants of (41), Hendry (1974) selected (11) as his preferred equation. The seasonal pattern for C_t seems to evolve whereas that for $\ln C_t$ does not (see Figs. 1 and 6 above) and hence the use of the untransformed data appears to have been one factor determining Hendry's choice. Further since C/Y was relatively constant over the period to 1967, the inclusion of an intercept in all the models considered by Hendry would greatly reduce the partial significance of four-period lagged variables. Both of these effects favour the incorrect selection of the evolving seasonals model as the best description of the data. Moreover, it is interesting that if a model like (39) is assumed as a data generation process, and w_t is highly correlated with w_{t-1} then regressing x_t on w_t and x_{t-1} will yield estimates like those in (12) when the data are *not* prior seasonally adjusted, and the true partial coefficient of x_{t-1} is zero. In summary, therefore, (41) seems to have the requisite properties to explain why previous researchers' methodologies led to their published conclusions.

Finally, in terms of the levels of the variables, equation (39) becomes:

$$x_t = k^* + \beta_1 w_t + (\gamma - \beta_1) w_{t-4} + (1 - \gamma) x_{t-4} + v_t. \quad (42)$$

Such an equation can be approximated closely by:

$$x_t = k^{**} + \beta_1 w_t + u_t \quad \text{where} \quad u_t = (1 - \gamma) u_{t-4} + e_t. \quad (43)$$

The mis-specification of (42) as (43) entails restricting the coefficient of w_{t-4} to be $(\gamma\beta_1 - \beta_1)$ instead of $(\gamma - \beta_1)$. This mis-specification will be negligible for small γ and $\beta_1 > 0$. Consequently, it is easy to approximate incorrectly the four period dynamics by fourth-order autocorrelation. Since γ is small, imposing the further restriction that the autocorrelation coefficient is unity will not noticeably worsen the fit and provides an alternative sequence whereby an incorrect differenced model might be selected (for a more general discussion of this last issue see Hendry and Mizon, 1978).

IX. INFLATION EFFECTS

Deaton (1977) has presented evidence for a disequilibrium effect of inflation on Consumers' Expenditure, which he interprets as consumers mistaking unanticipated changes in inflation for relative price changes when sequentially purchasing commodities. Since the forecast period contains inflation rates which are considerably greater than any observed during the sample used for estimation (the graph of $\Delta_4 \ln P_t$, where P_t is the implicit deflator of C_t, is shown in Fig. 7), Deaton's analysis offers a potential explanation for the poor forecast performance of all the estimated models.

In view of the functional form of the models (24) and (41), the regressors $\Delta_4 \ln P_t$ and $\Delta_1 \Delta_4 \ln P_t$ were included to represent the level and rate of change of inflation. Retaining the same sample and forecast periods yielded the results shown in equations (44) and (45) respectively (for comparability, we have chosen the log equivalent of (24)):

$$\begin{aligned}\Delta_4 \ln \hat{C}_t = {} & \underset{(0{\cdot}04)}{0{\cdot}022} + \underset{(0{\cdot}05)}{0{\cdot}34}\Delta_4 \ln Y_t - \underset{(0{\cdot}05)}{0{\cdot}16}\Delta_1 \Delta_4 \ln Y_t + \underset{(0{\cdot}003)}{0{\cdot}01}\Delta_4 D_t^0 \\ & - \underset{(0{\cdot}07)}{0{\cdot}21}\Delta_4 \ln P_t - \underset{(0{\cdot}14)}{0{\cdot}15}\Delta_1 \Delta_4 \ln P_t,\end{aligned} \tag{44}$$

$$R^2 = 0{\cdot}81, \quad \hat{\sigma} = 0{\cdot}0055, \quad \text{dw} = 1{\cdot}8, \quad z_1(20) = 146, \quad z_2(16) = 15;$$

$$\begin{aligned}\Delta_4 \ln \hat{C}_t = {} & \underset{(0{\cdot}04)}{0{\cdot}47}\Delta_4 \ln Y_t - \underset{(0{\cdot}05)}{0{\cdot}21}\Delta_1 \Delta_4 \ln Y_t - \underset{(0{\cdot}02)}{0{\cdot}10} \ln (C/Y)_{t-4} \\ & + \underset{(0{\cdot}003)}{0{\cdot}01}\Delta_4 D_t^0 - \underset{(0{\cdot}07)}{0{\cdot}13}\Delta_4 \ln P_t - \underset{(0{\cdot}15)}{0{\cdot}28}\Delta_1 \Delta_4 \ln P_t,\end{aligned} \tag{45}$$

$$R^2 = 0{\cdot}77, \quad \hat{\sigma} = 0{\cdot}0061, \quad \text{dw} = 1{\cdot}8, \quad z_1(20) = 21{\cdot}8, \quad z_2(12) = 19.$$

Both equations confirm Deaton's result that inflation was significantly reducing Consumers' Expenditure prior to 1971. Also, the inclusion of inflation effects in (45) has resolved the forecast problem: the considerable fall in the *APC* after 1971 (see Fig. 3) can be explained by the sharp increase in inflation and the five year ahead ex-post predictions from (45) satisfy the parameter stability test (Fig. 8 shows the plots of $\Delta_4 \ln C_t$ and $\Delta_4 \widehat{\ln C_t}$ over the period to 1975(iv)). Nevertheless, simply including the two additional regressors does *not of itself* guarantee an improved forecasting performance as z_1 in (44) shows. This outcome is easy to understand on the hypothesis that (45) constitutes the "true" model, since the behaviour of C/Y is negatively influenced by changes in P_t and so the approximation of C/Y by a constant is very poor over the forecast period.

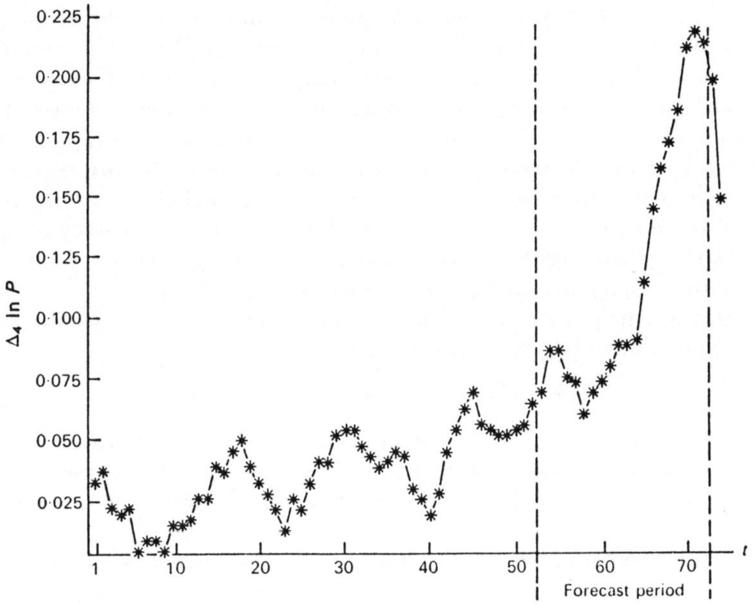

Fig. 7. Annual rate of change of prices.

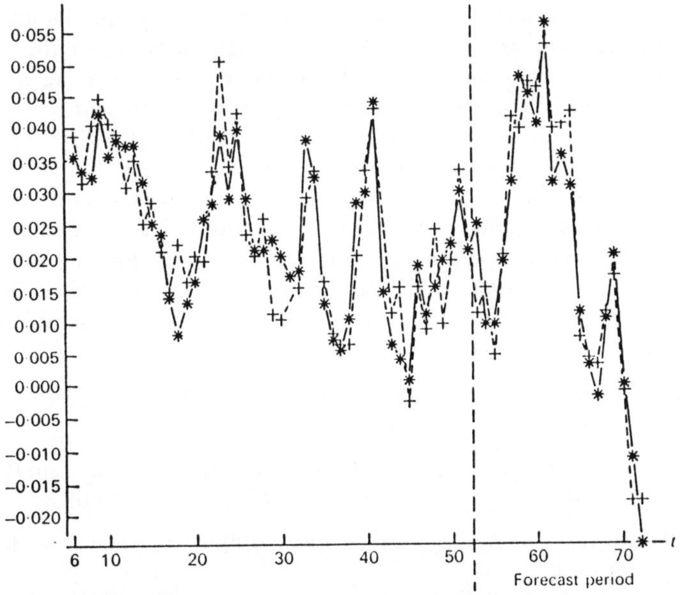

Fig. 8. Actual and predicted values of annual change in consumption.
——, $\Delta_4 \ln \hat{C}$. +——+, $\Delta_4 \ln C$.

Consonant with this argument, and illustrating the robustness of the parameter choice in (41), the only parameter estimate to be substantially altered by the inclusion of $\Delta_4 \ln P_t$ and $\Delta_1 \Delta_4 \ln P_t$ is the coefficient of $\ln (C/Y)_{t-4}$. The fact that (44) has a lower value of $\hat{\sigma}$ than (45) is evidence against suppressing the intercept, and indeed an intercept is significant if added to (45). However, $\ln (C/Y)_{t-4}$ loses significance if this is done and $z_1(20) = 137$. Thus, (44) and (45) exhibit an interesting conflict between goodness of fit and parameter stability as criteria for model selection. Bearing in mind that the forecast period is very different in several respects from the estimation period, the predictive accuracy of (45) is rather striking. Adding this to the earlier theoretical arguments, we have no hesitation in dropping the constant term instead of $\ln (C/Y)_{t-4}$.

On a steady-state growth path with constant annual real income growth rate g and inflation rate μ, (45) yields the solution:

$$C = KY \quad \text{where} \quad K = \exp(-5{\cdot}3g - 1{\cdot}3\mu). \tag{46}$$

When $g = 0{\cdot}02$ and $\mu = 0{\cdot}05$ (as roughly characterised the 1960s) $K = 0{\cdot}84$, whereas if μ increases to $0{\cdot}15$, K falls to $0{\cdot}74$ (which is similar to the 1970s). Variations in the rate of inflation induce substantial changes in the ratio of C to Y.

There are a number of theories in addition to Deaton's which would lead one to anticipate significant inflation effects in (45). For example, during periods of rapid inflation, the conventional measure of Y_t ceases to provide a good proxy for "real income" (note that equation (9) above holds when capital gains and losses are accounted for in Y_t) and $\Delta_4 \ln P_t$, etc., "pick up" this effect. Models like (10) based on the *LCH* but transformed to eliminate wealth, should manifest negative inflation effects of the form $\Delta_4 \ln P_t$ through the erosion of the real value of the liquid assets component of A_t. Although one might expect agents to alter the composition of their wealth portfolio by shifting into real assets such as housing when inflation is rapid, it is not clear how this would affect expenditure decisions. In terms of empirical evidence, Townend (1976) found a real Net Liquid Assets variable (N) to be significant in his specification of the consumption function together with negative inflation effects (based on Almon lags). Using Townend's data for N_t (1963(iii)–1975(i), retaining the last two years' data for a forecast test) the only form which yielded significant results when added to (45) was $\Delta_1 \ln N_t$ (which could be due in considerable measure to the joint endogeneity of C_t and N_t):

$$\begin{aligned}\Delta_4 \ln \hat{C}_t = {} & \underset{(0{\cdot}04)}{0{\cdot}47}\Delta_4 \ln Y_t - \underset{(0{\cdot}05)}{0{\cdot}28}\Delta_1 \Delta_4 \ln Y_t - \underset{(0{\cdot}02)}{0{\cdot}05} \ln (C/Y)_{t-4} \\ & - \underset{(0{\cdot}17)}{0{\cdot}27}\Delta_1 \Delta_4 \ln P_t + \underset{(0{\cdot}003)}{0{\cdot}008}\Delta_1 D_t^0 + \underset{(0{\cdot}05)}{0{\cdot}11}\Delta_1 \ln N_t + \underset{(0{\cdot}06)}{0{\cdot}01}\Delta_4 \ln P_t,\end{aligned} \tag{47}$$

$$R^2 = 0{\cdot}86, \quad \hat{\sigma} = 0{\cdot}0059, \quad \text{dw} = 1{\cdot}8, \quad z_1(8) = 41, \quad z_2(12) = 26.$$

The main impacts of adding $\Delta_1 \ln N_t$ to (45) are the halved coefficient of $\ln (C/Y)_{t-4}$ (in an *LCH* framework, these are proxies) and the dramatic change to almost zero in the coefficient of $\Delta_4 \ln P_t$, consistent with the hypothesis that

$\Delta_4 \ln P_t$ is a proxy for the erosion of the value of liquid assets from inflation. Nevertheless, the effect of accelerating inflation retains a large negative coefficient. The marked deterioration in the forecast performance of (47) suggests an incorrect specification and hence we decided to omit N_t from further consideration, attributing its significance in (47) to simultaneity.[1]

To test the validity of the various restrictions imposed on (45) (price level homogeneity, exclusion restrictions and the unit income elasticity) we estimated the general unrestricted model:

$$\ln C_t = \sum_{j=0}^{5} (\alpha_j \ln Y_{t-j} + \beta_j \ln P_{t-j}) + \sum_{j=1}^{5} \lambda_j \ln C_{t-j} + \epsilon_t. \tag{48}$$

The results are shown in Table 3, and Table 4 records the equivalent values derived from the restricted model (45) (it seemed spurious to include five lagged values of D_t^0 in (48), although doing so does not greatly alter the results, $\hat{\sigma}$ falling to 0·0059). The restrictions are not rejected on a likelihood ratio test, and indeed the two sets of estimates are rather similar. Moreover, to two decimal digits, $\Sigma\hat{\beta}_j = 0$ and $\Sigma\hat{\alpha}_j \simeq 1 - \Sigma\hat{\lambda}_j$ favouring the hypotheses of price homogeneity and a unit elasticity for income.

Finally, re-estimation of (45) assuming $\Delta_4 \ln Y_t$, $\Delta_1 \Delta_4 \ln Y_t$, $\Delta_4 \ln P_t$ and $\Delta_1 \Delta_4 \ln P_t$ to be endogenous and using instrumental variables[2] yielded the outcome shown in (45)*:

$$\Delta_4 \ln \hat{C}_t = \underset{(0\cdot04)}{0\cdot48}\Delta_4 \ln Y_t - \underset{(0\cdot06)}{0\cdot20}\Delta_1 \Delta_4 \ln Y_t - \underset{(0\cdot07)}{0\cdot12}\Delta_4 \ln P_t$$
$$- \underset{(0\cdot18)}{0\cdot28}\Delta_1\Delta_4 \ln P_t - \underset{(0\cdot02)}{0\cdot09} \ln (C/Y)_{t-4} + \underset{(0\cdot004)}{0\cdot007}\, \Delta_4 D_t^0, \tag{45*}$$

$$\hat{\sigma} = 0\cdot0061, \quad dw = 1\cdot7, \quad z_1(20) = 22, \quad z_2(12) = 19, \quad z_3(10) = 16,$$

where $z_3(l)$ is the test for validity of the choice of instrumental variables discussed by Sargan (1964) and is distributed as χ_l^2 in large samples when the instruments are independent of the equation error. It is clear that the coefficient estimates and the goodness of fit are hardly altered, providing no evidence of simultaneity biases.

An interesting result emerges from estimating (45) over the entire sample period (to 1975 (iv)):

$$\Delta_4 \ln \hat{C}_t = \underset{(0\cdot03)}{0\cdot48}\Delta_4 \ln Y_t - \underset{(0\cdot04)}{0\cdot23}\Delta_1 \Delta_4 \ln Y_t - \underset{(0\cdot01)}{0\cdot09} \ln (C/Y)_{t-4}$$
$$+ \underset{(0\cdot002)}{0\cdot006}\Delta_4 D_t^* - \underset{(0\cdot02)}{0\cdot12}\Delta_4 \ln P_t - \underset{(0\cdot10)}{0\cdot31}\Delta_1 \Delta_4 \ln P_t, \tag{45**}$$

$$R^2 = 0\cdot85, \quad \hat{\sigma} = 0\cdot0062, \quad dw = 2\cdot0, \quad z_2(12) = 23.$$

[1] Other regressors which were added to (47) without yielding significant results were unemployment, the relative price of durables to non-durables and short-term interest rates. The largest t value was for $\Delta_1\, \Delta_4$ ln (unemployment) and Bean (1977) reports a significant value for this variable in a variant of (45). Note that, if the significance of $\Delta_1 \ln N_t$ *is* due to simultaneity, then the vanishing of the *direct* effect of $\Delta_4 \ln P_t$ on $\Delta_4 \ln C_t$ provides *no* evidence on the "erosion of the value of real liquid assets" hypothesis.

[2] The instruments used were $\ln Y_{t-j}$ ($j = 1, \ldots, 5$), $\ln P_{t-j}$ ($j = 1, 4, 5$), $\ln F_{t-j}$, $\ln E_{t-j}$, $\ln I_{t-j}$ ($j = 0, 4$) (where F_t, E_t, I_t respectively denote the real value of current government expenditure, exports and gross domestic fixed capital formation) and the predetermined variables in the regression.

D_t^* is D_t^0 extended to allow for the introduction of VAT – see footnote 1, p. 674. Manifestly, the coefficient estimates and $\hat{\sigma}$ are hardly changed from (45), as would be expected given the value for $z_1(20)$ on equation (45). R^2 has, therefore, increased, and the coefficient standard errors are smaller, especially for $\Delta_4 \ln P_t$. However, the equivalent long period estimates of (44) alter considerably, with $\hat{\sigma}$ increasing to 0·0063 and $z_2(16)$ to 28. Thus, the overall data set does not offer much evidence against deleting the intercept, and strongly favours retaining $\ln (C/Y)_{t-4}$. From the longer sample period, a significant coefficient for $\Delta_4 \ln Y_{t-2}$ also can be established, creating a "smoother" distributed lag of C_t on Y_t.

Table 3

Unrestricted Estimates of (47)

j	0	1	2	3	4	5
$\ln C_{t-j}$	—	0·12 (0·17)	0·02 (0·04)	−0·06 (0·04)	0·98 (0·05)	−0·11 (0·17)
$\ln Y_{t-j}$	0·25 (0·06)	0·10 (0·08)	−0·06 (0·07)	0·11 (0·07)	−0·18 (0·07)	−0·16 (0·08)
$\ln P_{t-j}$	−0·59 (0·21)	0·50 (0·29)	−0·23 (0·24)	0·12 (0·24)	0·44 (0·28)	−0·24 (0·21)

$R^2 = 0·997$, $\hat{\delta} = 0·0062$, dw = 2·2.

Table 4

Solved Estimates from (45)

j	0	1	2	3	4	5
$\ln C_{t-j}$	—	0	0	0	0·90	0
$\ln Y_{t-j}$	0·26	0·21	0	0	−0·16	−0·21
$\ln P_{t-j}$	−0·41	0·28	0	0	0·41	−0·28

X. SUMMARY AND CONCLUSIONS

A simple dynamic model which conforms with a range of theoretical requirements and matches all of the salient features of the data was used to explain various recently published relationships between Consumers' Expenditure on Non-durables and Disposable Income. Extended to allow for the effects of inflation noted by Deaton (1977), the model produces an acceptable set of post-sample predictions over twenty quarters using the actual data for incomes and prices. While noting the implications of the analyses of Leamer (1974, 1975) for an exercise like that described above, we feel that our "prejudiced search for an acceptable model" has not been fruitless. We conclude that it is worth while trying to explain the *complete* set of existing findings; that restrictions derived from economic theories can be valuable in econometric modelling if correctly implemented to restrict the *model* but not the *data*; that seasonal adjustment of data can confuse the *selection* of an appropriate dynamic specification; that "multicollinearity" is not necessarily resolved by *restricting* the parameter space rather than by *enlarging* it, and that econometric relationships can predict accurately over periods in which the behaviour of the regressors is sufficiently different that mechanistic time-series methods will fail. However, we do not conclude that our model represents the "true" structural relationship since there are several important issues which have not been considered (including changes in income distribution and direct wealth effects). Hopefully, our methods, models and results will facilitate future work on these problems.

London School of Economics

JAMES E. H. DAVIDSON
DAVID F. HENDRY
FRANK SRBA
STEPHEN YEO

Date of receipt of final typescript: March 1978

References

Ando, A. and Modigliani, F. (1963). "The 'Life Cycle' Hypothesis of Saving: Aggregate Implications and Tests." *American Economic Review*, vol. 53, pp. 55–84.

Ball, R. J. and Drake, P. S. (1964). "The Relationship between Aggregate Consumption and Wealth." *International Economic Review*, vol. 5, pp. 63–81.

—— Boatwright, B. D., Burns, T., Lobban, P. W. M. and Miller, G. W. (1975). "The London Business School Quarterly Econometric Model of the U.K. Economy." Chapter 1 in Renton (1975).

Bean, C. R. (1977). "More Consumer Expenditure Equations." Unpublished paper AP(77)35, H.M. Treasury.

Bispham, J. A. (1975). "The NIESR Model and its Behaviour." Appendix to chapter 3 in Renton (1975).

Bock, M. E., Yancey, T. A. and Judge, G. C. (1973). "Statistical Consequences of Preliminary Test Estimators in Regression." *Journal of the American Statistical Association*, vol. 68, pp. 109–16.

Box, G. E. P. and Jenkins, G. M. (1976). *Time Series Analysis Forecasting and Control*, rev. ed. San Francisco: Holden-Day.

—— and Pierce, D. A. (1970). "Distribution of Residual Autocorrelations in Autoregressive-Integrated Moving Average Time Series Models." *Journal of the American Statistical Association*, vol. 65, pp. 1509–26.

Brown, T. M. (1952). "Habit Persistence and Lags in Consumer Behaviour." *Econometrica*, vol. 20, pp. 355–71.

Byron, R. P. (1970). "Initial Attempts in Econometric Model Building at NIESR." Chapter 1 in *The Econometric Study of the United Kingdom* (ed. K. Hilton and D. F. Heathfield). London: Macmillan.

Central Statistical Office (1976). *Economic Trends*, Annual Supplement (1976). London: H.M.S.O.

Davidson, J. E. H. (1975). "Studies of the Measurement Error Problem with Special Reference to the Specification and Estimation of the Consumption Function." Unpublished M.Sc. Dissertation, London School of Economics.

Davis, N., Triggs, C. M. and Newbold, P. (1977). "Significance Levels of the Box-Pierce Portmanteau Statistic in Finite Samples." *Biometrika*, vol. 64, pp. 517–22.

Deaton, A. S. (1972). "Wealth Effects on Consumption in a Modified Life-Cycle Model." *The Review of Economic Studies*, vol. 39, pp. 443–54.

—— (1977). "Involuntary Saving Through Unanticipated Inflation." *American Economic Review*, vol. 67, pp. 899–910.

Duesenberry, J. S. (1949). *Income, Saving and the Theory of Consumer Behaviour*. Cambridge: Harvard University Press.

Durbin, J. (1970). "Testing for Serial Correlation in Least Squares Regression When Some of the Regressors are Lagged Dependent Variables." *Econometrica*, vol. 38, pp. 410–21.

Fisher, F. M. (1962). *A Priori Information and Time Series Analysis*. Amsterdam: North Holland.

Friedman, M. (1957). *A Theory of the Consumption Function*. Princeton: Princeton University Press.

Garganas, N. C. (1975). "An Analysis of Consumer Credit and its Effects on the Purchases of Consumer Durables." Chapter 19 in Renton (1975).

Granger, C. W. J. (1966). "The Typical Spectral Shape of an Economic Variable." *Econometrica*, vol. 34, pp. 150–61.

—— and Newbold, P. (1974). "Spurious Regressions in Econometrics." *Journal of Econometrics*, vol. 2, pp. 111–20.

Hendry, D. F. (1974). "Stochastic Specification in an Aggregate Demand Model of the United Kingdom." *Econometrica*, vol. 42, pp. 559–78.

—— (1977*a*). "The Behaviour of Inconsistent Instrumental Variables Estimators in Dynamic Systems with Autocorrelated Errors." Discussion Paper A14, London School of Economics. *Journal of Econometrics* (forthcoming)

—— (1977*b*). "On the Time Series Approach to Econometric Model Building." In *New Methods in Business Cycle Research* (ed. C. A. Sims). Federal Reserve Bank of Minneapolis.

—— and Anderson, G. J. (1977). "Testing Dynamic Specification in Small Simultaneous Systems: An Application to a Model of Building Society Behaviour in the United Kingdon." *Frontiers in Quantitative Economics*, vol. IIIA (ed. M. D. Intriligator). Amsterdam: North Holland.

—— and Mizon, G. E. (1978). "Serial Correlation as a Convenient Simplification Not a Nuisance: A Comment on a Study of the Demand for Money by the Bank of England." ECONOMIC JOURNAL, vol. 88, pp. 549–63 (September).

Houthakker, H. S. and Taylor, L. D. (1970). *Consumer Demand in the United States, 1929–1970*. Harvard: Harvard University Press.

Johnston, J. (1972). *Econometric Methods*. New York: McGraw-Hill.

Leamer, E. A. (1974). "False Models and Post-Data Model Construction." *Journal of the American Statistical Association*, vol. 69, pp. 122–31.

—— (1975). "'Explaining Your Results' as Access Biased Memory." *Journal of the American Statistical Association*, vol. 70, pp. 88–93.

Modigliani, F. (1975). "The Life Cycle Hypothesis of Saving Twenty Years Later." In *Contemporary Issues in Economics* (ed. M. Parkin and A. R. Nobay). Manchester: Manchester University Press.

Pesaran, M. H. and Deaton, A. S. (1978). "Testing Non-Nested Non-Linear Regression Models." *Econometrica*, vol. 46, no. 3, pp. 677–94 (May).

Pierce, D. A. (1971). "Distribution of Residual Autocorrelations in the Regression Model with Autoregressive-Moving Average Errors." *Journal of the Royal Statistical Society* B, vol. 33, pp. 140–6.

Prothero, D. L. and Wallis, K. F. (1976). "Modelling Macroeconomic Time Series (with Discussion)." *Journal of the Royal Statistical Society* A, vol. 139, pp. 468–500.

Renton, G. A. (ed.) (1975). *Modelling the Economy*. London: Heinemann Educational Books.

Sargan, J. D. (1964). "Wages and Prices in the United Kingdom: A Study in Econometric Methodology." In *Econometric Analysis for National Economic Planning* (ed. P. E. Hart, G. Mills and J. K. Whitaker). London: Butterworths Scientific Publications.

Sargent, T. J. (1977). "Observations on Improper Methods of Simulating and Teaching Friedman's Time Series Consumption Model." *International Economic Review*, vol. 18, pp. 445–62.

Savin, N. E. (1977). "The Wald Test and the *S* Procedure." Cambridge, July (unpublished).

Shepherd, J. R., Evans, H. P. and Riley, C. J. (1975). "The Treasury Short-Term Forecasting Model." Chapter 2 in Renton (1975).

Sims, C. A. (1974). "Seasonality in Regression." *Journal of the American Statistical Association*, vol. 69, pp. 618–26.

Theil, H. (1971). *Principles of Econometrics*. London: John Wiley.

Townend, J. C. (1976). "The Personal Saving Ratio." *Bank of England Quarterly Bulletin*, vol. 16, pp. 53–61.

Wall, K. D., Preston, A. J., Bray, J. W. and Peston, M. H. (1975). "Estimates of a Simple Control Model of the U.K. Economy." Chapter 14 in Renton (1975).

Wallis, K. F. (1974). "Seasonal Adjustment and Relations Between Variables." *Journal of the American Statistical Association*, vol. 69, pp. 18–31.

Williams, R. A. (1972). "Demand for Consumer Durables: Stock Adjustment Models and Alternative Specifications of Stock Depletion." *The Review of Economic Studies*, vol. 39, pp. 281–95.

Zellner, A. and Palm, F. (1974). "Time Series Analysis and Simultaneous Equation Models." *Journal of Econometrics*, vol. 2, pp. 17–54.

[25]

Econometrica, Vol. 55, No. 5 (September, 1987), 1035-1056

ASYMPTOTIC PROPERTIES OF LEAST SQUARES ESTIMATORS OF COINTEGRATING VECTORS

BY JAMES H. STOCK

Time series variables that stochastically trend together form a cointegrated system. In such systems, certain linear combinations of contemporaneous values of these variables have a lower order of integration than does each variable considered individually. These linear combinations are given by cointegrating vectors. OLS and NLS estimators of the parameters of a cointegrating vector are shown to converge in probability to their true values at the rate $T^{1-\delta}$ for any positive δ. These estimators can be written asymptotically in terms of relatively simple nonnormal random matrices which do not depend on the parameters of the system. These asymptotic representations form the basis for simple and fast Monte Carlo calculations of the limiting distributions of these estimators. Asymptotic distributions thus computed are tabulated for several cointegrated processes.

KEYWORDS: Cointegration, error correction models, unit roots.

1. INTRODUCTION

IT IS WIDELY OBSERVED that many time series of economic interest follow a nondeterministic trend in levels or in logarithms, but that these variables appear to be stationary after first differencing. At the same time, however, these variables often trend together: certain linear combinations of contemporaneous observations seem to be stationary in the sense that they do not require further differencing to exhibit limited dependence. This article examines the asymptotic properties of least squares estimators of the parameters of these linear combinations. Using the theory of cointegrated process, I show that these estimators have asymptotic properties different from those of least squares estimators in stationary time series models: convergence to their probability limits occurs faster than usual, and their limiting distribution is nonnormal. If the view of variables stochastically trending together (in the formal sense described below) is correct, then these results suggest that a reexamination of statistical inferences based on such common macroeconomic regressions as aggregate consumption on aggregate income is in order.

Casual observation suggests that the phenomenon of economic time series variables stochastically trending together might be widespread. For example, real GNP and Federal tax receipts have both grown sharply in the postwar U.S. economy. However, the ratio of tax receipts to GNP has fluctuated but has remained in the neighborhood of 19 per cent over the past three decades. As a second, somewhat more formal example, it can be argued that the permanent income hypothesis suggests that in the long run there is a unit income elasticity of consumption. If this is so, then one would expect deviations of consumption from the "long run" level—the level implied by the unit elasticity condition—to be a process with a short memory, even though real consumption expenditures

[1] The author thanks Christopher Cavanagh, Robert Engle, Clive Granger, Andrew Harvey, Thomas Rothenberg, Mark Watson, and an anonymous referee for helpful suggestions concerning this research, and Suzanne Sowinski for her careful preparation of the manuscript. The research was supported in part by the National Science Foundation, Grant No. SES-84-08797.

and disposable income have grown considerably over the postwar period. Accordingly, the difference between log consumption and log income might reasonably be modeled as being stationary, although these variables, each taken individually, cannot be.

Recently there has been increased interest in error correction models, a class of models in which it is explicitly assumed that two or more time series variables stochastically trend together. In these models, deviations from a long run "equilibrium condition" (e.g., that the long run income elasticity of consumption is one) feed back into short run dynamics so that the long run relation tends to be maintained. This "error correction" mechanism ensures that the variables possess a common stochastic trend. Imposing the unit elasticity condition, Davidson, Hendry, Srba, and Yeo (1978) estimate an error correction model of aggregate consumption in the postwar United Kingdom.[2]

Granger (1983), Granger and Weiss (1983), and Engle and Granger (1987) have recently provided a unified framework for the analysis of error correction models and of time series processes in which the variables stochastically trend together. In this framework, a process is called "cointegrated" (CI) if there are one or more linear combinations of contemporaneous time series variables which have a lower order of integration than do any of the individual random variables which comprise the system. Adopting Engle and Granger's (1987) terminology, a vector that reduces the order of integration of the system is referred to as a cointegrating vector. From the perspective of error correction models, these cointegrating vectors describe the long run "equilibrium conditions" to which the variables tend to return.

The cointegrated process/error correction model is summarized in Section 2. Cointegrated processes have strikingly different properties from stationary time series, and the asymptotic theory presented here reflects those differences. With stationary time series, the expectation of a squared error objective function attains its minimum at the true value of an identifiable parameter (at least asymptotically); the objective function has a finite but larger expectation for other values of the parameter. However, this is not true for some squared error objective functions with CI processes: while the linear combinations of contemporaneous values of the data formed using cointegrating vectors are stationary and have a finite second moment, all other linear combinations are nonstationary and have an infinite unconditional second moment. This suggests first that least squares should produce relatively precise estimators of CI vectors, and second that standard asymptotic results will not apply to these estimators.

The results of this paper confirm this intuition. In Section 3, the properties of the ordinary least squares estimator of the identifiable elements of the CI vector obtained from a contemporaneous levels regression are examined. The main result is that, if each element of the vector X_t is integrated of order one, and if

[2] See Hendry and Richard (1983) for a further discussion of error correction models. One theoretical justification for considering error correction models is reviewed by Salmon (1982), who describes their derivation from linear quadratic economic optimization problems with normally distributed errors.

there is a cointegrating vector such that the linear combination formed using this vector is integrated of order zero, then the OLS estimator of this vector is consistent (subject to an identification condition) and converges in probability faster than $T^{1-\delta}$ for any positive δ. This contrasts sharply with conventional asymptotic results in which the rate of convergence is $T^{1/2}$.

A nonlinear least squares estimator of the CI vector is examined in Section 4. This estimator is obtained by applying nonlinear least squares to a regression of first differences of an element of X_t on lagged first differences of itself and of the other variables in the system, and on lagged levels of X_t, combined using the cointegrating vector. This NLS estimator corresponds to an unconstrained version of Davidson, Hendry, Srba, and Yeo's (1978) estimator.[3] In this section, it is shown that the NLS estimator is consistent and converges at the same rate as the OLS estimator.

The behavior of least squares estimators of the parameters describing the short run dynamics of the CI process are discussed in Section 5. Using the results of the previous two sections, I argue that these estimators converge to limiting normal random variables at the usual rate, $T^{1/2}$. Indeed, because of the fast rate of convergence of the estimators of the CI vector, the short run parameter estimators are asymptotically independent of the estimators of the CI vector and their distribution is well approximated by the standard output of OLS packages.

In Section 6, a technique to stimulate the distribution of these estimators is described and implemented for several CI systems. This technique is based on asymptotic representations of the OLS and NLS estimators in terms of two matrix-valued random variables which are multivariate generalizations of the numerator and denominator of the standardized OLS estimator of the first autoregressive coefficient in a scalar AR(1) process with a unit root. As White (1958) showed, the limit distribution of this estimator is nonnormal when there is a unit root. Similarly, the limiting distribution of the standardized (by T) least squares estimators of the CI vector will also be nonnormal. Despite this complication, the asymptotic representations greatly simplify the task of approximating the distribution of the estimators using Monte Carlo techniques.

2. COINTEGRATED PROCESSES AND ESTIMATORS OF COINTEGRATING VECTORS

The Model

Engle and Granger (1987) define a N dimensional time series variable X_t to be cointegrated of orders d and b ($CI(d, b)$) if it satisfies two conditions: (i) each component of X_t, when considered individually, is integrated of order zero after differencing d times; and (ii) there exists at least one (and possibly r) "cointegrating vectors" α_i such that the linear combination $\alpha_i' X_t$ is integrated of order zero after differencing $d-b$ times. Note that, for the vector α_i in (ii) to be consistent with criterion (i), if $b>0$ then the cointegrating vector must have

[3] These authors constrain the long run income elasticity of consumption to be one. If bequests are a luxury good, then the long run income elasticity of consumption would be less than one. Whether this is so is an empirical question.

at least two nonzero elements. In this paper, attention is restricted to the special case discussed in the introduction, $d = b = 1$.

Two different representations of cointegrated processes will be useful in the development below. The first involves the Wold moving average representation of the (mean zero) first differences of X_t:

$$\Delta X_t = C(L)\varepsilon_t \tag{2.1}$$

with $\Delta \equiv 1 - L$, where L is the lag operator and $C(L)$ is a matrix of lag polynomials. I shall assume that the errors ε_t have a nonsingular covariance matrix G and finite fourth moments:

$$\varepsilon_t \text{ are i.i.d. } (0, G), \quad E|\varepsilon_{it}\varepsilon_{jt}\varepsilon_{kt}\varepsilon_{lt}| \leq \mu < \infty \qquad (i, j, k, l = 1, \ldots, N). \tag{2.2}$$

Engle and Granger (1987) show that, if X_t is cointegrated, then $C(1)$ is singular. Furthermore, the cointegrating vectors are those linear combinations of the rows of $C(1)$ that yield the zero vector: $\alpha_i' C(1) = 0$, $i = 1, \ldots, r$. Since $C(1)$ is singular, the spectral density matrix of ΔX_t is singular at zero frequency. This singularity is the restatement in the frequency domains of the time domain notion that, as a result of the error correction mechanism, the components of the CI process stochastically trend together.

The second representation of cointegrated processes is in terms of an error correction model (ECM). In a single equation ECM with a single "equilibrium error", the change in one variable (e.g. ΔX_{1t}) is written as a linear function of lagged changes of X_t plus a lagged weighted difference of levels of X_t. This lagged difference in levels is the "error correction" term of the ECM. From a time series perspective, if ΔX_{1t} is not integrated, this error correction term clearly cannot be integrated since it enters into the expression for ΔX_{1t}. Thus this equilibrium error must be that linear combination of the integrated variables comprising X_t that is itself *not* integrated, i.e. $\alpha' X_t$. Extending this reasoning to multiple equations, with $r = 1$ the ECM representation for ΔX_t is

$$A^*(L)\Delta X_t = -\gamma\alpha' X_{t-1} + d(L)\varepsilon_t \tag{2.3}$$

where $A^*(0) = I_N$, the $N \times N$ identity matrix, γ is a $N \times 1$ vector, and $d(L)$ is a lag polynominal. The intuition leading to (2.3) is formalized in Theorem 1 of Engle and Granger (1987). They prove that if X_t is cointegrated with $r = 1$ then it has the ECM representation (2.3), where γ is such that $C(1)\gamma = 0$ and $d(L)$ is a scalar lag polynominal with no unit roots. When $1 < r < N$, their theorem indicates that (2.3) still obtains with α and γ respectively being the $N \times r$ matrices with columns satisfying $\alpha_i' C(1) = 0$ and $C(1)\gamma_i = 0$, $i = 0, \ldots, r$.

The asymptotic analysis in the following sections proceeds conditional on $\varepsilon_s = 0$ for $s \leq 0$. This assumption facilitates a simple derivation of a useful representation of X_t and the equilibrium errors. Substituting backwards in (2.1) and rearranging,

$$X_t = C(1) \sum_{s=1}^{t} \varepsilon_s + C^*(L)\varepsilon_t, \tag{2.4}$$

where

$$C^*(L)=\sum_{j=0}^{\infty}\left[\sum_{i=0}^{j}C_i-C(1)\right]L^j=\sum_{j=0}^{\infty}\left[-\sum_{i=j+1}^{\infty}C_i\right]L^j.$$

Since $\alpha_i'C(1)=0$, (2.3) and (2.4) imply that

(2.5) $\quad z_{it}\equiv\alpha_i'X_t=\alpha_i'C^*(L)\varepsilon_t.$

The Normalized Cointegrating Vector

The cointegrating vectors are identifiable only up to a scale parameter: if $\alpha_i'X_t$ is stationary, then so too is $c\alpha_i'X_t$ for any constant c. I therefore adopt a normalization that extends the natural specification when $N=2$. For example, if consumption C_t and income Y_t are cointegrated so that $C_t-\theta Y_t$ is stationary, α can be written as $\alpha'=(1\ \ 0)+(0\ \ -1)\theta$. More generally, let the first element of α_i be 1, and assume that the remaining elements are linear combinations of k unknown identifiable parameters $\theta_{i1},\ldots,\theta_{ik}$, $k\leqslant N-1$. Let $e_{(i)}$ denote the N dimensional unit vector with a one in the same place as it appears in α_i and zeros elsewhere. With this normalization, the cointegrating vector can be written

(2.6) $\quad \alpha_i=e_{(i)}+R_i\theta_i \qquad (i=1,\ldots,r)$

where $\theta_i'=(\theta_{i1}\ \ \theta_{i2}\ \cdots\ \theta_{ik})$ and R_i is a $N\times k$ matrix of known constants.

The Estimators

In the consumption-income example, the ordinary least squares estimator of the identifiable element of the cointegrating vector is simply the slope coefficient estimated by regressing consumption on income. More generally, the OLS estimator $\hat{\theta}$ solves

(2.7) $\quad \min_{\theta}\sum_{t=1}^{T}(\alpha_i'X_t)^2,\quad \alpha_i=e_{(i)}+R_i\theta$

when the normalization (2.6) is adopted. If, for example, $\alpha_i=(1\ \ -\theta_{i1}\ \cdots\ -\theta_{iN-1})$, so that there were no restrictions on the elements of α_i other than the first, then (2.7) would simply result in the estimator obtained by regressing X_{1t} on the other elements of X_t.

I also study a nonlinear least squares estimator of θ. There are two reasons to examine this estimator. First, it generalizes the estimator used by Davidson, Hendry, Srba, and Yeo (1978).[4] Second, the OLS estimator uses only contemporaneous values of X_t, thereby foregoing potential gains in efficiency from

[4] Davidson, Hendry, Srba, and Yeo (1978) estimate the "consumption function,"

$$\Delta_4c_t=\beta_1(L)\,\Delta_4i_t+\beta_2(C_{t-4}-\theta i_{t-4})+\beta_3(L)'X_t+u_t$$

where c_t, i_t, X_t, and u_t are respectively log personal consumption, log disposable income, other variables (price deflators and a dummy), and an error term, and where $\beta_1(L)$ and $\beta_3(L)$ are lag polynomials. They constrain $\theta=1$; the NLS estimator estimates θ simultaneously with the other parameters of the equation.

simultaneously estimating the parameters of the short run dynamics and the long run "equilibrium condition."[5] The NLS estimator is based on a regression of X_t in first difference form. Let

$$\xi_t = (\Delta X_t' \ \Delta X_{t-1}' \cdots \Delta X_{t-p+1}')',$$

where p is fixed and finite. Also let $\gamma_j, j = 1, \ldots, N$, denote the elements of γ in (2.3). The NLS estimators $\tilde{\theta}$, $\tilde{\gamma}_1$, and $\tilde{\beta}$ solve:

$$\text{(2.8)} \qquad \min_{\theta, \gamma_1, \beta} \sum_{t=p+1}^{T} (\Delta X_{1t} - \beta' \xi_{t-1} + \gamma_1 \alpha' X_{t-1})^2$$

where β is the vector of parameters corresponding to the first row of $[I - A^*(L)]$ in (2.3).

If there is one cointegrating vector and if θ is exactly identified, then the NLS estimator can be computed directly from the OLS estimators of the coefficients on the lagged levels terms in the unconstrained ECM representation of the equation at hand. For example, if $N = 2$, then the first equation in the unconstrained ECM representation is

$$\text{(2.9)} \qquad \Delta X_{1t} = \beta' \xi_{t-1} + \delta_1 X_{1t-1} + \delta_2 X_{2t-1} + u_t$$

where δ_1 and δ_2 are scalar parameters. Under the normalization (2.6), $\alpha = (1 \ -\theta)'$, $\theta = -\delta_2/\delta_1$, and $\tilde{\theta} = -\hat{\delta}_2/\hat{\delta}_1$, where $\hat{\delta}_1$ and $\hat{\delta}_2$ are the OLS estimators from (2.9). More generally, the NLS estimators can be computed directly from the unconstrained OLS estimators if the dimensionality of θ is $N - 1$.

3. THE OLS ESTIMATOR

Using the normalization (2.6) and the first order conditions arising from (2.7), the OLS estimator can be written,

$$\text{(3.1)} \qquad \hat{\theta}_i - \theta_i = -V_T^{-1} U_T$$

where

$$\text{(3.2)} \qquad V_T = T^{-2} \sum_{t=1}^{T} R_i' X_t X_t' R_i, \qquad U_T = T^{-2} \sum_{t=1}^{T} R_i' X_t X_t' \alpha_i,$$

assuming that the inverse of V_T exists. In this section an asymptotic representation of V_T and TU_T is given in terms of Γ_T and Ψ_T, where

$$\Gamma_T = T^{-2} \sum_{t=1}^{T} Y_t Y_t',$$

$$\Psi_T = T^{-1} \sum_{t=2}^{T} Y_{t-1} \eta_t',$$

[5] This NLS estimator is generally not the full information estimator, however. The full information estimator would require imposing cross-equation constraints on the CI process and estimating the system subject to these constraints. Engle and Granger (1987) discuss these constraints.

where $Y_t = \sum_{s=1}^{t} \eta_s$, $\eta_s = G^{-1/2}\varepsilon_s$, and $G^{1/2}G^{1/2\prime} = G$.[6] This representation, given in Theorem 1, makes it possible asymptotically to express the OLS estimator as a function of parameters of the CI process and these two random matrices, the distribution of which is functionally independent of the CI process parameters. In Theorem 2, this representation is used to show that, for all $\delta > 0$, $T^{1-\delta}(\hat{\theta}_i - \theta_i)$ converges to zero in probability.

THEOREM 1: *If* $\sum_{u=0}^{\infty} |C_u^*| < \infty$, *then* $V_T - D_1' \Gamma_T D_1 \xrightarrow{p} 0$ *and* $TU_T - D_1' \Psi_T D_2 - M \xrightarrow{p} 0$, *where* $D_1' = R_i' C(1) G^{1/2}$, $D_2' = \alpha_i' C^*(1) G^{1/2}$, *and* $M = D_1' D_2' + R_i' \sum_{j=0}^{\infty} C_j^* G C_j^{*\prime} \alpha_i$.

Proofs of the theorems are given in the Appendix.

The definition of the cointegrating vector requires that z_t be integrated of order zero. Theorem 1 places a stronger requirement on the dependence exhibited by these equilibrium errors: that $C^*(L)$ be summable. This condition, however, is not very restrictive. For example, if $C(L)$ has a finite order q, then by (2.4) $C^*(L)$ has order $q-1$, so the summability condition automatically holds. More generally, if ΔX_t is a vector ARMA process of finite order, then $C^*(L)$ is absolutely summable.[7] The conditions that $C(L)$ and $C^*(L)$ be absolutely summable are not equivalent, however; for example, if $C_j = (j+1)^{-2} I$, then $C(L)$ is absolutely summable but $C^*(L)$ is not.

Theorem 1 expresses TU_T as a sum of mean zero random variables plus a vector of constants. Thus the asymptotic distribution of TU_T (if it exists) will in general have a nonzero mean. Given (3.1), this in turn suggests that the OLS estimator will have a bias of order $O(T^{-1})$. The bias in TU_T may initially seem surprising, for standardized consistent least squares estimators in conventional time series models generally have a limit distribution with mean zero. However, this nonzero limiting mean has a simple interpretation. Since X_t and z_t both consist in part of the same shocks ε_t, cov (X_t, z_t) will be of order $O(1)$. Were X_t stationary, implying a standardizing factor $T^{1/2}$ rather than T, the estimator would therefore be inconsistent. However, X_t follows a stochastic trend, so this bias enters as $O(T^{-1})$. In other words, the right hand variable $R_i' X_t$ is correlated with the errors in the regression resulting from (2.7). Since $R_i' X_t$ is nonstationary, this

[6] The random variables Γ_T and Ψ_T are the multivariate generalizations of random variables appearing in the representation of the standardized OLS estimator of the first autoregressive parameter when there is a unit root. Let $y_t = \rho y_{t-1} + \eta_t$, η_t i.i.d. $(0, \sigma^2)$. When $\rho = 1$, then the OLS estimator $\hat{\rho}$ of ρ can be written $T(\hat{\rho} - 1) = [T^{-2} \sum_{t=1}^{T-1} y_t^2]^{-1} [T^{-1} \sum_{t=2}^{T} y_{t-1} \eta_t]$ where y_t is a random walk. The numerator of this expression is the scalar version of Ψ_T; the denominator is the scalar version of Γ_T, minus the asymptotically negligible term y_T^2 / T^2.

[7] The one-sided filter $C(L)$ is m-summable if $\sum_{j=0}^{\infty} j^m |C_j| < \infty$. If $C(L)$ is 1-summable, then $C^*(L)$ is summable:

$$\sum_{j=0}^{\infty} |C_j^*| = \sum_{j=0}^{\infty} \left| - \sum_{i=j+1}^{\infty} C_i \right| \leq \sum_{j=0}^{\infty} \sum_{i=j+1}^{\infty} |C_i| = \sum_{i=1}^{\infty} \sum_{j=0}^{i-1} |C_i| = \sum_{i=1}^{\infty} i |C_i| < \infty.$$

If $C(L)$ is the moving average representation polynomial matrix implied by a finite ARMA model with stable roots, then $C(L)$ is m-summable for all finite m, from which it follows that $C^*(L)$ is summable.

correlation results in a nonzero limiting mean rather than in estimator inconsistency.

I now turn to the consistency of the OLS estimator.

THEOREM 2: *If the column space of R_i does not contain a cointegrating vector, then $T^{1-\delta}(\hat{\theta}_i - \theta_i) \xrightarrow{p} 0$ for all $\delta > 0$.*

The asymptotic representation of Theorem 1 provides a basis for examining the limiting distribution of $T(\hat{\theta}_i - \theta_i)$. Since Y_t is a vector random walk with i.i.d. increments, Donsker's Theorem can be used to write the limit of Γ_T and Ψ_T as functionals of Wiener processes. Let $\{B(t), 0 \leq t \leq 1\}$ denote the N dimensional Wiener process, and let $\Rightarrow$ denote weak convergence of the associated distributions (Billingsley (1968)). Then

$$\Gamma_T \Rightarrow \int_0^1 B(t)B(t)'\,dt \equiv \Gamma, \tag{3.3}$$
$$\Psi_T \Rightarrow \int_0^1 B(t)\,dB(t)' \equiv \Psi.$$

Invoking Theorem 1, $V_T \rightarrow D_1' \Gamma D_1$ and $TU_T \rightarrow M + D_1' \Psi D_2$. These results imply that the limiting distribution of the OLS estimator is independent of the distribution of ε_t.[8]

The consistency result of Theorem 2 suggests a reinterpretation of the large sample properties often associated with the slope coefficient in a regression of aggregate consumption against aggregate disposable income. Using a simple Keynesian model, Haavelmo (1943) argued that this regression will yield an inconsistent estimator of the long run marginal propensity to consume because of simultaneous equations bias. In contrast, according to Theorem 2, this estimator is consistent. Indeed, because the normalization of the cointegrating vector is inconsequential for Theorem 2, the inverse of the OLS estimator of the slope coefficient in the reverse regression of income on consumption will also be consistent for the long run marginal propensity to consume. This in turn implies that, as the sample size increases, the correlation between income and consumption (or any two cointegrated variables) will approach 1. Of course, in finite samples these two estimates will differ. The size of this difference will depend in large part on the term M, which arises from the correlation between the right hand variables and the error term in the OLS regression. Thus, if consumption

[8] In the univariate case, i.e., in the problem of the OLS estimator of a unit root, the possibility of using the invariance principle was noted by White (1958). Rao (1978) uses Donsker's Theorem to argue that his representation of the asymptotic distribution of the OLS estimator in the unit roots problem with normal errors is valid even if the errors are nonnormal but have finite variance. Solo (1984) uses a similar approach, expressing the LM statistic for testing for a unit root in terms of these functionals of scalar Brownian motion. Donsker's Theorem and the continuous mapping theorem for univariate processes are presented and proved in Billingsley (1968) and Hall and Heyde (1980). Subsequent to the submission of this paper, these results have been extended to multivariate processes by Phillips and Durlauf (1986) and Chan and Wei (1986).

and income are cointegrated, Haavelmo's simultaneous equations bias vanishes asymptotically but is present in the form of finite sample bias.

4. THE NLS ESTIMATOR

The normal equation for the NLS estimator $\tilde{\theta}_i$ solving (2.8) implies that

$$\tilde{\theta}i - \theta_i = -\tilde{V}_T^{-1}\tilde{W}_T \tag{4.1}$$

where

$$\tilde{V}_T = T^{-2}\sum_{t=p+1}^{T} R_i' X_{t-1} X_{t-1}' R_i,$$

$$\tilde{W}_T = T^{-2}\sum_{t=p+1}^{T} R_i' X_{t-1}(\Delta X_{1t} - \hat{\beta}'\xi_{t-1} + \tilde{\gamma}_1 z_{it-1})/\tilde{\gamma}_1,$$

assuming that $\tilde{\gamma}_1 \neq 0$. This estimator is motivated by considering a single equation in the ECM formulation of CI processes (2.3). The plan of this section is the same as Section 3. An asymptotic representation for $\tilde{V}_T$ and $\tilde{W}_T$ is given in Theorem 3 in the case that (2.8) is correctly specified, i.e., $d(L) = 1$. Consistency at the rate $T^{1-\delta}$ is proven in Theorem 4 even if $d(L) \neq 1$.

THEOREM 3: *If* $d(L) = 1$, $\gamma_1 \neq 0$, *and* $\sum_{u=0}^{\infty}|C_u^*| < \infty$, *then* $T\tilde{V}_T - D_1'\Gamma_T D_1 \xrightarrow{p} 0$ *and* $T\tilde{W}_T - D_1'\Psi_t D_3 \xrightarrow{p} 0$, *where* $D_3' = e_1' G^{1/2}\gamma_1^{-1}$ *and* $e_1' = (1\ 0\ \cdots\ 0)$.

If $d(L) \neq 1$, then the error term $d(L)\varepsilon_t$ will be correlated with the right hand variables. Even so, as long as $d(L)\varepsilon_t$ exhibits limited dependence, the NLS estimator will be consistent.

THEOREM 4: *Assume that* $\sum_{u=0}^{\infty}|C_u^*| < \infty$ *and that the column space of* R_i *does not contain a cointegrating vector. If either*:

(a) $d(L) = 1$ *and* $\gamma_1 \neq 0$; *or*

(b) $\sum |d_i| < \infty$ *and* $\tilde{\gamma}_1 \xrightarrow{p} \gamma_1^* \neq 0$;

then $T^{1-\delta}(\tilde{\theta}_i - \theta_i) \xrightarrow{p} 0$ *for all* $\delta > 0$.

Two remarks on these results are in order. First, using the argument sketched in Section 3, under the conditions of Theorem 3, $T\tilde{W}_T \to D_1'\Psi D_3$. Second, Theorem 3 indicates that if $d(L) = 1$, the limiting representation for $T\tilde{W}_T$ does not include a constant term like the matrix M appearing in the limiting representation of TU_T in Theorem 1. The reason is simple: in the case of the OLS estimator, $R_i'X_t$ is correlated with the error term in the regression, while in the NLS case with $d(L) = 1$ the right hand variables are uncorrelated with the error, ε_{1t}. This suggests that the NLS estimator might tend to exhibit less bias than the OLS estimator. It might, however, also exhibit a greater spread in its distribution: if γ_1 is small, then since $D_3 = G^{1/2\prime}e_1/\gamma_1$, the variability of $\tilde{\theta}_i$ will tend to be large.

5. PROPERTIES OF LEAST SQUARES ESTIMATORS OF OTHER ECM COEFFICIENTS

So far I have been concerned with estimating the parameters describing the long run dynamics of the CI process, i.e., the parameters of the cointegrating vector. The task still remains to estimate the parameters describing the short run dynamics of the system which, in the ECM representation with $d(L)=1$, are the coefficients on z_{t-1} and on lagged first differences of X_t. Two sets of estimators of the parameters describing the short run dynamics of the CI process are implicit in the previous sections. The first is a two-step estimator: in the first step, α is estimated by OLS as in Section 3, and in the second step z_t is replaced by $\hat{z}_t = \hat{\alpha}'X_t$ and the relevant parameters of the ECM representation are estimated equation by equation. The second procedure is the one step NLS procedure of Section 4.

I now examine the distributions of these two estimators of the parameters describing the short run dynamics. Compared to the estimators of θ, the asymptotics of these estimators are simple: both the NLS and the two step OLS estimators have a limiting normal distribution, converging at rate $T^{1/2}$. In addition, the covariance matrix of the limit distribution is estimated consistently by conventional least squares computer packages, and the two step OLS and NLS estimators are asymptotically independent of the respective estimators of the cointegrating vectors. It follows that the two estimators of the parameters describing the short run dynamics are asymptotically equivalent, even though the OLS and NLS estimators of the cointegrating vectors are not.

The second stage of the two step procedure consists of estimating (by OLS) equations of the form,

$$\Delta X_{1t} = \beta'\xi_{t-1} - \gamma_1 \hat{z}_{t-1} + \varepsilon_{1t} \tag{5.1}$$

where it is assumed that there is a single cointegrating vector and that $d(L)=1$. Letting $\hat{f}_t = (\xi_t' \quad -\hat{z}_t)$, $f_t = (\xi_t' \quad -z_t)'$, and $\phi = (\beta' \quad \gamma_1)'$, the estimator $\hat{\phi}$ of ϕ obtained by estimating (5.1) using OLS is:

$$\hat{\phi} = \hat{F}_T^{-1} T^{-1} \sum_{t=p+1}^{T} \hat{f}_{t-1} \Delta X_{1t}$$

so that

$$T^{1/2}(\hat{\phi} - \phi) = \hat{F}_T^{-1} T^{-1/2} \sum_{p+1}^{T} \hat{f}_{t-1}(f_{t-1} - \hat{f}_{t-1})'\phi + \hat{F}_T^{-1} T^{-1/2} \sum_{p+1}^{T} \hat{f}_{t-1}\varepsilon_{1t} \tag{5.2}$$

where $\hat{F}_T = T^{-1}\sum_{p+1}^{T} \hat{f}_{t-1}\hat{f}_{t-1}'$. Also let $\tilde{f}_t = (\xi_t' - \tilde{z}_t)'$ and $\tilde{F}_T = T^{-1}\sum_{p+1}^{T} \tilde{f}_{t-1}\tilde{f}_{t-1}'$, where $\tilde{z}_t = \tilde{\alpha}'X_t$ and $\tilde{\alpha}$ is the NLS estimator of α. Using the normal equations from (2.8), the NLS estimator $\tilde{\phi}$ of ϕ can similarly be written:

$$T^{1/2}(\tilde{\phi} - \phi) = \tilde{F}_T^{-1} T^{-1/2} \sum_{p+1}^{T} \tilde{f}_{t-1}(f_{t-1} - \tilde{f}_{t-1})'\phi + \tilde{F}_T^{-1} T^{-1/2} \sum_{p+1}^{T} \tilde{f}_{t-1}\varepsilon_{1t}. \tag{5.3}$$

Finally, let $\hat{\phi}^*$ denote the OLS estimator of ϕ based on f_t, i.e., the OLS estimator that would be used were α known. Then

$$T^{1/2}(\hat{\phi}^* - \phi) = F_T^{-1} T^{-1/2} \sum_{p+1}^{T} f_{t-1}\varepsilon_{1t} \tag{5.4}$$

where

$$F_T = T^{-1} \sum_{t=p+1}^{T} f_{t-1} f'_{t-1}.$$

Turning first to the two step OLS estimator, the scaled difference between $\hat{\phi}$ and $\hat{\phi}^*$ is

(5.5) $$T^{1/2}(\hat{\phi} - \hat{\phi}^*) = \hat{F}_T^{-1} T^{-1/2} \sum_{p+1}^{T} \hat{f}_{t-1}(f_{t-1} - \hat{f}_{t-1})'\phi$$
$$+ \hat{F}_T^{-1} T^{-1/2} \sum_{p+1}^{T} (\hat{f}_{t-1} - f_{t-1})\varepsilon_{1t}$$
$$+ (\hat{F}_T^{-1} F_T - I) F_T^{-1} T^{-1/2} \sum_{p+1}^{T} f_{t-1}\varepsilon_{1t}.$$

Unlike the moment matrices involving X_t, the sums in (5.5) involve either the stationary variables f_t and ΔX_{1t} or estimates of f_t based on $\hat{\alpha}$. Since $F_T \xrightarrow{p} F = Ef_t f'_t$ (a nonsingular covariance matrix) and since $T^{-1/2} \sum f_{t-1} \varepsilon_{1t}$ has a limiting distribution, sufficient conditions for $T^{1/2}(\hat{\phi} - \hat{\phi}^*) \xrightarrow{p} 0$ are that:

(5.6a) $$T^{-1/2} \sum_{p+1}^{T} (\hat{f}_{t-1} - f_{t-1})\varepsilon_{1t} \xrightarrow{p} 0,$$

(5.6b) $$\hat{F}_T \xrightarrow{p} F,$$

(5.6c) $$T^{-1/2} \sum_{p+1}^{T} \hat{f}_{t-1}(\hat{f}_{t-1} - f_{t-1})' \xrightarrow{p} 0.$$

(Note that (5.6b) implies that $\hat{F}_T^{-1} F_T \xrightarrow{p} I$.) Since $\hat{f}_t - f_t = (0' \; z_t - \hat{z}_t)'$, sufficient conditions for (5.6) to hold are that:

(5.7a) $$T^{-1/2} \sum (z_{t-1} - \hat{z}_{t-1})\varepsilon_{1t} \xrightarrow{p} 0,$$

(5.7b) $$T^{-1/2} \sum (z_{t-1} - \hat{z}_{t-1}) f_{t-1} \xrightarrow{p} 0,$$

(5.7c) $$T^{-1/2} \sum (\hat{z}_t^2 - z_t^2) \xrightarrow{p} 0.$$

Conditions (5.7) obtain by combining the argument in the proof of Theorem 1 that $T^{-1} \sum X_t \Delta X'_{t-j} = O_p(1)$ for fixed j with the result of Theorem 2 that $T^{1-\delta}(\hat{\theta} - \theta) \xrightarrow{p} 0$. Thus $T^{1/2}(\hat{\phi} - - \hat{\phi}^*) \xrightarrow{p} 0$. Note that this argument extends directly to the case that (5.1) contains an intercept as well.

The key observations in arguing that $T^{1/2}(\hat{\phi} - \hat{\phi}^*) \xrightarrow{p} 0$ are that certain random matrices not involving $\hat{\alpha}$ are of order $O_p(1)$ and that $T^{1-\delta}(\hat{\theta} - \theta) \xrightarrow{p} 0$. Because of the similarity between the formulas for $\hat{\phi}$ in (5.2) and for $\tilde{\phi}$ in (5.3), the preceeding argument can be repeated exactly with $\tilde{f}_t$, $\tilde{F}_T$, and $\tilde{\alpha}$ replacing $\hat{f}_t$, $\hat{F}_T$, and $\hat{\alpha}$. Thus $T^{1/2}(\tilde{\phi} - \hat{\phi}^*) \xrightarrow{p} 0$ if $T^{1-\delta}(\tilde{\theta} - \theta) \xrightarrow{p} 0$, which in turn follows from Theorem 4. In addition, it follows that $T^{1/2}(\tilde{\phi} - \hat{\phi}) \xrightarrow{p} 0$, so the two estimators of the short run dynamics are asymptotically equivalent.

These results are formal restatements of the economic distinction made between the short run dynamics embodied in ϕ and the long run relation embodied in α. The long run relation can be estimated in such a way that the convergence of these estimators is especially fast. However, the estimated parameters of the short run relation converge at the usual, slower rate. Moreover, because of the fast rate of convergence of the estimator of the CI vector, the distribution of the short run parameter estimator $\hat{\phi}$ is asymptotically well approximated by the distribution of $\hat{\phi}^*$, for which α is assumed known. If $d(L) = 1$, then $\hat{\phi}^*$ (and thus $\hat{\phi}$ and $\tilde{\phi}$) will be consistent. In addition, $\hat{\phi}$ and $\tilde{\phi}$ will be approximately normal, with a covariance matrix $G_{11}F^{-1}$ (where G_{11} denotes the (1, 1) element of G). This covariance matrix is consistently estimated by the usual OLS output from the second stage OLS regression.

6. ASYMPTOTIC DISTRIBUTIONS

Despite the convenient asymptotic representation of the OLS and NLS estimators in terms of the functionals in (3.3), the exact asymptotic distribution of the OLS estimators would be difficult to compute in the course of applied research (cf. Rao (1978), Evans and Savin (1981a)). In this section I propose an alternative approach to the distributional problem which may prove more practical than exact calculation. This approach is based on the representations of Theorems 1 and 3.

In the asymptotic representations, the parameters of the cointegrated process enter as additive and multiplicative factors. Thus it is not feasible to tabulate the distribution of the estimators for all potentially interesting cointegrated processes. In addition, direct simulation of the distribution of the estimators of the cointegrating system by bootstrap or Monte Carlo methods (using the estimated parameters as the basis for generating pseudo-data) would be excessively costly for common use. However, the representations suggest an alternative two step approach to obtaining numerical approximations to the distributions. In the first step, Monte Carlo draws of the random matrices Γ_T and Ψ_T are generated (with sufficiently large T) and stored. In the second step, pairs of (Γ_T, Ψ_T) can be drawn randomly from the many such pairs already created; using the asymptotic representation of $\hat{\theta}$ and $\tilde{\theta}$ and using known or estimated values of D_1, D_2, D_3, and M, the distribution of the OLS and NLS estimators can then be computed numerically. This technique has the advantage that, once the pairs (Γ_T, Ψ_T) have been created, it is inexpensive to evaluate the distributions of the OLS and NLS estimators for different values of the nuisance parameters.[9]

[9] An alternative approach to the distributional problem would be to obtain an integral expression for the distribution of the estimator using the limit representation in terms of the limit functionals of Brownian motion. This approach would entail generalizing the results of White (1958), Rao (1978, 1980), and Evans and Savin (1981a, 1981b), who variously derive and evaluate expressions for the limit distribution of the OLS estimator of the first autoregressive parameter when there is a unit root. Our proposal is in keeping with the Monte Carlo approach to the unit root problem taken by, for example, Dickey and Fuller (1979), Dickey, Hasza, and Fuller (1984), and Evans and Savin (1984).

I present two sets of results based on this numerical approach. First, the convergence of the distribution of the OLS estimator to the distribution of its asymptotic representation is investigated for a specific cointegrated process. Second, the asymptotic distributions of the OLS and NLS estimators are tabulated and compared for several cointegrated processes. These asymptotic distributions are studied using a three parameter family of CI processes in their ECM representation. This family is given by (2.3) with $N=2$, $r=1$, and

$$A^*(L)=(1-\rho L)I, \qquad G=I, \qquad d(L)=1,$$
$$\alpha'=(1\ \ -\theta), \qquad \gamma'=(\gamma_1\ \gamma_2). \tag{6.1}$$

The true value of the parameter to be estimated, θ, is taken to be 1. This family of CI processes is thus parameterized by γ_1, γ_2, and ρ.[10]

Monte Carlo distributions of the OLS estimator and its asymptotic approximation (computed using the true values of D_1, D_2, and M) are presented in Table I.[11] For the CI process investigated in this table, both the asymptotic distribution and the empirical Monte Carlo distribution of the standardized OLS estimator have a nonzero mean. The resultant bias in small samples can be considerable: for example, for $T=25$, the expectation of the OLS estimator is .833; the expectation of its asymptotic approximation is .827. Because of standardization at the rate T, this bias rapidly becomes small: for $T=200$, the OLS estimator has expectation .977. In addition to being biased, the distribution of the OLS estimator is strongly skewed. For $T=50$, the mean of the standardized OLS estimator is -4.27, while its median is -3.39. This skewness persists as T increases.

The results of Table I suggest that the asymptotic approximation performs well for small samples. Although the accuracy of the approximation improves slowly as the sample size increases, there are still discrepancies between the approximate and the true distribution at $T=200$. Still, the convergence in this case appears rapid enough to make the asymptotic approximations useful.

The asymptotic distribution of the standardized OLS estimator ($T=200$) is tabulated for various parameter values in Table II. These distributions vary greatly, depending upon the values of the three nuisance parameters of the CI process. For example, the medians of the standardized distributions range from $-.29$ to -13.96; the standard deviations range from 1.64 to 21.18. In all cases, however, the median of the distribution is less than zero, and in all cases but one the OLS estimator is biased towards zero.

The asymptotic distribution of the standardized NLS estimator, based on the representation of Theorem 3, is presented in Table III for $T=200$. When $\gamma_2=0$, the distribution of the NLS estimator is considerably less skewed than that of

[10] If $d(L)=1$ in (2.3), then a simple recursion can be used to compute $C(L)$ in terms of the parameters of the ECM representation. Using (2.1), (2.3), (2.4), and $\alpha' C(1)=0$, if $A^*(L)=I-\sum_{i=1}^{p} A_i^* L^i$, then $C_0=I$ and, for $j\geq 1$, $C_j=\sum_{i=1}^{j}(A_i^*-\gamma\alpha')C_{j-i}$, where A_i^* is set to zero for $i>p$.

[11] Multivariate normal errors were used to generate the cointegrated time series and the random variates Γ_T and Ψ_T. The simulated CI time series and the matrix variates were constructed from different noise vectors.

TABLE I

EMPIRICAL DISTRIBUTION OF STANDARDIZED OLS ESTIMATOR $T(\hat{\theta}-\theta)$ AND ITS ASYMPTOTIC APPROXIMATION

MODEL (6.1), $\rho = .25$, $\gamma_1 = .5$, $\gamma_2 = 0$, and $\theta = 1$.[a]

Estimator		Probability of a Smaller Value (p) .05	.10	.25	.50	.75	.90	.95	Moments Mean	Std. Dev.
$T=25$	$F^{-1}_{OLS}(p)$	−13.05	−10.20	−6.13	−3.11	−1.24	0.40	1.57	−4.17	4.77
	$F^{-1}_{asy}(p)$	−14.42	−10.61	−6.00	−3.04	−1.15	0.30	1.32	−4.32	5.22
	$F_{OLS}(F^{-1}_{asy}(p))$	.040	.088	.260	.509	.762	.891	.943	—	—
$T=50$	$F^{-1}_{OLS}(p)$	−13.00	−10.15	−6.07	−3.39	−1.31	0.37	1.40	−4.27	4.86
	$F^{-1}_{asy}(p)$	−14.17	−10.20	−5.84	−3.26	−1.27	0.19	1.31	−4.28	4.91
	$F_{OLS}(F^{-1}_{asy}(p))$	.039	.098	.226	.513	.755	.891	.946	—	—
$T=100$	$F^{-1}_{OLS}(p)$	−13.61	−10.05	−6.10	−3.28	−1.37	0.27	1.25	−4.31	4.79
	$F^{-1}_{asy}(p)$	−14.10	−10.69	−6.29	−3.32	−1.38	0.32	1.22	−4.55	5.32
	$F_{OLS}(F^{-1}_{asy}(p))$	.046	.086	.239	.494	.749	.902	.948	—	—
$T=200$	$F^{-1}_{OLS}(p)$	−13.70	−10.26	−6.60	−3.50	−1.44	0.13	1.10	−4.56	5.06
	$F^{-1}_{asy}(p)$	−14.31	−10.93	−6.52	−3.46	−1.36	0.07	1.01	−4.66	5.24
	$F_{OLS}(F^{-1}_{asy}(p))$	.041	.093	.253	.505	.757	.896	.948	—	—

[a] Based on 2000 replications each of $\hat{\theta}$, Γ_T, and Ψ_T, $T = 25, 50, 100, 200$. The distributions labeled "OLS" refer to Monte Carlo draws of $\hat{\theta}$; the asymptotic distributions were calculated using the two step numerical approach described in the text.

TABLE II

ASYMPTOTIC DISTRIBUTION OF THE STANDARDIZED OLS ESTIMATOR $T(\hat{\theta}-\theta)$ FOR MODEL (6.1), $T = 200$, AND $\theta = 1$.[a]

Model Parameters			Probability of a Smaller Value							Moments	
γ_1	γ_2	ρ	.05	.10	.25	.5	.75	.9	.95	Mean	Std. Dev.
.5	0	0	−24.24	−18.07	−10.72	−5.64	−2.60	−0.54	0.33	−7.93	8.47
		.25	−14.31	−10.93	−6.52	−3.46	−1.36	0.07	1.10	−4.66	5.24
		.5	−6.18	−4.77	−2.86	−1.37	−0.18	1.04	1.85	−1.69	2.64
		.75	−2.63	−1.91	−1.13	−0.35	0.52	1.55	2.47	−0.25	1.64
.2	0	0	−59.96	−44.70	−26.52	−13.96	−6.44	−1.34	0.81	−19.60	20.94
		.25	−41.35	−30.95	−18.43	−9.83	−4.32	−0.64	1.57	−13.44	14.61
		.5	−21.69	−16.81	−10.07	−5.23	−1.86	0.52	2.12	−6.92	8.10
		.75	−3.73	−2.63	−1.50	−0.29	1.16	3.06	4.88	0.03	2.70
.5	−.5	0	−35.38	−27.79	−16.01	−7.09	−2.79	−0.78	−0.03	−11.22	12.40
		.25	−22.16	−17.55	−9.82	−4.36	−1.67	−0.24	0.34	−7.02	7.96
		.5	−13.65	−10.50	−6.01	−2.61	−0.93	−0.05	0.35	−4.21	4.87
		.75	−5.97	−4.79	−2.75	−1.23	−0.51	−0.16	−0.05	−1.95	2.13
.2	−.2	0	−59.92	−44.27	−25.88	−10.78	−3.41	0.89	2.95	−17.59	21.18
		.25	−42.76	−31.98	−18.51	−7.67	−2.25	0.99	2.60	−12.57	15.34
		.5	−27.86	−20.62	−12.12	−4.98	−1.39	0.70	1.89	−8.12	10.00
		.75	−12.50	−9.83	−5.50	−2.43	−0.91	−0.10	0.27	−3.91	4.48

[a] Based on 2000 replications of (Γ_T, Ψ_T), $T = 200$.

TABLE III

ASYMPTOTIC DISTRIBUTION OF THE STANDARDIZED NLS ESTIMATOR $T(\tilde{\theta}-\theta)$ MODEL (6.1), $T = 200$, $\theta = 1$.[a]

Model Parameters			Probability of a Smaller Value							Moments	
γ_1	γ_2	ρ	.05	.10	.25	.5	.75	.9	.95	Mean	Std. Dev.
.5	0	0	−6.61	−4.56	−2.22	0.01	2.36	4.98	7.40	0.16	4.53
		.25	−4.96	−3.42	−1.66	0.01	1.77	3.73	5.55	0.12	3.40
		.5	−3.31	−2.28	−1.11	0.00	1.18	2.49	3.70	0.08	2.27
		.75	−1.65	−1.14	−0.55	0.00	0.59	1.25	1.85	0.04	1.13
.2	0	0	−16.53	−11.40	−5.54	0.02	5.90	12.45	18.51	0.40	11.33
		.25	−12.40	−8.55	−4.15	0.01	4.43	9.34	13.88	0.30	8.49
		.5	−8.27	−5.70	−2.77	0.01	2.95	6.22	9.25	0.20	5.66
		.75	−4.13	−2.85	−1.38	0.00	1.48	3.11	4.63	0.10	2.83
.5	−.5	0	−4.83	−3.31	−1.27	1.80	6.76	12.86	17.49	3.59	7.34
		.25	−3.62	−2.48	−0.95	1.35	5.07	9.65	13.12	2.70	5.50
		.5	−2.41	−1.65	−0.63	0.90	3.38	6.43	8.74	1.80	3.67
		.75	−1.21	−0.83	−0.32	0.45	1.68	3.22	4.33	0.90	1.83
.2	−.2	0	−12.07	−8.27	−3.16	4.51	16.89	32.16	43.72	8.99	18.34
		.25	−9.05	−6.20	−2.37	3.38	12.67	24.12	32.79	6.74	13.75
		.5	−6.03	−4.14	−1.58	2.25	8.45	16.08	21.87	4.49	9.17
		.75	−3.05	−2.08	−0.80	1.11	4.22	8.04	10.81	2.23	4.58

[a] Based on 2000 replications of (Γ_T, Ψ_T), $T = 200$.

the OLS estimator. In addition, in this case the NLS estimator is much closer to being unbiased than is the OLS estimator. However, for nonzero γ_2 and small γ_1, the standardized NLS estimator is not asymptotically unbiased; indeed, for small ρ, this bias can be substantial, although it typically is not as large in absolute value as is the bias of the OLS estimator. Finally, in most cases the asymptotic distribution of the NLS estimator has a smaller spread (as measured either by the interquartile range or by the standard deviation) than does the OLS estimator.

This numerical approach to computing the distributions of $\hat{\theta}$ and $\tilde{\theta}$ can be used as a basis for statistical inference. For example, to test a hypothesis on an element of θ, say $\theta_1 = \theta_1^0$ vs. $\theta_1 \neq \theta_1^0$, the other elements of θ and the nuisance parameters $C(L)$ and G (and thus D_1, D_2, D_3, and M) could be estimated consistently under the restriction on θ either by two step OLS or by NLS. The asymptotic distribution of $\hat{\theta}_1$ under the null hypothesis could then be computed using the proposed techniques, thereby obtaining the probability under the null of realizing a value of (say) $|\hat{\theta}_1 - \theta_1^0|$ at least as large as that estimated. The construction of confidence intervals for θ_1 would be more difficult, since it would entail computing the critical points of $\hat{\theta}_1 - \theta_1^0$ for many values of θ_1^0. An instructive approach would be to adopt Kendall and Stuart's (1967, p. 120) suggestion and to "invert" the test statistic graphically.

In summary, these results suggest three conclusions. First, the asymptotic representation theorems provide an accurate and fast means of obtaining numerical approximations to the otherwise complicated distributions of the NLS and OLS estimators. Second, these distributions depend strongly on the other parameters of the CI system. Thus the parameters of the entire CI process must be estimated before inferences can be made about the estimator of the CI vector. Third, the OLS and NLS estimators can be substantially biased, especially for small sample sizes. For the parameterizations considered here, the OLS estimator appears more prone to this bias than does the NLS estimator, although this need not be so in general. Thus researchers estimating the parameters of cointegrated processes should exercise caution when interpreting their estimates without first adjusting for bias.

7. SUMMARY

Two broad conclusions emerge from this analysis. First, if a vector of time series variables is cointegrated, then least squares estimators of the parameters of the cointegrating vector will have a nonnormal limiting distribution which resembles a multivariate generalization of the distribution of the estimated autoregressive coefficient when there is a unit root in a univariate series. This distribution will in general be skewed, and both the OLS and the NLS estimators can have limit distributions with nonzero means after standardization. Furthermore, these estimators converge to their limiting distributions at a fast rate.

Second, these results indicate that inference based on the standard least squares output can be misleading in time series regressions with both lagged differences and levels of the dependent variable appearing as explanatory variables. In this case, the moment matrix of the levels regressors converges to a limiting random variable, and the distribution of certain regression coefficients will not be well approximated by normality.

These results suggest a simple computational technique for evaluating these distributions. This technique is based on representing the estimators as a function of consistently estimable parameters and two matrix-valued random variables. Once these random matrices have been generated, the distribution of the OLS and NLS estimators is readily computed by Monte Carlo integration based on draws of these random matrices. The computational savings of this approach over a bootstrap or full Monte Carlo procedure is substantial, reducing the number of computations by a factor of T.

On an informal level, there is good reason to suspect that cointegration could be a widespread phenomenon in macroeconomic data. For example, Nelson and Plosser (1982) have presented evidence that many macroeconomic variables seem to follow a stochastic rather than a deterministic trend and that, after differencing, these variables often appear to be stationary. If in addition certain linear combinations of contemporaneous values of these variables are stationary without further differencing, then the system of these variables form a cointegrated process, and the usual distributional approximations will not apply. As a specific example, Engle and Granger (1987) present evidence supporting the application by Davidson et al. (1978) of an ECM model to consumption and income. Their finding suggests that researchers who have regressed aggregate consumption on aggregate income have erred when using the standard errors produced by conventional regression packages. Still, this regression of consumption on income is not spurious: under the assumption of cointegration, the OLS and NLS estimators of the cointegrating vector are consistent and, indeed, converge to their probability limits at a relatively fast rate.

The John F. Kennedy School of Government, Harvard University, Cambridge, MA 02138, U.S.A.

Manuscript received May, 1985; final revision received November, 1986.

APPENDIX

PROOFS OF THEOREMS

PROOF OF THEOREM 1: Let $C^{+}(L)=C^{*}(L)G^{1/2}$. From (2.4),

$$X_t=C(1)\sum_{s=1}^{t}\varepsilon_s+C^{*}(L)\varepsilon_t=C(1)G^{1/2}Y_t+C^{+}(L)\eta_t.$$

Thus:

$$V_T=T^{-2}\sum_{t=1}^{T}R_i'[C(1)G^{1/2}Y_t+C^{+}(L)\eta_t][C(1)G^{1/2}Y_t+C^{+}(L)\eta_t]'R_i$$

$$=R_i'C(1)G^{1/2}\left[T^{-2}\sum_{t=1}^{T}Y_tY_t'\right]G^{1/2\prime}C(1)'R_i$$

$$+R_i'C(1)G^{1/2}\left[T^{-2}\sum_{t=1}^{T}Y_t(C^+(L)\eta_t)'\right]R_i$$

$$+R_i'T^{-2}\sum_{t=1}^{T}(C^+(L)\eta_t)Y_t'G^{1/2\prime}C(1)'R_i$$

$$+R_i'T^{-2}\sum_{t=1}^{T}(C^+(L)\eta_t)(C^+(L)\eta_t)'R_i$$

so

$$V_T-D_1'\Gamma_TD_2=T^{-1}(D_1'H_1R_i+R_i'H_1'D_1+R_i'H_2R_i) \tag{A.1}$$

where

$$H_1=T^{-1}\sum_{t=1}^{T}Y_t(C^+(L)\eta_t)',$$

$$H_2=T^{-1}\sum_{t=1}^{T}(C^+(L)\eta_t)(C^+(L)\eta_t)'.$$

Similarly,

$$TU_T=T^{-1}\sum_{t=1}^{T}R_i'[C(1)G^{1/2}Y_t+C^+(L)\eta_t][C(1)G^{1/2}Y_t+C^+(L)\eta_t]'\alpha_i$$

$$=D_1'H_1\alpha_i+R_i'H_2\alpha_i$$

since $\alpha_i'C(1)=0$. Proceed by rewriting H_1, recalling that $\varepsilon_s=0$, $s\leq 0$:

$$H_1=T^{-1}\sum_{t=1}^{T}Y_t\left[\sum_{j=0}^{t-1}C_j^+\eta_{t-j}\right]' \tag{A.2}$$

$$=T^{-1}\sum_{t=1}^{T}\sum_{j=0}^{t-1}(Y_t-Y_{t-j})\eta_{t-j}'C_j^{+\prime}$$

$$+T^{-1}\sum_{t=1}^{T}\sum_{j=0}^{T-1}Y_{t-j}\eta_{t-j}'C_j^{+\prime}$$

$$=H_3-H_4+(\Psi_T+H_5)\sum_{j=0}^{T-1}C_j^{+\prime}$$

where

$$H_3=T^{-1}\sum_{j=0}^{T-1}\zeta_jC_j^{+\prime},\quad \zeta_j=\sum_{t=j+1}^{T}(Y_t-Y_{t-j})\eta_{t-j}',$$

$$H_4=T^{-1}\sum_{j=0}^{T-1}\phi_jC_j^{+\prime},\quad \phi_j=\sum_{t=T-j+1}^{T}Y_t\eta_t',$$

$$H_5=T^{-1}\sum_{t=1}^{T}\eta_t\eta_t'.$$

Thus

$$TU_T=D_1'\Psi_TD_2+D_1'H_5D_2+R_i'H_2\alpha_i \tag{A.3}$$

$$+D_1'(H_3-H_4)\alpha_i+D_1'(\Psi_T+H_5)\left[\left(\sum_{j=0}^{T-1}C_j^+\right)-C^+(1)\right]'\alpha_i$$

since $C^+(1)'\alpha_i=G^{1/2\prime}C^*(1)'\alpha_i=D_2$. The expressions (A.1)-(A.3) are exact, involving no asymptotic approximations. From (A.3), the representation for TU_T stated in the theorem obtains if it is shown that: (i) $H_2\xrightarrow{p}\sum_{j=0}^{\infty}C_j^*GC_j^{*\prime}$; (ii) $H_3\xrightarrow{p}0$; (iii) $H_4\xrightarrow{p}0$; (iv) $H_5\xrightarrow{p}I$. If in addition it is shown that (v) $T^{-\delta}\Psi_T\xrightarrow{p}0$ for all $\delta>0$, then, using (A.1), the representation for V_T also obtains.

Since η_t has finite fourth moments and identity covariance matrix, (iv) is immediate. Since $C(L)$ is summable, (i) is also immediate. I therefore turn to (ii), (iii), and (v), thereby completing the proof.

(ii) This will be shown using Chebyshev's inequality. Since $E\eta_s\eta_t'=0$, $s\neq t$, $E\zeta_j=0$. To show that $H_3 \xrightarrow{p} 0$, consider a typical element of H_3. The (l, k) element of H_3 is

$$(H_3)_{lk}=\sum_{m=1}^{N}\delta_{lmk} \quad \text{where} \tag{A.4}$$

$$\delta_{lmk}\equiv T^{-1}\sum_{j=0}^{T-1}(\zeta)_{lm}(C_j^+)_{km},$$

where $(\zeta_j)_{lm}$ is the (l, m) element of ζ_j. It will be shown that, under the stated conditions, each element of the sum (A.4) converges to zero in probability, and thus that $H_3 \xrightarrow{p} 0$. Since $E\zeta_j=0$, it is sufficient to show that $\text{var}(\delta_{lmk})\to 0$. Now

$$\text{var}(\delta_{lmk})=T^{-2}\sum_{j=0}^{T-1}\sum_{i=0}^{T-1}E(\zeta_i)_{lm}(\zeta_j)_{lm}(C_j^+)_{km}(C_i^+)_{km}$$

$$\leq T^{-2}\sum_{j=0}^{T-1}\sum_{i=0}^{T-1}|(C_j^+)_{km}||(C_i^+)_{km}|\times\max_{i,j,l,m}(E(\zeta_j)^2_{lm}, E(\zeta_i)^2_{lm}). \tag{A.5}$$

Also

$$E(\zeta_i)^2_{lm}=\sum_{t=j+1}^{T}\sum_{s=j+1}^{T}E(Y_{1t}-Y_{1t-j})(Y_{1s}-Y_{1s-j})\eta_{m,t-j}\eta_{m,s-j}$$
$$=j(T-j)$$

since $E\eta_{mt}\eta_{ls}=1$ if $m=l$ and $t=s$ and $=0$ otherwise. Thus

$$\max_{i,j,l,m}(E(\zeta_i)^2_{lm}, E(\zeta_j)^2_{lm})\leq[\max(j, i)][T-\min(j, i)]$$

so by (A.5),

$$\text{var}(\delta_{lmk})\leq T^{-2}\sum_{j=0}^{T-1}\sum_{i=0}^{T-1}|(C_i^+)_{km}||(C_j^+)_{km}|[\max(j, i)][T-\min(j, i)]$$

$$\leq 2\left[\sum_{j=0}^{T-1}(j/T)|(C_j^+)_{km}|\right]\left[\sum_{i=0}^{T-1}(1-i/T)|(C_i^+)_{km}|\right].$$

Since $C^*(L)$ is summable, $C^+(L)$ is summable and is therefore Cesaro summable (Anderson (1971), Lemma 8.3.1). Thus $\sum_{j=0}^{T-1}(1-j/T)|C_j^+|\to\sum_{j=0}^{\infty}|C_j^+|$ and $\sum_{j=0}^{T-1}(j/T)|C_j^+|\to 0$, so $\text{var}(\delta_{lmk})\to 0$ and $H_3 \xrightarrow{p} 0$.

(iii) This argument proceeds in the same manner as the argument for (ii). First,

$$EH_4=T^{-1}\sum_{j=0}^{T-1}E\phi_jC_j^{+\prime}=T^{-1}\sum_{j=0}^{T-1}(j-1)C_j^{+\prime}\to 0$$

by Cesaro convergence. Letting $\tau_{lmk}\equiv T^{-1}\sum_{j=0}^{T-1}(\phi_j)_{lm}(C_j^+)_{km}$, by the argument leading to (A.5),

$$\text{var}(\tau_{lmk})\leq T^{-2}\sum_{j=0}^{T-1}\sum_{i=0}^{T-1}|(C_j^+)_{km}||(C_i^+)_{km}|\max[\text{var}((\phi_i)_{lm}), \text{var}((\phi_j)_{lm})].$$

By direct calculation,

$$\text{var}[(\phi_j)_{lm}]=\sum_{t=T-j+1}^{T}\text{var}(Y_{lt}\eta_{mt})=(j-1)\mu_4+j(T-1)-j(j-1)/2$$

where $\mu_4=\max_j E(\eta_{jt}^4)$. Consequently

$$\text{var}(\tau_{lmk})\leq 2\left[T^{-2}\sum_{j=0}^{T-1}[(j-1)\mu_4+j(T-1)-j(j-1)/2]|(C_j^+)_{mk}|\right]$$
$$\times\left[\sum_{j=0}^{T-1}|(C_j^+)_{mk}|\right]\to 0$$

since

$$\sum_{j=0}^{T-1}(j^2/T^2)|C_j^+|\leq\sum_{j=0}^{T-1}(j/T)|C_j^+|\to 0.$$

(v) This result also obtains using Chebyschev's inequality. Note that $E\Psi_T=0$ and that var $(\Psi_{Tij})=T^{-2}\sum_{t=2}^{T}\sum_{s=2}^{T}E(Y_{it-1}Y_{is-1}\eta_{jt}\eta_{js})=T(T-1)/2T^2$. Thus var $(T^{-\delta}\Psi_{Tij})\to 0$, so $T^{-\delta}\Psi_T\xrightarrow{p}0$.

Q.E.D.

Proof of Theorem 2: Using (3.1), $T^{1-\delta}(\hat{\theta}_i-\theta_i)=-V_T^{-1}T^{-\delta}(TU_T)$. Consequently, $T^{1-\delta}(\hat{\theta}_i-\theta_i)\xrightarrow{p}0$ if (i) V_T^{-1} has a limiting distribution; and (ii) $T^{1-\delta}U_T\xrightarrow{p}0$.

(i) Using the representation of Theorem 1, $V_T^{-1}=[D_1'\Gamma_TD_1]^{-1}+o_p(1)$. Thus V_T^{-1}will have a limiting distribution if Γ_T^{-1} has a limiting distribution and if D_1 has full column rank. By Theorem 2.4 of Chan and Wei (1986) or Lemma 3.1 of Phillips and Durlauf (1986), $\Gamma_T\Rightarrow\Gamma$, where Γ is given in (3.3). By the continuous mapping theorem, Γ_T^{-1} thus has the limiting distribution of $\Gamma^{-1}=[\int_0^1 B(t)B(t)'\,dt]^{-1}$.

The condition that D_1 have full column rank can be restated as requiring that there not exist a vector b such that $b'R_i'C(1)G^{1/2}=0$. Since G is nonsingular, this is equivalent to requiring that there be no b^* such that $b^{*\prime}C(1)=0$, where $b^{*\prime}=b'R_i'$. If such a b^* were to exist, it would be by definition a cointegrating vector, say α^*. Thus V_T^{-1} has a limiting distribution if there is no α_j, $j=1,\ldots,r$, and vector b such that $R_ib=\alpha_j$. That is, the column space of R_i cannot contain a cointegrating vector.

(ii) By Theorem 1 and the result (v) obtained in its proof, $T^{-\delta}(TU_T)\xrightarrow{p}0$.

Q.E.D.

Proof of Theorem 3: Since $\tilde{V}_T=V_T-R_i'T^{-2}\sum_{t=1}^{p-1}X_tX_t'R_i-R_i'T^{-2}X_TX_T'R_i$, and since $T^{-2}\sum_{t=1}^{p-1}X_tX_t'\xrightarrow{p}0$ and $T^{-2}X_TX_T'\xrightarrow{p}0$, it follows from Theorem 1 that $T\tilde{V}_T-D_1'\Gamma_TD_1\xrightarrow{p}0$. Turning to $\tilde{W}_T$,

$$\begin{aligned}T\tilde{W}_T=&(D_1'\Psi_TD_3+R_i'G^{1/2}[T^{-1}\textstyle\sum\eta_t(C^*(L)\eta_{t-1})']'D_3)(\gamma_1/\tilde{\gamma}_1)\\&-R_i'(T^{-1}\textstyle\sum X_{t-1}\xi_{t-1}')(\tilde{\beta}-\beta)/\tilde{\gamma}_1\\&+R_i'(T^{-1}\textstyle\sum X_{t-1}z_{it-1})(\tilde{\gamma}_1-\gamma_1)/\tilde{\gamma}_1.\end{aligned}$$

Since β, γ_1, and θ are identifiable and since the objective function (2.8) asymptotically attains a minimum at the true parameter values, $\tilde{\beta}$, $\tilde{\gamma}_1$, and $\tilde{\theta}$ are consistent. Therefore, the theorem obtains if

(i) $T^{-1}\sum\eta_t(C^*(L)\eta_{t-1})'\xrightarrow{p}0$,

(ii) $\text{var}\,[(T^{-1}\sum X_{t-1}\xi_{t-1}')_{lm}]=0(1)$,

(iii) $\text{var}\,[(T^{-1}\sum X_{t-1}z_{it-1})_j]=0(1)$,

for typical elements (l, m) and j of the corresponding random variables.

Condition (i) can be demonstrated to hold if $C^*(L)$ is summable using the same arguments as in the proof of Theorem 1. Conditions (ii) and (iii) also follow from the proof of Theorem 1 upon simple rewriting. For condition (ii), a typical element of ξ_{t-1} is $\Delta X_{jt-k}=\Delta X_{t-k}'e_j$, where e_j is the jth canonical unit vector. Now

$$\begin{aligned}T^{-1}\textstyle\sum X_{t-1}\Delta X_{t-k}'e_j=&C(1)G^{1/2}T^{-1}\textstyle\sum Y_{t-1}(C(L)G^{1/2}\eta_{t-k})'e_j\\&+T^{-1}\textstyle\sum(C^+(L)\eta_{t-1})(C(L)G^{1/2}\eta_{t-k})'e_j.\end{aligned}$$

From the proof of Theorem 1, the first term has variance of order $0(\text{var}\,(\Psi_{Tik}))=0(1)$, and the second term converges in probability to $\sum C_{j+k-1}^*GC_j^{*\prime}$. Thus (ii) is satisfied. Condition (iii) follows analogously.

Q.E.D.

Proof of Theorem 4: Under both conditions (a) and (b), $\tilde{V}_T-D_1'\Gamma_TD_1\xrightarrow{p}0$. It follows from the representation (4.1) and result (i) in the proof of Theorem 2 that $T^{1-\delta}(\tilde{\theta}_i-\theta_i)\to 0$ if $T^{-\delta}\tilde{W}_T\xrightarrow{p}0$. I now demonstrate that $T^{-\delta}\tilde{W}_T\xrightarrow{p}0$ under both the conditions.

Allowing for general $d(L)$, $T\tilde{W}_T$ can be written as

$$\begin{aligned}T\tilde{W}_T=&[D_1'\Psi_TD_3+D_1'T^{-1}\textstyle\sum Y_{t-1}(d^+(L)\eta_{t-1})'D_3](\gamma_1/\tilde{\gamma}_1)\\&+R_i'T^{-1}\textstyle\sum[C^+(L)\eta_{t-1}][d(L)\eta_t]'D_3(\gamma_1/\tilde{\gamma}_1)\\&-R_i'(T^{-1}\textstyle\sum X_{t-1}\xi_{t-1}')(\tilde{\beta}-\beta)/\tilde{\gamma}_1\\&+R_i'(T^{-1}\textstyle\sum X_{t-1}z_{it-1})(\tilde{\gamma}_1-\gamma_1)/\tilde{\gamma}_1\end{aligned}$$

where $d^+(L)=(d(L)-d(0))L^{-1}$. Thus sufficient conditions for $T^{1-\delta}\tilde{W}_T \xrightarrow{p} 0$ are that:

(i) $T^{1-\delta}\Psi_T \xrightarrow{p} 0$,

(ii) $T^{-1-\delta}\sum Y_{t-1}[d^+(L)\eta_{t-1}]' \xrightarrow{p} 0$,

(iii) $T^{-1}\sum[C^+(L)\eta_{t-1}][d(L)\eta_t]' \xrightarrow{p} \sum_{j=1}^{\infty} C^*_{j+1}Gd_j < \infty$,

(iv) $T^{-1-\delta}\sum X_{t-1}\xi'_{t-1} \xrightarrow{p} 0$ and $(\tilde{\beta}-\beta)/\tilde{\gamma}_1 \xrightarrow{p} c_1$,

(v) $T^{-1-\delta}\sum X_{t-1}z_{it-1} \xrightarrow{p} 0$ and $(\tilde{\gamma}_1-\gamma_1)/\tilde{\gamma}_1 \xrightarrow{p} c_2$,

where c_1 and c_2 are finite constants.

Condition (i) was shown as condition (v) in the proof of Theorem 1. Condition (iii) follows from the assumed absolute summability of $C^*(L)$ and $d(L)$. The first parts of conditions (iv) and (v) are implied by conditions (ii) and (iii) in the proof of Theorem 3. The second parts of conditions (iv) and (v) hold under both the conditions (a) and (b), but for slightly different reasons. Under (a), $\tilde{\beta} \xrightarrow{p} \beta$ and $\tilde{\gamma}_1 \xrightarrow{p} \gamma_1 \neq 0$, so $c_1 = c_2 = 0$. Under (b), $\tilde{\beta} \xrightarrow{p} \beta^* \neq \beta$ in general and $\tilde{\gamma}_1 \xrightarrow{p} \gamma_1^* \neq \gamma_1$ in general; however, $\gamma_1^* \neq 0$ by assumption, so c_1 and c_2 are finite.

All that remains is to show that condition (ii) is satisfied. This is clearly so under assumption (a), for then $d^+(L)=0$. Under (b), note that $T^{-1}\sum Y_{t-1}[d^+(L)\eta_{t-1}]'$ has exactly the same form as H_1 in Theorem 1, with $d^+(L)I$ replacing $C^+(L)$, except for asymptotically negligible differences in the limits of the summations. Since $T^{-\delta}H_1 \xrightarrow{p} 0$ if $\sum|C_j^+|<\infty$, it follows immediately that $T^{-1-\delta}\sum Y_{t-1}[d^+(L)\eta_{t-1}] \xrightarrow{p} 0$ if $\sum|d_j^+|<\infty$. Since $\sum|d_j^+|<\sum|d_j|$, condition (ii) holds under both assumptions (a) and (b). *Q.E.D.*

REFERENCES

ANDERSON, T. W. (1971): *The Statistical Analysis of Time Series*. New York: Wiley.

BILLINGSLEY, P. (1968): *Convergence of Probability Measures*. New York: Wiley.

CHAN, N. H., AND C. Z. WEI (1986): "Limiting Distributions of Least Squares Estimates of Unstable Autoregressive Processes," manuscript, University of Maryland.

DAVIDSON, J. E. H., D. F. HENDRY, F. SRBA, AND S. YEO (1978): "Econometric Modelling of the Aggregate Time-Series Relationship Between Consumer's Expenditure and Income in the United Kingdom," *Economic Journal*, 8, 661-692.

DICKEY, D. A., AND W. A. FULLER (1979): "Distribution of the Estimators for Autoregressive Time Series With a Unit Root," *Journal of the American Statistical Association*, 74, 427-431.

DICKEY, D. A., D. P. HASZA, AND W. A. FULLER (1984): "Testing for Unit Roots in Seasonal Time Series," *Journal of the American Statistical Association*, 79, 355-367.

ENGLE, R. F., AND C. W. J. GRANGER (1987): "Co-Integration and Error-Correction: Representation, Estimation and Testing," *Econometrica*, 55, 251-276.

EVANS, G. B. A., AND N. E. SAVIN (1981a): "The Calculation of the Limiting Distribution of the Least Squares Estimator of the Parameter in a Random Walk Model," *Annals of Statistics*, 9 1114-1118.

——— (1981b): "Testing for Unit Roots: I," *Econometrica*, 49, 753-779.

——— (1984): "Testing for Unit Roots: II," *Econometrica*, 52, 1241-1260.

FULLER, W. A. (1976): *Introduction to Statistical Time Series*. New York: Wiley.

GRANGER, C. W. J. (1983): "Cointegrated Variables and Error—Correcting Models," University of California—San Diego Discussion Paper 83-13.

GRANGER, C. W. J., AND A. A. WEISS (1983): "Time Series Analysis of Error—Correcting Models," in *Studies in Econometrics, Time Series, and Multivariate Statistics*. New York: Academic Press, 255-278.

HAAVELMO, T. (1943): "The Statistical Implications of a System of Simultaneous Equations," *Econometrica*, 11, 1-12.

HALL, P., AND C. C. HEYDE (1980): *Martingale Limit Theory and its Application*. New York: Academic Press.

HENDRY, D. F., AND J. F. RICHARD (1983): "The Econometric Analysis of Economic Time Series," *International Statistical Review*, 51, 111-163.

KENDALL, M., AND A. STUART (1979): *The Advanced Theory of Statistics*, Vol. 2, Fourth edition. New York: MacMillan.

NELSON, C. R., AND C. I. PLOSSER (1982): "Trends and Random Walks in Macroeconomic Time Series: Some Evidence and Implications," *Journal of Monetary Economics*, 10, 139-162.

PHILLIPS, P. C. B., AND S. N. DURLAUF (1986): "Multiple Time Series Regression with Integrated Processes," *Review of Economic Studies*, 53, 473-496.

RAO, M. M. (1978): "Asymptotic Distribution of an Estimator of the Boundary Parameter of an Unstable Process," *Annals of Statistics*, 6, 615-629.

SALMON, M. (1982): "Error Correction Mechanisms," *Economic Journal*, 92, 615-629.

SOLO, V. (1984): "The Order of Differencing in ARMA Models," *Journal of the American Statistical Society*, 79, 916-921.

WHITE, J. S. (1958): "Limiting Distribution of the Serial Correlation Coefficient in the Explosive Case," *Annals of Mathematic Statistics*, 29, 1188-1197.

Part VII
Multivariate Models

[26]

Modeling Multiple Time Series With Applications

G. C. TIAO and G. E. P. BOX*

An approach to the modeling and analysis of multiple time series is proposed. Properties of a class of vector autoregressive moving average models are discussed. Modeling procedures consisting of tentative specification, estimation, and diagnostic checking are outlined and illustrated by three real examples.

KEY WORDS: Multiple time series; Vector autoregressive moving average models; Cross-correlations; Partial autoregression; Intervention analysis; Transfer function.

1. INTRODUCTION

Business, economic, engineering and environmental data are often collected in roughly equally spaced time intervals, for example, hour, week, month, or quarter. In many problems, such time series data may be available on several related variables of interest. Two of the reasons for analyzing and modeling such series jointly are

1. To understand the dynamic relationships among them. They may be contemporaneously related, one series may lead the others or there may be feedback relationships.
2. To improve accuracy of forecasts. When there is information on one series contained in the historical data of another, better forecasts can result when the series are modeled jointly.

Let

$$\{Z_{1t}\}, \ldots, \{Z_{kt}\}, \quad t = 0, \pm 1, \pm 2, \ldots \tag{1.1}$$

be k series taken in equally spaced time intervals. Writing

$$\mathbf{Z}_t = (Z_{1t}, \ldots, Z_{kt})', \tag{1.2}$$

we shall refer to the k series as a k-dimensional vector of multiple time series. Models that are of possible use in representing such multiple time series, considerations of their properties, and methods for relating them to actual data have been extensively discussed in the literature. See in particular Quenouille (1957), Whittle (1963), Hannan (1970), Zellner and Palm (1974), Brillinger (1975), Dunsmuir and Hannan (1976), Box and Haugh (1977), Granger and Newbold (1977), Parzen (1977), Wallis (1977), Chan and Wallis (1978), Deistler, Dunsmuir, and Hannan (1978), Hallin (1978), Jenkins (1979), Hsiao (1979), Akaike (1980), Hannan (1980), Hannan, Dunsmuir, and Deistler (1980), and Quinn (1980). There are, however, considerable divergences of view. The object of this article is to describe an approach to the modeling and analysis that we have developed over a considerable period of time and that we are finding effective. Our main emphasis will be on motivating, describing, and illustrating the various methods used in an iterative model building process. Much, if not all, of the underlying theory can be found in the references given and, therefore, will not be repeated. Section 2 presents a short review of the widely used univariate ($k = 1$) time series and transfer function models as developed in Box and Jenkins (1970). Section 3 discusses a class of vector autoregressive moving average models. Model building procedures are discussed in Section 4 and applied to two actual examples in Section 5. A comparison with some alternative approaches and some concluding remarks pertaining to the analysis of fitting results are given in Section 6.

2. UNIVARIATE TIME SERIES AND TRANSFER FUNCTION MODELS

When $k = 1$ we shall write $\mathbf{Z}_t = Z_t$ in (1.2). An important class of models for discrete univariate series originally proposed by Yule (1927) and Slutsky (1937) and developed by such authors as Bartlett, Kendall, Walker, Wold, and Yaglom are stochastic difference equations of the form

$$\phi_p(B)z_t = \theta_q(B)a_t, \tag{2.1}$$

where $\phi_p(B) = 1 - \phi_1 B - \cdots - \phi_p B^p$ and $\theta_q(B) = 1 - \theta_1 B - \cdots - \theta_q B^q$. In (2.1) the a_t's are independently identically and normally distributed random shocks (or white noise) with zero mean and variance σ^2; B is the back-shift operator such that $BZ_t = Z_{t-1}$; and $z_t = Z_t - \eta$ is the deviation of the observation Z_t from some convenient location η.

Relationships between k series $\{z_{1t}\}, \ldots, \{z_{kt}\}$ can sometimes be represented by linear *transfer function* models of the form

$$z_{ht} = \sum_{i \in k(h)} [\omega_{s_{hi}}(B)B^{b_{hi}}/\delta_{r_{hi}}(B)]\, z_{it} + [\theta_{q_h}(B)/\varphi_{p_h}(B)]\, a_{ht}, \quad (h = 1, 2, \ldots, k) \tag{2.2}$$

where $z_{0t} \equiv 0$, $k(h)$ is the set $(1, \ldots, h - 1)$; $\omega_{s_{hi}}(B)$, $\delta_{r_{hi}}(B)$, $\varphi_{p_h}(B)$, and $\theta_{q_h}(B)$ are polynomials in B;

* G.C. Tiao is Professor of Statistics and Business, and G.E.P. Box is Vilas Research Professor, Department of Statistics, University of Wisconsin, Madison, WI 53706. The authors are grateful to W.R. Bell, I. Chang, M.R. Grupe, G.B. Hudak, and R.S. Tsay for computing assistance. This research was partially supported by the U.S. Bureau of the Census under JSA 80-10, the Army Research Office, Durham, NC under Grant No. DAAG29-78-G00166, and the Alcoa Foundation.

December 1981, Volume 76, Number 376
Theory and Methods Section

the b_{hi}'s are nonnegative integers; and $\{a_{1t}\}, \ldots, \{a_{kt}\}$ are k independent Gaussian white-noise processes with zero means and variances $\sigma_1^2, \ldots, \sigma_k^2$. In particular, intervention models of this form with one or more of the z_h's indicator variables have proved useful (Box and Tiao 1975; Abraham 1980).

Transfer function models of the form (2.2), however, assume that the series, when suitably arranged, possess a triangular relationship, implying for example that z_1 depends only on its own past; z_2 depends on its own past and on the present and past of z_1; z_3 on its own past and on the present and past of z_2 and z_1; and so on. On the other hand, if z_1 depends on the past of z_2, and also z_2 depends on the past of z_1, then we must have a model that allows for this *feedback*.

3. MULTIPLE STOCHASTIC DIFFERENCE EQUATION MODELS

3.1 The Vector ARMA Model

A useful class of models obtained by direct generalization of the Yule-Slutsky ARMA models that allow for feedback relationships among the k series is obtained from (2.2) by letting $k(h)$ be the set $(1, \ldots, k)$ excluding h. These models can be alternatively expressed as the vector autoregressive moving average ARMA models (Quenouille 1957),

$$\boldsymbol{\varphi}_p(B)\mathbf{z}_t = \boldsymbol{\theta}_q(B)\mathbf{a}_t, \qquad (3.1)$$

where

$$\boldsymbol{\varphi}_p(B) = \mathbf{I} - \boldsymbol{\varphi}_1 B - \ldots - \boldsymbol{\varphi}_p B^p,$$

$$\boldsymbol{\theta}_q(B) = \mathbf{I} - \boldsymbol{\theta}_1 B - \ldots - \boldsymbol{\theta}_q B^q$$

are matrix polynomials in B, the $\boldsymbol{\varphi}$'s and $\boldsymbol{\theta}$'s are $k \times k$ matrices, $\mathbf{z}_t = \mathbf{Z}_t - \boldsymbol{\eta}$ is the vector of deviations from some origin $\boldsymbol{\eta}$ that is the mean if the series is stationary, and $\{\mathbf{a}_t\}$ with $\mathbf{a}_t = (a_{1t}, \ldots, a_{kt})'$ is a sequence of random shock vectors identically independently and normally distributed with zero mean and covariance matrix $\boldsymbol{\Sigma}$. We shall suppose that the zeros of the determinantal polynomials $|\boldsymbol{\varphi}_p(B)|$ and $|\boldsymbol{\theta}_q(B)|$ are on or outside the unit circle. The series $\mathbf{z}_t$ will be stationary when the zeros of $|\boldsymbol{\varphi}_p(B)|$ are all outside the unit circle, and will be invertible when those of $|\boldsymbol{\theta}_q(B)|$ are all outside the unit circle. Properties of such models have been discussed by, for example, Hannan (1970), Anderson (1971), and Granger and Newbold (1977).

Some Simple Examples. To illustrate the behavior of observations from these models, Figure 1 shows two series with 250 observations generated from the bivariate ($k = 2$) first order moving average [MA(1)] model, $\mathbf{z}_t = (\mathbf{I} - \boldsymbol{\theta}B)\mathbf{a}_t$, with

$$\boldsymbol{\theta} = \begin{bmatrix} .2 & .3 \\ -.6 & 1.1 \end{bmatrix} \quad \text{and} \quad \boldsymbol{\Sigma} = \begin{bmatrix} 4 & 1 \\ 1 & 1 \end{bmatrix}. \qquad (3.2)$$

Figure 2 shows two series with 150 observations generated from the bivariate first order autoregressive [AR(1)] model, $(\mathbf{I} - \boldsymbol{\varphi}B)\mathbf{z}_t = \mathbf{a}_t$, with

Figure 1. Data Generated From a Bivariate MA(1) Model With Parameter Values in (3.2)

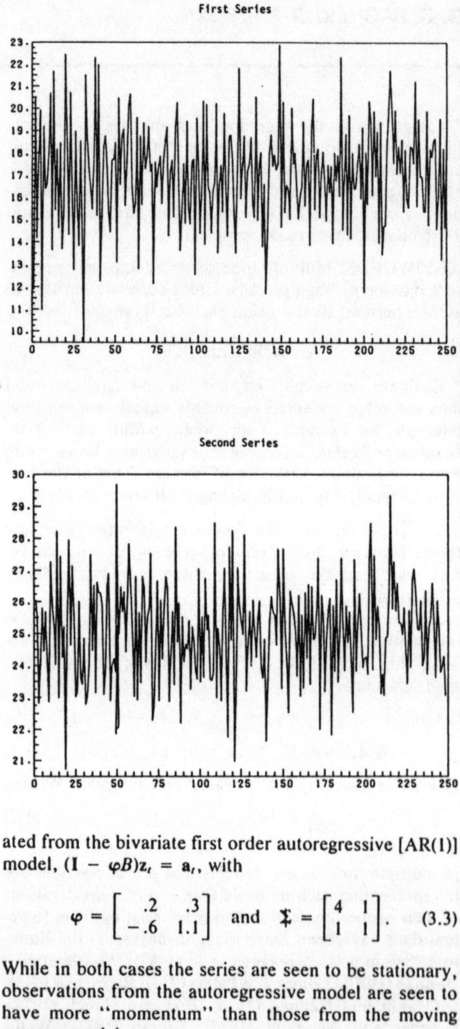

$$\boldsymbol{\varphi} = \begin{bmatrix} .2 & .3 \\ -.6 & 1.1 \end{bmatrix} \quad \text{and} \quad \boldsymbol{\Sigma} = \begin{bmatrix} 4 & 1 \\ 1 & 1 \end{bmatrix}. \qquad (3.3)$$

While in both cases the series are seen to be stationary, observations from the autoregressive model are seen to have more "momentum" than those from the moving average model.

In practice, time series often exhibit nonstationary behavior. When several such series are considered jointly, nonstationarity may be modeled by allowing the zeros of $|\boldsymbol{\varphi}(B)|$ in (3.1) to lie on the unit circle. A particular example is the model $(1 - B)\mathbf{z}_t = (\mathbf{I} - \boldsymbol{\theta}B)\mathbf{a}_t$, that is, after differencing each series we obtain a vector MA(1) model. This is a vector analog of the commonly used univariate nonstationary model $(1 - B)z_t = (1 - \theta B)a_t$. However,

Figure 2. Data Gerterated From a Bivariate AR(1) Model With Parameter Values in (3.3)

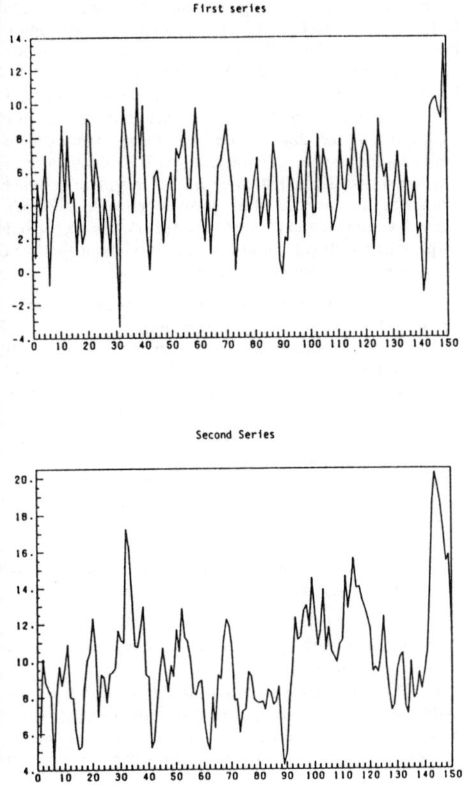

it should be noted here that for vector time series, linear combinations of the elements of $\mathbf{z}_t$ may often be stationary, and simultaneous differencing of all series can lead to unnecessary complications in model fitting. See, for example, the discussion in Box and Tiao (1977) and Hillmer and Tiao (1979).

Tranfer Function Model. For the vector model in (3.1), in general, all elements of $\mathbf{z}_t$ are related to all elements of $\mathbf{z}_{t-j}$ ($j = 1, 2, \ldots$) and there can be feedback relationships between all the series. However, if the $\mathbf{z}_t$'s can be arranged so that the coefficient matrices $\boldsymbol{\varphi}$'s and $\boldsymbol{\theta}$'s are all lower triangular, then (3.1) can be written as a transfer function model of the form (2.2). More generally, if the $\boldsymbol{\varphi}$'s and $\boldsymbol{\theta}$'s are all lower block triangular, then we obtain a generalization of the transfer function form of (2.2) in which both the input vector series and the output vector series are allowed to have feedback relationships. Furthermore, relationships between the vector transfer function model and the econometric linear simultaneous equation model have been discussed in Zellner and Palm (1974) and Wallis (1977).

3.2 Cross-Covariance and Cross-Correlation Matrices

For a stationary vector time series $\{\mathbf{Z}_t\}$ with mean vector $\boldsymbol{\eta}$, let $\boldsymbol{\Gamma}(l)$ be the lag l cross-covariance matrix

$$\begin{aligned}\boldsymbol{\Gamma}(l) &= E(\mathbf{z}_{t-l}\mathbf{z}'_t) \\ &= \{\gamma_{ij}(l)\}, \quad l = 0, \pm 1, \pm 2, \ldots \\ &\qquad\qquad i, j = 1, \ldots, k\end{aligned} \tag{3.4}$$

and let $\boldsymbol{\rho}(l) = \{\rho_{ij}(l)\}$ be the corresponding cross-correlation matrix.

When the vector ARMA model in (3.1) is stationary, it is well known that

$$\boldsymbol{\Gamma}(l) = \begin{cases} \sum_{j=l-r}^{l-1} \boldsymbol{\Gamma}(j)\boldsymbol{\varphi}'_{l-j} - \sum_{j=0}^{r-l} \boldsymbol{\psi}_j \boldsymbol{\Sigma} \boldsymbol{\theta}'_{j+l}, & l = 0, \ldots, r \\ \sum_{j=1}^{r} \boldsymbol{\Gamma}(l-j)\boldsymbol{\varphi}_j', & l > r, \end{cases} \tag{3.5}$$

where the $\boldsymbol{\psi}_j$'s are obtained from the relationship

$$\boldsymbol{\psi}(B) = \boldsymbol{\varphi}^{-1}(B)\boldsymbol{\theta}(B) = (\mathbf{I} + \boldsymbol{\psi}_1 B + \cdots),$$

$\boldsymbol{\theta}_0 = -\mathbf{I}$, $r = \max(p, q)$, and it is understood that (a) if $p < q$, $\boldsymbol{\varphi}_{p+1} = \cdots = \boldsymbol{\varphi}_r = \mathbf{0}$, and (b) if $q < p$, $\boldsymbol{\theta}_{q+1} = \cdots = \boldsymbol{\theta}_r = \mathbf{0}$.

In particular, when $p = 0$, that is, we have a vector MA(q) model, then

$$\boldsymbol{\Gamma}(l) = \begin{cases} \sum_{j=0}^{q-l} \boldsymbol{\theta}_j \boldsymbol{\Sigma} \boldsymbol{\theta}'_{j+l}, & l = 0, \ldots, q \\ \mathbf{0} & l > q. \end{cases} \tag{3.6}$$

Thus, all auto- and cross-correlations are zero when $l > q$. On the other hand, for a vector autoregressive model the auto- and cross-correlations in general will decay gradually to zero as $|l|$ increases.

3.3 A Determinantal Criterion for ARMA Models and the Partial Autoregression Matrices

From the moment equations in (3.5) for a stationary ARMA (p, q) model, we see that the autocovariance matrices $\boldsymbol{\Gamma}(l)$'s and the autoregressive coefficient matrices $\boldsymbol{\varphi}_1, \ldots, \boldsymbol{\varphi}_p$ are related as follows:

$$\begin{bmatrix} \mathbf{A}(p, m) & \mathbf{b}(p, m) \\ \mathbf{g}'(p, m) & \boldsymbol{\Gamma}(m) \end{bmatrix} \begin{bmatrix} \boldsymbol{\Phi}_{p-1} \\ \boldsymbol{\varphi}'_p \end{bmatrix} = \begin{bmatrix} \mathbf{c}(p, m) \\ \boldsymbol{\Gamma}(p + m) \end{bmatrix}, \quad m = q, q + 1, \ldots, \tag{3.7}$$

where

$$\mathbf{A}(p, m) = \begin{bmatrix} \Gamma(m) & \Gamma(m-1) & \cdots & \Gamma(m-p+2) \\ \Gamma(m+1) & \ddots & & \vdots \\ \vdots & & \ddots & \vdots \\ \vdots & & & \Gamma(m-1) \\ \Gamma(m+p-2) & \cdots & \Gamma(m+1) & \Gamma(m) \end{bmatrix},$$

$$\mathbf{b}(p, m) = \begin{bmatrix} \Gamma(m-p+1) \\ \vdots \\ \Gamma(m-1) \end{bmatrix},$$

$$\mathbf{c}(p, m) = \begin{bmatrix} \Gamma(m+1) \\ \vdots \\ \Gamma(m+p-1) \end{bmatrix},$$

$\mathbf{g}'(p, m) = [\Gamma(m + p - 1), \ldots, \Gamma(m + 1)]$, and $\mathbf{\Phi}'_{p-1} = [\varphi_1, \ldots, \varphi_{p-1}]$. Consider now the $k \times k$ matrix

$$\mathbf{D}(l, m) = [d_{ij}(l, m)] \qquad \begin{matrix} l = 1, 2, \ldots \\ m = 0, 1, \ldots, \end{matrix} \tag{3.8}$$

where $d_{ij}(l, m)$ is the determinant

$$d_{ij}(l, m) = \det \begin{bmatrix} \mathbf{A}(l, m) & \mathbf{c}_j(l, m) \\ \mathbf{g}'_i(l, m) & \gamma_{ij}(l + m) \end{bmatrix}, \qquad i, j = 1, \ldots, k$$

$\mathbf{c}_j(l, m)$ is the jth column of $\mathbf{c}(l, m)$, $\mathbf{g}'_i(l, m)$ is the ith row of $\mathbf{g}'(l, m)$, and $\gamma_{ij}(l + m)$ is the (i, j)th element of $\Gamma(l + m)$. It follows from (3.7) that for an ARMA (p, q) model

$$\mathbf{D}(l, m) = \mathbf{0} \quad \text{for} \quad l > p \quad \text{and} \quad m \geq q. \tag{3.9}$$

This provides a multivariate generalization of the results in Gray, Kelley, and McIntire (1978) for univariate ARMA models.

In the special case $m = q = 0$, (3.7) is a multivariate generalization of the Yule-Walker equations for autoregressive models in univariate time series. Analogous to the partial autocorrelation function for the univariate case, we may define a *partial autoregression matrix function* $\underset{\sim}{\mathcal{P}}(l)$ having the property that if the model is AR(p), then

$$\underset{\sim}{\mathcal{P}}(l) = \begin{cases} \varphi_l, & l = p \\ \mathbf{0}, & l > p \end{cases}. \tag{3.10}$$

From (3.7), we define $\underset{\sim}{\mathcal{P}}(l)$ as

$$\underset{\sim}{\mathcal{P}}'(l) = \begin{cases} \Gamma^{-1}(0)\Gamma(1), \; l = 1 \\ [\Gamma(0) - \mathbf{b}'(l, 0)\mathbf{A}^{-1}(l, 0)\mathbf{b}(l, 0)]^{-1} \\ [\Gamma(l) - \mathbf{b}'(l, 0)\mathbf{A}^{-1}(l, 0)\mathbf{c}(l, 0)], \; l > 1. \end{cases} \tag{3.11}$$

4. MODEL BUILDING STRATEGY FOR MULTIPLE TIME SERIES

The models in (3.1) contain a dauntingly large number $\{k^2(p + q) + \frac{1}{2}k(k + 1)\}$ of parameters, complicating methods for model building. It is natural that attempts have been made to simplify the general form in the model building process, for example by Granger and Newbold (1977) and Wallis (1977). While we sympathize with this aspiration, we feel that so far at least these attempts have not been successful. In some comparisons made later in Section 6, we argue that they do not result in genuine simplification, nor do they provide feasible methods when k is greater than 2 or 3. We see no alternative but to provide for direct initial fitting of models of the form (3.1). It must, however, be added

1. that often models of rather low order (p and q small) provide adequate approximation,
2. that occasionally knowledge of the system might allow simplification a priori, although even here prudent checking of the adequacy of the simplifcation would be necessary (see Zellner and Palm 1974),
3. that considerable simplification is almost invariably possible after an initial model has been fitted,
4. that 2 and 3 imply that provision should be made to allow models to be fitted in which certain parameters are fixed or constrained in some other way,
5. that other methods of seeking simplifications, for example principal component analysis or canonical analysis (see Box and Tiao 1977), will often prove effective.

In brief, we feel that although the full form (3.1) needs to be fitted initially, subsequent iterations will usually lead to simplification.

In what follows we sketch an iterative approach consisting of (a) tentative specification (identification), (b) estimation, and (c) diagnostic checking for the vector ARMA models in (3.1). A computer package to carry out this analysis has been completed (Tiao et al. 1979) consisting of three main programs: (a) Preliminary Analysis, (b) Stepwise Autoregression, and (c) Estimation and Forecasting.

4.1 Tentative Specification

The aim here is to employ statistics (a) that can be readily calculated from the data and (b) that facilitate the choice of subclass of models worthy of further examination.

Sample Cross-Correlations. The sample cross-correlations $\hat{\rho}_{ij}(l)$,

$$\hat{\rho}_{ij}(l) = \sum(Z_{it} - \bar{Z}_i)(Z_{j(t+l)} - \bar{Z}_j) / \{\sum(Z_{it} - \bar{Z}_i)^2 \sum(Z_{jt} - \bar{Z}_j)^2\}^{1/2}$$

where $\bar{Z}_i$ is the sample mean of the ith component series of $\mathbf{Z}_t$, are particularly useful in spotting low order vector moving average models, since from (3.6) $\rho_{ij}(l) = 0$ for $l > q$.

For the data shown in Figure 1, which were generated from a bivariate MA(1) model, Figures 3(a)–(c) show, respectively, the sample autocorrelations $\hat{\rho}_{11}(l)$ and $\hat{\rho}_{22}(l)$, and the sample cross-correlations $\hat{\rho}_{12}(l)$. The large values occurring at $|l| = 1$ would lead to tentative specification of the model as an MA(1). However, graphs of this kind become increasingly cumbersome as the number of series is increased. Furthermore, identification is not easy from a listing of sample cross-correlation matrices $\hat{\rho}(l)$ like that in Table 1(a), particularly when k is greater than 4 or 5.

In this circumstance, we have found the following simple device of great practical value. Instead of the numerical values, a plus sign is used to indicate a value greater than $2n^{-1/2}$, a minus sign a value less than $-2n^{-1/2}$, and a dot to indicate a value inbetween $-2n^{-1/2}$ and $2n^{-1/2}$. The motivation is that if the series were white noise, for large n the $\hat{\rho}_{ij}(l)$'s would be normally distributed with mean 0 and variance n^{-1}. The symbols can be arranged either as in Table 1(b) or as in Table 1(c). We realize that the variances of the $\hat{\rho}_{ij}(l)$'s can be considerably greater than $n^{-1/2}$ when the series are highly autocorrelated, so that these indicator symbols, if taken literally, can lead to overparameterization. However, we do not interpret these indicator symbols in the sense of a formal significance test, but as a rather crude "signal-to-noise ratio" guide. Taken together they can give useful and assimilable indicators of the general correlation pattern.

Table 2 shows sample cross-correlation matrices in terms of these indicator symbols for the series in Figure 2 generated from an AR(1) model. The persistence of large correlations suggests the possibility of autoregressive behavior. In general, the pattern of indicator symbols for the cross-correlation matrices makes it very easy to identify a low order moving average model.

Figure 3. Sample Auto- and Cross-Correlations for the Data in Figure 1

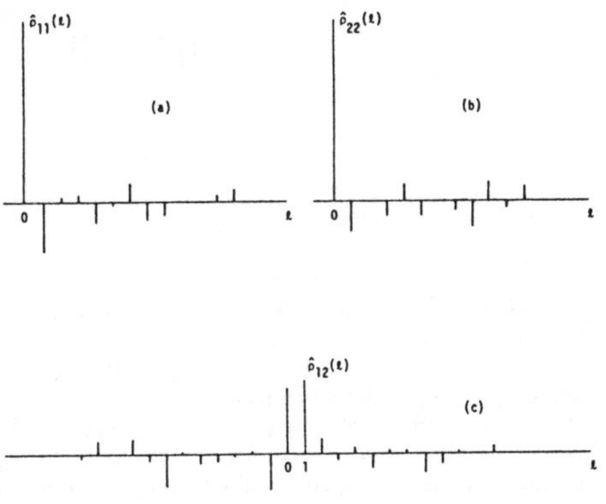

Sample Partial Autoregression and Related Summary Statistics. For an AR(p) process, the partial autoregression matrices $\mathcal{P}(l)$ in (3.11) are zero for $l > p$. They are therefore particularly useful for identifying an autoregressive model. Estimates of $\mathcal{P}(l)$ and their standard er-

Table 1. Cross-Correlations Matrices $\hat{\rho}$ (l) for the Data in Figure 1

(a) *Sample cross-correlation matrices $\hat{\rho}(l)$ for the data in Figure 1*

Lag 1-6

$$\begin{bmatrix} -.28 & .37 \\ -.21 & -.19 \end{bmatrix} \begin{bmatrix} .03 & .08 \\ .02 & .01 \end{bmatrix} \begin{bmatrix} .04 & -.03 \\ -.01 & -.08 \end{bmatrix} \begin{bmatrix} -.11 & .04 \\ -.03 & .09 \end{bmatrix} \begin{bmatrix} -.02 & -.09 \\ -.02 & -.08 \end{bmatrix} \begin{bmatrix} .10 & .01 \\ .01 & -.00 \end{bmatrix}$$

Lag 7-12

$$\begin{bmatrix} -.11 & .01 \\ -.17 & -.06 \end{bmatrix} \begin{bmatrix} -.09 & -.12 \\ -.03 & -.16 \end{bmatrix} \begin{bmatrix} .01 & -.06 \\ .08 & .10 \end{bmatrix} \begin{bmatrix} -.00 & .02 \\ .01 & -.04 \end{bmatrix} \begin{bmatrix} .03 & .00 \\ .08 & .08 \end{bmatrix} \begin{bmatrix} .06 & .04 \\ -.01 & .01 \end{bmatrix}$$

(b) $\hat{\rho}(l)$ in term of indicator symbols

Lag 1-6

$$\begin{bmatrix} - & + \\ - & - \end{bmatrix} \begin{bmatrix} \cdot & \cdot \\ \cdot & \cdot \end{bmatrix} \begin{bmatrix} \cdot & \cdot \\ \cdot & \cdot \end{bmatrix} \begin{bmatrix} \cdot & \cdot \\ \cdot & \cdot \end{bmatrix} \begin{bmatrix} \cdot & \cdot \\ \cdot & \cdot \end{bmatrix} \begin{bmatrix} \cdot & \cdot \\ \cdot & \cdot \end{bmatrix}$$

Lag 7-12

$$\begin{bmatrix} \cdot & \cdot \\ - & \cdot \end{bmatrix} \begin{bmatrix} \cdot & \cdot \\ \cdot & - \end{bmatrix} \begin{bmatrix} \cdot & \cdot \\ \cdot & \cdot \end{bmatrix} \begin{bmatrix} \cdot & \cdot \\ \cdot & \cdot \end{bmatrix} \begin{bmatrix} \cdot & \cdot \\ \cdot & \cdot \end{bmatrix} \begin{bmatrix} \cdot & \cdot \\ \cdot & \cdot \end{bmatrix}$$

(c) Pattern of correlations for each element in the matrix over all lags

	z_1	z_2
z_1	-	+ . . . .
z_2	- . . . . . -	- . . . . . . - . . . .

Table 2. Sample Cross-Correlation Matrices $\hat{\boldsymbol{\rho}}(l)$ for the Data in Figure 2 in Terms of Indicator Symbols

Lag 1-6

$$\begin{bmatrix} + & \cdot \\ + & + \end{bmatrix}\begin{bmatrix} \cdot & \cdot \\ + & + \end{bmatrix}\begin{bmatrix} \cdot & \cdot \\ + & + \end{bmatrix}\begin{bmatrix} \cdot & - \\ + & + \end{bmatrix}\begin{bmatrix} \cdot & \cdot \\ + & + \end{bmatrix}\begin{bmatrix} \cdot & \cdot \\ + & \cdot \end{bmatrix}$$

Lag 7-12

$$\begin{bmatrix} - & - \\ \cdot & \cdot \end{bmatrix}\begin{bmatrix} - & \cdot \\ \cdot & \cdot \end{bmatrix}\begin{bmatrix} \cdot & \cdot \\ \cdot & \cdot \end{bmatrix}\begin{bmatrix} \cdot & \cdot \\ \cdot & \cdot \end{bmatrix}\begin{bmatrix} \cdot & \cdot \\ \cdot & \cdot \end{bmatrix}\begin{bmatrix} \cdot & \cdot \\ \cdot & \cdot \end{bmatrix}$$

rors can be obtained by fitting autoregressive models of successively high order $l = 1, 2, \ldots$ by standard multivariate least squares.

It is well known (see, e.g., Anderson 1971) that for a stationary AR(p) model asymptotically the estimates $\boldsymbol{\varphi}'_1, \ldots, \boldsymbol{\varphi}'_p$ are jointly normally distributed. A useful summary of the pattern of the partials is obtained by listing indicator symbols, assigning a plus (minus) sign when a coefficient in $\hat{\boldsymbol{\Phi}}(l)$ is greater (less) than 2 (−2) times its estimated standard errors, and a dot for values in between.

To help tentatively determine the order of an autoregressive model, we may also employ the likelihood ratio statistics corresponding to testing the null hypotheses $\boldsymbol{\varphi}_l = \mathbf{0}$ against the alternative $\boldsymbol{\varphi}_l \neq \mathbf{0}$ when an AR(l) model is fitted. Let

$$\mathbf{S}(l) = \sum_{t=l+1}^{n} (\mathbf{z}_t - \hat{\boldsymbol{\varphi}}_1\mathbf{z}_{t-1} - \ldots - \hat{\boldsymbol{\varphi}}_l\mathbf{z}_{t-l}) \times (\mathbf{z}_t - \hat{\boldsymbol{\varphi}}_1\mathbf{z}_{t-1} - \ldots - \hat{\boldsymbol{\varphi}}_l\mathbf{z}_{t-l})' \tag{4.1}$$

Table 3. Indicator Symbols for Partial Autoregression and Related Statistics for Data in Figure 2

Lag l	Indicator symbols	$M(l)^{a}$ $\dot{\sim}\ \chi^2_4$	Diagonal elements of $\hat{\boldsymbol{\Sigma}}$
1	$\begin{matrix} \cdot & + \\ - & + \end{matrix}$	356.96	5.30 1.08
2	$\begin{matrix} \cdot & \cdot \\ \cdot & + \end{matrix}$	7.04	5.16 1.03
3	$\begin{matrix} \cdot & \cdot \\ \cdot & \cdot \end{matrix}$	2.63	5.07 1.03
4	$\begin{matrix} \cdot & \cdot \\ \cdot & \cdot \end{matrix}$	4.38	5.01 1.02
5	$\begin{matrix} \cdot & \cdot \\ \cdot & \cdot \end{matrix}$	2.42	4.95 1.01

[a] $\dot{\sim}$ means approximately distributed as.

be the matrix of residual sum of squares and cross products after fitting an AR(l). The likelihood ratio statistic is the ratio of the determinants

$$U = |\mathbf{S}(l)| / |\mathbf{S}(l-1)|. \tag{4.2}$$

Using Bartlett's (1938) approximation, the statistic

$$M(l) = -(N - \tfrac{1}{2} - l \cdot k)\log_e U \tag{4.3}$$

is, on the null hypothesis, asymptotically distributed as χ^2 with k^2 degrees of freedom, where $N = n - p - 1$ is the effective number of observations, assuming that a constant term is included in the model.

Finally, a measure of the extent to which the fit is improved as the order is increased is provided by the diagonal elements of the residual covariance matrices $\hat{\boldsymbol{\Sigma}}$ corresponding to the successive AR models.

For illustration, the matrices of summary symbols, the $M(l)$ statistics, and the diagonal elements of the residual covariance matrices for the series in Figure 2 are shown in Table 3 for $l = 1, \ldots, 5$. They indicate that an AR(1) or at most an AR(2) would be adequate for the data.

For the series shown in Figure 1, the pattern of the partials and related statistics are given in Table 4. Notice here that if we had confined attention to autoregressive models as is advocated in Parzen (1977), we would have needed p to be as high as 7. This is not surprising since with the MA(1) model of (3.2) written in the autoregressive form $\mathbf{z}_t = \boldsymbol{\pi}_1\mathbf{z}_{t-1} + \boldsymbol{\pi}_2\mathbf{z}_{t-2} + \ldots + \mathbf{a}_t$, we find

$$\boldsymbol{\pi}_1 = \begin{bmatrix} -.2 & -.3 \\ .6 & -1.1 \end{bmatrix}, \quad \boldsymbol{\pi}_2 = \begin{bmatrix} .14 & -.39 \\ .78 & -1.03 \end{bmatrix}, \ldots, \quad \boldsymbol{\pi}_6 = \begin{bmatrix} .23 & -.25 \\ .49 & -.51 \end{bmatrix}, \tag{4.4}$$

$$|\boldsymbol{\pi}_1| = .4, \quad |\boldsymbol{\pi}_2| = .16, \quad \ldots, \quad |\boldsymbol{\pi}_6| = .0041.$$

Thus, although the determinants $|\boldsymbol{\pi}_j|$ decrease rapidly towards zero as j increases, the elements of $\boldsymbol{\pi}_j$ converge to zero very slowly so that many autoregressive terms would be needed to provide an adequate approximation.

In general, the pattern of the partial autoregression matrices, the $M(l)$ statistic, and the diagonal elements of the residual covariance matrix are useful to distinguish between moving average and low order autoregressive models and to select tentatively the appropriate order for the latter.

808 Journal of the American Statistical Association, December 1981

Table 4. Pattern of Partial Autoregression and Related Statistics for Data in Figure 1

Lag	Pattern of $\hat{\mathscr{P}}(l)$	$M(l) \overset{a}{\sim} \chi_4^2$	‡
1	$\begin{bmatrix} - & - \\ + & - \end{bmatrix}$	123.2	4.78 1.88
2	$\begin{bmatrix} \cdot & \cdot \\ + & - \end{bmatrix}$	75.9	4.75 1.43
3	$\begin{bmatrix} + & \cdot \\ + & - \end{bmatrix}$	35.2	4.63 1.23
4	$\begin{bmatrix} \cdot & \cdot \\ + & \cdot \end{bmatrix}$	27.5	4.63 1.08
5	$\begin{bmatrix} \cdot & \cdot \\ + & \cdot \end{bmatrix}$	16.6	4.61 1.04
6	$\begin{bmatrix} \cdot & \cdot \\ + & \cdot \end{bmatrix}$	13.5	4.53 .98
7	$\begin{bmatrix} \cdot & - \\ + & \cdot \end{bmatrix}$	16.5	4.38 .94
8	$\begin{bmatrix} \cdot & \cdot \\ \cdot & - \end{bmatrix}$	8.1	4.31 .91

Sample Residual Cross-Correlation Matrices After AR Fit. After each AR(l) fit, $l = 1, \ldots, p$, cross-correlation matrices of the residuals $\hat{\mathbf{a}}_t$'s may be readily obtained. Table 5 shows indicator symbols for residual correlations after fitting AR(1) and AR(2) to the AR data plotted in Figure 2. Again a plus sign is used to indicate values greater than $2n^{-1/2}$, a minus sign for values less than $-2n^{-1/2}$, and a dot for in-between values. They verify that there is no need to go beyond an AR(2) model.

It is perhaps worth emphasizing here again that these indicator symbols are proposed as a rough preliminary device to help arrive at an initial model. They should not be treated as "exact significance testing." In a recent paper by Li and McLeod (1980), expressions have been obtained for the asymptotic distributions of the residual autocorrelations. As in the univariate case, the low order autocorrelations have variance considerably less than $n^{-1/2}$.

For mixed vector autoregressive moving average models in general, however, both the population cross-correlation matrices $\boldsymbol{\rho}(l)$ and the partial autoregression matrices $\mathscr{P}(l)$ decay only gradually toward $\mathbf{0}$. In some situations, the order of mixed models may be tentatively identified by inspection of patterns in residual cross-correlations after the AR fit, but in others study of residual correlations could be misleading. For illustration, consider the case of a stationary ARMA(1, 1) model

$$(\mathbf{I} - \varphi B)\mathbf{z}_t = (\mathbf{I} - \theta B)\mathbf{a}_t. \tag{4.5}$$

If an AR(1) model is fitted to $\{\mathbf{z}_t\}$, then the estimate $\hat{\varphi}$ will be biased. In fact, asymptotically $\hat{\varphi}$ converges in probability to

$$\hat{\varphi} \rightarrow \varphi_0 = \boldsymbol{\Gamma}'(1)\boldsymbol{\Gamma}(0)^{-1}. \tag{4.6}$$

Thus the residuals $\hat{\mathbf{a}}_t = \mathbf{z}_t - \varphi_0\mathbf{z}_{t-1}$ approximately follow the model

$$\hat{\mathbf{a}}_t = (\mathbf{i} - \varphi_0 B)(\mathbf{I} - \varphi B)^{-1}(\mathbf{I} - \theta B)\mathbf{a}_t. \tag{4.7}$$

Table 5. Indicator Symbols for Residual Cross Correlations for the AR (1) Data of Figure 2

AR (1) Lag 1-6	$\begin{bmatrix} \cdot & \cdot \\ \cdot & - \end{bmatrix}$	$\begin{bmatrix} \cdot & \cdot \\ \cdot & \cdot \end{bmatrix}$	$\begin{bmatrix} \cdot & \cdot \\ \cdot & \cdot \end{bmatrix}$	$\begin{bmatrix} \cdot & \cdot \\ \cdot & \cdot \end{bmatrix}$	$\begin{bmatrix} \cdot & \cdot \\ \cdot & \cdot \end{bmatrix}$	$\begin{bmatrix} + & \cdot \\ \cdot & \cdot \end{bmatrix}$
Lag 7-12	$\begin{bmatrix} - & \cdot \\ - & \cdot \end{bmatrix}$	$\begin{bmatrix} \cdot & \cdot \\ \cdot & \cdot \end{bmatrix}$	$\begin{bmatrix} \cdot & \cdot \\ \cdot & \cdot \end{bmatrix}$	$\begin{bmatrix} \cdot & \cdot \\ \cdot & \cdot \end{bmatrix}$	$\begin{bmatrix} \cdot & \cdot \\ \cdot & \cdot \end{bmatrix}$	$\begin{bmatrix} \cdot & \cdot \\ \cdot & \cdot \end{bmatrix}$
AR (2) Lag 1-6	$\begin{bmatrix} \cdot & \cdot \\ \cdot & \cdot \end{bmatrix}$	$\begin{bmatrix} \cdot & \cdot \\ \cdot & \cdot \end{bmatrix}$	$\begin{bmatrix} \cdot & \cdot \\ \cdot & \cdot \end{bmatrix}$	$\begin{bmatrix} \cdot & \cdot \\ \cdot & \cdot \end{bmatrix}$	$\begin{bmatrix} \cdot & \cdot \\ \cdot & \cdot \end{bmatrix}$	$\begin{bmatrix} + & \cdot \\ \cdot & \cdot \end{bmatrix}$
Lag 7-12	$\begin{bmatrix} \cdot & \cdot \\ \cdot & \cdot \end{bmatrix}$	$\begin{bmatrix} \cdot & \cdot \\ \cdot & \cdot \end{bmatrix}$	$\begin{bmatrix} \cdot & \cdot \\ \cdot & \cdot \end{bmatrix}$	$\begin{bmatrix} \cdot & \cdot \\ \cdot & \cdot \end{bmatrix}$	$\begin{bmatrix} \cdot & \cdot \\ \cdot & \cdot \end{bmatrix}$	$\begin{bmatrix} \cdot & \cdot \\ \cdot & \cdot \end{bmatrix}$

For $k = 1$, $\{\hat{a}_t\}$ follows an ARMA(1, 2) model so that the autocorrelations of $\hat{a}_t$ are

$$\rho_{\hat{a}}(j) = \varphi\rho_{\hat{a}}(j-1), j > 2 \tag{4.8}$$

and $\rho_{\hat{a}}(1)$ and $\rho_{\hat{a}}(2)$ are functions of φ and θ. Table 6 gives values of $\rho_{\hat{a}}(1)$ and $\rho_{\hat{a}}(2)$ for various combinations of values of φ and θ. For each combination, the first value is $\rho_{\hat{a}}(1)$ and the second $\rho_{\hat{a}}(2)$.

We see that if the true value of φ is large in magnitude, residual autocorrelations would lead to the choice of an MA(1) model for $\hat{a}_t$ and therefore the correct identification. For intermediate values of φ, a moving average of order 2 or higher might be selected, resulting in overparametrization.

In Gray, Kelley, and McIntire (1978) and Beguin, Gourieroux, and Monfort (1980), methods have been proposed to determine the order of univariate ARMA model. These methods are essentially equivalent to estimating, for $k = 1$, the determinant $D(l, m)$ in (3.8) using sample estimates of the autocovariances and selecting the orders of autoregressive and moving average polynomials on the basis of the property in (3.9). We are currently studying sampling properties of estimates of appropriate functions of $\mathbf{D}(l, m)$ in the vector case.

4.2 Estimation

Once the order of the model in (3.1) has been tentatively selected, efficient estimates of the associated parameter matrices $\boldsymbol{\varphi} = (\boldsymbol{\varphi}_1, \ldots, \boldsymbol{\varphi}_p)$, $\boldsymbol{\theta} = (\boldsymbol{\theta}_1, \ldots, \boldsymbol{\theta}_q)$, and $\boldsymbol{\Sigma}$ are determined by maximizing the likelihood function. Approximate standard errors and correlation matrix of the estimates of elements of the $\boldsymbol{\varphi}_j$'s and $\boldsymbol{\theta}_j$'s can also be obtained.

Conditional Likelihood. For the ARMA (p, q) model, we can write

$$\mathbf{a}_t = \mathbf{z}_t - \boldsymbol{\varphi}_1\mathbf{z}_{t-1} - \cdots - \boldsymbol{\varphi}_p\mathbf{z}_{t-p} + \boldsymbol{\theta}_1\mathbf{a}_{t-1} + \cdots + \boldsymbol{\theta}_q\mathbf{a}_{t-q}. \tag{4.9}$$

As in the univariate case discussed in Box and Jenkins (1970), the likelihood function can be approximated by a "conditional" likelihood function as follows. The series is regarded as consisting of the $n - p$ vector observations $\mathbf{z}_{p+1}, \ldots, \mathbf{z}_n$. The likelihood function is then determined from $\mathbf{a}_{p+1}, \ldots, \mathbf{a}_n$, using the preliminary values $\mathbf{z}_1, \ldots, \mathbf{z}_p$ and conditional on zero values for $\mathbf{a}_p, \ldots, \mathbf{a}_{p-q-1}$. Thus, as shown in Wilson (1973),

$$l_c(\boldsymbol{\varphi}, \boldsymbol{\theta}, \boldsymbol{\Sigma} \mid \mathbf{z}) \propto |\boldsymbol{\Sigma}|^{-(n-p)/2}\exp\{-\tfrac{1}{2}\operatorname{tr}\boldsymbol{\Sigma}^{-1}\mathbf{S}(\boldsymbol{\varphi}, \boldsymbol{\theta})\}, \tag{4.10}$$

where $\mathbf{S}(\boldsymbol{\varphi}, \boldsymbol{\theta}) = \sum_{t=p+1}^{n} \mathbf{a}_t\mathbf{a}'_t$. Properties of the maximum likelihood estimates obtained from (4.10) have been discussed in Nicholls (1976, 1977) and Anderson (1980).

It has been shown in Hillmer and Tiao (1979) that this approximation can be seriously inadequate if n is not sufficiently large and one or more zeros of $|\boldsymbol{\theta}_q(B)|$ lie on or close to the unit circle. Specifically, this would lead to estimates of the moving average parameters with large bias.

Exact Likelihood Function. For univariate ARMA models, the exact likelihood function has been considered by Tiao and Ali (1971), Newbold (1974), Dent (1977), Ansley (1979), and others. For vector models, this function has been studied by Osborn (1977) for the pure moving average case and by Phadke and Kedem (1978), Nicholls and Hall (1979), and Hillmer and Tiao (1979). It takes the form

$$l(\boldsymbol{\varphi}, \boldsymbol{\theta}, \boldsymbol{\Sigma} \mid \mathbf{z}) \propto l_c(\boldsymbol{\varphi}, \boldsymbol{\theta}, \boldsymbol{\Sigma} \mid \mathbf{z})l_1(\boldsymbol{\varphi}, \boldsymbol{\theta}, \boldsymbol{\Sigma} \mid \mathbf{z}), \tag{4.11}$$

where l_1 depends (a) only on $\mathbf{z}_1, \ldots, \mathbf{z}_p$ if $q = 0$ and (b) on all the data vectors $\mathbf{z}_1, \ldots, \mathbf{z}_n$ if $q \neq 0$. Estimation algorithms have been developed and incorporated in our computer package for the vector MA(q) model. For the general ARMA(p, q) model, it has been shown that a close approximation to the exact likelihood can be obtained by considering the transformation

$$\mathbf{w}_t = (\mathbf{I} - \boldsymbol{\varphi}_1 B - \cdots - \boldsymbol{\varphi}_p B^p)\mathbf{z}_t$$

so that (4.12)

$$\mathbf{w}_t = \boldsymbol{\theta}_q(B)\mathbf{a}_t$$

and then applying the results for MA(q) to $\mathbf{w}_t$, $t = p + 1, \ldots, n$.

Because estimation of moving average parameters using the exact likelihood is rather slow, we presently employ the conditional method in the preliminary stages of iterative model building and switch to the exact method towards the end.

4.3 Diagnostic Checking

To guard against model misspecification and to search for directions of improvement, a detailed diagnostic analysis of the residual series $\{\hat{\mathbf{a}}_t\}$, where

$$\hat{\mathbf{a}}_t = \mathbf{z}_t - \hat{\boldsymbol{\varphi}}_1\mathbf{z}_{t-1} - \cdots - \hat{\boldsymbol{\varphi}}_p\mathbf{z}_{t-p} + \hat{\boldsymbol{\theta}}_1\hat{\mathbf{a}}_{t-1} + \cdots + \hat{\boldsymbol{\theta}}_q\hat{\mathbf{a}}_{t-q}, \tag{4.13}$$

is performed. Useful diagnostic checks include (a) plots of standardized residual series against time and/or other variables and (b) cross-correlation matrices of the resid-

Table 6. Asymptotic Values of $\rho_{\hat{a}}$ (1) and $\rho_{\hat{a}}$ (2)

φ \ θ	−.95	−.50	.50	.95
−.95	—	.265 .085	−.381 −.03	−.481 −.036
−.50	.049 −.222	—	−.223 −.201	−.321 −.267
.50	.321 −.267	.223 −.201	—	−.049 −.222
.95	.481 −.036	.381 −.03	−.265 .085	—

Table 7. Pattern of Sample Cross-Correlations for the SCC Data

	Z_1 Stocks	Z_2 Cars	Z_3 Commodities
Z_1 Stocks	+ + + + + + + + ...	− − − − − − − − − − − − − − − − − − − −	− − − − − − − − − − − − − − − − − − − −
Z_2 Cars	. . . . + + +	+ + + + + + + + + + + + + + + ...	+ + + + + + + + + + + + + + ...
Z_3 Commodities	− − − − − − − . . . . + + + + +	+ + + + + + + + + + + + + + + + + + . .	+ + + + + + + + + + + + + + + + + . . .

uals $\hat{\mathbf{a}}_t$. As before, the structures of the correlations are summarized by indicator symbols. Overall χ^2 tests based on the sample cross correlations of the residuals have been proposed in recent papers by Hosking (1980) and Li and McLeod (1980). However, as is noted in Box and Jenkins (1970), such overall tests are not substitutes for more detailed study of the correlation structure.

5. ANALYSES OF TWO EXAMPLES

We now apply the model building approach introduced in the preceding section to the following sets of data:

1. The Financial Time Ordinary Share Index, U.K. Car Production and the Financial Time Commodity Price Index: Quarterly Data 3/1952–4/1967, obtained from Coen, Gomme, and Kendall (1969). This will be referred to as the SCC data.
2. The Gas Furnace Data given in Box and Jenkins (1970).

5.1 The SCC Data

The three series are

Z_{1t}: Financial Time Ordinary Share Index
Z_{2t}: U.K. Car Production
Z_{3t}: Financial Time Commodity Price Index

The authors of the original study were interested in the possibility of predicting Z_{1t} from lagged values of Z_{2t} and Z_{3t} using a standard regression analysis in which Z_{1t} was treated as a dependent variable and $Z_{2(t-6)}$ and $Z_{3(t-7)}$ as regressors or independent variables. For a critical evaluation of this approach, see Box and Newbold (1970). Here we consider what structure is revealed by the present multiple time series analysis, in which the three series are jointly modeled.

Tentative Specification. We see in Table 7 that the original series show high and persistent auto- and cross-correlations. Examination of the partials and related statistics in Table 8 shows that for $l > 2$ most of the elements of $\underset{\sim}{\mathcal{P}}(l)$ are small compared with their estimated standard errors and the $M(l)$ statistic fails to show significant improvement. Table 9 shows that the pattern of the cross-correlations of the residuals after AR(2) is consonant with estimated white noise. However, note that there is one large residual correlation at lag 1 after the AR(1) fit, suggesting also the possibility of an ARMA(1, 1) model.

Estimation. Both an AR(2) and an ARMA(1, 1) model were fitted using the exact likelihood method* but results are given only for the ARMA(1, 1) model, which produced a marginally better representation. For this model,

$$(\mathbf{I} - \boldsymbol{\varphi}B)\mathbf{Z}_t = \boldsymbol{\theta}_0 + (\mathbf{I} - \boldsymbol{\theta}B)\mathbf{a}_t, \qquad (5.1)$$

where $\boldsymbol{\theta}_0$ is a vector of constants, Table 10 shows the initial unrestricted fit and also the fits for two simpler models obtained by setting to zero those coefficients whose estimates were small compared to their standard errors.

Diagnostic Checking. Table 11 suggests that the restricted ARMA(1, 1) model provides an adequate representation of the data.

Implication of the Model. The final model implies that the system is approximated by

$$(1 - .98B)Z_{1t} = a_{1t} \qquad (5.2a)$$

$$(1 - .93B)Z_{2t} = .2 + a_{2t} \qquad (5.2b)$$

$$(1 - .83B)Z_{3t} = 2.8 + .40a_{1(t-1)} + (1 + .41B)a_{3t}. \qquad (5.2c)$$

Upon substituting (5.2a) into (5.2c), we get

$$(1 - .83B)Z_{3t} = 2.8 + .40(1 - .98B)Z_{1(t-1)} + (1 + .41B)a_{3t}. \qquad (5.2d)$$

Thus all three series behave approximately as random walks with slightly correlated innovations. From the point of view of forecasting, (5.2d) is of some interest since it implies that ordinary share $Z_{1(t-1)}$ is a *leading indicator* at lag 1 for the commodity index Z_{3t}. Its effect is small, however, as can be seen for example by the improvement achieved over the corresponding best fitting univariate model, which was

$$(1 - .78B)Z_{3t} = 3.63 + (1 + .53B)a_t, \sigma^2 = .151 \qquad (5.3)$$

The residual variance of .151 from the univariate model is not much larger than the value .134 for a_{3t} obtained

* For this example, estimates from the conditional likelihood for the ARMA(1, 1) case are very close to the exact results.

Table 8. Partial Autoregression and Related Statistics: SCC Data

Lag	Indicator Symbols for Partials	M(l) Statistic $\stackrel{\sim}{\rightarrow} \chi_9^2$	Diagonal Elements of $\hat{\Sigma} \times 10$
1	+ · · · + · · · +	301.3	.44 .89 1.62
2	− · · · · · − + −	18.6	.40 .84 1.23
3	· · · · · · · · ·	9.6	.37 .81 1.21
4	· · · · · · · · ·	3.6	.36 .79 1.19
5	· + · · + · · · ·	11.9	.32 .70 1.11

from the final vector model. Although the multiple time series analysis fails to reveal anything very surprising for this example, it shows what is there and does not mislead.

5.2 The Gas Furnace Data

The two series consist of (a) input gas rate and (b) output as CO_2 concentration at 9-second intervals from a gas furnace. We shall let Z_{1t} = gas rate + .057 and $Z_{2t} = CO_2 - 5.35$. This set of data was employed in Box and Jenkins (1970) to illustrate a procedure of identification, fitting, and checking of a transfer function model of the form (2.3) for $k = 2$ relating two time series one of which is *known* to be input for the other. Using this approach, the following models were found for the input Z_{1t} and the output Z_{2t};

$$(1 - 1.97B + 1.37B^2 - .34B^3)Z_{1t} = a_{1t}, \qquad \hat{\sigma}^2_{a_1} = .0353 \quad (5.4a)$$

$$Z_{2t} = \frac{\omega(B)}{\delta(B)} B^b Z_{1t} + \varphi(B)^{-1} a_{2t}, \; \hat{\sigma}^2_{a_2} = .0561, \quad (5.4b)$$

Table 9. Pattern of Cross-Correlation Matrices of Residuals: SCC Data

	Lag 1	2	3	4	5	6	7	8
(a) AR(1) model	· · + · · · · · ·	· · · · · · · · ·	· · · · · · · · ·	· · · · · · · · ·	· · · · · · · · ·	· · · · · · · · ·	· · · · · · · · +	· · · · · · · · ·
(b) AR(2) model	· · · · · · · · ·	· · · · · · · · ·	· · · · · · · · ·	· · · − · · · · ·	· · · · · · · · ·	· · · · · · · · ·	· · · · · · · · +	· · · · · · · · ·

Table 10. Estimation Results for the Model (5.1): SCC Data (exact likelihood)

	$\hat{\theta}_0$	$\hat{\varphi}$			$\hat{\theta}$			$\hat{\Sigma}$		
(1) Full Model	1.11	.81	.15	−.06	−.29	.23	.06	.037		
	(.64)	(.08)	(.07)	(.04)	(.15)	(.11)	(.07)			
	1.74	−.07	.98	−.09	−.45	.20	−.15	.022	.078	
	(.82)	(.10)	(.10)	(.05)	(.22)	(.17)	(.11)			
	4.08	−.32	.30	.76	−.79	.57	−.44	.013	.022	.129
	(1.47)	(.18)	(.17)	(.08)	(.28)	(.21)	(.13)			
(2) Restricted Model (intermediate)	.13	.90	.08					.042		
	(.09)	(.06)	(.06)	·	·	·	·			
	.59		.92	−.02				.022	.079	
	(.05)	·	(.04)	(.04)	·	·	·			
	2.48			.85	−.40		−.41	.017	.021	.131
	(1.10)	·	·	(.07)	(.23)	·	(.12)			
(3) Restricted Model (final)	.12	.98						.045		
	(.08)	(.03)		·	·	·	·			
	.24		.93					.024	.085	
	(.10)	·	(.04)	·	·	·	·			
	2.76			.83	−.40		−.41	.019	.023	.134
	(1.07)	·	·	(.06)	(.23)	·	(.12)			

Table 11. Pattern of Residual Cross-Correlations After Final Restricted ARMA(1,1) Model Fit: SCC Data

	$\hat{a}_1$	$\hat{a}_2$	$\hat{a}_3$
$\hat{a}_1$	. . . . –.	. . . .	. . . .
$\hat{a}_2$	. . . .	. . . .	. . . .
$\hat{a}_3$	. . . .	. . . . –.	. . . .

where $\omega(B) = -(.53 + .37B + .51B^2)$, $\delta(B) = 1 - .57B$, $\varphi(B) = 1 - 1.53B + .63B^2$, and the $\{a_{1t}\}$ and $\{a_{2t}\}$ series are assumed independent.

Particularly when we are dealing with econometric rather than engineering models, feedback relationships may not be known a priori; it is of interest, therefore, to analyze the data using the present approach where no distinction is made between an input and output variable and the fact that no feedback could occur in the system is not used.

Tentative Specification. In Table 12, we see that the auto- and cross-correlations of the original data in part (a) are persistently large in magnitude, ruling out low order moving average models; the $M(l)$ statistic (χ^2_4) in part (b) suggests that an AR(6) model might be appropriate; and the residual cross correlation pattern after an AR(6) fit in part (c) seems to verify the appropriateness of this model.

Estimation Results. Estimation results corresponding to an unrestricted AR(6) model

$$(\mathbf{I} - \varphi_1 B - \cdots - \varphi_6 B^6)\mathbf{Z}_t = \mathbf{a}_t \qquad (5.5)$$

are as follows:

$$\hat{\varphi}_1 = \begin{bmatrix} 1.93 & -.05 \\ (.06) & (.05) \\ .06 & 1.55 \\ (.08) & (.06) \end{bmatrix} \quad \hat{\varphi}_2 = \begin{bmatrix} -1.20 & .10 \\ (.13) & (.08) \\ -.14 & -.59 \\ (.16) & (.11) \end{bmatrix}$$

$$\hat{\varphi}_3 = \begin{bmatrix} .17 & -.08 \\ (.15) & (.09) \\ -.44 & -.17 \\ (.19) & (.11) \end{bmatrix} \quad \hat{\varphi}_4 = \begin{bmatrix} -.16 & .03 \\ (.15) & (.09) \\ .15 & .13 \\ (.19) & (.11) \end{bmatrix}$$

$$\hat{\varphi}_5 = \begin{bmatrix} .38 & -.04 \\ (.14) & (.08) \\ -.12 & .06 \\ (.18) & (.10) \end{bmatrix} \quad \hat{\varphi}_6 = \begin{bmatrix} -.22 & .03 \\ (.08) & (.03) \\ .25 & -.04 \\ (.11) & (.04) \end{bmatrix}$$

$$\hat{\Sigma} = \begin{bmatrix} .0345 & \\ -.0023 & .0566 \end{bmatrix}, \quad \hat{\rho}(a_1, a_2) = .045 \qquad (5.6)$$

If we let

$$\hat{\varphi}_l = \{\hat{\varphi}_{ij}{}^{(l)}\},$$

Table 12. Tentative Identification for the Gas Furnace Data

(a) Pattern of cross-correlations of the original data

	Z_{1t}	Z_{2t}
Z_{1t}	+ + + + + + + + + + + +	– – – – – – – – – – – –
Z_{2t}	– – – – – – – – – – . .	+ + + + + + + + + + + +

(b) M statistic for partial autoregression

Lag l	1	2	3	4	5	6	7	8	9	10	11
$M(l)$	1650	665	31.7	22.5	5.6	12.9	1.8	8.0	3.5	0	2.0

(c) Pattern of cross-correlations of the residuals after AR(6) fit

	$\hat{a}_{1t}$	$\hat{a}_{2t}$
$\hat{a}_{1t}$	. . . . –	. . . .
$\hat{a}_{2t}$	. . . .	. . . .

we see that $\hat{\varphi}_{12}{}^{(l)}$ are small compared with their standard errors over all lags, confirming (as in this case is known from the physical nature of the apparatus generating the data) that there is a unidirectional relationship between Z_{1t} and Z_{2t} involving no feedback. Also, $\hat{\varphi}_{21}{}^{(l)}$ is small for $l = 1, 2$, and the residuals $\hat{a}_{1t}$ and $\hat{a}_{2t}$ are essentially uncorrelated, implying a delay of 3 periods. It should be noted also that the variances for a_{1t} and a_{2t} are very close to those for a_{1t} and a_{2t} in (5.4), and their correlation is negligible.

To facilitate comparison with (5.4), we set $\varphi_{11}{}^{(l)} = 0$ for $l > 3$, $\varphi_{12}{}^{(l)} = 0$ for all l, $\varphi_{21}{}^{(l)} = 0$ for $l = 1, 2$, and $\varphi_{22}{}^{(l)} = 0$ for $l = 5, 6$. Estimation results for this restricted AR(6) model are then

$$\hat{\varphi}_1 = \begin{bmatrix} 1.98 & . \\ (.06) & \\ . & 1.53 \\ & (.06) \end{bmatrix} \quad \hat{\varphi}_2 = \begin{bmatrix} -1.38 & . \\ (.10) & \\ . & -.58 \\ & (.11) \end{bmatrix} \quad \hat{\varphi}_3 = \begin{bmatrix} .35 & . \\ (.06) & \\ -.53 & -.14 \\ (.07) & (.10) \end{bmatrix}$$

$$\hat{\varphi}_4 = \begin{bmatrix} . & . \\ .11 & .12 \\ (.16) & (.04) \end{bmatrix} \quad \hat{\varphi}_5 = \begin{bmatrix} . & . \\ -.04 & . \\ (.17) & \end{bmatrix} \quad \hat{\varphi}_6 = \begin{bmatrix} . & . \\ .21 & . \\ (.11) & \end{bmatrix}$$

$$\hat{\Sigma} = \begin{bmatrix} .0359 & -.0029 \\ & .0561 \end{bmatrix}, \quad \hat{\rho}(a_1, a_2) \doteq 0 \qquad (5.7)$$

Examination of the pattern of the cross-correlations of the residuals suggests that the model is adequate.

Implication of the Bivariate Model. The final AR(6) model (5.7) can be written

$$\begin{bmatrix} \varphi_{11}(B) & \\ \varphi_{21}(B) & \varphi_{22}(B) \end{bmatrix} \begin{bmatrix} Z_{1t} \\ Z_{2t} \end{bmatrix} = \begin{bmatrix} a_{1t} \\ a_{2t} \end{bmatrix}, \qquad (5.8)$$

where $\varphi_{11}(B) = 1 - 1.98B + 1.38B^2 - .35B^3$, $\varphi_{21}(B) = (.53 - .11B - .21B)B^3$, and $\varphi_{22}(B) = (1 - 1.53B + .58B^2 + .14B^3 - .12B^4)$. Assuming a_{1t} and a_{2t} are uncorrelated, the input model $\varphi_{11}(B)Z_{1t} = a_{1t}$ with $\text{Var}(a_{1t}) = .0359$ is essentially the same as (5.4a). Now the model relating the output Z_{2t} to the input Z_{1t} is

$$Z_{2t} = -\frac{\varphi_{21}(B)}{\varphi_{22}(B)} Z_{1t} + \frac{1}{\varphi_{22}(B)} a_{2t} \tag{5.9}$$

with $\text{Var}(a_{2t}) = .0561$. The noise model $\varphi_{22}^{-1}(B)a_{2t}$ is not very different from the corresponding one $\varphi^{-1}(B)a_{2t}$ in (5.4b), but the dynamic model $-\varphi_{21}(B)\varphi_{22}^{-1}(B)Z_{1t}$ at first sight appears markedly different from the first term on the right side of (5.4b). The reason is that in the form (5.9) the denominators of the dynamic model and of the noise model are constrained to be identical. This restriction is not present in the transfer function model (5.4b). The less restrictive form can however be written in the form of (5.9) if we set $\varphi_{22}(B) = \varphi(B)$ and $-\varphi_{21}(B) = \omega(B)B^b\{\varphi(B)\delta^{-1}(B)\}$. For this example, the factor $\varphi(B)\delta^{-1}(B) \doteq 1 - .96B$, and it is then seen that the models are in fact very similar. This may be confirmed by comparing the impulse response weights in Table 13, where $\omega(B)B^b\delta^{-1}(B) = \sum_{j=0}^{\infty} v_j B^j$ and $-\varphi_{21}(B)\varphi_{22}^{-1}(B) = \sum_{j=0}^{\infty} v^*_j B^j$.

Further Analysis of Stepwise AR Results. It is instructive to examine for this data the changes in the fitted autoregressive models as the order is increased. Using indicator symbols (and omitting the dots) Table 14 shows the situation for $p = 1, \ldots, 6$. The residual covariance matrix for each order is also given. The following observations may be made.

1. If only AR(1) or AR(2) were considered, one might be led to believe mistakenly that there was a feedback relationship between these two series.
2. The unidirectional dynamic relationship becomes clear when the order of the model, p, is increased to three. Since the input series Z_{1t} essentially follows a univariate AR(3) model, this suggests that the present procedure will correctly identify the one-sided causal dynamic relationship once the input model is appropriately selected.
3. The delay $b = 3$ emerges when the order p is increased to 4. Since only very marginal improvement in the fit occurs for $p > 4$, this is saying that the delay is correctly identified only when the model is specified essentially correctly.

Implications on General Time Series Model Building. The relative merit of the present procedure and more direct modeling of the system will depend on how much is known or how much we are prepared to assume. In some applications, particularly in engineering and most examples of intervention analysis, an adequate initial specification may be possible from knowledge of the nature of the problem. This may allow a flow diagram showing the feedback structure to be drawn and likely orders to be guessed for the various dynamic components. The resulting models can then be directly *fitted* in the manner described and illustrated in Box and MacGregor (1974, 1976) and Box and Tiao (1975). For a single input with feedback known to be absent, a prewhitening method is given in Box and Jenkins (1970) for *identifying* an unknown dynamic system, but extension of this identification method to multiple inputs is rather complex.

Particularly for economic and business examples, however, the feedback structure and orders of the multiple system are often unknown. The present multiple time series procedure has the great advantage that it allows *identification* of the feedback and dynamic structure. Furthermore,

1. A one-sided causal relationship, if it exists, will emerge in the identification process, and the stochastic structures of the input as well as the transfer function relationship between input and output will be modeled simultaneously.
2. Stochastic multiple input and multiple output situations are readily handled.
3. A useful method is provided for seeking leading indicators in economic and business applications. In this context it should be noted that a unidirectional dynamic relationship may not exist between two time series even when one variable is known to be the input for the other. One reason for this phenomenon is the effect of temporal aggregation. As shown in Tiao and Wei (1976), pseudo-feedback relationships could occur because of this temporal aggregation effect, and it would be a mistake to impose a transfer function model in such a situation.
4. However, when a simple transfer function structure of the form (2.2) *is* appropriate, the present multiple time series approach could rarely reproduce it directly—see, for example, (5.4b) and (5.9)—and some analysis of the fitted form might be necessary to reveal a more parsimonious and more easily understood structure.

6. COMPARISON WITH SOME OTHER APPROACHES AND CONCLUDING REMARKS

We have discussed various tools used in an iterative approach to modeling multiple time series and illustrated

Table 13. Impulse Response Weights for the Gas Furnace Data

	j = 0	1	2	3	4	5	6	7	8	9	10	11	12
v_j	·	·	·	−.53	−.67	−.89	−.51	−.29	−.17	−.09	−.05	−.03	−.02
v^*_j	·	·	·	−.53	−.70	−.77	−.48	−.26	−.09	−.01	.01	.00	−.01

Table 14. Successive AR Fitting Results for the Gas Furnace Data

Order of AR	φ_1	φ_2	φ_3	φ_4	φ_5	φ_6	$\boldsymbol{\Sigma}$
1	$\begin{bmatrix} + & + \\ - & + \end{bmatrix}$						$\begin{bmatrix} .102 & .090 \\ & .346 \end{bmatrix}$
2	$\begin{bmatrix} + & - \\ + & + \end{bmatrix}$	$\begin{bmatrix} - & + \\ - & - \end{bmatrix}$					$\begin{bmatrix} .037 & -.004 \\ & .069 \end{bmatrix}$
3	$\begin{bmatrix} + & \\ & + \end{bmatrix}$	$\begin{bmatrix} - & \\ - & - \end{bmatrix}$	$\begin{bmatrix} + & \\ & + \end{bmatrix}$				$\begin{bmatrix} .036 & -.002 \\ & .063 \end{bmatrix}$
4	$\begin{bmatrix} + & \\ & + \end{bmatrix}$	$\begin{bmatrix} - & \\ & - \end{bmatrix}$	$\begin{bmatrix} & \\ - & \end{bmatrix}$	$\begin{bmatrix} & \\ + & + \end{bmatrix}$			$\begin{bmatrix} .036 & -.003 \\ & .059 \end{bmatrix}$
5	$\begin{bmatrix} + & \\ & + \end{bmatrix}$	$\begin{bmatrix} - & \\ & - \end{bmatrix}$	$\begin{bmatrix} & \\ - & \end{bmatrix}$	$\begin{bmatrix} & \\ & \end{bmatrix}$	$\begin{bmatrix} & \\ & \end{bmatrix}$		$\begin{bmatrix} .035 & -.003 \\ & .058 \end{bmatrix}$
6	$\begin{bmatrix} + & \\ & + \end{bmatrix}$	$\begin{bmatrix} - & \\ & - \end{bmatrix}$	$\begin{bmatrix} & \\ - & \end{bmatrix}$	$\begin{bmatrix} & \\ & \end{bmatrix}$	$\begin{bmatrix} + & \\ & \end{bmatrix}$	$\begin{bmatrix} & - \\ + & \end{bmatrix}$	$\begin{bmatrix} .035 & -.002 \\ & .057 \end{bmatrix}$

how they work in practice. Much further work is needed, especially in the identification of mixed autoregressive moving average models and in developing faster estimation algorithms and better tools for diagnostic checking. In spite of the imperfections of the present tools and the preliminary nature of the approach, we have felt it appropriate to present them here in order to (a) illustrate the potential usefulness of vector autoregressive moving average models in characterizing dynamic structures in the data and (b) stimulate further development of modeling procedures. Several alternative approaches to modeling multiple time series have been proposed in the literature. It may be of interest to discuss briefly those proposed by Granger and Newbold (1977), Wallis (1977), and Chan and Wallis (1978).

In the Granger and Newbold approach, one begins by fitting univariate ARMA models to each series,

$$\varphi_{p_j}(B)Z_{jt} = \theta_{q_j}(B)C_{jt}, \quad j = 1, \ldots, k \tag{6.1}$$

and then attempts to identify the dynamic structure of the k white noise residual series $\{C_{jt}\}$ by examination of their cross-correlations. A model of the form (2.2) with $k(h)$ being the set $(1, \ldots, k)$ excluding h is then fitted to the k residual series. This model and the prewhitening transformations (6.1) then determine the model for the original vector series. As the authors themselves pointed out, the procedure is complex and difficult to apply for $k > 2$. One major difficulty arises from the fact that the parameters in the model for the residuals are subject to various complicated nonlinear constraints. Also, it can be readily shown that even if the vector series $\{\mathbf{Z}_t\}$ follows a low order ARMA model (3.1), the corresponding model for the residual vector $\{\mathbf{C}_t\}$ where $\mathbf{C}'_t = (C_{1t}, \ldots, C_{kt})$ can be complex and difficult to identify in practice.

The Wallis and Chan approach uses the form (6.1) for each individual series and the fact that the model (3.1) can be written as

$$|\,\boldsymbol{\varphi}(B)\,|\,\mathbf{Z}_t = \mathbf{H}(B)\mathbf{a}_t, \tag{6.2}$$

where $\mathbf{H}(B) = \mathbf{A}(B)\boldsymbol{\theta}_q(B)$, $\mathbf{A}(B)$ is the adjoint matrix and $|\,\boldsymbol{\varphi}_p(B)\,|$ the determinant of $\boldsymbol{\varphi}_p(B)$. As in the G and N approach, an individual model is first constructed for each series. From the degrees of the moving average polynomials $\theta_{q_j}(B)$ of these individual models, the degree of $\mathbf{H}(B)$ is determined. Next, models of the form

$$\mathbf{D}_l(B)\mathbf{Z}_t = \mathbf{H}(B)\mathbf{a}_t, \tag{6.3}$$

where $\mathbf{D}_l(B)$ is a diagonal matrix polynomial in B of degree l, are fitted successively for $l = r, r - 1, \ldots,$ where r is some specified maximum order, to determine an appropriate value for l. A likelihood ratio test is then performed to check whether the diagonal elements of $\mathbf{D}_l(B)$ are identical, that is, of the form (6.2). Finally, from the fitted $\mathbf{H}(B)$ and $|\,\boldsymbol{\varphi}(B)\,|$ or $\mathbf{D}_l(B)$, one guesses at the values of p and q in (3.1) and then proceeds to estimate the parameters in $\boldsymbol{\varphi}_p(B)$ and $\boldsymbol{\theta}_q(B)$. The efficacy of this approach is open to question on several grounds.

1. The degree of the polynomial $\mathbf{H}(B)$ in (6.2) can be higher than the maximum degree of $\theta_{q_j}(B)$ for the individual series. For example, suppose $k = 2$,

$$\mathbf{H}(B) = \begin{pmatrix} 1 & -h_1B \\ -h_2B & 1 \end{pmatrix}$$

and the two elements of $\mathbf{a}_t$ are independent. Then $q_1 = q_2 = 0$, but it would be a mistake to infer that $\mathbf{H}(B)$ is of degree zero.

2. For vector AR or ARMA models, the representation (6.2) is certainly nonparsimonious. Apart from the covariance matrix $\boldsymbol{\Sigma}$, for k series the maximum number of parameters in the original form (3.1) is $k^2(p + q)$, while the maximum number of parameters in the form (6.2) is $kp + [(k - 1)p + q]k^2$, representing an increase

of $pk(k-1)^2$ parameters. The increase could be even greater if the diagonal form (6.3) is employed. Thus, assuming the degree of $\mathbf{H}(B)$ is correctly specified, even for k as low as 3 or 4, a very large number of additional parameters will have to be estimated merely to identify correctly a low order vector AR model, say $p = 1$ or 2.

3. Since the correspondence between the degrees of the determinantal polynomial $|\boldsymbol{\varphi}(B)|$ and $\mathbf{H}(B)$ and the values of (p, q) is not necessarily one to one, it is not clear how one determines p and q in (3.1) from the form (6.2).

4. The approach is made even more computationally burdensome because the authors propose to employ the exact likelihood method for moving average parameters throughout the processes of model building. Our experience, however, suggests that because this method converges relatively slowly it is better to use it only in the final stage of the estimation process.

The chief distinction between our approach and the two alternatives just discussed is that we believe it better to tackle the dynamic relationships of the k series in their entirety, employing tools such as the estimates of cross-correlation matrices and partial autoregression matrices to shed light directly on the structure. Simplifications of one kind or another will then often follow. At least for the tentative specification of the vector autoregressive or the vector moving average model, our procedures seem far simpler to use in practice and do not require the multitude of steps these alternative approaches need to arrive at even a simple model.

To illustrate these points, we briefly consider the mink-muskrat example which Chan and Wallis used to illustrate their methods. They treat two series $Y_{1t}{}^*$ and $Y_{2t}{}^*$ obtained after "detrending" the muskrat and mink series by first and second degree polynomials respectively. Proceeding through the various steps outlined above, they eventually arrive at an AR(1) model. However, it will be seen that this same model is suggested immediately by the simple procedures we propose. Table 15(a) shows the partial autoregression results for $l = 1, 2$ and Table 15(b) the residual cross correlations after the AR(1) fit. A very similar analysis of this set of data is given in Ansley and Newbold (1979). For various reasons, we do not wish to sanctify this AR(1) model. These include the question of whether any linear structural model is adequate for these series (see Tong and Lim 1980). Also, the validity of the detrending procedures and the suspicious behavior of a high autocorrelation at lag 10 occurring in the residuals seem suspect. Our only point is to show that the circuitous route adopted by Chan and Wallis to arrive at this model is unnecessary.

Before concluding this paper, it is worth noting that in modeling as well as analysis of vector time series one often finds it useful to perform various eigenvalue and eigenvector analyses. Specifically, writing (3.1) in the form

$$\mathbf{z}_t = \hat{\mathbf{z}}_{t-1}(1) + \mathbf{a}_t, \tag{6.4}$$

Table 15. Identification of Muskrat-Mink Data

(a) Partial Autoregression and Related Statistics

Lag	Partials		$M(l) \overset{\sim}{\rightarrow} \chi_4^2$	Diagonal elements of $\hat{\boldsymbol{\Sigma}}$
1	+	−	111.7	.062
	+	+		.059
2	−	·	4.8	.0571
	·	·		.0572

(b) Cross-correlations of Residuals After AR(1) Fit

	a_1	a_2
a_1	············	·−··········
a_2	············	·········+··

where $\hat{\mathbf{z}}_{t-1}(1)$ is the one step ahead forecast of $\mathbf{z}_t$ made at time $t-1$, and denoting, for stationary series,

$$\boldsymbol{\Gamma}_z(0) = E(\mathbf{z}_t\mathbf{z}'_t)$$

and

$$\boldsymbol{\Gamma}_{\hat{z}}(0) = E(\hat{\mathbf{z}}_{t-1}(1)\hat{\mathbf{z}}_{t-1}(1)'),$$

it will often be informative to compute eigenvalues and eigenvectors of estimates of the following matrices:

$$(a)\ \boldsymbol{\Gamma}_z(0), \quad (b)\ \boldsymbol{\Sigma},$$

$$(c)\ \boldsymbol{\Gamma}_z(0)^{-1}\boldsymbol{\Gamma}_{\hat{z}}(0), \quad (d)\ \boldsymbol{\varphi}_l, \text{ and } \boldsymbol{\theta}_l.$$

Such analyses are described in Quenouille (1957), Box and Tiao (1977), and Tiao et al. (1979). Also, the eigenvalues and eigenvectors of the spectral density matrix of the model should also be considered (see Brillinger 1975). These techniques are useful in (a) detecting exact concurrent or lagged linear relations between series, and (b) facilitating understanding and interpretation of the fitted model. In our opinion, this is one of the most important and challenging topics for further research.

[*Received January 1981. Revised June 1981.*]

REFERENCES

ABRAHAM, B. (1980), "Intervention Analysis and Multiple Time Series," *Biometrika*, 67, 73–78.

ABRAHAM, B., and BOX, G.E.P. (1978), "Deterministic and Forecast-Adaptive Time Dependent Models," *Applied Statistics*, 27, 120–130.

AKAIKE, H. (1980), "On the Identification of State Space Models and Their Use in Control," in *Directions in Time Series*, eds. D.R. Brillinger and G.C. Tiao, Institute of Mathematical Statistics, 175–187.

ANDERSON, T.W. (1971), *The Statistical Analysis of Time Series*, New York: John Wiley.

——— (1980), "Maximum Likelihood Estimation for Vector Autoregressive Moving Average Models," in *Directions in Time Series*, eds. D.R. Brillinger and G.C. Tiao, Institute of Mathematical Statistics, 49–59.

ANSLEY, C. (1979), "An Algorithm for the Exact Likelihood of a Mixed Autoregressive Moving Average Process," *Biometrika*, 66, 59–65.

ANSLEY, C.F., and NEWBOLD, P. (1979), "Multivariate Partial Autocorrelations," *Proceedings of Business and Economic Statistics Section*, American Statistical Association, 349–353.

BARTLETT, M.S. (1938), "Further Aspects of the Theory of Multiple Regression," *Proceedings of the Cambridge Philosophical Society*, 34, 33–40.

BEGUIN, J.M., GOURIEROUX, C., and MONFORT, A. (1980), "Identification of a Mixed Autoregressive-Moving Average Process: The Corner Method," in *Time Series*, ed. O.D. Anderson, Amsterdam: North-Holland, 423–436.

BOX, G.E.P, and HAUGH, L. (1977), "Identification of Dynamic Regression Models Connecting Two Time Series," *Journal of the American Statistical Association*, 72, 121–130.

BOX, G.E.P., and JENKINS, G.M. (1970), *Time Series Analysis—Forecasting and Control*, San Francisco: Holden-Day.

BOX, G.E.P., and MACGREGOR, J.F. (1974), "The Analysis of Closed Loop Dynamic Stochastic Systems," *Technometrics*, 16, 391–398.

——— (1976), "Parameter Estimation with Closed-Loop Operating data," *Technometrics*, 18, 371–380.

BOX, G.E.P., and NEWBOLD, P. (1970), "Some Comments on a Paper by Coen, Gomme and Kendall," *Journal of the Royal Statistical Society*, Ser. A, 134, 229–240.

BOX, G.E.P., and TIAO, G.C. (1975), "Intervention Analysis with Applications to Environmental and Economic Problems," *Journal of the American Statistical Association*, 70, 70–79.

——— (1977), "A Canonical Analysis of Multiple Time Series," *Biometrika*, 64, 355–365.

BRILLINGER, D.R. (1975), *Time Series Data Analysis and Theory*, New York: Holt, Rinehart, and Winston.

CHAN, W.Y.T., and WALLIS, K.F. (1978), "Multiple Time Series Modelling: Another Look at the Mink-Muskrat Interaction," *Applied Statistics*, 27, 168–175.

COEN, P.G., GOMME, E.D., and KENDALL, M.G. (1969), "Lagged Relationships in Economic Forecasting," *Journal of the Royal Statistical Society*, Ser. A, 132, 133–163.

DEISTLER, M., DUNSMUIR, W., and HANNAN, E.J. (1978), "Vector Linear Time Series Models: Corrections and Extensions," *Advances in Applied Probability*, 10, 360–372.

DENT, W. (1977), "Computation of the Exact Likelihood Function of an ARIMA Process," *Journal of Statistical Computation and Simulation*, 5, 193–206.

DUNSMUIR, W., and HANNAN, E.J. (1976), "Vector Linear Time Series Models," *Advances in Applied Probability*, 8, 339–364.

GRANGER, C.W.J., and NEWBOLD, P. (1977), *Forecasting Economic Time Series*, New York: Academic Press.

GRAY, H.L., KELLEY, G.D., and McINTIRE, D.D. (1978), "A New Approach to ARMA Modelling," *Communications in Statistics*, B7, 1–77.

HALLIN, M. (1978), "Mixed Autoregressive-Moving Average Multivariate Processes with Time-Dependent Coefficients," *Journal of Multivariate Analysis*, 8, 567–572.

HANNAN, E.J. (1970), *Multiple Time Series*, New York: John Wiley.

——— (1980), "The Estimation of the Order of an ARMA Process," *Annals of Statistics*, 8, 1071–1081.

HANNAN, E.J., DUNSMUIR, W.T.M., and DEISTLER, M. (1980), "Estimation of Vector ARMAX Models," *Journal of Multivariate Analysis*, 10, 275–295.

HILLMER, S.C., and TIAO, G.C. (1979), "Likelihood Function of Stationary Multiple Autoregressive Moving Average Models," *Journal of the American Statistical Association*, 74, 652–660.

HOSKING, J.R.M. (1980), "The Multivariate Portmanteau Statistic," *Journal of the American Statistical Association*, 75, 602–607.

HSIAO, C. (1979), "Autoregressive Modeling of Canadian Money and Income Data," *Journal of the American Statistical Association*, 74, 553–560.

JENKINS, G.J. (1979), *Practical Experiences with Modelling and Forecasting Time Series*, Channel Islands: GJP Ltd.

LI, W.K., and McLEOD, A.I. (1980), "Distribution of the Residual Autocorrelations in Multivariate ARMA Time Series Models," TR-80-03, University of Western Ontario.

NEWBOLD, P. (1974), "The Exact Likelihood Function for a Mixed Autoregressive Moving Average Process," *Biometrika*, 61, 423–427.

NICHOLLS, D.F. (1976), "The Efficient Estimation of Vector Linear Time Series Models," *Biometrika*, 63, 381–390.

——— (1977), "A Comparison of Estimation Methods for Vector Linear Time Series Models," *Biometrika*, 64, 85–90.

NICHOLLS, D.F., and HALL, A.D. (1979), "The Exact Likelihood of Multivariate Autoregressive-Moving Average Models," *Biometrika*, 66, 259–264.

OSBORN, D.R. (1977), "Exact and Approximate Maximum Likelihood Estimators for Vector Moving Average Processes," *Journal of the Royal Statistical Society*, Ser. B, 39, 114–118.

PARZEN, E. (1977), "Multiple Time Series: Determining the Order of Approximating Autoregressive Schemes," in *Multivariate Analysis-IV*, ed. P. Krishnaiah, Amsterdam: North-Holland, 283–295.

PHADKE, M.S., and KEDEM, G. (1978), "Computation of the Exact Likelihood Function of Multivariate Moving Average Models," *Biometrika*, 65, 511–519.

QUENOUILLE, M.H. (1957), *The Analysis of Multiple Time Series*, London: Griffin.

QUINN, B.G. (1980), "Order Determination for a Multivariate Autoregression," *Journal of the Royal Statistical Society*, Ser. B, 42, 182–185.

SLUTSKY, E. (1937), "The Summation of Random Causes as the Source of Cyclic Processes," *Econometrika*, 5, 105–146.

TIAO, G.C., and ALI, M.M. (1971), "Analysis of Correlated Random Effects: Linear Model with Two Random Components," *Biometrika*, 58, 37–51.

TIAO, G.C., BOX, G.E.P., GRUPE, M.R., HUDAK, G.B., BELL, W.R., and CHANG, I. (1979), "The Wisconsin Multiple Time Series (WMTS-1) Program: A Preliminary Guide," Department of Statistics, University of Wisconsin, Madison.

TIAO, G.C., and WEI, W.S. (1976), "Effect of Temporal Aggregation on the Dynamic Relationship of Two Time Series Variables," *Biometrika*, 63, 513–523.

TONG, H., and LIM, K.S. (1980), "Threshold Autoregression, Limit Cycles and Cyclical Data," *Journal of the Royal Statistical Society*, Ser. B, 42, 245–292.

WALLIS, K.F. (1977), "Multiple Time Series Analysis and the Final Form of Econometric Models," *Econometrika*, 45, 1481–1497.

WHITTLE, P. (1963), "On the Fitting of Multivariate Autoregressions, and the Approximate Canonical Factorization of a Spectral Density Matrix," *Biometrika*, 50, 129–134.

WILSON, G.T. (1973), "The Estimation of Parameters in Multivariate Time Series Models," *Journal of the Royal Statistical Society*, Ser. B, 35, 76–85.

YULE, G.U. (1927), "On a Method of Investigating Periodicities in Disturbed Series, With Special Reference to Wolfer's Sunspot Numbers," *Philosophical Transactions of the Royal Society of London*, Ser. A, 226, 267–298.

ZELLNER, A., and PALM, F. (1974), "Time Series Analysis and Simultaneous Equation Econometric Models," *Journal of Econometrics*, 2, 17–54.

[27]

Journal of Econometrics 2 (1974) 17–54.

TIME SERIES ANALYSIS AND SIMULTANEOUS EQUATION ECONOMETRIC MODELS*

Arnold ZELLNER and Franz PALM

Graduate School of Business, University of Chicago, Chicago, Ill. 60637, U.S.A.

Received July 1973, revised version received November 1973

1. Introduction

In this paper we take up the analysis of dynamic simultaneous equation models (SEM's) within the context of general linear multiple time series processes such as studied by Quenouille (1957). As noted by Quenouille, if a set of variables is generated by a multiple time series process, it is often possible to solve for the processes generating individual variables, namely the 'final equations' of Tinbergen (1940), and these are in the autoregressive-moving average (ARMA) form. ARMA processes have been studied intensively by Box and Jenkins (1970). Further, if a general multiple time series process is appropriately specialized, we obtain a usual dynamic SEM in structural form. By algebraic manipulations, the associated reduced form and transfer function equation systems can be derived. In what follows, these equation systems are presented and their properties and uses are indicated.

It will be shown that assumptions about variables being exogenous, about lags in structural equations of SEM's, and about serial correlation properties of structural disturbance terms have strong implications for the properties of transfer functions and final equations that can be tested. Further, we show how large sample posterior odds and likelihood ratios can be used to appraise alternative hypotheses. In agreement with Pierce and Mason (1971), we believe that testing the implications of structural assumptions for transfer functions and, we add, final equations is an important element in the process of iterating in on a model that is reasonably in accord with the information in a sample of data. To illustrate these general points and to provide applications of the above methods, a

*Research financed in part by NSF Grant GS-2347 and by income from the H.G.B. Alexander Endowment Fund, Graduate School of Business, University of Chicago. Some of the ideas in this paper were presented in econometrics lectures and at a session of the Econometric Society's meeting in 1971 by one of the authors. The second author received financial support from the Belgian National Science Foundation.

dynamic version of a SEM due to Haavelmo (1947) is analyzed using U.S. post-World War II quarterly data.

The plan of the paper is as follows. In sect. 2, a general multiple time series model is specified, its final equations are obtained and their properties set forth. Then the implications of assumptions needed to specialize the multiple time series model to become a dynamic SEM for transfer functions and final equations are presented. In sect. 3, the algebraic analysis is applied to a small dynamic SEM. Quarterly U.S. data are employed in sects. 4 and 5 to analyze the final and transfer equations of the dynamic SEM. Sect. 6 provides a discussion of the empirical results, their implications for the specification and estimation of the structural equations of the model, and some concluding remarks.

2. General formulation and analysis of a system of dynamic equations

As indicated by Quenouille (1957), a linear multiple time series process can be represented as follows:[1]

$$\underset{p\times p}{H(L)}\ \underset{p\times 1}{z_t} = \underset{p\times p}{F(L)}\ \underset{p\times 1}{e_t}, \qquad t = 1, 2, \ldots, T, \tag{2.1}$$

where $z_t' = (z_{1t}, z_{2t}, \ldots, z_{pt})$ is a vector of random variables, $e_t' = (e_{1t}, e_{2t}, \ldots, e_{pt})$ is a vector of random errors, and $H(L)$ and $F(L)$ are each $p \times p$ matrices, assumed of full rank, whose elements are finite polynomials in the lag operator L, defined as $L^n z_t = z_{t-n}$. Typical elements of $H(L)$ and $F(L)$ are given by $h_{ij} = \Sigma_{l=0}^{r_{ij}} h_{ijl} L^l$ and $f_{ij} = \Sigma_{l=0}^{q_{ij}} f_{ijl} L^l$. Further, we assume that the error process has a zero mean, an identity covariance matrix and no serial correlation, that is:

$$Ee_t = 0, \tag{2.2}$$

for all t and t',

$$Ee_t e_{t'}' = \delta_{tt'} I, \tag{2.3}$$

where I is a unit matrix and $\delta_{tt'}$ is the Kronecker delta. The assumption in (2.3) does not involve a loss of generality since correlation of errors can be introduced through the matrix $F(L)$.

The model in (2.1) is a multivariate autoregressive-moving average (ARMA) process. If $H(L) = H_0$, a matrix of degree zero in L, (2.1) is a moving average (MA) process; if $F(L) = F_0$, a matrix of degree zero in L, it is an autoregressive (AR) process. In general, (2.1) can be expressed as:

$$\sum_{l=0}^{r} H_l L^l z_t = \sum_{l=0}^{q} F_l L^l e_t, \tag{2.4}$$

where H_l and F_l are matrices with all elements not depending on L, $r = \max_{i,j} r_{ij}$ and $q = \max_{i,j} q_{ij}$.

[1]In (2.1), z_t is assumed to be mean-corrected, that is z_t is a deviation from a population mean vector. Below we relax this assumption.

Since $H(L)$ in (2.1) is assumed to have full rank, (2.1) can be solved for z_t as follows:

$$z_t = H^{-1}(L)F(L)e_t, \tag{2.5a}$$

or

$$z_t = [H^*(L)/|H(L)|]F(L)e_t, \tag{2.5b}$$

where $H^*(L)$ is the adjoint matrix associated with $H(L)$ and $|H(L)|$ is the determinant which is a scalar, finite polynomial in L. If the process is to be invertible, the roots of $|H(L)| = 0$ have to lie outside the unit circle. Then (2.5) expresses z_t as an infinite MA process that can be equivalently expressed as the following system of finite order ARMA equations:

$$|H(L)|z_t = H^*(L)F(L)e_t. \tag{2.6}$$

The ith equation of (2.6) is given by:

$$|H(L)|z_{it} = \alpha_i' e_t, \qquad i = 1, 2, \ldots, p, \tag{2.7}$$

where α_i' is the ith row of $H^*(L)F(L)$.

The following points regarding the set of final equations in (2.7) are of interest:

(i) Each equation is in ARMA form, as pointed out by Quenouille (1957, p. 20). Thus the ARMA processes for individual variables are compatible with some, perhaps unknown, joint process for a set of random variables and are thus not necessarily 'naive', 'ad hoc' alternative models.

(ii) The order and parameters of the autoregressive part of each equation, $|H(L)|z_{it}$, $i = 1, 2, \ldots, p$, will usually be the same.[2]

(iii) Statistical methods can be employed to investigate the form and properties of the ARMA equations in (2.7). Given that their forms, that is the degree of $|H(L)|$ and the order of the moving average errors, have been determined, they can be estimated and used for prediction.

(iv) The equations of (2.7) are in the form of a restricted 'seemingly unrelated' autoregressive model with correlated moving average error processes.[3]

The general multiple time series model in (2.1) can be specialized to a usual dynamic simultaneous equation model (SEM) if some prior information about H and F is available. That is, prior information may indicate that it is appropriate to regard some of the variables in z_t as being endogenous and the remaining variables as being exogenous, that is, generated by an independent process. To represent this situation, we partition (2.1) as follows:

$$\begin{pmatrix} H_{11} & H_{12} \\ H_{21} & H_{22} \end{pmatrix}\begin{pmatrix} y_t \\ x_t \end{pmatrix} = \begin{pmatrix} F_{11} & F_{12} \\ F_{21} & F_{22} \end{pmatrix}\begin{pmatrix} e_{1t} \\ e_{2t} \end{pmatrix}. \tag{2.8}$$

[2]In some cases in which $|H(L)|$ contains factors in common with those appearing in all elements of the vectors α_i', e.g. when H is triangular, diagonal or block diagonal, some cancelling will take place. In such cases the statement in (ii) has to be qualified.

[3]See Nelson (1970) and Akaike (1973) for estimation results for systems similar to (2.7).

If the $p_1 \times 1$ vector y_t is endogenous and the $p_2 \times 1$ vector x_t is exogenous, this implies the following restrictions on the submatrices of H and F:

$$H_{21} \equiv 0, \quad F_{21} \equiv 0, \quad \text{and} \quad F_{12} \equiv 0. \tag{2.9}$$

With the assumptions in (2.9), the elements of e_{1t} do not affect the elements of x_t and the elements of e_{2t} affect the elements of y_t only through the elements of x_t. Under the hypotheses in (2.9), (2.8) is in the form of a dynamic SEM with endogenous variable vector y_t and exogenous variable vector x_t generated by an ARMA process. The usual structural equations, from (2.8) subject to (2.9), are:[4]

$$\underset{p_1 \times p_1}{H_{11}(L)} \underset{p_1 \times 1}{y_t} + \underset{p_1 \times p_2}{H_{12}(L)} \underset{p_2 \times 1}{x_t} = \underset{p_1 \times p_1}{F_{11}(L)} \underset{p_1 \times 1}{e_{1t}}, \tag{2.10}$$

while the process generating the exogenous variables is:

$$\underset{p_2 \times p_2}{H_{22}(L)} \underset{p_2 \times 1}{x_t} = \underset{p_2 \times p_2}{F_{22}(L)} \underset{p_2 \times 1}{e_{2t}}, \tag{2.11}$$

with $p_1 + p_2 = p$.

Analogous to (2.4), the system (2.10) can be expressed as:

$$\sum_{l=0}^{r} H_{11l} L^l y_t + \sum_{l=0}^{r} H_{12l} L^l x_t = \sum_{l=0}^{q} F_{11l} L^l e_{1t}, \tag{2.12}$$

where H_{11l}, H_{12l} and F_{11l} are matrices the elements of which are coefficients of L^l. Under the assumption that H_{110} is of full rank, the reduced form equations, which express the current values of endogenous variables as functions of the lagged endogenous and current and lagged exogenous variables, are:

$$y_t = -\sum_{l=1}^{r} H_{110}^{-1} H_{11l} L^l y_t - \sum_{l=0}^{r} H_{110}^{-1} H_{12l} L^l x_t + \sum_{l=0}^{q} H_{110}^{-1} F_{11l} L^l e_{1t}. \tag{2.13}$$

The reduced form system in (2.13) is a system of p_1 stochastic difference equations of maximal order r.

The 'final form' of (2.13), Theil and Boot (1962), or 'set of fundamental dynamic equations' associated with (2.13), Kmenta (1971), which expresses the current values of endogenous variables as functions of only the exogenous variables, is given by:

$$y_t = -H_{11}^{-1}(L) H_{12}(L) x_t + H_{11}^{-1}(L) F_{11}(L) e_{1t}. \tag{2.14}$$

If the process is invertible, i.e. if the roots of $|H_{11}(L)| = 0$ lie outside the unit circle, (2.14) is an infinite MA process in x_t and e_{1t}. Note that (2.14) is a set of 'rational distributed lag' equations, Jorgenson (1966), or a system of 'transfer

[4] Hannan (1969, 1971) has analyzed the identification problem for systems in the form of (2.10).

function' equations, Box and Jenkins (1970). Also, the system in (2.14) can be brought into the following form:

$$|H_{11}(L)|y_t = -H_{11}^*(L)H_{12}(L)x_t + H_{11}^*(L)F_{11}(L)e_{1t}, \tag{2.15}$$

where $H_{11}^*(L)$ is the adjoint matrix associated with $H_{11}(L)$ and $|H_{11}(L)|$ is the determinant of $H_{11}(L)$. The equation system in (2.15), where each endogenous variable depends only on its own lagged values and on the exogenous variables, with or without lags, has been called the 'separated form', Marschak (1950), 'autoregressive final form', Dhrymes (1970), 'transfer function form', Box and Jenkins (1970), or 'fundamental dynamic equations', Pierce and Mason (1971).[5] As in (2.7), the p_1 endogenous variables in y_t have autoregressive parts with identical order and parameters, a point emphasized by Pierce and Mason (1971).

Having presented several equation systems above, it is useful to consider their possible uses and some requirements that must be met for these uses. As noted above, the final equations in (2.7) can be used to predict the future values of some or all variables in z_t, given that the forms of the ARMA processes for these variables have been determined and that parameters have been estimated. However, these final equations cannot be used for control and structural analysis. On the other hand, the reduced form equations (2.13) and transfer equations (2.15) can be employed for both prediction and control but not generally for structural analysis except when structural equations are in reduced form [$H_{110} \equiv I$ in (2.12)] or in final form [$H_{11} \equiv I$ in (2.10)]. Note that use of reduced form and transfer function equations implies that we have enough prior information to distinguish endogenous and exogenous variables. Further, if data on some of the endogenous variables are unavailable, it may be impossible to use the reduced form equations whereas it will be possible to use the transfer equations relating to those endogenous variables for which data are available. When the structural equation system in (2.10) is available, it can be employed for structural analysis and the associated 'restricted' reduced form or transfer equations can be employed for prediction and control. Use of the structural system (2.10) implies not only that endogenous and exogenous variables have been distinguished, but also that prior information is available to identify structural parameters and that the dynamic properties of the structural equations have been determined. Also, structural analysis of the complete system in (2.10) will usually require that data be available on all variables.[6] For the reader's convenience, some of these considerations are summarized in table 1.

Aside from the differing data requirements for use of the various equation systems considered in table 1, it should be appreciated that before each of the equation systems can be employed, the form of its equations must be ascertained. For example, in the case of the structural equation system (2.10), not only must

[5] If some of the variables in x_t are non-stochastic, say time trends, they will appear the final equations of the system.

[6] This requirement will not be as stringent for partial analyses and for fully recursive models.

endogenous and exogenous variables be distinguished, but also lag distributions, serial correlation properties of error terms, and identifying restrictions must be specified. Since these are often difficult requirements, it may be that some of the simpler equation systems will often be used although their uses are more limited than those of structural equation systems. Furthermore, even when the objective

Table 1

Uses and requirements for various equation systems.

Equation system	Uses of equation systems: Prediction	Control	Structural analysis	Requirements for use of equation systems
1. Final equations[a] (2.7)	yes	no	no	Forms of ARMA processes and parameter estimates
2. Reduced form equations (2.13)	yes	yes	no	Endogenous–exogenous classification of variables, forms of equations, and parameter estimates
3. Transfer equations[b] (2.15)	yes	yes	no	Endogenous–exogenous classification of variables, forms of equations, and parameter estimates
4. Final form equations[c] (2.14)	yes	yes	no	Endogenous–exogenous classification of variables, forms of equations, and parameter estimates
5. Structural equations (2.10)	yes	yes	yes	Endogenous–exogenous variable classification, identifying information,[d] forms of equations, and parameter estimates

[a]This is Tinbergen's (1940) term.

[b]These equations are also referred to as 'separated form' or 'autoregressive final form' equations.

[c]As noted in the text, these equations are also referred to as 'transfer function', 'fundamental dynamic', and 'rational distributed lag' equations.

[d]That is, information in the form of restrictions to identify structural parameters.

of an analysis is to obtain a structural equation system, the other equation systems, particularly the final equations and transfer equations, will be found useful. That is, structural assumptions regarding lag structures, etc. have implications for the forms and properties of final and transfer equations that can be checked with data. Such checks on structural assumptions can reveal weaknesses in them and possibly suggest alternative structural assumptions more in accord with the information in the data. In the following sections we illustrate these points in the analysis of a small dynamic structural equation system.

3. Algebraic analysis of a dynamic version of Haavelmo's model

Haavelmo (1947) formulated and analyzed the following static model with annual data for the U.S., 1929–1941:

$$c_t = \alpha y_t + \beta + u_t, \tag{3.1a}$$

$$r_t = \mu(c_t + x_t) + \nu + w_t, \tag{3.1b}$$

$$y_t = c_t + x_t - r_t, \tag{3.1c}$$

where c_t, y_t and r_t are endogenous variables, x_t is exogenous, u_t and w_t are disturbance terms, and α, β, μ and ν are scalar parameters. The definitions of the variables, all on a price-deflated, per capita basis, are:

c_t = personal consumption expenditures,

y_t = personal disposable income,

r_t = gross business saving, and

x_t = gross investment.[7]

Eq. (3.1a) is a consumption relation, (3.1b) a gross business saving equation and (3.1c) an accounting identity.

In Chetty's (1966, 1968) analyses of the system (3.1) employing Haavelmo's annual data, he found the disturbance terms highly autocorrelated, perhaps indicating that the static nature of the model is not appropriate. In view of this possibility, (3.1) is made dynamic in the following way:

$$c_t = \alpha(L) y_t + \beta + u_t, \tag{3.2a}$$

$$r_t = \mu(L)(c_t + x_t) + \nu + w_t, \tag{3.2b}$$

$$y_t = c_t + x_t - r_t. \tag{3.2c}$$

In (3.2a), $\alpha(L)$ is a polynomial lag operator that serves to make c_t a function of current and lagged values of income. Similarly, $\mu(L)$ in (3.2b) is a polynomial lag

[7]In Haavelmo's paper, gross investment, x_t, is defined equal to 'government expenditures + transfers − all taxes + gross private capital formation', while gross business saving, r_t, is defined equal to 'depreciation and depletion charges + capital outlay charged to current expense + income credited to other business reserves − revaluation of business inventories + corporate savings'.

operator that makes r_t depend on current and lagged values of c_t+x_t, a variable that Haavelmo refers to as 'gross disposable income'. On substituting for r_t in (3.2b) from (3.2c), the equations for c_t and y_t are:

$$c_t = \alpha(L)y_t+\beta+u_t, \tag{3.3a}$$

$$y_t = [1-\mu(L)](c_t+x_t)-\nu-w_t. \tag{3.3b}$$

With respect to the disturbance terms in (3.3), we assume:

$$\begin{pmatrix} u_t \\ -w_t \end{pmatrix} = \begin{pmatrix} f_{11}(L) & f_{12}(L) \\ f_{21}(L) & f_{22}(L) \end{pmatrix}\begin{pmatrix} e_{1t} \\ e_{2t} \end{pmatrix}, \tag{3.4}$$

where the $f_{ij}(L)$ are polynomials in L, e_{1t} and e_{2t} have zero means, unit variances, and are contemporaneously and serially uncorrelated.

Letting $z_t' = (c_t, y_t, x_t)$, the general multiple time series model for z_t, in the matrix form (2.1), is:

$$\underset{3\times 3}{H(L)}\,\underset{3\times 1}{z_t} = \underset{3\times 1}{\theta}+\underset{3\times 3}{F(L)}\,\underset{3\times 1}{e_t}, \tag{3.5}$$

where $e_t' = (e_{1t}, e_{2t}, e_{3t})$ satisfies (2.2)–(2.3) and $\theta' = (\theta_1, \theta_2, \theta_3)$ is a vector of constants. In explicit form, (3.5) is:

$$\begin{bmatrix} h_{11}(L) & h_{12}(L) & h_{13}(L) \\ h_{21}(L) & h_{22}(L) & h_{23}(L) \\ h_{31}(L) & h_{32}(L) & h_{33}(L) \end{bmatrix}\begin{bmatrix} c_t \\ y_t \\ x_t \end{bmatrix} = \begin{bmatrix} \theta_1 \\ \theta_2 \\ \theta_3 \end{bmatrix} + \begin{bmatrix} f_{11}(L) & f_{12}(L) & f_{13}(L) \\ f_{21}(L) & f_{22}(L) & f_{23}(L) \\ f_{31}(L) & f_{32}(L) & f_{33}(L) \end{bmatrix}\begin{bmatrix} e_{1t} \\ e_{2t} \\ e_{3t} \end{bmatrix}. \tag{3.6}$$

To specialize (3.6) to represent the dynamic version of Haavelmo's model in (3.3) with x_t exogenous, we must have $\theta_1 = \beta$, $\theta_2 = \nu$,

$$\begin{array}{lll} h_{11}(L) \equiv 1 & h_{12}(L) \equiv -\alpha(L) & h_{13}(L) \equiv 0 \\ h_{21}(L) \equiv -[1-\mu(L)] & h_{22}(L) \equiv 1 & h_{23}(L) \equiv -[1-\mu(L)] \\ h_{31}(L) \equiv 0 & h_{32}(L) \equiv 0 & h_{33}(L) \end{array} \tag{3.7a}$$

and

$$f_{13}(L) \equiv f_{23}(L) \equiv f_{31}(L) \equiv f_{32}(L) \equiv 0. \tag{3.7b}$$

Utilizing the conditions in (3.7), (3.6) becomes:

$$\begin{bmatrix} 1 & h_{12}(L) & 0 \\ h_{21}(L) & 1 & h_{23}(L) \\ 0 & 0 & h_{33}(L) \end{bmatrix} \begin{bmatrix} c_t \\ y_t \\ x_t \end{bmatrix} = \begin{bmatrix} \theta_1 \\ \theta_2 \\ \theta_3 \end{bmatrix} + \begin{bmatrix} f_{11}(L) & f_{12}(L) & 0 \\ f_{21}(L) & f_{22}(L) & 0 \\ 0 & 0 & f_{33}(L) \end{bmatrix} \begin{bmatrix} e_{1t} \\ e_{2t} \\ e_{3t} \end{bmatrix}. \tag{3.8}$$

Note that the process on the exogenous variable is $h_{33}(L)x_t = f_{33}(L)e_{3t}+\theta_3$ and the fact that x_t is assumed exogenous requires that $h_{31}(L) \equiv h_{32}(L) \equiv 0$ and that $F(L)$ be block diagonal as shown in (3.8).

Table 2
Degrees of lag polynomials in final equations.

Final equation	Degrees of AR polynomials[a]	Degrees of MA polynomials for errors[b]		
		e_{1t}	e_{2t}	e_{3t}
(3.9): c_t	Maximum of r_{33} and $r_{12}+r_{21}+r_{33}$	Maximum of $r_{33}+q_{11}$ and $r_{33}+r_{12}+q_{21}$	Maximum of $r_{33}+q_{12}$ and $r_{33}+r_{12}+q_{22}$	$r_{12}+r_{23}+q_{33}$
(3.10): y_t	r_{33} and $r_{12}+r_{21}+r_{33}$	$r_{33}+q_{21}$ and $r_{33}+r_{21}+q_{11}$	$r_{33}+q_{22}$ and $r_{33}+r_{21}+q_{12}$	$r_{23}+q_{33}$
(3.11): x_t	r_{33}	—	—	q_{33}

[a] r_{ij} is the degree of h_{ij}. Note from (3.7a), $h_{21} \equiv h_{23} \equiv -[1-\mu(L)]$, and thus $r_{21} = r_{23}$.
[b] q_{ij} is the degree of f_{ij}.

In what follows we shall denote the degree of $h_{ij}(L)$ by r_{ij} and the degree of $f_{ij}(L)$ by q_{ij}.

From (3.8), the final equations for c_t and y_t are given by:

$$(1-h_{12}h_{21})h_{33}c_t = \theta'_1+(f_{11}-f_{21}h_{12})h_{33}e_{1t} +(f_{12}-f_{22}h_{12})h_{33}e_{2t}+f_{33}h_{12}h_{23}e_{3t} \tag{3.9}$$

and

$$(1-h_{12}h_{21})h_{33}y_t = \theta'_2+(f_{21}-f_{11}h_{21})h_{33}e_{1t} +(f_{22}-f_{12}h_{21})h_{33}e_{2t}-f_{33}h_{23}e_{3t}, \tag{3.10}$$

with $h_{21} \equiv h_{23}$ and θ'_1 and θ'_2 being new constants. Note that the AR parts of (3.9) and (3.10) have the same order and parameters. The degrees of the lag polynomials in (3.9) and (3.10) and in the process for x_t,

$$h_{33}x_t = f_{33}e_{3t}+\theta_3, \tag{3.11}$$

are indicated in table 2.

As mentioned above, the AR polynomials in the final equations for c_t and y_t are identical and of maximal degree equal to $r_{12}+r_{21}+r_{33}$, as shown in table 2, where r_{12} = degree of $\alpha(L)$ in the consumption equation, r_{21} is the degree of $\mu(L)$ in the business saving equation, and r_{33} is the degree of h_{33}, the AR polynomial in the process for x_t. Also, if the disturbance terms u_t and w_t are serially uncorrelated and if all the q_{ij} in table 2 are zero, the following results hold:

(i) In the final equation for c_t, the degree of the AR part is larger than or equal to the order of the MA process for the disturbance term; that is $r_{12}+r_{21}+r_{33} \geqq \max(r_{12}+r_{23}, r_{33}+r_{12})$, with equality holding if $r_{33} = 0$, since $r_{21} = r_{23}$, or if $r_{21} = r_{23} = 0$.

(ii) In the final equation for y_t, the degree of the AR polynomial is larger than or equal to the order of the MA process for the disturbance term; i.e., $r_{12}+r_{21}+r_{33} \geqq r_{33}+r_{21}$ with equality holding if $r_{12} = 0$. Thus if the process for x_t is purely AR and the structural disturbance terms u_t and w_t are not serially correlated, (i) and (ii) provide useful implications for properties of the final equations that can be checked with data as explained below.

Further, under the assumption that the structural disturbance terms u_t and w_t are serially uncorrelated, all q_{ij} other than q_{33} in table 2 will be equal to zero. If the process for x_t is analyzed to determine the degree of h_{33}, r_{33}, and of f_{33}, q_{33}, this information can be used in conjunction with the following:

(iii) In the final equation for c_t, the degree of the AR polynomial will be smaller than or equal to the order of the MA disturbance if $q_{33} \geqq r_{33}$. (Note $r_{21} = r_{23}$.) If $q_{33} < r_{33}$, the degree of the AR polynomial will be greater than the order of the MA disturbance term.

(iv) In the final equation for y_t, the degree of the AR polynomial will be greater than the order of the MA disturbance term given that $r_{12}+r_{33} > q_{33}$ and $r_{12} > 0$. They will be equal if $r_{12} = 0$ and $r_{33} \geqq q_{33}$ or if $r_{12}+r_{33} = q_{33}$. The latter will be greater if $r_{12}+r_{33} < q_{33}$.

In what follows, post-World War II quarterly data for the U.S., 1947–1972, are employed to analyze the final equations for c_t, y_t and x_t and to check some of the implications mentioned above.

From (3.8), the dynamic structural equations of the dynamized Haavelmo model are:

$$\begin{bmatrix} 1 & h_{12} & 0 \\ h_{21} & 1 & h_{23} \end{bmatrix} \begin{bmatrix} c_t \\ y_t \\ x_t \end{bmatrix} = \begin{bmatrix} \theta_1 \\ \theta_2 \end{bmatrix} + \begin{bmatrix} f_{11} & f_{12} \\ f_{21} & f_{22} \end{bmatrix} \begin{bmatrix} e_{1t} \\ e_{2t} \end{bmatrix}, \tag{3.12a}$$

or

$$\begin{pmatrix} 1 & h_{12} \\ h_{21} & 1 \end{pmatrix}\begin{pmatrix} c_t \\ y_t \end{pmatrix} = \begin{pmatrix} \theta_1 \\ \theta_2 \end{pmatrix} + \begin{pmatrix} 0 \\ -h_{23} \end{pmatrix} x_t + \begin{pmatrix} f_{11} & f_{12} \\ f_{21} & f_{22} \end{pmatrix}\begin{pmatrix} e_{1t} \\ e_{2t} \end{pmatrix}. \tag{3.12b}$$

From (3.12b), the transfer equations, the analogue of (2.15) are:

$$\begin{vmatrix} 1 & h_{12} \\ h_{21} & 1 \end{vmatrix}\begin{pmatrix} c_t \\ y_t \end{pmatrix} = \begin{pmatrix} \theta_1'' \\ \theta_2'' \end{pmatrix} + \begin{pmatrix} 1 & -h_{12} \\ -h_{21} & 1 \end{pmatrix}\begin{pmatrix} 0 \\ -h_{23} \end{pmatrix} x_t + \begin{pmatrix} 1 & -h_{12} \\ -h_{21} & 1 \end{pmatrix}\begin{pmatrix} f_{11} & f_{12} \\ f_{21} & f_{22} \end{pmatrix}\begin{pmatrix} e_{1t} \\ e_{2t} \end{pmatrix}, \tag{3.13}$$

or

$$(1-h_{12}h_{21})c_t = \theta_1'' + h_{12}h_{23}x_t + (f_{11}-f_{21}h_{12})e_{1t} + (f_{12}-f_{22}h_{12})e_{2t} \tag{3.14}$$

and

$$(1-h_{12}h_{21})y_t = \theta_2'' - h_{23}x_t + (f_{21}-f_{11}h_{21})e_{1t} + (f_{22}-f_{12}h_{21})e_{2t}, \tag{3.15}$$

where θ_1'' and θ_2'' are constant parameters that are linear functions of θ_1 and θ_2.

The following properties of the transfer equations, (3.14) and (3.15) are of interest:

(a) The AR parts of the two transfer equations are identical. Since h_{12} is of degree r_{12} and h_{21} of degree r_{21}, the order of the autoregression in each equation is $r_{12}+r_{21}$.

(b) In (3.14) the degree of the operator $h_{12}h_{23}$ hitting x_t is $r_{12}+r_{23} = r_{12}+r_{21}$, the same as that for the autoregressive part of the equation, $1-h_{12}h_{21}$.

(c) In (3.15), the degree of the lag operator, $-h_{23}$, applied to x_t is $r_{23} = r_{21}$, which is less than or equal to the degree of $1-h_{12}h_{21}$, the AR polynomial.

(d) The lag operator acting on x_t in the equation for c_t, $h_{12}h_{33}$, is a multiple of that acting on x_t in the equation for y_t and thus the former has degree larger than or equal to that of the latter.

(e) If the structural disturbance terms are serially uncorrelated, i.e. f_{ij} has degree zero in L for $i, j = 1, 2$, the orders of the MA error terms in (3.14) and (3.15) are $r_{12} \geqq 0$ and $r_{21} \geqq 0$, respectively. Thus for both equations, the order of the MA error process is less than or equal to the order of the AR part of the equation.

By use of appropriate statistical techniques and data, the transfer equations in (3.14)–(3.15) can be analyzed to determine the degrees of lag polynomials and to estimate parameter values. With these results in hand, it is possible to check the points (a)–(e) relating to the transfer equations associated with Haavelmo's dynamic model. Below the results of such calculations are reported.

4. Empirical analyses of final equations (3.9)–(3.11)

4.1. Analyses utilizing Box–Jenkins (BJ) techniques

In this subsection, we report the results of applying BJ identification and estimation procedures to the final equations of the dynamized Haavelmo model. Box and Jenkins (1970, p. 175) provide the following relations between the autocorrelation and partial autocorrelation functions associated with stationary stochastic processes for a single random variable:[8]

(1) For a purely AR process of order p, the autocorrelation function tails off and the partial autocorrelation function[9] has a cut-off after lag p.

(2) For a purely MA process of order q, the autocorrelation function has a cut-off after lag q and the partial autocorrelation function tails off.

(3) For a mixed ARMA process, with the order of the AR being p and that of the MA being q, the autocorrelation function is a mixture of exponential and damped sine waves after the first $q-p$ lags and the partial autocorrelation function is dominated by a mixture of exponentials and damped sine waves after the first $p-q$ lags.

Box and Jenkins suggest differencing a series until it is stationary and then computing estimates of the autocorrelation and partial autocorrelation functions. Using (1)–(3), it may be possible to determine or identify the nature of the process for the differenced series as well as values of p and q. Once the process or model and p and q have been determined, the model's parameters can be estimated, usually by use of a non-linear estimation procedure.

Plots of the data for the variables of Haavelmo's model, c_t, y_t, and x_t, are shown in fig. 1.[10] From this figure, it is seen that the variables apparently have trends and thus are non-stationary. First or second differencing of the variables may induce stationarity. For the reader's benefit, plots of the first differences of the variables are presented in fig. 2. It is clear from the plots of the first differences that they are less subject to trend than are the levels of the variables. However, a slight trend in the magnitudes of the first differences may be present if the levels are subject to a relatively constant proportionate rate of growth. For this reason, we also performed analyses based on second differences.

In fig. 3, we present the estimated autocorrelation function for the series $c_t - c_{t-1}$, the first difference of consumption.[11] Also indicated in fig. 3, is a $\pm 2\hat{\sigma}$ confidence band for the autocorrelations where $\hat{\sigma}$ is a large sample standard

[8]See Box and Jenkins (1970, pp. 64–65) for definition of this function.

[9]Autocorrelation functions have been formerly used in econometrics, see e.g. Wold (1953).

[10]The variables have been defined above. The data are seasonally adjusted quarterly, price-deflated, per capita aggregates, expressed in dollars at an annual rate, for the U.S. economy, 1947I–1972II, obtained from official sources cited in the appendix.

[11]The computer program employed was developed by C.R. Nelson and S. Beveridge, Graduate School of Business, University of Chicago.

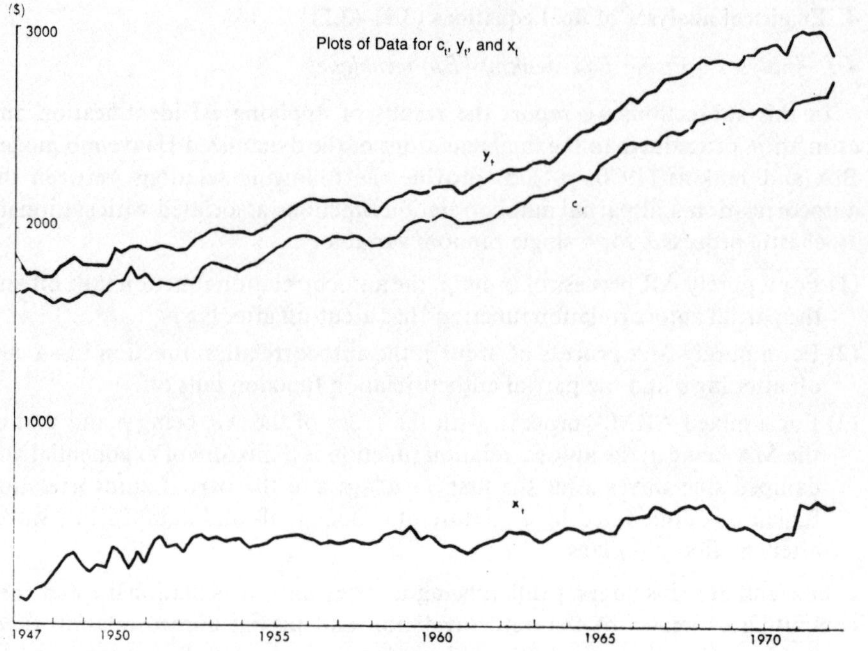
($)
3000
2000
1000
Plots of Data for c_t, y_t, and x_t
y_t
c
x_t
1947
1950
1955
1960
1965
1970

Fig. 1

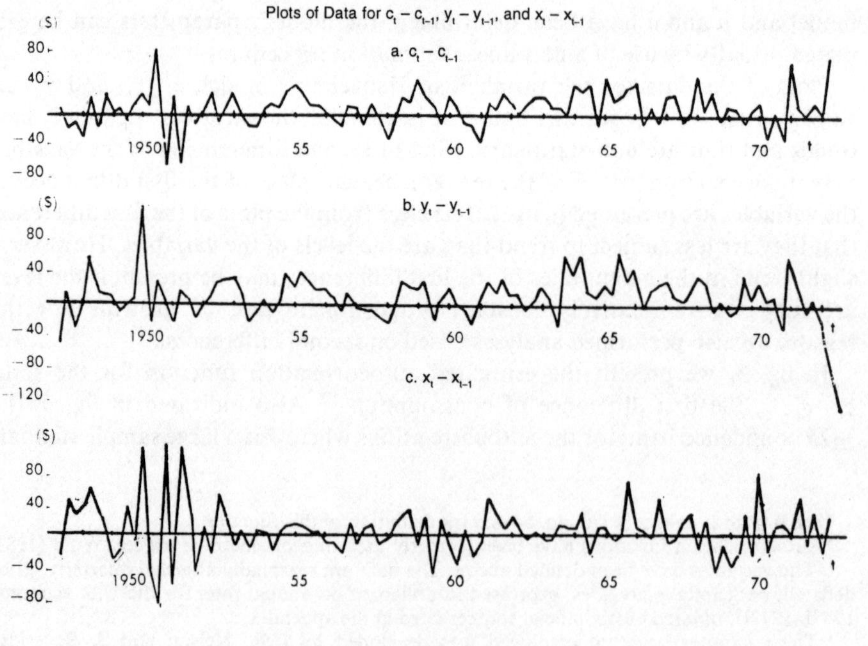
Plots of Data for c_t − c_{t−1}, y_t − y_{t−1}, and x_t − x_{t−1}
($)
a. c_t − c_{t−1}
80
40
− 40
− 80
1950
55
60
65
70
($)
b. y_t − y_{t−1}
80
40
− 40
− 80
−120
1950
55
60
65
70
c. x_t − x_{t−1}
($)
80
40
−40
−80
1950
55
60
65
70

Fig. 2

error for the sample autocorrelations.[12] It is seen that all estimated autocorrelations lie within the band except for that of lag 2. This suggests that the underlying process is not purely AR. If the autocorrelation estimate for lag 2 is regarded as a cut-off, the results suggest that a second order MA process may be generating the first differences of c_t. The estimated partial autocorrelation function, also shown in fig. 3, does not appear to contradict this possibility. Estimation of a second order MA model for the first differences of consumption, led to the following results using the BJ non-linear algorithm:

$$c_t - c_{t-1} = e_t + \underset{(0.101)}{0.0211}e_{t-1} + \underset{(0.101)}{0.278}e_{t-2} + \underset{(2.96)}{10.73} \qquad s^2 = 530, \tag{4.1}$$

where s^2 is the residual sum of squares (RSS) divided by the number of degrees of freedom and the figures in parentheses are large sample standard errors.

For income, y_t, a plot of the first differences is given in fig. 2. From the plot of the estimated autocorrelations for the first differences in fig. 4, it appears that none of the autocorrelations are significantly different from zero, a finding that leads to the presumption that the underlying model is not AR. Estimates of the partial autocorrelations for lag 4 and lag 10 lie close to the limits of the $\pm 2\hat{\sigma}$ band – see fig. 4. Other partial autocorrelations appear not to differ significantly from zero. If all autocorrelations and partial autocorrelations are deemed not significantly different from zero, then the conclusion would be that the first differences of income are generated by a random walk model which was estimated with the following results:

$$y_t - y_{t-1} = e_t + \underset{(8.336)}{10.03} \qquad s^2 = 842. \tag{4.2}$$

For the first differences of investment, $x_t - x_{t-1}$ – see plot in fig. 2 – the estimated autocorrelation and partial autocorrelation functions are given in fig. 5. The autocorrelations alternate in sign and show some significant values for lags less than or equal to 5 which suggests an AR model. The partial autocorrelation function has a cut-off at lag 4 supporting the presumption that the model is AR and indicating a 4th order AR scheme. Also, the partial autocorrelation function for the second differences has a cut-off at lag 3 while the autocorrelations alternate in sign for lags less than 11, findings which support those derived from analysis of first differences. In view of these findings, a 4th order AR model has been fitted with the data:

$$(1 + \underset{(0.0942)}{0.263}L - \underset{(0.0976)}{0.0456}L^2 + \underset{(0.0970)}{0.0148}L^3 + \underset{(0.0933)}{0.376}L^4)(x_t - x_{t-1}) \tag{4.3}$$

$$= e_t + \underset{(3.265)}{7.738} \qquad s^2 = 939.$$

[12] $\hat{\sigma}^2$ is an estimate of the following approximate variance of r_k, the kth sample serial correlation, given in Bartlett (1946). With $\rho_v = 0$ for $v > q$, var $(r_k) \doteq (1 + 2\Sigma_{v=1}^{q} \rho_v^2)/T$, for $k > q$. The $\pm 2\hat{\sigma}$ bounds for r_k, $k = 1, 2, \ldots, 12$, are calculated under the assumption, $\rho_v = 0$, $v > 0$. For $k > 12$, they are calculated assuming $\rho_v = 0$, $v > 12$.

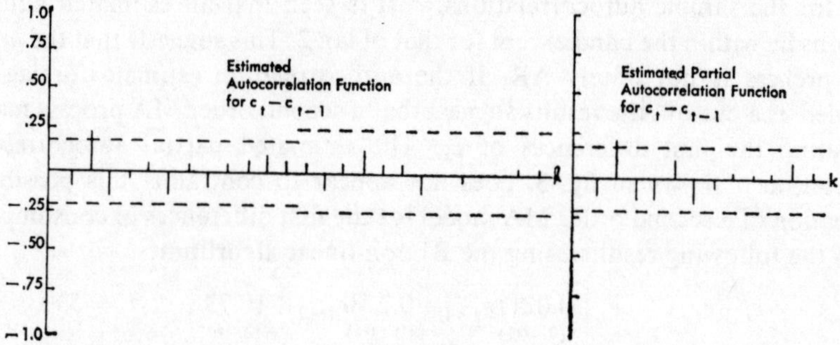

Fig. 3

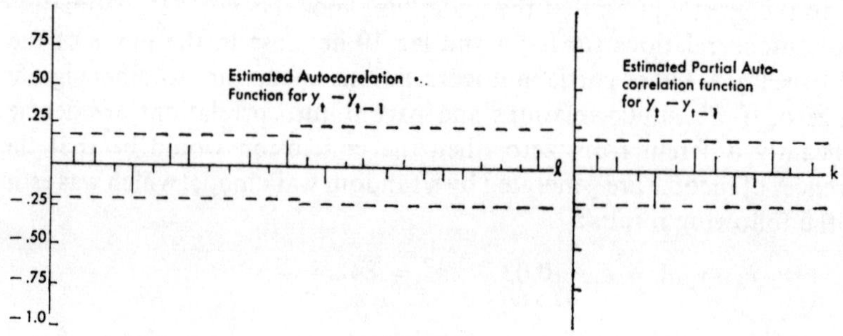

Fig. 4

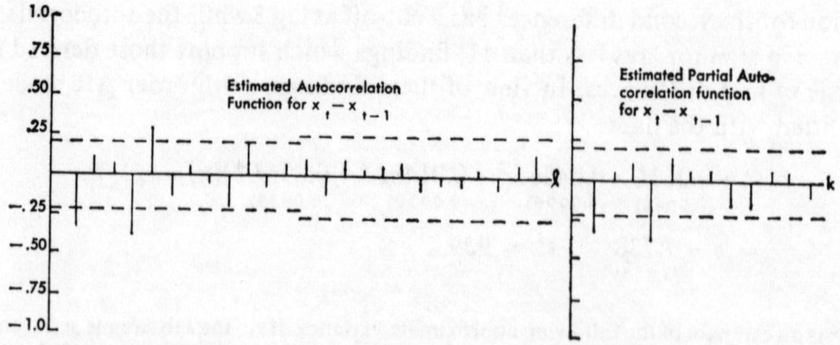

Fig. 5

Vertical axes of figs. 3–5 on the right: $\hat{\phi}_{kk}$, on the left: r_l.

In contrast to the processes for the first differences of c_t and y_t in (4.1) and (4.2), that for the first differences of investment, x_t, in (4.3) has an AR part. Thus the requirement of the structural form that all endogenous variables have identical AR parts of order equal to or greater than that for x_t – see (3.9)–(3.10) above – is not satisfied given the results in (4.1)–(4.3). Using the notation of table 2 with h_{ij} of degree r_{ij} regarded as an element of $H(L)/(1-L)$, the degree of the AR polynomial in (4.31) is $r_{33} = 4$ while that of the error process is $q_{33} = 0$. In the case where no cancelling occurs in (4.1)–(4.2), it is clear that the conditions (3.9) and (3.10) of table 2 can not be met. Even if h_{23} in (3.8) satisfies $h_{23} \equiv 0$ so that c_t and y_t are generated independently of x_t, the conditions on the final equations are not met by the results for the final equations in (4.1)–(4.3).[13] Thus while (4.1)–(4.3) appear to be consistent with the information in the data, they are not compatible with the dynamized Haavelmo model specified in sect. 3, eqs. (3.2a)–(3.2c).

At this point, the following are considerations that deserve attention:

1. Although the fits of the models in (4.1)–(4.3) are fairly good, it may be that schemes somewhat more complicated than (4.1)–(4.3) are equally well or better supported by the information in the data and are compatible with the implications of the Haavelmo model. This possibility is explored below.

2. To compare and test alternative final equations for each variable, it would be desirable to have inference methods that are less 'judgmental' and more systematically formal than are the BJ methods. In the next subsection, we indicate how likelihood ratios and posterior odds ratios can be used for discriminating among alternative final equation models.

3. It must be recognized that there are some limitations on the class of AR models that can be transformed to a stationary process through differencing. That is, only those AR models whose roots lie on the boundary or inside the unit circle can be transformed to stationary models by differencing. Other transformations, say logarithmic, have to be used for models with roots outside the unit circle.

4. Differencing series may amplify the effects of measurement errors present in the original data and seriously affect estimates of the autocorrelation and partial autocorrelation functions. Of course, this problem arises not only in the BJ approach but also in any analysis of ARMA processes, particularly those of high order.

4.2. Analyses of final equations utilizing likelihood ratios and posterior odds

The purpose of this section is to provide additional procedures for identifying or determining the forms of final equations. These procedures involve use of

[13] If $h_{23} \equiv 0$, then (4.1)–(4.2) imply $r_{12}+r_{21} = 1$; $r_{12}+q_{21}, q_{11}, q_{12}, r_{12}+q_{22} \leqq 2$ (with at least one equality); and $r_{21}+q_{11}, q_{21}, r_{21}+q_{12}, q_{22} \leqq 0$. These conditions imply $q_{11} = q_{12} = q_{21} = q_{22} = r_{21} = 0$, $r_{21} = 1$, and $r_{21} = 2$ which cannot hold simultaneously.

likelihood ratios and Bayesian posterior odds. After showing how to obtain likelihood ratios and posterior odds, some of the results are applied in the analysis of Haavelmo's model.

Consider the following ARMA model for a single random variable z_t,

$$\phi(L)z_t = \theta(L)\varepsilon_t, \qquad t = 1, 2, \dots, T, \tag{4.4}$$

where $\phi(L)$ and $\theta(L)$ are polynomials in L of degree p and q, respectively. Assume that the ε_t's are normally and independently distributed, each with zero mean and common variance, σ^2. Let $u_t \equiv \theta(L)\varepsilon_t$. Then given the 'starting values' for ε_t and z_t, ε_0 and z_0, the vector $\boldsymbol{u}' = (u_1, u_2, \dots, u_T)$ has a T-dimensional multivariate normal distribution with zero mean vector and covariance matrix Σ, that is:

$$p(\boldsymbol{u}|\boldsymbol{\phi}, \boldsymbol{\theta}, \sigma^2, z_0, \varepsilon_0) = (2\Pi)^{-T/2} \exp |\Sigma|^{-\frac{1}{2}} \left\{ -\tfrac{1}{2}\boldsymbol{u}'\Sigma^{-1}\boldsymbol{u} \right\}, \tag{4.5}$$

where $\boldsymbol{\phi}' = (\phi_1, \phi_2, \dots, \phi_p)$ and $\boldsymbol{\theta}' = (\theta_1, \theta_2, \dots, \theta_q)$. The matrix Σ is a $T \times T$ positive definite symmetric matrix with elements given by:

$$\begin{aligned} \sigma_{t,t-k} &= \sigma^2\Big(1 + \sum_{i=1}^{q} \theta_i^2\Big), && \text{for } k = 0, \\ \sigma_{t,t-k} &= \sigma^2\Big(-\theta_k + \sum_{i=k+1}^{q} \theta_{i-k}\theta_i\Big), && \text{for } 0 < k \leq q, \\ \sigma_{t,t-k} &= 0, && \text{for } k > q. \end{aligned} \tag{4.6}$$

Also, the joint probability density function (pdf) for the ε_t's, given by

$$\varepsilon_t = z_t - \phi_1 z_{t-1} - \dots - \phi_p z_{t-p} + \theta_1 \varepsilon_{t-1} + \dots + \theta_q \varepsilon_{t-q}, \qquad t = 1, 2, \dots, T, \tag{4.7}$$

is:

$$p(\boldsymbol{\varepsilon}|\boldsymbol{\phi}, \boldsymbol{\theta}, \sigma^2, \varepsilon_0, z_0) = (2\Pi\sigma^2)^{-T/2} \exp\left\{ -\frac{1}{2\sigma^2} \sum_{t=1}^{T} \varepsilon_t^2 \right\}. \tag{4.8}$$

Since the Jacobian of the transformation from the ε_t's to the z_t's is equal to one, the joint pdf for the z_t's, the likelihood function, is:

$$\begin{aligned} p(\boldsymbol{z}|\boldsymbol{\phi}, \boldsymbol{\theta}, \sigma^2, \varepsilon_0, z_0) = (2\Pi\sigma^2)^{-T/2} \exp\Big\{ -\frac{1}{2\sigma^2} \sum_{t=1}^{T} (z_t - \phi_1 z_{t-1} \\ - \dots - \phi_p z_{t-p} + \theta_1 \varepsilon_{t-1} + \theta_2 \varepsilon_{t-2} \\ + \dots + \theta_q \varepsilon_{t-q})^2 \Big\}. \end{aligned} \tag{4.9}$$

In this context, (4.9) is convenient since Marquardt's non-linear computational algorithm can be applied to obtain maximum likelihood (ML) estimates.

If we have an alternative ARMA model,

$$\phi_a(L)z_t = \theta_a(L)\varepsilon_{at}, \qquad t = 1, 2, \ldots, T, \tag{4.10}$$

where $\phi_a(L)$ is of degree p_a, $\theta_a(L)$ of degree q_a and the error process ε_{at} is $NID(0, \sigma_a^2)$, then the likelihood ratio, λ, for (4.4) and (4.10) is

$$\lambda = (\max_{\phi,\theta,\sigma} l(\phi, \theta, \sigma|z))/(\max_{\phi_a,\theta_a,\sigma_a} l(\phi_a, \theta_a, \sigma_a|z)), \tag{4.11}$$

where $l(\phi, \theta, \sigma|z)$ denotes (4.9) viewed as a function of its parameters and similarly for $l(\phi_a, \theta_a, \sigma_a|z)$. The ratio of maximized likelihood functions in (4.11) reduces to:

$$\lambda = (\hat{\sigma}_a^2/\hat{\sigma}^2)^{T/2}, \tag{4.12}$$

where

$$\hat{\sigma}^2 = \frac{1}{T}\sum_{t=1}^{T}(z_t - \hat{\phi}_1 z_{t-1} - \ldots - \hat{\phi}_p z_{t-p} + \hat{\theta}_1\hat{\varepsilon}_{t-1} + \ldots + \hat{\theta}_q\hat{\varepsilon}_{t-q})^2 \tag{4.13a}$$

and

$$\hat{\sigma}_a^2 = \frac{1}{T}\sum_{t=1}^{T}(z_t - \hat{\phi}_{1a} z_{t-1} - \ldots - \hat{\phi}_{p_a a} z_{t-p_a} + \hat{\theta}_{1a}\hat{\varepsilon}_{a,t-1} + \ldots + \hat{\theta}_{q_a a}\hat{\varepsilon}_{a,t-q_a})^2 \tag{4.13b}$$

are the ML estimates for σ^2 and σ_a^2.

If model (4.10) is nested in model (4.4), i.e. $p_a \leqq p$ and/or $q_a \leqq q$, with at least one strict inequality, and under the assumption that (4.10) is the true model, $2ln\lambda$ is approximately distributed as χ_r^2 with r being the number of restrictions imposed on (4.4) to obtain (4.10); that is, $r = p+q-(p_a+q_a)$ – see Silvey (1970, pp. 112–113). In choosing a significance level for this test, it is very important, as usual, to consider errors of the first and second kind. Rejecting the nested model when it is 'true' appears to us to be a less serious error than failing to reject it when the broader model is 'true'. That is, using the restricted model when the restrictions are not 'true' may lead to serious errors. Use of the broader model, when the restricted model is 'true', involves carrying along some extra parameters which may not be as serious a problem as giving these parameters incorrect values. This argues against using extremely low significance levels, e.g. $\alpha = 0.01$ or $\alpha = 0.001$. Also, these considerations rationalize somewhat the usual practice of some degree of over-fitting when the model form is somewhat uncertain. More systematic analysis and study of this problem would be desirable.

In order to compare (4.4) and (4.10) in a Bayesian context, we have to specify a prior distribution on the parameter space. In the problem of comparing *nested* models, this prior distribution has a mixed form with weights whose ratio is the prior odds on alternative models – see e.g. Jeffreys (1961, p. 250), Zellner (1971, p. 297ff.) and Palm (1972). Formally, the posterior odds ratio relating to (4.4) and (4.10) is given by:

$$K_{1a} = \frac{\Pi}{\Pi_a} \frac{\int p(\boldsymbol{\phi}, \boldsymbol{\theta}, \sigma) l(\boldsymbol{\phi}, \boldsymbol{\theta}, \sigma | z)\, \mathrm{d}\boldsymbol{\phi}\, \mathrm{d}\boldsymbol{\theta}\, \mathrm{d}\sigma}{\int p(\boldsymbol{\phi}_a, \boldsymbol{\theta}_a, \sigma_a) l(\boldsymbol{\phi}_a, \boldsymbol{\theta}_a, \sigma_a | z)\, \mathrm{d}\boldsymbol{\phi}_a\, \mathrm{d}\boldsymbol{\theta}_a\, \mathrm{d}\sigma_a}, \tag{4.14}$$

where K_{1a} is the posterior odds ratio, Π/Π_a is the prior odds ratio, and $p(\boldsymbol{\phi}, \boldsymbol{\theta}, \sigma)$ and $p(\boldsymbol{\phi}_a, \boldsymbol{\theta}_a, \sigma_a)$ are the prior pdf's for the parameters. Before (4.14) can be made operational, it is necessary to formulate the prior pdf's and to evaluate the integrals, either exactly or approximately.[14]

We now compute likelihood ratios to compare alternative formulations of the final equations of Haavelmo's model. The information in table 2 and empirical results in the literature on quarterly consumption relations suggest higher order AR and MA schemes than those fitted in sect. 4.1. For example, a 4th order AR model for the 2nd differences of consumption with 3rd order MA error terms is a scheme tentatively suggested by considerations presented in sect. 4.1. This scheme has been fitted with both the consumption and income data with results shown for c_t and y_t in tables 3 and 4 and those for x_t in table 5 with figures in parentheses being large sample standard errors. Also shown in table 3 are the results for the simple schemes of sect. 4.1 and results for several other specifications. It should be noted that use of the broader schemes for c_t and y_t results in decreases in the value of the residual sum of squares divided by degrees of freedom of about 8 to 12 per cent. However, it must be noted that the large sample standard errors associated with the point estimates are rather large in number of instances.

To put the comparison of alternative schemes on a more formal basis, likelihood ratios have been computed and are reported in table 6. Using these ratios as a basis for large sample χ^2 tests, it is found that it is possible to reject the simpler versions at reasonable significance levels. The results of the tests indicate that it is reasonable to retain the model (5, 1, 4) for consumption and income and

[14]Note however, as pointed out by Lindley (1961), the likelihood functions in the numerator and denominator of (4.14) can be expanded about ML estimates. If just the first terms of these expansions are retained, namely $l(\hat{\boldsymbol{\phi}}, \hat{\boldsymbol{\theta}}, \hat{\sigma}|z)$ and $l(\hat{\boldsymbol{\phi}}_a, \hat{\boldsymbol{\theta}}_a, \hat{\sigma}_a|z)$, and if the prior pdf's are proper, (4.14) is approximated by:

$$K_{1a} \doteq [\Pi/\Pi_a[l(\hat{\boldsymbol{\phi}}, \hat{\boldsymbol{\theta}}, \hat{\sigma}|z)/l(\hat{\boldsymbol{\phi}}_a, \hat{\boldsymbol{\theta}}_a, \hat{\sigma}_a|z)],$$

i.e. a prior odds ratio, Π/Π_a, times the usual likelihood ratio. As Lindley points out, additional terms in the expansions can be retained and the resulting expression will involve some prior moments of parameters. Thus on assigning a value to Π/Π_a, the prior odds ratio, the usual likelihood ratio is transformed into an approximate posterior odds ratio for whatever non-dogmatic, proper prior pdf's employed.

Table 3

Estimated final equations for consumption.

Model (p, d, q)[a]	RSS, residual sum of squares	DF	RSS/DF	Estimates of the AR part					Estimates of the MA part				Constant
				AR1	AR2	AR3	AR4	AR5	MA1	MA2	MA3	MA4	
1) (0, 1, 2)	52,012	98	530						−0.021 (0.101)	−0.278 (0.101)			10.727 (2.96)
2) (4, 2, 3)	45,807	92	497	−0.727 (0.365)	−0.199 (0.255)	−0.077 (0.178)	−0.123 (0.115)		0.354 (0.344)	0.258 (0.302)	0.452 (0.210)		0.283 (0.256)
3) (5, 2, 2)	48,411	92	525	−0.651 (0.458)	0.226 (0.142)	−0.0567 (0.160)	−0.230 (0.155)	0.0534 (0.162)	0.380 (0.452)	0.581 (0.409)			0.247 (0.164)
4) (5, 1, 4)	44,634	91	490	0.587 (0.101)	0.514 (0.199)	−0.166 (0.246)	−0.655 (0.0849)	0.075 (0.140)	0.678 (0.0958)	0.215 (0.198)	0.178 (0.246)	−0.684 (0.134)	6.751 (1.851)

[a] (p, d, q) denotes an ARMA model for the dth differences of a variable that has AR polynomial of degree p and MA polynomial of degree q.

Table 4

Estimated final equations for income.

Model (p, d, q)[a]	RSS, residual sum of squares	DF	RSS/DF	Estimates of the AR part					Estimates of the MA part				Constant
				AR1	AR2	AR3	AR4	AR5	MA1	MA2	MA3	MA4	
1) (0, 1, 0)	85,042	101	842										10.03 (8.336)
2) (0, 1, 4) + restrictions	79,362	99	797									0.302 (0.107)	10.90 (2.012)
3) (4, 1, 1)	78,546	95	823	0.0803 (0.353)	0.0861 (0.118)	−0.0156 (0.112)	−0.307 (0.110)		−0.016 (0.372)				12.182 (4.788)
4) (4, 2, 3)	78,827	92	821	−0.429 (0.418)	−0.154 (0.532)	0.222 (0.153)	−0.063 (0.120)		0.440 (0.384)	0.227 (0.423)	0.384 (0.580)		0.128 (0.395)
5) (4, 1, 4)	65,428	92	703	−0.225 (0.255)	−0.390 (0.244)	−0.437 (0.168)	−0.258 (0.224)		−0.295 (0.249)	−0.733 (0.215)	0.668 (0.210)	−0.057 (0.276)	22.545 (8.950)
6) (5, 1, 4)	65,351	91	705	0.0678 (1.207)	−0.552 (0.380)	−0.164 (0.771)	−0.211 (0.266)	−0.0048 (0.357)	0.0210 (1.214)	−0.833 (0.349)	−0.290 (1.073)	0.0417 (0.373)	18.834 (23.14)

[a] (p, d, q) denotes an ARMA model for the dth differences of a variable that has AR polynomial of degree p and MA polynomial of degree q.

Table 5

Estimated final equations for investment.

Model (p, d, q)[a]	RSS, residual sum of squares	DF	RSS/DF	Estimates of the AR part					Estimates of the MA part				Constant
				AR1	AR2	AR3	AR4	AR5	MA1	MA2	MA3	MA4	
1) (4, 1, 0)	90,519	96	939	−0.263 (0.0942)	0.0456 (0.0976)	−0.0148 (0.0970)	−0.376 (0.0933)						7.738 (3.265)
2) (4, 2, 3)	91,124	92	978	−0.653 (0.284)	−0.183 (0.294)	−0.0334 (0.132)	−0.325 (0.127)		0.587 (0.282)	0.301 (0.246)	0.115 (0.274)		−0.127 (0.232)
3) (5, 2, 1)	87,428	93	929	−0.247 (0.0924)	0.0395 (0.0991)	−0.0245 (0.0980)	−0.337 (0.0991)	0.106 (0.096)	1.014 (0.012)				−0.109 (0.102)
4) (5, 2, 2)	90,391	92	970	−0.659 (0.631)	−0.076 (0.192)	−0.0076 (0.127)	−0.364 (0.118)	−0.065 (0.276)	0.552 (0.609)	0.425 (0.630)			−1.04 (0.187)

[a] (p, d, q) denotes an ARMA model for the dth differences of a variable that has AR polynomial of degree p and MA polynomial of degree q.

(4, 1, 0) for investment. Given that these models are tentatively accepted, it is the case that the AR and MA polynomials for the consumption and income processes have identical degrees. However, the point estimates of the AR parameters of consumption and income processes are not very similar, a finding that must be tempered by the fact that standard errors associated with coefficient estimates are rather large, particularly for the AR parameters of the income process. It would be very desirable to develop joint estimation techniques for the two

Table 6

Results of large sample likelihood ratio tests applied to final equations of Haavelmo's model.

Models compared[a]	$\lambda = \frac{\mathcal{L}(X\|H_1)}{\mathcal{L}(X\|H_0)}$	$2 \ln \lambda$	r	Critical points for χ_r^2 $\alpha = 0.05$	$\alpha = 0.10$	$\alpha = 0.20$
1. *Consumption* c_t						
H_0: (0, 1, 2) vs. H_1: (4, 2, 3)[b]	573.547	—	—	—	—	—
H_0: (0, 1, 2) vs. H_1: (5, 1, 4)	2098.29	15.230	7	14.07	12.02	9.80
H_0: (5, 2, 2) vs. H_1: (4, 2, 3)[b]	15.871	—	—	—	—	—
H_0: (4, 2, 3) vs. H_1: (5, 1, 4)	3.654	2.592	2	5.99	4.61	3.22
2. *Income* y_t						
H_0: (0, 1, 0) vs. H_1: (0, 1, 4)[c]	31.697	6.912	1	3.84	2.71	1.64
H_0: (0, 1, 0) vs. H_1: (4, 1, 4)	4937.0×10^2	26.219	8	15.51	13.36	11.03
H_0: (0, 1, 0) vs. H_1: (5, 1, 4)	5236.0×10^2	26.337	9	16.92	14.68	12.24
H_0: (0, 1, 0) vs. H_1: (4, 2, 3)[b]	44.453	—	—	—	—	—
H_0: (4, 2, 3) vs. H_1: (5, 1, 4)	117.8×10^2	18.748	2	5.99	4.61	3.22
3. *Investment* x_t						
H_0: (4, 1, 0) vs. H_1: (5, 2, 1)[b]	5.678	—	—	—	—	—

[a] H: (p, d, q) denotes an ARMA model for the dth difference of a variable that has AR poly nomial of degree p and MA error polynomial of degree q.
[b] These are non-nested hypotheses.
[c] Here there are 3 restrictions on the parameters of the MA error process.

equations in order to increase the precision of estimation and joint test procedures for testing the hypothesis that the AR parameters are the same for the two processes.

What are the implications of retaining (5, 1, 4) models for c_t and y_t and a (4, 1, 0) model for x_t? As noted above, the empirical finding that first differencing appears adequate to induce stationarity for all three variables suggests that the model can be expressed in first difference form. That is, we rewrite (3.5) as follows:

$$\bar{H}(L)(1-L)z_t = \theta + F(L)e_t, \tag{4.15}$$

where $\bar{H}(L)$ has elements that are the elements of $H(L)$ divided by $1-L$. With the polynomials $h_{ij}(L)$ of degree r_{ij} considered elements of $\bar{H}(L)$ rather than $H(L)$ and if no cancelling occurs in (4.15), then under the restrictions imposed on the Haavelmo model in the preceding section (see table 2), we have $r_{33} = 4$; $q_{33} = 0$; $r_{12}+r_{21}+r_{33} = 5$;

$$r_{33}+q_{11}, r_{33}+r_{12}+q_{21}, r_{33}+q_{12}, r_{33}+r_{12}+q_{22},$$

$$r_{12}+r_{23}+q_{33} \leqq 4$$

and

$$r_{33}+q_{21}, r_{33}+r_{21}+q_{11}, r_{33}+q_{22}, r_{33}+r_{21}+q_{12}, r_{23}+q_{33} \leqq 4,$$

with at least one equality holding in both cases. These restrictions imply $r_{12}+r_{21} = 1$, all $q_{ij} = 0$ and $r_{12} = r_{21} = 0$, conditions that cannot hold simultaneously. Also, if we retain a (5, 2, 1) model for investment, we end up with a contradiction.

If we make the assumption that the joint process for Δc_t and Δy_t is independent of Δx_t, i.e. $h_{23} \equiv 0$ in (3.8), an assumption that may appeal to some Quantity of Money theorists but not to most Keynesians, the degrees of the polynomials reported in table 2 are reduced by r_{33} and we have the following restrictions on the degrees of the AR polynomials in the processes for Δc_t and Δy_t: $r_{12}+r_{21} = 5$; $q_{11}, q_{12}, r_{12}+q_{21}, r_{12}+q_{22} \leqq 4$; and $q_{21}, q_{22}, r_{21}+q_{11}, r_{21}+q_{12} \leqq 4$, with at least one equality holding in both cases. With further assumptions, e.g. $r_{12} = 2$ and $r_{21} = 3$, it is possible to determine compatible values for the degrees of the structural equations' lag polynomials and error term polynomials. However, this compatibility is attained only with the controversial assumption that the joint process for Δc_t and Δy_t is independent of the process for Δx_t, Haavelmo's investment variable.[15] A major implication of this last assumption is that the analysis of the transfer functions should reveal no dependence of either Δc_t or Δy_t on Δx_t, a point that is checked in the next section where we analyze the transfer equations (3.14)–(3.15).

An alternative way to achieve compatibility of the results of the final equation analyses with structural assumptions, is to assume that $h_{23}(L) \equiv h_{33}(L)$. This assumption implies that the investment variable influences Δc_t and Δy_t only through its disturbance term. With this assumption, h_{33} cancels in eqs. (3.9) and (3.10) and the empirical findings combined with the results in table 2, imply that $r_{33} = 4$, $r_{23} = r_{33} = 4$, by assumption, $q_{33} = 0$, $r_{12}+r_{21} = 5$,

$$q_{11}, q_{12}, r_{12}+q_{21}, r_{12}+q_{22} \leqq 4$$

and

$$q_{21}, q_{22}, r_{21}+q_{11}, r_{21}+q_{12} \leqq 4,$$

with at least one equality in each case. Further, the autoregressive parts of the

[15]In terms of (3.8), this assumption implies that $h_{23}(L) \equiv 0$. With this assumption, the structural equations are, from (3.3): $\Delta c_t = \alpha(L)\Delta y_t + \beta + u_t$ and $\Delta y_t = [1-\mu(L)]\Delta c_t - \nu - w_t$. That is, current and lagged values of y_t affect consumption and current and lagged consumption affect income.

final equations for c_t and y_t are identical to the autoregressive parts in their transfer equations. These implications of the assumption, $h_{23}(L) \equiv h_{33}(L)$, and of final equation findings for the forms of the transfer equations will be checked in the next section.

5. Empirical analyses of transfer equations (3.14)–(3.15)

We now turn to an analysis of the transfer functions, shown in (3.14)–(3.15), associated with the dynamized Haavelmo model. These equations express c_t and y_t as functions of their own lagged values, of current and lagged values of x_t, and of current and lagged error terms. The first step in the analysis of the transfer functions is the determination or identification of the degrees of the lag polynomials. In general a transfer function can be written as an infinite moving average process in exogenous variables plus an error term, u_t, with zero mean, that is,

$$y_t = v(L)x_t + u_t, \tag{5.1}$$

where $v(L) = \Sigma_{i=0}^{\infty} v_i L^i$. Often this infinite process can be well approximated by a finite distributed lag model of order k, that is $v(L) = \Sigma_{i=0}^{k} v_i L^i$. Solving the Yule–Walker equations for a kth order approximation, we obtain

$$Ey_t x_{t-\tau} = v_0 Ex_t x_{t-\tau} + v_1 Ex_{t-1} x_{t-\tau} + \ldots + v_k Ex_{t-k} x_{t-\tau}, \qquad \tau = 0, 1, 2, \ldots, k. \tag{5.2}$$

Rough estimates of the v_i's can be obtained by replacing the expectations in (5.2) by corresponding sample moments and solving for the v_i's. This is equivalent to regressing y_t on current and lagged values of x_t. Note too that $v(L)$ can be written as the ratio of two lag polynomials of degrees s and r, $\omega_s(L)$ and $\theta_r(L)$, as follows:

$$v(L) = [\omega_s(L)/\theta_r(L)]L^b, \tag{5.3}$$

with b some non-negative integer. Introduction of $b \neq 0$ allows for some 'dead time' in the response pattern of y_t to x_t. Using (5.3) and the preliminary estimates of the v_i's, obtained as described above, preliminary estimates of the parameters $\omega_s(L)$, ω_j's, $j = 0, 1, 2, \ldots, s$, and of $\theta_r(L)$, θ_i's, $i = 1, 2, \ldots, r$, can be found. As Box and Jenkins (1970, p. 378) point out, the v_j's, the impulse response weights consist of:

(1) b zero values, $v_0, v_1, \ldots, v_{b-1}$,
(2) a further $s-r+1$ values, $v_b, \ldots, v_{b+s-r}$, following no fixed pattern (if $s < r$, no such values occur), and
(3) values v_j, with $j \geqq b+s-r+1$, following a pattern given by an rth order difference equation with starting values $v_{b+s} \ldots v_{b+s-r+1}$.

Properties (1)–(3) can help to determine the values of b, s and r from the preliminary estimates of the v's. Then the residuals $\hat{u}_t = y_t - \hat{v}(L)x_t$ are analyzed to determine the degrees of the AR and MA parts of the error process using estimated autocorrelation and partial autocorrelation functions. Final estimation of the transfer function so determined can be accomplished in the BJ approach by use of Marquardt's non-linear algorithm.

It is important to observe that the results of final equation analyses can be employed to obtain some information about the degrees of transfer functions' lag polynomials. In fact, if assumptions regarding structural equations' forms are in accord with information in the data, there should be compatibility between the final equations' and transfer equations' forms that we determine from the data.[16] That is, final equation analysis led us to (5, 1, 4) processes for c_t and y_t and to a (4, 1, 0) process for x_t, namely, $\phi_{(4)}(L)\Delta x_t = e_t$, or $\Delta x_t = \phi_{(4)}^{-1}(L)e_t$. If we difference the transfer functions in (3.14) and (3.15) and then substitute $\Delta x_t = \phi_{(4)}^{-1}(L)e_t$, we obtain the final equations for c_t and y_t. To obtain compatibility with the empirically determined (5, 1, 4) final equations for c_t and y_t, the transfer functions must have polynomials hitting Δx_t with degree $s \leqq 3$ in the numerator and degree $r = 0$ in the denominator. In addition, the ratio of lag polynomials operating on the transfer functions' error terms should have a numerator of degree zero and denominator of degree one.

Under the assumption $h_{23}(L) \equiv h_{33}(L)$, introduced tentatively in the previous section, the final equation analyses yield the following implications for the transfer functions' lag structures in (3.14)–(3.15):

(1) The AR parts of both transfer functions are identical with the AR parts of the final equations and are of degree $r_{12}+r_{21} = 5$.

(2) The polynomial, h_{23}, hitting Δx_t in the transfer function for income is identical with the AR part of the final equation for x_t and has degree $r_{23} = r_{33} = 4$.

(3) The polynomial operating on Δx_t in the consumption transfer function has degree of at least 4.

(4) The order of the moving average error process in each transfer equation is equal to 4.

We shall check points (1)–(4) in the empirical analyses that follow. In this connection, it is the case that there is no assurance that the information in the data will be in accord with compatible findings for the final equations and transfer functions of the Haavelmo model since model specification errors, measurement errors, imperfect seasonal adjustment, etc., can affect analyses to produce incompatible results.

To determine the degrees of the lag polynomials in (3.14)–(3.15) and to get starting values for the v's, different values for k were employed in connection with (5.1)–(5.2) that provided preliminary estimates of the v's. For $k = 8$ and the first difference of c_t, the v_i's with $i = 0, 1$ and 6 appear to be significantly

[16] Here we abstract from the possibility that $h_{23}(L) \equiv 0$ since in this case transfer functions show no dependence on x_t, a point that is checked below.

different from zero and the behavior of the estimated v_i's is very irregular. The fact that v_0 is significantly different from zero implies that $b = 0$. With respect to determining values for r and s, the degrees of the polynomials in (5.3), the results are not very precise. The values indicated by our final equation analysis are used and starting values for the ω_i's are based on the estimates of the v_i's for alternative values of s and r. Further, the analysis of the residuals from an 8th order distributed lag model for the first difference of c_t suggests a mixed first order AR and second order MA error process. However, it is thought that this determination of the transfer function's properties is very tentative and thus it was thought worthwhile to proceed to estimate transfer functions in forms suggested by our final equation analyses. Some estimation results for these forms are shown in (5.4)–(5.5): with $s = 3$,

$$\Delta c_t = (\underset{(0.0689)}{-0.129} + \underset{(0.0704)}{0.188}L + \underset{(0.070)}{0.0875}L^2 - \underset{(0.068)}{0.037}L^3)\Delta x_t \qquad (5.4)$$
$$+ e_t/(1 + \underset{(0.105)}{0.0208}L) + \underset{(2.297)}{10.41},$$

with residual sum of squares (RSS) equal to 41,617, and with $s = 2$,

$$\Delta c_t = (\underset{(0.0685)}{-0.149} + \underset{(0.0709)}{0.172}L + \underset{(0.0677)}{0.0830}L^2)\Delta x_t \qquad (5.5)$$
$$+ e_t/(1 - \underset{(0.105)}{0.0047}L) + \underset{(2.34)}{10.03},$$

with RSS = 43,226.

Under the assumption $h_{23}(L) \equiv h_{33}(L)$, an estimate of the transfer function form suggested by the final equation analysis is:

$$\Delta c_t = -\frac{\underset{(0.068)}{0.0349} + \underset{(0.106)}{0.171}L + \underset{(0.102)}{0.264}L^2}{1 + \underset{(0.289)}{0.575}L - \underset{(0.480)}{0.187}L^2}\Delta x_t$$
$$+ \frac{1 - \underset{(0.388)}{0.550}L - \underset{(0.465)}{0.559}L^2}{1 - \underset{(0.327)}{0.484}L - \underset{(0.431)}{0.695}L^2 + \underset{(0.200)}{0.288}L^3} e_t + \underset{(8.573)}{10.55}, \qquad (5.6)$$

with RSS = 30,945.

With respect to the first differences of y_t, with $k = 8$, implementation of (5.1)–(5.2) resulted in just v_0 being significantly different from zero suggesting that $b = 0$. The estimated v_i's appear to follow a damped wave-like pattern. The difference between the values of r and s is thus thought to be small but this inference is very uncertain. In view of this, the values of s and r implied by the final equation analysis, $s \leqq 3$ and $r = 0$ have been employed along with a ratio of polynomials for the error process with numerator of degree 0 and denominator of degree 1. Some estimes reflecting these considerations follow.

For $s = 3$,

$$\Delta y_t = (\underset{(0.066)}{0.385} + \underset{(0.0675)}{0.139}L + \underset{(0.067)}{0.0938}L^2 - \underset{(0.0658)}{0.124}L^3)\Delta x_t + \frac{e_t}{(1 + \underset{(0.105)}{0.055}L)} + \underset{(2.15)}{10.83}, \tag{5.7}$$

with RSS = 38,908, and

for $s = 2$,

$$\Delta y_t = (\underset{(0.067)}{0.355} + \underset{(0.0696)}{0.121}L + \underset{(0.066)}{0.117}L^2)\Delta x_t + e_t(1 + \underset{(0.103)}{0.0077}L) + \underset{(2.301)}{10.01}, \tag{5.8}$$

with RSS = 41,547.

Under the assumption that $h_{23}(L) \equiv h_{33}(L)$, the transfer function for income suggested by the final equation analyses has been estimated with the following results:

$$\Delta y_t = \frac{\underset{(0.075)}{0.417} + \underset{(0.165)}{0.063}L + \underset{(0.163)}{0.068}L^2}{1 - \underset{(0.316)}{0.0628}L - \underset{(0.325)}{0.111}L^2 + \underset{(0.172)}{0.389}L^3}\Delta x_t + \frac{1 + \underset{(0.315)}{0.517}L}{1 + \underset{(0.303)}{0.551}L - \underset{(0.114)}{0.147}L^2}e_t + \underset{(2.396)}{11.02} \tag{5.9}$$

with RSS = 36.462.

The estimates reported in (5.4)–(5.9) are in accord with the implications of final equation analyses for the forms of the transfer functions. Further, we see that for (5.4)–(5.5) and (5.7)–(5.8), the AR polynomials for Δc_t and Δy_t are almost identical, a requirement that the transfer functions must satisfy given that the variables are generated by a joint process with x_t exogenous. Further, from (3.14), (a) the AR part of the transfer function for Δc_t should be identical, up to degree 1, to that operating on Δx_t in the same equation if the Haavelmo model is adequate, and (b) the lag operator acting on Δx_t in the equation for Δc_t should be a multiple of that for Δx_t in the income equation. The first of these requirements is not satisfied by the results in (5.4)–(5.5) since the polynomials acting on Δc_t and Δx_t have differing degrees. However, the requirements (a) and (b) are satisfied, as far as the degrees are concerned, for (5.6) and (5.9).[17]

Last, as mentioned above, one way to have the empirically determined final equations compatible with the dynamized Haavelmo model in (3.8) is to assume $h_{23} \equiv 0$, i.e. that the process for Δx_t is independent of the joint process for

[17]This suggests that the restriction $h_{21} \equiv h_{23}$, originally imposed, is probably not in accord with the information in the data.

Table 7

Estimated transfer functions for consumption.

Model	RSS	DF	RSS/DF	Estimates of the AR and MA parts of Δx_t	Estimates of the AR and MA parts of the error process	Constant
M_1	41,617	89	467.6	$\underset{(0.0689)}{-0.129}\ \underset{(0.0704)}{+0.188L}\ \underset{(0.070)}{+0.0875L^2}\ \underset{(0.068)}{-0.037L^3}$	$1/(1\underset{(0.105)}{+0.0208L})$	$\underset{(2.297)}{10.41}$
M_2	43,286	91	475.0	$\underset{(0.0685)}{-0.149}\ \underset{(0.0709)}{+0.172L}\ \underset{(0.0677)}{+0.0830L^2}$	$1/(1\underset{(0.105)}{-0.0047L})$	$\underset{(2.34)}{10.03}$
M_3	40,212	90	446.8	$\underset{(0.067)}{0.370}\ \underset{(0.068)}{+0.126L}\ \underset{(0.0677)}{+0.0829L^2}\ \underset{(0.066)}{-0.114L^3}$	$1\underset{(0.106)}{-0.0376L}$	$\underset{(2.202)}{10.62}$
M_4	37,941	84	451.7	$\dfrac{\underset{(0.074)}{-0.080}\ \underset{(0.108)}{+0.085L}\ \underset{(0.0897)}{+0.219L^2}}{1\underset{(0.351)}{+0.717L}\ \underset{(0.349)}{-0.143L^2}}$	$\dfrac{1\underset{(0.530)}{+0.495L}}{1\underset{(0.537)}{+0.445L}\ \underset{(0.117)}{-0.250L^2}\ \underset{(0.192)}{-0.003L^3}}$	$\underset{(2.83)}{10.16}$
M_5	36,504	82	445.2	$\dfrac{\underset{(0.0699)}{-0.111}\ \underset{(0.0767)}{+0.183L}\ \underset{(0.083)}{+0.0526L^2}\ \underset{(0.074)}{+0.123L^3}}{1\underset{(0.140)}{+0.111L}\ \underset{(0.114)}{+0.794L^2}}$	$\dfrac{1\underset{(0.334)}{-0.386L}}{1\underset{(0.320)}{-0.389L}\ \underset{(0.115)}{-0.236L^2}\ \underset{(0.122)}{+0.252L^3}}$	$\underset{(0.221)}{10.74}$
M_6	37,645	85	442.3	$\dfrac{\underset{(0.072)}{-0.129}\ \underset{(0.103)}{+0.050L}\ \underset{(0.076)}{+0.187L^2}}{1\underset{(0.246)}{+0.838L}\ \underset{(0.331)}{+0.275L^2}\ \underset{(0.203)}{+0.392L^3}}$	$\dfrac{1\underset{(0.219)}{+0.530L}}{1\underset{(0.212)}{+0.487L}\ \underset{(0.112)}{-0.204L^2}}$	$\underset{(2.601)}{10.75}$
M_7	33,453	83	403.1	$\dfrac{\underset{(0.068)}{-0.0349}\ \underset{(0.106)}{+0.171L}\ \underset{(0.102)}{+0.264L^2}}{1\underset{(0.289)}{-0.575L}\ \underset{(0.480)}{-0.187L^2}}$	$\dfrac{1\underset{(0.388)}{-0.550L}\ \underset{(0.465)}{-0.559L^2}}{1\underset{(0.327)}{-0.484L}\ \underset{(0.431)}{-0.695L^2}\ \underset{(0.200)}{+0.228L^3}}$	$\underset{(8.573)}{10.5}$

Table 8

Estimated transfer functions for income.

Model	RSS	DF	RSS/DF	Estimates of the AR and MA parts of Δx_t	Estimates of the AR and MA parts of the error process	Constant
M_1	38,908	89	437.2	$\underset{(0.066)}{0.385}+\underset{(0.0675)}{0.139L}+\underset{(0.067)}{0.0938L^2}-\underset{(0.0658)}{0.124L^3}$	$1/(1+\underset{(0.105)}{0.055L})$	10.83 (2.15)
M_2	41,547	91	456.6	$\underset{(0.067)}{0.355}+\underset{(0.0696)}{0.121L}+\underset{(0.066)}{0.117L^2}$	$1/(1-\underset{(0.103)}{0.0077L})$	10.01 (2.301)
M_3	43,149	90	479.4	$\underset{(0.0692)}{-0.145}+\underset{(0.0710)}{0.173L}+\underset{(0.071)}{0.075L^2}-\underset{(0.069)}{0.0265L^3}$	$1-\underset{(0.106)}{0.0127L}$	10.17 (2.34)
M_4	43,751	92	475.6	$\underset{(0.0683)}{-0.156}+\underset{(0.0706)}{0.164L}+\underset{(0.0676)}{0.088L^2}$	$1+\underset{(0.105)}{0.0046L}$	9.84 (2.33)
M_5	37,775	87	434.2	$\dfrac{\underset{(0.070)}{0.408}+\underset{(0.165)}{0.064L}}{1-\underset{(0.325)}{0.129L}-\underset{(0.164)}{0.168L^2}+\underset{(0.134)}{0.389L^3}}$	$\dfrac{1-\underset{(0.344)}{0.228L}}{1-\underset{(0.326)}{0.181L}-\underset{(0.107)}{0.172L^2}}$	11.11 (2.63)
M_6	42,819	89	481.1	$\dfrac{\underset{(0.075)}{0.390}-\underset{(0.292)}{0.110L}-\underset{(0.209)}{0.180L^2}}{1-\underset{(0.816)}{0.462L}-\underset{(0.620)}{0.637L^2}+\underset{(0.214)}{0.103L^3}}$	$1-\underset{(0.110)}{0.0364L}$	−13.41 (13.84)
M_7	36,462	85	429.0	$\dfrac{\underset{(0.075)}{0.417}+\underset{(0.165)}{0.063L}+\underset{(0.163)}{0.068L^2}}{1-\underset{(0.316)}{0.0628L}-\underset{(0.325)}{0.111L^2}+\underset{(0.172)}{0.389L^3}}$	$\dfrac{1+\underset{(0.315)}{0.517L}}{1+\underset{(0.303)}{0.551L}-\underset{(0.114)}{0.147L^2}}$	11.02 (2.396)

Δc_t and Δy_t. This implies no dependence of Δc_t and of Δy_t on Δx_t in the transfer equations. The dependence that has been found above might be interpreted as due to specification errors (e.g. x_t might not be exogenous) or to other complicating factors (e.g. measurement errors, poor seasonal adjustment, etc.). On the other hand, it may be that the alternative assumption $h_{23} \equiv h_{33}$ is more in accord with the information in the data. Note the substantial reduction in RSS associated with (5.6) and (5.9) relative to the RSS for other models.

Table 9

Results of large sample likelihood ratio tests applied to transfer functions of Haavelmo's model.

Models compared		$\lambda = \dfrac{L(y\|H_1)}{L(y\|H_0)}$	$2 \ln \lambda$	r	Critical points for χ_r^2		
					$\alpha = 0.05$	$\alpha = 0.10$	$\alpha = 0.20$
1. *Consumption*							
(1) H_0: M_2	H_1: M_1	6.66	3.79	1	3.84	2.71	1.64
(2) H_0: M_1	H_1: M_5	702.27	13.11	5	11.07	9.24	7.29
(3) H_0: M_2	H_1: M_4	678.89	13.04	5	11.07	9.24	7.29
(4) H_0: M_2	H_1: M_5	4679.79	16.90	6	12.59	10.64	8.56
(5) H_0: M_2	H_1: M_6	992.41	13.80	5	11.07	9.24	7.29
(6) H_0: M_3	H_1: M_5	126.11	9.67	5	11.07	9.24	7.29
(7) H_0: M_4	H_1: M_5	6.893	3.86	5	11.07	9.24	7.29
(8) H_0: M_2	H_1: M_7	3.5×10^5	25.56	5	11.07	9.24	7.29
(9) H_0: M_4	H_1: M_7	5.02×10^2	12.44	1	3.84	2.71	1.64
2. *Income*							
(1) H_0: M_2	H_1: M_1	26.609	6.563	1	3.84	2.71	1.64
(2) H_0: M_4	H_1: M_3	1.999	1.385	1	3.84	2.71	1.64
(3) H_0: M_4	H_1: M_6	2.935	2.153	3	7.81	6.25	4.64
(4) H_0: M_2	H_1: M_7	683.83	13.06	5	11.07	9.24	7.29
(5) H_0: M_4	H_1: M_7	9,065	18.22	5	11.07	9.24	7.29
(6) H_0: M_6	H_1: M_7	3,088	16.07	2	5.99	4.61	3.22
(7) H_0: M_5	H_1: M_7	5.86	3.54	1	3.84	2.71	1.64

To explore this last point more systematically, some alternative transfer function models, formulated without taking into account results of final equation analyses, have been estimated with results shown in tables 7 and 8. For comparison, results with models implied by the final equation analyses are also presented. A quick look at the residual sum of squares (RSS) indicates that for consumption, alternative model M_5 yields about a 12 per cent reduction in RSS relative to M_1 while M_7 yields about a 20 per cent reduction. For income, M_5 yields about a 3 per cent reduction in RSS relative to M_1 while M_7 provides the lowest RSS, about 6 per cent lower than for M_1.

For nested models, a large sample likelihood ratio test procedure has been employed to compare alternative formulations with results reported in table 9.

For consumption, M_2 is preferred to M_1 at the 5 per cent level. However, pairwise comparisons of M_2 against M_4, M_5 and M_6 favor the latter relative to M_2. However, in comparisons with M_7, both M_2 and M_4 are rejected. Thus the results of the likelihood ratio tests favor M_7, a model that is compatible with the results of the final equation analysis under the assumption $h_{23}(L) \equiv h_{33}(L)$. The results for income transfer functions, shown in the bottom of table 9, indicate that M_2 is rejected in favor of M_1 while M_4 performs better than M_3 or M_6. Compared with M_7, models M_2, M_4 and M_6 are rejected at the 5 per cent significance level, it appears that M_7 is not significantly different from M_5. The results of these comparisons suggest that it is reasonable to accept tentatively, models M_1, M_5 or M_7 as being in accord with the information in the data. If we retain models M_7 for consumption and M_7 for income,[18] we have $r_{12}+r_{21} = 5$ for the order of the AR polynomials acting on Δc_t and Δy_t, the degrees of the polynomials operating on Δx_t are of degrees, 5 and 4, respectively, and the error processes are each of order 4. Under the assumption that $h_{23}(L) \equiv h_{33}(L)$, these results are in accord with the requirements that the final equations must satisfy (see table 2).

6. Summary of results and implications for structural equations

In table 10, we present the preferred final equation and transfer function models for the dynamized Haavelmo model. From the information provided in table 10, the following are the implied restrictions on the lag structures appearing in the structural equations of the model where the r_{ij}'s refer to the degrees of elements of $\bar{H}(L)$, the matrix $H(L)$ divided by $(1-L)$:

1. $r_{12} = 1$; $r_{33} = r_{23} = r_{21} = 4$; $q_{11} = q_{12} = 0$; and $q_{21}, q_{22} \leqq 3$, with at least one equality holding.

2. The transfer functions show a dependence of Δc_t and of Δy_t on Δx_t. Under the assumption that $h_{23} \equiv h_{33}$, the final equations and transfer functions selected by the likelihood ratio tests are compatible insofar as the degrees of the relevant lag polynomials are considered.

3. Explicitly, a structural representation compatible with the results of the

[18]Other possibilities, e.g. M_7 for Δc_t and M_1 for Δy_t or M_7 for Δc_t and M_5 for Δy_t, lead to incompatibitilies with the requirements that the final and transfer equations must satisfy. In the first case, M_7 for Δc_t and M_1 for Δy_t, the AR parts of the transfer functions are not identical as required in (3.14)–(3.15) and even possible cancelling will not be sufficient to satisfy the condition on the polynomials hitting Δx_t in (3.14)–(3.15). If we retain M_7 for Δc_t and M_5 for Δy_t, their autoregressive parts have the same order, $r_{12}+r_{21} = 5$, and the degrees of the polynomials for Δx_t are respectively $r_{12}+r_{23} = 5$ and $r_{23} = 3$, implying $r_{21} = 2$. However, the assumption $h_{21}(L) \equiv h_{23}(L)$, implying $r_{21} = r_{23}$, is no longer satisfied. In addition, there is incompatibility with the analysis of the final equations requiring $r_{23} = 4$.

Table 10

Final equation and transfer function models for dynamized Haavelmo model.[a]

Systems of equations	Model	Order of AR part	Degree of lag polynomial for Δx_t	Order of MA error process
1. *Final equations*				
Δc_t	$(5, 1, 4)^b$	$r_{12}+r_{21} = 5$	–	$q_{11}, q_{12}, r_{12}+q_{21}, r_{12}+q_{22} \leqq 4$ (at least one equality holding)
Δy_t	$(5, 1, 4)^b$	$r_{12}+r_{21} = 5$	–	$q_{21}, q_{22}, r_{21}+q_{11}, r_{21}+q_{12} \leqq 4$ (at least one equality holding)
Δx_t	$(4, 1, 0)^b$	$r_{33} = 4$	–	$q_{33} = 0$
2. *Transfer functions*				
Δc_t	M_7^c	$r_{12}+r_{21} = 5$	$r_{12}+r_{23} = 5$	$q_{11}, q_{12}, r_{12}+q_{21}, r_{12}+q_{22} \leqq 4$ (at least one equality)
Δy_t	M_7^c	$r_{12}+r_{21} = 5$	$r_{23} = 4$	$q_{21}, q_{22}, q_{11}+r_{21}, q_{12}+r_{21} \leqq 4$ (at least one equality)

[a]It is assumed that $h_{23} \equiv h_{33}$.
[b]See tables 3–5 where estimated models are presented.
[c]See table 8 where estimated models are presented.

final equation and transfer function analyses is:

$$\begin{bmatrix} 1 & -\alpha^{(1)} & 0 \\ \mu_1^{(4)}-1 & 1 & \mu_2^{(4)}-1 \\ 0 & 0 & \mu_2^{(4)}-1 \end{bmatrix} (1-L) \begin{bmatrix} c_t \\ y_t \\ x_t \end{bmatrix} = \begin{bmatrix} \theta_1 \\ \theta_2 \\ \theta_3 \end{bmatrix} \tag{6.1}$$

$$+ \begin{bmatrix} f_{11}^{(0)} & f_{12}^{(0)} & 0 \\ f_{21}^{(\leqq 3)} & f_{22}^{(\leqq 3)} & 0 \\ 0 & 0 & f_{33}^{(0)} \end{bmatrix} \begin{bmatrix} e_{1t} \\ e_{2t} \\ e_{3t} \end{bmatrix},$$

where the superscripts in parentheses denote the degrees of lag polynomials that were determined from the final equation and transfer function analyses. Note that these polynomials are equal to the polynomials of the matrix $H(L)$ in (3.8) divided by a common factor $1-L$. The factor $1-L$ hitting the variables c_t, y_t and x_t puts them in first difference form, a transformation that appears adequate to induce stationarity in all three variables, a condition required for the correlogram analysis of the variables. That the same differencing transformation induces stationarity in all variables is not necessary for all models but is an empirical finding in the present case. Also, to achieve compatibility, it is necessary that $h_{11}(L) \equiv h_{22}(L) \equiv 1$, a special case of what was assumed in (3.7a). Last, it should be noted that $\mu_1^{(4)}(L)$ and $\mu_2^{(4)}(L)$ are not necessarily identical.

The system in (6.1) can alternatively be expressed in the form of (3.2a)–(3.2c) as follows:

$$\begin{bmatrix} 1 & 0 & -\alpha^{(1)} & 0 \\ -\mu_1^{(4)} & 1 & 0 & -\mu_2^{(4)} \\ -1 & 1 & 1 & -1 \end{bmatrix}(1-L)\begin{bmatrix} c_t \\ r_t \\ y_t \\ x_t \end{bmatrix} = \begin{bmatrix} \beta \\ v \\ 0 \end{bmatrix} + \begin{bmatrix} u_t \\ w_t \\ 0 \end{bmatrix}, \tag{6.2}$$

with u_t a serially uncorrelated disturbance term and w_t following a third order moving average process. Further, u_t and w_t will generally be correlated.

Using the identity, $\Delta y_t = \Delta c_t + \Delta x_t - \Delta r_t$, we can eliminate Δr_t from (6.2) to obtain:

$$\Delta c_t = \alpha_0 \Delta y_t + \alpha_1 \Delta y_{t-1} + \beta + u_t, \tag{6.3a}$$

and

$$\Delta y_t = (1-\mu_1^{(4)})\Delta c_t + (1-\mu_2^{(4)})\Delta x_t - v - w_t, \tag{6.3b}$$

$$= \sum_{i=0}^{4} \gamma_i \Delta c_{t-i} - v + w_t',$$

where $\alpha^{(1)} \equiv \alpha_0 + \alpha_1 L$, $1-\mu_1^{(4)} \equiv \Sigma_{i=0}^4 \gamma_i L^i$, and $-(1-\mu_2^{(4)})\Delta x_t = f_{33}^{(0)} e_{3t}$ have been used and $w_t' \equiv -(w_t + f_{33}^{(0)} e_{3t})$. The two equation system in (6.3) is a simultaneous equation model with dynamic lags and contemporaneously correlated disturbance terms, u_t and w_t', the former non-autocorrelated and the latter following a third order MA process. We can estimate the parameters of (6.3) employing 'single equation' or 'joint' estimation techniques as explained briefly below.[19]

For single equation estimation of (6.3a), we consider it in conjunction with the final equation[20] for y_t, namely a (5, 1, 4) ARMA process that we write as:

$$\Delta y_t = \sum_{i=1}^{5} \delta_i \Delta y_{t-i} + \phi_1 + \sum_{i=0}^{4} \lambda_{1i} a_{1t-i}, \tag{6.4}$$

where a_{1t} is a non-autocorrelated error with zero mean and constant finite

[19]These estimation procedures will be treated more fully in future work. A recent paper by Byron (1973) treats some of these problems from the likelihood point of view. Also, it will be noted that non-unique estimates for certain parameters are available from the final equation and transfer function analyses. In certain instances these latter estimates are obtained from estimates of ratios of lag polynomials and thus are probably not very reliable.

[20]Alternatively, the transfer function for Δy_t could be employed. However, it is not clear that use of the transfer function is to be preferred.

variance. The parameters of (6.4) have already been estimated above. We now substitute for Δy_t in (6.3a) from (6.4) to obtain

$$\Delta c_t = \alpha_0 \tilde{\Delta} y_t + \alpha_1 \Delta y_{t-1} + \beta' + v_{1t}, \tag{6.5}$$

where $\tilde{\Delta} y_t \equiv \Sigma_{i=1}^5 \delta_i \Delta y_{t-i}$, $\beta' \equiv \phi_1(\alpha_0+\alpha_1)$ and $v_{1t} \equiv w_t' + \alpha_0 \Sigma_{i=0}^4 \lambda_{1i} a_{1t-i}$ a fourth order MA process. Given consistent estimates of the δ_i's in $\tilde{\Delta} y_t$, we can calculate consistent estimates of α_0, α_1, β and parameters of the MA process for v_{1t}. The results of this approach are presented and discussed below.

With respect to single equation estimation of (6.3b), we consider it in conjunction with the (5, 1, 4) ARMA final equation for c_t that was estimated above and is expressed as:

$$\Delta c_t = \sum_{i=1}^{5} \eta_i \Delta c_{t-i} + \phi_2 + \sum_{i=0}^{4} \lambda_{2i} a_{2t-i}, \tag{6.6}$$

where a_{2t} is a non-autocorrelated error with zero mean and constant finite variance. Then on substituting for Δc_t in the second line of (6.3b) from (6.6), we have:

$$\Delta y_t = \gamma_0 \tilde{\Delta} c_t + \sum_{i=1}^{4} \gamma_i \Delta c_{t-i} + \nu' + v_{2t}, \tag{6.7}$$

where $\tilde{\Delta} c_t \equiv \Sigma_{i=1}^5 \eta_i \Delta c_{t-i}$, $\nu' \equiv \nu + \gamma_0 \phi_2$, and $v_{2t} \equiv w_t' + \gamma_0 \Sigma_{i=0}^4 \lambda_{2i} a_{2t-i}$, a fourth order MA process. Since consistent estimates of the η_i are available from the analysis of (6.6), they can be used in conjunction with (6.7) to obtain consistent estimates of the γ's, ν and the parameters of the process for v_{2t}.

As regards joint estimation of (6.5) and (6.7), single equation analysis yields residuals that can be used to estimate the covariance matrix for the disturbances, the v_{1t}'s and v_{2t}'s. For a two equation system, this matrix will be generally a $2T \times 2T$ matrix with four submatrices in the form of band matrices characteristic of MA processes. Let this matrix be denoted Ω and an estimate of it, $\hat{\Omega}$. Then with $\boldsymbol{v}' = (\boldsymbol{v}_1' \boldsymbol{v}_2')$, where the vector $\boldsymbol{v}_1$ has elements v_{1t} and $\boldsymbol{v}_2$ elements v_{2t}, minimization of $\boldsymbol{v}'\hat{\Omega}^{-1}\boldsymbol{v}$ can be done to provide joint estimates of the parameters.[21]

In table 11, we present various single equation consistent estimates of the parameters of the consumption equation in (6.3a). In the first line of the table, the final equation for Δy_t was employed to substitute for $\tilde{\Delta} y_t$ in the consumption function while in the second line the transfer function for Δy_t was employed.[22] It is seen that in both cases the point estimate for α_0 is negative. However, the standard errors are large so that a confidence interval at a reasonable level would include positive values. The estimates of α_1, the coefficient of Δy_{t-1} in (6.3a) are

[21]The new residuals can be employed to reestimate Ω and thus iteration of the process on Ω (and also on the parameters in $\tilde{\Delta} c_t$ and $\tilde{\Delta} y_t$) is possible.

[22]Note that the estimation of the consumption equation using the final equation expression for Δy_t is not linked to the assumption that Δx_t is exogenous whereas use of the transfer function expression for Δy_t is.

in the vicinity of 0.3 with a standard error of about 0.1.[23] That α_0 and α_1 are not very precisely estimated is probably due to collinearity of $\tilde{\Delta} y_t$ and Δy_{t-1}. Use of an informative prior distribution for α_0 and α_1 in a Bayesian analysis could help to improve the precision of inferences. To specify a prior distribution for α_0 and α_1 and also to interpret the results in table 11, it may be useful to regard Δc_t^p, the planned change in expenditures, including durables, to be linked to permanent income change, Δy_t^p, and transitory income change, Δy_t^t, as follows: $\Delta c_t^p = k\Delta y_t^p + \alpha_0 \Delta y_t^t + \alpha_1 \Delta y_{t-1}^t$. In planning consumption expenditures for the tth period, note that Δy_t^t is as yet *unrealized* transitory income whereas Δy_{t-1}^t is realized transitory income for period $t-1$. We believe that consumer reactions

Table 11

Single equation estimates of parameters of consumption equation (6.5).

1. *Using $\tilde{\Delta} y_t$ from final equation for Δy_t*

$$\Delta c_t = \underset{(0.180)}{-0.333}\,\tilde{\Delta} y_t + \underset{(0.111)}{0.251}\,\Delta y_{t-1} + \underset{(2.297)}{10.45} + (1 - \underset{(0.127)}{0.180}L + \underset{(0.128)}{0.022}L^2 - \underset{(0.118)}{0.375}L^3 - \underset{(0.119)}{0.079}L^4)a_{1t}$$

RSS = 40,701 DF = 86

Using $\tilde{\Delta} y_t$ from transfer function for Δy_t

$$\Delta c_t = \underset{(0.092)}{-0.034}\,\tilde{\Delta} y_t + \underset{(0.116)}{0.300}\,\Delta y_{t-1} + \underset{(2.240)}{7.216} + (1 - \underset{(0.129)}{0.258}L + \underset{(0.116)}{0.193}L^2 - \underset{(0.119)}{0.217}L^3 + \underset{0.115)}{0.003}L^4)a_{1t}'$$

RSS = 40,646 DF = 86

to realized transitory income will be much greater than that to as yet unrealized transitory income, i.e. $\alpha_1 > \alpha_0$ with α_0 small. Using $\Delta c_t = \Delta c_t^p + u_t$ and $\Delta y_t = \Delta y_t^p + \Delta y_t^t$ in connection with the relation for Δc_t^p above, we have $\Delta c_t = \alpha_0 \Delta y_t + \alpha_1 \Delta y_{t-1} + \beta + u_t$ with $\beta = (k - \alpha_0)\Delta y_t^p - \alpha_1 \Delta y_{t-1}^p$, assumed constant.[24] Within this framework, given the hypothesis that reaction to *unrealized* transitory income change, Δy_t^t is rather small, if not zero, while reaction to realized transitory income change Δy_{t-1}^t is positive, probably an α_1 between zero and one, the results in table 11 appear plausible.

In conclusion, we believe that the techniques presented above can be very helpful in checking the specifying assumptions of many existing linear or linearized models and in 'iterating in' on models that are suitable approximations to

[23] As explained below α_1 can be viewed as the coefficient of realized transitory income change and thus an estimate of α_1 in the vicinity of 0.3 seems reasonable.

[24] Alternatively, we could assume $(k - \alpha_0)\Delta y_t^p - \alpha_1 \Delta y_{t-1}^p = \beta + \varepsilon_t$, where ε_t is a non-autocorrelated random error with zero mean and constant variance.

the information in our data and that may predict well. Some topics that will receive attention in future work include further development of estimation techniques for different equation systems, joint testing procedures for nested and non-nested hypotheses, analyses of the comparative predictive performance of final equation, transfer function and structural equation systems, Bayesian procedures utilizing informative prior distributions, and applications. Finally, we cannot resist remarking that the present work lends support to the notion that so-called 'naive' ARMA time series models are not all that naive after all.

References

Akaike, H., 1973, Maximum likelihood identification of Gaussian autoregressive-moving average models, Biometrika 60, 255–265.

Bartlett, M.S., 1946, On the theoretical specification of the sampling properties of autocorrelated time series, J. Royal Stat. Soc. B 8, 27–41.

Box, G.E.P. and G.M. Jenkins, 1970, Time series analysis, forecasting and control (Holden-Day, San Francisco).

Byron, R.P., 1973, The computation of maximum likelihood estimates for linear simultaneous systems with moving average disturbances (Department of Economics, Australian National University) 19 pp. manuscript.

Chetty, V.K., 1966, Bayesian analysis of some simultaneous equation models and specification errors, Doctoral Dissertation (University of Wisconsin, Madison) unpublished.

Chetty, V.K., 1968, Bayesian analysis of Haavelmo's models, Econometrica 36, 582–602.

Dhrymes, P.J., 1970, Econometrics, statistical foundations and applications (Harper and Row, New York).

Haavelmo, T., 1947, Methods of measuring the marginal propensity to consume, Journal of the American Statistical Society 42, 105–122; reprinted in: W. Hood and T.C. Koopmans, eds., 1953, Studies in econometric methods (Wiley, New York).

Hannan, E.J., 1969, The identification of vector mixed auto-regressive-moving average systems, Biometrika 57, 223–225.

Hannan, E.J., 1971, The identification problem for multiple equation systems with moving average errors, Econometrica 39, 715–765.

Jeffreys, H., 1961, Theory of probability (The Clarendon Press, Oxford).

Jorgenson, D.W., 1966, Rational distributed lag functions, Econometrica 34, 135–149.

Kmenta, J., 1971, Elements of econometrics (MacMillan, New York).

Lindley, D.V., 1961, The use of prior probability distributions in statistical inference and decision, in: J. Neyman, ed., 1961, Proceedings of the fourth Berkeley symposium on mathematical statistics and probability, vol. I, 453–468.

Marschak, J., 1950, Statistical inference in economics, An introduction, in: T.C. Koopmans, ed., Statistical inference in dynamic economic models (Wiley, New York).

Nelson, C.R., 1970, Joint estimation of parameters of correlated time series (Graduate School of Business, University of Chicago) 41 pp. manuscript.

Palm, F., 1972, On mixed prior distributions and their application in distributed lag models, CORE Discussion Paper 7222 (University of Louvain).

Pierce, D.A. and J.M. Mason, 1971, On estimating the fundamental dynamic equations of structural econometric models, Paper presented at the Winter Meeting of the Econometric Society (New Orleans).

Quenouille, M.H., 1957, The analysis of multiple time series (C. Griffin and Co., London).

Silvey, S.D., 1970, Statistical inference (Penguin Books, Baltimore).

Theil, H. and J.C.D. Boot, 1962, The final form of econometric equation systems, Review of the International Statistical Institute 30, 136–152; reprinted in: A. Zellner, ed., 1968, Readings in economic statistics and econometrics (Little–Brown, Boston).

Tinbergen, J., 1940, Econometric business cycle research, Review of Economic Studies 7, 73–90.

Wold, H., 1953, Demand analysis: A study in econometrics (Wiley, New York).

Zellner, A., 1959, Review of 'The analysis of multiple time-series' by M.H. Quenouille, J. of Farm Economics 41, 682–684.
Zellner, A., 1971, An introduction to Bayesian inference in econometrics (Wiley, New York).

After completing this paper, the following Ph.D. Thesis, dealing with related topics, was brought to our attention by Dennis Aigner:

L.D. Haugh, 1972, The identification of time series interrelationships with special reference to dynamic regression models (Department of Statistics, University of Wisconsin, Madison).

Sources of data

Personal consumption expenditures, disposable personal income, gross investment data

Series 1946–65:

United States Department of Commerce/Office of Business Economics, 1966, The National Income and Product Accounts of the United States, 1929–65, Statistical Tables (Washington, D.C.).

Series 1966–72:

United States Department of Commerce/Office of Business Economics, Survey of Current Business (Washington, D.C.).

Consumer price index:

United States Department of Commerce/Office of Business Economics, Survey of Current Business (Washington, D.C.).

Population data:

U.S. Bureau of the Census, Current Population Reports: Population estimates, Series P-25 (Washington, D.C.).

[28]

Econometrica, Vol. 55, No. 2 (March, 1987), 251-276

CO-INTEGRATION AND ERROR CORRECTION: REPRESENTATION, ESTIMATION, AND TESTING

BY ROBERT F. ENGLE AND C. W. J. GRANGER[1]

The relationship between co-integration and error correction models, first suggested in Granger (1981), is here extended and used to develop estimation procedures, tests, and empirical examples.

If each element of a vector of time series x_t first achieves stationarity after differencing, but a linear combination $\alpha' x_t$ is already stationary, the time series x_t are said to be co-integrated with co-integrating vector α. There may be several such co-integrating vectors so that α becomes a matrix. Interpreting $\alpha' x_t = 0$ as a long run equilibrium, co-integration implies that deviations from equilibrium are stationary, with finite variance, even though the series themselves are nonstationary and have infinite variance.

The paper presents a representation theorem based on Granger (1983), which connects the moving average, autoregressive, and error correction representations for co-integrated systems. A vector autoregression in differenced variables is incompatible with these representations. Estimation of these models is discussed and a simple but asymptotically efficient two-step estimator is proposed. Testing for co-integration combines the problems of unit root tests and tests with parameters unidentified under the null. Seven statistics are formulated and analyzed. The critical values of these statistics are calculated based on a Monte Carlo simulation. Using these critical values, the power properties of the tests are examined and one test procedure is recommended for application.

In a series of examples it is found that consumption and income are co-integrated, wages and prices are not, short and long interest rates are, and nominal GNP is co-integrated with M2, but not M1, M3, or aggregate liquid assets.

KEYWORDS: Co-integration, vector autoregression, unit roots, error correction, multivariate time series, Dickey-Fuller tests.

1. INTRODUCTION

AN INDIVIDUAL ECONOMIC VARIABLE, viewed as a time series, can wander extensively and yet some pairs of series may be expected to move so that they do not drift too far apart. Typically economic theory will propose forces which tend to keep such series together. Examples might be short and long term interest rates, capital appropriations and expenditures, household income and expenditures, and prices of the same commodity in different markets or close substitutes in the same market. A similar idea arises from considering equilibrium relationships, where equilibrium is a stationary point characterized by forces which tend to push the economy back toward equilibrium whenever it moves away. If x_t is a vector of economic variables, then they may be said to be in equilibrium when the specific linear constraint

$$\alpha' x_t = 0$$

[1] The authors are indebted to David Hendry and Sam Yoo for many useful conversations and suggestions as well as to Gene Savin, David Dickey, Alok Bhargava, and Marco Lippi. Two referees provided detailed constructive criticism, and thanks go to Yoshi Baba, Sam Yoo, and Alvaro Ecribano who creatively carried out the simulations and examples. Financial support was provided by NSF SES-80-08580 and SES-82-08626. A previous version of this paper was entitled "Dynamic Model Specification with Equilibrium Constraints: Co-integration and Error Correction."

occurs. In most time periods, x_t will not be in equilibrium and the univariate quantity

$$z_t = \alpha' x_t$$

may be called the equilibrium error. If the equilibrium concept is to have any relevance for the specification of econometric models, the economy should appear to prefer a small value of z_t rather than a large value.

In this paper, these ideas are put onto a firm basis and it is shown that a class of models, known as error-correcting, allows long-run components of variables to obey equilibrium constraints while short-run components have a flexible dynamic specification. A condition for this to be true, called co-integration, was introduced by Granger (1981) and Granger and Weiss (1983) and is precisely defined in the next section. Section 3 discusses several representations of co-integrated systems, Section 4 develops estimation procedures, and Section 5 develops tests. Several applications are presented in Section 6 and conclusions are offered in Section 7. A particularly simple example of this class of models is shown in Section 4, and it might be useful to examine it for motivating the analysis of such systems.

2. INTEGRATION, CO-INTEGRATION, AND ERROR CORRECTION

It is well known from Wold's theorem that a single stationary time series with no deterministic components has an infinite moving average representation which is generally approximated by a finite autoregressive moving average process. See, for example, Box and Jenkins (1970) or Granger and Newbold (1977). Commonly however, economic series must be differenced before the assumption of stationarity can be presumed to hold. This motivates the following familiar definition of integration:

DEFINITION: A series with no deterministic component which has a stationary, invertible, ARMA representation after differencing d times, is said to be integrated of order d, denoted $x_t \sim I(d)$.

For ease of exposition, only the values $d = 0$ and $d = 1$ will be considered in much of the paper, but many of the results can be generalized to other cases including the fractional difference model. Thus, for $d = 0$ x_t will be stationary and for $d = 1$ the change is stationary.

There are substantial differences in appearance between a series that is $I(0)$ and another that is $I(1)$. For more discussion see, for example, Feller (1968) or Granger and Newbold (1977).

(a) If $x_t \sim I(0)$ with zero mean then (i) the variance of x_t is finite; (ii) an innovation has only a temporary effect on the value of x_t; (iii) the spectrum of x_t, $f(\omega)$, has the property $0 < f(0) < \infty$; (iv) the expected length of times between crossings of $x = 0$ is finite; (v) the autocorrelations, ρ_k, decrease steadily in magnitude for large enough k, so that their sum is finite.

(b) If $x_t \sim I(1)$ with $x_0 = 0$, then (i) variance x_t goes to infinity as t goes to infinity; (ii) an innovation has a permanent effect on the value of x_t, as x_t is the sum of all previous changes; (iii) the spectrum of x_t has the approximate shape $f(\omega) \sim A\omega^{-2d}$ for small ω so that in particular $f(0) = \infty$; (iv) the expected time between crossings of $x = 0$ is infinite; (v) the theoretical autocorrelations, $\rho_k \to 1$ for all k as $t \to \infty$.

The theoretical infinite variance for an $I(1)$ series comes completely from the contribution of the low frequencies, or long run part of the series. Thus an $I(1)$ series is rather smooth, having dominant long swings, compared to an $I(0)$ series. Because of the relative sizes of the variances, it is always true that the sum of an $I(0)$ and an $I(1)$ will be $I(1)$. Further, if a and b are constants, $b \neq 0$, and if $x_t \sim I(d)$, then $a + bx_t$ is also $I(d)$.

If x_t and y_t are both $I(d)$, then it is generally true that the linear combination

$$z_t = x_t - ay_t$$

will also be $I(d)$. However, it is possible that $z_t \sim I(d-b)$, $b > 0$. When this occurs, a very special constraint operates on the long-run components of the series. Consider the case $d = b = 1$, so that x_t, y_t are both $I(1)$ with dominant long run components, but z_t is $I(0)$ without especially strong low frequencies. The constant a is therefore such that the bulk of the long run components of x_t and y_t cancel out. For $a = 1$, the vague idea that x_t and y_t cannot drift too far apart has been translated into the more precise statement that "their difference will be $I(0)$." The use of the constant a merely suggests that some scaling needs to be used before the $I(0)$ difference can be achieved. It should be noted that it will not generally be true that there is an a which makes $z_t \sim I(0)$.

An analogous case, considering a different important frequency, is when x_t and y_t are a pair of series, each having important seasonal component, yet there is an a so that the derived series z_t has no seasonal. Clearly this could occur, but might be considered to be unlikely.

To formalize these ideas, the following definition adapted from Granger (1981) and Granger and Weiss (1983) is introduced:

DEFINITION: The components of the vector x_t are said to be *co-integrated of order d, b*, denoted $x_t \sim CI(d, b)$, if (i) all components of x_t are $I(d)$; (ii) there exists a vector $\alpha (\neq 0)$ so that $z_t = \alpha' x_t \sim I(d-b)$, $b > 0$. The vector α is called the *co-integrating vector*.

Continuing to concentrate on the $d = 1$, $b = 1$ case, co-integration would mean that if the components of x_t were all $I(1)$, then the equilibrium error would be $I(0)$, and z_t will rarely drift far from zero if it has zero mean and z_t will often cross the zero line. Putting this another way, it means that equilibrium will occasionally occur, at least to a close approximation, whereas if x_t was not co-integrated, then z_t can wander widely and zero-crossings would be very rare, suggesting that in this case the equilibrium concept has no practical implications.

The reduction in the order of integration implies a special kind of relationship with interpretable and testable consequences. If however all the elements of x_t are already stationary so that they are $I(0)$, then the equilibrium error z_t has no distinctive property if it is $I(0)$. It could be that $z_t \sim I(-1)$, so that its spectrum is zero at zero frequency, but if any of the variables have measurement error, this property in general cannot be observed and so this case is of little realistic interest. When interpreting the co-integration concept it might be noted that in the $N=2$, $d=b=1$ case, Granger and Weiss (1983) show that a necessary and sufficient condition for co-integration is that the coherence between the two series is one at zero frequency.

If x_t has N components, then there may be more than one cointegrating vector α. It is clearly possible for several equilibrium relations to govern the joint behavior of the variables. In what follows, it will be assumed that there are exactly r linearly independent co-integrating vectors, with $r \leq N-1$, which are gathered together into the $N \times r$ array α. By construction the rank of α will be r which will be called the "co-integrating rank" of x_t.

The close relationship between co-integration and error correcting models will be developed in the balance of the paper. Error correction mechanisms have been used widely in economics. Early versions are Sargan (1964) and Phillips (1957). The idea is simply that a proportion of the disequilibrium from one period is corrected in the next period. For example, the change in price in one period may depend upon the degree of excess demand in the previous period. Such schemes can be derived as optimal behavior with some types of adjustment costs or incomplete information. Recently, these models have seen great interest following the work of Davidson, Hendry, Srba, and Yeo (1978) (DHSY), Hendry and von Ungern Sternberg (1980), Currie (1981), Dawson (1981), and Salmon (1982) among others.

For a two variable system a typical error correction model would relate the change in one variable to past equilibrium errors, as well as to past changes in both variables. For a multivariate system we can define a general error correction representation in terms of B, the backshift operator, as follows.

DEFINITION: A vector time series x_t has an error correction representation if it can be expressed as:

$$A(B)(1-B)x_t = -\gamma z_{t-1} + u_t$$

where u_t is a stationary multivariate disturbance, with $A(0)=I$, $A(1)$ has all elements finite, $z_T = \alpha' x_T$, and $\gamma \neq 0$.

In this representation, only the disequilibrium in the previous period is an explanatory variable. However, by rearranging terms, any set of lags of the z can be written in this form, therefore it permits any type of gradual adjustment toward a new equilibrium. A notable difference between this definition and most of the applications which have occurred is that this is a multivariate definition which does not rest on exogeneity of a subset of the variables. The notion that one variable may be weakly exogenous in the sense of Engle, Hendry, and Richard (1983) may be investigated in such a system as briefly discussed below. A second notable difference is that α is taken to be an unknown parameter vector rather than a set of constants given by economic theory.

3. PROPERTIES OF CO-INTEGRATED VARIABLES AND THEIR REPRESENTATIONS

Suppose that each component of x_t is $I(1)$ so that the change in each component is a zero mean purely nondeterministic stationary stochastic process. Any known deterministic components can be subtracted before the analysis is begun. It follows that there will always exist a multivariate Wold representation:

$$(3.1) \qquad (1-B)x_t = C(B)\varepsilon_t,$$

taken to mean that both sides will have the same spectral matrix. Further, $C(B)$ will be uniquely defined by the conditions that the function $\det[C(z)]$, $z=e^{i\omega}$, have all zeroes on or outside the unit circle, and that $C(0)=I_N$, the $N\times N$ identity matrix (see Hannan (1970, p. 66)). In this representation the ε_t are zero mean white noise vectors with

$$\begin{aligned} E[\varepsilon_t\varepsilon_s'] &= 0, \quad t\neq s, \\ &= G, \quad t=s, \end{aligned}$$

so that only contemporaneous correlations can occur.

The moving average polynomial $C(B)$ can always be expressed as

$$(3.2) \qquad C(B) = C(1) + (1-B)C^*(B)$$

by simply rearranging the terms. If $C(B)$ is of finite order, then $C^*(B)$ will be of finite order. If $C^*(1)$ is identically zero, then a similar expression involving $(1-B)^2$ can be defined.

The relationship between error correction models and co-integration was first pointed out in Granger (1981). A theorem showing precisely that co-integrated series can be represented by error correction models was originally stated and proved in Granger (1983). The following version is therefore called the Granger Representation Theorem. Analysis of related but more complex cases is covered by Johansen (1985) and Yoo (1985).

GRANGER REPRESENTATION THEOREM: If the $N\times 1$ vector x_t given in (3.1) is co-integrated with $d=1$, $b=1$ and with co-integrating rank r, then:

(1) *$C(1)$ is of rank $N-r$.*

(2) *There exists a vector ARMA representation*

$$(3.3) \qquad A(B)x_t = d(B)\varepsilon_t$$

with the properties that $A(1)$ has rank r and $d(B)$ is a scalar lag polynomial with $d(1)$ finite, and $A(0)=I_N$. When $d(B)=1$, this is a vector autoregression.

(3) *There exist $N\times r$ matrices, α, γ, of rank r such that*

$$\alpha' C(1)=0,$$

$$C(1)\gamma=0,$$

$$A(1)=\gamma\alpha'.$$

(4) *There exists an error correction representation with $z_t=\alpha' x_t$, an $r\times 1$ vector of stationary random variables:*

$$A^*(B)(1-B)x_t=-\gamma z_{t-1}+d(B)\varepsilon_t \tag{3.4}$$

with $A^*(0)=I_N$.

(5) *The vector z_t is given by*

$$z_t=K(B)\varepsilon_t, \tag{3.5}$$

$$(1-B)z_t=-\alpha'\gamma z_{t-1}+J(B)\varepsilon_t, \tag{3.6}$$

where $K(B)$ is an $r\times N$ matrix of lag polynomials given by $\alpha' C^*(B)$ with all elements of $K(1)$ finite with rank r, and det $(\alpha'\gamma)>0$.

(6) *If a finite vector autoregressive representation is possible, it will have the form given by* (3.3) *and* (3.4) *above with $d(B)=1$ and both $A(B)$ and $A^*(B)$ as matrices of finite polynomials.*

In order to prove the Theorem the following lemma on determinants and adjoints of singular matrix polynomials is needed.

LEMMA 1: *If $G(\lambda)$ is a finite valued $N\times N$ matrix polynomial on $\lambda\in[0, 1]$, with rank $G(0)=N-r$ for $0\leq r\leq N$, and if $G^*(0)\neq 0$ in*

$$G(\lambda)=G(0)+\lambda G^*(\lambda),$$

then

(i) $\quad det\,(G(\lambda))=\lambda^r g(\lambda)I_N \quad$ *with $g(0)$ finite,*

(ii) $\quad Adj\,(G(\lambda))=\lambda^{r-1}H(\lambda),$

where I_N is the $N\times N$ identity matrix, $1\leq$ rank $(H(0))\leq r$, and $H(0)$ is finite.

PROOF: The determinant of G can be expressed in a power series in λ as

$$\det(G(\lambda))=\sum_{i=0}^{\infty}\delta_i\lambda^i.$$

Each δ_i is a sum of a finite number of products of elements of $G(\lambda)$ and therefore is itself finite valued. Each has some terms from $G(0)$ and some from $\lambda G^*(\lambda)$. Any product with more than $N-r$ terms from $G(0)$ will be zero because this will be the determinant of a submatrix of larger order than the rank of $G(0)$. The only possible non-zero terms will have r or more terms from $\lambda G^*(\lambda)$ and therefore will be associated with powers of λ of r or more. The first possible nonzero δ_i is δ_r.

Defining

$$g(\lambda)=\sum_{i=r}^{\infty}\delta_i\lambda^{i-r}$$

establishes the first part of the lemma since δ_r must be finite.

To establish the second statement, express the adjoint matrix of G in a power series in λ:

$$\operatorname{Adj} G(\lambda)=\sum_{i=0}^{\infty}\lambda^{i}H_i,$$

Since the adjoint is a matrix composed of elements which are determinants of order $N-1$, the above argument establishes that the first $r-1$ terms must be identically zero. Thus

$$\begin{aligned}\operatorname{Adj} G(\lambda)&=\lambda^{r-1}\sum_{r-1}^{\infty}\lambda^{i-r+1}H_i\\&=\lambda^{r-1}H(\lambda).\end{aligned}$$

Because the elements of H_{r-1} are products of finitely many finite numbers, $H(0)$ must be finite.

The product of a matrix and its adjoint will always give the determinant so:

$$\begin{aligned}\lambda^{r}g(\lambda)I_N&=(G(0)+\lambda G^*(\lambda))H(\lambda)\\&=G(0)H(\lambda)\lambda^{r-1}+h(\lambda)G^*(\lambda)\lambda^{r}.\end{aligned}$$

Equating powers of λ we get

$$G(0)H(0)=0.$$

Thus the rank of $H(0)$ must be less than or equal to r as it lies entirely in the column null space of the rank $N-r$ matrix $G(0)$. If $r=1$, the first term in the expression for the adjoint will simply be the adjoint of $G(0)$ which will have rank 1 since $G(0)$ has rank $N-1$. *Q.E.D.*

Proof of Granger Representation Theorem: The conditions of the Theorem suppose the existance of a Wold representation as in (3.1) for an N vector of random variables x_t which are co-integrated. Suppose the co-integrating vector is α so that

$$z_t=\alpha' x_t$$

is an r-dimensional stationary purely nondeterministic time series with invertible moving average representation. Multiplying α times the moving average representation in (3.1) gives

$$(1-B)z_t=(\alpha' C(1)+(1-B)\alpha' C^*(B))\varepsilon_t.$$

For z_t to be $I(0)$, $\alpha' C(1)$ must equal 0. Any vector with this property will be a co-integrating vector; therefore $C(1)$ must have rank $N-r$ with a null space containing all co-integrating vectors. It also follows that $\alpha' C^*(B)$ must be an invertible moving average representation and in particular $\alpha' C^*(1) \neq 0$. Otherwise the co-integration would be with $b=2$ or higher.

Statement (2) is established using Lemma 1, letting $\lambda = (1-B)$, $G(\lambda) = C(B)$, $H(\lambda) = A(B)$, and $g(\lambda) = d(B)$. Since $C(B)$ has full rank and equals I_N at $B=0$, its inverse is $A(0)$ which is also I_N.

Statement (3) follows from recognition that A(1) has rank between 1 and r and lies in the null space of C(1). Since α spans this null space, $A(1)$ can be written as linear combinations of the co-integrating vectors

$$A(1) = \gamma\alpha'.$$

Statement (4) follows by manipulation of the autoregressive structure. Rearranging terms in (3.3) gives:

$$[\tilde{A}(B) + A(1)](1-B)x_t = -A(1)x_{t-1} + d(B)\varepsilon_t,$$

$$A^*(B)(1-B)x_t = -\gamma z_{t-1} + d(B)\varepsilon_t,$$

$A^*(0) = A(0) = I_N$.

The fifth condition follows from direct substitution in the Wold representation. The definition of co-integration implies that this moving average be stationary and invertible. Rewriting the error correction representation with $A^*(B) = I + A^{**}(B)$ where $A^{**}(0) = 0$, and premultiplying by α' gives:

$$\begin{aligned}(1-B)z_t &= -\alpha'\gamma z_{t-1} + [\alpha' d(B) + \alpha' A^{**}(B)C(B)]\varepsilon_t \\ &= -\alpha'\gamma z_{t-1} + J(B)\varepsilon_t.\end{aligned}$$

For this to be equivalent to the stationary moving average representation the autoregression must be invertible. This requires that det $(\alpha'\gamma) > 0$. If the determinant were zero then there would be at least one unit root, and if the determinant were negative, then for some value of ω between zero and one,

$$\det(I_r - (I_r - \alpha'\gamma)\omega) = 0,$$

implying a root inside the unit circle.

Condition six follows by repeating the previous steps, setting $d(B) = 1$.

Q.E.D.

Stronger results can be obtained by further restrictions on the multiplicity of roots in the moving average representations. For example, Yoo (1985), using Smith Macmillan forms, finds conditions which establish that $d(1) \neq 0$, that $A^*(1)$ is of full rank, and that facilitate the transformation from error correction models to co-integrated models. However, the results given above are sufficient for the estimation and testing problems addressed in this paper.

The autoregressive and error correction representations given by (3.3) and (3.4) are closely related to the vector autoregressive models so commonly used in econometrics, particularly in the case when $d(B)$ can reasonably be taken to be 1. However, each differs in an important fashion from typical VAR applications. In the autoregressive representation

$$A(B)x_t = \varepsilon_t,$$

the co-integration of the variables x_t generates a restriction which makes $A(1)$ singular. For $r = 1$, this matrix will only have rank 1. The analysis of such systems from an innovation accounting point of view is treacherous as some numerical approaches to calculating the moving average representation are highly unstable.

The error correction representation

$$A^*(B)(1-B)x_t = -\gamma\alpha' x_{t-1} + \varepsilon_t$$

looks more like a standard vector autoregression in the differences of the data. Here the co-integration is implied by the presence of the levels of the variables so a pure VAR in differences will be misspecified if the variables are co-integrated.

Thus vector autoregressions estimated with co-integrated data will be misspecified if the data are differenced, and will have omitted important constraints if the data are used in levels. Of course, these constraints will be satisfied asymptotically but efficiency gains and improved multistep forecasts may be achieved by imposing them.

As $x_t \sim I(1)$, $z_t \sim I(0)$, it should be noted that all terms in the error correction models are $I(0)$. The converse also holds; if $x_t \sim I(1)$ are generated by an error correction model, then x_t is necessarily co-integrated. It may also be noted that if $x_t \sim I(0)$, the generation process can always be written in the error correction form and so, in this case, the equilibrium concept has no impact.

As mentioned above, typical empirical examples of error correcting behavior are formulated as the response of one variable, the dependent variable, to shocks of another, the independent variable. In this paper all the variables are treated as jointly endogenous; nevertheless the structure of the model may imply various Granger causal orderings and weak and strong exogeneity conditions as in Engle, Hendry, and Richard (1983). For example, a bivariate co-integrated system must have a causal ordering in at least one direction. Because the z's must include both variables and γ cannot be identically zero, they must enter into one or both of the equations. If the error correction term enters into both equations, neither variable can be weakly exogenous for the parameters of the other equation because of the cross equation restriction.

The notion of co-integration can in principle be extended to series with trends or explosive autoregressive roots. In these cases the co-integrating vector would still be required to reduce the series to stationarity. Hence the trends would have to be proportional and any explosive roots would have to be identical for all the series. We do not consider these cases in this paper and recognize that they may complicate the estimation and testing problems.

4. ESTIMATING CO-INTEGRATED SYSTEMS

In defining different forms for co-integrated systems, several estimation procedures have been implicitly discussed. Most convenient is the error correction form (particularly if it can be assumed that there is no moving average term). There remain cross-equation restrictions involving the parameters of the co-integrating vectors; and therefore the maximum likelihood estimator, under Gaussian assumptions, requires an iterative procedure.

In this section, we will propose another estimator which is a two step estimator. In the first step the parameters of the co-integrating vector are estimated and in the second these are used in the error correction form. Both steps require only single equation least squares and it will be shown that the result is consistent for all the parameters. The procedure is far more convenient because the dynamics do not need to be specified until the error correction structure has been estimated. As a byproduct we obtain some test statistics useful for testing for co-integration.

From (3.5) the sample moment matrix of the data can be directly expressed. Let the moment matrix divided by T be denoted by:

$$M_T = 1/T^2 \sum_t x_t x_t'.$$

Recalling that $z_t = \alpha' x_t$, (3.5) implies that

$$\alpha' M_T = \sum_t [K(B)\varepsilon_t] x_t' / T^2.$$

Following the argument of Dickey and Fuller (1979) or Stock (1984), it can be shown that for processes satisfying (3.1),

$$\lim_{T \to \infty} E(M_T) = M \quad \text{a finite nonzero matrix,} \tag{4.1}$$

and

$$\alpha' M = 0, \quad \text{or} \quad (\text{vec}\,\alpha)'(I \otimes M) = 0. \tag{4.2}$$

Although the moment matrix of data from a co-integrated process will be nonsingular for any sample, in the limit, it will have rank $N - r$. This accords well with the common observation that economic time series data are highly collinear so that moment matrices may be nearly singular even when samples are large. Co-integration appears to be a plausible hypothesis from a data analytic point of view.

Equations (4.2) do not uniquely define the co-integrating vectors unless arbitrary normalizations are imposed. Let q and Q be arrays which incorporate these normalizations by reparametrizing α into θ, a $j \times 1$ matrix of unknown parameters which lie in a compact subset of R^j:

$$\text{vec}\,\alpha = q + Q\theta. \tag{4.3}$$

Typically q and Q will be all zeros and ones, thereby defining one coefficient in each column of α to be unity and defining rotations if $r > 1$. The parameters θ

are said to be "identified" if there is a unique solution to (4.2), (4.3). This solution is given by

$$(4.4) \qquad (I \otimes M)Q\theta = -(I \otimes M)q$$

where by the assumption of identification, $(I \otimes M)Q$ has a left inverse even though M does not.

As the moment matrix M_T will have full rank for finite samples, a reasonable approach to estimation is to minimize the sum of squared deviations from equilibrium. In the case of a single co-integrating vector, $\hat{\alpha}$ will minimize $\alpha' M_T \alpha$ subject to any restrictions such as (4.3) and the result will be simply ordinary least squares. For multiple co-integrating vectors, define $\hat{\alpha}$ as the minimizer of the trace $(\alpha' M_T \alpha)$. The estimation problem becomes:

$$\begin{aligned} \operatorname*{Min}_{\alpha\, s.t. (4.3)} \operatorname{tr}(\alpha' M_T \alpha) &= \operatorname*{Min}_{\alpha\, s.t.\, (4.3)} \operatorname{vec} \alpha' (I \otimes M_T) \operatorname{vec} \alpha \\ &= \operatorname*{Min}_{\theta} (q + Q\theta)'(I \otimes M_T)(q + Q\theta), \end{aligned}$$

which implies the solution

$$(4.5) \qquad \hat{\theta} = -(Q'(I \otimes M_T)Q)^{-1}(Q'(I \otimes M_T)q), \quad \operatorname{vec} \hat{\alpha} = q + Q\hat{\theta}.$$

This approach to estimation should provide a very good approximation to the true co-integrating vector because it is seeking vectors with minimal residual variance and asymptotically all linear combinations of x will have infinite variance except those which are co-integrating vectors.

When $r = 1$ this estimate is obtained simply by regressing the variable normalized to have a unit coefficient upon the other variables. This regression will be called the "co-integrating regression" as it attempts to fit the long run or equilibrium relationship without worrying about the dynamics. It will be shown to provide an estimate of the elements of the co-integrating vector. Such a regression has been pejoratively called a "spurious" regression by Granger and Newbold (1974) primarily because the standard errors are highly misleading. They were particularly concerned about the non-co-integrated case where there was no relationship but the unit root in the error process led to a low Durbin Watson, a high R^2, and apparently high significance of the coefficients. Here we only seek coefficient estimates to use in the second stage and for tests of the equilibrium relationship. The distribution of the estimated coefficients is investigated in Stock (1984).

When $N = 2$, there are two possible regressions depending on the normalization chosen. The nonuniqueness of the estimate derives from the well known fact that the least squares fit of a reverse regression will not give the reciprocal of the coefficient in the forward regression. In this case, however, the normalization matters very little. As the moment matrix approaches singularity, the R^2 approaches 1 which is the product of the forward and reverse regression coefficients. This would be exactly true if there were only two data points which, of course, defines a singular matrix. For variables which are trending together, the correlation approaches one as each variance approaches infinity. The regression line passes nearly through the extreme points almost as if there were just two observations.

Stock (1984) in Theorem 3 proves the following proposition:

PROPOSITION 1: *Suppose that* x_t *satisfies* (3.1) *with* $C^*(B)$ *absolutely summable, that the disturbances have finite fourth absolute moments, and that* x_t *is co-integrated* (1, 1) *with r co-integrating vectors satisfying* (4.3) *which identify* θ. *Then, defining* $\hat{\theta}$ *by* (4.5),

$$T^{1-\delta}(\hat{\theta}-\theta) \xrightarrow{p} 0 \quad \text{for} \quad \delta>0. \tag{4.6}$$

The proposition establishes that the estimated parameters converge very rapidly to their probability limits. It also establishes that the estimates are consistent with a finite sample bias of order $1/T$. Stock presents some Monte Carlo examples to show that these biases may be important for small samples and gives expressions for calculating the limiting distribution of such estimates.

The two step estimator proposed for this co-integrated system uses the estimate of α from (4.5) as a known parameter in estimating the error correction form of the system of equations. This substantially simplifies the estimation procedure by imposing the cross-equation restrictions and allows specification of the individual equation dynamic patterns separately. Notice that the dynamics did not have to be specified in order to estimate α. Surprisingly, this two-step estimator has excellent properties; as shown in the Theorem below, it is just as efficient as the maximum likelihood estimator based on the known value of α.

THEOREM 2: *The two-step estimator of a single equation of an error correction system, obtained by taking* $\hat{\alpha}$ *from* (4.5) *as the true value, will have the same limiting distribution as the maximum likelihood estimator using the true value of* α. *Least squares standard errors will be consistent estimates of the true standard errors.*

PROOF: Rewrite the first equation of the error correction system (3.4) as

$$y_t = \gamma \hat{z}_{t-1} + W_t\beta + \varepsilon_t + \gamma(z_{t-1} - \hat{z}_{t-1}),$$

$$z_t = X_t\alpha,$$

$$\hat{z}_t = X_t\hat{\alpha},$$

where $X_t = x_t'$, W is an array with selected elements of Δx_{t-i} and y is an element of Δx_t so that all regressors are $I(0)$. Then letting the same variables without subscripts denote data arrays,

$$\sqrt{T}\begin{bmatrix} \gamma & -\gamma \\ \beta & -\beta \end{bmatrix} = [(\hat{z}, W)'(\hat{z}, W)/T]^{-1}[(\hat{z}, W)'(\varepsilon+\gamma)(z-\hat{z})]/\sqrt{T}.$$

This expression simplifies because $\hat{z}'(z-\hat{z})=0$. From Fuller (1976) or Stock (1984), $X'X/T^2$ and $X'W/T$ are both of order 1. Rewriting,

$$W'(z-\hat{z})/\sqrt{T}=[W'X/T][T(\alpha-\hat{\alpha})][1/\sqrt{T}],$$

and therefore the first and second factors to the right of the equal sign are of order 1 and the third goes to zero so that the entire expression vanishes asymptotically. Because the terms in $(z-\hat{z})/\sqrt{T}$ vanish asymptotically, least squares standard errors will be consistent.

Letting $S=\text{plim}\,[(\hat{z}, W)'(\hat{z}, W)/T]$,

$$\sqrt{T}\begin{bmatrix}\gamma & -\gamma\\ \beta & -\beta\end{bmatrix} \xrightarrow{A} D(0, \sigma^2 S^{-1})$$

where D represents the limiting distribution. Under additional but standard assumptions, this could be guaranteed to be normal.

To establish that the estimator using the true value of α has the same limiting distribution it is sufficient to show that the probability limit of $[(z, W)'(z, W)/T]$ is also S and that $z'\varepsilon/\sqrt{T}$ has the same limiting distribution as $\hat{z}'\varepsilon/\sqrt{T}$. Examining the off diagonal terms of S first,

$$\hat{z}'W/T - z'W/T = T(\hat{\alpha}-\alpha)'[W'X/T](1/T).$$

The first and second factors are of order 1 and the third is $1/T$ so the entire expression vanishes asymptotically:

$$\begin{aligned}(\hat{z}-z)'(\hat{z}-z)/T &= z'z/T-\hat{z}'\hat{z}/T\\ &= T(\hat{\alpha}-\alpha)'[X'X/T^2]T(\hat{\alpha}-\alpha)(1/T).\end{aligned}$$

Again, the first three factors are of order 1 and the last is $1/T$ so even though the difference between these covariance matrices is positive definite, it will vanish asymptotically. Finally,

$$(\hat{z}-z)'\varepsilon/\sqrt{T}=T(\hat{\alpha}-\alpha)'[X'\varepsilon/T]1/\sqrt{T},$$

which again vanishes asymptotically.

Under standard conditions the estimator using knowledge of α will be asymptotically normal and therefore the two-step estimator will also be asymptotically normal under these conditions. This completes the proof. *Q.E.D.*

A simple example will illustrate many of these points and motivate the approach to testing described in the next section. Suppose there are two series, x_{1t} and x_{2t}, which are jointly generated as a function of possibly correlated white noise disturbances ε_{1t} and ε_{2t} according to the following model:

$$x_{1t}+\beta x_{2t}=u_{1t}, \quad u_{1t}=u_{1t-1}+\varepsilon_{1t}, \tag{4.7}$$

$$x_{1t}+\alpha x_{2t}=u_{2t}, \quad u_{2t}=\rho u_{2t-1}+\varepsilon_{2t}, \quad |\rho|<1. \tag{4.8}$$

Clearly the parameters α and β are unidentified in the usual sense as there are no exogenous variables and the errors are contemporaneously correlated. The reduced form for this system will make x_{1t} and x_{2t} linear combinations of u_{1t} and u_{2t} and therefore both will be $I(1)$. The second equation describes a particular linear combination of the random variables which is stationary. Hence x_{1t} and x_{2t} are $CI(1, 1)$ and the question is whether it would be possible to detect this and estimate the parameters from a data set.

Surprisingly, this is easy to do. A linear least squares regression of x_{1t} on x_{2t} produces an excellent estimate of α. This is the "co-integrating regression." All linear combinations of x_{1t} and x_{2t} except that defined in equation (4.8) will have infinite variance and, therefore, least squares is easily able to estimate α. The correlation between x_{2t} and u_{2t} which causes the simultaneous equations bias is of a lower order in T than the variance of x_{2t}. In fact the reverse regression of x_{2t} on x_{1t} has exactly the same property and thus gives a consistent estimate of $1/\alpha$. These estimators converge even faster to the true value than standard econometric estimates.

While there are other consistent estimates of α, several apparently obvious choices are not. For example, regression of the first differences of x_1 on the differences of x_2 will not be consistent, and the use of Cochrane Orcutt or other serial correlation correction in the co-integrating regression will produce inconsistent estimates. Once the parameter α has been estimated, the others can be estimated in a variety of ways conditional on the estimate of α.

The model in (4.7) and (4.8) can be expressed in the autoregressive representation (after subtracting the lagged values from both sides and letting $\delta = (1-\rho)/(\alpha-\beta)$) as:

(4.9) $$\Delta x_{1t} = \beta\delta x_{1t-1} + \alpha\beta\delta x_{2t-1} + \eta_{1t},$$

(4.10) $$\Delta x_{2t} = -\delta x_{1t-1} - \alpha\delta x_{2t-1} + \eta_{2t},$$

where the η's are linear combinations of the ε's. The error correction representation becomes:

(4.11) $$\Delta x_{1t} = \beta\delta z_{t-1} + \eta_{1t},$$

(4.12) $$\Delta x_{2t} = -\delta z_{t-1} + \eta_{2t},$$

where $z_t = x_{1t} + \alpha x_{2t}$. There are three unknown parameters but the autoregressive form apparently has four unknown coefficients while the error correction form has two. Once α is known there are no longer constraints in the error correction form which motivates the two-step estimator. Notice that if $\rho \to 1$, the series are correlated random walks but are no longer co-integrated.

5. TESTING FOR CO-INTEGRATION

It is frequently of interest to test whether a set of variables are co-integrated. This may be desired because of the economic implications such as whether some system is in equilibrium in the long run, or it may be sensible to test such hypotheses before estimating a multivariate dynamic model.

Unfortunately the set-up is nonstandard and cannot simply be viewed as an application of Wald, likelihood ratio, or Lagrange multiplier tests. The testing problem is closely related to tests for unit roots in observed series as initially formulated by Fuller (1976) and Dickey and Fuller (1979, 1981) and more recently by Evans and Savin (1981), Sargan and Bhargava (1983), and Bhargava (1984), and applied by Nelson and Plosser (1983). It also is related to the problem of testing when some parameters are unidentified under the null as discussed by Davies (1977) and Watson and Engle (1982).

To illustrate the problems in testing such an hypothesis, consider the simple model in (4.7) and (4.8). The null hypothesis is taken to be no co-integration or $\rho = 1$. If α were known, then a test for the null hypothesis could be constructed along the lines of Dickey and Fuller taking z_t as the series which has a unit root under the null. The distribution in this case is already nonstandard and was computed through a simulation by Dickey (1976). However, when α is not known, it must be estimated from the data. But if the null hypothesis that $\rho = 1$ is true, α is not identified. Thus only if the series are co-integrated can α be simply estimated by the "co-integrating regression," but a test must be based upon the distribution of a statistic when the null is true. OLS seeks the α which minimizes the residual variance and therefore is most likely to be stationary, so the distribution of the Dickey-Fuller test will reject the null too often if α must be estimated.

In this paper a set of seven test statistics is proposed for testing the null of non-co-integration against the alternative of co-integration. It is maintained that the true system is a bivariate linear vector autoregression with Gaussian errors where each of the series is individually $I(1)$. As the null hypothesis is composite, similar tests will be sought so that the probability of rejection will be constant over the parameter set included in the null. See, for example, Cox and Hinkley (1974, p. 134–136).

Two cases may be distinguished. In the first, the system is known to be of first order and therefore the null is defined by

$$(5.1) \qquad \begin{array}{l} \Delta y_t = \varepsilon_{1t}, \\ \Delta x_t = \varepsilon_{2t}, \end{array} \quad \begin{bmatrix} (\varepsilon_{1t}) \\ (\varepsilon_{2t}) \end{bmatrix} \sim N(0, \Omega).$$

This is clearly the model implied by (4.11) and (4.12) when $\rho = 1$ which implies that $\delta = 0$. The composite null thus includes all positive definite covariance matrices Ω. It will be shown below that all the test statistics are similar with respect to the matrix Ω so without loss of generality, we take $\Omega = I$.

In the second case, the system is assumed merely to be a stationary linear system in the changes. Consequently, the null is defined over a full set of stationary autoregressive and moving average coefficients as well as Ω. The "augmented" tests described below are designed to be asymptotically similar for this case just as established by Dickey and Fuller for their univariate tests.

The seven test statistics proposed are all calculable by least squares. The critical values are estimated for each of these statistics by simulation using 10,000 replications. Using these critical values, the powers of the test statistics are computed by simulations under various alternatives. A brief motivation of each test is useful.

1. CRDW. After running the co-integrating regression, the Durbin Watson statistic is tested to see if the residuals appear stationary. If they are nonstationary, the Durbin Watson will approach zero and thus the test rejects non-co-integration (finds co-integration) if DW is too big. This was proposed recently by Bhargava (1984) for the case where the series is observed and the null and alternative are first order models.

2. DF. This tests the residuals from the co-integrating regression by running an auxiliary regression as described by Dickey and Fuller and outlined in Table I. It also assumes that the first order model is correct.

3. ADF. The augmented Dickey-Fuller test allows for more dynamics in the DF regression and consequently is over-parametrized in the first order case but correctly specified in the higher order cases.

4. RVAR. The restricted vector autoregression test is similar to the two step estimator. Conditional on the estimate of the co-integrating vector from the co-integrating regression, the error correction representation is estimated. The test is whether the error correction term is significant. This test requires specification of the full system dynamics. In this case a first order system is assumed. By making the system triangular, the disturbances are uncorrelated, and under normality the t statistics are independent. The test is based on the sum of the squared t statistics.

5. ARVAR. The augmented RVAR test is the same as RVAR except that a higher order system is postulated.

6. UVAR. The unrestricted VAR test is based on a vector autoregression in the levels which is not restricted to satisfy the co-integration constraints. Under the null, these are not present anyway so the test is simply whether the levels would appear at all, or whether the model can be adequately expressed entirely in changes. Again by triangularizing the coefficient matrix, the F tests from the two regressions can be made independent and the overall test is the sum of the two F's times their degrees of freedom, 2. This assumes a first order system again.

7. AUVAR. This is an augmented or higher order version of the above test.

To establish the similarity of these tests for the first order case for all positive definite symmetric matrices Ω, it is sufficient to show that the residuals from the regression of y on x for general Ω will be a scalar multiple of the residuals for $\Omega = I$. To show this, let ε_{1t} and ε_{2t} be drawn as independent standard normals. Then

$$(5.2)\qquad y_t = \sum_{i=1,t} \varepsilon_{1i}, \qquad x_t = \sum_{i=1,t} \varepsilon_{2i},$$

and

$$(5.3)\qquad u_t = y_t - x_t \sum x_t y_t / \sum x_t^2.$$

To generate y^* and x^* from Ω, let

$$(5.4)\quad \begin{aligned} \varepsilon^*_{2t} &= c\varepsilon_{2t}, \\ \varepsilon^*_{1t} &= a\varepsilon_{2t} + b\varepsilon_{1t}, \end{aligned}$$

where

$$c = \sqrt{\omega}_{xx}, \quad a = \omega_{yx}/c, \quad b^2 = \omega_{yy} - \omega^2_{yx}/\omega_{xx}.$$

Then substituting (5.4) in (5.2)

$$\begin{aligned} x^* &= cx, \quad y^* = ay + bx, \\ u^* &= y^* - x^*\textstyle\sum y^*_t x^*_t / \sum x^{*2}_t \\ &= ay + bx - cx\textstyle\sum (ay_t + bx_t)cx_t / \sum c^2 x^2_t \\ &= au, \end{aligned}$$

thus showing the exact similarity of the tests. If the same random numbers are used, the same test statistics will be obtained regardless of Ω.

In the more complicated but realistic case that the system is of infinite order but can be approximated by a p order autoregression, the statistics will only be asymptotically similar. Although exact similarity is achieved in the Gaussian fixed regressor model, this is not possible in time series models where one cannot condition on the regressors; similarity results are only asymptotic. Tests 5 and 7 are therefore asymptotically similar if the p order model is true but tests 1, 2, 4, and 6 definitely are not even asymptotically similar as these tests omit the lagged regressors. (This is analogous to the biased standard errors resulting from serially correlated errors.) It is on this basis that we prefer not to suggest the latter tests except in the first order case. Test 3 will also be asymptotically similar under the assumption that u, the residual from the co-integration regression, follows a p order process. This result is proven in Dickey and Fuller (1981, pp. 1065–1066). While the assumption that the system is p order allows the residuals to be of infinite order, there is presumably a finite autoregressive model, possibly of order less than p, which will be a good approximation. One might therefore suggest some experimentation to find the appropriate value of p in either case. An alternative strategy would be to let p be a slowly increasing nonstochastic function of T, which is closely related to the test proposed by Phillips (1985) and Phillips and Durlauf (1985). Only substantial simulation experimentation will determine whether it is preferable to use a data based selection of p for this testing procedure although the evidence presented below shows that estimation of extraneous parameters will decrease the power of the tests.

In Table I, the seven test statistics are formally stated. In Table II, the critical values and powers of the tests are considered when the system is first order. Here the augmented tests would be expected to be less powerful because they estimate parameters which are truly zero under both the null and alternative. The other four tests estimate no extraneous parameters and are correctly specified for this experiment.

From Table II one can perform a 5 per cent test of the hypothesis of non-co-integration with the co-integrating regression Durbin Watson test, by simply

TABLE I

THE TEST STATISTICS: REJECT FOR LARGE VALUES

1. The Co-integrating Regression Durbin Watson: $y_t = \alpha x_t + c + u_t$

   $\xi_1 = DW$. The null is $DW = 0$.

2. Dickey Fuller Regression: $\Delta u_t = -\phi u_{t-1} + \varepsilon_t$.

   $\xi_2 = \tau_\phi$: the t statistic for ϕ.

3. Augmented DF Regression: $\Delta u_t = -\phi u_{t-1} + b_1 \Delta u_{t-1} + \cdots + b_i \Delta u_t - p + \varepsilon_t$.

   $\xi_3 = \tau_\phi$.

4. Restricted VAR: $\Delta y_t = \beta_1 u_{t-1} + \varepsilon_{1t}$, $\Delta x_t = \beta_2 u_{t-1} + \gamma \Delta y_t + \varepsilon_{2t}$.

   $\xi_4 = \tau_{\beta 1}^2 + \tau_{\beta 2}^2$.

5. Augmented Restricted VAR: Same as (4) but with p lags of Δy_t and Δx_t in each equation.

   $\xi_5 = \tau_{\beta 1}^2 + \tau_{\beta 2}^2$.

6. Unrestricted VAR: $\Delta y_t = \beta_1 y_{t-1} + \beta_2 x_{t-1} + c_1 + \varepsilon_{1t}$, $\Delta x_t = \beta_3 y_{t-1} + \beta_4 x_{t-1} + \gamma \Delta y_t + c_2 + \varepsilon 2_t$.

   $\xi_6 = 2[F_1 + F_2]$ where F_1 is the F statistic for testing β_1 and β_2 both equal to zero in the first equation, and F_2 is the comparable statistic in the second.

7. Augmented Unrestricted VAR: The same as (6) except for p lags of Δx_t and Δy_t in each equation.

   $\gamma_7 = 2[F_1 + F_2]$.

NOTES: y_t and x_t are the original data sets and u_t are the residuals from the co-integrating regression.

checking DW from this regression and, if it exceeds 0.386, rejecting the null and finding co-integration. If the true model is Model II with $\rho = .9$ rather than 1, this will only be detected 20 per cent of the time; however if the true $\rho = .8$ this rises to 66 per cent. Clearly, test 1 is the best in each of the power calculations and should be preferred for this set-up, while test 2 is second in almost every case. Notice also that the augmented tests have practically the same critical values as the basic tests; however, as expected, they have slightly lower power. Therefore, if it is known that the system is first order, the extra lags should not be introduced. Whether a pre-test of the order would be useful remains to be established.

In Table III both the null and alternative hypotheses have fourth order autoregressions. Therefore the basic unaugmented tests now are misspecified while the augmented ones are correctly specified (although some of the intervening lags could be set to zero if this were known). Notice now the drop in the critical values of tests 1, 4, and 6 caused by their nonsimilarity. Using these new critical values, test 3 is the most powerful for the local alternative while at $\rho = .8$, test 1 is the best closely followed by 2 and 3. The misspecified or unaugmented tests 4 and 6 perform very badly in this situation. Even though they were moderately powerful in Table II, the performance here dismisses them from consideration.

Although test 1 has the best performance overall, it is not the recommended choice from this experiment because the critical value is so sensitive to the particular parameters within the null. For most types of economic data the differences are not white noise and, therefore, one could not in practice know

TABLE II

CRITICAL VALUES AND POWER

I MODEL: Δy, Δx independent standard normal, 100 observations, 10,000 replications, $p = 4$.

Statistic	Name	1%	5%	10%
	Critical Values			
1	CRDW	.511	.386	.322
2	DF	4.07	3.37	3.03
3	ADF	3.77	3.17	2.84
4	RVAR	18.3	13.6	11.0
5	ARVAR	15.8	11.8	9.7
6	UVAR	23.4	18.6	16.0
7	AUVAR	22.6	17.9	15.5

II MODEL: $y_t + 2x_t = u_t$, $\Delta u_t = (\rho - 1)u_{t-1} + \epsilon_t$, $x_t + y_t = v_t$, $\Delta v_t = \eta_t$; $\rho = .8, .9$, 100 observations, 1000 replications, $p = 4$.

Statistic	Name	1%	5%	10%
	Rejections per 100: $\rho = .9$			
1	CRDW	4.8	19.9	33.6
2	DF	2.2	15.4	29.0
3	ADF	1.5	11.0	22.7
4	RVAR	2.3	11.4	25.3
5	ARVAR	1.0	9.2	17.9
6	UVAR	4.3	13.3	26.1
7	AUVAR	1.6	8.3	16.3

Statistic	Name	1%	5%	10%
	Rejections per 100: $\rho = .8$			
1	CRDW	34.0	66.4	82.1
2	DF	20.5	59.2	76.1
3	ADF	7.8	30.9	51.6
4	RVAR	15.8	46.2	67.4
5	ARVAR	4.6	22.4	39.0
6	UVAR	19.0	45.9	63.7
7	AUVAR	4.8	18.3	33.4

what critical value to use. Test 3, the augmented Dickey-Fuller test, has essentially the same critical value for both finite sample experiments, has theoretically the same large sample critical value for both cases, and has nearly as good observed power properties in most comparisons, and is therefore the recommended approach.

Because of its simplicity, the CRDW might be used for a quick approximate result. Fortunately, none of the best procedures require the estimation of the full system, merely the co-integrating regression and then perhaps an auxiliary time series regression.

This analysis leaves many questions unanswered. The critical values have only been constructed for one sample size and only for the bivariate case, although recently, Engle and Yoo (1986) have calculated critical values for more variables

TABLE III

CRITICAL VALUES AND POWER WITH LAGS

MODEL I: $\Delta y_t = .8\Delta y_{t-4} + \epsilon_t$, $\Delta x_t = .8\Delta x_{t-4} + \eta_t$; 100 observations, 10,000 replications, $p = 4$, ϵ_t, η_t independent standard normal.

Statistic	Name	Critical Values 1%	5%	10%
1	CRDW	.455	.282	.209
2	DF	3.90	3.05	2.71
3	ADF	3.73	3.17	2.91
4	RVAR	37.2	22.4	17.2
5	ARVAR	16.2	12.3	10.5
6	UVAR	59.0	40.3	31.4
7	AUVAR	28.0	22.0	19.2

MODEL II: $y_t + 2x_t = u_t$, $\Delta u_t = (\rho - 1)u_{t-1} + .8\Delta u_{t-4} + \epsilon_t$, $y_t + x_t = v_t$, $\Delta v_t = .8\Delta v_{t-4} + \eta_t$; $\rho = .9, .8$. 100 observations, 1000 replications, $p = 4$.

Statistic	Name	Rejections per 100: $\rho = .9$ 1%	5%	10%
1	CRDW	15.6	39.9	65.6
2	DF	9.4	25.5	37.8
3	ADF	36.0	61.2	72.2
4	RVAR	.3	4.4	10.9
5	ARVAR	26.4	48.5	62.8
6	UVAR	.0	.5	3.5
7	AUVAR	9.4	26.8	40.3

Statistic	Name	Rejections per 100: $\rho = .8$ 1%	5%	10%
1	CRDW	77.5	96.4	98.6
2	DF	66.8	89.7	96.0
3	ADF	68.9	90.3	94.4
4	RVAR	7.0	42.4	62.5
5	ARVAR	57.2	80.5	89.3
6	UVAR	2.5	10.8	25.9
7	AUVAR	32.2	53.0	67.7

and sample sizes using the same general approach. There is still no optimality theory for such tests and alternative approaches may prove superior. Research on the limiting distribution theory by Phillips (1985) and Phillips and Durlauf (1985) may lead to improvements in test performance.

Nevertheless, it appears that the critical values for ADF given in Table II can be used as a rough guide in applied studies at this point. The next section will provide a variety of illustrations.

6. EXAMPLES

Several empirical examples will be presented to show performance of the tests in practice. The relationship between consumption and income will be studied in some detail as it was analyzed from an error correction point of view in DHSY and a time series viewpoint in Hall (1978) and others. Briefer analyses of wages and prices, short and long term interest rates, and the velocity of money will conclude this section.

DHSY have presented evidence for the error correction model of consumption behavior from both empirical and theoretical points of view. Consumers make plans which may be frustrated; they adjust next period's plans to recoup a portion of the error between income and consumption. Hall finds that U.S. consumption is a random walk and that past values of income have no explanatory power which implies that income and consumption are not co-integrated, at least if income does not depend on the error correction term. Neither of these studies models income itself and it is taken as exogenous in DHSY.

Using U.S. quarterly real per capita consumption on nondurables and real per capita disposable income from 1947-I to 1981-II, it was first checked that the series were $I(1)$. Regressing the change in consumption on its past level and two past changes gave a t statistic of +.77 which is even the wrong sign for consumption to be stationary in the levels. Running the same model with second differences on lagged first differences and two lags of second differences, the t statistic was −5.36 indicating that the first difference is stationary. For income, four past lags were used and the two t statistics were −.01 and −6.27 respectively, again establishing that income is $I(1)$.

The co-integrating regression of consumption (C) on income (Y) and a constant was run. The coefficient of Y was .23 (with a t statistic of 123 and an R^2 of .99). The DW was however .465 indicating that by either table of critical values one rejects the null of "non-co-integration" or accepts co-integration at least at the 5 per cent level. Regressing the change in the residuals on past levels and four lagged changes, the t statistic on the level is 3.1 which is essentially the critical value for the 5 per cent ADF test. Because the lags are not significant, the DF regression was run giving a test statistic of 4.3 which is significant at the 1 per cent level, illustrating that when it is appropriate, it is a more powerful test. In the reverse regression of Y on C, the coefficient is 4.3 which has reciprocal .23, the same as the coefficient in the forward regression. The DW is now .463 and the t statistic from the ADF test is 3.2. Again the first order DF appears appropriate and gives a test statistic of 4.4. Whichever way the regression is run, the data rejects the null of non-co-integration at any level above 5 per cent.

To establish that the joint distribution of C and Y is an error correction system, a series of models was estimated. An unrestricted vector autoregression of the change in consumption on four lags of consumption and income changes plus the lagged levels of consumption and income is given next in Table IV. The lagged levels are of the appropriate signs and sizes for an error correction term and are individually significant or nearly so. Of all the lagged changes, only the first lag of income change is significant. Thus the final model has the error correction term estimated from the co-integrating regression and one lagged change in income. The standard error of this model is even lower than the VAR suggesting the efficiency of the parameter restrictions. The final model passes a

TABLE IV

REGRESSIONS OF CONSUMPTION AND INCOME

Dep. Var.:	C	ΔEC	ΔEC	ΔC	ΔC
Y	.23 (123)				
$C(-1)$				−.19 (−2.5)	
$Y(-1)$				.046 (2.5)	
$EC(-1)$		−.22 (−3.1)	−.26 (−4.3)		−.14 (−2.2)
$\Delta C(-1)$				.092 (0.9)	
$\Delta C(-2)$				.017 (0.2)	
$\Delta C(-3)$				.16 (1.5)	
$\Delta C(-4)$				.009 (0.1)	
$\Delta Y(-1)$				.059 (1.8)	.068 (2.5)
$\Delta Y(-2)$				−.023 (−.7)	
$\Delta Y(-3)$				−.027 (−.8)	
$\Delta Y(-4)$				−.020 (−.7)	
$\Delta EC(-1)$		−.13 (−1.4)			
$\Delta EC(-2)$		.12 (1.4)			
$\Delta EC(-3)$		.03 (0.4)			
$\Delta EC(-4)$		−.13 (−1.6)			
CONST	.52 (85)			.10 (2.4)	.003 (2.6)
σ	.01628	.00999	0.01015	.01094	.01078
DW	.46	2.0	2.2	2.0	1.9

Dep. Var:	Y	ΔEY	ΔEY	ΔY	ΔY
C	4.29 (123)				
$C(-1)$				.15 (.67)	
$Y(-1)$				−.034 (.63)	
$EY(-1)$		−.23 (−3.2)	−.26 (−4.4)		−.053 (−1.1)
$\Delta C(-1)$				.79 (2.5)	.66 (2.4)
$\Delta C(-2)$				−.48 (−1.5)	
$\Delta C(-3)$				.68 (2.2)	
$\Delta C(-4)$				.56 (1.8)	.60 (2.1)
$\Delta Y(-1)$				−.027 (−.3)	
$\Delta Y(-2)$				−.051 (−.5)	
$\Delta Y(-3)$				.011 (.1)	
$\Delta Y(-4)$				−.23 (−2.5)	−.19 (2.1)
$\Delta EY(-1)$		−.13 (−1.5)			
$\Delta EY(-2)$		.12 (1.4)			
$\Delta EY(-3)$		.03 (0.4)			
$\Delta EY(-4)$		−.14 (−1.6)			
CONST	2.22 (−50)			−.071 (−.6)	.016 (4.6)
σ	.07012	.04279	.04350	.03255	.03321
DW	.46	2.0	2.2	2.1	2.2

NOTES: Data are from 1947-I to 1981-II. EC are the residuals from the first regression and EY are the residuals from the sixth regression. T ratios are in parentheses.

series of diagnostic tests for serial correlation, lagged dependent variables, nonlinearities, ARCH, and omitted variables such as a time trend and other lags.

One might notice that an easy model building strategy in this case would be to estimate the simplest error correction model first and then test for added lags of C and Y, proceeding in a "simple to general" specification search.

The model building process for Y produced a similar model. The same unrestricted VAR was estimated and distilled to a simple model with the error correction term, first and fourth lagged changes in C and a fourth lagged change in Y. The error correction is not really significant with a t statistic of -1.1 suggesting that income may indeed be weakly exogenous even though the variables are co-integrated. In this case the standard error of the regression is slightly higher in the restricted model but the difference is not significant. The diagnostic tests are again generally good.

Campbell (1985) uses a similar structure to develop a test of the permanent income hypothesis which incorporates "saving for a rainy day" behavior. In this case the error correction term is approximately saving which should be high when income is expected to fall (such as when current income is above permanent income). Using a broader measure of consumption and narrower measure of income he finds the error correction term significant in the income equation.

The second example examines monthly wages and prices in the U.S. The data are logs of the consumer price index and production worker wage in manufacturing over the three decades of 50's, 60's and 70's. Again, the test is run both directions to show that there is little difference in the result. For each of the decades there are 120 observations so the critical values as tabulated should be appropriate.

For the full sample period the Durbin Watson from the co-integrating regression in either direction is a notable .0054. One suspects that this will be insignificantly different from zero even for samples much larger than this. Looking at the augmented Dickey Fuller test statistic, for p on w we find $-.6$ and for w on p we find $+.2$. Adding a twelfth lag in the ADF tests improves the fit substantially and raises the test statistics to .88 and 1.50 respectively. In neither case do these approach the critical values of 3.2. The evidence accepts the null of non-co-integration for wages and prices over the thirty year period.

For individual decades none of the ADF tests are significant at even the .10 per cent level. The largest of these six test statistics is for the 50's regressing p on w which reaches 2.4, which is still below the 10 per cent level of 2.8. Thus we find evidence that wages and prices in the U.S. are not co-integrated. Of course, if a third variable such as productivity were available (and were $I(1)$), the three might be co-integrated.

The next example tests for co-integration between short and long term interest rates. Using monthly yields to maturity of 20 year treasury bonds as the long term rate (R_t) and the one month treasury bill rate r_t as the short rate, co-integration was tested with data from February, 1952 to December, 1982. With the long rate as the dependent variable, the co-integrating regression gave:

$$R_t = 1.93 + .785\, r_t + ER_t, \quad DW = .126; \quad R^2 = .866,$$

with a t ratio of 46 on the short rate. The DW is not significantly different from zero, at least by Tables II and III; however, the correct critical value depends upon the dynamics of the errors (and of course the sample size is 340—much greater than for the tabulated values). The ADF test with four lags gives:

$$\underset{}{\Delta ER_t} = -\underset{(-3.27)}{.06}\; ER_{t-1}$$

$$+ \underset{(4.55)}{.25}\, \Delta ER_{t-1} - \underset{(-4.15)}{.24}\, \Delta ER_{t-2} + \underset{(-4.15)}{.24}\, \Delta ER_{t-3} - \underset{(-1.48)}{.09}\, \Delta ER_{t-4}.$$

When the twelfth lag is added instead of the fourth, the test statistic rises to 3.49. Similar results were found with the reverse regression where the statistics were 3.61 and 3.89 respectively. Each of these test statistics exceeds the 5 per cent critical values from Table III. Thus these interest rates are apparently co-integrated.

This finding is entirely consistent with the efficient market hypothesis. The one-period excess holding yield on long bonds as linearized by Shiller and Campbell (1984) is:

$$EHY = DR_{t-1} - (D-1)R_t - r_t$$

where D is the duration of the bond which is given by

$$D = ((1+c)^i - 1)/(c(1+c)^{i-1}$$

with c as the coupon rate and i the number of periods to maturity. The efficient market hypothesis implies that the expectation of the EHY is a constant representing a risk premium if agents are risk averse. Setting $EHY = k + \varepsilon$ and rearranging terms gives the error correction form:

$$\Delta R_t = (D-1)^{-1}(R_{t-1} - r_{t-1}) + k' + \varepsilon_t,$$

implying that R and r are co-integrated with a unit coefficient and that for long maturities, the coefficients of the error correction term is c, the coupon rate. If the risk premium is varying over time but is $I(0)$ already, then it need not be included in the test of co-integration.

The final example is based upon the quantity theory equation: $MV = PY$. Empirical implications stem from the assumption that velocity is constant or at least stationary. Under this condition, log M, log P, and log Y should be co-integrated with known unit parameters. Similarly, nominal money and nominal GNP should be co-integrated. A test of this hypothesis was constructed for four measures of money: $M1$, $M2$, and $M3$, and L, total liquid assets. In each case the sample period was 1959-I through 1981-II, quarterly. The ADF tests statistics were:

$M1$	1.81	1.90
$M2$	3.23	3.13
$M3$	2:65	2.55
L	2.15	2.13

where in the first column the log of the monetary aggregate was the dependent variable while in the second, it was log GNP. For only one of the $M2$ tests is the test statistic significant at the 5 per cent level, and none of the other aggregates are significant even at the 10 per cent level. (In several cases it appears that the DF test could be used and would therefore be more powerful.) Thus the most stable relationship is between $M2$ and nominal GNP but for the other aggregates, we reject co-integration and the stationarity of velocity.

7. CONCLUSION

If each element of a vector of time series x_t is stationary only after differencing, but a linear combination $\alpha' x_t$ need not be differenced, the time series x_t have been defined to be co-integrated of order (1, 1) with co-integrating vector α. Interpreting $\alpha' x_t = 0$ as a long run equilibrium, co-integration implies that equilibrium holds except for a stationary, finite variance disturbance even though the series themselves are non-stationary and have infinite variance.

The paper presents several representations for co-integrated systems including an autoregressive representation and an error-correction representation. A vector autoregression in differenced variables is incompatible with these representations because it omits the error correction term. The vector autoregression in the levels of the series ignores cross equation constraints and will give a singular autoregressive operator. Consistent and efficient estimation of error correction models is discussed and a two step estimator proposed. To test for co-integration, seven statistics are formulated which are similar under various maintained hypotheses about the generating model. The critical values of these statistics are calculated based on a Monte Carlo simulation. Using these critical values, the power properties of the tests are examined, and one test procedure is recommended for application.

In a series of examples it is found that consumption and income are co-integrated, wages and prices are not, short and long interest rates are, and nominal *GNP* is not co-integrated with $M1$, $M3$, or total liquid assets, although it is possibly with $M2$.

Department of Economics, University of California—San Diego, La Jolla, CA 92093, U.S.A.

Manuscript received September, 1983; final revision received June, 1986.

REFERENCES

BHARGAVA, ALOK (1984): "On the Theory of Testing For Unit Roots in Observed Time Series," manuscript, ICERD, London School of Economics.

BOX, G. E. P., AND G. M. JENKINS (1970): *Time Series Analysis, Forecasting and Control.* San Francisco: Holden Day.

CAMPBELL, JOHN Y. (1985): "Does Saving Anticipate Declining Labor Income? An Alternative Test of the Permanent Income Hypothesis," manuscript, Princeton University.

COX, D. R., AND C. V. HINKLEY (1974): *Theoretical Statistics.* London: Chapman and Hall.

CURRIE, D. (1981): "Some Long-Run Features of Dynamic Time-Series Models," *The Economic Journal*, 91, 704–715.

DAVIDSON, J. E. H., DAVID F. HENDRY, FRANK SRBA, AND STEVEN YEO (1978): "Econometric Modelling of the Aggregate Time-series Relationship Between Consumer's Expenditure and Income in the United Kingdom," *Economic Journal*, 88, 661–692.

DAVIES, R. R. (1977): "Hypothesis Testing When a Nuisance Parameter is Present Only Under the Alternative," *Biometrika*, 64, 247–254.

DAWSON, A. (1981): "Sargan's Wage Equation: A Theoretical and Empirical Reconstruction," *Applied Economics*, 13, 351–363.

DICKEY, DAVID A. (1976): "Estimation and Hypothesis Testing for Nonstationary Time Series," PhD. Thesis, Iowa State University, Ames.

DICKEY, DAVID A, AND WAYNE A. FULLER (1979): "Distribution of the Estimators for Autoregressive Time Series With a Unit Root," *Journal of the American Statistical Assoc.*, 74, 427–431.

——— (1981): "The Likelihood Ratio Statistics for Autoregressive Time Series with a Unit Root," *Econometrica*, 49, 1057–1072.

ENGLE, ROBERT F., DAVID F. HENDRY, AND J. F. RICHARD (1983): "Exogeneity," *Econometrica*, 51, 277–304.

ENGLE, ROBERT F., AND BYUNG SAM YOO (1986): "Forecasting and Testing in Co-integrated Systems," U.C.S.D. Discussion Paper.

EVANS, G. B. A., AND N. E. SAVIN (1981): "Testing for Unit Roots: 1," *Econometrica*, 49, 753–779.

FELLER, WILLIAM (1968): *An Introduction to Probability Theory and Its Applications, Volume I.* New York: John Wiley.

FULLER, WAYNE A. (1976): *Introduction to Statistical Time Series.* New York: John Wiley.

GRANGER, C. W. J. (1981): "Some Properties of Time Series Data and Their Use in Econometric Model Specification," *Journal of Econometrics*, 121–130.

——— (1983): "Co-Integrated Variables and Error-Correcting Models," unpublished UCSD Discussion Paper 83-13.

GRANGER, C. W. J., AND P. NEWBOLD (1977): *Forecasting Economic Time Series.* New York: Academic Press.

——— (1974): "Spurious Regressions in Econometrics," *Journal of Econometrics*, 26, 1045–1066.

GRANGER, C. W. J., AND A. A. WEISS (1983): "Time Series Analysis of Error-Correcting Models," in *Studies in Econometrics, Time Series, and Multivariate Statistics.* New York: Academic Press, 255–278.

HALL, ROBERT E. (1978): "A Stochastic Life Cycle Model of Aggregate Consumption," *Journal of Political Economy*, 971–987.

HANNAN, E. J. (1970): *Multiple Time Series.* New York: Wiley.

HENDRY, DAVID F., AND T. VON UNGERN-STERNBERG (1981): "Liquidity and Inflation Effects on Consumer's Expenditure," in *Essays in the Theory and Measurement of Consumer's Behavior*, ed. by A. S. Deaton. Cambridge: Cambridge University Press.

JOHANSEN, SOREN (1985): "The Mathematical Structure of Error Correction Models," manuscript, University of Copenhagen.

NELSON, C. R., AND CHARLES PLOSSER (1982): "Trends and Random Walks in Macroeconomic Time Series," *Journal of Monetary Economics*, 10, 139–162.

PAGAN, A. R. (1984): "Econometric Issues in the Analysis of Regressions with Generated Regressors," *International Economic Review*, 25, 221–248.

PHILLIPS, A. W. (1957): "Stabilization Policy and the Time Forms of Lagged Responses," *Economic Journal*, 67, 265–277.

PHILLIPS, P. C. B. (1985): "Time Series Regression with Unit Roots," Cowles Foundation Discussion Paper No. 740, Yale University.

PHILLIPS, P. C. B., AND S. N. DURLAUF (1985): "Multiple Time Series Regression with Integrated Processes," Cowles Foundation Discussion Paper 768.

SALMON, M. (1982): "Error Correction Mechanisms," *The Economic Journal*, 92, 615–629.

SARGAN, J. D. (1964): "Wages and Prices in the United Kingdom: a Study in Econometric Methodology," in *Econometric Analysis for National Economic Planning*, ed. by P. E. Hart, G. Mills, and J. N. Whittaker. London: Butterworths.

SARGAN, J. D., AND A. BHARGAVA (1983): "Testing Residuals from Least Squares Regression for Being Generated by the Gaussian Random Walk," *Econometrica*, 51, 153–174.

SHILLER, R. J., AND J. Y. CAMPBELL (1984): "A Simple Account of the Behaviour of Long-Term Interest Rates," *American Economic Review*, 74, 44–48.

STOCK, JAMES H. (1984): "Asymptotic Properties of Least Squares Estimators of Co-Integrating Vectors, manuscript, Harvard University.

WATSON, MARK W., AND ROBERT ENGLE (1985): "A Test for Regression Coefficient Stability with a Stationary AR(1) Alternative," forthcoming in *Review of Economics and Statistics.*

YOO, SAM (1985): "Multi-co-integrated Time Series and Generalized Error Correction Models," manuscript in preparation, U.C.S.D.

[29]

Econometrica, Vol. 58, No. 1 (January, 1990), 113–144

INFERENCE IN LINEAR TIME SERIES MODELS WITH SOME UNIT ROOTS

BY CHRISTOPHER A. SIMS, JAMES H. STOCK, AND MARK W. WATSON[1]

This paper considers estimation and hypothesis testing in linear time series models when some or all of the variables have unit roots. Our motivating example is a vector autoregression with some unit roots in the companion matrix, which might include polynomials in time as regressors. In the general formulation, the variable might be integrated or cointegrated of arbitrary orders, and might have drifts as well. We show that parameters that can be written as coefficients on mean zero, nonintegrated regressors have jointly normal asymptotic distributions, converging at the rate $T^{1/2}$. In general, the other coefficients (including the coefficients on polynomials in time) will have nonnormal asymptotic distributions. The results provide a formal characterization of which t or F tests—such as Granger causality tests—will be asymptotically valid, and which will have nonstandard limiting distributions.

KEYWORDS: Cointegration, error correction models, vector autoregressions.

1. INTRODUCTION

VECTOR AUTOREGRESSIONS have been used in an increasingly wide variety of econometric applications. In this paper, we investigate the distributions of least squares parameter estimators and Wald test statistics in linear time series models that might have unit roots. The general model includes several important special cases. For example, all the variables could be integrated of order zero (be "stationary"), possibly around a polynomial time trend. Alternatively, all the variables could be integrated of order one, with the number of unit roots in the multivariate representation equaling the number of variables, so that the variables have a VAR representation in first differences. Another special case is that all the variables are integrated of the same order, but there are linear combinations of these variables that exhibit reduced orders of integration, so that the system is cointegrated in the sense of Engle and Granger (1987). In addition to VAR's, this model contains as special cases linear univariate time series models with unit roots as studied by White (1958), Fuller (1976), Dickey and Fuller (1979), Solo (1984), Phillips (1987), and others.

The model and notation are presented in Section 2. Section 3 provides an asymptotic representation of the ordinary least squares (OLS) estimator of the coefficients in a regression model with "canonical" regressors that are a linear transformation of Y_t, the original regressors. An implication of this result is that the OLS estimator is consistent whether or not the VAR contains integrated components, as long as the innovations in the VAR have enough moments and a

[1] The authors thank Lars Peter Hansen, Hal White, and an anonymous referee for helpful comments on an earlier draft. This research was supported in part by the National Science Foundation through Grants SES-83-09329, SES-84-08797, SES-85-10289, and SES-86-18984. This is a revised version of two earlier papers, "Asymptotic Normality of Coefficients in a Vector Autoregression with Unit Roots," March, 1986, by Sims, and "Wald Tests of Linear Restrictions in a Vector Autoregression with Unit Roots," June, 1986, by Stock and Watson.

zero mean, conditional on past values of Y_t. When an intercept is included in a regression based on the canonical variables, the distribution of coefficients on the stationary canonical variates with mean zero is asymptotically normal with the usual covariance matrix, converging to its limit at the rate $T^{1/2}$. In contrast, the estimated coefficients on nonstationary stochastic canonical variates are nonnormally distributed, converging at a faster rate. These results imply that estimators of coefficients in the original untransformed model have a joint nondegenerate asymptotic normal distribution if the model can be rewritten so that these original coefficients correspond in the transformed model to coefficients on mean zero stationary canonical regressors.

The limiting distribution of the Wald F statistic is obtained in Section 4. In general, the distribution of this statistic does not have a simple form. When all the restrictions being tested in the untransformed model correspond to restrictions on the coefficients of mean zero stationary canonical regressors in the transformed model, then the test statistic has the usual limiting χ^2 distribution. In contrast, when the restrictions cannot be written solely in terms of coefficients on mean zero stationary canonical regressors and at least one of the canonical variates is dominated by a stochastic trend, then the test statistic has a limiting representation involving functionals of a multivariate Wiener process and in general has a nonstandard asymptotic distribution.

As a special case, the results apply to a VAR with some roots equal to one but with fewer unit roots than variables, a case that has recently come to the fore as the class of cointegrated VAR models. Engle and Granger (1987) have pointed out that such models can be handled with a two-step procedure, in which the cointegrating vector is estimated first and used to form a reduced, stationary model. The asymptotic distribution theory for the reduced model is as if the cointegrating vector were known exactly. One implication of our results is that such two-step procedures are unnecessary, at least asymptotically: if the VAR is estimated on the original data, the asymptotic distribution for the coefficients normalized by $T^{1/2}$ is a singular normal and is identical to that for a model in which the cointegrating vector is known exactly *a priori*. This result is important because the two-step procedures have so far been justified only by assuming that the number of cointegrating vectors is known. This paper shows that, at a minimum, as long as one is not interested in drawing inferences about intercepts or about linear combinations of coefficients that have degenerate limiting distributions when normalized by $T^{1/2}$, it is possible to avoid such two-step procedures in large samples. However, when there are unit roots in the VAR, the coefficients on any intercepts or polynomials in time included in the regression and their associated t statistics will typically have nonstandard limiting distributions.

In Sections 5 and 6, these general results are applied to several examples. Section 5 considers a univariate AR(2) with a unit root with and without a drift; the Dickey-Fuller (1979) tests for a unit root in these models follow directly from the more general results. Section 6 examines two common tests of linear restrictions performed in VAR's: a test for the number of lags that enter the true VAR and a "causality" or predictability test that lagged values of one variable do not enter the equation for a second variable. These examples are developed for a trivariate system of integrated variables with drift. In the test for lag length, the F test has a chi-squared asymptotic distribution with the usual degrees of freedom. In the causality test, the statistic has a χ^2 asymptotic distribution if the process is cointegrated; otherwise, its asymptotic distribution is nonstandard and must be computed numerically. Some conclusions are summarized in Section 7.

2. THE MODEL

We consider linear time series models that can be written in first order form,

$$(2.1) \qquad Y_t = AY_{t-1} + G\Omega^{1/2}\eta_t \qquad (t = 1, \ldots, T),$$

where Y_t is a k-dimensional time series variable and A is a $k \times k$ matrix of coefficients. The $N \times 1$ vector of disturbances $\{\eta_t\}$ is assumed to be a sequence of martingale differences with $E[\eta_t | \eta_1, \ldots, \eta_{t-1}] = 0$ and $E[\eta_t \eta_t' | \eta_1, \ldots, \eta_{t-1}] = I_N$ for $t = 1, \ldots, T$. The $N \times N$ matrix $\Omega^{1/2}$ is thought of as the square root of the covariance matrix of some "structural" errors $\Omega^{1/2}\eta_t$. The $k \times N$ constant matrix G is thought of as known *a priori*, and typically contains ones and zeros indicating which errors enter which equations. Note that because N might be less than k, some of the elements of Y_t (or more generally, some linear combinations of Y_t) might be nonrandom. It is assumed that A has k_1 eigenvalues with modulus less than one and that the remaining $k - k_1$ eigenvalues exactly equal one. As is shown below, this formulation is sufficiently general to include a VAR of arbitrary finite order with arbitrary orders of integration, constants and finite order polynomials in t. The assumptions do not, however, allow complex unit roots so, for example, seasonal nonstationarity is not treated.

The regressors Y_t will in general consist of random variables with various orders of integration, of constants, and of polynomials in time. These components in general are of different orders in t. Often there will be linear combinations of Y_t having a lower order in probability than the individual elements of Y_t itself. Extending Engle and Granger's (1987) terminology, we refer to the vectors that form these linear combinations as *generalized cointegrating vectors*. As long as the system has some generalized cointegrating vectors, the calculations below demonstrate that $T^{-p}\Sigma Y_t Y_t'$ will converge to a singular (possibly random) limit, where p is a suitably chosen constant; that is, some elements of Y_t will exhibit perfect multicolinearity, at least asymptotically. Thus we work with a transformation of Y_t, say Z_t, that uses the generalized cointegrating vectors of Y_t to isolate those components having different orders in probability. Specifically, let

$$(2.2) \qquad Z_t = DY_t.$$

(Note that in the dating convention of (2.1) the actual regressors are Y_{t-1} or, after transforming by D, Z_{t-1}.) The nonsingular $k \times k$ matrix D is chosen in such a way that Z_t has a simple representation in terms of the fundamental stochastic and nonstochastic components. Let $\xi_t^1 = \Sigma_{s=1}^t \eta_s$, and let ξ_t^j be defined recursively by $\xi_t^j = \Sigma_{s=1}^t \xi_s^{j-1}$, so that ξ_t^1 is the N-dimensional driftless random walk with innovations η_t and ξ_t^j is the j-fold summation of η_t. The transformation D is chosen so that

(2.3)

$$Z_t = \begin{bmatrix} Z_t^1 \\ Z_t^2 \\ Z_t^3 \\ Z_t^4 \\ \vdots \\ Z_t^{2g} \\ Z_t^{2g+1} \end{bmatrix}$$

$$= \begin{bmatrix} F_{11}(L) & 0 & 0 & 0 & \cdots & 0 & 0 \\ F_{21}(L) & F_{22} & 0 & 0 & \cdots & 0 & 0 \\ F_{31}(L) & F_{32} & F_{33} & 0 & \cdots & 0 & 0 \\ F_{41}(L) & F_{42} & F_{43} & F_{44} & \cdots & 0 & 0 \\ \vdots & \vdots & & & & \vdots & \vdots \\ F_{2g,1}(L) & F_{2g,2} & \cdots & \cdots & \cdots & F_{2g,2g} & 0 \\ F_{2g+1,1}(L) & F_{2g+1,2} & \cdots & \cdots & \cdots & F_{2g+1,2g} & F_{2g+1,2g+1} \end{bmatrix} \begin{bmatrix} \eta_t \\ 1 \\ \xi_t^1 \\ t \\ \vdots \\ t^{g-1} \\ \xi_t^g \end{bmatrix}$$

$$\equiv F(L)\nu_t$$

where L is the lag operator and $\nu_t = (\eta_t' \cdots \xi_t^{g\prime})'$. Note that the stochastic and deterministic elements in ν_t alternate and that ν_t has dimension $(g+1)N + g$. The variates ν_t will be referred to as the canonical regressors associated with Y_t. In general, $F(L)$ need not be square even though D will be. In addition, for specific models fitting in the general framework (2.1), some of the rows given in (2.3) will be absent altogether.

The lag polynomial $F_{11}(L)$ has dimension $k_1 \times N$, and it is assumed that $\Sigma_{j=0}^{\infty} F_{11j} F_{11j}'$ is nonsingular. Without loss of generality, F_{jj} is assumed to have full row rank k_j (possibly equal to zero) for $j = 2, \ldots, 2g+1$, so that $k = \Sigma_{j=1}^{2g+1} k_j$. These assumptions ensure that, after appropriate rescaling, the moment matrix $\Sigma Z_t Z_t'$ is (almost surely) invertible—i.e., no elements of Z_t are perfectly multicolinear asymptotically—so that the OLS estimator of AD^{-1} is unique.

From (2.2) and (2.3), it is clear that D must be chosen so that its rows select linear combinations of Y_t that are different orders in probability. Thus some of the rows of D can be thought of as generalizations of cointegrating vectors: partitioning $D = [D_1' \cdots D_{2g+1}']'$, so that $Z_t^j = D_j Y_t$, D_1 forms a linear combination of Y_t such that Z_t^1 has mean zero and is $O_p(1)$; D_2 forms a linear combination with mean F_{22} that is also $O_p(1)$. The linear combinations formed with D_3 are $O_p(t^{1/2})$, those formed with D_4 are $O_p(t)$, and so on. In this framework these linear combinations include first differences of the data, in addition to including cointegrating vectors in the sense of Engle and Granger

(1987). The row space of $D_1, \ldots, D_{2g}$ is the subspace of $\Re^k$ spanned by the generalized cointegrating vectors of Y_t.

Derivation of (2.2) *and* (2.3) *from the Jordan Form of A*

Specific examples of (2.2) and (2.3) are given at the end of this section and in Sections 5 and 6. As these examples demonstrate, D and $F(L)$ in general are not unique, although the row spaces of $D_1, [D_1' \; D_2']'$, etc. are. This poses no difficulty for the asymptotic analysis; indeed, it will be seen that only the blocks along the diagonal in $F(L)$ enter into the asymptotic representation for the estimator and F statistic. This nonuniqueness means that in many cases a set of generalized cointegrating vectors can be deduced by inspection of the system, and that $F(L)$ is then readily calculated. For completeness, however, we now sketch how (2.2) and (2.3) can be derived formally from the Jordan canonical form of A.

Let $A = B^{-1}JB$ be the Jordan decomposition of A, so that the matrix J is block diagonal with the eigenvalues of A on its diagonal. Suppose that the Jordan blocks are ordered so that the final block contains all the unit eigenvalues and no eigenvalues less than one in modulus. Let J_1 denote the $k_1 \times k_1$ block with eigenvalues less than one in modulus, let J_2 denote the $(k - k_1) \times (k - k_1)$ block with unit eigenvalues, and partition B conformably with J so that $B = (B_1' \; B_2')'$. The representation (2.2) and (2.3) can be constructed by considering the linear combinations of Y_t formed using B. Let $Z_t^1 = B_1 Y_t$. These definitions and (2.1) imply that

(2.4) $$Z_t^1 = J_1 Z_{t-1}^1 + B_1 G \Omega^{1/2} \eta_t.$$

Because the eigenvalues of J_1 are less than one in modulus by construction, Z_t^1 is integrated of order zero and the autoregressive representation (2.4) can be inverted to yield

(2.5) $$Z_t^1 = F_{11}(L)\eta_t,$$

where $F_{11}(L) = (I - J_1 L)^{-1} B_1 G \Omega^{1/2}$. Thus (2.5) provides the canonical representation for the mean zero stationary elements of Z_t.

The representation for the integrated and deterministic terms comes from considering the final Jordan block, J_2. This block in general has ones on the diagonal, zeros or ones on the first superdiagonal, and zeros elsewhere; the location of the ones above the diagonal determines the number and orders of the polynomials in time and integrated stochastic processes in the representation (2.3). The structure of this Jordan block makes it possible to solve recursively for each of the elements of $B_2 Y_t$. Because J_2 consists of only ones and zeros, each element of $B_2 Y_t$ will be a linear combination of polynomials in time and of partial sums of $\{\eta_s\}$. Letting $\tilde{F}$ denote the matrix of coefficients expressing these linear combinations, one obtains the representation for the remaining linear combinations of Y_t:

(2.6) $$B_2 Y_t = \tilde{F}\tilde{\nu}_t \qquad \text{where} \qquad \tilde{\nu}_t = (1\; \xi_t^{1\prime}\; t\; \xi_t^{2\prime} \cdots \xi_t^{g\prime})'.$$

Elementary row and column operations need to be performed on (2.6) to put $\tilde{F}$ into the lower reduced echelon form of (2.3). Let $\tilde{D}$ be the $(k-k_1)\times(k-k_1)$ invertible matrix summarizing these row and column operations, so that

$$(2.7)\qquad \begin{bmatrix} Z_t^2 \\ \vdots \\ Z_t^{2g+1} \end{bmatrix} = \tilde{D}B_2Y_t = \begin{bmatrix} F_{22} & \cdots & 0 \\ \vdots & & \vdots \\ F_{2g+1,2} & \cdots & F_{2g+1,2g+1} \end{bmatrix} \tilde{\nu}_t \equiv \tilde{D}\tilde{F}\tilde{\nu}_t.$$

The representation (2.2) and (2.3) obtains from (2.5) and (2.7). Let

$$(2.8)\qquad D = \begin{bmatrix} I_{k_1} & 0 \\ 0 & \tilde{D} \end{bmatrix} B \quad \text{and} \quad F(L) = \begin{bmatrix} F_{11}(L) & 0 \\ 0 & \tilde{D}\tilde{F} \end{bmatrix},$$

where $\nu_t = (\eta_t' \, \tilde{\nu}_t')'$ as in (2.3). Combining (2.5), (2.7), and (2.8) yields

$$(2.9)\qquad Z_t = DY_t = F(L)\nu_t,$$

which is the desired result.

This derivation warrants two remarks. First, when an intercept is included in the regression, D can always be chosen so that $F_{21}(L)=0$ in (2.3). Because excluding an intercept is exceptional in applications, it is assumed throughout that $F_{21}(L)=0$ unless explicitly noted otherwise. Second, it turns out that whether $F_{j1}(L)=0$ for $j>2$ is inessential for our results; what matters is that these lag polynomials decay sufficiently rapidly. When D is obtained using the Jordan form, (2.8) indicates that these terms are zero. Because D is not unique, however, in practical applications (and indeed in the examples presented below) it is often convenient to use a transformation D for which some of these terms are nonzero. We therefore allow for nonzero $F_{j1}(L)$ for $j>2$, subject to a summability condition stated in Section 3.

Stacked Single Equation Form of (2.2) *and* (2.3)

The first order representation (2.1) characterizes the properties of the regressors Y_t. In practice, however, only some of the k equations in (2.1) might be estimated. For example, often some of the elements of Y_t will be nonstochastic and some of the equations will be identities. We therefore consider only $n \leqslant k$ regression equations, which can be represented as the regression of CY_t against Y_{t-1}, where C is a $n\times k$ matrix of constants (typically ones and zeros). With this notation, the n regression equations to be estimated are:

$$(2.10)\qquad CY_t = CAY_{t-1} + CG\Omega^{1/2}\eta_t.$$

Let $S_t = CY_t$, $\tilde{A} = CA$, and $\Sigma^{1/2} = \mathrm{C}G\Omega^{1/2}$ (so that $\Sigma^{1/2}$ is $n\times N$). Then these regression equations can be written

$$(2.11)\qquad S_t = \tilde{A}Y_{t-1} + \Sigma^{1/2}\eta_t.$$

The asymptotic analysis of the next two sections examines (2.11) in its stacked single equation form. Let $S = [S_2\, S_3 \,\cdots\, S_T]'$, $\eta = [\eta_2\,\eta_3\,\cdots\,\eta_T]'$, $X =$

$[Y_1 \; Y_2 \cdots Y_{T-1}]'$, $s = \mathrm{Vec}(S)$, $v = \mathrm{Vec}(\eta)$, and $\beta = \mathrm{Vec}(\tilde{A}')$, where $\mathrm{Vec}(\cdot)$ denotes the column-wise vectorization. Then (2.11) can be written

$$(2.12) \qquad s = [I_n \otimes X]\beta + [\Sigma^{1/2} \otimes I_{T-1}]v.$$

The coefficient vector δ corresponding to the transformed regressors $Z = XD'$ is $\delta = (I_n \otimes D'^{-1})\beta$. With this transformation, (2.12) becomes

$$(2.13) \qquad s = [I_n \otimes Z]\,\delta + [\Sigma^{1/2} \otimes I_{T-1}]\,v.$$

Thus (2.13) represents the regression equations (2.10), written in terms of the transformed regressors Z_t, in their stacked single-equation form.

An Example

The framework (2.1)–(2.3) is general enough to include many familiar linear econometric models. As an illustration, a univariate second order autoregression with a unit root is cast into this format, an example which will be taken up again in Section 5. Let the scalar time series variable x_t evolve according to

$$(2.14) \qquad x_t = \beta_0 + \beta_1 x_{t-1} + \beta_2 x_{t-2} + \eta_t \qquad (t = 1, \ldots, T),$$

where η_t is i.i.d. (0, 1). Suppose that a constant is included in the regression of x_t on its two lags, so that Y_t is given by

$$(2.15) \qquad Y_t = \begin{bmatrix} x_t \\ x_{t-1} \\ 1 \end{bmatrix} = \begin{bmatrix} \beta_1 & \beta_2 & \beta_0 \\ 1 & 0 & 0 \\ 0 & 0 & 1 \end{bmatrix} \begin{bmatrix} x_{t-1} \\ x_{t-2} \\ 1 \end{bmatrix} + \begin{bmatrix} 1 \\ 0 \\ 0 \end{bmatrix} \eta_t.$$

Suppose that $\beta_0 = 0$, $\beta_1 + \beta_2 = 1$, and $|\beta_2| < 1$, so that the autoregressive polynomial in (2.14) has a single unit root. Following Fuller (1976) and Dickey and Fuller (1979), because $\beta_0 = 0$ (2.14) can be rewritten

$$(2.16) \qquad x_t = (\beta_1 + \beta_2)x_{t-1} - \beta_2(x_{t-1} - x_{t-2}) + \eta_t$$

so that, since $\beta_1 + \beta_2 = 1$, x_t has an AR(1) representation in its first difference:

$$(2.17) \qquad \Delta x_t = -\beta_2 \Delta x_{t-1} + \eta_t.$$

Although the transformation to Z_t could be obtained by calculating the Jordan canonical form and eigenvectors of the companion matrix in (2.15), a suitable transformation is readily deduced by inspection of (2.16) and (2.17). Because x_t is integrated and Δx_t is stationary with mean zero, (2.16) suggests letting $Z_t^1 = \Delta x_t$, $Z_t^2 = 1$, and $Z_t^3 = x_t$. Then $k_1 = k_2 = k_3 = 1$ and (2.14) can be rewritten

$$(2.18) \qquad x_t = \delta_1 Z_{t-1}^1 + \delta_2 Z_{t-1}^2 + \delta_3 Z_{t-1}^3 + \eta_t,$$

where $\delta_1 = -\beta_2$, $\delta_2 = \beta_0$, and $\delta_3 = \beta_1 + \beta_2$. In the notation of (2.10), (2.18) is $CY_t = (CAD^{-1})Z_{t-1} + \eta_t$, where $C = (1\ 0\ 0)$, $\Sigma^{1/2} = 1$ and A is the transition matrix in (2.15). The transformed variables are $Z_t = DY_t$, where

$$D = \begin{bmatrix} 1 & -1 & 0 \\ 0 & 0 & 1 \\ 1 & 0 & 0 \end{bmatrix}.$$

The transformed coefficient vector is $CAD^{-1} = (\delta_1\ \delta_2\ \delta_3) = \delta'$; note that $\beta = D'\delta$.

A straightforward way to verify that D is in fact a suitable transformation matrix is to obtain the representation of Z_t in terms of ν_t. Write $\Delta x_t = \theta(L)\eta_t$, where $\theta(L) = (1 + \beta_2 L)^{-1}$, and use recursive substitution to express x_t as $x_t = \theta(1)\xi_t^1 + \theta^*(L)\eta_t$, where $\theta_i^* = -\sum_{j=i+1}^{\infty}\theta_j$ (i.e. $\theta^*(L) = (1-L)^{-1}[\theta(L) - \theta(1)]$). Thus for this model (2.3) is:

$$\begin{bmatrix} Z_t^1 \\ Z_t^2 \\ Z_t^3 \end{bmatrix} = \begin{bmatrix} \theta(L) & 0 & 0 \\ 0 & 1 & 0 \\ \theta^*(L) & 0 & \theta(1) \end{bmatrix} \begin{bmatrix} \eta_t \\ 1 \\ \xi_t^1 \end{bmatrix}. \tag{2.19}$$

3. AN ASYMPTOTIC REPRESENTATION OF THE OLS ESTIMATOR

We now turn to the behavior of the OLS estimator $\hat{\delta}$ of δ in the stacked transformed regression model (2.13),

$$\hat{\delta} = (I_n \otimes Z'Z)^{-1}(I_n \otimes Z')s. \tag{3.1}$$

The sample moments used to compute the estimator are analyzed in Lemmas 1 and 2. The asymptotic representation of the estimator is then presented as Theorem 1. Some restrictions on the moments of η_t and on the dependence embodied in the lag operator $\{F_{j1}(L)\}$ are needed to assure convergence of the relevant random matrices. For the calculations in the proofs, it is convenient to write these latter restrictions as the assumption that $\{F_{j1}(L)\}$ are g-summable as defined by Brillinger (1981). These restrictions are summarized by:

CONDITION 1: (i) $\exists$ some $\mu_4 < \infty$ such that $E(\eta_{it}^4) < \mu_4$, $i = 1, \ldots, N$. (ii) $\sum_{j=0}^{\infty} j^g |F_{m1j}| < \infty$, $m = 1, \ldots, 2g+1$.

Condition 1(ii) is more general than necessary if (2.2) and (2.3) are obtained using the Jordan canonical form of A. Because $F_{11}(L)$ in (2.3) is the inverse of a finite autoregressive lag operator with stable roots, (ii) holds for all finite g for $m = 1$; in addition, (ii) holds trivially for $m > 1$ when Z_t is based on the Jordan canonical representation, since in this case $F_{m1}(L) = 0$. Condition 1(ii) is useful when the transformation D is obtained by other means (for example by inspection), which in general produce nonzero $F_{m1}(L)$. In the proofs, it is also assumed that $\{\eta_s\} = 0$, $s \leqslant 0$. This assumption is a matter of technical convenience. For example, Z_0^i, $i = 1, 3, 5, \ldots, 2g+1$ could be treated as drawn from some distribution without altering the asymptotic results. (For a discussion of various assumptions on initial conditions in the univariate case, see Phillips (1987, Section 2).)

The first lemma concerns sample moments based on the components of the canonical regressors. Let $W(t)$ denote a n-dimensional Wiener process, and let $W^m(t)$ denote its $(m-1)$-fold integral, recursively defined by $W^m(t) = \int_0^t W^{m-1}(s)\,ds$ for $m \geq 1$, with $W^1(t) \equiv W(t)$. Also let $\Rightarrow$ denote weak convergence of the associated probability measures in the sense of Billingsley (1968). Thus:

LEMMA 1: *Under Condition* 1, *the following converge jointly*:

(a) $T^{-(m+p+1/2)}\Sigma_1^T t^m \xi_t^{p\prime} \Rightarrow \int_0^1 t^m W^p(t)'\,dt, \qquad m \geq 0,\ p \geq 1,$

(b) $T^{-(m+p)}\Sigma_1^T \xi_t^m \xi_t^{p\prime} \Rightarrow \int_0^1 W^m(t) W^p(t)'\,dt, \qquad m, p \geq 1,$

(c) $T^{-(m+p+1)}\Sigma_1^T t^{m+p} \to (m+p+1)^{-1}, \qquad m, p \geq 0,$

(d) $T^{-(p+1/2)}\Sigma_1^{T-1} t^p \eta_{t+1}' \Rightarrow \int_0^1 t^p\,dW(t)', \qquad p \geq 0,$

(e) $T^{-p}\Sigma_1^{T-1}\xi_t^p \eta_{t+1}' \Rightarrow \int_0^1 W^p(t)\,dW(t)', \qquad p \geq 1,$

(f) $T^{-1}\Sigma_1^T (F_{m1}(L)\eta_t)(F_{p1}(L)\eta_t)' \xrightarrow{p} \Sigma_{j=0}^\infty F_{m1j}F_{p1j}',$

$m, p = 1, \ldots, 2g+1,$

(g) $T^{-(p+1/2)}\Sigma_1^T t^p (F_{m1}(L)\eta_t) \Rightarrow F_{m1}(1)\int_0^1 t^p\,dW(t),$

$p = 0, \ldots, g;\ m = 1, \ldots, 2g+1,$

(h) $T^{-p}\Sigma_1^T \xi_t^p (F_{m1}(L)\eta_t)' \Rightarrow K_p + \int_0^1 W^p(t)\,dW(t)' F_{m1}(1)',$

$p = 1, \ldots, g;\ m = 1, \ldots, 2g+1;$

where $K_p = F_{m1}(1)'$ *if* $p = 1$ *and* $K_p = 0$ *if* $p = 2, 3, \ldots, g$.

Similar results for $m, p \leq 2$ or for $N = 1$ have been shown elsewhere (Phillips (1986, 1987), Phillips and Durlauf (1986), Solo (1984), and Stock (1987)). The proof of Lemma 1 for arbitrary m, p, N relies on results in Chan and Wei (1988) and is given in the Appendix.

Lemma 1 indicates that the moments involving the different components of Z_t converge at different rates. This is to be expected because of the different orders of these variables; for example, ξ_t^p is of order $O_p(t^{p-1/2})$ for $p = 1, 2, \ldots$. To handle the resultant different orders of the moments of these canonical regressors, define the scaling matrix,

$$\Upsilon_T = \begin{bmatrix} T^{1/2}I_{k_1} & & & & & 0 \\ & T^{1/2}I_{k_2} & & & & \\ & & TI_{k_3} & & & \\ & & & \ddots & & \\ & & & & T^{g-1/2}I_{k_{2g}} & \\ 0 & & & & & T^g I_{k_{2g+1}} \end{bmatrix}.$$

In addition, let H denote the $nk \times nk$ "reordering" matrix such that

$$H(I_n \otimes Z') = \begin{bmatrix} I_n \otimes Z_1' \\ I_n \otimes Z_2' \\ \vdots \\ I_n \otimes Z_{2g+1}' \end{bmatrix}$$

where $Z_j = XD'$. Using Lemma 1, we now have the following result about the limiting behavior of the moment matrices based on the transformed regressors, Z_t.

LEMMA 2: *Under Condition* 1, *the following converge jointly*:
(a) $\Upsilon_t^{-1}Z'Z\Upsilon_T^{-1} \Rightarrow V$, *where*

$$V_{11} = \Sigma_{j=0}^{\infty} F_{11j}F_{11j}',$$

$$V_{12} = V_{21}' = \Sigma_{j=0}^{\infty} F_{11j}F_{21j}',$$

$$V_{1p} = V_{p1}' = 0, \qquad p = 3,\ldots,2g+1,$$

$$V_{22} = F_{22}F_{22}' + \Sigma_{j=0}^{\infty} F_{21j}F_{21j}',$$

$$V_{mp} = F_{mm}\textstyle\int_0^1 W^{(m-2)/2}(t)W^{(p-1)/2}(t)'\,dtF_{pp}',$$

$$m = 3,5,7,\ldots,2g+1;\ p = 3,5,7,\ldots,2g+1,$$

$$V_{mp} = F_{mm}\textstyle\int_0^1 t^{(m-1)/2}W^{(p-1)/2}(t)'\,dtF_{pp}' = V_{pm}',$$

$$m = 2,4,6,\ldots,2g;\ p = 3,5,7,\ldots,2g+1,$$

$$V_{mp} = \frac{2}{p+m-2}F_{mm}F_{pp}', \qquad m = 2,4,6,\ldots,2g;\ p = m+2,\ldots,2g.$$

(b) $H(I_n \otimes \Upsilon_T^{-1})(I_n \otimes Z')(\Sigma^{1/2} \otimes I_{T-1})v \Rightarrow \phi$, *where* $\phi = (\phi_1'\,\phi_2' \cdots \phi_{2g+1}')'$, *where*

$$\phi_m = \operatorname{Vec}\left[F_{mm}\textstyle\int_0^1 W^{(m-1)/2}(t)\,dW(t)'\Sigma^{1/2\prime}\right], \qquad m = 3,5,7,\ldots,2g+1,$$

$$\phi_m = \operatorname{Vec}\left[F_{mm}\textstyle\int_0^1 t^{(m-2)/2}\,dW(t)'\Sigma^{1/2\prime}\right], \qquad m = 4,6,\ldots,2g,$$

$$\phi_2 = \phi_{21} + \phi_{22}, \qquad \textit{where} \quad \phi_{22} = \operatorname{Vec}\left[F_{22}W(1)'\Sigma^{1/2\prime}\right] \qquad \textit{and}$$

$$\begin{bmatrix} \phi_1 \\ \phi_{21} \end{bmatrix} \sim N(0,\Psi), \quad \textit{where} \quad \Psi = \begin{bmatrix} \Sigma \otimes V_{11} & \Sigma \otimes V_{12} \\ \Sigma \otimes V_{21} & \Sigma \otimes (V_{22} - F_{22}F_{22}') \end{bmatrix}$$

and where (ϕ_1, ϕ_{21}) *are independent of* $(\phi_{22}, \phi_3, \ldots, \phi_{2g+1})$. *If* $F_{21}(L) = 0$, $\phi_2 = \phi_{22}$ *and* ϕ_{21} *does not appear in the limiting representation.*

The proof is given in the Appendix.[2]

Lemma 2 makes the treatment of the OLS estimator straightforward. Let M be an arbitrary $n \times n$ matrix, and define the function $\Phi(M, V)$ by

$$\Phi(M, V) = \begin{bmatrix} M \otimes V_{11} & \cdots & M \otimes V_{1,2g+1} \\ \vdots & & \vdots \\ M \otimes V_{2g+1,1} & \cdots & M \otimes V_{2g+1,2g+1} \end{bmatrix}.$$

We now have the following theorem.

THEOREM 1: *Under Condition* 1, $H(I_n \otimes \Upsilon_T)(\hat{\delta} - \delta) \Rightarrow \delta^*$, *where* $\delta^* = \Phi(I_n, V)^{-1}\phi$.

PROOF: Use $\hat{\delta} = (I_n \otimes Z'Z)^{-1}(I_n \otimes Z')s$ and (2.13) to obtain

$$\begin{aligned} H(I_n \otimes \Upsilon_T)(\hat{\delta} - \delta) &= H(I_n \otimes \Upsilon_T)(I_n \otimes Z'Z)^{-1}(I_n \otimes \Upsilon_T) \\ &\quad \times (I_n \otimes \Upsilon_T^{-1})(I_n \otimes Z')(\Sigma^{1/2} \otimes I_{T-1})v \\ &= \left[H\left(I_n \otimes \left[\Upsilon_T^{-1}(Z'Z)\Upsilon_T^{-1}\right]\right)H^{-1}\right]^{-1} \\ &\quad \times \left[H\left(I_n \otimes \Upsilon_T^{-1}\right)(I_n \otimes Z')\left(\Sigma^{1/2} \otimes I_{T-1}\right)v\right] \\ &\Rightarrow \left[H(I_n \otimes V)H^{-1}\right]^{-1}\phi = \Phi(I_n, V)^{-1}\phi \end{aligned}$$

where Lemma 2 ensures the convergence of the bracketed terms after the second equality. *Q.E.D.*

This theorem highlights several important properties of time series regressions with unit roots. First, $\hat{\delta}$ is consistent when there are arbitrarily many unit roots and deterministic time trends, assuming the model to be correctly specified in the sense that the errors are martingale difference sequences. Because the OLS estimator of β in the untransformed system is $\hat{\beta} = (I_n \otimes X'X)^{-1}(I_n \otimes X')s = (I_n \otimes D')\hat{\delta}$, $\hat{\beta}$ is also consistent.

Second, the estimated coefficients on the elements of Z_t having different orders of probability converge at different rates. When some transformed regressors are dominated by stochastic trends, their joint limiting distribution will be nonnormal, as indicated by the corresponding random elements in V. This observation extends to the model (2.1) results already known in certain univariate and multivariate contexts; for example, Fuller (1976) used a similar rotation and scaling matrix to show that, in a univariate autoregression with one unit root and some stationary roots, the estimator of the unit root converges at rate T, while the estimator of the stationary roots converges at rate $T^{1/2}$. In a somewhat

[2] In independent work, Tsay and Tiao (1990) present closely related results for a vector process with some unit roots but with no deterministic components. While our analysis allows for constants and polynomials in t, not considered in their work, their analysis allows for complex unit roots, not allowed in our model.

more general context, Sims (1978) showed that the estimators of the coefficients on the mean zero stationary variables have normal asymptotic distributions. When the regressions involve X_t rather than Z_t, the rate of convergence of any individual element of $\hat{\beta}$, say $\hat{\beta}_j$, is the slowest rate of any of the elements of $\hat{\delta}$ comprising $\hat{\beta}_j$.

Third, when there are no Z_t regressors dominated by stochastic trends—i.e., $k_3 = k_5 = \cdots = k_{2g+1} = 0$—then $\hat{\delta}$ (and thus $\hat{\beta}$) has an asymptotically normal joint distribution. $H(I_n \otimes \Upsilon_T)(\hat{\delta} - \delta) \xrightarrow{\mathscr{L}} N(0, \Sigma \otimes V^{-1})$, where V is nonrandom because the terms involving the integrals $\int_0^1 W^p(t) W^m(t)' \, dt$ and $\int_0^1 W^p(t) \, dW^m(t)'$ are no longer present. In addition, V is consistently estimated by $\Upsilon_T^{-1} Z'Z \Upsilon_T^{-1}$, from which it follows that the asymptotic covariance matrix of $\hat{\beta}$ is consistently estimated by the usual formula. There are several important cases in which $k_3 = k_5 = \cdots = k_{2g+1} = 0$. For example, if the process is stationary around a nonzero mean or a polynomial time trend, this asymptotic normality is well known. Another example arises when there is a single stochastic trend, but this stochastic trend is dominated by a nonstochastic time trend. This situation is discussed by Dickey and Fuller (1979) for an AR(p) and is studied by West (1988) for a VAR, and we return to it as an example in Section 5.

Fourth, Theorem 1 is also related to discussions of "spurious regressions" in econometrics, commonly taken to mean the regression of one independent random walk with zero drift on another. As Granger and Newbold (1974) discovered using Monte Carlo techniques and as Phillips (1986) showed using functional central limit theory, a regression of one independent random walk on another leads to nonnormal coefficient estimators. A related result obtains here for a single regression ($n = 1$) in a bivariate system ($N = 2$) of two random walks ($k_3 = 2$) with no additional stationary components ($k_1 = 0$) and, for simplicity, no intercept ($k_2 = 0$). Then the regression (2.4) entails regressing one random walk against its own lag and the lag of the second random walk which, if $\Omega = I_2$, would have uncorrelated innovations. The two estimated coefficients are consistent, converging jointly at a rate T to a nonnormal limiting distribution.

4. AN ASYMPTOTIC REPRESENTATION FOR THE WALD TEST STATISTIC

The Wald F statistic, used to test the q linear restrictions on β,

$$H_0\colon R\beta = r \qquad \text{vs.} \qquad H_1\colon R\beta \neq r$$

is

$$F = (R\hat{\beta} - r)' \left[R \left(\hat{\Sigma} \otimes (X'X)^{-1} \right) R' \right]^{-1} (R\hat{\beta} - r)/q. \tag{4.1}$$

In terms of the transformed regressors Z_t the null and alternative hypotheses are

$$H_0\colon P\delta = r \qquad \text{vs.} \qquad H_1\colon P\delta \neq r$$

where $P = R(I_n \otimes D')$ and $\delta = (I_n \otimes D'^{-1})\beta$. In terms of P, δ, and Z, the test statistic (4.1) is

$$(4.2)\qquad F=(P\hat{\delta}-r)'\left[P\left(\hat{\Sigma}\otimes(Z'Z)^{-1}\right)P'\right]^{-1}(P\hat{\delta}-r)/q.$$

The F statistics (4.1), computed using the regression (2.12), and (4.2), computed using the regression (2.13), are numerically equivalent.

As in Section 3, it is convenient to rearrange the restrictions from the equation-by-equation ordering implicit in P to an ordering based on the rates of convergence of the various estimators. Accordingly, let $P=\tilde{P}H$, where H is the reordering matrix defined in Section 3, so that $\tilde{P}$ contains the restrictions on the reordered parameter vector $H\delta$. Without loss of generality, $\tilde{P}$ can be chosen to be upper triangular, so that the (i, j) block of $\tilde{P}$, $\tilde{P}_{ij}$ is zero for $i>j$, where $i, j=1,\ldots,2g+1$. Let the dimension of $\tilde{P}_{ij}$ be $q_i\times nk_j$, so that q_1 is the number of restrictions being tested that involve the nk_1 coefficients on the transformed variables Z_t^1; these restrictions can potentially involve coefficients on other transformed variables as well. Similarly, q_2 is the number of restrictions involving the nk_2 coefficients on Z_t^2 (and perhaps also $Z_t^3,\ldots, Z_t^{2g+1}$), and so forth, so that $q=\Sigma_{j=1}^{2g+1}q_j$.

In the previous section, it was shown that the rates of convergence of the coefficients on the various elements of Z_t differ, depending on the order in probability of the regressor. The implication of this result for the test statistic is that, if a restriction involves estimated coefficients that exhibit different rates of convergence, then the estimated coefficient with the slowest rate of convergence will dominate the test statistic. This is formalized in the next theorem.

THEOREM 2: *Under Condition* 1, $qF\Rightarrow\delta^{*\prime}P^{*\prime}[P^*\Phi(\Sigma^{-1},V)^{-1}P^{*\prime}]^{-1}P^*\delta^*$, *where* δ^* *is defined in Theorem* 1 *and*

$$P^*=\left[\begin{array}{cc|ccc}\tilde{P}_{11} & \tilde{P}_{12} & & 0 & \\ 0 & \tilde{P}_{22} & & & \\ \hline & & \tilde{P}_{33} & & 0\\ & 0 & & \ddots & \\ & & 0 & & \tilde{P}_{mm}\end{array}\right].$$

PROOF: First note that, since $P=\tilde{P}H$ by definition, $P(I_n\otimes\Upsilon_T^{-1})=\tilde{P}H(I_n\otimes\Upsilon_T^{-1})=\tilde{P}(\Upsilon_T^{-1}\otimes I_n)H=\Upsilon_T^{*-1}P_T^*H$, where Υ_T^* is the $q\times q$ scaling matrix

$$\Upsilon_T^*=\begin{bmatrix}T^{1/2}I_{q_1} & & & & & \\ & T^{1/2}I_{q_2} & & & 0 & \\ & & TI_{q_3} & & & \\ & & & \ddots & & \\ & 0 & & & T^{g-1/2}I_{q_{2g}} & \\ & & & & & T^{g}I_{q_{2g+1}}\end{bmatrix},$$

and where $\{P_T^*\}$ is a sequence of $q \times nk$ nonstochastic matrices with the limit $P_T^* \to P^*$ as $T \to \infty$, where P^* is given in the statement of the theorem. (The matrix H reorders the coefficients, while $(I_n \otimes \Upsilon_T^{-1})$ scales them; $H(I_n \otimes \Upsilon_T^{-1}) = (\Upsilon_T^{-1} \otimes I_n)H$ states that these operators commute.) Thus, under the null hypothesis,

$$\begin{aligned}
qF &= (P\hat{\delta} - r)'\left[P\left(\hat{\Sigma} \otimes (Z'Z)^{-1}\right)P'\right]^{-1}(P\hat{\delta} - r) \\
&= \left[P(I_n \otimes \Upsilon_T^{-1})(I_n \otimes \Upsilon_T)(\hat{\delta} - \delta)\right]' \\
&\quad \times \left[P(I_n \otimes \Upsilon_T^{-1})(I_n \otimes \Upsilon_T)(\hat{\Sigma} \otimes (Z'Z)^{-1})(I_n \otimes \Upsilon_T)(I_n \otimes \Upsilon_T^{-1})P'\right]^{-1} \\
&\quad \times \left[P(I_n \otimes \Upsilon_T^{-1})(I_n \otimes \Upsilon_T)(\hat{\delta} - \delta)\right] \\
&= \left[\Upsilon_T^{*-1} P_T^* H(I_n \otimes \Upsilon_T)(\hat{\delta} - \delta)\right]' \\
&\quad \times \left[\Upsilon_T^{*-1} P_T^* H\left(\hat{\Sigma} \otimes \left(\Upsilon_T (Z'Z)^{-1} \Upsilon_T\right)\right) H' P_T^{*\prime} \Upsilon_T^{*-1}\right]^{-1} \\
&\quad \times \left[\Upsilon_T^{*-1} P_T^* H(I_n \otimes \Upsilon_T)(\hat{\delta} - \delta)\right] \\
&= \left[P_T^* H(I_n \otimes \Upsilon_T)(\hat{\delta} - \delta)\right]' \\
&\quad \times \left[P_T^* H\left(\hat{\Sigma} \otimes \left(\Upsilon_T^{-1} Z'Z \Upsilon_T^{-1}\right)\right)^{-1} H' P_T^{*\prime}\right]^{-1} \\
&\quad \times \left[P_T^* H(I_n \otimes \Upsilon_T)(\hat{\delta} - \delta)\right] \\
&\Rightarrow (P^*\delta^*)'\left[P^* H(\Sigma \otimes V^{-1})H' P^{*\prime}\right]^{-1}(P^*\delta^*)
\end{aligned}$$

where the last line uses Lemma 2, Theorem 1, $P_T^* \to P^*$, and $\hat{\Sigma} \xrightarrow{p} \Sigma$ (where the consistency of $\hat{\Sigma}$ follows from the stated moment conditions). The result obtains by noting that $H(\Sigma \otimes V^{-1})H' = H(\Sigma^{-1} \otimes V)^{-1}H' = \Phi(\Sigma^{-1}, V)^{-1}$. *Q.E.D.*

Before turning to specific examples, it is possible to make three general observations based on this result. First, in the discussion of Theorem 1 several cases were listed in which, after rescaling, the estimator $\hat{\delta}$ will have a nondegenerate jointly normal distribution and V will be nonrandom. Under these conditions, qF will have the usual χ_q^2 asymptotic distribution.

Second, suppose that only one restriction is being tested, so that $q = 1$. If the test involves estimators that converge at different rates, only that part of the restriction involving the most slowly converging estimator(s) will matter under the null hypothesis, at least asymptotically. This holds even if the limit of the moment matrix $Z'Z$ is not block diagonal or the limiting distribution is nonnormal. This is the analogue in the testing problem of the observation made in the previous section that a linear combination of estimators that individually converge at different rates has a rate of convergence that is the slowest of the various constituent rates. In the proof of Theorem 2, this is an implication of the block diagonality of P^*.

Third, there are some special cases in which the usual χ^2 theory applies to Wald tests of restrictions on coefficients on integrated regressors, say Z_t^3. An example is when the true system is $Y_{1t} = \rho y_{1t-1} + \eta_{1t}$, $|\rho| < 1$, and $Y_{jt} = Y_{jt-1} + \eta_{jt}$, $j = 2, \ldots, k$, where $E\eta_t\eta_t' = \text{diag}(\sigma_1^2, \Sigma_{22})$. In the regression of Y_{1t} on $\gamma_0 + \beta_1 Y_{1t-1} + \beta_2 Y_{2t-1} + \cdots + \beta_k Y_{kt-1}$, $(\hat{\beta}_2, \ldots, \hat{\beta}_k)$ have a joint asymptotic distribution that is a random mixture of normals and the Wald test statistic has an asymptotic χ^2 distribution; for more extensive discussions, see for example Johansen (1988) and Phillips (1988). The key condition is that the integrated regressors and partial sums of the regression error be asymptotically independent stochastic processes. This circumstance seems exceptional in conventional VAR applications and we do not pursue it here.

5. UNIVARIATE AUTOREGRESSIONS WITH UNIT ROOTS

Theorems 1 and 2 provide a simple derivation of the Fuller (1976) and Dickey-Fuller (1979) statistics used to test for unit roots in univariate autoregressions. These results are well known, but are presented here as a straightforward illustration of the more general theorems. We consider a univariate second order autoregression, first without and then with a drift.

EXAMPLE 1—An AR(2) with One Unit Root: Suppose that x_t is generated by (2.14) with one unit root $(\beta_1 + \beta_2 = 1)$ and with no drift $(\beta_0 = 0)$, the case described in the example concluding Section 2. Because a constant term is included in the regression, $F_{21}(L) = 0$ and V is block diagonal. Combining the appropriate elements from Lemma 1 and using $F(L)$ from (2.19),

$$\Upsilon_T(\hat{\delta} - \delta) \Rightarrow \left\{ \begin{array}{c} \delta_1^* \\ \begin{bmatrix} 1 & \theta(1)\int W(t)\,dt \\ \theta(1)\int W(t)\,dt & \theta(1)^2 \int W(t)^2\,dt \end{bmatrix}^{-1} \begin{bmatrix} \int dW(t) \\ \theta(1)\int W(t)\,dW(t) \end{bmatrix} \end{array} \right\},$$

where $\delta_1^* \sim N(0, V_{11}^{-1})$, with $V_{11} = \Sigma_{j=0}^{\infty}\theta_j^2 = (1 - \beta_2^2)^{-1}$ and $\theta(1) = (1 + \beta_2)^{-1}$. Thus the coefficients on the stationary terms (Z_{1t} and Z_{2t}) converge at the rate $T^{1/2}$, while $\hat{\delta}_3$ converges at the rate T. In terms of the coefficients of the original regression, $\beta_2 = -\delta_1$ and $\beta_1 = \delta_1 + \delta_3$. Since $T^{1/2}(\hat{\delta}_3 - \delta_3) \xrightarrow{p} 0$, both $\hat{\beta}_1$ and $\hat{\beta}_2$ have asymptotically normal marginal distributions, converging at the rate $T^{1/2}$; however, $\hat{\beta}_1$ and $\hat{\beta}_2$ have a degenerate joint distribution when standardized by $T^{1/2}$.

While the marginal distribution of $\hat{\delta}_1$ is normal, the marginal distribution of $\hat{\delta}_2$ (the intercept) is not, since the "denominator" matrix in the limiting representation of $(\hat{\delta}_2, \hat{\delta}_3)$ is not diagonal and contains random elements, and since $\int W(t)\,dW(t)$ has a nonnormal distribution. Thus tests involving $\hat{\delta}_1$, or $\hat{\delta}_1$ in combination with $\hat{\delta}_3$, will have the usual χ^2 distribution, while tests on any other coefficient (or combination of coefficients) will not.

In the special case that $\beta_0 = 0$ is imposed, so that an intercept is not included in the regression, V is a diagonal 2×2 matrix (here $F_{21}(L) = 0$ even though there is no intercept since ΔX_t has mean zero). Thus, using Theorem 1, the limiting distribution of the OLS estimator of δ_3 has the particularly simple form

$$T(\hat{\delta}_3 - \delta_3) \Rightarrow \int W(t)\, dW(t) \Big/ \left[\theta(1) \int W(t)^2\, dt\right],$$

which reduces to the standard formula when $\beta_2 = 0$, so that $\theta(1) = 1$.

The limiting representation of the square of the Dickey-Fuller t ratio testing the hypothesis that x_t has a unit root, when the drift is assumed to be zero, can be obtained from Theorem 2. When there is no estimated intercept the F statistic testing the hypothesis that $\delta_3 = 1$ has the limit,

$$F \Rightarrow \left[\int W(t)\, dW(t)\right]^2 \Big/ \int W(t)^2\, dt. \tag{5.1}$$

As Solo (1984) and Philips (1987) have shown, (5.1) is the Wiener process limiting representation of the square of the Dickey-Fuller "$\hat{\tau}$" statistic, originally analyzed by Fuller (1976) using other techniques.

EXAMPLE 2—AR(2) with One Unit Root and Nonzero Drift: Suppose that x_t evolves according to (2.14), except that $\beta_0 \neq 0$. If $\beta_1 + \beta_2 = 1$ then the companion matrix A in (2.15) has 2 unit eigenvalues which appear in a single Jordan block. Again, D and $F(L)$ are most easily obtained by rearranging (2.14), imposing the unit root, and solving for the representation of x_t in terms of the canonical regressors. This yields

$$x_t = \delta_1 Z^1_{t-1} + \delta_2 Z^2_{t-1} + \delta_4 Z^4_{t-1} + \eta_t$$

where $Z^1_t = \Delta x_t - \mu$, $Z^2_t = 1$, $Z^4_t = x_t$, $\delta_1 = -\beta_2$, $\delta_2 = \beta_0 - \mu\beta_2$, and $\delta_4 = \beta_1 + \beta_2$, where $\mu = \beta_0/(1 + \beta_2)$ is the mean of Δx_t. In addition,

$$\begin{bmatrix} Z^1_t \\ Z^2_t \\ Z^4_t \end{bmatrix} = \begin{bmatrix} \theta(L) & 0 & 0 & 0 \\ 0 & 1 & 0 & 0 \\ \theta^*(L) & 0 & \theta(1) & \mu \end{bmatrix} \begin{bmatrix} \eta_t \\ 1 \\ \xi^1_t \\ t \end{bmatrix},$$

where $\theta(L) = (1 + \beta_2 L)^{-1}$ and $\theta^*(L) = (1 - L)^{-1}[(1 + \beta_2 L)^{-1} - (1 + \beta_2)^{-1}]$, so $k_1 = 1$, $k_2 = 1$, $k_3 = 0$, and $k_4 = 1$. Because there are no elements of Z_t dominated by a stochastic integrated process, $\hat{\delta}$ has an asymptotically normal distribution after appropriate scaling, from which it follows that $\hat{\beta}$ has an asymptotically normal distribution.

If a time trend is included as a regressor, qualitatively different results obtain. Appropriately modifying the state vector and companion matrix in (2.15) to include t, the transformed regressors become:

$$\begin{bmatrix} Z_t^1 \\ Z_t^2 \\ Z_t^3 \\ Z_t^4 \end{bmatrix} = \begin{bmatrix} \theta(L) & 0 & 0 & 0 \\ 0 & 1 & 0 & 0 \\ \theta^*(L) & 0 & \theta(1) & 0 \\ 0 & 0 & 0 & 1 \end{bmatrix} \begin{bmatrix} \eta_t \\ 1 \\ \xi_t^1 \\ t \end{bmatrix}.$$

In this case, $\hat{\delta}_2, \hat{\delta}_3$ and $\hat{\delta}_4$ have nonnormal distributions. The F statistic testing $\delta_3 = 1$ is the square of the Dickey-Fuller "$\hat{\tau}_\tau$" statistic testing the hypothesis that x_t has a unit root, when it is maintained that x_t is an AR(2) and allowance is made for a possible drift; its limiting representation is given by direct calculation using Theorem 2, which entails inverting the lower 3×3 diagonal block of V. The (nonstandard) limiting distribution of the F statistic testing the joint hypothesis that $\delta_3 = 1$ and $\beta_0 = 0$ can also be obtained directly using this framework.

6. VAR'S WITH SOME UNIT ROOTS

Many hypotheses of economic interest can be cast as linear restrictions on the parameters of VAR's. This section examines F tests of two such hypotheses. The first concerns the lag length in the VAR, and the second is a test for Granger causality. These tests are presented for a trivariate VAR in which each variable has a unit root with nonzero drift in its univariate representation. Four different cases are considered, depending on whether the variables are cointegrated and whether time is included as a regressor. We first present the transformation (2.2) and (2.3) for these different cases, then turn to the analysis of the two tests.

Suppose that the 3×1 vector X_t obeys

$$X_t = \gamma_0 + A(L)X_{t-1} + \eta_t \qquad (t = 1, \dots, T), \tag{6.1}$$

where $n = N = 3$, where $A(L)$ is a matrix polynomial of order p and where it is assumed that γ_0 is nonzero. When time is not included as a regressor, (6.1) constitutes the regression model as well as the true model assumed for X_t; when time is included as a regressor, the regression model is

$$X_t = \gamma_0 + \gamma_1 t + A(L)X_{t-1} + \eta_t \tag{6.2}$$

where the true value of γ_1 is zero.

Suppose that there is at least one unit root in $A(L)$ and that, taken individually each element of X_t is integrated of order one. Then ΔX_t is stationary and can be written,

$$\Delta X_t = \mu + \theta(L)\eta_t \tag{6.3}$$

where by assumption $\mu_i \neq 0$, $i = 1, 2, 3$. This implies that X_t has the representation

$$X_t = \mu t + \theta(1)\xi_t^1 + \theta^*(L)\eta_t. \tag{6.4}$$

Thus each element of X_t is dominated by a time trend. When time is not included as a regressor, Y_t is obtained by stacking $(X_t', X_{t-1}', \ldots, X_{t-p+1}', 1)$; when time is included, this stacked vector is augmented by t. Note that, if X_t is not cointegrated, then $\theta(1)$ is nonsingular and $A(L)$ contains 3 unit roots. However, if X_t has a single cointegrating vector α (so that $\alpha'\mu = \alpha'\theta(1) = 0$), then $\theta(1)$ does not have full rank and $A(L)$ has only two unit roots.

As in the previous examples, it is simplest to deduce a suitable transformation matrix D by inspection. If the regression equations do not include a time trend, then (6.1) can be written

$$X_t - A^*(L)(\Delta X_{t-1} - \mu) + [\gamma_0 + A^*(1)\mu] + A(1)X_{t-1} + \eta_t, \tag{6.5}$$

where $A_j^* = -\sum_{i=j+1}^{p} A_i$, so that $A^*(L)$ has order $p-1$. If the regression contains a time trend, then (6.2) can be written as

$$\begin{aligned} X_t = {} & A^*(L)(\Delta X_{t-1} - \mu) + [\gamma_0 + \gamma_1 + A^*(1)\mu] \\ & + A(1)X_{t-1} + \gamma_1(t-1) + \eta_t. \end{aligned} \tag{6.6}$$

Note that, if X_t is not cointegrated, then $A(1) = I$, $\theta(L) = [I - A^*(L)L]^{-1}$, and $\mu = [I - A^*(1)]\gamma_0$, while if X_t is cointegrated $A(1) - I$ has rank 1.

The part of the transformation from Y_t to Z_t involving X_t depends on whether the system is cointegrated and on whether a time trend is included in the regression. Using (6.5) and (6.6) as starting points, this transformation, the implied $F(L)$ matrix, and the coefficients in the transformed system are now presented for each of the four cases.

CASE 1—No Cointegration, Time Trend excluded from the Regression: Each element of X_t is (from (6.4)) dominated by a deterministic rather than a stochastic time trend. However, because μ is 3×1 there are two linear combinations of X_t that are dominated not by a time trend, but rather by the stochastic trend component ξ_t^1. Thus Z_t^4 can be chosen to be any single linear combination of X_t; any two linearly independent combinations of X_t that are generalized cointegrating vectors with respect to the time trend can be used as a basis for Z_t^3. To be concrete, let:

$$Z_t^1 = \begin{bmatrix} \Delta X_t - \mu \\ \vdots \\ \Delta X_{t-p+2} - \mu \end{bmatrix}, \qquad Z_t^2 = 1,$$

$$Z_t^3 = \begin{bmatrix} X_{1t} - (\mu_1/\mu_3)X_{3t} \\ X_{2t} - (\mu_2/\mu_3)X_{3t} \end{bmatrix}, \qquad Z_t^4 = X_{3t}.$$

Using (6.4), the two nonstationary components can be expressed as

$$Z_{it}^3 = \phi_i(1)\xi_t + \phi_i^*(L)\eta_t, \qquad i = 1, 2, \tag{6.7a}$$

$$Z_t^4 = \mu_3 t + e_3'\theta(1)\xi_t^1 + e_3'\theta^*(L)\eta_t, \tag{6.7b}$$

where $\phi_i(1) = [e_i - (\mu_i/\mu_3)e_3]'\theta(1)$, $\phi_i^*(L) = [e_i - (\mu_i/\mu_3)e_3]'\theta^*(L)$, and where

e_j denotes the jth 3-dimensional unit vector. The $F(L)$ matrix is thus given by

$$(6.8)\qquad \begin{bmatrix} Z_t^1 \\ Z_t^2 \\ Z_t^3 \\ Z_t^4 \end{bmatrix} = \begin{bmatrix} F_{11}(L) & 0 & 0 & 0 \\ 0 & 1 & 0 & 0 \\ \phi^*(L) & 0 & \phi(1) & 0 \\ e_3'\theta^*(L) & 0 & e_3'\theta(1) & \mu_3 \end{bmatrix} \begin{bmatrix} \eta_t \\ 1 \\ \xi_t^1 \\ t \end{bmatrix}$$

where $\phi^*(L) = [\phi_1^*(L)\;\; \phi_2^*(L)]'$ and $\phi(1) = [\phi_1(1)\;\; \phi_2(1)]'$, and where $k_1 = 3(p-1)$, $k_2 = 1$, $k_3 = 2$, and $k_4 = 1$.

To ascertain which coefficients in the original regression model (6.1) correspond to which block of Z_t, it is convenient to let ζ_t denote the transformed variables in (6.7), so that

$$(6.9)\qquad \zeta_t = WX_t, \qquad W = \begin{bmatrix} 1 & 0 & -\mu_1/\mu_3 \\ 0 & 1 & -\mu_2/\mu_3 \\ 0 & 0 & 1 \end{bmatrix}.$$

Because $A(1)X_t = A(1)W^{-1}\zeta_t$, the coefficients on Z_t^3 and Z_t^4 can be obtained by calculating $A(1)W^{-1}$. Upon doing so, the regression equation (6.5) becomes,

$$(6.10)\qquad X_t = A^*(L)(\Delta X_{t-1} - \mu) + [\gamma_0 + A^*(1)\mu]Z_{t-1}^2 + [A(1)e_1\; A(1)e_2]Z_{t-1}^3 + A(1)[(\mu_1/\mu_3)e_1 + (\mu_2/\mu_3)e_2 + e_3]Z_{t-1}^4 + \eta_t$$

which gives an explicit representation of the coefficients in the transformed regression model in terms of the coefficients in the original model (6.1).

CASE 2—No Cointegration, Time Trend Included in the Regression: When time is included as a regressor, a natural choice for Z_t^4 is t; for F_{44} to have full rank, all elements of X_t will appear, after a suitable transformation, in Z_t^3. Thus Z_t^1 and Z_t^2 are the same as in Case 1, $Z_t^3 = X_t - \mu t = \theta(1)\xi_t + \theta^*(L)\eta_t$, and $Z_t^4 = t$ so that

$$(6.11)\qquad \begin{bmatrix} Z_t^1 \\ Z_t^2 \\ Z_t^3 \\ Z_t^4 \end{bmatrix} = \begin{bmatrix} F_{11}(L) & 0 & 0 & 0 \\ 0 & 1 & 0 & 0 \\ \theta^*(L) & 0 & \theta(1) & 0 \\ 0 & 0 & 0 & 1 \end{bmatrix} \begin{bmatrix} \eta_t \\ 1 \\ \xi_t^1 \\ t \end{bmatrix}.$$

In contrast to the previous case, now $k_3 = 3$ and $k_4 = 1$. Solving for the implied coefficients on the transformed variates as was done in Case 1, the regression equation (6.6) becomes

$$(6.12)\qquad X_t = A^*(L)(\Delta X_{t-1} - \mu) + [\gamma_0 + A^*(1)\mu]Z_{t-1}^2 + A(1)Z_{t-1}^3 + \mu Z_{t-1}^4 + \eta_t.$$

CASE 3—Cointegration, Time Trend Excluded from the Regression: When X_t is cointegrated with a single cointegrating vector, the 2×3 matrix $F_{33} = \phi(1)$ in

(6.8) no longer has full row rank, so an alternative representation must be developed. Informally, this can be seen by recognizing that, if X_t is cointegrated and if there is a single cointegrating vector, then there can only be two distinct trend components since there is some linear combination of X_t that has no stochastic or deterministic trend. Thus $k_3 + k_4$ will be reduced by one when there is a single cointegrating vector, relative to Case 1. A formal proof of this proposition proceeds by contradiction. Suppose that X_t has a single cointegrating vector α (so that $\alpha' X_t$ is stationary) and that $k_3 = 2$. Let $\alpha = (1\ \alpha_1\ \alpha_2)'$, so that $\alpha'\mu = 0$ implies that α can be rewritten as $\alpha = [1\ \alpha_1\ (-\alpha_1\mu_2 - \mu_1)/\mu_3]'$. Now consider the linear combination of Z_t^3:

$$\begin{aligned} Z_{1t}^3 + \beta Z_{2t}^3 &= [X_{1t} - (\mu_1/\mu_3)X_{3t}] + \beta[X_{2t} - (\mu_2/\mu_3)X_{3t}] \\ &= [1\ \beta\ (-\beta\mu_2 - \mu_1)/\mu_3]\, X_t = \alpha' X_t \end{aligned}$$

where α_1 has been set to β in the final equality. Since $\alpha' X_t$ is stationary by assumption, $Z_{1t}^3 + \alpha_1 Z_{2t}^3$ is stationary; thus $(1\ \alpha_1)\phi(1) = 0$. Since $\phi(1) = F_{33}$, this violates the condition that F_{33} must have full row rank.

To obtain a valid transformation, W must be chosen so that $\zeta_t = W X_t$ has one stationary element, one element dominated by the stochastic trend, and one element dominated by the time trend. To be concrete, let

$$W = \begin{bmatrix} 1 & \alpha_1 & \alpha_2 \\ 1 & 0 & -\mu_1/\mu_3 \\ 0 & 0 & 1 \end{bmatrix},$$

where it is assumed that $\alpha_1 \neq 0$ so that X_{2t} enters the cointegrating relation. Accordingly, let

$$\begin{aligned} \zeta_{1t} &= \alpha' X_t = \alpha'\theta^*(L)\eta_t, \\ \zeta_{2t} &= X_{1t} - (\mu_1/\mu_3)X_{3t} = [e_1 - (\mu_1/\mu_3)e_3]'\theta^*(L)\eta_t \\ &\quad + [e_1 - (\mu_1/\mu_3)e_3]'\theta(1)\xi_t, \\ \zeta_{3t} &= X_{3t} = \mu_3 t + e_3'\theta(1)\xi_t + e_3'\theta^*(L)\eta_t. \end{aligned}$$

Now let

$$Z_t^1 = \begin{bmatrix} \Delta X_t - \mu \\ \vdots \\ \Delta X_{t-p+2} - \mu \\ \zeta_{1t} \end{bmatrix}, \qquad Z_t^2 = 1, \qquad Z_t^3 = \zeta_{2t}, \qquad Z_t^4 = \zeta_{3t},$$

and use the notation $\phi_1^*(L)$ and $\phi_1(1)$ from (6.7a) to obtain:

$$\text{(6.13)}\qquad \begin{bmatrix} Z_t^1 \\ Z_t^2 \\ Z_t^3 \\ Z_t^4 \end{bmatrix} = \begin{bmatrix} F_{11}(L) & 0 & 0 & 0 \\ 0 & 1 & 0 & 0 \\ \phi_1^*(L) & 0 & \phi_1(1) & 0 \\ e_3'\theta^*(L) & 0 & e_3'\theta(1) & \mu_3 \end{bmatrix} \begin{bmatrix} \eta_t \\ 1 \\ \xi_t \\ t \end{bmatrix}$$

so that $k_1 = 3(p-1)+1$, $k_2 = 1$, $k_3 = 1$, and $k_4 = 1$. Expressed in terms of the transformed regressors, the regression equation becomes

$$(6.14)\quad \begin{aligned} X_t &= A^*(L)(\Delta X_{t-1} - \mu) + A(1)(e_2/\alpha_1)\zeta_{1t-1} + [\gamma_0 + A^*(1)\mu] Z^2_{t-1} \\ &\quad + A(1)(e_1 - e_2/\alpha_1) Z^3_{t-1} \\ &\quad + A(1)[(\mu_1/\mu_3)e_1 - ([\alpha_2 + (\mu_1/\mu_3)]/\alpha_1)e_2 + e_3] Z^4_{t-1} + \eta_t. \end{aligned}$$

The $F(L)$ matrix in (6.13) and the transformed regression equation (6.14) have been derived under the assumption that there is only one cointegrating vector. If instead there are two cointegrating vectors, so that there is only one unit root in $A(L)$, then $k_3 = 0$ so that there is no Z^3_t transformed regressor. In this case (studied in detail by West (1988)) all the coefficient estimators will be asymptotically normally distributed, and all test statistics will have the usual asymptotic χ^2_q distributions.

CASE 4—Cointegration, Time Trend Included in the Regression: The representation for this case follows by modifying the representation for Case 3 to include a time trend. Let

$$\begin{aligned} \zeta_{1t} &= \alpha' X_t = \alpha'\theta^*(L)\eta_t, \\ \zeta_{2t} &= X_{1t} - \mu_1 t = e_1'\theta^*(L)\eta_t + e_1'\theta(1)\xi_t, \\ \zeta_{3t} &= X_{3t} - \mu_3 t = e_3'\theta^*(L)\eta_t + e_3'\theta(1)\xi_t, \end{aligned}$$

and let

$$Z^1_t = \begin{bmatrix} \Delta X_t - \mu \\ \vdots \\ \Delta X_{t-p+2} - \mu \\ \zeta_{1t} \end{bmatrix}, \qquad Z^2_t = 1, \qquad Z^3_t = \begin{bmatrix} \zeta_{2t} \\ \zeta_{3t} \end{bmatrix}, \qquad Z^4_t = t.$$

Letting $\pi^*(L) = [e_1'\theta^*(L)\ e_3'\theta^*(L)]'$ and $\pi(1) = [e_1'\theta(1)\ e_3'\theta(1)]'$, one obtains:

$$(6.15)\quad \begin{bmatrix} Z^1_t \\ Z^2_t \\ Z^3_t \\ Z^4_t \end{bmatrix} = \begin{bmatrix} F_{11}(L) & 0 & 0 & 0 \\ 0 & 1 & 0 & 0 \\ \pi^*(L) & 0 & \pi(1) & 0 \\ 0 & 0 & 0 & 1 \end{bmatrix} \begin{bmatrix} \eta_t \\ 1 \\ \xi_t \\ t \end{bmatrix}$$

so that $k_1 = 3(p-1)+1$, $k_2 = 1$, $k_3 = 2$, and $k_4 = 1$. The transformed regression equation is

$$(6.16)\quad \begin{aligned} X_t &= [A^*(L)(\Delta X_{t-1} - \mu) + A(1)(e_2/\alpha_1)\zeta_{1t-1}] \\ &\quad + [\gamma_0 + A^*(1)\mu] Z^2_{t-1} \\ &\quad + [A(1)(e_1 - e_2/\alpha_1)\zeta_{2t-1} + A(1)(-\alpha_2 e_2/\alpha_1 + e_3)\zeta_{3t-1}] \\ &\quad + A(1)\mu Z^4_{t-1} + \eta_t. \end{aligned}$$

These transformations facilitate the analysis of the two hypothesis tests.

EXAMPLE 1—Tests of Lag Length: A common problem in specifying VAR's is determining the correct lag length, i.e., the order p in (6.1). Consider the null hypothesis that $A(L)$ has order $m \geqslant 1$ and the alternative that $A(L)$ has order $p > m$:

$$H_1: A_j = 0, j = m+1, \ldots, p, \quad \text{vs.} \quad K_1: A_j \neq 0, \text{ some } j = m+1, \ldots, p.$$

The restrictions on the parameters of the transformed regression model could be obtained by applying the rotation form Y_t to Z_t, as discussed in general in Section 4. However, in these examples the restrictions are readily deduced by comparing (6.10), (6.12), (6.14), and (6.16) with (6.5) and (6.6). By definition $A_{j+1} = A^*_{j+1} - A^*_j$ and $A^*_p = 0$; thus $A_j = 0$ for $j \geqslant m+1$ implies and is implied by $A^*_j = 0$, $j \geqslant m$. In terms of the transformed regression model, H_1 and K_1 therefore become

$$H_1^*: A_j^* = 0, j = m, \ldots, p-1, \quad \text{vs.}$$

$$K_1^*: A_j^* \neq 0, \text{ some } j = m, \ldots, p-1.$$

In each of the four cases, the restrictions embodied in H_1^* are linear in the coefficients of the Z_t^1 regressors. Since the regression is assumed to include a constant term, $F_{21}(L) = 0$ in each of the four cases. Thus in each case V is block diagonal, with the first block corresponding to the stationary mean zero regressors. It follows directly from Theorem 2 that (q times) the corresponding test statistic will have the usual $\chi^2_{3(p-m)}$ distribution.

EXAMPLE 2—Granger Causality Tests: The second hypothesis considered is that lags of X_{2t} do not help predict X_{1t} given lagged X_{1t} and X_{3t}:

$$H_2: A_{12j} = 0, \ j = 1, \ldots, p, \quad \text{vs.} \quad K_2: A_{12j} \neq 0, \text{ some } j = 1, \ldots, p.$$

In terms of the transformed regression models, this becomes

$$H_2^*: A_{12}(1) = 0 \quad \text{and} \quad A^*_{12j} = 0, \ j = 1, \ldots, p-1, \quad \text{vs.}$$

$$K_2^*: A_{12}(1) \neq 0 \quad \text{or} \quad A^*_{12j} \neq 0, \text{ some } j = 1, \ldots, p-1.$$

As in the previous example, the second set of restrictions in H_2^* are linear in the coefficients of the Z_t^1 regressors in each of the four cases. However, H_2^* also includes the restriction that $A_{12}(1) = 0$. Thus whether the F statistic has a nonstandard distribution hinges on whether $A_{12}(1)$ can be written as a coefficient on a mean zero stationary regressor.

In Case 1, $A_{12}(1)$ is the (1,2) element of the matrix of coefficients on Z_t^3 in (6.10), and it does not appear alone as a coefficient, or a linear combination of coefficients, on the stationary mean zero regressors. It follows that in Case 1 the restriction on $A_{12}(1)$ imparts a nonstandard distribution to the F statistic, even though the remaining restrictions involve coefficients on Z_t^1. In Case 2, inspection of (6.12) leads to the same conclusion: $A_{12}(1)$ appears as a coefficient on Z_t^3, and $A_{12}(1) = 0$ implies and is implied by the corresponding coefficient on Z_t^3 equaling zero. Thus the test statistics will have a nonstandard limiting distribution. However, because F_{22}, F_{33}, and F_{44} differ between Cases 1 and 2, the distributions of the F statistic will differ.

In both Case 1 and Case 2, the distribution of the F test depends on nuisance parameters and thus cannot conveniently be tabulated. However, since these nuisance parameters can be estimated consistently, the limiting distribution of the test statistic can be computed numerically. Since V is block diagonal, in both cases the statistic takes on a relatively simple (but nonstandard) asymptotic form. Let $\tilde{V}$ denote the (random) lower $(k_2+k_3+k_4)\times(k_2+k_3+k_4)$ block of V and let $\tilde{P}_{11}$ and $\tilde{P}_{33}$ denote the restrictions on the coefficients corresponding to the transformed regressors Z_1 and Z_3 in the stacked single-equation form, respectively, as detailed in Section 4. Then a straightforward calculation using Theorem 2 shows that $pF \Rightarrow F_1+F_2$ where $F_1=(\tilde{P}_{11}\delta_1^*)'[\tilde{P}_{11}(\Sigma\otimes V_{11}^{-1})\tilde{P}_{11}']^{-1}(\tilde{P}_{11}\delta_1^*)\sim\chi^2_{p-1}$ and $F_2=(\tilde{P}_{33}\delta_3^*)'[\tilde{P}_{33}\Phi(\Sigma^{-1},\tilde{V})^{-1}\tilde{P}_{33}']^{-1}(\tilde{P}_{33}\delta_3^*)$, where the elements of F_2 consist in part of the functionals of Wiener processes given in Lemma 2 and where the block diagonality of V and Lemma 2(b) imply that F_1 and F_2 are independent.

In Cases 3 and 4, X_t is cointegrated and the situation changes. In both (6.14) and (6.16), $A_{12}(1)$ appears as a coefficient on ζ_{1t}, the "equilibrium error" formed by the cointegrating vector. Since ζ_{1t} is stationary with mean zero, the estimator of $A_{12}(1)$ will thus be asymptotically normal, converging at the rate $T^{1/2}$, and the F-test will have an asymptotic χ^2_p/p distribution.[3]

At first glance, the asymptotic results seem to depend on the arbitrarily chosen transformations (6.8), (6.11), (6.13), and (6.15). This is, however, not so: while these transformations have been chosen to make the analysis simple, the same results would obtain for any other transformation of the form (2.2) and (2.3). One implication of this observation is that, since X_{1t}, X_{2t}, and X_{3t} can be permuted arbitrarily in the definitions of ζ_t used to construct D and $F(L)$ in the four cases, the F statistic testing the exclusion of any one of the regressors and its lags will have the same properties as given here for X_{2t-1} and its lags.

The intuition behind these results is simple. Each element of X_t has a unit root —and thus a stochastic trend—in its univariate autoregressive representation. In Cases 1 and 2, these stochastic trends are not cointegrated and dominate the long run relation among the variables (after eliminating the effect of the deterministic time trend) so that a test of $A_{12}(1)=0$ is like a test of one of the coefficients in a regression of one random walk on two others and its lags. In contrast, when the system is cointegrated, there are only two nondegenerate stochastic trends. Including X_{1t-1} and X_{3t-1} in the regression "controls for" these trends, so that a test of $A_{12}(1)=0$ (and the other Granger noncausality restrictions) behaves like a test of coefficients on mean zero stationary regressors.

[3] This assumes that $\alpha_1\neq 0$, so that there is a linear combination involving X_{2t} which is stationary. If $\alpha_1=0$, there is no such linear combination, in which case the test statistic will have a nonstandard asymptotic distribution.

7. PRACTICAL IMPLICATIONS AND CONCLUSIONS

Application of the theory developed in this paper clearly is computationally demanding. Application of the corresponding Bayesian theory, conditional on initial observations and Gaussian disturbances, can be simpler and in any case is quite different. Because the Bayesian approach is entirely based on the likelihood function, which has the same Gaussian shape regardless of the presence of nonstationarity, Bayesian inference need take no special account of nonstationarity. The authors of this paper do not have a consensus opinion on whether the Bayesian approach ought simply to replace classical inference in this application. But because in this application, unlike most econometric applications, big differences between Bayesian and classical inference are possible, econometricians working in this area need to form an opinion as to why they take one approach or the other.

This work shows that the common practice of attempting to transform models to stationary form by difference or cointegration operators whenever it appears likely that the data are integrated is in many cases unnecessary. Even with a classical approach, the issue is not whether the data are integrated, but rather whether the estimated coefficients or test statistics of interest have a distribution which is nonstandard if in fact the regressors are integrated. It will often be the case that the statistics of interest have distributions unaffected by the nonstationarity, in which case the hypotheses can be tested without first transforming to stationary regressors. It remains true, of course, that the usual asymptotic distribution theory generally is not useful for testing hypotheses that cannot entirely be expressed as restrictions on the coefficients of mean zero stationary linear combinations of Y_t. These "forbidden" linear combinations can thus be characterized as those which are orthogonal to the generalized cointegrating vectors comprising the row space of D_1, i.e. to those generalized cointegrating vectors that reduce Y_t to a stationary process with mean zero. In particular, individual coefficients in the estimated autoregressive equations are asymptotically normal with the usual limiting variance, unless they are coefficients of a variable which is nonstationary and which does not appear in any of the system's stationary linear combinations.

Whether to use a transformed model when the distribution of a test of the hypothesis of interest depends on the presence of nonstationarity is a difficult question. A Bayesian approach finds no reason ever to use a transformed model, except possibly for computational simplicity. Under a classical approach, if one has determined the form of the transformed model on the basis of preliminary tests for cointegration and unit roots, use of the untransformed model does not avoid pretest bias because the distribution theory for the test statistics will depend on the form of the transformation. One consideration is that tests based on the transformed model will be easier to compute. Tests based on the two versions of the model will, however, be different even asymptotically, and might have different power, small-sample accuracy, or degree of pretest bias. We regard comparison of classical tests based on the transformed and untransformed models as an interesting open problem.

To use classical procedures based on the asymptotic theory, one must address the discontinuity of the distribution theory. It can and will occur that a model has all its estimated roots less than one and the stationary asymptotic theory (appropriate if all roots are in fact less than one) rejects the null hypothesis of the maximal root being greater than, say, .98, yet the nonstationary asymptotic theory (appropriate if the maximal root is one) fails to reject the null hypothesis of a unit root. In practice it may be usual to treat something like the convex closure of the union of the stationary-theory confidence region and the unit root null hypothesis as if it were the actual confidence region. Is this a bad approximation to the true confidence region based on exact distribution theory? We should know more than we do about this.

When nonstationarity itself is not the center of interest or when the form and degree of nonstationarity is unknown, the discontinuity of the asymptotic theory raises serious problems of pretesting bias. As we have already noted, in order to test a null hypothesis of Granger causal priority with the classical theory one must first decide on whether nonstationarity is present and, if so, its nature. To the extent that the results of preliminary tests for nonstationarity and cointegration are correlated with results of subsequent tests for causal priority, interpretation of the final results is problematic. When the preliminary tests suggest a particular nonstationary form for the model but at a marginal p-value of, say, .10 or .15, one could consider tests of the hypotheses of interest both under the integrated and nonintegrated maintained hypotheses. Results are likely often to differ, however, and this asymptotic theory offers no guidance as to how to resolve the differences with formal inference.

This paper provides the asymptotic distribution theory for statistics from autoregressive models with unit roots. Now that these difficulties are resolved, it appears that a new set of issues—related to the logical foundations of inference and the handling of pretest bias—arise to preserve this area as an arena of controversy.

Dept. of Economics, University of Minnesota, Minneapolis, MN 55455, U.S.A.
Kennedy School of Government, Harvard University, Cambridge, MA 02138, U.S.A.
Dept. of Economics, Northwestern University, Evanston, IL 60208, U.S.A.

Manuscript received January, 1987; final revision received March, 1989.

APPENDIX

PROOFS OF LEMMAS 1 AND 2

PROOF OF LEMMA 1: The proof of this lemma uses results developed in Chan and Wei (1988, Theorem 2.4), who consider the convergence of related terms to functionals of Wiener processes and to stochastic integrals based on Wiener processes. Throughout we condition on $\{\eta_s = 0\}$, $s \leqslant 0$. This is done for convenience, and could, for example, be weakened to permit the initial conditions for Z_t^1 to be drawn from a stationary distribution.

(a) First consider $m = 0$:

$$T^{-(p+1/2)}\sum_{1}^{T}\xi_t^p = T^{-(p+1/2)}\sum_{t=1}^{T}\sum_{s=1}^{t}\xi_s^{p-1}$$

$$= T^{-1}\sum_{t=1}^{T}\left[T^{-(p-1/2)}\sum_{s=1}^{t}\xi_s^{p-1}\right].$$

Thus, if $T^{-(p-1/2)}\Sigma_{s=1}^{t}\xi_s^{p-1} \to W^p(\tau)$, where $\tau = \lim(t/T)$, then

(A.1) $$T^{-(p+1/2)}\sum_{s=1}^{t}\xi_s^p \to W^{p+1}(\tau) \quad \text{or} \quad T^{-(p+1/2)}\xi_t^{p+1} \to W^{p+1}(\tau)$$

by the Continuous Mapping Theorem (for the univariate case, see Hall and Heyde (1980, Appendix II); for the multivariate case, see Chan and Wei (1988)). Letting $\xi_t^0 \equiv \eta_t$ and using Chan and Wei's (1988) results, $T^{-1/2}\xi_t^1 = T^{-1/2}\Sigma_{s=1}^{t}\xi_s^0 \Rightarrow W(\tau)$ so (A.1) follows by induction.

For $m > 0$,

$$T^{-(m+p+1/2)}\sum_{1}^{T}t^m\xi_t^p = T^{-1}\sum_{1}^{T}(t/T)^m\left[T^{-(p-1/2)}\xi_t^p\right] \Rightarrow \int_0^1 \tau W^p(\tau)\,d\tau.$$

(b) $$T^{-(m+p)}\sum_{1}^{T}\xi_t^m\xi_t^{p\prime} = T^{-1}\sum_{1}^{T}\left(T^{-(m-1/2)}\xi_t^m\right)\left(T^{-(p-1/2)}\xi_t^p\right)'$$

$$\Rightarrow \int_0^1 W^m(\tau)W^p(\tau)'\,d\tau$$

where we use (a) for the convergence of $T^{-(p-1/2)}\xi_t^p$.

(c) Obtains by direct calculation.

(d) $$T^{-(p+1/2)}\sum_{1}^{T}t^p\eta_{t+1}' = T^{-1/2}\sum_{1}^{T}(t/T)^p\eta_{t+1}' \Rightarrow \int_0^1 t^p\,dW(t)',$$

(e) $$T^{-p}\sum_{1}^{T}\xi_t^p\eta_{t+1}' = T^{-1/2}\sum_{1}^{T}\left(T^{-(p-1/2)}\xi_t^p\right)\eta_{t+1}' \Rightarrow \int_0^1 W^p(t)\,dW(t)'$$

where the convergence follows using Theorem 2.4 (ii) of Chan and Wei (1988) for $p = 1$ and using their Theorem 2.4 (i) for $p > 1$.

(f) This follows, using Chebyschev's inequality, from $\Sigma|F_{11j}| < \infty$ and bounded 4th moments.

(g) The approach used to prove (g) and (h) extends the argument used in Solo (1984). (We thank an anonymous referee for substantially simplifying our earlier proofs of (g) and (h).) First consider the case $p = 0$. From Lemma 1(d) and Condition 1(ii) it follows that:

$$T^{-1/2}\sum_{1}^{T}F_{m1}(L)\eta_t = F_{m1}(1)\left(T^{-1/2}\xi_T\right) + T^{-1/2}F_{m1}^*(L)\eta_T \Rightarrow F_{m1}(1)\int_0^1 dW(t)$$

where $F_{m1j}^* = -\Sigma_{i=j+1}^{\infty}F_{m1i}$, yielding the desired result.

The general case is proven by induction. Let $H(L)$ be a matrix lag polynomial. Assume that if

$$\sum_{0}^{\infty}j^k|H_j| < \infty \qquad (k = 0,\ldots,p-1),$$

then

$$T^{-(k+1/2)}\sum_{1}^{T}t^kH(L)\eta_t \Rightarrow H(1)\int_0^1 t^k\,dW(t) \qquad (k = 0,\ldots,p-1).$$

Now note that $F_{m1}(L)\eta_t = F_{m1}(1)\eta_t + F^*_{m1}(L)\Delta\eta_t$, so that the term in question can be written,

$$\text{(A.2)}\qquad T^{-(p+1/2)}\sum_1^T t^p F_{m1}(L)\eta_t = F_{m1}(1)\left[T^{-(p+1/2)}\sum_1^T t^p\eta_t\right] + T^{-(p+1/2)}\sum_1^T t^p F^*_{m1}(L)\Delta\eta_t$$

$$= F_{m1}(1)\left[T^{-(p+1/2)}\sum_1^T t^p\eta_t\right] + T^{-1/2}F^*_{m1}(L)\eta_T$$

$$+ T^{-(p-1/2)}\sum_1^{T-1}\left[t^p-(t+1)^p\right]F^*_{m1}(L)\eta_t$$

$$= F_{m1}(1)\left[T^{-(p+1/2)}\sum_1^T t^p\eta_t\right] + T^{-1/2}F^*_{m1}(L)\eta_T$$

$$+ \sum_{k=0}^{p-1} d_k T^{-(p-k)}\left[T^{-(k+1/2)}\sum_1^{T-1} t^k F^*_{m1}(L)\eta_t\right]$$

where $\{d_k\}$ are the constants from the binomial expansion, $t^p-(t+1)^p = \Sigma_{k=0}^{p-1} d_k t^k$.

The first term in (A.2) has the desired limit by Lemma 1(d). The second term in (A.2) vanishes in probability by condition 1(ii). The final p terms in (A.2) converge to zero by the inductive assumption if $\Sigma_{j=0}^{\infty} j^k|F^*_{m1\,j}| < \infty$ for all $k = 0,\ldots, p-1$. To verify this final condition, note that

$$\text{(A.3)}\qquad \sum_{j=0}^{\infty} j^k|F^*_{m1\,j}| \leqslant \sum_{i=0}^{\infty}\sum_{j=0}^{i-1} j^k|F_{m1i}| \leqslant C_{k+1}\sum_{j=0}^{\infty} j^{k+1}|F_{m1\,j}|,$$

where C_{k+1} is a finite constant. The final expression in (A.3) is bounded by assumption (Condition 1(ii)) so the result obtains under the inductive assumption. Since the inductive assumption is satisfied for $p=0$, the result follows for $p = 0,1,\ldots, g$.

(h) We prove the lemma for $F_{11}(L)$, showing the result first for $p=1$. Following Stock (1987), write

$$T^{-1}\sum_1^T \xi_t(F_{11}(L)\eta_t)' = H_3 - H_4 + \left(T^{-1}\sum_1^T \xi_{t-1}\eta_t' + H_5\right)\sum_0^{T-1} F'_{11\,j}$$

where

$$H_3 = T^{-1}\sum_0^{T-1}\rho_j F'_{11\,j},\qquad \rho_j = \sum_{j+1}^T(\xi_t-\xi_{t-j})\eta'_{t-j},$$

$$H_4 = T^{-1}\sum_0^{T-1}\phi_j F'_{11\,j},\qquad \phi_j = \sum_{T-j+1}^T \xi_t\eta_t',$$

$$H_5 = T^{-1}\sum_1^T \eta_t\eta_t'.$$

Now, $H_5 \xrightarrow{p} I$ and $T^{-1}\Sigma\xi_{t-1}\eta_t' \Rightarrow \int_0^1 W(t)\,dW(t)'$. In addition, Stock (1987) shows that $H_3 \xrightarrow{p} 0$ and $H_4 \xrightarrow{p} 0$ if $\Sigma|F_{11\,j}| < \infty$, which is true under Condition 1. Thus, for $p=1$,

$$T^{-1}\sum_1^T \xi_t(F_{11}(L)\eta_t)' \Rightarrow F_{11}(1)' + \int_0^1 W(t)\,dW(t)'F_{11}(1)',$$

which is the desired result.

The case of $p \geqslant 2$ is proven by induction. Let $H(L)$ be a lag polynomial matrix with $\Sigma_0^{\infty} j^k|H_j| < \infty$, $k = 1,\ldots, p-1$, and assume that

$$T^{-k}\sum_1^T \xi_t^k(H(L)\eta_t)' \Rightarrow K_k + \int_0^1 W^k(t)\,dW(t)'H(1)',\qquad k = 1,\ldots, p-1,$$

where K_k is given in the statement of the lemma with $H(1)$ replacing $F_{m1}(1)$. Now write

$$(A.4)\qquad T^{-p}\sum_1^T \xi_t^p[F_{m1}(L)\eta_t]' = T^{-p}\sum_1^T \xi_t^p\eta_t' F_{m1}(1)' + T^{-p}\sum_1^T \xi_t^p[F_{m1}^*(L)\Delta\eta_t]'$$

where $F_{m1j}^* = -\sum_{i=j+1}^{\infty} F_{m1i}$.

Consider the first term in (A.4). Noting that $\xi_t^p = \eta_t + \sum_{k=1}^{p} \xi_{t-1}^k$, one obtains:

$$(A.5)\qquad T^{-p}\sum_1^T \xi_t^p\eta_t' F_{m1}(1)' = T^{-p}\sum_1^T \xi_{t-1}^p\eta_t' F_{m1}(1)' + T^{-p}\sum_1^T \eta_t\eta_t' F_{m1}(1)'$$
$$+\sum_{k=1}^{p-1} T^{-(p-k)}\left[T^{-k}\sum_1^T \xi_{t-1}^k\eta_t'\right] F_{m1}(1)'.$$

Since $p \geqslant 2$, Lemma 1(e) and Condition 1(ii) ensure that all but the first terms in (A.5) vanish in probability. Applying Lemma 1(e) to the first term in (A.5), one obtains (for $p \geqslant 2$):

$$T^{-p}\sum_1^T \xi_t^p\eta_t' F_{m1}(1)' \Rightarrow \int_0^1 W(t)\,dW(t)' F_{m1}(1)'.$$

All that remains is to show that the second term in (A.4) vanishes in probability. Now

$$(A.6)\qquad T^{-p}\sum_1^T \xi_t^p[F_{m1}^*(L)\Delta\eta_t]' = T^{-p}\sum_{t=1}^T\sum_{s=1}^t \xi_s^{p-1}[F_{m1}^*(L)\Delta\eta_t]'$$
$$= T^{-p}\sum_{s=1}^T \xi_s^{p-1}\left[\sum_{t=s}^T F_{m1}^*(L)\Delta\eta_t\right]'$$
$$= T^{-p}\sum_{s=1}^T \xi_s^{p-1}[F_{m1}^*(L)\eta_T]' - T^{-p}\sum_{s=1}^T \xi_s^{p-1}[F_{m1}^*(L)\eta_{s-1}]'$$
$$= \left[T^{-(p-1/2)}\sum_1^T \xi_t^{p-1}\right][T^{-1/2}F_{m1}^*(L)\eta_T]'$$
$$- T^{-p}\sum_1^T \eta_t[F_{m1}^*(L)\eta_{t-1}]'$$
$$- \sum_{k=1}^{p-1} T^{-(p-k)}\left[T^{-k}\sum_{t=1}^T \xi_{t-1}^k(F_{m1}^*(L)\eta_{t-1})'\right].$$

The first term in (A.6) vanishes by Lemma 1(a), the inequality (A.3), and condition 1(ii). The second term vanishes by Chebyschev's inequality and Condition 1(ii). The remaining $p-1$ terms in (A.6) vanish by the inductive assumption if $\sum j^k|F_{m1j}^*| < \infty$, but this final condition is implied by (A.3) and Condition 1(ii). Since the inductive assumption was shown to hold for $p = 1$, the result for $p \geqslant 2$ follows.

PROOF OF LEMMA 2: We calculate the limits of the various blocks separately. The joint convergence of these blocks is assured by Theorem 2.4 of Chan and Wei (1988).

(a) Consider $(\Upsilon_T^{-1}Z'Z\Upsilon_T^{-1})_{pm}$ for

(i) $p = m = 1$,

(ii) $p = 1$, $m = 2, 4, 6, \ldots, M$,

(iii) $p = 1$, $m = 3, 5, 7, \ldots, M-1$,

(iv) $p = 3, 5, 7, \ldots, M-1$, $m = 3, 5, 7, \ldots, M-1$,

(v) $p = 2, 4, 6, \ldots, M$, $m = 3, 5, 7, \ldots, M-1$,

(vi) $p = 2, 4, 6, \ldots, M$, $m = 2, 4, 6, \ldots, M$,

where M is an even integer.

(i) $p = m = 1$:

$$\left(\Upsilon_T^{-1} Z' Z \Upsilon_T^{-1}\right)_{11} = T^{-1}\Sigma\left(F_{11}(L)\eta_t\right)\left(F_{11}(L)\eta_t\right)'$$
$$\xrightarrow{p} \sum_0^{\infty} F_{11j} F_{11j}' \equiv V_{11} \qquad \text{by Lemma 1(f).}$$

(ii) $p = 1, m = 2$:

$$\left(\Upsilon_T^{-1} Z' Z \Upsilon_T^{-1}\right)_{12} = T^{-1}\Sigma\left(F_{11}(L)\eta_t\right)\left(F_{21}(L)\eta_t + F_{22}\right)'$$
$$= T^{-1}\Sigma\left(F_{11}(L)\eta_t\right)\left(F_{21}(L)\eta_t\right)' + T^{-1}\Sigma F_{11}(L)\eta_t' F_{22}'$$
$$\xrightarrow{p} \sum_0^{\infty} F_{11j} F_{21j}' \equiv V_{12}$$

by Lemma 1(f) and (g), using $\Sigma_0^{\infty} |F_{21j}| < \infty$.

$p = 1,\ m = 4, 6, \ldots, M$:

$$\text{(A.7)} \qquad \left(\Upsilon_T^{-1} Z' Z \Upsilon_T^{-1}\right)_{1m} = T^{-m/2}\Sigma\left(F_{11}(L)\eta_t\right)\left(F_{mm} t^{(m-2)/2} + F_{mm-1}\xi_t^{(m-2)/2} + \cdots + F_{m2} + F_{m1}(L)\eta_T\right)'$$
$$= T^{-(m-2)/2-1}\Sigma\left(F_{11}(L)\eta_t\right) t^{(m-2)/2} F_{mm}'$$
$$+ T^{-(m-2)/2} T^{-1}\Sigma\left(F_{11}(L)\eta_t\right)\xi_t^{(m-2)/2'} F_{mm-1}'$$
$$+ \cdots + T^{-(m-2)/2} T^{-1}\Sigma\left(F_{11}(L)\eta_t\right) F_{m2}'$$
$$+ T^{-(m-2)/2} T^{-1}\Sigma\left(F_{11}(L)\eta_t\right)\left(F_{m1}(L)\eta_t\right)'.$$

Each of the terms in (A.7) converges to zero in probability by Lemma 1(g), (h), and (f) (using $\Sigma |F_{m1j}| < \infty$) respectively, for $m > 2$. That the omitted intermediate terms converge to zero in probability follows by induction. Thus $(\Upsilon_T^{-1} Z' Z \Upsilon_T^{-1})_{1m} \xrightarrow{p} 0$, $m = 4, 6, 8, \ldots, M$.

(iii) $p = 1,\ m = 3, 5, 7, \ldots, M - 1$:

$$\text{(A.8)} \qquad \left(\Upsilon_T^{-1} Z' Z \Upsilon_T^{-1}\right)_{1m} = T^{-m/2} Z_1' Z_m$$
$$= T^{-m/2}\Sigma\left(F_{11}(L)\eta_t\right)\left(F_{mm}\xi_t^{(m-1)/2} + F_{mm-1} t^{(m-3)/2} + \cdots + F_{m2} + F_{m1}(L)\eta_t\right)'$$
$$= T^{-1/2} T^{-(m-1)/2}\Sigma\left(F_{11}(L)\eta_t\right)\xi_t^{(m-1)/2'} F_{mm}'$$
$$+ T^{-1/2} T^{-((m-3)/2+1)}\Sigma\left(F_{11}(L)\eta_t\right) t^{(m-3)/2} F_{mm-1}'$$
$$+ \cdots + T^{-(m-2)/2} T^{-1}\Sigma\left(F_{11}(L)\eta_t\right) F_{m2}'$$
$$+ T^{-(m-2)/2} T^{-1}\Sigma\left(F_{11}(L)\eta_t\right)\left(F_{m1}(L)\eta_t\right)'.$$

Each of the terms in (A.8) vanish asymptotically by application of Lemma 1(h), (g), and (f) (using $\Sigma |F_{m1j}| < \infty$), for $m \geqslant 3$. By induction, the intermediate terms also vanish thus $(\Upsilon_T^{-1} Z' Z \Upsilon_T^{-1})_{1m} \xrightarrow{p} 0$, $m = 3, 5, 7, \ldots, M - 1$.

(iv) $p, m = 3, 5, 7, \ldots, M - 1$:

$$\text{(A.9)} \qquad \left(\Upsilon_T^{-1} Z' Z \Upsilon_T^{-1}\right)_{mp} = T^{-(m-1)/2} T^{-(p-1)/2} Z_p' Z_m$$
$$= T^{-(m+p-2)/2}\Sigma\left(F_{mm}\xi_t^{(m-1)/2} + F_{mm-1} t^{(m-3)/2} + \cdots + F_{m1}(L)\eta_t\right)$$
$$\times\left(F_{pp}\xi_t^{(p-1)/2} + F_{pp-1} t^{(p-3)/2} + \cdots + F_{p1}(L)\eta_t\right)'.$$

The leading term in (A.9) converges to a random variable:

$$\text{(A.10)} \qquad F_{mm} T^{-(m+p-2)/2}\Sigma\xi_t^{(m-1)/2}\xi_t^{(p-1)/2'} F_{pp}' \Rightarrow F_{mm}\int_0^1 W^{(m-1)/2}(t) W^{(p-1)/2}(t)' \, dt F_{pp}'$$

by Lemma 1(b). We now argue that the remaining terms in (1.3) converge to zero in probability. First, it follows from (A.10) that the cross terms in $(\xi_t^{(i-1)/2}, \xi_t^{(j-1)/2}) \xrightarrow{P} 0$ for $i \leqslant m$, $j \leqslant p$, and $i+j<m+p$. Second, the terms in $(\xi_t^{(i-1)/2}, t^{(j-3)/2})$ and $(t^{(i-3)/2}, \xi_t^{(j-1)/2})$ vanish for $i \leqslant m$, $j \leqslant p$. For example,

$$T^{-(m+p-2)/2}\Sigma F_{mm}\xi_t^{(m-1)/2}t^{(p-3)/2}F'_{pp-1}$$
$$= F_{mm}T^{-1/2}T^{-[(m-1)/2+(p-3)/2+1/2]}\Sigma\xi_t^{(m-1)/2}t^{(p-3)/2}F'_{pp-1} \xrightarrow{P} 0$$

by Lemma 1(a). Finally, the cross terms of $(\xi_t^{(i-1)/2}, F_{p1}(L)\eta_t)$ and $(t^{(i-3)/2}, F_{p1}(L)\eta_t)$, $i \leqslant m$, all converge in probability to zero using the arguments in (ii) and (iii) above. Thus, for $p, m = 3,5,7,\ldots, M-1$,

$$\left(\Upsilon_T^{-1}Z'Z\Upsilon_T^{-1}\right)_{pm} \to F_{pp}\int_0^1 W^{(p-1)/2}(t)W^{(m-1)/2}(t)'\,dtF'_{mm}.$$

(v) $p = 2,4,6,\ldots, M$; $m = 3,5,7,\ldots, M-1$:

$$\text{(A.11)}\quad \left(\Upsilon_T^{-1}Z'Z\Upsilon_T^{-1}\right)_{pm} = T^{-(p+m-2)/2}\Sigma\left(F_{pp}t^{(p-2)/2} + F_{pp-1}\xi_t^{(p-2)/2} + \cdots + F_{p1}(L)\eta_t\right)$$
$$\times\left(F_{mm}\xi_t^{(m-1)/2} + F_{mm-1}t^{(m-3)/2} + \cdots + F_{m1}(L)\eta_t\right)'$$
$$= T^{-(p+m-2)/2}\Sigma F_{pp}t^{(p-2)/2}\xi_t^{(m-1)/2\prime}F'_{mm} + \text{cross terms.}$$

The arguments in (ii)–(iv) imply that the cross terms in (A.11) converge to zero in probability. Applying Lemma 1(a) to the leading term in (A.11), $(\Upsilon_T^{-1}Z'Z\Upsilon_T^{-1})_{pm} \Rightarrow F_{pp}\int_0^1 t^{(p-2)/2}W^{(m-1)/2}(t)'\,dtF'_{mm}$.

(vi) $p, m = 2,4,6,\ldots, M$, $m+p>4$:

$$\text{(A.12)}\quad \left(\Upsilon_T^{-1}Z'Z\Upsilon_T^{-1}\right)_{pm} = T^{-(p+m-2)/2}\Sigma\left(F_{pp}t^{(p-2)/2} + F_{pp-1}\xi_t^{(p-2)/2} + \cdots + F_{p1}(L)\eta_t\right)$$
$$\times\left(F_{mm}t^{(m-2)/2} + F_{mm-1}\xi_t^{(m-2)/2} + \cdots + F_{m1}(L)\eta_t\right)'$$
$$= T^{-(p+m-2)/2}\Sigma F_{pp}t^{(p-2)/2+(m-2)/2}F'_{mm} + \text{cross terms}$$
$$\xrightarrow{P} \left[(p+m-4)/2+1\right]^{-1}F_{pp}F'_{mm} = 2/(p+m-2)F_{pp}F'_{mm}$$

where the leading term in (A.12) converges nonstochastically using Lemma 1(c) and the remaining cross terms $\xrightarrow{P} 0$ by repeated application of Lemma 1, $\Sigma|F_{m1\,j}| < \infty$, and the arguments in (ii)–(iv) above. The expression for V_{22} obtains directly.

(b) Let $v^+ = [\Sigma^{1/2} \otimes I_{T-1}]v$ and let $M = 2g+1$, so that

$$H(I_n \otimes \Upsilon_T^{-1})(I_n \otimes Z')v^+ = \begin{bmatrix} T^{-1/2}(I_n \otimes Z_1')v^+ \\ T^{-1/2}(I_n \otimes Z_2')v^+ \\ \vdots \\ T^{-(M-1)/2}(I_n \otimes Z_M')v^+ \end{bmatrix}$$

where $(I_n \otimes Z_m')v^+ = \operatorname{Vec}(\Sigma Z_t^m \eta'_{t+1}\Sigma^{1/2\prime})$. Thus consider:

(i) $\quad T^{-(m-1)/2}\Sigma Z_t^m\eta'_{t+1}\Sigma^{1/2\prime} \qquad m = 3,5,7,\ldots, M,$

(ii) $\quad T^{-(m-1)/2}\Sigma Z_t^m\eta'_{t+1}\Sigma^{1/2\prime} \qquad m = 2,4,6,\ldots, M-1,$

and $T^{-1/2}(I_n \otimes Z_1')v^+$.

(i) $m = 3,5,7,\ldots, M$:

$$\text{(A.13)}\quad T^{-(m-1)/2}\Sigma Z_t^m\eta'_{t+1}\Sigma^{1/2\prime} = T^{-(m-1)/2}\Sigma\left(F_{mm}\xi_t^{(m-1)/2} + F_{mm-1}t^{(m-3)/2}\right.$$
$$\left.+ \cdots + F_{m1}(L)\eta_t\right)\eta'_{t+1}\Sigma^{1/2\prime}$$
$$= F_{mm}T^{-(m-1)/2}\Sigma\xi_t^{(m-1)/2}\eta'_{t+1}\Sigma^{1/2\prime}$$
$$+ F_{mm-1}T^{-1/2}T^{-[(m-3)/2+1/2]}\Sigma t^{(m-3)/2}\eta'_{t+1}\Sigma^{1/2\prime}$$
$$+ \cdots + T^{-(m-3)/2}T^{-1}\Sigma\left(F_{m1}(L)\eta_t\right)\eta'_{t+1}\Sigma^{1/2\prime}.$$

The leading term in (A.13) converges to a nondegenerate random variable by Lemma 1(e), while the remaining terms vanish asymptotically by Lemma 1(d), (e), and (f), and by induction. Thus, for $m = 3, 5, 7, \dots, M$,

$$T^{-(m-1)/2}\Sigma Z_t^m \eta'_{t+1}\Sigma^{1/2\prime} \Rightarrow F_{mm}\int_0^1 W^{(m-1)/2}(t)\, dW(t)'\Sigma^{1/2\prime}.$$

(ii) $m = 4, 6, \dots M-1$:

$$\text{(A.14)} \quad T^{-(m-1)/2}\Sigma Z_t^m \eta'_{t+1}\Sigma^{1/2\prime} = T^{-(m-1)/2}\Sigma\big(F_{mm}t^{(m-2)/2} + F_{mm-1}\xi_t^{(m-2)/2} + \cdots + F_{m1}(L)\eta_t\big)\eta'_{t+1}\Sigma^{1/2\prime}$$

$$= F_{mm}T^{-(m-1)/2}\Sigma t^{(m-2)/2}\eta'_{t+1}\Sigma^{1/2\prime} + \text{cross terms}$$

$$\Rightarrow F_{mm}\int_0^1 t^{(m-2)/2}\, dW(t)'\Sigma^{1/2\prime}$$

where the cross terms in (A.14) vanish using the result in (ii) above and the g-summability of $F_{m1}(L)$ for $m = 4, 6, \dots, M-1$.

For $m = 2$, the expression in (A.14) is:

$$\text{(A.15)} \quad T^{-1/2}\Sigma Z_t^2 \eta'_{t+1}\Sigma^{1/2\prime} = T^{-1/2}\Sigma\big(F_{21}(L)\eta_t\big)\eta'_{t+1}\Sigma^{1/2\prime} + F_{22}T^{-1/2}\Sigma\eta'_{t+1}\Sigma^{1/2\prime}.$$

Suppose that both terms in (A.15) have well-defined limits, so that $\text{Vec}[T^{-1/2}\Sigma Z_t^2\eta'_{t+1}\Sigma^{1/2\prime}] \Rightarrow \phi_2 = \phi_{21} + \phi_{22}$, where ϕ_{21} and ϕ_{22} correspond to the two terms in (A.15). Since the second term in (A.15) converges to $F_{22}W(1)'\Sigma^{1/2\prime}$, $\phi_{22} = \text{Vec}[F_{22}W(1)'\Sigma^{1/2\prime}]$. Thus it remains only to examine ϕ_{21} and ϕ_1.

The first term in (A.15) has a limiting distribution that is jointly normal with the term for $m = 1$. Using the CLT for stationary processes with finite fourth moments,

$$\begin{bmatrix} \text{vec}\big[T^{-1/2}\Sigma\big(F_{11}(L)\eta_t\big)\eta'_{t+1}\Sigma^{1/2\prime}\big] \\ \text{vec}\big[T^{-1/2}\Sigma\big(F_{21}(L)\eta_t\big)\eta'_{t+1}\Sigma^{1/2\prime}\big] \end{bmatrix} \Rightarrow \begin{bmatrix} \phi_1 \\ \phi_{21} \end{bmatrix} \sim N(0, \Psi),$$

where

$$\Psi = \begin{bmatrix} \Sigma\otimes\Sigma_j F_{11j}F'_{11j} & \Sigma\otimes\Sigma_j F_{11j}F'_{21j} \\ \Sigma\otimes\Sigma_j F_{21j}F'_{11j} & \Sigma\otimes\Sigma_j F_{21j}F'_{21j} \end{bmatrix}$$

$$= \begin{bmatrix} \Sigma\otimes V_{11} & \Sigma\otimes V_{12} \\ \Sigma\otimes V_{21} & \Sigma\otimes(V_{22} - F_{22}F'_{22}) \end{bmatrix}.$$

Theorem 2.2 of Chan and Wei (1988) implies that (ϕ_1, ϕ_{21}) are independent of $(\phi_{22}, \phi_3, \dots, \phi_{2g+1})$.

REFERENCES

BILLINGSLEY, P. (1968): *Convergence of Probability Measures*. New York: Wiley.

BRILLINGER, D. R. (1981): *Time Series Data Analysis and Theory*. San Francisco: Holden-Day.

CHAN, N. H., AND C. Z. WEI (1988): "Limiting Distributions of Least Squares Estimates of Unstable Autoregressive Processes," *Annals of Statistics*, 16, 367–401.

DICKEY, D. A., AND W. A. FULLER (1979): "Distribution of the Estimators for Autoregressive Time Series With a Unit Root," *Journal of the American Statistical Association*, 74, 366, 427–431.

ENGLE, R. F., AND C. W. J. GRANGER (1987): "Co-Integration and Error-Correction: Representation, Estimation and Testing," *Econometrica*, 55, 251–276.

FULLER, W. A. (1976): *Introduction to Statistical Time Series*. New York: Wiley.

GRANGER, C. W. J. (1983): "Co-Integrated Variables and Error-Correcting Models," Discussion Paper #83-13, University of California—San Diego.

GRANGER, C. W. J., AND P. NEWBOLD (1974): "Spurious Regressions in Econometrics," *Journal of Econometrics*, 2, 111–120.

HALL, P., AND C. C. HEYDE (1980): *Martingale Limit Theory and Its Applications*. New York: Academic Press.

JOHANSEN, S. (1988): "Statistical Analysis of Cointegration Vectors," *Journal of Economic Dynamics and Control*, 12, 231–254.
PHILLIPS, P. C. B. (1986): "Understanding Spurious Regressions in Econometrics," *Journal of Econometrics*, 33, 311–340.
——— (1987): "Time Series Regression With a Unit Root," *Econometrica*, 55, 277–302.
——— (1988): "Optimal Inference in Cointegrated Systems," Cowles Foundation Discussion Paper No. 866, Yale University.
PHILLIPS, P. C. B., AND S. N. DURLAUF (1986): "Multiple Time Series Regression with Integrated Processes," *Review of Economic Studies*, 53, 473–496.
SIMS, C. A. (1978): "Least Squares Estimation of Autoregressions with Some Unit Roots," Center for Economic Research, University of Minnesota, Discussion Paper No. 78-95.
SOLO, V. (1984): "The Order of Differencing in ARIMA Models," *Journal of the American Statistical Association*, 79, 916–921.
STOCK, J. H. (1987): "Asymptotic Properties oi Least Squares Estimators of Cointegrating Vectors," *Econometrica*, 55, 1035–1056.
TSAY, R. S., AND G. C. TIAO (1990): "Asymptotic Properties of Multivariate Nonstationary Processes with Applications to Autoregressions," forthcoming, *Annals of Statistics*, 18, March.
WEST, K. D. (1988): "Asymptotic Normality, When Regressors Have a Unit Root," *Econometrica*, 56, 1397–1418.
WHITE, J. S. (1958): "The Limiting Distribution of the Serial Correlation Coefficient in the Explosive Case," *Annals of Mathematical Statistics*, 29, 1188–1197.

[30]

Journal of Economic Dynamics and Control 12 (1988) 231–254. North-Holland

STATISTICAL ANALYSIS OF COINTEGRATION VECTORS

Søren JOHANSEN*

University of Copenhagen, DK-2100 Copenhagen, Denmark

Received September 1987, final version received January 1988

We consider a nonstationary vector autoregressive process which is integrated of order 1, and generated by i.i.d. Gaussian errors. We then derive the maximum likelihood estimator of the space of cointegration vectors and the likelihood ratio test of the hypothesis that it has a given number of dimensions. Further we test linear hypotheses about the cointegration vectors.

The asymptotic distribution of these test statistics are found and the first is described by a natural multivariate version of the usual test for unit root in an autoregressive process, and the other is a χ^2 test.

1. Introduction

The idea of using cointegration vectors in the study of nonstationary time series comes from the work of Granger (1981), Granger and Weiss (1983), Granger and Engle (1985), and Engle and Granger (1987). The connection with error correcting models has been investigated by a number of authors; see Davidson (1986), Stock (1987), and Johansen (1988) among others.

Granger and Engle (1987) suggest estimating the cointegration relations using regression, and these estimators have been investigated by Stock (1987), Phillips (1985), Phillips and Durlauf (1986), Phillips and Park (1986a, b, 1987), Phillips and Ouliaris (1986, 1987), Stock and Watson (1987), and Sims, Stock and Watson (1986). The purpose of this paper is to derive maximum likelihood estimators of the cointegration vectors for an autoregressive process with independent Gaussian errors, and to derive a likelihood ratio test for the hypothesis that there is a given number of these. A similar approach has been taken by Ahn and Reinsel (1987).

This program will not only give good estimates and test statistics in the Gaussian case, but will also yield estimators and tests, the properties of which can be investigated under various other assumptions about the underlying data generating process. The reason for expecting the estimators to behave better

*The simulations were carefully performed by Marc Andersen with the support of the Danish Social Science Research Council. The author is very grateful to the referee whose critique of the first version greatly helped improve the presentation.

than the regression estimates is that they take into account the error structure of the underlying process, which the regression estimates do not.

The processes we shall consider are defined from a sequence $\{\varepsilon_t\}$ of i.i.d. p-dimensional Gaussian random variables with mean zero and variance matrix Λ. We shall define the process X_t by

$$X_t = \Pi_1 X_{t-1} + \cdots + \Pi_k X_{t-k} + \varepsilon_t, \qquad t = 1, 2, \ldots, \tag{1}$$

for given values of $X_{-k+1}, \ldots, X_0$. We shall work in the conditional distribution given the starting values, since we shall allow the process X_t to be nonstationary. We define the matrix polynomial

$$A(z) = I - \Pi_1 z - \cdots - \Pi_k z^k,$$

and we shall be concerned with the situation where the determinant $|A(z)|$ has roots at $z = 1$. The general structure of such processes and the relation to error correction models was studied in the above references.

We shall in this paper mainly consider a very simple case where X_t is integrated of order 1, such that ΔX_t is stationary, and where the impact matrix

$$A(z)|_{z=1} = \Pi = I - \Pi_1 - \cdots - \Pi_k$$

has rank $r < p$. If we express this as

$$\Pi = \alpha\beta', \tag{2}$$

for suitable $p \times r$ matrices α and β, then we shall assume that, although ΔX_t is stationary and X_t is nonstationary as a vector process, the linear combinations given by $\beta' X_t$ are stationary. In the terminology of Granger this means that the vector process X_t is cointegrated with cointegration vectors β. The space spanned by β is the space spanned by the rows of the matrix Π, which we shall call the cointegration space.

In this paper we shall derive the likelihood ratio test for the hypothesis given by (2) and derive the maximum likelihood estimator of the cointegration space. Then we shall find the likelihood ratio test of the hypothesis that the cointegration space is restricted to lie in a certain subspace, representing the linear restrictions that one may want to impose on the cointegration vectors.

The results we obtain can briefly be described as follows: the estimation of β is performed by first regressing ΔX_t and X_{t-k} on the lagged differences. From the residuals of these $2p$ regressions we calculate a $2p \times 2p$ matrix of product moments. We can now show that the estimate of β is the empirical canonical variates of X_{t-k} with respect to ΔX_t corrected for the lagged differences.

The likelihood ratio test is now a function of certain eigenvalues of the product moment matrix corresponding to the smallest squared canonical correlations. The test of the linear restrictions involve yet another set of eigenvalues of a reduced product moment matrix. The asymptotic distribution of the first test statistic involves an integral of a multivariate Brownian motion with respect to itself, and turns out to depend on just one parameter, namely the dimension of the process, and can hence be tabulated by simulation or approximated by a χ^2 distribution. The second test statistic is asymptotically distributed as χ^2 with the proper degrees of freedom. It is also shown that the maximum likelihood estimator of β suitably normalised is asymptotically distributed as a mixture of Gaussian variables.

2. Maximum likelihood estimation of cointegration vectors and likelihood ratio tests of hypotheses about cointegration vectors

We want to estimate the space spanned by β from observations X_t, $t = -k+1, \ldots, T$. For any $r \leq p$ we formulate the model as the hypothesis

$$\mathrm{H}_0: \quad \mathrm{rank}(\Pi) \leq r \quad \text{or} \quad \Pi = \alpha\beta', \tag{3}$$

where α and β are $p \times r$ matrices.

Note that there are no other constraints on $\Pi_1, \ldots, \Pi_k$ than (3). Hence a wide class containing stationary as well as nonstationary processes is considered.

The parameters α and β can not be estimated since they form an overparametrisation of the model, but one can estimate the space spanned by β.

We can now formulate the main result about the estimation of sp(β) and the test of the hypothesis (3).

Theorem 1. The maximum likelihood estimator of the space spanned by β is the space spanned by the r canonical variates corresponding to the r largest squared canonical correlations between the residuals of X_{t-k} and ΔX_t corrected for the effect of the lagged differences of the X process.

The likelihood ratio test statistic for the hypothesis that there are at most r cointegration vectors is

$$-2\ln(Q) = -T \sum_{i=r+1}^{p} \ln(1-\hat{\lambda}_i), \tag{4}$$

where $\hat{\lambda}_{r+1}, \ldots, \hat{\lambda}_p$ are the $p-r$ smallest squared canonical correlations.

Proof. Before studying the likelihood function it is convenient to reparametrise the model (1) such that the parameter of interest Π enters explicitly. We write

$$\Delta X_t = \Gamma_1 \Delta X_{t-1} + \cdots + \Gamma_{k-1} \Delta X_{t-k+1} + \Gamma_k X_{t-k} + \varepsilon_t, \qquad (5)$$

where

$$\Gamma_i = -I + \Pi_1 + \cdots + \Pi_i, \qquad i = 1, \ldots, k.$$

Then $\Pi = -\Gamma_k$, and whereas (3) gives a nonlinear constraint on the coefficients $\Pi_1, \ldots, \Pi_k$, the parameters $(\Gamma_1, \ldots, \Gamma_{k-1}, \alpha, \beta, \Lambda)$ have no constraints imposed. In this way the impact matrix Π is found as the coefficient of the lagged levels in a nonlinear least squares regression of ΔX_t on lagged differences and lagged levels. The maximisation over the parameters $\Gamma_1, \ldots, \Gamma_{k-1}$ is easy since it just leads to an ordinary least squares regression of $\Delta X_t + \alpha\beta' X_{t-k}$ on the lagged differences. Let us do this by first regressing ΔX_t on the lagged differences giving the residuals R_{0t} and then regressing X_{t-k} on the lagged differences giving the residuals R_{kt}. After having performed these regressions the concentrated likelihood function becomes proportional to

$$L(\alpha, \beta, \Lambda) = |\Lambda|^{-T/2} \exp\left\{ -\tfrac{1}{2} \sum_{t=1}^{T} (R_{0t} + \alpha\beta' R_{kt})' \Lambda^{-1} (R_{0t} + \alpha\beta' R_{kt}) \right\}.$$

For fixed β we can maximise over α and Λ by a usual regression of R_{0t} on $-\beta' R_{kt}$ which gives the well-known result

$$\hat{\alpha}(\beta) = -S_{0k}\beta(\beta' S_{kk}\beta)^{-1}, \qquad (6)$$

and

$$\hat{\Lambda}(\beta) = S_{00} - S_{0k}\beta(\beta' S_{kk}\beta)^{-1}\beta' S_{k0}, \qquad (7)$$

where we have defined product moment matrices of the residuals as

$$S_{ij} = T^{-1} \sum_{t=1}^{T} R_{it} R'_{jt}, \qquad i, j = 0, k. \qquad (8)$$

The likelihood profile now becomes proportional to

$$|\hat{\Lambda}(\beta)|^{-T/2},$$

and it remains to solve the minimisation problem

$$\min |S_{00} - S_{0k}\beta(\beta' S_{kk}\beta)^{-1}\beta' S_{k0}|,$$

where the minimisation is over all $p \times r$ matrices β. The well-known matrix relation [see Rao (1973)]

$$\begin{vmatrix} S_{00} & S_{0k}\beta \\ \beta' S_{k0} & \beta' S_{kk}\beta \end{vmatrix} = |S_{00}|\,|\beta' S_{kk}\beta - \beta' S_{k0} S_{00}^{-1} S_{0k}\beta|$$

$$= |\beta' S_{kk}\beta|\,|S_{00} - S_{0k}\beta(\beta' S_{kk}\beta)^{-1}\beta' S_{k0}|$$

shows that we shall minimise

$$|\beta' S_{kk}\beta - \beta' S_{k0} S_{00}^{-1} S_{0k}\beta| / |\beta' S_{kk}\beta|$$

with respect to the matrix β.

We now let D denote the diagonal matrix of ordered eigenvalues $\hat{\lambda}_1 > \cdots > \hat{\lambda}_p$ of $S_{k0}S_{00}^{-1}S_{0k}$ with respect to S_{kk}, i.e., the solutions to the equation

$$|\lambda S_{kk} - S_{k0} S_{00}^{-1} S_{0k}| = 0, \tag{9}$$

and E the matrix of the corresponding eigenvectors, then

$$S_{kk} E D = S_{k0} S_{00}^{-1} S_{0k} E,$$

where E is normalised such that

$$E' S_{kk} E = I.$$

Now choose $\beta = E\xi$ where ξ is $p \times r$, then we shall minimise

$$|\xi'\xi - \xi' D \xi| / |\xi'\xi|.$$

This can be accomplished by choosing ξ to be the first r unit vectors or by choosing $\hat{\beta}$ to be the first r eigenvectors of $S_{k0}S_{00}^{-1}S_{0k}$ with respect to S_{kk}, i.e., the first r columns of E. These are called the canonical variates and the eigenvalues are the squared canonical correlations of R_k with respect to R_0. For the details of these calculations the reader is referred to Anderson (1984, ch. 12). This type of analysis is also called reduced rank regression [see Ahn and Reinsel (1987) and Velu, Reinsel and Wichern (1986)]. Note that all possible choices of the optimal β can be found from $\hat{\beta}$ by $\beta = \hat{\beta}\rho$ for ρ an $r \times r$ matrix of full rank. The eigenvectors are normalised by the condition $\hat{\beta}' S_{kk} \hat{\beta} = I$ such that the estimates of the other parameters are given by

$$\hat{\alpha} = -S_{0k}\hat{\beta}(\hat{\beta}' S_{kk}\hat{\beta})^{-1} = -S_{0k}\hat{\beta}, \tag{10}$$

which clearly depends on the choice of the optimising β, whereas

$$\hat{\Pi} = -S_{0k}\hat{\beta}(\hat{\beta}' S_{kk}\hat{\beta})^{-1}\hat{\beta}' = -S_{0k}\hat{\beta}\hat{\beta}', \tag{11}$$

and

$$\hat{\Lambda} = S_{00} - S_{0k}\hat{\beta}\hat{\beta}'S_{k0} = S_{00} - \hat{\alpha}\hat{\alpha}', \tag{12}$$

and the maximised likelihood as given by

$$L_{\max}^{-2/T} = |S_{00}| \prod_{i=1}^{r} (1 - \hat{\lambda}_i), \tag{13}$$

do not depend on the choice of optimising β.

With these results it is easy to find the estimates of Π and Λ without the constraint (3). These follow from (6) and (7) for $r = p$ and $\beta = I$ and give in particular the maximised likelihood function without the constraint (3):

$$L_{\max}^{-2/T} = |S_{00}| \prod_{i=1}^{p} (1 - \hat{\lambda}_i). \tag{14}$$

If we now want a test that there are at most r cointegrating vectors, then the likelihood ratio test statistic is the ratio of (13) and (14) which can be expressed as (4), where $\hat{\lambda}_{r+1} > \cdots > \hat{\lambda}_p$ are the $p - r$ smallest eigenvalues. This completes the proof of Theorem 1.

Notice how this analysis allows one to calculate all p eigenvalues and eigenvectors at once, and then make inference about the number of important cointegration relations, by testing how many of the λ's are zero.

Next we shall investigate the test of a linear hypothesis about β. In the case we have $r = 1$, i.e., only one cointegration vector, it seems natural to test that certain variables do not enter into the cointegration vector, or that certain linear constraints are satisfied, for instance that the variables X_{1t} and X_{2t} only enter through their difference $X_{1t} - X_{2t}$. If $r \geq 2$, then a hypothesis of interest could be that the variables X_{1t} and X_{2t} enter through their difference only in all the cointegration vectors, since if two different linear combinations would occur then any coefficients to X_{1t} and X_{2t} would be possible. Thus it seems that some natural hypotheses on β can be formulated as

$$\mathrm{H}_1: \quad \beta = H\varphi, \tag{15}$$

where $H(p \times s)$ is a known matrix of full rank s and $\varphi(s \times r)$ is a matrix of unknown parameters. We assume that $r \leq s \leq p$. If $s = p$, then no restrictions are placed upon the choice of cointegration vectors, and if $s = r$, then the cointegration space is fully specified.

Theorem 2. The maximum likelihood estimator of the cointegration space, under the assumption that it is restricted to sp(H), *is given as the space spanned by the canonical variates corresponding to the r largest squared canonical correlations between the residuals of* $H'X_{t-k}$ *and* ΔX_t *corrected for the lagged differences of* X_t.

The likelihood ratio test now becomes

$$-2\ln(Q) = T\sum_{i=1}^{r} \ln\{(1-\lambda_i^*)/(1-\hat{\lambda}_i)\}, \tag{16}$$

where $\lambda_1^*, \ldots, \lambda_r^*$ *are the r largest squared canonical correlations.*

Proof. It is apparent from the derivation of $\hat{\beta}$ that if $\beta = H\varphi$ is fixed, then regression of R_{0t} on $-\varphi' H' R_{kt}$ is still a simple linear regression and the analysis is as before with R_{kt} replaced by $H'R_{kt}$. Thus the matrix φ can be estimated as the eigenvectors corresponding to the r largest eigenvalues of $H'S_{k0}S_{00}^{-1}S_{0k}H$ with respect to $H'S_{kk}H$, i.e., the solution to

$$|\lambda H'S_{kk}H - H'S_{k0}S_{00}^{-1}S_{0k}H| = 0.$$

Let the s eigenvalues be denoted by λ_i^*, $i = 1, \ldots, s$. Then the likelihood ratio test of H_1 in H_0 can be found from two expressions like (13) and is given by (16), which completes the proof of Theorem 2.

In the next section we shall find the asymptotic distribution of the test statistics (4) and (16) and show that the cointegration space, the impact matrix Π and the variance matrix Λ are estimated consistently.

3. Asymptotic properties of the estimators and the test statistics

In order to derive properties of the estimators we need to impose more precise conditions on the parameters of the model, such that they correspond to the situation we have in mind, namely of a process that is integrated of order 1, but still has r cointegration vectors β.

First of all we want all roots of $|A(z)| = 0$ to satisfy $|z| > 1$ or possibly $z = 1$. This implies that the nonstationarity of the process can be removed by differencing. Next we shall assume that X_t is integrated of order 1, i.e., that ΔX_t is stationary and that the hypothesis (3) is satisfied by some α and β of full rank r. Correspondingly we can express ΔX_t in terms of the ε's by its moving average representation,

$$\Delta X_t = \sum_{j=0}^{\infty} C_j \varepsilon_{t-j},$$

for some exponentially decreasing coefficients C_j. Under suitable conditions on these coefficients it is known that this equation determines an error correction model of the form (5), where $\Gamma_k X_{t-k} = -\Pi X_{t-k}$ represents the error correction term containing the stationary components of X_{t-k}, i.e., $\beta' X_{t-k}$. Moreover the null space for $C' = \sum_{j=0}^{\infty} C_j'$ given by $\{\xi | C'\xi = 0\}$ is exactly the range space of Γ_k', i.e., the space spanned by the columns in β and vice versa. We thus have the following representations:

$$\Pi = \alpha\beta' \quad \text{and} \quad C = \gamma\tau\delta', \tag{17}$$

where τ is $(p-r)\times(p-r)$, γ and δ are $p\times(p-r)$, and all three are of full rank, and $\gamma'\beta = \delta'\alpha = 0$. We shall later choose δ in a convenient way [see the references to Granger (1981), Granger and Engle (1985), Engle and Granger (1987), or Johansen (1988) for the details of these results].

We shall now formulate the main results of this section in the form of two theorems which deal with the test statistics derived in the previous section. First we have a result about the test statistic (4) and the estimators derived in (11) and (12).

Theorem 3. Under the hypothesis that there are r cointegrating vectors the estimate of the cointegration space as well as Π and Λ are consistent, and the likelihood ratio test statistic of this hypothesis is asymptotically distributed as

$$\operatorname{tr}\left\{\int_0^1 \mathrm{d}BB'\left[\int_0^1 BB'\,\mathrm{d}u\right]^{-1}\int_0^1 B\,\mathrm{d}B'\right\}, \tag{18}$$

where B is a $(p-r)$-dimensional Brownian motion with covariance matrix I.

In order to understand the structure of this limit distribution one should notice that if B is a Brownian motion with I as the covariance matrix, then the stochastic integral $\int_0^t B\,\mathrm{d}B'$ is a matrix-valued martingale, with quadratic variation process

$$\int_0^t \operatorname{var}(B\,\mathrm{d}B') = \int_0^t BB'\,\mathrm{d}u \otimes I,$$

where the integral $\int_0^t BB'\,\mathrm{d}u$ is an ordinary integral of the continuous matrix-valued process BB'. With this notation the limit distribution in Theorem 3 can be considered a multivariate version of the square of a martingale $\int_0^t B\,\mathrm{d}B'$ divided by its variance process $\int_0^t BB'\,\mathrm{d}u$. Notice that for $r = p-1$, i.e., for testing $p-1$ cointegration relations one obtains the limit distribution with a one-dimensional Brownian motion, i.e.,

$$\left(\int_0^1 B\,\mathrm{d}B\right)^2 \Big/ \int_0^1 B^2\,\mathrm{d}u = \left(\left(B(1)^2 - 1\right)/2\right)^2 \Big/ \int_0^1 B^2\,\mathrm{d}u,$$

Table 1

The quantiles in the distribution of the test statistic,

$$\operatorname{tr}\left\{\int_0^1 \mathrm{d}B B' \left(\int_0^1 B(u)B(u)'\mathrm{d}u\right)^{-1} \int_0^1 B\,\mathrm{d}B'\right\},$$

where B is an m-dimensional Brownian motion with covariance matrix I.

m	2.5%	5%	10%	50%	90%	95%	97.5%
1	0.0	0.0	0.0	0.6	2.9	4.2	5.3
2	1.6	1.9	2.5	5.4	10.3	12.0	13.9
3	7.0	7.8	8.8	14.0	21.2	23.8	26.1
4	16.0	17.4	19.2	26.3	35.6	38.6	41.2
5	28.3	30.4	32.8	42.1	53.6	57.2	60.3

which is the square of the usual 'unit root' distribution [see Dickey and Fuller (1979)]. A similar reduction is found by Phillips and Ouliaris (1987) in their work on tests for cointegration based on residuals. The distribution of the test statistic (18) is found by simulation and given in table 1.

A surprisingly accurate description of the results in table 1 is obtained by approximating the distributions by $c\chi^2(f)$ for suitable values of c and f. By equating the mean of the distributions based on 10,000 observations to those of $c\chi^2$ with $f = 2m^2$ degrees of freedom, we obtain values of c, and it turns out that we can use the empirical relation

$$c = 0.85 - 0.58/f.$$

Notice that the hypothesis of r cointegrating relations reduces the number of parameters in the Π matrix from p^2 to $rp + r(p-r)$, thus one could expect $(p-r)^2$ degrees of freedom if the usual asymptotics would hold. In the case of nonstationary processes it is known that this does not hold but a very good approximation is given by the above choice of $2(p-r)^2$ degrees of freedom.

Next we shall consider the test of the restriction (15) where linear constraints are imposed on β.

Theorem 4. The likelihood ratio test of the hypothesis

$$\mathrm{H}_1:\quad \beta = H\varphi$$

of restricting the r-dimensional cointegration space to an s-dimensional subspace of R^p is asymptotically distributed as χ^2 with $r(p-s)$ degrees of freedom.

We shall now give the proof of these theorems, through a series of intermediate results. We shall first give some expressions for variances and their limits, then show how the algorithm for deriving the maximum likelihood estimator can be followed by a probabilistic analysis ending up with the asymptotic properties of the estimator and the test statistics.

We can represent X_t as $X_t = \Sigma_{j=1}^{t} \Delta X_j$, where X_0 is a constant which we shall take to be zero to simplify the notation. We shall describe the stationary process ΔX_t by its covariance function

$$\psi(i) = \text{var}(\Delta X_t, \Delta X_{t+i}),$$

and we define the matrices

$$\mu_{ij} = \psi(i-j) = \text{E}(\Delta X_{t-i} \Delta X'_{t-j}), \qquad i, j = 0, \dots, k-1,$$

$$\mu_{ki} = \sum_{j=k-i}^{\infty} \psi(j), \qquad i = 0, \dots, k-1,$$

and

$$\mu_{kk} = - \sum_{j=-\infty}^{\infty} |j| \psi(j).$$

Finally define

$$\psi = \sum_{j=-\infty}^{\infty} \psi(j).$$

Note the following relations:

$$\psi(i) = \sum_{j=0}^{\infty} C_j \Lambda C'_{j+i},$$

$$\psi = \sum_{j=0}^{\infty} C_j \Lambda \sum_{j=0}^{\infty} C'_j = C \Lambda C',$$

$$\text{var}(X_{t-k}) = \sum_{j=-t+k}^{t-k} (t-k-|j|) \psi(j),$$

$$\text{cov}(X_{t-k}, \Delta X_{t-i}) = \sum_{j=k-i}^{t-i} \psi(j),$$

which show that

$$\mathrm{var}(X_T/T^{1/2}) \to \sum_{i=-\infty}^{\infty} \psi(i) = \psi,$$

and

$$\mathrm{cov}(X_{T-k}, \Delta X_{T-i}) \to \sum_{j=k-i}^{\infty} \psi(j) = \mu_{ki},$$

whereas the relation

$$\mathrm{var}(\beta' X_{T-k}) = (T-k) \sum_{j=-T+k}^{T-k} \beta'\psi(j)\beta - \sum_{j=-T+k}^{T-k} |j|\beta'\psi(j)\beta$$

shows that

$$\mathrm{var}(\beta' X_{T-k}) \to \beta'\mu_{kk}\beta,$$

since $\beta' C = 0$ implies that $\beta'\psi = 0$, such that the first term vanishes in the limit. Note that the nonstationary part of X_t makes the variance matrix tend to infinity, except for the directions given by the vectors in β, since $\beta' X_t$ is stationary.

The calculations involved in the maximum likelihood estimation all center around the product moment matrices

$$M_{ij} = T^{-1} \sum_{t=1}^{T} \Delta X_{t-i} \Delta X'_{t-j}, \qquad i, j = 0, \ldots, k-1,$$

$$M_{ki} = T^{-1} \sum_{t=1}^{T} X_{t-k} \Delta X'_{t-i}, \qquad i = 0, \ldots, k-1,$$

$$M_{kk} = T^{-1} \sum_{t=1}^{T} X_{t-k} X'_{t-k}.$$

We shall first give the asymptotic behaviour of these matrices, then find the asymptotic properties of S_{ij} and finally apply these results to the estimators and the test statistic. The methods are inspired by Phillips (1985) even though I shall stick to the Gaussian case, which make the arguments somewhat simpler.

The following lemma can be derived by the results in Phillips and Durlauf (1986). We let W be a Brownian motion in p dimensions with covariance matrix Λ.

Lemma 1. *As $T \to \infty$, we have*

$$T^{-1/2}X_{[Tt]} \xrightarrow{\text{w}} CW(t), \tag{19}$$

$$M_{ij} \xrightarrow{\text{a.s.}} \mu_{ij}, \qquad i, j = 0, \dots, k-1, \tag{20}$$

$$M_{ki} \xrightarrow{\text{w}} C\int_0^1 W \mathrm{d}W' C' + \mu_{ki}, \qquad i = 0, \dots, k-1, \tag{21}$$

$$\beta' M_{kk}\beta \xrightarrow{\text{a.s.}} \beta' \mu_{kk}\beta, \tag{22}$$

$$T^{-1}M_{kk} \xrightarrow{\text{w}} C\int_0^1 W(u)W'(u)\,\mathrm{d}u\, C'. \tag{23}$$

Note that for any $\xi \in R^p$, $\xi' M_{kk}\xi$ is of the order in probability of T unless ξ is in the space spanned by β, in which case it is convergent. Note also that the stochastic integrals enter as limits of the nonstationary part of the process X_t, and that they disappear when multiplied by β, since $\beta' C = 0$.

We shall apply the results to find the asymptotic properties of S_{ij}, $i, j = 0, k$, see (8). These can be expressed in terms of the M_{ij}'s as follows:

$$S_{ij} = M_{ij} - M_{i*}M_{**}^{-1}M_{*j}, \qquad i, j = 0, k,$$

where

$$M_{**} = \{M_{ij},\ i, j = 1, \dots, k-1\},$$

$$M_{k*} = \{M_{ki},\ i = 1, \dots, k-1\},$$

$$M_{0*} = \{M_{0i},\ i = 1, \dots, k-1\}.$$

A similar notation is introduced for the μ_{ij}'s. It is convenient to have the notation

$$\Sigma_{ij} = \mu_{ij} - \mu_{i*}\mu_{**}^{-1}\mu_{*j}, \qquad i, j = 0, k.$$

We now get:

Lemma 2. *The following relations hold*

$$\Sigma_{00} = \Gamma_k \Sigma_{k0} + \Lambda, \tag{24}$$

$$\Sigma_{0k}\Gamma_k' = \Gamma_k \Sigma_{kk}\Gamma_k', \tag{25}$$

and hence, since $\Gamma_k = -\alpha\beta'$.

$$\Sigma_{00} = \alpha(\beta'\Sigma_{kk}\beta)\alpha' + \Lambda \quad \textit{and} \quad \alpha = -\Sigma_{0k}\beta(\beta'\Sigma_{kk}\beta)^{-1}. \tag{26}$$

Proof. From the defining eq. (5) for the process X_t we find the equations

$$M_{0i} = \Gamma_1 M_{1i} + \cdots + \Gamma_{k-1}M_{k-1,i} + \Gamma_k M_{ki} + T^{-1}\sum_{t=1}^{T}\varepsilon_t \Delta X'_{t-i}, \tag{27}$$

$i = 0, 1, \ldots, k-1$, and

$$M_{0k} = \Gamma_1 M_{1k} + \cdots + \Gamma_{k-1}M_{k-1,k} + \Gamma_k M_{kk} + T^{-1}\sum_{t=1}^{T}\varepsilon_t X'_{t-k}. \tag{28}$$

Now let $T \to \infty$, then we get the equations

$$\mu_{00} = \Gamma_1\mu_{10} + \cdots + \Gamma_{k-1}\mu_{k-1,0} + \Gamma_k\mu_{k0} + \Lambda, \tag{29}$$

$$\mu_{0i} = \Gamma_1\mu_{1i} + \cdots + \Gamma_{k-1}\mu_{k-1,i} + \Gamma_k\mu_{ki}, \qquad i = 1, \ldots, k-1, \tag{30}$$

$$\mu_{0k}\beta = \Gamma_1\mu_{1k}\beta + \cdots + \Gamma_{k-1}\mu_{k-1,k}\beta + \Gamma_k\mu_{kk}\beta. \tag{31}$$

If we solve the eq. (30) for the matrices Γ_* and insert into (29) and (31), we get (24), (25), and (26).

We shall now find the asymptotic properties of S_{ij}.

Lemma 3. For $T \to \infty$, *it holds that, if* δ *is chosen such that* $\delta'\alpha = 0$, *then*

$$S_{00} \overset{\text{a.s.}}{\to} \Sigma_{00}, \tag{32}$$

$$\delta' S_{0k} \overset{\text{w}}{\to} \delta' \int_0^1 \mathrm{d}W\, W' C', \tag{33}$$

$$\beta' S_{k0} \overset{\text{a.s.}}{\to} \beta'\Sigma_{k0}, \tag{34}$$

$$T^{-1} S_{kk} \overset{\text{w}}{\to} C\int_0^1 W(u)W'(u)\,\mathrm{d}u\, C'. \tag{35}$$

$$\beta' S_{kk}\beta \overset{\text{a.s.}}{\to} \beta'\Sigma_{kk}\beta. \tag{36}$$

Proof. All relations follow from Lemma 1 except the second. If we solve for Γ_* in the eq. (27), insert the solution into (28), and use the definition of S_{ij} in terms of the M's, then we get

$$S_{0k} = T^{-1}\sum_{t=1}^{T} \varepsilon_t X'_{t-k} + \Gamma_k S_{kk} - \sum_{i=1}^{k-1}\sum_{j=1}^{k-1} T^{-1}\sum_{t=1}^{T} \varepsilon_t \Delta X'_{t-i} M^{ij} M_{jk}. \tag{37}$$

The last term goes a.s. to zero as $T \to \infty$, since ε_t and $\Delta X'_{t-i}$ are stationary and uncorrelated. The second term vanishes when multiplied by δ', since $\delta'\Gamma_k = -\delta'\alpha\beta' = 0$, and the first term converges to the integral as stated.

Lemma 4. The ordered eigenvalues of the equation

$$|\lambda S_{kk} - S_{k0} S_{00}^{-1} S_{0k}| = 0 \tag{38}$$

converge in probability to $(\lambda_1, \ldots, \lambda_r, 0, \ldots, 0)$, *where* $\lambda_1, \ldots, \lambda_r$ *are the ordered eigenvalues of the equation*

$$|\lambda \beta' \Sigma_{kk} \beta - \beta' \Sigma_{k0} \Sigma_{00}^{-1} \Sigma_{0k} \beta| = 0. \tag{39}$$

Proof. We want to express the problem in the coordinates given by the p vectors in β and γ, where γ is of full rank $p-r$ and $\gamma'\beta = 0$. This can be done by multiplying (9) by $|(\beta, \gamma)'|$ and $|(\beta, \gamma)|$ from the left and right, then the eigenvalues solve the equation

$$\left| \lambda \begin{bmatrix} \beta' S_{kk} \beta & \beta' S_{kk} \gamma \\ \gamma' S_{kk} \beta & \gamma' S_{kk} \gamma \end{bmatrix} - \begin{bmatrix} \beta' S_{k0} S_{00}^{-1} S_{0k} \beta & \beta' S_{k0} S_{00}^{-1} S_{0k} \gamma \\ \gamma' S_{k0} S_{00}^{-1} S_{0k} \beta & \gamma' S_{k0} S_{00}^{-1} S_{0k} \gamma \end{bmatrix} \right| = 0.$$

We define $A_T = (\gamma' S_{kk} \gamma)^{-1/2}$ so that by (35), $A_T \xrightarrow{P} 0$. Then the eigenvalues have to satisfy the equation

$$\left| \lambda \begin{bmatrix} \beta' S_{kk} \beta & \beta' S_{kk} \gamma A_T \\ A_T' \gamma' S_{kk} \beta & I \end{bmatrix} - \begin{bmatrix} \beta' S_{k0} S_{00}^{-1} S_{0k} \beta & \beta' S_{k0} S_{00}^{-1} S_{0k} \gamma A_T \\ A_T' \gamma' S_{k0} S_{00}^{-1} S_{0k} \beta & A_T' \gamma' S_{k0} S_{00}^{-1} S_{0k} \gamma A_T \end{bmatrix} \right| = 0.$$

The coefficient matrices converge in probability by the results in Lemma 3, and the limiting equation is

$$\left| \lambda \begin{bmatrix} \beta' \Sigma_{kk} \beta & 0 \\ 0 & I \end{bmatrix} - \begin{bmatrix} \beta' \Sigma_{k0} \Sigma_{00}^{-1} \Sigma_{0k} \beta & 0 \\ 0 & 0 \end{bmatrix} \right| = 0,$$

or

$$|\lambda\beta'\Sigma_{kk}\beta - \beta'\Sigma_{k0}\Sigma_{00}^{-1}\Sigma_{0k}\beta|\,|\lambda I| = 0,$$

where I is an identity matrix of dimension $p-r$, which means that the equation has $p-r$ roots at $\lambda = 0$. It is known that the ordered eigenvalues are continuous functions of the coefficient matrices [see Andersson, Brøns and Jensen (1983)], and hence the statement of Lemma 4 is proved.

We shall need one more technical lemma before we can prove the more useful results. We decompose the eigenvectors $\hat{\beta}$ as follows: $\hat{\beta}_i = \beta\hat{x}_i + \gamma\hat{y}_i$, where $\hat{x}_i = (\beta'\beta)^{-1}\beta'\hat{\beta}_i$ and $y_i = (\gamma'\gamma)^{-1}\gamma'\hat{\beta}_i$. Let $\hat{x} = (\hat{x}_1, \ldots, \hat{x}_r) = (\beta'\beta)^{-1}\beta'\hat{\beta}$. Note that although we have proved that the eigenvalues λ_i are convergent, the same cannot hold for the eigenvectors $\hat{\beta}_i$ or $\hat{x}_i$, since if the limiting eq. (39) has multiple roots then the eigenvectors are not uniquely defined. This complicates the formulation below somewhat. Let

$$S(\lambda) = \lambda S_{kk} - S_{k0}S_{00}^{-1}S_{0k}.$$

Lemma 5. For $i = 1, \ldots, r$, we have

$$\gamma' S(\hat{\lambda}_i)\gamma/T \overset{w}{\to} \lambda_i\gamma' C\int_0^1 WW'\,\mathrm{d}u\, C'\gamma, \tag{40}$$

$$\hat{y}_i \in O_P(T^{-1}), \qquad \hat{x} \in O_P(1), \qquad \hat{x}^{-1} \in O_P(1), \tag{41}$$

$$\beta' S(\hat{\lambda}_i)\beta\hat{x}_i \in O_P(T^{-1}), \tag{42}$$

$$\gamma' S(\hat{\lambda}_i)\beta\hat{x}_i = -\gamma'\left[T^{-1}\sum_{t=1}^{T} X_{t-k}\varepsilon_t'\right]\Sigma_{00}^{-1}\Sigma_{0k}\beta\hat{x}_i + o_P(1). \tag{43}$$

Proof. The relation (40) follows directly from (35) in Lemma 3, since by Lemma 4, $\hat{\lambda}_i \overset{P}{\to} \lambda_i > 0$.

The normalisation $\hat{\beta}' S_{kk}\hat{\beta} = I$ implies by an argument similar to that of Lemma 4 for the eigenvalues of S_{kk} that $\hat{\beta}$ and hence $\hat{x}$ is bounded in probability. The eigenvectors $\hat{\beta}_i$ and eigenvalues $\hat{\lambda}_i$ satisfy

$$\beta' S(\hat{\lambda}_i)\beta\hat{x}_i + \beta' S(\hat{\lambda}_i)\gamma\hat{y}_i = 0, \tag{44}$$

$$\gamma' S(\hat{\lambda}_i)\beta\hat{x}_i + \gamma' S(\hat{\lambda}_i)\gamma\hat{y}_i = 0. \tag{45}$$

Now (40) and (45) imply that $\hat{y}_i \in O_P(T^{-1})$, and hence from (44) we find that $\beta' S(\hat{\lambda}_i)\beta\hat{x}_i \in O_P(T^{-1})$, which shows (42), and also from the normalising condition, that $\hat{x}'\beta' S_{kk}\beta\hat{x} \xrightarrow{P} I$. Hence $|\hat{x}|^2|\beta' S_{kk}\beta| \xrightarrow{P} 1$, which implies that also $\hat{x}^{-1}$ is bounded in probability, which proves (41). From (37) it follows that

$$\gamma' S_{k0} + \gamma' S_{kk}\beta\alpha' = \gamma' T^{-1}\sum_{t=1}^{T} X_{t-k}\varepsilon_t' + o_P(1).$$

Now replace $\alpha = -\Sigma_{0k}\beta(\beta'\Sigma_{kk}\beta)^{-1}$ [see (26)] by the consistent estimate $-S_{0k}\beta(\beta' S_{kk}\beta)^{-1}$, then

$$\gamma' S(\hat{\lambda}_i)\beta\hat{x}_i = \gamma' S_{kk}\beta(\beta' S_{kk}\beta)^{-1}(\hat{\lambda}_i\beta' S_{kk}\beta - \beta' S_{k0}S_{00}^{-1}S_{0k}\beta)\hat{x}_i$$

$$-\gamma' T^{-1}\sum_{t=1}^{T} X_{t-k}\varepsilon_t'\Sigma_{00}^{-1}\Sigma_{0k}\beta\hat{x}_i + o_P(1).$$

The first term contains the factor $\beta' S(\hat{\lambda}_i)\beta\hat{x}_i$ which tends to zero in probability by (42). This completes the proof of Lemma 5.

We shall now choose δ of dimension $p\times(p-r)$ such that $\delta'\alpha = 0$ [see (17)] in the following way. We let $P_\alpha(\Lambda)$ denote the projection of R^p onto the column space spanned by α with respect to the matrix Λ^{-1}, i.e.,

$$P_\alpha(\Lambda) = \alpha(\alpha'\Lambda^{-1}\alpha)^{-1}\alpha'\Lambda^{-1}.$$

We then choose δ of full rank $p-r$ to satisfy

$$\delta\delta' = \Lambda^{-1}(I - P_\alpha(\Lambda)).$$

Note that $\delta'\alpha = 0$, and that $\delta'\Lambda\delta = I$ of dimension $(p-r)\times(p-r)$. Note also that $P_\alpha(\Lambda) = P_\alpha(\Sigma_{00})$ since Σ_{00} is given by (26). This relation is well-known from the theory of random coefficient regression [see Rao (1965) or Johansen (1984)].

Lemma 6. For $T\to\infty$, we have that $T\hat{\lambda}_{r+1},\dots,T\hat{\lambda}_p$ converge in distribution to the ordered eigenvalues of the equation

$$\left|\lambda\int_0^1 BB'\,\mathrm{d}u - \int_0^1 B\,\mathrm{d}B'\int_0^1 \mathrm{d}B\,B'\right| = 0, \tag{46}$$

where B is a Brownian motion in $p-r$ dimensions with covariance matrix I.

Proof. We shall consider the ordered eigenvalues of the equation

$$\left|\begin{bmatrix} \beta' S_{kk}\beta/T & \beta' S_{kk}\gamma/T \\ \gamma' S_{kk}\beta/T & \gamma' S_{kk}\gamma/T \end{bmatrix} - \mu \begin{bmatrix} \beta' S_{k0}S_{00}^{-1}S_{0k}\beta & \beta' S_{k0}S_{00}^{-1}S_{0k}\gamma \\ \gamma' S_{k0}S_{00}^{-1}S_{0k}\beta & \gamma' S_{k0}S_{00}^{-1}S_{0k}\gamma \end{bmatrix}\right| = 0.$$

For any value of T the ordered eigenvalues are

$$\hat{\mu}_1 = \left(T\hat{\lambda}_p\right)^{-1}, \ldots, \hat{\mu}_p = \left(T\hat{\lambda}_1\right)^{-1}.$$

Since the ordered eigenvalues are continuous functions of the coefficients, we find from Lemma 3 that $\hat{\mu}_1, \ldots, \hat{\mu}_p$ converge in distribution to the ordered eigenvalues from the equation

$$\left|\begin{bmatrix} 0 & 0 \\ 0 & \gamma' C \int_0^1 WW' \,\mathrm{d}u\, C'\gamma \end{bmatrix} - \mu \begin{bmatrix} \beta'\Sigma_{k0}\Sigma_{00}^{-1}\Sigma_{0k}\beta & \beta'\Sigma_{k0}\Sigma_{00}^{-1}F \\ F'\Sigma_{00}^{-1}\Sigma_{0k}\beta & F'\Sigma_{00}^{-1}F \end{bmatrix}\right| = 0,$$

where F is the weak limit of $S_{0k}\gamma$.

This determinant can also be written as

$$|\mu\beta'\Sigma_{k0}\Sigma_{00}^{-1}\Sigma_{0k}\beta| \Big| \gamma' C \int_0^1 WW' \,\mathrm{d}u\, C'\gamma$$
$$- \mu F' \left[\Sigma_{00}^{-1} - \Sigma_{00}^{-1}\Sigma_{0k}\beta\left(\beta'\Sigma_{k0}\Sigma_{00}^{-1}\Sigma_{0k}\beta\right)^{-1}\beta'\Sigma_{k0}\Sigma_{00}^{-1}\right] F \Big|, \tag{47}$$

which shows that in the limit there are r roots at zero. Now apply (24) and (25) of Lemma 2 and find that

$$\Sigma_{00}^{-1} - \Sigma_{00}^{-1}\Sigma_{0k}\beta\left(\beta'\Sigma_{k0}\Sigma_{00}^{-1}\Sigma_{0k}\beta\right)^{-1}\beta'\Sigma_{k0}\Sigma_{00}^{-1}$$

equals

$$\Sigma_{00}^{-1}(I - P_\alpha(\Sigma_{00})) = \Lambda^{-1}(I - P_\alpha(\Lambda)) = \delta\delta',$$

and hence that the second factor of (47) is

$$\left| \gamma' C \int_0^1 WW' \,\mathrm{d}u\, C'\gamma - \mu F'\delta\delta' F \right|,$$

which by (33) equals

$$\left|\gamma' C\int_0^1 WW'\,\mathrm{d}u\,C'\gamma - \mu\gamma' C\int_0^1 W\mathrm{d}W'\,\delta\,\delta'\int_0^1 \mathrm{d}W\,W'C'\gamma\right|. \tag{48}$$

Thus the limiting distribution of the $p-r$ largest μ's is given as the distribution of the ordered eigenvalues of (48).

The representation (17): $C=\gamma\tau\delta'$ for some nonsingular matrix τ now implies, since $|\gamma'\gamma|\neq 0$ and $|\tau|\neq 0$, that

$$\left|\delta'\int_0^1 WW'\,\mathrm{d}u\,\delta - \mu\delta'\int_0^1 W\mathrm{d}W'\,\delta\delta'\int_0^1 \mathrm{d}W\,W'\delta\right| = 0. \tag{49}$$

Now $B=\delta' W$ is a Brownian motion with variance $\delta'\Lambda\delta = I$, and the result of Lemma 6 is found by noting that the solutions of (46) are the reciprocal values of the solutions to the above equation.

Corollary. The test statistic for H_0: $\Pi=\alpha\beta'$ given by (4) will converge in distribution to the sum of the eigenvalues given by (46), i.e., the limiting distribution is given by (18):

$$\operatorname{tr}\left\{\int_0^1 \mathrm{d}B B'\left(\int_0^1 BB'\,\mathrm{d}u\right)^{-1}\int_0^1 B\,\mathrm{d}B'\right\}.$$

Proof. We just expand the test statistic (4),

$$-2\ln(Q) = -T\sum_{i=r+1}^{p}\ln(1-\hat\lambda_i) = \sum_{i=r+1}^{p} T\hat\lambda_i + o_P(1),$$

and apply Lemma 6.

We can now complete the proof of Theorem 3.

The asymptotic distribution of the test statistic (4) follows from the above corollary, and the consistency of the cointegration space and the estimators of Π and Λ is proved as follows. We decompose $\hat\beta = \beta\hat x + \gamma\hat y$, and it then follows from (41) that $\hat\beta\hat x^{-1} - \beta = \gamma\hat y\hat x^{-1} \in O_P(T^{-1})$. Thus we have seen that the projection of $\hat\beta$ onto the orthogonal complement of sp(β) tends to zero in probability of the order of T^{-1}. In this sense the cointegration space is consistently estimated. From (11) we find

$$\hat\Pi = -S_{0k}\hat\beta\left(\hat\beta S_{kk}\hat\beta\right)^{-1}\hat\beta' = -S_{0k}\hat\beta\hat x^{-1}\left((\hat\beta\hat x^{-1})' S_{kk}\hat\beta\hat x^{-1}\right)^{-1}(\hat\beta\hat x^{-1})',$$

which converges in probability to

$$-\Sigma_{0k}\beta(\beta'\Sigma_{kk}\beta)^{-1}\beta' = \alpha\beta' = \Pi.$$

From (12) we get by a similar trick that

$$\hat{\Lambda} = S_{00} - S_{0k}\hat{\beta}(\hat{\beta}'S_{kk}\hat{\beta})^{-1}\hat{\beta}'S_{k0}$$
$$\xrightarrow{\mathrm{P}} \Sigma_{00} - \Sigma_{0k}\beta(\beta'\Sigma_{kk}\beta)^{-1}\beta'\Sigma_{k0} = \Sigma_{00} - \alpha(\beta'\Sigma_{kk}\beta)\alpha',$$

which by (26) equals Λ. This completes the proof of Theorem 3.

In order to prove the Theorem 4 we shall need an expansion of the likelihood function around a point where the maximum is attained. We formulate this as a lemma:

Lemma 7. Let A and B be $p \times p$ symmetric positive definite matrices, and define the function

$$f(z) = \ln\{|z'Az|/|z'Bz|\},$$

where z is a $p \times r$ matrix. If z is a point where the function attains its maximum or minimum, then for any $p \times r$ matrix h we have

$$f(z+h) = f(z) + \operatorname{tr}\{(z'Az)^{-1}h'Ah - (z'Bz)^{-1}h'Bh\} + \mathrm{O}(h^3).$$

Proof. This is easily seen by expanding the terms in f using that the first derivative vanishes at z.

We shall now give the asymptotic distribution of the maximum likelihood estimator $\hat{\beta}$ suitably normalised. This is not a very useful result in practise, since the normalisation depends on β, but it is convenient for deriving other results of interest.

Lemma 8. The maximum likelihood estimator $\hat{\beta}$ has the representation

$$T\left[\hat{\beta}(\beta'\hat{\beta})^{-1}\beta'\beta - \beta\right]$$
$$= \gamma(\gamma'S_{kk}\gamma/T)^{-1}\gamma'\left[T^{-1}\sum_{t=1}^{T} X_{t-k}\varepsilon_t'\right]\Sigma_{00}^{-1}\Sigma_{0k}\beta(\beta'\Sigma_{k0}\Sigma_{00}^{-1}\Sigma_{0k}\beta)^{-1}$$
$$\times\beta'\Sigma_{kk}\beta + \mathrm{o}_P(1), \qquad (50)$$

which converges in distribution to

$$\gamma\left(\int_0^1 UU'\,\mathrm{d}u\right)^{-1}\int_0^1 U\,\mathrm{d}V',$$

where U and V are independent Brownian motions given by

$$U=\gamma' CW, \tag{51}$$

$$V=\beta'\Sigma_{kk}\beta\left(\beta'\Sigma_{k0}\Sigma_{00}^{-1}\Sigma_{0k}\beta\right)^{-1}\beta'\Sigma_{k0}\Sigma_{00}^{-1}W. \tag{52}$$

The variance of V is given by

$$\operatorname{var}(V)=\beta'\Sigma_{kk}\beta\left(\beta'\Sigma_{k0}\Sigma_{00}^{-1}\Sigma_{0k}\beta\right)^{-1}\beta'\Sigma_{kk}\beta-\beta'\Sigma_{kk}\beta. \tag{53}$$

Note that the limiting distribution for fixed U is Gaussian with mean zero and variance

$$\gamma\int_0^1 UU'\,\mathrm{d}u\,\gamma'\otimes\operatorname{var}(V).$$

Thus the limiting distribution is a mixture of Gaussian distributions. This will be used in the derivation of the limiting distributions of the test statistics [see Lemma 9].

Proof. From the decomposition $\hat{\beta}_i=\beta\hat{x}_i+\gamma\hat{y}_i$ we have from (45)

$$T\left(\hat{\beta}_i-\beta\hat{x}_i\right)=T\gamma\hat{y}_i=-T\gamma\left(\gamma' S(\hat{\lambda}_i)\gamma\right)^{-1}\left(\gamma' S(\hat{\lambda}_i)\beta\right)\hat{x}_i.$$

It follows from (40) and (43) in Lemma 5 that this can be written as

$$\gamma\left(\gamma' S_{kk}\gamma/T\right)^{-1}\gamma'\left[T^{-1}\sum_{t=1}^{T}X_{t-k}\varepsilon_t'\right]\Sigma_{00}^{-1}\Sigma_{0k}\beta\hat{x}_i\hat{\lambda}_i^{-1}+\mathrm{o}_P(1).$$

Hence for $\hat{x}=(\hat{x}_1,\dots,\hat{x}_r)=(\beta'\beta)^{-1}\beta'\hat{\beta}$ and $\hat{D}_r=\operatorname{diag}(\hat{\lambda}_1,\dots,\hat{\lambda}_r)$,

$$T(\hat{\beta}-\beta\hat{x})$$
$$=\gamma\left(\gamma' S_{kk}\gamma/T\right)^{-1}\gamma'\left[T^{-1}\sum_{t=1}^{T}X_{t-k}\varepsilon_t'\right]\Sigma_{00}^{-1}\Sigma_{0k}\beta\hat{x}\hat{D}_r^{-1}+\mathrm{o}_P(1). \tag{54}$$

Now multiply by $\hat{x}^{-1}$ from the right and note that it follows from (42) that

$$\beta' S_{kk}\beta\hat{x}\hat{D}_r - \beta' S_{k0}S_{00}^{-1}S_{0k}\beta\hat{x} \in o_P(1),$$

which shows that

$$\hat{x}\hat{D}_r^{-1}\hat{x}^{-1} \xrightarrow{P} \left(\beta'\Sigma_{k0}\Sigma_{00}^{-1}\Sigma_{0k}\beta\right)^{-1}\beta'\Sigma_{kk}\beta.$$

Now insert this into (54) and we obtain the representation (50), which converges as indicated with U and V defined as in (51) and (52). The variance matrix for V is calculated from (52) using the relation (26). Similarly the independence follows from (26).

Lemma 9. The likelihood ratio test of the hypothesis of a completely specified β *has an asymptotic representation of the form*

$$-2\ln(Q) = T\,\mathrm{tr}\Big\{\mathrm{var}(V)^{-1}\Big(\hat{\beta}\big(\beta'\hat{\beta}\big)^{-1}\beta'\beta - \beta\Big)' \times S_{kk}\Big(\hat{\beta}\big(\beta'\hat{\beta}\big)^{-1}\beta'\beta - \beta\Big)\Big\} + o_P(1), \tag{55}$$

which converges weakly to

$$\mathrm{tr}\left\{\mathrm{var}(V)^{-1}\int_0^1 \mathrm{d}V\,U'\left(\int_0^1 UU'\,\mathrm{d}u\right)^{-1}\int_0^1 U\,\mathrm{d}V'\right\}, \tag{56}$$

where U *and* V *are given by (51) and (52).*

The statistic (56) has a χ^2 *distribution with* $r(p-r)$ *degrees of freedom.*

Proof. The likelihood ratio test statistic of a simple hypothesis about β has the form

$$T\{\ln[|\beta'(S_{kk} - S_{k0}S_{00}^{-1}S_{0k})\beta|/|\beta' S_{kk}\beta|] - \ln[|\hat{\beta}'(S_{kk} - S_{k0}S_{00}^{-1}S_{0k})\hat{\beta}|/|\hat{\beta}' S_{kk}\hat{\beta}|]\}.$$

Now replace $\hat{\beta}$ by $\hat{\beta}\hat{x}^{-1} = \tilde{\beta}$, say, which is also a maximum point for the likelihood function. Then the statistic takes the form $T\{f(\beta) - f(\tilde{\beta})\}$ for $A = S_{kk} - S_{k0}S_{00}^{-1}S_{0k}$ and $B = S_{kk}$ [see Lemma 7]. By the result in Lemma 7 it follows that this can be expressed as

$$T\,\mathrm{tr}\left\{(\tilde\beta'A\tilde\beta)^{-1}(\tilde\beta-\beta)'A(\tilde\beta-\beta)-(\tilde\beta'B\tilde\beta)^{-1}(\tilde\beta-\beta)'B(\tilde\beta-\beta)\right\}$$

$$+\mathrm{O}_P\left(T(\tilde\beta-\beta)^3\right)$$

$$=T\,\mathrm{tr}\left\{\left[(\tilde\beta'A\tilde\beta)^{-1}-(\tilde\beta'B\tilde\beta)^{-1}\right](\tilde\beta-\beta)'S_{kk}(\tilde\beta-\beta)\right\}$$

$$-T\,\mathrm{tr}\left\{(\tilde\beta'A\tilde\beta)^{-1}(\tilde\beta-\beta)'S_{k0}S_{00}^{-1}S_{0k}(\tilde\beta-\beta)\right\}+\mathrm{O}_P\left(T(\tilde\beta-\beta)^3\right).$$

Now use the result from Lemma 8 that $\tilde\beta-\beta\in\mathrm{O}_P(T^{-1})$ to see that the last two terms tend to zero in probability. We also get

$$[\tilde\beta'(S_{kk}-S_{k0}S_{00}^{-1}S_{0k})\tilde\beta]^{-1}-[\tilde\beta'S_{kk}\tilde\beta]^{-1}$$

$$\xrightarrow{\mathrm{P}}[\beta'(\Sigma_{kk}-\Sigma_{k0}\Sigma_{00}^{-1}\Sigma_{0k})\beta]^{-1}-[\beta'\Sigma_{kk}\beta]^{-1}=\mathrm{var}(V)^{-1}.$$

Finally we note that $T(\tilde\beta-\beta)'S_{kk}(\tilde\beta-\beta)$ converges in distribution to

$$\int_0^1 \mathrm{d}V\,U'\left(\int_0^1 UU'\,\mathrm{d}u\right)^{-1}\int_0^1 U\,\mathrm{d}V'.$$

Now use the fact that for given value of U the $(p-r)\times r$ matrix $\int_0^1 U\mathrm{d}V'$ is Gaussian with mean zero and variance matrix

$$\int_0^1 UU'\,\mathrm{d}u\otimes\mathrm{var}(V),$$

hence the distribution of (56) for fixed U is χ^2 with $(p-r)r$ degrees of freedom. Since this result holds independently of the given value of U it also holds marginally. This basic independence and the conditioning argument is also used in the work of Phillips and Park (1986b) in the discussion of the regression estimates for integrated processes.

We can now finally give the proof of Theorem 4.

We want to test the hypothesis H_1: $\beta=H\varphi$.

We now choose ψ $(s\times(s-r))$ to supplement φ $(s\times r)$ such that (ψ,φ) $(s\times s)$ has full rank. We can choose ψ such that $H\psi=\gamma\eta$ for some η $(p-r)\times(s-r)$.

The test statistic (16) can be expressed as the difference of two test statistics we get by testing a simple hypothesis for β. Thus we can use the representation (55) and (50) for both statistics and we find that it has a weak limit, which can be expressed as

$$-2\ln(Q) \xrightarrow{w} \operatorname{tr}\left\{\operatorname{var}(V)^{-1}\int_0^1 \mathrm{d}V\,U'\left(\int_0^1 UU'\,\mathrm{d}u\right)^{-1}\int_0^1 U\,\mathrm{d}V'\right.$$
$$\left. -\operatorname{var}(V_H)^{-1}\int_0^1 \mathrm{d}V_H\,U_H'\left(\int_0^1 U_H U_H'\,\mathrm{d}u\right)^{-1}\int_0^1 U_H\,\mathrm{d}V_H'\right\},$$

where

$$U_H = \psi' H' C W = \eta'\gamma' C W = \eta' U,$$

and

$$V_H = \varphi' H' \Sigma_{kk} H\varphi\left(\varphi' H' \Sigma_{k0}\Sigma_{00}^{-1}\Sigma_{0k} H\varphi\right)^{-1}\varphi' H' \Sigma_{k0}\Sigma_{00}^{-1} W = V.$$

Thus

$$-2\ln(Q) \xrightarrow{w} \operatorname{tr}\left\{\left[\int_0^1 \mathrm{d}V\,U'\left(\int_0^1 UU'\,\mathrm{d}u\right)^{-1}\int_0^1 U\,\mathrm{d}V'\right.\right.$$
$$\left.\left. -\int_0^1 \mathrm{d}V\,U'\eta\left(\eta'\int_0^1 UU'\,\mathrm{d}u\,\eta\right)^{-1}\eta'\int_0^1 U\,\mathrm{d}V'\right]\operatorname{var}(V)^{-1}\right\}.$$

For fixed value of U the $(p-r)\times r$ matrix

$$Y = \left(\int_0^1 UU'\,\mathrm{d}u\right)^{-1/2}\int_0^1 U\,\mathrm{d}V'\operatorname{var}(V)^{-1/2}$$

is Gaussian with variance matrix $I \otimes I$. Let $\tilde{\eta} = (\int_0^1 UU'\mathrm{d}u)^{-1/2}\eta$, then the decomposition into independent components, given by

$$\operatorname{tr}\{Y'Y\} = \operatorname{tr}\left\{Y'\left(I - \tilde{\eta}(\tilde{\eta}'\tilde{\eta})^{-1}\tilde{\eta}'\right)Y\right\} + \operatorname{tr}\left\{Y'\tilde{\eta}(\tilde{\eta}'\tilde{\eta})^{-1}\tilde{\eta}'Y\right\},$$

shows that each term is χ^2 distributed with degrees of freedom $r(p-r)$, $r(p-s)$ and $r(s-r)$, respectively. Thus the limiting distribution of $-2\ln(Q)$ is for fixed U a χ^2 distribution with $(p-s)r$ degrees of freedom. Since this result does not depend on the value of U it holds marginally. Thus the proof of Theorem 4 is completed.

References

Ahn, S.K. and G.C. Reinsel, 1987, Estimation for partially nonstationary multivariate autoregressive models (University of Wisconsin, Madison, WI).

Anderson, T.W., 1984, An introduction to multivariate statistical analysis (Wiley, New York).

Andersson, S.A., H.K. Brøns and S.T. Jensen, 1983, Distribution of eigenvalues in multivariate statistical analysis, Annals of Statistics 11, 392–415.

Davidson, J., 1986, Cointegration in linear dynamic systems, Mimeo. (London School of Economics, London).

Dickey, D.A. and W.A. Fuller, 1979, Distribution of the estimators for autoregressive time series with a unit root, Journal of the American Statistical Association 74, 427–431.

Engle, R.F. and C.W.J. Granger, 1987, Co-integration and error correction: Representation, estimation and testing, Econometrica 55, 251–276.

Granger, C.J., 1981, Some properties of time series data and their use in econometric model specification, Journal of Econometrics 16, 121–130.

Granger, C.W.J. and R.F. Engle, 1985, Dynamic model specification with equilibrium constraints, Mimeo. (University of California, San Diego, CA).

Granger, C.W.J. and A.A. Weiss, 1983, Time series analysis of error correction models, in: S. Karlin, T. Amemiya and L.A. Goodman eds., Studies in economic time series and multivariate statistics (Academic Press, New York).

Johansen, S., 1984, Functional relations, random coefficients, and non-linear regression with application to kinetic data, Lecture notes in statistics (Springer, New York).

Johansen, S., 1988, The mathematical structure of error correction models, Contemporary Mathematics, in press.

Phillips, P.C.B., 1985, Understanding spurious regression in econometrics, Cowles Foundation discussion paper no. 757.

Phillips, P.C.B., 1987, Multiple regression with integrated time series, Cowles Foundation discussion paper no. 852.

Phillips. P.C.B. and S.N. Durlauf, 1986, Multiple time series regression with integrated processes, Review of Economic Studies 53, 473–495.

Phillips, P.C.B. and S. Ouliaris, 1986, Testing for cointegration, Cowles Foundation discussion paper no. 809.

Phillips, P.C.B. and S. Ouliaris, 1987, Asymptotic properties of residual based tests for cointegration, Cowles Foundation discussion paper no. 847.

Phillips, P.C.B. and J.Y. Park, 1986a, Asymptotic equivalence of OLS and GLS in regression with integrated regressors, Cowles Foundation discussion paper no. 802.

Phillips, P.C.B. and J.Y. Park, 1986b, Statistical inference in regressions with integrated processes: Part 1, Cowles Foundation discussion paper no. 811.

Phillips, P.C.B. and J.Y. Park, 1987, Statistical inference in regressions with integrated processes: Part 2, Cowles Foundation discussion paper no. 819.

Rao, C.R., 1965, The theory of least squares when the parameters are stochastic and its applications to the analysis of growth curves, Biometrika 52, 447–458.

Rao, C.R. 1973, Linear statistical inference and its applications, 2nd ed. (Wiley, New York).

Sims, A., J.H., Stock and M.W. Watson, 1986, Inference in linear time series models with some unit roots, Preprint.

Stock, J.H., 1987, Asymptotic properties of least squares estimates of cointegration vectors, Econometrica 55, 1035–1056.

Stock, J.H. and M.W. Watson, 1987, Testing for common trends, Working paper in econometrics (Hoover Institution, Stanford, CA).

Velu, R.P., G.C. Reinsel and D.W. Wichern, 1986, Reduced rank models for multiple time series, Biometrika 73, 105–118.

Name Index